Edinburgh Jazz Enlightenment

The Story of Edinburgh Traditional Jazz

– GRAHAM BLAMIRE –

An environmentally friendly book printed and bound in England by
www.printondemand-worldwide.com

Mixed Sources
Product group from well-managed
forests, and other controlled sources
www.fsc.org Cert no. TT-COC-002641
© 1996 Forest Stewardship Council

FSC

PEFC Certified
This product is
from sustainably
managed forests
and controlled
sources
www.pefc.org

PEFC
PEFC/16-33-415

This book is made entirely of chain-of-custody materials

i

www.fast-print.net/store.php

Edinburgh Jazz Enlightenment –
The Story of Edinburgh Traditional Jazz
Copyright © Graham Blamire 2012

ISBN 978-178035-290-9

First published 2012 by
FASTPRINT PUBLISHING
Peterborough, England.

About The Author

Graham Blamire

(from the collection of the author, photographer unknown)

The author is a double bass player who began playing traditional jazz in Edinburgh in the late 1950s, starting before he had left school. Over the course of more than 50 years, he has played with many of the local bands and has had many opportunities to play with well-known visiting jazz musicians. A habitual keeper of notes and scrap books, he accumulated a wealth of information and anecdotes about his own playing experiences and about those with whom he played. After the advent of home computers, he began compiling and organising a data bank about the individual jazz musicians and bands during his time in Edinburgh. He also began collecting information from others involved, including some who remembered jazz in Edinburgh well before his time. A member at one time or another of the well-known Edinburgh bands 'Old Bailey and his Jazz Advocates', 'The Scottish Jazz Advocates', 'The Louisiana Ragtime Band' and 'The Spirits of Rhythm', he played innumerable gigs and festivals and made a number of recordings, broadcasts and television appearances. For over 25 years, he has led the four-piece 'Maid of the Forth Stompers', entertaining passengers on the cruise boat 'The Maid of the Forth', sailing from South Queensferry on the Firth of Forth.

Dedication

This book about Edinburgh traditional jazz is dedicated to the 'punters', those loyal, enthusiastic and much-valued followers of local jazz who, over the years and decades, turned up in support at the pubs, clubs and jazz events. Without them there would have been no real local jazz scene at all and nothing for me to write about.

JGB 2011

Lino cut by and with the permission of Ian Boyter

Author's Foreword and Acknowledgements

In writing this book, I had the support and assistance of many people. Many of my jazz colleagues willingly (as far as I knew) gave of their time as I ransacked their memories, sometimes of events that had taken place anything up to 60 years ago. I am particularly grateful to those who were able to tell me about pre-1960s Edinburgh jazz, which largely pre-dated my personal experience. They included: Billy Alison, Jim Baikie, Dougie Campbell, Ron Carruthers, Roger Craik, Peter Davenport, Jim Douglas, Fionna Duncan, Iain Forde, Fraser Gauld, Jimmy Gavin, George Hewitt, Dizzy Jackson, Dave Keir, Pete Kerr, Ralph Laing, Andrew Lauder, Jake McMahon, Kenny and Violet Milne, Fred Murray, Jim Petrie, Mike Pollett, Ronnie Rae, Ken Ramage, Bill Salmond, Bobby Stewart, Norrie Thomson, Jim Walker, Jack Weddell, Brian Weld and Jim Young.

A great deal of information was made freely available to me by John Latham of the Sandy Brown Society, Ian Maund who runs the Sandy Brown Jazz website and Jim Keppie of the Edinburgh Jazz Archive Group. I also received support and help from writers who have published material about Edinburgh jazz, including Alastair Clark, John Gibson, Kenny Mathieson and Tony Troon, and the local newspapers, the Scotsman and Edinburgh Evening News. I also wish to acknowledge the help and encouragement that I received from Mike Hart, Founding Director of the Edinburgh International Jazz and Blues Festival. I wish to acknowledge the power of meticulous work put in by Norrie

Thomson in compiling the discography appendix. I must also mention Donald 'Chick' Murray, school pal and so often rhythm section comrade-in-arms, without whose prompting (ie nagging) I might never have got started.

This is not a critical account but is intended as an affectionate look at the story of traditional jazz in a City that bred so many fine jazz musicians and supported the music over so many decades. The book traces a chronological sequence from about 1920 until the first decade of the 21st Century. Throughout the book are profiles of many of the personalities who made Edinburgh traditional jazz what it was and is; the profiles are usually placed chronologically, either at the point where an individual first appeared on the jazz scene or when he or she made their greatest impact. The profiles vary greatly in length. This should not be taken as a measure of an individual's significance but merely as the product of how much information was available and the extent to which his story reflects a particular period. The sharp-eyed will undoubtedly spot a few anomalies and contradictions and, in an account that has relied on memories stretching back over many decades, who could wonder at that?

I have made no attempt to cover the development in Edinburgh of modern jazz, by which I mean jazz which stems from the harmonic and rhythmic advances of bebop and post-bebop jazz. Although I have included a number of jazz musicians who were able to play in both the traditional and more modern forms, I am simply not qualified, either by playing or listening experience, to do justice to the development of these important and more modern forms. It is my hope that someone else will write the story of Edinburgh modern jazz, perhaps as a companion to this volume.

Every effort has been made to identify and acknowledge copyright holders of material referred to or reproduced in this book, and I apologise for any omissions. To my regret, all efforts to trace the current holders of copyright in respect of two books by James Lincoln Collier, 'The Making of Jazz' and 'Louis Armstrong – a biography', have been unsuccessful. In addition, it has also proved impossible to trace the current copyright holders of Sinclair Traill's book

'Concerning Jazz', published in 1957 by Faber and Faber. A number of the photographs date from many years ago and, in many cases, the identity of the photographer has long been forgotten. Never-the-less, the efforts of these photographers in ensuring that the Edinburgh jazz scene of their time was put on the record is acknowledged and I apologise for the lack of individual acknowledgement.

I also wish to acknowledge the support and forbearance of my wife, Liz, and the rest of my family who, for over two years, became accustomed to my normal (or perhaps I should say usual) behaviour being replaced by a sort of mental and physical limbo, while I researched and struggled to write this account.

To all of these I am grateful for their patience, kindness, interest and support. So many people told me that the story of Edinburgh traditional jazz had to be written sometime. I hope I have done it justice.

Graham Blamire, December 2011.

Foreword by Mike Hart MBE

Founding Director, Edinburgh International Jazz and Blues Festival

There can be no doubt that the story of Edinburgh traditional jazz deserved to be written down. The City has had a long link with the music which, although it began as a purely American phenomenon, has become, over the last hundred years or so, perhaps the most significant musical development of the 20th century. Jazz now straddles the whole world but, like any worthwhile art form, continues to operate at all levels: from international to local, from amateur to professional, from high art to playing for personal pleasure, from the great concert halls to the local pub. Edinburgh traditional jazz has all of these and a jazz history that has now lasted for almost a hundred years. It is that story that this book is all about. It traces the major developments, the notable events, the memorable bands and, most of all, the personalities that made the story. It is sometimes assumed that jazz in Edinburgh began in the 1940s. However, this is not so and it is interesting and surprising to be able to read something of the Edinburgh jazz world of the 1920s and 30s. That this early period is covered is one indication of just how much work has gone into the writing of this book.

There have been, of course, a number of well-known high points in the history of Edinburgh traditional jazz. These include the pioneering days of the 1940s and early 1950s, which produced an astonishing number of fine players, such as Sandy Brown, Al Fairweather, Stan Greig, Archie Semple and Alex Welsh, who were to make their mark in both UK and world terms. There was also the spell during the 1980s, when the Edinburgh International Jazz Festival was graced by the presence of some of the legends of middle period jazz, including players of the stature of Harry 'Sweets' Edison, Buddy Tate, Teddy Wilson, Jay McShann, George Chisholm, Earle Warren, Dick Hyman, Al Grey, Milt Hinton and Doc Cheatham.

However, this book is about much more than the great names and great times. Notable as these were, it is good to have the emphasis on the jazz musicians and bands which made the jazz scene of Edinburgh surely one of the most active and buoyant in the UK, if not in the whole of Europe. Jazz is a music that demands character in both the music itself and the people who play it and Edinburgh jazz has had plenty of both. Who could forget the drive and excitement of the playing of Tello (Ian Telford), Dave Paxton, Jim Petrie or John McGuff? What about the sheer musicality of Alex Shaw's piano playing? Or the rumbustious humour and energy of Charlie McNair? Or, for that matter, the commitment and dedication of those, including all the above, who played jazz in their chosen style, because they believed it to be a music of great worth, with a tradition that should be kept alive?

Edinburgh has been fortunate in having so many jazz musicians, so many jazz bands and so much jazz. However, none of it would have meant much without the support it received from the public and it is good to see that this book is dedicated to the jazz followers. I said that the story of Edinburgh traditional jazz deserved to be written down. Now it has been and Graham Blamire has done the Edinburgh jazz world a service. I wish the book well.

Mike Hart, Edinburgh, December 2011

Contents

Chapter I

Prelude to a Tidal Wave

This book is primarily concerned with the story of traditional jazz in Edinburgh since the mid-nineteen forties; that is, traditional jazz played in and around Edinburgh by local jazz musicians and bands. It is not much concerned with jazz played in and around Edinburgh by visiting bands, professional or otherwise, except in passing and when such bands have had a marked effect on local jazz, this being especially the case in the early years. Similarly, the significant number of local jazz musicians who went on to become distinguished or even famous professional players at a UK or international level, will primarily be discussed in respect of their careers when playing in Edinburgh in local bands, rather than their contributions in a wider and better known context. In some cases, the wider reputations will be covered more than adequately in more resounding publications than this.

Jazz, as a recognisable form of music, appears to have emerged in the USA sometime during the last decade of the 19th century and the first decade of the 20th century. Over the years since, the music, in the first place a product of many cultures, developed in a number of ways and in a number of places. The result was that different styles of jazz became recognisable. These included, for example, the classic New Orleans styles of the 1920s as played by Joe 'King' Oliver, Louis Armstrong, Sydney Bechet and Jelly Roll Morton, although not necessarily played exclusively in New Orleans. There was a style that developed in Kansas City

1

and was typified by the bands of Benny Moten and later, Count Basie. In Harlem, jazz was played by stride piano players such as James P Johnston, Willie 'The Lion' Smith and Fats Waller and the band of Duke Ellington in the 1920s and 1930s. A group of white youngsters in Chicago, inspired by the great black bands and a white trumpet player called Bix Beiderbecke, founded what came to be known as Chicago jazz. Another predominately white style, which came to be called Swing in the mid-1930s and early 1940s, was exemplified by the music of Benny Goodman, Tommy Dorsey, Artie Shaw and their big bands. By then, jazz had spread to many countries, particularly to France and the UK, and had become recognised as an artistic phenomenon which was to be the major influence in 20th century popular music.

Of course, jazz in the early days (or 'jass' as it was apparently then spelt) had not been welcomed with open arms by everybody. It was a new and, to many, an alarmingly aggressive sound. In addition, it was no longer safely obscure but, because of the new-fangled radio and phonograph machines, suddenly in everybody's ears. Established standards of music and taste were being challenged and swept aside; musical mayhem and anarchy had arrived. Even in New Orleans, its apparent birthplace, it was hardly surprising that a music that had close associations with the Red Light district was going to upset the city fathers. Jim Godbolt, the jazz writer and historian, in his book 'The World of Jazz - in printed ephemera and collectibles'[1], reports that a 1918 edition of the New Orleans 'Times-Picayune' referred to jazz as a *'form of musical vice'* and said *'Its musical value is nil, and its possibilities of harm are great'*. Jim also adds that, as early as 1921, the Ladies Home Journal posed the question *'Does jazz put the sin in syncopation?'* and reports that *'...children of all ages, removed the 'J' from posters'* when bands were advertised as 'jass bands'. There are other accounts of such unflattering terms as 'unspeakable jazz' and 'filthy jazz', which, in all probability, simply acted as a major motivator towards jazz

---

[1] Godbolt J,, 'The World of Jazz in Printed Ephemera and Collectibles', Studio Editions Ltd, 1990, by permission of Jim Godbolt

for the rebellious youth of the time. However, these Blimpish reactions were hardly a new phenomenon in society and were to be repeated at intervals throughout the history of 20th Century music even, perhaps more surprisingly, within jazz itself, whenever the more radical developments took place.

Sometime around the late 1930s or early 1940s, there began two dramatic and opposite developments, one looking forward to the future and one looking back to the past. These were firstly, the advent of new concepts of rhythm and harmony which led to the development of bebop and the later variations of modern jazz. Secondly, there arose what the distinguished American musicologist and critic, James Lincoln Collier, called '*a tidal wave of traditional jazz*'[2] – a world-wide movement back towards earlier forms of jazz and a rejection of Swing and the modern developments of bebop. This 'tidal wave' came to be called the Revival. It is principally what took place in Edinburgh in the wake of the Revival, from the mid-1940s on, with which this book is concerned. However, before exploring that, what had been Edinburgh's jazz history up to that point?

It seems perfectly clear that there was jazz activity in Edinburgh before the mid-1940s, although not a great deal is known about it. At the time of writing in 2011, it seems unlikely that there are many people alive who will remember much about those now distant days. There are however, a few sources of information.

In particular, there was one jazz musician who was active in Edinburgh in the 1950s and who, as a professional journalist, occasionally produced articles about jazz. One or two of these give a brief account of the pre-war period. He was the late George Crockett, a drummer who played in Edinburgh in the 1940s and 50s and who later moved to work and live in the west of Scotland. Much of the information in this chapter is taken from his published work. Although George had left Edinburgh by the time I

---

[2] Collier J L, 'The Making of Jazz – a Comprehensive History' Granada Publishing 1978. Every effort has been made to trace the current holder of copyright for this work but without success.

was making my way into the Edinburgh jazz scene in about 1959, I met him several times and played in a band with him on at least one occasion. In particular, I remember meeting him in 1988 when he turned up at a gig at which I played with Bill Salmond's Louisiana Ragtime Band in the Harbour Arts Centre in Irvine, on the Ayrshire coast. George did not play on that occasion but, in his capacity as a journalist, he wrote a review of the gig in a local paper. It seemed to me that he was a jazz enthusiast whose interest extended beyond listening and playing into the historical and sociological background of the music.

According to George in an article[3] published in the Edinburgh Weekly in 1966, there had been an interest in jazz in Edinburgh since the end of the Great War in 1918. With the possible exception of the days of the so-called 'trad boom' in the early 1960s, jazz generally has been a minority interest since the World War II. However, George considered that the time when jazz enjoyed its greatest local popularity was as a new and novel form of dance in the early 1920s. He says that the first person to bring jazz to Edinburgh was a piano player called **Symon Stungo**. Stungo formed a five-piece band inspired by the Original Dixieland Jazz Band (ODJB), the white American band which had an enormous impact when they came from the USA to take London by storm at the Hammersmith Palais in 1919. Stungo's band, like the ODJB, had trumpet, clarinet, trombone, piano and drums. It is not clear from George's writing where the Stungo band was based and they may have come from elsewhere to play in Edinburgh. It appears that the band was called **Symon Stungo and his Jazz-maniacs** and George speculates that Edinburgh must have taken to jazz much as London had taken to the ODJB.

Reports of the time tell us that the ODJB had come as something of a shock to polite London society of 1919. They had opened at Albert de Courville's 'Joy Bells' at the Hippodrome but these self styled 'musical anarchists' did

---

[3] Crockett G, Edinburgh Weekly, 22 December 1966, 'From the Twenties to the Sixties – All That Jazz in Edinburgh'. All efforts to trace the copyright holder of this article have failed but the author wishes to acknowledge the valuable record that this article represents. Information used by kind permission of Eileen Mack, closest living relative of George Crockett.

not last long there.   The comedian George Robey was apparently on the bill and it was at his instigation that the ODJB were hastily removed from the programme.   Robey, who is said to have regarded them as an abomination, seems just as likely to have been highly miffed at being upstaged by these brash newcomers.   Whatever, the ODJB went on to a very successful nine month run at the Hammersmith Palais and twentieth century music was never to be the same again.   I have no doubt that the impact of Stungo's outfit on staid Edinburgh society would be similar - the punk rockers of their day, upsetting those you would expect and delighting the returning survivors of the war who would, no doubt, take all the cathartic, social amusement they could get, after the tensions and repressions of 'the war to end all wars'.   The so-called Jazz Age of the 1920s had begun, even in staid old Edinburgh. George Crockett goes on to tell us that, in Edinburgh, a friend of Stungo's converted an old drill-hall into the Wemyss Ballroom, where he intended to feature jazz.   This was apparently at a time when other Edinburgh dance halls still had notices instructing that there was *'No jazzing allowed'*, no doubt to the relief of local George Robeys and stately Edinburgh matrons with their knickers in a twist.

Stungo had been asked by this friend to bring his band to play in Edinburgh.   This suggests that he was based elsewhere but it does sound fairly likely that they were a Scottish band and, indeed, it seems that Stungo may well have run more than one band.   Apparently, the popularity of the Stungo band or bands was not confined to Edinburgh and George Crockett says that they *'...opened the Tay Street Palais in Dundee and the Aberdeen Music Hall dances'.* They also played at the Bobby Jones Ballroom in Ayr.   In Edinburgh, Stungo had bands at the North British Hotel (now the New Balmoral but still the NB), the Oak Room Cafe in the New Picture House (apparently where Marks and Spencers shop was situated in Princes Street in 1966) and at the Havana night club, which by 1966 had become the Pibroch Restaurant.   These venues, particularly the North British Hotel, were prestigious places and it seems reasonable to assume that Stungo ran bands of some quality and reputation.   Al Stewart, an Edinburgh dance band and jazz musician who was playing in Edinburgh in the 1920s and still active in the 1990s, gives a slightly different account. Al, in an article published in an Edinburgh jazz magazine, The Scottish Jazz News, in the early 1990s, says *'The first jazz band imported from London in 1926 was Symon Stungo's Jazz Maniacs which contained Nick Ivanoff* (an Edinburgh musician). *They played in the Marine Gardens for wages of, believe it or not, £25 a week each. I'll leave you to work out what that would be at today's values'*[4].

Apparently, it was from the Havana Club that Stungo's band was included in a list of bands for some early broadcasting which George Crockett says presented *'...a form of jazz or let's settle for jazz-oriented dance music'*. Stungo managed to attract show business stars from the old Empire Theatre or the King's Theatre to drop in at the club after their shows, when he gave them a champagne supper and would persuade them to do a spot. Some, at least, appear to have been jazz musicians as, on one occasion, Symon Stungo persuaded Coleman Hawkins, the great American tenor sax player, to visit the club. George estimates that this must have been in the early 1930s, when Hawkins was touring Britain with the Jack Hylton band. Thanks to the work of Jim Keppie and the Edinburgh Jazz Archive Group, we know that Symon Stungo had attended the Royal High School of Edinburgh. This was the school which was later to gain considerable renown in the jazz world as the producer of an almost incredible number of jazz musicians, some of them of international stature. In particular, the 1940s and 1950s would see the school produce so many jazz musicians that they became known collectively as the 'Royal High School Gang', of whom we will hear a great deal more later in this book. Jim Keppie, himself a former pupil of the school, also tells us that Symon Stungo, in his eighties at the time, played ragtime piano at a concert at the Old Royal High School on 30th November 1974, accompanied by two rather younger alumni of his old school, Dizzy Jackson (bs) and John

---

[4] Stewart A, Scottish Jazz News, Volume 2, issue 5 , July/August 1990

Nicholson (drms)[5]. It looks as if Symon Stungo was the very first of the Royal High School jazz musicians that we know about, the first of what was to be a long and distinguished line.

George Crockett goes on to comment that the depression years of the early thirties *'put jazz in the doldrums'*. However, when the Swing craze swept the USA in the mid to late 1930s, *'Britain was unmoved in the mass but collectors of jazz recordings were multiplying and most large cities had rhythm clubs'*. George had access to some copies from 1935 of a magazine called Swing Music which, even when he was writing in 1966, was long defunct. These magazines carried reports from the rhythm clubs and, although there were such clubs in Glasgow and a thriving one in Dundee, there was no mention of a rhythm club in Edinburgh at that time. George's own introduction to live jazz, rather than on gramophone records or the meagre ration provided by BBC radio, was when he heard the great Fats Waller in early 1939, at the old Empire Theatre. Fats shared the bill with a programme of variety troupers including comedians and acrobats. George reports that the theatre was half empty and that two elderly ladies sitting near him read out *'Fats Waller, rhythm pianist'* in the programme and wondered *'Who's he?* When Fats made his appearance, he apparently made little impression on the elderly ladies but certainly impressed George.

Fats Waller was, of course, already a legend in jazz by that time and was renowned for working hard, living hard and playing hard. Fats' manager at the time, Ed Kirby, recalled an incident during this 1939 visit to Edinburgh when, after his show was over, Fats paid a visit to the Havana Club, where he consumed a generous quantity of his favourite brand of gin. Ed and Fats had later left the club in the 'wee sma' hours', got into a taxi and headed for wherever they were staying. As the taxi was heading up the Mound, a steep and winding street leading off Princes Street, Fats somehow contrived to fall out of the taxi. Ed Kirby is reported as saying *'I shouted to the taxi driver to*

---

[5] Later known as the actor, John McGlynn

stop the damn cab. I was glad to see Fats pick himself up and catch up with the cab as if nothing had happened.'

Also early in 1939, Coleman Hawkins made another visit to Edinburgh, this time on a private tour sponsored by the Selmer saxophone company, and a private show for the local trade took place at the Kintore Rooms. George comments that he considered this to be *'more like it'* and that Hawkins blew in front of a local rhythm section which, he reports, *'acquitted themselves very well'*. As far as he was able to recall, the rhythm section included Bill Stark, who was later to play with the Vic Lewis band, on bass, Eddie Canelli on guitar, George Buchanan on piano and a *'very fine Edinburgh drummer'* called Jackie McHardie. Jackie McHardie was later to pursue his musical career in the south and George reports that, in about 1965, he was playing with George Chisholm's Jazzers in the Black and White Minstrel Show (how non-PC can you get?) at London's Victoria Palace Theatre. Apparently there was a *'hip audience'* present for the show at the Kintore Rooms and this inspired Hawkins to an excellent performance. George Crockett commented that he was always glad to have heard this performance, because Coleman Hawkins was at the peak of his creative ability during this period.

Another journalistic source of information about the 1930s is an article written by the Scotsman newspaper jazz writer and critic Tony Troon, in the programme notes for the Edinburgh International Jazz Festival in 1986. In this article, Tony reports that *'Edinburgh has a strong jazz and dance-band tradition and in the thirties supported no fewer than 36 dance halls. Visiting American musicians, like Fats Waller, Coleman Hawkins and Benny Carter, played one-night stands here during that decade'*[6].

Al Stewart, whom we have already met, was born in about 1909. We know this because he wrote to the local 'Scottish Jazz News' in January 1990, to thank everyone who had helped make his surprise eightieth birthday party, at the Blue Lagoon pub, such a success. Al played both double bass and alto saxophone and was still active as a

---

[6] Troon A, 'The Second Chorus Factor', McEwen's Edinburgh International Jazz Festival programme, 1986

regular 'sitter in' on the Edinburgh jazz scene in the 1990s. He also contributed three brief articles to the Scottish Jazz News[7], recording his memories of jazz and dance music in pre-WWII Edinburgh. By the mid-1920s, Al was already on the road to becoming an active musician and, when he was around fifteen years old, he had already tried *'putting some beat'* into tunes like 'Alexanders', 'Who's Sorry Now?' and 'Dinah' on his mouth organ. While at Boroughmuir High School, he had received a few lessons on double bass, which he said was *'very rare in those days'*, presumably meaning the lessons rather than the double bass. Sometime during the next couple of years, he managed to buy a clarinet for 7/6d (about 35 pence in today's money) and started to play at socials and Boys Brigade dances the next week. He also tells us that music had started to change around that time, with bands like the Harlem Foot Warmers, 'Henderson', 'Lunceford' and 'Armstrong' heralding what was to become 'swing music', and adds that *'...jazz as we know it today really took off'*. In Edinburgh, Al reports, the people responsible were *'...Frankie Smith (trumpet), Nick Ivanoff (tenor sax), Bill Landles (alto sax) and at least half a dozen more, really good jazz men'*. He adds that probably the best of them all was Jimmy Miller (violin) who was *'as good as Venuti'* (Joe Venuti, the great American jazz violinist) and suggests that George Chisholm would verify this, having played a few gigs with Miller in Edinburgh in the early 1930s. The piano and accordion wizard was apparently Chrissie Colette and the guitar ace was Eddie Canale. Al goes on tell us that the place to be was the New Dunedin, which was half way down the steps off the Lawnmarket. After the war, this venue became known as the Anchor Palais and was owned by Billy Fawcet. Fawcet was a bass player for whom Al sometimes deputised ('depped' in jazz parlance), as he could not play and run the ballroom at the same time. Others whom Al remembers as having played at this venue were Derick McLean (alto), Bobby Stewart senior (drums), Archie McLean, brother of Derick (piano), Jimmy Miller (violin), Eddie Canale (guitar), Bobby Jack (sax), Allan Thompson (sax) and a trumpet

---

[7] Stewart A, Scottish Jazz News, Volume 2 issues 5 and 7, Volume 3 issue 3, 1990

player whose name Al could not recall. Apparently, everyone in town who could play jazz went along to this place to sit in, including Chrissie Colette (piano), Chick Knox (trumpet), Alfie Bell (drums), Tom, Reg and Jack Rutherford who were all drummers, Al Wilson (piano), Nick Ivanoff (ten sax), Bill Landles (alto sax), Bertie Roy (alto sax) and many others.

Another venue of the time was the Star Cafe, which was at the bottom of Easter Road *'in one of the tunnels on the left'*. Al remembers that, in the early days, the bandstand at this place was high up on the wall, with an old tram spiral stair to climb up! Later, the bandstand was shifted to the floor, as the previous arrangement had only been safe for piano, drums and four musicians, although Al recalls *'...seeing eight up there and, Dagostino, who was the owner couldn't do much about it. On a bottle of whisky a day, he couldn't see that far'!* The personnel at the Star Cafe were Nick Ivanoff (tenor-fiddle, leader), Alfie Bell (drums), Al Weston (piano) and Al Stewart himself on bass and alto sax. Many other musicians also played there, including Angus Mailland and Chick Know (trumpets), someone called 'Melville' instrument unknown, Chrissie Colette (piano and accordion), Bill Landles, Bertie Roy, Andy 'Choo' Richardson and Jock Wright (reeds). Al Stewart finished his 1990 memoir by saying *'All these people, and many more, beyond my memory now, played a lot of jazz there in the early thirties'*.

As already stated, by the 1940s, jazz had already developed a number of quite recognisable styles, not surprising in a music that had, by then, had the best part of half a century in which to develop. The jazz history books tell us that it was the re-discovery of a number of almost forgotten New Orleans based veterans that sparked off the Revival. However, as time was to demonstrate, the Revival would itself both reflect and, to some extent at least, replicate some of the stylistic changes that had appeared in the first forty to fifty years of jazz history. Of course, the question arises as to what style (or styles) of jazz was to appear in Edinburgh in the mid 1940s, when the Revival, James Lincoln Collier's *'tidal wave of traditional jazz'*, first arrived in town. That and what followed it, is what the rest of this book will be about.

Another question that is worth asking is what was the attitude to jazz at the time of the Revival? In art, there is often a tension between a very earnest, 'art for art's sake' approach on the one hand and a populist, usually more commercially slanted, showmanship on the other, with all degrees in between. Jazz was and is certainly no different. A glance at jazz writings around the time of the Revival, such as those of Rudi Blesh in the USA and Rex Harris in the UK, will quickly demonstrate that it was a time of earnest research and romantic, nostalgic reflection.

Further information about Edinburgh jazz at that time comes from the recollections of the redoubtable Jackie MacFarlane, a remarkable and resilient character who had a career in the City Cleansing Department and had fought in the Spanish Civil War. Jackie was around the Edinburgh jazz scene and sang with many bands in Edinburgh, from the 1940s through to his death in 1993. Happily for us, Jackie recorded many of his memories when he was interviewed for a feature in the programme of the 1980 Edinburgh International Jazz Festival[8]. It appears that he had kept a *'voluminous scrapbook'* about his jazz experiences in Edinburgh and, with the help of this, was able to recall events back to *'about 1940 when he went to see Fats Waller in the Empire Theatre'*. It seems likely that this was, in fact, the visit of Fats Waller in 1939, as described above in George Crockett's recollections. Jackie remembered an advertisement for the Edinburgh Rhythm Club, which was to meet in the studios at Methven Simpson's music shop in Princes Street. As this was after Jackie returned from war time service in the forces, it was probably around the middle 1940s. At this club, he met a young man called David Mylne, later to become a noted collector of and authority on recorded jazz, especially the work of Sydney Bechet. The meetings of the Edinburgh Rhythm Club, according to Jackie, were at first sessions which featured only recordings of jazz, which contrasts with

---

[8] The Edinburgh International Jazz Festival 1980 programme, page 23 'Jackie looks back'

George Crockett's account above. He goes on to say that live jazz first appeared after the war, at the YWCA in Reigo Street and that this involved such names as Sandy Brown, Al Fairweather, Stan Grieg and Archie Semple. Jackie, who was a life-long teetotaller, reports sardonically that tea and lemonade were served and that *'the really bad boys had to go across the road to the pub for stronger stuff'*. As the next few decades were to demonstrate more than adequately, Jackie's *'really bad boys'* must have rapidly achieved a dominant role, which was soon to establish the pub as the natural habitat of local jazz activity.

Yet another good source of information about the late 1940s and early 1950s is George Hewitt, one of the remarkably large group of Royal High School of Edinburgh pupils, who were at the heart of the traditional jazz Revival in Edinburgh. George Hewitt, a trombone player is, at the time of writing in 2011, still playing and putting on a monthly jazz concert in the Harbour Arts Centre in Irvine, Ayrshire. George, in a memoire written in 2008, like George Crockett and Jackie MacFarlane, gives information about the Edinburgh Rhythm Club in which he says:

"According to Stu Eaton (and who would want to disagree with him?), the Edinburgh Rhythm Club had its first meetings in the mid-1940s in a room above Methven Simpson's in Princes Street (SBSoc, NL, 58)[9]. The next location seems to have been at 20 Hill Street (SBSoc, NL,117&118). Thereafter there were the David Mylne sessions, already described (see later), followed, it would appear, by a similar set up at the Lidop Hotel at Douglas Crescent (SBSoc, NL, 135). By 1952-53 the Crown Bar known as the 'Stud Club' in Lothian Street, was one jazz centre while another was the India Buildings in Victoria Street where Dave Milne operated on Sundays. I can recall playing there at least a couple of times in 1955-56 with the Eagle Jazzmen – I think that great character and ubiquitous figure Jackie MacFarlane insisted on singing with us – but other 'survivors' e.g. Dizzy Jackson and Mike Hart are much better sources for both these venues than myself."

John Latham, who was to be instrumental in establishing the Sandy Brown Society (SBS) in 1996, told

---

[9] Sandy Brown Society (SBS), Newsletter 58

me that he seems to remember Stuart Crockett[10] saying that the room used by the Rhythm Club in 20 Hill Street was also used by Orkney and Shetland islanders as a social club.

Jackie MacFarlane also says that in 1950, the Archie Semple Band was formed and played regularly at monthly Jazz Band Balls in the Oddfellows Hall in Forrest Road. Jackie was what he called a *'purveyor of peace'* or bouncer at these events. On occasions he shared this task with an ex-art college male model called 'Big Tam' Connery, later to achieve world-wide fame as the film actor Sean Connery. The next venue for live jazz was the Escom Jazz Club, named by Archie Semple after a well known building in Johannnesburgh (why is not recorded), and located in the Tolbooth Hall in the High Street. Jackie reports that, during these years, there was a Musician's Union ban on foreign bands and it was the early 1950s before the first of the touring bands appeared in the form of Graeme Bell's Australian Jazz Band. This was an event which took place in the West End Cafe in Shandwick Place, near the west end of Princes Street. Another band to appear was Mick Mulligan's Magnolia Jazz Band, with a very young singer called George Melly. Freddie Randall, the 'Deb's Delight', and his band regularly appeared alongside the Sandy Brown Band, as did Joe Daniels and his Hot Shots, with whom Jackie made several guest appearances. Jackie also recalled a period when the Edinburgh Jazz Club had difficulty finding premises, having been thrown out of one venue after another (see also Chapter VII). At one point, the only home available to them was the basement of a pet shop in London Road where they were surrounded by the pet shop stock including flying foxes, snakes, rabbits and budgies. The banjo and guitar player, Mike Hart, also recalled playing there while being watched by a large flying fox, a type of bat, hanging upside down from a nearby shelf.

The MacFarlane scrapbook is said to have included some *'rather embarrassing photos'* said to have shown a fifteen year old Mike Hart (later founder and Director of the Edinburgh International Jazz Festival) *'playing drums with*

---

[10] See chapter IV

Sandy Brown, Charlie McNair, Dizzy Jackson et al on a tram returning from a gig in Musselburgh'.

Apparently the drums kept rolling off the driver's platform onto the road and the tram had to be stopped about three times, much to the annoyance of the 'clippie'.

The Oddfellows Hall in 2010 – scene of many an early Jazz Band Ball (photograph by the author)

It is unclear whether the above implies that the various musicians were actually playing jazz on the tram or simply travelling on it with their instruments but it would not surprise me if they had been playing. Concerts around that time in the Usher Hall featured big names such as Billy Eckstine, Frankie Laine, Big Bill Broonzy, Josh White and Sarah Vaughan and it was Jackie's habit to go back stage to meet the stars. On the dance band side, The Palais de Dance featured bands such as those of Harry Roy, Bert

Ambrose, Lew Stone and *'the excellent resident band led by Basil Kirchin'*.

It seems clear from the memories referred to above that, although there had been some interest in jazz before that time, there was a major increase in jazz activity in the years just following the second World War. By the mid-1940s local interest in jazz and, more significantly, interest in playing jazz, was really on the move and accelerating, but would it last and would it lead to anything? As it turned out, James Lincoln Collier's *'tidal wave of traditional jazz'*, the Revival, had unleashed a flood tide in Edinburgh. The result was to be a burgeoning local traditional jazz scene, which would produce many fine jazz musicians and bands and, as it happens, quite a bit of mayhem and general falling about as well, very much in the tradition already established by Fats Waller. Traditional jazz in Edinburgh was to continue to flourish for many decades to come.

Chapter II

The Revival

Edinburgh, in the latter half of the twentieth century, was to gain a well-deserved reputation as a major centre of traditional jazz. The world-wide renewal of interest in earlier forms of jazz that arose in the 1940s, which came to be known as the **Revival**, had a particularly notable impact in Edinburgh. This resulted in, not only a lively and active coterie of local, amateur jazz players, but the emergence of a number of musicians who went on to make a career in jazz, some with reputations at an international level. Local traditional jazz was to thrive and continue for many decades (as did more modern forms of jazz) and was to receive added impetus from a second (and more populist) resurgence of interest in the early 1960s, the so-called 'Trad Boom'. Yet another boost came with the creation, in the late 1970s, of the Edinburgh International Jazz Festival. The foundations for what was to come later were laid down by a remarkable group of local jazz musicians, together with their followers and supporters, that arose in the late 1940s and early 1950s.

At the heart of this group were a surprisingly large number of individuals who were pupils at the City's Royal High School. Jazz history already had its Austin High School Gang, a group of enthusiastic youngsters with an interest in jazz in 1920s Chicago, which included Bud Freeman (ten), Jim Lannigan (bs), Jimmy McPartland (tpt), Dick McPartland (bjo), Frank Teschemacher (clt) and others. They all attended the Austin High School, most of them

16

started in music on the violin before switching to something more suited to jazz and several of them became notable jazz musicians. The precedent was there in the jazz books and it was natural that the Edinburgh group became known as the **Royal High School Gang**. Two prominent individuals in the Royal High School Gang were an aspiring clarinet player called Sandy Brown and a trombone player, later to switch to trumpet, Al Fairweather.

The members of the Royal High School Gang were not the only ones involved however, and there was another, equally significant group, not associated with any one school, which was just as active. They were grouped around a pair of brothers who played clarinet and trumpet, Archie and John Semple respectively, and a trumpet player called Alex Welsh. Both groups were engaged in playing traditional jazz but, from accounts of the time, it appears that even then, they were reckoned to play different forms of the music.

The singer and writer, George Melly, in his vastly entertaining autobiographical book 'Owning Up'[11], makes a clear distinction between two separate forms of jazz which emerged at the time of the Revival, both of which he says claimed the name **New Orleans Jazz**. Melly allocates separate names to each, in the interests of clarity. The renewal of interest in early jazz as played by the top New Orleans professional musicians, such as Louis Armstrong, Jelly Roll Morton and Joe 'King' Oliver, although in fact mostly played and recorded in Chicago and elsewhere, he calls **revivalist jazz**. The other form, based on the music of rediscovered veterans such as Bunk Johnson and George Lewis who had, for the most part, remained in New Orleans, he calls **traditional jazz**. I can understand Melly's reasoning on this but, for me, his terms are unsatisfactory, mainly because <u>both</u> forms arose from the Revival and it is therefore confusing to call one of them 'revivalist jazz'. For myself and for greater clarity, I would prefer to replace Melly's terms with classic jazz and fundamentalist jazz respectively. However, although I consider 'fundamentalist'

---

[11] 'Owning Up' by George Melly (Copyright © George Melly, 1965) Reprinted by permission of A. M. Heath and Co ltd

to be the term that best expresses the 'back to the source' principle of this kind of jazz, the term does seem to carry a politically negative flavour nowadays. As I do not wish to use the term in this negative way, I am going to use instead 'purist jazz', a term that was in common usage for this type of jazz in the 1950/60s, reflecting the desire to play the music in its pure form, unsullied by commercialism. I will therefore use the terms **classic jazz** (deriving from Armstrong, Oliver, Morton et al) and **purist jazz** (deriving from Johnson, Lewis et al), when referring to the two forms of New Orleans jazz that emerged within the Revival.

As we will see later, as time went on, the purist style won the battle of names and claimed the term **New Orleans jazz** for itself. This came about, I believe, because so much post-Revival jazz in the UK followed the purist style, rather than the classic style, and this trend was apparent even by the late 1950s and early 1960s. This is reinforced by the excellent Phillip Larkin who, writing in 1962, gave the credit to Ken Colyer, saying *'That British traditional jazz turned from the Armstrong-Oliver pattern to that offered by George Lewis and the modern New Orleans bands was largely the work of Ken Colyer, who visited the Crescent City as a seaman and brought back the inspiration that is the foundation of Barber and Bilk today'*[12]. At the time of writing in 2010, I believe that it is this purist style that is in the best health of any of the traditional forms. There are still hundreds of bands across the UK and on the Continent playing in this style and there are whole jazz festivals devoted to presenting it.

In addition, I will use the term **traditional jazz** to mean all jazz music, including Swing and other big band jazz, that sprang from the older harmonic and rhythmic tradition that pre-dated the advent of the new harmonic and rhythmic directions of bebop in the 1940s, the greatest and most dramatic change of direction in jazz history. Of course, Edinburgh had its bebop developments too but this seems to me to have had a separate life of its own. For this reason, plus the fact that I am by no means qualified to do so, this book will not attempt to cover Edinburgh's bebop

---

[12] Larkin P, 'All What Jazz?', pages 55-56, published by Faber and Faber, 1970

and other modern jazz developments. When required, I will use the collective term **modern jazz** to cover all of bebop and the post-bebop jazz developments.

Inevitably, the term **contemporary jazz** will crop up but it is a term fraught with peril. I remember Humphrey Lyttelton once, on his radio show 'The Best of Jazz', saying that he had received a letter criticising him for the lack of contemporary jazz in his weekly selections of recordings. Humph then announced that the next record would put that right. The next record turned out to be by the Ken Colyer Band playing, as always, jazz of an uncompromising purist variety. After the record had finished, Humph pointed out that it had been recorded just three weeks previously and '...*you can't get much more contemporary than that*!'

Happily, the George Crockett article from 1966, referred to in the last chapter, also gives a little information about the Edinburgh jazz scene during the 1939-1945 war years and just after. It seems that, in contrast to the situation in 1935, there was a thriving Rhythm Club in Edinburgh during the war years. In the nature of things at that troubled time, both the members and the players involved were mostly itinerant and it was apparently 1945 and the end of the war, before the local jazz scene assumed a more settled state. George Crockett reports that the Rhythm Club did not just function on a diet of recorded jazz but also featured a live band. He describes the band as '*enthusiastic amateurs playing the traddiest of trad*' and recalls that there was one individual who played the tuba until the mouth piece went missing! This band contained some local jazz talent which would make a substantial mark in a wider context in the not so distant future. Beyond '*traddiest of trad*' George Crockett does not give any further information about the style of this band. However, George Melly writes of visits to Edinburgh in the early 1950s and says that the Edinburgh jazz scene was divided into two separate cliques. Describing one of these, he goes on: '*There were the purists led by a clarinet player called Sandy Brown and a trumpet player called Al Fairweather. They played at that time Ken Colyer music at its most uncompromising and they listened to our* (ie The Mick Mulligan Band's) *brand of Dixieland with*

19

glowering disapproval'. Ken Colyer was, of course, the English trumpeter who remained faithful, throughout his entire career, to the early traditions of New Orleans jazz, that is, purist jazz. In many ways, he was one of the prime movers in the surge of traditional jazz that developed in the UK in the 1940s, 50s and 60s. Melly even goes so far as to say that Ken Colyer *'...invented British traditional jazz',* which may sound like an exaggeration but seems to me, at least in terms of purist jazz, to be not all that far from the truth.

Melly's view that Brown and Fairweather *'...played Ken Colyer music at its most uncompromising'* I find hard to believe. It may be that Al and Sandy did start off playing music inspired by the rediscovered veterans but the evidencc seems to me to make that very unlikely. I played a few of times with Sandy, with Al on a greater number of occasions and I have listened to their recordings throughout most of my life. In my experience, most jazz musicians retain in their playing at least a little of their original inspiration. I was never aware of the slightest discernable George Lewis influence in Sandy's playing and heard not the remotest trace of a Bunk Johnson sound in Al's. Jim Godbolt, who acted as agent for Sandy and Al in the 1950s, and who therefore should have known what he was talking about, wrote *'Clarinettist Sandy Brown and trumpeter Al Fairweather first played together in Edinburgh, their band based entirely on the classic Louis Armstrong Hot Five and Hot Seven records'*[13]. Brian Lemmon, who played piano with Sandy for many years, said of him *'To me the only obvious influence was Johnny Dodds, in sound and phrasing.'* Stu Eaton, an Edinburgh trumpet player and early associate of both Sandy and Al, says *'The early standards were Dodds for Sandy and Louis for Al'*[14]. Further evidence comes from Sandy Currie who was one of the Royal High School Gang. He says, on the sleeves notes to a CD issued around 1998[15], that it was not until the time that this recording was made

---

[13] Godbolt J, 'All This and Many a Dog', page 75, Northway Publications revised edition 2007 and by permission of Jim Godbolt

[14] Eaton S, Sandy Brown Society Newsletter No 99, March 2005

[15] Sleeve note by Sandy Currie, 'Sandy Brown – The Historic Usher Hall Concert 1952', Lake Records LACD94

in 1952, that the purist revival was underway, with *'...people trying to play like the recently discovered and recorded Bunk Johnson, George Lewis and many others who had never left New Orleans.'* Currie goes on to say that Sandy Brown's band remained true to their original ideal of King Oliver's Creole Jazz Band and Louis Armstrong's Hot Five. All this seems to me to be spot on. Certainly, judging by the recordings of Sandy and Al, especially those made in the early 1950s, there can be no doubt that Sandy's early inspiration was Johnny Dodds, the clarinettist on most of Louis Armstrong's seminal 1920s 'Hot Five' and 'Hot Seven' recordings. Similarly, Al's playing clearly arises directly from early Louis Armstrong with perhaps a bit of Tommy Ladnier, who recorded with Sydney Bechet, in there as well.

All this evidence is in accord with the accounts of Dave Paxton, another great Edinburgh clarinettist, and a contemporary of Sandy and Al. I played with Dave for a number of years in the Edinburgh bands the New Society Syncopators and Bill Salmond's Louisiana Ragtime Band. Dave Paxton was closely associated with the Sandy and Al group in their early days and he was absolutely clear that both he and Sandy had their early roots in the playing of Dodds. Dave Paxton seemed to me to be little interested in the clarinet playing of George Lewis and, on several occasions, made it clear that he considered the influence of the purist school to have arrived considerably later than his own formative years in Edinburgh. In fact, he seemed to consider it primarily a 1950s influence in the UK and I remember him, on at least one occasion referring, without much warmth, to the British purist influence as *'That 1950s stuff'*. In addition, when Dave and I played with the Louisiana Ragtime Band in Holland in 1987, I brought home a review of the band from a local newspaper. I later had it translated and well remember Dave's indignant reaction when he discovered that he had been accredited with playing in the style of George Lewis, whom he certainly did not rate as highly as Johnny Dodds.

Regarding George Melly's comment, it seems to me to be much more likely that the *'glowering disapproval'* of the Brown band was directed at the performance of the

Mulligan band, rather than that they failed to play 'Ken Colyer music'.

The other, equally important, Edinburgh jazz grouping of the time, that centred around **Alex Welsh and the Semple brothers**, was clearly considered to play in a different style to that of the Brown/Fairweather crowd. Although George Melly says that *'The Brown-Fairweather axis and the Welsh-Semple clique hardly communicated'*, it is clear from early, locally made recordings, that there was in fact quite a bit of mixing between the two groups. Pete Davenport, a trumpet player later to form and lead a jazz band at the Edinburgh Art College, told me in 2010 that, although there was quite marked intolerance between advocates of the two styles, this was much more prevalent amongst the followers than amongst thc musicians themselves.

Melly says of the Welsh/Semple clique that they *'played Condon music'*, by which he means that they followed the path of the white Chicagoans around the guitar player Eddie Condon. Jim Young, a fine New Orleans style bass player who played a leading role in Edinburgh jazz from the mid-1950s, recognised this in conversation with me in 2010, but said that he considered that the Revival had quickly divided into three separate styles. Jim identified the three as classic jazz, purist jazz and the Chicagoan/Condon style of the Welsh/Semple groups. However, having thought hard about this, I feel that in fact there was basically a division into only two styles. The bands led by Eddie Condon (born 1905) had themselves followed in the footsteps of Oliver, Armstrong and the white cornet player Bix Beiderbecke (born 1903). They were barely a generation younger than Oliver (born 1885) and Morton (born 1890), not all that much younger than Armstrong himself (born 1900 or 1901), and their music pre-dated by many years the re-discovery of the New Orleans veterans. Their music seems to me to have derived directly from the classic jazz tradition and they were, therefore, themselves part of that tradition. Applying this theory to the Edinburgh jazz scene of the 1940s, it seems to me that, in spite of the clear differences between the Brown/Fairweather group and the Semple/Welsh group, they both belonged squarely within the classic jazz part of the Revival. I suppose, by the judgemental standards of the time, the Welsh/Semple clique were seen to be moving off down an off-shoot of the classic style and perhaps they were even considered to be compromising it.

As in the case of Sandy Brown and Al Fairweather, I certainly never detected the slightest trace of a purist influence in the playing of Alex Welsh, who seemed to me to have modelled his playing on that of Bix Beiderbecke and Wild Bill Davison. A lack of purist influence was also true of Archie Semple, whose playing reflected that of both Ed Hall and Pee Wee Russell, both frequent associates of the so-called Chicagoans. The recordings made years later, when Welsh and Semple had long-since moved to a London base, certainly confirm their Chicago style, with no trace of a purist influence. However, even in the early days, they were clearly off down a path that was different from that of Brown and Fairweather. It seems that, as early as the late 1940s, the classic jazz tradition of the Revival was already sub-dividing.

Further confirmation that the Edinburgh jazz of the late 1940s and early 1950s was inspired by classic jazz and not the purist school, comes from trombonist Mike Pollett who was active in Edinburgh jazz between 1951 and 1958, during which time he was a member of the Climax Jazz Band. I met with him in 2010 when working on this book and, with no prompting from me, Mike volunteered the information that he had belonged to '...the New Orleans school, as inspired by Bunk Johnston and George Lewis'. He also made a point of saying that the purist influence had not been felt in Edinburgh until the 1950s, the formation of the Climax Jazz Band being a result of this. Although Mike Pollett was clearly familiar with the music of Sandy Brown and Al Fairweather and Alex Welsh, he had not been part of the groups around them and was clear that his involvement in Edinburgh jazz was both different and later than theirs. Illustrating this he said that he had never, to his knowledge, met Archie Semple.

So what was it that really separated the classic and purist categories and had seemed so important in the early days of the Revival? It certainly was not simply the race or colour of the originals, as Afro-Americans, white Americans

23

and Creoles of French or Spanish ancestry had all played prominent roles in New Orleans. It seems to have been perceived as a divide between the music of those who had stayed on in New Orleans and those who had moved away to find success elsewhere, such as Chicago or New York. This suggests a divide between those who saw commercial opportunities for themselves elsewhere and did something about it and those who stayed behind in New Orleans. The purist concept seems to have been that, by moving away for commercial reasons, the music was contaminated by the need to be commercial. The very use of the term purist jazz implies an adherence to an early form of jazz, uncontaminated by commerce or non-New Orleans influences. There is no doubt whatsoever that the followers of this style sincerely believed that this was so and believed that this older, unspoiled and 'pure' form represented something of particular artistic merit, a far from unreasonable perception.

Looking back now, it seems to me that the main <u>musical</u> difference was that the purist school used a lot of ensemble playing (ie simultaneous improvising) and virtually no arranged passages, whereas the classic style increasingly moved towards a music dominated by soloists and a tendency towards sometimes quite elaborate arrangements. Whether this represented contamination by commercialism or simply an increasing sophistication of the music is a matter for the individual to consider. In addition, many recordings give the clear impression that the technical abilities of the classic jazz musicians were of a considerably higher standard overall, than those of the purist persuasion. However, this is a technical rather than an artistic distinction and does not, in my view, diminish the artistic value of the less technically accomplished playing. In any case, it has to be recognised that some of the re-discovered veterans were getting on a bit in years by the time they were rediscovered and given the chance to record. In addition, some of them had played little in their immediate past. We should simply be thankful that their playing was put on record before it was too late. Their important influence in Edinburgh will be the subject of Chapter VII – The Jazz Purists.

It must be remembered that, when George Melly spoke of two forms of jazz within the Revival, he was speaking only about two forms of <u>New Orleans</u> jazz and not all of jazz. The path of jazz during the first half of the 20th Century had already demonstrated the organic development that would be expected of any living art form. These changes came about as individuals, groups of individuals and even the geographical spread of the music, exerted their influence. It seems likely to me that, if an art form failed to grow organically in this way, failed to develop and change, it would rapidly stagnate and die.

Although the original inspiration behind the Revival seems to have been a turning back to the origins and a rejection of many of the organic developments that had taken place, it does not seem to me that the Revival, in the end, can be said to have achieved this. What really seems to have happened was that the organic changes simply started all over again, demonstrating once again that change was inevitable. By the time I became actively involved in the Edinburgh traditional jazz scene, some fifteen years or so after the mid-1940s Revival, there were plenty of local jazz musicians whose styles reflected influences well outside the classic and purist models. These included musicians whose inspiration arose, for example, from such as Jack Teagarden and Dickie Wells (tbn), Bobby Hackett and Muggsy Spannier (tpt), Coleman Hawkins and Lester Young (ten) and the Ellington musicians. Few of these could be said to belong to either of the Revival categories and most were not New Orleans musicians at all but came from various other centres of jazz, including Kansas City, Chicago, New York and even Texas. The local jazz musicians they inspired, however, were active <u>within</u> the Revival movement and inevitably, had an effect upon it. These musicians had simply discovered that jazz had a wider stylistic base than New Orleans alone, even if they themselves had been originally attracted by the jazz of the Revival. The 1940s Revival was itself no more capable of freezing jazz at a point in time than the first half of the twentieth century had been. Having started out as a New Orleans concept, the Revival itself was changing (degenerating some would have said) and other stylistic variations of traditional jazz re-appeared, to an extent reflecting and replicating the developments of the first half century of jazz.

Later on, terms descriptive of these changes, some of which had been in use in jazz long before the Revival, became commonplace. These included the already mentioned **Chicago style**, which was said by French writer Jean Pierre Lion to be *'...an energetic and fierce adaptation of the New Orleans style'*[16]. The term Chicago style was often replaced by the term **Condon music**, a tribute to the key role played by Eddie Condon, who, for so long, had kept the flame of small band traditional jazz alive in his bands and clubs.

A term which became closely allied to this style was **dixieland**. This rather awkward term, which in the USA was often used to denote any small group traditional jazz, in the UK was used to describe traditional jazz of the white school. Unfortunately, it was also sometimes used, especially by those who believed that only Afro-Americans could play jazz, as a derogatory term implying an inferior, superficial type of jazz. This is illustrated by the 'Guinness Jazz A – Z' which said of dixieland *'...to many it still suggests white jazz, and the revivals of the 1940s tended to perpetuate the error (if it may be termed an error – or is it just another case of usage dictating?). The revival of traditional jazz idioms, complete with banjos, pumping tubas and four-square rhythms, was often done under the name of Dixieland, frequently by white bands in such places as Nick's in New York, where it was inevitably referred to as Nicksieland jazz. In the widest possible sense, it now embraces all traditional styles, but there is a clear need for clarification of what one intends by using the name'*[17]. These are wise words and, in this book, I will use the term in a purely descriptive, non-derogatory way, meaning jazz inspired by the Chicagoan tradition, exemplified by the

[16] Lion J P, 'Bix - The Definitive Biography of a Jazz Legend', pub 2007, Reproduced by permission of the Continuum International Publishing Group Ltd

[17] Clayton P, Hammond P, 'The Guinness Jazz A – Z', Guinness Superlatives 1986, by kind permission of Guinness World Records Ltd

predominately white group of musicians of the 1920s, gathered around the organizing figure of Eddie Condon.

Another term was the **European tradition**, usually relating to music derived from the music of Django Reinhardt and the 'Hot Club of France', the first truly original European contribution to the development of jazz. **Rhythm and blues** or **R & B** referred to a predominantly black, blues based music that was to become one of the most important building blocks of rock music. The music of small, extrovert and very 'jumping' bands was sometimes called **jump** or **jump jive**. The term **trad**, which was really just an abbreviation of traditional jazz, came to be used, rather slightingly, for the music of British traditional jazz bands during the 'Trad boom' of the late 1950s and early 1960s. An even more derogatory term, **traddy pop** was used to describe recordings by trad bands with the aim of selling vast number of records and getting into the Top Twenty, which they sometimes did.

There was also an interesting, middle-of-the-road term, which was **mainstream**. This was apparently invented in the 1950s by the jazz writer and critic, Stanley Dance. According to the 'Guinness Jazz A – Z'[18], Dance described this as *a kind of jazz which, while neither 'traditional' nor 'modern', is better than both'*. However, it must be remembered that Dance's definition belongs to the 1950s and relates to jazz of that time. The 'Guinness Jazz A – Z' goes on to say that mainstream was employed to describe *'...the music of jazz musicians who were by no means past their prime but who had formed their styles and made their reputations before or during the Swing era and found themselves short of work when the jazz audience divided itself into modern and traditional, paying scant attention to what lay in between'*. Another term, **small band swing**, was almost synonymous with mainstream, and was used to describe the music of bands of around six to eight musicians who had spent most of their time playing in the big Swing bands. Certainly, by the 1980s, when I was involved in a band that styled itself mainstream, I thought

---

[18] Clayton P, Hammond P, 'The Guinness Jazz A – Z', Guinness Superlatives 1986, by kind permission of Guinness World Records Ltd

of it as meaning the kind of small group music played by middle period jazz musicians such as Buck Clayton, Dickie Wells, Teddy Wilson, Benny Goodman and Johnny Hodges, many of whom had made their names in big bands during the 1930s and 1940s.

The term **Swing** itself, of course, referred to the music of the big, predominately white bands of the period between about 1935 and the late 1940s, such as those of Benny Goodman, Artie Shaw and the Dorsey brothers. There was one band, however, that seems to me to deserve a term of its own and that is the band of Duke Ellington, which has always seemed to me best described as a **jazz orchestra**.

Finally, in this explanation of terms, I should add that, throughout this book, I have used the term **'jazzer'** to embrace all those who populate the jazz scene, including all enthusiasts, supporters, listeners, organisers and writers, as well as those who play the music; in other words the whole jazz crowd. The term **'punter'** will also crop up. The term is not in any way derogatory but is widely and affectionately used by the players to identify those who turn out to support bands, act as volunteers at festivals, run events, distribute publicity and produce newsletters, articles, magazines and websites: all those, in fact, without whom the jazz scene would be a sad and empty place. All these terms and others, imprecise and over-lapping as they undoubtedly are, will be of use as we follow the course of Edinburgh traditional jazz over the second half of the twentieth century.

Reading some of the above, it may seem that the Revival had been a bit of a waste of time and that everything simply returned to how it had been before the Revival, but this was not so. The Revival was a major, world-wide renewal of interest in the earlier forms of jazz and perhaps the most important part of it was the large number of these new enthusiasts who actually started playing the music. Another important factor was that many of the early generations of jazz musicians were still alive and still playing and suddenly found themselves back in demand. In addition there were some, like Bunk Johnson (tpt) and Kid Ory (tbn), who were no longer playing but were located, given help to resume playing (including the provision of new false teeth!) and found themselves with a new career in jazz. The Revival, in spite of petty squabbles, parochialism and some fairly dire music along the way, re-invigorated traditional jazz. It brought back great and almost forgotten figures from the past and it provided the music with, literally, fresh blood. A great deal of notable music resulted, some of it locally in Edinburgh, where gifted musicians played originally and eloquently, not slavishly copying, but producing inspired music within their chosen idiom. Because of the Revival, traditional jazz, instead of just fizzling out, was able to continue as a vital, vigorous music, not really in competition with modern jazz but alongside and in parallel with it. I doubt that this would have been possible without the Revival.

Chapter III

The Classic Jazz Pioneers

Most accounts of traditional jazz in the UK credit the Red Barn, a pub in Barnehurst, Kent, as the birth place of the Revival in the UK. Presumably, this means the birth place of the *active playing* of traditional jazz, as there were clearly plenty of Rhythm Clubs around before this, where listening to recorded jazz was the norm. The Red Barn sessions featured a band called the George Webb Dixielanders. During the early years of WWII, while working in the Vickers-Armstrong munitions factory, the leader of this band, pianist George Webb, had founded the Bexleyheath Rhythm Club. Sometime after this, and after taking piano lessons, he began rehearsing with a like-minded trumpeter called Owen Bryce. Together they formed the George Webb Dixielanders and fixed up a regular gig in the basement of the Red Barn pub. The band went on to make some recordings, broadcast on the radio and play concerts in various cities in the UK but disbanded in early 1948. Several members of the band went on to make names for themselves in years to come, in particular the trumpeter Humphrey Lyttelton and clarinettist Wally Fawkes.

George Webb, who was sometimes called the 'father of British jazz', was born on 8th October 1917 and died on 10th March 2010, at the age of 92. There is no doubt of the importance in British jazz of this band, but whether it was in fact the first to start playing Revival jazz in the UK is not clear and does not really matter much. What does matter is that, in a number of centres around the country, similar efforts to form bands to play traditional jazz were gathering pace. It seems very unlikely that these well-scattered efforts were inspired by the George Webb Dixielanders, given that there would be few recordings of British traditional bands at that time. In addition, there would be little jazz communication across the country in these days, before much in the way of a jazz press existed. In fact, all around the country, interest in early jazz was burgeoning and, following the example of revivalist bands such as that of Lu Waters and Turk Murphy et al in the USA, people were learning to play instruments and bands were being formed. The jazz writer Sinclair Traill, in his book 'Concerning Jazz'[19], says that *The band which first took up cudgels on behalf of traditional jazz in this country was George Webb's Dixielanders'* but goes on to name other early bands. Traill lists them as the bands of Chris Barber and Ken Colyer in London, The Saints Jazz Band in Manchester, The Merseysippi band in Liverpool and significantly, Sandy Brown and Alex Welsh who were pioneering traditional jazz in Edinburgh.

As we have already seen, the early revivalists in Edinburgh in the early to late 1940s were organised into two groups, one centred on clarinettist Sandy Brown and the other on fellow clarinettist Archie Semple with his brother John Semple and Alex Welsh, both of whom played trumpet. As we have already heard, the group associated with Sandy Brown had come to be identified as the **Royal High School Gang (RHS Gang)**, because so many of the group had attended the city's Royal High School. It is hard to be precise about just how many Royal High scholars were actively involved in jazz in Edinburgh in the 1940s but it is clear that there were quite a few. It seems likely that there were somewhere between twenty and thirty of them actively playing or attempting to play the music, ranging from a few who would become internationally famous in jazz, through a good number who would establish lengthy local careers, to others who were only active briefly, before dropping out.

---

[19] Traill S, 'Concerning Jazz', page 136, Faber and Faber 1957. All attempts to trace the current copyright holder of this book have been unsuccessful.

There was clearly a central group of talented musicians, who led the way, but it is equally clear that there were many others who also played an important part. Amongst the latter, there would be some who were less committed, perhaps less able, musicians and certainly many who were non-playing enthusiasts. However, there can be no doubt that they, collectively, comprised a self-sustaining jazz movement, both within and beyond the school, the effects of which are around to this day. This jazz movement at the Royal High School may even have had something of a crusade about it, a sense of pursuing and supporting an earlier and more worthwhile form of jazz, something that added up to a cause worthy of commitment. Jazz, like any other organic entity, needs a suitable environment in which to grow and the doings of the whole group collectively – musical, organisational or just turning up to listen – seems to have provided just that environment. It did not end there either and, in the following decades, there would be many other jazzers, younger but just as committed, from the Royal High School jazz production line.

Just when the appellation, the Royal High School gang, first came to be used is uncertain but I think it must have been fairly early on. Certainly, I was aware of the term shortly after I came into the Edinburgh jazz scene around 1960 and the drummer, Kenny Milne and trumpeter Andrew Lauder, whose Edinburgh jazz histories go back beyond mine, also remember the term from early in their careers. I can remember established jazzers with whom I played, such as Archie Sinclair and Jack Duff, not only using the term but relishing its links to the music of the Austin High School Gang, a form of jazz with which each had much in common. Going still further back, the drummer Bill Strachan, who was a school contemporary of the group associated with Sandy Brown, has also confirmed that he remembers the collective term RHS crowd or gang being used quite early on in his jazz career, as early as the late 1940s or early 1950s. I have also heard the term used in a variety of ways, from the quite specific, meaning only the early Sandy Brown band, to a more generic inclusion of the entire Royal High School jazz crowd of the 1940s and 50s. It is worth noting that there were even some who, like

Dave Mylne and Ian Arnott whom we shall meet shortly, did not actually attend the Royal High School but were so closely involved with the Gang that they were often assumed to be a part of it. The most common usage, in my early experience, was to use it as a collective tag for the jazz musicians from the school, although at that time, we would not have thought of putting a capital G on gang, often just saying the Royal High gang or crowd. In my view, the term is such an obvious one, given the jazz precedent of the Austin High School Gang in Chicago, that I think that it is extremely likely that it was 'invented' on a number of occasions, by different people, at different times and in different places. The first published use of the term of which I am aware, was by jazz critic Tony Troon, writing in The Scotsman after Al Fairweather's death in 1993, when he referred to Al as *'...one of the Royal High School 'gang' of musicians of the early Fifties...'*[20].

The term was also used by John Latham, about whom we will hear more shortly, in an article headed 'The Royal High School Gang' which appeared in the May 1996 edition of Jazz Journal'[21]. The article pointed out that, in the New Orleans jazz revival of the 1940s, jazz bands were springing up all over the UK and not just in London. Latham explains that Sandy Brown's band, then playing in the West End Cafe and including Sandy's old school mates Al Fairweather and Stan Grieg, could be described as the Royal High School Gang. The article goes on to describe the early recording activities of Sandy and the others and finishes by reiterating that *'...very important music was being created in Scotland and that far from being centred in London, the British jazz movement sprang to life simultaneously at several independent locations, of which one of the most important was Edinburgh'*. In this book, it will be in its widest and most general sense that I shall use the term. The Royal High School Gang (the RHS Gang) seems to me a term that embraces the whole spectrum of components that make jazz on any scale a communicative art form – players,

---

[20] Troon Anthony, 'Al Fairweather: jazz trumpeter', The Scotsman, 22nd June 1993

[21] Latham J, 'The Royal High School Gang', Jazz Journal May 1996, by permission of Jazz Journal www.jazzjournal.co.uk

organisers, listeners, recorders of sounds and images and, no doubt, critics as well – and they all seem to me to have played their part and earned their place.

Amongst the RHS Gang who were already playing instruments in the mid-1940s, were Sandy Brown (clt and pno), Al Fairweather (tbn), Stu Eaton (tpt), Neil Pringle (pno) and Ronnie Geddes (drms). An RHS pupil, who was not an active player but a keen jazz follower, was Jim Walker. Jim, who came to Edinburgh from Peterculter near Aberdeen at the age of seven, was a contemporary of several of the musicians, including Al Fairweather, Stu Eaton and Bob Craig who were in his year, and Sandy Brown who was in the year below. Dave Paxton was a couple of years ahead and Stan Greig was about three years behind him. In about 1990, Jim Walker wrote a memoire about these early days in which he said *'Jazz must have oozed out of the walls in the old Royal High School building during the war years because it seemed that just about everybody in my year and the year below was a jazz fan'*. Jim put much of this enthusiasm down to the influence of Sandy Brown and adds that there may have been a touch of a *'one in the eye for authority'* gesture about it. Jim's introduction to jazz came through a talk given by Sandy at the literary and debating society, which was illustrated with a selection of recordings. His interest was furthered by his pal, Stu Eaton, who was more knowledgeable than Jim was about jazz and encouraged him. A group of these young jazz followers would invade Clifton's Record Shop in Princes Street on Saturday mornings to hear the latest jazz releases, mostly on the rhythm series from Parlophone. Apparently, each 78 rpm record cost five shillings and four pence half-penny, which is only about twenty seven pence in today's money, but was considered a fortune at the time. The secret was to attach yourself to someone who had a bit of cash and could buy a record. Jim recalls how impressed he was by Sandy Brown's ability to hear a boogie woogie record only a couple of times, before he was able to play it in full on the RHS gym piano. A jazz band of variable membership would practice in the school gym, including a few who were not RHS pupils. Even at that time, Sandy seemed to have *'been born note perfect'* on the clarinet, never playing anything less than fluently, although he tended to impose his own high standards on others. When novices showed some promise and a willingness to take advice, Sandy could be encouraging and tolerant but Jim remembers him once telling an aspiring trombone player *'I could make a better sound with my arse'*? The drummer Bill Strachan has also said that, at times, Sandy could be quite brutal in his criticism of others and remembers the banjo player, Norrie Anderson, being reduced to a quivering wreck by Sandy's complaints about the chords he was playing, saying despairingly *'I suppose I must be playing the wrong chords but I am playing them properly'*? The front-line of the school gym band was often Stu Eaton on trumpet, Sandy on clarinet and Al Fairweather on trombone while Bob Craig, modest and still very unsure of himself, would try out his trombone quietly in the background.

The RHS gym band, however, was not the only active traditional jazz band around and Jim Walker remembers a group of rather older musicians who, around 1945, played at the Edinburgh Rhythm Club, located in the rehearsal room above Methven Simpson's music shop in Princes Street. This group included Bob Fairley (tpt), Drew Bruce (ten and sometimes, sop sax), Drew's mother Ma Bruce (pno) and Bill McGregor (bjo) and we will meet some of them, in a little more detail, in the next chapter. George Crockett was also associated with this group, playing drums both at Methven Simpsons and a few years later, when the band reconstituted itself in new premises at the YWCA in Riego Street. Sandy and Al Fairweather were quickly drawn into the group at the Rhythm Club, although the main business was listening to a record recital, with the live music almost an impromptu afterthought at the end of the session. Around this time, another band was formed by Archie Semple (clt) and his brother John who, Jim Walker says, played a strong if not very original lead on trumpet, with George Crockett on drums. Their main interest was in the white Chicago jazz of the Eddie Condon type and we will hear much more about them in Chapter V.

In UK terms, **Sandy Brown (clarinet, piano, vocals)** was clearly into early revivalist action, his profile on the Sandy Brown Jazz website saying that he formed his first band in

1943[22]. Many years later in the mid-1990s, long after Sandy's death and mainly through the sterling work of Dr John Latham, a Senior Lecturer in International Economic History at the University of Wales in Swansea, a Sandy Brown Society (SBS) was formed to celebrate his life. In about 1996 the SBS began publishing regular newsletters and the special 99th Edition newsletter, published in March 2005, the 30th anniversary of Sandy's death, gives some indication of dates. In John Latham's summary of Sandy's career, he states *'It is said that Sandy Brown formed his first band as early as 1943, and the latest Sandy Brown Discography shows him to have been recording in 1946'*[23]. These early activities also involved Sandy's near contemporaries Stu Eaton (tpt), Alastair (Al) Fairweather (tbn and later, tpt), Bob Craig (tbn), Dave Paxton (clt) and Stan Grieg (drms and pno). They, like Sandy, attended the Royal High School, Stan the year behind Sandy and Al and Bob a couple of years ahead, John Latham telling us that both Stan and Al were members of Sandy's early bands.

Stu Eaton has said[24] that he, Al and Bob all started school together in October 1932 and that the three of them, when they were about 12 years old, had started *'fooling around with music'* in his mother's basement. He adds that Sandy, whom he says was *'the catalyst'*, joined them about two or three years later. Eaton also tells us that Sandy played an Albert system clarinet, as he then considered that the more modern Boehm system was only for *'classical stuff, wimps and Benny Goodman'*. However, it seems that he may not have stuck with his original model of clarinet. Jim Walker has recalled that Sandy, at some point, had said goodbye to *'...his old Albert clarinet (all held together with insulating tape and bits of string with a decided droop in the middle) and had acquired a new Boehm'*. Sandy used a very hard reed, in an attempt to sound as much like Johnny Dodds as possible, and there is a story that Wally Fawkes, having inspected one of Sandy's reeds, asked him what he used, suggesting that it might be floor boards!

---

[22] http://sandybrownjazz.co.uk
[23] SBS Newsletter No. 99, March 2005
[24] SBS Newsletter No. 7, June 1997

Eaton throws some light on the issue of Sandy's teeth, telling us that they were *'less than dazzling'* and, before starting to play, he would smoothly convey them to his pocket with one sweep of his handkerchief, without his audience being much the wiser. Stu Eaton also says that Sandy's clarinet mouth piece was *'very marked'*[25], by which he presumably means that the surface was pitted by tooth marks. Just how this came about is something of a mystery, in the light of Sandy being known to remove his false teeth before playing – unless he had gums like iron! The answer may lie in information from the sax player, Tony Coe, who revealed in a SBS Newsletter[26] that it was only Sandy's upper teeth that were missing and confirmed that it was these that he removed to play clarinet. Like so many jazz musicians, Sandy was self taught on his instrument and John Latham, in Sandy's biography in the Oxford Dictionary of National Biography, says that the absence of formal training was crucial to his unique approach to the clarinet[27].

John Latham also gives details about Sandy's place of birth and his arrival in Edinburgh. Jazz reference books consistently give Sandy's date and place of birth as 25 February 1929 in Izatnagar in India. He was the second son of John Brown, a railway engineer and his wife, Minnie Henderson. In recent years, doubts have been raised by some of Sandy's contemporaries about his place of birth. However, Latham's research into the matriculation registers for the Royal High School of Edinburgh shows that Sandy entered the school on 2 October 1933 at the age of four and that his previous school was the infant school, Garahkpur. Latham quotes Sandy's book, 'The McJazz Manuscripts: A Collection of the Writings of Sandy Brown' (Ed. David Binns, Faber and Faber, London and Boston, 1979), as giving his place of birth as Izatnagar near Bareilly in India, where his father had been an engineer on the railway network. Latham also refutes the tale that Sandy's mother was

[25] SBS Newsletter No. 7, June 1997
[26] SBS Newsletter No 90, June 2004
[27] Oxford Dictionary of National Biography: Oxford Dictionary of National Biography Index of Contributors by Colin Matthew and Brian Harrison (2004) p4-5 Volume 8 (not verbatim), by permission of Oxford University Press, www.oup.com

Indian and quotes Sandy's cousin Elsie, who told Stan Grieg that Sandy's mother (Elsie's Auntie Minnie) was as Scottish as she was. This is given further weight as the Royal High School records indicate that he was staying with his maternal grandmother, Mrs Henderson, which does not sound much like an Indian surname to me! Apparently, Sandy did sometimes say that his mother was Indian and, indeed, in the 'McJazz Manuscripts', he claims that she was Muslim and had turned Christian on her marriage. Certainly, judging by his looks, Sandy could have had Indian blood in him. However, it looks as though this story has to be put down to the idiosyncratic Brown sense of humour. On the family's return to Scotland in the early 1930s, they lived at first in Wishaw before moving to Edinburgh. It appears that Sandy's father had been unwell and that he died in about 1936, when Sandy was still very young. Latham also confirms that Sandy spent all his school days at the Royal High School and had lived at 4 Abercorn Crescent, which is off Willowbrae Road, in the Jock's Lodge area of Edinburgh.

Drawing by Patricia Davenport of Sandy Brown in the Crown Bar in 1954 (by kind permission of Peter and Patricia Davenport)

Sinclair Traill, in his 1957 'Concerning Jazz' already quoted, gives an interesting verbatim statement of Sandy's which gives us a good idea of his views early in his jazz career:

'I've always tried to have a <u>hot</u> band because that is what jazz has to offer. It means playing real blues with a beat – and I don't mean just 12 bar themes; the blues is part of all jazz that I like. For that reason I don't like British jazz much. For another reason too: most British players can't play very well technically, so they never attempt what they don't feel they can do. The result is light music, which I hate, and they ought to. Fairweather and I compose a lot of the band's repertoire – it makes us think what we're doing, and creation is always apt to be better than emulation. I don't agree with the theory that jazz shouldn't be <u>sung</u>. The dearth of jazz singers here is no argument. It means only that there is a dearth of jazz singers! I like the vocal blues harmonies, and generally oppose the "Brass Band" theory that seems to have the traditionalist world by the throat today.'[28]

Small wonder then that the music produced over the years by Sandy Brown and Al Fairweather was to be some of the most original and hottest traditional jazz ever heard in Britain. Small wonder either that John Latham, in a May 1996 article in the magazine 'Jazz Journal'[29], emphasises this early activity in Edinburgh when he says *'We have to realise that very important music was being created in Scotland and that far from being centred on London, the British jazz movement sprang to life simultaneously at several independent locations, of which one of the most important was Edinburgh.'*

This book will not presume to attempt a fully detailed biography of any of the jazz musicians mentioned, but it is interesting to consider what sort of people they were, especially in the early days of the Revival. For a glimpse of Sandy Brown as a young man, we are again indebted to the SBS. In the SBS Newsletter No 99 already alluded to, some

---

[28] Traill S, 'Concerning Jazz', page 140, Faber and Faber 1957. All attempts to trace the current copyright holder of this book have been unsuccessful.
[29] Latham J, 'Jazz Journal' 'The Royal High School Gang', May 1996, www.jazzjournal.co.uk

of Stu Eaton's recollections are recorded and he describes Sandy as *'a standout at school'*. He goes on to say that Sandy was *'highly visible and audible'* and was the leading light of a group who broke the rules and indulged in jokes *'practical and impractical'*! He also says that Sandy and Al Fairweather were seen as a pair, not just because they played jazz together, but because they were considered to be equally good. Eaton considered Al to be the hotter player while Sandy was the bluer player, meaning of course, that Sandy's playing was suffused by the influence of the blues. The blues influence was certainly apparent in all of Sandy's playing and 'The McJazz Manuscripts' lists an early recording by Sandy (made privately in 1948) of a tune called 'Emigratin' Blues'. On this recording, Sandy plays piano, accompanying the blues singing of Drew Bruce. Drew Bruce was a clarinet and sax player and was described by Stan Grieg as *'a blues singer of great talent'*[30]. His mother, known as 'Ma' Bruce, played piano around the Edinburgh jazz scene in the 1940/50s, although said by Stu Eaton to *'...read all her music'*[31].

Al Fairweather and Sandy Brown
(by kind permission of Peter Davenport)

---

[30] SBS Newsletter No. 56, August 2001
[31] SBS Newsletter No 91, July 2004

After leaving school, Sandy did his National Service with the Royal Army Ordnance Corps in the years 1948/49 and then went on to the Edinburgh College of Art, where he trained as an architect, eventually specialising in acoustic architecture. His jazz activities continued while he was a student and in 1952, his band played a famous concert at the Usher Hall, when they supported the Mississippi blues singer, Big Bill Broonzy, an occasion we shall look at in more detail in the next chapter. There was a second Usher Hall appearance the next year, supporting the Freddy Randall band and, also in 1953, the band travelled to London to take part in a National Jazz Federation concert at the Royal Festival Hall.

Amongst the jazz memorabilia in the possession of Jim Walker was one particularly unexpected and delightful relic. This was a 78 rpm record, on the Wildcat label, with 'Oh, Didn't he Ramble' printed on one side and just the name Sandy Brown on the other. The labels are quite simply printed although not, I would say, home-made, there is no serial number and the titles on the labels are typed, as by an ordinary, old-fashioned type writer. This seems to have been quite a usual practice at the time, when recordings were often made privately by some local recording firm. The labels on the Swarbrick and Mossman recordings made by the early Sandy Brown band, about which we will hear later, are also typed in this way. On one side of the disc, the recording of 'Oh, Didn't he Ramble' is hot and driving, with a band apparently consisting of trumpet, clarinet, trombone, banjo, bass and drums. The trumpet is clearly Al Fairweather and the clarinet is obviously Sandy, still in his early Doddsian mode. The trombonist sounds like Bob Craig and it seems likely that the banjoist is Norrie Anderson. Dizzy Jackson, in 2012, told me that he had no recollection of being on this particular recording. The track has the usual 'Oh, Didn't He Ramble' out of tempo introduction, complete with the 'Ashes to Ashes, Dust to Dust' spiel, spoken by Sandy I think, followed by some quite convincing howls of grief and mourning from the rest of the band. The drums pick up the tempo and are followed by two ensemble choruses, a chorus each from clarinet, trombone and trumpet, then two closing ensemble choruses. It is a good spirited stuff but it is the other side of the record that is really fascinating.

Jim Walker says that this reverse side is a recording of Sandy being interviewed on the radio programme 'In Town Tonight', an occasion which he remembers, and says that Sandy's interview followed one with Boris Karlof! Jim reports that he found the record in a charity shop somewhere and, as it is precious and fragile, he had copied it onto tape, a copy of which he gave me. Because the interview gives such a good account of what Sandy and his band were up to at the time, it is well worth giving the whole story. There is a brief single chorus of a blues played by the band and then the BBC interviewer (I) begins:

I   *That music was by Sandy Brown and his band from Edinburgh* (actually, what he says is 'That was Sendy Brown and his Bend from Aidinburgh'). *The band is paying its first visit to London and here's its leader, architect and clarinet player Sandy Brown. Well, what are you doing in London apart from playing jazz Mr Brown?*

SB *Well, we came down to take part in the National Jazz Federation annual concert at the Festival Hall the other day.*

I   *Uhhu*

SB *That was particularly interesting to me musically and architecturally.*

I   *I can well imagine it. All the eight members of your band – do they all have different jobs?*

SB *Oh yes. The drummer's a surveyor, the bass player's a law student, the trumpet player's an artist and so on.*

I   *A very versatile bunch. When did you first get together?*

SB *It really started at school then we did our time in the services and when we came out, three years ago, we decided to learn our instruments seriously.*

I   *Where have you played?*

SB *In Scotland of course and several times in Paris. Every summer we play there. The first year when we were there the boys gave me a nasty shock.*

I   *Really? What did they do?*

SB   *We were booked to play in a cafe but they all got lost except the trombone player and myself. So we decided we couldn't carry on by ourselves so we had to run round the streets of Paris frantically searching for unemployed French musicians. As a report for duty, it was the strangest assortment of instrumentalists ever assembled.*

I   *Well, what did you do? How long did you play?*

SB   *We played all the night there and the people in the cafe were delighted with what they thought an all Scottish band.*

I   *Where as it was French with just a dash of Scotch, eh? What are you going to play for us?*

SB   *Well, we've been celebrating Louis Armstrong's birthday today and appropriately, we'd like to play a number of his he recorded twenty years ago and it's still popular today - When You're Smiling.*

(The band plays)

I   *Well, hot music from hot Scotland eh? Thank you very much Sandy Brown and your band.*

The band then plays a couple of choruses of ensemble on 'When you're Smiling', and the interviewer, for all his awful BBC accent, was quite right – it is hot. As to the line-up of the band on this side of the record, in the interview Sandy refers to the drummer as 'a surveyor' and Ralph Laing, a near contemporary of the RHS Gang and later to be a fine jazz piano player, confirms that this description would fit Farrie Forsyth. The bass player is said by Sandy on the recording to be law student, which puzzled me at first, until I was tipped off by John Latham. John told me that it was Dizzy Jackson, who had been a law student before changing course and becoming a teacher and a quick phone call to Dizzy confirmed this. He added that, in addition to Boris Karloff, the black pianist 'Hutch' had also made an appearance on the show. Hutch was a Grenadian who had been one the biggest cabaret stars of the 1920/30s and whose full name was Leslie Arthur Julien Hutchinson.

Just why the interviewer refers to *'all the eight members of your band'* is not at all clear, unless he simply miscounted. Dizzy recalls that the line-up for the recording was Al Fairweather (tpt), Bob Craig (tbn), Sandy (clt), Norrie Anderson (bjo), Dizzy (bs) Dru Paterson (pno) and Farrie Forsyth (drms). Apparently, Stan Greig, who would have otherwise played piano, was on National Service at the time and could not always get away to play. It sounds like only a six-piece band on the recording and, although there may well be a piano as well, I cannot convince myself that I can hear one. This recording is certainly a fascinating peep into the distant past but how on earth did it come to be on a 78 rpm record? Perhaps the BBC gave them a recording of their efforts as a memento and, of course, there would be few readily available recordings on tape then, but who knows what its origins were? The mention in Sandy's interview of Louis Armstrong's birthday, at that time believed to be 4th July, would seem to fix the day and Sandy's reference to coming out of the services three years ago should make it 1952/53, so it seemed likely that the BBC recording was made on the 1953 trip mentioned above. Dizzy has confirmed that it was 1953, although he also said that the recording was made on his birthday, which would make it the 14th of July rather than on Louis' birthday on the 4th.

There is other information that relates very closely to the above and further confirms the line-up of Sandy's band on the broadcast. Dizzy has confirmed it was on this same trip that Sandy's band made some other recordings. These were made for the Esquire label and are listed in Sandy's discography[32] as having been recorded on 11th July 1953. The tunes recorded were 'Dr Jazz' (two takes), 'Four or Five Times' (two takes) and 'Wild Man Blues' (single take). The band line-up is given as Al Fairweather (tpt), Sandy Brown (clt), Bob Craig (tbn), Dru Paterson (pno), Norrie Anderson (bjo), Dizzy Jackson (bs) and Farrie Forsyth (drms). There is an additional recording[33], made for Esquire on 11th July 1953, this being two takes of 'King Porter Stomp', which

---

[32] Bielderman G et al, Sandy Brown Discography, Eurojazz Discos No. 5

[33] Bielderman G et al, Stan Greig Discography, Eurojazz Discos No. 45, Nov 1995, Sandy Brown's Jazz Band, Esquire 20-022, EP28,333, recorded London, 11th July 1953. A footnote says that Stan Greig does not appear on five other titles from this session, presumably the other Esquire tracks discussed above.

were made by the same line-up but with Stan Greig on drums, to the exclusion of Farrie Forsyth.

Al Fairweather stayed on in London about this time, with Alex Welsh taking his place in the Brown band back in Edinburgh. A year or so later in 1954, Sandy joined the lengthening list of Edinburgh jazz musicians who had moved to London. There he joined up again with Al Fairweather and went on to further great success in jazz and in his professional career, but these London based happenings are beyond the scope of this book. On 29th September 1954, Sandy married Flo' Armstrong, a legal secretary. Happily Sandy's later career is well covered in recordings and jazz publications, including his own 'The McJazz Manuscripts'. Both the recordings and the 'Manuscripts' are amongst the very best and most original ever produced in British jazz and are highly recommended to everyone who likes their jazz (and their reading) original, hot and exciting.

I played with Sandy Brown on a few occasions, probably not more than half a dozen in all, when he sat in with our band, Old Bailey and his Jazz Advocates. This was when he was visiting Edinburgh back in the 1960s, but I cannot say that I knew him as a person. My impression was of a strong-minded individual with a formidable intellect and the most ferocious musical attack of any jazz musician I ever played with. The only other with an attack comparable to Sandy's was the American trumpeter, Wild Bill Davison, with whom I played a couple of times in the mid-1970s. As Bill Davison was elderly by the time I played with him, perhaps I should declare it a draw between the two most open, honest and expressive musicians I ever heard live. Both clearly played straight from the heart and both set about the music with a fierce, emotional drive that was utterly gripping. I once heard Sandy give an opinion on an up and coming young jazz musician and the main thrust of his view was that the youngster's playing *'had no balls'*. No one could have ever accused Sandy's playing of lacking balls; it was one of the most forth-right and vigorous sounds in all of jazz.

Another story which gives a good picture of Sandy's character, according to John Latham, originated with the jazz critic and writer Alun Morgan. He had been at a concert in Canterbury, Kent, which featured a number of jazz reed players, including Sandy. Morgan was compering the show, and after announcing a young modern jazzer who played unaccompanied soprano sax, he retired to the bar. Sandy was there, a glass of whisky in one hand and a glass of water in the other. The sound of far-out, unaccompanied soprano sax came over the PA. Sandy took a sip from each of his glasses in turn then remarked *'While I respect the courage and determination of young men who push the boundaries of music further out, I retain the right to not f- - king well listen'*[34].

Later, the Fairweather-Brown band moved towards a more mainstream style, a move perhaps not meeting with everyone's approval, but it remained exciting and original music, even if it had shed some of the rough magic of their earlier approach.

It has been reported that Sandy once calculated that the average life span of a jazz musician was somewhere in the mid forties. His prediction was to be horribly accurate in his own case, for Sandy was to die of malignant hypertension at the tragically young age of 46, on 15 March 1975, while watching on TV, Scotland lose to England in a rugby Calcutta Cup match. His death was a huge loss to jazz, to his professional field of architecture and, of course, to his family and friends. He was truly a great clarinet player, perhaps the most distinguished and original jazz musician Britain has ever produced, certainly in the traditional field. What he might have gone on to achieve if his health had held up, we shall never know, but it seems unlikely that he would ever have been willing to rest on the laurels of his past.

Although I hardly knew Sandy as a person, I was fortunate enough to get to know **Al Fairweather (trumpet)** quite well, after he had returned to Edinburgh in the late 1980s. Al was born in Edinburgh on 12 June 1927 and brought up in the Portobello area of the city. Like Sandy Brown, he attended the RHS and discovered jazz while in secondary school. With Sandy and others of the RHS Gang,

---

[34] Sleeve note by Alun Morgan on HEP LP 2017

he was already actively involved in playing jazz by the mid-1940s, starting out, not on the trumpet on which he would make his name, but on the trombone. Another one of the Gang, Sandy Currie, says that Al was stuck with trombone *'having lost on the toss of a coin'* to Stu Eaton, when they both wanted to play trumpet[35]. Al's original trombone is still around. It was made in Czechoslovakia, probably before WWI, and has a shamrock on the bell. It has been in the possession of yet another, but rather younger, RHS pupil, trombonist George Hewitt, since he bought it from Al in the early 1950s. George had had to return the 'Boosey and Hawkes' trombone, on which he started out, when he left school in 1952 and he raised the £7 that Al wanted for his instrument by working at a harvest camp near Coldstream. Al's former trombone has been resident in George Hewitt's attic in Irvine for many years. George got it with a battered wooden case which had replaced the oilskin wrapping that Al had originally used. Al's old trombone was brought to Edinburgh in 2010 to be an exhibit in an exhibition celebrating Edinburgh jazz.

George Hewitt says that it was Sandy Brown who persuaded Al to switch to the trumpet. Al's initial attempts on trumpet did not immediately impress Jim Walker, who wondered if a horrible mistake had been made. Jim remembers that at first, Al hardly ever moved out of the lower register, had a coarse, unattractive tone and every one missed his trombone playing. However, Jim also says that, although his early lack of technique was obvious, Al had retained his superb phrasing, the total cohesion of his solos and his drive in the ensembles. Jim highlighted Al's joined-up playing beautifully by saying *'When other soloists often play unrelated phrases, Al played in sentences, which made up a paragraph which in turn contributed to the whole story of the tune'.* Jim recalled that the band had made its first recording only about six weeks after Al had started on trumpet and, although his comparative lack of technique was apparent, his imagination and jazz feeling shone through.

---

[35] Sleeve note by Sandy Currie, 'Sandy Brown – The Historic Usher Hall Concert 1952', Lake Records LACD94

Like Sandy, Al went on to Edinburgh College of Art, where he gained a diploma in painting and drawing. He was clearly a talented artist, as well as an outstanding jazz musician, and a portrait by Al of Sean Connery, retained in the Art College collection, appeared in the centenary show at the Edinburgh College of Art in 2007 and got a mention in the Times. This dated from a time, long before his 007 days, when the then Big Tam Connery acted as a 'bouncer' at the Jazz Band Balls held at the Oddfellows Hall in the evenings and posed as a model at the Art College during the day.

In late 1953, a year before Sandy had finished his course at Art College, Al went to live in London. There he joined the band of Cy Laurie, another Johnny Dodds inspired clarinet player, with whom he made some excellent recordings. A year or so later, when Sandy too moved south, the two great Edinburgh players teamed up again and went on to produce a series of wonderful, original recordings, mostly featuring compositions and arrangements by Al and Sandy. In my view, these recordings were the absolute zenith of British traditional jazz, never bettered to this day. Later, while Sandy concentrated on his architectural affairs, Al spent a number of years with Acker Bilk's band, where he joined up with another great British original, the alto sax and clarinet player, Bruce Turner, in what many would consider to have been the best band that Bilk ever had. Later still, in the late 1980s, when Al's health was causing serious problems, he returned to Edinburgh where he teamed up with his contemporaries Bob Craig and Dave Paxton and others, with whom he continued to produce terrific music.

I liked Al Fairweather a lot. He was friendly, totally modest, indeed incredibly self deprecating considering his achievements, and encouraging to me personally. In the late 1980s, I was involved in a five piece band, which we called the Jazz Masters, playing a mainstream form of jazz. Al, as well as sitting in with us quite frequently, was also happy to dep with us when we were short handed, and was endlessly encouraging about what we were trying to do musically.

Al Fairweather's original trombone and other memorabilia in a showcase at an exhibition at the Central Library to mark the setting up of an Edinburgh Jazz Archive, in 2010 (photograph by the author)

He was also kind enough to give me arrangements of two tunes that he had written. The band folded before we got these numbers into our repertoire and, as these were numbers that Al told me he had never done anything with himself, I believe they remain to this day two originals by a great jazz musician that have never been played or heard. Writing this has prompted me to do something about this and they may yet make their belated appearance on the Edinburgh jazz scene[36].

I was always struck by how genuinely modest and self-deprecating Al was about his own abilities and achievements. In addition to being a great trumpet player, he had written and arranged some of the most original and exiting material ever played by British jazz bands - and yet he told me what a struggle it had been. He said that he was a poor and slow reader and writer of music and everything he had done had cost him a huge amount of time and effort.

---

[36] One of them, 'Bonzo Bounce', we brought into our repertoire in 2011

Al wrote in a letter to Stuart Carter '...*I have been doing some arranging. I don't know if you have ever tried it (I suspect you have) but it is one of the most difficult things to attempt. I've been doing it for some years now and it doesn't get any easier – it seems that the mind seizes up when you are faced with a blank manuscript and ideas don't come very readily. The funny thing is, the ideas come quickly enough if you were playing!*'[37]

You would never have guessed his difficulty with reading and writing music from the results. Even in the early days in Edinburgh, it is clear that Al was a friendly, encouraging and laid back sort of person. George Hewitt tells of how Al, already an established name in local jazz, was none-the-less willing to go along and fill-in at rehearsals with the schoolboy band in which George was playing at the time, when their young trumpeter Kenny Jack was unable to make it. Many years later, Al was to return to Edinburgh and to playing jazz on the local jazz scene, where we will catch up with him in a later chapter. Al Fairweather died in Edinburgh on 21st June 1993.

Stan Greig (piano and drums) was born in Edinburgh on 12th August 1930. His father, Artie, was a piano tuner, a trade that Stan would also follow later, and had a piano shop in the Jock's Lodge part of Edinburgh. Artie Greig also played drums and Stan's mother taught English and played piano. Stan was educated at the RHS and, according to 'The Rough Guide to Jazz'[38], he joined Sandy Brown's band in 1945. Like others of the RHS Gang, he lived in the Joppa/Portobello district of Edinburgh. Dizzy Jackson, who was later to play bass in the Brown band, tells us[39] that Sandy always had a problem because Stan was both the best piano player and the best drummer available but, of course, could not play both at once. Stan made his first recordings with the Brown band in 1949 and 1950, recording for the Swarbrick and Mossman (S & M) label.

---

[37] SBS Newsletter No. 66, June 2002

[38] Carr, Fairweather and Priestly 'The Rough Guide to Jazz', 3rd Edition May 2004, Rough Guides Ltd, distributed by the Penguin Group

[39] SBS Newsletter No. 11, November 1997

Stan was not only a versatile musician but was clearly an effective proselytiser on behalf of jazz. George Hewitt recollects that he and Kenny Jack, both slightly younger RHS pupils, had become acquainted with Stan and he was to be a major musical influence on them. Stan had left the RHS some years before this and was serving an apprenticeship at Henry Robb's Shipyard in Leith, intent on becoming a ship's engineer. More relevantly to Hewitt and Jack, he was the piano player in the Sandy Brown band with whom he played at jazz dances at the Oddfellows Hall, regular spots at the West End Cafe and at gigs in the Crown Bar, which was host to the 'Stud Club'. They used to meet him on Sundays in an Italian cafe on the Portobello seafront, where Stan would enthuse volubly about jazz and let them borrow some of the records that he brought along with him.

After completing his apprenticeship, Stan was called up for National Service, joining the Royal Engineers (Inland Water Transport) and found himself in charge of a floating crane at Marchwood Camp, near Southampton. John Latham tells the story of Stan being discovered to be a 'crack shot' and being chosen to compete in the Royal Engineers rifle team. Happily Stan, realising what the outcome of this would be, brought his potential career as a sniper to an abrupt end by deliberately aiming off target![40] On his return to Edinburgh in 1952 after being de-mobbed, he rejoined the Brown band, playing at a famous Usher Hall concert in 1952 supporting Big Bill Broonzy, making further recordings with them for S and M, and broadcasting with the band on BBC Scotland in 1952.

Stan went to London in 1954 where he worked with Ken Colyer (on drums), Humphrey Lyttelton, the Fairweather–Brown band, Bruce Turner's band, Acker Bilk and the John Chilton Footwarmers with George Melly, before returning for another eight years with the Lyttelton band. Between about 1966 and 1968, when Stan was with Acker Bilk's band, his Edinburgh colleague Al Fairweather was on trumpet. I remember Bruce Turner, back in the 1960s, telling me how

---

[40] Latham J, Lee R and Bielderman G, 'Stan Greig Discography', Eurojazz Discos No. 42, 2nd Edition April 2001

51

highly he rated Stan's drumming, emphasising his formidable ability to swing a band, and expressing a wish that he could persuade him back into his own band. Ralph Laing, himself a fine piano player, once told me that he felt that Stan was very much under-rated as a piano player. He pointed out that Stan's playing had an authentic blues feel, which was quickly recognised by American musicians who were always keen to have Stan backing them. An example of this was Stan's inclusion as the only non-American in several tours of Europe in the 1980s with the stellar Harlem Jazz and Blues. Ralph considered Stan's playing to be endlessly thoughtful, never playing two choruses the same way and constantly responding to the playing of those whom he was accompanying.

Stan remained a major player in the British jazz world over the next four or five decades, continuing to put in time and recording with most of the prominent British jazz bands. He also led bands of various sizes, ranging from a trio to the 1975 London Jazz Big Band which included, amongst others, Al Fairweather. As well as playing trumpet, Al was the main arranger for the band. In fact, this band was of considerable stature, playing every week at the 100 Club and was a formidable aggregation, including many of the top players of the day. In the 1980s and 90s, after a four year spell with George Melly and a return to Humphrey Lyttelton's band, Stan played mostly as a solo pianist in clubs, pubs and jazz festivals. Sadly, Stan was affected by Parkinson's disease in later life and it was the disabilities associated with this debilitating condition, although he tried to hide it, which brought an end to his second spell with the Lyttelton band. Ralph Laing, who knew him well, has said that, in spite of his difficulties, Stan never stopped trying and late in his career, kept stoically working with Laurie Chescoe's band, while he still had reasonable movement in his hands. In addition, it was during this difficult period in his life that Stan helped Jools Holland to develop the bluesy piano playing, for which he would become famous.

For readers who wish to follow Stan's later career, there is an excellent biography, written by John Latham, in the 'Stan Greig Discography' published by 'Eurojazz Discos', which gives a detailed account of his career as a professional jazz musician[41]. A further mark of Stan's major impact on jazz is the fact that, by Ralph Laing's calculations, he has no fewer than one hundred and five LP recording sessions listed. Stan Greig was made President of the Sandy Brown Society from its inception in 1996 and in 2010, still held that office.

Bob Craig (trombone) was, for a period spanning six decades, one of the great stalwarts of the Edinburgh traditional jazz scene. He was born in Edinburgh in 1927, the son of a publican who ran a pub on Nicholson Street in the Southside of the town. Bob's schooling was at the RHS, where he was in the same class as Stu Eaton and Al Fairweather. A profile of Bob on the Sandy Brown Jazz website[42] tells us that the three of them became friends and, during the years of WWII when they were in their teens, they began both to listen to jazz and to learn to play the music. They also got together with Sandy Brown, who was in the year below them. Bob, who had for some reason acquired the nickname of 'Bugs', had taken up the trombone and, when Al Fairweather switched to trumpet, became the trombone player in the Brown band. After school, there were the usual interruptions of those days when National Service affected all of them at one time or another and Bob, who was in the RAF, grew what was to become his trademark handlebar moustache. Trumpeter and band leader Charlie McNair, reminiscing years later, recalled how in the 1960s, after Bob had appeared on STV, presenter Bill Tennant had remarked on the moustache and said that Bob was the Jimmy Edwards of the music business.

In the early 1950s, when Fairweather and Brown left for London, Bob stayed on in Edinburgh, where he had completed his BSc in engineering at Edinburgh University.

---

[41] Latham J, Lee R and Bielderman G, 'Stan Greig Discography', Eurojazz Discos No. 42, 2nd edition 2001
[42] www.sandybrownjazz.co.uk/profilebobcraig.html

SANDY BROWN (Clt.), AL FAIRWEATHER (Tpt.), BOB CRAIG (Tbn.), JIMMY FORSYTH (Drs.), NORRIE ANDERSON (Bjo.), CHARLIE JACKSON (Bass).

(from the collection of Peter Davenport, photographer unknown)

The trumpeter and journalist, Alastair Clark, who wrote Bob's obituary[43] when he died in 1998 at the age of 71, referred to him as *'the most modest of men'* and said that Bob *'never reckoned that he could compete at the highest level'* in jazz. It may have been for that reason that he did not move to London with his band colleagues but London's loss was to be very much Edinburgh's gain.

A story about Bob that went the rounds at one time, was that he had gone with others of the Gang to hear the Louis Armstrong All Stars, on one of their infrequent visits to the UK. Bob and the others had inveigled themselves by some means into the band room and had even managed to have a word or two with Louis himself. The clarinettist with the band was the great Barney Bigard, who had made his name as one of Duke Ellington's star sidemen throughout the 1930s. I suppose as much to have something to say to Louis as anything else, Bob mentioned what many jazz followers in those days were saying, which was that Bigard, great player though he was, was not the ideal clarinettist for the Armstrong band. Apparently, Louis was not greatly taken with this view and the story went that he continued publically to castigate Bob, whom he apparently referred to

---

[43] Clark A, 'Bob Craig', The Scotsman obituaries, 5 August 1998

as 'Bops' Craig, whenever he introduced Bigard during the rest of their tour.

After Sandy's and Al's departure, Bob continued to be very active around the local jazz scene and at various times, led bands of his own and played in many of the other Edinburgh bands, including those of Charlie McNair and Mike Hart. He later became part of an outstanding front line, comprising Ian 'Tello' Telford (trumpet), Dave Paxton (clarinet) with Bob himself on trombone, in the band that got together when Paxton returned to Edinburgh in the mid-1960s. This band later metamorphosed into 'Mike Hart's Society Syncopators' and I played with them for a couple of years in the 1970s, when the original bass player, Donald McDonald, went off to play saxophone. What made this front line so good was the unerring instinct the three of them had for their respective roles in a traditional jazz band. All three of them played a style that came direct from the music of King Oliver and early Louis Armstrong, each was master of that style and that frontline gelled magnificently. I consider that, of all the front lines with whom I played over a fifty year career in local jazz, none played together so naturally and convincingly as this one and the ensemble passages, when all three horns played together, were a joy to hear. As Alastair Clark said years later, Bob's trombone playing consisted of, *'nothing flashy, just the hot, punchy, chordal fundamentals that provided a marvellous platform for other horn players to take off on'*[44]. His playing always reminded me of that of the great Kid Ory, the trombonist on many of the classic Louis Armstrong 'Hot Five' and 'Hot Seven' recordings, recordings which Bob and his colleagues certainly considered to be the pinnacle of traditional jazz.

In the early recordings of the Sandy Brown Band, made before Sandy, Al and Stan Greig departed for the south, Bob's playing stands up well alongside that of the others, playing the traditional role of the trombone to perfection, just as he was to do across six decades in Edinburgh jazz. He was also to make much memorable music in the 1980s with his old pals Dave Paxton and Al Fairweather, both

---

[44] Clark A, 'Bob Craig', The Scotsman obituaries, 5 August 1998

home again after many years away, and bass player Dizzy Jackson, who like Bob had remained in Edinburgh. Bob was also to put in a lengthy spell in the 1980s with Bill Salmond's Louisiana Ragtime Band and he remained an active player right up to his death in 1998.

Another of the Gang, and another who was to be an important Edinburgh musician into the 1990s, was **Dave Paxton (clarinet)**. With a date of birth of 16 April 1926, he was fairly close to Al and Bob Craig in age and had attended Portobello High School, before joining the others at the RHS. A SBS Newsletter[45], with information courtesy of Edinburgh's Jim Keppie, tells us that Dave left school at fifteen and completed a course at the Leith Nautical College. This enabled him to join the RAF in 1942, as an apprentice. Eyesight problems prevented him from making air crew but he served for four years before returning to Edinburgh in 1948. Dave was self taught on clarinet and, like Sandy, was an ardent follower of the great Johnny Dodds. He also admired the playing of two other great American clarinetists, Omar Simeon and Jimmy Noone. I remember Dave telling me that he also had a lot of time for the great Swing clarinetists, Benny Goodman and Artie Shaw, although he said he could never decide which of these two he preferred. Dave often played with Sandy and Al at the Edinburgh Jazz Club in Riego Street, which had previously been known as the Rhythm Club, a period Jim Walker recalls as a golden age. The Jazz Band Balls in the Oddfellow's Hall had also started around this time and, although plenty came to dance, many came along just to listen. Jim recalls that the music seemed to get better and better. One night, Sandy's band took a break which seemed to go on and on and then a clarinettist, unknown to Jim Walker, got up on the band stand and played one lyrical solo after another, accompanied only by piano. This was Dave Paxton and Jim remembers the occasion as *'pure magic'*.

After working as an insurance clerk in Edinburgh, Dave went out to the Persian Gulf in about 1951, to work in the oil industry, and did not return to Edinburgh permanently

---

[45] SBS. Newsletter 150, June 2009

until the mid-1960s. He then rapidly re-established himself as a major player in the local jazz scene. I remember Al Fairweather telling me that Dave, a hard working and conscientious musician himself, had constantly urged Sandy Brown to practice hard at his clarinet playing. I had also been aware for many years of the famous story, a legend of Edinburgh jazz, about the weekend spent by Sandy and Dave in a wooden hut in the Pentland Hills. Bill Strachan says that the hut was at Ravelrigg junction, on the railway line just to the west of Balerno, and was one of a group of holiday huts, all of them made from old, wooden, railway goods wagons. Apparently, the two clarinetists had taken themselves off to this remote spot and there they had spent an entire weekend (Jimmy Keppie reports that it was a whole week) practicing together. Their programme had followed a pattern: practice scales all morning; then practice blues choruses all afternoon, providing criticism of each other, before moving on to playing call and response phrases in the evening. They were said to have survived for the entire duration on nothing but eggs!

Sandy, of course, would go on to become an internationally renowned jazz musician, a player whose abilities and originality saw him acclaimed as a genius, but he was not the only outstanding player amongst these pioneers. Dave Paxton, in my view, was a talent comparable to Al Fairweather's. Both were very good indeed, both were under rated; Al because of his constant association with Sandy, and Dave, both because of association with Sandy and by the fact that he never played full time or made anything like the number of recordings that his ability deserved. In addition, and unlike Al, Dave had fewer opportunities to play with musicians whose talents matched his own. I knew, admired and played with Dave for many years and we will hear much more about him later in this book, after his return from the Middle East.

These then, were amongst the more prominent of the Royal High School Gang but they were by no means all of them. There were many more who were contemporary with those mentioned above and then a whole line of others over the years to come. We will meet many of them in the next chapter.

Chapter IV

The RHS Jazz Production Line

Another in the same school year at the RHS as Al Fairweather and Bob Craig was **trumpeter Stu Eaton** who was a significant figure on the early jazz scene. As a clue to Stu Eaton's style, John Latham tells us that Eaton, responding to the comment that his playing was too 'white', retorted *'Well, I am white.'* As John Latham goes on to say, this was an interesting comment from someone who believed that only Negroes, Jews and Scots could play jazz, and who personally qualified on two counts![46] Stu Eaton emigrated to Canada in 1954 where he still lives at the time of writing in 2010. Eaton had played initially with a band that included fellow trumpeter Bob Fairley, Bill McGregor (bjo), Drew Bruce (rds) and Drew's mother, 'Ma' Bruce (pno). It is not clear just how early this band was, although we know from Jim Walker that it was already playing in 1945. As a group, they were older than the RHS Gang. There was however, another early RHS jazzer around at this time as well. He was Edward 'Teddy' Gage, who played the soprano sax and was later to become an art teacher at Fettes School, a senior lecturer at Napier University and a distinguished art critic with The Scotsman. By 1946/47, Eaton was playing trumpet in one of Sandy's earliest bands, with Al

---

[46] SBS Newsletter No. 2, August 1996

Fairweather (tbn), George Crockett (drms), Ma Bruce (pno) and Drew Bruce who played sax and sang[47].

Jim Walker says that **Drew Bruce (reeds, vocals)**, while not impressing him as a sax player, made up for it with his infectious enthusiasm for the music and was also a good vocalist with a very earthy sound. Jim thinks that Drew would have been about ten years older than most of the RHS crowd. According to Bill Strachan, Drew Bruce's father had a market garden in York Road in the Trinity area of Edinburgh (others have said it was near Orchard Brae) where, during the years of WWII, they grew vegetables as part of the war effort. A further benefit of the market garden was that it put Drew in a reserved occupation, thus allowing him to avoid being called up. Bill Strachan says that Drew was something of an opportunist, putting him in mind of Private Walker in 'Dad's Army', the TV series about the Home Guard. Apparently, Drew was a gifted wheeler dealer, using the Three Tuns pub in Hanover Street, then sometimes known ironically as the Exchange, as his personal market place. There he did very well, bartering vegetables for fags and clothes from members of the American forces. Bill recalls that some of the RHS Gang would occasionally work at the Bruce market garden to earn a bit of extra pocket money. Another enterprising venture of Drew's was an attempt to make some illicit hooch, trying to create alcohol by fermenting some of his vegetable products with invert sugar. Someone produced an equally illicit, small still affair and a quantity of very rough spirit was obtained. When tasted by Bob Craig, it almost slew him on the spot and the experiment was not repeated. Ma Bruce is said to have owned copies of the sheet music of all Jelly Roll Morton's compositions but her collection was lost when their house was sold.

Bill McGregor (banjo), who was born on 2nd September 1910 and educated at George Watson's College, was a generation older than any of the RHS Gang. Bill had a grocer's shop in the Marchmont area of Edinburgh, a shop which his son Kenny, continued to run as a grocers until

---

[47] SBS Newsletters Nos. 7 Jun 1997, 31 Jul 1999, 54 Jun 2001, 58 Oct 2001, 144 Dec 2008, 145 Jan 2009

2006. Clearly a man of parts, Bill was also involved with a water polo club at Warrender Baths, not far from his shop. Jim Walker remembers him as being a very solid banjo player. As an interesting historical aside, Bill Strachan reports that Bill McGregor owned, not only a wax cylinder of Caruso singing, but also the requisite machine on which to play it. This is confirmed from an unexpected source. I had known Kenny McGregor since he was a school boy, and when I met with him in 2011 to talk about his father's career in jazz, he lent me a letter received by his father, dated 12th December 1946. This letter is signed by Gerald Lascelles and is almost completely about their mutual interest in jazz. The letter makes it clear that they had already corresponded a lot but gives no hint as to how the two came to know each other.

The Honourable Gerald Lascelles (1924 - 1998) was the younger son of the 6th Earl of Harewood and Mary, the Princess Royal and daughter of King George V. The Princess Royal was thus sister to both Edward XIII and George VI and her son, Gerald Lacelles, first cousin of our present Queen. More pertinently to us, Lascelles was well known as a passionate jazz enthusiast and supporter in his day and his name turns up quite regularly in jazz writings of the time. He was certainly a significant figure in British jazz, particularly in the 1940/50s and, like his fellow aristocratic jazz buff, the Marquis of Donegal, was greatly valued as an opener of jazz clubs and festivals, when his name was a guarantee of copious press coverage.

In the letter, Lascelles congratulates Bill on his recent acquisition of an Edison cylinder gramophone, which he describes as 'a bit primitive, but very amusing', and goes on to say that his brother once had some cylinders lent to him '...but they were all opera and sounded grim'. He also says that he did not know of anyone who had any cylinders at that time but '...will enquire in case I can chance upon one of the fabulous Bolden ones on Blue Ambriol'[48]. It seems that

---

[48] Lascelles probably meant Blue Amberol Records, a trademarked name for cylinder recordings made by the Eddison Co of the USA between1912 and 1929. They originally produced 2 minute wax cylinders, then changed to 4 minute black wax 'Amberol' cylinders from 1908. They then changed again to 'indestructible'

Lascelles knew his jazz history and, interestingly, this is the only reference, of which I am aware, in which the legendary, and still untraced, Buddy Bolden recordings are said to be on a named recording label. Bill had apparently been filling up his record collection with '... *some choice Bix and Bessie, not to mention Morton*', which gives us a fairly clear picture of his tastes in jazz. Lascelles goes on to say that, while he saw (Jelly Roll) Morton recordings as '...*very much an acquired taste*', he had liked all he had heard to date. However, he did not approve of the Yerba Buena Band, although he had never heard them, and found it '...*hard to accept their instrumentation*'. In spite of never having heard them, and only had them '*preached at me*', he speculated that they had a somewhat coarse tone or, at least, '...*I found this to be the case on hearing the Webb Dixielanders who I think have much the same instrumentation*'.

Lascelles then goes on to write about his ongoing career in the 2nd Battalion, the Rifle Brigade, British Army of the Rhine, in which he was serving. He had been made Education Officer for the battalion and part of this role was to run what he calls a 'Rhythm Club'. He explains that this was mostly about dishing out a certain amount of jazz and jive on records, to anyone who wished to hear it. The most popular records are reported to be the Muggsy Spaniers followed by the (Benny) Goodman Sextet and his other small groups. He also '*lashes out a little piano music on wax – Hines and Waller mostly*'. Lascelles reports that he had attended a live broadcast at BFN (British Forces Network), as a member of the audience, and had bumped into a sergeant who ran the Swing Club. In the true spirit of the Revival, he says that the Swing Club was '...*not as bad as its name implies as they play Mezz/Ladnier and Muggsy and Bix on occasions*'. The meeting with the sergeant had provided an opportunity for Lascelles to bring back some records, when he returned from leave, followed by the chance to participate in a broadcast, which he hoped '...*might be a good chance to put over a line of really first-*

'Blue Amberol' cylinders, which lasted approx 4 minutes and were made of celluloid with a Plaster of Paris core and were blue in colour (Wikipedia) *class jazz to those who want it'.* The crusading spirit of the Revival!

Lascelles own record buying had been fairly extensive and he had acquired records '*...ranging from the Mary Lou Williams Sextet on Asch to some real gems of piano and blues singing on early and I think unheard-of labels from the USA, which I got through the MM* (presumably, the Melody Maker) *and a charming man who is selling out his collection of almost entirely piano jazz, mostly solos which I think you disapprove of!*' On British labels he had contented himself with Bechet's 'Texas Moaner' and *'the Bunk'*, which he had not as yet heard, as it was at home. He had also got hold of some Josh White on Brunswick and (Wingy) Manone's 'Ain't Got Nobody', which was not as good as he had hoped. He had liked Mel Powell's piano playing on the Goodman Sextet's 'Ain't Misbehavin'' and the *'classic Stardust by Waller on BB, which is now one of my favourite discs'.* He goes on to report that *'The wax my brother brought back from the States is really terrific, especially some of the Commodore sides, and that beautiful* (Art) *Hodes 'Selections from the Gutter'.* Finally with regard to his record collection, he says that he had had the great misfortune to lose the entire catalogue of his collection and was having to make a new one, '*...more or less on a card index principle, as it is the best way of sorting out all the information in the most get-attable form!*' Lascelles final paragraph in the letter gives a marvellous insight to the thinking in jazz circles of the time and is worth quoting in full. He writes:

'The revival of jazz is in sight – so you say – but I wonder just how much of it is revival and where the decline comes in. Frankly with this Rebop around the corner, and name bands breaking up all over the States, it is hard to say where one stands. Certainly swing has had it in no mean manner, but whether jazz or some bastard music will replace it is a risky thing to bet on right now. People like jazz in large numbers – but they don't really appreciate it in the full sense of the word, and regard it as just another phenomenon of the popular music world, which is never a good thing in my opinion. The ban on foreign musicians is another serious deterrent to any serious attempt to revise our views and

standards of jazz in GB. This will no doubt be lifted in time, but it may be too late then.'

Gerald Lascelles' letter is a wonderful time capsule of the jazz world of the mid-1940s. It is a microcosm of the times, expressing many of the hopes and fears of a music, in the dying days of Swing, in the process of splitting itself in two – the two parallel channels of the future: Revivalist jazz and the bebop revolution. It certainly demonstrates that the fabled feuds of the 1940s were very real at the time and gives life to the stories of the two camps haranguing each other in bitter and fierce rivalry. This battle royal between the beboppers and the 'Mouldy Fygges', as they called the traditionalists, was to an extent still around when I came on the jazz scene of the late 1950s but had diminished to an occasional irritable lack of tolerance.

Kenny McGregor, to whom I am especially grateful for allowing me access to Lascelles letter, remembered nothing of his father's jazz playing. It seems that Bill McGregor had stopped playing, either before Kenny was born or early in his life. He had kept his banjo though, which Kenny still has, and I remember Bill McGregor letting me see the instrument back in the 1960s, when I told him that I was involved in jazz. Kenny does however, remember his Dad listening to recordings of the bands of Duke Ellington, Count Basie and Louis Armstrong and going with him to hear the Ellington band in concert in Newcastle in 1969, a concert that I too managed to attend. Kenny also remembers his Dad complaining that none of the jazz greats seemed to come to play in Edinburgh. Bill McGregor, one of the earliest Edinburgh jazzers that we know about, died in 1970, in his sixty first year.

Bob Fairley (trumpet) seems to have had a weak lip for trumpet and could only manage a few numbers before his embouchure failed him. Jim Walker recalls that Bob had a lovely tone and imaginative phrasing, rather reminiscent of Bix Beiderbecke.

**An Edinburgh jazz band, location unknown but probably in the 1940s.
Drew Bruce (clarinet), Bob Fairley (trumpet), Bill McGregor (banjo), Ma Bruce (piano) Drummer unknown but it could be a young Bob Craig on trombone (photo from the collection of Kenny McGregor, photographer unknown)**

Stu Eaton would sometimes take over from Bob Fairley when his lip gave out and gradually Drew Bruce took more of a back seat. Ma Bruce, however, continued for a while and was renowned for hammering out chords on the key board, to the extent that Jim Walker felt with her around, there was hardly a need for a drummer.

A sign of Revival activity elsewhere was a visit, by Stu Eaton, Drew Bruce, Bill McGregor and Bob Fairley, to Hawick on 4th April 1946 to hear the George Webb Dixielanders with their new addition, Humphrey Lyttelton on trumpet, and Wally Fawkes on clarinet. This was apparently Humph's first gig with the Webb band and the event was further distinguished by Drew Bruce joining the band to sing a couple of numbers, including 'Winin' Boy'[49].

---

[49] SBS Newsletter No 141, Sept 2008

Apparently, Wally Fawkes was required to judge the Belle of the Ball and Pretty Ankle competitions! An even more adventurous visit by Eaton and others of the RHS Gang, was to Paris in the following year, when they met the great New Orleans clarinet and soprano sax player, Sydney Bechet[50]. This and a second visit to Paris, is vividly described in Sandy Brown's 'The McJazz Manuscripts'[51]. There seems to have been a surprising amount of travelling around by the Edinburgh jazz crowd in the early days. Jim Walker tells the tale of one trip by an early Edinburgh band to Manchester, where they were warned against setting foot in a certain area because there was a wild and dangerous gang around. Inevitably, the band found its way to the danger area and, sure enough, the dreaded gang hove into view. The band immediately started singing 'I Belong to Glasgow' and the wild and dangerous gang quietly melted away!

The earliest drummer with Sandy Brown's bands is believed to have been journalist **George Crockett (drums)**, into whose published information on pre-WWII jazz in Edinburgh we have already delved in Chapter I. It is clear that he had an interest in jazz before 1940 and, having been born in Galashiels on 16th July 1920, he was about half a generation older than most of the RHS Gang. Crockett seems to have been one of the earliest musicians to be involved in the Revival in Edinburgh and he played and recorded with Sandy Brown in his earliest period. According to Derek Copland, in a memoire published on the Sandy Brown Jazz website[52], the earliest recordings by the Brown band, were made in 1946/47. They were made privately and recorded on acetate and George Crockett was the drummer on these recordings. A Sandy Brown Society Newsletter[53] gives the line-up on these early recordings as Stu Eaton (tpt), Sandy Brown (clt), Ma Bruce (pno), Billy Neill (gtr), Bruce (in fact, Bill) McGregor (bjo) and Gerald (in fact, George) Crockett (drms). The first of these Glasgow

---

[50] SBS Newsletter No. 141, Sept 2008
[51] Binns D (editor), 'The McJazz Manuscripts – A Collection of the Writings of Sandy Brown', Faber and Faber, 1979, by kind permission of David Binns
[52] Copland D, http://sandybrownjazz.co.uk/profilegeorgecrockett.html
[53] SBS Newsletters No 54, June 2001 and No 58, October 2001

recording dates is given in October 1946 and the tunes were 'Yellow Dog Blues', 'untitled', 'Doctor Jazz' and 'Shoe Shiner's Drag'. The same line-up is said to have made further recordings, again in Glasgow, on 3rd January 1947, when the tunes were 'Careless Love' with Div (presumably Drew) Bruce (voc) and 'Bill Bailey'. Then, on 25th January 1947, they recorded 'Buddy Bolden's Blues', 'Jazz Me Blues', 'Sad Ole Blues', 'Royal Garden Blues' (on which Bob Fairley was added on trumpet) and 'Joe Turner's Blues' with Drew Bruce on vocal. Finally, a session on 4th July 1947 produced 'I Ain't Gonna give Nobody None of my Jellyroll' and 'Careless Love'. Apparently, a copy of these old acetate recordings was taken by discographer and Sandy's old commanding officer, Horace Meunier Harris, to the National Sound Archive to find out if they could be cleaned up but, unfortunately, they were beyond restoration.

Although he had played and recorded with Sandy Brown, George Crockett seems to have been drawn to the more Dixieland oriented music of the group around Alex Welsh and Archie Semple. Certainly, his later playing was to be mostly with Welsh, Semple and others of the *'more Dixieland'* persuasion, and we will hear more of him in Chapter V.

Another by the name of Crockett, **Stuart 'Stu' Crockett (tbn)**, had played trombone with trumpeter Stu Eaton in his earliest days. Although I had been told that they were not related, it has also been reported that Stu and George Crockett were cousins. The bass player, Dizzy Jackson, tells us that Stu Crockett was at one time band manager for the Sandy Brown band and, amongst other duties, organized a two week tour around gigs in London in 1953, including one at the Royal Festival Hall and one at Wood Green. Many years later, Stu Crockett was to be a member of the committee which was responsible for organizing a memorial plaque to Sandy Brown and Al Fairweather[54]. Stu Crockett, one of the RHS Gang, died in the Edinburgh area on the sixteenth of February 2012 at the age of 87.

Sandy Currie, also an RHS scholar, has already been mentioned and seems to have been one of those invaluable

---

[54] SBS Newsletter No 4

enthusiasts around the jazz scene who contribute a great deal through their willingness to organize, keep notes and even make recordings. It appears that Sandy also got actively involved in playing as the Edinburgh drummer, Kenny Milne, says that he can remember him playing bass with one of Charlie McNair's bands in the 1950s. Sandy Currie had been secretary and treasurer of the Edinburgh Jazz Club when it was run by another notable enthusiast, Dave Mylne. It is to Sandy Currie's heroic efforts that we owe the recording of a historic and important concert at the Usher Hall in February 1952, involving the Sandy Brown band and the great Mississippi Blues singer, Big Bill Broonzy, of which more later. Sandy Currie too, in the 1990s, was on the various committees responsible for memorial plaques to Sandy Brown and Al Fairweather at the Royal High School, the Usher Hall and London's 100 Club. I met him when I was playing with Old Bailey and his Jazz Advocates in the 1960s and, after a gig, he insisted on me and several others accompanying him back to his flat in the Morningside district of town. There, we listened to jazz records and much reminiscing from Sandy, until I made my escape to stagger home, bleary eyed and shivering from cold and lack of sleep, as the dawn broke over the early morning milk carts and paper boys delivering the day's news. I only wish now, that I had been better prepared to listen and take note of what Sandy Currie had to say; it would have been extremely interesting and a valuable source of information for this book.

It may be that Sandy Currie's boundless enthusiasm was a bit much for at least one jazz musician. There was a story around that someone Sandy knew was to make a trip to Paris. Sandy insisted that he should look up a famous American jazz musician, then resident in the French capital. *'I know him well'* Sandy Currie had said *'I spent a lot of time with him when I was in Paris recently myself. Just say you know me.'* His friend duly made his way to the house of the famous American, said he had been recommended to call by his friend, Sandy Currie - and promptly had the door slammed in his face and was told to f- - k off in no uncertain terms! I have no idea if this was true or not, but it is a good story. Sandy Currie died in Edinburgh on 15th January 2011.

Dave Mylne was associated with the RHS Gang, although not a pupil of the school. He was a great enthusiast for classic jazz, an enthusiastic collector of jazz records and something of an entrepreneur. He was to become an architect, based, I understand, in Duns in the Scottish Borders. In the 1940s, his father was headmaster of a private school then located in Dalhousie Castle, now a posh hotel, out on the south side of Edinburgh near Bonnyrigg. Apparently, the Brown band played quite regularly for weekend dances at the school and the band members were also allowed access to a collection of jazz records and books, presumably belonging to either Mylne senior or junior. This information comes from another Sandy Brown Jazz website profile of another member of the Brown band, Willie Burns[55], who replaced George Crockett on drums in the later 1940s. Malcolm Burns, son of Willie, told me that his Dad used to talk about how they had to travel to Dalhousie Castle, complete with drum kit, by public transport.

Dave Mylne himself clearly had aspirations to get involved in the playing side of jazz and tried his hand at drumming. A photograph, sent in by Drew Landles and shown in an SBS Newsletter[56], shows him playing drums in a band at the Oddfellows Hall, with Bob Craig, Stu Eaton, Drew Bruce and Drew Landles himself on piano. Dave Mylne was much involved in promoting jazz in Edinburgh during the Revival, had presented many record sessions and, by 1950, was running the Edinburgh Rhythm Club. He later became known as an authority on classic jazz, particularly the playing of Sydney Bechet. Unfortunately, the impressive and extensive record collection which he had built up was auctioned off and broken up after his death. As this collection apparently included a lot of Edinburgh based jazz, it is a great pity that there was no Edinburgh jazz archive at that time, into which it could have been placed.

---

[55] http://sandybrownjazz.co.uk/profilewillieburns.html
[56] SBS Newsletter No. 88, April 2004

Willie Burns (drums) did not attend the RHS but had arrived in Edinburgh with his parents, who had come originally from Stornoway, on the Isle of Lewis in the Hebrides. The profile of Willie on the Sandy Brown Jazz website alluded to above (which is packed with interesting information and is highly recommended to all readers of this book), tells us that his parents had emigrated to Australia, where Willie was born on 5th November 1932. They then returned to Scotland and eventually ended up in Edinburgh, sometime in the later 1930s. On arrival in Edinburgh, Willie was enrolled at George Watson's College but by good fortune, his family put down their roots in Joppa, not far from several members of the RHS Gang, including Stan Grieg and Johnny Twiss (banjo and guitar), both of whom played with the early Brown band. Stan and Johnny Twiss were pals of Willie's older brother Malcolm, known as Mal, and through this connection Willie also got to know them.

Willie was keen on music and had learned to play drums with a local pipe band. He was apparently an extroverted character and he may well have volunteered himself as a drummer, when he found himself in contact with the members of the Brown band. It is reported that these youngsters were able to rehearse in the Burns family home in Esplanade Terrace, in Joppa, and even give impromptu public performances. When the weather was good, the big bay windows of the upstairs room would be wide open and holiday makers from the beach would find themselves being treated to an unofficial jazz concert. Willie's son, Malcolm Burns, told me that there was a story in his family, which he remembers hearing when he was young, that Willie was already playing with the band in Rose Street pubs when he was only 14 years old. If this was so, then it would have been in about 1947, which would certainly tie in nicely with the time scale of the early Sandy Brown band. It would also, of course, fit in with the future development of the Edinburgh jazz scene, which came to rely on the pubs for regular playing venues.

The Sandy Brown Band
Johnny Twiss (bjo), Stan Greig (pno), Sandy Brown (clt),
Al Fairweather (tpt), Willie Burns (drms)
(from the collection of Malcolm Burns, photographer
unknown)

A record from the time tells us that the band on 29th October 1949 was Al Fairweather, Sandy Brown, Stan Greig, Johnny Twiss on banjo, Will Redpath on bass and Willie Burns on drums. This was also the line up for the band's first studio recording session, the results of which were issued in 1950 on S & M (Swarbrick and Mossman) Records, with the serial numbers S&M 1001 and 1002. The tunes were *Melancholy Blues, Irish Black Bottom, Alexander* and *Of All the Wrongs You You've Done to Me.* These recordings are now very rare and if anyone has a copy, they are very fortunate. Willie's son Malcolm has a copy of one of the old 78 rpm records but unfortunately it is in two pieces and has been for a long time, the breakage dating from before Malcolm's mother handed it on to him!

Willie became a teenage engineering apprentice, serving his time in Henry Robb's yard in Leith. Willie's family returned to Stornoway in 1950, when his father (yet another Malcolm) 'retired' to run a small Harris Tweed business, and

Willie completed his engineering apprenticeship there before, in the 1950s, becoming a ship's engineer. George Hewitt says that Willie was eventually replaced in the Brown band, at different times, by Farrie Forsyth and Bill Strachan. Malcolm Burns believes that his father never played again with the Brown band after his return to Stornoway. However, he remembers his mother saying that they used to meet up and hang out with Sandy and the band, when they played in Glasgow in the late 1950s, by which time Willie and his wife were living there. Malcolm also remembers a story about Sandy showing off his false teeth, which were apparently split in two to help his blowing technique or something of the sort. Given Sandy's later reputation and the many stories about his teeth, it seems a shame that no enterprising salesman has tried to market special Sandy Brown dentures, already split in two, to help clarinet disciples play like Sandy!

Willie Burns died, at the age of 60, on 5th May 1993, having suffered a heart attack. After he died, Stan Greig got in touch with his wife Barbara and Willie's son Malcolm, visited Stan in London. Several members of Willie's family had an interest in music, including his son who took up guitar in the 1970s, and several grandchildren who sing, play guitar or bagpipes. One granddaughter won a prize for her singing and has a saxophone playing grandfather on her mother's side of the family. His name is Jim Galloway but this is not the Jim Galloway from Ayrshire, who was to be great success in the Edinburgh International Jazz Festivals of the 1980/90s, but another reeds player of the same name who came from Kirkcaldy. He attended Edinburgh College of Art and played jazz on the sax and clarinet, sometimes leading bands, from the late 1950s on, playing in the bebop style. Later, he lived in London and Manchester, where he became involved in playing with big bands. He now, in 2011, lives near Glenrothes, where he has continued to play, and has appeared in Glasgow with the Michael Deans band.

Rather endearingly, **Will Redpath (bass)**, who played bass on the S&M recordings, described himself, as *'the*

World's worst bass player'[57]. In the profile on Dizzy Jackson on the Sandy Brown Jazz website[58] (another profile well worth reading), there is another good story about Will Redpath, who clearly did not mind telling stories against himself. Firstly, Dizzy Jackson tells us *'Someone once told me that Will used to play with a pair of leather gloves on. I don't know if that's true.'* Will then goes on to explain *'The story about me wearing gloves (or rather one on my right hand) – or Elastoplast - is true. I had taken up the bass because I was desperate to participate in this music I loved, but I quickly found out that I was no musician and had to do feverish mental calculations when the boys decided to change key, which they did instinctively. I had bought the double bass from a pawn shop for £5. It leaked, so that I had to pull the strings very hard. This resulted in shredding my fingers and producing a noise dominated by the string hitting the wood. The whole episode was one that I would rather have forgotten'.* (Note: Will was not alone in his suffering, or his solutions. When I first got into skiffle music in the late 1950s, I started on the washboard and found that (a) I could not keep the thimbles on my fingers and that (b) when the thimbles flew off, I was left scrubbing away with my bare fingers. This had an effect like a cheese grater and clearly could not be allowed to continue as I was beginning to have visions of being left fingerless. I too wore gloves, with thimbles riveted on, which partly solved the problem (the rivets hurt my fingers inside the gloves) but left me looking a bit of a prat).

Jim Walker remembers what he describes as a tremendous party at Will Redpath's house in Morningside Place. This took place at the time when Graeme Bell's Australian Jazz Band was in town and the pianist from that band turned up at the party. Jim recalls that the pianist *'played until his fingers must have been raw'* and that Sandy Brown, who was *'...incredibly drunk, was propped up against the door post with his clarinet and played some of the most marvellous music I have ever heard'.* However poorly he rated his own bass playing, Will was clearly an

---

[57] SBS Newsletter No. 95, November 2004
[58] http://www.sandybrownjazz.co.uk/profiledizzyjackson.html

enthusiastic jazzer and we know that he came from a creative family, Jim Walker telling us that he was the nephew of the famous Scottish painter, Anne Redpath. Jim also says that Will had taken up bass after a *'valiant struggle with the sousaphone'*. I would like to have met Will Redpath. I think I would have liked him and, after all, whatever he might say about his own contribution, he did record with several of the legendary figures of British traditional jazz, something that not everyone can claim.

Charles 'Dizzy' Jackson (bass), who was born in Edinburgh on 14th July 1932 and attended the RHS, replaced Will Redpath in the Brown band. He had acquired his nickname because he could waggle his ears in imitation of a 'B' movie actor of the time, who was called Dizzy. He was a little younger than Sandy, Al and Bob, who were already active with their earliest jazz band, and Dizzy recalled that he heard them play in the school playground during a mock election project. Dizzy noted that Sandy was *'the dominant figure in the band – as ever!'* Later, Dizzy and some friends started going regularly to listen to jazz at the West End Cafe in Shandwick Place, the street that is a continuation of the west end of Princes Street. This establishment crops up constantly in tales of the Revival in Edinburgh and Dizzy's memory of the place is recorded in his profile on the Sandy Brown Jazz website mentioned above[59]. He says *'It had an ornate entrance and you would go down a long corridor where you could get coffee, to a huge room at the back. The room was about twenty feet high with a stage at the back. There was no alcohol served, just coffee with waitress service at the tables. I can remember hearing the Graeme Bell Band and many others there.'*

Again we are indebted to the profile of Dizzy on the Sandy Brown Jazz website for the tale of how he came to replace Will Redpath. Jimmy Gavin, a close associate of the RHS Gang, apparently told Dizzy that the band was looking for a bass player, as Will Redpath had left. Jimmy apparently informed Dizzy that as he, Dizzy, had played violin at school, he ought to be able to handle a double bass! Having given this some thought, Dizzy bought himself

---

[59] http://www.sandybrownjazz.co.uk/profiledizzyjackson.html

a bass for £20 at Gordon Simpson's music shop, which was in Stafford Street, just round the corner from the West End Café. Like so many in jazz history, Dizzy commenced to teach himself how to play and went along to practice with the band. Help from Stan Greig, regarding chord structure and musical intervals, enabled Dizzy to make progress and he soon became a regular member of the band, playing with them in the West End Café and at other gigs. Incidentally, he bought well and in 2011 he is still playing the same double bass. It would be interesting to know its value now.

Dizzy has recalled how astounded he was (gobsmacked is the word he used) by the trumpet playing of Al Fairweather and says that he was moved to tears by the quality of Al's playing, particularly his hot tone and musical ideas. Al, Dizzy reported, always had something to say and the numbers would get increasingly hotter and hotter, as the ensemble playing developed. He also tells of playing at the Art Revels, an annual dance of incredible wildness run by the students at the Edinburgh College of Art. It was at this gig that Al Fairweather once removed an irritating invader of the band stand by shifting his trumpet to his left hand and belting the invading nuisance with his right. I can also vouch for the wildness of the Art Revels, having played at the event on many occasions in the 1960s. It was a fancy dress dance and once, just as I was arriving, a reveller turned up dressed in a large cardboard tube with balloons at his feet. Asked by the doorman what he was supposed to be, he responded that he was an erect penis and was most indignant to be refused entry on the grounds of obscenity. Nothing if not resourceful, he stamped on his balloons and was allowed in as a rocket.

Dizzy is listed as a member of the Brown band that played at the Big Bill Broonzy concert at the Usher Hall in 1952, mentioned above and recorded by Sandy Currie. Many years later, in 1998, a transcription from Sandy Currie's recording of the concert was released by Lake Records (LAKE CD94). This recording reveals just how good the Brown band was at this early point in its history. The band line-up is given on the CD sleeve as Sandy Brown, Al Fairweather, Bob Craig, Stan Greig (who played both piano and drums during the concert), Norrie Anderson (banjo),

Dizzy Jackson (bass) and Farrie Forsyth (drums). Although Sandy Currie's original recording tape had deteriorated, the recording had at some time been copied onto acetate, and it was possible to clean this up to a condition suitable for general release. Sandy's profile on the Sandy Brown Jazz website says that the band played the first half of the concert and Broonzy the second half[60]. However, this is not what the printed programme for the concert says. The programme gives the running order as:

1. Sandy Brown's Jazz Band set the pace for tonight (list of tunes)
2. Big Bill Broonzy and his guitar ramble through a selection of Folk songs, guitar solos and spirituals (list of tunes)

Intermission

3. The Jazz Band returns to the fray (list of tunes)
4. Big Bill's Skiffle Party ends the evening during which he and the band will play a completely unpredictable choice of blues (list of tunes)

As indicated in the above extract, the programme lists the tunes that the band would play and the tunes from which Broonzy would select his songs for the evening. Of course, on the night either Broonzy or the band or both may well have deviated from this plan and, given the improvisatory nature of jazz and the blues, this seems not unlikely.

Dizzy Jackson's place in the band at this concert has been questioned by some who believe that it was a bass player called John Rae who played. This includes a contemporary, Bill Strachan, who also says that it was he who played drums at this concert and not Farrie Forsyth. Jazz enthusiast the late Janol Scott also believed that Bill Strachan and John Rae were the drummer and bass player respectively. In addition, John Rae's widow, Jacqueline Rae, wrote about this to the SBS in October 2000[61], making a convincing case that it had been her late husband who

---

[60] http://sandybrownjazz.co.uk/sandybrown.html
[61] SBS Newsletter No. 16 April 1998, 46 October 2000

played bass. John Rae, who died in 1976, was a medical student who played with Al and Sandy in about 1951-52. George Hewitt, however, believes it was Dizzy he heard that night and Dizzy himself is adamant that it was he who played. Dizzy has said[62] *'I played the '52 concert on bass. I had already been with the band for a year when the concert took place. I actually still have a visual memory of being on the stand in the hall and playing and got particularly excited at Sandy's solo in High Society. I can even remember signing the visitor's book in the Shakespeare Bar next to the Usher Hall as visiting artists did and getting a free drink. What musician would forget that? Bob and Stan are quite certain it was me playing. Farrie was already the regular drummer when I joined the band'.* Jim Young, another long serving Edinburgh bass player whom we will meet later, was also at the concert and confirms that he remembers Dizzy Jackson playing bass that night and this is also the view of trombonist Mike Pollett, who was another attending the concert.

I thought that I might have been able to throw some light on the situation when I managed to get hold of a copy of the printed programme for the concert from trumpeter Peter Davenport, but no such luck. The programme, although detailed in other respects, does not give the line-up of the band. On the back of the programme, there are several advertisements, including one for a Jazz Band Ball, featuring Sandy's band, at the Oddfellows Hall the following Friday. This does list the band line-up but, frustratingly, shows Stan Grieg as 'piano and drums' but does not list any other drummer and lists no bass player at all! We already know that Stan played both piano and drums at the Broonzy concert because, clearly audible on the CD, Sandy announces, rather condescendingly in my view, that Stan is going to have *'an attempt'* on the drums. Stan had been playing piano up to this point and there is clearly another drummer playing at the same time. The advert for the Jazz Band Ball also lists Hoss Ross on washboard but there is no trace of a washboard on the CD recording of the concert. All very mysterious!

---

[62] SBS Newsletter No. 16, April 1998

The sleeve notes for the CD of the concert, issued by Lake Records, were written by Sandy Currie himself and he certainly lists Dizzy as the bass player. However, Sandy Currie himself later contributed to the uncertainty, when he sent to the SBS, a photograph of the band setting up prior to the concert and identifies a figure in the photo as John Rae[63]. This certainly reinforces the doubt about the identity of the bass player. Further to this, Sandy Currie pointed out that there were in fact, not one but two concerts at the Usher Hall, involving the Sandy Brown Band. The second concert took place in January 1953, a year after the Big Bill Broonzy concert, with the Brown Band supporting, on this occasion, the Freddy Randall Band. Perhaps the source of the confusion lies here and, remembering that these two concerts took place a very long time ago in the early 1950s, memories of who played at which concert may well have become hazy. As anyone who has tried interviewing people about times in the past will know, it is quite amazing how memories, with absolutely no ulterior motive, will differ in accounts of the same events. It seems to me totally understandable that memories vary, sometimes quite substantially, about events of more than fifty years ago. I played with the Old Bailey band in the Usher Hall on 1st April 1966 (45 years ago at the time of writing) when we played as support band to the touring Alex Welsh band with Earl Hines. This was our equivalent to the Brown band Usher Hall concerts in 1952 and 1953, and yet, incredibly, I can remember almost nothing about it. This seems utterly ridiculous but it is absolutely true. Furthermore, one member of our band who played that night remembered it as Earl Hines actually playing with us, which he certainly did not, playing only with the Welsh band. As Stu Eaton apparently once said *Time has a way of distorting the past*!!

In a final effort to resolve the question of who played at the Usher Hall concerts of 1952 and 1953, in 2011 I went to the Shakespeare Bar, still next to the Usher Hall as described by Dizzy, and asked if they still had visitor's books from the 1950s. The manager said that she had no knowledge of any such books but suggested they may have

---

[63] SBS Newsletter No. 20, Aug 1998

been handed over to the Usher Hall itself or to the City Central Library. Both would have been suitable depositories for what were, after all, interesting local historical documents but there was record of them at either location. It remains to be resolved but for the moment at least, it must remain a mystery.

Dizzy also took part in the London tour in 1953, mentioned above, and recalls that *'Sandy and Al were now colossal and Bob Craig was at his prime'*. He also says that Wood Green was a marvelous gig. Trombonist Archie Sinclair, of whom we will hear much more later in this book, was down from Edinburgh and he, Dizzy and Ken Colyer went home by tube *'more than a little drunk'*. Ken tried to demonstrate the single-handed way to roll a cigarette and covered the floor in tobacco and fag paper. Archie was sick, then fell asleep in a toilet cubicle and had to be rescued by Al Fairweather, who had appeared from somewhere, and who climbed over the cubicle door and released him.

After Dizzy had completed his National Service, in about 1956, he was invited by Sandy and Al to move to London to join up with them again. However, Dizzy was in the throes of completing his degree at Edinburgh University and did not feel like moving to London in any case, so he turned down the offer and stayed where he was. Dizzy Jackson, in his 'day job', was a school teacher and later a Headmaster and, like Bob Craig, he remained for decades a much valued and active player of jazz in Edinburgh. He will appear again later in this book, when he played with important Edinburgh bands such as 'Charlie McNair's Jazz Band', the 'Spirits of Rhythm' and 'Dave Keir's Hot Five' and eventually on into the twenty first century.

Jimmy Gavin (trumpet), who had been instrumental in encouraging Dizzy Jackson to take up the double bass, was born in Duns in the Borders in 1928 but moved with his family to Edinburgh when he was only three weeks old. Although he was to be closely involved with the RHS Gang and the rest of the Edinburgh jazz crowd of the 1940/50s, he did not attend the Royal High School but was educated at James Clark's School. On leaving school, Jimmy worked as a draughtsman surveyor with the Ordnance Survey and then, when he was twenty seven, he entered the Edinburgh

College of Art. He was later to become an artist and lecturer in art at the Carlisle College of Art, now part of the University of Cumbria. He had heard jazz on the radio from an early age and had been captivated by it right away. By the age of sixteen or seventeen, Jimmy had acquired a trumpet and proceeded to teach himself how to play it, commenting to me in 2011 that, while he thought that he had a good tone, he considered his technical skills to have been fairly limited. His first model on trumpet was Bix Beiderbecke, soon to be followed by Louis Armstrong. Technically limited or not, he was soon associating with other like-minded jazzers, including Mike Hart (then playing drums), the trombone player Jimmy Hilson, clarinettists Norrie Sinclair and Ian 'Daz' Arnott and pianist Drew Landles, some of whom will feature later in this book. In time, he formed a band of his own, **Gavin's Gloryland Jazz Band**, which, at one time or another, had Mike Hart on drums, Jimmy Hilson on trombone and Daz Arnott on clarinet. Jimmy remembers the band playing gigs in Musselburgh Town Hall and at a church hall in Liberton.

Gavin's Gloryland Jazz Band playing at the 1950 or '51 student's rag week parade. Jimmy Gavin (tpt), Jimmy Hilson (tbn), Norrie Sinclair (clt) and Mike Hart (drms). Jazz band leader-to-be Archie Sinclair gazes out from the foreground. (from the collection of Jimmy Gavin, photographer unknown)

Amongst Jimmy's other jazz related memories is one which concerns a visit to Paris in the 1950s. Jimmy and Dizzy Jackson were in a Paris pub when Dizzy said that he thought that a man standing at the end of the bar looked like Albert Nicholas, the great Creole clarinettist. Nicholas, born in New Orleans in 1900, was an almost exact contemporary of Louis Armstrong and one of the finest and most mellow clarinet players in all of jazz. Like his childhood friend Sydney Bechet, he had found his star on the rise again in the context of the post-WWII traditional jazz revival and had settled in France in 1953. Greatly daring, Jimmy Gavin approached the chap at the bar who confirmed that he was indeed Albert Nicholas and, after a few drinks together, invited Dizzy and Jimmy back to his flat where he cooked them the famous New Orleans dish of red beans and rice. What an experience for two young Edinburgh jazzers who must have felt that one of their Gods was walking the Earth. Although Jimmy Gavin's career as an active jazz musician was to be fairly brief, his interest in jazz was to be life-long and in 2011, now in his eighties, he was still turning up at Edinburgh jazz gigs, his enthusiasm for the music undimmed.

Jim 'Farrie' Forsyth (drums), according to George Hewitt, played drums with just about every band there was in Edinburgh and Glasgow in the 1950s and 60s. George describes him as an *'excellent Baby Dodds style drummer with an infectious brand of humour'*. Lenny Herd, a fine trumpet player from Paisley, has a photo of Farrie playing with Glasgow's George Penman's Jazzmen in 1961 and he also played with George Hewitt and Ralph Laing (then playing trumpet but later a well-known piano player and writer) in the Eagle Jazz Band, which was west coast based, in 1955/56. This band also included the banjo player Brian Weld, who is still (in 2011) playing regularly in Edinburgh. George Hewitt also says that Farrie played on some of the sides made with the S&M recording people. Farrie eventually departed to London, where he played with jazz musicians of the calibre of Ken Sims, a top trumpet player who put in time with Acker Bilk's famous band. Farrie Forsyth died in December 1999.

Two other close associates of the Gang, although not RHS scholars, were **Norrie Anderson (banjo)** and Ian 'Daz' Arnott, yet another of the long list of good Edinburgh clarinet players. Norrie Anderson, tall and red haired, was a contemporary of Sandy Brown and Al Fairweather at Art College and replaced Johnny Twiss in the Brown band in about 1951. He continued to play on a regular basis through 1951/52 and played with the band at the famous Big Bill Broonzy Usher Hall concert in 1952. He also, according to George Hewitt, appeared with the band on various recordings issued by Swarbrick and Mossman, Lake and Esquire. Norrie Anderson died in December 2009. Unfortunately, I have been unable to unearth any information about the earlier banjo player, Johnny Twiss.

Ian 'Daz' Arnott (clarinet), although not RHS educated, was closely associated with the RHS Gang and played in 1951/52 with a 'second line' RHS band, **Kenny Jack's Jazzmen**. This band was run by Kenny Jack while still a schoolboy and its membership included Kenny Jack (tpt), George Hewitt (tbn), Ian 'Daz' Arnott (clt), George Patterson (pno), Alec Wilson (bjo) and Fraser Bowman (drms/washboard). Apparently this band actually made a recording. The tunes were 'Muskrat Ramble' and 'Buddy's Habit' and the recording took place at Graham's Recording Studios in Haddington Place, Edinburgh. Ian Arnott failed to turn up and George Hewitt describes the recordings as probably sounding like the Buddy Bolden Band on a very bad day.

Later, Ian played with Mike Hart and also various short-lived bands formed by George Hewitt and Ralph Laing in about 1953/54. He was a great admirer of the playing of Sandy Brown, trying determinedly to emulate Sandy's Doddsian tone and even striving to imitate Sandy's way of holding his clarinet and his characteristic 'bull neck' when playing. Allegedly, he and Sandy Brown once went up Arthur's Seat (non-Edinburgh readers will be relieved to hear that this refers to a hill and not to a person) for an alfresco duet. Ian also played occasional duets with Sandy at the West End Café, before he emigrated to Canada in about 1954. There is story that he and Sandy Brown were supposed to record some duets in London but Ian failed to turn up (was this becoming a habit?), as he had burned his fingers trying to repair a faulty car exhaust. Ian occasionally re-appeared in Edinburgh thereafter, but spent most of his life in Toronto, where both Stu Eaton and Ralph Laing played with him and were impressed.

In Canada, Ian played with many great jazz names including Buck Clayton, Ruby Braff, Vic Dickenson, Edmund Hall, Jimmy Rushing, Pee Wee Russell, Cootie Williams, Rex Stewart, Dickie Wells, Lil Hardin, Paul Barbarin, George Lewis, Willie 'The Lion' Smith, Wingy Manone and Ben Webster. He was a member of the Imperial Jazz Band in Toronto and Dr McJazz, led by expatriate Glasgow trumpeter Charlie Gall, and also played with a Canadian Climax Jazz Band. Ian was invited to join Turk Murphy's band but was unable to do so, because of union rules. He also played classical music. George Hewitt describes him as a fine Johnny Dodds styled player and likens his playing to that of Dave Paxton. Ian Arnott came over as a soloist to play at the 1981 Edinburgh Jazz Festival and played with the Scottish Jazz Advocates, in a venue in Hanover Street called Refreshers. I played at this session but, for reasons I would now rather draw a veil over, I can remember next to nothing about it and regrettably, nothing about Ian's playing. Not his fault but mine, but I can remember others in our band talking about what a good player he was. Late in life, Ian Arnott suffered heart problems and he died in Canada in May 2006.

Another drummer with the Brown band was the aforementioned **Bill Strachan (drums)**, who was born in Edinburgh in 1928 and attended the RHS, a year or two after Sandy Brown. Although not attending the same school, during his school days Bill was friendly with John and Archie Semple. Bill began playing drums in the local Boys Brigade Band and was with them from the age of 15 until he was 18. He was introduced to jazz on record and began buying one record each month, an early favourite being Muggsy Spanier. A friend, Bill Roberts, worked on Salveson's whaling ships and was able to bring back many records which were not then available locally. Another source of good listening was a school friend called Janol Scott, who had managed to get hold of a lot of Jelly Roll

Morton recordings. Bill soon started going along to the Edinburgh Rhythm Club, then in Methven Simpson's music shop, where he met and heard some of the early jazzers, including Drew Bruce and Bill McGregor. These were clearly interesting times and Bill remembers some of the jazz crowd going to Edinburgh's only Indian restaurant, near the Crown Bar, where they could only afford the cheapest item on the menu, a cup full of rice tipped onto a plate with a hard-boiled egg covered in curry sauce.

National Service followed in 1948/49, during which time he never left the UK because he was in the army rugby team! Back in Edinburgh, when Willie Burns dropped out of the Sandy Brown Band in about 1950, Bill became the drummer, the line up at that time being Sandy Brown (clt), Al Fairweather (tpt), Bob Craig (tbn), Norrie Anderson (bjo), Johnnie Rae (bs), and Stan Grieg, who played both piano and drums with the band. Soon after this, business and rugby dominated Bill's life and he moved to live in the west of Scotland, not returning to Edinburgh until 1977.

Interested in reviving his jazz career, a vacancy in Bill Salmond's Louisiana Ragtime Band, created by the departure of drummer Iain Forde, led to Bill joining this band, with whom he stayed for about a year. Later he was to play in Jim Petrie's band in Basin Street, a popular and busy jazz lounge in the Haymarket Station Bar. Later still, in the late 1980s, he played with his fellow RHS Gangsters Bob Craig and Dizzy Jackson together with Al Fairweather, who had also returned to town by then. These veterans of the early days were joined by Jack Graham (clt), Graham Scott (pno) and Jock Westwater (bjo), all of whom we will meet in later chapters. Bill says that, for a spell, Kenny Milne, better known as a drummer, played second trumpet in this band, which had a regular spot at the Glen Elg Hotel, at the foot of Leamington Terrace. He also played another regular, although short-lived, spot with Jim Petrie's band, which at that time include the clarinet player Dick Lee, at a pub in Auchendinny, a village near Penicuik. Other gigs that were regular for a while were with a band in the Nelson Hotel in Nelson Street and in the Royal Hotel in Royal Terrace but then, sometime in the early 1990s, Bill retired from playing. At the time of writing in 2011, he continues to meet up regularly with other veteran jazzers involved in the Edinburgh Jazz Archive Group and with them, he played a part in the successful setting up of an archive of Edinburgh jazz in the Central Library.

St Andrew's Rag Day 1954
Ian Arnott (clt), unknown (pno), Ralph Laing (tpt),
George Hewitt (tbn), Jim Goudie (bjo)
(from the collection of George Hewitt, photographer
unknown)

Kenny Jack (trumpet) attended the RHS from 1946-52 and, with contemporary **George Hewitt (trombone)**, formed the school boy band Kenny Jack's Jazzmen, with the line-up given above. Later, Farrie Forsyth played drums with the band and Dizzy Jackson sometimes played bass. Kenny Jack's health was to break down in later life and he died in the 1980s. George Hewitt, whose recollections of the 1940s and 50s have contributed so much to this account already, had started to play trombone in his third year at the RHS, when both he and Kenny Jack had lessons from an elderly brass band conductor, John Faulds. The tuition took place in the Brass Band Hall in Hanover Street. Here Mr Faulds demonstrated his abhorrence of girls wearing any form of makeup, the lessons being punctuated by abrasive comments on 'painted women' observed from the Hall window. George and Kenny were given welcome encouragement by Stan Greig and they were invited to rehearsals of the Brown band at Stan's parent's house in Morton Street, Portobello. They also went along to the West End Café and to Dave Mylne's record sessions, when Mylne would deliver talks on various aspects of jazz, illustrated with recordings from his extensive collection.

George Hewitt recalls that the Kenny Jack Jazzmen were rehearsing in the Brass Band Hall by 1952 and a whole afternoon spent trying to get a single tune right was not at all unusual. They eventually began to get a few gigs, including an interval spot at the RHS summer dance, probably the first time jazz had been heard in the hallowed precincts of the RHS preparatory school. Occasionally they hit the big time and played as second band to the Sandy Brown band at Jazz Band Balls, held at the Oddfellow's Hall. George later moved to live in Ayrshire where, after continuing to make the long journey to and from Edinburgh for band rehearsals for a time, he joined up with Ralph Laing, who played trumpet at that time, and they formed first the Ayrshire Jazz band and, later, the Eagle Jazz Band. At the time of writing in 2011, George Hewitt continues to play trombone with his 'New Orleans Joymakers' at monthly jazz concerts at the Harbour Arts Centre in Irvine, a band that includes Lenny Herd (tpt), Tom Taylor (clt), Tony Lang (bjo) and Hamish Hendry (drms), all from the west of Scotland, and Graham Blamire (bs), who travels through from Edinburgh. In spite of the generally parlous state of traditional jazz in 2011, it is good to be able to report that these sessions are consistently well supported, with many regulars making sure of their tickets by booking well in advance.

Now come two names who will make much more major appearances later in this book, **Mike Hart (drums, banjo later)** and Charlie McNair (trumpet), both of whom were RHS schoolboys, although a year or two younger than the original Gang.

The Sandy Brown Band playing at Pete Davenport's 21st Birthday party. Bob Craig, Al Fairweather, a youthful Mike Hart, Sandy Brown, Farrie Forsyth (by kind permission of Peter Davenport)

Mike, who was born in Inverness on 23 March 1934, originally appeared as a drummer and first played with a band led by Jimmy Gavin, Gavin's Gloryland Band in 1949, when only in his mid-teens. He then went on to play drums with the Sandy Brown band between 1950 and 1952.

One night in the West End Café, Sandy had come up to Mike and asked him if he would like to sit in with the band. Mike recalls that he *'nearly fell over but immediately accepted and I did a number of gigs with Sandy over the years'*. Mike also says of Sandy that *'He was not an easy person to play with, in that his musical direction was conveyed to me via Al Fairweather and Stan Greig. He never spoke to me at all. His standards were so high that I used to feel extremely nervous. He was virtually a God to us young chaps'*[64]. Mike has also said how much he was influenced in his jazz career by his early association with Sandy, Al Fairweather and Stan Greig. With the Brown band, Mike made a trip to London in 1952 when they played several gigs including the 'Big Jazz Show', run by Maurice Kinn at the Royal Albert Hall. The band that made the trip was Al

---

[64] SBS Newsletter No. 68, August 2002

Fairweather (tpt), Sandy Brown (clt), Bob Craig (tbn), Stan Greig (pno), Norrie Anderson (bjo), Dizzy Jackson (bs) and Mike on drums. Stan Greig played a couple of numbers on drums at the Albert Hall but was probably a bit handicapped, as the bass drum pedal had broken while Mike was playing. (NB This story will be of particular interest to the many drummers whom Mike castigated for banging the bass drum too hard, later in his career!) Among the other bands taking part were the Mick Mulligan band with George Melly, the Sid Phillips band and the Yorkshire Jazz Band. Mike later, of course, switched to banjo and guitar and went on to play a very major part in Edinburgh jazz for the next six decades. The frequent appearance of his name throughout this book will be a tribute to his work and influence.

Charlie McNair (trumpet), who was a couple of years older than Mike Hart, started playing in the early 1950s and rapidly established himself as a band leader. It was Charlie's band that Dizzy Jackson joined when he turned down the chance to go to London to rejoin Sandy and Al. Later in this book, we will pick up Charlie's long and successful career as an Edinburgh band leader.

We now come to a unique and ubiquitous figure, not RHS but another associate of the Gang, and one who was to be a constant presence in the local jazz scene from the mid-1940s until his death in 1993. His name was **Jackie MacFarlane (vocals)**, into whose early recollections we have already dipped in Chapter I. Jackie was around the jazz scene in the early days of the Brown band and, unable to play an instrument, clearly decided that his way into active participation was by becoming a singer. In addition to his habit of popping up at gigs volunteering a song or two, a habit he would maintain across six decades, Jackie also served as 'bouncer' at various locations at which jazz was presented. He is particularly remembered for his 'bouncer' duties at the Oddfellow's Hall, duties shared with Tam (later Sean) Connery, when he was reckoned to be a much more effective bouncer than Connery. Sandy Brown attributed Jackie's 'bouncering' effectiveness to his experiences when he fought in the Spanish Civil war[65]. By 1954 Jackie was acting as master of ceremonies at the Sunday evening gigs at the Condon Club in India Buildings. In spite of his success as a bouncer, Jackie was a good natured and kind hearted chap. There was at least one occasion when an Edinburgh jazzer had had to put one of his musical instruments into hock and Jackie, who could not have been all that well-off for cash himself, immediately offered to pay to retrieve the instrument, allowing the jazzer to continue to play his gigs. I can also remember Bob Craig habitually introducing Jackie, who was of generous girth, as '..*our resident globe...*', with Jackie chortling away, enjoying the joke as much as anyone.

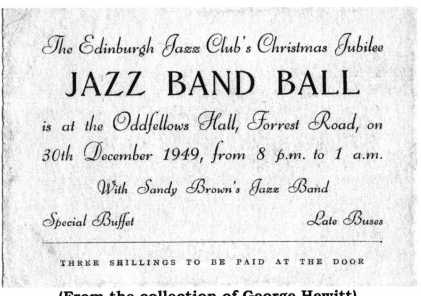

The Edinburgh Jazz Club's Christmas Jubilee

JAZZ BAND BALL

is at the Oddfellows Hall, Forrest Road, on 30th December 1949, from 8 p.m. to 1 a.m.

With Sandy Brown's Jazz Band

Special Buffet   Late Buses

THREE SHILLINGS TO BE PAID AT THE DOOR

(From the collection of George Hewitt)

There were a number of locations where all this jazz activity took place. According to George Hewitt, the Edinburgh Rhythm Club had its first meetings, in the mid-1940s, above Methven Simpson's music shop, which was then in Princes Street. Later, the club moved to 20 Hill Street followed by a similar set up at the Lido Hotel in Douglas Crescent. By 1952/53, the Crown Bar in Lothian

---

[65] Binns D (editor), 'The McJazz Manuscripts - A collection of the writings of Sandy Brown', Faber and Faber 1979, by kind permission of David Binns

Street was functioning as 'The Stud Club' and another jazz centre was 'The Condon Club', meeting on the top floor of India Buildings in Victoria Street. The bass player, Jim Young, recalls that it was mostly the Archie Semple/Alex Welsh band that played there and their Dixieland/Chicagoan style certainly ties in with the name 'Condon Club'. Rather disappointingly, the name 'The Stud Club' did not make any reference to the general virility of the jazz crowd but was just an abbreviation of 'The Student Club', and was initially run by Sandy Brown.

Lothian Street, where the Crown Bar was situated, is now long gone, swept away during the development of the area around the McEwan Hall. The Crown Bar was still going strong as a jazz venue in the 1960s when I first appeared around the jazz scene and I remember gigs there with a band led by the trumpeter Jim Petrie and also with the band put together in the mid-1060s for the return from abroad of Dave Paxton. In addition to these, as we have already seen, jazz had been featured in the West End Café (later to become the 'New Yorker') in Shandwick Place and, as we have already heard, there were the 'Jazz Band Balls' in the Oddfellow's Hall in Forrest Road. The West End Café seems, at least for a while, to have thrived on jazz events. As we have already noted, quite a number of touring bands appeared there including the Freddie Randall Band, Mick Mulligan's Band with George Melly and Graeme Bell's Jazz Band from Australia.

The very fact that so many, and so many good, jazz musicians were produced by a single High School in such a short period of time of course begs the question 'Why?' That the school itself encouraged jazz seems at least uncertain and there are some indications that it may have displayed a disapproving attitude. However, accounts vary, even amongst those who were involved at the time. Dizzy Jackson says *'jazz was not generally encouraged at the school*[66]. Dickie Alexander, an Edinburgh town councillor who was involved in the work to set up the memorial plaque to Sandy Brown and Al Fairweather, in a letter to the Scotsman in 1996, subsequently included in a Sandy

[66] www.sandybrownjazz.co.uk/profiledizzyjackson.html

90

Brown Society Newsletter, said *'The thrawn resistance to flair and innovation goes back a long way. At the old Royal High School, Edinburgh, pupils were forbidden to play jazz, so Sandy Brown and his pals played in the school lavatories out of earshot of the music master'.* Dickie, who was writing in support of the plan to create a memorial to Sandy Brown and Al Fairweather, then goes on to propose *'Let's put a plaque outside the old school lavatories at the Calton Hill building. That's where it all began!'*[67]

On the other hand, George Hewitt who, along with Kenny Jack, had been invited by Bill Bowie, the head of music at the school, to learn to play the trombone and trumpet respectively, with a view to joining the school orchestra, gives a rather different slant. George says *'...Bill Bowie had never objected to Kenny and myself being involved in jazz since he reckoned it improved our playing for the classical stuff.'* Another Royal High pupil from the 1940s, Jim Walker, is also very much of the view that the school, if not quite giving jazz an official blessing, at least did nothing to put obstacles in its way. Jim felt that one speaker at the ceremony when the memorial plaque was put in place had given a clear impression that the school had been highly discouraging towards jazz. Jim rejects this view and points out that, as no one stepped in to stop the use of the gym for jazz band practices and a jazz band in full cry is not the easiest of things to keep dark, there was at least a degree of tacit approval from within the school.

It seems to me that the most likely thing is that the world-wide awakening of interest in traditional jazz had impacted on some of the youngsters at the school, just as things new and probably a bit rebellious, would always intrigue the young. What perhaps was different, was that one or two of the youngsters, Sandy Brown particularly but also Al Fairweather, Stu Eaton, Dave Paxton, Bob Craig and Stan Greig, were not only sufficiently strong characters to influence their peers but were quickly good and successful enough to encourage others and keep the movement going. What remains surprising is the sheer number of

---

[67] SBS Newsletter No 1, July 1996, from letter by Dickie Alexander to 'The Scotsman', 14th June 1996

youngsters, RHS and associated others, who got involved, the astonishing quality of the best of the music they produced and just how long their influence was to last. The supply of jazz musicians from the RHS (and increasingly from other sources in Edinburgh) did not finish with the RHS Gang of the 1940s and early 1950s. Several more from the RHS were to come along over the next decade or so, including Jack Duff, Bill Salmond and John Nicholson, later well known as the actor John McGlynn, who starred in the famous TV series 'All Creatures Great and Small'.

As we have already noted, there was a second group of pioneers around who, even in the 1940s, had started to go down a different musical track. This was the group which formed around the trumpeter Alex Welsh and the clarinetist Archie Semple. They were almost exact contemporaries of the RHS Gang and although Alex, Archie and the trombone player Dave Keir played at various times with the RHS Gang, their loyalties and music belonged to a slightly different version of the classic jazz tradition, as described in Chapter II. They were to become known as the Dixielanders and they too were to make a major impact on the world of traditional jazz. It is to them that we will turn our attention next.

Chapter V
The Dixieland Pioneers

It is an astonishing fact that Edinburgh produced, not only the RHS Gang which was to provide several high quality British jazz musicians but, more or less simultaneously, a second group which was to have a similar impact. Although this group could not claim a handy label arising from a common scholastic background, they did come to be distinguished from the RHS Gang by being referred to as the **Dixielanders**. This term, used in the descriptive, non-derogatory manner described in Chapter II, seems to me a reasonable title for them, as their principle inspiration was the music played by the so-called Chicagoans associated with Eddie Condon. The Edinburgh Dixielanders of the late 1940s and early 1950s were centred on a pair of brothers, Archie (clt) and John Semple (tpt) and another trumpeter, Alex Welsh. The Semple/Welsh grouping, the Dixielanders, has a place in Edinburgh's jazz history just as significant and long lasting, as that of Sandy, Al and the RHS Gang.

Chronologically, the first of the Dixielanders around the Edinburgh jazz scene was the journalist **George Crockett (drums)**, born in 1920, whom we have already met through his published works and his involvement with the RHS Gang. We know from George Hewitt and others that Crockett seemed more interested in the *'more dixieland'* style of jazz, and this seems to me to make chronological sense. George Crockett's writings demonstrate that he was already interested in jazz by the middle to late 1930s, when he heard both Fats Waller and Coleman Hawkins play in

Edinburgh. In other words, Crockett's interest pre-dated the Revival and it is clear that he was listening to both the live and the recorded jazz of the 1930s. In the 1930s, George would have been an impressionable teenager and, like most of us, it is likely that the music he heard in his teenage years would tend to establish his musical leanings. As this was an era when the cutting edge of jazz was in the hands of people such as Benny Goodman, Artie Shaw, Teddy Wilson and others of their generation, in addition to the slightly older musicians such as Louis Armstrong and Duke Ellington, it would seem logical that Crockett's tastes in jazz were already well formed before the Revival really took hold. In addition to the great Swing Bands, he would almost certainly have been aware of the smaller group music of the Chicago musicians and others, many of whom would have made their living playing in the sections of the big Swing bands.

Although George Crockett was involved, to the extent of making recordings, with the Sandy Brown Band, when the time was ripe, he seems to have been a key factor in the formation of the first Edinburgh band that played in the Dixieland style. This was the band which was to function under Archie Semple's leadership and usually called **Archie Semple's Dixielanders**. This band was later to metamorphose into the **Nova Scotia Jazz Band**, often called simply the Nova Scotians. Both George Hewitt and trumpeter Pete Davenport believe that George Crockett was instrumental in ensuring that a band in the Dixieland style continued after the point when Archie Semple departed Edinburgh for the south. This view is endorsed by Edinburgh trumpeter Andrew Lauder, who joined the Nova Scotians in the mid-1950s, when George Crockett was still active in Edinburgh and still playing in the band. It appears that John Semple also dropped out at about the time his brother left for the south, to be replaced on trumpet by Alex Welsh. It also seems likely that George Crockett, having been instrumental in founding the new band, did not actually lead it but left this duty to someone better suited to leading, even if only because of playing one of the front-line instruments. Later, George was to move to live in Ayrshire, where he continued his career in journalism, and where, in the late 1980s or early 1990s, he hosted a regular jazz programme on West Sound radio. He used the broadcasts to play his favourite records and to interview local musicians and jazz followers. Derek Copland, who knew him well all the years he was in Ayrshire, told me that George continued to play drums and in his final years was playing with Jimmy McCullough and his Scottish Country Dance Band. George Crockett died in Ayr, on 5th January 1996.

Trombonist Dave Keir had moved from the Sandy Brown band to join the Archie Semple led band, reporting that its membership when he joined was John Semple (cnt), Archie Semple (clt and ldr), Dave Keir (tbn), Percy Pegg (pno), Jimmy Mooney (gtr), Mike Samuels (bs) and George Crockett (drms). It was to be Dave Keir who assumed the leadership of the band after Archie's departure and he also reports that he named it the Nova Scotia Jazz Band. The reason for using a band name not based on the name of an individual was because the new trumpeter, Alex Welsh, felt that, if it was to continue but under a new leader's name, it would lose any reputation it had built up. Apparently this had happened previously. Dave Keir says that the original membership of the Nova Scotians was Alex Welsh (tpt), Dave Keir (tbn, ldr), Jack Graham (clt), Drew Landles (pno), Jimmy Mooney (gtr), Dickie Alexander (bs) and George Crockett (drms). When Dave Keir, in his turn, set off to join the Mick Mulligan band in London in early 1953, Alex Welsh became leader of the Nova Scotians, thus continuing Edinburgh's Dixieland alternative to the fairly strict classicism of the Sandy Brown band.

Amongst the hundreds of papers that I read when writing this book, there was a copy of a part of a letter that had been published in a newspaper or magazine. Unfortunately, there was no clue to the publication, no date given and the name of the writer was missing from the copy. However, the same letter is quoted in a SBS Newsletter[68] and it is clear that it was written by the Edinburgh piano player Ronnie Carruthers. The letter says that students of the jazz scene in Edinburgh would be interested in what it

---

[68] SBS Newsletter No. 31, July 1999

calls *'...the seminal events that occurred in the city's Braid Crescent.'* This street is in the Morningside area of Edinburgh and number 1 Braid Crescent was the home of the Semple family. Ronnie goes on to say that a corporate decision was taken by the family that a band be formed to further the jazz interests of the two boys, John and Archie. A band was duly formed and the line-up is given as Ian Brown (instrument unspecified), Jack McDonald (t – presumably trumpet), John Semple (bugle), Archie Semple and Sandy Brown (clts), Archie Deacon (d – presumably drums) and letter writer, Ronnie Carruthers himself, on piano. Whether this is the Ian Brown, who later played bass around Edinburgh, is uncertain and just how John was going to play jazz on a bugle is not explained. However, this is very early evidence of collaboration involving Sandy Brown and the Semple brothers. Ronnie tells us that, at the start, the combined knowledge of those involved was two tunes and that he could *'...still see the sad twittering of the those Morningsider's curtains as they realized that another day of rest was not to be once the band began to strut their stuff'*. The hostile stirrings from the neighbours unfortunately seem to have alarmed the previously supportive Semple parents, and Ronnie records that, after many happy Sundays, the sessions were suddenly abandoned. He goes on to note however, that *'...the seeds of jazz were truly sown as a result of those unfettered sessions'*. This seems to signal the start of the Semple brothers jazz playing careers and it seems likely that this episode was in the early to mid-1940s, when John would have been in his later teens and Archie and Sandy Brown in their early teens.

John Semple (cornet, piano, drums) was born in Edinburgh around 1925. He and his younger brother Archie developed an early interest in jazz and both brothers took up instruments, John, cornet (he may later have also played trumpet) and piano, and Archie, both trumpet and clarinet. The Semple family moved to South Africa for a while but, before long, returned to Edinburgh. John Semple followed a career as a photographer, working for a firm called Edinburgh Cameras, having served his apprenticeship with Yerburys, the famous Edinburgh photographers, for many years based up on Churchill, in the Morningside area of the town. However, the Semple brothers interest in jazz continued and, away from the day job, John played in a variety of bands, organised and led by Archie or John himself. There was a degree of friendly rivalry but also cooperation, with the other contemporary group of Edinburgh jazzers which included Sandy Brown, Al Fairweather, Stan Greig and others of the RHS Gang. The friendship and cooperation between the two groups is demonstrated by the personnel listings for the recording sessions shown below. Later, when Alex Welsh came along to play trumpet, John Semple switched to piano.

Unlike Alex Welsh and his brother Archie, John was not interested in pursuing a career in full time music. He seems to have been unwilling, for a number of reasons, to consider a move to London, a move which appears to have been considered a pre-requisite for full-time, professional jazz. In addition, it seems that he was modest about his playing abilities, Dave Keir telling me that John was aware of what he saw as his own limitations and had told his brother that, if he found better, he would step down from the trumpet chair. Around the time in the early 1950s when Archie and Alex Welsh departed for the south, John gave up regular playing and concentrated on his career in photography. His interest in jazz continued however, attending concerts and taking a great interest in his brother's and Alex Welsh's successful professional jazz activities in the south. Later on, he played in sessions involving friends, usually playing keyboard or drums. However, it is clear that John Semple had been a significant figure in the early days of Revival jazz in Edinburgh, playing an important part in building the foundations of the traditional jazz hotspot that Edinburgh was to become. John Semple died in Edinburgh, in his late sixties, in 1993.

Archie Semple (clarinet), brother of John, was born in Edinburgh on 31st March 1928. According to John Chilton's 'Who's Who of British Jazz', when he was in his teens, Archie played trumpet as well as clarinet. This would explain why Archie, who was to make a great name for himself as a clarinet player, is listed on trumpet on one of the recordings listed below. Chilton says that Semple

97

served in the Royal Navy in 1946-48 and, by Autumn 1949, was leading a band in Edinburgh called the **Escom Jazz Band**, which later became known as the **Capitol Stompers** and then the **Capitol Jazzmen**. There were clearly several band names in use as there are also accounts of Archie's band being called **Archie Semple's Dixielanders** and **Archie Semple's Capital Jazzmen**.

**The Castle Jazz Band, probably at Dalhousie Castle
Believed to be Stu Crockett (tbn), John Semple (tpt),
Archie Semple (clt), Willie Burns (drms), Johnny Twiss
(gtr) and Stan Greig (pno)
(from the collection of Malcolm Burns, photographer
unknown)**

In Spring 1952, Archie moved to London to take up an invitation to join Mick Mulligan's Jazz Band. Later, he was to move to the Freddy Randall band, with whom he played from January 1953 until August 1954. This was followed by a spell in pianist/trombone player Norman Cave's jazz band in late 1954. After that, Archie teamed up again with his Edinburgh colleague Alex Welsh, who had followed him to London, and he remained in this, the first great Alex Welsh band, from February 1955 until March 1963. With that band, Archie made many memorable recordings, in which he beautifully complements the Welsh trumpet, and features on many wonderful tracks. Unhappily, the various pressures of playing jazz for a living started to take their toll on an already less than robust personality, otherwise he might have gone on for very much longer as a member of what was by then, the finest Dixieland band that the UK had ever produced. John Latham, writing in 1993[69], says that when he heard this early version of the Alex Welsh band, Archie was the outstanding player. He describes his tone as having a sweeter and truer edge than that of Pee Wee Russell, noting how effectively Archie could use the bottom register of the clarinet, especially when playing ballads.

Archie Semple seems to have been a vulnerable sort of chap and, to help us understand something of his personality, we are fortunate to have the recollections of Roy Crimmins, a fine trombone player from Perth, recorded in a 1998 article written by John Latham[70]. Roy Crimmins first met Archie in 1951, when Archie's Capitol Jazzmen were support band to the Mick Mulligan band, in which Crimmins was playing. He records that the whole Mulligan band was *'knocked out'* by Archie's playing and that Mulligan asked his bandsmen to take a cut in their already meagre pay, so that Archie could join them. Later, after Alex Welsh came down to London in 1954, both Crimmins and Archie became members of the Alex Welsh band, thus reversing the leader/sideman relationship that Archie and Alex had in Edinburgh. Roy Crimmins says that it soon became obvious that Archie was far from well and, during a strenuous month-long spell at the New Orleans Bierbar in Dusseldorf, his health broke down and he had to return to the UK. Archie's playing at that time, according to Crimmins, was based on that of the great Ed Hall, with a bit of Pee Wee Russell's influence in there as well. However, as Archie became less well, his style became pure Pee Wee Russell. Crimmins recounts that it was not only Pee Wee's musical style that appeared but also some other

---

[69] Latham J, 'Archie Semple', Foot Tappers News (Cardiff), March/April 19930
[70] Latham J, 'Archie Semple (1928-1974) - Roy Crimmins remembers', Jazz Rag, March/April 1998

mannerisms. Archie, when striving for the right words, would sometimes stammer and tap his teeth with his right forefinger. Years later when Crimmins was touring with Pee Wee Russell, he found to his amazement that Pee Wee did exactly the same thing. What made this extraordinary was that Archie could not have known about this habit of Pee Wee's until that tour, as they had never previously met.

Sadly, Crimmins says that *'slowly Archie cracked up again'* and his playing got more and more like that of Pee Wee Russell. The 'Rough Guide to Jazz'[71] describes Archie as *'a spiritual son of Ed Hall, then Pee Wee Russell'*. This change in Archie's style did not please Alex Welsh, who would make pointed comments that Ed Hall was his favourite clarinet player. Understandably, this made Archie more and more uncomfortable. He had spent most of his life following Ed Hall, whose playing he adored, but as Crimmins said, he just could not help playing like Pee Wee. In the end, there was a shockingly unhappy experience during a BBC broadcast, that left Archie devastated. During the run-through, the producer came into the studio to say that the clarinet player was not, under any circumstances, to play any solos. If ever there was a statement that indicated a complete ignorance of what jazz was about, this was surely it. Archie was then in his Pee Wee Russell phase and Pee Wee's style was one of the most idiosyncratic in all of jazz, full of unexpected twist and turns, bent notes, croaks, wheezy inflections and growls. He has been described by Gunther Schuller[72], a great admirer of Russell's playing and one of the USA's most distinguished musicologists, as *'...a unique, wondrously self-contained musical personality'* and *'...also one of the most touching and human players that jazz has ever known'*. However, Schuller also admits that *'At first hearing, one of those Russell solos tended to give the impression of a somewhat inept musician, awkward and shy, stumbling and muttering along in a rather directionless fashion'*. To an

[71] Carr, Fairweather and Priestly, 'The Rough Guide to Jazz', 3rd Edition May 2004, Rough Guides Ltd, distributed by the Penguin Group
[72] 'The Swing Era: The Development of Jazz, 1930-1945 (History of Jazz)': by Gunther Schuller (1992) 49 words p610, by permission of Oxford University Press, www.oup.com

uninitiated listener, such as this hapless BBC producer, there is little doubt that the playing of Archie Semple in his Pee Wee mode, would sound strange and even alien. Unfortunately, the BBC producer that day was not only unfamiliar with jazz, and therefore unsuitable to be involved with this broadcast, but seems also to have been an extremely insensitive individual. In Archie's hearing, he added to his first comment that the clarinet player was not to solo, saying '...*not on my programme, he just can't play*'. A much more robust personality than Archie would have been severely shaken by this crass statement. Roy Crimmins, describing Archie's reaction, says '*He was broken. He started shaking with nerves and embarrassment, and he couldn't move or talk. I walked over and took him to the gents where we both had a very large Scotch....He was now a very frightened man in the band*'.

Whether this horrible incident caused it or not, Archie's fragile nervous health deteriorated and he started missing gigs with the band. Eventually, he was unable to return to the band, although Alex Welsh continued to pay him. In 1964 he returned briefly to lead his own quartet, but his health broke down once again and he was forced to retire from playing. The 'Rough Guide' says of him '*A charming man but with a deeply nervous disposition, Semple suffered a breakdown on stage at the 1964 Richmond jazz festival and never really played again*'. Archie Semple, yet another great Edinburgh jazz man to die young, died in London on 26 January 1974, at the age of only forty five.

Alex Welsh (cornet and trumpet/cornet) was born in Leith on 9th July 1929, the eldest child of Alexander Welsh, a coal merchant, and his wife, Ann Livingstone Plank. The family lived at 2 Lorne Square, just off Leith Walk. John Chilton's 'Who's Who of British Jazz'[73] tells us that Alex played accordion while at Broughton Secondary School and, after leaving school, took up a position of clerk with the Ministry of Works. Alex's girlfriend during his years in Edinburgh was Frances Maxwell, who later married and became the mother of a fine Edinburgh jazz musician of a

---

[73] John Chilton 'Who's Who of British Jazz', second edition 2004, reproduced by permission of Continuum International Publishing Group

later generation, John Burgess. Speaking in 2011, Frances could not recall Alex working with the Ministry of Works but does remember him working for the Scottish Widows, the major life insurance company, in St Andrew's Square. Later, he had lessons on the cornet from one Bill Taverner and started playing with the Leith Silver Band. He seems to have developed an early interest in jazz, modeling his style on that of Bix Beiderbecke, and by 1951, Alex was playing cornet with Archie Semple's Dixielanders. Again, there seems to be some doubt about the name of this band, the internet Wikipedia naming the band as Archie Semple's Capital Jazz Band. The band included Dave Keir on trombone who, like Archie Semple, played in the Chicago style associated with Eddie Condon, a style which would have been entirely compatible with Alex's Bix Beiderbecke inspired trumpet playing. Some recordings were made by this band on the Glasgow based S & M (Swarbrick and Mossman) label.

At some point in 1952, at the time when Archie Semple left go to London, the band that was to be called the Nova Scotians was formed, and Alex played cornet with them for a while. The Nova Scotians seem to have been built originally from the remnants of the Archie Semple band. Dave Keir, who played trombone in this band, tells us that Alex had come in on trumpet to replace John Semple and they also had Dickie Alexander on bass, who was later replaced by Pat Malloy. Sometime after this, Alex Welsh joined Sandy Brown's Blue Five, replacing Al Fairweather, who had moved to London in late 1953. In retrospect, it all sounds a bit like a game of musical chairs.

There was clearly quite a bit of movement generally amongst the Edinburgh jazz musicians at this time and it is hard to be certain about who played in which band and when. However, it is probably correct to assume that there was a pool of jazz musicians who got together in various combinations at various times. Documentation that was with a collection of early acetate recordings, presumably made privately and now in the ownership of Ishbel Semple, includes 'tentative' personnel listings. The tracks are shown as having been recorded between 1945 and 1952 and the personnel listings give an idea of those involved.

They also demonstrate that there were many different combinations of musicians, but give no indication about the permanency or otherwise of these groupings. It seems likely that some of the aggregations were simply set up for the purpose of a recording session, rather than representing permanent bands. Those involved are listed as:

Trumpet/cornet	John Semple, Alex Welsh, Stu Eaton, Archie Semple
Clarinet	Archie Semple, Sandy Brown
Trombone	Stuart Crockett, Dave Keir
Piano	Stan Greig, Drew Landles
Guitar	Ken Duncan, Jimmy Mooney
Bass	Pat Malloy
Drums	Willie Burns, George Crockett
Vocals	Jackie MacFarlane, Jack Thomson

Some of the above recordings were apparently taken from a broadcast, introduced by Steve Race, who gives the line up as John Semple (tpt), Archie Semple (clt), Dave Keir (tbn), Percy Pegg (pno), Jimmy Mooney (gtr or bjo), Mike Samuels (bs) and George Crockett (drms).

Alex Welsh is described in the Oxford Dictionary of National Biography as *'short and dapper, with a perky demeanor'*[74]. He walked with a pronounced limp, the result, I have always believed, of polio when he was young although others have suggested it was caused by an injury. Like Sandy Brown and Al Fairweather, a single hearing left little doubt as to where Alex's musical roots lay. The music that Alex loved beyond all others was clearly the free-wheeling, driving music of the so-called Chicagoans. In fact, this might be better termed 'Condon music', meaning the jazz played by the group of American musicians who, in the 1930s and 1940s, grouped themselves around the guitar player Eddie Condon, as many of them were not from Chicago at all. In particular, as his playing developed, Alex's trumpet style seemed to have common roots with the

---

[74] Oxford Dictionary of National Biography: Oxford Dictionary of National Biography Index of Contributors by Colin Matthew and Brian Harrison (2004) 7 words p84 Volume 58, by permission of Oxford University Press, www.oup.com

group of trumpeters associated with Condon - Wild Bill Davison, Muggsy Spannier and Jimmy McPartland. Like their playing, Alex's was a wonderful mix of the lyricism of Bix Biederbecke, spiced up with the aggressive attack and rough edges that Davison especially, liked to add to his sound. This style, of course, was itself derived from the classic jazz laid down in the 1920s, by Louis Armstrong and King Oliver, strongly enhanced by the influence of Beiderbecke. Like Sandy Brown and Al Fairweather, Alex was aided and abetted by other Edinburgh musicians of a like mind, creating wonderful music locally, but also forging the skills that enabled him, and his colleagues Archie Semple and Dave Keir, to pursue professional careers in jazz, from a London base.

Alex moved to London in May 1954, to join the band of Dave Keir who had already moved south. However, Alex left Dave's band after only three weeks, to form a band under his own name, which first appeared in June 1954. Sinclair Traill, in his 'Concerning Jazz'[75], published in 1957, comments on how many Scottish jazz musicians there were in British traditional bands and goes on to say *'The Scots, it would seem, take to jazz music'*. Traill gives the personnel of the first London based **Alex Welsh Jazz Band** as including two other Scots, trombonist Roy Crimmins (from Perth) and Archie Semple on clarinet. He goes on to say *'The brand of jazz the Alex Welsh band play is strictly from Dixie. Bright, clean and well rehearsed, the band portray the music of the white musician, as opposed to the coloured man's music from New Orleans. This policy has resulted in some quite undeservedly harsh criticism from those purists who can only see one facet of jazz, namely New Orleans music. The band play Dixieland music, a type of jazz which has its followers the world over. As long as they play it well, let's be fair and give credit where credit is due.'* This last sentence seems to me just a little bit patronizing and perhaps reveals something of his own preferences. It certainly sounds a bit dismissive now, in the light of the

---

[75] Traill S, 'Concerning Jazz', pages 143-144, Faber and Faber 1957. All attempts to trace the current copyright holder of this book have been unsuccessful.

great music the Welsh band was to play over the coming years.

Alex Welsh went on to run an extremely successful band over the next twenty five years. They were frequently selected to accompany famous visiting Americans, including Ruby Braff (cnt), Red Allen and Wild Bill Davison (tpt), Bud Freeman (ten) and Earl Hines (pno). All of these regarded the band, which had steadily moved towards embracing a more mainstream style of playing, as world class. In addition, Alex led his band to America in 1968, when they were invited to play at the prestigious Newport Jazz Festival, to considerable critical acclaim. Later, in the 1970s and early 1980s when his health began to give way, Alex was forced to disband for a while but was able to resume playing in September 1981. However, by the middle of the next year, his health was once again failing and he played what was to be his final gig on 10 June 1982. The Alex Welsh band was revered as the best in its style, a reputation that remains to this day. At one time or another, it featured top class musicians such as Roy Crimmins and Roy Williams (tbn), Archie Semple, Al Gay and Johnny Barnes (rds), Fred Hunt (pno), Jim Douglas (gtr), Ronnie Ray and Ron Mathewson (bs) and Lenny Hastings (drms). Alex was offered but declined, a place in the band of the great American trombonist Jack Teagarden. Bud Freeman, the famous tenor sax playing Chicagoan, said of the Welsh band that they were *'the best small band of their kind in the world'*[76]. George Melly, who knew all the London based bands well, also praised the Welsh band saying *'...one of the most grown up bands, musically speaking, that this country has yet produced – hot yet controlled, exciting yet intelligent, professional yet uncompromising, unswayed by fashion but the opposite of obscurantist'*[77].

Throughout his career, Alex Welsh remained faithful to the music of the Chicagoans, veering at times into a mainstream style. In addition to Alex's trumpet playing, his

---

[76] Carr, Fairweather and Priestly, 'The Rough Guide to Jazz', 3rd Edition May 2004, Rough Guides Ltd, distributed by the Penguin Group

[77] Simpson N, Bielderman G, 'Alex Welsh Discography', Eurojazz Discos No.20, September 2007 edition

band always included musicians of the highest class and the band's style, captured on many recordings, remains a model of its kind. If at times his sidemen stole the solo honours, Alex unfailingly played a great lead and created several great bands in succession, all of which were regarded with great esteem and affection by several generations of jazz followers in the UK and abroad. Like the Fairweather – Brown band, the Welsh band were never really part of the populist 'Trad Boom' of the late 1950s and early 1960s, eschewing fancy uniforms and a showy presentation in favour of straight-ahead Dixieland jazz and great playing. As John Latham says of Alex in the Oxford Dictionary of National Biography, '...his real contribution was in holding together for more than twenty years, a band of the highest professional quality, and providing a platform for other more creative but volatile personalities'[78]. Unfortunately, Alex Welsh was to be yet another of Edinburgh's Revival jazz musicians to die young. After what the 'Rough Guide to Jazz' refers to as a long, debilitating illness, he died in London at the age of 52, on 25th June 1982, and is buried in Ruislip Cemetery.

Alex's near contemporary, **Dave Keir (tbn, tpt, euphonium, rds and pno)**, was a remarkably versatile musician and, once again, we are indebted to the Sandy Brown Jazz website[79] for a great deal of relevant information. Dave was born on 9th April 1928 in Townhill, a small mining village two miles north of Dunfermline in Fife. His father worked in the dockyard at Rosyth, about four miles from their home. Dave's first exposure to music was to the playing of his mother who, through her own determination, had taught herself to play hymns and light classics on an old harmonium. At the age of about ten, Dave started to learn to play the cornet, receiving free tuition from a miner who played with the local miners' brass band. After this, he began to improvise to his mother's playing, something that he considers good training for the

[78] Oxford Dictionary of National Biography: Oxford Dictionary of National Biography Index of Contributors by Colin Matthew and Brian Harrison (2004) 30 words p84 Volume 58, by permission of Oxford University Press, www.oup.com
[79] http://sandybrownjazz.co.uk/profiledavekeir.html

jazz sounds to which he would later turn. Dave attended secondary school in Dunfermline where the music teacher, 'Pop' Gardiner, being short of trombone players, provided him with a bass trombone pitched in the key of G, together with a 'teach yourself' manual. Dave taught himself to play the instrument in six weeks and was able to take his place in the school orchestra. As Dave found it easy to 'busk' (ie improvise) everything, he never found the time to become a good reader of music.   Later, he managed to procure a trombone of his own and began to play with a local dance band in the evenings.

Later still in the 1940s, inspired by seeing the Bing Crosby film 'Birth of the Blues', he developed a fancy for leading a jazz band on clarinet. As a result of this, he bought himself an old Albert system clarinet and, once again, taught himself how to play it.   During National Service in the RAF, whilst posted in Yorkshire, he played in a dance band which gave him the opportunity to play alto saxophone and clarinet and he also had the chance to play euphonium in the station band. Unfortunately he missed out on an opportunity to get together with Monty Sunshine, later to gain fame as clarinetist in the Chris Barber Band who, unknown to Dave, was stationed in the same camp.

On returning to Dunfermline, Dave started a course of study at Edinburgh University and played with two local bands, the Creole Belles Jazz Band and Jock Turner's Jazz Band, with whom he went to London to play some jazz club gigs. Moving to lodgings in Edinburgh, he soon discovered the Sandy Brown band, with whom he was allowed to sit in on clarinet, which must have been an unnerving experience alongside the highly competitive Sandy.   Later, this association brought him the chance to join the Brown band, although on trumpet, replacing Stu Eaton. At this stage, Al Fairweather was away on National Service and was, in any case, still playing trombone. Al's return brought about a switch of roles, with Al becoming the band's trumpeter and Dave moving to the trombone chair. Dave relates how Sandy had heard Al play someone's trumpet and was so impressed by the sound he made, considering Al to be a 'natural' on trumpet, that he persuaded Al to make a permanent change to trumpet.

Sandy's aim of achieving the sound of the Louis Armstrong Hot Five resulted in him bringing in Bob Craig to play trombone in the required Kid Ory style, and Dave moved over to join Archie Semple's Dixielanders. He found their Chicago style much more to his taste and, when Archie Semple moved south to join Mick Mulligan's band in London, as we have heard, Dave took over leadership of the band and gave it a new name, the Nova Scotians[80]. Alex Welsh had just replaced John Semple on trumpet, Pat Malloy soon took over from Dickie Alexander on bass and Jack Graham, who was to become an important Edinburgh jazz musician over the next five decades, was recruited to take Archie Semple's place on clarinet. It should be pointed out that this Dickie Alexander is not the same Dickie Alexander who was a Town Councillor and who was to be a member of the committee which organized a memorial plaque to Sandy Brown and Al Fairweather in the 1990s. After about a year, Dave Keir himself departed south to join Archie Semple in the Mulligan band and Alex Welsh became leader of the Nova Scotians.

Dave Keir went on to have a successful career as a professional jazz musician, mostly playing trombone, in a number of good bands, including those of Freddy Randall and Bruce Turner, in addition to leading a number of bands of his own. In 1957, he went to Moscow with Bruce Turner's band. He also played a variety of instruments when gigging with other bands, including those of Sid Phillips, Bobby Mickleburgh, Johnny Parker and Ken Colyer's Omega Brass Band, before joining a band led by clarinetist Dick Charlesworth and again, setting up bands of his own. When the popularity of 'trad bands' began to wane around 1964, Dave returned to Edinburgh to complete his degree, became a teacher of mathematics and physics and then, for the next twenty years or so, hardly played at all. However, he was to return to playing jazz many years later and we shall catch up with Dave Keir again, later in this book, when we reach the 1980s.

---

[80] http://sandybrownjazz.co.uk/profiledavekeir.html

NOVA SCOTIA JAZZ BAND
ALEC WELSH (Cor. or Tpt.), JACKIE GRAHAM (Clt.), DAVE KEIR (Tbn.), JIMMY MOONEY (Gtr. and Bjo.)
DICK ALEXANDER (Bass), GEORGE CROCKETT (Drs. and leader), DREW LANDLES (Pno.)
DAVE KEIR has since left the band to join Mick Mulligan's Magnolias. His place has been taken by IAN ANDERSON.
Trumpet spot is now occupied by STU EATON.

Nova Scotia Jazz Band business card, probably around 1953 (from the collection of Peter Davenport, photographer unknown)

The departure of Alex Welsh, Archie Semple and Dave Keir, like that of Sandy Brown, Al Fairweather and Stan Greig, left the band more than a bit short handed. However, they did not all disappear at the same time and replacements were found as required. The band, now known as the Nova Scotians, soldiered on and the Dixieland tradition remained alive and well in Edinburgh. George Crockett was still around playing drums with the band and it may well have been his efforts again that kept the band going.

Dave Keir tells us[81], in his profile on the Sandy Brown Jazz website that, when Archie Semple moved away to London, **Jack Graham (clarinet, alto sax, vocals)** took over his place in the Nova Scotians. Frances Burgess (nee Maxwell), Alex Welsh's girlfriend in the 1950s, speaking in 2011, says that she remembers Jack being there at the

---

[81] http://www.sandybrownjazz.co.uk/profiledavekeir.html

meeting at which the band was formed. The line-up of the band now included Alex Welsh (tpt), Dave Keir (tbn), Jack Graham (clt), George Crockett (drms) and Pat Malloy from Dunfermline, who had replaced Dickie Alexander on bass. I remember Dave Keir telling me that Jack Graham just seemed to appear at the right time and no one was really very sure where he had come from. Jack was born in 1929 and, like Dizzy Jackson and Bob Craig, was to remain a major player in the Edinburgh jazz scene for a very long time. I was fortunate enough to play in several bands with Jack over many years and got to know him well. He was a gifted musician with a remarkable musical ear and he had the ability to fit smoothly into bands, from New Orleans to Swing, which played in widely differing styles. In many ways, it was this versatility and ability to fit in so readily, that was to make him made him such a well-loved and respected player.

After his spell with the Nova Scotians, Jack put in lengthy service with Charlie McNair's Jazz Band, Old Bailey and his Jazz Advocates, Mike Hart's Society Syncopators, The Scottish Jazz Advocates and The Scottish Society Syncopators, all major local bands, all of which made their mark on Edinburgh jazz. Jack also occasionally ran bands under his own name. We will hear more about these bands later, as well as the fine four piece band, The Diplomats of Jazz, led by trumpeter Jim Petrie, in which Jack played through most of the 1990s. He also played a great deal of dance music over the years and was never short of gigs. Jack was an accomplished clarinet player, a fact that always made me wonder how he, a man renowned for his liking for a quiet life, ever raised enough energy to learn to play such a difficult instrument so fluently. In fact, I suspect that he may well have learned to play the clarinet while doing his National Service.

Jack was one of the most laid back individuals I ever met and, at times, he gave every indication of complete lethargy. He had a career as a telephone engineer but always seemed to be suffering from a chronic shortage of cash, a state which seemed to give him an air of gentle bewilderment. His sinuous and graceful playing was much admired, not only around the Scottish jazz scene, but also in a wider context when, in the 1980s, he played at many jazz festivals in the UK, the USA and in Europe. His style was sometimes likened to that of the great Ed Hall but, in fact, his sound and style were very much his own. He did, however, share with Ed Hall a raspy, agile approach that was instantly recognisable, his supple and responsive playing nicely complementing the trumpet lead and enhancing the ensemble. I was aware, from early in our acquaintance, that Jack had once been voted the best clarinet player in Scotland. This was at some competitive jazz event in the 1950s, and I knew about it because Archie Sinclair, the trombonist who led the Old Bailey band when both Jack and I were members, often made reference to this achievement when introducing him.

In addition to his general air of somnolence, Jack was also very fond of his food and there were many legends about his capacity to stuff himself, particularly when there was access to free food. On one occasion, when playing with the Old Bailey band at a barbecue event on the harbour side at Dunbar, the band was supplied with a filled roll apiece. A single roll was never going to be enough for Jack, although he was very pleased to discover that the filling was a whole kipper, a favourite of his. Brian Sinclair, a young bass player from Dunfermline (and now an extremely able bass player based in the USA), was depping for me on this gig, and was much less chuffed to find a kipper in his roll. With a grunt of disgust, Brian threw his kipper to the flock of gulls circling about the harbour. Andrew Lauder was on this gig and said that the kipper only just escaped Jack's clutching hands as it flew through the air. Jack then turned in wrath on the astounded Brian, whom he subjected to many bitter recriminations about wasting good food that would have been a lot better disappearing down Jack's gullet than a gull's. Andrew, not to mention Brian, was absolutely amazed. *'I thought he was going to have a seizure.'* Andrew said afterwards, *'I never thought he could move that fast. He damn nearly caught the kipper before the gull got to it'.*

In character, Jack was a friendly, quiet man and the type around whom many affectionate anecdotes, such as those above, tended to gather. He was a much valued member of every band he adorned, even if he drove every band leader for whom he ever worked half demented with his skill, indeed genius, for arriving at the very last minute for every gig. He made quite a number of recordings with the various bands with which he played including Charlie McNair's band, Old Bailey's Jazz Advocates, Mike Hart's Scottish Society Syncopators, the Scottish Jazz Advocates and the Diplomats of Jazz[82]. These recordings, many of which will be found listed in the discography appendix, remain to remind us of his talent and musicianship. Later in life, Jack had serious health problems requiring major surgery. Happily, he made a good recovery and was able to resume playing. Jack Graham eventually retired to Spain where he died, on 26th of January 2005, at the age of 77.

There were, of course, many others who played with the bands led by Archie Semple and the Nova Scotians, in the late 1940s and early 1950s. Some we have already met in earlier chapters in association with the RHS Gang, including Sandy Brown himself, Stu Eaton, Stan Grieg, Willlie Burns and Jackie MacFarlane, again emphasising that there was some mixing between the two groupings. Others who played and even recorded, were pianists Ronnie Carruthers and Drew Landles, bass player Pat Malloy, vocalist Jack Thomson and guitarists Ken Duncan and Jimmy Mooney.

Drew Landles (piano) was born in 1928 in Hawick, where he spent his early years, and was introduced to piano by his mother, an accomplished player herself. Drew went on to gain the Advanced Preparatory Certificate with Honours from the Trinity College of Music. After National Service in the Royal Navy, he arrived in Edinburgh in 1948 to attend Art College, where he studied architecture. In town, he lived with Will Redpath, and Stu Eaton, both jazzers we have already met, and someone he describes as *'an eccentric American Forces jazz enthusiast'* called Lee Cross. Bill Strachan also knew this character and tells the tale of an attempt to go to Paris on a jazz seeking trip, the transport being Lee Cross' motor bike. Apparently, they got only as far as Dunbar before the motor bike packed in,

---

[82] See discography appendix

Cross having never put any oil in it. They did make it to Paris however, although only by hitching lifts the whole way. Bill also tells the story of an episode which started with a pie eating contest in Paddy's Bar in Rose Street. Lee Cross had the motor bike with him and they decided to head for the West End Café. According to Bill, about seven of them somehow got onto the bike and went roaring off down Rose Street. Hardly surprisingly, they were stopped when they reached a police box and were escorted to the police station in the High Street, where a police doctor was called to check their alcohol content. When the doctor got to Lee Cross, he immediately declared his American citizenship and stated that he was in Scotland to learn to play the bagpipes. This was apparently partly true and the incident came to an end with Lee Cross being invited to go along to a rehearsal with the Edinburgh Police Pipe Band and the rest of them allowed to make their way home, with no charges laid.

Around this time, while he was an Art College student, Drew Landles also met Sandy Brown, Al Fairweather, Stan Greig and Bob Craig and was invited to go along to their practice sessions. He also became friendly with John and Archie Semple and Alex Welsh around the same time, and began to play gigs with them. One of the high-lights of this musical association was an appearance on the second of three BBC jazz concerts, this one being devoted to Chicago style jazz. A short while after this, the band was paired with the Mick Mulligan band from London and, with them, they toured in Scotland and the north of England. Drew apparently played piano rather in the manner of Swing pianists, such as the great Teddy Wilson who had made his name with the Benny Goodman small groups in the 1930s. It was this fluent style that made him a popular choice on piano in bands involving both the Brown/Fairweather gang and the Semple brothers. After qualifying as an architect in 1953, Drew was transferred to London by the company with whom he had secured a job. There, he gradually lost touch with the active music scene and his playing career ended in about 1956, as he concentrated on developing his architectural practice.

Much later in 2010, long retired and back in Edinburgh, Drew was one of the Edinburgh Jazz Archive Group (EJAG)[83], which planned and organized an exhibition and the establishment of an archive of Edinburgh jazz, in the Edinburgh Central Library. The contribution which Drew brought to the work of the EJAG was largely the story of his involvement with the Alex Welsh and Archie Semple group and, to an extent, the Sandy Brown and Al Fairweather group, back in the 1940s and 50s. Drew Landles saw the successful fulfillment of the Archive Group's projects in 2010 but, sadly, died in Edinburgh just a few weeks later, on September 21st 2010. Drew's contribution, late in his life, to the work of the EJAG must have given him a great deal of satisfaction. It was good too that Drew's personal contribution, as an active and influential player in Edinburgh jazz, was recorded and preserved by the work of EJAG, from which much of the above information about Drew has been taken.

Pat Molloy (bass) came from Dunfermline where, according to George Melly in 'Owning Up', he had been an insurance agent. Melly describes him as of Irish origin and very small with '...*a classic Irish face with black curly hair and a complicated mouth full of teeth*'[84]. Pat had joined the Archie Semple Dixielanders, at the suggestion of Dave Keir who shared his Dunfermline background, replacing Mike Samuels whose lecturing duties at the University were causing him to miss gigs. Later, Pat Malloy and Archie Semple went off south to join the Mick Mulligan band at about the same time as another Edinburgh jazzer, the **guitarist Jimmy Currie**, who was later to become well known as solo guitarist in the 'Lonnie Donegan Skiffle Group'. Jimmy Currie seems to have been something of an all-rounder. In addition to his jazz and skiffle playing, George Melly describes him as a convinced modernist but also says that he had worked out a cabaret act which

---

[83] Edinburgh Jazz Archive Group 2010 - Jim Keppie, Bll Strachan, Donald 'Chick' Murray, Drew Landles

[84] 'Owning Up' by George Melly, (Copyright © George Melly, 1965) Reprinted by permission of A. M. Heath & Co Ltd

required him to dress up as a Mexican and deliver what Melly describes as *'abysmal patter'*!

Another Edinburgh jazzer who appeared around the late 1940s and early 1950s was **pianist Ronnie Carruthers**. Ronnie came from a musical family, his Granny having been the pianist who played for silent movies in the building in Shandwick Place which became the West End Café. Although most of Ronnie's musical career was to be with the dance bands of Edinburgh, he was involved in the earliest activities of the Revivalists in Edinburgh and, as we have heard, he was one of the group that gathered at the Semple household at 1 Braid Crescent when the Semples, Sandy Brown and others were just beginning to make their way in jazz[85]. There is a photograph, sent in by Ronnie, and shown in a SBS Newsletter, which shows Archie Semple accompanied by Archie Deacon on drums and Ronnie on piano[86].

Before the end of the war, Ronnie was a visitor at 4 Hillside Crescent, where a number of like-minded musicians gathered to play, including Jimmy Walker, Duncan Campbell, Stan Reynolds and others from the Palais Dance Band. Later on, in common with many musicians involved in dance music, Ronnie's interest in jazz moved towards the mainstream and modern forms, rather than more traditional jazz. He was a founding member of the Modern Jazz Club, which functioned between 1945 and 1954 on Sunday afternoons on the top floor of 1 India Buildings, after the New Orleans practice session earlier in the day had finished. Ronnie describes this as *'...a proper club with a membership register and membership cards, which was just as well as it was frequently raided by police who were looking for drink and drugs'*. Apparently the police harassment became quite serious, until Dr Selby Wright, the well-known and much respected minister of the Canongate Church, remonstrated with them on behalf of the club. Ronnie seemed to have a knack of settling into residencies that were to last. For example, he was with Tony Fusco's band in Tony's Ballroom in Picardy Place from

---

[85] SBS Newsletter No. 31, July 1999
[86] SBS Newsletter No. 35, November 1999

1949 to 1953 and with Alex Ferguson's band at the Leith Assembly Rooms from 1955 to 1959. However, his longest residency was to be his weekly solo piano spot at Henderson's vegetarian restaurant in Hanover Street, which began in 1990 and was still going strong more than twenty years later. Another long term and successful gig for Ronnie was his place in the resident rhythm section at monthly jam sessions run by the drummer, Roger Craik. At these sessions, which took place at the Starbank Hotel in Newhaven, guest horn players were invited by Roger to feature with the rhythm section and they regularly drew a good and enthusiastic crowd. A decade into the twenty-first century, Ronnie Carruthers, now in his eighties, was still playing regularly around town, and played wonderfully well in a piano, guitar and drums trio, later joined by John Burgess on tenor sax, which graced the opening of the exhibition on Edinburgh jazz in the Central Library on 31st July 2010.

Chapter VI

Moves towards Mainstream in the 1950s

The departure southwards in 1954 of Alex Welsh, left the 'Nova Scotians' short of a trumpet player and, as far as I have been able to find out, Stu Eaton, whom we have already met with the RHS Gang, and then **Bob Harley (cornet)** were the replacements. Eaton's name appears on a Nova Scotians photographic band card, which actually shows Alex Welsh, but has a foot note which says *'Trumpet spot now occupied by Stu Eaton'.* The same foot note also states that *'Dave Keir has since left the band to join Mick Mulligan's Magnolias. His place has been taken by Ian Anderson'.* Bob Harley seems to have originated from Kirkcaldy in Fife and Andrew Lauder, who would eventually replace him in the Nova Scotians, remembers him as *'...a fine Dixieland styled player. He didn't play in the manner of Bobby Hackett or Wild Bill Davison but was perhaps a bit like Jimmy McPartland in his sound and style'.* Andrew thinks that, when Bob left the band, it was to go to London to seek a career in jazz.

At some point, a second reeds player joined the Nova Scotians. This was **Johnny Winters (tenor sax and clarinet)** who came from Stenhousemuir, near Stirling, to attend Edinburgh University, where he studied economics as a mature student. Both the drummer Roger Craik and trumpeter Andrew Lauder have said that Winters was really a tenor sax player, rather than clarinet, and Roger described him as playing in the manner of Eddie Miller, a fine American tenor player who made his name with the

Bob Crosby Band. Winters played tenor sax with band until Jack Graham left, when he switched to clarinet and, for a time, led the band. Roger Craik and Andrew Lauder both remarked that Johnny Winters had an interest in the more modern forms of jazz. Andrew, who also described him as a good player, added that Winters, while initially keen on the Eddie Condon or Chicagoan style of jazz, later became interested in the clarinet playing of Jimmy Giuffre, although he never actually seemed to play in this style himself.

Johnny Winters was active on the Edinburgh traditional jazz scene while he remained at University but, after he had graduated, he moved away from Edinburgh. He did, however, take part in a private recording session arranged by Roger Craik in June 1969. I was involved in this session, playing bass, along with Andrew Lauder (tpt), Graeme Robertson (tbn), Alan Anderson (pno) and Roger Craik himself on drums. The recording quality is not great but, from what can be heard through the rather jumbled sound, it is clear that Johnny Winters was indeed a fine player. I can remember him complaining at this session that he was badly out of practice. He said, after we had been playing for a while, that his lips felt so tired and jelly-like that he was afraid to blow hard, as it felt as if his lips were going to go flying right down the outside of the barrel of the clarinet! Johnny Winters died in the mid-1990s.

In 1956, the afore-mentioned **Andrew Lauder (trumpet)** came in to replace Bob Harley. Andrew had been introduced to jazz by his brother, who had a number of New Orleans recordings, and Andrew says that he can remember being puzzled by the music he was hearing, recalling that he could not hear the tune. He reports that it was hearing a Sid Phillips record that enabled him to make sense of what was going on and how the various instruments played their part. He found himself homing in on what the trumpeter was playing and, around his eighteenth birthday in 1955, he bought himself an old trumpet. He discovered that there was a jazz club, called the Condon Club, which operated in India Buildings in Victoria Street. This was a function hall high up in the building, with a caretaker who lived on the top floor. A drummer called Alan Hastie, who worked with Andrew in the organ building trade, introduced him and he became a member, later becoming a member of the club committee. Andrew started to go the regular Sunday evening sessions and got to know the band and their arrangements.

India Buildings in Victoria Street the home of much early Edinburgh jazz activity (photo by the author)

The band was the Nova Scotians whose line up by this time was: Bob Harley (tpt), Ian Anderson (tbn), Johnny Winters (ten sax and co-leader), Jack Graham (clt), Bert Murray, who was from Fife (pno), Jim Baikie (gtr), someone who Andrew thinks was called Bert Paterson (bs) and George Crockett (drms and co-leader). The band also used the services of a couple of vocalists, the already mentioned drummer Alan Hastie and Brenda New, whose real name was Brenda Tosh. Sometimes, Alan Hastie would bring his drum kit along and there would be a number featuring two drummers. Changes in the band brought in Norman Skinner on piano and a black Grenadian, Len Barclay, who replaced Ian Anderson. Ian Anderson was apparently 'something in the City' and he could be seen on occasions during the day wearing a bowler hat and carrying a brolly! He later moved to London. Andrew Lauder described Len Barclay as a nice smooth trombonist but not really a Dixieland player. Jack Graham eventually left the band but was not replaced, Johnny Winters, as we have already heard, switching to clarinet. The Condon Club also featured interval bands at these sessions, including more modern players such as Dougie Campbell (gtr), Johnny Smith (tpt) and Ronnie Carruthers (pno).

Andrew, as a member of the committee, would arrive early at the club, to set up the lighting and get the place ready, and this led to opportunities for him to sit in. When Bob Harley took the road to London in 1956, Andrew, just ten months after starting on trumpet, was invited to take his place in this well established band. Around this time, in about 1956, Andrew started to meet other jazzers around town, including trumpeters Charlie McNair and Jim Petrie and trombonist Archie Sinclair, whom he first came across in the West End Café and with whom he was later to have a lengthy musical partnership. He also became aware of the Climax Jazz Band, of whom we will hear much more in the next chapter, and remembers other bands led by Mike Hart and Bob Craig, although he thinks that Mike may have been playing with the Climax band at this time. Eventually, Andrew says, the Nova Scotians sadly just faded out, a common enough fate for local jazz bands, but a shame in the case of a band which had started out under Archie Semple's leadership and carried the local Dixieland banner for a decade or more.

At this point, as with so many of the jazzers in the 1940 and 50s, Andrew was called up to do his National Service which he spent in the RAF, serving in, amongst other places, the Middle East. Here he bumped into another Edinburgh musician, Bill Marshall, later to make a local reputation in folk and country music, before still later re-inventing himself as a clarinet player on the jazz scene. On his return from the Forces, Andrew was approached to play with a new band being organized by **Pete Kerr (clarinet)**, who was from Haddington, where he had previously run a band. The new band was called **Pete Kerr's Capital Jazz Band** and the purpose of forming it was a bid to play full time. The band that Kerr got together was: Andrew Lauder (tpt), Johnny McGuff (tbn). Pete Kerr (clt and leader), Alex Shaw (pno), Jim Douglas (bjo and gtr), Ian Brown (bs) and George Crockett (drms) and it was clearly another band in the Dixieland tradition. This band went off to Germany on a tour that lasted from November 1960 to early 1961, as we will hear shortly, and then the band folded, bringing to an end Andrew's short-lived professional career.

Pete Kerr's Capital Jazz Band, like Pete himself, had its origins, not actually in Edinburgh itself but in Haddington, the county town of East Lothian, about twenty miles east of the capital, and we can follow the band's history from the recollections of their **banjo and guitar player, Jim Douglas**. Jim was born near Gifford, a small East Lothian town not far from Haddington, on 13th May 1942. His father was a drummer in the Royal Army Medical Corps pipe band and his mother a shepherd's daughter who was in service at Newton Hall, where his father's regiment was billeted. Jim's education took place mostly at Yester Primary School and then at the famous Knox Academy at Haddington, which was where he met a fellow pupil, Pete Kerr. Jim had become interested in the current craze for skiffle and, after successfully pestering his mother into buying him a guitar, he had got down to some serious practice which, he claims, bored both his immediate family and his uncle, who became his severest critic. Jim then became a member of the local 'Tynesiders Skiffle Group', which took its name from the East Lothian River Tyne and not the Newcastle one, until he heard the Chris Barber Jazz Band, an experience which promptly changed his musical allegiance. Soon afterwards, in his own words, he was *'completely wrapped up in traditional jazz'*.

It was not long before he was finding his way into the Edinburgh jazz scene of the late 1950s, where he began visiting the Royal Mile Cafe in the High Street to listen to the Royal Mile Jazz Band, led by trumpeter Eric Rinaldi. This band included drummer Sandy Malcolm who, like Jim himself, would later put in some time with the famous Clyde Valley Stompers. Another member of the band was guitarist Alex Marshall, at whose house Jim would sometimes stay after the jazz sessions. It was Alex who introduced Jim to the music of Django Reinhardt and to whom Jim gives considerable credit for laying the foundations of his whole future career in jazz. His enthusiasm for jazz well and truly established, Jim then found himself helping school pal Pete Kerr to form the 'Hidden Town Dixielanders', the 'Hidden Town' being Haddington. They soon had a band together which included, in addition to Pete on clarinet and Jim on guitar, Jack Blair (tbn), Kimber Buglass (tpt), John Logan (bs) and Bob Sandie (drms).

The Hidden Town Dixielanders was clearly quite a talented outfit and, after winning the local heat of the 'Carroll Levis Discoveries Show', they were rewarded with a trip to London to take part in a broadcast. However, with success came change and, within a few months, Ken Ramage came in on trombone, Alastair Clark on trumpet, George Crockett on drums and a piano player, Bob McDonald, was recruited. In addition, the band's name was changed to Pete Kerr's Dixielanders. A couple of recordings were issued (about which we will hear more shortly, when we meet Alastair Clark) and, as the band grew in popularity, they were approached by an impresario based in Germany. He was John Martin, who owned the Storyville Club in Cologne and, having heard the band on the recordings, he offered them a chance of a couple of months playing, with the possibility of other work in Germany to follow. This, however, meant the band becoming a professional outfit and, inevitably, this brought more changes in personnel, most of them bringing in names which would become well known in jazz circles. The talented trombonist Ken Ramage had already turned professional, heading south to join the Charlie Gall band, and his replacement had been Johnny McGuff. Trumpeter Alastair Clark's burgeoning journalistic career precluded any professional ambitions in jazz and it was this that brought Andrew Lauder into the band. Bob McDonald was studying medicine in Edinburgh and vacated the piano chair in favour of Alex Shaw and Ian Brown came in on bass to replace John Logan, who worked in the printing trade. Jim Douglas himself had just been taken on as an apprentice potter with Castle Wynd Potteries and, although somewhat reluctant to give up a promising career, in the end, with the brave encouragement of his disappointed mother, he took the plunge and moved into the world of professional jazz.

The German adventure brought a month in Cologne's 'Storyville', followed by a further month in Mannheim's 'Schwabinger Kunstler Keller'. However, the work was hard, Pete Kerr recalling that they were required to play from 8.00pm to 2.00am all seven nights of the week, with additional matinees on Saturdays and Sundays. Unfortunately, further work in Germany did not materialize, Pete commenting that beat groups from the UK were beginning to move in on the German clubs, and the band returned to the UK after their original two months were completed. None-the-less, in spite of the hard work and the lack of further work, the time in Germany had allowed them to enjoy some wonderful musical experiences. Amongst these were gigs when they accompanied bongo/conga player and vocalist Frank Holder, who had played and sung with the Johnny Dankworth band, and some gigs accompanying the fine veteran American reeds man, Benny Waters. There was also, to the astonished delight of drummer George Crockett, the chance to meet the great modern jazz drummer, Art Blakey. When the band returned to the UK in February 1961, it was to find that the Trad Boom was in full swing and they expected this to bring them a lot of work. However, several Scottish bands had already been making forays into England and the London agents approached by Pete did not deem an invasion by yet another one as necessary. Sadly, they decided to disband and returned northwards and homewards, to pick up the pieces.

However, for some of the band at least, all was far from lost. Forrie Cairns, star clarinetist with the Scotland's famous Clyde Valley Stompers, had decided – like others before him – to leave and form his own band. Pete Kerr was invited to replace him, his recruitment coinciding with the band moving its permanent base from Glasgow to London. Shortly afterwards, the Scottish nature of the band was further maintained by the recruitment of Jim Douglas.

Pete Kerr's Dixielanders in Germany 1960/61
In checked shirts from the left – Pete Kerr, Alex Shaw,
Andrew Lauder, Ian Brown, George Crockett
(Photo by permission of Jim Douglas)

As it turned out, this new version of the Stompers was also to have an unsettled time, with the leader, trombone player Ian Menzies, sadly having to stop playing because of health issues. What, in fact, happened was that, although Ian Menzies retired to Jersey and later to Canada, he retained a controlling interest in the band by forming a company called Clyde Valley Stompers Ltd with London agent Lyn Dutton, whose office acted both as the band's booking agent and as business managers of the limited company. Pete Kerr took over leadership of the band and brought in Johnny McGuff to replace Menzies and added pianist Bert Murray. When the re-jigged Stompers took the road under Pete's leadership, the line-up was Malky Higgins and later Joe McIntyre (tpt), Pete Kerr (clt), Johnny McGuff (tbn), Bert Murray (pno), Jim Douglas (bjo/gtr), Bill Bain (bs) and Robbie Winter (drms). This edition of the Stompers, through its constant touring all over the UK, set about extending the loyal fan base that earlier line-ups had established in the band's west of Scotland heartland. In 1962, the Stompers recorded their biggest-selling single recording, featuring an arrangement, largely by Bert Murray, of Prokopiev's 'Peter and the Wolf', with ex-Syd

Phillip's sideman Joe McIntyre on trumpet. This recording, made for the Parlophone company under the direction of one George Martin, later to become famous for his work with the Beatles, made it to the very edge of the revered Top Twenty pop charts. The popularity of this record led to the Stompers becoming, for a time, the most televised jazz band in Britain, with regular spots on such top network programmes as 'Thank Your Lucky Stars', 'Cool for Cats' and 'The Morecambe and Wise Show'. Film work also beckoned, with an appearance in Tommy Steele's 'It's All Happening' followed by an invitation to provide the title music for Norman Wisdom's 'On the Beat'. The band's contribution to the soundtracks of these movies was taped, like their Parlophone records, at EMI's famous Abbey Road Studios and again produced by George Martin. However, despite such unprecedented success, this version of the Clyde Valley Stompers, in its time Scotland's most successful traditional jazz band, did not last much longer. The choice of band personnel lay with the business managers, giving rise to concerns being raised by Pete about how this might reflect on musical policy. The resulting discord ultimately led to Ian Menzies withdrawing use of the Clyde Valley Stompers name, ownership of which he had retained, and the Pete Kerr led version of the band came to an end.

The Clyde Valley Stompers phase of their jazz careers over, Pete Kerr and Jim Douglas returned to Edinburgh and the formation of the last of Pete's bands, this time under the name Pete Kerr's Scottish All Stars. The personnel of this band had an average age of less than twenty one and included the exceptional young bass player from Shetland, Ron Mathewson, and an excellent young Edinburgh drummer, Billy Law. However, with the decreasing demand for live jazz, the band was obliged to travel, quite literally, the length and breadth of Britain to stay in business, once trekking overnight from an engagement in Southampton to Glasgow for a radio broadcast, followed immediately by a dance in Hawick and another overnight drive to a gig in Thurso! They also made a couple of extended play recordings[87] at the Craighall Studios in Edinburgh, 'Jazz at the Capital' in 1963 and 'More Jazz at the Capital' in 1964. These were released on Waverley Records, the company with which Pete Kerr had made his recording debut some five years previously. The full line-up of the band on these recordings was Mike Scott (tpt), Pete Kerr (clt), Eddie Lorkin (tbn), Mike Oliver (pno), Jim Douglas (bjo/gtr), Ron Mathewson (bs) and Billy Law (drms).

Sadly, this band too had a short life, coming to an end when Pete Kerr took up an offer from EMI to become a record producer. Pete's career in record production was a successful one, most of his two hundred or so recordings being of music with a Scottish flavour but also including three albums by the Alex Welsh band, recorded at the Craighall Studios, 'Alex Welsh at Home', 'Alex Welsh Vintage 1969' and 'The Alex Welsh Dixieland Party'. However, the biggest selling record produced by Pete was that of 'Amazing Grace' by the Royal Scots Dragoon Guards, recorded at Redford Barracks, Edinburgh, which became an international number one hit, going on to sell some thirteen million copies still, in 2012, the highest selling instrumental single of all time. Years later, the talented and versatile Pete Kerr was to embark on yet another successful career, this time as an author, publishing a number of books, both travel writing and fiction, including 'Snowball Oranges', 'Thistle Soup' and 'The Gannet Has Landed'[88].

While Pete was developing his career away from playing jazz, Jim Douglas and Billy Law headed south and eventually, after a fairly lean time, Billy joined the band led by clarinet player Terry Lightfoot and Jim, at first covering for Diz Disley, went on to become a permanent member of the Alex Welsh band. Jim and Billy moved into a famous jazz house at Fawley Road, West Hampstead, sharing the accommodation with well known jazzers Brian Lemon, Colin Purbrook, Keith Ingham and Tony Bayliss, with the added attraction of having Sandy Brown living just round the corner. Jim recalls having the great good fortune to be

---

[87] See discography appendix
[88] www.peter-kerr.co.uk

asked by Sandy to play at his Christmas parties where, he says, '...*the measures became legendary*'!

Jim Douglas remained with the Alex Welsh band for all of eighteen years, all of course well documented and all delightfully happy years for Jim, playing with some of the finest jazz musicians ever produced in this country. The band played at the famed Newport Jazz Festival in the USA in 1968, made many notable recordings and accompanied some of the great names of jazz on tour. It is well worth listing some of these great players as they give some idea of the stature of the Welsh band of that time – Henry 'Red' Allen, Wild Bill Davison, Earl Hines, Ruby Braff, Willie 'The Lion' Smith, Pee Wee Russell, Eddie 'Lockjaw' Davies, Eddie Miller, Ben Webster, Dickie Wells, Rex Stewart, Peanuts Hucko, Bob Wilbur, Dick Wellstood, Billy Butterfield, Pee Wee Erwin, Sammy Price, Johnnie Mince, Yank Lawson, Vic Dickenson and others – a roll call of some of the finest players of the middle period of jazz.

Since the untimely death of Alex Welsh in 1982, Jim Douglas' career has taken many twists and turns, involving bands led by Digby Fairweather, Keith Smith, Val Wiseman, Pete Strange and Dave Shepherd. He also played a number of concerts with Stephane Grapelli, played a gig with the South Rampart Street Paraders, which included the great drummer Nick Fatool, and toured Europe with Bob Haggard, Bob Barnard and an Alex Welsh tribute band, which Jim was instrumental in putting together. Jim married Alex Welsh's widow, Margaret in 1983 and, when their son Will was young and '...*when the road got too long*', he also pursued a career as a chef. He retired from playing in 2009 but in 2011, with his family responsibilities nicely under control, he was able to return to playing, when the drummer Laurie Chescoe asked him to join his re-union band. With Laurie's band, Jim Douglas appeared at the 2011 Edinburgh International Jazz and Blues Festival. I was lucky enough to play in the band that alternated with them at the Mardi Gras in the Grassmarket, and it was great to hear Jim playing as well as ever, a tower of strength both in the rhythm section and in his solo playing.

However, we must return to the 1950s and again pick up the story of what was happening in the Edinburgh jazz world of the time. After his brief professional career, Andrew Lauder was to join another Edinburgh band, one which was to have a long and successful run. This was Old Bailey and his Jazz Advocates, a band of which we will later hear much more. I played more with Andrew than I did with any other musician: from 1964 to 1970 and 1975 to January 1981 with the Old Bailey band, from January 1981 to 1984 with the Scottish Jazz Advocates and then, from 1987 to date (ie 2011), in a four piece band, The Maid of the Forth Stompers, which played on a cruise ship. Over this long period, I reckon I got to know his playing almost as well as he knew it himself. Andrew did not play in the hot, driving style aspired to by most traditional jazz trumpeters. His style was cooler, lyrical and thoughtful, his roots drawing on the model laid down by Bix Biederbecke and continued by trumpeters such as Bobby Hackett, Jimmy McPartland, Ruby Braff and even Chet Baker.

In particular, it was always said that Andrew had modeled himself on the playing of the white American Bobby Hackett, whose playing Andrew revered above all others. Andrew himself credited the Glasgow based trumpet player, George Ogilvie (still playing in Glasgow in 2011), for turning his attention towards Hackett. However, I believe that, in fact, his approach to improvisation was rather different to that of Hackett. Leonard Feather, the distinguished jazz musician and writer, in his 'The Book of Jazz'[89], defines three approaches to melodic improvisation used by jazz musicians. The first and simplest is where '...the original melody is respected completely; the only change lies in the lengthening or shortening of some notes, repetition of others, use of tonal variations and dynamics to bring out its in conformity with the personality of the interpreter.'

The second is where '...the melody remains completely recognizable but its phrases are subject to slight additions and changes; here and there a note is added or subtracted and perhaps a whole phrase is transmuted, but to the layman listener the original melody remains perceptible

---

[89] Feather, L 'The Book of Jazz', pub. 1957 by Arthur Barker Ltd, an imprint of The Orion Publishing Group, London

throughout either in the actual statement or by indirection.'
Gunther Schuller, in his scholarly book 'Early Jazz - its
roots and development' gives a similar view from the veteran
clarinet player, Buster Bailey. Bailey, commenting on his
own clarinet playing around 1917, said *'I...was embellishing
around the melody. At that time, I wouldn't have known
what they meant by improvising. But embellishing was a
phrase I understood'*[90]. In the same book, Schuller also
adopts a term previously applied to this form of improvising
by the French jazz writer Andre Hodier, which is
'paraphrase improvisations'. He explains that this is a type
of improvisation *'...based primarily on embellishment or
ornamentation of the original melodic line'*[91].

Feather's third category is where *'...the soloist departs
entirely from the melody; in fact rather than using it as a
point of departure, he uses instead the chord pattern of the
tune.'* This is given further strength by James Lincoln
Collier who, after pointing out Louis Armstrong's advances
in technical ability and confidence in the mid-1920s, goes
on to say *'Third – and this is extremely significant – he uses
the written melody less and less as a guide and embarks
more and more on wholly original voyages, navigating only
on the chord changes – the song's underlying harmonies.
Where in the Oliver solos he followed a preset line and in the
Henderson solos frequently paraphrased the melody, he is
now, as the Hot Five series progresses, throwing the
frequently pedestrian melodies the scornful glance they
deserve and inventing entirely new melodies'*[92]. Schuller
also comments on this where he says *'In all the early New
Orleans performances the original composition played a
predominant role in "improvisation". The younger men like
Armstrong, Sidney Bechet and Johnny Dodds gradually*

---

[90] 'Early Jazz: Its Roots and Musical Development (The History of Jazz)', by Gunther
Schuller (1968) 25 words p66, by permission of Oxford University Press,
www.oup.com

[91] 'Early Jazz: Its Roots and Musical Development (The History of Jazz)', by Gunther
Schuller (1968) 13 words p323, by permission of Oxford University Press
www.oup.com

[92] Collier J L, 'Louis Armstrong – a Biography', Pub. Michael Joseph Ltd, 1984. Every
effort has been made to trace the current holder of copyright of this work but
without success.

broke away from the theme improvisation concept, and, after the mid-twenties solo improvisation, with few exceptions, came to mean extemporizing on chords rather than melodies'[93].

While I do not think that jazz improvisers necessarily fall neatly into a single one of these three categories, but may well fit in somewhere between them or even move between them, they none-the-less help us understand how improvisation may be approached.

Bobby Hackett was not only a trumpet player but also an able, professional guitarist, the significance of which is recognized by James Lincoln Collier when he points out *'As a guitarist, Hackett was more familiar than many horn players with how chords fit together.'* He then goes on to contrast Hackett's playing with that of Max Kaminsky and says *'Where Kaminsky was a minimalist, playing perhaps only one of the notes of a chord, Hackett very frequently played all of them.'[94]* Hackett certainly frequently plays tumbling, graceful lines through the chord changes, with an ease that indicates a comprehensive familiarity with their makeup and relationship to each other. To that extent, he seems to me to be a player who improvised on the chord pattern of the tunes, albeit constructing wondrously melodic choruses, in the manner of Leonard Feather's third category of improvising. Andrew does not seem to me to improvise that way. He has a terrific ear for harmony and seemed to me always to work from the melody, his gifted ear enabling him to find notes that altered and enhanced the melody line. Andrew himself always maintained that he did not know the theory of chord construction or the musical relationship between different chords. However, whatever were the differences in their approaches, like Bobby Hackett, Andrew was a graceful, lyrical player who always sounded musicianly and controlled. He was probably the

---

[93] 'Early Jazz – Its Roots and Musical Development (The History of Jazz)' by Gunther Schuller (1968) 52 words p80, by permission of Oxford University Press, www.oup.com

[94] Collier, J L, 'The Making of Jazz – a Comprehensive History', Granada Publishing Ltd, 1978 Every effort has been made to trace the current holder of copyright of this work but without success.

best player of melody with whom I ever played, with a great ability to expose the real beauty of a melody, particularly when the tune was a ballad. He was to remain an important player in Edinburgh for over fifty years.

Jim Baikie (guitar) was born in India and came to Edinburgh in 1944, where he was educated at George Watsons College. While at school, he took up the ukelele and met Roger Craik, later to be a well-known local jazz drummer. It was while at University between 1949 and 1952, that Jim developed an interest in jazz. Hearing about jazz sessions at India Buildings, he went along and, outside the venue, bumped into George Crockett and helped him in with his drum kit. This was to be Jim's first experience of live jazz and it seems likely to have been the band led by Archie Semple, prior to his departure for London. Later, of course, the band became the Nova Scotians and, by now playing guitar, Jim got the chance to sit in with the band and, as he puts it, other variations of the group. He remembers playing at this time with Alex Welsh, Johnny McGuff (tbn), Archie Semple, Dicky Alexander (bs), Jimmy Mooney (gtr) and George Crockett (drms). Jim later played 'on the boats', the term used by musicians to denote work in bands which were employed to provide music on trans-Atlantic liners.

Jim became a very able guitar player and this, plus his good singing voice and easy empathy with audiences, made him a natural band leader. He set up and led a dance band which worked steadily in town for over thirty years, a band which included musicians such as Ronnie Carruthers (pno), Alfie Seely (accordion), Derek Lawton or Eric Rinaldi (tpt), Ronnie Dunn (bs) and Ian Gillan (drms). Many of them, including Jim himself, were interested in jazz and played in jazz combos as well as dance bands. Jim's love for and interest in jazz continued and, much later, beginning in the 1990s and continuing until 2010, he was to be a regular in the resident rhythm section organized by Roger Craik, which hosted monthly jazz sessions at the 'Starbank Inn' in Newhaven and featured invited guest horn players.

After the demise of the Nova Scotians, the Dixieland tradition was to be kept alive in Edinburgh by **The Royal Mile Jazz Band**, which played in the Chicagoan tradition.

This band, according to Andrew Lauder, played at the Royal Mile Café, which was owned by the mother of the band's trumpet player, Eric Rinaldi. Others who played in this band included Jack Duff and Joe Smith on reeds, David 'Eed' Smith who played both trombone and banjo (although presumably not at the same time), Tom Finlay on piano and Sandy Malcolm on drums.

'Boosey and Hawkes', the musical instrument makers, sponsored a 'National Trad Band Contest' in 1962 and the local heat took place in the Edinburgh Palais de Dance, in December of that year. This competition was very much a sign of the times, as the infamous 'Trad Boom' was upon us and trad jazz records were featuring in the Pop charts. The Contest Rules included the statement *'Any musical instrument may be used but each group must contain at least one trombone, one trumpet, one banjo and one clarinet'* – a sign of the times indeed! I took part in this contest, playing with a schoolboy band, the **Mound City Jazz Band** and, at that stage of our collective development, we were really just there to make up the numbers. However, the Royal Mile Jazz Band also took part and, hardly surprisingly considering their line-up, were serious contenders, eventually finishing as runners up to Old Bailey and his Jazz Advocates. The local heat was reviewed in the Edinburgh Evening News and the reviewer, John Gibson, reported that the Royal Mile band sounded well rehearsed and seemed engrossed in a Condon-type sound. They played *'I've Found a New Baby'*, *'Mood Indigo'* and *'My Gal Sal'*. Gibson also noted that *'...clarinetist Jack Duff and drummer Sandy Malcolm emerged as two of the evening's outstanding musicians'*[95]. This was not surprising as these two went on to have full time careers in jazz, in Jack Duff's case, a lengthy and distinguished one.

Another journalist and a colleague of John Gibson, was **Alastair Clark (trumpet)**, who had become interested in jazz through hearing the Sid Phillips band on the wireless in the mid-1950s. In Alastair's case, his interest in jazz was very much a personal thing. He was not involved in any jazz gang, nor was he taken to jazz sessions or persuaded to

---

[95] Gibson J, Edinburgh Evening News, 4th December 1962.

buy jazz records by already committed friends. He simply got into jazz on his own, without even wondering if there were others around with the same interests. He was not even aware that Edinburgh was already considered something of a hot spot for jazz. He had been educated at Daniel Stewart's College and, while at school, saved up £6 with which he bought a trumpet from Mev Taylor's shop at Haymarket. He then persuaded the school to allow him to have trumpet lessons from the brass teacher, who played trumpet in the Empire Theatre pit band. Alastair was taught the rudiments but was finally caught out by his tutor who said *'You're faking'* as he battled his way through 'Baa Baa Black Sheep'. The tutor was correct, Alastair was playing by ear, not reading the music, and that is the way it was to stay.

Alastair's interest, at this time, was in black music, much influenced by the writings of the Frenchman Hugues Panassie, and Alastair strove to achieve a sound like that of Louis Armstrong – a laudable aim if ever there was one! After practice at home, when he played into a cupboard full of clothes to muffle the sound, he went to his first live gig after being told by a pal that there were jazz sessions in the Crown Bar in Lothian Street. Here he not only heard Sandy Brown but discovered that were others who shared his interest in hot music. Alastair was knocked out by Sandy's playing, considering him to be better than any clarinetist that he had ever heard on record. Attending the Crown sessions also brought him into contact with the bass player Jim Young, who arranged for him try out for a band he was forming. This was followed by several makeshift bands and then came what Alastair has called his *'big break'*. Al Fairweather followed by Sandy Brown had departed for London and trombonist Bob Craig, intent on filling in the gaps to keep the band playing, offered Alastair the trumpet slot. Alastair describes this as a fabulous experience and recalls that Dougie Campbell, whom he describes as a great guitarist, was in the band. Even without Al and Sandy, the band under Bob Craig's leadership continued to be successful and played some important gigs, including one in the Usher Hall when they were the warm up band for the Chris Barber band. This gig was sold out and Pat Halcox,

133

Barber's fine trumpeter, afterwards complimented Alastair on his playing.

Later, Alastair was to play trumpet with **Pete Kerr's Dixielanders**, a band with whom he made a couple of singles records. I have a copy of one of these recordings and the lineup is Alastair Clark (tpt), Pete Kerr (clt and leader), Ken Ramage (tbn), Bob McDonald (pno), Jim Douglas (bjo), Johnny Logan (bs) and George Crockett (drms). The tunes are *'Stars and Stripes for Ever'* on one side and *'Ice Cream'* on the other and it is was on Waverley Records, No. SPL 505[96]. The band sounds quite fiery and Alastair, playing well himself, was clearly in good company. Later, he had to leave the band to concentrate on his career in journalism, when Pete Kerr had a stab at playing full time, taking the band to Germany under the name Pete Kerr's Capital Jazz Band, as described earlier. As we have already heard, Andrew Lauder was the replacement for Alastair. Later still, after National Service, Alastair returned to Edinburgh, switched to alto saxophone, and formed a band with Ian 'Tello' Telford on trumpet, Donald McDonald on bass and Dennis Morton on drums. This band played *'mainstreamy, swingy stuff'*, according to Alastair, and had a fortnightly gig at the Art College, where they attracted a good following.

Alastair went on to have a successful career in journalism, becoming a senior journalist with the 'Scotsman' newspaper and, although the pressures of his work put an end to his jazz career, he looks back on his playing days as the happiest of his life. He is of the view that jazz is the most creative form of art because it is instant and *'you live or die by what you come up with in the next 30 seconds'*. He also points out how many jazzers were creative in other ways, in addition to their music, and considers that jazz is the ultimate platform for creativity. He tempers this, however, in terms of more recent developments in jazz, believing that some of the heart has gone out of the music, feeling that attempts to be more ludicrously virtuosic than the next guy have taken over. Alastair Clark stopped playing far too soon and his

---

[96] See Discography Appendix

Armstrong inspired trumpet (and his alto sax playing, although I never heard this) was a serious loss to Edinburgh traditional jazz.

The trombonist who recorded the *'Stars and Stripes/ Ice Cream'* single with the Pete Kerr band was **Ken Ramage (trombone and later, drums)**. He was born in 1937 and educated at Leith Academy, where he learned to play violin in the school orchestra. A viewing of the 'bio-pic' 'The Glen Miller Story' in 1953 awakened in him an ambition to play jazz trombone and he was quickly into action, one of his first gigs being at the Stud Club, then located on St John's Hill off the Pleasance. At this gig he met local jazzers Peter Davenport, Jim Petrie and Jim Young. In 1959, Ken played with Johnny Keating's Big Band, which played regularly in a venue called the Harmony Inn in the Canongate. Keating, who was also involved in the running of the famous Ted Heath Band, had suggested that Ken be recruited for this band. However, in the end, although Ken's jazz playing was well up to the standard required, Keating came to the conclusion that his music reading was not and reluctantly felt that he could not put Ken's name forward.

Not long after this, Ken decided that he wanted to pursue a professional career in jazz and joined Charlie Gall's band, touring Germany with them in 1959. On the return of the band to London, it was to find that the so-called Trad Boom was underway and everything in the traditional jazz world had moved towards a more commercial approach. Ken, by now a player with a formidable technique, found himself fired *'...for playing too many notes'!* Ken interpreted this as a conflict between Dixieland, which was his preferred style, and New Orleans jazz, which was very much in fashion, and, as Ken put it, *'...trombone players were expected to sound like Jim Robinson again'!* Jim Robinson, who played very much in the early tailgate manner, was of course the trombone player in the George Lewis band whose style was followed by many of the successful British traditional bands. The few British bands which played outside this model, such as Alex Welsh's band and the Sandy Brown and Al Fairweather band, were never really a part of the Trad Boom and had something of a struggle to find gigs while the boom lasted. I should add, for the sake of accuracy, that the Kenny Ball band, which followed a white dixieland model rather than a New Orleans one, was also extremely successful during the boom. However, this was mostly because they followed a notably commercial policy of producing jazzed-up versions of catchy, well-known tunes, many of them from shows and films, such as 'Samantha', 'The Green Leaves of Summer' and '88 Days in Peking'.

After his exit from the Charlie Gall band, Ken joined the band of Eggy Ley and stayed with them for about a year. Eggy Ley, whose real name was Derek William Ley, was a London born reeds player who ran a number of bands, which worked mainly on the Continent, and who later became a radio producer. With the Eggy Ley band in 1961, Ken toured and recorded with Benny Waters, a legendary reeds player from the USA who had played and recorded with Joe 'King' Oliver in the 1930s.

Ken himself then organized a band, the Ken Ramage Dixielanders, to tour in Germany in 1962, and this he regards as the best of all the many bands with which he played. This is not a surprising view given the quality of the line-up which included Per Hansen on trumpet, Edinburgh's own Jack Duff and Alec Shaw on reeds and piano respectively, George Cole on drums and an outstanding bass player, Ron Mathewson from Shetland. The band was not only good but also successful, making a number of live broadcasts on BFN (British Forces Network) and AFN (American Forces Network) while they were in Germany. Ken remembers that this band was, at the time, the only professional jazz band which was playing the terrific material written by Sandy Brown and Al Fairweather other than, of course, the Fairweather-Brown band itself. The young bass player, Ron Mathewson, was to go on to have a major jazz career, firstly with the Alex Welsh band and then into more modern forms of jazz with Ronnie Scott, amongst many others. I remember Ron Mathewson arriving in Edinburgh from Shetland in the very early 1960s and, even then, his playing scared me to death. He was to become an awesome player, with an amazing technique, who seemed to be able to play at the speed of light. His brother Matt Mathewson was a fine pianist who played in Edinburgh for a while in the 1950s.

The Ken Ramage Dixielanders later broke up while still based in Germany and Ken was briefly stranded there. However, out of the blue came a chance to join an American band, which was playing the Storyville Club in Frankfurt. This band was called the Route Two Tooters and they had won the American Inter-Collegiate Band National Contest, a win which had led to a tour in Europe. Illness had resulted in the departure of their trombone player and Ken was on the spot at just the right time to be offered his place in the band, an offer he was only too pleased to accept. He then sailed with the band as they headed back to the USA, fulfilling the next part of their contract by playing on the liner as it sailed across the Atlantic. A final perk of his spell with the Rout Two Tooters was the chance to record with them for the famous Riverside Records in New York, although sadly the recordings were never released. It was during this recording session that Ken became aware that the great modern jazz trumpeter, Dizzy Gillespie, was in the next studio. Later, when most of the Route Two Tooters had departed back to college, Ken, with help from an American trumpet playing friend, made his way to Albany, in up-state New York, where he played part-time with the local Dixieland band. He also worked in the golf course business for a while, where his Scots accent came in handy, many of the green keepers in those days being Scots! The trumpet player who had assisted Ken was Superintendent of the Albany Country Club and it turned out that Dizzy Gillespie, who was apparently keen on horses, went there quite regularly to do some riding when he was in the area. A happy outcome of this was that Ken got to know the famous bebopper quite well.

Ken returned to Edinburgh in 1967 to take over the family shop, his father having gone into local politics. He set about forming various jazz groups, sometimes four-piece sometimes a sextet, and held down regular gigs at The White Cockade in Rose Street and The Yellow Carvel in Hunter's Square, behind the Tron Church. Both of these were good and popular jazz venues, supporting many bands over the years, including that of Charlie McNair. Ken Ramage also did a lot of work with dance bands and in the clubs. This latter term tends to mean the likes of Working

Men's Clubs, Miner's Clubs and so on, there being a lot of them scattered around Fife and in the Borders.

Ken also played a series on STV with piano player Alec Shaw, a fine guitarist called Bill Mulholland, Ronnie Rae on bass and on drums Davie Dunn, who was to emigrate to Australia. The series was called 'A Touch of Jazz' and it was shortly after this TV work that he went back on the boats, cruising to the Bahamas and the Caribbean area generally. When working on the boats, each musician was expected to play two instruments, presumably to increase the versatility of the bands. The Edinburgh drummer Kenny Duff was in the boat band and Ken Ramage would take over on the drum kit whenever Kenny Duff was taking his breaks. Because of this, Ken nominated drums as his second instrument, a portent of the future because, as we will see later in this book, Ken Ramage was later to suffer dental problems that would result in him having to stop playing trombone and to switch to drums. He would also later return to the Edinburgh jazz scene.

The reeds player in the band nominated by Ken Ramage as the best he ever ran, was **Jack Duff (reeds, piano)**. Jack was born in Edinburgh on 13th August 1940 and was educated at the Royal High School. He started on piano at the age of seven and took up clarinet at fifteen, later adding all the various saxes to his musical armoury. Although ten years or so younger than the original RHS Gang, he was much influenced by them, particularly by the playing of Sandy Brown. Jack was also influenced by the great tenor saxist Coleman Hawkins and was certainly more oriented towards middle period jazz and Swing than New Orleans jazz. He first appeared on the Edinburgh jazz scene in the late 1950s and, as a teenager, played with the Charlie McNair band and the Royal Mile Jazzmen. He then went on to play full time with the local dance band leader, Cam Robbie, and then in 1959, with the Geraldo Orchestra.

Jack was and remained throughout his career, a great enthusiast and was an inveterate sitter-in whenever the chance came up. Often the first sign that he was around would be a hopeful face smiling round the edge of the door and you knew that Jack had arrived and was looking for a sit-in. This happened so often when I was playing with the

Old Bailey band in the early 1960s, that band leader Archie Sinclair gave him the nickname 'Face'! He was a terrific musician and was always welcome. When I first met him in the early 1960s, he was particularly enthused by the playing of Paul Gonzalves, the tenor sax player with the Duke Ellington band, and I remember going to Newcastle with Jack and several others to hear the Ellington band in concert, still with all the great names playing as wonderfully well as ever.

Jack joined the band that Ken Ramage put together to tour Germany in 1962, the band Ken said was his best ever. At the end of this tour, he returned to London and then moved to Jersey in 1964, where he worked with another Edinburgh exile, the bass player Gerry Rossi, and led his own band. Jack became the leading jazz player on Jersey and his band accompanied many international stars including Johnny Griffiths, Sonny Stitt, Harry Edison, Kenny Davern, Kay Starr, Jimmy Witherspoon, Roy Eldridge, Benny Waters and Joe Harriot. During this period of his career, he recorded three albums, including one with trumpeter Kenny Wheeler as guest. Jack's yearly programme, when based on Jersey, was to remain there during the six-month long summer seasons, then play full time on the ocean liners, including the Queen Elizabeth and the Canberra, in the winters. His ability as a more than competent jazz pianist was a great asset during the work on the boats. He maintained this pattern for more than twenty years, visiting many exotic destinations in the USA, Australia and the Caribbean. At various other times, Jack also put in time with the Sid Lawrence Orchestra, played with the fine American clarinet player Peanuts Hucko at the Jersey Jazz Festival in the late 1970s and with Humphrey Lyttelton at the 1982 Edinburgh Jazz Festival.

Jack eventually returned to Edinburgh in 1990, when he quickly slotted in as if he had never been away, working both as a soloist and setting up bands under his own leadership. He was a featured soloist with Hamish McGregor's Fat Sam's Band (see chapter XIV) and became the reeds player with Mike Hart's Scottish Society Syncopators, making many festival appearances with these bands, both in the UK and abroad. He was a consummate and extremely versatile musician for whom music was his whole life. He was completely at home in most jazz styles and this enabled him to sustain a full time career in the music over a long period. One of the many admirable things about Jack was, whatever his own actual preferences may have been in jazz, he never gave less than his enthusiastic best, whoever he was playing with. In addition to his musicianship, Jack had a full, rounded tone on all the reed instruments that he played and he enhanced the sound of every band with whom he played. Sadly, after only ten years back in his home city, his health began to give problems and Jack Duff died in Edinburgh at the age of only sixty, on 30th September 2000. There was however, to be an odd little tail piece to Jack's story.

In the Edinburgh Evening News of 11th December 2000[97], there appeared an article by John Gibson which described the unique way in which Jack's widow, Erika, had managed to scatter his ashes just where he would have wished. Jersey, in the Channel Islands, had been a special place in Jack's life and he had a tremendous affection for the island that had been his home and provided his living, for so many years. Erika decided that it was from the coast of Jersey that Jack's ashes should be scattered into sea. There was however, a problem; the Jersey authorities were very much against the ashes of anyone but current residents being scattered there. Nothing daunted, it did not take long for the ever-resourceful Erika to come up with a scheme to get round the problem and, in the process, share a last laugh with Jack. Erika had been invited to Jersey to attend a memorial concert to Jack and decided this was the time to smuggle his ashes back to the island. She accomplished this by adding the ashes to the content of a bottle of Jack Daniels whisky, a favourite tipple that the two of them had shared on many an occasion! It was this, of course, that gave rise to John Gibson's witty heading of 'My fond farewell with a bottle of Jack...'! The memorial concert, which featured the Jersey Big Band and the playing of two fine London jazzers, Kathy Stobart and Digby Fairweather,

---

[97] Gibson J, 'My fond farewell with a bottle of Jack...', Edinburgh Evening News, December 11 2000

was presented in the Grand Hotel in St Helier and was a great success, with the proceeds going to charity. On the morning following the concert (although probably not all that early!), Erika quietly made her way down to the shore in front of the hotel and scattered the contents of the bottle into the bay. Erika had reported that, although she had shed the odd tear, she did so with a smile, knowing how much Jack would have appreciated the memorial event, the location and, perhaps most of all, the sheer audacity and humour of this final act of his long and successful jazz career.

Roger Craik (drums) was born in 1940 and was introduced to pipe band drumming while at George Watson's College. He was also introduced to jazz when at school and played in the George Watson's Jazz Babies, with fellow pupils Hamish Hay (clt) whom Roger describes as talented, 'Vally' Valentine (tpt), Chick Mooney (bjo), Bobby Kidd (bs) and Roger himself, by now playing a full drum kit. Roger reports that the Headmaster eventually put a stop to the jazz activities, a far from unfamiliar story!

Roger's older brother, Gus, played guitar and through him, Roger came into contact with a group of Edinburgh University musicians, which included Jim Baikie (gtr) and Johnny Winters (rds). As Roger remembers it, many of the jazz musicians who were around the Edinburgh scene at this time played a great deal of dance music but took every chance they could to play jazz. Apparently, there was a division between the University players and the Edinburgh players, the two groups tending to keep apart. Roger found himself more involved with the University group and was a frequent dep with the band that Jim Baikie put together. He also did a season up in the Trossachs with a trio which included his brother Gus and a pianist called Bob McDonald, who was a medical student. This trio played what Roger describes as Swing oriented dance music.

Roger was also involved in a residency at the Student's Union, near the McEwan Hall, where he played with a band which included Charlie McNair. This band featured Charlie on trumpet, Bill Skinner on clarinet, Laurie Gardner, another medical student, on piano, Norrie Gray on guitar, Charlie McCourt, whom Roger remembers as a postman, on bass and Roger himself on drums. Many years later, in the 1980s, Roger was a member of the band called The Festival City Jazz Band, which played at the Clarenden Hotel and included Ian Scott, who was the band leader, on piano, Jimmy Shortreed (clt), Andrew Lauder (tpt), Bill Smith (tbn) and Jim Baikie (gtr). Later still, in July 1996, Roger was to set up the very successful monthly jazz sessions at the Starbank Inn in Newhaven, where he had a resident rhythm section which backed invited horn players.

Although there were occasional temporary changes, the resident rhythm section at the **'Starbank' sessions** was Roger (drms), Jim Baikie (gtr and vocals), and the 'two Ronnies' – Ronnie Caruthers (pno) and Ronnie Dunn (bs). These sessions were popular with both audience and musicians, always well attended, and provided a showcase for top Edinburgh horn players including Jack Duff, Jack Graham, Hamish McGregor, Tom Chalmers, Jimmy Woods Keith Edwards and Dick Lee (rds), John McGuff (tbn), Andrew Lauder and Colin Steele (tpt), Dougie Campbell (gtr) and also the popular singer, Jean Mundell. Also deserving of a mention is the owner of the 'Starbank Inn', Scott Brown, a long time supporter of jazz, whose goodwill and on-going support was crucial to the success of these Sunday afternoon sessions.

Roger Craik modestly described himself to me as a having been a *'sort of permanent dep'* during his early days, when he often helped out the bands of the time when they were short of a drummer. Saying this, he gave the impression that he did not consider himself good enough to hold down a regular place in a band. In fact, he was a skillful drummer who was extremely knowledgeable about jazz and who always did a fine job when he was called on to play. Roger had a high-flying career in the legal profession, becoming a Queen's Counsel and a Sheriff, and I suspect that his jazz playing was restricted by his studies when he was at University and then later, by a busy and demanding career.

An early enthusiast of tape recordings, not the least of his many contributions to the Edinburgh jazz scene were the many recordings he made, carefully catalogued and stored, of many of the Edinburgh bands. Sometimes he would bring together a selected band for a recording session and these recordings too, are part of Roger's extensive collection. It would be good to think that, sometime in the future, these recordings will become part of an archive of Edinburgh jazz[98]. Roger Craik has also written articles on jazz for various jazz publications, including one published in the September 2010 edition of the Journal of the International Association of Jazz Record Collectors[99], entitled 'The Legacy of Alex Welsh', for which he got an award from the Association.

Ronnie Dunn (bass), who played bass for many years at Roger Craik's Starbank sessions, became interested in jazz around 1954 when he was thirteen years old, largely because his two elder brothers were interested and had an extensive record collection. Most of the material he heard was the music of Art Tatum, Louis Armstrong and, eventually, Charlie Parker and Dizzy Gillespie. Around the same time, Ronnie began playing cornet in his local Boys Brigade band and then, in 1957, he went to the Usher Hall to hear the Gerry Mulligan Quartet with Bob Brookmeyer, Joe Benjamin and Dave Bailey. After that, as he has said, he was totally hooked on jazz.

Local jazz also attracted his attention and he started going to the West End Cafe on Sunday nights to hear the Dickie McPherson Quintet with McPherson (tpt), Robbie Richardson (ten sax), Alex Shaw (pno), Gerry Rossi (bs) and Billy Allison (drms). Ronnie first played the double bass when, at Leith Academy, a show was to put on and they had everything they needed except a bass player. He volunteered and borrowed the school bass and, as he put it, *'started mucking around with it'*. Trombone player Ken Ramage was a fellow pupil at the school and, when he heard that Ron was playing bass, he invited him to join his band which was playing at the Condon Club in India Buildings. At these sessions, Ron met Jack Duff (rds) for

---

[98] An archive of Edinburgh jazz was launched at the Edinburgh Central Library on 30th July 2010, largely thanks to the sterling work of Jim Keppie, Donald Murray, Bill Strachan and Drew Landles. The evening also featured a small exhibition about the history of jazz in Edinburgh and a quartet led by pianist Ron Carruthers

[99] IAJRC Journal – Journal of the International Association of Jazz Record Collectors, published quarterly

the first time and remembers that Ken McCullough was the guitar player.

Things started to move rapidly after that and, over the next year or so, Ron made contact with a host of jazzers who were involved in the more modern reaches of local jazz, including Jim Baikie, Roger and Gus Craik, Tom Finlay (pno) who had just appeared from Cowdenbeath, Dougie Campbell (gtr), Norman Skinner (pno), Alan Hastie (drms) and the vocalist Jimmy Gilmore, who at that time was playing clarinet and tenor sax. However, there was obviously a strong local traditional jazz scene around as well and Ron found himself going to the Royal Mile Cafe on Sunday evenings. There he heard jazzers such as Eric Rinaldi, (tpt) Jack Duff, Johnny McGuff (tbn), Forbes Laing (bs) and Sandy Malcolm (drms) amongst others. When the Finlay-Gentleman Quintet was formed in 1960, Ron was the bass player with Alec Gentleman (ten sax), Tom Finlay, Johnny Smith (tpt) and Ian McDonald (drms). This band was to become popular and played at a number of venues around town, as well as playing at the likes of the Art College Revels. At this event, the Quintet played as the opening band before the big name bands came on. These included the Johnny Dankworth Big band and the Tubby Hayes Quintet and it was at an Art Revels that Ron met, for the first time, the fine Scottish trumpeter, Jimmy Deuchar.

In 1961 or 1962, the London based modern sax player Ronnie Scott opened a jazz venue in Edinburgh, located behind John Knox's house in the High Street. Here the Finlay-Gentleman band played as openers for a succession of London bands including those of Joe Harriot, Ronnie Scott himself, Les Condon, Tubby Hayes and Phil Seaman. Then, at the end of 1963 , Ronnie together with Tom Finlay and drummer Billy Allison signed up for 'Geraldo's Navy', the bands run by the Geraldo organisation to play on cruise liners, and the three of them spent six months playing on the Empress of Canada, cruising between New York and the West Indies. This brought them the wonderful experience of three nights every two weeks in New York, when they were able to hear Miles Davis, Wes Montgomery, Al Cohn, Zoot Sims, John Bunch, Woody Herman, Lionel Hampton, Dizzy

Gillspie, the Gerry Mulligan Concert jazz band and a host of others.

After returning to Edinburgh, Ron gigged around town with the Finlay-Gentleman and Jim Baikie bands and with the brothers from Shetland, pianist Matt and bass player Ron Mathewson. In 1967, Ron left Edinburgh for Scone in Perthshire and there was a gap in his playing career. He did, however, cover the trip to the Sacramento Jazz Festival with the Scottish Jazz Advocates in 1981, when I was unable to get away from the day job to make the trip. Then, in 1987 the guitarist Dougie Campbell persuaded him out of retirement and they got together in a duo which, as late as 2010, still made occasional appearances. In addition to this, Jimmy Deuchar, also based in the Perth area, brought Ron into his Quintet with which Ron played until Deuchar's death in 1993. Since then Ron has stayed in action, mostly playing gigs as a dep, but also putting in time with bands backing Edinburgh singers Edith Budge and Jean Mundell. Ron also played with bands put together to back visiting jazzers such as Martin Taylor, Eddie Thompson, Benny Waters, Joe Temperley, trombonist Joe Wilson from the Woody Herman band and a good number of others, visiting from a London base.

From the above account, it will be clear that Ronnie Dunn's interest and playing was mostly in the sphere of more modern styles of jazz rather than the jazz styles with which this book is principally concerned. However, he is typical of a group of able and versatile Edinburgh jazzers, such as Jack Duff, Tom and Jack Finlay, Dougie Campbell and Jim Baikie who, to a significant degree, were active across the spectrum of local jazz. Not the least of Ronnie's contributions to Edinburgh jazz, was the part he played in the Starbank sessions. These sessions were almost unique in Edinburgh jazz, providing a forum for local jazzers to get together in the time honoured jam session setting and proved to be an extremely popular Sunday afternoon gig for many years. Sadly, while I was engaged in writing this piece about him, Ronnie Dunn died suddenly, in Perth at the age of 69, on 17th October 2010.

Now we come to two particularly distinguished Edinburgh figures, both of whom were amongst the best of their generation on any instrument. Both favoured middle period jazz and both were highly respected professional musicians with formidable reputations. Both had long and successful careers and, simply because they made their first mark in Edinburgh jazz in the late 1950s and early 1960s, I have included them in this chapter.

The first is **Ronnie Rae (bass)**, who was born 1938 in Edinburgh and was brought up in the Musselburgh area. Ronnie started playing tuba when he was eleven years old and was encouraged by a school friend to join the Musselburgh and Fisherrow Brass Band. It was during his spell with this band that he won a prize as the best tuba player in Scotland. Later, health problems interfered with his tuba playing and he switched to the double bass, attending Johnnie Keating's School of Music from 1957-1958, where he learned the basics of the instrument under the tutelage of another great Edinburgh bass player, Jimmy Luke. Ronnie played his first gig on bass in the Crown Hotel in Hawick with Edwin Holland's band and remained with this band for a number of months. A fellow member of the band was trombonist Johnnie McGuff, who would also go on to a notable career in jazz. Later, Ronnie worked with the Palais bands in Edinburgh and Glasgow. He also worked with another fine trombone player Ken Ramage, and as a member of the Alex Shaw trio, in gigs around Edinburgh during the 1960s.

In the 1960s, Ronnie began his professional career as a jazz musician, moving south to play with the Alex Welsh Band, then in its great years, and completing two spells with this band, one in 1963 and the other in 1965. During his time with the Welsh band, Ronnie played, broadcast and made recordings with some of the great jazz names who toured with the band. These included Ruby Braff, Ben Webster, Bill Coleman, Eddie Miller, Eddie 'Lockjaw' Davis, Bud Freeman, Wild Bill Davison and Earl Hines.

On his return to Edinburgh, Ronnie played seven nights a week with pianist Alex Shaw in the Mount Royal Hotel. It was during the course of this work that Ronnie again backed the great piano player Earl Hines, in the Chimes Casino in Edinburgh. Although now back in Scotland, Ronnie remained a bass player with an international

146

reputation and, from his Edinburgh and later Glasgow bases, he worked as a 'free lance', touring and playing gigs with a host of great jazz men. Their names read like a 'Who's Who' of middle period jazz – Ray Bryant, George Chisholm, Al Cohn, Georgie Fame, Art Farmer, Tal Farlow, Buddy de Franco, John Griffin, Barney Kessel, Lee Konitz, Humphrey Lyttelton, Red Norvo, Shorty Rogers, Buddy Tate, Scott Hamilton, Warren Vache, Teddy Wilson, Louis Stewart, Spike Robinson and many more – the list just goes on and on. He played all over the world, including many of the most famous jazz festivals, at Sacramento, San Diego, Los Angeles, Palm Springs, Toronto, Calgary, Vancouver, Switzerland, Jakarta in Indonesia, Bali and Bangkok, Germany, China, Russia and, nearer home, Cork, Glasgow and Edinburgh.

Added to all that, Ronnie was bass player in residence at the Fife Summer Jazz School for ten years and for six years taught and played at the Scottish Arts Council and Lottery funded 'Fionna Duncan Vocal Jazz Workshops', which took place across Scotland. A Scottish Arts Council grant in 1999 enabled him to take sufficient time out from playing to write and arrange eleven of his own compositions. This led to him forming a band called Scotia Nostra, to perform his compositions on a concert tour around Scotland.

A great double bassist, Ronnie has had an illustrious career in jazz, much of it in what would now be seen as the mainstream of jazz, and he played, toured and recorded on numerous occasions with some of the finest jazz musicians that ever played. Those wishing to trace Ronnie's playing should turn to the professional jazz catalogues which contain many fine recordings featuring his playing in stellar company. Ronnie was, and is, such an accomplished player that he was perfectly capable of playing any form of jazz and, a true professional, he never gave anything other than a great performance, whoever he played with and wherever he played. He was even willing to deputise for me with the Old Bailey band and the Scottish Jazz Advocates, going on tour with them to the Sacramento Jazz Jubilee in 1982 and 1983, when I was unable to make the trips, something that makes me feel very humble to this day. Perhaps my only claim to any sort of note in the jazz world is that, according to Fionna Duncan, it was my calling off from a trip to Sacramento that brought Ronnie and Fionna together, a partnership still going strong almost thirty years on.

I can remember very clearly the awe with which I and the other local bass players, always regarded him and this remains true even in 2011, with Ronnie now in his seventies. Throughout his long career in jazz, Ronnie has remained Scotland's number one bass player and is also Scotland's most experienced and most in demand bassist. The huge repertoire he has built up over the years made him the ideal choice to lead the all-star trio that has hosted the official Late Night Jam Sessions at the Glasgow International Jazz Festival.

Not the least of Ronnie's many contributions to Scottish jazz was his founding of a jazz dynasty, all of his family of two sons and four daughters making their mark in the contemporary jazz world. Their interest in music was hardly surprising given Ronnie's stature as a bass player and the fact that their mother, Margaret, was a music teacher. Between them, the young Raes, who chose which instruments they wished to study at about the age of eight, played piano, cornet, guitar, drums, violin, French horn and oboe. All four daughters are accomplished singers, elder son Ronnie junior is a fine jazz pianist and younger son John a highly rated jazz drummer and composer. Three of the girls, Cathie, Gina and Sylvia, perform together as The Rae Sisters, as well as appearing individually, and youngest sister Gillian is also a fine singer, although seldom heard in public. The achievements and stature of the younger Rae's are reflected in their high reputations in contemporary jazz and jazz promotion and administration and are a great credit to Ronnie. However, their jazz styles and activities are well beyond the scope of this book and this is not the place to explore their careers. Readers who wish to know more about Scotland's biggest and best known contemporary jazz family should refer to their family website[100] and seek opportunities, live and recorded, to enjoy the astonishing talents of this gifted family.

---

[100] http://raefamilyjazz.com

The second of these two great Edinburgh players is **Alex Shaw (piano)**, and he, like Ronnie Rae, he was one of finest and most versatile Edinburgh jazz musicians of his generation. Indeed, Alex was another of the Edinburgh jazzers who could hold his own with anyone and he should have been a much better known figure on the UK jazz scene than is the case. Alex's interest in jazz began in the early 1940s when he heard a 78 rpm recording of the great pianist Art Tatum and from then on, jazz was to be his music. It is strange and not a little sad that Alex does not feature in the standard British jazz references book and left very few recordings to remind us of his brilliance. He did however, along with Ronnie Rae, record with the brilliant, modern American clarinet player Buddy de Franco, the recording including, rather unexpectedly, an almost straight version of the Scottish tune 'The Dark Island'.

On the few occasions when Alex moved away from Edinburgh to play, for example when he went to play in Germany with Pete Kerr's Capital Jazz Band in 1960, he found it difficult to cope with life on the road. Well aware of this, he was to settle for a life playing jazz at home in Edinburgh. Although this deprived the wider world of Alex's scintillating playing, it was greatly to Edinburgh's benefit and, although he had plenty of offers to play elsewhere, including invitations to play in the USA, he turned them all down. He was once approached to record for the prestigious Hep Records but, when it transpired that he would have to undertake a tour to promote the recording, he again said no. Similarly, although he occasionally appeared on a more formal stage, particularly at the Queen's Hall when the Scottish jazz organization Platform was at its most active in the 1980s, Alex was most at home playing in more informal settings, such as his long-running residencies at the George Hotel and in the Platform One bar, in the Caledonian Hotel.

In Edinburgh, Alex was a jazz institution and a by-word for quality jazz. His forte was the standard repertoire of quality popular tunes and an Alex Shaw residency was a Mecca for local followers of top-notch piano playing and visiting jazz musicians alike. His knowledge of the twentieth century song book was vast and his sensitive and always swinging interpretations a joy to hear. His Platform One residency was followed by others at the Drum and Monkey and then the Dome in George Street, where he played until shortly before his death. He usually played with a trio, adding bass and drums to his piano, and over the years his frequent companions were musicians of the caliber of bass players Ronnie Rae and Brian Shiels and drummers Mike Travis and Dave Swanston.

He was to be a fixture on the Edinburgh International Jazz Festival (EIJF) programme, even in its earliest days, being included in the second Festival in 1980 when it was said that his trio was as far as the then very traditional programme would go towards modern jazz. The performance of the Alex Shaw trio was hailed the following year as *'...a popular and refreshing break from the hot music which made up the main part of the programme'*[101]. From then on, Alex and his trio would become the accompanists of choice for scores of distinguished visiting jazzers and they were often the house trio for the late night jam sessions during the EIJF. When jazz journalist Kenny Mathieson wrote Alex's obituary in the Scotsman he said *'If Shaw knew the tunes, he knew how to play them. His command of jazz phrasing and rhythm was complete, his melodic invention never flagged, and he sailed through the most fearsome tempo with unruffled assurance'*[102]. Mathieson also recounted how, when Alex suffered a broken arm in the late 1980s, and was unable to play for a while, a benefit evening held at Calton Studios attracted a large proportion of the Edinburgh jazz crowd and a substantial number from elsewhere.

Alex was held in the highest respect and affection by everyone and, as Ronnie Rae reminded me recently, was affectionately known as 'Faither', a tribute to his pre-eminent position on the Edinburgh jazz scene. In the early post-WWII decades, both he and Ronnie Rae would without a doubt, have been regarded as modern jazz musicians. Now, in 2011, it is easy to understand that they were in fact right in the mainstream of jazz: versatile, thoroughly

---

[101] The Edinburgh International Jazz Festival 1980 programme
[102] Mathieson K, 'Alex Shaw', The Scotsman, April 2000

capable and creative. Both made wonderful music, as Ronnie still does, both gave enormous encouragement to other jazzers and Edinburgh jazz was greatly enriched by their playing. By a happy chance, Alex lived in the flat above the young Gordon Cruikshank, later to be one of Edinburgh's best mainstream tenor sax players. Gordon could hear Alex practicing in the room above and eventually, when he was about twelve years old, he approached Alex to ask what this music was that he could hear. Alex explained and played the youngster some recordings by the likes of Cannonball and Nat Adderley. The rest, as they say, is history. Gordon could not get enough of the music after this and was destined for a notable career in jazz. Alex, in a town that had more than its fair share of fine jazz piano players, was a revered figure who should have been better known nationally and was one of Edinburgh's finest ever. Alex Shaw, pianist and gentleman and one of the most modest and likeable of all Edinburgh jazzers, died at home in Edinburgh, on 2nd April 2000.

It will have become clear in the chapters on the Royal High Gang and the Semple/Welsh Dixielanders and from the accounts of others like Alex Shaw and Ronnie Rae, just how many of the early post-WWII generation of Edinburgh jazzers had a go at a full time career in jazz. George Melly, in 'Owning Up', speculates on just why there were so many Scottish jazzers when he says *'Why are there so many Scots jazz musicians and, come to that, why so many good ones? Sandy Brown, a convinced Scottish Nationalist, has a theory that it's to do with the fact that Scottish folk music is still a reality'*[103]. Bruce Turner also ruminated on this very point when he stayed with us, during a playing visit to Edinburgh with his Jump Band back in the 1960s. It does seem to me that there is some kind of affinity between Scots and jazz but just why, I do not know. I suppose some sort of link could be found between the deprived, down-trodden nature of the early jazzers, especially the black musicians in the southern states of the USA, and the Scots' perceptions of

---

[103] 'Owning Up' by George Melly, (Copyright © George Melly, 1965) Reprinted by permission of A. M. Heath & Co Ltd

their own history of subjugation and disadvantage (and an inferiority complex!) compared to a stronger southern neighbour, but it sounds a tenuous link to me. Perhaps it's a rhythmic thing, with Scottish country dance and ceilidh music a lively and top-tapping tradition. However, what I do know is, and it will probably bring down derision on my head, I sometimes detected in Sandy Brown's impassioned clarinet playing something of the unbuttoned wildness of the bagpipes.

Chapter VII

The Jazz Purists

Although there were many fine players left in Edinburgh, the departure of musicians of the calibre of Sandy Brown, Al Fairweather, Stan Greig, Alex Welsh, Archie Semple, Dave Paxton and Dave Keir would have left a large hole in any local jazz scene. However, hardly had these great players disappeared down the A1, or in Dave Paxton's case, the road to Bahrain, than belatedly and quite surprisingly, there was another jazz renewal. Out of the blue and almost a decade later than the classic jazz part of the Revival, the missing purist element arrived in Edinburgh. What follows in this chapter is a series of profiles of some of the major jazzers involved, with their accounts of the bands and venues of the time. Inevitably and hardly surprisingly, with more than sixty years having gone by, there are a few contradictions in these accounts but these hardly matter. What does matter is the picture they paint of a lively jazz scene, still with that pioneering, almost crusading spirit that was such a big part of the Revival.

Perhaps the first sign of purist jazz activity in Edinburgh came with a band formed by someone who was not from Edinburgh at all. **Peter Davenport (trumpet)**, who was born in 1931, came from Staffordshire in the English Midlands. Peter, towards the end of the war, had been listening to recordings of the Sid Phillips band, which he says he found quite exciting and then, because he was intrigued by the name, he bought a recording of Bunk

Johnston playing 'When the Saints go Marching In'. Bunk Johnson, an elderly trumpeter who had been rediscovered after years out of music was, of course, an iconic figure in purist jazz and his rediscovery was perhaps the key to the whole purist jazz movement. Peter was to be much influenced by this kind of jazz but this was to come later, after his National Service.

His National Service was with the North Staffordshire regiment and he found himself posted to Trieste. There he discovered that his Education Sergeant was one Diz Disley, later to become a noted guitar player with several British jazz bands, including some particularly fine recordings with Sandy Brown and Al Fairweather. Eventually Disley, a mercurial character, was to become a member of Stephane Grappelli's band. This gives some indication of Disley's stature as a guitarist, as he was following in the footsteps of one of Europe's most resounding jazz names, the great Django Reinhardt. However, at the time of their encounter in the army, Diz Disley was to have no impact on the future jazz career of Peter Davenport, who had not, at this time, begun to play an instrument. Disley did, however, contrive to create a lasting impression. Later in his jazz career, he was to establish a reputation as something of wanderer, whose habit seemed to be to create or join bands and then disappear.

His wandering tendencies were certainly to the fore while he was stationed in Trieste. Apparently, he went walk about and succeeded in crossing a border into Yugoslavia, then under the stern communist rule of Marshall Tito. Here he was promptly arrested and clapped in jail, no doubt with the intention of subjecting him to close and severe interrogation. Diz Disley, a man of pronounced left wing views, was more than a match for the situation. Deftly turning the tables on his captors, he lectured them on their luke-warm brand of communism, pointing out that they were not running it at all properly and proffering enthusiastic advice on how to mend their ways. It was all too much for his bemused captors who hastily dispatched him back to Trieste, clearly greatly relieved to be shot of him and, no doubt, well and truly chastened by the experience.

After his National Service was completed, Peter Davenport arrived in Edinburgh in 1949 to attend Art College. There he studied drawing and painting, the same course undertaken by Al Fairweather, but a year or so after Al, joining the 1949 intake a term late in January 1950. This meant that Peter was at Art College around the same time as Sandy Brown, who was studying architecture. Peter's future wife, Patricia, was also at college and, like Peter, was studying painting and drawing. He discovered that there were dances every month, which everybody tried to attend. Cam Robbie, for many years a successful Edinburgh dance band leader, had his band in the downstairs hall, while there was jazz in the upstairs hall. Through this and later visits to the Crown Bar, Peter became aware of what he describes as the great music of Sandy Brown and Al Fairweather.

He and a group of fellow students were greatly enthused by this and went, as a group, to Rosenblume's shop at the top of Victoria Street, where there was a plentiful supply of second-hand musical instruments for sale. Eventually, each became the proud owner of an instrument: Peter had acquired a trumpet, Andrew Gilmour a clarinet, both Ian Gordon and Mike Duncan had bought banjos, Baxter Cooper had a drum kit, Jimmy Lane a trombone and, in addition, there was Colin Bennett who played piano and who later took up the double bass. Together they formed the **Art College Jazz Band** and their first gig was at a hall near Blackhall, on the west side of Edinburgh. Just how soon it was after the band was formed that this gig took place is not clear but it was probably quite soon, enthusiasm likely to have been more vital than musical expertise. On a personal note on this topic, in the late fifties, when I was starting, I played my first gig on double bass before I had really found out how to tune the instrument properly and well before I had ventured above the Bb note on the first string or attempted to use the fourth string at all. This was the result of pressure from other band members who were well ahead of me and had no intention of waiting until I caught up, if I ever would.

Things then began to conspire to encourage the young, aspiring trumpet playing Davenport in finding his way around the jazz world. Sandy Brown soon became aware of the Art College band and Peter has said how kind and encouraging he found both Sandy and Al Fairweather. Friendly and welcoming though Al was, Peter was completely intimidated by his ability as a trumpeter, to the extent that he never once dared to play on a band stand alongside him. Perhaps because of this, Peter came to know Sandy better than Al. Once, Sandy dragooned Peter into driving him and the visiting Wally Fawkes, already a famous name with the Humphrey Lyttelton band and a cartoonist of renown, around Glasgow, so that Wally could view some buildings of which he required to draw cartoons.

Peter's mother was French and this led to visits to relatives in France. A cousin there was the girlfriend of the trumpeter with Claude Luter's famous jazz band and she was able to sneak Peter in free to hear the great Sidney Bechet guesting with the band. By this time, the Art College band had starting listening with great interest to recordings arriving from the USA of the George Lewis band. When talking about this, Peter pointed out that this was the time of what he called *the Ken Colyer thing* in the UK. Colyer, of course, was the Norfolk born trumpet player who was to dedicate his entire playing career to the music of the rediscovered veterans like Lewis and Bunk Johnson. His influence in the UK was to be very considerable. At the time of writing 60 years on, there remains in Britain an extremely healthy purist jazz movement with many bands, festivals, recordings and publications, largely inspired by Colyer's efforts. There were also, for many years after Colyer's death in 1988, a Ken Colyer Trust and a Ken Colyer Trust Jazz Band, still delivering Colyer's message – a fine tribute to a sincere and dedicated jazzer.

Their interest in the Lewis band recordings and the 'Colyer thing' was to take the Art College band down a very different jazz track compared to that of Sandy and Al or for that matter, Alex Welsh and Archie Semple. The Art College band became what was to become known as 'purist' jazz musicians, a label denoting those who were inspired by the music of George Lewis and his New Orleans veterans, the music of early New Orleans.

Pete Davenport's Jazz Band
L to R: Mike Pollett (tbn), Pete Davenport (tpt), Baxter Cooper (drms*), Ian Arnott (clt), Mike Duncan (bjo), Colin Bennett (pno) (*Cooper is playing Farrie Forsyth's drums) (From the collection of Peter Davenport, photographer unknown)

In due course, Peter and the others completed their courses and left Art College but the band continued in Edinburgh, now known as **Pete Davenport's Jazz Band**. The membership of the band had inevitably changed over time and the post-Art College band included at times Chris Cook or 'Squire' Hartley on clarinet, Mike Pollett and later Jack Weddell on trombone, Farrie Forsyth, Baxter Cooper and later Kenny Milne on drums, Colin Bennett and later Jim Young on bass. Baxter Cooper now, in 2011, lives in Glenfarg but has been inactive in jazz for many years. There was also a piano player around, whom Peter only remembered as Paterson but who I think, on the basis of information from Mike Hart, was probably Johnny Paterson.

Peter stayed on in Edinburgh until around 1956/57, during which time the band made a visit to play in London, which seemed to have been an irresistible attraction to aspiring jazzers in those days. The trip was arranged by either Jim Young or Farrie Forsyth and they played three gigs there: one at Woodgreen, one at the Ken Colyer Club and one other, the location of which is lost in the mists of time. At one of the gigs *'dozens of chaps clutching washboards'* arrived and asked to sit in with the band. The band, which had at this time never heard of skiffle, were fairly taken aback by this and also by the arrival of the sax player Dick Heckstall-Smith, who also sat in. Heckstall-Smith, a musician with modernist tendencies, had already played with Sandy Brown and A Fairweather, who were by now London based, and he was also a bit taken aback by the purist style of the Davenport band. He had assumed that all Edinburgh bands would play like Sandy and Al and the pronounced difference in style must have been quite a shock.

In the late 1950s, Peter took himself off to Argyllshire to pursue a career as a painter of abstracts but, when this provided less than boundless riches, he got himself into farming as well. This period had about zero jazz content but, after a return to Edinburgh in 1960, he began again, sitting in with various Edinburgh bands. He then found the delightful Tullybannocher in Comrie, Perthshire and moved there, farming about 250 acres with a further investment in 1972 in a restaurant. As before, local jazz activity was practically nil but Peter continued to make visits to Edinburgh, where he was again welcomed as a sitter-in with bands, including those of Archie Sinclair, Charlie McNair and Mike Hart. Peter remembers that Archie Sinclair in particular, was always pleasant and made him very welcome. Later, from 1980 to 1990, the restaurant was let out to Crawfords but, in 1990, Peter took it back under his own management, which enabled him to start the Tullybannocher jazz evenings. These went on to become very successful over the next twenty years or so, and were a favourite annual gig for many bands from Edinburgh and elsewhere. About once a year, Peter would put together a band of invited veterans and featured them as his 'Re-union Jazz Band'. The monthly Tullybannocher jazz nights ran on a Friday evening and were a nicely balanced combination of jazz and a buffet supper, with the option of dancing if people were so inclined. They continued on after Peter had retired from the business and, although reduced in number, they continued to feature Peter's re-union band.

The Pete Davenport Art College band, purist in style, had disappeared from the Edinburgh scene by 1957 but that, by no means, meant the end of purist jazz in town. Other bands in the same tradition were to appear and these were to include some of the jazzers who had played in Peter Davenport's bands. The purist tradition was to remain in good hands and some of the musicians were to make big reputations for themselves in their field.

Mike Hart (banjo/guitar), whom we last met playing drums with the Sandy Brown band when little more than a school boy, had gone off to do his National Service in the RAF between 1952 and 1954 and had continued to play drums when in the services. It is all too easy to forget nowadays what an impact National Service had in the 1950s. I was only about half a generation younger than jazzers who played in the 1940s and 50s and National Service had ceased by the time I left school, but people only a year or two older than me had had to do their bit. Many of the earlier jazzers have commented on how the early bands were constantly being disrupted by people being called up, replacements being sought and returning people fitted back into bands. It was clearly a time not only of post-war austerity and rationing but also of major disruption to people's lives.

When Mike returned to Edinburgh in 1954, it was to discover that Charlie McNair had formed a jazz band. Mike had by this time taken up the banjo and he joined the McNair band as banjoist and also played any one-off gigs that were around. However, Mike was then, as ever, a man of some ambition and energy, not to mention being of an entrepreneurial bent, and it was inevitable that he would lead bands of his own. Around this time, he set up the first of his **Blue Blowers**, a band name he would continue to use over many years. This first version was a proper 'jug band', as befitted the name, no doubt in the tradition of the Mound City Blue Blowers, led in Chicago by Red McKenzie and Eddie Condon. This kind of band, in addition to the odd legitimate instrument, used kazoos, paper and comb, washboards and jugs, which could be blown into to produce convincing tuba-like bass notes. Mike's Blue Blowers had jug, washboard, guitar, banjo and trumpet, which was played by Ian 'Tello' Telford. Mike played several of these instruments, sometimes playing washboard and jug or banjo and jug simultaneously, the jug held on a special stand to leave his hands free. The Blue Blowers played in the Shoestring Café, which was in the High Street opposite the Canongate Church, and had been set up by the minister of that church, the Rev Dr Selby Wright. Around the same time, Mike also ran a skiffle group. This was called 'The Ravers' and included in its number was Dougie Campbell, later to become one of Edinburgh's best jazz guitarists.

Starting in jazz about the same time as Mike, was a young piano player called Johnny Paterson who, as we have heard, had played with the Pete Davenport band. He apparently played in the stride piano tradition and later emigrated to New York. Mike Hart was studying to go to engineering college at this time and his father, knowing that Paterson was a gifted engineer, employed him to give Mike some extra tutoring. This noble effort by Hart senior to build a respectable career in engineering for his son sadly came to nothing. Mike and Johnny Paterson used the money Mike's father had paid for tutoring to go drinking instead! Mike was clearly already very active around the local jazz scene but soon another band came along, the Climax Jazz Band, in which he was to play a founding role, along with several other jazzers who were to have long and important careers in Edinburgh jazz.

Mike Pollett (trombone) was born in Bombay on 23rd August 1934 and later moved with his family back to Scotland, settling in Edinburgh. He was educated at George Watson's Boy's College where there was no jazz influence whatsoever but he believes that singing bass in the school choir may well have created an affinity for trombone parts in traditional jazz bands. Attracted to jazz, he became a frequent visitor to the West End Café and the Stud Club and found himself, in his own words, completely captivated by the jazz of Sandy Brown and Al Fairweather. Having taken up trombone, he joined Pete Davenport's band in 1955, making a front line with Pete (tpt), Squire Hartley (clt) and with a rhythm section of Mike Duncan (bjo), Colin

Bennett (pno) and Farrie Forsyth or Baxter Cooper (drms). He also played with an early Charlie McNair band, which included Joe Smith on clarinet, with which band he played a winter of Sunday nights at the jazz club in India Buildings. The band also played on stage in a cinema in Rodney Street, during the interval of a public showing of a film, which may have been 'The Five Pennies', a bio-pic of the life of cornetist Red Nichols. With the McNair band, Mike appeared on a Beltona recording of two numbers made at a Scottish Jazz Band championship held in Glasgow, the two tracks being Hiawatha Rag and Meadow Lane Stomp[104] about which we will hear more in chapter XIII.

An early version of the Climax Jazz Band playing in the Moir Hall
Jim Young (bs), Al Hanney (clt), Kenny Milne (drms), Jim Petrie (tpt), Mike Hart (bjo), Mike Pollett (tbn) (from the collection of Jim Petrie, photographer unknown)

---

[104] See discography appendix

Mike Pollett, like Mike Hart, then became a founder member of the Climax Jazz Band in 1956. The band played at the Stud Club, which was variously located in a number of venues including the Roman Eagle Hall at 1 Johnstone Terrace, the Moir Hall on St John's Hill in the Pleasance, a venue in York Place, the Dofos Pet Shop on the corner of Leith Walk and London Road and in the basement of bass player Jim Young's house in Viewforth. The early Climax line-up with which Mike Pollett played was Jim Petrie (tpt), Stewart Pitkethly and later Alistair Hanney (clt), Mike himself on trombone, Jim Young (bs), Mike Hart (bjo) and Kenny Milne (drms). This early Climax band practiced in the Pollett parents' house and played Climax Rag as its signature tune. Mike says that this was the inspiration for the name of the band but there are at least two other versions of this, to which we will come shortly.

Later, Jake McMahon also came into the band on clarinet and Mike recalls that Jim Young was stage leader of the band, an arrangement that seems to indicate that, while Jim was the front man, the band was run on a cooperative basis. Apparently Jim Young was also the owner of a large motor car which was big enough to transport the band to gigs, with the double bass strapped to the roof - or not, as the case may be. On one particularly memorable occasion, the bass was left unstrapped and, at the first corner, the car turned but the bass went straight on and was smashed to fragments on the road! I remember once, in the 1960s, sitting in on a bass that Jim Young was playing and noticed that it was an unorthodox shape and size. I am sure that this was the unfortunate fragmented bass, lovingly restored to playing condition, if not its original shape and size, by the ever resourceful Jim Young. Many years later, while I was writing this book, I was reminiscing with Jim and the topic of this reconstructed instrument came up and I told Jim that I remembered thinking that it was the Quasimodo of the double bass!

Another memorable occasion for Mike Pollett was when he played with one of the Edinburgh bands, not the Climax band but probably either that of Charlie McNair or Pete Davenport, at a concert at the St Andrew's Hall in Glasgow, where they were the support band for the Dave Brubeck

Quartet. In 1958, after Mike completed his training as a Chartered Accountant, he went into the army for National Service, which included a spell in Portsmouth when he played with trumpeter Cuff Billet, a fine player later to be a prominent name in jazz. After demob, Mike departed to Singapore where he briefly played with a local cosmopolitan band, including a trumpet player from the USA embassy, at up-market functions.

Looking back in 2011, Mike thought that he probably had quite a significant impact on the development of interest in the purist variety of Revivalist jazz in Edinburgh. He had discovered a shop in the West Bow which sold records and remembers that it had broken 78 rpm records pinned up on the wall, by way of advertising. There he bought a number of recordings on the HMV label by the Bunk Johnson band, including a recording of the tune I Wish I Could Shimmy Like My Sister Kate. With these records in his possession, Mike was able to let others hear what we now know were seminal recordings in the development of purist jazz in the UK and he believes that this played an important part in the rise of interest in this type of jazz in Edinburgh. This is corroborated by drummer Kenny Milne who told me that the fact that they were able to listen to Mike Pollett's collection of recordings in the purist style was crucial in the formation of the Climax band's style. Mike's first important individual contact in Edinburgh jazz had been with Mike Hart and, soon after this, he was in touch with others including trumpeter Jim Petrie and, a bit later, the bass player, Jim Young. Although Mike was very much attracted to purist jazz for its own sake, an interest that remains intact in 2011, he also speculated that a part of the attraction at the time, in terms of trying to play jazz, was the fact that there seemed to be fewer technical demands than in what was perceived as the more advanced music of the likes of Louis Armstrong and Jelly Roll Morton. In particular, there seemed no need to be able to read written music and this was a major help in encouraging these enthusiastic youngsters in making a start in jazz. Although Mike Pollett is, at the time of writing, back living in Scotland near Kinross, he no longer plays.

Kenny Milne (drums and later trumpet) was born on 1st May 1937 and educated at Broughton High School, where he was one of a group of school pupils who got together to listen to jazz records in the school gym. Apparently Sandy Brown, who was already an active jazz musician, turned up in the gym one day, having heard the sound of the records as he was passing the school. In about 1951, at the instigation of one of the group, Graeme Robertson, they decided to form a jazz band which they called the Broughton School Jazz Band. The band included Graeme Robertson, who was later to play both trombone and bass, Karl Ekeval (clt), Stewart Sangster (washboard), Andy Cockburn (bjo) and Kenny Milne (drms). Graeme Robertson once brought to school the sheet music for the famous jazz tune Hello Central, Give Me Dr Jazz which they proceeded to hand over to their music teacher, with a request that he play it. Thinking back on this after about sixty years, Kenny Milne said that he seemed to remember that the music teacher had been unable to play it. However, Graeme Robertson remembers it differently and assures me that he could handle it without any bother, having been much involved in the dance band world when he was a student. Graeme remarked that he had been pleasantly surprised to find that his music teacher was a lot more 'hip' than he had expected and this is partly mirrored in a similar experience I and my fellow jazz followers had while at school. A former pupil of the school had returned to teach music and, having been known as a serious student of music even as a schoolboy, the expectation was that he would be little interested in our awakening jazz enthusiasms. However, we were wrong. He not only took an interest but, when he heard that we were going to hear the Humphrey Lyttelton band in the Place Jazz Club, he arranged with us to get hold of a ticket for him. He duly came along to the Place, taking a keen interest in the music and even prepared to ask us about the way a jazz band could maintain an organized sound when there was clearly a great deal of improvisation goingon. We were fairly green ourselves, at that point in our jazz education, but he seemed genuinely interest and said nothing to make us feel that we were being in any way patronized. It was a

164

particularly impressive version of Humph's band that we heard that night, including both Danny Moss (ten) and Joe Temperley (bar) in its line-up.

However, we need to get back to Broughton High School in the early 1950s and its group of budding jazzers. From Sandy Brown, the group had discovered that he and others played at the West End Café and the Crown Bar in Lothian Street. Kenny Milne ventured along to the Crown one night and heard **Bob Craig's Jazz Band**, which had Bob on trombone, with Ian 'Daz' Arnott on clarinet, Farrie Forsyth on drums, Kenny Wheatley on bass and, as far as Kenny can remember, Al Clark on trumpet. Another band that Kenny remembers from this time played in the Crown Bar on Monday evenings and had a two-trumpet line up, the two being Ian 'Tello' Telford and Kenny Jack, whom Kenny describes as sounding like Joe 'King' Oliver. The two trumpeters apparently had fights about the music, something that is confirmed by Pete Davenport, who remembers them arguing heatedly over which notes they should each be playing! Iain Forde, whom we will meet shortly, also remembers traumas involving Tello and Kenny Jack, whom he remembers as 'Jacko'. In a later band, in which Iain Forde played trombone and Karl Ekeval clarinet, they discovered that their two trumpeters had learned all the famous two-trumpet breaks from the 1920s 'King' Oliver records. Unfortunately, they had copied them from old recordings which did not play in accurate pitch, resulting in them learning them in ridiculous and totally unreasonable keys such as B natural and Gb. This, not surprisingly, completely foxed Iain and Karl Ekeval, rendering all Tello's and Jacko's hard work unusable!

By the time of his visits to the Crown Bar, Kenny Milne had become aware of a style of New Orleans jazz in which much of the music played consisted of ensemble passages, with all the front line instruments playing simultaneously. This was in contrast to other jazz he had heard on recordings of Louis Armstrong and Jelly Roll Morton, which included a lot of solo playing.

In the meantime, Kenny Milne had discovered for himself that Revival jazz was split into the two different ways of playing, classic and purist jazz. He bought some records which included one by George Lewis and his New Orleans Stompers on the Vogue label, and describes how, on hearing it, the hairs stood up on the back of his neck. From that point on, Kenny's main jazz interest was to be the purist style.

Visits to the West End Café made him aware of others who turned up regularly, among them was one called Jack Weddell and a tall, thin individual with a mop of black hair, who turned out to be called Jim Petrie. Later, Kenny attended a party for Sandy Brown, who was leaving for London, and met Mike Hart, who introduced him to Weddell and Petrie. This was to be a fruitful meeting as it led to a decision to get a band together. Andy Cockburn, who had played banjo with the Broughton School Jazz Band, had disappeared by this time, so the band formed included Mike Hart. The band they put together was to be called the **West Richmond Street Stompers**, the original line up including Jim Petrie (tpt), Jack Weddell (tbn), Kenny Milne (drms) and a piano player whom Kenny only remembers as 'Walter'. Later, Joe Smith, who was already playing clarinet with Charlie McNair's band, came in on bass. Just how long the West Richmond Street Stompers were in existence is not clear, but around 1956, much the same group of jazzers was to be involved in the formation of a band that was to have a long and distinguished history in Edinburgh. This was the Climax Jazz Band.

Kenny Milne moved to London in 1960, to further his career in pharmacy, and there he played with many of the best UK New Orleans jazzers including Cuff Billett (tpt), Pete Dyer (tbn) and Bill Greenow (rds). He also replaced the famous band leader and drummer, Barry 'Kid' Martyn, in the Kid Martyn Band, when Barry Martyn went off to New Orleans. Kenny Milne was to return to Edinburgh in 1977, where we will meet him again later, taking up trumpet as well as continuing as one of the finest New Orleans style drummers in the UK.

Jack Weddell (trombone and vocals), who was born in Edinburgh in 1937, had sung as a boy soprano in his school choir. His interest in jazz was sparked off by hearing a recording, quite a well known and commercially successful recording in fact, of the Pee Wee Hunt band

166

playing 'Twelfth Street Rag'. This was quite a corny record by any standards and may seem an unfortunate early exposure for a budding jazzer. However, Jack survived this to become a key and long-term member of the decidedly purist Climax Jazz Band. He had received trombone lessons while at school and was in an early jazz band with trumpeter Jim Petrie by the time he was fourteen, making this about 1951. Later, he played in a band with Petrie, Kenny Milne (drms), and Karl Ekeval (clt), playing in a variety of clubs, many of which he remembers as being run by Jim Young. He was already one of the group that was later to form the core of the Climax band, but he also put in time as trombonist with the bands of the two trumpet playing band leaders, Pete Davenport and Charlie McNair.

As with all his contemporaries, Jack was called up for National Service when he was about nineteen and played bass trombone while in the RAF band. Here he experienced great trouble reading the parts and blithely busked his way through most of the music. Loss of his teeth caused a temporary hiatus in his trombone playing, resulting in a switch to bass drum and cymbal in the military band. Happily for Edinburgh jazz, the problem with his teeth was overcome and he returned to Edinburgh at the age of twenty one, where he replaced Mike Pollett with the Climax band. A move to London in 1962 brought the opportunity to play with various bands and to make some recordings with the legendary Kid Sheik Colar in a band which also included top rank players such as Sammy Rimmington (clt), Paul Sealley (bjo), Barry Richardson (bs) and Barry Martyn (drms).

After a spell back in Edinburgh from 1967, when he re-joined the Climax band, Jack was again in London from 1977 to 1982, and then returned once more to both Edinburgh and the Climax band. He later also joined a new Edinburgh band of which we will hear much more, the Spirits of Rhythm and he continued to play with these bands for many years. Throughout Jack's career, there were also many gigs with parade bands. These were marching bands in the New Orleans tradition and amongst those with whom Jack played were the Excelsior band in London and the Auld Reekie and Criterion parade bands in

Edinburgh. Jack also toured in Holland, Germany and Switzerland with the Climax band and, much later, was on the Australian tour with the Climax Re-union Band in 1992.

Jack was a fine player in the early New Orleans school of trombone playing and an able and appealing singer. It so happened that many of the songs he sang were of a melancholy and quite sentimental nature and I can remember depping with the Spirits of Rhythm when Kenny Milne referred to them as '*Jack's weepies*'. Later on, for some personal reason, Jack stopped playing earlier than most of his contemporaries, and his playing and singing were a real loss around the Edinburgh jazz scene.

Jim Petrie (trumpet and vocals), born on 14th April 1937, was a player who was to be a mainstay of Edinburgh jazz for decades and was to make a big name for himself in New Orleans jazz. Jim was educated at Tynecastle School, where a fellow pupil was Jack Weddell, and where they both were offered a chance to join the school band. While Jack chose the trombone, Jim went for the cornet. The instrument he was allocated was an Eb Cornet, which Jim still maintains ruined his lip for the rest of his life! Jim had lessons from a Jimmy Pennel, a tutor who visited the school and who played in Alexander's Dance Band, at the Leith Assembly Rooms. Jim and Jack were lent records by Jack's brother in law, including some by the trombone playing band leader, Pee Wee Hunt.

Jim left school in 1952 and, with his interest in jazz like Weddell's stimulated by the recorded music, the two of them began going along to the West End Café where the first band that Jim heard was Graeme Bell's Australian Jazz Band. Many years later, Jim was to play a session in the Bruntsfield Links Hotel with Bell, when the Australian was on a visit with Preacher Hood's band. Jim also found his way to the Jazz Club functioning in India Buildings, where he heard the Sandy Brown band playing the first hour and a band including Alex Welsh playing the second. The Crown Bar soon drew their attention too and it was there in 1954, at the farewell party for Sandy Brown who was leaving for London, that Mike Hart introduced Jim and Jack to Kenny Milne and clarinetist Karl Eckvall. More or less immediately, plans were put in place to get a jazz band together and, as we already know, it was this group that was to be the core of the West Richmond Street Stompers. This band with Jim, Jack, Kenny Milne on drums and Jim Young on bass, was soon into action with jazz club gigs at the Dofos Pet Shop in London Road, in premises in York Place and the Eagle Lodge, as the club moved about, seeking a reliable home.

Sometime during these years, Jim was given a record by his brother John who told him that, although he did not much care for the music himself, Jim might like it. The record was of the Bunk Johnson band playing Tishomingo Blues and Jim was an instant convert to what was becoming known as purist jazz. Like others who experienced similar immediate conversions to jazz or a specific style of jazz, he still describes his reaction to hearing the Bunk record vividly and says he can remember the reaction he felt as clearly today as he did all those years ago. From then on, he was to model his style on the playing of the re-discovered early New Orleans trumpeters, including Bunk Johnson of course and also Avery 'Kid' Howard, who played with the George Lewis band.

In 1955, when plans to form the Climax Jazz band came along, Jim was to be a founder member and he remembers the original band as himself on trumpet, Mike Pollett (tbn), Chris Cook (clt), Mike Hart (bjo), Jim Goudie (bs) and Kenny Milne (drms), although Mike Pollett is certain that Jim Goudie never played bass in the Climax band when he was a member. Although in and out of the band several times, including a gap in 1957-59 when he was away on National Service, Jim was to put in a lot of time with the Climax band in the late 1950s and early 1960s. Amongst the many venues at which Jim remembers the band playing were the Moir Hall, Jim Young's jazz club in the cellar of his home in St Peter's Place and the Crown Bar. Jim also played with the band in the Scottish Jazz Band Championship in Glasgow in 1957. In the 1960s, with the departure to London of many of the original members, the Climax band continued to be as active as ever under Jim's leadership with Alan Quinn (tbn), George Gilmour (clt), Bill Salmond (bjo), Willie Mack (bs) and Jimmy Elliott (drms).

Jim Young (double bass/brass bass) was born in Edinburgh on 7th June 1933 but was to spend much of his school years in Canada. He had been brought up on classical music, meaning in his case, music up to 1790, but learned to play sousaphone in his school brass band in Canada. Jim says that he was to become aware of a similarity between jazz and baroque, especially in the up and down movements of fugues. He later returned to the UK and, in the Grand Cinema in Stock Bridge in 1945, he saw a short film about the revival of interest in early jazz. He can remember how the rhythm affected him and, like Kenny Milne, he felt the hairs on the back of his neck rise. From that point on, it was to be rhythm and swing that mattered to Jim. In the film, there was a clip of the Original Dixieland Jazz Band making a recording, in which each member of the band played into a very large, white trunk or funnel affair, about five or six feet long and shaped like a trumpet bell. This apparently was to ensure proper separation of the sound of each instrument as it was transmitted to the mechanical recording device. Jim also went to the West End Café, where he heard Graeme Bell's Australian Jazz Band and made his way to hear the Sandy Brown band in the Oddfellow's Hall. He was also at the Usher Hall concert when the Brown band supported Big Bill Broonzy and is sure that Dizzy Jackson played bass and Farrie Forsyth drums on that famous occasion. Another jazz venue he visited was in India Buildings, where it was mostly the bands involving Alex Welsh that he heard.

Jim was called up for National Service in the RAF and Bomber Command, where he played brass bass in the military band and with this band, he played at the Queen's coronation in 1953. While still in the RAF, Jim started to learn to play the trumpet. By way of recruiting musicians into the RAF band, they were allowed a brief chance to ask new comers if they played an instrument as they got off the bus. Amongst these new comers was one called Mike Hart, who reported that he had played drums in Edinburgh. Jim remembered having seen the band on a student Charities Parade and got out a photograph he had taken and there was Mike in the photo. After National Service was over in 1954 and they were back in Edinburgh, Mike Hart contacted Jim who was now playing trumpet but, he says, very badly. Mike had by then made his switch to banjo and they put a band together with Jim on trumpet and Mike on banjo. Also included was one Richard Robertson, known as Big Richard, who was supposed to play drums but, according to Jim, could actually only play on wood blocks. Alastair 'Shorty' Gauld, brother of the trumpet playing Fraser who would later make his mark in Edinburgh jazz, was another who played banjo with the band, presumably with Mike also on banjo. The impression is that bands at that time tended to recruit who they could from the limited number around, even if it meant that two people played the same instrument.

At some point, Jim also had a go at playing trombone, playing in a band which had Al Clark on trumpet and Chris Cook on clarinet, and which played interval spots to Pete Davenport's Art College Jazz Band. The Stud Club had been initiated by Sandy Brown at the Crown Bar in Lothian Street some time before and Jim, an energetic organizer, became involved in running this in a number of other locations. It was based successively at the Orkney Rooms, the Dofos Pet Shop at the top of London Road, then the Caithness Rooms, the Roman Eagle Hall at 1 Johnston Terrace and the Moir Hall, which was in the Pleasance. Jim remembers great trouble when trying to run the various jazz clubs, as the police were very wary of them and kept trying to have them closed down. I can remember this problem clearly and, when I first ventured into the jazz clubs around 1960, many of them were run on a membership basis, with membership cards that had to be shown to gain entry, in an attempt to satisfy the police that the club was legitimate.

The question of just why the police were so against any attempt to run a jazz venue is an interesting one. Jim reports that the Stud Club, then on Wednesday evenings in the 'Crown Bar', was shut down by the police, after a policeman's daughter told her father that she had paid to get in and he ordered it closed. Apparently, only sixpence was charged so that the band could be given something at the end of the session.

(By permission of Jim Young)

Jim and Bob Craig then tried to run it as proper club with rushed-out membership cards, but again the police took action, telling the publican that he might lose his license the next year if they did not stop. The publican was unhappy about the club closing but, as if in compensation, allowed the band to buy the piano at a very low cost.

Peter Davenport then found a venue for the Stud Club at the Orkney Rooms in Hill Street where jazz flourished for a few months. This was followed by the move to the cellar of the pet shop, where several different bands played. However, once again it was not to last and the pet shop owner's license was threatened by the police. This initiated a move to the cellar of the Blenheim Café next door, where they again lasted a few months before yet another visit from the police. The café owner was told that she would have a visit from the Health Inspector if the jazz club was not closed down. As banjo player Brian Weld recalls it *'An officious police inspector from Gayfield Square police station forced the jazz cellar to quit. We never knew why and he wouldn't say, because there was absolutely no alcohol or drugs, the young musicians and audience being perfectly well behaved. No drunks ever came in that I remember – revival New Orleans jazz in those days was very much a young person's peccadillo'.*

Jim Young
(by permission of the late Alan Quinn)

Jim Young made a trip to Gayfield Square police station and saw a superintendent who told him that he would shut down any premises he opened on his patch. Another venue tried, in York Place, was followed by short spells at the Roman Eagle Hall and then two years at the Moir Hall in the Pleasance. Jim then moved the Stud Club to the cellar of his home in St Peter's Place. This ran for two years until, in July 1960, they got notice to quit, this time not from the police but from the Town Council, in a document signed by the Town Clerk, no less. The document stated that Jim was running an illegal club in a private house and that he could be fined £20 for every day the notice to quit was ignored. The actual offence was described as '...*the partial change of use of a dwelling house at 19 St Peter's Place, Edinburgh, to a club has been carried out without the grant of planning permission...*'.

Jim later discovered from a jazz follower who had been a trainee policeman, that the police thought that he was running a house of ill repute! They had set up a watch in the house opposite and watched for two weeks but saw nothing, which was hardly surprising. The Edinburgh jazzers were nothing if not determined and even the loss of Jim Young's cellar venue did not stop them. An undated newspaper cutting reported that *'Members of the Stud Jazz Club, Edinburgh – closed by order – jived again last night...in the middle of the Firth of Forth. The club hired the M.V. Second Snark, took along a band and for two hours they rocked the boat. The club met in the basement of band leader Jim Young's Edinburgh home until banned by the Corporation'.*

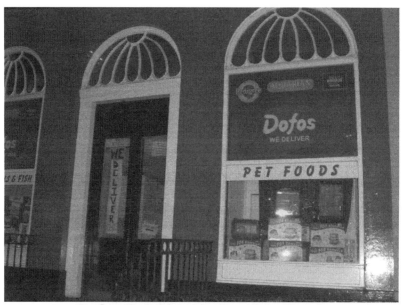

Dofos Pet Shop in London Road
Once home to the Stud Club and still flourishing in
2010 (Photo by the author)

Presumably the police had the laws of the time on their side but what on earth was all the paranoia about? Was it a fear that there was illegal drinking going on? Or drugs? What nameless health threats did a jazz band carry that would require the Health Inspector to be called in? Suspecting the existence of a brothel seems fairly bizarre

174

but they were obviously very suspicious. Surely they could have simply checked to see if there was any illegal drinking or drugs or prostitution? If paying at the door was the issue, why not just sort that out? But no, they seemed to have been determined to close down any attempt to put on jazz that was open to the public. Nowadays, I am sure it would be seen as harassment. It certainly seems to have had the flavour of an official kill-joy attitude about it. Perhaps it was in tune with stern Scottish Presbyterianism; a glowering, authoritarian disapproval of anyone having the temerity to enjoy themselves. It must have seemed as if the Ten Commandments had been specially abbreviated until there was only one left reading 'THOU SHALT NOT!!!!'

Of course, this was only the 1950s and the war years, with their aura of strict control of everything, were not that long gone. Perhaps the shades of grim war time restrictions remained in the attitudes of the authorities of the day, with a belief that society, unless rigidly controlled, would go on the rampage. Perhaps we should be grateful that the 1960s, with new attitudes and a willingness to cock a snoot at authority, especially by the younger generation, were just around the corner.

Jim Young had taken up double bass by accident. He had been at the jazz club one evening when the Pete Davenport band was playing. The band had someone who was learning to play double bass but he had not turned up that night. By good fortune however, the bass was there. Pete Davenport spotted Jim and called over to him *'You know about music, pick up that bass and play it. It has the notes marked on it so you should have no problem!'* Jim did as instructed and that was the start of his career as a double bassist. Later, in 1955, a lack of bass players led him to acquire a double bass of his own and he played for while with a band led by Jim Petrie, the Crescent City Jazz Band, which included, besides Jim Petrie on trumpet, Jack Weddell on trombone and Kenny Milne on drums.

After a spell in London, Jim returned to Edinburgh, where the early versions of the **Climax Jazz Band** began to appear. These early versions of this important Edinburgh band involved a number of musicians including Jim Petrie on trumpet, Mike Pollett on trombone, Chris Cook, Stewart

175

Pitkethly or Alistair Hanney on clarinet, Mike Hart on banjo, Jim Goudie or Jim Young on double bass and Kenny Milne on drums. The music the band played was strictly in the purist style and most of these players were to remain with the band for a number of years. Jim Young stayed with the Climax band, playing a leading part, until 1963 when he went abroad, returning in 1967 to re-join the band, and remaining active with them throughout the 1970s.

Kenny Milne reports that the early rehearsals of the Climax Jazz Band took place in Mike Pollett's house in Craigmillar or at Mike Hart's garage, which was near the Meadows. Mike Pollett was well supplied with recordings of the Bunk Johnson and George Lewis bands, and these formed the basis of the band's style. I had always assumed that Climax band acquired its name because of the famous Climax sessions recorded by the George Lewis band, but apparently this may not have been so. Mike Pollett's version, as we have heard, was that the name came from the tune 'Climax Rag'. However, at least one later member of the band claims that the name came about because, when the band was rehearsing in its early days, someone noticed that there was work to remove tram lines going on outside which involved a 'Climax' compressor! You pays your money and you takes your choice!

As with all the bands at this time, there were to be changes brought about by National Service and other factors, and Jim Goudie, who had played bass for a while, took the well-worn road to London, where later he could be found playing with the Mike Peters band. Kenny's brother, Jimmy Milne, was for a time manager of the Climax band and they played at jazz clubs at Ayr, Glenrothes, and Dundee but, in the early days, they did not have a residency in Edinburgh. At some point around 1956, Mike Hart left and was replaced by Brian Weld on banjo. Later changes brought in Dougie Boyter on banjo, Tom Wood on piano, Dougie Goodall on clarinet and Jack Weddell on trombone, as National Service continued to be an issue. Tom Wood was later to emigrate to Australia and was to play an important part in the re-union tour of Australia, made by the specially re-formed Climax band, in the early 1990s.

When Jim Petrie went off to complete his stint in the army, Charlie Malley who was from Falkirk or Jake Simpson from Glasgow, played trumpet in his place. Inevitably, there were some band politics as well and, for a while, Kenny Milne and Stewart Pitkethly left the band. Stewart Pitkethly was replaced on clarinet by Alastair Hanney, who was later to become an eminent academic in Norway, and Kenny Milne was replaced on drums by Colin Cant. When Jim Petrie returned from National Service, he also returned to the band and this paved the way for the return of both Stewart Pitkethly and Kenny Milne.

When Mike Hart left the Climax band, he had been replaced for a time by **Brian Weld (banjo and tenor guitar)**. Brian's day job was civil engineering and he had taken up banjo in about 1952, after being introduced to jazz by the drummer Farrie Forsyth. Farrie had played a Bunk Johnson recording to him in a record shop booth and Brian reports that he was totally captivated by the sound and swing of the band and, in particular, by the playing of the banjo player Lawrence Marrero. As a result, he bought a banjo from Gordon Simpson's Music Shop in Stafford Street, where he was allowed to pay it up with no written agreement and no interest charged. Incidentally, this is by no means the only story of Gordon Simpson's kindness to budding musicians, several others commenting on various small favours done by a decent man who seemed genuinely concerned to help musicians. I remember once when, before a gig, our band met in a pub in William Street and found Gordon Simpson there. When our banjo player discovered he had forgotten to bring his spare banjo strings with him, Gordon Simpson was good enough to return to his shop and open it up to supply him with strings.

Another in the same vein was **Pete Seaton (accordion)** who at one time worked in Gordon Simpson's music shop but, later, set up on his own music shop, over on the south-side of town. Pete had taken up accordion in 1942 and, after taking lessons from a Miss Sutherland, had become a highly proficient player. Although he played Scottish country dance music, it was not the sort of music that appealed to him, having a preference for a wider repertoire. He worked in the music shop during the day and played accordion in the evenings, making a big name for himself as a top class dance band musician. He was resident in the Palais when the BBC came to film heats for the television programme 'Come Dancing' and then went on to a six nights a week residency at the George Hotel, playing for dinner dances. He remained there from 1950 until 1960 and, during this time, he performed on radio with the Swedish Royal Concert Orchestra in 1960.

Pete was always interested in jazz and it showed in his playing, of which he said *'You couldn't play the same tune a hundred times without exploring alternative themes'*. Pete also played in the West End Café and was the arranger for the third one of a series of BBC jazz concerts, the third being devoted to modern jazz. He was also a member of the band for that concert, the line-up of which was Jim Walker (rds), Pete Seaton (accordion), Dave Simpson (pno), Dickie Alexander (bs) and Kenny Duff (drms). Later, Pete played piano in the bar of the Caledonian Hotel. Like Gordon Simpson, Pete was a greatly respected figure around the Edinburgh dance and jazz scene and there are many examples of his willingness to assist musicians. When my double bass was burned in a fire at the Manhattan Jazz Club in the mid-1960s, Pete allowed me a new instrument from his shop, not only before I could pay for it, but before I had any idea of how I was going to raise the money.

The trombonist, Bill Munro, also paid tribute to Pete Seaton. Bill found himself without an instrument, when he had to return a trombone to the works silver band with whom he had been playing. Having failed to pick up anything suitable on the second hand market, he found what he wanted in Pete's music shop, a nice Selmer instrument priced at £26. It turned out that Pete was supplier to the afore-mentioned silver band and, not only did he knock the price down to £21, he would not take a deposit saying *'Ach well, you can pay it up out of any gig money you get'*. Bill was not even in a band at this point but did eventually manage to pay it off, with Pete charging him no interest whatsoever. A fine musician with a real interest in jazz, Pete Seaton was always willing to extend a helping hand, as well as endless encouragement, to his fellow musicians. Pete's son, Murray Seaton, was later to open a music shop specializing in drums in the Newington area of town.

Meanwhile, Brian Weld, whom we left the proud owner of his first banjo, fixed up some lessons from someone he described as an elderly banjo player in Edinburgh, and got started in jazz, playing in one of Charlie McNair's practice bands. This was followed by a spell with a band led by Bob Craig at the Crown Bar and some gigs with Pete Davenport's band, including some private recordings. As Brian tells it, Bob had taken over the Sandy Brown band when Sandy went off to London. Al Fairweather had also departed for the south and Al Clark had replaced him on trumpet, with Brian taking over from Norrie Anderson on banjo. The Crown Bar gig closed when new owners put up the rent, making it financially no longer viable, and the Bob Craig band moved to what Brian calls 'the fabulous jazz cellar in Blenheim Place'. Apparently the cellar was beautifully decorated with murals of some of the jazz greats, including Louis Armstrong, Fats Waller, and Bessie Smith. The murals had been painted by Farrie Forsyth whom Brian says had turned out to be a very talented mural painter as well as a great New Orleans drummer. The rent for the cellar was covered by a very small entrance fee, similar to that charged at the Crown Bar. Brian played there quite a bit, mostly with pick-up bands involving well known jazzers such as Ian 'Tello' Telford and Charlie McNair, but does not remember ever being paid more than a few shillings.

When, as we have already heard, the jazz cellar was forced to close by the police, the Bob Craig band moved to a church hall in High School Yards, a street just off and parallel to the Canongate, where they played every week for a year or two, the band including Bob, Brian, Jim Young, Farrie Forsyth and Pete Davenport. Later still, Brian was to play with Charlie McNair's band at the 1957 Scottish Jazz Band Championships in Glasgow. The later 1950s must have been a particularly busy period for him as he played simultaneously with a couple of Glasgow based bands and the Climax band in Edinburgh. However, it sounds as if this all got too much for him as he retired from playing in 1959 and was not to re-appear as an active jazzer until the early 1980s, where we will catch up with him later.

The Climax Jazz Band
Violet Milne (voc), Jim Young (bs), Dougie Boyter (bjo),
Jim Petrie (tpt), Kenny Milne (drms), Jack Weddell (tn),
Jake McMahon (clt), Tom Wood (pno)
(From the collection of Jim Petrie, photographer
unknown)

More changes in the Climax band occurred in about 1958/59, when the excellent clarinet player, Jake McMahon and Allan Ritchie, who played the banjo left-handed, came into the band. A further change came about when Kenny Milne, who had qualified as a pharmacist in July 1960, went to London to work, and he was replaced by Allan Ritchie's brother, Pete Ritchie. Further changes, as the band moved on into the 1960s, were to bring in, for a varying lengths of time, Brian Smith on trumpet, Alan Quinn on trombone, Bill Salmond on banjo and Jimmy Elliott or George Hutchinson on drums.

It seems clear that, by this time, there was an increased number of jazz musicians available locally and, of course, when National Service was abandoned in 1960, this further eased the pressure on bands. There was another band around in the mid-1950s which played in approximately the same style as the Climax band. This band was led by **Iain Forde (drums, trombone, piano)** who played trombone at this time. A photograph of the time confirms that the band was called the Excelsior Ragtime Band, at least at one point in its history. Notes about recordings made by this band show a changing line-up which included at one time or another:

Trumpet:	M Underwood or Fraser Gauld
Trombone:	Iain Forde
Clarinet:	Graham 'Willie' Cairns or Sandy Gracie or Jake McMahon
Banjo:	Fraser Gauld or A Davidson or Allan Ritchie
Bass:	Graham 'Willie' Cairns
Drums:	Graham Orr or Pete Ritchie

The recordings were made between 1956 and 1960, the period when Iain was at art College studying architecture, and in a variety of locations including Coatbridge Terrace, an Ann Street cellar and Victoria Buildings. It is tedious to keep listing band personnel in this manner, but what the list above illustrates is that there was a certain amount of switching between instruments going on. It has to be assumed that the musicians were trying out various instruments until they found one on which they could settle. Iain Forde himself, on trombone on all the above recordings, was later to become a successful drummer. The Ritchie brothers and Jake McMahon were all to be lured away from the Iain Forde band by the chance to play in the already well established Climax band.

Iain Forde had started in a skiffle group in 1956 with, among others, the future trumpet player Fraser Gauld, and was to become something of a multi-instrumentalist in his search for his best niche in traditional jazz, playing, at various times, tuba, banjo, trombone, drums and piano. He also played bagpipes.

Iain Forde's 'Excelsior Ragtime Band' in the 1950s
Back row: Willie Cairns (bass), Graham Orr (drums),
Alan Davidson (banjo)
Front row: Sandy Gracie (clarinet), Fraser Gauld
(trumpet), and Iain Forde (trombone)
(from the collection of Fraser Gauld, photographer
unknown)

I never heard of him trying bagpipes in a jazz context, although I would not have put it past him! Iain claims to have converted to purist beliefs on the advice of Stewart Pitkethly and, as a result, threw away all his 'modernist' records of people like Louis Armstrong and Kid Ory!

In 1965 Iain heard that there was a band playing in the Woolpack pub in Bristo Place. He went along to hear them and, within a few weeks, found himself playing trombone in a band that included Fraser Gauld, Bill Salmond and Jim Young. However, it was not to be all that long before Jack Weddell returned from the south and the band decided that Jack would come in on trombone and Iain would play drums. As he recalls, the drum kit at first consisted of a snare drum and a cardboard box but he was later to inherit a proper drum kit that had belonged to Colin Cant. It was to be on drums in fact, that Iain was to make a considerable impact and he was later to put in time as drummer with a number of quality Edinburgh bands, including bands led by banjoist Bill Salmond and the Climax band. A man with a subtle and delightful sense of humour, Iain Forde could be very funny. Clarinetist Gerard Dott tells the story of a jazz gig in an Edinburgh pub when Iain was on drums and Simon Carlyle on sousaphone. A punter who was a regular drinker in the place but who usually left before there was any danger of the band starting to play, was still there one night when the band was setting up. He looked on in incredulous disbelief as Simon Carlyle assembled the enormous brass complexities of his sousaphone. Clearly unable to believe his eyes, the punter asked *'Is that thing heavy?'* Before Simon could respond, Iain Forde replied *'Well you see, it is hollow inside so that makes it a bit lighter'!*

The account above, describing the many changes in the composition of the Edinburgh jazz bands, is undoubtedly more than a bit confusing and rather resembles tales of the Swing era in the USA, when bands competed ferociously for musicians, when better known bands raided lesser bands for recruits and there was a never-ending movement of musicians from one band to another. However, in the 1950s jazz world of Edinburgh, there would not have been very much of a financial reward on offer, if any, and most of the changes would no doubt have been on the basis of perceived prestige, band politics and who happened to be on good terms with whom, at the time. George Melly, in 'Owning Up', writes about how there are always changing loyalties and friendships in touring bands and says *'...a musician who is a friend can become an enemy, someone to be avoided at all costs, and then, a week later, become a friend again. As in medieval Europe the pattern of alliances is always changing.'*[105] I have no doubt that this was true but, in my experience it can happen just as readily in a local, amateur or semi-pro band. Melly is correct too, I am

---

[105] 'Owning Up' by George Melly, (Copyright © George Melly, 1965) Reprinted by permission of A. M. Heath & Co Ltd

sure, in pointing out that it is often the most trivial of things that can count, for or against.

The power of advertising in the 1950s!
(by permission of Jim Young)

Jim Young tells the story of one Hogmany (New Year's Eve, for any uncivilized people reading this) when he had been playing with the Climax band at the Tempo Club, situated next to John Knox's house in the High Street. Sharing the bill with them was Barry 'Kid' Martyn's Jazz Band from London and, at the end of the gig, they got the two bands together and went to the nearby Tron Kirk, where they marched round and round, playing as a marching band. There was a huge crowd already gathered there, the Tron being a traditional meeting place at Hogmany. Jim recalls that the police were remarkably cooperative, this being quite surprising at a time when jazz seemed to be ranked about equal with gun running or worse in police circles. After a bit, the joint bands marched off round the town, gathering a bigger and bigger crowd as they went. Jim reckoned that, with this resounding success to their credit, the Climax band had a good claim to be the originators of the famous Edinburgh Hogmany parties of later years!

At one point in the early 1960s, so many members and ex-members of the Climax band had moved to London that the band re-formed as a London based Edinburgh Climax Jazz Band and played in the White Hart pub in Drury Lane. This pub is reputed to be the oldest licensed premises in London. Included in the London version of the band were Jim Young, Kenny Milne, Jake McMahon, Jack Weddell and Allan Ritchie – Edinburgh must have seemed quite empty of 'purist' jazzers for a while. Happily, a recording of the London band was made during a rehearsal in 1965 and this was preserved. The Edinburgh jazzers on the recording were the above, but without Allan Ritchie. They were joined by Christer Fellows, a French trumpet player, and Lars Edregran, a piano player from Sweden. As is typical of jazz band rehearsals in my experience, some of the musicians arrived late, after the recording had begun, and both Jack Weddell and Kenny Milne only appear on some of the 16 sides recorded[106].

While Jim Young was London based, he soon established himself as a much-in- demand bass player and played with the bands of Mike Peters and Bill Brunskill. Jim can remember a gig in Bristol with the Mike Peters band when the interval band was that of Acker Bilk. Amongst his many other gigs, there was an occasion when he was called in by the famous band leader, Chris Barber, to play brass bass on a recording of New Orleans style parade band jazz.

Jake McMahon (clarinet and tenor sax), born in Edinburgh on 21st January 1941, was several years younger than the group which had founded the Climax Jazz Band. He was educated at Tynecastle School and went on to have a very successful career as an accountant before retiring when he was 52, as Finance Director of a multinational company. He was to become yet another in the long line of outstanding clarinet players that Edinburgh produced. His interest in jazz was sparked off by a visit to India Buildings, where he heard a band led by Bob Craig. This band included, in addition to Bob, Alastair Clark (tpt), Johnny Winters (clt) and Eed Smith and Brian Weld, both on banjos. This was followed by another visit to the same

---

[106] See Discography Appendix

venue when he heard Charlie McNair's band, with Joe Smith on clarinet and Jimmy Hilson on trombone. Jake then discovered the Stud Club, at that time located at the Moir Hall, and it was through this that he fell under the spell of George Lewis.

It seems likely that it was the Climax Jazz Band, playing in their customary George Lewis style, that Jake heard at the Stud Club. Jake describes the Climax band of that time as a 'moveable feast', on account of constant changes in band membership, mostly because of National Service. Inspired by the jazz he had heard, Jake started on clarinet. He took a few lessons from someone who played with the Post Office band, but he considers himself largely self-taught. By 1958, at the age of 17, he was playing sufficiently well to join a band led by Iain Forde, then on trombone, with Fraser Gauld on trumpet, Allan Ritchie on banjo and Donald Macdonald on bass. After serving an apprenticeship with this band, Jake then graduated to the Climax band, replacing Dougie Goodall who had gone to South Africa, and joining trumpeter Jim Petrie and trombonist Jack Weddell in a strong front-line.

A great high-light for Jake was the chance to play, on his 18th birthday, with the George Lewis band on their visit to Edinburgh in 1959. Jake stayed with the Climax band until 1963, when he moved to London to further his career in accountancy. There he met up with other Climax expatriates and played in the London version of the band, before joining the band of trumpeter Bob Wallis. This band is notable in retrospect, as it had on drums Ginger Baker, later to be a major star as a rock drummer with the supergroup 'Cream'. Later, Jake was to play with Pete Dyer's band with Cuff Billett on trumpet and then had a long spell with Keith Smith's band. With this band he toured the continent, accompanying famous musicians such as Memphis Slim, Sammy Price and Champion Jack Dupree.

**Jim Young and Jake McMahon
(photo from the collection of the late Alan Quinn,
photographer unknown)**

In 1975, Jake formed a quartet of his own, playing mostly tenor sax, a venture that lasted for 17 years. A move from London to Derbyshire in 1993 led to a new quartet there, which in 2010 was still gigging, and to Jake running Dexter's Jazz Club in Nottingham. During all the years in London and Derbyshire, Jake continued to stay closely in touch with the Edinburgh jazz scene, returning frequently to play, often in association with the Edinburgh Jazz Festival, which was launched in 1979. These visits brought him opportunities to play with famous visiting musicians like Kenny Davern, Harry Allen, Ken Peplowski, Spike Robinson, Jim Galloway and Mose Allison. Staying in contact with the Edinburgh jazz scene also enabled him to tour in Germany and the USA as a member of Mike Hart's Society Syncopators. He also toured Australia in 1992, as a member of the Climax Re-union Jazz Band, returning there for further touring as a single the following year.

Jake was and is a top-notch reeds player, whether on clarinet or sax, and a worthy successor to earlier men like Sandy Brown, Archie Semple and Dave Paxton. Always a powerful player with a big sound, his playing grew and developed over the years. He became a versatile player, at home in many different jazz settings, although he never lost the authentic early New Orleans sound that had inspired his early playing. At least one other notable Edinburgh clarinet player considers him the best he ever heard in the George Lewis tradition.

The Climax Jazz Band was one of the most prominent Edinburgh bands when I took my first hesitant steps into the local jazz scene in about 1959. I remember the band of that time well, feeling greatly in awe of them, intimidated by their reputation as seriously purist in outlook and perhaps not likely to take kindly to a young 'traddy' like me. I thought the band was terrific, the front line of Jim Petrie, Jack Weddell and Jake McMahon hot, exciting and well-integrated and the rhythm section, which included Jim Young and the Ritchie brothers when I first heard them, pounding along in great style. I was most impressed by the power with which Jim Young played and, to a large extent, tried to play like him in my early days.

I seem to remember noticing that they played a lot of ensemble passages, which is as it should be in this kind of traditional jazz band. The emphasis on ensemble playing is, to me, the outstanding characteristic of this early form of jazz, something that needs a special skill. Later, as the influence of Louis Armstrong and Sidney Bechet took hold, bands started to feature more and more solo work. Soon, most jazz performances became, in effect, a series of solos, topped and tailed with ensemble or arranged passages at the start and finish. In the Swing bands of the 1930/40s, this was still true but the ensemble playing was replaced with passages from the brass and reeds sections in a call and response pattern. Later still, when bebop arrived in the 1940s, the introductory and ending choruses were usually played in unison by the horns, with a string of lengthy solos in between. It is all too common today to hear good bands, playing in the purist tradition, but falling into the common pattern of strings of solos. There was always some solo playing in jazz but the development of fine ensemble playing seems to me to be the great achievement of purist jazz. It would be sad if this special skill faded away.

Kenny Milne once told me about the Climax band taking part in the 1957 Scottish Jazz Band Championship, when they had been heavily marked down by the judges on 'presentation'. In addition, when an East of Scotland heat of the 1962 'Boosey and Hawkes' sponsored 'National Trad Band Contest' was reviewed by John Gibson of the Edinburgh Evening News, he said that the Climax Jazz Band was *purist and too idealist for this type of competition*[107]. In retrospect, I consider that both of these comments should be interpreted, not negatively, but as a positive reflection on a band which was serious about its music and preferred a degree of dignity to some of the embarrassing excesses of presentation and material that were around at the time of the so-called 'Trad Boom'. I played in the latter contest and can remember some of what passed for band uniforms. Of one band, which will remain nameless, John Gibson said '*...had it sunk to a vote on band uniforms, they would have lost any poll*'. As I recall, they were dressed in white laboratory coats.

So Edinburgh, in addition to being a hot-house for jazzers of the classic jazz persuasion had, in the mid-1950s, become a nursery for a formidable purist tradition as well. As time has gone on, it seems the purist style of traditional jazz has won the battle for ownership of the term 'New Orleans jazz'. At the time of writing this in 2011, New Orleans jazz in this sense, has perhaps the largest following of any form of traditional jazz. This seems to be especially so in Europe, where a number of jazz festivals are devoted to this style. As with the earlier crowd around Sandy Brown, Al Fairweather, Alex Welsh and the Semple brothers, Edinburgh had again produced players of considerable calibre in their field, including some such as Jim Young, Jim Petrie, Kenny Milne, Jack Weddell and Jake McMahon who made big reputations for themselves and were and are highly rated. Their status is confirmed by their many invitations to back and record with touring New Orleans veterans and to play at New Orleans styled jazz festivals in the UK and abroad. Again, like the earlier jazzers, the tradition did not stop with the originators but was to march

---

[107] Edinburgh Evening News, 5th December 1962.

on, with younger musicians and new bands coming along to play in the same style. We will meet many of them in the next chapter.

Chapter VIII

The Great Communicators

The late 1950s and early 1960s were a very odd time for traditional jazz generally in the UK and Edinburgh was no different. By one of these inexplicable changes in the public taste, traditional jazz suddenly became popular. In fact jazz (or a certain kind of jazz) was probably more popular with the general public in the UK than it had ever been, with the possible exception of the great Swing craze of the 1930/40s. This seems to have been a peculiarly British phenomenon because, although traditional jazz continued to have a large following on the continent, there it seemed to be more a music for the committed jazz fan, rather than the general public.

Just why this UK upsurge in interest happened is hard to say. George Melly, in his perceptive book 'Revolt into Style'[108], points out that the Trad Boom was both unexpected and untypical (in terms of general popularity) because its practitioners were '...*far older than the norm and had been around much longer; the emphasis was instrumental rather than vocal and the sexual aspect was almost non-existent*' (presumably this latter comment refers to Trad's appeal, rather the behaviour of its practitioners!) Melly credits Chris Barber as being the great populariser and it is certainly true that the Barber band had an enormous following, playing to packed houses everywhere it

---

[108] 'Revolt into Style – The Pop Arts in Britain' by George Melly, (Copyright © George Melly, 1970) Reprinted by permission of A M Heath & Co Ltd.

went. Also, the Barber band recording of Sydney Bechet's 'Petite Fleur', featuring clarinettist Monty Sunshine, made its way into the Pop charts in April 1959. However, two other bands, in the end, were to have a much greater Pop following than Barber. These were the bands of Kenny Ball, who played a strong, Dixieland style and the inimitable Acker Bilk who, with his folksy, rustic approach, brilliantly enhanced by a contrasting Edwardian presentation, became the central figure of the 'Trad Boom'.

In fact, the first significant UK post-war traditional jazz hit was Humphrey Lyttelton's recording of a blues piece, 'Bad Penny Blues', with Stan Grieg on piano, which was recorded in April 1956 and entered the Pop charts later that year. However this recording, in retrospect, seems a genuinely accidental 'one-off'. Certainly, Humph never seems to have made any attempt to flirt with Pop success again, nor does it seem to have provoked any sudden, general increase in the popularity of traditional jazz. In contrast, the success of Barber, Bilk and Ball was to spark off a remarkable movement across the country, with bands springing to prominence at both local and national level. Bands were already in place of course, because of the Revival, but what had changed was the sudden demand from what seemed to be the general public. For local bands, there was suddenly the opportunity to get out of the pubs and into the local limelight.

What Melly does not say much about, is the relationship between 'Trad' and skiffle. Melly does give an outline description of what skiffle was and says *'Originally the word had been used, during the 20s, to describe a sort of jazz in which some or all the legitimate instruments were replaced by kazoos, washboards or broom-handle bass fiddles. Later there was, in British skiffle, a resurrection of the music within the traditional meaning of the term, but at first the word was deliberately misapplied to mean a folk-spot within the context of an evening of traditional jazz'*[109]. Skiffle in the UK, in the first place, was indeed an off-shoot of traditional jazz. Ken Colyer once again had led the way, featuring a

---

[109] 'Revolt into Style – The Pop Arts in Britain', by George Melly, (Copyright © George Melly 1970) Reprinted by permission of A.M. Heath & Co Ltd.

skiffle session in the middle of his jazz sessions, the skiffle group made up from within his band. The music was fairly simple, drawing mostly on the folk-blues of the southern states of the USA, especially the songs of Huddie Ledbetter, better known as 'Leadbelly'.

Chris Barber had been a member of Colyer's band and, after he left and formed a band of his own, he retained the idea of skiffle sessions. Barber's skiffle sessions were centred on the singing of his Glasgow born banjo player, Lonnie Donegan, who had also been with Colyer. Out of the blue, a track originally on a Chris Barber LP then issued as a single, became a hit, climbing to Number 1 in the Pop charts in May 1956. This was a version of an old American railroad song, associated with Leadbelly, called 'Rock Island Line'. Why this recording should have taken off as a major seller is unclear but its success led to Donegan going off on his own. He went on to have a string of popular hits in the late 1950s, although gradually moving away from the American inspired original material and becoming more and more like an old time music hall act.

Part of the appeal of skiffle was certainly the ease with which enthusiasts could get in on the act. As George Melly said in 'Revolt into Style': *There was the 'Anyone can do it' side to it; a few chords on the guitar and you were away'*. This was certainly the attraction for me and, at the age of about fifteen, I was soon making a start as a skiffler, my initial instrument being the washboard. I was not alone. There were many other local skifflers and, across the whole UK, many thousands, all scrubbing away earnestly on washboards, guitars, banjos, tea-chest basses and any other article with the capacity to make a reasonably rhythmic noise.

Several of my local contemporaries, who started in skiffle, went on to establish themselves in the Edinburgh jazz scene. Among them were Mike Travis, later a top modern jazz drummer, and clarinettist Gerard Dott. Bill Salmond, who was to become a long-serving Edinburgh band leader, was a Lonnie Donegan follower and started a skiffle group in about 1957. For us and, I am sure, for hundreds like us, the next step after skiffle had been almost inevitable; we got increasingly interested in the music of the bands from which skiffle had sprung. Gradually, proper instruments were acquired, rudimentary skills put in place and a batch of new jazzers was added to the Edinburgh jazz pool. In addition, a number of skifflers moved the other way, towards folk music, and were to be a factor in the burgeoning folk music movement of the next couple of decades.

The move into traditional jazz was logical – skiffle had not only sprung from the bosom of the traditional jazz bands but also shared much of its cultural roots and, above all, the same rhythmic base. Skiffle, like traditional jazz, was at its best when it was played with a swinging beat. In addition, of course, traditional jazz was carrying a high profile with the younger generation, because of the success of Barber, Bilk and Ball, and there is no denying that this was attractive to many of us. I have always believed that the easy start that skiffle provided was a key factor in enabling a healthy number of new jazz musicians to come flooding into local jazz around 1960. It was hardly on the scale of the Revival but the 'Trad Boom', for all its absurdities, with its influx of new blood, was another shot in the arm for traditional jazz. It was certainly right up the street of two Edinburgh band leaders in particular – Charlie McNair and Archie Sinclair. Both were serious jazzers who cared about the music, both understood the history of jazz but, above all, they were both born communicators and both thrived on having an audience.

Charlie McNair (trumpet and vocals), who was born in 1932, had been around the Edinburgh jazz scene for some time. Charlie worked in the grocery business and was at one time manager of a Lipton's shop at Tolcross but, later in his career, he ran a Delicatessen of his own in Forrest Road. Charlie was educated at the Royal High School and was thus a fully-paid-up member of the RHS Gang, although a year or two younger than the Sandy Brown and Al Fairweather crowd. Probably through school contacts, he found out about jazz sessions in Riego Street, near Tolcross, went along and heard Sandy and Al playing. His interest in jazz blossomed and he took up trumpet, being self taught like so many of his generation. There was a story around at one time, that Mike Hart had found an old trumpet on a rubbish heap somewhere and had sold it to Charlie for 7/6d, but this is unsubstantiated.

Apparently, his early practice attempts at home were not much appreciated by at least one neighbour, who pushed anonymous letters objecting to the noise through the letterbox, greatly upsetting Charlie's mother who interpreted these as death threats! Another Charlie story from a bit later, concerns his role in Big Bill Bronnzy's appearance in Edinburgh. Charlie was in Shrewsbury when on National Service and had made a habit of visiting Liverpool on a regular basis. There he had met up with Broonzy at a club which was almost certainly the Cavern, later to be famous as the early home of the Beatles, and had had a chance to speak with the great blues singer. Big Bill, finding out that Charlie was from Edinburgh, told him he was coming up to play at the Usher Hall, but was much bothered by the prospect of being harassed on his arrival by hordes of newspaper men.

Charlie was already in regular touch with Sandy Currie, who was still in Edinburgh, and between them they hatched a plot to kidnap Big Bill off his train at Haymarket Station. This was the stop before Big Bill's destination of Waverley Station, where the paparazzi would be lying in wait. The plan is said to have worked perfectly and the two of them whisked a grateful Big Bill off his train at Haymarket and off to the Shakespeare Bar, next door to the Usher Hall, where they no doubt celebrated in a suitable manner. As I know of no other appearance by Big Bill Broonzy in Edinburgh in the 1950s, if the story is true, this must have been before the famous concert in 1952, when the Sandy Brown band was also on the bill.

It was not long before Charlie, a man of indomitable enthusiasm and optimism, was into the business of putting a band together and he was to become one of the longest serving of all Edinburgh jazz band leaders. As we have already heard, trombonist Mike Pollett played in a band led by Charlie in the mid-1950s and, with that band, made a couple of recordings on the 'Beltona' label[110]. This was a 78 rpm record (BL2670), with Hiawatha on one side and

[110] See Discography appendix

Meadow Lane Stomp on the other[111]. Apparently, the name of the second of the titles arose from the location of Mike Hart's father's garage in Meadow Lane, where the band held its practice sessions. Inexplicably, the name of the band on the 78 single is 'Charlie McNair's Skiffle Group', inexplicable because it is clearly a straight ahead traditional jazz band! At the time of writing, the recording of Hiawatha is available on the internet site, You Tube. When I met with Mike Pollett in 2011, I asked him to cast his mind back over sixty years to this recording and who had been in the band. Mike was certain that, in addition to Charlie McNair trumpet and Mike himself on trombone, the band also included Joe Smith on clarinet and probably Mike Hart on banjo. He was less certain about the identity of the drummer but thought that it was likely to have been Sandy Malcolm. He was unable to recall who, if anyone, had played bass. The two tracks had been recorded at a Scottish Jazz Band Championship at the St Andrew's Hall in Glasgow and it seems that the McNair band competed in this event at least four times, in 1955, '56, '57 and '58. By a process of elimination, we were able to fix the year of the recording as 1955, as there is other information about this same competition in the years 1956 and 1957 which precludes Mike Pollett's involvement in these years.

On 30th June 1956, at the next Championship, again in the St Andrew's Hall in Glasgow, Charlie's band again competed. This time they were again recorded, contributing a single track, 'Oh, Didn't He Ramble', to a Beltona 10" LP (ABL 519) featuring the bands that took part. The LP was called 'Scots Traditional Jazz Concert' and was apparently the first live recording of a jazz concert in Scotland. The sleeve notes are by Sandy Brown and the other tracks are by Alan Mason's Jazzmen and an early version of the famous Clyde Valley Stompers who, with vocalist Mary McGowan, are said on the sleeve to have won the 1955 Scottish Traditional Jazz Band Championship a year previously. The line-up of the McNair band is given on the LP cover as Charlie (tpt), Jimmy Hilson (tbn), Joe Smith

---

[111] See Discography appendix

(clt), Mike Hart and Eed Smith (bjos), and Sandy Malcolm (drms). There is no mention of a bass player.

In the Edinburgh Jazz Archive, there is a printed programme for the third Scottish Jazz Band Championship in which the McNair band competed. This was again held in the St Andrew's Hall and was on Sunday, 31st March 1957. This event was under the aegis of the Evening Times and the Glasgow Jazz Club and, on this occasion, the McNair band had Charlie (tpt), Joe Smith (clt), Archie Sinclair (tbn), Brian Weld (bjo), Gerry Rossi (bs) and Arthur Ferguson (drms). As far as I have been able to find out, there was no recording made that year.

Charlie's band competed in the Championship yet again the next year, 1958, and was listed among the twelve competing bands in a special edition of the Glasgow Evening Times on Friday, 5th September 1958. The Evening Times and the Glasgow Jazz Club were, once again, joint sponsors of the event. This special edition of the newspaper was apparently not on general sale but only available at the jazz championship venue, the St Andrew's Halls. The covering article[112] gives a comprehensive preview of the event, firstly announcing that the twelve bands comprised no fewer than eighty-four musicians. Several of the competing bands were from Edinburgh, the full list being: Chic Chisholm's Jazz Men (Castlemilk), Bob Craig's Jazz Band (Edinburgh – Stud Club), Jack Duff's Jazz Men (Edinburgh – Stud Club), Charlie Gall and his Modern Dixieland Band (Glasgow – Woodend Club), Charlie McNair's Jazz Band (Edinburgh – West End Cafe Club), Bill Miller's Jazz Men (Glasgow), George O'Donnell and his Dixieland All-Stars (Cupar, Fife), The Omega Jazz Men (Dundee – Dundee Jazz Club), the Stateside Jazz Men (Paisley – Delta Jazz Club), the Storyville Jazz Band (Glasgow – Pan Club), the Vernon Jazz Band (Glasgow – Pan Club, Low Roof Jazz Club) and the Royal Mile Jazz Band (Edinburgh – Royal Mile Cafe Club).

Charlie McNair's resident spot at the West End Cafe was said to be '...one of Edinburgh's busiest clubs where they

---

[112] Reproduced with permission of Herald and Times Group, Glasgow Evening Times, 'The boys are rarin' to go', MacDougall J, 5th September 1958

regularly pull in 600' and Bob Craig's band is described as *'One of the longest established Edinburgh groups, some of whose past members have made the big time'*. The Royal Mile band is described as *'...one of the pioneer groups'* while Jack Duff's band unfortunately gets short shrift, being hailed only as *'Another Edinburgh group'!* Charlie McNair's band played 'Hot Lips', Big House Blues' and 'Yama Yama Man', Bob Craig's band played 'Atlanta Blues', Ain't Misbehavin" and 'Monday Date', while the Jack Duff band played 'Pennies from Heaven', 'Tin Roof Blues' and 'At the Jazz Band Ball'. The Royal Mile band is listed as playing 'Clarinet Marmalade' but their other selections are illegible in the rather battered available copy of the newspaper.

A review article from the Evening Times[113], published after the championship, announced that the Vernon Jazz Band, led by trombonist Mark Bradley, had been the winners for 1958, with three bands tying for second – Bob Craig's band, George O'Donnell's band and a band that was not even listed in the preview article, Laurie Dunlop's Esquire Band, from Glasgow. This presumably accounts for the increased participation figures quoted, which are given as thirteen bands and ninety musicians. The winning band got £40 and the three runners-up shared £60. In the individual awards, the best performance of the evening went to banjoist Mike Hart of Charlie McNair's band. The individual instrumental awards went to trombonist George O'Donnell, clarinettist Jack Graham and trumpeter Bob Harley, both of Bob Craig's band, and the Vernon band's rhythm section was judged best rhythm section. Best performance was rewarded with £5, donated by the Glasgow Record Shop, and the best individual instrumentalists each got £5, donated variously by McCormacks, Ken-dals Shirts and the Clydesdale (presumably the bank, rather than a horse). The best rhythm section got a £6 voucher, donor unspecified. The judges were listed as 'jazz authority' Lord Donegal, Decca's manager Dick Rowe and London bandleader Mickey Ashman. The judges had agreed that the jazz standard was higher than they had expected and

---

[113] Reproduced with permission of Herald and Times Group, Glasgow Evening Times, 'Vernon Band are the jazz champions', 6th September 1958

they were also surprised at the strength of the jazz movement in Scotland! Three of the Edinburgh bands had phoned the venue at the starting time to say that they were fog-bound and unlikely to make the contest, however they had eventually arrived just in time to compete. All of which, I think you will agree, adds up to a fascinating glimpse of Scottish jazz, circa 1958.

As Irene McNair, Charlie's wife, remembers it, Charlie had a band in about 1956/57, which was similar in line-up to those shown above and it included Charlie (tpt), Joe Smith (clt), Archie Sinclair (tbn) and Mike Hart (bjo). As Irene recalls, David 'Eed' Smith was later added on a second banjo and Bob Craig came in to replace Archie Sinclair. It is clear from the above that Charlie's band was already extremely active by the middle 1950s and that there were many changes in the band personnel along the way.

Charlie McNair's Jazz Band sometime in the 1950s
Dizzy Jackson, Al McPake, Bill Skinner, Sandy Malcolm,
Charlie McNair, Mike Hart, Archie Sinclair
(From the collection of Mike Hart, photographer
unknown)

By 1958, Charlie had established himself as Master of Ceremonies at the West End Cafe Sunday evening sessions. At this gig, the band included Charlie, Bob Craig, Jack

199

Graham (clt), Mike Hart (bjo), Al McPake (gtr), Dizzy Jackson (bss) and either Sandy Malcolm or Bobby Stewart (drms). This seems to have continued as a regular gig through 1959 and 1960. At that time, as throughout his long career in jazz, Charlie was able to attract well known personalities from the British jazz scene and the West End Cafe was usually full of young, Coke swilling, coffee drinking jazz fans hoping to see the likes of Sandy Brown, Al Fairweather and George Chisholm (tbn), as a free bonus. I should perhaps explain that the word 'Coke' above refers to the fizzy drink Coca Cola and not, in those innocent days, anything of a more potent nature!

Another feature of the West End Cafe sessions was a cabaret spot starring the ever enterprising Mike Hart. Apparently, Mike did a spot in the cafe programme which he called 'Dr Strabismus, whom God preserve, of Utrecht', this act consisting of Mike touring around the punter's tables delivering a performance involving a tuba, a violin and vocal. This continued every week, to the great enjoyment of the band but not, it is feared, the punters, until the manager promised to fire the band unless it stopped forthwith. It is perhaps too much to hope for, but it would be wonderful if the Edinburgh Jazz Festival board could prevail on Mike to reprise this cultural gem in the next year or two, before it is lost forever.

Sometime in the late 1950s (possibly the early 1960s), Charlie's band recorded again, this time on the Edinburgh based label 'Waverley Records'. There were two records, a single which had 'Colonel Bogey March' on one side and 'My Journey to the Sky' on the other, and a second single with 'The Fish Man' and 'Big House Blues' (Waverley Records SLP 502 & 504)[114]. The line up for this recording was Charlie, Bob Craig (tbn), Jack Graham (clt), Mike Hart (bjo), Dizzy Jackson (bss) and Bobby Stewart (drms).

In 1961, the Charlie McNair band, now known as **Charlie McNair's Confederate Jazzmen**, complete with appropriate uniforms, made an appearance at a Jazz Band Ball at Anchor Close. Other bands on same the bill were the Finlay Gentleman Quintet and the Bill Stronach Four,

---

[114] See discography appendix

both of which played in a modern jazz style. The Finlay Gents, as they were often called, featured Tom Finlay on piano and Alec Gentleman, a sax player from Falkirk, while the vibes player, Bill Stronach, led the other band. Bill Stronach used to adopt an exaggerated, hunched posture as he applied himself to his vibes keyboard, with the result that we christened him 'The Praying Mantis'. The ever enterprising Charlie had meanwhile initiated away fixtures for which he ran buses taking band followers to venues far enough away from Edinburgh to qualify as Bona-fide travellers. This was to get round the Sunday drinking laws of the time which insisted that only bona-fide travellers could be served alcohol on a Sunday. Still in the early 1960s, there was a National Trad Band Contest late in 1961 and Charlie's band competed in the local heat. The band included clarinettist Bill Skinner who, John Gibson in the Evening News reported, *'caught the ear'*[115] and Dougie Campbell, who at this time was playing both guitar and banjo with the band.

Dougie Campbell (guitar), who was born in Fife on 26th May 1925, had established himself as a fine musician and guitarist by the 1950s. He was a versatile player who was capable of playing in a wide range of styles in both jazz and dance music. He had been influenced early in his career by the playing of Charlie Christian, the great American guitarist who made his name with Benny Goodman in the late 1930s and early 1940s, before his early death from TB. Dougie also played sax and was to develop into a notable and greatly respected arranger, even early in his career providing several local bands with well-crafted and thoughtful arrangements. Dougie, as an extremely able and flexible player, knew and had played with all the Edinburgh jazz musicians and, even when they moved south, many would stay in touch with him. This included Sandy Brown and, between the 1950s and the 1970s, Dougie produced a number of arrangements for the Sandy Brown band, now of course London based.

His musical interest was wide and certainly tended towards the more modern and progressive forms of jazz.

---

[115] Gibson J, Edinburgh Evening News, December 1961

His first public performances had been in a venue which he describes as *'up a close off the Grassmarket'* with Ron Gilbertson (tenor sax), Ian Brown (bass) and Sandy Malcolm (drums). He later moved on to the 88 Club, which was then *'up a close off the High Street'*, by which time Dizzy Jackson was on bass. Dougie joined the Charlie McNair band in 1957 and, at the same time, was playing a regular Art College gig with Gilbertson, Jackson and Bobby Stewart, who had replaced Sandy Malcolm on drums. By the early 1960s, Dougie had become more involved with club and dance work and had developed his arranging skills to the point where as well-known a band as that of Humphrey Lyttleton was using his arrangements. Examples of his work can be found on Humph's LP 'I Play as I Please', which includes a number of Dougie's arrangements.

The piano player Ralph Laing recalls Stan Greig telling him that, when he was playing in the Humphrey Lyttelton band, he had spoken with Lyttelton about bringing Dougie into the band, which at that time had no guitarist. Lyttelton made the offer of a place in his band but, not wishing to move to London, Dougie turned down the offer and stayed on in Edinburgh. Speaking with Dougie in 2010, he said that this was something that he had later come to regret, recalling that, had he joined the Lyttelton band, the first tour would have been around Europe in the company of the great Sydney Bechet. As his reputation as an arranger spread, Dougie was commissioned to arrange material for other well-known band leaders including Johnny Dankworth and Kenny McIntosh, who ran a big band in the Wimbledon area, and for whom Dougie wrote a number of commercial arrangements.

As his career progressed, Dougie remained as adaptable as ever and featured with a number of R and B groups in the late 1960s. In the 1970s and 1980s, he was invited to play with Jimmy Deuchar, the famous Dundee born trumpeter who had made his name with the bands of Johnny Dankworth, Oscar Rabin, Geraldo, Ronnie Scott, Tubby Hayes and Jack Parnell, amongst many others. Deuchar had moved back to Scotland in the later part of his career and Dougie would sometimes cover for Deuchar's piano player, playing with Deuchar's small group that also included Edinburgh's Ronnie Dunn on bass. The association with Deuchar also brought Dougie the opportunity to play with the band at a number of jazz festivals in the west of Scotland, including those at Rothesay and Dunoon. The work with the Deuchar band had been an experience that Dougie had greatly enjoyed, saying how much he had admired Jimmy Deuchar's playing. In the 1980 and early 1990s, much of Dougie's playing was in a guitar/bass duo, again working with Ronnie Dunn, a lot of the gigs being in pubs, restaurants and lounges. He also worked for a time in a trio setting with Al Fairweather, recently back in Edinburgh, and the former professional bass player, Lindsay Cooper. In addition, he continued to enjoy guitar and bass duo work, often with the fine bass player, Kenny Ellis.

Dougie remained a highly respected Edinburgh jazzer throughout his lengthy playing career, always welcome as a guest or sitter-in with both traditional and more modern Edinburgh bands. He had, and I am sure has, a pawky and dry sense of humour with a nice line in sending up the hip language of the day, referring to his fellow jazz musicians, in a broad, vernacular Edinburgh accent, as 'they caats'. At the time of writing in 2011, Dougie Campbell is still active in local music after a career that has already spanned seven decades, from the 1940s to the 2000s. His current musical activity he describes as 'odd gigs' as and when they arise. In 2010, he was working with the small, modern styled band of the pianist Roger Cull. He played with this group, together with guest trumpeter Colin Steele, at the Balerno Music Festival in September 2010 attracting, as always, a great deal of praise that had everything to do with the quality of his playing and nothing to do with his age. At the age of 84, Dougie Campbell can look back on a career as one of the most capable and flexible jazz musicians that Edinburgh has ever produced, a true elder statesman of Edinburgh jazz.

Before looking at the career of Dougie Campbell, we had left the Charlie McNair band just entering the hectic 1960s. Over the next few years, Charlie continued to run his band with his customary enthusiasm, with changes in personnel along the way. I can remember playing in support of his band, with a band called **Fred Terry's Capital Jazz Band,** on Friday evenings at the Jazz Gallery Club which was located in a bakers shop and restaurant in Hanover Street. As I recall, the McNair band at this time had Bob Craig or sometimes Graeme Robertson (tbn), Bill Skinner (clt), Frank Gifford (bjo), Kenny Wheatley (bss) and Bobby Stewart (drms) and was playing very much in the traditional mode. The Jazz Gallery was run by a promoter called Noel McNally and was quite an ambitious project. The bill often had two Edinburgh bands, usually the bands of Charlie McNair and Fred Terry, and sometimes featured a guest band, such as the West Nile Jazz Band from Glasgow.

The drummer Mike Travis and I had graduated, in early 1962, from our school boy band, the **Mound City Jazz Band** to Fred Terry's band, which had Fred (tpt), Grant Liddell (clt), Alan Quinn (tbn) and John Yuill (bjo). The band was short lived, breaking up later the same year when Fred went south to further his day job career, but was quite a busy band during its short life span. The promoter, Noel McNally, had further ambitions and ran a Jazz Gallery Promotions event at the Eldorado Ballroom in Leith on 16th April 1962. This show had an extensive bill and was billed as an 'All Night Rave'. The bill included the Al Fairweather – Sandy Brown All Stars, now of course a London based band, Alex Harvey's Big Soul Band, and the Charlie McNair and Fred Terry bands. The Al and Sandy band was by then in its mainstream phase and the line up was Al, Sandy, Tony Milliner (tbn), Brian Lemon (pno), Brain Prudence (bs) and Jackie Dougan (drms). Later, McNally relocated his Jazz Gallery Club to the Lotus Club in Musselburgh, where he combined jazz bands with Pop groups including the Dean Hamilton Combo and the Roadsters.

It was at a Jazz Gallery gig that Charlie McNair's band had a contretemps with the Lothians and Borders Constabulary. The police staged a raid on the club one Friday evening, although what they thought they might find was not clear. The place was not licensed and the most they might have found was a hip flask or the odd screw top of pale ale, which we were perfectly entitled to carry. In any case, Charlie's band, which was in full cry when the police arrived, was required to stop playing while the police prowled about looking suspiciously into every corner. When at last the police departed, Charlie's sense of humour got the better of him and the band broke into a version of the 'Z Cars Theme', the signature tune of a then current cops and robbers TV series. The police were clearly not amused and got their revenge on Charlie and some of the band by hanging about until the gig had finished and then catching them drinking after hours in some pub.

Charlie McNair, at some point in the mid-1960s, also made changes in his band in pursuit of a more mainstream sound. Graeme Robertson, whom we last met as a jazz crazy schoolboy at Broughton High School in the company of Kenny Milne et al, came in on trombone, with Dougie Campbell now on guitar and Bill Skinner on clarinet. Bill Skinner was a fine reeds player who later emigrated to South Africa, a sad loss to the Edinburgh scene. Charlie replaced him with a sax player with modernist tendencies, Ron Gilbertson and then further enhanced the mainstream sound by starting to play flugelhorn himself.

At the end of the 1960s, Charlie made a move in the direction of populist appeal, this being the era of Pop culture, flower power and psychedelic happenings, and re-named the band **The Purple Eyes Jazz Noise**! The line-up for this band was Charlie, Gerard Dott (clt), David 'Eed' Smith (tbn), Alex Marshall (gtr), Norrie Bell (bs) and Pete Drummond (drms). Eed Smith also sometimes played feature numbers on banjo. Gerard Dott recalls that Charlie formed this band after he had had a year or so out of jazz, although Irene McNair does not remember Charlie ever having such a break. I have never really discovered why the trombonist and banjo player David Smith was called Eed. The nearest to a consensus amongst those who knew him is that it may have derived from the second syllable of David. Apparently Charlie and Eed planned to turn the band into a cabaret act complete with carefully rehearsed comedy spots featuring the two of them. Gerard Dott says that they did actually get as far as rehearsing material and even bought some slapstick-type effects, such as custard pies, for the act! It seems that these plans eventually came to nothing and the band settled down as a traditional jazz band again.

Charlie had an amazing, natural gift for fronting a band and for communicating with the punters. He had an original and very rapid wit and could extemporise convoluted and very funny announcements, about tunes and band members, like no one else I ever heard. He had a highly inventive way of introducing members of his band and Irene McNair remembers how he would introduce the guitar player Al McPake as Pete McPoke! Gerard Dott, who played clarinet with him some years later and was of a quiet and retiring disposition, would be introduced as *'Leader of The Morningside Tongs'* or on occasion, *'...mild mannered Clarke Kent'*, the alter ego of Superman. He had a sharp eye for personal characteristics and facial expressions and quickly would pick out something that enabled him to put a label on people. I suspect that, in the same way that cartoonists work, Charlic would work on the image of an individual until the punters thought that they too, could see what Charlie could see. Thus, over the years, Johnnie Harper became Biffo the Bear, Pete Ritchie was Doris Day, George Howden was Ethel and Colin Archbold, who came in later on bass guitar, was Corporal Smegma!.

Gerard Dott remembers Charlie, when the band had two simultaneous residencies, one in an up-market hotel and the other in a shabby, run-down pub where incredibly, the drinks were dearer than they were in the posh hotel, telling the punters in the run-down place to remember that they were *'...paying for the surroundings'!*. Gerard also speculates that the band may well have lost the residency in the end, because of Charlie's frequent reference to the price of the beer! It was at this pub too, that Charlie would refer to its location in his best Bronx accent, saying that they were situated at the *'...carner of Bread and Spittal'*, meaning on the corner between Bread Street and Spittal Street.

Trombonist George Howden told me about an evening when the McNair band was booked to play in one of those rather bleak village halls, somewhere north of the Highland line. As the band was getting ready to play, George noticed that there were only four or five punters in the hall and no sign that there were to be any more. George mentioned this to Charlie, saying that this looked like their lot for the evening. Apparently the four or five punters were sitting in a solemn line along one of the walls and, after the first number, Charlie announced through the PA system *'The doctor will see you soon'!* George also tells the tale of another time when a punter approached Charlie asking the clarinettist's name, as he would like to have a word with him. The clarinettist was Gerard Dott, not one of the world's most loquacious individuals and someone who, very sensibly, tended only to speak when absolutely necessary. Charlie pointed at Gerard and told the enquiring punter *'That's him over there but don't get talking to him or you'll never get away'!*

Whenever I saw him at one of his many pub residencies, I was struck by how much at home he always looked; the jazz pub was Charlie's natural habitat. Charlie had a genius for involving his audience and absolutely revelled in the camaraderie and rapport that he was able to establish so readily. He would get so involved in the whole business that he would be most reluctant to stop playing when the end time came. Gerard Dott remembers that, when the pub licensing hours were changed in Scotland and pubs could stay open until 11.00 pm instead of 10.00 pm, Charlie expected the band to be delighted, in spite of the fact that they had to play an extra hour for no increase in the already miserable money! At one pub residency, the band was officially supposed to stop at 11.00pm and playing on after this was liable to incur the wrath of sundry neighbours. Gerard also remembers that sometimes, following mysterious negotiations, the endlessly enthusiastic Charlie would announce in triumphant tones *'We can play until 11.30 (or 12.00 or 12.30) tonight!'*

Most Charlie gigs had a tendency to start a bit late and finish quite a bit late. This was particularly galling for the more indolent amongst Charlie's bandsmen, such as Jack Graham, whose ideal would have been to start a quite bit late and finish quite a bit early. When the band had started late, Charlie would genially assure any concerned punters that all would be well – the band would play everything a bit faster until they had caught up! Charlie continued successfully to lead his band in his own inimitable fashion for many years and we shall meet them again later in this book, when we have a look at the next few decades.

In December 1959, Mike Hart and **Archie Sinclair (trombone)** got together with a view to setting up a new band. Archie Sinclair was born in Leith on 8th June 1933 and educated at George Heriot's School. He started his working life with the Bank of Scotland, before emigrating to Canada in 1953. While working for a Toronto bank in 1954, he met and married Betty, also from Leith and also like Archie, of Shetland ancestry. Then in 1955 and still in Canada, he took up the trombone. When a group of fellow Scots exiles decided to form a band and found themselves short of a trombone player, Archie knew exactly what he had to do. He walked into a second hand shop and bought a trombone, not in the least deterred by the fact that he had no idea how to play it. As John Gibson of the Edinburgh Evening News was to say *'Cursed with a landlady who had no ear for jazz in its embryonic state, Archie was forced to practise at night in the bank – until the police were called to investigate the strange noises which someone thought were part of some devilish plot to rob the bank'*[116].

Another ex-pat Scot, Stu Eaton, relates[117] that he played trumpet with the Imperial Jazz Band in Toronto in about 1955/56. This band included Ian 'Daz' Arnott on clarinet, and Stu Eaton has said that they were later joined by Archie Sinclair on trombone. By the time Archie returned to Edinburgh in 1956, he was getting a better sound from the trombone, found a job in advertising and soon made his way around the jazz spots, sitting in whenever he had the opportunity.

The story goes that Mike Hart and Archie, having brought together the personnel for a band, as yet unnamed, were walking through the business part of town when they spotted a brass nameplate outside an impressive doorway. This plate bore the name of some respected, legal gentleman together with the word Advocate. They immediately adopted the name Jazz Advocates for the new band and then later, added the name Old Bailey. One tale is that Archie added this bit after reading about the Lady Chatterley's Lover book trial at the Old Bailey in London. However, Archie himself

---

[116] Gibson J, programme for 'Tribute to Archie Sinclair Concert', 27 February 1970.
[117] SBS Newsletter No. 163, July 2010

208

liked to tell people that *'I had a habit of standing at the bar, so why not 'Old Bailey?'* The band therefore, became known as **Old Bailey and his Jazz Advocates** and, whatever the truth about the origin of the name, it was to go on to be one of Edinburgh's most successful and best loved bands. Although Archie was to be the key figure in the success of the band, tribute must again be paid to Mike Hart who, as was so often the case, was again a part of a new development in Edinburgh jazz.

The original line up of the new band included Ian 'Tello' Telford (tpt), Jack St Clair (clt), Archie Sinclair (tbn), Mike Hart (bjo and gtr), Donald Macdonald (bs) and Bobby Stewart (drms). Archie, like Charlie McNair, had a genius for communicating with people. As the journalist and drummer George Crockett was to say in an article published in 1966 *'What I have always respected about Archie, or 'Old Bailey', as he has become known to us all, is the fact he combines a musical integrity with a sense of humour. And in a jazz scene that has all too often been dour and humourless, this commendable combination has somehow got through to all who have enjoyed listening or dancing to his band for the past six years.'*[118]

Of course, the time was ripe for jazz bands fronted by great communicators like Archie Sinclair and Charlie McNair. The 'Trad Boom' was well established with the general public and traditional jazz bands were flavour of the month as far as bookings for local gigs were concerned. In addition, the local and national press were running regular weekly jazz columns and other articles, often written by knowledgeable and supportive journalists like John Gibson (Edinburgh Evening News), Alastair Clark (The Scotsman), Dougie Middleton (Edinburgh Evening News) and George Crockett (Edinburgh Weekly).

One report in the Evening News[119] said *'The Eighty Eight Club, situated in Henderson Place (off Henderson Row) is probably Edinburgh's nearest approach to a typical London*

---

[118] Crockett G, Edinburgh Weekly, December 1966, all efforts to trace the copyright holder of this article have failed but the author wishes to acknowledge the valuable record that this article represents.

[119] Edinburgh Evening News, 'Jazzman this is for you', undated, probably 1960

jazz haunt, with its discreet lighting and decor, slick seating, and generally intimate atmosphere. Local groups provide the music – modern on Fridays and Saturdays from 9.30pm to 2am, and traditional on Sundays from 8 to 11.30pm.....Pulling in the crowds on Sundays are 'Old Bailey and his Jazz Advocates', who, although only two months 'old', are finding plenty of work with their brand of 'trad' which is going down particularly well with Bilk fans. The Edinburgh based Advocates play at Hawick Town Hall every second Saturday and are due at the Haddington Corn Exchange to-morrow'.

Another undated article[120] from about the same time reported *'The Eighty Eight Club, Edinburgh jazz haunt gutted by fire three weeks ago, is to be re-built. Work will begin soon on the Pitt Street site and the club, which is run by Londoners Paul and Brian Waldman, should be ready by the end of April. Meanwhile, Old Bailey and his Jazz Advocates, who were the resident Sunday evening band at the 'Eighty Eight', have switched to the Tempo Club in the High Street for Wednesday evening sessions. The Tempo is also owned by the Waldman brothers'.* As the above articles had been kept by Carol Telford, it seems likely that they date from the time Tello was with the Old Bailey band in 1960. Around the same time, the Old Bailey band was proving to be a popular draw at the Premier Club in Dunbar, and in Coldstream and Hawick in the Border country.

The Old Bailey Band, as it came to be called, had rapidly established itself as one of the most able and entertaining of the local jazz bands, not only in Edinburgh but also in Scotland generally. The personnel of the band did not remain stable and, as is often the case with new bands, there were several changes before the band settled down. However, thanks to Archie Sinclair and Mike Hart, the band's policy and presentation remained steady and successful. The diary was well filled with local and more distant gigs and residencies were fixed up. At the time that the McNair band was in the Jazz Gallery, the Old Bailey Band was resident in the Tempo Club in the High Street and The Place Jazz Club at 4 India Buildings, Victoria

---

[120] Edinburgh Evening News, '88 Club will be rebuilt', undated, probably 1960

Street and run by the Waldman brothers. India Buildings, the former home of the Edinburgh Jazz Club, seems to have had an affinity with jazz.

Tello did not stay for long and, by as early as March 1961, he had left to be replaced by Andrew Lauder. Andrew joined on a 'temporary trial basis' which he claims, with the Old Bailey band still getting together for re-union gigs in 2011, has still not been ratified by either the band or himself after 50 years! Andrew was to stay for the remainder of the band's first existence, which lasted until 1970, and then throughout its various reincarnations in the 1970s and 80s. Other early changes saw Charlie Welch come in on drums, Graeme Robertson, Gerry Rossi and Forbes Laing had spells on bass and Jack St Clair was replaced by Jack Graham on clarinet. Unfortunately, the band made few recordings, just a single[121] with 'Teddy Bear's Picnic' on one side and 'Beale Street Blues' on the other, made in the Place Jazz Club in about 1963 and a single track, 'Hey Look Me Over', on the Student Charities record in about 1966[122].

The departure from the Old Bailey band in 1962 of **Jack St Clair (clarinet)**, resulted in Jack setting up his own band, firstly as a four piece then a full six piece, the **Jack St Clair Jazz Band**. This more or less coincided with the breakup of the Fred Terry band and Jack recruited me and John Yuille, on bass and banjo, from the Fred band. Later, Johnnie Harper came in on banjo and Donald 'Chick' Murray on drums. Jack also recruited Bill Munro on trombone and two trumpet players in succession, firstly Alec Fleming in June 1962 then, when Alec went abroad in 1963, an Irishman called Mervyn Morrison. In early 1964, there were disagreements in the Jack St Clair band and Mervyn, Gerard Dott, Bill Munro, Johnnie Harper, me and Chick Murray all left to set up a short lived band called the **New Savoy Jazz Band**. At first, we intended to call the band the New Savoy Jump Band, because the name sounded different, until someone asked if we were actually

---

[121] See Discography appendix
[122] Ibid

211

going to play jump style jazz. On reflection, we decided that we were not and hastily changed to Jazz Band.

The New Savoy band entered for the National Jazz Federation Jazz Band Contest in July 1964 and succeeded in getting through the local heat to take part in the 12 band Scottish finals in Ayr. It was at the Edinburgh heat of this competition that the band was complimented by one of the judges who said that it was *'Honestly the best amateur traditional band we have come across in Scotland and one of the best in the whole contest'*. Chick Murray says it was Max Jones of the Melody Maker, while I remember him as being called John Gee, but it does not really matter who it was, it was just nice to be complimented. Unfortunately, we played badly at the Scottish finals and were unplaced. Bill Munro decided to stop playing for a while in September 1964 and no sooner had Dave Margaroni (tbn) been lined up to replace him, than the short history of the New Savoy Jazz Band came to an end. This was because three of us had been invited to join the Old Bailey band, and once again it was all change. Jack St Clair meanwhile kept his band running by bringing in Jim Petrie on trumpet and Alan Quinn on trombone among others, but eventually, Jack departed for the south where he soon established himself and once more got a band together, somewhere in Oxford area.

The Old Bailey band had been enjoying a reasonably stable period but, in Autumn 1964, Jack Graham, Forbes Laing and Charlie Welch all departed for reasons that varied depending on who was telling the story. One version was that it was a row about punctuality (certainly believable in Jack Graham's case!), another was that the three of them were not happy about a new late night residency that the band had taken on. Whatever the cause, there were vacancies on clarinet, bass and drums and these were filled by Gerard Dott, me and Donald 'Chick' Murray respectively.

The Old Bailey band had remained very popular and, in addition to plenty of local work, was also playing gigs all over Scotland. In my view, there is little doubt about why the band was such a popular success. The band had always been musically capable and played very much in the currently popular manner, however, it was Archie's personality that was the key. Archie was good looking, good natured, friendly and gregarious and, like Charlie McNair, he had a ready wit. He was always willing to chat to the punters in a friendly way and, again like Charlie, he spoke to them from the bandstand in a way that made them feel involved. He was a natural showman with a warm personality that drew people to him and made them like him and, liking him, they tended also to like the band.

Archie lived in the Trinity area of Edinburgh but considered himself to be a passionate 'Leither', that is a native of Leith, with a formidable loyalty to the port. He was also an enthusiast for the Hibernian Football Club, an institution also identified with Leith, and had a certain pride in his own ability as a footballer. On at least one occasion, he allowed himself to be persuaded to turn out for a 'show biz XI'. This was a popular gimmick of the time, when sundry hopefuls, with sometimes fairly sketchy connections to show business, would turn out against other celebrity opposition, usually in the name of some charity. Andrew Lauder used to say that Archie could have been a reasonable footballer, if only he had been able to run. Certainly, when I once went along to watch, he seemed to spend most of the game falling over, especially when the ball came anywhere near him. He was very keen though, although I have to say he is the only footballer I ever saw who habitually dribbled the ball without actually moving in any direction. Archie's great football heroes were the 'Famous Five', the legendary Hibs forward line of Eddie Turnbull, Willie Ormond, Lawrie Reilly, Bobby Johnstone and Gordon Smith. Of these, it was Gordon Smith he particularly worshipped and I fancy that, in the midst of his static dribbles, in his mind's eye he was acting out his vision of the great Hibs winger.

Gordon Smith was, of course, one of the great names in Scottish football in the late 1940s and 1950s, perhaps the most loved and admired of the 'Famous Five'. He remains to this day something of a legend who, although winning only eighteen caps for Scotland, played for all of eighteen years with Hibs, before enjoying further success late in his career with Heart of Midlothian and Dundee Football Clubs. A player of great skill and grace of movement, Gordon Smith played his part in three Scottish League titles with Hibs, another League title and the League Cup with Hearts and, in a final flourish, yet another League title with Dundee. Even I, a rugby playing product of a rugby playing school, was aware that this was a special footballer who inspired, not just admiration but reverence, in a whole generation of football followers. Indeed, after I became a member of the Old Bailey Band, I could hardly have failed to be aware of the prowess of Gordon Smith. In his cups, often in the bandwagon, when Archie was waxing lyrical about his enthusiasms, it could sometimes be hard to keep track of when we had left New Orleans and entered the Easter Road stadium. Sometimes it sounded as if the Famous Five had included Jack Teagarden or that Willie Ormond had made his finest recordings as a member of the Ellington band. In fact, if Archie had only known it, there seems to have been a valid connection between Gordon Smith and jazz.

In 2011, there was an article by Paul Forsyth in the sports section of 'Scotland on Sunday'[123] celebrating the publication of a book[124] about Gordon Smith by his son, Tony, a professional pianist. The book was called 'Gordon Smith: Prince of Wingers'. The article picked out a number of interesting facts from the book, including Gordon Smith's liking for the music of Fats Waller and Leadbelly and indeed '...all things jazz and blues'. Gordon Smith's interest in jazz is further confirmed by trombonist and drummer Ken Ramage, another HIbs follower, who told me that Gordon would often turn up at the Barnton Hotel in the 1970s, when the Festival City Jazz Band was playing. In his book, Tony Smith goes on to relate how, when on a holiday in France, Gordon Smith had discovered that Sydney Bechet was a guest at the same hotel. Apparently, the Scottish footballer and the great New Orleans clarinet and soprano sax player quickly became firm friends. So much so, that Bechet was soon providing Smith with tickets to some of his performances and they shared a number of early morning swims in the blue waters of the Mediterranean, before settling down to relax in the sun. It was reported that

---

[123] Forsyth P, 'Star among the Stars', Scotland on Sunday, 4 September 2011
[124] Smith Tony, 'Gordon Smith: Prince of Wingers', Black and White Publishing 2011

Bechet had said *'I can hear music in the sound of those waves, Gordon. The waves are talkin' to me man. You must be able to hear it.'* What a shame that Archie never knew about this friendship, he would have been ecstatic and the bandwagon tales would have become still more confusing.

The late night residency, which may well have caused the departure of Jack Graham, Forbes Laing and Charlie Welch, was up on the Calton Hill, at the east end of Princes Street. This was basically an Italian restaurant, the Candlelight Rooms, which had opened a jazz club on its top floor and called it the Manhattan Club. This was something of a departure for Edinburgh jazz. Most of the jazz venues had been in pubs, which closed at 10.00pm at that time, or other, non-licensed premises, which were available in the evening. This new jazz venue did not open until 10.00pm and ran on into the early hours of the morning, 2.00 am as I recall. Although slow to begin with (Mario, the manager, bought us a drink the first night he made a profit!), the club eventually caught on and attracted a good sized crowd.

Quite often, the Old Bailey band played as support band at functions involving touring jazz bands and sometimes members of the visiting bands were persuaded to come on to the Manhattan Club for a late night blow. An extraordinary night took place on 3rd September 1965, when there were an astonishing number of jazz musicians present. This was because it was the Edinburgh Festival time and a couple of famous bands were in town. The Bruce Turner Jump Band, with Sandy Brown guesting, was at Bungy's Night Spot in the High Street and the Chris Barber Band with Ottilie Patterson was doing a late night Fringe Show at the Playhouse. Elsewhere, Danny Moss was playing in a band with Ron Mathewson on bass. Something of a jazz geek even then, I took a note of who was there and who played. The list, with those that played marked*, was :

Trumpets: Pat Halcox*, Ray Crane*, Tommy Lister*, Johnny Smith, Pete Martin, George Roy, Charlie McNair, Pete Davenport
Trombones: Archie Sinclair*, Graeme Robertson*, Harry Cadger

Reeds: Gerard Dott*, Jack Graham*, Hamish McGregor, Sandy Brown*, Bruce Turner

Piano: Alex Shaw*, Ronnie Gleaves*, Jack Finlay, Ian Scott*

Guitar/banjo: Ruan O'Loughlan*, Johnnie Harper*, Mike Hart*, Stu Morrison, John Slaughter, Lachlan McColl

Bass: Ron Mathewson*, Ronnie Rae*, Malcolm Rees*, Graham Blamire*, Dave Buchan*, Jimmy Luke

Vibes: Bill Stronach

Drums: Graham Burbidge*, Laurie Chescoe*, Chick Murray*, Eddie Smith*, Duncan Docherty*, Mike Travis*

Archie and Mike had, of course, made sure that all the visiting jazzers knew that the Manhattan session was on and that they were all invited. It certainly was an incredible night, perhaps unprecedented in the history of Edinburgh traditional jazz. Archie had also made sure that the event was announced in the press. He was quoted as saying *'They are going to have the biggest rave of all time in Edinburgh. After midnight, all these musicians will be joining me at my resident club, the Manhattan, at Calton Hill. I can only forecast that Edinburgh will never have experienced anything like it. It is a celebration of my first anniversary at the club. At any time during night, the boys will be arriving and taking the stand as they feel like it. There could be something like 20 top musicians having a blow together.'*[125]
Another reason for the big turnout of local jazzers was probably because the club was supposed to be closing and this had been billed as the last night. In fact, the club re-opened exactly one week later, with not a Saturday missed! The Manhattan Club continued to run successfully until 21st September 1966, when it mysteriously burned down in the middle of the night. My bass and Chick Murray's drums were burned in the fire, causing complicated insurance claims. It had been a great venue and had

---

[125] Edinburgh Evening News, September 3rd, 1965

become a regular late night drop-in spot for many visiting jazzers, although seldom to the extent of the famous event described above. Earl Hines, Al Fairweather, Sandy Brown, Ray Kart, Dickie Kart and Bob van Oven of the Dutch Swing College band, George Chisholm and others had all dropped in and played at one time or another. The Manhattan Club, with its late night policy, had been a welcome innovation in Edinburgh, giving the jazz scene something it had never had before, but it was gone and nothing like it was to come along until the still distant days of the Edinburgh Jazz Festival.

The Old Bailey band, however, continued, keeping very busy, many times playing in support of famous, professional bands, such as those of Acker Bilk, Kenny Ball, Alex Welsh and the Dutch Swing College. Other gigs were in venues such as the Cephas Club, which was in the vaults beneath St George's Church in Shandwick Place, and numerous other gigs both in and out of town. A particularly memorable gig was a concert in the Usher Hall on 1st April 1966, when the band played second to the Alex Welsh band with the great Earl 'Fatha' Hines on piano.

In 1965, Mike Hart had gone abroad for a while and Johnnie Harper took over on banjo and guitar. Gerard Dott had dropped out in October 1965, after a year with the band, and had been succeeded by Hamish McGregor. Hamish tells the story of one gig when the band was making heavy weather of it, probably just one of those times when things were not going as smoothly as usual. Archie, with his advertising executive's instinct for style and presentation, turned to Hamish and said out of the corner of his mouth *'Smile – or you're fired!'*. Then, in August 1966, Hamish left to form a band of his own, allowing the return of Jack Graham, presumably now forgiven for any transgressions in the past! Another change in 1967 was the temporary departure of Andrew Lauder who went off to play a dance residency at the Cavendish Ballroom and was replaced for time by Jim Petrie. Jim stayed for a number of months and then Andrew came back into the fold.

Old Bailey and his Jazz Advocates c 1969
L-R Graham Blamire, Chick Murray, Archie Sinclair,
Johnnie Harper, Jack Graham, Andrew Lauder
(from the collection of the author, photographer
unknown)

In January 1969, it seemed as though the days of Archie leading the Old Bailey band were over. I was studying in Glasgow as this time and, although I was home most nights and still a member of the band, I was not around the Edinburgh jazz scene to the extent I had been. However, there had been pressure from Archie's employers about his high jazz profile and an increasing need for him to put more time into his work activities. Whatever was at the back of it, an article in the 'Evening News' announced that *'Old Bailey (off the stand he's Archie Sinclair, 35 year old director of an advertising firm in the West End) has blown his last note as trombonist-leader of the Jazz Advocates'*[126].

The article went on to explain that the band had been founded by Archie and Mike Hart in 1960 and that, over the

---

[126] 'Edinburgh Evening News', 'Fond ta-ta to Old Bailey', January 1969

years, they had been one of Scotland's busiest semi-pro bands, saying *'Now OB is quitting because of business commitments'*. Archie was quoted as saying *'I'm handling over leadership to another Edinburgh trombonist, Kenny Ramage, who's got professional experience and who, I am sure, will do a grand job. The band is otherwise carrying on as before'*. Archie's final blow with the band was to be at Johnnie Harper's wedding in January 1969. I missed most of this period with the band, being away in Glasgow a lot of the time, tied up with my final professional exams, with Dave Margaroni depping for me on bass. However, the new arrangement was to have a fairly short life as Ken Ramage, a professional musician who naturally needed more than the Old Bailey band could provide to make a living, returned to work on the boats a few months later. As it turned out, clearly missing playing and unable to keep away, Archie by then felt able to return and, by the late Summer of 1969, he was back playing his trombone and leading the Old Bailey band as before. Now clear of exams, I too was able to return to the band that summer. Sadly, this was to be a tragically short come-back for Archie because, on Saturday 29th October 1969, things came to a horrible and shocking halt.

The band had played at the YMCA in South St Andrew's Street, which had succeeded the Manhattan Club as a residency. Afterwards, Archie Sinclair and several others had gone out to Andrew Lauder's house in Ratho Station for a bit of a party. On the way back into town, their car hit a stationary lorry on the Glasgow Road, near the City boundary. All four in the car were killed. Archie left a widow, Betty, and two young children, a host of grieving friends and colleagues, and a shocked and numbed jazz band. In retrospect, it was a tragedy that he had ever started to play again.

With Betty Sinclair's full support, the band played a gig to which it was committed the next night, with Dave Margaroni coming in on trombone. After much discussion and again with Betty's support and encouragement, the band decided to continue, changing the name slightly to **Old Bailey's Jazz Advocates** (instead of Old Bailey and his Jazz Advocates), but after a year or so, disbanded in 1970.

There had been a benefit night in memory of Archie in Eaglesham, run by the Glasgow promoter Andy Daisley with strong support from the George Penman Jazzmen, and a concert in the Odeon Cinema in Edinburgh, which featured the Chris Barber band, the Old Bailey band, the New Society Syncopators and the McCalmans Folk group. In the end, for the members of the band, Archie was irreplaceable and, although the band was to get together again in the future, it was right to stop when we did.

Of the others in the Old Bailey band of the early 1960s, **Bobby Stewart (drums)** was born on 17th January 1938 and educated at James Gillespie's and Tynecastle schools in Edinburgh. After school, he made his living as an electronics and radar engineer. He had followed in the footsteps of his father who was also a drummer. His father, Bobby senior, who was clearly something of a character, mostly played drums in dance music and became quite well-known for his method of playing the last tune at each session. His habit, as the final number got going, was to steadily dismantle his drum kit while continuing to play until, by the end of the tune, everything was neatly packed up but for the snare drum and perhaps one cymbal on which he had continued! Bobby senior, at one time, played for dancing in the Star Cafe in Leith Street and their music was relayed by some mysterious means to dancers in another venue some considerable distance away. Whether or not they were paid double for this extraordinary arrangement, is not known.

Bobby junior, in spite of having a drummer for a father, was self-taught and never received any drum tuition from his Dad. While most of his contemporaries did their couple of years National Service, Bobby signed up as a Regular and was in the RAF for three years, during which he played in both military and dance bands. It was during this period that Bobby learned to read music and he played side drum in the military band and a full drum kit in the dance band. He got a lucky break when he was stationed in Baghdad, the established drummer in the station band, which played a mixture of jazz and dance music, departing on the plane on which Bobby had just arrived. Bobby was immediately drafted into the band for the Christmas Concert and remembers that the first tune he was required to play was 'Intermission Riff'.

On his return in 1959 to Edinburgh after his service in the RAF, Bobby joined the band of Charlie McNair. Bobby recalls an appearance in the Usher Hall when the McNair band was playing as support band to the Clyde Valley Stompers. When the interval ended and the McNair band was due to start the second half of the show, half of the band were still in the Shakespeare Bar and the remainder took the stage with only the banjo, bass and Bobby on drums. Not in the least thrown by finding themselves reduced to a trio, they extemporised on Bob Haggart's 'Big Noise from Winnetka', a tune which is economical in its instrumental needs, until their missing comrades eventually slunk onto the stage. Bobby remained with the McNair band for a year or two then moved on to the newly formed Old Bailey and his Jazz Advocates, with which band he remained for about a year, before giving way to Charlie Welch.

For a time, Bobby had shared a flat with another drummer, Sandy Malcolm, and they shared out gigs too, when necessary. By this time, he had developed a liking for more modern forms of jazz and Swing and increasingly played with others of a similar persuasion, including Ron Gilbertson (reeds and flute), Bill Stronach (vibes), Dougie Campbell (guitar) and Dizzy Jackson (bass). With these musicians, and others including Joe Capaldi (reeds) and Eric Rinaldi (trumpet), he played many small group sessions in the Royal Mile Cafe, which belonged to the Rinaldi family. He also put in some time playing regular gigs with the Alex Shaw Trio, in which he and Alex were joined by the excellent bass player, Jimmy Luke. Bobby's interest in the more modern forms of jazz is reflected in the drummers whom he considers have influenced his style. These include Joe Hodge, who played with the Dave Brubeck combo and was his main influence, Joe Morello, Jo Jones and Buddy Rich, although he also adds '... and all the drummers of the Swing era'. Between 1965 and 1967, Bobby went off to play music full-time, playing on cruise liners which sailed between South Africa and Australia, when his ability to read music came in more than handy.

The boat gigs came Bobby's way through the good offices of the Edinburgh piano player, Ronnie Bates, whom, it will surprise nobody to learn, was known as Master Bates.

Bobby's later career in Edinburgh jazz was to include work, in venues including the Athenian and the Laughing Duck, with a group fronted by trombonist Ken Ramage and which included Jack Finlay (pno), Dave Margaroni (bs) and vocalist Kenny Charleston. This group later led to the formation of the Jack Finlay Trio, in which Bobby played with bassists Ken Macdonald and, later, Kenny Ellis. This top class trio became a regular backing group, for more than a decade, for many of the mainstream jazzers who came to play at the Edinburgh International Jazz Festival. He also made a further contribution to local and Scottish jazz when he served for a while as secretary of Platform, the jazz promoting organisation, replacing the southwards-heading Charlie Alexander and working with treasurer Jack Finlay. However, although he was much involved in the more contemporary forms of jazz, not all of Bobby's playing was to be with mainstream and modern jazz musicians. On many occasions he returned to the more traditional style, playing quite regularly with Mike Hart's Society Syncopators and a variety of other Edinburgh jazz bands over the years. His long career in Edinburgh jazz (which he describes as his *'chequered career'*) also included spells with the award winning 'Musician's Union Big Band', Pete Seaton's Band and Fat Sam's Band. In the 2000s, he was a member of the 'Mellotones', a group specialising in the music of the great singer Mel Torme, with Alan Anderson on piano and Jimmy Taylor on vocals and bass, playing weekly sessions in the Jazz Bar, a venue in Chambers Street. In 2011, at the time of writing, although complaining of a number of *'aches and pains'*, Bobby Stewart remains one of Edinburgh's best drummers, as comfortable and competent in the role of traditional jazz drummer as he is in the more rarefied atmosphere of mainstream and modern forms of jazz.

Donald Macdonald (bass, reeds), the original bass player in the Old Bailey band, was born in 1939 and educated at George Heriot's School but was not involved in jazz while at school. Donald was to become an architect, a profession that seems to have contributed more than its fair share of Edinburgh jazzers. After school, he found himself playing a 'home built' bass and says that he was press ganged into playing in a band with Fraser Gauld (tpt), Jake McMahon (clt) and Alan Ritchie (bjo). He was a founder member of the Old Bailey band but soon left to concentrate on his final year of architectural studies at Edinburgh College of Art. Later, in the 1970s, he was to play bass with an outstanding band, the New Society Syncopators, put together by Mike Hart and about which we will hear in the next chapter. In the early 1970s, Donald gave up playing bass for a while and took up saxophone, mostly playing alto sax but later played the seldom heard bass sax. Later still, he made a return to his original instrument to play bass with a top class band put together by Hamish McGregor in the 1980s, Fat Sam's Band. Donald played with this band from 1981 to 1988, playing at many festivals and touring extensively.

Donald Macdonald was the first of what was to become a bass playing dynasty, one brother Ken also playing bass, another brother Angus playing brass bass for a time and Ken's son Owen, was to be yet another bass player. Donald senior, father of Donald, Ken and Angus, was a long-term loyal follower of the jazz scene and skilled artist who drew many memorable cartoons which featured in jazz publications and Edinburgh Jazz Festival programmes.

Donald 'Chick' Murray (drums), born in 1943, was a school contemporary of Gerard Dott and me at George Heriot's School but, although interested in drumming, was never a member of the school pipe band. He was unusual in the Edinburgh traditional jazz world as his inspiration was neither classic nor purist jazz, but the music of the Swing era, especially that of Benny Goodman and his star drummer, Gene Krupa. He had been captivated by the bio-pic of Krupa's life, the 'Gene Krupa Story' and had been to see it five times in a single week! He then attended Keating's School of Music in 1960/61 and, after some work in dance bands, first appeared around the jazz scene in 1962, encouraged by his links with me and Gerard Dott. His interest in Swing made his style quite a bit different from most of the local traditional jazz drummers, who were more concerned to sound like Baby Dodds or Zutty

Singleton, and this had a major impact on every band with whom he played. His playing was rock steady and, although quite a powerful player, the tight, crisp sound he got, gave any rhythm section in which he played a controlled, well organised feel.

He had come up by way of Jack St Clair's Jazz Band and then the New Savoy Jazz Band, before joining the Old Bailey band at the same time as me in 1964. He was to stay with the Old Bailey band until it broke up in 1970 but was again with the band when it reformed in the mid-1970s. The interim period remained busy for Chick, who played with both four-piece and six-piece bands led by Ken Ramage at the White Cockade (the Ken Ramage Jazz Advocates), before moving on to Seven Up, a band put together by Hamish McGregor. Chick later played at the Old Smiddy Inn in Pencaitland with Edwin Holland, whom he rates as one of the best arranger/musicians of the time, and this experience enabled him to become established on the dance band circuit. In 1974 he returned to the jazz scene when he joined the Charlie McNair band, becoming part of a strong line-up with Charlie, Jack Graham or Gerard Dott (rds), Ian McCauley (tbn), Johnnie Harper (bjo and mouthorgan), Johnnie Phillips (gtr) and Colin Archbold (bs).

Chick has fond memories of periods when this band was augmented by two guest musicians, Ally Dawson, a professional guitarist from Edinburgh who had been working in South Africa, and the one and only Sandy Brown, who was back in town on alternate weeks while working on the acoustics of the Festival Theatre. Sadly, this would be almost the last that Edinburgh would see and hear of Sandy, who was to die in March 1975. We will pick up Chick's 1970/80s jazz career in later chapters, when we follow the adventures of the re-formed Old Bailey Band, its metamorphosis into the Scottish Jazz Advocates and his playing with a new band, the Jazz Masters. He eventually retired from playing in the early 1990s, although he continued to make occasional appearances with various dance bands and at Old Bailey re-union gigs.

Chick was, however, to make another, and important, contribution to Edinburgh jazz when, in the mid-2000s, he became part of a small group of veteran jazzers who met regularly in town to chew the fat and reminisce about the old days. It was not long before this group came up with a notable project. Their plan was to organise an exhibition celebrating Edinburgh jazz and to pursue both the setting up of an archive and the writing of a history of Edinburgh jazz. As their plans became increasingly focused, this group became known as the Edinburgh Jazz Archive group (EJAG) and we will hear much more about them later in this book[127].

The **clarinet and piano player Gerard Dott**, born on 14th February 1943 and educated at George Heriot's School, had started in skiffle in the late 1950s, first of all playing guitar and then saving up to buy a clarinet. At first he listened to the playing of Monty Sunshine of the Chris Barber band, before moving on to an appreciation of the music of the Duke Ellington Orchestra, particularly the playing of the great clarinettist, Barney Bigard. Like Chick Murray, Gerard's style developed in a way that was markedly different from most of his fellow clarinet players, many of whom had been inspired by Johnny Dodds, George Lewis or the British 'trad' clarinettists, such as Acker Bilk. Gerard had started with the schoolboy band, the Mound City Jazz Band and then graduated by way of the New Savoy Jazz Band to the Old Bailey band in 1964. He also had a spell when he played piano with the Climax band in the early 1960s, when they had residencies in the Crown Bar, the Imperial Hotel at the top of Leith Street and in the North Merchiston Boy's Club, in Watson Crescent.

Gerard was also drawn into a band led by a young trumpeter, not long out of school, called Pete Martin, whom we will meet shortly. Both Gerard and Chick Murray were to become long term Edinburgh jazzers, with both later putting in substantial spells with the Charlie McNair band, in Gerard's case joining Charlie's band in 1966. It was at the end of this period in 1972, after six years with the McNair band, that Gerard caused a minor sensation when he suddenly went off to play full time with a remarkable folk-rock band, the Incredible String Band. They included Mike Heron, who had been at school with me, Gerard and

---

[127] See Chapter XVII

Chick, and Robin Williamson, who had been the banjo player in the schoolboy Mound City Jazz Band. In time, Robin Williamson, who was born on 24th November 1943, was to make a big name for himself in the world of traditional Scottish and Irish culture as a multi-instrumentalist, musician, singer, song writer and storyteller.

In the String Band, Gerard played several instruments, including the clarinet, tenor sax, keyboard, bass guitar and the five-string or Bluegrass banjo. Gerard stayed with them, touring in the USA and elsewhere, for about a year, before he returned to the Edinburgh jazz scene. On his return, he played for a while in a Folk Group called Carterbar with which I was also involved, again playing several instruments, as well as with a short-lived band called The Granton Jass Works, in a residency at the White Cockade in Rose Street. Later, in the 1970s, he was to play with the Nova Scotia Jazz Band at the Hailes House Hotel and then in a four piece off-shoot of this band with Gus Ferguson (tpt), Johnnie Harper (bjo and gtr) and me, before re-joining the Charlie McNair band. After his second stint with the McNair band, he took a break from playing for a while in the early 1980s, then returned to play a band led by Jim Petrie at the Glenelg Hotel and also a pub in Elm Row. This was a fairly short term engagement and was followed by Gerard becoming a member of a band initially led by Donald Macdonald at Basin Street. Later, after Donald left, Bob Craig took over the running of the band and, when Al Fairweather returned to Edinburgh, Bob brought his old colleague into the band. However, in about 1987, disillusioned with the jazz scene, Gerard stopped playing, a break from music that was to last for all of eighteen years, before he made a belated but welcome return in 2006.

In the interest of completeness, I had better give some information about myself, **Graham Blamire (bass),** born in Edinburgh on 10th March 1943 and educated at George Heriot's School. I became involved in music by way of skiffle in about 1957, mostly through being in the Scouts, and my first tentative efforts were on the washboard. The skiffling crowd with whom I was involved included Colin

Oswald, Mike Travis and Gerard Dott, the latter two, like me, going on the develop their musical interests into jazz. A short-lived effort to play guitar went nowhere but, when the first attempt to put a jazz band together came along, it was clear that there was a vacancy for a double bass player. I managed to cajole my parents into buying me a double bass from Methven Simpson's music shop. This first instrument was a Selmer bassette which, although it had a normal finger board and strings, had a considerably reduced body or sound box. This, while making it easier to transport, did tend to make it look as if a normal bass has shrunk.

I followed much the same path as Gerard Dott, moving on from the school-boy Mound City Jazz Band to play, in succession, with Fred Terry's Jazz Band, Jack St Clair's Jazz Band and the New Savoy Jazz Band, before joining the Old Bailey band in September 1964. This was the occasion of the great upheaval in the Old Bailey band, when Jack Graham (clt), Forbes Laing (bs) and Charlie Welsh (drms) all departed, their places taken by Gerard Dott, me and Chick Murray respectively. The membership of the Old Bailey band at this time thus included, in addition to us three newcomers, Andrew Lauder (tpt), Archie Sinclair (tbn) and Mike Hart (bjo). This was a time of great popularity for this band and it was an extremely busy period, with gigs all over Scotland as well as occasional forays into the north of England.

After the break-up of the Old Bailey band in 1970, I went on to play folk music with the Caiystane and Carterbar folk groups, while simultaneously playing jazz with the Granton Jass Works. There was also a particularly rewarding year or so with the Society Syncopators, then still in their early format, with Ian Telford, Dave Paxton, Bob Craig and Mike Hart still in the band. The resurrection of the Old Bailey band, arranged by Hamish McGregor in 1975, brought me back into the Old Bailey fold and I was to remain with the band for the rest of its history, including its re-birth as the Scottish Jazz Advocates in 1981. This brought opportunities to play with many famous visiting jazzers, particularly concerts with Bud Freeman and Wild Bill Davison in the Dominion Cinema 1976, and a host of others in the early years of the EIJF.

A disappointment was missing out on trips with the band to the Sacramento Jazz Festival, caused by my college teaching commitments of the time, although I did manage the trip to play at the Eindhoven Jazz Dagen in 1983. In the late 1970s, I took over organising the Nova Scotia Jazz Band, an off shoot of the Old Bailey band with a residency at the Hailes House Hotel in the Kingsknowe area of town, and then the four-piece version of this band which played at the Original Hotel in Roslin. Later, I was to play a lengthy spell with Bill Salmond's Louisiana Ragtime Band and be instrumental in forming the Jazz Masters and Maid of the Forth Stompers, bands which we will meet later.

When he was nine years old, finding a broken banjo in his grandmother's attic (could she have been a banjo player? Perhaps an old banjo should be called a granjo?) was the unlikely start for another Edinburgh jazzer who was to make a career in jazz. **Johnnie Harper (guitar, banjo, bass guitar)** was born in Edinburgh on 4th December 1944 and attended Daniel Stewart's College. Johnnie's interest in jazz was awakened by listening to jazz records belonging to school pals, the first that he remembers being a recording by Louis Armstrong of St Louis Blues, which was on both sides of a 78 rpm record. After this, he moved on to the recordings of Bix Beiderbecke and the Eddie Condon bands, thus following a 'Chicago' route, rather than one oriented towards New Orleans bands. After repairing the attic banjo, he set about learning to play it, receiving some assistance with a few chords from Fraser Gauld, who was to become a prominent local trumpeter. Like many of us of this generation, Johnnie first got into skiffle, at the early age of about eleven. This was followed, when he was about fifteen or sixteen, by the formation of his first 'band', which included, in addition to his own banjo playing, a trumpeter, a clarinet player, a guitarist and someone playing a tea chest bass[128].

---

[128] For those too young to remember or so old that they have forgotten, a tea chest bass consisted of a large plywood box (the tea chest) stood open side down, with a string leading from the centre of the upper side to the top of a pole (which was usually a brush handle). The lower end of the pole was set on corner of the upper surface of the tea chest and, by plucking the string while tightening or loosening

Johnnie's first experience of live jazz came in about 1958/59, when he went along to the West End Cafe, where he heard Charlie McNair's Confederate Jazz Band. Although it was a long time ago, he thinks that the band was made up of Charlie (tpt), Jack Graham (clt), Archie Sinclair (tbn), Mike Hart (bjo), Dizzy Jackson (bs) and Sandy Malcolm (drms). His second exposure to live jazz, also in the late 1950s, was at the Royal Mile Cafe in the High Street, where it was the Royal Mile Jazz Band that played, with Eric Rinaldi on trumpet and, again, Archie Sinclair on trombone. The others in the band he cannot now recall but he does remember that Bill Marshall sat in with the band, playing a mandolin.

Later, Johnnie went along to a 'Bring Your Instrument' event at the Place Jazz Club where he was heard by Chick Murray. Chick, clearly impressed, invited him to a practice of the Jack St Clair band which, being short of a banjo player at just the right time, soon recruited him. This was followed by the formation of the New Savoy Jazz Band and then, when Mike Hart went abroad in 1965, Johnnie rejoined Chick Murray and me, this time making up the Old Bailey rhythm section. Johnnie remained with the Old Bailey band until its breakup in 1970, after which he played in a rock band with his guitar playing brother Mike. Too good a player to be long without a jazz gig, he was soon recruited by trombonist Ken Ramage and later became a member of the Charlie McNair band, with which he remained until the Old Bailey band was reformed in the mid-1970s, of which we will hear more later. Other Edinburgh bands that Johnnie played with, before beginning his professional career, included the Charleston Trio (late 1960s) which consisted of Johnnie, Mike Hart and singer Liz Stewart, Seven Up led by Hamish McGregor (early 1970s), Johnny Horne and the Hornets (early 1970s), Tangerine (1970-72) which included his brother Mike on guitar, and the Nova Scotia jazz Band and Nova Scotia Quartet, both in the mid to later 1970s.

---

the tension on the pole, different notes could be produced in imitation of a double bass. This 'instrument', though crude, could be surprisingly effective

Although the first period in the history of Old Bailey's Jazz Advocates came to an end when the band broke up in 1970, it was not to be long before the band name returned to the Edinburgh jazz scene. When Ken Ramage, who had already led the band for a spell in 1969, returned to town from his latest stint on the boats in the early 1970s, he brought the Jazz Advocates name back into use, putting together a band under the name of the **Ken Ramage Jazz Advocates**. The band he formed was a strong one and included Jim Petrie on trumpet, Ken himself on trombone, Johnnie Harper on banjo and Chick Murray on drums. As usual with local bands, there were to be a number of changes in the line-up as time went on, with Jack Graham, Hamish McGregor or Gerard Dott playing reeds at one time or another and similarly with Dave Margaroni, Norrie Bell or Jimmy Luke playing bass. The drum chair was later occupied by Pete Ritchie or Bill Weston, who was not a native of Edinburgh but a visitor and whom Ken remembers as a very good drummer. When Johnnie Harper went off to join the Charlie McNair band, Colin Warwick, a relative newcomer whom we shall meet more fully in a later chapter, was recruited on banjo. All of these changes maintained a strong line-up and the band did very well, with residencies at Lucky McLeucher's Howf, which was actually in the Doric Hotel, and at Jean Ferguson's long-established jazz spot, the White Cockade in Rose Street. Records kept by both Ken himself and Colin Warwick, who played with the band, indicate that the Ken Ramage Jazz Advocates came to an end sometime in 1971. In any case, once again the lure of full time playing beckoned for Ken Ramage and, by 1973, he was back on the road.

The clarinettist Gerard Dott, who had put in about a year with the Old Bailey band in the 1960s, also played with an enterprising band which played in a mainstream style and was led by **trumpeter Pete Martin**. Pete Martin was born in Edinburgh on 25 June 1947 and attended George Watson's College before going on to Edinburgh University. He recalls that the late 1950s and early 1960s was the time of the 'trad boom' and, because of this, it was relatively easy to hear 'jazz type' sounds, giving as an example the fact that the girl next door had a Chris Barber EP! Pete started playing trumpet when he was aged nine, although he did not come from a musical family, and was shown how to play scales by the school janitor. Later, he was to have some lessons on reading music from reed player Jack Duff but was otherwise self taught and very much influenced by jazz recordings in all styles.

Looking back almost fifty years later, Pete remembers that there were positive reasons for his early interest in mainstream jazz. His thinking was (and to some extent still is) that both Dixieland and bebop relied heavily on conventions, which placed considerable limitations on what a soloist could do. In contrast, Pete considered that middle period jazz was of a relatively uncluttered nature, which allowed plenty of space for a soloist to express himself. He also felt that it encouraged a melodic way of playing. Speaking with Pete in 2010 while writing this book, he said that he believed that this approach had allowed him to remain open to a wide range of jazz styles and he emphasised that he still takes genuine pleasure from hearing players from all styles and periods of jazz. Pete's open approach was fairly unusual amongst aspiring jazzers around 1960, when most of us were Hell bent on aping the 'trad' sound we were hearing on the radio and television. However, he was far from alone in his jazz tastes and, even at school, he was associating with a group of young jazz musicians who shared his views.

They included a couple of fine guitarists, Lachlan McColl and Charles Alexander who would continue in mainstream jazz throughout their playing careers, and Allen Skinner who played drums. Pete began sitting in with local bands in the early 1960s and Gerard Dott remembers when the young Pete, clutching a trumpet and looking about twelve years old, turned up at a gig and was allowed to sit in. Apparently, even then he was well advanced and he astounded the band with his already accomplished and rapid technique. After this, Pete played some gigs with the equally young Hamish McGregor and continued to look for sit-in opportunities

By 1964, Pete had formed a band of his own, the **Pete Martin All Stars** which he continued to run until about 1968. This was a good, enthusiastic band, willing to go its own way when everyone else was playing 'trad', playing broadly in the tradition of the Duke Ellington small groups. In addition to Pete and Gerard Dott, the All Stars included Lachlan McColl (gtr), Alan Skinner (drms), Brian Keddie then Dave Margaroni and later, George Howden, (tbn), Dave Buchan (bs) and, occasionally, Jack Finlay (pno). Looking back, in 2010, Pete felt that the name of the band was not quite as cringe making then as it is now! He explained that they had settled on the name because everybody in the band had played in other bands already.

At various times between 1964 and 1968, the band had residencies at the Crown Bar, Rutherford's Bar, which was in the High Street on the other side and just uphill from John Knox's house, the Woolpack opposite the McEwan Hall and at The Athenian in Howe Street. Latterly, frequent guests with Pete's band included Gordon Cruikshank on tenor and Howard Copland on alto sax. Around about the winter of 1964/65, Pete was playing the interval spot at the Manhattan Club, where the Old Bailey band was resident, with a quartet, which, if memory serves me right, was a cut down version of his All Stars band. Pete also played with Hamish McGregor's band The Memphis Road Show around 1967 to 1969 and with a band put together by pianist Jack Finlay, the Jack Finlay Quintet. Unfortunately, Pete was then lost to Edinburgh jazz, his career taking him of south of the border in 1969, where he became a Senior Lecturer at the University of Manchester.

He continued to be very active in jazz and, over the years, played with some great names including Jimmy Witherspoon, Eddie 'Cleanhead' Vinson, Roy Williams, Danny Moss, Bobby Wellins, Don Weller, Eddie Thompson, Henry Lowther, Gary Boyle, and Nikki Iles, amongst others. He also made recordings with the Don Rendell/Joe Palin Trio and the Alan Hare Big Band. Pete lists his favourite jazz musicians as *Louis Armstrong, Count Basie and Clark Terry then* and *Kenny Wheeler, Woody Shaw and Duke Ellington later*. When he told me this, I was surprised that he put Duke Ellington in his 'later' list, as I had always associated Pete with a great regard for the music of Duke Ellington, even when he first appeared on the Edinburgh jazz scene in the early 1960s.

The Pete Martin band's **guitarist, Lachlan MacColl**, was born in 1946 and spent much of his early childhood in Shetland, Orkney and Lanarkshire, before coming to Edinburgh, where he attended George Watsons Boys College between 1959 and 1964. Thereafter, he went on to study sculpture at Edinburgh College of Art before starting a career in teaching art in 1970. His mother was musical and a good singer and Lachlan, always in interested in sound, found himself particularly attracted towards stringed instruments. His older brother too, exerted an influence on his developing interests, when he brought home some recordings of Django Reinhardt and Mile Davis. Looking back, Lachlan says that he made an immediate connection with this music. He considers that he must have been at just the right age to begin to absorb the rich expressiveness and emotion, in what he describes as *'this timeless, powerful music'*, although the Reinhardt and Davis recordings were made almost twenty years apart. He also comments that he was unable to find the same depth of communication in the then popular 'trad', nor was he able to embrace the Rock 'n Roll, or beat music as it was then called, that he heard on Radio Luxembourg.

Lachlan was given a guitar by an older friend, who was already playing in a 'Shadows' type of band (ie modelled on the backing group of the singer Cliff Richard, the Shadows). This does not seem to have been a particularly distinguished instrument as he notes that, at that time, cheap, mail order guitars were not for the faint hearted! However, he got stuck in, made some progress and was eventually rewarded with the acquisition of better instrument. Lachlan was fortunate to be at school just a year behind Charles Alexander, already an accomplished guitarist and bass guitarist who was to have distinguished career in jazz. Charles Alexander gave the young Lachlan some invaluable initial guidance and advice and then he just got on with it; listening and learning and trying to pick out the sound of the acoustic guitar on jazz big band recordings. He also became aware of the solo guitarists, those whose guitars were electrically amplified, noting particularly the influential Charlie Christian, who made his name initially with Benny Goodman, and the wonderfully lyrical George Barnes, who was to make so much memorable music with the cornet player, Ruby Braff. Lachlan cites as his main influences, guitarists such as Jim Hall who could accompany sensitively on electric guitar and the excitement and percussive drive of Herb Ellis, particularly when Ellis was with the Oscar Peterson trio. The dynamic playing of Wes Montgomery, a highly influential guitarist especially in the 1960s, was also to leave its mark on Lachlan's own playing and he treasures memories of hearing Montgomery in 1965 and Jim Hall in 1966, both in Ronnie Scott's Club in London, trips that he made with Charles Alexander.

It will have become clear from the above, that Lachlan MacColl's jazz interests and playing really put him beyond the scope of this book. However, he was another of these versatile and able musicians, like Ronnic Rae and Tom Finlay, who were more than capable of straddling the line between the older forms of jazz and the later music coloured by the changes brought by bebop. His own playing certainly reflects what he says above about guitarists who could accompany sensitively and he was, and is, a quietly effective rhythm player and soloist who always seemed to me to enhance and bring out the best in the musicians around him. Back in the 1960s when I first heard and played with Lachlan and the Pete Martin band, I thought of them as very much in the 'modernist' camp and moving in a different direction, away from the traditions of jazz and the music I was trying to play. Now in 2011, it is perfectly clear that their music was right in the main stream of jazz development, informed by and reflecting the more complex harmonies and rhythms of post-bebop jazz. They were just as concerned with lyrical improvisation, the characteristic altered pitch and sounds of jazz, expressive communication and swing, as were any of the earlier jazz stylists. In 2011, Lachlan MacColl remains a stalwart of the wider Edinburgh jazz community, still the thoughtful, sensitive guitarist he has been for almost fifty years in local jazz.

Charles Alexander (guitar), who was also associated with the group around Pete Martin, was born in Edinburgh on 10th May 1946 and, like several of the others, attended George Watson's Boys College. He had access to a ukulele when he was about eleven years old but had graduated to a guitar by the time he was thirteen. He was to be largely self taught and, like most youngsters, he was at first attracted by the pop music of the day, teaching himself to play tunes associated with the Shadows and the American guitarist, Duane Eddy. He then found himself recruited into a school beat group called Unit 1, in which he was to play bass guitar. This was just before the Beatles era and the music they played mostly took the form of 'covers' of the recordings of popular stars of the day, including the Everley Brothers and the Shadows. This brought him into contact with another bass guitar player, Alastair 'Atty' Watson and also Mike Heron, the guitarist and singer later to make his name as a founder member of the Incredible String Band. Then was to come a seminal experience. Atty Watson let him hear some recordings of Django Reinhardt and he experienced one of these eureka moments, the like of which will crop up many times in this book, and his musical world was changed forever. This first exposure to the music of Django Reinhardt he found an overwhelming experience and the impact was such that he '...almost slid off the sofa'. Jazz was henceforth to be the music for Charles and he did not take long to acquire some Django LPs of his own.

His interest in jazz established, he was soon in contact with Pete Martin and Lachlan MacColl, both a year behind him at school, and quickly became involved in their early jazz activities. Although he was not really a member of the band, he remembers playing with the Pete Martin band at their first resident spot, at Rutherford's Bar in the High Street. I am fairly sure that these would be the sessions that Gerard Dott has spoken about, when he recalled playing with Pete's band at pub gigs when he was the only one in the band who was over the legal age for drinking! It was with Pete Martin and the group around him, that Charles was to develop his knowledge and interest in jazz.

It was not long before Charles made contact with many other Edinburgh jazzers, amongst whom was the pianist Alan Anderson who recruited him to play in his quartet. Keen to advance his playing, Charles fixed up a number of lessons with Dougie Campbell and was greatly taken, not only with Dougie's skill as a guitar player and teacher, but also his pawky humour. Apparently, Charles had landed a gig with an accordion player with whom he had never played but, one lunchtime in Paddy's Bar in Rose Street, discovered that Dougie had played with him. When he asked Dougie what the accordion player was like, Dougie's response was that he had never got over the death of George Formby! Speaking with Charles when writing this account, I was struck by a very perceptive comment made by him. He said that, not only had Dougie Campbell given him great encouragement, but it was also from him that he *had learned how to learn*.

By now becoming very keen on jazz, although he had no thoughts at the time of ever making a career of it, he also took other musical work that came along and played many commercial gigs with the drummer Duncan Lonie, who ran a dance band. Others with whom Charles became involved were, not surprisingly, jazzers who were interested in the more modern and contemporary forms including Jack Finlay, Ronnie Dunn and Bill Mulholland, another fine guitarist and very capable jazz musician, although he also played other forms of music. Mulholland played in a top local beat group, the Dean Hamilton Combo, and his expertise and playing was a major influence on Charles who sometimes depped for Alan Coventry, the Dean Hamilton Combo's bass guitarist. There was plenty of jazz around in the Edinburgh of the middle 1960s and others with whom Charles would play many gigs were the trombonists Ken Ramage and Brian Keddie, bass player Ronnie Rae, vocalists Jimmy Gilmour and Jimmy Leslie and drummer, George Crookes.

Charles had attended Edinburgh University, where he ran the University Jazz Club, before graduating with a law degree, although he was never to practise in this field. A module in this course of study was in forensic medicine which brought him into further contact with Dougie Campbell, who worked in this field. In fact Charles' career was to be in music and jazz and in 1973, he left Edinburgh for the south where, for nine years, he was to be Director of the Jazz Society in London. With this organisation he produced hundreds of jazz events, from weekly jazz club meetings to major jazz festivals, including the Camden Jazz

Week. After his stint with the Jazz Society, he concentrated on his own playing career and was soon one of the leading jazz guitarists in London. His other major interest was in jazz education and he was to become jazz guitar tutor at the Richmond Adult Community College. In 1984, he was to found Jazzwise Publications, which markets instructional books on jazz, software and DVDs and which, later, was to publish the monthly Jazzwise Magazine and organise the annual Jazzwise Summer school.

Broadcasting was also to open its doors to this versatile and extremely able proselytiser on behalf of jazz and he presented seven series of BBC Radio 2's Six Silver Strings programmes and was to write and present the 12-part series The Guitar in Jazz for BBC Radio 3. His many and varied talents far from exhausted, Charles also ventured into the world of writing and in 1999 his book Masters of the Jazz Guitar was published by Balafon Books and, in addition, he was to co-author two books with Nick Freeth, The Acoustic Guitar and The Electric Guitar. A player of his calibre was bound to make many recordings and amongst his more recent have been the CDs When Lights Are Low (Deep River Records) and A Handful of Stars, on both of which he played with the saxophonist, Jeffrey Benson and Comparing Notes (33 Records) featuring his jazz guitar duo with Andy Robinson.

It may that some readers will see Charles Alexander's jazz activities as outwith the main subject of this book but, to my mind, like others we have heard about, he belongs right in the centre of the broad spectrum of jazz. His early inspiration came from Django Reinhardt and, partly through the influence of Brian Keddie and Pete Martin, he was soon captured by the wonderful music of the Basie and Ellington orchestras. The iconic jazz series broadcast by the BBC, Jazz 625, was another fertile source of inspiration and opened up the world of international jazz for Charles, as it did for so many of us in the 1960s. His contribution to jazz was immense, embracing jazz administration, publishing, writing and broadcasting, all in addition to his own fine playing and recording career. At the time of writing in 2011, Charles Alexander remains as active and busy as ever, thirty eight years on from leaving his home city and still London based. The attractions and opportunities of London were so often to act as a magnet, pulling south so many of Edinburgh's finest jazz talents but, when their influence and impact on a wider world of jazz is considered, it would be small-minded to be too parochial about it.

For a very long time, Edinburgh saw nothing of Pete Martin or the band then, as a result of an invitation from Roger Spence who was working with the Edinburgh International Jazz Festival, he got his All Stars band together for a re-union concert at the 2010 Festival. The re-union band with Pete (tpt), Gerard Dott (clt), George Howden (tbn), Lachlan McColl (gtr), Tim Pharoah (bs) and Allen Skinner (drms), was very close to the 1960s line-up. Jack Finlay was there too and played a few numbers with the band. They played extremely well, the concert was a sell-out and, for a little while at least, it was the 1960s again for some of us. Apart from anything else and unlike the rest of us, Pete still managed to look much as he had in the 1960s, if no longer quite 'about twelve'! With a bit of luck the Pete Martin All Stars will be back for more Festival appearances in the near future.

The 1960s was a mad time for most of us, the years of Pop Art and Carnaby Street, Flower Power and hippies smoking pot, love-ins and 'Ban the Bomb', but a good time too. There was plenty of traditional jazz around and a big following to go with it, even if most of them had little interest in or knowledge of jazz history. The 'Trad Boom' did not last all that long and was more or less over at a national level by 1962 and the advent of the Beatles. However, at a local level, 'Trad' remained popular and, whatever else it had done to the music, it had brought in a good number of new players. The excesses of some UK bands at the height of the craze, with daft uniforms and funny hats, tunes with little scope for jazz interpretation and little regard for what jazz really was, was sad and a bit depressing, but there was a good side as well. There was nothing to be lost and everything to be gained by a good humoured, lively presentation and the encouragement of the participation of the jazz punters who came along to listen. These two unforgettable Edinburgh band leaders excelled at this – Charlie McNair and Archie Sinclair, the great communicators - and the great entertainers.

Chapter IX

Return of a 'Gangster'

As the sixties rumbled on, the established Edinburgh bands rumbled on too then, in 1966, there came welcome news of the impending return of one of the great Edinburgh Revivalist pioneers. **Dave Paxton**, one of the original RHS Gang, had been working in the middle-east for about fifteen years, based variously in Bahrain, Italy and Lebanon, mostly in the oil industry. His main job had apparently been as a Stillman which, although it sounds as if he might have been making whisky, actually meant he was engaged in commissioning new refineries and training local personnel to operate them. There was a great sense of anticipation in the Edinburgh jazz scene when news of his imminent return spread, especially amongst those who remembered his playing in the 1940s. Those of us who were too young to remember these early days were left in no doubt that this was the return of very high class jazzer.

If my memory serves me right, preparations were made in advance to have a band ready assembled for him when he eventually arrived. It seems likely that Mike Hart and Bob Craig, fellow RHS Gangsters, and Ian Telford, would have been involved in this, and had agreed with Dave to have a band assembled, ready for his return. Whatever was going on in preparation, I remember being aware that a **Dave Paxton Jazz Band** was about to appear. Sure enough, the band duly appeared and I know that I depped on bass with them in the Crown Bar in June 1966. As I recall, the band was Ian 'Tello' Telford (tpt), Dave Paxton (clt), Bob Craig (tbn), Mike Hart (bjo/gtr), Donald Macdonald (bs – for whom I was depping) and Iain Forde (drms). I had been an established member of the Old Bailey band for a couple of years by this time and was well accustomed to playing with good players, but this was some band. Dave must have felt almost as if he had never been away.

The front line was outstanding, built around **Ian 'Tello' Telford's (trumpet)** fiery, early Armstrong inspired lead, with both Dave, playing wonderfully well, and Bob Craig integrating with the trumpet lead as to the manner born. Tello was the hottest trumpet player of my time in the Edinburgh jazz scene. Having said that, I have to acknowledge that I never heard Al Fairweather during his early days in Edinburgh and, by the time Al returned in the late 1980s, his health had deteriorated and he was a more subdued trumpeter than the glories of his playing on the 'McJazz' and other recordings. Tello was born in Glasgow in 1933 and came to live in Edinburgh at the age of eleven, after his father had died. He had a cousin called Norrie Sinclair for whom Tello's uncle had fixed up piano lessons. The cousin was not all that keen and sometimes, when he was supposed to be practicing tunes, Tello would take over on the piano and play the tune by ear, better than his cousin could manage from the written music. This was reassuring for the uncle until he came through one day and discovered that it not his son but his nephew who was playing. Clearly a kindly man, the uncle offered to pay for piano lessons for Tello who, however, turned down this musical opportunity.

Later, clearly of a musical bent and with a good ear and after completing his National Service in the RAF in 1954/55, Tello took up the cornet, teaching himself how to play. Shortly after this, he started to play in a band that Bob Craig was running and also with Mike Hart's Blueblowers, in the Shoestring Cafe. Speaking in 2010 with Tello's widow, Carol, she recalled that he had been keen to try a flugelhorn, and when his daughter Karen was offered a chance to play in her school band, Tello persuaded her to ask to try out a flugelhorn. He then appropriated the instrument for a try-out of his own! Later, liking the mellow sound of the bigger instrument, he bought one for himself.

Tello was clearly a player of considerable open-mindedness, interested in trying new things, and keen to explore the ins and outs of how jazz worked. Peter Davenport remembers hearing Tello and fellow trumpeter Kenny Jack experimenting with a two trumpet partnership, of the type used by Joe 'King' Oliver and the young Louis Armstrong in the Creole Jazz Band, and arguing furiously about who should play which notes.

Tello's confidence in the late 1950s was now sufficient to allow him to set up a band of his own and he put together an outfit with himself on trumpet, Karl Eckeval on clarinet, Clive Hamilton on guitar, Donald Macdonald on bass and Colin Cant on drums. Then, in 1960, came the formation of the Old Bailey band, of which Tello was the first choice and original trumpet player, as described in Chapter VIII. He left this band after about a year and again put together a band of his own, again including Karl Eckeval, Donald Macdonald and Colin Cant. This band played at monthly dances which took place in the common room of the Edinburgh College of Art. Iain Forde recalls that Karl Eckeval was replaced in this band by Al Clark, now playing sax, the reason being that Karl did not have a phone and could not be contacted about gigs! Quite understandably, he was not very happy about this and complained about it quite bitterly for some time!

In the meantime, Tello had met Dave Paxton on his occasional visits home from his work in the Middle East. Dave had complained of being starved of jazz records out East, and Tello had been sending a selection out to him. An article in the Edinburgh Evening News[129], unfortunately not dated, refers to Dave Paxton sitting in with the Charlie McNair band and playing a farewell to Rhythm Club members at a session where he was '...backed by trumpeter Iain Telfer (sic), Mike Hart and the nucleus of the resident group'. The article goes on 'Dave, who works in the Bahrain oil refineries, has come to the end of his three-month vacation during which time he has played with Old Bailey and the Climax band. Dave and Ian Telfer (sic) were renewing an old partnership at the club on Wednesday, as the last time Dave

---

[129] 'Edinburgh Evening News', 'Jazz about Town', undated

was on leave – two years ago – they formed a very successful group'. It sounds very much as if the seeds of the future Dave Paxton Jazz Band, which was to become the New Society Syncopators, had been sown during Dave Paxton's spells of home leave.

The secret of the integrated togetherness of the Tello, Dave Paxton and Bob Craig front line, I am certain, was their complete familiarity with the style in which they were playing. Many years later in 2010, when I was a member of an Edinburgh Jazz Festival discussion panel on Edinburgh traditional jazz, someone from the floor contributed a comment that, in the early days, enthusiasts listened very intently to jazz records, until they knew every nuance and detail of the recordings. I am sure this was true and I can remember being astonished at the detailed knowledge that people like Tello, Dave and Bob had of the early Armstrong records. They knew every note played, every inflection, every subtlety, and were able to apply this, in arranged and improvised passages, to their own playing. Alastair Clark, in his obituary on Bob Craig in 1998, said about Bob and Dave that their playing partnership *'...was a particularly symbiotic and fruitful one, for Paxton, like Bob, felt that the creative apogee of 'traditional jazz' had been reached by the Armstrong Hot Five and Hot Seven groups'*[130].   This perceptive comment also applied, exactly in my view, to the equally symbiotic and fruitful partnership of Bob, Dave and Tello in this band of the late 1960s and early 1970s. The three of them had listened to and loved the same style of jazz all their lives, their knowledge of it was profound, and consequently they gelled completely as a playing unit. There was not much wrong with the rhythm section either, which also played as a proper unit, and romped along in good style.

Just what happened after this is lost in the mists of time. Dave Paxton was a magnificent player but never, to my knowledge, had any sort of hankering after a band leader's role, with all its trials and tribulations.

---

[130] Clark A, 'The Scotsman', 5th August 1998

**Dave Paxton – master clarinettist
(photo by permission of Jim Walker)**

Playing was his thing and I think that it would have been his playing on which he would have wanted to concentrate. Mike Hart, as so often, was really the driving force behind the organisation of the band and Bob Craig, not Dave Paxton, led the band on the bandstand. Eventually, the band changed its name and became known as the New Society Syncopators and it was under this name that they really established themselves in Edinburgh. They rightly became very popular and had a big following, with a number of pub based residencies and plenty of away gigs. The band was to become known affectionately as The Syncs.

In the early 1970s and after the breakup of the 1960s version of the Old Bailey band, I was fortunate enough to have a spell of about a year playing with the Syncs in their early form. The bass player, Donald Macdonald, had decided to take up saxophone and had gone off to concentrate on this, and I took his place. By this time, there were changes in respect of the drummer as well and Chick Murray came in for a while. However, great drummer though he was, his Swing style was not really right for this band and after a while, Billy Alison replaced him, and then a drummer called Vic Reynolds. These two were both fine drummers, in Billy Alison's case an exceptional one, but again their more modern styles were not really right for the band. In the end, Iain Forde, whose style was just right, came back into the band. He had only left in the first place because, for a while, he was unable to play all the gigs because of work and family commitments. Apparently Iain's welcome return came about at the behest of Alastair Clark, who was about to present the band on Radio Scotland from the BBC studios in Queen Street. Alastair was in a position to stipulate that Iain and Donald Macdonald, both of whom had not long left the band, should return for the broadcast, so that the band was as it had been when the broadcast was first arranged. This took place in late 1969 and 1970 and, although I had just replaced Donald, it was absolutely right that he returned for the radio show. The broadcast resulted in some recordings which are still around and which, I believe, were simply made by someone recording from their radio. It is a great shame that these recordings have never been made available more generally, as the music is terrific. Donald Macdonald played, not me, so I have no stake in saying this; in my view they are among the best recordings made by an Edinburgh band in my time. They only exist, as far as I know, on the private copies made of the radio programme and it is unlikely that they will have survived in the BBC archives. Iain Forde gave me a copy of a few of the tracks, and the whole band, but Dave Paxton in particular, is in top form.

Drummer Billy Alison, who was born in 1933, was another of the Edinburgh jazzers who had a broad interest in jazz and was able to play in both traditional and more modern forms of the music. He had learned pipe band drumming when in the Scouts, when he was ten years old. In 1947, at age only fourteen, he had toured in Holland with his Scout band, the 148th Troop St Cuthbert's, and had recorded at Radio Hilversun. After leaving the Scouts, Billy bought a drum kit, put in some serious practice, then went along to a 'come as you please' session at the Palais de Dance in Fountainbridge. Here he sat in with the Jimmy Walker Quintet, on Kenny Duff's drum kit. Kenny Duff, impressed with Bill's playing, soon handed on a gig at St Cuthbert's Hall, near the Art College, at which Billy made his debut. After this, Bill teamed up for a while with an accordion player called Johnny Robertson.

By 1951, he was playing at a modern jazz club in India Buildings with Ron Carruthers and Alex Tait but was then called up for National Service and posted to Germany. Here he formed what he called 'a camp trio' (the mind boggles - just how camp were they?!) which played at mess dances and other gigs outside the camp. Back home again after demob, Billy joined Tony Fusco's dance band, which played in the Picardy Place Hall, and was involved in other dance gigs with Fred Murray (bs) and Fred Duligal (ten sax), who later went to Canada. He also played at American bases both with and for, keyboard player Bert Valentine. In 1956 Billy joined Pete Seaton and bass player Gerry Rossi at the Berkeley Restaurant in Lothian Road and then moved to the Pallais de Dance, with the Hal Collins Quartet, again with Seaton and Rossi and leader Hal Collins on guitar. Later he was with Pete Seaton again, this time at the George Hotel, where he remained for the next thirteen years.

It was during this time that Billy had some time off for various sessions with the BBC including, in 1962, programmes such as 'Variety Ahoy!', which went out from the naval dockyard at Rosyth, and 'Piano Provided', which went out from the Queens Street studios. There was a four month break in 1963 from the George Hotel when Billy, together with Edinburgh jazzers Tom Finlay (pno) and Ronnie Dunn (bs), went cruising to the West Indies, playing as a Latin American Trio, teamed up with an orchestra as part of what many musicians on the boats were to call 'Geraldo's Navy'. In 1965, Billy recorded the programme 'For Your Entertainment', again from the BBC studios in Queens Street. Much later, in the 1970s, Billy was joined at the George Hotel by pianist Alex Shaw and bassist Ronnie Rae, in what was obviously a high class jazz trio. By 1973, this trio had moved to Henry Spurway's hotel, the Elm Tree, in West Calder and, during this period, recorded at the STV Gateway studios in Leith Walk for Bill Tennant's 'Come Tuesdays' programme. In addition, there were a number of University lunch time sessions when Billy accompanied some of the British modern jazz aristocracy, including Tubby Hayes and Joe Harriot. There was also work with various small groups between 1983 and 1986, during the Edinburgh International Jazz Festivals.

Never really a traditional jazz musician, Billy was, like the guitarist Dougie Campbell, one of the Edinburgh musicians who were flexible enough to play in many styles. He was to demonstrate this flexibility much later when, at the turn of the 1980s, he played with Al Fairweather, Dave Paxton, trombonist Bill Smith and pianist Ian Scott, at the Ritz Hotel in Grosvenor Street at Haymarket. Technically excellent, Billy Alison was much admired by fellow drummers and was a tower of strength in any band with whom he played.

Geraldo's Navy
Tom Finlay, Billy Alison, Ronnie Dunn
(from the collection of Billy Alison, photographer unknown)

As well as their various residencies in venues such as The Wee Windies in the High Street and the Lochewe Hotel in Royal Terrace, the Syncs played many away gigs and, on one of a series of gigs at Ledlannet House in Fife, the band shared the bill with the American mouth organ maestro, Larry Adler. Sometimes the indefatigable Jackie MacFarlane was added to the band as vocalist and there was one memorable night when the band, with Jackie, played at Stirling University. This was while I was a member of the band and we shared the bill with a very good but exceptionally loud rock band called, if memory serves me right, Tear Gas. The event was absolutely packed but even the students wilted in the face of the rock band's volume and they all hastily retreated to the bar in the next room. When we went on, by comparison with the rock band's awesome stage presence, we must have looked really feeble and pathetic. The six of us standing there, with just one microphone and a tiny combo amplifier for Jackie's vocals, and surrounded by several acres of rock band gear.

Alastair Clark wrote it up in the Scotsman the next weekend and said *'There were four staccato foot stomps and the New Society Syncopators, fired by the hot coals of Ian Telford's trumpet, were surging forward like a steam engine that shows no sign of ever stopping'*. To the amazement of the band, the students came pouring back into the hall, packed themselves about twelve deep around the bandstand, cheering and yelling their approval. As Alastair Clark reported[131], the students roared appreciation *'...and finally hoisted Jackie MacFarlane shoulder-high and carried him out of the hall like the conquering hero he was'*. Clark then described the band's Thursday night residency in the Royal Mile Centre saying *'There's a curious quality of incipient decadence rather than revival about this setting, but the jazz is as rich and meaty as any you can find in these islands'*. He then continued *'The Syncopators take Jelly Roll Morton, the King Oliver Band and the Armstrong Hot Five and Hot Seven as favoured prototypes and the reproduction is uncannily accurate and vibrantly alive in numbers like 'Snake Rag' and 'Wild Man Blues''*. Alastair also compared

---

[131] Clark A, 'Trad crosses the sound barrier', 'Scotsman' September 1972

the vigorous heat of the Syncs performance to some recordings of British trad bands during the 'Trad Boom', commenting on how 'namby-pamby' the latter had become.

It is hard now to track just what happened within the ranks of the New Society Syncopators after this, not helped by the fact that I had dropped out of the band at the end of 1972, to be replaced by Norrie Bell. Gradually the original personnel left the band, beginning with Tello, and the sound of the original band was lost forever. Mike Hart was running the band and, as the originals left, he was able to bring in top class replacements but, being jazz musicians, each had his own style and sound and inevitably, with every change in personnel, the band sound changed. The band, in spite of the changes, was to continue very successfully through the 1970s until they amalgamated with the re-born Old Bailey band, but that is story for another chapter.

Later, Tello played in a band at the White Cockade in Rose Street, a band which included Donald Macdonald, now on sax, and Ken Macdonald, Donald's brother, on bass. Carol Telford recalls that this band 'went modern'! After this, Tello joined the Charlie McNair Jazz Band, playing second trumpet to Charlie. I remember hearing the band at this time and noticing how well Tello understood the role of the second trumpet, no doubt the outcome of his much earlier experiments in a two trumpet line-up with Kenny Jack. Other Edinburgh bands tried two trumpets, but none in my view managed to use the system as convincingly as when Tello was involved. Ian 'Tello' Telford died on 5th April 2002 at the age of 68, following a lengthy period of ill health and after being inactive in jazz for a number of years.

Bill Salmond (banjo and guitar), who was born in Edinburgh in May 1941, had attended the Royal High School but was not influenced at all by the notable jazz heritage of the school. In the mid-1950s, in common with so many of his generation, he became interested in skiffle music and Lonnie Donegan, and this led to him forming a skiffle group in about 1957. In 1958, a friend took him to the Moir Hall in the Pleasance, where he heard the early Climax Jazz Band. Then, a year later, he went through to Glasgow to hear the George Lewis band, then on tour in the UK, and this was to be the major influence on his playing and playing career. Bill was to remain loyal to the purist style for the rest of his career and, as a banjo player, he took for his main models, George Lewis' banjoist Lawrence Marrero and two other Americans, George Guesnon and Emanuel Sayles.

As the 1950s came to an end and the 1960s began, Bill played with several bands, including one run by the trombone player Bill Munro, and another led by the clarinet player, Jack St Clair. Later, he had a shot at running a band under his own name. I remember playing with one of his bands in 1961, under the name **The Savoy New Orleans Jazz Band**, in Rutherford's Bar in the High Street and at the Lotus Club in Musselburgh. This band included a fine trumpet player called Brian Smith who had put in a spell with the Climax band and who, unfortunately, soon departed for London. In addition, there was Grant Liddell who played clarinet, a drummer called Gordon Thompson and a trombone player called Alan Quinn who, like Bill, was still an important Edinburgh jazzer several decades later, although in Alan's case with a lengthy break in the middle. I can remember going to a practice session with this band of Bill's. Rather oddly, it took place in the basement of the Edinburgh Stock Exchange, entry to which, if I remember rightly, had been arranged by Grant Liddell. I also remember this band of Bill's playing alongside the Climax band at the Mardi Gras Club, which was located in the North Merchiston Boy's Club in Watson Crescent and, I think, run by the Climax band bass player, Jim Young.

The Climax band had a residency at that time in the cellar of Jim Young's house and, not surprisingly Bill, with his interest in purist jazz, used to go along to listen. When the banjo player Alan Ritchie left the Climax to go to London, Bill was the obvious replacement and he joined the band in late 1961, joining Jim Petrie (tpt), Jack Weddell (tbn), Jake McMahon (clt), Jim Young (bs) and Pete Ritchie (drms). This was a strong line-up and the Climax remained a formidable band in the purist tradition. When speaking of this time in his jazz career, Bill, like others, made the point that there had been constant changes in the local bands, as National Service interrupted the playing lives of the older band members. However, it was now the early 1960s and

National Service had become a thing of the past, allowing the Climax band to settle down. Bill was to remain with the band until 1968 when he finally moved on, his departure from the band triggered by one of those typical squabbles that can break out even in the most settled of bands. On this occasion, it was something to do with the band being asked to play over the agreed time at a gig and one band member refusing, because he had to get home to allow the baby sitter to go off duty! Bill was not involved directly in this particular uproar but I suspect that, with his earlier experience of band leading, he was already beginning to think it was time once more to put together a band of his own.

It was then, in early 1969, that Bill put together the first of his bands under the name **The Louisiana Ragtime Band**, the band which he was still running 40 years later. The first version of the band had Fraser Gauld (tpt), Gerard Dott (clt), George Howden (tbn), Willie Mack (bs) and Chick Davis (drms) in addition to Bill himself on banjo. The new band's first gig was in the Cephas Club in February 1969, practices took place during the next month and they started on their first residency on 17th March 1969, in the Lothian Bar in Lothian Road. Chick Davies dropped out after just a few months and was replaced by Iain Forde and then Pete Ritchie, before John Nicholson (later known as John McGlynn) took over. Clarinettist Gerard Dott left in about July 1970, to be replaced by George Gilmour. Other residences held by the band around this time were at Merryman's Cellar in Hanover Street, between March and July 1970, after which they moved on to the Haymarket Bar. Many other gigs were played, including the Cephas Club, which was a regular every month for a while, the YMCA and the Kirkcaldy Jazz Club. Later, while holding down a gig at the Carlton Hotel, a trumpeter from Dundee, Robin 'Gus' Ferguson, came into the band for a while. Later still, Bill featured his first 'trumpetless' front line, a formula that he was to use many times in the future, when the clarinettist George Duncan and trombonist Jack Weddell fronted the band and shared the lead duties.

It is much to Bill's credit that, if he was unable to find a player who suited the style he was pursuing, he would often do without, rather than compromise the band sound. Bill also had an unusual strategy he occasionally used to recruit new band members. If there was no one around that seemed a good fit, he was perfectly prepared to create a suitable candidate, by persuading someone interested in the music to take up an instrument. It was by this method that Bill acquired his bass player, Willie Mack and drummer, Eric Jamieson and in both cases, he even put them in touch with appropriate local assistance while they were starting. In 1972, Bill also had the initiative to place an advert in the Evening News for a piano player. He had two applicants, both with the surname Scott and both came for an audition. As a result of this, Graham Scott, then still a schoolboy, got the job.

Bill Salmond's Louisiana Ragtime Band or the LRB as it became known, became a fixture on the Edinburgh jazz scene and, although there were quite a number of changes in the band over the years, it was always a good, driving band, firmly committed to early New Orleans jazz. It would be impossible now to list in chronological order, all the various changes in personnel, especially as some musicians had several separate spells with the band. However, a listing of those who played with the band gives an idea of Bill's success in keeping his band going for so long:

Trumpet: Fraser Gauld, Gus Ferguson, Dave Strutt, Kenny Milne, Brian Robertson
Reeds: Gerard Dott, George Duncan, Dave Paxton, George Gilmore, Ian Boyter
Trombone: George Howden, Jack Weddell, Alan Quinn, Simon Carlyle, Bob Craig, Martin Bennett
Piano: Graham Scott
Banjo/gtr: Bill Salmond (leader)
Bass: Jim Young, Adrian Bull, Willie Mack, Robin Galloway, Graham Blamire, Bill Brydon
Drums: Chick Davis, Iain Forde, Pete Ritchie, John Nicolson (McGlynn), Jimmy Elliott, Kenny Orr, Roy Dunnett, Eric Jamieson, Kenny Milne

I played with the band between 1985 and 1991 and was fortunate to be with the band when it reached several high spots in its history. Dave Paxton, who had left the Society Syncopators, had come in on clarinet and was to stay with the LRB for eighteen years, still playing wonderfully well. Bob Craig was on trombone for quite a lengthy period and then he was replaced by Martin Bennett, a vastly experienced English trombone player, who was also a good singer. Bill had recruited a young, inexperienced trumpet player who was to be with the band for some years, before going on to lead bands of his own. He was Brian Robertson and, with Martin Bennett directing the front line, Dave, Martin and Brian made a good and compatible unit.

In 1987, Bill took the band to the Enkhuisen Jazz Festival in Holland, and I never heard the band play better than on this occasion. We also made several trips to play at the new Bute Jazz Festival, on the Isle of Bute in the Firth of Clyde, where the band helped to launch this new venture and establish it on the Scottish jazz festival rota. This came about largely because Phil Mason, a red-hot New Orleans trumpet player from the south, had moved up to live on the Isle of Bute. Phil had been at University in Dublin with Martin Bennett and had played for years with the famous Max Colllie Rhythm Aces and then the Pete Allen Band, before basing himself in Scotland, from where he toured with his own band. Phil made many trips to play with the LRB, mostly at their residency in the Navaar House Hotel in Newington. This was always a well-attended gig and Phil's presence did us no harm at all and, I feel sure, was a positive factor in Brian Robertson's rapid progress on trumpet. Phil had founded the Bute Jazz Festival, a very popular festival that was to be a fixture in the Scottish jazz calendar for many years.

Over the years, the LRB played at festivals on the Continent (Enkhuisen, Gothenburg, Celerina, Davos) and toured in both Holland and Sweden. They were to be stalwarts of the Edinburgh International Jazz Festival and also featured at other UK jazz festivals including Orkney, Bute, Keswick, Largs and Kirkcudbright. They were selected to back a number of visiting stars, including pianist Alton Purnell, drummer Barry Martyn, trumpeter Kid Shiek Colar and sax players Sam Lee and Benny Watters. The famous American pianist Johnny Guarnieri played with the band on one occasion and, at the Navaar House Hotel, the drummer Barrett Deems and bass player Arvel Shaw, both former members of the Louis Armstrong All Stars, turned up one evening and sat in with the band. After over forty years, Bill Salmond's Louisiana Ragtime Band remains a Scottish jazz institution and shows no signs of stopping.

In finding **Graham Scott (piano)** through a newspaper advert, Bill Salmond introduced a jazzer who was to make a solid impact and who, almost as much as Bill himself, was to be a constant presence in the LRB. Graham was born in Australia on 27th March 1954 and was educated at Edinburgh's Daniel Stewart's College. He had piano lessons from age seven until he was fourteen and, at school, played bass drum in the pipe band. He was only seventeen when he was taken on by Bill and had responded to the newspaper advert which had asked for a 'bluesy piano player', which, naturally, we used to pretend to believe was actually for a 'boozy piano player'. In fact, Graham's playing was very much influenced by the blues and he had played a selection of 'Boogie Woogie' tunes at his audition. He had clearly listened to Boogie Woogie piano players such as Meade Lux Lewis and played a strong, two handed style which always reminded me of the playing of the American, Art Hodes. In addition to playing piano, Graham's experience of playing the bass drum made him a valuable addition to the various parade bands that often featured at outdoor events. These were marching brass bands in the New Orleans tradition, and usually organised by Jim Young (The Auld Reekie Parade Band) or the drummer, Kenny Milne (The Criterion Parade Band).

As well as his long term loyalty to the LRB, Graham also played with an excellent band put together in the 1980s by the returning Al Fairweather and then, in the 1990s, with Mike Hart's Edinburgh Ragtimers. As well as making all the festival gigs with the LRB, he also toured in the 1980s in Germany, Holland, Belgium and Switzerland with the band of Colin 'Kid' Dawson, a well known New Orleans styled trumpeter from Newcastle and did the annual Ascona Festival in Switzerland with the Criterion Parade Band. He joined the LRB in 1971 and forty years later in 2011, he was still there.

Bill Salmond's Louisiana Ragtime Band in Basin Street in 1987
L-R Graham Scott (pno), Dave Paxton (clt), the author (bs), Bill Salmond (bjo), Roy Dunnett (drms), Brian Robertson (tpt), Martin Bennett (tbn)
(from the collection of the author, photographer unknown)

Willie Mack (bass) was born in Douglas in Lanarkshire on 10th November 1943 and had a grandfather and father who both played pedal organ. His early interest in jazz came about through hearing the music of the British traditional bands during the 'trad boom' of the late 1950s and it led to a particular interest in the music of George Lewis, one of the great figures of the New Orleans Revival. Long before he ever played bass, Willie was approached by Bill Salmond's father, Bill Salmond senior, who enquired if he might be interested in playing bass in the Climax band, in which Bill junior was playing. I suspect that this was an example of Bill junior's laudable willingness to seek recruit's to the music he loved by encouraging individuals to take up an instrument. Take up the bass Willie did and, before long, he made his debut with the Climax band in 1965 and also played with a folk dance band called the Reivers, led by Adrian Bull. Adrian Bull was also to make an appearance on the Edinburgh jazz scene as a bass player but played mandolin in the Reivers.

Willie Mack then became a founder member of Bill Salmond's Louisiana Ragtime Band in the late 1960s and from 1980 to 1985 was also to be a member of the Spirits of Rhythm, splitting the bass playing duties with Robin Galloway. With these established purist styled bands, he had welcome opportunities to play with New Orleans greats Alton Purnell (pno), Kid Shiek Colar (tpt), Sammy Lee and Capt. John Handy (sax) and Teddy Riley (tpt). Willie visited New Orleans in 1970 and sat in with a band of veteran jazzers in Preservation Hall, including Kid Thomas Valentine (tpt), Andrew Morgan (ten sax), Orange Kellin (clt), Earl Humphrey (tbn), Las Edegran (pno) and the English ex-pat Barry Martyn (drms). Willie recorded with both the LRB and the Spirits[132] and was on the Spirits' LP 'Sam Lee meets the Spirits of Rhythm' in 1974. A banker in his day job, Willie Mack retired from playing, although not from listening to jazz, in 1985 and remains an active supporter of the local jazz scene.

George Gilmour (clarinet) was born in Edinburgh in March 1947, took up clarinet at the age of eighteen and later added both soprano and alto saxophones to his musical armoury. His playing was inspired and influenced by the playing of Sydney Bechet and later by the playing of George Lewis. He was recruited into the Climax band in the mid-1960s, replacing the London bound Jake McMahon, before joining Bill Salmond's Louisiana Ragtime Band. George had been invited for an audition with Bill Salmond before being offered a place in the band and recalls that, after playing some clarinet pieces, he began to open up his soprano sax case. Bill, at that time a strict New Orleans man to whom saxophones were anathema, said quietly but

---

[132] See discography Appendix

firmly *'You won't be needing that '* and George, just as quietly, shut the soprano back in its case again!

His style was ideal for both bands and he was a worthy successor to Jake McMahon in the Climax band. He was also active in the parade band scene and, being a very strong player with a big sound, he always sounded marvellous soaring over the typical hot, brassy ensemble of the parade bands. Powerful though his playing was, George was also able to play with great tenderness and feeling and I have always felt that he was an extremely soulful player. From the age of about thirty, George worked as a light house keeper and spells of two years in the west of Scotland and six years in the Orkney Islands, kept him out of jazz for about twelve years. However, a posting to the St Abb's Head light in East Lothian followed by a spell on the relief rota allowed him to begin playing in Edinburgh again around 1990. He re-joined the Climax band and, with them, made three trips to play at the Ascona Jazz Festival in Switzerland. He also played with Violet Milne's Spirits of Rhythm and, at one point, was playing with them on Sundays between 1.00pm and 4.00pm at the Stair Arms Hotel near Pathhead, before driving into Edinburgh to play with the Climax band, at a venue in Royal Circus, in the evening. In 1991, he replaced Dave Paxton in Bill Salmond's Louisiana Ragtime Band, with whom he played at the Gothenburg Jazz Festival in Germany in 1994. George stayed with this band for about seventeen years, eventually leaving in 2008. Since then, he has mostly played occasional gigs with a variety of bands but still, at the time of writing in 2011, plays regularly with Kenny Milne's Criterion Brass Band.

One of the drummers who played with the Louisiana Ragtime Band was **John Nicolson (drums)**. He was born on 8th September 1953 and was yet another in the long line of Royal High School jazzers, John recalling that was he at school with *'...a scary number of other musos'*. It was at school that he began his career as a drummer, becoming a member of the school pipe band, although, reflecting on this in 2011, he remarked that he had no idea why he had joined, adding *'...it wasn't for the clothes...'*. As far as jazz was concerned, his first drum influence was Joe Morello, the partially blind drummer who made his name with the Dave Brubeck quartet. In spite of this decidedly modern model, John's first Edinburgh jazz gig was with the Louisiana Ragtime Band in 1969, in the Lothian Bar, Lothian Road. This gig was a regular Monday evening spot for the band and John remembers the reward for his weekly contribution as '...ten bob (50p), a pint and a pie'. Other Louisiana gigs were in the Cephas Club, under St George's West Church in Shandwick Place, and an appearance at the Usher Hall, where they played in front of two thousand Girl Guides!

Rapidly establishing his reputation as an able drummer, John soon began to expand his playing activities and it was not long before he started in the more general run of gigs, playing for weddings, dance bands, the infamous miners' clubs and what he describes as 'cocktail stuff' in various Edinburgh hotels. His spell with the Louisiana band was followed by work with the Charlie McNair band, Ken Ramage's band and, in a more modern jazz setting, gigs with the fine sax player, Gordon Cruikshank. In addition, he played with piano player Jimmy Hendry in a swinging trio that included Ronnie Rae on bass, this gig being in what was then the Dragonara Hotel, at Belford Bridge. Further jazz gigs were with the Society Syncopators and the Jazz Advocates, both in their Old Bailey format and their later manifestation, the Scottish Jazz Advocates. It was with this latter band that John made trips to the Sacramento Jazz Jubilee in 1983 and 1984, depping for Chick Murray, and also appearing on the Scottish Jazz Advocates 1984 recording, 'All in Perfect Working Order'[133], on which he plays on two tracks along with Ronnie Rae, who also made the trip, covering for me on bass. In the 1980s, John was a regular in the programme of the Edinburgh International Jazz Festival (see chapter XII), in which he had some great jazz experiences, playing with famous names including reeds man Benny Waters, trombone legend George Chisholm, the great piano player Teddy Wilson, bebop trumpeter Red Rodney and the inimitable Humphrey Lyttelton. He Canada he played with

---

[133] See discography appendix

258

clarinetist Peanuts Hucko and, in Sacramento, played briefly with Bob Haggard, one time bass player with Bob Crosby's Bobcats, famous for his bass and drums feature with Ray Baduk, 'Big Noise from Winnetka'.

Although a highly capable and well-regarded jazz drummer, John had few other chances to record in jazz settings but his versatility enabled him to make many recordings in a wide range of other styles including Country and Western, rock and pop and radio commercials. Having embarked on an acting career in 1975, John also performed in musical theatre with Young Lyceum, Wildcat and 7:84. He later changed his name to **John McGlynn**, for professional purposes, and appeared in a range of TV series including 'Taggart', 'Soldier Soldier', 'Silent Witness' and 'All Creatures Great and Small'. John eventually left Edinburgh, basing himself in the London area, his departure a considerable loss to the Edinburgh jazz scene. After more than twenty five years in the south, he turned up again on a visit to Edinburgh in 2011, when he came along to the Jazz and Jive Club (see chapter XVII). He sat in with my band, the Maid of the Forth Stompers, demonstrating that he had lost none of his ability to swing or his energetic ability to drive a band along.

We have just met someone who moved away from Edinburgh but our next jazzer moved in the opposite direction. **Simon Carlyle (trombone, sousaphone)** was born in Cambridge on 10th September 1945 and moved with his family to Bristol when he was about four years old. He attended Bristol Grammar School before embarking on a six year course in Veterinary Medicine at Cambridge University, followed by a further three years completing a PhD. He then became a lecturer in veterinary pharmacology at the Royal Dick Veterinary College in Edinburgh from 1973 to 2006. His musical activities began when, as Simon puts it, his parents '...*inflicted piano lessons on him...*' at the age of about six. However, he had managed to escape from this to the Sea Mills Junior School Brass Band, when he was in about primary five. Here he became one of two cornet players under the enthusiastic direction and tuition of a Mr Ellison. Later, at Grammar school, he was to find sitting counting innumerable silent bars waiting for the next trumpet entry to be less than stimulating and, after a while, gave up on his budding orchestral career.

However, he was not to be lost to music for long and soon began to listen to some jazz and blues around Bristol, including the Acker Bilk band, in addition to which he also picked up on recorded jazz on the radio. One recording that particularly made an impression was the King Oliver band recording of 'Riverside Blues', which he heard on a history of jazz programme, and he lost little time in purchasing some jazz records of his own. A Chris Barber recording of 'Brownskin Mama' was one of the first, to be followed by EPs[134] featuring Bunk Johnson and Louis Armstrong. Shortly after this, an English teacher at his school started up a school jazz band as an evening club, and Simon, hastily recalling his brass playing skills, joined on cornet. This was clearly a fairly eclectic outfit, as Simon recalls them attempting written arrangements of material ranging from Fats Waller's 'Shortnin' Bread' to Thelonious Monk's 'Blue Monk'. However, it was to be at University where his career in traditional jazz kicked off in earnest.

Someone put up a notice asking for volunteers to form a band for the College's Rag Day float and Simon, discovering that one Dick Wharton was ahead of him with his trumpet, volunteered to get his father to send up an ancient trombone that had been liberated from the Bristol University's lumber room. He has little recall of the Rag Day event, apart from the grief they had to endure from the music shop from which they had hired the tuba. Apparently they were less than delighted about the large number of dents that it had acquired from pennies thrown into it by the crowd. Clearly undaunted by this unfortunate experience, the band decided to continue as the South Side Jazz Band and they struggled on with a late 1920s repertoire that Simon describes as 'both eclectic and

---

[134] It has just occurred to me that some readers made be flummoxed by this term. While 78 rpm records played at 78 rpm and had one track on each side, EPs were 'extended play' records that played at 45 rpm and usually had 4 tracks, 2 on each side. LPs, or long play records, were even more impressive, playing at $33^{1}/_{3}$ rpm and having anything up to 6 or 7 tracks on each side. My English teacher at school, 'Kipper' Heron, was greatly taken by EPs, referring to them enthusiastically as '4 sided records'!'

esoteric', including such immortal gems as 'Barataria', 'Bring it on Home to Grandma' and 'Root Hog, or Die', as well as better known stuff like 'Sobbin' Blues' and 'Diga Diga Doo'. Later, when Dick left, he switched back to cornet and the band did several May Balls and other gigs, during which they warmed up for Lulu, played as support to the Chris Barber band and even spotted a young Prince Charles in the audience at one point.

Simon was eventually the only one left of the University band, his nine years being an unusually lengthy student career, and he began playing gigs with some of the town bands. As all of these were well supplied with trumpet and trombone players, he borrowed a double bass and re-launched his playing career with the Savoy Jazz Band. This does not seem to have gone all that well, as he lasted only the one session. However, a man of considerable tenacity and fortitude, he found that a month's practice '...*increased his mean survival time dramatically...*' and was soon playing quite regularly again. On completion of his PhD, he departed for his lecturing career in Edinburgh.

Simon says that he did not really model his playing on anyone in particular, which is not all that surprising as he would have needed a whole list of models to cover all the instruments he had tried. However, he did listen to a lot of recordings of the early recording bands including those of King Oliver, Armstrong, Jelly Roll Morton, Armand Piron, Fletcher Henderson, Jabbo Smith and many others. When pushed, he selected the great trombonist J C Higginbotham, whose huge sounding, shouting playing was such a wonderful feature of the Luis Russell band of the late 1920s and early 1930s, and believes that he developed his own tendency towards declamatory phrasing from him.

Now in Edinburgh, it was not long before he found his way into the local jazz scene, tracking down a band playing in the upstairs room of a pub on the Royal Mile, which seemed to be run by Mke Hart and included Jim Petrie (tpt) and Jack Weddell (tbn). Simon's first Edinburgh gig was in the famous White Cockade in Rose Street and was a jam session in which he found himself playing trumpet alongside Charlie McNair. This experience persuaded him into beating a hasty and prudent retreat to the trombone and it was on this instrument that he found himself sitting in with Bill Salmond's Louisiana Ragtime Band, at their sessions in the Minto Hotel. What became quite regular sittings in clearly went well and it was not long before he was invited to join the band. This was during one of the LRB's periods when they did not use a trumpeter and Simon was required to play lead on trombone. At first George Duncan played beside him on clarinet and then he was replaced by Dave Paxton. Simon described sitting next to Dave Paxton as a period he looks back to as both a pleasure and a privilege. The band played about twice a week and moved around a number of venues over the next few years. Eventually, Kenny Milne came into the band on trumpet and, after a brief period of experimentation with the expanded front-line, Simon found himself surplus to requirements allowing him, as he says, '...to spend more time with my family...'

The next opening for Simon came when Jim Young assembled his Auld Reekie Parade Band, in which Simon played trombone, but when Kenny Milne started up his Criterion Brass Band, it was time to dust off the old sousaphone he had picked up for next to nothing in Cambridge and had had in the attic ever since. This seems to have been around the time that the French band, L'Orpheon Celeste was making a big impression in the Edinburgh Jazz Festival (which puts it around 1979/80) and Simon believes that it was their example that inspired the the first version of the Diplomats of Jazz. This new four-piece echoed the format of the French band, with Jim Petrie (tpt, vocs), Andy Hampton (clt), Jock Westwater (bjo) and Simon on sousaphone. Rehearsals in Jock's print shop in Juniper Green gave Simon a chance to work out what he should be doing on his brass bass before they launched themselves on the Edinburgh public. Simon spent a couple of years with the Diplomats before being replaced by Bill Brydon. From that point on, his playing became less, except for a couple of years around 2000, when he played with Mike Westwater's Tweed Valley band. Currently, in 2011, his most regular gigs are with the Criterion Brass Band, although he adds wryly that he does occasional depping jobs with other bands, especially if it is an outside gig with a chance of rain.

Arriving from the south, Simon Carlyle had soon established himself on the Edinburgh jazz scene and, although he was really a multi-instrumentalist, it was on the scarce sousaphone that he really made his mark. However, it was on trombone that he played on the LRB's 1976 recording, which has become something of a New Orleans collector's item. He was also on a number of recordings made by the Criterion Brass Band, which will be found in the discography, and on some jazz festival recordings made by the Tweed Valley band. He has also played in other forms of music and has recorded Early Music CDs with the Edinburgh Renaissance Band and, in 2005, played with a klezmer band called She'koyokh, on Czech radio. Happily, in 2011, he is still around and recently filled in for me with the Maid of the Forth Stompers. Soon, I hope to persuade him along to a session or two to sit in, although on which instrument that will be must remain a mystery until he actually turns up.

Chapter X

How to eat Stovies While Singing 'Georgia on my Mind'

Before leaving the 1960s, a look at the career of **Alan Anderson (piano)** will give a very good insight into the Edinburgh jazz world, particularly the University jazz scene, of that time and beyond. It also gives a good indication of the wider jazz context in which Edinburgh traditional jazz existed, both in terms of the more modern forms of the music and geographically, in the neighbouring Border counties. Although Alan himself was to play mostly in the more modern styles, he did play in traditional bands and he was yet another of that versatile, able group of jazzers who were equipped to play in a broad range of styles. Alan was born in Ilfracombe in Devon on 22nd June 1943 but, by the time he was three months old, the family had moved to Scotland. His early schooling was at a variety of junior schools in the south of the country, before he settled in at Berwickshire High School in Duns. From there, he was to advance to Edinburgh University, from which he would eventually graduate with a law degree. Both the Anderson parents were interested in music, Alan's mother playing piano and church organ and his father keen on the dance band music of his era.

Alan can remember hearing jazz on the radio, later realising that this would have been BBC Jazz Club which, in those days, followed the football results on a Saturday afternoon. He had piano lessons between the ages of seven and thirteen, which he loathed, and never sat any exams or got any grade passes. However, his future as a piano player was saved by his 'ear', which enabled him to play some of the pop songs he heard on the radio, and he even started to write some little arrangements in a manuscript book provided by one of his despairing piano teachers. One of these arrangements recently came to light and its date is nicely indicated, the tune being the 'Ballad of Davy Crockett', a song that was an enormous success in the mid-1950s. By then, Alan's reading was good enough for him to attempt some of the simpler classics, as well as ragtime and boogie-woogie pieces popularised by Winnie Atwell. His blossoming talents on the piano came to the notice of his school music teacher who soon had him involved with the school orchestra, an experience from which Alan feels he gained a lot. Later, a school jazz band was formed and, dressed like the Acker Bilk band, they were included in the end of term concert. It looks as if the Border schools were a bit more tolerant of jazz than those in Edinburgh, where so many school jazz activities had rapidly hit the buffers of scholastic disapproval.

At University, Alan went along to the Fresher's Conference where he soon discovered one Roger Craik, sitting behind a desk labelled Rhythm Club. When he discovered that Alan could play piano, Roger invited him to a Fresher's audition at the SRC hall in Chambers Street. He must have done alright because, just a week or two later, he found himself in the same venue at the Fresher's Concert, playing Honky-tonk Train Blues and, as an encore, Bad Penny Blues, accompanied by Roger on drums and Ronnie Dunn on bass. Rather poignantly, Alan reports that, having played his own first gig with Ronnie, they were again playing together nearly fifty years later, on 16th October 2010, the day before Ronnie's sudden and unexpected death at the age of sixty nine.

Then came what Alan calls a 'sudden lurch' in his jazz appreciation when, having only managed to take in shows by Humphrey Lyttelton and the Chris Barber bands while at school, he discovered that the University Rhythm Club was running a bus to Glasgow. Ever the enthusiast, he rapidly made sure he was included, without having much of a clue as to who he was going to hear. It turned out to be a stellar bill featuring the Dizzy Gillespie Quintet, with Lalo Schifrin on piano, and the show was opened by the John Coltrane Quintet, including Eric Dolphy, McCoy Tyner and Elvin Jones. Alan remembers the Coltrane group's playing of My Favourite Things, which lasted for half an hour, with Coltrane's solo accounting for at least half of that!

Back in Edinburgh, he quickly made contact with local jazzers through the Rhythm Club and soon began to pick up gigs with bands run by Jim Baikie and Duncan Lonie, although this was mostly dance work. This type of experience, as it did for many musicians, resulted in him learning a vast repertoire of material in a very short space of time. The norm was to play a lot of medleys and the horn players in these bands, people like saxist Ron Gilbertson and trumpeter Derek Lawton, would simply signal the key of the next tune and Alan would have to follow, whatever the key and whatever the tune. He also played a lot of University gigs and was a frequent sitter-in at local jazz spots. After a year or so, Alan became first choice piano player with Roger Craik's Swing Six, a band which often included Eric Rinaldi (tpt), Jack Graham (rds), Dizzy Jackson (bs) and Roger himself on drums and which made at least one LP recording. He also became involved in the Rhythm Club administration as treasurer and helped book some of the big names including Tubby Hayes, for lunch-time University gigs, when they were in town for other bookings. The Rhythm Club also featured regular record sessions, as well as live presentations.

Late night parties and jam sessions at drummer Sandy Malcolm's flat, at the corner of George Street and Hanover Street, were a feature of this time, with the result that Hanover Street, with good reason, was soon re-christened Hangover Street. There were many clubs featuring jazz in town at this time and among those that Alan visited were: The Roost (Leith Street), The Manhattan Club (Calton Hill), The Place later to become Nicky Tam's and The Gamp Club (both Victoria Street), Rutherford's Bar and Bungy's (both the High Street), the Coda Club, The New Yorker (Shandwick Place), The Athenian later to become The Laughing Duck (Howe Street), The Rainbow Rooms, the Royal Chimes Club and Moby Dick's. One great gig that remains bright in Alan's memory was at the Gamp Club, when Tubby Hayes was backed by Dougie Campbell (gtr), Ronnie Rae (bs) and Billy Alison (drms), all of course Edinburgh jazzers. The Manhattan was the home of Old Bailey's Jazz Advocates, with Archie Sinclair (tbn), Andrew Lauder (tpt), Mike Hart (bjo), Graham Blamire (bs) and Chick Murray (drms) and Alan recalls how the band's sense of humour, particularly that of band leader Archie Sinclair, made these sessions memorable, as well as Andrew Lauder's renowned collection of wild life photographs.

Alan later became secretary of the University Rhythm Club, a post he was to hand over, two years later, to guitarist Charles Alexander. It is clear that, in the 1960s and onwards, University jazz was fairly heavily dominated by the more modern forms of the music, while the rest of Edinburgh jazz remained largely in the hands of the traditionalists. This rather emphasises the point made earlier by Roger Craik, that these sub-divisions of the local jazz scenes tended to operate quite separately, without a lot of mixing. However modern in its leanings or not, guest jazzers who were featured by the Rhythm Club demonstrate a more eclectic choice as they included Ronnie Ross (bari sax), Sandy Brown (clt), Al Fairweather (tpt), Joe Harriott (alto sax) and, would you believe it, The Temperance Seven! Alan himself played quite a bit with a quartet which included, at various time, Johnny Hope (bs gtr), Dave Margaroni (bs), Brooke Coventry (drms) and Ivor Shalovsky (drms). After graduating in 1965, Alan remained in Edinburgh for a time and continued his jazz activities, including much socialising and the late night parties and jam sessions which continued to thrive, often in the company of others interested in contemporary jazz, such as Jack and Tom Finlay and Bobby Stewart. Also around much of the time was Duncan Lonie, then best known as a dance band leader and drummer and now, in 2011, a director of the Edinburgh International Jazz festival, about which we shortly will hear much more. In those days too, Paddy's Bar, run by Paddy Crossan in Rose Street, was the meeting place greatly favoured by the jazz fraternity every Saturday lunch time. Alan reports that, in the mid-2000s and almost fifty years on, Paddy was still around, frequently turning up at Saturday afternoon jazz sessions at 80 Queen Street.

Although Alan Anderson joined his father's legal practice in Coldstream, he continued to spend a lot of his time, especially at weekends, in Edinburgh. However, by about the mid-1070s, a jazz scene began to come together in the Border country, starting with jam sessions in Berwick and Kelso, and Alan, a party and jam session animal if ever there was one, was soon involved. In time, a Borders Big Band was formed and Alan was to dep with them on a number of occasions. There was also a band, which included Francis Cowan on bass as well as Alan, which was called Border Crossing and which played the then fashionable 'crossover' music, combining jazz with rock and also including standards and Latin-based material.

Alan was also to become involved with the jazz promotion organisation Platform and soon set up a Borders branch, which promoted many jazz events over the years, featuring some high class jazz names such as Martin Taylor, Tommy Whittle, Benny Waters, Danny Moss and his wife singer Jeanie Lamb, Joe Temperley, Jimmy Deuchar, Alex Welsh and his Band and Blues Night with Alexis Korner. A Platform jazz weekend at Melrose featured local jazzers, together with the Gateway Jazz Band from Carlisle, accompanying George Chisholm (tbn), and the Dave Shepherd Quartet. Sadly, after putting on their most ambitious project, a concert show-casing the great vibes player Red Norvo with guitarist Tal Farlow and bassist Ronnie Rae, funding became a problem and the Borders Branch of Platform had to be wound up.

Alan Anderson was to make many more contributions to Edinburgh jazz, traditional and modern, over the coming decades, frequently playing at the Edinburgh International Jazz Festival in the 1980s and '90s, playing with the Old Bailey band and with the Wooltown Re-visited Jazz Band, a reincarnation of Hawick's famous Wooltown Jazz Band. His Edinburgh jazz festival gigs also included backing work with a trio including bassist Ronnie Dunn and drummer Ken Mathieson, when he had the opportunity to play with visiting alumni such as Jim Galloway, Roy Williams, Jim Douglas and, from the USA, Benny Waters and Dick Carey.

In the 1990s, after moving to live in North Berwick, he even managed a regular Edinburgh gig at, successively, Preservation Hall in Victoria Street, Morrison's Bar in Morrison Street and Harry's Bar in Randolph Place, with a band put together by drummer Toto McNaughton. This was clearly a good band and included at times Alex Gentleman (ten), Dougie Campbell (gtr), trumpeters Donald Corbett and Colin Steele and bass players Roy Percy and Lindsay Cooper. This band attracted many quality sitters-in, including Tommy Smith and Gordon Cruikshank (both ten sax) and singer Danny Street, the gig eventually coming to an end for Alan around the year 2000.

Later he was to play keyboard with the Royal British Legion Big Band, rehearsing with them at the Lady Haig Poppy factory at Canonmills every week. At the time of writing in 2011, Alan remains with this band, which underwent a couple of name changes, firstly to the slightly less daunting moniker, RBLS Big Band and then to The Sound of Seventeen Big Band. He now serves as its treasurer, and has played with the band at the famous North Sea Jazz Festival at the Hague in 2002 and at the even more prestigious Montreux Jazz Festival the following year, followed by other Festival appearances at Derry and Cork, the Edinburgh International Jazz Festival and on the Fringe. Alan Anderson remains an extremely active jazz musician, playing regularly in Edinburgh at good venues like the Tron Bar, Henry's Jazz Cellar, The Bridge and The Jazz Bar, the latter two run by the fine Edinburgh modern jazz drummer, Bill Kyle, although sadly The Bridge was destroyed by a disastrous fire in 2002. He also plays and arranges in a trio with bass player and vocalist Jimmy Taylor and Bobby Stewart or Dave Swanson on drums. They are called the Mellotones and focus mainly on the music of Mel Torme. With this trio, Alan has played long residencies at the Caledonian Hotel, 80 Queen Street and the Jazz Bar and says that, in 2011, he considers Edinburgh one of the best places in the UK for jazz.

Alan Anderson's jazz career exemplifies an issue which has surfaced again and again as I have been writing this book and which, I have to admit, has now become less clear than it seemed when I started off – just where do the fault lines, if they exist at all, occur in jazz? Musicians like Alan may have a preference for the more modern and contemporary sounds but, looking back at the time of writing, the music they play does not seem to me to be anything like as different from 'traditional jazz', as once seemed the case. Even within what is more clearly the traditional jazz bag, there are so many subdivisions and categories, that it is really much easier to see all of it as a continuum of jazz, in which you just have to find the bit you like best. Perhaps Alan Anderson would feel, like me, that he loves and respects all of jazz but likes some forms of the music more than others. Live and let live seems a reasonable philosophy!

The 1970s started with Edinburgh jazz in good shape. Although the Old Bailey band had disbanded in 1970 and the Pete Martin All Stars had broken up when Pete left town in about 1969, Mike Hart's Society Syncopators, the Climax Jazz Band, the Louisiana Ragtime Band and Charlie McNair's Jazz Band, played on as strongly as ever. Some of the Climax boys were back in town after their various sojourns in London, although that did not include Jake McMahon or Kenny Milne, both of whom unfortunately remained in the south. The Climax band had several residencies in the 1970s including one at the Bruntsfield Links Hotel, run by publican Ian Whyte in Whitehouse Loan, and another at the White Cockade, a long term jazz venue in Rose Street.

Johnnie Harper, who was to join the Charlie McNair band in the early 1970s, and Gerard Dott who was on clarinet at that time, recall that Charlie's band played residencies at quite a few pubs, clubs and hotels in the 1970s. These included The Place, a large establishment on several floors, going down from the top of Victoria Street to the level of the Cowgate far below. The Place had been a mainstay of jazz in the 1960s and later, re-named Nicky Tams, was to become a popular venue for folk music. There was also Bungy's, located in a close off the Royal Mile, run by the Waldman brothers, and another long term jazz venue. The Cephas Club, which functioned as a sort of youth club in the crypt of St George's church in Shandwick Place, was presumably run by the church and sometimes featured jazz. The Gallery Club in Hanover Street was another hang-over from the 1960s, and there was also the Lochewe Hotel and the Festival Tavern in Lothian Road.

Charlie also played in two other pubs and it was at these that I remember Charlie building a very large and devoted following, almost a cult following, particularly amongst the student population. These were the White Cockade in Rose Street and the Yellow Carvel, a pub with a sea-faring theme, situated in Hunter's Square, behind the Tron Church. To drop into one of these sessions when Charlie was in full cry, was a lesson in how to establish a rapport with the crowd, as Charlie exchanged banter and a great deal of almost surreal wit with the punters, bar staff and band.

In the late 1960s and into the 1970s, the McNair band still had Eed Smith on trombone, although he occasionally reverted to banjo for special comedy features such as 'Out of the Dawn There Came a Moonbeam'. There was also a strong rhythm section of Alex Marshall (gtr), Jimmy Luke (bs) and Pete Ritchie (drms), in which the vastly experienced Jimmy Luke would constantly shout instructions to Pete Ritchie about what he should be playing, such as when he should move on to the high hat cymbal and when he should hit a back beat. Pete, placid and long suffering soul that he was, did not seem to mind. By now the Purple Eyes Jazz Noise image, cultivated by Charlie at an earlier point, was in abeyance and the band was becoming again a tight little Dixieland band, kicked along by its excellent rhythm section.

Around this time too, the McNair band took on a regular spot at the Kirkcaldy Jazz Club, which was held in the Rose Bowl in Anthony's Hotel. This was an impressive circular ballroom and the gig became famous for the stovies, which were served free to everyone at the interval. Once, when the stovies were late to appear, Charlie was inspired to offer a demonstration of how to eat a bowl of stovies while singing 'Georgia on my Mind', which he did although none too successfully! It was here too, that Charlie's limerick habit started. An earnest young man approached Charlie one evening and asked if the band ever did any 'Jazz and Poetry', at that time the height of fashion in serious jazz circles. Charlie, equally earnestly, assured him that just

271

such an event was planned for the second half. When the moment came, the band struck up an impressive twelve bar riff and Charlie marched up to the microphone to declaim *'There was a young man from Winnukta.....'!* The bass player, Tim Pharoah, was often with the band on these Kirkcaldy gigs and apparently Tim, too, developed a taste for Limericks, he and Charlie often spending the journey home swapping their favourites.

By the time the McNair band were established in their residencies at the Yellow Carvel and the White Cockade, the band had Charlie (tpt), Gerard Dott (clt), George Howden (tbn), Johnnie Harper (bjo), Colin Archbold (bs gtr) and Pete Ritchie (drms).   Johnnie Harper had replaced Jock Westwater who had himself replaced Alec Marshall, after the latter went off to London to become a band manager/impresario.   Gerard remembers this as a particularly good period for the McNair band and believes that the healthy following built up amongst students and young people in general, may have owed something to George Howden's involvement with the rock group, Mama Flyer. In addition, the band's repertoire at that time included several numbers with a rock flavour, including 'Revival' and the Beatles song, 'Norwegian Wood'. A particularly popular feature of the White Cockade sessions were Charlie's regular slanging matches with the formidable female publican, who had an awesome command of invective. She was the redoubtable Jean Ferguson, whom Charlie routinely referred to as *'our resident madam'!*

I remember once depping with Charlie's band in the Yellow Carvel and being faced with a request from a punter for 'Big Noise from Winetka'. This tune is a feature for bass and drums only and was made famous by its creators, Bob Haggart and Ray Bauduc of the 'Bob Crosby Bobcats'. Charlie knew I had sometimes played the tune with the Old Bailey band and suggested I played it with his drummer, Pete Ritchie. Pete indicated that he was only vaguely familiar with the tune but off we went nonetheless. I should have known better. 'Big Noise' is usually started by the drummer playing a sort of sprightly rattle on the rim of a drum. Unfortunately Pete brought it in at a tempo that would have been suitable for a fairly melancholy blues. It was my fault, I should have set the tempo for Pete and our rendering of the tune (that is rendering as in 'to tear apart') was a total disaster. The tune never got off the ground and was greeted with a stony silence by the punters. Charlie offered comfort by suggesting that the world was not yet sufficiently artistically advanced for such a novel and musically challenging departure from tradition. He asked for a round of applause for our courage and, of course, being Charlie, got it.

Alastair Clark, in an article in the 'Scotsman' in 1972[135] said of the McNair band *'The band are* (sic) *tough, rumbustious, versatile – capable of leapfrogging the years from trad to groovy, riff-borne rock-and-soul without apparently causing any bewilderment among the audience or themselves. They're at their best in a throbbing version of Herbie Hancock's "Blind Man" which takes them well out of the traditional bag'.* He went on to comment on Charlie himself saying *'Charlie McNair, on trumpet, typifies the eclecticism of the band, blowing in a breezy hotch-potch of styles that somehow manages to accommodate comfortably New Orleans, Dixieland, main-stream, bop and Blood Sweat and Tears. His singing covers an equally broad area, from Big Bill Broonzy to Frank Sinatra. It all hangs together'.* The photo accompanying this article shows Charlie's band of the time, with Jack Graham (clt), Charlie, George Howden (tbn) and Johnny Phillips (bs gtr), all in action in the Yellow Carvel.

During the 1970s, Charlie made many changes to the line-up of his band. He snapped up Johnnie Harper and Chick Murray when they became available and there were many other changes, which are too many to chronicle accurately. Johnnie Harper remembers the main changes and compiled the following list, noting that some of the musicians left the band for a while but made a comeback at a later date:

Trumpet: Charlie McNair

---

[135] Clark A, 'Trad crosses the sound barrier', 'The Scotsman', September 1972

Reeds:	Gerard Dott, Jack Graham, someone called Stewart who had 'big hair'!, George Duncan, Sandy Brown
Trombone:	George Howden, Ian 'Olly' McAulay, Bill Munro, John Arthur
Banjo:	Jock Westwater, Johnnie Harper, Harald Vox
Bass:	Jimmy Luke, Johnnie Harper (on bass guitar), Norrie Bell, Tim Pharoah, Colin Archbold
Drums:	Pete Ritchie, Chick Murray, Tom 'Toto' McNaughton

Around 1971, Charlie began featuring a solo guitarist in the band and took on in turn Johnnie Fitzsimmons, Ally Dawson, Mike Harper and Johnnie Phillips. The solo guitar was dropped at the end of the seventies. Another innovation was the use of bass guitar instead of the more traditional double bass. A surprising name in the above list is that of Sandy Brown. Sandy had returned to the Edinburgh area for a while in the early seventies, while he was establishing a business base in South Queensferry, and played with the McNair band whenever he could.

A regular in the McNair band towards the end of the 1960s and into the early 1970s was **George Howden (trombone)**, who was born in Edinburgh in 1948. George had learned to play trombone with the Salvation Army when he was about 12 years old. Whilst at school, he played with the Leith Silver band, his school orchestra and the Edinburgh Youth Orchestra. In the mid-1960s, George formed his own band before, in the late 1960s, joining the Pete Martin All Stars, the young and progressive Edinburgh mainstream band. Next came his years in the Charlie McNair band, George crediting Charlie with being a big influence on his subsequent career in jazz. Towards the end of the decade, he also joined the jazz/rock band, Mama Flyer.

Charlie McNair's Jazz Band
L-R Harald Vox, Bill Munro, Toto McNaughton, Colin
Archbold, George Duncan, Charlie McNair
(from the collection of Harald Vox, photographer
unknown)

In 1974, he left Edinburgh for the bright lights of London where he again formed a band of his own, Howden's Hotshots, with the help of his great friend and former colleague in the McNair band, the guitar player Alex Marshall. The Hotshots played at venues all over the UK and on one occasion, supported the Alex Welsh band at the 100 Club in Oxford Street. A regular gig was at the Kensington Hilton where, over a seven year period, George played with many famous jazzers including Stan Greig and Mike Cotton. Later in the mid-1970s George and his band put in a couple of months playing at a venue in Cadaques, Spain and, during this run, they were invited to play for the surrealist painter Salvador Dali and his wife. They also found time to record a single of 'Ice Cream' and to record some jazz sessions for BBC Radio 2. During his years based in the south, George played and recorded with many of the best known British jazzers of the day including Alan Elsdon, Tony Pitt, Brian Lemon, Keith Smith, Laurie Chescoe, Al Gay, Jim Douglas and, not long before he died, Edinburgh's Alex Welsh. It was to be all of 35 years and

2009 before George Howden returned to Scotland, when he and his wife based themselves in the Scottish Borders. Happily, this enabled him to make the 50 mile journey to Edinburgh for gigs and he was soon back in action in the Edinburgh jazz scene as if he had never been away.

Another who was to be long-term stalwart of the Charlie McNair band was **Colin Archbold (bs gtr)**, who joined the band after an extensive career in rock music. Colin was born on 14th November 1944 and educated at the Edinburgh Academy and his first job on leaving school was to train as a window dresser with St Cuthbert's Co-operative Store in Bread Street. He started his musical career as a bass guitarist with a band called the Sabres, for whom he auditioned successfully in 1961, and with them he toured US army bases all over Scotland and played the Star Club in Germany, as well as gaining a considerable local reputation. 1965 saw him a member of the Roadsters and, by 1968 he had made a move into jazz oriented music, playing in Hamish McGregor's Memphis Road Show. More time in rock music followed with Brody, a band which was on the verge of signing up to an important recording contract which sadly fizzled out at the last moment. Time with other rock groups, including Gasoline Alez and Chaktra, followed before he joined the McNair band in the early 1970s, a band with which he would remain for nearly thirty years. Colin Archbold was a man with a considerable zest for life and, in addition to his musical activities, he ran a building firm, had an enormous enthusiasm for fast cars and was a extremely enthusiastic cricketer, turning out for the Woodcutter's Club, who played at Bangholm Sports Ground, near Goldenacre.

Particularly memorable was Colin's ready ability to play up to the inventive wit and general anarchy that flowed from the irrepressible Charlie McNair and it was no surprise that his stint with the McNair band was to be a long one. He was to share in many of the best years of the McNair band's lengthy service in Edinburgh jazz, including the years when Charlie flirted with a rock influence and became something of an Icon of Anarchy for the Student population. Unfortunately, by 2001, Colin Archbold was experiencing serious health problems which brought an end to his playing and, on 4th June 2005, he died in Edinburgh at the early age of just sixty. His obituary by Alasdair Steven appeared in the Scotsman of 10th August 2005[136].

A new but short-lived band started up in the early 1970s, with Fraser Gauld (tpt), Gerard Dott (clt), Paul Munro (tbn), Jock Westwater (Bjo), Iain Forde (drms) and me on bass. Paul Munro's wife, Jacqui, sang with the band which, like Charlie McNair's band, had a residency in the White Cockade in Rose Street. The band adopted the name of **The Granton Jass Works**, a name which makes me cringe to this day. Iain Forde recalls that this band later 'morphed' into a slightly different form, with Donald Macdonald, now playing sax, and Ovin Helseth (bs) coming in. Iain also reports that they practiced in Donald Macdonald's house behind a wall of instrument cases, as a defence against Donald's Dalmatian dog, which had developed a strong desire to eat Jock Westwater!

Jock Westwater (banjo), a member at times of both the McNair band and the 'Granton Jass Works', had been around the scene for a number of years. Jock was born in Edinburgh in 1949 and educated at Daniel Stewart's College. He was lucky enough to have an uncle who was a regular at the West End Cafe and Jock developed an interest in jazz through listening to his uncle's collection of 78 rpm records. His interest in playing banjo came a bit later, after he got out into the local scene and heard the local bands, in particular, the playing of Mike Hart. Jock claims to have been bullied into *'bashing out chords'* for his brother Mike, when he took up clarinet in 1962, although I find it hard to believe that Jock was ever being bullied into anything by anyone!. He had played with a succession of bands in the 1960s, including some involving his brother, and a variety of small combos led by the trombonist, Ken Ramage. Jock also had a spell with the long established Climax band on his CV.

One of the bands, involving his brother and clarinettist George Duncan, was given the name **Jock Strap and his Two Swingers**, another was the **Bash Street Kids** and yet

---

[136] Steven A, 'Colin Archbold', The Scotsman, 10th August 2005, by permission of Alasdair Steven

another was the only jazz band whose name began with an apostrophe, the **....'king Great Band**. There seems to me to be a common thread running through this sequence of band names and it makes me strongly suspect that Jock Westwater was responsible for the 'Granton Jass Works' moniker as well. Jock also played with a band called **The Great Northern Jook Band**. This was a jug and washboard band that played 1920s jug and country blues material and songs associated with Jim Kweskin, the American jug band leader. In the later 1970s, Jock again played with a fair number of bands including the **Jack Graham Jazz Band**, the **Criterion Jazz Band** led by drummer Kenny Milne and **Jim Petrie's Jazz Band**. All of these bands had comparatively short lives but the association with Jim Petrie was to lead to the formation of a top class and long lasting band, the **Diplomats of Jazz**, some years later in the 1980s. The 1980s would also bring Jock the opportunity to play in two very good bands put together by two returned Edinburgh veterans - Al Fairweather and Dave Keir, but the story of these bands is for a later chapter. Jock Westwater was a man of many bands. Why he moved about so much I do not know but it seemed to suit him. His expertise on the banjo and his experience of so many bands, gave him a huge repertoire of material which made him a particularly versatile and able player to have as a dep.

After a year or two in the early 1970s away playing on the boats, the trombonist, Ken Ramage returned to the Edinburgh jazz scene and it was not long before he was back in action. A band had been put together by a piano player called Ian Scott, which he called the **Festival City Jazz Band**. Ken Ramage not only joined this band but 'fronted' it - that is led the band on the bandstand. The full line-up of the band was Charlie Malley (tpt), Jimmy Shortreed (clt and alto), Ken Ramage (tbn), Colin Warwick (bjo), Kenny Burns (bs) and Russ Cessford (drms). This band commenced on a very successful and well supported residency at the Barnton Hotel. Ken Ramage stayed with the band for the next eight and half years and then his trombone playing came to an unfortunate and sudden stop. It was understandably a sad and traumatic business for

Ken, so much so that he can recall in detail exactly what happened. He had been having increasing dental problems for some time and, on Easter Sunday 1983, while playing 'Tishomingo Blues' in the Barnton Hotel, his teeth gave way altogether, and that was the end of his trombone career. He was obviously distressed by this and his accomplished playing was a sad loss to the Edinburgh scene. However, he had another string to his bow and, in time, he was able to develop this and, some years later after a spell living in the USA, he was able to return to active playing in Edinburgh as a drummer.

The Festival City Jazz Band had meanwhile moved to a new residency in the Crest Hotel on the Queensferry Road, near Blackhall. They also, for some reason, changed their name and became the **Capital Jazz Band**, although this was often given as the **Capital City Jazz Band**. It seems likely that the name change came about when the band leader, Ian Scott, dropped out of the band. Ken Ramage had continued to play and front the band but, after he was forced to stop playing, Graham Robertson came in on trombone and Kenny Burns, the bass player, took over running the band. Others who played with the 'Capital Jazz Band' around this time included a top class **reeds player, Jock Graham** who was from Fife. Jock Graham was a vastly experienced player who not only played all the reed instruments but was also an accomplished flute and violin player, and he had played for years with the big band led by Fife's famous band leader and arranger, Tommy Sampson. Jock Graham's son, Dave Graham, also played piano with the Capital band for a while and a very good former professional jazz drummer, Billy Law, came in on drums. This was another successful and well supported gig and there were often other Edinburgh jazzers dropping in for a sit-in with the band.

The **banjo player Colin Warwick**, who played with both the Festval City and Capital Jazz Bands, was a late starter in jazz. Colin was born in Edinburgh on 20th July 1942 and attended Bruntsfield Primary and Boroughmuir Senior Secondary Schools. He went on to have a long career with the Royal (Dick) School of Veterinary Education, where he was on the technical staff, providing a photographic and graphic service. On his retirement in 2005, he was awarded an MBE for services to veterinary education and, in 2011, was continuing his involvement with the 'Dick Vet', now as an Honorary Fellow of the University of Edinburgh, working on veterinary history. Colin's first exposure to jazz came about through hearing LP recordings of the Stan Kenton band, back in the 1950s. This was followed by his first purchase of a 78 rpm record when, as he puts it *'...not knowing any better, I bought 'Truckin'' by the showman and drummer, Eric Delaney'.* Happily he seems to have soon recovered from this unpromising start and went along to hear the Ken Colyer band at the Tollcross Central Hall in early 1954, when the band still included Chris Barber and Lonnie Donegan, a session which also included some skiffle music. Later, at the same venue, he was to hear the Mick Mulligan band with singer George Melly. Now well and truly hooked on traditional jazz and with the Trad Boom in full swing, Colin soon found his way to the various Jazz Band Balls held at the Fountainbridge Palais where, as well as the local jazz bands, he heard the bands of Sandy Brown, Terry Lightfoot and Acker Bilk. Another source of memorable jazz experiences was the Usher Hall, where he heard George Lewis, Big Bill Broonzy, Earl Hines, Oscar Peterson and Sister Rosetta Tharpe, who was touring with the Chris Barber band.

At that time, Colin had never imagined that he would actually play in a jazz band but eventually, he purchased a second hand zither banjo, disposed of the unwanted fifth string and learned a few chords. Soon he was playing at impromptu sessions in his flat in East Preston Street, sessions which included friends and work colleagues with an interest in music. It was through one of these that Colin met the banjo player Jock Westwater who, as Colin remembers it, was playing at the time with Jim Petrie's Quartet. By then getting more and more into his playing, Colin spotted a newspaper advert for a 'Bacon and Day' 1930 vintage banjo and bought it for the princely sum of £25. In spite of his scant experience of playing, it was not long before he landed his first gig which was in 1970 with the Climax Jazz Band, in the Haymarket Station Bar. Colin remembers the line-up of this edition of the Climax band as

Jim Petrie (tpt), Jack Weddell (tbn), George Gilmour (clt), Jim Young (bs) and firstly Iain Forde then John Nicholson (drms), with Colin himself on banjo. He then became a member of the Ken Ramage Jazz Advocates, which was resident in the White Cockade pub in Rose Street. The line-up of this band when Colin became a member, was Jim Petrie (tpt), Ken Ramage (tbn), Hamish McGregor (rds), Colin Warwick (bjo), Jimmy Luke then Norrie Bell (bs) and Donald 'Chick' Murray (drms). As Colin remembers it, Ken Ramage led this band during the period around late summer and autumn 1971, which was probably squeezed in between Ken's various spells away playing on the transatlantic liners.

When his spell with the Ken Ramage band came to an end, Colin joined the newly formed West End Jazz Band, of which we will hear more later, and was with them at their resident spot in the Ailsa Craig Hotel in Royal Terrace. The line-up of the band at this time was Alec McIntosh (tpt), Angus Macdonald (tbn), Eddie Hamilton (clt), Tom Bryce (pno and ldr), Colin Warwick (bjo), Charlie McCourt (bs) and Roy Dunnett (drms). During his spell with the West End band came the move, in 1978, to the band with which Colin was to spend many years: the Festival City Jazz Band, later to be re-named the Capital Jazz Band. This band played in the Dixieland style and was resident at the Barnton Hotel, on the outskirts of town on the Queensferry Road and had an experienced line-up, with Charlie Malley (tpt), Ken Ramage (tbn), Jimmy Shortreed (rds), Ian Scott (pno), Colin on banjo, Ken Burns (bs gtr) and Russ Cessford (drms). This was a very well supported gig and the band regularly played to packed houses each Sunday afternoon. In 1982, after a personnel shuffle, the band, as we have heard, changed its name to the Capital Jazz Band. By that time, Graeme Robertson had replaced Ken Ramage, the excellent Jock Graham had arrived from Fife to play reeds, George Cavaye had taken over on piano, Ken Burns had added a tuba to his armoury and the fine drummer, Billy Law, had joined the band. In 1986, the band made their move to the Crest Hotel, further into town along the Queensferry Road, where they continued to draw good crowds. In addition to his banjo playing, Colin sometimes regaled the crowd with a vocal or two, sometimes 'Hello Central Give Me Dr Jazz' and sometimes a harmony version of 'Dapper Dan', in partnership with bass player Ken Burns.

I always felt that one of the reasons for the success of both the Barnton and the Crest Hotel sessions, lay in the policy of the band to welcome other jazzers and invite them to sit in. Often a pianist such as Danny Dorrian or George Bartleman would play during the band's break and, in the second half, great variety and interest would be added by some high class guests. These often included players of the calibre of Jack Duff (rds), Al Fairweather (tpt), Johnny McGuff (tbn), Ralph Laing and Stan Greig (pno) and, a future major star of more modern forms of jazz, the young Tommy Smith (ten). In addition to these distinguished names, even I sat in once or twice, the band's tolerance sufficient to allow one of my vocal efforts. They also welcomed proper singers and these included Blanche Calloway, the daughter of the famous American band leader and singer Cab Calloway, Jean Mundell, Liz McEwan, the blues singer Tam White and the indefatigable Jacky MacFarlane, now quite advanced in years but still teetotal and still travelling everywhere by bus.

Colin Warwick also played briefly with Angus Macdonald's Deep South band, John Arthur's Dr McJazz and the Dave Keir Quartet and depped with most of the Edinburgh jazz bands at one time or another. I remember an occasion in the 1990s when Colin depped on the Cruise boat, the Maid of the Forth and, when I arrived, it was to find him displaying a hither too unknown talent, playing bagpipes for the punters on the Hawes Pier! He counts amongst his best jazz memories playing with the Festival City band in support of George Chisholm with Keith Smith's Hefty Jazz at an evening session at the Barnton Hotel in 1986 and a number of gigs in far-flung parts of the country such as Dumfries, Bute, Peebles and Kintore. There was also a blustery weekend in 1989 at the Cork Jazz Festival with a band improbably called the BP Old Boilers, courtesy of trumpeter Charlie Malley who worked in the oil industry.

The advent of the Edinburgh International Jazz Festival in 1979 was to bring him many more gigs and the chance to play with top class visitors like Roy Williams (tbn) and the reeds men, John Barnes and Jim Galloway. It also brought him, like the rest of us, priceless opportunities to hear and sometimes to meet, some of the great names of jazz, in Colin's case including Sandy Brown, Benny Waters, Teddy Wilson, Dick Hyman, Stephane Grappelli and many more. His regrets include never hearing Louis Armstrong live, missing out on the Edinburgh jazz scene of the 1950s when some of the big names were still around and being unaware of the Stud Club when it was in St Peter's Buildings, just down the road from his parent's house. Colin Warwick stopped playing in 1996 after a local jazz career of twenty six years but still has his banjo. Who knows, we may not yet have seen and heard the last of a late starting but enthusiastic and popular jazzer.

We have already met the **trombone and bass player Graeme Robertson** back in chapter VII, when we heard that his interest in jazz had begun, when still at school, in the company of drummer Kenny Milne and clarinet player, Karl Ekeval. Graeme was born in the Granton area of Edinburgh on 26th November 1935 and attended Wardie Primary School and Broughton High School. He did his National Service in the RAF between 1954 and 1956, based at Uxbridge in North West London. Continuing to live in the London area after NS and now married, he undertook a course at Houndslow Teacher Training College, Middlesex, in 1956/57 before embarking on a varied career which included spells as an engineer, an insurance agent, a door to door salesman and a shop assistant in a legal forms firm. On his return to Edinburgh in 1961, he worked with the Ministry of Power and as a taxi driver. As a youngster, he had been interested in the radio and books and, the youngest of six, discovered an interest in music through listening to records, mostly of Swing music, which were brought home by his brothers on pay day.

His interest in music now awakened and his listening having expanded to take in Louis Armstrong's Hot Five, on which he heard the playing of trombonist Kid Ory, he proceeded to teach himself to play trombone. With Kenny Milne and Karl Ekeval, Graeme had started playing in a school boy jazz band, although it had a somewhat unorthodox line-up at first, including Karl Ekeval on accordion and Graeme himself on kazoo. His first public playing experience came while he was in the RAF, where he was fortunate enough to fall in with one Jack Potts, a multi-instrumentalist from Newcastle whose main instrument was cornet, who taught him a lot about jazz. Graeme later attended the famous Parker's Brass Studio in London, where he honed his developing playing skills. Early gigs included a regular spot in the Queen's Arms, Uxbridge and, after he had completed his spell in the RAF, with a band called the Apex Jazz Band at a club run by the band itself, in Penge, in South London. This band was attached to an agent who arranged gigs for the band in the Ken Colyer Club and other venues in London. Graeme's first professional work was with the Mike Peters Jazz Band in 1959 and, when he returned to Edinburgh in 1961, his replacement with the Peters band was none other than Roy Williams, later to make a great name of himself with the Alex Welsh and Humphrey Lyttelton bands and to become recognised as one of the finest trombonists in jazz.

Graeme lists his jazz and trombone influences as Kid Ory in the early days, followed by Jack Teagarden, then on to the modern playing of Charlie Parker and two of the giants of modern jazz trombone, J J Johnson and Kai Winding. However, a man with a broad appreciation of jazz, he told me his listening taste was very wide and he considers that his own playing, in the end, was *influenced by just about everybody*. Certainly, after I became aware of Graeme's playing in the early 1960s, it was clear that he had already abandoned the New Orleans tradition and was already firmly in the mainstream of jazz. In fact, his playing always struck me as cool in style, with a thoughtful, musicianly approach. He was to further expand his musical knowledge, as time went on, taking a course in trombone at Napier College of Music, from which he graduated in 1975 with a diploma in both playing and teaching. He also became interested in writing and arranging music and this was to play a larger and larger part of his musical activities.

Graeme's return to Edinburgh saw him, in 1962, form a band under his own leadership, a band to which he gave the unlikely name of **Sam Pig and his Trotters**. Besides Graeme on trombone, the line-up included Al Clark (tpt), old school pal Karl Ekeval (clt), Frank Gifford (bjo) and Sandy Malcolm (drms). His next move came about through fairly unusual circumstances, involving a sudden and unplanned switch of instrument. Graeme had been at an 'after gig' party one night, a party which was also attended by some of members of the recently formed Old Bailey and his Jazz Advocates. At some point the Old Bailey bass player departed, leaving his bass to be collected the next day. Graeme, who had 'fooled about' on someone's bass when he was very young, picked up the bass and played as best he could in a jam session with some of the remaining Old Bailey crowd. To his astonishment, this led to a visit a day or two later from Archie Sinclair and Mike Hart, who invited him to join OB on a regular basis! Nothing loath, he bought himself a bass, fixed up some help from bass player Ian Brown, accepted the invitation and found himself a member of what was fast becoming Edinburgh's busiest jazz band, doubling his future potential for gigs into the bargain.

In the mid-1960s, Graeme joined the Charlie McNair band before, as he put it, *'going commercial'*. By this, he meant moving out into the wider gig world and taking on work with various dance bands, including that of Jimmy Mitchell in the Cavendish Ballroom and work in Tiffany's, a night club with cabaret, which was part of the Mecca empire. He also put in almost ten years playing in the band at the Plaza, a famous Edinburgh dance hall. He clearly built a successful career in this more commercial world, mostly playing bass. Answering an advertisement in the Melody Maker led to six months in the Gulf Hotel in Bahrain, and other work included a cruise on a P & O liner and a summer season with Jack Duff in Jersey. He also picked up commercial gigs recording radio jingles for Radio Edinburgh and other work involving composing and arranging music. The late 1960s and early 1970s saw him move into the field of folk music, when he played and recorded, again on bass, with such groups as The Cairn, The Islanders, The Humble Bums and Bread, Love and Dreams.

Other regular work included playing in Working Men's Clubs, a setting renowned as a fertile source of muso's anecdotes and Graeme Robertson was no exception. He told me of gig at one of these clubs when the evening was begun by the resident Social Convenor who, after much tapping and blowing into the microphone to make sure it was working, set the tone for the evening's entertainment. *'As some o' youse a'ready ken, last week saw the sad death of auld Wullie, a regular attender o'the Club for many years, who always sat in that chair over there. We will now have a minute's silence in memory of auld Wullie'.* There followed a respectful silence until the Social Convenor felt time was up: *'Now, movin' on tae a more serious subject, it has came to the Committee's attention that some o' youse are pissin' on the back wall o' the car park.........'.*

Graeme's trombone and jazz playing was not neglected over the years either and included jazz gigs with Jack Duff and bass player Lindsay Cooper, work with the Finlay-Gentleman Quintet and playing time with a rehearsal band that played weekly sessions in Nicky Tams, formerly known as the 1960s jazz spot, The Place. He would also become a member of the Capital Jazz Band, taking over the trombone chair from Ken Ramage and playing and singing with the band for many years, when they were resident in the Esso Hotel, on the Queensferry Road. The years 1972 to 1980 saw him heavily involved as an instrumental teacher with the Education Dept of Edinburgh City Council and this led to the formation of several youth bands, playing in the Swing style, including, in the early 1980s, the first youth band to be featured at the Edinburgh International Jazz Festival. There were also appearances for the youth band at the King's Theatre, with the Gang Show. The mid-1980s saw him become a member of Hamish McGregor's fledgling Fat Sam's Band, in which Graeme's son Nick, another talented musician, was also to appear, as vocalist. With Fat Sam's Band, Graeme played at jazz festivals in Cork, Lille, Bruges and Sacramento, further expanding his impressive and varied CV. He made a number of jazz recordings with the Fat Sam and Capital bands, which will be found in the discography appendix.

Graeme Robertson was one of the most versatile and busy jazzers throughout his long career as both trombonist and bass player in Edinburgh jazz, before finally bringing his active gig playing to a halt around 2003. At the time of writing in 2011, he and his wife are living in retirement in Bo'ness in West Lothian, while Graeme keeps up his musical interest by running a rehearsal band in the Corstorphine area of Edinburgh, for which he writes, arranges and directs. A serious and hard-working musician, Graeme Robertson brought to Edinburgh jazz a trombone style that was outwith the usual traditional jazz style and, as a teacher, he leaves a legacy of well-tutored young musicians who will help keep up Edinburgh's strong reputation as a musical centre well into the 21st Century.

Billy Law (drums) was born in Edinburgh on 1st August 1940, educated at Sciennes and Darroch schools and began pipe band drumming in the Boys Brigade when he was twelve years old. An avid listener to radio and records, Billy soon developed an interest in jazz, although he recalls that there was very little jazz on the radio in the early 1950s. He began going along to the Condon Club in India Buildings almost every Sunday evening and it was there that he heard the Alex Welsh band for the first time. Now competent on a drum kit, Billy began playing jazz and dance music with like-minded, local youngsters in the mid-1950s, although he did not become a member of a jazz band until later. The guitarist Jim Baikie gave him his start in playing with good musicians around 1957 and he remembers these times as being surrounded by people who helped him make progress. In 1960, the trombone player Ken Ramage recommended Billy to a Danish band, the Jazz Cardinals, and he started his career as a professional jazz drummer with them, touring in West Berlin, Denmark and Sweden. After returning to Scotland, he became a member of the Clyde Valley Stompers, then under the leadership of clarinettist Pete Kerr. He stayed on with Pete Kerr, when the clarinettist returned to Scotland after his spell leading the Stompers, and became a member of his new band, Pete Kerr's All Stars. With this band, in the early 1960s, Billy made two extended play records at the Waverley Studios in Edinburgh. In March 1964, he joined the band of another clarinet player, Terry Lightfoot, and in the same year, played with blues singer Long John Baldry. He was also to play with the jazz bands of Bob Wallis, Max Collie and Charlie Galbraith, Billy recalling that it was all very

287

enjoyable but work was scarce. He did, however, manage to buy a houseboat, in which he lived at the famous Eel Pie Island on the Thames.

A short period co-leading a band with a star of the future, the famous rock singer Rod Stewart, was followed by him joining Alec Harvey's Big Soul Band in 1965. Apparently, time with this band was extremely entertaining, the chief mirth-maker being one Bob Nimmo, who is said to have almost made Billy ill with laughter. This was followed by a spell gigging with bands such as pianist Lennie Felix's trio, Colin Smith's Sextet and the Alex Welsh Band. Billy greatly admired the Welsh band, especially its drummer Lennie Hastings, who was his favourite drummer in the Dixieland idiom. He then became a member of another fine band, the band led by trumpeter Alan Elsdon. Although the Alex Welsh band was the usual choice to back visiting American jazzers, the Elsdon band got a look in too. Billy missed their tour with trumpeter Wingy Manone but was with them for a tour with clarinettist Albert Nicholas. Unfortunately, this was an unhappy tour but the next was clearly a knock out.

The guest this time was none other than Ed Hall, one of the greatest of jazz clarinettists, who in his time had played in the clubs owned by gangsters, put in five years with the Louis Armstrong All Stars without a single rehearsal, and who, in Billy's words *'had seen it all'*. For the three weeks of the tour, Billy had the pleasure of driving a car with Ed Hall sitting beside him and listening to all Ed's stories. The whole Elsdon band loved Ed for his kindness and generosity to all of them and he once called Billy *'a Goddamn life saver'*, when the drummer saved a particularly messy ending. An especially appreciated habit of Ed Hall's was always to make a point of praising the band to the audience. Although the band was not aware of it at the time, they were recorded at one of the concerts with Ed Hall and two CDs were issued. This had been a happy time for the Alan Elsdon band, which was in good form and feeling refreshed. Billy considers that the CDs are a great reminder of that good time and, in his words, are *'not too bad'*, although like all jazzers he *'would like a re-take'!*

After leaving the Elsdon band in 1969, Billy returned to Edinburgh, where he played for a number of years in the pit band at the King's Theatre. In addition, he played many gigs with Edinburgh jazz and dance bands, including the spell with the Capital Jazz Band described above, and he took part in a Clyde Valley Stompers re-union tour in 1982. In the 1980s and 1990s, Billy was to play with bands organised by Al Fairweather and Ralph Laing, after these two veterans had returned to Scotland. Billy's father, Willie Law, was a 'weel kent' face around the Edinburgh jazz scene for many years, always welcome when he made one of his regular appearances at jazz gigs all round the town, a loyal supporter of the local bands and not only those in which his son was playing. Writing this in 2011, it is sad to relate that Billy Law has not played for many years, a loss to the Edinburgh jazz scene of one of its best ever drummers.

Another with several bands to his name was **Hamish McGregor (reeds, trombone, Hammond organ, vocals)**, who was born in 1946 and educated at Merchiston Castle School. He had developed an interest in traditional jazz, which was at the height of its 'Trad Boom' popularity at the time, while still at school. As a school boy, Hamish was already getting bands together to make recordings and getting to know the local Edinburgh jazz scene. It was soon clear that he was an enterprising and determined individual with a flair for presentation and there was little doubt that he would go on to be a successful band leader and a major force in the local scene. He came from a musical family and had started out playing clarinet, with trombone as his second instrument. There are some privately made recordings of a band put together for the recording session and featuring his trombone playing and singing. Hamish recruited a trumpet player from Dunfermline, Tommy Lister, together with Jack Graham (clt), Johnnie Harper (bjo), me (bs) and Charlie Welch, the Old Bailey drummer, for this recording session. The recording, it has to be said, is very much of its time, most of the material being the sort of novelty tunes associated with the 'Trad Boom' years. Hamish seemed to give up trombone after this and concentrated on clarinet although, in time, he played all the various saxes, tending to favour the alto sax.

After his year with the Old Bailey band, of which we have already heard, Hamish had led several bands of his own in the later 1960s, each lasting about two years, including a band he called **Hamish McGregor and his Clansmen**, which played in the style of the famous Alex Welsh Band. This band included trumpet player Tommy Lister, Dave Margaroni on trombone and the excellent Jack Finlay on piano. The Clansmen band was followed by what Hamish describes as a ten piece soul band, the **Memphis Road Show**, which included Tommy Lister plus Pete Martin on trumpets and bringing in a high class tenor saxophonist, Gordon Cruikshank. In turn, this was followed by a band called **Seven Up** which Hamish put together in 1969, just about the time the Old Bailey band broke up. This enabled him to recruit Andrew Lauder, Dave Margaroni, Johnnie Harper and Chick Murray from the Old Bailey band along with Johnnie Harper's brother, Mike, on solo guitar. In spite of the past histories of the musicians involved, the band played as an R and B combo, rather than as a traditional jazz band. This band broke up in 1971 and, for a few years, Hamish ran a series of combos featuring many of the above jazzers and, sometimes, Hamish on the Hammond organ.

In 1975, Hamish McGregor, now resident in South Queensferry, assembled a band to play a residency in the Forth Bridge Hotel in the village. The band he finally assembled included Andrew Lauder (tpt), Johnnie Harper (bjo and gtr), Chick Murray (drms) and me on bass. This band, it was clear, was going to have a strong flavour of the Old Bailey band as it had been when Archie Sinclair died. In addition, Hamish had signed up Sam Smith, a newcomer to the Edinburgh scene, to play trombone. **Sam Smith (trombone, vocals)**, whose full name, we discovered later, was actually Alastair Salmond-Smith, had been born in Edinburgh on the 15th of September 1940. He had been born with a kyphosis of the spine, an abnormality that had resulted in a hunched posture and short stature. He had started playing trombone when at the Royal College of Art in London, where he became a graphic designer, and his first band, while still at college, had been Colin Whale's Jazz Band. He had played with Dick Charlesworth and his City

Gents when he was about twenty five and many other bands, before making his way to Cumbria where he gigged with the well known Mick Potts Jazz Band around Carlisle. Eventually he had returned to Edinburgh, where Hamish got to hear of him and invited him to join the new band. In addition to being a good trombone player with a nice mellow sound and a particularly effective way of playing in the ensemble, Sam was a good singer rather in the style of Acker Bilk. He was also something of a character, with a remarkable capacity for gin, was soon popular with the crowds and fitted into the new band very well.

Since the break-up of the Old Bailey band in 1970, Andrew Lauder had done most of his playing in the dance band world, playing with the bands of Jim Baikie and Cam Robbie, and had also been involved with the George Hotel house band. This was run by Alec Walker who, in fact, no longer played himself but held the contract with the hotel to provide a band for dinner dances six nights a week. Andrew did these events on Wednesdays, Fridays and Saturdays for about five years. However, when the chance came to get together with most of the Old Bailey crowd, Andrew was up for it. The residency in Queensferry was not to last long and soon the band, by now once more calling itself **Old Bailey's Jazz Advocates**, had moved to the Fountain Inn, situated behind the Barnton Hotel in Whitehouse Road.

This gig became remarkably popular and at one stage, punters were arriving a full hour before the band was due to start, simply to secure a good seat. The 'Jazz News' pamphlet for the Edinburgh International Jazz Festival for 1979 referred to the Fountain Inn as '..a veritable Mecca for Scots (nay, international) jazz freaks'. What was also remarkable was the number of followers of the band from the 1960s who turned up and became regulars again. This residency continued very successfully and then, in March 1976, the Old Bailey band was selected by promoter Ed Baxter to back Bud Freeman, the famous Chicagoan tenor sax star, in concerts at the Dominion Cinema in Morningside. These were followed by further concerts with Freeman and then a couple more with the great American trumpeter Wild Bill Davison, also in the Dominion, in

August and September 1976. The band was augmented by Tom Finlay on piano for these concerts and his playing greatly impressed the visitors, both of whom would have liked to take Tom with them for the rest of their solo tours.

The Freeman concert in August was reviewed by Alastair Clark in the Scotsman where he said *'A dapper, likable little man,* (Bud Freeman) *was on stage for something like three hours and was still blowing hot choruses round about 2 a.m. He was, of course, in canny fettle, rarely extending his improvisations beyond familiar territory and enthusiastically seeing to it that ever member of the supporting Old Bailey's Jazz Advocates had an abundance of solo space.....Tom Finlay played some super piano... notably when backing Freeman in a swingy quartet setting'.*

The Old Bailey band also took on a second residency in March 1977 at the Hailes House Hotel, in the Kingsknowe area of town but, when Hamish McGregor, Andrew Lauder and Chick Murray decided they did not want to take this on and dropped out, the band took on the name **The Nova Scotia Jazz Band**. The spaces were filled by bringing in Gus Ferguson on trumpet, Gerard Dott on clarinet and Dave Rae on drums. The choice of name was in a way unfortunate, as there was no real connection with the much better known band of the same name from the 1950s. After a while, banjoist Johnnie Harper also dropped out and his place was taken by first, Jock Westwater and then the banjo player originally from Germany, Harald Vox. This became another well attended residency and it lasted until June 1979.

Another off-shoot of the Old Bailey/Nova Scotia bands was a four piece band, the **Nova Scotia Quartet**, that took on a residency at the Original Hotel, Roslin. This was my doing and it came about because I had been greatly taken by two sets of recordings of American jazz quartets. These were the well known 'Big Four' recordings by a four piece including Muggsy Spannier and Sydney Bechet and a wonderful set of only four tracks made by Rex Stewart, Barney Bigard and Billy Taylor of the Duke Ellington band together with Django Reinhardt, when Ellington was on tour in France. The early membership of the Nova Scotia Quartet briefly included Andrew Lauder and John McGregor on clarinet but soon settled down with Gus Ferguson (trumpet), Gerard Dott (clarinet, Johnnie Harper (guitar and banjo) and Graham Blamire (bass).

Harald Vox (banjo) was born in Berlin on 25th November 1938 and began playing piano at age seventeen and then banjo at nineteen. His first band was Old Bucket's Jazz Band, which was based at Lake Constance, followed by several other bands, one of which he describes as *'an oompah band'*, in Southern Germany around Ravensburg, Ull, Stuttgart and Hanover. Harald then moved to the UK to attend teacher training college, where he played in a local non-jazz quartet. He then moved to Edinburgh in 1970, where he was introduced to the local jazz scene through hearing the Old Bailey band, becoming friendly with the Old Bailey banjo player Johnnie Harper, and picking up a few gigs. When Johnnie Harper left the Old Bailey off-shoot, the Nova Scotia Jazz Band, Harald was on hand to take over and, around the same time, he put in spells with the West End Jazz Band and the Spirits of Rhythm.

Harald had established himself around the Edinburgh scene at just the right time, as Johnnie Harper had left town in the late 1970s to make a full-time career for himself in jazz, and Harald was there to fill the gap. In 1978, he joined the Charlie McNair band, with whom he was to stay until the mid-1990s, and also played with a band called Dr McJazz. Clearly very busy, Harald was also playing with Frank Birnie's East Coast Jazz band at the Blue Lagoon on Monday evenings, where he was to stay for many years. Between 1992 and 1997, Harald played with the Maid of the Forth Stompers and then started playing through in Glasgow with Muldoon's Jazz and Blues Band.

By this time, there was much more cross-over between the Edinburgh and Glasgow jazzers, mainly because of the diminishing number of traditional jazz musicians around, and quite a number of Edinburgh musicians were involved with Glasgow bands, including Dave Strutt, Gus Ferguson, Andrew Lauder and the bass player, Dick Walink. Harald Vox then became a member of the well known George Penman Jazzmen with whom he was to stay until George Penman's death in 2009, after which he was to play a major part in keeping the band together as Penman's Jazzmen, with whom he continues to play at the time of writing in 2011.

Meanwhile, picking up our story where we left it in the late 1970s, the Old Bailey band itself was still pulling in good crowds at the Fountain in Barnton. The guitar and banjo player, Johnnie Harper had been with the band between 1965 and 1970 and then again from 1975, when the band reformed. In mid-summer 1978, Johnnie took the step we have already heard about, which was one that he had been contemplating for a while; the decision to try to make a living as a full time jazz musician. He left the Old Bailey band, in which he had made a big reputation for himself, and pursued a professional career which saw him play with the bands of Steve Mason, Jumbo Richford and Colin Dawson. Later, he was to be a member of the French four piece band which had been a great success in Edinburgh in 1978, L'Orpheon Celesta and then the band of the outstanding English clarinet player, Sammy Rimmington.

A move to Norway in 1984 led to work with the Magnolia Jazz Band, the Ophelia Ragtime Orchestra, Jazzade and the Roshnes Jazz Band. On several occasions, he made return visits to play in Edinburgh, particularly during the Edinburgh International Jazz Festivals of which we will hear much more in the next chapter. This included the Festival of 1979, when he returned to play the whole of the Festival with the Old Bailey band. When Johnnie left the Old Bailey band in 1978, his replacement was the man he himself had replaced in 1965, band founder member Mike Hart. Mike was still running his own band, now called Mike Hart's Society Syncopators, and this new arrangement was bound to lead to times when gigs clashed and indeed, this was the reason that Johnnie Harper had played the 1979 Festival with the Old Bailey band.

Then, in October 1979, the Old Bailey band acquired a second musician whom they were sharing with the Syncs, pianist Tom Finlay. This, in turn, led to Tom's piano playing brother Jack covering the 1980 Edinburgh Jazz Festival with the Old Bailey band, with an American banjo player, Ed Turner, covering for Mike Hart. This was clearly not an ideal situation as, just when the band needed to be at its best, things were disrupted by having to get deps up to speed with arrangements and routines, excellent though the deps were. This was a real issue as the band had been building more and more arrangements and new material into its repertoire, under the enthusiastic leadership of Hamish McGregor. This can be appreciated by a listen to an LP recorded by the band in 1980 and called 'Complete with Bum Notes'. This recording was eventually reviewed by Ray Coleman in the Melody Maker who noted that *'Scotland has always had a strong reputation for fiery traditional jazz bands'*. The review also picked out Andrew Lauder's trumpet playing for its *'outstanding tone and authority'* and referred to Sam Smith's trombone contribution as a *'rasping joy'*[137]. Meanwhile, the residency at the Fountain Inn came to an end, when the place was sold, and the band took on a succession of other residencies including the Maybury Road House and The George Hotel in George Street, with others coming along as they moved into 1980s. In 1980, they worked with George Melly on an STV film about the Edinburgh Jazz Festival, made some radio broadcasts and went to the Dunkirk Jazz Festival. Here they became European Amateur Jazz Champions for 1980, succeeding the Syncs who had won the title in 1979. However, the problem of sharing musicians with another band remained. It was not to be resolved until January 1981.

The **Society Syncopators** had continued under the leadership of Mike Hart but inevitably the band sound had altered a great deal, as the band line-up changed. Tello was the first of the Old Guard to leave, followed by Dave Paxton and Bob Craig. The replacements were Gus Ferguson, a trumpeter from Dundee, Jack Graham on reeds and Johnny McGuff on trombone, all of whom were with the band by the mid to late 1970s and the piano player, Tom Finlay, had been added around the same time. These were top class jazz musicians and the band was to continue on its successful course throughout the seventies.

Robin 'Gus' Ferguson (trumpet, flugelhorn) was born in Dundee on 26th September 1942 and educated at the Harris Academy. After starting with piano lessons at the

137 Coleman R, 'Melody Maker', December 5, 1981

age of seven, he switched to trumpet when he was eleven years old and had a half hour formal lesson every school-day lunch time until he was sixteen. The formal teaching of a legitimate method presumably accounts for the technical assurance with which he handles the trumpet and his ability to read music, a relatively rare craft amongst the traditional jazz fraternity. He played in the Dundee Schools Brass Band and Dundee Schools Orchestra. Gus also put in some time with the Tay Division Royal Naval Reserve Band, the Bobby Hayes Sextet and the Domino Dance Band. The Domino Dance Band featured a combination of Scottish country dance music and current popular hits. Each week the Dominoes would buy the sheet music of the latest Top Twenty hit and practice it in the car on the way to their next gig. Their gigs were in village halls and hotels all over Perthshire and Angus.

An early influence on Gus was the show trumpeter Eddie Calvert. Gus then began to listen to recordings of Louis Armstrong and the bands of Kenny Ball, Chris Barber and Acker Bilk, who were all getting a fair amount of air time on radio and TV, and this prompted him into starting to play that kind of music. Gus was particularly impressed by Kenny Ball's technical excellence on the trumpet and also admired the Ball band, which he considered had a bright, new sound and was more up-to-date in its approach than other bands. When he was about nineteen, he started playing in a Dixieland band on Saturday lunch times in the Top Hat pub in Princes Street, Dundee. The band later became known as the Top Hat Seven, a band of which Gus became the leader.

In December 1968, Gus's day job moved him to Edinburgh, where he soon made an impact on the local jazz scene, and formed a band which included Jimmy Shortreed on clarinet, Johnnie Harper on banjo and John Nicholson on drums. When talking about his early days in Edinburgh, Gus made the point that many local jazz musicians were active in several bands simultaneously and did not confine their playing to a single band. The Gus Ferguson Jazz Band eventually developed into a band which Gus named the **Rhythm Method**[138] and they had a Saturday lunch time residency in a hotel in Princes Street. Jackie MacFarlane would often drop in for a song or two and it is likely that Bill Smith was on trombone in this band.

Shortly after this, jazz enthusiast Dave Mylne persuaded Gus to disband his own outfit and join Mike Hart's Society Syncopators. The Syncs, who were later to adopt the name **The Scottish Society Syncopators**, had just lost the services of trumpeter Ian 'Tello' Telford and Gus was the replacement. At first, Gus played in the front line with Dave Paxton and Bob Craig but, by the late 1970s, both Dave and Bob had moved on to be replaced by Jack Graham and Johnny McGuff. The line up of the band was completed by Tom Finlay on piano, Mike Hart who led the band on banjo and guitar, Ken Macdonald on bass and Bobby Stewart on drums. This was the line up when the band made its first LP, recording 'Jazz Tattoo', in March 1980. The LP included a couple of Scottish tunes, 'My Ain Folk' and 'Loch Lomond', both sung by Jack Graham, and in his sleeve note, Dave Mylne said *'It is courageous that they include such traditional Scottish items as 'Loch Lomond' and 'My Ain Folk'. There are pitfalls in such a policy, but the band treat their folk music with such good taste and good humour that it is completely successful'*[139].

Mylne also pointed out that this was not the only notable activity of the band around this time and says *'In 1978 the band entered the Dunkirk jazz contest and came second in the traditional section. In 1979 they carried off the first prize with trombonist Johnny McGuff winning the "individual musician of the competition" award. Fired with enthusiasm from these successes in France, Mike landed an invitation to take the band, with all expenses paid, to the Sacramento Jubilee in 1979. They were a resounding success and were there again in 1980 to join the sixty other bands that make the festival so unique'.* Mylne went on to report *'As one fan from Reno wrote to an English friend, after hearing the*

---

[138] A band called 'Bill Jones' Rhythm Method', led by trombonist Bill Jones, is listed in the 1980 EIJF programme apparently having chosen a similar name.

[139] Mylne D, sleeve note on 'Jazz Tattoo', 'Mike Hart's Scottish Society Syncopators', Parsnip Records PR1001 (See discography appendix)

Syncopators in California – "You would do yourself well to go out of your way to hear these guys. They stole the show, as it were. The way these boys in their kilts played Dixieland, you would think they invented the stuff". High praise indeed, but well deserved. A hearing of the 'Jazz Tattoo' LP confirms that this was a very good band playing a wide choice of material with considerable fire and feeling.

Others who played with the Syncs during this period included Charlie Malley, the trumpeter from Falkirk who had been with the Climax band for a spell in the 1950s, and Dave Strutt, a top class trumpeter, who came originally from Colchester. Gus Ferguson reckons that, as he was unable to make the trips to Dunkirk in 1978/79, due to business commitments, it must have been one of these two who were with the Syncs when they competed. Gus Ferguson was to remain a major player on the Edinburgh jazz scene for years to come and we will catch up with him again in the 1980/90s, when he was an original member of another important group, Fat Sam's Band.

Mike Hart's Society Syncopators

EUROPEAN JAZZ CHAMPIONS - DUNKIRK 1979

For Bookings:
MIKE HART
1 St Stephen Place
Edinburgh 5
Scotland, UK
Tel: 031-226-3736

Ken Macdonald, Johnny McGuff, Charlie Malley, Jack Graham, Frank Birnie, Mike Hart, Tom Finlay (by permission of Mike Hart)

The piano player with both the Syncs and the re-formed Old Bailey band, **Tom Finlay (piano)**, was born in Fife in 1939 and came to Edinburgh to study accountancy in 1959. He had already been taking piano lessons in Fife, where he ran a band but in Edinburgh, he enrolled at Johnny Keating's School of Music in 1961, to further develop his playing. He soon formed a band in Edinburgh which included Colin Terris (French horn), Jimmy Gilmore (tenor sax), Kenny Wheatley (guitar) and Robin Kelso (bass). They played one gig in the Papingo Club but, perhaps because it was at the height of the 'Trad Boom', their more modern style was not successful. At Keating's School, Tom met Alec Gentleman, a jazzer from Falkirk who was studying tenor sax, and this led to him joining a band run by Ken Ramage (trombone) which had Alec Gentleman on tenor sax and Ronnie Dunn on bass. When Ken Ramage went abroad, the band continued but took a new name, the 'Finlay Gentleman Quartet'.

This band soon established itself and was popular with the 'non-trad' section of the Edinburgh jazz public. It was frequently the support band for London based mainstream and modern jazzers visiting Edinburgh and, in September 1963, Tom Finlay together with Ronnie Rae on bass and Billy Alison on drums, were included in an Edinburgh group that backed the West Indian sax player Joe Harriot in the Student's Union. At that time, young jazz musicians tended to get together at the Tempo Club, which was in the High Street behind John Knox's house, and the 369 Club which was also in the High Street. The band, which was playing in the jazz funk idiom, found some work through the Art College and Edinburgh University, where there were lunch time sessions. In addition to his work in the more modern forms of jazz, Tom had, of course, also played with the Chicagoan styled Royal Mile Jazzmen, with the likes of reeds man Jack Duff and drummer Sandy Malcolm, as we heard in Chapter VI. Then, in 1964, Tom went off to play on the transatlantic liners and a couple of years later in 1966, went on a world cruise with Graeme Robertson, now playing bass, and Bobby Stewart on drums. This brought them the chance to hear many great American musicians in

New York, musicians that up until then they had only heard on record.

The constant playing required on these trips had another benefit too; having started as enthusiastic amateurs, the ceaseless practice made polished professional musicians of them. This stood them in good stead and they found plenty work, in both dance and jazz combos, when they returned to Edinburgh. Tom Finlay was to become one of the most versatile and respected of all of Edinburgh's jazzers, a man who could play as easily with top flight visiting musicians as he could with local jazz bands of any type. The list of top-flight jazz musicians with whom Tom played is a very lengthy one, too long to give here, but amongst them were reeds men Peanuts Hucko, Bob Wilber, Scott Hamilton and Bud Freeman, and trumpeters Doc Cheatham, Harry 'Sweets' Edison and Red Rodney, who had played with the Charlie Parker Quintet between 1949 and 1951 – a distinguished list from the main stream of jazz, some of whom did not appear in Edinburgh until the advent of the Edinburgh International Jazz Festival in late 1970s. It was in the 1970s too, that Tom was persuaded by Mike Hart to join the New Society Syncopators and he was with the band on their successful trips to Dunkirk. He was to remain an important Edinburgh jazzer for many years and at the time of writing in 2010, is as active and admired, both as a band pianist and solo, as ever.

Chapter XI

New Orleans Jazz in the 1970s

Things were happening in the Edinburgh purist jazz world in the 1970s as well, although by then, this form of the music was usually called New Orleans jazz. **Violet Milne (piano, vocals)**, wife of drummer Kenny Milne and mother of trumpeter Finlay, had been born in Glasgow in 1936. She had started singing with the Vintage Jazz Band in Glasgow in 1958, a band that included Farrie Forsyth on drums. After moving to Edinburgh, she sang with the Climax band and then, after moving to London, sang with the Kid Martyn Ragtime Band. There followed a period living in Essex, when she was not active in jazz while raising her family and then, in 1971, she took up piano. This led to gigs with various bands before she became a member of the Essex based Criterion Jazz Band in about 1975. In 1977, Violet and Kenny returned to Edinburgh. Back on home territory, in December 1979, Kenny was instrumental in forming a band for a one-off gig supporting the touring Freddy Kohlman Band from New Orleans, and they played alongside the Kohlman band at the Adam Rooms.

The new band, which they christened the **Spirits of Rhythm**, sounded so good and had played so well that, after the gig, they decided to keep the band together. The original line-up was Fraser Gauld (tpt), George Duncan (ct), probably Bill Jones (tbn), Violet (pno), Willie Mack (bs) and Kenny on drums. There was also a banjo player whose pony tail hair style has proved more memorable than his name! Kenny had taken up trumpet around 1970, about the same time as his son Finlay began on the same instrument. At the time the Spirits of Rhythm were formed, Kenny was already heavily committed playing trumpet with Bill Salmond's Louisiana Ragtime Band and, with Kenny unable to spare the time, Violet took over the running of the new band. The Spirits, as the band was to become known, was to become an Edinburgh institution and would be the band with whose name Violet would always be associated.

The band was immediately successful and was included in the second Edinburgh International Jazz Festival in 1980. Over the next couple of years, there were a few changes in the band but by 1984, the line up had stabilised, with Ian Boyter replacing George Duncan, Jack Weddell coming in on trombone, Brian Weld on banjo and Robin Galloway on bass, a line up that was to last. The Spirits had several very successful residencies and amongst them was La Grenouille in the New Town, Sorbonne in the Cowgate, Nobles Bar in Constitution Street in Leith, the Stair Arms out beyond Dalkeith near Pathhead and the Haymarket Bar and Basin Street, both of which were near Haymarket Station. Basin Street is of particularly fond memory for many local jazzers as it was, for years, a major venue for local jazz with jazz bands featured almost every evening of the week. It was located in the upstairs bar of the Haymarket Station Bar and had reproduction posters of old time jazz bands and musicians on the walls of the stairway. At one time the Spirits following was such that it allowed them to feature at Basin Street on two consecutive evenings each week.

The Spirits, throughout their long (and continuing) history, played in the New Orleans style and played a major part in keeping this type of traditional jazz alive and well in Edinburgh. The band's reputation, coupled with that of Kenny Milne who had a well-deserved reputation as a drummer in New Orleans circles, enabled them to play at many jazz festivals, both in the UK and on the Continent. Included in these were the Ascona and Arosa Jazz Festivals in Switzerland and, in the UK, jazz festivals at Glasgow, Peebles, Dundee, Kirkcudbright, Girvan, Bute, Orkney, Keswick and Bude, in addition to the Edinburgh International Jazz Festival (EIJF). In the latter, they became an essential component of the programme and, at the time of writing in 2010, the Spirits can claim with pride, that they have featured in the EIJF every year since their debut in 1980. This makes a still growing total of thirty one consecutive appearances at the EIJF, the only one they missed being the very first in 1979, hardly their fault as it took place four months before the band was formed. The Spirits also made several tours in Switzerland, mostly playing in hotels, and a particularly memorable event in their history was an invitation to play at the World Economic Forum at Davos, also in Switzerland, where they shared the lime light with US President Bill Clinton.

The band also made several recordings, the first being an LP which featured them with guest tenor saxophonist Sam Lee, who had been born in Napoleonville in Louisiana in 1911 and moved to New Orleans in 1926. This LP was recorded in April 1984 at the Hart Street Studios in Edinburgh and the band line-up was the stabilised one given above, but with the bass playing duties shared between Robin Galloway and Willie Mack. The Spirits also appeared on a compilation tape recorded at the Keswick Jazz Festival, issued by Lake Records, and appeared on another compilation recording, called 'Jazz Around the World', issued by Jazz Crusade. In addition, Kenny's investment in some high class recording gear has enabled the issue of several other CDs, produced by the band themselves[140].

In the nature of bands, the passing years brought some changes in personnel. After Fraser Gauld stopped playing, Violet often used just a two-piece front line, with Ian Boyter on reeds and Jack Weddell on trombone sharing the lead role, although the fine trumpeter Dave Strutt played with them for an extended period in the 1990s. The obvious choice on trumpet would, of course, have been Violet's and Kenny's son Finlay, who became a very good player, but unfortunately, Finlay's work in television took him away from Edinburgh. Jack Weddell was in and out of the band at least three times before he eventually retired from playing. Brian Weld also left, to be succeeded by Nigel

---

[140] See Discography Appendix

303

Porteous, but later made a return to the band. On bass, after Robin Galloway left Edinburgh, Fred Murray, Roy Percy, Dizzy Jackson and Graham Blamire all played with the Spirits for spells. At the end of the first decade of the twenty first century, the Spirits of Rhythm continue to play in their mellow, warm and relaxed New Orleans style, with a line-up that is remarkably similar to that of the early 1980s – Violet and Kenny Milne, Ian Boyter, Alan Quinn on trombone (who sadly was to die in early 2011), Brian Weld and the veteran bass player, Dizzy Jackson.

Fraser Gauld (trumpet), the Spirits' original trumpeter, was born on 10th May 1940, educated at Daniel Stewart's College and was to become a computer programmer in his 'day job'. He had violin lessons at school and played in the school orchestra but soon decided that the violin did not suit him. His older brother, Alastair 'Shorty' Gauld, was already involved in jazz and played banjo in Mike Hart's Blue Blowers, playing alongside Mike and Ian Telford on trumpet, at the Shoestring Cafe in the Royal Mile. Apparently, the older Gauld had a recording of Bunk Johnson playing 'Tishomingo Blues' and when Fraser heard this he was hooked. He decided that he wanted to play clarinet but, as no clarinet was available at school, he managed to borrow a school trumpet from someone in the school orchestra. Like so many of us of that generation, he then proceeded to teach himself to play his instrument. Bunk Johnson was to remain Fraser's model throughout his jazz career.

The next step was obviously to start a band and Fraser soon got together with others at school to begin their playing careers in one of the junior school classrooms, which happened to have a piano. The original little group had Fraser, who knew enough to play a little piano, Sandy Gracie on clarinet and one or two others. Another pupil at the school was Iain Forde, already playing trombone, who looked in and intimated that he was interested in joining them. According to Iain Forde, Fraser was musically the key member of this group. This was because he was the only one who knew anything about chords and was able to demonstrate on piano and, because his brother owned a banjo, on that instrument as well. However, the jazz pioneers of Daniel Stewart's College were to go the way of so many similar attempts in those unenlightened times. The Headmaster, Dr Robbie, got to hear of their efforts and proclaimed that it must stop forthwith, and of course it did. However, salvation was at hand in the person of the school chaplain, a Mr Chisholm, who took pity on them and arranged for them to practice in a church storage hall, next to John Knox's house in the High Street.

Fraser and the others practiced like mad and soon organised a jazz concert, inviting all their friends from school and even one of the teachers. They obviously used their limited manpower with great skill and versatility and were able to present, not only the jazz band, but a skiffle group and a jug band as well. The cost of a ticket was kept down to one penny and all unsold tickets were put in the bell of the school tuba, from where they made regular but unscheduled appearances for years afterwards, to the general mystification of successive generations of Daniel Stewarts College tuba players. The invited teacher duly attended and wrote a report on the concert, which stated that the music had been terrible and, in a critique of the jug band's performance, added that '...for some reason Stuart McGregor spat into a jug'. Nothing daunted, two of the intrepid band, Fraser himself and Willie Cairns, set themselves to making a full-size, plywood replica of the school's double bass. Fraser proudly reports that this was accomplished, 'complete with the curly bit on top', presumably meaning the scroll. Unfortunately, although the result 'looked perfect', it turned out to sound like a tea chest. Even this did not deter them, and they began to practice in Iain Forde's mother's house in Ann Street.

After leaving school, enthusiasm intact in spite of Headmasterly opposition, instrument manufacturing set-backs and typical jazz critic negativity, Fraser and Iain Forde met up with others with jazz playing aspirations. These were Jake McMahon and two brothers, Alan and Peter Ritchie, whom they met at the Stud Club, then functioning in St John's Hill, and they soon formed a band. Willie Cairns dropped out and, having found a replacement in the person of Donald Macdonald, they turned their carpentry skills towards manufacturing a trolley on which

305

to transport the bass to his house in Portobello. (It does not surprise me in the slightest that a trolley was required for the home made double bass. When I was in the Scouts at about the same time, lack of any real instruments inspired us to make a guitar from a kit. It too, looked alright but turned out to be of incredible weight, as well as having a feeble sound which was inaudible at a distance of about three feet. It came in useful at camp to stop things blowing away in a strong wind.) Fraser and company meanwhile started holding practices in India Buildings.

There followed a bit of a gap in Fraser's jazz career as, while he was at Edinburgh University, he did little playing. However, by 1964 he was free from studies and joined Bill Salmond's band, with whom he played residences at the Woolpack, the Lothian Bar and at the Cephas Club, situated in the crypt of St Georges West church in Shandwick Place. Although a church establishment, this latter venue turned out to be a dangerous place. One night, a mob of aggressive young yobs turned up and invaded the band room. At the time, this room was being shared with a group of Gillespie's school girls who were getting changed into dancing outfits for a dance demonstration. The girls ignored the yobs and continued changing. This impressive display of coolness under fire and stiff upper lip was too much for the yobs who, according to Fraser, were *'dumbstruck'*. However, their yobbishness soon reasserted itself and shortly afterwards, they switched off all the lights and began to throw bottles at the band stand, before making off into the night with the till.

In the 1970s, Fraser played with a succession of bands with peculiar names including the Granton Jass Works and the 'king Great Band, which had Jock Westwater (bjo), Walt Smith (clt), Paul Munro (tbn) and Dave Rae (drms). He also played with a band called Deep South, which played in the Nelson Hotel and included Angus MacDonald (tbn), Andy Hampton (clt), Colin Warwick (bjo), Robin Galloway (bs) and again, Dave Rae (drms). None of these bands lasted for very long and, at the end of the 1970s, Fraser became a member of Violet Milne's new band, The Spirits of Rhythm, and this one did last.

**The Spirits of Rhythm in Basin Street at Haymarket
Back row: Kenny Milne (drms), Violet Milne (pno), Brian
Weld (bjo), Fred Murray (bs),
Front row: Ian Boyter (rds), Fraser Gauld (tpt), Jack
Weddell (tbn)
(by permission of Ian Boyter)**

With the Spirits, Fraser played at their residency in La
Grenouille and he remembers that Brian Weld, who had
played the banjo with the Climax Jazz Band back in the
1950s, happened to be passing the venue one evening,
heard the band, came in into the pub and was more or less
immediately recruited to play banjo. Although Brian had
not played for twenty five years, he soon rediscovered his
previous skills and was quickly back in the swing of things.
Fraser was on the recording that the Spirits made with
Sammy Lee and whoever wrote the sleeve notes paid Fraser
a well-deserved compliment, saying that he was *'nicknamed
'Phraser' because of his electrifying runs'*. While playing
with the Spirits Fraser also played with a band put together
by the trombonist, Alan Quinn. This band was based at the
Temple Hall, a hotel in the Portobello area, and adopted the
name of the hotel, calling themselves the Temple Hall

Stompers. The band, in addition to Fraser and Alan Quinn, had Eddie Hamilton (clt), Beverly Knight (bjo), Jimmy Tunnah (bs) and Roger Hanley (drms).

Meanwhile, Fraser went with the Spirits to play at a couple of Ascona Jazz Festivals but, just before a third visit in 1987, his playing came to a sad and premature end. There was a history of the ear trouble, tinnitus, in Fraser's family and unfortunately, he found himself afflicted with this debilitating condition. The medical advice was to keep away from loud noises and it was soon apparent that the sound of a New Orleans band in full cry came well within the medical concept of loud noises. Fraser had no option but to stop playing. He made an attempt some twenty years later to play again, but the tinnitus quickly returned and the attempt came to nothing. The loss of Fraser's trumpet playing was a major blow to Edinburgh jazz and especially to the Spirits of Rhythm. He was an assured, hot player with a delicious sense of timing and swing, in both his lead work and his soloing. The extent of the loss is well illustrated by the difficulty the Spirits had in replacing him, often choosing to play without trumpet than to settle for less than the standard that Fraser Gauld had set.

George Duncan (clarinet, alto sax) was born in Edinburgh 9th September 1945 and, after early schooling at Flora Stevenson's School near the foot of Orchard Brae, transferred to George Watsons College when he was twelve. His family was not a particularly musical one, although his father liked the singing of Bing Crosby, and it was his Crosby records that first attracted the young George to music. His older brother Billy had some jazz records, including some by the George Lewis band and the Louis Armstrong All Stars, and these soon attracted George's interest. The Lewis recordings, from around 1952, included Burgundy Street Blues, a tune that George was later to play many times, together with Mamma Don't Allow and Yaka Hula Hickey Dula. His interest in jazz now established, George, at the age of thirteen, decided to take up clarinet and, after a few introductory lessons, taught himself how to play.

His first venture into active playing came about because his mother, convinced she had a musical prodigy on her hands, responded to an advert and arranged an audition for him. This was in the Spring of 1962 and, at the age of about sixteen, George duly attended his audition in a church hall in Constitution Street in Leith. It turned out that this was an attempt to form a jazz band to be called the 'Stories Alley Jazz Band', after a lane off the Kirkgate in Leith. This was because one of the band had managed to filch the street sign bearing the words Stories Alley and had set it up on the bass drum. The only one of the band, most of whom were in their mid-twenties, whose name George was able to remember was the drummer, George Hutchison, known as Hutch. George's audition was successful and, although it was really just a practice band, he also played a couple of gigs with them. However, his mother, who had arranged it in the first place, now got cold feet. Mindful of his approaching school higher exams, she put pressure on him and George resigned. George's mother probably felt she had been right, as his school results were good enough to allow him to go off to study pharmacy at Robert Gordon's College (now University) in Aberdeen, a period when he did little playing.

Before going to Aberdeen, George had made further contacts within the Edinburgh jazz scene and had played at the Woolpack pub, near the McEwan Hall, with one of Bill Salmond's early bands, a band which included Alan Quinn on trombone. On his return to Edinburgh in 1969, he soon got back in touch with Bill and, in 1970, began playing regularly with Bill's band which also included Dave Strutt (tpt), George Howden (tbn), Willie Mack (bs) and Kenny Orr (drms). This was in a residency in the Haymarket Station Bar (later to become Basin Street) which lasted until 1971 after which the band, now with Gus Ferguson on trumpet and Graham Scott on piano, moved to a new spot in the Carlton Hotel on the North Bridge. The Carlton gig came to an end in 1972 but by then the band had taken on another spot, at the Canmore Lounge. This pub stood at the crossroads between the Grange and Causewayside, and the residency was to continue until 1974. This gig was followed by a move to the St Clair Hotel in Minto Street, by which time Bill had dropped the trumpet and was using a two piece front line, with George often playing the lead on alto sax. George's Edinburgh jazz career then came to a temporary halt as he moved to London, where he teamed up with two other Edinburgh exiles, Kenny Milne and Dougie Boyter, in Kenny's Criterion Jazz Band. George also played with a band run by a drummer called John Petters and, with the latter band, George played with two fine trumpeters, Ken Sims and Freddie Randall.

George's return to Edinburgh in 1979 put him in the right place at the right time. Kenny and Violet Milne had also returned to town and George joined the new band put together by Violet, the Spirits of Rhythm, with whom he would stay until 1982. After the three years with the Spirits, George was to join the band with whom he was to stay for the next seventeen years, the band of Charlie McNair.

Ian Boyter (reeds), was born in 1943 in St Andrews but later moved to Edinburgh, where he attended Boroughmuir Senior Secondary School. Ian was to become a graphic designer. He was self taught on alto sax and, at the age of sixteen, started playing in rock bands including The Outlaws and Ricky and the Eagles. However, when he was twenty two, he stopped playing altogether and was not to resume until he was thirty five. This time, it was the jazz scene that attracted him and his first band was to be the Spirits of Rhythm, replacing George Duncan in time for the 1983 Edinburgh Jazz Festival. In addition, Ian soon started his own band, the Gumbo Jazz Band, which bore a strong family likeness to the Spirits of Rhythm, with a line-up of Finlay Milne and later, Donald Corbett (tpt), Bill Jones (tbn), Violet Milne (pno), Tony Sergent (bs), Kenny Henderson (bjo) and Roger Hanley (drms). The Gumbo band had a residency in the Spider's Web, in Morrison Street.

Ian, by this time, had added clarinet to his armoury, although he always regarded sax as his main instrument. He soon proved his worth in a jazz context, being a natural improviser with a strong, muscular sound on tenor sax and a warm, woody tone on clarinet. He was ideally suited to the New Orleans style and, after starting with them in 1983, was to remain loyal to the Spirits for almost thirty years at the time of writing in 2011. Ian also frequently played as a dep around town, but was also to become a member of other bands at various times, an example being Jim Petrie's Diplomats of Jazz. The Spirits, however, always had first call on his services. In the 2000s, he played for a time with the Maid of the Forth Stompers and also became a member of Bill Salmond's Louisiana Ragtime Band.

Over the years, Ian broadened his experience and style and was always keen to take every playing opportunity. In 2010, he set up his own jazz band website and is able and willing to put together bands from duos up to full seven-piece New Orleans bands. He also plays in a singer-led Swing band, 'Swing Supreme'. He has tried his hand at writing tunes and constantly works on extending his musical knowledge. However, the New Orleans style always seemed to me to be Ian's natural jazz habitat, with his preference for a free improvising setting, whether demonstrating his ability to play the orthodox role of the reeds as secondary to a trumpet lead or taking the lead role himself.

No account of Edinburgh traditional jazz would be complete without a look at another aspect of the New Orleans influence – the bands which were sometimes called **Parade Bands**, sometimes Marching Bands and, especially in the USA, Brass Bands. These bands generally played at outdoor events and were very much part of the New Orleans jazz tradition. William J Schafer's book, 'Brass Bands and New Orleans Jazz'[141] explains that *'The brass band in nineteenth century America was as ubiquitous in its time as juke boxes and electric music systems in ours'*. What he is referring to here is, of course, not the brass band in a jazz context but the fact that *'When even large cities could not raise a symphony orchestra, every village had its silver cornet band and bandstand in the square'*. Shafer goes on to explain that the brass band was a major contributor amongst the many and varied sources that went to create jazz in the late nineteenth and early twentieth century. He goes on to say *'If we look carefully at early New Orleans music in milieu and time, the brass band emerges as a major source, a gene pool, for jazz'*. Thus, along with sundry other

---

[141] Schafer W J, 'Brass Bands and New Orleans Jazz', pages 8 and 9, ISBN 0-8071-0282-2 pbk, by permission of Louisiana State University Press, 1977

sources such as complex African rhythms and 'blue' tonality, European notions of harmony and form, Ragtime, French and Spanish rhythms and American folk traditions, the music and even the actual form of the nineteenth century American town and city brass bands, must be seen as a significant component in the heady mix that went into the making of jazz. Schafer, quoting an observer of the black music milieu after the civil war, also tells us that, as early as 1878, *'New Orleans has several fine brass bands among its coloured population'*. It seems unlikely that these bands would sound like the New Orleans Parade Bands of today. It is probable that they were marching bands, using principally brass instruments, modelled on the military bands of the time, and designed to provide suitably rousing music, when municipal pride demanded it.

However, it seems that, as time went by, the tide of influence turned, and the New Orleans Parade Bands became more and more influenced by jazz music. From then on, it seems, the parade bands of New Orleans increasingly adopted the mores of jazz: improvisation, particularly simultaneous improvisation, a tendency to bend or 'blue' the pitch of notes and, above all, the sensuous rhythmic nuances that came to be called swing. This latter factor is perhaps the most telling of all, providing what Schafer calls *'...a tension between the march's strong, striding 1-and-3 beat emphasis with the Afro-American penchant for 2-and-4 accents'*. Part of this development seems to have been a move away from the formality of the nineteenth century brass bands, with their use of written parts, towards a looser, much more informal and extemporised performance, albeit with a clear discipline that determined the role of each instrument in producing a coherent, integrated ensemble. Rex Harris, writing in his book 'Jazz' in the 1950s, says *'..."jazzing" of marches was achieved partly by the trick of shifting the accent from the strong to the weak beat and partly by allowing solo players to "decorate" the melody they were playing – solo improvisation; or several players to indulge in their extemporisation simultaneously – collective improvisation'*[142].

---

[142] Harris R, 'Jazz', 4th edition, page 57, Penguin Books, 1956

In other words, the New Orleans parade bands became less like military bands in character and more like a New Orleans jazz band, but on the move rather than static.

Schafer points out that the brass bands provided a training ground for many great jazzmen such as King Oliver, Bunk Johnson, Kid Ory and Louis Armstrong. However, he also says that brass band playing in New Orleans, in addition, produced a cadre of men who persisted with the brass band tradition after 1920 and regarded themselves as different from jazz musicians, still playing from written scores and not 'ear men' like the jazzers. The names of some of the famous New Orleans Parade Bands have come down the years to us: the Allen Brass Band (1907-1950) led by the father of the great trumpeter, Henry 'Red' Allen, the Eureka Brass Band which started in 1920, the Excelsior Brass Band active between 1880 and 1931, Kid Howard's Brass Band of 1945-1950 and, more recently, the Olympia Brass Band and the revived Onward Brass Band of about 1960. The personnel listed by Schafer for these bands and many others, are scattered with the names of famous New Orleans jazz musicians.

The first key figure in the development of Parade Bands in Edinburgh was the double bass player Jim Young of the Climax band who, thanks to his military band training, also played both tuba and sousaphone. We have already heard, in Chapter VII, the story of the first marching band in Edinburgh, when the combined Climax and Kid Martyn bands took themselves from the Tempo Club in the High Street to play for Hogmanay revellers at the Tron Church. This is the first record of which I am aware of a marching jazz band in Edinburgh, although it was really just two existing jazz bands getting together to play out of doors. The venture was so successful that the Climax band repeated it at Hogmanay for several years. As for the marching aspect, Jim says that a better description might be that they shuffled along!

Jim Young then spent some time, between 1963 and 1967, based in London, where the strong New Orleans jazz movement had already led to the formation of a number of Parade Bands. Jim's ability to play brass bass ensured that his services were much in demand and he was soon involved, playing many Parade Band gigs in London and on the Continent. He also recorded with several of these bands, one of which was Casimir's Paragon Brass Band, which also included Edinburgh's Jake McMahon on E-flat clarinet. Jim made a second LP with the Paragon band, recorded live on the streets of Rouen in France, on November 22nd 1970. He was also on the LP 'Dejan's Olympia Brass Band in Europe', which was recorded in Berlin on 4th August 1868, the cover of which has a photo of the band including Jim, on the steps of St Paul's Cathedral. Jim was also present on some tracks on a second LP made by this band, which was recorded in London at St Martin's in the Field and St Paul's Cathedral, on 26th July 1968. Chris Barber too, called on Jim's services, when he made a double LP of Parade Band jazz. This was issued as 'Chris Barber Special' on Black Lion Special recordings (BLP 20108/9), in 1975 and features the Beatles tune, 'All My Loving'.

On his return to Edinburgh, Jim Young was soon into action forming a proper marching band in the New Orleans tradition, which he called the **Auld Reekie Parade Band**. This band proved very popular and played at the Edinburgh Students' Charities Processions, where it was heard by the very large crowd that used to turn out for this annual event. At that time, in the late 1970s, the Edinburgh New Orleans bands had an annual Hogmanay Jazz Band Ball and it became the tradition that the bands would exit just before midnight, before making a grand entry as a marching band, bringing in the New Year with suitable flourish. The Auld Reekie band was also involved in the early Edinburgh Jazz Festivals and, indeed, featured at the opening event of the very first Festival, in Tiffany's Ballroom, in St Stephen Street, in 1979. The Auld Reekie Parade Band of that year can be heard playing 'St Louis Blues' on the special compilation LP that was issued to celebrate the 1980 Festival. Playing with them were two visitors from New Orleans, drummer Andrew Hall and tenor saxist Teddy Johnson.

Jim Young describes the classical line-up for a Parade band as: two trumpets, two trombones, one brass bass (tuba or sousaphone), an E-flat clarinet, one or two saxophones, a snare drum and a bass drum. It was traditional to have someone in a sort of drum major role at the head of the band where, instead of a drum major's mace, he was equipped with a brolly and a whistle. Apparently this was more for show than any real musical function, although he would use the whistle to call the band to attention before moving off. Kenny Milne, like Jim Young much involved with Parade Bands, claims that it was the function of the brolly man to draw the attention of the band to potential hazards in their path, such as holes in the road or piles of horse or dog poo lying about! A parade band was, in fact, governed by the snare drummer and the senior trumpeter. When the band was on the move but not playing, the snare drummer's job was to tap out the beat on the snare, so the band could march (or shuffle!) along in time. At the point when the band was to begin to play again, the trumpeter would play a short phrase that told the band the tune they were to play and its key. It was then the function of the snare drummer to play an introductory pattern of ratta-tat-tats, after which the band would burst into action. The usual marching formation had the trombones at the front, followed by the two trumpets with the brass bass between them, then the reeds, and finally the two drummers. The tradition, started in New Orleans, was for a 'second line' of people to march along behind the band, some with brollys, all moving in time with the beat of the band and making a colourful and lively display.

Jim recruited for the 'Auld Reekie' band among the Edinburgh traditional jazzers, most of whom played in the band at one time or another. They included Jim himself (brass bs), Jim Petrie, Fraser Gauld and Kenny Milne (tpts), Jack Weddell, Bob Craig and Sam Smith (tbns) and George Gilmour and George Duncan (rds). Sometimes Kenny Milne, Pete Ritchie or Bill Warden would play the snare and sometimes others had to be dragooned into the band at short notice when they were short. Kenny Milne remembers being back in Edinburgh on holiday and being hastily recruited by Jim Young to play the bass drum. On that occasion, the Auld Reekie band was augmented by a group of Musicians Union members, which Kenny Milne remembers as including Jimmy Shortreed (clt), George Roy (tpt) and Russ Cessford (drms). Apparently this came about because the M.U. had been asked to put together a Parade Band, probably for the Charities procession, and they had turned to Jim Young for help. Kenny's unexpected stint on bass drum ended with him *'completely knackered and covered with blood from where he had knocked his knuckles off against the bass drum'!* On another occasion, an alarmed Kenny Macdonald was hauled out of the crowd at the start of a parade to play the bass drum.

Kenny Milne says that Parade Bands generally had become much less dependent on written music, *'less dots oriented'* was his description, as time went on and by about the 1970/80s, they played as almost totally improvising bands. However, it was by no means a musical free for all. The role of each instrument within the eight to ten piece band was clearly understood, so that the whole made an integrated sound, much in the same way as in the traditional New Orleans bands' ensemble playing. Kenny himself founded Edinburgh's second parade band, which he called the **Criterion New Orleans Brass Band**, in time for the second Edinburgh Jazz Festival in 1980. He drew on much the same pool of musicians as had Jim Young, and Jim himself sometimes played bass drum with them when Graham Scott, the regular bass drummer, was unavailable.

Kenny recalls that they sometimes greatly increased the size of the band for especially demanding jobs, when extra power was needed, such as the annual Jazz Festival parade along Princes Street, when they would sometimes have a band of sixteen to twenty, including five trumpeters. A former next door neighbour of the Milne family when they lived in Essex, Edwin Adcock, often came up take on the role of the drum major brolly man, more correctly called the Grand Marshall. In New Orleans, parade bands were often accompanied by dancers and Kenny and Violet Milne's daughter Jennifer, her pal Cathy McInally and Margaret Cut, a long time supporter of Edinburgh jazz, often took on this job. Jennifer and Cathy in particular, became quite well known as dancers, dressing for the part and strutting their stuff with considerable flair and enthusiasm, which always took a trick at parade time.

The Criterion Brass Band became successful in the long term, the longest serving of Edinburgh's parade bands. They played at many Edinburgh Jazz Festivals, as well as jazz festivals on the Continent at Ascona, Davos, and Celerina, usually travelling as an eight or nine piece band, including the two dancers. They also became regulars at other jazz festivals in Scotland, including those at Peebles and Glasgow, as well as frequent gigs at gala days at South Queensferry and Loanhead and even played at a few funerals. The band's publicity pamphlet listed their gigs as including Galas, openings, barbecues, concerts, product launches, sports events, car rallies, fund-raising events and corporate entertainments, all of which in the past had been enlivened by the band's infectious beat and raunchy music. The repertoire is described as including rags, stomps, spirituals, dirges, blues, popular melodies and traditional jazz marches. Typical tunes played are given as When the Saints Go Marching In, Doctor Jazz, Panama Rag, The Old Rugged Cross, Down in Honky Tonk Town and Basin Street Blues. At the time of writing in 2010, the Criterion Brass Band have issued three CDs of their music. Musicians who played with the Criterion Brass Band included:

Trumpets:	Kenny Milne, Finlay Milne, Fraser Gauld, Jim Petrie, Adam Latto and Colin Dawson
Trombones:	Jack Weddell, Bob Craig and Sam Smith
Reeds:	Ian Boyter, George Gilmour, George Duncan and Cameron Greig
Brass bass:	Symon Carlyle, Jim Young and Dick Staughan (from Newcastle)
Snare drum:	Kenny Milne, Eric Jamieson, Mac Rae (from Newcastle)
Bass drum:	Graham Scott, Bill Salmond, Bill Martin, Jim Young and Beverly Knight

Adam Latto also sometimes played bass drum, sousaphone or euphonium. Sometimes, a Parade Band would be improvised on the spot, when the occasion demanded it. I can remember members of the Spirits of Rhythm and the Louisiana Ragtime Band forming up as a Parade Band to lead us all from the ferry to the Stromness

Hotel, at the start of the Orkney Jazz Festival in the late 1990s.

The Criterion Brass Band in full cry
Graham Scott (bass drum), George Gilmour (clt), Alan
Quinn (tbn), Simon Carlyle (sousa)
(photo courtesy of Peter Davenport)

A third Edinburgh Parade band, which was to be called the **Honestas Brass Band**, was formed in 1987 by Adam Latto. **Adam Latto (cornet, trumpet, tuba, euphonium, sousaphone and bass drum)** was born in Fisherrow on 22 November 1937 and educated at Mussellburgh Grammar School, where a class mate was the bass player, Ronnie Rae. Adam was very much a Musselburgh man, indeed something of an authority on the history of the town, and the band's name came from Musselburgh's reputation as the 'Honest Toun'. Adam by day was an antiquarian book seller and for many years, he traded from his book shop, by the side of the River Esk, in Musselburgh. He returned from National Service around 1958, at the age of twenty one, and started cornet lessons with the local brass band, Musselburgh and Fisherrow Trades Prize Band. He had always had an interest in jazz but it was not until he heard Kenny Milne's Criterion Brass Band that he decided to get actively involved. The Honestas Brass Band first got together to practice in March 1987 and this was followed by a marching rehearsal along at the Old Grange Mining Museum at Prestongrange, just to the east of Musselburgh. Over the years, Adam used many musicians in the Honestas band and the stalwarts who were the mainstay of the band, are shown below:

Trumpet: Adam Latto, Graham McArthur, Jimmy Welsh, Gus Ferguson
Trombone: Andrew Mulhern, Alan Quinn, Sandy Barclay, Gavin Dawson
Reeds: Eddie Hamilton, Bob Busby, Bob McDowell, Alex Munro, George Mitchell
Snare drum: Roy Dunnett, Eddie Hamilton, Roger Hanley, Ian Forrest
Bass drum: Bill Salmond, Beverly Knight, Brian Weld, Adam Latto
Brass bass: Bill Brydon, Lindsay Cooper, Fred Freyling-Kelly, Adam Latto

In addition, long-serving Edinburgh jazz followers Gerry and Cathie Brennan were recruited to act as Grand Marshalls in the New Orleans tradition, always leading the way with great flair and panache.

The Honestas band played its first gig at Wallyford Miner's Gala on 6th June 1987 and remained in action until 1989, when there was a two year break in its history, largely because several key members became unavailable. However, Adam got the band together again in 1992 and over the next fourteen years, the band was never short of gigs. They played at many Edinburgh Jazz Festival events, taking part in the Mardi Gras in the Grassmarket on numerous occasions and in the Festival opening parade. In seven consecutive years, 1996 to 2002, they played at the Hawick Jazz Festival. Other gigs were at the Danderhall Gala, the Leith pageant, the Leith Jazz Festival from 1992 to 2002, the St Stephen Street Festival and, on one occasion, a funeral at the Corstorphine Hill cemetery.

**Caricature of Adam Latto by trumpeter Jimmy Welsh
(from the collection of Adam Latto, by permission of
Jimmy Welsh)**

They even played at a Chinese Dragon Boat Race at Leith
Docks and a Hibs v Hearts match at Easter Road, although
which was the more bizarre event, I cannot say! As time
went by, of course, there were times when Adam had to fill
gaps in the band and many of the well known Edinburgh
jazzers made appearances, including the leaders of
Edinburgh's other two parade bands, Jim Young and Kenny
Milne. Adam himself had to play both snare and bass drum
at times when availability was a problem. Adam Latto
retired to live in the Border country in 1993, living just over
the border near Berwick upon Tweed, but kept the
Honestas Brass Band going until 2006, when their final gig
was the Edinburgh International Jazz Festival Mardi Gras.
While living near Berwick, Adam played sousaphone in the
Tweed River Jazz band for twelve years.

The purist or New Orleans tradition was and is a very
strong part of Edinburgh jazz. Starting in the 1950s, when
the Climax Jazz Band made its first appearance, right
through the 1960s and 70s with the Louisiana Ragtime
Band and the Spirits of Rhythm and on into the 1980s and

90s when, in addition to the jazz bands, there was the strong marching band presence with the Auld Reekie, Criterion and Honestas Brass bands, New Orleans jazz was an integral part of the Edinburgh jazz scene. At the time of writing in 2011, the New Orleans tradition remains the strongest part of Edinburgh traditional jazz, with the Edinburgh Jazz and Jive Club featuring the Spirits, the Louisiana Ragtime Band, Brian Robertson's Forth River Ragtimers, Jim Petrie's Diplomats of Jazz and the Criterion Brass Band, all still around and all with their roots firmly in the New Orleans tradition. There is even a latter day revival of the spirit of the Climax band itself, styling themselves the Anti-Climax Jazz Band!

Chapter XII

The Edinburgh International Jazz Festival

Not for the first time, Mike Hart had an idea in his head and it concerned the setting up of some sort of notable and regular jazz event in Edinburgh. He had heard that there was a festival of traditional jazz held in Sacramento in California and, interested to find out more, made a special visit, flying out there in 1978. The Sacramento event had been founded in 1973 and was called the Sacramento Jazz Jubilee, later to become the Sacramento Jazz Festival. The founder was a trumpeter called Bill Borcher, who led a band called the Oregon Jazz Band. Clearly a man of wide interests, Bill Borcher also had connections with one of the bigger breweries and was a basketball coach. The original plan which Borcher had contrived, had been to get hold of all the traditional jazz band leaders that he knew who owned or ran their own jazz clubs, and ask them if they would be interested in playing at the Jazz Jubilee for nothing! Borcher then arranged for the brewers to provide beer, also for nothing, for the entire weekend of the event. His next move was to arrange for members of his basketball association to serve in the local bars, where they sold the beer, and used the proceeds to fund the event and pay the invited foreign bands. While this scheme may seem wildly unlikely, Bill Borcher had brought it off and the Jazz Jubilee had run very successfully, since its inception in 1973. In addition to the American bands which appeared for nothing, guest bands from all over the world were also featured, although they were paid.

322

Mike met with Bill Borcher, picked his brains, had a good look at the Jazz Jubilee, and returned home Hell-bent of starting something similar in Edinburgh. Mike was not one to let the grass grow under his feet and, later that same year, he was already able to launch his first mini-festival. This first attempt to get something going was really a small-scale trial run and can be seen now as just the forerunner of what was to become a major event in the world jazz festival programme – The Edinburgh International Jazz Festival (EIJF).

This initial event took place in Stewart's Ballroom on Abbeyhill, off Regent Road and not far from Holyrood Palace. Mike had managed to persuade the owner to put up £500 to fund a jazz event that was to run over a Friday, Saturday and Sunday in the summer of 1978. The bands that Mike booked were all local and were his own New Society Syncopators, Jim Petrie's Jazz Band and Bill Salmond's Louisiana Ragtime Band. In addition, guest artistes were booked to appear with the Syncs and they were the fine tenor sax player from London, Al Gay and Edinburgh's own RHS Gangster, pianist and drummer, Stan Greig. Assessing it afterwards, Mike considered that the event had been reasonably successful. He had certainly learned a lot and was sufficiently encouraged to start planning immediately for a much more ambitious project in the following year. It was from 1979 rather than 1978 that the history of the Edinburgh Jazz Festival really began and certainly, when the Silver Jubilee celebrations for the first twenty five years took place in 2003, the twenty five began with the 1979 Festival.

For **1979**, Mike approached local brewers Drybroughs, who agreed to sponsor a 'pub trail', and christened the whole event **The Edinburgh Jazz Festival**. An organising committee, or board of directors, was formed. This included Ian Nelson, representing Drybroughs, and a good number of the local jazzers, including both musicians and non-musicians. Sam Smith, the Old Bailey band trombone player, for example, was recruited to handle much of the programme design and text, on the basis of his experience in graphic design work, and Donald McDonald, the bass and sax player, took on the job of organising the running order at gigs. A printed programme was produced, for which advertisers were attracted, and an ambitious programme it proved to be. The 1979 Jazz Festival was to run from Sunday 26th to Thursday 30th August and it started with a Festival Jazz Ball in Tiffany's Ballroom in St Stephen's Street, the programme for which included the local Russ Moore's Big Band, Old Bailey's Jazz Advocates and the Auld Reekie Parade Band. There were also three guest bands: L'Orpheon Celesta from France, the Onward Jazz Band from Newcastle and the special guests, the Oregon Jazz Band, led by Bill Borcher. The pub trail sponsored by Drybourghs was an especially ambitious part of the programme, as it was mostly free and featured a frequent, indeed frenetic, change-over of bands.

The 12 venues for the Festival were the George Hotel (Bar I and Bar II) in George Street, the Claremont Hotel in Claremont Crescent, Calton Studios in Calton Road, La Grenouille in Abercromby Place, The Northern bar at Canonmills, the Hopetoun Bar in Morrison Street, the Tankard Lounge in Rose Street, the Abercorn Inn in Piershill, Tramps near Tollcross, the St Vincent Bar in St Vincent Street and the Broughton Bar in Broughton Street. As far as I remember, the two venues in the George Hotel and Calton Studios were paying venues, but the rest were free. All of the venues operated throughout the five days of the Festival and, while some of the venues featured evenings only programmes, many also had lunchtime sessions. It was later announced that over 20,000 people took part[143]. To give a flavour of the programme, here are a couple of extracts:

George Hotel - 'Bar I' - Tuesday 28th August

3.30-4.15	Savannah Syncopators
4.15-4.45	L'Orpheon Celesta
4.45-5.30	Savannah Syncopators
7.30-8.45	Savannah Syncopators
8.45-9.45	Onward Jazz band
9.45-10.45	Mike Hart's Society Syncopators

---

[143] Edinburgh International Jazz Festival 1980 programme

10.45-11.30   L'Orpheon Celesta

Tankard Lounge – Monday 27th August

6.30-7.30   Old Bailey's Jazz Advocates
7.30-8.45   Deep South
9.00-10.00   Charlie McNair's Jazz Band
11.00-12.00   The Rhythm Method

The Northern Bar – Thursday 30th August

12.30-2.00   Onward Jazz Band
7.30-8.30   Louisiana Ragtime Band
9.30-11.30   Old Bailey's Jazz Advocates

The above extracts demonstrate an ambitious and quite intricate piece of planning, with the bands involved in short sets. However, what the above extracts do not show, is the fact that the bands were appearing at several venues each evening. As an example, I was playing with the Old Bailey band and our programme for Wednesday 29th August was:

6.30-7.30   Tramps
8.15-9.30   Abercorn Inn
10.15-11.30   George Hotel (Bar One)

Those familiar with the geography of Edinburgh will appreciate that these three venues are a long way apart, involving much travelling between spots. In addition, there was a lot of gear to shift, including amplifiers, large instruments such as double basses and drums, as well as all the musicians. I can testify to the fact that this type of programme was extremely hard work, however there was a great pioneering spirit and it was also great fun – even if I would not like to undertake anything this strenuous now-a-days! We probably would not have managed at all if it had not been for the heroic efforts of the couriers and drivers, volunteers who were there to help with moving gear, finding parking spaces and even calming down over-stressed and temperamental bandsmen. The full line-up of bands for this first Edinburgh Jazz Festival numbered 18 (ten

325

Edinburgh bands and 8 from elsewhere) and the 1979 Roll of Honour was as follows:

Guest bands -	Edinburgh bands –
L'Orpheon Celesta (France)	Russ Moore Big Band
Onward Jazz Band (Newcastle)	Old Bailey's Jazz Advocates
Oregon Jazz Band USA)	Auld Reekie Parade Band
Savannah Syncopators (England)	Bill Salmond's Louisiana Ragtime Band
Cooper/Hayton Duo	Mike Hart's Society Syncopators
George Penman Jazzmen (Glasgow)	Climax Jazz Band
Gateway Jazz Band (Carlisle)	Charlie McNair's Jazz Band
Deep South	Rhythm Method
	West End Jazz Band
	Djangology

One of the bands listed above is **Djangology**, a new band which grew, completely unintentionally, out of guitarists Neil Munro and Johnny Harper and reeds man Gerard Dott getting together for practice sessions at Neil Munro's house. Apparently, the Jazz Festival organizers had heard of this activity and, without consulting any of them, included them in the Jazz Festival programme. They also bestowed on them the name Djangology, in recognition of the Reinhardt influence in Neil's playing. Johnny Harper was unable to make the Festival gigs because of other playing commitments and they became a four piece band with a membership of Gerard Dott, Neil Munro on solo guitar, Ian Aitken, who was to go on to play with the pop star Shakin' Stevens, on rhythm guitar, and Johnny Phillips on bass guitar. Later, they had a residency at Le Grenouille and made a brief TV appearance during the Festival playing 'Fascinating Rhythm'. Sadly, the band only lasted a couple of years, disbanding in 1980. Neil Munro had never been happy with the imposed name, apparently considering it to be too type casting in character and, by its nature, unnecessarily restricting their musical freedom. In protest, when the time came for their final gig, Neil had them billed as The Norman Hitler Big Band!

There is no intention in this book of attempting a detailed account of the Edinburgh Jazz Festival and its developments over the many years to come. Rather, I will give an outline account of the early years, the main developments and the increasingly impressive list of great jazz names who took part, as the Festival established itself, becoming, in a surprisingly sort time, a premier event on the international jazz stage.

In **1980**, the Jazz Festival was to run from 24th to 28th August and was now styled **The Edinburgh International Jazz Festival** (EIJF). It was again in association with Drybroughs and the programme stated that *'...the festival broadens its wings geographically and stylistically but still retains an emphasis on hot traditional jazz and undiscovered musicians. Twenty-one bands and five soloists from six different countries, playing at sixteen venues and performing over 200 sessions'.* It was also announced that *'the programme's character has developed considerably to include some of the creators of the music alongside a number of exciting new discoveries. There are more events, more spontaneous guests, a much bigger marching parade – and no electric pianos!'*[144] Other innovations were that the BBC was to broadcast some sessions from the George Hotel and that a Jazz Bus would provide free transport between venues. Festival T-shirts were available, as was an All Venues Badge. A 1980 Jazz Festival LP was available at £4.50 which featured eleven different bands including Edinburgh's Auld Reekie Parade Band, the Storyville Five, the Louisiana Ragtime Band, the Charlie McNair Jazz Band, Mike Hart's Society Syncopators and Old Bailey's Jazz Advocates. Guest bands featured on the LP were L'Orpheon Celesta, WASO, George Penman's Jazz Band with Fionna Duncan, the Savannah Syncopators and the Sammy Rimmington Jazz Band.

Star visitors for 1980 included the remarkable reeds player Benny Waters, who had been born on 23 January 1902, had played and recorded with 'King' Oliver and Fletcher Henderson, and who was still playing as dynamically as ever. Benny was to continue his amazing playing career until after his 95th birthday in 1997, on which occasion he recorded an album called 'Live at Ninety Five' for Bluenote, and finally died on 11 August 1998. Other notable visitors included drummer Andrew Hall and trumpeter Teddy Riley from New Orleans, blues singer Jan Sutherland from Merseyside, trombonist Roy Williams from

---

[144] Edinburgh International Jazz Festival 1980 programme

Luton, the Bourbon Street Jazz Band from Denmark, the New Black Eagle Jazz Band from the USA,, Sammy Rimmington's Jazz Band from London, a gypsy band called WASO from Belgium, who played in the Django tradition, and a banjo virtuoso from the USA, Ed Turner. In addition, there were several returners from 1979 including L'Orpheon Celesta, the Savannah Syncopators and Kid Dawson's Onward Jazz Band. All of the 1979 local bands appeared but, in addition, there were Bill Jones' Rhythm Method, the Corstorphine Jazz Youth Orchestra, the Storyville Five and Violet Milne's Spirits of Rhythm.

A welcome inclusion was that of Edinburgh's own piano maestro, Alex Shaw with his trio, said to be '...as far as the Festival goes towards "modern" jazz'. There was again an extensive free pub trail, featuring an increased number of venues. The bands had extremely demanding schedules once again, with three gigs in a day commonplace. However, a great compensation for several of the local bands was a number of sessions where they backed one of the guest solo stars. Below is a day's programme for one of the George Hotel venues; as an example of how the Festival had grown in all ways:

George Hotel I – Tuesday 26ᵗʰ August 1980

12.30-2.00pm	Alex Shaw Trio with Benny Waters
12.15-3.00pm	L'Orpheon Celesta
3.00-4.00pm	WASO
4.15-5.00pm	New Era Jazz Band
5.30-6.30pm	Corstorphine Jazz Youth Orchestra
7.00-8.00pm	George Penman's Jazz Band with Fionna Duncan
10.15-11.30pm	Festival All Stars – Teddy Riley, Benny Waters, Roy Williams, Stan Greig, Billy Law, Ronnie Rae

Once again, there was a great atmosphere and a sense of supporting something very worthwhile. There were really enormous crowds turning out, right through from the opening Parade along Princes Street to the closing sessions on Thursday 28th August. Things were looking and sounding good.

The **1981 EIJF** ran from 23rd to 27th August 1981 and was again sponsored by Drybroughs. Iain Nelson, Drybrough's Sales and Marketing Director, said in the printed programme *'We at Drybroughs are delighted with the continued growth, both physically and conceptually of the Edinburgh International Jazz Festival....Through the use of Drybroughs pubs and hotels in Edinburgh as mainly free entry venues, we feel that the original concept of live jazz at grass roots level is being maintained. The Drybroughs Youth Jazz Band Trophy will be awarded for the first time this year following a competition involving nine youth bands. It is vital that young talent is recognized and encouraged in order to assure the future of Jazz in Scotland."*[145] Mike Hart, also in the programme, said *'This year looks as if it will be the most exciting yet, with four great bands from the USA, one from Denmark, one from France, one from Belgium and a whole host of bands and top class solo musicians from the UK'.*

The Youth Jazz competition, to be held in the Queen's Hall, was a particularly welcome innovation, with several prizes on offer. In addition to the Drybourgh's Trophy for the most promising band, there were to be prizes for individual merit, including the Pete Seaton Shield for the best young musician and other prizes donated by Gordon Simpson's Music Shop and the Musician's Union. The youthful competitors included the Tommy Smith Quintet, the Midnight Blues Band, Twang, the Wester Hailes Education Centre Syncopators and the Corstorphine Youth Jazz Orchestra. No one knew then, of course, that the young tenor saxist, Tommy Smith, was to become a world famous jazz musician within a few short years. Tribute was paid to Platform, the Scottish jazz promotion organisation who had organised jazz groups and classes under the guidance of Gordon Cruikshank, for generating *'...a whole new youth jazz scene with all sorts of different aspects of jazz music finding its way into the curriculum'.*

There were again many returning, successful bands from previous years, with new guests including The Jazz Society

---

[145] Official Programme, 1981 EIJF

from the north of England, the Batchelors of Jazz from Glasgow, the Watergate 7 + 1 from France, and the Golden West Syncopators and the High Sierra Jazz Band and the Tarnished Six from the USA.   New solo visitors included clarinetist Ian Arnott, whom we last met as a young associate of the RHS Gang in the early 1950s, banjo player Johnny Harper briefly home from his travels, pianist Fred Hunt and trumpeter Digby Fairweather.   The established favourites Benny Waters and Roy Williams were back again. There were several new local bands making a first appearance as well, including Swing 81, the Apothecaries of Jazz who were a composite band from all over the UK, the Festival City Jazz Band and the Scottish Jazz Advocates. A number of unattached local jazzers were featured as soloists guesting with various bands, including vocalist Jackie MacFarlane, drummer Dave Swanson, Gus Ferguson, Donald McDonald and Alex Shaw.   The Festival again kicked off with a parade along Princes Street and two major Jazz Band Balls were held, one on the opening night and the other, billed as a Grand Farewell Ball, on final night in the Big Top Marquee at Prestonfield House Hotel. The latter was to culminate with a Great Breakfast Jam Session, timed to finish at 4.30am!   Ian Nelson of Drybourghs, writing in the next year's programme, said of the 1981 Festival *'The response from bands and enthusiasts alike was staggering – venues throughout the town were bulging at the seams and the overall atmosphere was absolutely fantastic'.*

The **fourth EIJF** took place between Sunday 29th August and Thursday 2nd September **1982** and was billed as the **Drybourghs Edinburgh International Jazz Festival**. Mike Hart, in his Message from the Director said of the Festival to come *'We are unique, because 60% of our venues are free, we are taking jazz to the people. We are unique because, unlike many other festivals, we do not require "name" artistes to "put bums on seats", we invite performers for their excellence, enthusiasm and good humour. Lastly, we are unique because our setting is Edinburgh – need I say more!'*[146]   Mike also paid a particular tribute to Donald

[146] Edinburgh International Jazz Festival 1982 programme

McDonald saying that his '...*effort and dedication has been beyond the call of duty.*'

Once again, the programme had been expanded, with bands from the USA, Canada, Poland, Austria, West Germany, France, Denmark, England and Scotland. Again, many old favourites were back but with many new comers, including the Carol Kidd Trio, the Ralph Laing All Stars, the Royal Society Jazz Orchestra, the Ness River Rhythm Kings, the Hot Antic Jazz Band, the Merseysippi Jazz Band, the Seatown Seven, the South Frisco Jazz Band, the Traditional Jazz Four, the Trevor Richards Trio, the Bluenote Seven and the Dave Donohoe Band. The programme listed a total of 32 bands, with one new Edinburgh band making its first appearance. This was the **Gumbo Jazz Band** which featured Finlay Milne, trumpet playing son of Kenny and Violet, Ian Boyter (rds), Dave Bradford (tbn), Tony Sergent (bs) and Mac Rae (drms). Although this was to be quite a short lived band, with a couple of musicians who were not Edinburgh based and presumably brought in for the Festival, it marked the first appearance of Ian Boyter who was to become a long serving Edinburgh jazzer. Unfortunately, the talented Finlay Milne was not to become an Edinburgh fixture. His work in TV took him to the south, although happily he was to make fairly regular return visits in the future.

However, impressive though the list of bands was, it was the number and quality of the solo guests that demonstrated just how far the EIJF had come in four short years. Old favourites like Benny Waters, Al Gay and Roy Williams were there again, as were Fred Hunt and Digby Fairweather, but added to them was a positive feast of great names. The new comers were headed by the great Teddy Wilson, surely one of the finest jazz pianists in all of jazz and the versatile Dick Carey, the original pianist with the Louis Armstrong All Stars, who was equally adept on trumpet and alto horn. From Canada were singer Jodie Drake and sax man Jim Galloway, an ex-pat Scot from Ayrshire. From the UK there was the one and only Humphrey Lyttelton, pianist Eddie Thompson, guitarist Jim Douglas once of Gifford in East Lothian, the reeds maestros Johnny Barnes and Dave Shepherd, bass player Paul Sealey and Roy Crimmins, trombone player in one of the late Alex Welsh's best bands. In addition, there was a host of Scottish based musicians who were making guest appearances with many of the bands. It was some programme and it was some Festival. The pub trail was as big as ever, and there was an increase in the pay-to-get-in venues. Ian Nelson, in the programme for the next year said of the 1982 EIJF *'I asked if 1982's Jazz Festival could possibly follow the success of the previous one. The answer was resounding, pulsating, exciting and definite. The Festival really took off, and for four days, Edinburgh rang out to hot sounds played by musicians from countries as far apart as Poland and the USA, but sharing a common bond, a love for jazz'*[147].

However, it did not come without cost. The work done and the problems faced by the organizers can be gauged from Mike Hart's comments in EIJF 1983 programme: *'We have made it to our fifth year! It never ceases to amaze me how it all comes together, after battling through what seemed to be insurmountable odds. This year we had to overcome the cancellation of our biggest attraction, which was to be held at Murrayfield Stadium – The Jazz Pavilion, four weeks prior to the Festival. This meant a frantic search for a site, ranging from farmer's fields to ice rinks! We are extremely fortunate in acquiring the Sports hall at Meadow Bank Stadium thanks to the kind assistance of the Director of Recreation and Leisure'*. The Festival was once again sponsored by Drybroughs although, sadly, this was to be their final year.

The **1983 EIJF** started, as had become the tradition, with the jazz parade along Princes Street followed by the Youth Jazz Band competition, which continued to attract a good number of quality entries. There were eight entries this year and the prizes made up an impressive list:

The Drybrough Cup for the best Youth Band
The Pete Seaton Shield for the best Young Musician
The Musician's Union Prize for the best Young Drummer

---

[147] Edinburgh International Jazz Festival 1983 programme

The Gordon Simpson Prize for the Most Promising Young Musician
The Alex Welsh Trophy for the Most Promising Young Trumpeter.

The Festival dates this year were Sunday 28th August to Friday 2nd September 1983. Yet again, there had been expansion, with nineteen guest bands from across the world and fifteen from Scotland. Again, the list of solo performers was quite remarkable. Newcomers from the USA included trumpeter Adolphus 'Doc' Cheatham who had worked with Chick Webb, Teddy Wilson, Cab Calloway and Benny Goodman, Count Basie's lead alto saxophonist Earle Warren and Al Casey, who had made his name as guitarist with Fats Waller and his Rhythm. From the UK came the fine piano players Brian Lemmon and Dill Jones and clarinetist Acker Bilk. Given that the likes of Benny Waters, Roy Williams, Jim Galloway, Fred Hunt, and Dave Shepherd were back again, together with a host of Scottish jazzers, it meant that, yet again, the organizers had put together an appetising array of talent. Newcomers amongst the visiting bands were the Natural Gas Jazz Band, the Rosie O'Grady Band, the Climax Band from Canada, the Pete Allen Jazz Band, the Hot Club of London, Kid Boyd's New Orleans Jazz Band and Tommy Burton's Sporting House Four. In addition, Humph was back but with his full band this time, as usual packed with star names, and there was the band of a terrific trumpeter from Australia, Bob Barnard, the first band from Oz to appear at the EIJF.

BBC Radio Scotland had presented an engraved bowl to be awarded to the band chosen by a panel of judges as the best in the festival, with bands of four or more members and with no professional musicians eligible to compete. The 1983 winners were to be the Hot Antic Jazz Band from France. Among the Edinburgh bands new to the Festival were the Jack Finlay Trio and the East Coast Jazz Band led by drummer, Frank Birnie. The band included some illustrious local names including Jimmy Shortreed on reeds (what else?!) and trombonist Johnny McGuff, whose main band was now the Scottish Jazz Advocates. The 1983 EIJF programme totaled twenty eight listed as solo guests and an incredible thirty three bands.

A band, although not one from Edinburgh, that should be mentioned is the **Apothecaries of Jazz**. This band was made up of jazz-playing pharmacists from across the UK and was an advertising venture sponsored by the pharmaceutical companies, the Winpharm Group and Hobbypharm. They played in the New Orleans style and described themselves a 'Dispensers of Fine Jazz'. The band was led by banjoist Bernard Hardisty and varied from seven to as much as thirteen-piece, including a couple of vocalists and a Grand Marshall. Two Edinburgh pharmaceutical jazzers, Kenny Milne (tpt) and George Duncan (rds), were involved and had played with the Apothecaries at the EIJF in 1981/82/83 and were to do so again in 1986. This band travelled widely on behalf of their sponsors and, in addition to many jazz events in the UK, appeared in Hong Kong, Malta and Hawaii as well as making a number of appearances on TV.

There were many local benefits from the EIJF and not least among them, was the fact that so many ordinary followers, with perhaps, only a casual liking for the noise that traditional jazz bands make, had become familiar, not only with some of the biggest names in jazz, but also saw that some of the top local musicians were no slouches either. In addition, there were some people, visitors and locals alike, attracted to the EIJF, who had no previous interest in jazz whatsoever but rapidly became converts.

It was sad that Drybroughs, who had given such terrific support over the first five years, felt it was time to drop out. Without their support there would have been no EIJF, or at best, a very much less ambitious one, and their withdrawal could have spelt the end of a great project. As Mike Hart was to say in the 1984 programme *'After the withdrawal of our previous sponsors, in February of this year, I did not know if we were in a position to continue. At the eleventh hour, however, Edinburgh's foremost suppliers of 80/- ale came to the rescue'*. It had been a near thing but the sixth EIJF show was to go on.

The new sponsors for 1984 were to be another famous name in Scottish brewing, **Scottish Brewers** and their sponsorship of the EIJF was to be under the banner of their famous brand name, **McEwens**. Like their predecessors, McEwens were to put their weight behind the pub trail which, in the eyes of many including a lot of the local musicians, had been one of the great successes of the early Festivals. Mike said *'I would also like to thank the owners and managers of our new free trade venues for their enthusiastic support. Without them the jazz festival would have been but a shadow of its former self'*. This meant, of course, a whole new list of pub venues which were part of the McEwens empire and, although some good venues were lost, it was exciting to be playing in new places and attracting people local to the pubs. The Scottish Brewers Chairman himself, Alastair Mowat, was involved and on the Board of Directors of the EIJF, which seemed an encouraging sign of the new sponsors commitment, and he said *'As a company, Scottish Brewers strongly believe that we should support those who support us and we are therefore equally delighted to have been able to save this now well established and very popular event which has become such a prominent supporting feature of the Edinburgh Festival'*. It should also be mentioned that Alastair Mowat was to be a consistent and generous supporter of the EIJF over many years. A jazz enthusiast himself, his contributions to the festival went far beyond his business involvement and were to include a sizeable personal donation to the EIJF funds. With friends of that calibre, the future of the EIJF looked to be secure for a long time to come.

The programme for the **1984 McEwen's EIJF (19th to 24th August)** was, as had become usual, to start with the Youth Jazz Band Competition on the morning of the opening Sunday. The Sunday afternoon saw the now traditional closing of Princes Street for the Jazz Parade, this year featuring no less than nineteen floats, which continued to attract thousands of spectators. The Sunday night and small hours of Monday morning were devoted to the traditional Opening Jazz Band Ball at the Jazz Pavilion in Meadowbank Stadium. The same venue was to host other special events including a Salute to Humphrey Lyttelton, a Tribute to Count Basie, a Midnight Folly, a Take me Back to

New Orleans Carnival and the Grand Farewell Ball. There was also another innovation, a Jazz Tap and Jive competition. In addition to the main venues at the Meadowbank Stadium and the George Hotel, there were fifteen pubs and hotels on the still mostly free pub trail.

This year the programme listed thirty-three bands, an impressive array of solo stars and an even longer list of Scottish jazzers, making guest appearances. Once again, there were many familiar and welcome faces, who had appeared in earlier festivals, and the list of new comers featured some resounding jazz names. Amongst them was Count Basie's great tenor sax star Buddy Tate, pianist Red Richards, tap dancer Will Gaines and cornetist Warren Vache, all from the USA. From the UK there was Kenny Baker, one of the country's finest ever trumpeters, the inimitable trombonist George Chisholm, one of Europe's best ever jazz musicians, and singer Beryl Bryden. New comers amongst the bands included Monty Sunshine's Jazz Band, the Frog Island Jazz Band with clarinetist Cy Laurie, Bob Kerr's Whoopee Band and the Midnight Follies Orchestra, all from south of the border, Sweden's Sveriges Jazz Band, the Hot Cotton Jazz Band from the USA, the Jazz Classics from West Germany and the Sensation Band from Canada. From the Continent came Italy's Milano Jazz Gang and Leonardo Pedersen's Jazz Kadel from Denmark. There could be no doubt that the EIJF was living up with a vengeance to the International part of its title.

More locally, there were a couple of new bands, the **Jack Graham Jazz Band**, a new departure for the perennial side-man Jack Graham, and the **Alan Anderson Band**, from their base in the Border country and playing in a mainstream style. A band specially put together for the festival was **The Rising Sons**, a band of youngsters, some of whom were offspring of well known jazzers, including trumpeter Finlay Milne, son of Kenny and Violet, Sammy Rimmington junior, a clarinetist like his Dad and Emile Martyn, drummer son of the well-known Barry. Carol Kidd, a great singer with a growing international reputation, and Dave Batchelor were over from Glasgow and, of course, there were all the usual suspects from Edinburgh. The

EIJF continued to go from strength to strength and the new sponsors had settled in comfortably.

So the first six years, from 1979 to 1984, of the EIJF had been and gone. So far, it was clear that each year had been better than the last, the choice greater, the number and quality of the guests becoming more and more impressive. In the Programme for the 1986 McEwen's EIJF, the Scotsman jazz writer and critic, Tony Troon, wrote *'...it was in 1980 that the EIJF began to operate a policy which transformed the event over succeeding years, giving it breadth and serious purpose to stand alongside its other quality of providing foot-tapping entertainment. This policy was the hiring of individual jazz stars to mix into the broth, giving jazz patrons some evidence of creative origins to counterbalance the derivative hordes. (A few of these derivative bands, however, were undeniably good)'* [148]. There may be a hint of an 'art for art's sake' stance in Tony's comments (although as one undoubtedly numbering amongst the derivative hordes, I am glad he added the last bit), none the less, in essence, he was quite right. He was also correct, later in his article, when he hailed the EIJF policy of inviting jazz musicians who were *'...below the level of mega-stardom that dominates the popular arts'* but were musicians of *'...great ability and individuality who should not be overlooked'*. He gave as examples of this, the not obvious choices of Teddy Riley and Benny Waters, the first such guests of the EIJF.

However, it must be pointed out that, if it had not been for the efforts of the foot-tapping entertainers, a vast number of the people who turned out to support the early Festivals would not have turned out, the Festival could well have shriveled and died and the followers would never have had the chance to hear the distinguished visitors. Tony Troon also paid tribute to what he called 'The Second Chorus Factor' – the fact that many musicians who had spent years buried in the sections of bands were musicians who, as Tony said, had huge quantities of bottled up creative talent. He gave, as examples of this factor,

---

[148] Troon A, 'The Second Chorus Factor', McEwen's Edinburgh International Jazz Festival programme, 1986

musicians such as Fats Waller's guitarist Al Casey and trumpeter Doc Cheatham, both wonderful players who made an enormous impact in their performances at the EIJF.

The EIJF was now in the midst of what, for many, were to be especially memorable years. With hindsight, it is fairly clear why this should be so. The EIJF had been created, in the first place, to be a festival of traditional jazz. This meant, of course, traditional jazz in its broadest sense, embracing any of the many strands of jazz in its pre-bebop form. Later, as the years went by, the spectrum was to widen and increasingly, more modern forms of jazz were to be presented (Edinburgh's Tommy Smith was to be prominent amongst them), as were jazz influenced performers with a more general public appeal, such as Georgie Fame and Van Morrison. However, in the mid-1980s, that trend was only just beginning and the EIJF was still very much oriented to the earlier forms of jazz. What was clear from the history of jazz, of course, was that, from the late 1940s on, by far the greater number of new, young, cutting-edge jazz musicians, especially amongst the Afro-Americans, was playing in the bebop and post-bebop style. By the mid-1980s, this shift had been going on for about forty years and, inevitably, the great names from the pre-bebop world who were still around and active, were getting fewer and fewer.

The first generation of post-bebop jazzers were, by the 1980s, themselves becoming veterans, so it was hardly surprising that the surviving pre-bop greats were well into the twilight of their careers. There were also many great players who had come into jazz post-bebop, who were not really revivalists, but had been content to stay more or less within the mainstream, pre-bebop style. These included players such as Ruby Braff, Scott Hamilton, Ken Peplowski, Kenny Davern, and others, but the pool of the older players was inevitably contracting. In the mid-1980s, however, there were still some of these pre-bebop veterans to invite to the EIJF, still playing wonderfully well and providing a late but privileged opportunity to hear them. It would be true, I think, to say that the 1980s represented the last flowering of the middle period of jazz; the playing of jazzers who had themselves been inspired by and had built on, the earlier forms of the music and who had added greater technical and musical knowledge and skill. As a measure of the quality of the EIJFs of the mid-1980s, it is worth running the eye down those who featured as solo guests, some real veterans others much younger, in the years 1983-1987. The years in which they appeared are shown:

Buddy Tate 1984/85/86/87
Al Casey 1983
Red Richards 1984
Warren Vache 1984/85
Doc Cheatham 1983/84
Earle Warren 1983
Benny Waters 1983/84/85/86
Jim Galloway 1983/84/85/86/87
Henri Chaix 1983
Acker Bilk 1983
Fred Hunt 1983
Len Skeat 1983
Dave Shepherd 1983/84/85/86
Kenny Baker 1984
George Chisholm 1984
Roy Williams 1983/84/85/86/87
Will Gaines 1984
Brian Lemon 1983/84/85/86
Paul Sealley 1983/84
Al Casey 1985/87
Al Fairweather 1985/86
Carl Fontana 1985
Gus Johnson 1985/86
Jane Jarvis 1985
Milt Hinton 1985/86
Ray Bryant 1985/86
Spanky Davis 1985/86
Tommy Smith 1985/87
Bruce Adams 1986/87
Bill Aldred 1986/87
John Barnes 1986/87
Harry Edison 1986/87

Jack Fallon 1986
Stan Greig 1986/87
Al Grey 1986
Dick Hyman 1986
Humphrey Lyttelton 1986/87
Fapy Lafertin 1986
Johnny Parker 1986/87
Dave Newton 1986
Jack Parnell 1986/87
Lillian Boutte 1987
Janusz Carmello 1987
Wally Fawkes 1987
Ray Foxley 1987
Al Gay 1987
Dave Green 1987
Reggie Johnson 1987
Oliver Jackson 1987
Brain Kellock 1987
Thomas L'Etienne 1987
Johnny Letman 1987
Jay McShann 1987
Grover Mitchell 1987
Danny Moss 1987
Mike Peters 1987
Antti Sarpila 1987
Mark Shane 1987
Ralph Sutton 1987
Bruce Turner 1987
Martin Taylor 1987
Al Cohn 1987
Bob Wilber 1987

Of course, the above list is by no means the end of the story of these vintage years. Some listed as guests in the above were there in other years but featured, not as solo guests, but as band leaders, for example Humphrey Lyttelton. Also not shown above is the host of bands, some of them very notable, which appeared in the same years. Nor does the list include the talented array of local bands and soloists who played their usual crucial role, particularly on the vastly popular pub trail. It would be tedious to try to list everyone who played and every special session that took place, but perhaps the above does demonstrate the quality, as well as the sheer quantity, of jazz on offer in the mid-1980s. This is not to imply that the earlier Festivals were any less memorable or that there were not terrific Festivals to come but for many, and I believe this includes Mike Hart himself, these years were the peak.

But it was not only the increasingly impressive list of solo stars and bands that made the mid-1980s EIJFs so memorable. There were also some new developments that demonstrated the increasing ambition and confidence of the event and its organisers. In **1985 (18th to 23rd August)**, the special tribute events continued, in this case celebrating the centenaries of both Joe 'King' Oliver and Jelly Roll Morton. In addition, there were more sessions featuring all-star groups brought together from among the guest list, usually under the leadership of one of the great names, and international groups, bringing together jazzers from all over the world. The line-up of the Festival All Stars at the Opening Ball in 1985 of Buddy Tate (ten sax), Spanky Davis (tpt), Carl Fontana (tbn), Ray Bryant (pno), Al Casey (gtr), Milt Hinton (bs) and Gus Johnson (drms), would have enhanced and added lustre to any jazz event in the world.

Other All–star sessions were led by Buddy Tate, Warren Vache, Al Fairweather, Carl Fontana and Roy Williams. Top Scottish jazzers, including Ronnie Rae (bs), Tony McLennan (drms), Jack Finlay (pno), Kenny Ellis (bs) Dave Swanson (drms) and Francis Cowan (bs), were fittingly included in some of the All-Star bands. For the first time, there was a collaborative venture with the Scottish National Orchestra, arranged jointly by the McEwen's EIJF and the Edinburgh International Festival, including the premier of a new work specially commissioned by the EIJF. This was described in the programme as the climax of the Festival and took place in the Usher Hall under the baton of Russell Gloyd. The new work, entitled 'Hot and Suite', had been written by Jim Galloway and was described as *'...a fantasia for orchestra and jazz ensemble with the concept being a loose chronological look at some of the major signposts on the journey that jazz has made since its beginnings'*[149]. The performers and signposts were introduced throughout the evening by Humphrey Lyttelton.

Thirty three bands were listed in 1985, and there were twenty venues which, happily, still included fourteen free venues on the pub trail, although a couple of them were only free for lunch time sessions, tickets being required in the evening. Locally, 1985 was marked by the first EIJF appearance of Hamish McGregor's new band, Fat Sam's Band, playing in a jump jive, R 'n B and Swing style, a band which was to become a long-term fixture on the Edinburgh jazz scene and which was to build for itself, an international reputation. Another local new comer was the Gordon Cruikshank Quartet, playing in a modern style, with Gordon fronting on tenor sax, backed by Dave Newton (pno), Brian Shields (bs) and Mike Travis (drms).

In **1986 (17ᵗʰ to 23ʳᵈ August)**, again sponsored by McEwens, the EIJF was to host a total of thirty seven bands, not including the various star-studded bands put together for special sessions. It also featured an increase in the number of paying venues, with seven of these dubbed Gold Star Venues, for which tickets were required. The free pub trail remained in good health, with thirteen venues well scattered across the town. Important events included another major Usher Hall concert. Mike Hart introduced this in the Programme by saying *'I am delighted to announce that, due to the great success of our joint concert with Edinburgh Festival last year, our closing production will be held again in the Usher Hall, titled 'the Golden Age of Jazz' presented by Dick Hyman'*[150].

---

[149] Introduction, McEwen's Edinburgh International Jazz Festival programme, 1985.
[150] Edinburgh International Jazz Festival programme 1986

The Opening Ball at Meadowbank was graced by one of the put-together bands and again, it was like one of those bands we used to put together in our imaginations when we were young. This one had a real flavor of the old Count Basie band with a line-up of Harry Edison (tpt), Al Grey (tbn), Buddy Tate (ten sax) and the same wonderful rhythm section that had enthralled everybody the previous year, Ray Bryant (pno), Milt Hinton (bs) and Gus Johnson (drms). It was billed as Harry Edison's Harlem Stampede and throughout the seven days, it made several appearances with one or other of the legends nominated as leader. There was also a 1986 Festival All Stars which had Spanky Davis (tpt), Roy Williams (tbn), Jim Galloway (rds), Johnny Parker (pno), Jack Fallon (bs) and Jack Parnell (drms).

Milt Hinton was a revelation on bass. I remember standing with a group of other bass players, which from memory included Ronnie Rae, Roy Percy and Jerry Forde, by the side of the band stand at Meadowbank, listening to him play with the other legends. Without exception, we were utterly captivated by his playing. In the case of one of us, I believe that the experience of listening to Milt Hinton radically altered his whole concept of what the double bass was capable of and changed his whole approach to his instrument from then on. Apart from his outstanding solo work, I was struck by Milt Hinton's seemingly effortless power and swing. Every note was so well centred, so well placed and moved so seamlessly through the structure of each tune, that the rest of the extremely distinguished band seemed simply to lie back on his beat and be carried along with it.

The **1987 McEwen's EIJF** ran for eight days, from 15th to 22nd August. Mike Hart, writing his customary introduction in the official programme[151], said *'This year's Festival has taken another stride towards being one of the most exciting events in the World's Jazz Calendar. I have included some interesting new faces along with some of the old favourites, plus some of the American Jazz Giants who deserve more recognition in Europe'*. It had seemed clear that there had been some broadening of scope over several

---

[151] Edinburgh International Jazz Festival programme 1987

years, but there was a definite and conscious acceleration of the process in 1987. This was high-lighted by the journalist Kenny Mathieson, then of WIRE magazine, who headed his article in the 1987 official Programme *'So What Happened to Edinburgh's Trad Bash?'* He answered his own question by saying *'Simple, it has moved with the times – Mike Hart hasn't been letting the grass grow under his feet. From its humble origins in an Edinburgh Ballroom, with a full two guests from the international jazz scene – well, okay , from England – the Festival has not only grown in size, reputation and merit, it has also steadily diversified in the process, if never quite to the extent evident as this year.'* [152]

The heading for Kenny Mathieson's article sounded, as was probably intended, a bit provocative. 'Trad Bash' is hardly a complimentary term and there seemed to be a hint that, to achieve artistic and critical respectability, the EIJF had seen a need to embrace a wider spectrum of jazz. With hindsight, although not at the time, I think he was correct. As the great veteran originals of the middle period of jazz faded away, there would have to be an increasing reliance on the reproduction by others of earlier forms of jazz. There would soon be much less scope to present originals, even if some were well past their prime. I think this is partly the point that Tony Troon was making in the 1986 Programme when he spoke of *'...giving jazz patrons some evidence of creative origins to counterbalance the derivative hordes'*[153]. The ability to present evidence of creative origins in the future was going to require an opening of the door to more modern and contemporary jazz musicians. The message from both Tony Troon and Kenny Mathieson to the EIJF seemed to me to be something like – by all means celebrate the jazz glories of the past but jazz is not just the past, it has a present and a future as well. It is only fair to add that both Kenny Mathieson and Tony Troon had a great many good things to say about the EIJF, to the extent that Tony headed his 1987 Programme article *'The Ninth in an Increasingly Impressive Series'*.

---

[152] Mathieson K, Edinburgh International Jazz Festival programme, 1987
[153] Troon A, Edinburgh International Jazz Festival Programme, 1986

Of course, as years went by, the tendency to look backwards was to continue with a policy of laying on tribute packages, where musicians were expected to represent the styles of past masters. However, generally it was the bands and band arrangements that represented the style being celebrated, with soloists free to play as they pleased. In addition, although the concept was by definition derivative in nature, the tributes did sometimes feature musicians who had been involved with the originals. A notable example of this was the presence of Buddy Tate in the Tribute to Count Basie in 1984. The big event for 1987 was The King of Swing, a tribute to Benny Goodman, which featured some of the original Goodman big band scores and was presented by the great clarinetist, Bob Wilber. These were, of course, notable anniversaries and well worth marking in this way and, backward looking or not, they were of a very high standard.

Equally sincere and welcome were events dedicated to the memory of jazz musicians who had recently died, including Alex Welsh, Fred Hunt and Gordon Dillon, trumpeter with the George Penman Jazzmen from Glasgow. Perhaps ringing slightly less true and with a more obvious commercial slant, were presentations in years to come under titles such as 'Joe Bloggs plays the music of Louis Armstrong'. On a personal note, it always seemed to me that, in a jazz context, Joe Bloggs should play the music of Joe Bloggs. However, I am well aware that it is easy for me to say that, when I did not have to worry about selling tickets and filling venues. Speaking of venues, 1987 saw the advent of two new major ones, a 1000 capacity Jazz Big Top on the Meadows and the Jazz Amphitheatre in Lothian Road. In total, there were eight Gold Star venues and fourteen free venues on the pub trail.

There really can be little doubt that there was a clear case, and probably a need, to open up the EIJF to contemporary and more modern forms of jazz and, in 1987, the EIJF board had taken decisive action to widen the range of jazz on offer. The programme included the Tommy Chase Quartet, described as *selling hard-driving bop to the youthful club goers of London'*, the Dave Newton Band, the Clark Tracey Quintet who *'delivered melodic jazz in the modern style'* and the Stan Tracey Trio, all of whom were firmly in the modern camp. It was also good to see local representatives of the more modern approach, with the inclusion of the John Burgess Band, fronted by John Burgess on tenor sax, who had been a winner in a previous Youth Jazz Competition. The EIJF had come a long way since the early years and the coy comment in the 1980 programme that Alex Shaw and his trio were *'...as far as the Festival goes towards "modern" jazz'*.

Also featuring as a name in an EIJF programme for the first time, was **Brian Kellock**, then aged around twenty-five and having just finished his Bachelor of Music degree at Edinburgh University. Brian was to go on to become one of the finest jazz musicians Edinburgh had ever produced, a world renowned piano player, with the interest and capability to play wonderfully well in virtually any form of jazz. His career is really beyond the scope of this book and his many recordings will be found listed in the major catalogues. However, in 1987, due presumably to a typo, it was not as Brian <u>Kellock</u> that he appeared in the Programme but Brian <u>Kellog</u>. What an opportunity he had, had he been so inclined; he could have formed a band in the Spike Jones tradition and had a major career as Brian Kellog and the Corn Flakes!

In the **1988 McEwen's EIJF** Programme, Mike Hart said *'For our tenth anniversary year we have over 400 musicians from all over the world performing in 23 venues sponsored by Scotland's leading brewer'*[154]. There were now twelve Gold Star venues, two concert venues but the free venues had dropped to just nine and, for the first time, the pay-to-get-in venues were outnumbering the free venues. Mike also stressed the fact that he was featuring great artistes who had been brought in for their excellence and not necessarily for what he called their show biz appeal. A fascinating Hall of Fame was included in the Programme, which listed all the individual performers and bands who had been featured over the ten years. The Hall of Fame came to the remarkable total of 294 bands and individuals who had appeared in the Programmes. Heaven knows what the total

---

[154] Edinburgh International Jazz Festival programme 1988

number of individual musicians would have been, taking into account that many of those listed were bands of anything up to twelve or fourteen piece.

1988 saw the return of many established favourites but also a good number of distinguished newcomers from the pre-Bebop end of the spectrum, including Scott Hamilton (ten sax), Art Hodes (pno), Jake Hanna (drms), Howard Alden (gtr), Dan Barrett (tbn), Dave McKenna (pno), Jack Lesberg (bs), Bob Barnard (tpt) and Tommy Whittle (ten sax). There were around forty seven bands listed in the Programme, of which some twenty one were new comers to the EIJF. New bands included seven from England, three from the USA, one each from Holland, Australia, Canada, Portugal and Germany and, encouragingly, half a dozen from Scotland. It was good to see amongst the English contingent, a band called Dix Six Plays Bix, not because of the fairly excruciating name, but because the tradition associated with Bix Biederbecke always seemed to be a bit under-represented in jazz generally. It was also good to see Fionna Duncan, who had sung in many EIJFs as a band singer, featuring with a band under her own name. Fionna's band was notable too as it included not only her musical partner, Ronnie Rae, on bass but Ronnie's sons, Ronnie junior on piano and John on drums. The trend towards more modern artistes continued with the Courtney Pine Quintet, Peter King (alto sax) and the John Rae Collective. This last was a real pointer towards things to come, featuring not only John Rae himself but Brian Kellock (pno), Kenny Ellis (bs), Kevin McKenzie (gtr), Colin Steele (tpt) and Phil Bancroft (ten sax), every one of them representing the future of Scottish contemporary jazz, and every one a name to note.

An innovation that was to be a significant pointer to future festivals was the inclusion of a number of blues specialists including Louisiana Red (gtr/vocs), the Beaker Blues Band, the Johnny Mars Blues Band and, featuring Edinburgh's own remarkable blues singer, the Tam White Band. There was also a special blues event called Really the Blues.

A concert in the Queen's Hall was given the title Djangology and focused on the musical tradition of Django

Reinhardt, with Fapy Lafertin, the remarkable gypsy band WASO and a special expansion of Edinburgh's Swing 88 into the Swing 88 Big Band. The 10th Anniversary Concert in the Usher Hall was A Tribute to Woody Herman and starred the NY Jazz Orchestra and the Concord All Stars, with Warren Vache, Scott Hamilton, Dan Barrett (tbn), Dave McKenna, Jack Lesberg, Jake Hanna and Howard Alden. The show also featured Doc Cheatham and the Harlem Blues and Jazz Band. It was said of this band in the Programme *'This band brings together, under the leadership of maestro Doc Cheatham, a selection of veteran jazz and blues musicians whose careers reach back to the flowering of classic jazz in the 20s and 30s'*. The line-up was terrific and included old EIJF favourite, guitarist Al Casey. Some band, some Programme and some Festival. Things continued to look good.

And that is as far as this book will track the EIJF year by year. We have looked at the developments over the first ten years and noted the remarkable growth from small beginnings to a place in the international jazz calendar. We leave it with its future, at least in the meantime, assured. The future, however, would bring many changes. The amount of more modern forms of jazz would increase gradually and the introduction of specialist blues artistes would lead, in 1997, to a change in the name to the Edinburgh International Jazz and Blues Festival (EIJBF). Gradually too, the free pub trail, an immensely popular part of the early Festivals, would diminish and disappear and with that would come a gradual decline in the part played by the local Edinburgh traditional bands. This was a great pity and was greatly mourned by many supporters but, in the end, they had had the solution in their own hands. The free pub trail fell by the wayside because, although the punters turned out in droves in the pubs, there was a tendency for them to sit and enjoy the music but a lack of a tendency to buy many drinks. Both the major sponsors dropped out because, in the end, their pubs just did not do enough business.

The Festival had started as an event simply celebrating traditional jazz and, while it was that and that alone, its success was plain to see. However, it was always inevitable that its character would change as time went on and it grew bigger. Mike Hart had started with quite a small, hard-working committee, drawn mostly from people already involved in the local traditional jazz scene. As the Festival grew, the numbers required to plan and run the event had to get bigger. As the Festival grew, more sponsors were required and the Edinburgh City Council took a stake in it. It was necessary to find ways to attract more people, sell more tickets and find ways for the Festival itself to generate more in the way of funds. Names with more clout with the general public began to appear, less pure in jazz terms perhaps, but always with a jazz orientation. New and still more ambitious venues came along, including the Festival Theatre and even St Giles Cathedral. Major changes like these did not exist in a vacuum, they brought their own changes. New people, new sponsors and new interests brought new ideas and influences and changes in policy and direction. Change was inevitable but there is no doubt that the early Festivals, those from 1979 and through the 1980s into the 1990s, are looked back upon with a great deal of affection by an awful lot of people, musos and punters alike.

However, the involvement of local bands in the EIJBF did not stop by any means. Some like Bill Salmond's Louisiana Ragtime Band, Violet Milne's Spirits of Rhythm, Jim Petrie's Diplomats of Jazz, Hamish McGregor's Fat Sam's Band and Mike Hart's Scottish Society Syncopators continued to appear in the Programme virtually every year. As the pub trail diminished, new free events appeared including the Mardi Gras, a spectacular outdoor celebration of jazz, held on the first Saturday to launch the Festival and staged in the historic Grassmarket. Jazz on a Summer's Day, another free open air event, took place in Princes Street Gardens, in the heart of the City and nestled below Edinburgh Castle. This latter event particularly, was an enormous success and reputably drew the biggest crowds of any jazz event in the UK. These were major events within the Festival, with big name bands involved, and with the accent still on traditional jazz.

Jumping forward many years, a glance at the Programme for the 2009 EIJBF demonstrates just how far the Festival

348

had come over its first 31 years, especially if compared with the examples, given earlier, of the Programmes in the first few years. In 2009, the Festival Chairman, Brian Fallon, introduced things by saying that the Programme included '...all the styles of jazz and blues, from every era of the music. You can hear the most exciting contemporary jazz groups, and the world's leading exponents of the earliest jazz piano styles, and all the stages in between'[155]. What was described as straight ahead jazz highlights included American trumpeter Roy Hargrove, Courtney Pine presenting his new project based on the music of Sydney Bechet and trumpeter Ryan Kisor, blowing up a storm with a special quintet. Atomic, The Thing and Konrad Wiszniewski represented the modern jazz zone and there was a new funk programme, featuring New Orleans drummer Stanton Moore, Elephant and Ibrahim Electric. Jack Bruce, Eric Burden and Maggie Bell were welcomed back. Singer Sinne Eeg made her Scottish debut, while Carol Kidd and Barabra Morrison returned to the Festival. A series of concerts was to take place featuring Dwayne Dopsie and the Zydeco Hellraisers, Colin Steele's Stramash and Paris Washboard.

There was a strong Scottish element too, with blues singer Tam White, Borderer David Milligan, a composer and pianist who was to write scores for the first ever Edinburgh Jazz Festival Orchestra, and baritone saxist Joe Temperley, now in his eightieth year and late of the Ellington Orchestra. Dick Hyman, now Hon President of the EIJBF, was returning as were tenor saxists Phil Bancroft and Tommy Smith, Colin Steele, Graeme Stephen, Konrad Wisziewski and Kenny Mathieson's Classic Jazz Orchestra. Several bands were described as defining the Edinburgh music scene including Fat Sam's Band, Melting Pot and Moishe's Bagel. There were shows dedicated to the music or influence of Duke Ellington, Robert Burns and Chet Baker.

Traditional jazz was featured at the Heriots Rugby Club Pavilion, courtesy of the 'Edinburgh Jazz 'n Jive Club', whose home it was throughout the year. There was also

---

[155] Edinburgh International Jazz and Blues Festival 2009

traditional jazz elsewhere with Phil Mason's New Orleans All Stars, Tricia Boutte, Edith Budge, the Batchelors of Jazz, Bill Salmond's Louisiana Ragtime Band, Swing 2009 and the Spirits of Rhythm with Thomas L'Etienne, all appearing. However, there was no doubt that by 2009, the main component of the programme was contemporary and modern forms of jazz. There were eighteen pay-to-get-in venues, for many of which booking in advance was essential, the pub trail was long gone and the only free outlets were Jazz on a Summer's Day in Princes Street Gardens and the Mardi Gras, in the Grassmarket.

Another interesting trend had been started in the 1999 EIJBF, when there was a re-union presentation of Old Bailey's Jazz Advocates. This was not a celebration of famous Edinburgh jazzers who had made their name on the National or International stage, but simply of a local band that had, in its day, been popular on a local level. The concert took place in the Hub, up on the Royal Mile near the Castle and, in addition to the Old Bailey band, featured Fionna Duncan, the George Penman Jazzmen and The Wolverines from Sweden. The response was gratifyingly enthusiastic and the show was a sell-out. This successful venture was to be developed much further in 2003, with a Silver Jubilee of Edinburgh Traditional Jazz in the Queen's Hall. This was a celebration of, not only the first twenty five years of the EIJBF, but also of the important part that the local bands had played and we will explore it in more detail later in this book. The re-union policy apropos local bands was to continue and, in the 2010 EIJBF, there were successful re-union concerts featuring the Old Bailey band, the Climax band and Pete Martin's All Stars. It was as if 1965 was alive and well and living in Edinburgh.

By the 1990s, a Board of Directors had long ago replaced the committee of local jazz enthusiasts and included several Edinburgh Councillors and figures from the world of business. By 2010, Mike Hart was styled Founding Director and there were two professional producers, Fiona Alexander and Roger Spence. Changed days indeed, but the EIJBF was clearly in good shape and was still up there with the best of European jazz events. There were regrets of course. Many mourned the early Festivals with their great

350

atmosphere, accent on entertainment and amateur enthusiasm. Many mourned the loss of the free pub trail venues – even if they had seldom bought more than a half pint of beer all evening! But the EIJBF was still a vibrant event with an International reputation, great musicians still came to play at it, local jazz was still there in greater strength than ever, if different in character. I wonder what Sandy Brown would have made of it? Would he have approved, or at least accepted it, in its 2010 form? I think he would have recognized that any art form, or festival celebrating an art form, that was to remain properly alive, had to change, had to recognize change and allow the new generations to take the lead.

But none of it, early days or later, would have happened at all without a lot of effort and goodwill from a lot of people. Particularly in the early days, scores of local jazz people gave their time and effort freely, as planners, organizers, couriers, designers and musicians - and even more of them as the essential 'bums on seats' too. Even in the first EIJF in 1979, Dryboroughs, although the principle sponsor, were not the only ones who contributed. The 1979 Festival Committee's thanks to the good number of local businesses and friends who had donated equipment, assistance, and finance were recorded in the Official Programme. Trophies were donated by the Musicians Union and the local music shops and suppliers. Even after Dryboroughs dropped out and McEwens became the major sponsor, there were many others whose contributions were crucial, including companies, both local and national, and individuals who took advertising space in the printed programmes.

There were also those at the heart of it all, the Committee and later, the Board, members whose responsibility it was to plan, organise, promote and run the EIJBF. By 1986, there had to be a special page of Acknowledgements in the Programme, to record all those who had played a part, with a special mention for what was called 'a vast volunteer army'. However, this is not the place to attempt to pay tribute to the all those whose input and hard work made the EIJBF possible. Nor am I going to attempt to acknowledge all those, both individual and corporate, who donated funds and equipment or helped in so many other ways. For those who wish to find out about all this, it is all recorded in the Official Programmes, many copies of which are still around. It is hoped that a full set of these will eventually be lodged in the Edinburgh Central Library Jazz Archive, launched in 2010[156] by the Edinburgh Jazz Archive Group[157].

However there is, of course, one person whose contribution underpins that of everyone else. Without Mike Hart's vision, energy and sheer bloody-mindedness, it is probable that nothing would have happened at all and there would have been no EIJBF. Mike's involvement in Edinburgh jazz began in the early post-WWII days, when Sandy, Al, Stan, Bob Craig, Dave Paxton, Archie and John Semple, Alex Welsh and all the rest of the pioneers, were laying the foundations of what was to become Edinburgh's reputation as a major jazz centre. Later, Mike was to be a factor, sometimes the crucial factor, in many of the key events in Edinburgh jazz developments - a founder member of the Climax Jazz Band, joint founder of the Old Bailey band and involved in the creation of the band that was formed for Dave Paxton's return from the Middle East. In addition, Mike was to be a key figure in the Scottish Jazz Advocates and leader of the Scottish Society Syncopators. He was an early pioneer of Edinburgh bands traveling abroad to play at festivals and to tour, and an extremely effective proselytizer on behalf of Edinburgh jazz. In addition to all of which he was, for over half a century, one of the most active musicians on the Edinburgh jazz scene.

It was Mike who created the Edinburgh International Jazz and Blues Festival. Without the EIJBF, few of us would have heard great players like Benny Waters, Doc Cheatham, Harry Edison, Buddy Tate, Milt Hinton, Carl Fontana and many more, certainly not on our own doorstep. Fewer still would ever have had the chance to actually play with these visiting stars. I still find it hard to believe that I played with a musician, Benny Waters, who

---

[156] Central Library Jazz Archive, Edinburgh Central Library, www.edinburgh.gov.uk/greenpencilaward
[157] Edinburgh Jazz Archive Group 2010 - Jim Keppie, Bill Strachan, Donald 'Chick' Murray and Drew Landles

had played and recorded with Joe 'King' Oliver. In terms of the EIJBF, Mike began as simply Director of a small jazz event in 1979 and continued in this role as the EIJBF grew and developed and, sometime around 1989, became a charitable limited company. For years, Mike worked in a voluntary capacity and it was a long time before he was employed by E.I.J.F Ltd and paid a salary as Artistic Director. His sterling efforts on behalf of jazz in Scotland were recognized in 1995, when he was awarded an MBE in the Queen's Birthday Honours List. The citation said *'Michael Warner Hart, for services to jazz in Scotland'*. Mike said in response *'I am extremely flattered by this honour and accept it on behalf of all the musicians and volunteers who have helped me to achieve a high profile for Scottish jazz'*. It was appropriate that the citation said Scottish jazz, because the success and fame of the Edinburgh event spurred many others across Scotland into action and jazz festivals have sprung up all over the country.

A further recognition of Mike's achievement in founding and driving the EIJBF was a citation from the City of Sacramento in 2008, in celebration of the thirtieth anniversary of the EIJBF. Headed 'Resolution by the City Council', as well as congratulating both Mike and the City of Edinburgh itself, the document concluded by saying:

'Now, therefore, be it resolved, by the Mayor and Council of the City of Sacramento, that we do hereby recognize the Edinburgh Jazz and Blues Festival on the occasion of its 30th Anniversary and do hereby extend our best wishes for a wonderful, fun-filled music celebration.'

Later, as others took stakes in the EIJBF, Mike was able to hand over responsibility for parts of the event to others and, as he moved into his seventies, his direct influence necessarily lessened. By 2010, now styled Founding Director, he remained on the Board and continued to exert a positive force on behalf of jazz, in an economic climate where the whole world seemed to be obsessed with commercial issues.

Mike Hart MBE
Founding Director of the EIJF
(cartoon by Neil Kempsill[158] 2003, from the collection of
Mike Hart)

Mike at times, like many effective people, could be controversial, confrontational, short-fused and infuriating but he also had vision, energy, tenacity, utter determination and, when he wanted to, a great deal of charm. Without him, Edinburgh jazz would have been greatly the poorer.

---

[158] All efforts to trace Neil Kempsill have failed but his original work in producing this excellent caricature is acknowledged

Chapter XIII

The Boom Years Begin

The 1980s, invigorated by the success of the EIJF, was to be a busy and productive decade for the Edinburgh jazz scene. So healthy was the local scene, that many bands were able to run more than one residency a week and few bands in those days were sharing musicians with another band. The jazz following was numerous and enthusiastic enough to support, at least for a while, the publication of a local jazz magazine. This was called simply **Jazz Magazine** and the first edition appeared in November 1983. In charge of advertising was Jan Hill, whose idea the magazine was, and the editor was Andrew Pattison. The front cover was graced by a caricature of Bill Salmond, hair awry, strumming his banjo, stomping his foot and filling the air with noxious fumes from a large cigar. There was an editorial that explained the magazine's purpose and future plans, which were to include space for reader's letters. A selection of beautifully drawn jazz cartoons, produced by Donald Macdonald senior, father of the Macdonald bass playing dynasty, brightened up the pages. There were many adverts, some of which advertised local bands, jazz venues and jazz associated businesses.

Regular features included a Pub Survey which gave a critical review of a selected jazz venue, the one featured in this first edition being the amazing Basin Street at Haymarket, where there was jazz every night except Friday. A Hot Club News feature gave an update on the Hot Club, a non-profit making venture which existed '...*to promote New*

Orleans jazz in Edinburgh'. Platform News was written by Roger Spence and explained that Platform was *'..a grouping of seven non-profit making jazz promoting clubs with a base in Edinburgh'* and gave a comprehensive account of their activities and promotions to come. Gordon Cruikshank had contributed Jazz Train, an article describing how schismatic jazz was and focusing mostly on post-Bebop jazz. There was the first of what was to be a series on Legends of Jazz, the first subject being Bix Beiderbecke. Another regular feature was to be a Jazz Horoscope, written by Violet Milne, setting out our predicted fortunes under the signs of the Zodiac and indicating the best dates for recording, buying hi-fi equipment, socialising, creativity, looking for work, using your initiative, putting a band together, new projects and new gigs. There was even a Speakeasy News which seemed to be a slot in which new talent was described, this first one being about an eleven year old drummer, David Stewart, who had been sitting in at various jazz gigs. Most interesting of all in retrospect are the two pages headed Edinburgh Scene[159] and listing the regular jazz gigs around town. This gives such a clear account of the venues of the time and the sheer number of jazz gigs, that it is well worth showing in full.

Edinburgh jazz gigs in November 1983:

Monday

East Coast Jazz Band	Blue Lagoon Lounge	9.00 to 12.00
St Stephen Street Stompers	Raffels Bar	8.30 to 11.00
Grange Band	Grange Hotel	8.30 to 11.00
Bob Craig Jazz Band	Preservation Hall	8.30 to 11.00
Guitar Duo	Basin Street	8.30 to 11.00

Tuesday

Louisiana Ragtime Band	Navaar Hotel	8.30 to 11.00
East Coast Jazz Band	Sovereign Bar	8.30 to 11.00
George Roy Jazz Band	Oliver's bar	8.30 to 11.00
Jazz Machine	Preservation Hall	9.00 to 11.30
West End Jazz Band	Basin Street	8.30 to 11.00

Wednesday

Cottontoes	Argyll Bar	9.00 to 11.00
Louisiana Ragtime Band	Basin Street	8.30 to 11.00
'Band'	Northern Bar	8.30 to 11.00

---

[159] 'Jazz Magazine', Issue 1, November 1983, by kind permission of Jan Hill.

Charlie McNair Jazz band	Goblet Bar	9.00 to 12.00
Capital City Jazz band	Magna Carta	8.30 to 11.00
Bill Waugh Jazz Band	Preservation Hall	8.30 to 11.00

Thursday

West End Jazz Band	Ailsa Craig Hotel	8.30 to 11.00
Spirits of Rhythm	Basin Street	8.30 to 11.00
Scottish Jazz Advocates	Platform 1	8.30 to 11.00
Blue Swing	Calton Studios	8.30 to 11.00
Afton Trio	Afton Hotel	8.30 to 11.00
Bob Craig Jazz Band	Glenelg Hotel	9.00 to 12.00
Nite Life	Royal British Hotel	8.30 to 11.00

Friday

3 D	Calton Studios	8.30 to 11.00
Spirits of Rhythm	La Sorbonne	8.30 to 11.00
Jazz Machine	Eglinton Hotel	8.30 to 11.00
Phil Bancroft Trio	Clarinda's Wine bar	8.30 to 11.00
Neil Munro Trio	Basin Street	8.30 to 11.00
Edinburgh Jazz Quartet	Magna Carta	8.30 to 11.00
Blue Swing	Traverse Theatre	8.30 to 11.00

Saturday

Swing 83	Calton Studios	9.00 to 11.00
George Roy Jazz Band	Oliver's Bar	1.00 to 3.00
St Stephen Street Stompers	Raffles Bar	2.00 to 5.00
Alex Shaw Trio	Platform 1	12.00 to 2.00
Jack Graham	Eglinton Hotel	8.15 to 11.15
Blue Swing	La Sorbonne	8.30 to 11.00
See note*	Basin Street	8.30 to 11.00
Border Crossing	Nicky Tams	2.00 to 5.00

Sunday

Alex Shaw Trio	Platform 1	12.00 to 2.30
Capital City Band	Barnton Hotel	1.00 to 4.00
Festival City	Westfield Function Suite	1.00 to 3.00
Jazz Machine	Eglinton Hotel	2.15 to 5.15
Scottish Jazz Advocates	Platform 1	8.30 to 11.00
Old Reekie Footwarmers	Glenburn Hotel	8.30 to 11.00
Charlie McNair Jazz band	Granary Bar	8.30 to 11.00
Blue Swing	Black Hart Bar	8.30 to 11.00
Jack Graham	Basin Street	8.30 to 11.00
Royal Jazz Band	Royal Hotel, Portobello	8.30 to 11.00

The above listing reveals a total of forty nine regular, weekly jazz gigs. Added to that, the same magazine carries an advert placed by Platform, which shows that they were running weekly, late night jazz events at the Queens Hall. It is hard to credit now that there were so many venues, so many regular gigs, so many bands and enough followers to go round. In addition, of course, a large number of bands require a large number of jazz musicians to fill them. In fact, the Edinburgh jazz scene had again received a timely injection of new blood – or to be strictly accurate, fairly old blood. We have already seen the reasons for the first two expansions in the local jazz scene – firstly the Revival in the 1940s and secondly, the 'trad boom' in the late 1950s and early 1960s. Both of these stemmed from quite sudden and unexpected increases in the popularity of jazz but this time the reason was very different: it arose primarily because, of all things, the discotheque.

The late 1960s and the 1970s had seen the rise of the disco and the subsequent drop in the employment of live dance bands. This mainly affected the all-purpose dance bands which offered a menu of traditional dances such as fox trots and quicksteps and waltzes, spiced up a bit with versions of tunes from the current Top Twenty. The more specialised dance bands, such as those playing Scottish Country Dance music, were less affected but it was becoming clear that the old style dance bands by no means suited the generations that had been raised on the Beatles and the Rolling Stones. The youngsters wanted something that sounded like the music they heard on the radio, television and juke boxes. They did not want to dance to somebody playing Beatles tunes on a violin or accordion, they wanted to dance to the music of Beatles themselves, or something very like it. There were two ways to achieve this. One was to book local rock bands imitating the music of their heroes and the other was to dance to the recordings of the heroes themselves.

Recording and playback technology had, of course, been developing at a furious pace and, by the 1960s, was well able to deal with the demands of playing records for dancing, even in quite a major way and in sizable venues. The days of dinner-jacketed musicians solemnly playing formal programmes of traditional dance music would never be the same again and the days of the manic, fast talking disc jockey had arrived. Locally, dozens of dance band musicians - piano and accordion players, trumpeters and reeds players, drummers and double bass players - accustomed to plenty of regular work, began to find themselves confronted by increasingly empty booking diaries. Many of them were enthusiastic musicians who wanted to keep playing and some of them turned to the jazz scene.

Jazz and dance music were historically closely related and there were many who considered jazz, particularly the traditional variety, primarily to be dance music. As late as the 1930s Swing era, band leaders like Benny Goodman considered their bands to be dance bands. Goodman's huge popularity had been, at least partly, founded on his band's appearance on a regular radio broadcast call 'Let's Dance' and his signature tune at that time had the same name. Goodman, expressing his admiration for piano player Teddy Wilson, called him the finest dance band musician in the USA. Even if, at a local level, some dance band music was 'light music' of the kind abhorred by Sandy Brown, even if some of it was churned out on autopilot in an artless, soulless and swingless manner, it was certainly not all like that. Nor was it all po-faced, some of the dance bands being just as good at falling about as were the jazz bands. There is an authentic story of one Edinburgh dance band that arrived to play at a quite high-powered gig. On being directed to where they were to play, they were delighted to be told that there was a drink for the band on the bandstand. When they clambered onto the bandstand, they were even more delighted to find a crate of beer and six assorted bottles of spirits, including a rather nice malt. Being the band they were, they naturally ignored the beer and got laced in amongst the spirits. They were sent home in disgrace after the spot dance for having drunk all the prizes.

There were plenty local musicians playing in dance bands whose first love was jazz. There were many local jazzers who took as much dance band work as was offered, simply to be playing, including musicians of the calibre of Andrew Lauder, Tom Finlay, Johnny McGuff and Jim Baikie. Jim Baikie was, in fact, at that time, much more active on the dance scene than on the jazz one and ran one of the busiest and most popular dance bands around. There were others too, such as trumpeter George Roy and reeds man Jimmy Shortreed who, although most of their playing had been in dance work, were more than capable jazzers. One result of the collapse of the dance band scene was an influx of musicians to the local jazz scene, even if some made the transition with more success than others, just when the local jazz scene, spurred on by the success of the EIJF, was burgeoning.

Meanwhile, Issue 2 of the Jazz Magazine was published, covering December 1983 and January 1984. The regular feature Pub Survey this time was about the Westfield Function Suite, where the Festival City Jazz Band, led by pianist Ian Scott, had a regular spot. Hot Club News reported a successful Speakeasy event at the Magna Carta Lounge which congratulated those attending on their 1930s gear, for which prizes had been awarded. The Hot Club Hogmany Jazz Party was to be held in the Minto Hotel Function Room on 31st December and tickets were available from the secretary, Terry Jamieson. Platform News told us that *'On January 16th, the young Edinburgh saxophonist Tommy Smith should fly of to the USA, taking up his scholarship to Berklee College in Boston'*. There was to be a benefit concert, featuring Tommy, Martin Taylor and George Chisholm, on 12th January to raise funds towards the £6000 that Tommy required to pay for his studies. Warren Vache was appearing at the 'Platform' gig at the Queen's Hall on 20th January and it was noted *'...it's still rare to have a major new artist who takes his inspiration from the style which pre-date Parker and Gillespie's be-bop revolution'*. Gordon Cruikshank's article spoke of the Edinburgh based Hep, which he reported was Scotland's only jazz specialist jazz label, and which had issued a recording called 'Songs for Sandy', recorded live at the Queen's Hall by trumpeter Digby Fairweather. The recording *'...portrayed the life and musical personality of clarinettist the late Sandy Brown...and shows why he, along with Bruce Turner, is* (sic – presumably Gordon meant 'was') *about the best pre-bop clarinettist/saxophonist in Britain today'*. The Record Review feature told how the Louisiana Ragtime Band had issued their first LP, 'Louisiana Ragtime', which was now a recognised collector's item, about seven years previously, and reviewed their new recording which was called 'Linger Awhile'. The new LP was recommended as a Christmas gift.

Issue 3 of Jazz Magazine, in March 1984, included a Pub Survey of the Blue Lagoon where drummer Frank Birnie led the East Coast Jazz Band every Monday evening. Hot Club News announced their first 'do' for 1984, a night at the Sorbonne. Those attending were invited to wear a costume portraying a song title and there were to be prizes for guessing what the title was. A Hot Club invitation to the French band, the Hot Antic, had been withdrawn because of the ridiculous fee demanded. The Edinburgh Scene gig guide showed that regular weekly gigs had dropped slightly, to thirty nine per week. Platform was putting on concerts at the Queen's Hall on 2nd March (Jimmy Feighan Quartet), 9th March (Al Cohn), 16th March (Stewart Forbes Quartet), 19th March (Eddie Prevost Quartet), 23rd March (Joe Temperley with the Bruce Adams Quartet) and 30th March (George Keiller Quartet and Festival City Jazz Band). The coming EIJF was previewed and Humphrey Lyttelton was profiled.

The Speakeasy feature contained a perceptive review, written by a visiting Australian sax player called Lew Smith, of one of Platform's shows in the Queen's Hall. This, in fact, was the benefit concert in aid of Tommy Smith's educational venture to the USA, which had been advertised in Issue 2. Lew Smith, after telling of his long wait in a draughty corridor for tickets, had been impressed by the young Tommy and wrote '*As a saxophonist, I had never heard anyone with the control, range and fluency displayed at such a tender age. As a jazz player I was amazed at his maturity and constant flow of ideas. Sure, he's derivative, but the prospect in five to fifteen years of a major performer in the world of jazz is a very bright one indeed. His demeanour was modest, and he thoughtfully thanked all his backers and the audience for their support for his campaign*'. Prophetic words indeed. Although Tommy's style puts him beyond the reach of this book, he had been taken by his father, Tommy Smith senior, to jazz gigs all over Edinburgh where he was encouraged by the musicians and allowed to sit in, when at his earliest stage of development. Later, when there was a television documentary about Tommy, Jimmy Shortreed, who played clarinet with the Festival City Jazz Band, appeared and spoke of the young Tommy who, in turn, confirmed that Jimmy had been one of his early inspirations. Tommy came from the Wester Hailes area of the city and the story of the support given to him by the local community and the Edinburgh jazzers, is a heart warming one.

And that is where the Jazz Magazine seems to end. The March 1984 issue is the last that I have and I am sure I would have bought and kept any further issues. It was an ambitious project and very well produced but, perhaps, too ambitious to survive, even in the healthy jazz climate of 1980s Edinburgh. However, it has left a detailed record of what the Edinburgh jazz scene was like in the early 1980s, when the EIJF was young and the town pulsed every week to the sound of forty nine jazz gigs.

Jazz Magazine may have come to an abrupt end but the Edinburgh jazz scene had never been healthier, at least in terms of the sheer volume of jazz being played. The renewed energy deriving from the EIJF not only gave the established bands a welcome boost, it also fuelled the formation of several new bands. One of the established bands had in fact been around since the early 1970s when it had been put together by Falkirk trombonist John Arthur, but at first had played mostly in the Falkirk area. He gave the band the name **Dr McJazz** and, as the 1970s moved towards the 1980s, they increasingly became a feature of the Edinburgh pub jazz scene. The original line-up included Des Monaghan (tpt), Bob Busby (rds), John Arthur himself (tbn), Gus McKay (bs gtr) and his wife Helen McKay on vocals. The other rhythm players varied but included Harald Vox on banjo and Roger Hanley or Johnny Johnson on drums. Later changes brought in George Duncan on clarinet, when Bob Busby went overseas, and a photograph of the time shows a young Martin Foster playing clarinet with the band. A band flyer from the 1970s has the foot note *'The total height of the band is 38 feet and 2 inches'!*

The Dr McJazz Band played in a number of the established Edinburgh jazz pubs, including the Glenelg Hotel, later to be called Young's Hotel, in Leamington Terrace. It was when this hotel changed hands and became a Chinese restaurant that their residency there came to a halt. As Norrie Thomson was to say on a Dr McJazz CD sleeve note *'The new owners didn't want any Cornet Chop*

Suey on the menu? The band was also to hold a very successful resident spot for about four years on Saturday evenings at Basin Street, in the Haymarket Station Bar, in the 1980s. The band also played at many jazz festivals over the years, including those in Edinburgh and Leith.

As we have already heard, the Edinburgh traditional jazz scene had been extremely active in the 1970s and **John Arthur (trombone)** was as busy as anyone. John was born on 27th October 1930 and played piano during his teens, with local small dance bands around Falkirk. Later he completed his National Service but continued to be involved in music of one kind or another. He taught at the Falkirk College, in the electrical engineering department, and, after attending Edinburgh University for three years during which he stopped playing, he returned to the Falkirk College to teach in the English and Communication Studies Department. He retired from the college in 1993. John had taken up trombone in the 1950s and, in the 1960s, joined Andy Lothian's Dundee based jazz band, before joining the Vernon Jazz Band in Glasgow. John travelled widely with this band and also took part in a number of Radio broadcasts from Glasgow on the 'Come Thursday' programme. It was when the Vernon Jazz Band folded, around 1969/70, that John formed the Dr McJazz Band, at first playing mostly around Falkirk but later becoming established in Edinburgh.

John's trombone heroes were the great Jack Teagarden and, in the UK, Chris Barber, and it was on the Barber band that the Dr McJazz Band was to model its style. That style can be heard on a couple of recordings, retrospectively issued on CD, 'The Incredible McJazz', recorded in 1992 but issued in 2003, and 'Doctor McJazz – A Miscellany', issued in 2009, many years after the band had ceased to be active[160]. In addition to playing with the McJazz band, John also put in time with Jim Petrie's band in the Glenelg Hotel, with the West End Band in the Ailsa Craig Hotel and, for a time, played in the Blue Lagoon (later to become the Caley Sample Room) on Thursdays with pianist Ian Scott's band. John also played with Charlie McNair's Jazz Band

---

[160] See discography Appendix

during their Wednesday evening residency in Preservation Hall in Victoria Street. He was also to undertake a week-long tour in the south of England with a band led by Dumfries based trumpeter, John Cowan, during which they had the famous Kenny Ball as guest trumpeter. At the time of writing, John Arthur, now just into his eighties, continues to play trombone, at the Edinburgh Jazz and Jive Club, with Brian Robertson's Forth River Ragtimers and Fred Murray's Club House Seven.

The clarinet player who played an important part in the formation of the Dr McJazz band was **Bob Busby (reeds),** who was born on 17th December 1935 in Edinburgh. Early in Bob's life, his family moved to Falkirk, where he received his schooling and where he also received classical training on piano up to Grade 8. His introduction to jazz came in 1952 when a friend Max Murray, later to play centre forward for the Glasgow Rangers, played him a recording of the Humphrey Lyttelton band playing 'Get Out of Here and go on Home'. A year later, now switched on to jazz, Bob gave up piano and bought a clarinet. By 1957 he was proficient enough to form a Falkirk based jazz band which included Charlie Malley on trumpet and Arthur Ferguson on drums, to which they gave the name the Memphis Jazz Band. Later, when Bob was studying chemistry in Glasgow, he met up with Graham Stark at jam sessions at the Glasgow Tech, where they formed the Tech Jazz Band. Graham Stark was then playing piano and was later to become a well-known Glasgow based piano and trumpet player, for many years associated with the Kit Carey Jazz Band. Bob remained with the Tech Jazz Band until 1961, when Graham Stark left. After this, Bob played only occasional gigs, mostly with Stark or trombonist John Arthur, another Falkirk based jazzer. Then, in 1969, Bob joined Dr McJazz, the band which had been formed by John Arthur.

At first, in the early 1970s, the new Dr McJazz band played mostly in the Falkirk area but then, in about 1975, Charlie Malley, the Falkirk based trumpet player then playing with Mike Hart's band in Edinburgh, invited both Bob and John Arthur through to Edinburgh and they began to be offered gigs in the city. They both played in the

Glenelg Hotel with Jim Petrie's band, which also included Jock Westwater, Dizzy Jackson and Iain Forde, in the latter part of 1977 and made a CD. However, for Bob this came to an end when, in September 1978, he left for Oman where he remained until his return to the UK in 1982.

After his return, he joined the West End Jazz Band, which we will hear more about shortly, and remained with them through 1982 to 1984 when he again went abroad, this time to Saudi Arabia, where he stayed until 1986. His return this time saw him play from 1986 to 1988 with the Yelly Dug Jazz Band, apparently named after a dog at the cafe where they played, the Ca Va in the High Street. The proprietress of the pub had heard Bob play at Basin Street and asked him to put a band together like the one she had heard. The Yelly Dug band, in addition to Bob on reeds, included Jim Petrie (trumpet), Bob Craig (trombone), Jock Westwater (banjo), Dizzy Jackson (bass) and Iain Forde (drums). They remained at the Ca Va on a weekly basis for a few months and then lost the spot when the cafe changed hands. Shortly after this, the Saturday evening spot at Basin Street became available and Bob was invited to put a band in. This he was happy to do and he was to hold the Basin Street residency until about March 1988. The band continued to use the name the Yelly Dug Jazz Band but there had been changes in the line-up by this time, with Beverley Knight taking over on banjo and Roger Hanley replacing Forde on drums. Two CDs were made by the Yelly Dug Jazz Band around this time. Bob was then abroad again between 1988 and 1997, when he managed to play occasional gigs in Africa and Abu Dhabi, before again returning to the UK. 1997 saw him join Dave Keir's Hot Five, with which band he remained until 2002, after which he joined Jim Petrie's Diplomats of Jazz in 2003.

To my ears, Bob's style on clarinet has always seemed to have a discernable Sandy Brown influence, hot phrasing and a sharp edge to his tone giving him an attack in the Sandy manner. Alongside the equally hot trumpets of Dave Keir and Jim Petrie in the late 1990s and 2000s, Bob's playing provided a very compatible counterpoint, enhancing their lead on trumpet and matching them in his commitment to hot jazz. Bob made a couple of recordings with the Dave Keir band, 'Stomp Stomp Stomp' in 1999 and 'Redman Blues' in 2002, details of which can be found in the Discography and both of which nicely demonstrate his playing[161].

Tom Bryce (piano) was born in Maddiston, a village just outside Falkirk, in 1940 and attended the local primary school and Falkirk Technical School. After leaving school, he began an apprenticeship at Bonnybridge Power Station and became an electrical power engineer, studying at a number of technical colleges, including the Paisley Tech, through in the west of Scotland. His father was an accomplished piano player with certificates to his name and he saw to it that Tom began piano lessons at the age of eight years which continued until he was twelve. His father was clearly a man of good sense and he told Tom not to bother about certificates but to play piano with the object of enjoying himself. Tom was also fortunate in having a piano teacher who was as open minded as his father and who encouraged him to play a wide variety of music from light classics to pop. By the early 1950s, Tom was listening to the Light Programme on a crystal set and found himself attracted to the music of the big bands and jazz bands of the day. After this, he began to find himself automatically trying to put some swing into his piano playing (he says he still is) and it was not long before he latched onto the fact that there was a something of a jazz revival in the offing. At first, he listened to the British traditional bands, including those of Chris Barber and Ken Colyer, but it was not to be long before he found himself greatly taken by the music of the George Lewis band. He also bought many music books that included the works of W C Handy, Jelly Roll Morton, Duke Ellington and the ragtime pianists. A bit out of this particular jazz bag, he also had and has, a fondness for the piano playing of George Shearing, who was in the process of becoming one of the great names of modern jazz.

Tom moved to Edinburgh in the mid-1960s and, with a friend who also worked with him at the Cockenzie Power Station, he began to find his way into the Edinburgh jazz scene, listening to the Climax band at the White Cockade in

---

[161] See Discography Appendix

Rose Street and Bill Salmond's band at the Hopetoun Lounge, in Morrison Street. Later, in the 1970s, he added to his rota the Hailes House Hotel in the Kingsknowe area, where he heard the Nova Scotia Jazz Band. At the White Cockade, Tom met Alec McIntosh who, like Tom himself, worked for the Electricity Board and, discovering that Toshy played trumpet, they began to get together to play some music. A notice in the Evening News brought to Tom's attention that the YWCA had a small modern piano, which they considered underused, and were looking for people interested in playing it. On the back of this, he went to along to a meeting, arranged by one Amie Jamieson of the YWCA, and soon declared his interest in jazz and the piano. This led to a group of interested individuals getting together at the YWCA, which they were all required to join (I don't know about anyone else but I have never thought of Tom as a young Christian woman), and it soon became clear that they had the makings of a jazz band.

In addition to Tom and Alec McIntosh, there was Dave Galloway who played trombone and Dave's bass playing son Robin Galloway, who had learned on a bass which he had made himself. A banjo player, who was a pupil at the Rudolf Steiner school, also came along but did not stay long. However, before he disappeared, he had arranged for another banjo player to take his place, who turned out to be Harald Vox, then a teacher at the same school. Soon, the gradually expanding group was joined by Bill Martin on drums and then Eddie Hamilton came along, acting on a tip off from Dave Paxton, who had heard that there was a new band looking for a clarinet player. In fact, the YWCA sessions, which were originally intended to be just people getting together for a blow, attracted rather more than was needed for a single band and there quite a few others who also came along as well, including some women folk. The YWCA was located in Randolf Place in the West End of Edinburgh and, after each session, the whole gang would hasten across to the nearby West End Bar to revive themselves. It was therefore natural that, when the time came to decide on a name, they chose to call themselves the **West End Jazz Band**. The name West End, of course, also had a resonance with New Orleans, as a place name on the nearby Lake Pontchartrain, and appeared famously in the title of the Joe 'King' Oliver tune, made famous by Louis Armstrong, West End Blues.

The band's first residency was at the Loch Ewe Hotel in Royal Terrace and they started there on 17th August 1978 with a line-up that had now settled down as Alec McIntosh (tpt), Eddie Hamilton (clt), Angus Macdonald (tbn), Tom Bryce (pno), Bill Somerville or Colin Warwick (bjo), Charlie McCourt (bs) and Roy Dunnett (drms). They then moved to another hotel under the same ownership, the Ailsa Craig also in Royal Terrace, where they were to play on Thursdays for about three years, before taking on a second weekly spot on Tuesdays, at the famous Basin Street at Haymarket, where they were to stay until 1989. It was while at the Ailsa Craig that they arrived one Thursday to find the place full of Welshmen, up for the rugby international at Murrayfield. Late in the evening, a Welshman asked to borrow the microphone and proceeded to make an emotional announcement about a colleague, the highlight of whose life had been the biennial visit to Edinburgh for the rugby. Apparently this chap had died, leaving instructions that his ashes were to be scattered on the Murrayfield turf after a Welsh win, and his pals had a casket containing his ashes with them. Unfortunately for their plans, Scotland beat Wales on the Saturday and when the band arrived the following Thursday, there was the casket of ashes, returned to the hotel bar, on a shelf with the many bottles of whisky, ('resting with the spirits', as the Evening News put it), and there it remained until the next Welsh victory several years later.

In between the longer residencies, there were a number of other, briefer residencies for the West End band in venues including the Northern Bar at Canonmills, the Grange Hotel in Grange Loan and the Dell Inn at Slateford. In addition to their successful and well supported gigs, the West End band became a regular feature of the EIJF, making their debut in 1979 and remaining in the programme for many years. In one EIJF programme, it was said of the band: *'Under the eagle eye of Tom Bryce, part-time custodian of the nation's power supply, this bizarre collection of painters (Hitler type), whisky samplers, post oafish officials, aviators,, etc have a common desire to play unpretentious, good time, sing along interpretations of the jazz standards'*

Tom Bryce looks back on the 1980s as a great time for Edinburgh jazz and so it was, with jazz sounds bursting out of pubs all over the City and more bands than you could count. As well as his own West End band, he was to put in a little time with other bands too, playing for a while with the Climax band, during their residency at the Black Bull in the Grassmarket. Of course, in the nature of bands, there were changes in personnel along the way in the West End band and both Bill Smith and John Arthur played trombone at various times, Dennis Morton played drums, Gus Mckay came in on banjo, Des Monaghan from Polmont on trumpet and, in 1982, Bob McDowell replaced Eddie Hamilton. Although Bob did not stay all that long before going off to the West Indies to work, this was to be a significant change in the future of the band. In the meantime, Bob Busby followed by George Duncan replaced Bob McDowell and the band played on until 1989 when, with the Ailsa Craig gig long gone, Basin Street stopping its jazz policy and Tom Bryce involved in the complexities of a change of job, a new marriage and building a new house, the West End Jazz Band came to a halt.

It was not until 1998 that the band got together again, this renaissance being triggered off by the return of Bob McDowell to live in Linlithgow, County town of West Lothian. Bob contacted Tom Bryce to suggest that they reform and it was agreed that Bob would take on the running of the band, which from then on was to be Linlithgow based. They also agreed a policy of trying to involve West Lothian based jazzers and, already having Bob from Linlithgow and Tom from Faucheldean, they were able to recruit Andrew Lauder from Threemiletown (tpt), Bill Smith (Livingston) or John Arthur (Falkirk) for trombone, Dick Walink from Broxburn (bs) and, West Lothian apparently being a banjo free zone (which should help the local housing market), Kenny Henderson from Dunfermline, on banjo.

"THE BAND HAS JUST PLAYED THE BASIN STREET BLUES EXCEPT FOR
EDDIE WHO WAS UP BEALE STREET FOR A WHILE."

**Cartoon of West End Jazz Band by Donald Macdonald
snr
Charlie McCourt (bs), Eddie Hamilton (clt), Roy Dunnett
(drms), Alec McIntosh (tpt), Colin Warwick (bjo), Tom
Bryce (pno), Angus Macdonald (tbn)
(by permission of Ken Macdonald)**

There was to be a succession of drummers, including
Malcolm Brown, Roy Dunnett and Kenny Milne, before a
very promising local youngster called Jack Wilson was also
recruited.

Bob McDowell had definite ideas about promoting jazz
and he soon set up the Linlithgow Jazz club, whose first
home was the Masonic Hall next to the Burgh Hall, right in
the heart of the town. Later the Club moved into the Burgh
Hall itself, where they enjoyed a long and successful run.
Unfortunately, this was to come to an end after a lengthy
refurbishment programme, when it was decided that the
premises were likely to be required for the like of wedding
receptions and the Jazz Club found itself homeless. Bob
McDowell made strenuous efforts to find a new venue and
at various times, the Club functioned in the Linlithgow
Rugby Club and the West Lothian Golf Club premises but
with many trials and tribulations along the way. At the
time of writing, they seem to have settled in the Queen
Margaret Hall, at the east end of the town, and it is hoped

that this lively and well-supported jazz club continues to flourish, as it deserves.   The Linlithgow Jazz Club has featured many famous guests over the years, including the likes of Warren Vache, Bob Barnard, Roy Williams, Johnny Barnes, Jeff Barnhart and Martin Litton and the West End band itself has featured at the Keswick Jazz Festival, in Cumbria.

Tom Bryce, thinking back over his playing career, said that his real interest was in creating a platform for the front line players and that he was never really all that much concerned with the piano's solo potential. He felt that the West End Jazz Band had, in the main, lived up to his hopes that its members could play as long as they wished, could leave when they wished and remain friends, so that they could return in the future when the opportunity arose. Tom said that he had felt it to have been a great privilege to be a part of the Edinburgh jazz scene, to have known and played with so many great people and to have been part of the West End Jazz Band that he founded, a band that has already lasted for over thirty years.

Bob McDowell (reeds) was born on 16th March 1956 in Belfast and educated at Belfast Royal Academy and Queen's University, Belfast, becoming a chemical engineer and, latterly, a wine merchant. A visit to hear a live jazz band at the Glenmachen Hotel, just outside Holywood, County Down, when he was seventeen, resulted in him becoming 'totally hooked' on jazz – and how often have we heard similar stories in this book already? Bob had learned to play clarinet at school but says that it only 'became alive' for him after hearing jazz. He reckons that he listened to just about everybody he could but, if pushed, he would have to name Sydney Bechet as a special favourite. When he moved to Edinburgh in the course of his work, he got a lucky break, arriving to listen to a West End Jazz Band session and having a sit in with the band, on the very night their clarinet player was leaving. This was in 1982 and he was soon a member of the band with which he was to stay until 1988, his tenure only coming to an end because he moved away to work in the West Indies.

When he returned to live in Linlithgow in 1998, it was not long before the West End Jazz Band, which had ceased to play in the early 1990s, was re-born with Bob taking on the leadership of the band. Under Bob's hard working lead, not only did the West Lothian based band thrive but so did the Linlithgow Jazz Club, which he founded. As always with new ventures, there were problems to be solved and developments that took time. For example, at first there was no drummer in the reformed band, as there was no room in the Masonic Hall in Linlithgow, the club's first home, but there was more room when they moved to the Burgh Hall in 2001. In addition to the long list of solo stars already given above, the Club played host to an impressive array of visiting bands which included three from Australia, two each from Norway and Sweden, and four each from France and the USA. However, there were other important aspects to Bob's jazz endeavors. Certainly not the least of his many contributions to local jazz, and to jazz in general, was his securing of an Art's Council grant which was used to pay for *'half the piano'* for the jazz club and to fund educational visits to eighteen primary schools. These visits, providing youngsters with what would often be their first experience of jazz and its history, were a great success and Bob has said that the youngsters were *'the best audience ever'*.

The bass player with the West End Jazz Band, after they became West Lothian based, was **Dick Walinck (bass)**. Dick was born on 3rd December 1955 and, after attending George Heriot's School, went on to study at the Kirkcaldy Technical College, Edinburgh's Stevenson College and Napier University, before going on to become a senior software engineer in the computer industry. Dick was self-taught on guitar and first got involved in playing in public in 1974 when, with some of his pals from university, he formed a band called Jasper Morgan and The Chams, which played Latin American music. This band had a fairly short career but was the cause of Dick changing instruments when, finding that the Chams had too many guitarists, Dick found himself forced to buy and play a bass guitar. His involvement in jazz came about after he had gone along to hear the Festival City Jazz Band in a hotel in Princes Street and, finding himself as relaxed as a newt, allowed himself to be persuaded into having a sit-in with the band. In spite of, by his own account, *'making a mess of it'*, the experience awoke in him a determination to learn about jazz chord sequences. When, just a week or so later he sat in again, the bass player with the band, Kenny Burns, invited him to provide holiday cover at the band's regular gig at the Barnton Hotel.

In spite of his conversion to jazz, Dick continued to play bass guitar until, one night at a party, the drummer Frank Birnie discovered that Dick had a double bass at home. This soon resulted in not very subtle pressure to switch to double bass, which he did, and it was not long before he established himself as a bass player on the Edinburgh jazz scene. However, he was to remain interested in other forms of music and, over the years, he played many gigs with bands playing folk and Celtic music, including Norfolk, Callenish and Drombeg. In the Edinburgh jazz world, he soon became a member of Frank Birnie's East Coast Jazz Band, playing between 1980 and 1995 at their popular and well-supported Monday evening residency at the Blue Lagoon (later to be called the Sample Room), in Angle Park Terrace. A particularly memorable night at the Blue Lagoon was when the exceptional guitarist Martin Taylor, who had played with the great violinist Stephane Grappelli between 1979 and 1990 and later led the famous Spirit of Django band, sat in with the East Coast Jazz Band.

It was in 1998, when the West End Jazz Band was re-formed by Bob McDowell as a West Lothian based band, that Dick became a member and he has remained with the band ever since. This band, driven along by Bob's organizing energy from their Linlithgow Jazz Club base, brought Dick the chance to play with a number of the famous guests that Bob managed to attract to the club, including trombone maestro Roy Williams, American cornetist Warren Vache, reeds man John Barnes and the great Australian trumpeter, Bob Barnard. Later, from 2002, Dick was to be one of a number of Edinburgh jazzers who made regular trips across country to play with the Glasgow jazz bands, in his case trombonist Hugh Muldoon's Jazz and Blues Band, then playing in Laurie's Bar in the Candleriggs. In 2005, when this band spilt in two, Dick was to stay with the part of the band that stayed on in

Laurie's Bar to become banjo player Davie Wilson's Uptown Shufflers. He was also to play with another Glasgow jazz band, the Witnesses, which included the well-known Glasgow trombone player and vocalist Jackie Murray, in a fortnightly residence at the Three Judges pub at Partick Cross. Dick Walinck, to whom I was often grateful for his willingness to cover for my holidays, made a number of recordings including 'Scotsounds' in 1979 and 'Thingummygig' on STV in 1978, both with Norfolk and in the jazz field, with the Uptown Shufflers in 2008, on a CD called 'Live at Glasgow River Festival'. In 2011, as well as providing a bit of Edinburgh culture in the Glasgow jazz scene, he continues to help keep the jazz flame alive in West Lothian, with the West End Jazz Band.

Eddie Hamilton (clarinet) was born on 8th July 1937 and educated at Craiglockhart and Tynecastle schools. To trade, he was a painter and decorator and later became a postman. His musical background he describes as 'mostly classical' but he became switched on to jazz through going to see Chris Barber and George Lewis, when he was twenty. Inspired by this experience, he made his way to Mev Taylor's music shop, in Clifton Terrace near Haymarket, where he purchased his first clarinet. When he was asked if he wanted a case to go with the instrument, he said that he did but was astonished when he saw that the case was *'square and not long'!* However, undaunted, he took instrument and case home and, when he opened it, was dismayed to discover that the musical instrument inside was in four pieces. Believing that a clarinet was supposed to be all in one piece, he went back to Mev Taylor's a couple of days later to seek elucidation. The people in the shop were amazed that anyone who had bought a clarinet did not know how to assemble it, let alone play it. However, they showed Eddie what to do to turn the four pieces into a clarinet and gave him a book on how to play it. This had pictures showing black for closed and white for open holes and, after that, it was simply a matter of practice.

Eddie then bought some George Lewis records and set about learning the Lewis style, becoming in the process a devoted fan of the New Orleans clarinetist. His active playing of jazz began when he started going round jazz gigs in town and met Dave Paxton, then playing with the Louisiana Ragtime Band, who told him about a group who were looking for a clarinet player, in the hope of forming a jazz band. Eddie discovered that this group held rehearsals in a café in Randolph Place, near the West End of Princes Street. He went along on a cold dismal night and arrived to find himself in the company of a piano player called Tom Bryce, a trumpeter called Alex McIntosh and a few others. He was welcomed with open arms and became a regular member of the group. This group was to become the West End Band and their first gig was in 1978, at the Lochewe Hotel in Royal Terrace, with a line-up of Eddie, Alex McIntosh, Tom Bryce, Dave Galloway (tbn), Harald Vox (bjo), Robin Galloway (bs) and Bill Martin (drms). Eddie stayed with them until 1982, when he left the band.

Later that same year, he was asked to play with what he calls a 'makeshift band', at the Stockbridge Festival in St Stephen Street. However, foul weather put a stop to this gig and the band retired, as bands do, to the nearest hostelry, the Baillie on the corner of the street. There they met the owner of Raffles Bar, a pub near the other end of St Stephen's Street. This gentleman asked them to play the rest of the afternoon in his pub, an invitation which they accepted with alacrity. They got a great reception and, to their delight, found themselves with a regular Saturday spot. They quickly decided to call themselves the **St Stephen Street Stompers** and the band that day was Eddie, Alex McIntosh, Angus Macdonald (tbn), Colin Warwick (bjo) and Frank Birnie (drms). The gig went well, lasting for about a year and half, although the personnel of the band was to change as time went on. Dave Strutt, Brian Robertson and Andrew Lauder all played trumpet at one time or another, Kenny Henderson and Beverley Knight had a spells on banjo, Jimmy Tunnah and Roy Percy played bass, Bill Brydon sousaphone and Roger Hanley drums, with Hugh Smith playing washboard at other times. Sometimes special guests were persuaded along and these included Mac Rae from Newcastle, who played both drums and trumpet, the well-known clarinetist Brian Carrick also from Newcastle, the trumpet and trombone team of Pam and Llew Hird and, more locally, Jim Petrie.

After the demise of the Raffles sessions, Eddie fixed up a regular spot for a couple of years at the Cavern in Leith, where he reduced the band to a quartet to suit the cramped space, with a line-up that was for the most part Eddie, Dave Strutt, Beverley Knight and Bill Brydon. The highlight of the St Stephen Street Stompers career was their appearance in August 1985, on a live broadcast of the Radio 2 show, Brian Matthews Round Midnight. This show went out from the Caledonia hotel during the EIJF for several years and often featured bands appearing at the festival. Eddie still treasures a taped copy of the show, the band at the time having, in addition to Eddie, Brian Robertson (tpt), Kenny Henderson (bjo), Angus Macdonald (tba) and Hugh Smith (washboard). Eddie remembers the occasion as very enjoyable and never to be forgotten. Eddie seemed to have an affinity with bands called 'Stompers' and he was to go on to play with Alan Quinn's Templehall Stompers, followed by ten years when he was with Brain Robertson's Ellwyn Stompers. At the time of writing in 2011, he is still in regular action, still playing and singing in his inimitable and sincere fashion, with Brian Robertson's Forth River Ragtimers.

November 1980 saw the first gig for a major new Edinburgh band, which was not only almost unique in drawing its main influence from a European model, but would go on to establish itself with a reputation that extended far beyond Edinburgh. This band was formed jointly by guitarist John Russell and trumpeter Dave Strutt and was inspired by the gypsy band WASO, which had made the first of several appearances at the EIJF in summer 1980. John Russell had been a long term admirer of the music of Django Reinhardt and had, as he puts it, *'been living for years'* on a diet of the recorded output of the great Belgian gypsy guitarist. He confesses to being thunderstruck by the experience of hearing the Django style live, in the form of WASO. John and Dave Strutt lost no time in searching out local musicians who would be able to play in this style and, in a few short months, had their new band ready.

Their choice of a name was an inspired one, christening the band **Swing 1980** but with the plan of updating the name incrementally with each passing year. Of course, a regularly changing band name poses a problem for a writer concerned with tracing the band over time but, for the purposes of this book, I will refer to the band simply as Swing 1980-2011. The original line-up was John Russell (rhythm gtr), Dave Strutt (tpt), Dick Lee (rds), Neil Munro (solo gtr) and Fergus Currie (bs). John Russell says that the band policy was democratic decision making (which he qualifies by adding the word Machiavellian!) and always having a regular residency, which serves to keep everyone focused and reminds them of their first band choice. Wise words these, especially the latter part and, I am sure, a sensible way of building band loyalty in a world where even jazz musicians in established bands are sometimes tempted to take the first gig that comes along.

A quality outfit from the start, Swing 1980-2011 were never short of gigs and, over the years, held residencies in a number of good venues including La Grenouille, the Cygnet Lounge, Bannerman's in the Cowgate and the Malt Shovel in Cockburn Street. This last residency was to become established as the longest running of any held by an Edinburgh jazz band and, in 2011, Swing 1980-2011 had completed, with only the shortest of breaks, an incredible total of twenty seven years at the Malt Shovel. Their success was well deserved, the whole band always committed to the best playing they could produce and, when required, always recruiting high class musicians. This is, in many ways, a tribute to John Russell who, together with Dick Lee has been with the band throughout its thirty year history. One of the finest ever rhythm guitarists from Scotland, John, in addition to his own fine playing, has been a sort of guardian of the band's quality throughout.

There were changes of course, but always with good players replaced by other good players. On bass, after short spells from Fergus Currie, who now lives and plays classical music in Athens, and Ian Hope, Jerry Forde played from 1982 to mid-1987 before handing over to Roy Percy, who remains with the band in 2011. Neil Munro played from 1980 to 1984 and was succeeded in turn by three other fine solo guitarists, Martin Leys from 1984 to 1990, Phil Adams from 1992 to 2002 and Stephen Coutts, from the west of Scotland, who joined the band in 2002 and remains in place in 2011. Stephen's early musical career was spent studying classical violin and it is perfectly clear that classical music's loss was very much a major gain for jazz. He is an exceptional guitarist with many gigs with great jazz musicians on his CV, both in Europe and in Canada. With his background in violin playing and his skill as a guitarist, it is not surprising that, when the chance came along, he struck up a friendship with the great French jazz violinist, the late Stephane Grappelli. Stephen Coutts is described by his colleagues, with every justification, as a 'musician's musician'. I once played a gig with Stephen, in a trio led by Ayrshire's outstanding trumpeter Mike Daly and, once I had come to terms with feeling more than a bit out-classed, I was considerably knocked out by Stephen's apparently effortless ability to play any tune suggested and his endlessly creative and beautiful improvisations.

Swing 1980-2011 have made a number of recordings issued on CD, their first being 'Live at the Cygnet' from 1984, with others issued in 1986, 1998, 1999, 2002, 2005 and 2009[162]. These recordings give a good account of a remarkable band which, in addition to jazz standards and pieces associated with the Django Reinhardt tradition, always included a great deal of unusual material in their repertoire. Dick Lee, who was a highly active musician involved in all sorts of jazz and Scottish musical traditions, including many interesting fusions of styles, was always a highly original player and a fertile source of compositions and arrangements. The band also made a number of radio broadcasts over the years, amongst which were Round Midnight in 1985, a number of 'arts programmes' on radio Scotland in the 1990s and Stephen Duffy's 'Jazz Train', which went out live, in 2008.

Edinburgh jazz folk lore includes a number of versions of a story involving Swing 1980-2011 and a fabled trip to China. Here, at last, is the true version, provided by John Russell. Dick Lee had come up with the idea of the band going to play in China and, the band being supportive, in

---

[162] See discography Appendix

1986 they started raising money to fund the trip. Money was raised by various means including the band's own efforts, sponsorship from private business and Edinburgh Council, who were supportive because of twinning arrangements with Xian and seeing it as a cultural trip. After a great deal of difficult and shambolic communication, the band, which at the time had John, Dick Lee, Martin Leys and Jerry Forde, set off for China in July 1987. It should be mentioned that Roy Percy had by this time taken over from Jerry Forde on bass but, because the planning had been going on while Jerry was in the band, Roy stood aside for the trip.

Swing 2011 outside their long-term residency, The Malt Shovel
Roy Percy (bs), John Russell (gtr/ldr), Stephen Coutts (solo-gtr), Dick Lee (rds)
(by permission of John Russell)

They arrived and had been in Beijing for a week after which they were to fly to Xian to give what John called a *'huge concert'*. There was also a plan to get the band to

Shanghai before returning to Beijing, presumably so that they could play in all three cities, although this was not clear to the band. Wherever the band went in their extensive travels round the tourist itinerary in Beijing, they found themselves accompanied by a team of three - a translator, a guide and a driver - who took them around in an air-conditioned mini-bus. They then discovered, after a few days, that they were picking up the tab, not only for their own expenses, but also those of their Chinese team. Hasty calculations revealed that this was going to put them well beyond their planned expenditure. Protests directed at their translator got them nowhere as he indicated that he was not in a position to change anything until several committees had approved any changes to the programme. At this point, the band became convinced that the Chinese, a notably inventive people, must have invented bureaucracy.

A contingency plan of simply heading for Xian and their concert came to naught when bad weather closed in and all flights were cancelled. A series of hair-tearing meetings resolved nothing and the band decided to get themselves off the hook and get an early flight home. With a great deal of hard work on the part of the band and a certain amount of luck, they managed to get an Air France flight and fled after ten days of mind-boggling frustration. John confesses having his hitherto positive and democratic feelings towards the People's Republic somewhat diminished by the experience and says that it had been like being on another planet. So there we have the true story from the horse's mouth and, as John says, if anyone asks *'Did Swing 1980-2010 play jazz in China?'* the answer is no, except in their hotel room. And I thought that it was a right hassle depping in Glasgow pubs. Born in 1980, Swing 1980-2011 shows no sign of ever stopping; let us hope that there will be many more annual increments added to the name of this remarkable Edinburgh jazz band.

John Russell (guitar), the heart beat of Swing 1980-2011, was born in Edinburgh on 28th April 1945, attended St Ignatius and St Anthony's schools and became a college lecturer. His early exposure to jazz came from hearing British trad bands on the radio but it was when he heard a recording of the great Django Reinhardt that he was struck by his personal musical thunderbolt. This was his music and it has remained so over the half century plus that has passed since. Not surprisingly, he took up guitar, on which he was self taught. It is equally unsurprising that, although he numbers all the jazz greats amongst those he regards as his jazz heroes, it is the great guitarists which interest him most. John's early playing experience was with various dance bands in the early 1960s. He also had a band of his own, Jason and the Argonauts, which he led between 1961 and 1966 and with whom he *did the Beatles and Rhythm and Blues thing'*.

His early ventures into the Edinburgh jazz scene were in the 1970s, when he sat in with the bands of Charlie McNair and Hamish McGregor. Later, of course, his playing was dominated by his work with Swing 1980-2011 but he also managed to fit in work with a number of other bands, all of them of considerable quality. These included the Ralph Laing All Stars in 1995, the Alex Yellowlees Hot Club around 1999/2000 and the Scottish Jazz All Stars between 2006 and 2008. The latter was a band put together by Glasgow trombone player Dave Batchelor, mostly to work at jazz festivals, and which included some stellar Scottish jazz names in its membership, including Lennie Herd (tpt), Forrie Cairns (clt), Brian Kellock (pno) and Ronnie Rae (bs). Forrie Cairns had, of course, initially made his name with the Clyde Valley Stompers and had the distinction of being the only clarinettist whom Sandy Brown, in 'The McJazz Manuscripts', acknowledged as a possible challenger. I made a trip to play on the Isle of Arran with both Lennie Herd and Forrie Cairns in 2007 and, although Forrie was by then in his seventies, he was still playing wonderfully well, as indeed was Lennie.

With Swing 1980-2011, John Russell made many recordings which show to great advantage his sterling rhythm guitar work, providing a clean, crisp chordal sound of impeccable tempo, worthy of the Basie band's Freddie Green himself. The Swing 1980-2011 recordings can be found in the discography Appendix but John made a couple of other recordings with the Alex Yellowlees Hot Club, 'Hot Club Live' in 1999 and 'Hot Club Style' in 2000. His work with Swing 1980-2011 brought him opportunities to play with many renowned jazzers, amongst them reeds man Benny Waters, trumpeters Warren Vache and Digby Fairweather, trombonist Roy Williams, guitarists Howard Alden, Marty Grosz and Diz Disley and piano player Brian Kellock who has also recorded with Swing 1980-2011. It must have pleased John a great deal also to play, on many occasions, with the guitarist that he considers to be Django Reinhardt's true successor – Fapy Lafertin.

The reeds player with Swing 1980/2011 throughout its entire existence to date, has been **Dick Lee (clarinet, bass clarinet, recorder, soprano sax)**. Dick was born in Kenilworth, Warwickshire, on 20th April 1951 and was educated at Leamington College for Boys. Dick occasionally worked on building sites, on the oil rigs, as a groundsman and, in what he says must be the worst job in the world, checking for pressing faults on LP records, hot off the presses at the Polydor factory in Walthamstow. This task may seem straightforward but it had its hidden perils. It involved sampling the record surface by lifting the needle every sixty seconds or so but also entailed, to save time, having to play the 33 rpm records at 45 rpm – sheer torture for a musician of any sensitivity. In this job, he did 8 hour shifts, changing all the time, and with a mind-numbing preponderance of James Last and Herb Alpert, it's a wonder that he survived. However, it seems that the oilrig work had notable compensation, his clarinet sounding amazing when played in the leg of an oil rig which, according to Dick, had a reverb like the Taj Mahal! However, he was to be and was to remain, a full time musician. I say musician rather than jazzer advisedly, fine jazzer although he is, as Dick was to be an astonishingly wide ranging player, embracing an impressive spectrum of different forms of music.

Dick's parents always loved music, including classical, jazz and an array of other forms, and he feels fortunate that, from an early age, they surrounded him with music. Not only did his parents take him to City of Birmingham Symphony Orchestra concerts from the age of six but they also bought him a clarinet and sent him to the Birmingham School of Music, for clarinet lessons with the CBSO principal clarinettist, John Fuest. However, in the end, it was jazz that was to enthral him, although he never had any jazz lessons. He did, however, manage to pack in a lot of listening, every week for many years his mother sending him cassettes of Jazz Record Requests and Sounds of Jazz, recorded from the radio. All this listening soon enabled Dick to distinguish jazzers whom he particularly liked, his main influences forming an eclectic line-up of Joe Venuti, Adrian Rollini, Django Reinhardt, Lester Young, Benny Goodman, Don Ellis, Charlie Parker and Johnny Dodds.

The first encounter of the young Dick Lee with Edinburgh jazz took place, not in Edinburgh, but in Ardfern in Argyll in about 1978, when he heard and sat in with the New Society Syncopators (later, of course, to be known as Mike Hart's Scottish Society Syncopators). This was the first time he had ever played with a real jazz band. He cannot remember the full line-up of the band on this memorable occasion but does remember the inimitable Jackie MacFarlane in top form. He also remains grateful to Mike Hart for allowing *an unknown chancer* to get up and play with the band, something he considers to have been a life-changing experience. In 1980, Dick moved to live in Edinburgh where he joined a band called the Southside Strutters, which included one Robin Harper, later to be well-known as a Green MSP in the Scottish Parliament, on rhythm guitar. Then he joined Swing 1980.

To an extent, Dick's jazz career, from then on, was to be that of Swing 1980/2011 but there were many other ventures along the way. He formed a couple of bands under his own leadership, Dick Lee's Chamber Jazz between 1989 and 1997, No No Nonet from 1990 to 1996 and Dick Lee's Septet, from 1999 to 2005. However, he continued throughout to play with Swing 1980/2011, as they established themselves as one of Edinburgh's and the UK's finest small jazz combos. A busy man, Dick Lee, but that was far from all. He also managed to fit in a great deal of playing with other musical combinations, including some ground-breaking fusions of jazz with Celtic music, playing and recording with bagpiper Hamish Moore, ex-Pentangle guitarist John Renbourn, the approximately thirty-six piece La Banda Europa and the innovative folk styled quintet, Bag o' Cats. His other jazz outings kept him busy too and, in addition to appearing on all the Swing 1980/2011 recordings, he also played and recorded with drummer Kenny Mathieson's Classic Jazz Orchestra, a terrific band playing Kenny's arrangements of classic jazz of the 1920s and '30s, with whom he appeared on the albums 'Jelly's New Clothes' and 'The Classic Jazz Orchestra Salutes the Kings of Jazz'. In 2011, Dick was working and recording with accordionist David Vernon, with whom he has toured and produced the recordings 'Reeds United' and, their most recent album, 'Airlocked'.

When asked about the great players with whom he had played, he listed tenor sax players Benny Waters and Konrad Wyzniewski and Edinburgh's own trumpeter Jim Petrie, for whose playing Dick has a great deal of respect and a warm admiration. In 2011, Dick Lee is still as busy as ever, his latest venture his band Dr Lee's Prescription, his playing still agile and quirky, one of the most refreshingly original of all Scotland's jazz musicians.

The third bass player with Swing 1980/2011, was **Jerry Forde (bass)**, who was born in Edinburgh on 27th November 1961. Jerry had a proper Edinburgh jazz pedigree, his father being Iain Forde, who had made a notable contribution to Edinburgh jazz over several decades, mainly as a drummer. Jerry attended Bruntsfield Primary School, before completing his education at James Gillespie's High School, and later graduated as a civil and structural engineer, having studied at Napier and Edinburgh Universities. With a father already heavily involved in jazz, it was inevitable that the young Forde would have an early exposure to the music, Jerry claiming that his first personal response to jazz came at an Anita O'Day and Johnny Dankworth concert in London in 1961 when, still in the foetal state, he gave his mother a good kicking during the performance! Jerry shared with me membership of the 38th Edinburgh scout troop, although quite a number of years apart, and his earliest musical efforts included playing banjo-ukelele and 'a bit of trumpet' at scout camps.

Jerry reports that *'other than pre-natal foot tapping and dancing'*, his earliest memories of jazz were of his father playing the music of the great names of jazz at a generous volume, on 78 rpm and vinyl LP records and a Ferrograph reel to reel tape recorder. Oddly, Jerry has no memory of Iain playing drums in the house, although he is sure this must have taken place, but he does recall a number of band practices in their basement, in Warrender Park Road. His Dad also played a lot of jazz piano in the house and they had a pianola, complete with a selection of piano rolls, most of which were of music hall tunes. Jerry discovered that these could be 'jazzed up' by pedalling like mad and playing them very fast. Apparently the pianola was actually owned by the clarinet player George Gilmour who, at that time earning his living as a light house keeper, had found that there was no room for it in the light house! Many of the piano rolls belonged to the bass player Jim Young. Jerry's early memories of life at home include hearing the records and admiring the album covers, of the likes of Fats Waller, Louis Armstrong, Bunk Johnson, Johnny Dodds and many others. Yet another early exposure to jazz was Jerry's attendance, on his twelfth birthday in 1973, at the last appearance in Scotland of Duke Ellington with his orchestra.

Jerry had piano lessons from the age of 7 and slowly worked his way through the various grades. His final tutor, Stan Banigan, was keen to encourage him to try some fairly unusual material, including less well known Scott Joplin rags, Erik Satie and Debussy, plus what Jerry calls some *'very quirky material from a variety of sources'*. Obviously a go-getting sort of character, Jerry managed to purloin an acoustic guitar which had been bought for his sister Emily and then managed to purchase steel and a twelve string guitars, on which he learned both chord and line playing. By about 1976, he had begun swapping pop guitar chords and had made a number of musical connections and friendships, still in the 1980s pop music idiom. Other early musical activity during school days was playing *'reluctant tuba'* and using his guitar playing skills, on both rhythm and bass guitar in teenage bands, playing a strange mixture of *'progressive rock, punk and new wave'*, whatever that might be.

However, the latent family interest in jazz was about to make itself felt. He started to have a go at jazz bass, still on the bass guitar, and his first *'very tentative'* gig was with

Jim Petrie's band in the Glenelg Hotel. He reports that he *'got through, just about'*. Having made a start and probably with encouragement from his Dad and other jazzers, he then bought a double bass from Ken Macdonald, who also provided a few lessons. He was soon reached a decent level of competence and found that his ability to read music from his piano playing days helped him a great deal, although when he reads bass music he has to mentally transcribe it from the piano, commenting that it is just as well that it is light on crochets! From then on, Jerry's progress was down to practice and playing gigs, finding plenty of motivation from increasingly taking on work with several of the Edinburgh bands. Some early experience was with Bill Salmond's Louisiana Ragtime Band, with which he gradually built up his volume and stamina. However, in spite of experience in the New Orleans style, he decided against attempting to learn the slap style, partly because he preferred to use steel, rather than gut, strings.

Joining Swing 1982 in March of that year, brought a whole load of new challenges, with Jerry having to learn a lot of new material, new techniques and quite tricky key and tempo changes, plus having to brush up his sight reading. He was with the band when they were awarded the 'Best Band Award' at the EIJF in 1983 and made the famous, if ultimately abortive, trip to China in 1987, described above. He also owed a lot to his friend and mentor, the late Francis Cowan, whom Jerry describes rightly as *'a formidably real musician'*, with whom Jerry did a lot of rehearsing and playing. Playing with Francis brought him huge gains in bass technique, helping him cope with difficult rhythmic patterns and sight reading and extend his range on the instrument, including some arco (bow) work. Recently, at about the time of writing in 2011, he has made a partial return to his roots, digging out his bass guitar in response to the demanding writing of Dick Lee for a new band, Dr Lee's Prescription with Dick himself, Phil Adams and Marcus Ford, having to learn some fairly fiendish parts. This includes some very fast, very high playing with a range of shifting time signatures, although still *'just about'* within the jazz tradition. And to think that I used to find Muskrat Ramble and Basin Street Blues quite hard enough.

Jerry now plays his third double bass, his first having been returned to Ken Macdonald in about 1985, for the use of Owen Macdonald in his early bass playing years. His second had belonged to the late Tony Sargent and this instrument, although Tony played left-handed, was actually strung for right-handed playing, with Tony standing on the 'wrong' side of the bass. Talk about making things difficult for yourself! Apparently Tony's bass, although made by an amateur, had a really good carved front and an ebony fingerboard. Jerry eventually bought a top-class instrument in 1999, had it set up by Ken Macdonald, and is still playing it in 2011.

When asked about his bass playing models, Jerry points to a whole line of great players - Ray Brown, Walter Page from the Basie band, a number of fine bassists who played with the band of Duke Ellington, Niels-Henning Orsted Pederson, Percy Heath, Gary Karr (a virtuoso classical double bass player), the one and only Milt Hinton and Jaco Pastorius. You would be hard pushed to improve on that list. A bass player with a serious and conscientious attitude to his music, Jerry Forde's Edinburgh jazz CV embraces spells with the Louisiana Ragtime Band 1980 to '81, Swing 1982 to '87 (and on-going deps for Roy Percy), the Bill Jones Quartet, the Alan Yellowlees trio/Quartet, Mike Hart's Scottish Society Syncopators, Le Jazz Hot, duos, trios, quartets, quintets and big band jazz with Francis Cowan from 1984 to '96 and the Marcus Ford trio from 1996 to the present. With the Syncopators, he toured in the USA and Poland in 1986, in the company of Dave Strutt and Andrew Lauder (tpts), Johnny McGuff (tbn), Tom Finlay (pno), Frank Birnie (drms) and band leader Mike Hart himself, on banjo and guitar.

His career has also brought him into the recording studios and he has made recordings with Swing 1984, the Society Syncopators (1986) and Le Jazz Hot (2001)[163]. Asked about great players he has played with, he lists Milt Hinton in the sessions at the Edinburgh International Jazz

---

[163] See discography appendix

Festival called 'The Judge Meets the Section', when 9 bassists played together and he recalls that he had to 'detune' his bass to play the lowest part required. There was also an occasion when he claims he *played for Ray Brown'*. This turning out to be a gig in 1999, when Jerry played in Suruchi's Indian Restaurant, and Ray Brown came in for a meal! There were also gigs involving Fapy Lafertin, with Swing 1985 and sits-in with Al Fairweather's band with Jerry's Dad, Iain, on drums. One of the few second generation Edinburgh jazzers, Jerry Forde remains a fine player and one of the younger musicians (ie under the age of fifty!) who are involved in Edinburgh traditional jazz. On such as he, depends the future of the music. In fact, he may be a link to a third generation from the same family, his youngest daughter Lauren playing alto sax and, according to Jerry, having a *'good jazzy/bluesy ear'* and his brother Miles having two sons, Robbie and Jamie, who are keen piano players with a wide musical interest, including jazz. I liked Jerry's final comment on bass playing – *'Ah, contra-basso, eso se toca contrabajo!'* (a Spanish word play on the similarity of double bass and hard-work). He never spoke a truer word.

Roy Percy (bass) was to be, not only a very good bass player, but also a man of many bands, all of them of a high calibre, often being a member of several of them at the same time. He first began to make a name for himself in the mid-1980s, particularly when, in November 1986, he took over from Jerry Forde in Swing1986. He joined the band when they were already well established and with a burgeoning reputation for swinging and extremely well-played jazz. The takeover was gradual, as we have already heard, with Jerry Forde playing out a number of gigs already in his diary before he departed for the south, where his day job had taken him. Roy was remain with the band in the long term and is still there at the time of writing in 2011, when the band is, of course, known as Swing 2011.

When vocalist Craig McMurdo broke up his first band, the Gooseberries, and formed a new outfit to be called That Swing Thang in 1986, Roy jumped at the chance of playing with the new band. Initially playing in the jump jive style of Louis Prima and Louis Jordan, with some jazz standards and Nat 'King' Cole material in the mix as well, the band swiftly grew from its original vocalist, two guitars and double bass format to become a 'full sized' band with vocalist, trumpet, sax, trombone, guitar, piano, bass and drums. With That Swing Thang, Roy made many appearances on television, including Blue Peter, Pebble Mill at One and This Morning, in addition to countless Grampian TV's Art Sutter Shows and a good number of Hogmany shows. He stayed with the band until around 2004/04 but still makes occasional appearances with Craig McMurdo when the singer resurrects his smaller combo to perform the jump jive and Nat Cole material. In 1988, Roy also became a member of the trio put together by reeds man Martin Foster, Le Jazz Hot. This was a peppy little band, originally with Raymond Gillespie on guitar, capable of playing with considerable fire, although in fact playing a wide spectrum of material, embracing everything from ragtime to lounge music. With them, Roy appeared on a televised TV show called 'The Big Break' and remained with the band until 1992, although he has continued to make occasional appearances with the band right up to the present time in 2011. Another band with its roots in jump jive, Hamish McGregor's nine-piece Fat Sam's Band, also recruited Roy's services in 1998. With them, he travelled twice to play at the Sacramento Jazz Jubilee, in 1998 and 2000, to the Los Angeles Sweet and Hot Festival in 2001, a Middle East tour in 1999 and a number of forays to Scandinavia, before eventually leaving the band in 2005.

A highly versatile player, as befits a bass player with a living to make from the music, Roy also ventured into the purist style, joining the famous Climax Jazz Band in the late 1980s and remaining with them until around 1992. With them, he played at the Ascona Jazz Festival in 1990 and made a number of trips to play with the band in Holland. Still in purist mode, Roy also put in a number of spells with the Spirits of Rhythm, playing with them more or less continuously from 1990 to 2000. Still in the realm of New Orleans jazz but in the classic style, Roy played for a time with Al Fairweather's Sundowners in the early 1990s, where he found himself alongside Al's fellow veterans Bob Craig and Dave Paxton. Not surprisingly, Roy's skill and versatility brought him many depping gigs with other Edinburgh bands, including Mike Hart's Society Syncopators, Bill Salmond's Louisiana Ragtime Band and the Maid of the Forth Stompers. At the time of writing, Roy has been playing and recording with a tidy four-piece band led by the outstanding trumpet player from Ayrshire, Mike Daly, a band which includes John Burgess on clarinet and Duncan Findlay on banjo. Many other recorded examples of Roy's playing, with a variety of bands, can be found in the discography appendix.

As a fellow bass player, I naturally never played in a band with Roy, but I was interested to watch his development from his early days until the present, when he is one of the most sought after bass players in the country. It has always seemed to me that he was very much influenced by the playing of the great Milt Hinton when he made his appearances at the EIJF in 1985 and 1986. Hinton was a wonderful player, not only a rock solid powerhouse in the rhythm section but a terrific and melodic soloist as well. Roy was already a good player but, after hearing Hinton, he seemed to me to make major strides forward, even managing to master some of the tricky double and triple slap techniques that were such an appealing feature of the American's style. No one worked harder than Roy Percy in developing his technique and style and he has become deservedly successful as a professional musician. It is gratifying to see top class younger jazzers, such as Roy, Mike Daly and John Burgess, although more than capable players of more modern forms of jazz, clearly valuing the older styles and helping to keep the main stream of the music alive and well in the twenty-first century.

Chapter XIV

Advocates, Syncopators and Fat Sam

The re-formed **Old Bailey's Jazz Advocates** had enjoyed a remarkable run of success since getting together again in 1975 and they entered the 1980s in good shape, with a line-up of Andrew Lauder (tpt), Hamish McGregor (rds), Sam Smith (tbn), Tom Finlay (pno), Mike Hart (bjo), Graham Blamire (bs) and Donald 'Chick' Murray (drms). A residency at Waterman's Bar in the Grassmarket between June and November 1980 was followed by a move in January 1981 to the Garrick Bar, in Spittal Street, near the Usher Hall. However, the band was still sharing both Mike Hart and Tom Finlay with Mike's band, the Scottish Society Syncpators, and the time had come to resolve the situation. At the start of 1981, the two bands in effect merged. The new line-up was an eight piece band with Andrew Lauder, Hamish McGregor and Sam Smith being joined in the front line by Jack Graham and a rhythm section of Tom Finlay, Mike Hart, Graham Blamire and Chick Murray. In addition, the famous jazz singer from Glasgow, Fionna Duncan, joined the band and a new recording was planned.

After some debate, the new band was given the title the **Scottish Jazz Advocates**. Alastair Clark, in his Sounds Around column in the Scotsman, announced the new band by writing *'Happily, Edinburgh's home-based trad musicians never die – they just reshuffle themselves into a different permutation. The latest chapter in a long and complex history involves Old Bailey's Jazz Advocates and Mike Hart's Scottish Society Syncopators, formerly the New Society*

Syncopators. Are you with me so far? Well, they've merged under the title of the Scottish Jazz Advocates and the new eight piece band can be heard tomorrow at the first of a series of free sessions at the Caledonian Hotel, Edinburgh'[164]. Alastair was quite right and on 25th January 1981, the new band took up a residency in the Caledonian Hotel, at the West End of Princes Street. John Gibson also announced the merging of the two bands and his article in the Evening News provides an interesting comment on the times, giving the price of a pint of beer as fifty nine pence, lager at sixty two pence and whisky at fifty nine pence[165].

The Caledonian Hotel, one of the great nineteenth century railway hotels, was a prestigious venue and the new band's residency was to be for a four week trial in the first place, with success promising a permanent gig. In fact, by May, John Gibson was able to write in the Evening News, *'Business has been so brisk for the Scottish Jazz Advocates at the Caledonian Hotel on Sunday night since they took their trad music there in March that the sessions have been extended to Thursdays'*[166]. John Gibson also announced that the Caledonian Hotel, or the Caley as it was known, was to be added to the list of venues for that year's EIJF. He also wrote that the Advocates were to fly to California the next week for concerts, radio and TV spots and to plug their new album which was called Live at the Caley, which featured Fionna Duncan on several numbers. The recording was made in March 1981, live in the Caley, as the name said. Unfortunately, it was recorded the day after a Scottish rugby international against Ireland and the well-oiled Irish rugby supporters packed into the bar tended to make their presence felt throughout the entire proceedings! There followed a trip to play at the Sacramento Jazz Festival, where the band made a good impression with strong prospects of an invite for the next year. 1982 brought a BBC Radio 1 Jazz Club broadcast, when the band

---

[164] Clark A, 'Sounds Around', The Scotsman, 24th January 1981

[165] Gibson J, 'Joining up for the sound of jazz', Edinburgh Evening News, 24 January 1981

[166] Gibson J, 'More gigs for the Advocates', Edinburgh Evening News, 7th May 1981

played as support band to the Clyde Valley Stompers, who were on a re-union tour with Fionna Duncan. Fionna sang with both bands on the broadcast.

The jazz **vocalist, Fionna Duncan**, was born at Garelochhead, Dunbartonshire, on 5 November 1939. In 1950, she joined the school Ballad and Blues Club, while she was attending Rutherglen Academy, and from second year at school, she sang the soprano lead in several Gilbert and Sullivan operas run by the very go-ahead music department. These included 'The Dukes Dilemma' and 'Country Girl' and she further extended her activities by joining 'The Bankhead Players', a well known amateur drama group, with whom she appeared around Glasgow and the surrounding area. All this experience was to be of great value to Fionna in her career in music, gaining her not only a solid foundation in music but also in stage presentation and, in addition, she was to leave school with a pass in Higher Music. Her brother Ian was a piano player and, at only seventeen years old, Fionna sang with his modern jazz group, the Lindsay McDonald Quartet, at the Glasgow University Student's Union and became resident singer in the Glasgow University Snug Bar, singing every Saturday evening. In 1956, while on a business trip to the USA, she sang on TV, did several radio programmes and turned down a prestigious recording contract with Riverside Records. The contract would have required her to move to live in the USA permanently, and she turned it down because of this.

On returning to Scotland, Fionna auditioned for the BBC in Glasgow and, for the following two years, she had a regular Saturday morning radio broadcast with the Joe Gordon Folk Four on a show called 'Skiffle Club'. Next came another Saturday morning radio show, 'Saturday Club'. Around this time, she also became vocalist with Glasgow's Steadfast Jazz Band and then, after winning a talent contest, joined Forrie Cairns' All Stars. This was followed by Fionna signing up to sing with the famous Clyde Valley Stompers, which also included Forrie Cairns on clarinet, and she was with them when the band played long summer residencies on the Isle of Arran, great times which were to become something of a legend. I did a gig on Arran on 2007, in a quartet featuring Forrie Cairns, Lennie Herd (tpt) and Alastair McDonald (bjo/vocs), and was amazed by the endless number of punters who came up to speak with Forrie and reminisce about the great days of the Stompers on Arran, almost fifty years after the events. After her time with the Stompers, Fionna returned to a band led by Forrie Cairns, and was to be a member of his Clansmen, until 1964. This was followed by a tour in Germany as a solo singer and then she took up a residency at the Georgian Club in London, a gig which lasted from about 1964 to 1970 (the Who's Who of British Jazz says 1966 until 1971). This night club gig, which entailed a show of ninety minutes every evening during which she sang with the Georgian Dixielanders, provided Fionna with a terrific opportunity to extend her repertoire and style and she has said that it was a great learning experience. The evening sessions were a draw for many of the leading 'Show Biz' personalities of the time and, although the show was directed by Billy Petch and Bobby Chandler from Talk of the Town, it afforded Fionna more invaluable show experience, as she organised the rehearsals, sorted out the lighting and was involved in auditioning new acts. All this added up to a performer right on top of her game, with a thorough understanding of how to project and with formidable stamina.

Fionna returned to Scotland around 1970 as a full time vocalist, touring in Europe and the USA. By 1977, she was singing with the Glasgow based George Penman's Jazzmen, an arrangement which continued until 1981, when she began singing with the Scottish Jazz Advocates. Later, she was to make guest appearances with the Eggy Ley band between 1984 and 1986. In 1985, she formed her own trio, with musical partner Ronnie Rae on bass, Ronnie's son John on drums and Brian Kellock on piano, a top class group featuring the finest players in Scotland. With this stellar Trio, Fionna made many international festival appearances and toured in Canada and Switzerland. Fionna was to continue to work successfully with the trio and as a solo singer throughout the 1990s, starred at the EIJF and other festivals and, from 1995, ran many successful jazz vocal workshops. The workshops developed rapidly over the next few years and became an important fixture on the Scottish jazz calendar, providing an invaluable training ground for aspiring young vocalists. This part of her career must have given Fionna, and her team of professional tutors and musicians, a vast amount of satisfaction. Her career was dotted with recordings, many of which are still available today, all of them demonstrating her consummate ability as a jazz singer with style, energy and a remarkable sense of timing. Fionna Duncan, with a jazz career now in excess of forty five years, remains a major Scottish jazz name and, in the 2000s, was as popular as ever and continued to be one of the biggest draws on the Scottish jazz scene.

The Scottish Jazz Advocates c 1984
L-R Hamish McGregor, Johnny McGuff, Graham Blamire,
Chick Murray, Andrew Lauder, Tom Finlay, Mike Hart
(from the collection of the author, photographer
unknown)

Meanwhile, the Jazz Advocates Caledonian Hotel gig, in spite of being located in a very large lounge, continued to draw packed crowds on both the Thursday and Sunday evenings. Early in 1983, Jack Graham left the band and was not replaced, reducing the band to seven piece plus Fionna Duncan. Also in 1983, the Jazz Advocates made a trip to London where they played at a wonderful jazz pub, the Prince of Orange in Rotherhythe, and the famous 100

Oxford Street, a jazz club since the 1950s. May and June of that year saw another trip to Sacramento followed by a tour in California at the end of which, the trombone player Sam Smith, decided to stay on and the band came home without him. The replacement for Sam was Johnny McGuff, who fitted in immediately and added a formidable soloist to the band's line-up. The Caledonian Hotel, impressed with the success of the two jazz nights they hosted each week, then developed part of their premises into a special live music lounge. The Caley had originally been a railway hotel in the great days of rail travel, and the area they developed had once been the left luggage department of the Caledonian Station. They called the new lounge Platform 1 and it was up and running in time for the 1983 EIJF. Platform 1 became the venue for the Jazz Advocates sessions and was also added to the EIJF venues. The EIJF that year attracted BBC Radio and Brian Matthew, a well known DJ and broadcaster, presented his nightly show Round Midnight from the Caledonian Hotel. The Jazz Advocates took part in several of these radio shows and, as in previous EIJFs, the band played host to a number of distinguished guests including Jim Galloway, Acker Bilk and Count Basie's famous lead alto sax player, Earle Warren. Later that year, the band went to Holland to play at the Jazz Dagen in Eindhoven, a three day jazz festival where they again met and played with Earle Warren.

In March 1984, the band recorded yet another album, this one given the title 'All in Perfect Working Order'. As this was again targeted at the American market, it was given a Scottish flavour and included Johnny McGuff's remarkably agile playing of the Scottish march 'The Black Bear', complete with a chorus on bagpipes! August 1984 brought the usual packed EIJF programme for the band and then, shortly after this, the Scottish Jazz Advocates came to an end. Hamish McGregor had plans to put together a different kind of band and he left the Jazz Advocates in September 1984. There was a brief period when plans were discussed to keep the band together but, in November 1984, the Scottish Jazz Advocates were wound up. The demise of the Jazz Advocates brought the opportunity for Mike Hart to get the **Scottish Society**

Syncopators together again, which he did, including Andrew Lauder, Johnny McGuff, Tom Finlay and Mike himself from the Jazz Advocates and bringing in Jack Graham, Francis Cowan (bass) and Frank Birnie (drums).

Francis Cowan (bass, guitar, cello, lute, composer, arranger, teacher), who was born in Duns in 1940, was a remarkable musician who made his mark across a wide spectrum of Scottish music. Perhaps best known for his work as a jazz guitarist, he also performed in the classical and folk fields and was a well-known and respected instrumental teacher. In addition to his excellent work on guitar and bass, he also played cello and lute and had made a name for himself as a writer and arranger. During his brief stay on bass with the Syncs in the early 1980s, he contributed a number of excellent arrangements and recorded with the band on their 1985 album "Huntin', Shootin' and Jazz'n", a recording which includes a rarity in traditional jazz, a bowed bass solo. His many other involvements in Edinburgh music included a lengthy spell in a duo with the singer Melanie O'Reilly, as well as performing solo and leading a number of bands from trios up to eight-piece. A technically accomplished and extremely versatile musician, Francis was much respected for his unfailing musicality, enthusiasm and likeable personality. Tragically, Francis was to die in a road accident on 20th September 1996 at the age of only fifty six, leaving a huge gap in Scottish music generally, as well as in Edinburgh jazz. As another bass player, I never played a gig with Francis and did not know him well but knew enough to like him and hold him in great regard as a musician. I wish to acknowledge the excellent obituary contributed to the Scotsman by Kenny Mathieson, from which some of the details in this brief account have been taken[167].

Mike Hart soon found a Sunday lunchtime venue for the reconstituted Syncs in the Learmonth Hotel, just over the Dean Bridge, and this was soon established as another successful jazz gig. The hotel ran this session as a jazz brunch and one of the local newspapers was able to say

---

[167] Mathieson K, 'Francis Cowan', The Scotsman, September 1996

that it was a success from day one. The article reported that the music was right, the room was right and so were the encouragingly big crowd and the food and drink prices. The final stamp of approval had been provided by the indestructible Jackie MacFarlane who was there, impromptu and unpaid as ever! By the early days of 1985, Mike had expanded the band to include a second trumpeter, this being the excellent Dave Strutt. The Scottish Society Syncopators, with many changes in personnel along the way, were to continue as one of Edinburgh's top bands, playing at jazz festivals in the UK, North America and Europe, recording and broadcasting right through the 1990s and into the new century. Among those who later played with the reformed Syncs were Jake McMahon, Jack Duff and Martin Foster (reeds), Bruce Adams (trumpet) and Ken Macdonald, Gerry Forde and Ricky Steele (bass).

Both the Scottish Jazz Advocates and the Scottish Society Syncopators were graced by the playing of Johnny McGuff on trombone. **Johnny McGuff (trombone)**, who was born in Edinburgh on 13th February 1932, was one of the most remarkable of all Edinburgh jazzers. He came from a musical family and, at age twelve, he started lessons on trombone with a tutor called Bill Tabener. He made rapid progress and, after some early experience playing with the Arniston Brass Band from Gorebridge and the Newtongrange Brass Band, he was playing with local dance bands within a year of beginning lessons. One of his very first appearances in public was when he sat in with a dance band in which his father, Gordon McGuff, was playing drums. When he was just thirteen, he featured in a concert at Newbattle Abbey, for troops stationed in the area. After leaving school, Johnny completed an apprenticeship as a bricklayer before serving his National Service in the Royal Artillery, when he played with army bands and at any dance band gigs he was offered. After discharge from the army, he was soon in action with some of the leading Scottish dance bands of the time, including bands led by Edwin Holland, Tommy Sampson, Johnny Kildare, Pete Seaton and Cam Robbie. Later there was to be a spell at the Locarno Ballroom in Liverpool, regular broadcasts with the BBC, the teaching of music in schools in Dalkeith and Gorebridge and a stint with Ken McIntosh's band.

Johnny McGuff drew his inspiration from three sources: Jack Teagarden, Don Lusher and George Chisholm. The trad boom of the late 1950s and early 1960s put his technically accomplished and inventive playing very much in demand and he found himself playing with the Clyde Valley Stompers, during the period when they were led by clarinettist Pete Kerr. With this band, he made many TV appearances, including the famous Morecambe and Wise Show. Later, Johnny played with Terry Lightfoot's Jazz Band before returning to Edinburgh. Back on home ground, he was soon snapped up by Mike Hart to play with the Society Syncpators, with whom he travelled to the Dunkirk Jazz Festival in 1979. There, in addition to the band's success, Johnny won the award for best soloist in the competition. He then became one of the Scottish Jazz Advocates, replacing Sam Smith when he decided not to return from California, after the Sacramento Jazz Festival in 1983. Johnny stayed with the Jazz Advocates for the remainder of the band's existence and then, when Mike Hart reformed his Scottish Society Syncopators in November 1984, he became a member of that band.

Over the years, Johnny made many trips with these bands to play at jazz festivals in the UK, Europe and the USA. He was always a major draw at these events, his blistering attack, agile technique and inventiveness catching the ear of jazz fans wherever he played. His reputation led to him being invited to the USA to take part in a specially assembled international all-star band. He also won the best trombonist award in Radio Two's 1991 Big Band competition. It must have pleased him that he was presented with this award by one of his own heroes, the great Don Lusher. Johnny was always a terrific all-round musician, and he was as comfortable playing with a brass band, a theatre pit band, a ballroom orchestra and the Scottish country dance bands of Jim Mcleod and Bobby Colgan, as he was in a jazz setting. He was endlessly versatile and, as Ken Mathieson was to point out in his obituary on Johnny in 2005 '...he was even able to combine the two styles (ie jazz and Scottish country dance music) in *his feature number, "The Black Bear", which went down equally well at jazz concerts and jazz gigs. No mean feat.'*[168] When top jazz musicians toured Scotland as soloists, Johnny was always first on their list when a band was being assembled to play with them and, in this context, he played with jazzers such as Acker Bilk, Alex Welsh, Kenny Ball, Humphrey Lyttelton, Yank Lawson, Wild Bill Davison and Jim Galloway. He was always one of the select group of local jazzers who were picked, and were good enough, to play in the genuine all-star bands that were assembled during the EIJFs.

It is impossible to write about Johnny McGuff without mentioning his sense of humour, as he was consistently one of the funniest raconteurs around the Edinburgh jazz scene, his stories told with great good humour and enthusiasm. Ken Mathieson gave a couple of examples and they are too good to leave out now. As Ken wrote in Johnny's obituary *'John's habit of taking an afternoon snooze on tour meant he sometimes missed band meals, so when the merits of French cuisine were being discussed in the tour bus, John said "I much preferred the meal I didn't get in France to the one I missed in Germany".* The other came about when Johnny was on tour in the USA and, as Ken reports, *"He once emerged blinking into the California sunshine and observed "Newtongrange has a great day for the Gala".'*

In the course of his long career, Johnny amassed a fund of wonderful tales of bands and gigs and his telling of these tales, in his own inimitable fashion, brightened many a weary journey. He claimed that, at the end of one gig when the crowd had been less than ecstatic about the band, one trusting member of the band had enthusiastically told the rest of them that they would have a return booking the following winter. This seeming unlikely, he was queried about the source of his information and, according to Johnny, reported that he had heard one of the punters say *'It'll be a cauld day before we have that band back again'!* Another tale, my favourite amongst the McGuff collection of anecdotes, concerned one of his innumerable appearances

---

[168] Mathieson K, 'John McGuff' obituary, The Scotsman, 14 July 2005

in the 'clubs', the Working Men's and Miner's Welfare institutes that once peppered the southern half of Scotland. Johnny was playing in a band, as part of an evening of entertainment, and the interval act was a young female singer, who was struggling to make herself heard or appreciated. Accompanied by a keyboard player, she was rapidly losing the attention of the crowd, from which arose a mounting hubbub of conversation. In the middle of her spot, the club social convener suddenly leapt up on stage and started banging a tin tray to get attention. In mid-song, the hapless singer's voice faltered and faded away. *"Now then ladies and gen'lemen,"* said the social convener firmly *"In this club we have a great tradition of showing the same respect for the bad acts as we do for the good yins, so let's have a bit of order if you please'.* Then, turning to the singer with an encouraging wave of his hand *'On you go hen'*!

Johnny's career continued until December 2004, when his playing came to an end because of cancer. He died on 11th July 2005 and Mike Hart, with whom he had played so often, said *'He was the most outstanding musician in the band. He was the man who made the band sound the way it did. He was of huge importance. Johnny was an amazing comedian and kept us laughing all the time. He was one of those guys who didn't have a enemy in the world. He will be sorely missed.'* For myself, I never played with anyone whose playing and company gave me more pleasure and it was a great privilege to have known him. Johnny McGuff featured on a number of recordings made by the Scottish Jazz Advocates and the Scottish Society Syncopators, which remain to remind us of one of the best jazz musicians that Edinburgh ever produced.

Dave Strutt (trumpet, mellophone, vocals), who was to play with the Syncs throughout most of the 1980s and well into the 1990s, was born in 1942 at Colchester in Essex. This was a part of the country under heavy attack from German bombers at the time but, hard as Hitler tried, he failed to wipe out the young Strutt.

Mike Hart's Scottish Society Syncopators
Tom Finlay, Jack Duff, Murray Smith, Dave Strutt,
Ricky Steele, Johnny McGuff, Mike Hart
(from the collection of Mike Hart, photographer
unknown)

In fact, Dave not only survived but can still recall the street party that greeted the end of the war in 1945, describing it as potentially a great gig, if only the war had lasted another fifteen years! Dave was educated at Colchester Royal Grammar School where, with a group of like-minded friends, he tried to start a school jazz society, only to be thwarted by an obstructive headmaster (and how often have we heard similar stories throughout this book?) Dave had already joined the local town band with a view to getting his hands on an instrument and in this he was successful, being allocated a trombone. However, this project too came to a sad end because of an official abhorrence of jazz, when one day the bandmaster stood up and announced *'I hope none of you young lads is going to go off and play this jazz stuff'*. Recognising a less than sympathetic environment, Dave abandoned this attempt but was rather more encouraged by an enlightened examination board which set him an essay on Louis Armstrong, when he sat his 'O' level English!

Dave traces his interest in jazz to his older brother Ray, who thwarted his attempts to listen to Children's Hour on the radio, insisting instead on tuning in to the American Forces Network, which broadcast from Germany. Apparently, this station featured an announcer who introduced each record in a dead-pan voice and included in his selection some recordings of the great Sarah Vaughan. Dave claims that his brother was in love with Sarah Vaughan, which he says surprised him, as he himself was unable to distinguish between one singer and the next. He does however acknowledge that all this unwilling exposure to jazz oriented broadcasts may have helped him to develop an ear for sounds, something he considers the absolute essential for appreciating jazz.

Looking back now, Dave regrets that he never had the benefit of any proper training. He had bought himself a battered trumpet in Soho when on a day trip to London and, as he says wryly, being aware that there were ample opportunities to play for even the fairly incompetent in the 1950s, he simply relied on his ear and taught himself. By this time, Dave too had fallen in love, not with Sarah Vaughan but with the playing of Louis Armstrong, which he henceforth took as his model. In those days, the art colleges tended to be hotbeds of jazz enthusiasm, as we have already witnessed in Edinburgh, and Dave discovered that, at the Colchester Art School, there was a pianist called John Addyman and a clarinet player called Bernard Watson. He had the good fortune to become involved with these two, who were the first adults he had come across who were prepared to be encouraging and help him to acquire some playing experience. Dave soon widened his interest in jazz, next discovering the magic of Bix Beiderbecke and then, with his pal Dick Mayhew, spending a great deal of time searching out records by Jelly Roll Morton. They knew that Morton was important in jazz history but found that his recordings were very hard to track down. This will ring bells for many who sought jazz recordings in the 1940s and 50s, when nearly all the early recordings had been deleted from the catalogues. The days of endless re-issues and compilations were still years ahead and collectors still grubbed about in dusty junk shops, searching out the precious (and incredibly fragile) 78 rpm relics of the twenties and thirties.

Dave, for some reason no longer clear to him, did not become caught up in the burgeoning, Ken Colyer inspired, enthusiasm for the purist music of Bunk Johnson and George Lewis and his interest remained with the music of the 1920s. Reminiscing recently, he recalled with great pleasure the happy hours, crouched over a tiny gramophone in Dick Mayhew's front room, trying to distinguish the playing of Louis Armstrong from that of King Oliver, on one of the re-issue London label ten inch LPs.

Dave's next move was to Leeds University, at which he says he was a *'tragically incompetent student'*, but where he discovered one saving grace – there was plenty of jazz! He found himself playing with a student band called Casey's Hot Seven, with whom he played at the Moorside Working Men's Club to what he describes as *'...a capacity audience of pissed students'*. However, alleged academic incompetence and pissed students apart, University life was to bring him into contact with what he describes as *'...a lot of intense and varied jazz influences'*. Dave has been known to say in retrospect that going to University was the biggest mistake of his life but he also recognises that it had a deeply defining influence on him. Looking back now, he says that he *'...discovered the wider horizons of jazz - saw some really great players and wasted an awful lot of time (possibly) in dank cellars filled with fragrant vapours from the cigarettes of bleary eyed hipsters'* which, the great players excepted, sounds to me a bit like Easter Road on a bad day.

After he escaped from Leeds academia in 1969, Dave hitched a lift up to Scotland with his girlfriend, who had managed to get a job at Edinburgh University. At that point, his plan was to stay for an indeterminate but limited time. The 'indeterminate but limited time' turned out to be thirty five years, a period which included one marriage and two children. After that length of time and with two children born and raised in Scotland, it is hardly surprising that he considers himself to be an adopted Scot. Scotland in general and the Edinburgh jazz scene in particular was, in my view, extremely lucky to have him. Dave was an integral part of the Edinburgh jazz scene for most of my jazz career, he was and is a very fine trumpet player and an extremely likeable bloke. If he was on trumpet, it was likely to be a good gig and he was easy to get along with. Yet, in spite of all that, there was one occasion when he found himself excluded from a gig at which he would have loved to have played. The reason given for his omission was, of all ludicrous things, that Dave was not a Scot! The gig was a Sandy Brown memorial event, and Dave was told that it was absolutely essential to recruit a Scottish trumpet player and he was therefore, unsuitable. Dave was undoubtedly hurt by this exclusion and I wonder what Sandy Brown would have had to say? According to George Melly in 'Owning Up', Sandy was a *'convinced nationalist'*[169], by which I guess he means a Scot with a great regard and loyalty towards all things Scottish, perhaps even with a belief that Scotland should be independent in the political sense, probably even very nationalist when Scottish and English teams are tearing lumps off each other at Murrayfield or Hampden Park. I can certainly believe all of that of Sandy but so what? Sandy was a jazzer who played international music, loved the blues of the Afro-Americans beyond any other music, lived and played much of his music in the south and sought out and revered others for what they could play, not for where they came from. I really do not think Sandy would have cared a damn if the trumpet player at the memorial concert had come from Mars, as long as he could really play.

Dave found the Edinburgh of the 1970s full of opportunities to play traditional jazz and one of his first associations was with a band called the Doon By Jazz Band. This band included Jock Westwater on banjo, Gerard Dott on clarinet, George Howden on trombone and, apparently, me on bass, although I have absolutely no memory of the band. I do, however, remember the ramifications of Dave's difficulty with the local accents. He claims that his untutored English ears had great difficulty with my rather awkward name, as spoken by Jock Westwater, and that he heard it as Grimble Mire, which he continued to believe was

---

[169] 'Owning Up' by George Melly, (Copyright © George Melly, 1965) Reprinted by permission of A. M. Heath & Co Ltd

my name for some considerable time. I was quite puzzled to find myself addressed as Grimble, although in an entirely friendly way, and remember wondering what part of the world he came from. It had quite a vogue for a while and I even thought of adopting it as a nom de plume, if I ever actually managed to start writing about jazz. Even now it occasionally turns up, usually when Bill Salmond is around, when he not infrequently greets me with a dignified and welcoming *'Ah, Grimble'*. In spite of finding myself renamed Grimble, I was much impressed by the playing of this newly arrived trumpeter but I was rather put out by his then current habit of holding his trumpet so that it pointed to the floor when he played. At that time, I liked my trumpet players to point their trumpets skywards, in the best Hollywood manner, like Danny Kaye in the Five Pennies film. Later on, he not only continued to play beautifully but also took to holding his trumpet in the approved way. I wonder now if I ever said anything but I hope not.

In 1980, during the EIJF and in the company of John Russell, Dave heard the wonderful guitar playing of Fapy Lafertin with gypsy band WASO. This had a profound influence on the two of them and they made an almost on-the-spot decision to attempt something along the same lines. Showing remarkable energy and speed-off the-mark for jazzers, it was no time at all before the band that was to be Swing 1980 was born, the history of which we have already explored. Of course, the EIJF had given an enormous boost to Edinburgh jazz and, in paying tribute to the sterling work of Mike Hart in this context, Dave picks out in particular the opportunities that the Festival brought, not only to hear but actually to play with some great players. Like me, he finds it almost incredible that we played with Benny Waters, a man who had played with King Oliver in the 1920s and whose career marched with that of jazz itself. Like many others, Dave considers that the EIJF was no ordinary festival, it was something unique and within it were some never to be repeated experiences.

After leaving Swing 1985 in that year, Dave joined Mike Hart's Scottish Society Syncopators, at first in a two trumpet team with Andrew Lauder and later in partnership with the outstanding trumpeter from Glasgow, Bruce Adams. His move from Swing 1985 to the bigger band was partly to build up his experience of playing in a traditional line-up, deciding that after five years he needed more freedom and less pressure than he was finding in the smaller band. His tongue in the cheek explanation now is that, inside the cultured small group man, there was a brash, extrovert Dixieland horn player struggling to get out! The other reason for his move was the chance that the Syncs offered to get to jazz festivals elsewhere and he went on to play with the band in Sacramento, Vancouver, Dresden and in the South of France. The Syncs also brought him the opportunity to record with the great Wild Bill Davison. This was on an LP that is now considered something of a collector's item, as it turned out to be just about Wild Bill's final recording session. This recording was to produce a particularly satisfying moment when, years later in France, someone played him a track from this album and he was able to say *'Oh yes! That's me!'*, to general stupefaction.

After his stint with the Syncs, Dave was one of the first Edinburgh based jazzers to make regular trips across the country to play with Glasgow based bands, in his case, George Penman's Jazzmen. The Penman band, then as always, was a sturdy band very much in the mould of the successful British trad bands but it brought Dave a chance that he particularly savoured – playing alongside George Kidd, one of the finest trombone players that Scotland ever produced. The Penman experience also introduced Dave to what he describes as the surreal world of West of Scotland bowling clubs, a sort of lost world of archaic social mores, replete with such carefully preserved customs as *'Gentlemen, you may now remove your jackets'*! Other enjoyable west coast gigs were those with George Hewitt's New Orleans Joymakers, at their monthly gigs at the Harbour Arts Centre in Irvine, and the Glasgow City Centre pub gigs with the band of trombonist, Hugh Muldoon. He particularly enjoyed the totally relaxed and unrehearsed approach of these bands, something I would endorse, having also played many times with both of these bands.

When he finally departed the Penman band Dave, given his complete lack of any Bunk Johnson pedigree, was surprised to find himself offered the trumpet chair in Violet Milne's Spirits of Rhythm. I, too, was with the Spirits around this time and, while it could be said that there was a certain stylistic anomaly between the band's asserted style and Dave's Bixian trumpet playing, I thought the band sounded great. Like me, Dave thoroughly appreciated the drive and swing of Kenny Milne's work on the drums and, looking back now, he picks out the playing of Ian Boyter, hailing him rightly as *'...a man with an amazing innate sense of swing and a listening ear'*. With the Spirits, Dave made regular trips to Switzerland and a couple of expeditions to the Orkney Jazz Festival.

Dave's long Edinburgh sojourn was at last to come to an end when, in 2004, he departed to live in rural France. There, at the time of writing and in spite of a dearth of local jazzers, he still manages to play in what he describes as *'...some great little venues'*. These include the Jazz Cafe at Reveillon, run by British trumpeter Bob Tinker, the Cafe de Routes at Alencon, where the delightful and generous host Dominique Destombes plays bass, and even a jazz club in Caen which is held on the back of a lorry! An unexpected meeting, which also led to some gigs, was with a pianist whom Dave discovered playing outside a cafe at the national Fete de Musique. This turned out to be one Cal Finnegan, whom Dave had last met forty five years previously at university! Dave Strutt's move to France deprived Edinburgh of one of its best and most versatile trumpet players, but our loss was France's gain and it is good to know that he is still in regular action and keeping his chops in trim.

Bruce Adams (trumpet) was a professional jazz trumpeter who played with the Syncs for a while after Andrew Lauder dropped out. This preserved for a time the two trumpet format, with Bruce in partnership with Dave Strutt, and Dave has said what an inspiration it was to play alongside him. According to John Chilton's 'Who's Who of

British Jazz'[170], Bruce Adams was born in Birkenhead on 3rd July 1951 and came from a show biz family which had been involved in the music hall world, before setting up home in Glasgow a year or two after Bruce was born. Bruce's father was a comedian, guitarist and vocalist and his mother a dancer. He made an early start on trumpet and won the TV talent series Opportunity Knocks when he was fourteen years old. After leaving school, he toured in variety with his father and played at Expo '67 in Montreal. He also completed a tour in Aden with the great comedian, Tony Hancock, which must have been a memorable experience. Later work included spells on the liners QE2 and Canberra before he returned to his Glasgow base from where he undertook freelance work and worked with saxophonist Bill Fanning. By the early 1980s, Bruce had picked up a number of jazz awards and, by 1984, was featuring as a solo artiste in the EIJF programmes. He was included in the Syncs line-up for the EIJF in 1987, '88, '89 and '91. An international jazz name with a big reputation, Bruce Adams has toured and played extensively and appeared at many festivals across the world. Among the many notable names with whom he has played are Dick Hyman, Benny Carter, Bob Wilber, Bill Aldred, Alan Barnes, and Pascal Michaux, as well as frequently leading bands of his own.

As an extra attraction, the Society Syncopators sometimes featured the excellent singing of **Wendy Weatherby (vocals, cello, composer).** Wendy was and is something of an all-rounder in music, as capable of swinging along with a traditional jazz band as in exploring the haunting folksongs of Scotland or the glorious works of Robert Burns. With rather more of an academic background in music than the average traditional jazzer, she graduated from the Royal Scottish Academy of Music and Drama in 1983. Her wide musical interests have taken her all round the world to sing and play at festivals in the UK, the continent of Europe, the USA and the former Soviet Union. She has worked, both as a cellist and a singer, with some of

[170] Chilton J, 'Who's Who of British Jazz', 2004 edition, reproduced by permission of Continuum International Publishing Group

the most notable names in Scottish music including Hamish Moore, Billy Jackson, The Pearlfishers, Michael Marra and Phil Cunningham. Her theatre credits include 'The Ship' and 'The Big Picnic' (Bill Bryden), John Bett's adaptation of Robert Burns' 'The Jolly Beggars' for Wildcat, Catherine Wheels 'The Story of the Little Gentleman' and Wee Stories' 'Arthur' and 'Tam O' Shanter', Wendy composing the music for this latter production. She also composed the music for the film scores of 'A Thief in the Night', 'Tickets for the Zoo' and 'Saved', which appeared on Channel 4 and BBC-2. In 2001, Wendy landed a commission from Celtic Connections which led to the creation of 'Daybreak at the World's Edge', the poems of William Soutar set for four cellos and three male voices. A further major achievement was another larger scale work in 2004, based on Lewis Grassic Gibbons 'Sunset Song'. With 'Cloud Howe' and 'Grey Granite' in 2005, Wendy completed the famous Gibbons trilogy 'The Scots Quair', which was performed at the 2007 Celtic Connnections festival, in the Glasgow City Halls. In 2010, Wendy was nominated as Scots Traditional Singer of the Year and, although she did not win the title, she would have got my vote if I had had one.

In addition to her performing activities, Wendy is also active in the teaching field and has hosted many workshops in both cello and singing. She teaches cello at RSMAD, the School of Excellence in Plockton, Newcastle University and the Adult Learning Scots Music Group in Edinburgh. She also features regularly with Dr Fred Freeman's illustrated lectures on Robert Burns, when she has performed alongside Marc Duff (ex-Capercaillie), John Morran (Deaf Shepherd), and Sandy Brechin (Jimmy Shandrix Experience). Wendy continues to be in demand all over the world, as both cellist and singer, and has a host of recordings to her name, some solo and some with others. Her website[171] is packed with information about her career, recordings and all her other music and drama activities and is commended to all jazzers who remember her singing with the Society Syncopators and other Edinburgh jazz bands.

---

[171] http://wendyweatherby.co.uk

With all these multifarious calls on her time, it is surprising that she ever managed to find time to sing with jazz bands but, when she did, she brought a cheery, joyful personality, great musicality and no mean ability to swing.

The Sync's long-serving **drummer, Frank Birnie**, was a relatively late arrival on the Edinburgh traditional jazz scene. Frank was born in Edinburgh on 31st March 1936 and educated at Balgreen Primary and then Saughton (later to be called Carrickvale) Secondary School. After leaving school, he began an apprenticeship in marine engineering, at Robb's Shipyard in Leith, just a few years after Stan Greig had followed the same route. After completing his apprenticeship, he went into the merchant navy and his first trip abroad, which paid £46 a month, was to last for all of two years! He loved the life at sea and appreciated the opportunities it brought to see the world, visiting far flung places such as Japan, Singapore and Hong Kong, among many others. His interest in music had begun early when he played 'drums' on a kitchen chair, accompanying his Uncle Jock who played a five-row button accordion. He acquired his first real drum kit, which consisted of a snare drum and bass drum and cost £15, when he was fifteen. Frank had another musical uncle, Uncle Bertie, who was lead drummer in the Granton Gas Works Pipe Band, and it was he who taught Frank the rudiments of drumming. When he started to play in public, it was with his Uncle Jock and another accordion player called Alec McKenzie, playing Scottish Country dance music, performing at weddings and similar functions, and Frank remembers having to transport his drums by bus to these gigs.

Later, he was to expand his playing into the club scene, often backing cabaret acts in the company of Clive Greathead who played organ. Once, playing in Billy's Bar, a large establishment in Prestonpans, they were accompanying a singer who was in full cry when they were approached by what Frank describes as a 'wee wuman'. This lady turned out to be the treasurer who had come to hand over the band's wages, which she insisted on doing, including having Clive sign a receipt, while he continued to back the somewhat bemused singer! As it turned out, this eccentric behaviour was considered the normal procedure and it continued throughout their tenure at the venue. Around this time, Frank found other playing opportunities in dance work, including a couple of years at the Heart's Supporter's Club in Craigmillar.

Sometime in the 1970s, Frank ventured into the jazz scene and became a regular at the Yellow Carvel pub, where he listened to the Charlie McNair band and had the occasional sit in. It was not long before he decided that he fancied playing more of their kind of music. Eventually, sometime around 1977, he was offered a jazz gig. This was at the New Liston Arms in Kirkliston and it came about through the trombonist, Sam Smith. Sam was playing there in a band that included Andrew Lauder (tpt), Jack Graham (rds), Tom Finlay (pno) and Mike Hart (bjo) and, when he arrived, Frank realised that he knew none of them, except Sam himself. After several numbers, the little trombonist turned to him and said *'You're spoiling us!'* Thinking that he was making a mess of things, Frank began apologising when Sam interrupted saying *'No, no, I mean you are swinging'.* This led to Frank becoming a permanent part of the band and his jazz career had begun.

Things moved rapidly and by 1978 he had visited the Dunkirk Jazz Festival with Mike Hart's Society Syncopators, where they came second in the traditional jazz category of the band championship. In 1979 the band, including Frank, returned to Dunkirk and this was the year they were crowned European Champions in the same category and, later that same year, he went with the band to play at the Sacramento Jazz Jubilee in California. However, his involvement with the band was to come to an abrupt halt in 1980, when the Society Syncopators amalgamated with Old Bailey's Jazz Advocates, thus creating the Scottish Jazz Advocates. Nothing daunted, Frank kept playing with other bands and when, only a year or two later, the Jazz Advocates broke up, Frank was again included in Mike's re-formed band, now to be called the Scottish Society Syncopators. This time, his stay was to be a prolonged one and was to include several more visits to Sacramento, tours in France, Germany and Poland (they were there when the Chernobyl nuclear disaster occurred) and a number of recordings. It was on one of these trips that the band, and

Mike Hart in particular, began to invent pseudo-Germanic names, in the German style of combining nouns. A duck became known as a 'quackinpecker', a handkerchief a 'snotterviper', a friendly dog was a 'barkinschnuffler' and a savage one a 'barkinschnapper'. The game apparently became less popular with the banjo section when Dave Strutt decided that a banjo player was an 'arschenclanger'! A cherished memory from the trip to California came when Frank was introduced to the well-known American drummer, Nick Fatool. When Fatool realised who Frank was he exclaimed *'Shit man! You're in the Scottish band. They tell me you kick a mean set of skins!'* The records that Frank made with the Syncs included their excellent 'Huntin', Shootin' and Jazz'n' album and also the particularly memorable LP that included as guests, the ex-patriot Scot Jim Galloway (rds) and the great American trumpeter, Wild Bill Davison[172].

A big, strongly built man who was a powerful drummer, Frank later formed the East Coast Jazz Band which played an extremely successful ten-year residency at the Blue Lagoon, continuing well through the 1990s. This was a gig at which sitters-in were always made welcome by the amiable drummer and which was to become a popular Monday night drop-in spot for many of the Edinburgh jazz musicians. Frank Birnie played on well into the 2000s, finishing his playing career in mid-decade when playing with Jim Baikie's Jimjammers at the Sheraton Hotel.

Ken Macdonald (bass), was born in 1948 and attended George Heriot's School but was not involved in any jazz activity at school. There was marked musical interest in his family, with elder brother Donald already active as a bass player on the Edinburgh jazz scene, and Ken first tried his hand as a guitar player in a folk group. Ken's interest in jazz was ignited when he went along to the Loch Ewe Hotel in Royal Terrace, where he heard the Society Syncopators. This was the Syncs in their original form, with the Telford/Paxton/Craig front line and Ken's brother Donald on bass, with Mike Hart and Iain Forde completing the rhythm section. A bit later, when he was attending

---

[172] See discography appendix

Aberdeen School of Architecture, Ken followed in Donald's footsteps and set about learning to play double bass. At first he played an old bass of Donald's on which he had fitted a new plywood front, already showing an aptitude for the instrument repair work by which he would eventually make his living. However, when Ken returned to Edinburgh in 1975, he found that Donald's bass was available. Donald had, for the time being at least, abandoned bass in favour of playing sax, and Ken switched to using Donald's instrument. Donald then persuaded Ken to play a couple of numbers with the Syncs, who were playing at a party in Iain Forde's house, and there he was heard by Jim Petrie. Jim was looking for a bass player for the Climax band at the time and invited Ken along to play with the band.

Ken's first Climax gig was in 1975 in the Yellow Carvel and he was clearly a success. He was promptly taken on permanently and was to remain with the band for three years. In 1978 he joined Mike Hart's Society Syncopators and recorded with them on their album 'Jazz Tattoo', recorded on 9th March 1980. He was also with the band when they made their triumphant visits to the Dunkirk Jazz Festival, coming second in the traditional jazz section in 1978 and taking first place in 1979. Ken was to stay with the Syncs until 1983, when the band merged with the Old Bailey band to become the Scottish Jazz Advocates. Shortly after this, Ken left Edinburgh to undertake a violin making course at the Violin Making School in Newark, in Nottinghamshire. After completing the course, he made his living for a year or so in musical instrument work but then joined a local architectural firm part time, dividing his time between the two very different occupations. Ken was to remain in the south, playing gigs around the Midlands with many professional musicians, until his return to Edinburgh in 1989. Back home, he at first combined free lance architecture with instrument repair work but later, was able to concentrate fully on the latter, mostly specialising in the double bass.

After his return to Edinburgh, Ken was also soon in demand as a bass player, playing many gigs with a wide variety of bands over the years. He played about six years with Jim Petrie's Diplomats of Jazz, when they were resident in Leslie's Bar, a beautifully preserved Victorian bar in Causewayside. He was also very active backing visiting musicians at jazz festival time and in small group work, often with guitarist Dougie Campbell, and Tom or Jack Finlay. A spell of several years in the 1990s with a band led by Alan Quinn at the Templehall Hotel in Portobello, was followed by playing with a quintet, led by trumpeter Brian Robertson, in the Elwyn Hotel in Portobello Road, a residency that continued for about ten years, before ending in 2009. This in turn paved the way for Ken to remain with Brian Robertson when he formed his seven piece band, the Forth River Ragtimers in 2000, a band with which he was still playing in 2011. Ken would also make a brief return to the Climax band when they got together for a re-union concert, alongside the similarly re-formed Old Bailey band, during the 2010 EIJBF. Ken's son Owen is now continuing the family tradition of producing high quality bass players. Owen, like Ken himself, is a creative and flexible bass player, well able to play in traditional jazz bands, although his preference is naturally for more contemporary jazz, and he is much involved in work with trios and quartets, often backing singers.

The bass player who succeeded Ken Macdonald with the Syncs was **Ricky Steele (bass)**, who was born in Edinburgh on 8th January 1960 and attended Perth High School, before qualifying as an accountant. While still at primary school, Ricky's attempts to teach himself to play his older sister's trumpet came to an abrupt halt when he was caught and taken up to the 'big school', to which the trumpet belonged. Expecting to be in trouble, he was instead asked to play something for the trumpet tutor who, clearly quite impressed, provided him with some early lessons. After moving to secondary school in Perth, he continued with his trumpet tuition and played for the school band, before graduating to the county orchestra. This was followed by some gigs with the Perth Theatre pit orchestra, before moving on to play cornet with the Perth Silver Band. Clearly a promising and enterprising musician, he also taught himself to play guitar, which opened up the opportunity for him to play in a rock band while still at school. In addition, he played both guitar and trumpet in a dance band and then, when he was in his late teens and early twenties, he switched to playing bass guitar with both the rock band and the dance band.

Going along to listen to a local jazz band brought Ricky his first chance to hear a double bass up close. It did not take him long to decide that this was the instrument for him and, hastily swapping a Gibson 175 guitar for a double bass, he proceeded to teach himself to play it. He was soon a member of the local jazz band, staying with them for a year or two, before becoming part of a new band which started a regular Sunday gig in Perth. This was clearly a band of some quality, as their regular trombonist was the excellent George Kidd and another two famous jazzers from Glasgow, Carol Kidd and Fionna Duncan, appeared as guest vocalists. Carol Kidd was obviously impressed by Ricky's playing and, after the death of her regular bass player Alec Moore, she booked Ricky to play in her own three piece backing group. Ricky, whose jazz heroes have included bass players Scott la Faro and Ray Brown, then came down to Edinburgh to play a gig with a Scottish jazz legend, Edinburgh's Alex Shaw. This was to be the start of his long involvement with the Edinburgh jazz scene and the beginning of a twenty five year run at the EIJF. In 1986, he moved to live in Edinburgh and, after depping with many of the local bands, he became a member of Mike Hart's Society Syncopators, with whom he remained until the early 2000s. Ricky recorded with the Syncs and also made a number of recordings with the Tom Finlay Trio, including three CDs made in Cuba which included a number of Cuban musicians. An extremely able and versatile bass player, Ricky Steele worked with too many top jazzers to list in total but noting just Al Cohn, Warren Vache, Milt Hinton, Bob Barnard, Doc Cheatham, Roy Williams and Red Rodney as examples, gives some idea of the quality of jazz with which he was involved.

Another jazz musician who, like Ricky Steele, arrived from Perth and was to be a notable addition to the Edinburgh jazz resources, was **Campbell Normand (piano)**. Campbell was born in Perth in 1962 and educated at Perth High School. He had formal piano lessons up to grade five from the age of seven and lessons in playing the organ from age twelve.   A talented musician, Campbell also played tenor horn in the Perth Silver Band and, briefly, the French horn in the Tayside Schools Orchestra.   By the age of fourteen, he had made a start on his keyboard career and was playing organ in club bands around Perth. His interest in jazz was triggered by visits to Sunday jazz sessions at the Murrayshall House Hotel, near Perth, where he was eventually given the chance to sit in with the resident jazz band and, in no time at all, he was hooked on the music, citing his favourite jazz pianists as Oscar Peterson and Monty Alexander.

In 1980, Campbell moved to Edinburgh where he attended Edinburgh University before graduating as a lawyer, specialising in civil litigation.   Not surprisingly, he was attracted to the playing of Alec Shaw, attending many of the great Edinburgh pianist's trio sessions at Platform One, the entertainment lounge in the Caledonian Hotel. Campbell's first experience of playing in the EIJF came in 1988, when he made up a fine rhythm section with Ricky Steele (bs) and Kenny Mathieson (drms)[173], backing the well known trumpeter Bob Wallis and Glasgow's Forrie Cairns on clarinet.   It was also around this time that he joined a band of which we will hear more very shortly, Hamish McGregor's Fat Sam's Band, staying for about three years and with which band he has continued to dep ever since. After his spell with Fat Sam's Band, most of Campbell's playing has been with small bands and trios, as well as working with various vocalists.   He has, of course, remained busy, as befits a player of his quality and versatility, playing several times a month, another of the group of able Edinburgh musicians who are able to play across a wide spectrum of jazz styles.

1982 saw a winter jazz event which was billed as 'Mardi Gras – Grand Carnival Masquerade - Jazz Band Ball'. This seems to have been a one-off venture and it took place on Tuesday 23 February 1982 in the Astoria Ballroom in Abbeymount.   The programme stated that the intention was to '...*brighten up the dull month of February and get*

---

[173] This is Kenny Mathieson, the well known drummer and band leader from the west of Scotland and not the journalist of the same name.

people back to life after recovering from the New Year period'.
The event was to feature six bands playing continuously for
five and a half hours in two ballrooms, plus guest stars and
musicians. There was to be something for everyone from
'...hot dance music to pure Dixieland' to *'Ory's Creole Eating
House'* for meals and snacks and patrons were invited to
wear Carnival costume or fancy dress and masks. The
guest bands were the eleven piece Savannah Syncopators
from the north-east of England, the Severnside Jazz Band
who were normally resident at the Shrewsbury Jazz Club
and the Bourbon Jazzmen from the west of Scotland, led by
Glasgow based trumpeter, Dave Mathews. The local bands
on the bill were the Festival City Jazz Band, Jim Petrie's
Jazz band and the West End Jazz Band. Solo attractions
were Fionna Duncan and Edinburgh's own Mr Five by Five,
the inimitable Jackie MacFarlane, who were to sing with
several of the bands.

Drummer Frank Birnie, then leading the East Coast Jazz
Band, also made a guest appearance and both Frank and
bass player Dick Walink were thanked for lending
instruments. As well as giving details about the Mardi
Gras, the programme gives an interesting snapshot of
Edinburgh jazz in the winter of 1982, carrying
advertisements for some of the venues then supporting jazz,
including the Grange Hotel, the Ailsa Craig Hotel (both the
West End Jazz Band), the Black Bull (the Climax Jazz
Band), the Caledonian Hotel (the Scottish Jazz Advocates),
the Hopetoun Bar (the Louisiana Ragtime Band), the
Barnton Hotel (the Festival City Jazz Band), the Bonnington
Bridge Bar (Frank Birnie's Jazz Band), the Glenelg Hotel
(Jim Petrie's Jazz Band), the Garrick Bar featuring both the
Charlie McNair Jazz Band and Swing '81 (sic), who
according to this publication, appeared to have forgotten to
update their name. There was also a full page advert for the
Goblet in Rose Street, which styled its sessions featuring
the Charlie McNair Jazz Band, the Goblet Jazz Club. This
latter advert included a wonderful picture of a debonair
Charlie McNair in a DJ, complete with buttonhole
carnation, cigar and trumpet, and looking like one of those
pictures of jazzers like Bix Beiderbecke and Frankie
Trumbauer in the early 1920s. There was also a

photograph of an extremely relaxed looking Mike Hart clutching pint and grinning like a Cheshire cat, the caption of which said *'Happiness is a Jazz Festival Director on the last night!'*

When Hamish McGregor left the Scottish Jazz Advocates in October 1984, he was soon into action forming his new band. What he had planned, was a band that would play in the 'jump-jive' tradition of Louis Jordan. He recruited Gus Ferguson on trumpet, Graeme Robertson on trombone, Bill Simpson on tenor and soprano saxes, Tom Finlay on piano, Tony Howard on guitar, Bobby Miller on bass guitar, Kenny Mathieson on drums and Nick Robertson (son of Graeme) on vocals. Hamish set himself to think up a name for the new band and came up with the moniker **Fat Sam's Band**. The name came from a song title, 'Fat Sam from Birmingham', which had been recorded by Louis Jordan and was, in fact, the only song Jordan ever recorded with a big band. After rehearsing, the band played its first gig on St Valentine's Day, the 14th of February 1985. The venue, formerly known as the Capercaillie, was to re-open on that date as The Elephant and Castle.

Fat Sam's Band was to go on to be extremely successful, playing all over the world from its Edinburgh base and, in addition to all the foreign gigs, was to be just as busy in Edinburgh. About a year and a half after the band was formed, Hamish negotiated a residency with Edinburgh businessman John Edmonds, which was to be in a new venue just opening. This was an American styled restaurant located in the old Edinburgh Meat Market building, on the corner of Fountainbridge and Semple Street, and the venue adopted both the band's name and logo. Fat Sam's Downtown Diner became a fashionable and very popular eatery, famous not only for its food and music, but also for Percy the Piranha, a large and ferocious looking fish, which swam about in a tank just inside the door. The band celebrated the 9th anniversary of its launch in 1995 in Fat Sam' eatery' on 16th February 1994, and the programme included a re-union of Old Bailey's Jazz Advocates and another Edinburgh band we will meet shortly, the Jazz Masters. The restaurant, which at its peak was especially popular as a venue for youngster's birthday celebrations, eventually closed in 2000. In 1990, the band appeared on the television programme Opportunity Knocks, hosted by the comedian, Les Dawson. They sounded and looked very good on the programme (I still have a video recording of their spot) and were placed third out of the seven competing acts. There is little doubt that, on talent alone, they should have been placed higher than this, perhaps even first, but jazz was not riding high in general popularity at that time.

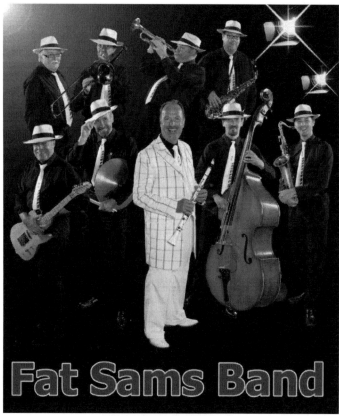

Fat Sam's Band
(by permission of Hamish McGregor)

Over the years, the membership of the nine-piece Fat Sam's Band inevitably changed from time to time and, at one time or another, the following were members of the band:

Trumpet:	Gus Ferguson, Tom McNiven, Bill Hunter
Trombone:	Graeme Robertson, Jimmy Mann
Clarinet/Alto sax:	Hamish McGregor
Ten sax:	Bill Simpson, Tom Chalmers, Jack Duff, Steve Meeker, John Burgess, Iestyn Evans, Gordon McNeill
Baritone sax:	Martin Foster, Jack Duff
Keyboard:	Tom Finlay, Campbell Normand
Guitar:	Tony Howard, Phil Adams
Bass:	Donald McDonald, Lindsay Cooper, Roy Percy
Drums:	Kenny Mathieson
Vocals:	Nick Robertson, Hamish McGregor

The list of festivals alone at which they played, never mind all the other gigs, gives an idea of their popularity and their ability to attract bookings from all over the world. On the band website[174] in 2010, the list of festivals at which the band had played included fourteen in the UK, two in Ireland, nineteen in Europe, one in the Middle East, one in Canada and four in the USA. Bearing in mind that quite a few of these were visited many times, some indeed on an annual basis, this is some list. In addition, by the end of 2011, they had made six recordings, issued on CD as 'Fat Sam's Band' and packaged as volumes I to VI, and it is likely that there will be many more to come. On the website, the versatility of the band is emphasised, with three speciality programmes on offer for different occasions:

- *'A Tribute to Louis Jordan'*, the King of Jump Jive
- *'A Night at the Cotton Club'*, featuring the music of early Ellington and Calloway – 1920's and 30's
- *'An Evening of Jump-Jive – Boogie – Swing – Jazz – Blues – R and B'*, from Glenn Miller and Duke Ellington to Fats Domino and the 'Blues Brothers'

The website declares that *'Versatility and variety is the band's bye-line and is such that it offers a wide variety of*

---

[174] www.fatsamsband.com

421

musical sounds and styles in its performance. Allied to a strong presentation, the band is both a highly polished jazz-based Showband and a serious interpreter of mainstream jazz'. Fat Sam's Band was always a highly professional outfit, always well rehearsed and exciting and without doubt, the most commercially successful of the Edinburgh bands within the traditional jazz style. Hamish McGregor was, right from the start, a talented, natural showman with a real flair for presentation and he was the key factor in the band's success. Fat Sam's Band celebrated its Silver Jubilee on February 14th 2010 with a show in the Queen's Hall, as high-octane and dynamic as ever and, at twenty five years old, showed no signs of ever stopping.

Chapter XV

Bands Old and New and Returning Veterans

The early 1980s had already seen the continuation of several of the established bands and the formation of a number of new ones. The **Climax Jazz Band** was still going as strongly as ever and had found a good new residency. The Queen's Hall had opened in about 1979, as a major new concert venue, and Jim Young's firm had fitted out their kitchen. Jim had casually talked about the band to someone at the Hall when the work was going on and the happy result of this was that the Climax band landed a residency, playing every Friday evening, not in the main hall, but in the bar. The residency lasted about a year but another happy outcome of the gig was that they were able to celebrate the band's twenty-fifth anniversary in 1981, by staging a Silver Jubilee concert in the Queen's Hall. Another band in the purist traditional, the **Spirits of Rhythm**, had been formed in the dying days of 1979, as we have already heard. As the new decade began, they had quickly established themselves as a major new attraction and were to go on to become another of Edinburgh's long serving bands.

The **Charlie McNair Jazz Band** had stormed into the 1980s with Charlie in his usual ebullient form. Early in the decade, Charlie had residencies at the Goblet Lounge in Rose Street and the prestigious Granary Bar, part of the Dragonara Hotel, beside the Dean Bridge. The band by this time had, in addition to Charlie himself, Bill Munro (tbn), Gerard Dott (clt), Harald Vox (bjo), Johnny Fitzsimmons (bs gtr) and Kenny Milne (drms). At other times, it was Dizzy Jackson, Johnny Phillips or Peter Gordon–Smith on bass. At some point, Gerard Dott dropped out of the Goblet gig and George Duncan came in on clarinet and, by late 1982, George was playing all of Charlie's gigs. Gerard Dott moved on to play with a band at the Haymarket Station Bar. At first this band was led by Donald MacDonald, now playing a variety of saxes, with Bob Craig (tbn) and a rhythm section of Graham Scott (piano) together with two original RHS Gangsters, Dizzy Jackson (bss) and Bill Strachan (drums). Gerard joined the band after sitting in one evening and recalls that Bob was amazed that he wanted to join on clarinet as Gerard had been doing a lot of piano playing at this time, mostly depping in the Louisiana Ragtime band, when Graham Scott was unavailable. Over time, Bob gradually became the band leader and then, in the late 1980s, Al Fairweather returned to Edinburgh and joined the band, a move that was later to lead to a residency at the Glenelg Hotel in Leamington Terrace, off Gilmore Place.

Meanwhile, Charlie McNair also moved residencies and had taken on what was to become his main gig from 1983 to 1994, Preservation Hall in Victoria Street. Preservation Hall, a venue clearly named with jazz in mind, provided several other bands with a residency as well, including George Roy and his Jazzmen and the East Coast Jazz Band. In his various residencies, perhaps especially at Preservation Hall, Charlie's usual ability to charm his audience ensured him a packed house on most nights and the devoted following of a large group of regulars, again largely composed of students. Other 1980s residencies for the McNair band were in Harry's Bar, near the West End, Bentley's in Rose Street (which he played using only a quartet) and Pierre Victoire in Dock Place, Leith.

Gerard Dott tells the story of the time when Charlie had a new banjo player who, although he would become a good player, at the time was lacking in both experience and confidence. Because of this, he had developed the alarming habit of sometimes panicking if he was unexpectedly thrown a banjo solo and simply stopping dead in his tracks, leaving the rest of the band to thunder on. Never one to miss an opportunity for a good laugh, Charlie hatched a plot with the rest of band. They picked a fairly complicated tune, with which they knew the banjo player was already struggling and on which, if he was signalled to take a solo, they knew he would go into sudden stop mode. At the pre-arranged moment, Charlie suddenly and dramatically signalled for the banjo solo and as expected, the banjo player stopped dead. At the same moment, the entire band also stopped dead. They then solemnly counted the bars of a completely silent banjo chorus before coming in a right place, as if nothing had happened, which indeed had been the case! Charlie McNair, already the great survivor across four decades of Edinburgh jazz, was in fine fettle as the 1980s wore on.

The McNair band trombonist of the 1980s was **Bill Munro (trombone)**, who was born in Ayrshire on 4th February 1936 and attended Ayr Academy. His family was musical and Bill has described his mother as playing piano *'like an angel'* and his father as a having a fine baritone voice. Early piano playing lessons came to nothing because of *'lack of both interest and manual dexterity'*, Bill much preferring rugby and cricket. Sometime around 1951, he remembers being knocked out by some music he heard on a radio station called A.F.N. This stood for American Forces Network and the music broadcast was by the likes of the bands of Paul Whiteman, Benny Goodman, Glenn Miller, Artie Shaw and Tommy Dorsey. Shortly after this, a friend let him hear some scratchy old 78 rpm recordings of the Louis Armstrong Hot Five and Seven and King Oliver's Creole Jazz Band. Brought up on classical music, Bill had no idea that such exciting music existed and from that point on, he was hooked on jazz. Around the same time, he heard the Humphrey Lyttelton band with Wally Fawkes on clarinet and Johnny Parker on piano and thought they were wonderful.

His introduction to live jazz came around 1954 when the Clyde Valley Stompers played a gig at Ayr Pavilion. The Stompers were extremely popular in the west of Scotland at that time and Bill was impressed by their trumpeter, Charlie Gall, and the leader and trombonist, Ian Menzies. The Stompers had a singer with them, a *'real belter of a red hot mama'* according to Bill, and she was called Mary

MacGowan. He also remembers that, good though they were, the Stompers were sometimes referred to disparagingly as 'white dixielanders' by the more purist inclined jazz followers. This I find an interesting comment from such an informed source, as it has always been my impression that, while very strong in Edinburgh, the purist movement never seemed to have had as much influence in Glasgow and the west of Scotland. Bill's next exposure to live jazz came when the Chris Barber band played Ayr Town Hall when as Bill says, *'the joint nearly erupted'*. The Barber band was then the top British traditional jazz band and the crowd would not let them leave the stage until they had played umpteen encores. They certainly had a major impact on Bill Munro who, from then on, set his heart on learning to play jazz trombone.

In 1956, Bill moved to Edinburgh where he worked as an apprentice engineer with McTaggart Scott and Company and pursued his professional studies at the Bristo Tech and Heriot Watt Colleges. An opportunity came up to listen in to a rehearsal of the works silver band, at which Bill discovered that they had a spare trombone. He was quick to express an interest and was duly invited to become what they called a 'learner'. Things went quite well for a while and then he was promoted to play in the real band. The band was under the direction of a Yorkshire army band master who took exception to Bill's habit of tapping his foot while playing. Bill received a severe Yorkshire-type bollocking from this worthy along the lines of *'I'm the fooking conductor here tha' knows. Tha' sits to attention in my fooking band'*. This led to a sad parting of the ways, although ameliorated by Bill sneakily managing to hang on to the trombone. Valiant efforts to progress on the instrument led to skirmishes with a less than thrilled land lady, who objected to dying cow noises from the bedroom, forcing Bill to drive his vintage Riley to the Pentland Hills on wet Sundays, where he serenaded the bemused sheep with the trombone slide sticking out of the car window.

By 1957, Bill had begun to find his way into the Edinburgh jazz scene. At India Buildings on Sunday evenings he heard Archie Sinclair and Johnny Winters while, at another regular Sunday gig at the West End Cafe, he came across Charlie McNair, Jim Young and Mike Hart. He also made his way to the jazz club then running in Jim Young's basement in St Peters Place, where the great George Lewis and Jim Robertson put in an appearance, and to the Stud Club during its sojourn in the Pleasance, where he met Jim Petrie, amongst others. Another jazz haven was at the Royal Mile Cafe where trumpeter Eric Rinaldi, son of the cafe owner, had a regular Saturday night gig. Clearly making his way successfully into the local jazz scene, disaster then struck the budding jazz trombonist. An untimely audit was conducted within the ranks of the silver band which revealed the absence of the trombone which Bill had neglected to return and he had no option but to hand it over. Fruitless attempts to purchase a second hand horn led eventually to the purchase of a new trombone, courtesy of the generosity and support of Pete Seaton, of which we have already heard. Disaster circumnavigated, Bill was back in action.

Sometime around 1959, he was approached by a young trumpeter, Fred Terry, who informed him that a pal was trying to put a band together and was short of a trombone player. The pal turned out to be the clarinet player Jack St Clair, and Bill went along for an audition at the Pooles Synod Hall. The audition clearly worked out well and the band began regular practices before Jack announced their first public engagement. This was the interval spot at the West End Cafe, where they supported the resident band. This did not work out quite as intended. Although trombone player Bob Craig congratulated them on their playing of Chimes Blues, which he said was the best he had heard from an amateur band, the acclaim they had received from the punters offended the resident band to the extent that they were not permitted to play the second interval! Nothing daunted, the Jack St Clair band soon had a number of gigs in the back room of the Crown Bar of fond memory but again, not without unforeseen problems. One gig there in 1959 culminated in woeful humiliation, with the band having to organise a whip round to raise 5/- (25 pence in today's money) towards the hall rental. This was all of thirty bob (£1.50) and, as they had charged 1/- (5 pence) entrance money, it would seem that they had attracted only twenty five punters. Bill had recently married and his wife, Chris, was less than impressed by this financial embarrassment, especially as she had had to shell out to get in, commenting *'Huh, I thought you guys were supposed to be a big draw'.*

Bill reports that the band was improving by this time and sometimes even managed to play almost in tune, this technical breakthrough no doubt assisting them in securing a weekly gig at the Place Jazz Club in Victoria Street. By now it was the early 1960s and I had joined Bill in the Jack St Clair Band. Around this time, there was one away booking that both Bill and I both recall with a certain affection, if not with great clarity. This was at the Inchnacardoch Hotel on the banks of Loch Ness. The band had been booked to play at the local village hall on the Friday evening and then, for the entertainment of owner's guests, at the hotel itself on the Saturday night. We had a horrendous journey up from Edinburgh in foul weather and arrived very late for the Friday gig, something that seemed to bother the Highland punters not one whit. They merely waited patiently until we had arrived, made a commensurate adjustment in the finishing time and on we went. Saturday was spent sleeping and drinking in about equal proportions and then we played all evening and all night, until about six in the morning. We did not play continuously, of course, and there were hazy interludes during which a barman, who was a confusing mixture of black Barbadian and Highland teuchter, sang incomprehensible Gaelic songs with the local Ghillie. An accordion player also appeared at some point and in an excess of enthusiasm, I tried to play bass along with him. I think I got sworn at for my efforts although, as this was in Gaelic, it is just possible, although unlikely, that it was complimentary. At six in the morning it was broad daylight and at least half the band, reeling from lack of sleep and Highland hospitality, took advantage of our host's generosity to go splashing about on Loch Ness in the hotel rowing boat, to our extreme peril. The other half, I believe, went out on the ponies from the hotel's pony trekking stable but as none of them would ever speak about this experience, I have no idea what happened. Everything else about the weekend is a blank.

Bill stayed with the Jack St Clair band for a while and then stayed on when it became, sans Jack, the New Savoy Jazz Band. However, by 1964, pressures of family and work responsibilities led to him stopping playing and he sold his trombone, not resuming playing, with a new trombone, until 1980. His services were soon snapped up and he was to spend most of the 1980s with the Charlie McNair band, during one of its best periods as already described above, before finally retiring from music in 1990 and later moving back to live in Girvan in Ayrshire. Bill lists as his favourites and influences many of the great Americans including Armstrong, Ory, Ellington, Oliver, Bechet and Morton and amongst, the UK jazzers, Lyttelton, Sandy Brown and Chris Barber. His own playing was much in the Barber style, itself founded on Ory, and he was a particularly fine ensemble player. I played quite a bit with Bill in the early 1960s and what stays in the memory is his enthusiastic attack, which never failed to drive the band along in good style. He had a nice mellow tone and a sure musical ear, both of which were a sad loss to the Edinburgh jazz scene during the years when he was inactive.

Although there must be a large number of punter-made private recordings featuring Bill, especially during his 1980s time with the McNair band, there seems to be a lack of any professional recordings to remind us of his playing. Bill himself remembers the recording of a session with Jim Petrie's band in the Crown Bar in about 1960 but I have not been able to trace this. There was also a BBC recording made at the Queen's Hall in about 1983 with the Charlie McNair band. This included the tunes *Buddy's Habit*, *Weary Blues*, *Apex Blues*, *If You's a Viper*, and *Yes, Yes in Your Eyes*, but it seems likely that this was a broadcast recording and not made for general release. Bill has a taped copy and, although he says that he did not think much of it at the time, on hearing it more recently, he felt that the band had generated a lot of atmosphere. He once played this recording for his daughter Claire, who expressed herself as most impressed, saying *'Bloody magic Dad, I had no idea you guys were as good as that'*. Bill suspects that she was after a loan at the time.

Bill Salmond's Louisiana Ragtime Band had long ago demonstrated their ability to keep a residency going in the long term, keeping the Hopetoun Lounge in Morrison Street busy from June 1976 until April 1983. The band, which by now had the major attraction of Dave Paxton in the clarinet chair, then moved on to the Navaar House Hotel, on the south side of town, in June 1983. This was a gig that was to become something of an institution and it was to continue until February 1999. In fact, so successful was the Navaar gig, that it became another of these residencies where loyal and regular followers would arrive long before the band, determined to ensure they got a seat. It actually went a bit further than that, as many of them were anxious to secure, not just a seat, but their <u>usual</u> seat, and would look a bit miffed if it was already taken. There was also a sensibly supportive landlord who not only supplied a decent piano, but made sure that it was kept in tune. The bar was invariably packed each Tuesday evening, with many spilling out into the hallway and listening through the doorway behind the piano. Bill had many contacts throughout the world of New Orleans jazz and he was often able to invite visiting players to join the band at their Tuesday evening sessions. In the early 1980s, Kenny Milne was Bill's trumpeter and when Kenny left, Bill replaced him with a new comer, Brian Robertson.

Brian Robertson (trumpet), who was born in Edinburgh on 31st December 1955 and educated at Portobello High School, had been a regular follower at the Hailes House Hotel sessions, where the Nova Scotia Jazz Band of the late 1970s played. These sessions stimulated Brian into taking up the trumpet and he took lessons for a couple of years from trombonist and brass teacher, Graeme Robertson. He soon got fed up playing scales and arpeggios and set out to learn the rest of what he needed on his own, keen to start playing jazz as soon as possible. A common story this – conscientious music teachers must shudder when their pupils start to show an interest in jazz. Brian says that Graeme Robertson was a very able teacher but had soon realised that Brian was *'not very good at dots'* and just wanted to play jazz! Brain's original inspiration had been Gus Ferguson, then of the Nova Scotia band, and Brian's first sortie in public, in a highly nervous condition, was a sit in with that band at the Hailes House Hotel. Shortly after this, he teamed up with trombonist Andy Mulhern and formed the **Darktown Jazz Band**, whose first gig was at the Parkside Bowling Club in Edinburgh. After this, they soon found themselves making headway in the Edinburgh jazz scene but the Darktown Jazz Band came to an end when Brian joined Bill Salmond's Louisiana Ragtime Band in early 1986.

In spite of his early liking for the Dixieland style of the Nova Scotia Jazz Band, Brian soon transferred his allegiance to the purist form of jazz, forming a lasting admiration for the music of the Ken Colyer band. In particular, he cites as his ideal the Colyer rhythm section when it consisted of John Bastable (banjo), Ray Foxley (piano), Ron Ward (bass) and Colin Bowden (drums), asking *'How could a front line fail with a rhythm section like that?'*. He also admires the trumpet playing of Bix Beiderbecke and the American west coast revivalist, Lu Waters. In addition, he cites Louis Armstrong, Tommy Ladnier, Red Allen and Muggsy Spannier as favourites but says that Ken Colyer was the main influence on his own style. Speaking with Brian Robertson in 2010, he said what a privilege it had been to have played with local musicians, the 'local greats' he called them, such as Dave Paxton, Al Fairweather, Johnny McGuff, Jimmy Shortreed, Bob Craig, Andrew Lauder, George Gilmour and Kenny Milne. He also expressed his fears for the future of the music, pointing out that these great players, many of them already gone, were not being replaced, raising the possibility that Edinburgh traditional jazz, so strong for more than half a century, would just fizzle out. However, Brian himself was to do what he could to bolster the local jazz scene, going on later to form and run a band of his own and to remain a force on the local scene for decades to come.

Brian, in my view, probably learned quite a bit in his early days from the fiery, New Orleans styled trumpeter, Phil Mason. Phil, a professional jazz musician with Max Collie's Rhythm Aces, had taken up residence on the Isle of

Bute and later formed a touring band of his own. In addition to touring from his Isle of Bute base, Phil quite frequently made the trip over to Edinburgh, where he was a regular visitor at Bill Salmond's Navaar House gig. A colleague of Phil's, the trombonist Martin Bennett, also moved up to Scotland for a while in the 1980s, living on his hundred year old sailing ship, berthed at Irvine. Martin became a member of Bill's band and his authoritative playing and ability to direct a front line were also useful pointers for Brian. Martin stayed with the Louisiana Ragtime Band for more than two years between 1985 and 1987, when the line-up was Brian Robertson (trumpet), Martin Bennett (trombone), Dave Paxton (clarinet), Graham Scott (piano), Bill Salmond (banjo), Graham Blamire (bass) and either Roy Dunnett or Eric Jamieson (drums). In this form, the band made annual trips in the later 1980s to play at the Bute Jazz Festival, which had been founded by Phil Mason and which was to become an important event in the Scottish Jazz calendar.

In May 1987, Bill took his band over to Holland to play at the Enkhuizen Jazz Festival. By then, the band had been blessed with a stable line-up for some considerable time, enabling it to play in the well-integrated manner that is so essential to the New Orleans style. When Martin Bennett left to return south, the replacement was Bob Craig who, several years later, gave way to Alan Quinn. The Louisiana Ragtime Band ended the 1980s as it had entered the decade, with a strong line-up and in great demand.

One of the Louisiana Ragtime Band's regulars was **Roy Dunnett (drums).** Roy was born in Edinburgh on 22nd August 1941 and made his start on playing drums with a Boys Brigade pipe band. In his teens in the 1950s, like so many of us of that generation, he was attracted to skiffle music and soon found himself playing washboard in a skiffle group. Later, he played drums in a variety of dance bands before moving on to rock music, in which style he played with a group with the glorious name of the Screaming Citizens and another rock band, the Rapiers. The bass guitarist in the latter was Scott Murray, brother of jazz and dance band bass player Fred Murray, and with this band Roy was to play in the Locarno Ballroom in Slateford Road and the Palais de Dance, in Fountainbridge.

Roy's debut in jazz came in the 1970s when he joined Bill Salmond's Louisiana Ragtime Band, with whom he played at their residency in the Hopetoun Lounge in Morrison Street. Roy was later to be replaced in the LRB by Eric Jamieson but had returned to the band by 1986 and played with the band at its residencies at the Navaar House Hotel, the Sands Hotel in Joppa and at Basin Street, in the Haymarket Station Bar. He also made the trips to play at the Enkhuizen Jazz Festival in Holland and the Isle of Bute Jazz Festival, both in 1987, as well as playing with the band at several EIJFs. A spell out of jazz followed but by the late 1990s, Roy had reappeared on the Edinburgh jazz scene and in the 2000s was playing regularly with Brian Robertson's Forth River Ragtimers and a band led by the bass player, Fred Murray, Fred's Clubhouse Seven. Roy was something of a character and I have to say, I liked him a lot. I remember a phone call from him which came right out of the blue. He had a habit of beginning new conversations as if you were in the middle of an on-going verbal interaction. *'Oh, by the way'* he said, when I answered the phone *'I've just phoned you for a chat. I'm bored with the speaking clock and I've fallen out with the Samaritans, so I thought I'd give you a ring'.* An indefatigable conversationalist, Roy Dunnett's presence in the car to or from a gig ensured that there would be no awkward silences.

Eric Jamieson (drums), born in Edinburgh on 19th September 1940 and educated at Tynecastle School, had become interested in jazz by his mid-teens, through listening to records and the radio. In particular, he became interested in the music of the George Lewis band and, when he was about fifteen years old in the middle 1950s, he began to venture out into the Edinburgh jazz scene. He soon found his way to the Condon Club, which was located in India Buildings in Victoria Street, and amongst the bands he remembers from around that time was the Climax Jazz Band, with Jim Petrie on trumpet. Eric remained a regular listener and jazz supporter around the Edinburgh jazz scene for many years, with no thought of becoming a musician, and then, in the 1970s, he began going to the Hopetoun Lounge in Morrison Street, where the attraction was Bill Salmond's Louisiana Ragtime Band. At that time, Kenny Milne was playing trumpet with the band but there was frequently no drummer. Knowing Bill Salmond's commitment to the pure New Orleans style, I am sure that this was because there was no one around and available at the time who played drums in the style that would have suited the band. Bill, with a clear view of how he wanted his band to sound, would certainly have chosen to do without a drummer, rather than compromise the band's style. Kenny Milne would have been ideal of course, but, as he was already playing trumpet in the band, he could hardly play drums as well. However, Kenny was to come up with a solution and it was he who approached Eric Jamieson and asked him if he had ever considered having a go at drums. Although this had never crossed Eric's mind, it was not to be long before Kenny had persuaded him into going along to the Milne house on Liberton Brae, where Kenny took him under his wing and they began a series of drum lessons. In addition to working on the rudiments of drumming and probably to help him develop a proper feel for jazz drumming, Kenny soon encouraged Eric to start playing in a band setting and, with the young Finlay Milne already developing his skills on trumpet plus Kenny Henderson on banjo, there was soon a practice band in full cry at Liberton Brae.

Eric's first real gig was with the LRB at the Hopetoun Lounge, when the band included Bill, Kenny, Dave Paxton, Symon Carlyle then playing trombone, Graham Scott and Willie Mack on bass, and later he made the move with the band to their new residency at the Navaar House Hotel. As we have already heard, Eric was to alternate with Roy Dunnett a number of times but he was with the LRB when they made their recording 'Way Down Yonder in New Orleans'[175]. He was also to play with the band at a number of jazz festivals, among them Edinburgh, Bute, Keswick, Dumfries and Orkney. Speaking with Eric now, he remembers with particular affection the early EIJFs and the

---

[175] See discography appendix

434

opportunities they brought play with visiting players of the calibre of trumpeter Teddy Riley from New Orleans and the great veteran reeds man, Benny Waters. He also has fond memories of playing with another New Orleans legend, the sax player Sammy Lee. Eric played on for a number of years, mostly with the LRB but also putting in a lengthy spell with Alan Quinn's Templehall Stompers, at the Templehall Hotel in Portobello but sadly, his playing came to a stop in the late 1990s, because of health problems. However, his interest in jazz continues at the time of writing in the second decade of the twenty-first century and it would not surprise me in the least if we have not seen the last of Eric Jamieson, jazz drummer.

When Kenny Milne left his trumpet playing slot with the Louisiana Ragtime Band in 1986, he had no intention of allowing his trumpet playing to come to an end. Of course, he continued to be very busy as drummer with the Spirits of Rhythm but it was not long before he put together a new band, built around his trumpet lead. This he called the **Criterion Jazz Band**[176] and the original membership included Jack Weddell (tbn), Ian Boyter (rds), Jock Westwater (bjo) and, a newcomer to the Edinburgh jazz scene, Bill Brydon on sousaphone. Later on, Bill Smith would replace Jack Weddell on trombone while reeds man Jimmy Shortreed and banjo players Brian Weld and Beverley Knight would also put in time with the band. In the bustling jazz climate of the mid-1980s, it was not long before the Criterion band was filling its bookings diary. They landed a plumb gig at the prestigious golfing centre of Gleneagles, where they played a 'Sunday Jazz Brunch' engagement in the Gleneagles Hotel for about three years. Closer to home, there was another run of gigs associated with the serving of food, at Fat Sam's Eatery in Fountainbridge, where for a couple of years the band played two evenings a week. All this playing at restaurants was not without its side effects and Kenny Milne, recalling that the Fat Sam's Eatery gigs included a meal as part of the deal, reckoned he had put on about a stone in weight

---

[176] Not to be confused with the Criterion Brass Band, a parade or marching band, also led by Kenny Milne

during this period! The Criterion Jazz Band played on, regularly and successfully, well into the 1990s and, even at the time of writing in 2010, still occasionally gets together when suitable gigs come up.

Another two new bands, with a close relationship to each other, appeared on the local scene in the later 1980s. In 1986, a five piece band was formed with the intention of playing in the so-called 'mainstream' style. At first there was no name for this band but with its first gig imminent, a temporary name had to be found and it appeared in the Merlin, a pub in Morningside Road, as the Rhythm Aces. Not only was this name inappropriate to the style of music played but it was also the established name of a full time touring band, Max Collie's Rhythm Aces, so the name was hastily dropped. The Merlin gig did not last long, and by March 1987 the band had moved to a slot at Basin Street. Basin Street was the upstairs lounge of the Haymarket Station Bar, next door to Haymarket Station, and was one of the best jazz pubs that Edinburgh ever had. The upstairs bar had been designed for jazz sessions, with old jazz posters and photographs on display in the stairway and the lounge walls decorated with murals depicting New Orleans scenes. For years, Basin Street hosted jazz six, or even seven, nights a week and was an important venue during the EIJF. The new band appeared at the 1987 EIJF as 'Graham Blamire's Jazz Band', as a permanent name had still not been chosen, but at last and after what seemed endless discussions, the somewhat immodest sounding title of **The Jazz Masters** was agreed. The membership of the band was Andrew Lauder (tpt and flugelhorn), Jimmy Shortreed (rds), Jack Finlay (pno), Graham Blamire (bs) and Donald 'Chick' Murray (drms). The material played was, in the main, a combination of small band Swing tunes, many of them associated with the Benny Goodman small groups, and tunes from the Duke Ellington repertoire. There was also some original material, with Andrew Lauder writing a couple of tunes and Graeme Robertson and Al Fairweather contributing both original tunes and arrangements.

Jack Finlay (piano), brother of fellow pianist Tom, was born in Fife in 1944 and was to become a Chartered Accountant. Jack and Tom were born into a musical family

436

which encouraged interest in playing musical instruments but, in spite of this, Jack only received one piano lesson, which took place when he was seven years old. This is hard to believe considering how proficient a piano payer he was to be but, apparently, the experience was so off putting, that he did not return to the piano keyboard until he was thirteen years old, when he set out to teach himself! There was plenty of music in the house to influence him, including recordings of Benny Goodman, Ruby Braff, Vic Dickenson and other jazz greats. Jack was to move to Edinburgh where his first gig was with the Pete Martin All-Stars in Rutherford's Bar. He also played with vibes player Bill Stronach and then was with the Charlie McNair band when it had, in addition to Jack and Charlie, Graeme Robertson (tbn), Robbie Robertson (rds), Dougie Campbell (gtr), Kenny Wheatley (bs) and Bobby Stewart (drms). This was the period when the McNair band was pursuing something of a mainstream policy, and it was already clear that Jack's interest was towards the more modern end of the jazz spectrum. Spells with Hamish McGregor's bands, the Clansmen and the Memphis Road Show, followed and then Jack moved to Jersey, where he played two summer seasons with Edinburgh's Jack Duff who was then resident in Jersey. A return to Edinburgh in 1970 saw him join the Ken Ramage Quartet and later, another quartet with Brian Keddie (tbn), Ian Croal (bs) and Bill Kyle (drms).

Jack, along with Kyle, Croal and guitarist Charlie Alexander, became a founding member of the jazz organisation Platform, which started in Edinburgh but later had branches in Glasgow, Aberdeen and Dundee. Platform did an enormous amount of good work in the jazz field, including bringing the Duke Ellington Orchestra to the Usher Hall in 1973. Jack had become a highly capable jazz piano player, well up to the demanding roles he took on during the EIJFs, when he accompanied the likes of Benny Waters, Harry Edison, Art Farmer, Joe Temperley and various other big jazz names. Benny Waters in particular, was greatly impressed by Jack's playing and regularly requested that Jack backed him on his many visits. As well as a sparkling solo player, Jack was always a particularly sensitive accompanist when backing horn players and singers. He playing was also much appreciated by bass players because of his incisive attack and sparing, open, left hand work that kept the rhythm sound light and airy, leaving plenty of space for everyone to be heard.

Jack claims that he was *'corrupted by the traddies'* in the guise of the present writer and Chick Murray when, in 1986, he was a founder member of the new Jazz Masters. In our defence, it has to be pointed out that this band was not all that 'traddy' and soon built up a repertoire of material associated with Goodman, Ellington and even some fairly modern jazzers, including Gerry Mulligan and Benny Golson. After the Jazz Masters finished in the early 1990s, Jack returned to work in trios and duos of his own, often in the company of like-minded musicians such as Kenny Ellis and Kenny McDonald (bs) and Bobby Stewart (drms). A piano player whose style was influenced by Teddy Wilson, Bill Evans and Oscar Peterson, in 2011 Jack Finlay was as busy as ever, a versatile and much respected pillar of the Edinburgh jazz scene.

In April 1987, the Jazz Masters became a six piece band for a while when the fine trombone player, Brain Keddie, came in. Brian also contributed a number of tight, swingy arrangements but, unfortunately, his stay was a short one, as he moved off to work in Paris in June of the same year. There was quite a bit of interest in the band from other musicians and many came along as invited guests or just to sit in at the Basin Street gig, amongst them trumpeters Al Fairweather and Dave Strutt, pianist Ralph Laing, singers Liz McEwen and Fionna Duncan, reeds man Dick Lee, trombonists Dave Keir and Graeme Robertson and tenor saxists Gordon Cruikshank and Dave Roberts. As the band was only five piece, in contrast to most of the others which were six or seven piece, it had been possible to negotiate a small amount of extra money to allow guests to be invited on a paid basis, every week or two. Later, after Brian Keddie had disappeared to France, the Jazz Masters again became six piece for a spell, this time the addition being John Bancroft who, when his medical duties allowed it, played vibes with the band. John was a medical consultant, who played both vibes and piano, and was the father of three youngsters, all of whom were to make their considerable mark on jazz. Sophie was a fine singer and the twins, Tom and Phil, who were born in 1967, were to become important jazz musicians at the highest level in contemporary jazz, going on to make international names for themselves. Tom played drums and Phil tenor sax but both were talented writers and arrangers as well, and both came along to sit in with the Jazz Masters, Tom in addition once depping for Chick Murray at one of the regular gigs.

A guest who made a number of appearances with the Jazz Masters, both at Basin Street and during the EIJF, was **singer Liz MacEwan**. The presence of Jack Finlay on piano, who had often worked with Liz and was familiar with her material, meant that we could find common ground with the greatest of ease and I remember us wishing that she could sing with us all the time. Liz was already established as one of Scotland's best jazz singers, with a great personality and a fine, adaptable voice. She had started in Tiffany's Nightclub in Edinburgh away back in the 1970s, with The Band of Gold, and had sung all types of music, all over the world. This included a tour with Demis Roussos and singing in US Army bases in West Germany, her wide musical experience enabling her to build up a formidable repertoire of songs from all genres. In addition to her free lance career, Liz also sang for four years in the 1980s alongside Edinburgh's blues legend, Tam White, with his band, the Dexters, and worked with them on a number of albums and BBC broadcasts. Liz also worked as a backing singer with the well-known Scottish band, Runrig and toured with another legend, Van Morrison. Her appearances at the EIJF were many and in particular, included sell-out success with her 'Tribute to Peggy Lee' shows. Liz also worked for a time on the luxury liner the QE2 before returning to Edinburgh in 1990 and, a thoroughly experienced professional, she has continued to be in demand across the country ever since. Accompanied by her pianist, she has performed at well-known Edinburgh venues such as the Dome, Centotre and Cafe Grande and the Balmoral Hotel. Her success continued with appearances at Aberdeen's The Albyn and the Jamhouse in Edinburgh, where she was often accompanied by the Jack Finlay Trio. She also notched up successes in company with the Frank Holden Experience, an eighteen piece Swing band featuring the best of Glasgow's horn players. A class act and as well-liked and respected by musicians as she is popular with her audiences, Liz MacEwan, in the 2000s, remains one of the countries' best and most sensitive singers.

The Jazz Masters' Basin Street gig lasted until December 1988, after which residencies were tried at the Postillion pub, near the St Andrew's Square bus station, where Fionna Duncan, Sophie Bancroft and Edith Budge all sang with the band, and at the Westbury Hotel in Corstorphine, but neither of these lasted long. After this, the Jazz Masters survived mostly on one-off gigs into the 1990s, when there was a spell when they played regularly at Fat Sam's Downtown Diner. The band played in the EIJFs in 1995 and 1996 but, by late 1996, the band had ceased to play. There were several reasons for this. Although there had been encouragement and even some enthusiasm for their mainstream style from many of the local jazz musicians, especially Al Fairweather, Gordon Cruikshank and Graeme Robertson, this was not matched by support from the jazz followers. The local jazz crowds preferred a more New Orleans or Dixieland oriented sound and found the music of the Jazz Masters less familiar and less to their taste. On one notable but depressing occasion, a regular jazz follower approached one of the band (me) at Basin Street and said quite aggressively *I thought this was supposed to be a jazz band?*' On being assured that that was so and asked what his problem was, he replied with some heat *'There's no banjo and no trombone'* In the face of this character's apparent belief that he had a divine right to define jazz, there did not seem much point in arguing with him. The other reason for the band's demise lay in the other commitments of the band members and in particular, the increasing activity of another band, formed at around the same time, and drawing three-quarters of its members from the Jazz Masters.

A cruise boat sailed every summer from the Hawes Pier in South Queensferry, taking passengers around the picturesque islands of the Firth of Forth, where they could enjoy the scenery and wildlife, as well as admire the great

Forth Bridge from water level. This was the Maid of the Forth and its owner had added jazz cruises to his programme in 1986. In summer 1987, the owner, John Watson, contacted me to offer the gig on a regular basis. A band was put together which included three of the Jazz Masters, Andrew Lauder (trumpet), Jimmy Shortreed (reeds) and Graham Blamire (bass), who, with the addition of Bill Salmond (banjo), were to be the band which would eventually play under the name of the boat as **The Maid of the Forth Stompers**. This was to become one of Edinburgh's longest running resident gigs and by 2011, the band were in its twenty-fifth consecutive season. Early in the band's history, they began taking gigs ashore, in addition to the boat work, sometimes expanding for special occasions to five or six piece.

Jimmy Shortreed (reeds), the reeds player with both the Jazz Masters and the Maid of the Forth Stompers, was born in Hawick on 22nd November 1922. Jimmy bought his first clarinet, for which he had saved for three years, when he was twelve years old in 1934, and later added alto sax to his repertoire. His impressionable teenage years were, of course, in the 1930s when the great Swing era was in full cry and the bands of Benny Goodman, Artie Shaw and the Dorseys were at the peak of their popularity. In particular, the Swing era had been dominated to a large extent by the virtuoso clarinet playing of Goodman and Shaw and it was Benny Goodman who was to be Jimmy's inspiration. This brought about a strange anomaly many years later, when Jimmy became fully involved in the Edinburgh traditional jazz scene. Jimmy was about half a generation older than the Revivalists of the 1940s and his clarinet style and tastes in jazz, had already been formed by the time the 1940s came along. Because of this, and unlike clarinettists such as Sandy Brown, Dave Paxton, Ian Arnott and Jake McMahon, his playing was not influenced by either of the two dominant styles of the Revival. The anomaly was that, although Jimmy was older than the Revivalist clarinet players, he was actually playing a style that, in terms of jazz history, was younger and more recent than that of the Revivalists. The roots of Jimmy's style lay in the second half of the 1930s, rather than in the period between 1920 and 1935.

**Jimmy Shortreed in 1996
(photo by the author)**

During his war service between 1941 and 1945, Jimmy played in RAF dance bands and, after the war, most of his playing was in local small dance bands and in the reeds sections of various big bands, which also played for dancing. Although his main musical love was jazz and Swing, he would see no contradictions in playing dance music. The big band Swing craze of the 1930s was primarily seen as jazz based dance music and, throughout his career, in addition to his dance band work, Jimmy quite often helped out with the Edinburgh jazz bands. As with so many of the dance band regulars, Jimmy found himself short of playing, when the discos decimated the dance bands in the 1960s and '70s, and it was then that he became increasingly directly involved in the Edinburgh jazz scene. He was one of the dance band regulars who made the switch to jazz playing with a natural ease, where some

442

of the others struggled. He was drawn into the Festival City Jazz Band through his pal, the piano player Ian Scott, who had also found himself short of dance work, and he played with them in the Barnton Hotel from about 1975. Later, Jimmy was a regular for many years at drummer Frank Birnie's East Coast Jazz Band sessions, on Monday evenings at The Blue Lagoon. Then in 1986, he was invited to join the new band just being put together, the Jazz Masters. This was my doing and it was because, as well as very much liking Jimmy's playing, I reckoned that he would make an ideal partnership with the trumpet playing of Andrew Lauder. That partnership worked out very well and was continued when the Maid of the Forth Stompers band came along. Jimmy played out the rest of his career with the latter band, starting on the cruise boat in 1987 and eventually retiring from playing after the cruising season ended in autumn 2001, just a week or two before his seventy ninth birthday.

Jimmy was a gentle, courteous man, universally liked among the Edinburgh jazzers, both musicians and followers. His playing, its roots in the playing of Benny Goodman always obvious, featured a lovely, singing tone and a fluent, lyrical way of improvising. After Jimmy died, I wrote an appreciation of him for the Scotsman[177] and, referring to the Blue Lagoon sessions in particular, said *'His melodic and very accessible playing made him a great favourite with the loyal and sizable crowds that turned out every week and his feature numbers were a weekly highlight...He brought to his music a friendly and open joyfulness that touched everyone who listened'*. That last point was well illustrated by a regular at the Blue Lagoon who, when explaining why he liked Jimmy's clarinet playing so much, said *'...there always seems to be a smile in his playing'*. The only commercial recordings of his playing are a set made by the Maid of the Forth Stompers in 1995. However, there is another set of studio quality recordings, unfortunately never yet issued, with the Jazz Masters. These show Jimmy in the type of small band Swing setting

---

[177] Blamire G, 'Jimmy Shortreed – an appreciation', The Scotsman, 12th January 2006

443

which suited him very well and several tracks show very good examples of his playing. The excellent Gordon Cruikshank also guests on tenor sax on some of the tracks and even now, more than twenty years after they were recorded, it would be good to see them made available. Jimmy Shortreed died at the age of eighty three, on December 11 2005 and Artie Shaw's beautiful recording of Stardust, one of Jimmy's all time favourites, was played at his funeral.

A jazzer mentioned above and whom few would classify in the traditional category nonetheless deserves his place in this book, because of his staunch support for all forms of jazz and the time he put in with at least a couple of the more traditional jazz bands, including the Jazz Masters with whom he made the recordings[178] spoken of above. He was **Gordon Cruikshank (reeds)**, who was born on 12th September 1949. Gordon had been encouraged in his interest in jazz by a neighbour, the fine piano player Alex Shaw, and had played flute at school, before taking up the various saxophones. He had been active in the Edinburgh modern jazz and rock scenes in the late 1960s, as well as playing with Hamish McGregor's Memphis Road Show. He also worked with the blues singer Tam White and, in the 1970s, was to collaborate with many jazz musicians interested in the more modern forms of jazz, including Lachlan McColl, Brian Keddie, Dave Newton, Kenny Ellis, Bill Kyle and Tony McLennan. Gordon made a big reputation for himself in his chosen style and accompanied many visiting jazz musicians from south of the border and the USA as well as becoming a member of Head, the leading Scottish 'jazz fusion' band. He also made a career for himself as a broadcaster, presenting 'Take the Jazz Train' and 'Jazz Junction' on Radio Scotland and 'Sound of Jazz' on Radio 2, when it was broadcast from Scotland. In addition, he founded and directed a jazz school which flourished principally at Broughton High School in Edinburgh. This organisation was attended by many up and coming jazz musicians and was active in introducing to

---

[178] Studio quality recordings made in 1988 in Finger's Piano Bar, Edinburgh, these at 2010 had not yet been made available on general release

jazz and helping to develop many later prominent jazz musicians including Tommy Smith, Phil and Tom Bancroft and John Rae.

Although as a player, Gordon belonged with the mainstream/modern end of jazz, he was, in fact, interested in the whole of jazz and knew a great deal about the music and its history. He showed an eclectic taste in his record selections on the 'Jazz Train' and took an interest in the whole Edinburgh jazz scene, modern and traditional. He frequently would remind his listeners about jazz gigs, of all schools, and made a habit of dropping in for a blow at the Jazz Masters sessions at Basin Street. I had many a chin wag with him in his favourite Morningside boozer, Bennetts Bar in Maxwell Place, where we would chew the fat about jazz in general and the Edinburgh scene in particular. He once told me how nervous he felt when he was included in one of the specially assembled big bands during an EIJF and found himself sitting between Buddy Tate and Benny Waters in the reeds section. What always came over was his love for all of jazz and his genuine admiration for great local players such as Sandy Brown, Al Fairweather, Alex Shaw and Dave Paxton. Gordon Cruikshank made a great contribution to jazz in Edinburgh and Scotland in several fields and it was a tragedy when, after moving to York in the 1990s, his health broke down and he died in 2002 at the age of only 52.

There were two highly significant returns to the Edinburgh jazz scene in the 1980s, both concerned jazzers who had been big Edinburgh names in the early post-war years, both had made careers for themselves as jazz musicians in the south and both were to make their mark all over again in Edinburgh jazz. They were Dave Keir and Al Fairweather. **Dave Keir** was the first to return. After his career as a professional jazz musician, Dave had become a school teacher, making use of his degree and teaching mathematics and physics, and had remained in this profession for more than twenty years. In all that time, he had played almost no music, only once playing with a school band at one of the schools. He had played no jazz whatsoever and he did not resume his jazz career until after he had taken early retirement from teaching and returned

445

to Edinburgh. His return to playing came as a result of a chance meeting with Mike Hart in 1980. Mike was of course, by then running the Edinburgh International Jazz Festival, and he invited Dave to sit in with his band. This signalled a return to regular playing and during the early 1980s he played in Edinburgh with Charlie McNair's Jazz Band, Frank Birnie's East Coast Jazz Band, The Capital Jazz Band and Mike Hart's Edinburgh Ragtimers. He was also a welcome sitter-in at other sessions and, in the later 1980s, would quite frequently turn up at Basin Street at Haymarket to sit in with the mainstream styled Jazz Masters. At first Dave, a multi-instrumentalist, pursued his come-back on trombone, the instrument on which he had made his name but later, in the 1990s, he decided to make a change which I remember him telling me he had long intended, making the trumpet his main instrument.

The other veteran to return was **Al Fairweather** who, after about thirty five years in the south, came back to his home city in the late 1980s. He had started to think about returning in about 1982, when he had played in Edinburgh with a band organised by pianist Ralph Laing. The Bluenote Jazzmen from Bristol had made a late withdrawal from the EIJF that year and Mike Hart had asked Ralph, then living near Bristol, to arrange a replacement. He put together a band which was to play as the Ralph Laing All Stars and, with the inclusion of Al on trumpet, it was intended that the band would play some of the McJazz material, that is the music written and arranged by Al and Sandy Brown in the mid-1950s. The band was clearly a good one with some resounding names, including Micky Cooke (tbn), Nick Cooper (rds), Wayne Chandler (gtr), Harvey Weston (bs) and Tony Allen (drms), in addition to Al and Ralph himself. The band came north, opened with a gig in the Perth vicinity, then worked their way through two gigs a day at the EIJF. They also played a number of gigs on their way back south and Ralph Laing recalls how Al had enjoyed all this. He was in the midst of family troubles, the most serious of which was his wife's multiple sclerosis, and he was unhappy in his teaching post. However, the short tour north had been a success, the band had played well and Al had said to Ralph '...*we must keep doing this*'.

The band then did a few jobs in the south at venues such as London's 100 Club and, in the following Spring of 1983, they made a BBC Jazz Club broadcast and undertook another short Scottish tour. This time the band included two other Scottish jazzers, Johnny McGuff on trombone and Francis Cowan, an extremely able Edinburgh bass player. This time, the itinerary included a gig at the Queen's Hall and one south of the border, in Carlisle.

Unfortunately, Al suffered a serious heart attack later in 1983, which was to stop him playing for a year, and he required to be fitted with a heart pace maker. To add greatly to his troubles, his wife Judy then died after a long period of deteriorating health. Realising perhaps that there was little now to keep Al in the south, Ralph Laing pointed out to him that, as properties in Edinburgh were then selling at a much lower rate than in London, he should be able to sell up in Harrow, return to Edinburgh and have a decent nest egg into the bargain. Happily for Edinburgh jazz, Al was to take Ralph's advice and he returned permanently to Edinburgh in 1987.

Less happily, he was still not in the best of health and the heart attack in 1983 had clearly taken its toll of his energy and confidence. The journalist and trumpeter Alastair Clark was later to write that it had been a distinctly subdued Al who returned to Edinburgh[179]. However, while I am sure that this was true, it was not long before he was making his way back into active playing. I have already, in an earlier chapter, written of how modest Al was about his achievements in jazz, nevertheless, it bears repeating now when he soon showed himself more than willing to get involved around the local jazz scene, playing again, as in his early days, with Edinburgh bands in Edinburgh pubs. An early regular gig seems to have been organised by Al's old sparring partner, Bob Craig, who soon took the chance to bring Al into the band that was playing on Sunday evenings in Basin Street. The line-up of this band, in addition to Al and Bob, included Gerard Dott (clt), Graham Scott (pno) and two other veterans of the 1940/50s, Dizzy Jackson (bs) and Bill Strachan (drms).

---

[179] Clark A, ' Bob Craig', 'Scotsman' obituaries, 5 August 1998

After the Basin Street gig folded, there was a gap before Bob fixed up a replacement venue. When he did, he phoned Gerard Dott to invite him to play at the new venue, only to discover that he had decided to stop playing and Gerard has confirmed that this was in 1988. Gerard's decision to stop playing was, of course, a significant loss for the Edinburgh jazz scene that would not be reversed until 2006, but it does seem to have opened the door to bring together a notable front-line partnership - Al, Bob and their fellow RHS Gangster, Dave Paxton. The new gig that Bob had arranged was at Young's Hotel, formerly the Glenelg Hotel, in Leamington Terrace, and henceforth, the band was to play under Al Fairweather's name. There is a photograph dated 1989, shown on Dave Paxton's profile on the Sandy Brown Jazz website[180], which shows the band playing there with a line-up of Al, Bob and Dave with Graham Scott (pno), Jim Young (bs) and Kenny Milne (drms), clearly a formidable line-up, dominated by veterans from the 1940s and '50s. The caption below the photograph on the website suggests that the band may have played under the name of Fairweather Friends. However, Jim Walker has a number of privately made recordings of the band in Young's Hotel around this time on which the band is given as the Sundowners and are all dated 1989 and 1990.

I remember going to hear the band on a number of occasions and they sounded marvellous. Just like the Dave Paxton, Ian Telford and Bob Craig front line of the Society Syncopators in the early 1970s, this front line too benefitted from same extraordinary compatibility of the three horn players – Al, Dave and Bob gelling as to the manner born. It was a great privilege to hear this band and, although we were not to know it then, it was just about the last chance to hear three of the original RHS gang playing together regularly. It must have been a great gig musically for the whole band but it brought an added non-musical bonus for Bob and Jim Young, both of whom lived within about a hundred yards of the hotel!

---

[180] http://www.sandybrownjazz.co.uk/profiledavepaxton.html

**Al Fairweather's Sundowners – Young's Hotel 1989
Jim Young, Dave Paxton, Al Fairweather, Kenny Milne,
Bob Craig
(by permission of Jim Walker)**

Al was to also to take on a number of other gigs on a regular basis, among them Frank Birnie's Monday evening spot at the Blue Lagoon, and he played for a time at the Clarenden Hotel where Roger Craik, in August 1988, both played in the band and made a recording of a session. The journalist Tony Troon, writing in the Scotsman after the untimely deaths of both Dave Paxton and Al Fairweather in 1993[181], said how much the partnership of the two veterans was relished around the Edinburgh jazz scene, commenting that *'Fairweather-Paxton was an act to catch'*. He had previously sought information in his regular jazz column as to whether anyone had any recordings of the two of them playing together. He had received two positive responses, one jointly from Jim Walker and Bill Todd and the other from Roger Craik. Tony Troon says how much he was impressed by a recording that featured not only Al and Dave but also Bob Craig in a band that also included Jock Westwater on banjo. Tony picked out a *'...very fine version of 2.19 Blues and a typically intricate Paxton reading of*

---

[181] Troon A, 'Fairweather and friends', The Scotsman, 1993

449

Black and Blue with simple and telling muted trumpet by Fairweather'. Of the session recorded by Roger Craik, Tony said *'You could hardly remain unaffected by the ideal pairing – a trumpeter who deals in powerful, clear statements and a clarinettist supplying intricate embellishment'.*

Jim Walker who recorded the other set, had pointed out that *'Al constructed his phrases in coherent paragraphs while Dave set off Al's directness with wonderful embroideries and confidently taken breaks'.* Tony summarises his thoughts by saying *'... each understands his role perfectly and never runs short of an original statement. Made for each other'.* These are eloquent tributes to two great players and it was Edinburgh's extraordinary good fortune to have them playing together, often in the company of Bob Craig, as their distinguished careers drew to a close. Unfortunately, these were simply private recordings made by punters at regular pub sessions and they were not intended, nor of a suitable recording quality, for general release.

Al Fairweather - 1989
(by permission of Jim Walker)

450

We all knew, of course, that Al had been in poor health for some years when he returned to Edinburgh in 1987, but it was still a real shock when he died suddenly in 1993, following a second heart attack. He had been commissioned to paint a portrait of the wife of a fellow local musician, the drummer Billy Law, and she had gone round to collect it. Al had gone into the next room to fetch the painting and she heard him fall. In his will, Al left most of his written band arrangements to Ralph Laing who has handed them on to the British Jazz Archive, which is based in Loutham in Essex. Steve Voce, a distinguished jazz critic, wrote Al's obituary in the 'Independent'[182] and said that Humphrey Lyttelton had gone to some trouble to point out that Al had been an influence on his own playing. Humph had said *'When I first heard him he scared me to death. He had a wonderful tone derived from Armstrong's playing which was unique to Al'*. That was quite a compliment coming from another of the UK's top trumpeters.

Another trumpeter and journalist, Alastair Clark, wrote[183] that it had been a subdued Al who had returned from the south and, while this was undoubtedly true, he was a still a very fine player and it was a great privilege and pleasure to get to know him and to play with him back in his home town. Dave Paxton was only sixty seven when he died and Al only sixty six. We could have hoped for many more years from them but, sadly, it was not to be. But what a joy and privilege it was hear Al, Dave and Bob playing together, during those precious six years between Al's return in 1987 and 1993.

Al's friend and musical collaborator, **Ralph Laing (piano)**, was born in Sanquhar in Dumfriesshire in 1936 and was educated at Kilmarnock Academy, before going on to St Andrew's University. Ralph believes that his interest in jazz must have begun at a very early age as, when he was only just able to walk, his party trick was to go over to the stack of 78 rpm records at home, pick out Duke Ellington's recording of 'Ring Dem Bells' and insist on it being played.

---

[182] Steve Voce, obituary 'Al Fairweather', 'The Independent', 24 June 1993
[183] Clark A, 'Obituaries – Bob Craig', 'Scotsman', 5 August 1998

He also remembers hearing a recording of Fats Waller's 'Alligator Crawl' when he was about eight or nine years old and considers that it was this that got him hooked on jazz. He was later to meet up with the Edinburgh born trombonist and RHS gangster, George Hewitt, who shared Ralph's interest in jazz and was living in Irvine in Ayrshire. Ralph had received piano lessons while he was at school but later took up trumpet and got involved with the local Burgh Band, with which he had some trumpet lessons. His heart however, was in jazz rather than the Burgh Band. A Glasgow jazz band with the wonderful name of St Mungo's Disciples then came to play in Kilmarnock on the Saturday of a student rag week. This band included trumpeter George Ogilvie, trombonist Bob Nummey and reeds player Maurice Rose, the first two of whom are still playing regularly in Glasgow at the time of writing in 2011. Ralph went along to hear them and, having taken along his trumpet, he asked for a sit in, as did George Hewitt, who had appeared with a trombone.

Together Ralph and George formed a couple of jazz bands, firstly the Ayrshire Jazz Band and then the Eagle Jazzmen. However, Ralph's career on trumpet was to be short and he was soon to return to the piano, on which he was to make his reputation in jazz. He was also to become well known as an erudite and knowledgeable jazz critic and a frequent writer of sleeve notes. In addition, he wrote quite a number of jazz related articles and features, the most significant of which was perhaps the two volume 'Jazz Records – the Specialist Labels', which he and Chris Sheridan published in 1979/80 and which, thirty years on, remains in print today. Ralph, who held a high ranking post with Rolls Royce, retired to Edinburgh in February 1991 and soon established himself as a highly respected contributor to the local jazz scene.

He kept his Groove Juice band going until 1993, with Al Fairweather contributing many arrangements, and continued to do some work with the band on the Continent, although Al only took part in a few of these trips. Ralph also put together bands to play at the EIJF, all high quality outfits, one of them having a line-up of Al, Jack Duff (rds), Bob Wilson from Nottingham (tbn), Lindsay Cooper (bs) and

Richie Bryant (drms), with Ralph himself on piano. He also took responsibility for the rhythm section that hosted the EIJF jam sessions, using the same line-up as above. Another joint project between Ralph Laing and Al Fairweather was the writing of a musical version of Kingsley Amis's Lucky Jim. When Al died, the musical score was complete but there was no script. However, this has now been written although the work has yet to be performed. In 2011, Ralph Laing continues to live in Edinburgh and plays whatever gigs come along, a fine player with a long and distinguished jazz pedigree.

A new development in 1987 was the starting up of a new, independent, local jazz festival. This was a 'single venue' festival set up and run by **Ken Ramage**, the former trombone player now playing drums, and it was run on the basis of no charge to the punters. David Stewart, of the company D M Stewart, had negotiated sponsorship with one of the breweries and then fixed up an agreement with Ken to put on a week long programme of evening jazz events in the Guildford Arms, in West Register Street, close to the east end of Princes Street. This was one of the pubs run by the Stewart family and not only was it in a central and prestigious location, it was also one of Edinburgh's finest surviving Victorian pubs. Believed to date back to about 1890, it featured enormous sand blasted windows, wood panelling on the walls, a complex and beautifully decorated ceiling and a lounge bar perched on a balcony. It says much for the quality of the Guildford Arms decor that it managed to exist literally next door to the sumptuous Cafe Royal, another marvel of Victorian pub design, without being in any way diminished by its neighbour's splendid marble floors, ceramic murals and sculptured ceilings. Sponsorship in the early years, without which the event could not have taken place, came from the Harviestoun and Atlas Breweries.

Ken's jazz festival, which became known as the **Guildford Arms Jazz Festival**, was to present jazz of the traditional to mainstream type and was to become a successful annual event. The programme originally ran for a week, taking place each evening from 9.00pm to 12.00 midnight and generally the first two nights coincided with

453

the last two nights of the EIJF. Each evening featured a band built around Ken's own drumming, filled out with invited jazz musicians, mostly local but also including an impressive list of guests from further afield. Typically, there would be a piano, bass and drums rhythm section fronted either by a team of horn players carefully selected to blend well together or a guest soloist.

It is not possible to list all the many local jazzers who played a part but a random selection of names will give some idea of the quality and style of jazz that graced the Guildford over the years. The Edinburgh scene contributed the likes of pianists Tom and Jack Finlay, Ron Carruthers and George Cavaye, trumpeters Al Fairweather, who played all the Guildford Arms festivals between 1988 and 1992, Andrew Lauder, Gus Ferguson and Jim Petrie, bass players Ken Macdonald, Kenny Ellis, Ronnie Dunn and Dizzy Jackson, guitarist Lachlan MacColl, reeds men Jimmy Shortreed, Jack Graham, Bill Simpson, Jimmy Woods and Phil Bancroft, trombonist Graeme Robertson, vocalists Wendy Weatherby and Jean Mundell and many others. Guests from elsewhere in Scotland included pianists Frank Tinson and Jimmy Martin, bass player John Hartley from Aberdeen, tenor sax player Dave Roberts from Inverurie, another tenor man, Robbie Richardson, from the Borders and trumpeter Al Gibson from West Lothian. Glasgow provided trumpeter George Ogilvie and the major attraction of vocalist Fionna Duncan.

The guest list from further afield was just as impressive and must be headed by the great trombonist Roy Williams, a star of both the Alex Welsh and Humphrey Lyttelton bands, who was to be an ever-present attraction over a span of twenty four years (and still counting). The London jazz scene was further represented by trumpeter Terry Meechan, clarinettist Ian Christie who was the guest star at the very first Guildford Jazz Festival in 1987, another Welsh and Lyttelton alumnus in reeds player John Barnes, guitarist Jim Douglas and the fine alto sax and clarinet player Bruce Turner, who made many appearances. Ken Ramage also sometimes arranged additional gigs or even little tours for his guests from the south, when he would take them, along with his backing trio, to venues in the north of Scotland.

454

Speaking with Ken in 2011, he recalled one such trip when the guest soloist was Bruce Turner who asked him to make a detour on the way home to visit Pitreavie Castle, where Bruce had been stationed during the war.

In addition to the Guildford event and the north of Scotland gigs, Ken was also active in arranging jazz weekends and charity jazz band balls through the year, some of which took place in the Masonic Club at Shrubhill, a very large venue which he was able to fill for a number of years. Al Fairweather, a great supporter of local jazz since his return from the south, played at all the early Jazz Band Ball events run by Ken as did pianist Alex Shaw, although Alex never managed to play the Guildford Arms Festivals. Sadly, Al Fairweather, who had been a constant support for Ken's various projects between 1988 and 1992, died just before a Jazz Band Ball run by Ken in the Leith Ex-serviceman's Club in June 1993. In a well-deserved gesture, Ken then ran the event as a tribute to Al, with Roy Williams on trombone, Jack Duff on reeds and Andrew Lauder coming in on trumpet in Al's place. Another trumpeter, George Ogilvie, sometimes brought his whole band over from Glasgow to play at the Jazz Band Balls. As a further contribution to the success of his various ventures, Ken and his wife Viv (who sadly died in 2010) would often provide accommodation for visiting jazzers, thus cutting costs in a budget that none-the-less usually ended up over-stretched. What should certainly be mentioned is that there was always a collection in aid of children with cancer at the Guildford events and the proceeds from the various jazz band balls went towards the annual Edinburgh Taxi Trade Handicapped Kiddies Outing. It was small wonder that Ken was able to count on the support of so many jazzers from Edinburgh and elsewhere for these events.

The first run of Guildford Jazz Festivals continued until 1992 but this sequence of seven years actually included nine festivals, as Ken ran two festivals in both 1990 and 1991. However, that brought the Guildford Jazz Festval to an end for the time being as Ken made a return to the USA, where he was to stay for the next nine years. Happily, his return to Edinburgh saw the resumption of his partnership with David Stewart and the Guildford Arms, with the first of a new series of festivals taking place in 2003. Since then, the Guildford Jazz Festival has again been an annual event, with sponsorship provided by the excellent Orkney Brewery, which brought the name 'Orkney Jazz at the Guildford Arms'. Many well-known jazzers from Edinburgh and elsewhere have taken part in the series of festivals beginning in 2003, their number including many who had already played a part in the first series, together with others such as reed players Gerard Dott, George Duncan, and Martin Foster, trombonists Alan Quinn and Dave Batchelor and many others. Guests from further afield have included reeds man Jim Galloway from Toronto and, in 2010, Frank Perowsky, a top tenor sax man who had played with the likes of Woody Herman, Peggy Lee, Sarah Vaughan and Billy Eckstine.

In the year of writing of 2011, the Guildford Jazz Festival continues to flourish, still attracting good crowds and still delivered without cost to the punters. It now takes place over no fewer than thirteen evenings and is advertised as part of a package: The Guildford Arms Free Fringe Music, the jazz festival being followed by Caledonian Folk and Blues at the Guildford. Like the rest of Edinburgh jazz, the Guildford Arms Jazz Festivals continued to be affected by losses among its regular contributors, with both Ronnie Dunn and Alan Quinn dying in the months following the 2011 event. However, others filled the gaps and the 2011 Guildford Arms jazz programme went ahead from 5th to 17th August and was, as usual, a well-attended success. It featured various combinations under the names the Ken Ramage Trio and the Ken Ramage Dixie Six and was again headed by the ever loyal and popular Roy Williams. The singer Freddie King also appeared, as did Jim Petrie's Diplomats of Jazz. The 'cast' for 2011 was billed as Keyboard: Jack Finlay, Campbell Normand, Dave Graham, Graham Scott and Steve Grossart; Trumpet: Jim Petrie, Andrew Lauder and Brian Robertson; Trombone: George Howden; Reeds: Dick Lee, Bob Busby, Bill Marshall and Andy Hampton; Bass: Ken Macdonald, Kenny Ellis, Owen Macdonald and Graham Blamire; Banjo: Bev Knight; Vocalist: Patsy Hindley and Drums: Ken Ramage. The

Guildford Jazz Festival, after twenty four years, albeit with a break of about ten years, showed no signs of stopping for as long as the now seventy-four year old Ken Ramage, who had worked so hard to organise the festivals as well as annually knocking his pan in at the drum kit, wanted to keep it going.

The 1980s had certainly been a busy decade. Traditional jazz in the pubs and elsewhere and the EIJF were thriving and there were plenty of punters willing to turn out and support both. As a demonstration of just how vigorous the jazz scene was in the later 1980s, a list published in April 1987 shows the following:

Jazz in Edinburgh – 8.30-11.00 unless stated – April 1987

Monday	Starbank, Newhaven	Jim Petrie J.B.	9-12
	Blue Lagoon, Angle Park Tce	East Coast J.B.	
	Fingers Bar	Jazz pianist	
	Malt Shovel	Sophie Bancroft and trio	
Tuesday	Basin Street	West End J.B.	
	Navaar House Hotel	Louisiana Ragtime Band	
	Handsel, Stafford St.	Lachlan McColls trio	
	L'Attache	Liz McEwan, Brian Keddie	
	Struan Hotel (Zoo)	Darktown J.B.	
	Malt Shovel	Swing 1987	
	Fingers Bar	Jazz pianist	
Wednesday	Basin Street	Louisiana Ragtime Band	
	Preservation Hall, Victoria St.	Charlie McNair J.B.	9-12
	Scotty, Piershill	Darktown J.B.	
	Fingers Bar	Jazz pianist	
	Maxie's Bistro	'Take Three'	
	Fat Sam's	Fat Sam's Band	
	Royal Hotel, Roslin	Martin Leys Quartet	
Thursday	Basin Street	Graham Blamire J.B.	
	Templehall, Esplanade, Portobello	Templehall Stompers	
	Fingers Bar	Jazz pianist	
	Cassis, Abercromby Place	The Jazz Machine (Joe Capaldi)	9-12
Friday	Basin Street	Spirits of Rhythm	
	L'Attcahe, Rutland Hotel	Fionna Duncan with Ronnie Rae Trio and Bruce Adams	
	Fingers Bar	Jazz pianist	
	Ellersley House Hotel	Frank Tinson Trio	
Saturday	Preservation Hall	Toto McNaughton J.B.	2-4
	Platform 1 (Caledonia Hotel)	Alec Shaw Trio	12-3
	The Shore Bar, Leith	Geoff Byrne trio (Lunchtime)	
	Basin Street	Yelly Dug J.B.	

	L'Attache	Fionna Duncan and Trio	
	Clarendon Hotel, Grosvenor St.	Festival City J.B.	
	Fingers Bar	Jazz pianist	
Sunday	Learmonth Hotel	Society Syncopators	1-4
	Sheraton Hotel	Mike Hart J.B (brunch)	1-3
	Crest Hotel, Blackhall	Capital City J.B.	2-5
	Platform 1	Ronnie Rae Trio	
	L'Attache	Fionna Duncan Trio	
	Haymarket	Jean Mundell and the Embers	
	Grosvenor Hotel	Alexander's Big Band (dancing)(£2)	
	Fingers Bar	Jazz Band	

The above list shows that there were forty-two regular jazz spots each week, with a remarkably wide choice of styles on offer. Almost all were free, with only the Grosvenor Hotel charging at the door, although you were supposed to buy 'brunch' at the Sheraton. The total of forty-two regular weekly gigs is not far off the total of forty nine shown in Chapter XII in respect of November 1983. As Edinburgh traditional jazz ended the 1980s, it was clearly still in robust good health.

Chapter XVI

Millennium Done Been Here and Gone

The 1990s began with a good number of established bands still in vigorous action including the Louisiana Ragtime Band, the Spirits of Rhythm, Mike Hart's Scottish Society Syncopators, Fat Sam's Band, the Climax Jazz Band, the Criterion Brass Band (now billed in the EIJF programme as the Criterion New Orleans Parade Band), Dr McJazz, the Templehall Stompers, the Jazz Masters, Swing 1980-2010, Charlie McNair's Jazz Band, the Maid of the Forth Stompers and the Alex Shaw Trio. Although the Jazz Masters stopped playing early in the decade, most of these long serving bands were to continue for many years to come, although inevitably with some changes in their ranks. The West End Band too, after disappearing for a year or two, got together again later in the decade under reeds player Bob McDowell's leadership, the band playing from a Linlithgow base, with many of its members living in West Lothian.

Trumpeter and vocalist Jim Petrie had continued to be extremely active in Edinburgh jazz since his debut in the 1950s and he had remained involved with the Climax Jazz Band throughout most of the 1960s. In the early 1970s, Jim played in the White Cockade pub in Rose Street with a band led by trombonist Kenny Ramage, a residency that lasted for a couple of years. This band was the successor to the short-lived Ken Ramage's Jazz Advocates that Kenny had led in 1969. Jim also played for over two years in another band involving Kenny, this being the Festival City

Jazz Band. This band was based in the Barnton Hotel and included Jim, Kenny, Jimmy Shortreed (rds), the nominal leader of the band Ian Scott (pno), Colin Warwick (bjo), Ken Burns on (bs) and Russ Cessford (drms). When the Ramage band finished at the White Cockade, Jim continued with the Tuesday evening spot for a further five years or so, fronting the Climax Jazz Band, which had Jack Weddell (tbn), George Gilmour (clt), Colin Warwick (bjo), Ken Macdonald (bs) and Roy Dunnett (drms).

Through the later 1970s and early 1980s, Jim led a succession of bands which appeared under a variety of names. Most of these bands were built around a core of players, drawing on Edinburgh's now large population of experienced jazzers. Jim was in the Black Bull pub in the Grassmarket for five years with a band that included Bob Craig (tbn), George Duncan (clt), Tom Bryce (pno), Harald Vox (bjo) and Jim Young (bs). Other successful residencies were at the Golden Rule in Yeaman Place, off Fountainbridge, and at the Glenelg Hotel, where he played with a band that included Bob Craig or John Arthur (tbn), Andy Hampton (rds), Jock Westwater (bjo), Dizzy Jackson (bs) and Iain Forde (drms). Jim's band had appeared as the Jim Petrie Jazz Band in the very first Edinburgh Jazz Festival in 1978 and again in 1980. In 1983 they appeared as the Jim Petrie Quartet, with a line-up of Jim on (tpt), Andy Hampton (rds), Jock Westwater (bjo) and Simon Carlyle (sousa). By 1986 they had become the Vindaloo Stompers (I detect the hand of Jock Westwater in this name), with the same personnel as 1983 but with the addition of Gerard Dott also on reeds and Iain Forde on drums. By 1987 they had become Jim Petrie's Chinese Jazz Band (Jock again, I'll bet) with Jim, Andy Hampton and Bob Busby (rds), Jock Westwater (bjo) as before and Simon Carlyle (sousa). In the late 1980s and into the early 1990s, Jim continued to be involved with the Climax band, which played at the Claret Jug in Great King Street and another venue in Drumsheugh Gardens, the band at this point in its long history, having Jim, Jack Weddell, George Gilmour, Jock Westwater and a young Roy Percy making his debut on bass. Unusually, the band did without a drummer at this time.

However, in 1988, the band which Jim was to lead for the next twenty years and more was formed, growing out of the bands Jim had led in the earlier 1980s. The original line-up of the new band, which was to be called the **Diplomats of Jazz** and which would become a major and long term Edinburgh band, was Jim Petrie (tpt and vocs), Andy Hampton (rds), Jock Westwater (bjo) and Simon Carlyle (sousa). Jim had, of course, started in the 1950s as a strong adherent of the purist/New Orleans school of traditional jazz. Originally with a style based on early New Orleans trumpet players such as Bunk Johnson and Avery Kid Howard, later in his career Jim was to make a deliberate change in his style, unconvinced that his existing style really suited the new quartet setting. He had listened to the playing of great trumpeters belonging to the classic jazz tradition and, in particular, took on board the influences of early Louis Armstrong and Jabbo Smith. Jim himself came to describe his playing from then on as belonging to the classic tradition and, in my view, he made a great success of the re-modelling of his style. Jazz orthodoxy has it that jazz musicians will have set their style and reached their creative peak early in their careers, as early as in their twenties or thirties. In my view, Jim Petrie was able, very successfully, to reinvent his style as he grew older and, always a fiery player, was still extending his expressive range in middle age. His playing was greatly admired by many, in particular one American visitor. This jazz enthusiast had toured around the Edinburgh jazz pubs and was intrigued to find Jim playing in many of them with different bands. He told Jim *'Man, you sure wear a lotta hats!'* and declared him to be *'A National Treasure'*, a notable and well deserved tribute to a long serving and sincere jazzer.

The Diplomats of Jazz had their first gig at the Palmerston Hotel and then moved on to play Sunday afternoons at the Ettrick Hotel in the Polwarth area for all of eight years. They also had successful residencies at various times at the Glencairn Hotel in Royal Circus on Sunday evenings, a spell at the Bank Hotel opposite the Tron Church and four and a half years in the Golden Rule in Yeaman Place. There were changes in the Diplomats in the early 1990s with Jack Graham taking over on reeds from Andy Hampton, Bill Brydon replacing Symon Carlyle on sousaphone and Beverley Knight coming in on banjo to replace Jock Westwater, eventually leaving Jim as the only original member.

Another adventure for Jim was a re-forming of the early Climax Jazz Band from the 1950s, for a long distance tour. This came about through the efforts of Tom Wood, who had played piano with the early Climax band in the Stud Club in 1959, and had subsequently emigrated to Australia, where the tour was to take place. The band that made the trip in 1992 as the Climax Re-union Jazz Band was as close to the original line-up as possible with Jim Petrie (tpt and vocs), Jack Weddell (tbn and vocs), Jake McMahon (clt), Mike Hart (bjo), Jim Young (bs) and Kenny Milne (drms). Their old colleague from the 1950s, Tom Wood, who was then playing with the New Zenith Jazz Band, joined up with them in Australia. The tour was a great success and was celebrated by a recording, made after their return home, with Tom Finlay deputising on piano for Tom Wood[184].

A clear signal of the way things were to go appeared in the mid-1990s. Traditionally, there had been a jazz scene in Edinburgh and another, almost completely separate one, in Glasgow. However, in the mid-1990s came the first indications of a decline in the number of active jazz musicians and the Edinburgh and Glasgow jazzers began to be more involved with each other. Jim Petrie was one of the first, joining the Glasgow based George Penman Jazzmen in 1995 after depping with them on many occasions, succeeding Alec Dalgleish as Penman's trumpeter, an arrangement that was to last for seven years. Later, other Edinburgh jazzers would follow Jim into the Penman band, including trombonist Johnny McGuff, trumpeter Gus Ferguson, who eventually replaced Jim Petrie, and the banjo player, Harald Vox. Indeed, Harald Vox was to take over the running on the Penman band after George Penman died in 2009.

---

[184] See discography Appendix

The Diplomats of Jazz in the late 2000s
Bill Brydon (sousa), Jim Petrie (tpt), Bev Knight (bjo),
Bob Busby (rds)
(from the collection of Jim Petrie, photographer
unknown)

The Penman band in fact had gone a stage further even than using cross-City musicians; they actually had a band residency in Edinburgh, at the Fairmile Inn, once called the Ski Lodge, at Fairmilehead. At the time, clearly suffering an attack of acute parochialism, I remember feeling astounded by their brass neck and thinking that it was like having aliens from outer space living in your street.

Eventually other west coast based jazzers started to appear playing Edinburgh gigs, alhough this tended to be small bands made up mainly of jazzers from the west, rather than Glasgow jazzers making up the numbers in Edinburgh bands. Those who later played regularly in the capital included the exceptional trumpeter from Ayr, Mike Daly, who both ran and played at regular resident spots at the Sheraton Hotel and the Dome, a large pub occupying a magnificent former bank building in George Street. Banjo player Kit Carey, trumpeter Graham Stark and clarinetist Duncan Nairn were three west based jazzers who made frequent appearances at these city centre gigs. Jim Petrie, after his stint with the Penman band, even set up a band that was called the Two Cities Jazz Band. This band was jointly led by Jim and the Glasgow clarinet player Ivan Henderson, who had played with the Penman band for many years. Jim and Ivan, together with the Glasgow banjo player and entertainer Alastair McDonald, made many weekend trips to play in Denmark. Here they were joined by a Danish bass player and drummer to make up a five piece band which was highly rated in Denmark. The movement west to east of Glasgow jazzers to play with Edinburgh bands was much less marked, which seems to indicate that, by then, Edinburgh had a greater number of available, active jazz musicians than Glasgow.

Meanwhile, the Diplomats had gone from strength to strength in their various resident spots through the 1990s and on into the new century. Jack Graham would eventually leave the band when he moved away to live in Spain and his replacement was the experienced clarinet player from Falkirk, Bob Busby, still playing in his hot, spikey style. Jim Petrie and Bob made an exciting combination and, with the by now long established rhythm team of Bev Knight and Bill Brydon, the Diplomats were to remain a popular and feisty band, punching well above their four-piece weight. Over the years, the Diplomats played at many jazz festivals and Bob Busby tells the tale of a gig at the Leith Jazz Festival when a lady approached the band to say how much she had enjoyed their performance and asked Bob his name. When he told her, she said 'Bob who?' causing Bill Brydon to invent a mythical jazz publication 'Bob Who's Who's Who of Jazz'!

Later, the Diplomats were to move to a two year spot in Leslie's Bar, one of the finest of Edinburgh's historic pubs with a wonderful Victorian interior, and later to the Reverie, formerly the Wine Glass, on Newington Road. The Diplomats of Jazz made several CDs[185] over the years, two of them featuring Jack Graham's agile and sympathetic

---

[185] See discography Appendix

clarinet weaving its spells round Jim Petrie's peppy trumpet line, wonderful reminders of one of Edinburgh's long line of great clarinettists.

The Diplomats long-serving **banjo player, Beverley Knight**, was born in Dundee on 20th August 1959 and attended the city's Craigie High School, before coming to Edinburgh to study at Napier University and Moray House College of Education. There had always been music playing in the house when she was young, her father keen on classical music, her mother singing at concert parties, and it was as a teacher of music and brass instruments that Bev was to make her living. Bev's interest in music had begun early, learning to sing harmonies along with her mother, and she was to begin guitar lessons when she was still at primary school. Later, at secondary school, she moved on to euphonium and spent a lot of time while at school taking part in concerts and shows, something she would continue while studying in Edinburgh. In the early 1980s, Bev had a friend who owned a banjo and she became fascinated by the instrument. She managed to buy herself a cheap, 5-string banjo and a book on how to play Bluegrass style but in retrospect describes her attempts as a 'total failure'! However, salvation was at hand when a friendly barman scribbled down some G banjo chord shapes for her and she was away. Her earlier experience on guitar meant that she had an understanding of how chords worked and she was quickly able to pick up the basic chords on the banjo.

As a youngster, Bev had listened to all sorts of music, including jazz, and had developed a wide musical taste which remains to this day. However, about the time of the early banjo experiments, Bev's interest in jazz increased and she began to expand her knowledge of chords, greatly helped by getting out around the Edinburgh jazz scene to listen to the local bands. She also found that listening to recordings of bands from the 1920s and 1930s helped her to form her style of playing. In jazz terms, her particular liking is for the classic jazz of the twenties and thirties. However, when asked about her favourites, it is bands rather than individuals she quotes, naming the famous bands of Louis Armstrong, Jimmy Noone and Fletcher Henderson but also citing less well-known names such as

McKinney's Cotton Pickers and Charlie Johnstone's Paradise Orchestra.

Bev's jazz career in Edinburgh was kick-started by a lucky chance. She was walking to her school teaching job one morning, when a supply teacher asked her if anyone in the music department played banjo. I shudder to think what response such a question would have received if it had been directed to the music department when I was at school but happily, times had changed. It turned out that the supply teacher's husband, John Keenan, played double bass in a band and they were short of a banjo player. It did not take long for Bev to offer her services, together with what she describes as her 'few chords', and she found herself a member of the St Stephen Street Stompers. This was in the 1980s and the Edinburgh pubs were alive with jazz bands. Before long, Bev had established herself in the usual way, by depping with as many bands as she could, and soon built up her experience and her repertoire of chords. She also made a point of getting round the pubs to hear the variety of styles on offer and eagerly took the chance offered by the 1980s EIJFs to listen to the fabulous mix of jazz available, finding this a wonderful way to add to her jazz experience.

It was not long before the jazz scene cottoned on to the fact that there was a new and able banjo player about and a musically educated female one at that, which made a nice change. In the 1980s, Bev was to play with many of the local bands including the Templehall Stompers, Charlie McNair's Jazz Band, the Centurion Jazz Band, the Spirits of Rhythm, Kenny Ramage's band and Al Fairweather's Sundowners, sometimes in depping arrangements which could go on for months. Her reputation as a good player soon reached Glasgow and she was also to play with the George Penman Jazzmen and the band led by clarinet player Ivan Henderson, through in the west.

In 1993, Bev joined the band with which she would remain for many years, replacing Jock Westwater in Jim Petrie's Diplomats of Jazz. This was to be the band with which Bev would be most identified and, with them, she made her debut on record. She was on the Diplomats 'Body and Soul' recording in 1995 with Jim Petrie, Jack Graham and Bill Brydon and, over the next fifteen years or so, made many other recordings with the band, all of which will be found in the discography appendix. She also recorded with the Ivan Henderson band, which included Jim Petrie on trumpet, appearing on their CDs 'Midnight with Scotland's Two Cities Jazz Band' in 2000 and 'Ivan Henderson's All Stars Play at Goldenacre' in 2007. Bev's jazz career also brought her the opportunity to play with some well known jazzers from elsewhere, including Martin Litton, Norman Field, Annie Hawkins, Colin Bowden, Phil Mason, Roy Williams and Fionna Duncan. She considers herself to have been very fortunate to have started when Edinburgh was buzzing with jazz every night and having so many opportunities to play with so many bands, some of them of a very high calibre. After nearly twenty years with the band, Bev Knight remains an indispensible stalwart of the Diplomats of Jazz and of the Edinburgh jazz scene.

In 1990, another jazz festival had sprung up within the City boundaries and, as in the case of the EIJF, we will explore it in outline, looking only at the major developments over its years of existence. Leith, although incorporated with Edinburgh in 1929 and sometimes called Edinburgh's port, quite rightly prides itself in being an independently minded, lively and forward looking town in its own right. Famous for its waterside pubs, eateries and extensive docks, Leith also made its mark as a jazz town when it ran its own **Leith Jazz Festival** in the 1990s.

In **1990**, the annual Leith Festival, Pageant and Gala included, for the first time, a jazz event which featured sixteen bands in nine venues, every one of which offered free entrance. The jazz schedule was featured as a special section in the Leith Festival printed programme. It was headed Leith Jazz, and was to take place over three days, from Friday 15th to Sunday 17th June. The programme announced that Leith jazz was organised by the Leith Visitor Development Group with the help of Mike Hart of the EIJF. The jazz event was funded by the pubs involved and an impressive list of around twelve sponsors. The nine venues were The Tattler in Commercial Street, the Waterfront in Dock Place, the Trading Post and The Shore Bar both on the Shore, Todd's Tap and the Cavern Bar both in Bernard Street, the Chequers and Port o' Leith both in Constitution Street and McKirdy's in Assembly Street. The list of sixteen bands included some familiar local names in the Wendy Weatherby Trio, the Diplomats of Jazz, Charlie McNair's Jazz Band, the Fionna Duncan Trio, the Ken Ellis Trio, Dr McJazz, the Jazz Masters, the Spirits of Rhythm, Hip Replacement, Swing 1990 and newcomers Le Jazz Hot. From Glasgow came the George Penman Jazzmen and from south of the Border, Brian Carrick's Heritage Hall Stompers. The biggest name was that of the exceptional trumpeter from the USA, Warren Vache, who was to appear with the Brian Kellock Trio at McKirdy's on the Friday and the Trading Post on the Saturday. The Saturday programme included a parade in the Shore area which featured The Criterion Parade Band, the Auld Reekie Parade Band and the Falkirk Foot Tappers.

For **1991**, the event was billed as the Leith Jazz Festival (LJF) in its own right, rather than merely as a part of the wider Leith festival, and had expanded to include over fifteen venues in bars and restaurants. There were twenty performers, with Mike Hart's St Louis Ragtimers, Jack Duff's Band, the Louisiana Ragtime Band, Le Jazz Hot, Swing '91 and Ralph Laing's Jazzmen with Wendy Weatherby among the local additions. Some bands with a more contemporary style were also included, with Mike Travis' EH15, the Jan Swanson Quartet and the Sylvia Rae Quartet all appearing. There was no big international name for 1991 but visitors from elsewhere included the West Jesmond Rhythm Kings from Newcastle. An expanded list of over thirty sponsors had contributed and the LJF issued its own printed programme, instead of relying on a section within that of the Leith Festival.

A similar pattern was in place for the **1992 LJF** but it was announced that, this time round, the event was in association with Burton Ale. Although there was a drop in venues to ten, it was a full and ambitious programme, with events on the Friday evening, lunchtime, early evening and late evening gigs on the Saturday and Sunday, and an afternoon street parade each day. Newcomers included John Burgess Jazz, Jeanie Maxwell and the Jazzwegians, Making Waves, the Jelly Roll Band, Swing Palace, Annie

McNichol and Jazz Therapy and the well known singer, Danny Street.

During one of these early LJFs, I remember playing on an outdoors bandstand on the Shore, perched above the Water of Leith just at the point where the river enters the waters of Leith Docks. I was speaking through the microphone, which means that it must have been with the Jazz Masters, when Mike Hart drew up driving his tiny three wheeled vintage car. He was dressed very stylishly in period gear with a leather helmet and goggles and when I greeted him over the PA as Biggles and commented that I thought people usually had two roller skates, he shook his fist at me.

The association with Burton Ale continued in **1993** and **1994**, when the new acts in 1993 included the Sophie Bancroft Trio, Freddie King, the Tees Valley Jazz Men, the Two Step Ticklers, The Goodbye Look (this sounds a defeatist sort of name to me – I wonder if they got any more bookings?), the Eddie Severn Duo, Edith Budge and Friends, and the Martin Foster Quartet, with an expanded Le Jazz Hot, styling itself a jazz orchestra. There were also to be 'Strolling Players and Street Performers' each afternoon and a notable new venue was the Cruise Ship Edinburgh, a large vessel permanently moored at The Shore. The 1993 street parade was to include, in addition to the Criterion and Auld Reekie Parade Bands, the George Heriot's Swing Band, Picante, the Jackson Five (not that one surely?) and the popular and decorative Brolly Dollies. Additional attractions were an Antique and Craft Fair, a Kite Spectacular and Kite Flying Display and a Street Party, which featured some of the parade bands plus Dr McJazz, the Louisiana Ragtime Band and Jazz Company. The 1994 programme had a slightly increased number of venues and brought in the Kevin Dorrian Quartet, Jim Baikie's Jim Jammers and Carol Clegg and Speakeasy and the Honestas Parade Band made its first appearance.

By **1996**, the LJF was in association with Caledonian 80/- Ale and introduced itself proudly as the '...*only entirely free Jazz Festival in Scotland'*. There were eleven venues and top of the bill was a guest from Canada, Mose Scarlett, described as a crooner and raconteur whose '...*musical*

469

cache includes countless gems of Jazz, Blues, Ragtime and Swing'. Most of the old favourites returned and included for the first time, amongst many others, were the local Broughton High School Big Band, the Porky Boys, the Dave Keir Quartet, the Jean Mundell Trio and the Edinburgh University Big Band with Fionna Duncan. Other newcomers were the Jazz Ecosse All Stars and the Duck Fat Jazz Band with both the Lochwinnoch Carnival Orchestra and the New Orleans Wanderers joining the parade bands out on the streets.

The LJFs for **1997**, **1998** and **1999** continued the association with the Caledonian Brewery and kept faith with many of the stalwarts from previous years. Welcome additions were the Dougie Campbell Trio, the Liz MacEwan Quartet and the Portobello High School Jazz Band, with Brian Carrick's Heritage Hall Stompers making a return after an absence of several years. 1998 saw the debut of the local Yelly Dug Jazz Band, Eddie Hamilton's St Stephen Street Stompers, the Jack Duff Band and the Jack Finlay Trio. Other debutants included Blues Incorporated, the Dana Dixon Blues Band, Dr Chicago, Some Days are Diamonds and another band with a slightly discouraging sort of name, Mud in Your Ear! This reminds me of Eddie Condon's famous question when contrasting some of the less harmonious of the bebop sounds with older jazz. Condon asked *'Does it enter the ear like broken glass or like honey?'* but I wonder what would he have made of jazz entering the ear like mud?! In addition, the 1998 street events were augmented by a Big Band Extravaganza and the Edinburgh Samba School, both scheduled for Tower Place. Local first timers for 1999 were the Gus Ferguson Fast Five, the Rootsie Tootsie Blues Band, the West End Jazz Band, the Roy Percy Trio and a band simply billed as Mike Hart's Jazz Band. Other newcomers included the Arhoolies, the Chilli Dogs, Jazz Incident, Quintet East, Sugar House, Swing Bridge and Le Vieux Jazz Men.

The 1999 LJF was followed by two blank years when there was no festival but happily **2002** saw a resumption of activities. Caledonian Brewery seemed to have dropped out as sponsors but the printed programme had an introductory spiel by Lord Provost of Edinburgh, Lord

470

Lieutenant and Admiral of the Forth Eric Milligan who said that the Council was '...*delighted to be supporting the Festival along with a number of commercial sponsors*'[186]. In fact, the organisation of the LJF seemed to be in slightly different hands, a statement in the programme announcing that the 'Leith Jazz Festival is a Mike Hart Festival Production' with an organising committee chaired by Paul Nolan, Councillors Tom Ponton and Brian Fallon in the role of organising secretaries with Mike Hart himself and his colleague Jim Thomson as treasurer, representing 'Mike Hart Festival Productions'. Tribute was paid to Lord Provost Eric Milligan, Councillors Steve Cardownie and Phil Attridge, Sir Tom Farmer and Norrie Thomson's volunteers, '...*without whom the festival could not have taken place*'. There was a new spread of venues this year as well, which included Ocean Blue, Mariachi, the Cameo Bar, Club Java, the Persevere Bar, the Waterline, Nobles, the Central Bar, the Waterfront, Ocean Terminal and Next Generation, with a street parade and another outdoor event at Commercial Quay. A free jazz bus, supplied by Lothian Buses and featuring 'some fine music' was to tour the venues at thirty minute intervals. The programme continued to feature many of the bands which had played over the first ten years of the LJF while a number of new faces included Delta Croft Review, the Louisiana Shakers, the Pat Quin Four, Rev Doc, the Standard Bearers, the Todd Gordon Quartet, Vent D'est, Joe Gordon's Banjos and the local Roger Hanley's Jazz Hounds.

Sadly, the 2002 Leith Jazz Festival was to be the last of what had been a very worthwhile and innovative project. The lack of major sponsorship from a brewer meant that there was no longer a list of the brewer's pubs as convenient venues and for 2002, there had been a scramble to secure a suitable scatter of suitable premises. In spite of strenuous efforts to attract new sponsors and supporters, it became clear that the Leith Jazz Festival was no longer financially viable. Reluctantly, the organisers accepted the inevitable and Scotland's only completely free jazz festival came to an end. It had been a brave and highly successful

---

[186] Milligan Rt Hon Eric, Leith Jazz Festival programme for 2002

venture in spite of being cursed by several years of foul weather and, given that it was free to the punters, it had done extraordinarily well to run for a total of eleven years. In my view, a view I know was shared by many jazzers, Leith, with its historic waterfront, old pubs of character and picturesque streets, was a highly atmospheric and conveniently compact location for a jazz festival. Perhaps it would not be too fanciful to say that it was possible to feel something of the romance and waterside image of New Orleans. Its demise was a sad loss and it was to be greatly missed by musicians and punters alike for whom it felt like a gaping hole in the annual jazz panorama, as we moved on into the first decade of the new century.

The trio **Le Jazz Hot** had turned up in the inaugural Leith jazz event in 1990 and was led by **reeds player Martin Foster**. Martin had been born in Edinburgh in 1962 and his early interest in jazz had been sparked by listening to some of his Dad's records, which featured the likes of the Chris Barber and Sid Phillips bands. He took up the clarinet when he was still at school, after hearing the American clarinetist Peanuts Hucko playing with the Syd Lawrence Orchestra in the Usher Hall. Hucko was, of course, a very fine reeds player who had played with many great bands, including those of Glenn Millar, Benny Goodman and Eddie Condon. He had also been a member of the Louis Armstrong All Stars for a couple of years in the late 1950s. I remember once hearing him described as a sort of 'Dixieland Benny Goodman', which I considered unfairly dismissive of a very good player, although he certainly processed some of the smooth technical ease of Goodman. It is perhaps not surprising then, to hear that Martin found himself attracted to the playing of Goodman himself and that of his fellow great Swing stylist, Artie Shaw. Very much in the same stylistic pattern, Martin told me that, once he had started sitting in with some of the Edinburgh bands in the late 1970s, he reckoned that he had picked up some useful tips from Jimmy Shortreed, another clarinetist firmly in the Swing tradition, whom he considered an early and encouraging influence.

Martin also took up the alto saxophone and developed his playing by becoming a member of the Edinburgh Youth

Jazz Orchestra, run by Jimmy Grossart, before moving onto soprano and later baritone sax. Not content with playing these instruments, he was to go on adding new ones, finally playing all the members of the sax family, from the tiny sopranino right through to the enormous bass sax, as well as bass clarinet and flute. With an impressive array of instruments at his command, he was well able to take on the demanding role of the only horn fronting a trio and, in 1989, he formed Le Jazz Hot, together with Raymond Gillespie on guitar and Roy Percy on bass, making their mark at the LJF in 1990 as we have heard. This same band was included in the EIJF in 1991, when the official Programme hailed **Raymond Gillespie (guitar)** as a player who '...*in spite of his tender years has already graduated from being a Reinhardt clone to develop his own unique style*'.

The combination of a large range of instruments as well as the ability and flexibility of his co-conspirators in the rhythm section to respond to changes in style and dynamics, meant that even within the apparent limitations of a trio, Le Jazz Hot was particularly known for its wide-ranging repertoire and versatility. Inspired by the approach of the small groups of the twenties led by the likes of Joe Venuti, Le Jazz Hot featured a truly eclectic repertoire, influenced by the sounds of Bechet, Gerry Mulligan, Goodman, Adrian Rollini, Ellington, and Mozart, along with occasional flurries of Klezmer and Tango. As Roy Percy once said, the music of Le Jazz Hot featured '...*everything from Ragtime to lounge music*' - often within a single number. It was once described as the biggest three-piece band in the country. The 1991 EIJF Programme also alerted readers to look out for the expanded Le Jazz Hot Orchestra at the Cotton Club. This was a line-up which occasionally augmented the trio with trumpet, trombone, tenor sax and drums. It played a variety of music from the early Ellington repertoire through to touches of Spike Jones and his City Slickers.

It would be sometime in the early 1990s that I first heard Martin and what struck me, as it did everyone who heard him play, was his fleet-fingered ability to play his instruments at great speed. This was to be further demonstrated years later when, at a concert in the Queen's Hall in 2003, he astonished everyone by playing the traditional clarinet chorus from High Society, a renowned test piece for clarinet, on the bass sax!

As well as keeping various versions of le Jazz Hot going, Martin moved into other jazz settings and, over the years, featured with Francis Cowan, Fat Sam's Band, the Tommy Samson Big Band, the Dick Lee Septet and Ken Mathieson's Classic jazz Orchestra. Although he describes himself as a clarinetist at heart, Martin Foster has continued to play all the saxes but with a penchant for the baritone and bass, as it is his contention that '...*with sax, size really does matter*'!

Bill Salmond's Louisiana Ragtime Band entered the 1990s seven years into their long Navaar House residency, which was to continue for many years yet. The line-up of the band at the start of the decade was Brian Robertson (tpt), Dave Paxton (clt), Graham Scott (pno), Bill himself (bjo), Graham Blamire (bs), Roy Dunnett (drms) with Bob Craig (tbn) being replaced in 1990 by Alan Quinn. **Alan Quinn (trombone, piano)** had been born in Leith on 9th May 1943 and always considered himself to be a 'Leither'. He attended Holy Cross Academy and was to become a structural engineer. Alan had two elder brothers, Tommy who was some fifteen years older and Jimmy about twelve years older, who were both musicians. Tommy played saxophone and Jimmy piano and, while both of them played a lot of dance music, both were interested in and played early Be-bop jazz, frequently with Johnny Smith, another Leither, on trumpet. The two elder Quinns also played in resident dance bands at the Maybury Roadhouse out on the Glasgow Road, Tommy playing with Danny Dorrian's band in one hall while Jimmy played a couple of evenings each week, in another hall in the same building.

When he was five years old, Alan's father made him a model tin sax and this, plus his brothers' playing, stimulated an early interest in music. His first real instrument was piano and he had some piano lessons from both brother Jimmy and Danny Dorrian.

Bill Salmond, Alan Quinn and Ian Boyter
When Kit Carey sent this photo to Ian Boyter he said 'I
noticed the notice behind you and noticed that you had
taken no notice of the notice'!
(by permission of Kit Carey)

However, an accident which left him with tendon damage in an arm put an end to his career as a pianist and, at about seventeen, after hearing Acker Bilk's Paramount Jazz Band on the radio, he bought himself a trombone. As a budding trombonist, Alan was taken under the wing of the famous Leith Silver Band, which provided him with some tuition and with whom he played alongside a trumpeter called Donald Bremner. Donald Bremner, like Alan, would also become involved in the Edinburgh jazz scene when he played, albeit for only a short time in 1961, with the schoolboy Mound City Jazz Band, which included the clarinettist Gerard Dott, drummer Mike Travis and the present writer on double bass.

It was not long before Alan made his debut in Edinburgh jazz, joining an early Bill Salmond band called the Savoy Jazz band, followed by Jack St Clair's band and also playing with the Climax Jazz band, in which he replaced Jack Weddell during his time away in London. Alan was to find himself drawn into the purist New Orleans style of jazz, although he says that this was not really through any conscious choice on his part. He reports that it came about as *'almost an accident'* through playing with Bill Salmond's band and the Climax band, both bands in the New Orleans tradition. However, an allegiance to New Orleans jazz suited him very well as it introduced him to the Deep South sound of George Lewis's trombone player, Jim Robinson, who was to remain Alan's model for the rest of his playing career. Alan was to remain associated with the New Orleans style of jazz throughout his long, although interrupted, career in Edinburgh jazz. He reckons that his Bebop inclined brothers must have been fairly taken aback by his adherence to an early form of jazz but, if they were, they put no obstacles in his path. However, another force was soon to put a stop to his jazz playing.

Keen to play, Alan soon discovered that there was an active dance band scene in Edinburgh in which he saw the potential for more playing opportunities. Clearly feeling that the trombone was not all that much in demand in the dance bands, in 1967 Alan bought himself a bass guitar, taught himself how to play it and, for the next sixteen years, confined his playing to dance band gigs. It was not to be until 1983 that he was to return to jazz. It came about through going to listen to clarinettist Eddie Hamilton's band, the St Stephen Street Stompers, where he jumped at the chance of a sit-in with the band and found himself hooked again. In the mid-1980s, he formed a band of his own, the Templehall Stompers, named after their residency in the Portobello area of town, the Templehall Hotel. This was clearly again to be a band in the New Orleans tradition, the original line-up including Fraser Gauld (tpt), Eddie Hamilton (clt), Beverley Knight (bjo), Jimmy Tunnah (bs) and Eric Jamieson (drms). Later, after the sad death of Jimmy Tunnah, Lindsay Cooper played bass for a while before Ken Macdonald came in. Further changes would bring in Brian Robertson on trumpet and Bill Salmond on banjo, while Jim Petrie also did some sessions with them on trumpet.

While continuing to play with his own band at the Templehall Hotel, Alan was to join Bill Salmond's Louisiana

Ragtime Band in 1990 in which, as we have heard, he replaced the veteran RHS gangster, Bob Craig. The LRB line-up that Alan joined was Brian Robertson (tpt), Dave Paxton (clt), Graham Scott (pno), Bill Salmond (bjo), Graham Blamire (bs) and Roy Dunnett (drms). A few years later, when Brian Robertson left the LRB, Alan played on in a two man front-line, first of all in partnership with Dave Paxton, then, when Dave left, with George Gilmour. The LRB two man front-line, sharing the lead between clarinet and trombone, would continue for most of the next two decades, right through to the end of the long-running Navaar House Hotel gig in 1999 and beyond, well through the first decade of the new century.

Later, when the Templehall Hotel changed hands and the gig came to an end and the successful replacement gig at Miller's Foundry Bowling Club also ended, Alan gave up band leading, feeling that he simply needed a break. As the 2000s moved on and the number of active jazzers around the Edinburgh jazz scene became fewer, Alan was to find himself in ever greater demand, eventually playing simultaneously with the LRB, the Spirits of Rhythm, the Anti-Climax Jazz Band and also playing some jazz in a mainstream style with the reeds player, Ian Boyter. Always a player with a great sense of swing and a vigorous, full sound, Alan was also a good singer and an entertaining band leader with a particularly nice line in humour. His sixteen year sabbatical between 1967 and 1983 was a major loss to Edinburgh jazz but it was good in 1983 to welcome back to the fold a player who always seemed to me to have a natural affinity for jazz. An endlessly good humoured and very likeable personality and a gifted communicator, Alan's comeback to Edinburgh jazz was highly successful and, for almost another thirty years, his playing and singing was something to be sought for on the Edinburgh jazz scene, always adding great drive and swing to all the bands with which he played. Sadly, Alan Quinn, one of the best liked of all Edinburgh jazzers, died of cancer on 4th February 2011, at the age of only sixty seven.

I had played bass with the Louisiana Ragtime Band, in addition to the Jazz Masters, between 1985 and 1992 and, when I left, it was Bill Brydon who took over. **Bill Brydon**

(sousaphone, double bass) was born in Edinburgh on 30th December 1963 but was to attend school in the Border country, at Galashiels Academy, and go on to have career as a Director of Human Resources. His conversion to jazz came about through a friend at University who let him hear a recording of Jelly Roll Morton's 'The Chant' and Bill reports that he was *'hooked instantly'*. It is extraordinary how frequently descriptions of a 'Eureka Moment' have cropped up when gathering data for this book. Many jazzers have reported similar immediate turnings on to jazz through a single exposure to the music. Both bass player Jim Young and drummer Kenny Milne have spoken of how they had felt the hairs on the back their necks rise, when they first heard certain jazz recordings and it was the same in my case. It happened for me at school when, late one summer term, our English teacher, 'Kipper' Heron, invited the class to bring in favourite records to play and explain to the class why we liked them. I remember taking a skiffle record but it was the playing of someone else's choice, a recording of the Kid Ory band playing Swanee River, that was my instant turn-on to jazz. I lost no time in buying a copy of the LP for myself and I still have it which, even after more than fifty years, still has the power to remind me of that first magical realization that this was the music for me. In common with Jim Young, it was the rhythm that affected me and, to this day, I consider swing to be the one really indispensible ingredient of jazz.

Bill Brydon had started in music by learning to play cornet in his school band before eventually switching to the tuba. In time, he transferred his brass bass expertise to the tuba's bigger brother, the sousaphone. It was on this enormous instrument that Bill made his first appearances on the Edinburgh jazz scene, playing in Kenny Milne's Criterion Jazz Band from 1986 until 1993. The sousaphone that Bill played had an interesting history, having been played in an Edinburgh professional band called Leslie Jeffries' Rialto Orchestra, which had made a number of recordings in the 1920s. Bill joined Jim Petrie's four-piece band, the Diplomats of Jazz, in 1990 and remains a member of this band more than twenty years on, in 2011. Later, with the encouragement of Bill Salmond, Bill added the double bass to his musical weaponry and opened up a second and parallel jazz career for himself, continuing to play sousaphone with the Diplomats and joining Bill Salmond's Louisiana Ragtime band on string bass. Bill replaced me with the LRB when I left in the early 1990s and he has managed to accommodate the demands of both these successful bands over many years, appearing on a number of recordings with each[187].

Like Bev Knight, Bill quotes bands rather than individuals when he talks about his jazz influences, listing amongst them McKinney's Cotton Pickers, the Fletcher Henderson Orchestra and King Oliver's Dixie Syncopators. When asked about great names he had played with, he said that there were none, although he had stood in an Edinburgh pub queue once with the great bass player, Milt Hinton! Bill had taken the chance to ask him about Tiny Parham's Bluesicians, a band with whom Hinton had recorded in the 1930s. On another occasion, he had got close enough to Benny Waters to ask him about arrangements he had written for the Charlie Johnson Paradise Orchestra in the mid-1920s. Asked about memorable gigs he had played, he cited an occasion when, with Bill Salmond's band, he had played in a beautiful, wooden-built, 17th century church in Sweden, recalling that, when the audience got to their feet, the ancient wooden balconies had started to bounce up and down, causing a certain amount of consternation in the band.

In playing both brass and string bass, Bill Brydon reflects what was once the norm in jazz, when early players with a responsibility for the bass line, like Pops Foster and John Kirby, routinely played whichever was required by the band's musical arrangements. The important difference in Bill's case was that he played the two instruments in separate bands and very wise too, in my opinion. Even with modern transport, the thought of carrying both a sousaphone and a double bass to every gig is a daunting one, fraught with the risks of prolapsed inter-vertebral discs and worse, and how they managed in the early days is beyond me.

---

[187] See discography Appendix

The trumpeter Brian Robertson, who had been with Bill Salmond's Louisiana Ragtime Band since 1986, left the band sometime in 1994. However, while still playing with the LRB, in 1987 he had begun playing with Alan Quinn's Templehall Stompers, at their residency in the Templehall Hotel. This was another well supported gig and they usually packed the place on Thursday evenings. When the Templehall gig finally folded and the band moved to a new regular spot at the Millers Foundry Bowling Club in Parker Terrace, off Portobello Road, Brian went with them. The new place was just as successful as the Templehall had been, as the crowd moved with the band, and the tradition of packed Thursday evenings continued until 2000, when this residency too came to an end. Anxious to keep a regular spot going, Brian Robertson went to the nearby Ellwyn Hotel in Portobello Road and asked if there was any possibility of playing there. Perhaps aware that the band had been bringing in good business at the bowling club, the answer was yes. However, as Alan Quinn had decided to take a break, Brian found himself putting a band into the Ellwyn Hotel himself, thus beginning his career as a band leader.

Initially, he put in a four piece band with himself, Eddie Hamilton, Brian Weld on banjo and Bill Brydon on bass. When the veteran Brian Weld took a break from playing for a while, his temporary replacement was Andrew Mulhern, who had by then added banjo playing to his skills on trombone. Brian Robertson later decided to expand the bands scope and expanded it into a five-piece by adding Graham Scott on piano. The Ellwyn gig attracted a very loyal following, including some who came along for a sit in with the band, regulars being Jimmy Welsh with his trumpet, and Bill Brown on banjo, each of whom seldom missed a night over the all the years the gig lasted. They always got a sit in, this adding greatly to the atmosphere of a friendly and welcoming gig. Drummer Frank Birnie, at his long-running gig at the Blue Lagoon, followed the same policy, actively looking for sitters in, and there is no doubt at all that it added to the popularity of the gig, as well as encouraging jazzers who seldom played. At the Ellwyn, other regulars to play with the band were Alan Quinn and the afore-mentioned Andrew Mulhern, on trombone this time, who would often arrive with their horns and usually end up playing the whole night. After a while, the bass player Bill Brydon left the band and Owen Macdonald, son of Ken and the latest in the seemingly endless line of bass playing Macdonalds, came in. Owen was a student at the time and Brian remembers that he would sometimes set up a music stand with his University notes on it and get on with his studies, while Owen himself and the rest of the band were playing! The punters apparently just assumed that he was reading the music. After Owen left, his dad, Ken, took over on bass.

Brian had called the band the **Ellwyn Stompers** and they made a CD in 2002 to which he gave the name 'The Ellwyn Stompers (almost) Live at the Ellwyn Hotel'[188]. The Ellwyn residency ran for a good ten years or so, only ending in May 2010, to the lasting regret of its many regulars, or as Brian says, those who had not already gone to the great Preservation Hall in the Sky! In fact, Brian had put his finger on a serious and increasing problem. Just as the average age of the bands tended to increase by one for every year that passed, so did that of the punters. Just as there were very few young musicians coming into traditional jazz, so there was a sad lack of young punters coming along. I think we all knew it, although nobody had any answer for it and, as far as the pub residencies were concerned, the writing was beginning to appear all too clearly on the wall.

Brian Robertson was to form a second band in 2000, this one for the purposes of making recordings and playing club gigs and festivals, rather than with any intention of seeking a residency. Regular gigs included Pete Davenport's jazz nights at Tullbannocher in Comrie and also evenings at Mugdock, a country park north of Milnegavie near Glasgow, which put on jazz nights several times a year. I did several of these latter nights with the band and thoroughly enjoyed the tiny and always well-filled theatre, which had good acoustics and a great atmosphere. The new seven-piece band Brian called the **Forth River Ragtimers** and its membership was Brian himself on trumpet and vocals,

---

[188] See discography Appendix

Sandy Barclay from the Borders who played trombone until about 2007 when he was replaced by John Arthur, Eddie Hamilton (clt), Graham Scott (pno), Brian Weld (bjo), Ken Macdonald (bs) and, persuaded out of retirement, Roy Dunnett (drms). Between 2000 and 2009, the Forth River Ragtimers produced four CDs[189], with a fifth due to be recorded in early 2011.

A sad but inevitable effect of the passing years became all too clear in 1993, which saw the deaths of three Edinburgh jazz stalwarts. **Dave Paxton**, who had been playing latterly with Jim Petrie's band, became ill and died on 19th April 1993, just a few days after his sixty seventh birthday. A band was put together to play at Dave's funeral and it included Al Fairweather, Jim Petrie and Dave Strutt (tpts), Bob Craig and Dave Keir (tbns), Jack Graham and Jack Duff (rds), Mike Hart (bjo) and Dizzy Jackson (bs). An obituary by Tony Troon appeared in the Scotsman in which he, rightly, called Dave a *'rare talent'*[190]. I also contributed an appreciation in which I hailed him a *'master of the classic jazz clarinet'*, remarking on the great enthusiasm he brought to his music and emphasising his ability to play *'...originally and personally within a long established idiom, allowing it to continue as a living tradition rather than mere reproduction of a past era'*[191].

Al Fairweather, as well as playing in the band, had also spoken eloquently at Dave's funeral and it was a considerable shock when Al himself died, just a few weeks later, on 21st June 1993, at the age of sixty six. Tony Troon again contributed an obituary in the Scotsman and commented on Al's recorded output, noting that his performances stood out as *'...adventurous and unusual in the catalogue of traditional-mainstream jazz'*. Tony also remarked on Al's talent as an arranger, particularly noting his work with the Brown-Fairweather band of the 1950s, when his skill at *'...placing new ideas in a context which had to win over a basically conservative audience, managed to*

---

[189] See discography Appendix

[190] Troon A, 'Dave Paxton: Jazz Clarinettist', The Scotsman, April 1993

[191] Blamire G, 'A master of the classic jazz clarinet', The Scotsman', 26th April 1993

assert itself against the odds'[192]. John Gibson also paid tribute, linking Al's name with that of Sandy Brown, and pointing out that *'A stack of recordings, many of which do not sound dated today, is their legacy, along with memories galore to be cherished by jazz fans and friends here and countless musicians down south, who held their music in the highest esteem'[193].*

The third blow of a sad year came in December when **Jackie MacFarlane** died at the age of seventy three. Again there were tributes in the Scotsman and the Evening News and there were letters to the newspapers too, which spoke of him as a natural charmer and said how much he would be missed. One letter said that Jackie had been one of the nicest and kindest people that the writer had ever known. We have already heard how, in the early days, Jackie and Sean Connery were fellow bouncers at the Jazz Band Balls in the Oddfellows Hall in Forrest Road. I understand that, after Jackie died, a newspaper reported that the former Lord Provost, Eleanor MacLaughlin, who had supervised Connery's investiture as a Freeman of the City, had got in touch with the film star's agents to tell them of the loss. To her surprise, she shortly afterwards received a phone call and a voice said *'Hello Eleanor, its Sean here....'.* Connery explained that film contracts prevented him from getting back for the funeral but he subsequently sent a sympathetic letter which was passed on to Jackie's family. John Gibson, in an article in the Evening News, said *'A man who brought much pleasure to music lovers is to get his own memorial in the city'[194].* This was a reference to the setting up of a bench in Nicholson Square with a plaque which, it was planned, would say *'In memory of Edinburgh's Mister Jazz, from his fellow artists, friends and music lovers'.* Charlie McNair, Dave Strutt, Bob Craig, Dave Keir, Mike Hart and Dizzy Jackson all played in the band at Jackie's funeral. Years later, in 1998, I was asked to write an article about Jackie for a south side local magazine and I ended it

---

[192] Troon A, 'Al Fairweather: jazz trumpeter', The Scotsman', 22nd June 1993

[193] Gibson John, 'City loses top jazzman Al', The Edinburgh Evening News, 22nd June 1993

[194] Gibson John, 'Jackie's melodies linger on', Edinburgh evening News, December 1993

by saying '...*he was unique and, whatever else, a lot of people thought well of him'*.

Plaque on Jackie MacFarlane's memorial seat in Nicholson Square (photograph by the author)

As the years passed, the losses continued with the death of **Bob Craig** at the age of seventy on 4th August 1998. Towards the end of his life, Bob had tended to confine his playing to the Criterion Brass Band, the Edinburgh marching band run by Kenny Milne. Bob had played with that band at the EIJF Mardi Gras in the Grassmarket just a couple of days previously and had seemed well and in good form. However, sadly, he collapsed after suffering a stroke at home the next day and died in the Royal Infirmary just a day later. Bob had been an integral part of the Edinburgh jazz scene for fifty years and, with his death, we lost a real character. John Gibson paid tribute in the Evening News and quoted Bob's long time friend and colleague, Dizzy Jackson, as saying '*At his peak, Bob was well-rated and was ever ready to blow. He never had a bad word to say about anybody and nobody had a bad word for him. He* *plunged into the Mardi Gras with typical enthusiasm'.* John also quoted Charlie McNair as saying *'Bob played in my band off and on for five years. He was just a lovely bloke'*[195]. The Criterion Brass band played at Bob's funeral, which was a simple grave side ceremony, Bob having not been a religious man. It was strange to see the band without Bob at the front with his trombone. Members of his family paid tribute to him as did his former classmate Bill Strachan, and a recording of Bob playing the tune 'Ory's Creole Trombone' with an early Sandy Brown band, was played. He was a huge miss on the local jazz scene, not only because of his playing, but also because of his cheery, good-natured and endlessly optimistic personality. As Alastair Clark put it, *'A truly lovely man'*[196].

The importance of the jazz followers, the punters, should never be underestimated. Without them there would be no scene at all or, at best, sad and lonely musicians playing for their own amusement behind closed doors. In fact, in the case of quite a number of the punters, their contribution went far beyond simply turning up to support bands. Many were willing helpers at the EIJF, taking on all manner of responsibilities, acting as couriers, drivers, venue organisers and, minders (especially for some of the more elderly visiting jazzers), and generally making sure that all the unseen and sometimes thankless tasks were covered. However, there were several loyal and hard-working punters whose efforts went still further. In March 1989, Bill Bruce and Elliott Davies launched a publication called The Scottish Jazz News. This was to be a regular free production, sent out to all EIJF volunteers and with supplies of copies available at all the regular jazz venues. In addition, for only £2 a year, you could have a copy mailed to you. The venture was, at least in part, subsidised by advertising, but I suspect that Bill and Elliott carried some of the costs themselves, particularly at the start. The main content at first was a comprehensive gig listing, covering all the many weekly jazz gigs in Edinburgh, with

---

[195] Gibson John, 'Sadness as jazz legend dies', Edinburgh Evening News, August 1998
[196] Clark A, 'Obituaries – Bob Craig', 'Scotsman', 5 August 1998

additional information about one-off gigs. Listings and one-off information were also given for Glasgow, Saltcoats, Kilmarnock, Ayr, Greenock, Inverness, Dumfries, Perth, even Belfast and Tyne and Wear and many more areas would be added later. There was a letters page, a couple of articles, news about jazz festivals in the offing and even a competition, which offered EIJF tapes as prizes.

The intended circulation dates were unclear but it was hoped at the start to have the next edition out in May of that year. In fact, the organizers beat that date with an edition in April which included all the previous features and appealed for contributors such as writers, cartoonists and cross word puzzle compilers. There was a leading article on the forthcoming Glasgow Jazz Festival and a review of the Bude Jazz Festival. With some trepidation I also ventured into print in this issue, albeit anonymously. I had written sleeve notes for the Scottish Jazz Advocates LP 'All in Perfect Working Order', which had a tartan theme designed for the American market. In the sleeve notes, I had developed the tartan theme, lampooning the band, writing each member up under a pseudo-Scottish Mickey-taking name which purported to caricature their personalities. The drummer Chick Murray, of a mildly grumbly and critical disposition, was given the name Crabbit McGrump and pianist Tom Finlay, supposedly a hard headed businessman, was Graspin McCash. For the Jazz News, I invented an environment called the Edinburgh Jazz Jungle and populated it with a whole range of strange, musical, animal inhabitants under the tile 'The Bestiary of Jazz'. The series was prefaced with the statement *'This exciting, fascinating, serialised account will take you, for the first time, into real contact with the inhabitants of a unique and highly specialized habitat – the Edinburgh Jazz Jungle'.*

I dug out these writings recently and I have to say they are fairly cringe-making in retrospect. Trombone playing Bob Craig with his trademark moustache appeared under the genus 'Glissinfartinsliders', with his specific name of 'Raspinroarin Raftache', and poor old Mike Hart, banjo player and antique dealer, came out as 'Djanglemikehart Junkenhustler'. Looking at these 'portraits' now, I was lucky not to be lynched although, in my defence, I did clear them with each victim before they went to print. In addition to my efforts, the second edition of Jazz News also reported that the graffiti on the Basin Street ladies' loo wall included the announcement *'I love Kenny Milne – he plays a mean drum'*. The perpetrator of this public declaration of affection is unfortunately not known but it does remind me of my favourite bit of pub graffiti. Sometime in the 1960s, one of the Rose Street pubs, clearly fed up with graffiti all over the loo walls, invested in a blackboard. This was put up on the wall in the men's loo, handily placed above the urinals, and complete with a little wooden ledge for the chalk. It was a sad failure. The next time I went in, the blackboard was completely blank and beside it, scored about an inch deep into the wall, were the words 'Where is the f- -king chalk?'

Jazz News did very well, each edition containing more and more information about the Scottish jazz scene and attracting plenty of letters of encouragement, some of them even from remote and barely civilised places like Australia and Glasgow. Issue number three came out in June and number four appeared in August 1989, in good time to include a EIJF flyer outlining that year's programme. The magazine was also a very useful means of communication amongst the jazz crowd, helping ambitious punter-trips to be organized to as far-flung a jazz festival as the Sacramento Jazz Jubilee. The magazine itself became more ambitious too, arranging reviewers for all the Scottish jazz festivals and making sure that new jazz ventures were given maximum publicity, often assuring a good turnout even on opening nights. Letters poured in, many of them reminiscing about days gone by, and giving news of jazz elsewhere. Articles appeared about great historical jazz figures such as Jelly Roll Morton and Pee Wee Russell. An interesting slant on the times can be gleaned from the listings, which were headed 'Regular Free Venues'. Jazz News issue number four, dated August 1989, shows an almost incredible fifty-two free weekly gigs in Edinburgh, with ten gigs each Saturday, which I think probably represents the highest point of jazz activity that the City ever reached. By October that year the total had dropped to fifty but on Wednesday evenings, there was a choice of no fewer than twelve venues offering jazz, including Fat Sam's Band at Fat Sam's eatery, Fairweather Friends at Young's Hotel, and Fionna Duncan with the Jack Finlay Trio at the Fairmile Inn, out on the Biggar Road. I have come across no records that show a greater concentration of jazz in Edinburgh than at this time, and almost all of it was free!

Unfortunately, it proved impossible to maintain the Jazz News production rate. In 1990, which saw the commencement of Volume Two of the magazine, with issue numbers one to five appearing in consecutive months between March and July. However, the sixth issue seems not to have appeared until well on in the year and contained an apology from the editors citing pressure of work (ie day job type work) as the reason for the delay. Around this time, the issues also stopped carrying a date, which I think was probably a sign that the editors could not be certain when they would be able to issue it. Number seven of that Volume was also delayed and seems not to have appeared until after April 1991, judging by the reports of events included. The new Volume Three started sometime in 1991 but probably not much before the EIJF in August, instead of March when it should have begun, and it appears that only three more issues came out. The last I have, issue three of Volume Three, seems to have been issued sometime between April and August 1992 and, as I am sure I would have kept any others that appeared, that seems to have been the last one.

It was a pity that the venture came to a halt. It was great while it lasted, full of useful information about regular gigs, one-off events, jazz festivals and a forum where jazzers could express their views and reminisce about old times. It even began to print quite prickly letters, indicative of ruffled feathers, the first issue of Volume Three including a letter complaining bitterly about upheavals in the membership of Glasgow's George Penman band. Both George and the apparent victims of the upheaval went into print with explanations designed to calm the multitudes, but it was good to see a bit of spice amongst the more common epistles of praise and fond memories; more of such spice would have been very welcome, in my view. The Scottish Jazz News was a noble effort and was to be much missed but I think it probably came to an end for an all too common reason. Nearly all good ideas of this sort are driven by the selfless dedication of a very small number of people, in this case hardly more than two or three. Energies are bound to run down, work and family concerns are bound to exert pressure and enthusiasms can become eroded. There needs to be recognition of the real pressures of driving an ambitious project like this and some sort of 'succession planning' put in place. Bill Bruce and Elliott Davies, both alas now gone, did the Edinburgh jazz scene proud, and were to do so again, but what a pity some of us did not read the clear warning signs that they were feeling the pressure. Some of us could have pitched in with a bit of help or even an offer to take over the show for a while, allowing them to ease out, at least temporarily. However, Jazz News came to an end, as all good things do, and it has to be said, there would soon be other signs that the boom years were passing too.

There was another jazz punter driven initiative in the late 1990s. Again it involved Elliott Davies but this time in partnership with another loyal and long-term supporter of the Edinburgh jazz scene, Roy MacGregor. By 1997, the EIJF had been around for about eighteen years and, not unnaturally, there had been a number of changes in both direction and format. Mike Hart was still at the helm but it had been necessary to add a number of others to the festival board, including Assembly Direct as co-promoters, and there was no doubt that the proportion of more modern and contemporary jazz had increased. It was in 1997 too that the jazz festival was to restyle itself the Edinburgh International Jazz and Blues Festival (EIJBF), although a separate Blues Festival had run in tandem with the EIJF for year or two prior to this. In addition to new influences on policy and programming, the part played by the local traditional jazz bands was now less prominent and there seems to have been a fear that, with the withdrawal of the McEwan's sponsorship in the mid-1990s, the free pub trail would be very much diminished or even disappear completely. This seems to have been a realistic fear as the 1995 EIJF had included a McEwan's Pub Trail with seven venues all offering free admission and both lunch time and evening sessions whereas, by 1997, the EIJF had replaced the free pub trail with two free outdoor events, the Commonwealth Mardi Gras in the Grassmarket and the Commonwealth Jazz on a Summer's Day, set around the Ross Theatre in Princes Street Gardens.

Concerned and unhappy about these changes, the energetic Davies and MacGregor set out to demonstrate that there was still a large number of faithful supporters who wanted to listen to the local bands in free venues and that they would turn up in sufficient numbers to keep the publicans happy. Accordingly, a mini-festival was set up to run concurrently with the EIJBF, offering a programme of ten bands playing in a couple of venues, both free of charge. The two venues were the Caley Sample Room, formerly the Blue Lagoon and a year-round jazz pub, and the Royal Ettrick Hotel, only a short walk from the Sample Room and another regular jazz venue. The programme was quite ambitious in that it was to run over eight days from the 4th to the 10th of August, and the organisers managed to book most of the local traditional bands. Those who played in the mini-festival that year were the Spirits of Rhythm, Bill Salmond's Louisiana Ragtime Band, Jim Baikie's Jim-jammers, Dr McJazz, the St Stephen Street Stompers, Le Jazz Hot, the Dave Keir Jazztet, Charlie McNair's Jazz Band, the Diplomats of Jazz, Bill Marshall's Dixie Elastic Band and a twelve-piece band put together by bass player Fred Murray. In addition, there was the Tweed Valley Jazz Band from the Borders and a special guest appearance of a group of Sengalese Drummers.

The Caledonian Brewery had been approached and chipped in with a form of sponsorship which took the shape of kegs of their beer provided free to the venues, the sale of which which helped pay for the bands. Further support without charge came from reeds man Ian Boyter, a graphic designer to trade, who provided the art work for the programme free, as a gesture of support. The printed programme stated that *'Our aim is to offer traditional jazz free, during the official Edinburgh Jazz Festival'* and was headed up the 'Sizzling Summer Festival of Jazz'. There was also a further statement which said *'Jazz in Edinburgh owes a large debt to Sandy Brown and Al Fairweather in*

490

particular. Many of their contemporaries are playing in the bands listed here and our hope is that the music will inspire future musicians'. Although there were only evening sessions, the venture was popular and very well supported and was a definite success.

Encouraged by their first venture, the organisers put on a second program in 1998, this time billed as the Edinburgh Jazzcrawl, and again supported by the Caledonian Brewery. In the programme blurb, the previous year was justifiably celebrated by the organisers who said *'Last year we were delighted by the support the venture received. You seemed very happy and filled the venues'.* There was a change in the venues with the Gillsland Hotel replacing the Royal Ettrick and the addition of a third venue, this being W J Christie's, a pub in the West Port, near the Grassmarket. The Jazzcrawl ran over nine days between 31st July and 8th August and featured seventeen bands, including many of the previous year's participants. Newcomers included Alan Quinn's Templehall Stompers, the Yelly Dug Jazz Band, Fay Levey and her Quartet and the Maid of the Forth All Stars. The new venue W J Christie's apparently did not attract quite the support of the other two, perhaps because it was not within walking distance of the others and also because it featured pay-at-the-door events on the first two evenings. In spite of the odd hiccup, the Jazzcrawl was a success, just like its predecessor of 1997, and was again well supported. However, that was to be the end of the experiment and, indeed, it seems very clear that there was never any intention of establishing a long-term rival to the EIJF. The principle objective had been to demonstrate that traditional jazz played in pubs, mostly by the local bands, remained a major draw and, satisfied that they had achieved this, Elliott Davies and Roy MacGregor left it at that.

There is no doubt at all that the free pub trail had been a very popular part of the EIJF but it has to be remembered that it was only free as far as the punters were concerned; the bands still had to be paid. It only existed because of the support and sponsorship of major brewers and it appears that, from the brewer's point of view, it ran at a loss. As we have already noted, a large turnout and a packed lounge does not necessarily mean that there is an equivalent increase in the bar sales. However, Elliot Davies and Roy MacGregor were happy that a point had been made and, even if there would be no return to the heady days of a free pub trail with a generous scattering of venues all over the City, traditional jazz and the local bands would continue to play their part in the future EIJFs, although it was to be the early 2000s before there was much evidence of this. Elliot Davies, endlessly supportive follower of Edinburgh traditional jazz, whose characteristic laugh could so often be heard ringing out even over the sound of a jazz band in full cry, died in the summer of 2010 and a band organized by Bob McDowell played at his funeral.

The name of the Ayrshire trumpeter Mike Daly has already appeared in this chapter, as has that of reeds player John Burgess. These two would eventually get together in a band set up by John Burgess in 2009, the Nova Scotia Jazz Band, the third Edinburgh based band of that name after the 1950s band started by George Crockett and the 1970s version, which had been an off-shoot of the Old Bailey band and played in the Hailes House Hotel. **John Burgess (reeds)** was born in Haddington on the 25th of August 1967 and attended James Gillespie's High School in Edinburgh, between 1979 and '84. Although he was to make a relatively late start as a jazz musician, his interest in jazz had a solid background through his mother Frances, who had been Alex Welsh's girlfriend throughout his years in Edinburgh, the two of them having got together even before Alex met up with Archie Semple and joined Archie's band. Frances had been very much immersed in Edinburgh jazz, through her friendship with Alex, and had known all the 1950s jazz crowd and, although they had drifted apart, had remained friends with Alex right up to time of his death in 1982. She had kept what John calls *'a small but select'* LP collection which included recordings by the likes of Fats Waller, Louis Armstrong, Muggsy Spannier and Jelly Roll Morton, in addition to the recordings of the Alex Welsh band. John Burgess's interest in jazz stemmed from that of his mother and, by 1982 at the age of fifteen, he had volunteered as a helper at the Edinburgh International Jazz Festival.

This was during what many would consider to have been the apogee of the EIJF and gave John the chance to hear many great jazzers at close range. He was particularly taken by the playing of Buddy Tate, Warren Vache and Earle Warren but also recalls with great admiration bands such as Kusbandet, the Hot Antic, the New Black Eagle and the Swedish Jazz Kings, all of which had a major effect on him. He was also an eager listener to the recordings and stories of the Edinburgh jazz greats from the 1950s, which he describes as having been a huge thing for him and his future in jazz. In 1985, when he was seventeen, John managed to procure a clarinet, courtesy of Mike Hart, and from another source, a plastic alto saxophone. He had, in fact, intended to take up the cornet but the secondhand model on which he had his eye in Mev Taylor's shop had been sold when he went back and he was persuaded to buy the alto sax instead. John made the typical jazzer's self-taught start but also took a few lessons from Gordon Cruikshank and reinforced his early learning by transcribing solos from sheet music.

John made a start to his active music career after only a few weeks of playing, when he formed a band with Alex Poots, who now runs the Manchester Festival. I remember him turning up at the 1986 EIFJ young musician's competition in 1987, a year when I was on the judging panel. Once again demonstrating my nerdish tendencies, I still have my notes from that occasion from which I see that the nineteen year old John, by this time playing tenor sax, was leading a quartet called 'Jazz Monk'. I had also jotted down that he played '...very measured, confident tenor' and also displayed confidence in his presentation. There was stiff competition among the more modern youthful presentations that year in the form of the young trumpeter Colin Steele fronting another quartet, 'First Light'. Regarding Colin, I had noted '...very good trumpet with a nice tone and little vibrato' and his '...good, fat tone and smooth execution on flugelhorn'. Both John Burgess and Colin Steele were, of course, to go on to notable success in jazz and I cringe now to think that I once sat in judgement on them but, no matter how convenient it would be, none of us can really escape our past!

The programme for that youth jazz competition included the information that John was already gravitating between Edinburgh and London and, also in 1987, he was to move full time to London. There he played and recorded with many top notch jazz names, too many to list in full but including Alan Skidmore, Jim Mullen, Maggie Nichols, Roy Williams, Forrie Cairns and Brian Kellock. He also appeared at festivals and clubs in Spain, Germany, Finland, Sweden, Denmark, Norway, Italy, the Czech Republic, North Africa and the Middle East and, in 1989, his trio won the prestigious NFMS Special Concert Artist Award.

The boy from Haddington was certainly going places fast and, in 1994, he left London to study under George Garzone at the Berklee School of Music in Boston, USA and also took private tuition from Jerry Bergonzi. This was followed by a move across the USA to San Francisco, where he studied with Joe Henderson, before moving north to Seattle and then settling in Vancouver. A return to Edinburgh in the later 1990s saw John put in four years with Hamish McGregor's Fat Sam's Band, where he sat alongside another great Edinburgh reeds man, Jack Duff, and took part in a couple of recordings[197]. He also did some work with a band put together by pianist Ralph Laing which, as John has noted, *'..happily included Al Fairweather'*. John returned permanently to the UK and Edinburgh in 2005, where he became briefly a member of Bill Salmond's Louisiana Ragtime Band and free lanced with a number of well-established Edinburgh jazzers, including Gus Ferguson, Martin Foster, Tom Finlay and Hamish McGregor, as well as playing with Edinburgh's famous blues man, Tam White with whom he stayed until Tam's untimely death in 2010.

Talking with John Burgess in 2011 was to discover a man who had played in an impressive spectrum of musical styles. Apart from playing with his own groups and the bands mentioned above, he had also played improvised music with 'GIO', smooth jazz with 'Blue Soul Groove', modern classical music with 'Music from the Brewhouse' and post bop jazz with the 'Chris Wallace Quartet'. He had also collaborated with stellar names such as the New York

---

[197] See discography appendix

494

pianist and Hammond organ player Gary Valente and bassist John Webber. In addition to all of that, in 2009 he formed the afore-mentioned Nova Scotia Jazz Band which included Mike Daly on trumpet, Duncan Findlay on guitar and banjo and first Roy Percy and then Ken Macdonald on bass. With John Burgess's jazz history in mind, it may seem surprising that this band played in the classic jazz tradition but it was obvious from speaking with John that his regard for jazz was exceptionally wide in its range. He nominated, in chronological order, his jazz influences as Muggsy Spannier, Wild Bill Davison, Archie Semple, Ben Webster, Johnny Hodges and Zoot Sims, a solid and impressive set of milestone musicians in jazz history. He spoke of his admiration for the playing of Dave Paxton, as well as that of the other big names of 1940s/50s Edinburgh jazz. It was clear that he had retained a huge regard for the Alex Welsh band, in whose footsteps the Nova Scotia Jazz Band followed. Indeed, John confirmed that he had based his clarinet playing on that of Archie Semple, the great Edinburgh clarinetist who made his name with the early Alex Welsh band of fond memory. He also spoke of his pride in belonging to a town that had produced, not only the core of the Welsh band but '...guys like Sandy Brown, Al Fairweather, Stan Greig, Dave Keir et al' and, successful modern player though he most certainly is, there was not the slightest doubt about his sincerity. At the time of writing in 2011, John has recorded over seventy times as a 'side man' and has issued seven albums as a leader. With all this behind him and every sign of a long and promising career to come, John Burgess is a worthy name in the long list of high class jazz musicians from the Edinburgh area, a man with a deep knowledge of and respect for jazz of all eras.

Now we come to something of a rarity in Edinburgh traditional jazz; a jazz musician who was born as late as 1987! **Jack Wilson (drums)** must have got heartily sick of constantly being referred to as 'Young Jack Wilson', as if he had been baptized that way, but the truth was that, by the age standards of Edinburgh traditional jazz, he seemed virtually embryonic when he first appeared. Jack was born on 8th May 1987 and was educated at Woodlands High

School and then its replacement, Braes High School, both in Falkirk. There was little in the way of jazz to be heard around his home although his parents, who were young in the 1960s, provided him with plenty of exposure to 1960s music, such as that of the Beatles, the Hollies and Rod Stewart. In addition, his relatively rural environment also provided plenty of Ceilidh and Scottish Country Dance music, plus what Jack has called *'a liberal sprinkling of bits and pieces like Val Doonican and Kenneth McKellar'*. Not perhaps the most promising background for a future traditional jazzer but Jack believes that this eclectic musical hotch-potch may well have made him a bit more open minded about music than most of his contemporaries.

His opportunity to start playing drums came in his second year at high school but only because it was a part of the syllabus for S2 students in music, not because he had sought it out. In fact, Jack considers that, if the opportunity had not presented itself in this way, it is quite likely that he would never have played drums. As it was, he turned out to have something of a flair for the instrument and, with an offer of free tuition for Standard Grade students of music, he was able to continue through his third and fourth years and, for three years, he received tuition from Stewart Blackwood, who taught percussion around the Falkirk schools.

Jack's first contact with jazz came through, of all unlikely institutions, the Church of Scotland. Innes Duncan, a family friend and a member of Torphichen Kirk, had organized a band to give young people in the church a chance to play. Amongst them were Innes Duncan's two daughters, each of whom played an instrument and both of whom went with their father to Monday evening sessions in Linlithgow, run by Bob McDowell, to give youngsters the chance to try their hand at playing jazz. Jack soon found himself with an invitation to go along with the Duncan family to one of these sessions. This was the first time young Jack (there I go again) was to play this kind of music and he had no idea what to expect. As a result, he went along with only a pair of drumsticks and ended up battering away on a collection of instrument cases! In attendance at the session, were Tom Bryce, Andrew Lauder and banjo player Hans Koal, all giving up their time to encourage these fortunate youngsters to take an interest in traditional jazz. It was as a result of these sessions that Jack was given the chance to play at the Linlithgow Jazz Club's Christmas party, when he sat in with the West End band on Malcolm Brown's drum kit. Jack was fourteen years old at the time.

His first proper gig was when he was asked to dep for Kenny Milne with the West End band at Gardening Scotland, a horticultural show at the Royal Highland Show ground at Ingliston. He must have done well on his debut because he continued to dep for Kenny over the next year or so and was also given every chance to sit in on Kenny's kit at the Jazz Club. Later, when Kenny stood down from the West End band, Jack was taken on as their regular drummer. Asked about highlights of his years with the band, he picked out gigs when he played with star guests trumpeters Duke Hietger and Bob Barnard and pianist Jeff Barnhart, saying he would be glad to play with them every day, as indeed would most of us. Playing with another fine trumpeter, Enrico Tomasso, in a show at the Falkirk Town Hall was another special gig.

I was interested to hear what Jack had to say about his influences and was not all that surprised when he named, not contemporary rock or jazz drummers, but two jazz drummers representative of earlier styles and from very different environments. One was Gene Krupa, the great Chicagoan who made his name with the Benny Goodman band, picked out by Jack for his endlessly hard-working but not intrusive playing, especially when with the smaller combos, such as the Goodman trios and quartets or the famous McKenzie and Condon Chicagoans. Jack's other influence came from Edinburgh's own Kenny Milne, Dean of New Orleans drummers, to whose playing Jack had listened through his formative years. He could hardly have had a better model and, to this day, Kenny remains someone to whom Jack looks up and whose approval matters to him. Another influence, although not from a drummer, came from banjo player Harald Vox, who put in a number of years with the West End band. At a band rehearsal Harald, fairly unceremoniously, pointed out to Jack just how loudly he was playing and advised that he should cut down the volume pronto. Thereafter Harald, a kindly and considerate individual, continued to encourage Jack to play in a light manner, something for which Jack remains grateful, commenting that he regularly receives compliments from musicians and punters alike, on his ability play quietly. Quite rightly, Jack values such compliments, saying that he would much rather be perceived as a quiet, sensitive player than a portable Blitzkrieg!

Later in his career but still only in his late teens and early twenties, Jack was to join the throng of cross-country travellers, playing in Glasgow with Hugh Muldoon's Jazz and Blues Band in 2005/06 and Davie Wilson's Uptown Shufflers from 2006, while continuing to play with the West End Jazz Band in Linlithgow. Jack is one of the very few recruits from his generation to join the Edinburgh traditional jazz scene. He rapidly gained a deserved reputation as a fine drummer and, by the end of the first decade of the new century, this was reflected in invitations to dep with established Edinburgh bands such as Bill Salmond's Louisiana Ragtime Band, the Maid of the Forth Stompers, Swing Supreme, Mike Hart's Scottish All Stars and John Burgess' Nova Scotia Jazz Band. Jack's career and progress in jazz, with early encouragement at school, the opportunity provided through the church youth activities and then further chances arising via Bob McDowell's sterling work in West Lothian, demonstrate just what can be done to stimulate interest in jazz, even among youngsters in the early twenty first century. However, if traditional jazz is to thrive in the future, there is no doubt that we will need many more like Jack Wilson, not the least of whose contributions to the Edinburgh jazz scene has been to reduce the average age of any band in which he plays by a fair number of years!

Chapter XVII

I Can't Get Finished

The importance of the contributions to jazz of Sandy Brown and Al Fairweather, not just in Edinburgh but internationally, had long been recognised and was well documented in jazz literature. However, by the mid-1990s and with both Sandy and Al by then gone, there was still no formal mark of their achievements in their native city. It was to take the initiative and energy of a Swansea based clarinet player and long time admirer of Sandy's playing to get things moving. He was, of course, Dr John Latham and he wrote to The Scotsman newspaper on 12 June 1996. In his letter, he pointed out that Sandy was *'arguably the most original and innovative British post-war jazz musician'* and added that *'Together with Al Fairweather and Stan Grieg he revolutionised British jazz when he left Edinburgh for London in the mid-1950s'*. Latham then went on to make the case for some form of memorial saying *'...there is no memorial to him in his home town, no museum, no archive, statue, not even a plaque. Is it not time that the jazz fraternity in Scotland planned a suitable scheme in his memory?'*[198] It did not take long for others to express their support and, by the end on the month, Jack Duff, Janol Scott and Dickie Alexander had all written in to the paper.

Clearly not a man to let things slide, John Latham invited anyone interested in the proposal to meet with him

---

[198] SBS Newsletter No 1, July 1996, from letter of John Latham to 'The Scotsman', 12 June 1996

in the bar of the Royal Circus Hotel (previously the Glencairn Hotel) on Saturday 3 August 1996, when he was to be in Edinburgh. This meeting was a great success, with a good turnout including, amongst many others, Sandy's widow, Flo' Brown, and his old colleagues, Stan Grieg and Bob Craig. Dickie Alexander, a recently retired City Councillor, had persuaded the Lord Provost to take an interest and, after the 3rd of August meeting, a committee was formed with the resounding title of 'The Lord Provost's Sandy Brown Memorial Society'. Members who attended the first meeting of the committee were Dickie Alexander (appointed secretary and later, chairman), Bob Craig, Stuart Crockett, Sandy Currie, Mike Hart, Charles 'Dizzy' Jackson, Ralph Laing and Janol Scott, with apologies from Flo' Brown, D Kerr, A Rowan, and D Michie. Others who subsequently joined the committee were Dave Keir, Jack Duff and David Michie, the emeritus Professor of painting from the Edinburgh College of Art. Rightly and logically, it was agreed that the memorial would refer to both Sandy and Al Fairweather, and not Sandy alone. Further meetings followed and a bank account was set up for donations.

After considering several options, it was decided that a plaque would be the most fitting memorial. There were extensive discussions about where the plaque should be placed and various locations were discussed, including the frontage of the India Buildings, which had been the location of an early Edinburgh jazz club, the frontage of the Oddfellow's Hall, where so many jazz events had taken place, and the site of the long-gone West End Cafe in Shandwick Place, where the Brown band had held a lengthy residency. However, a near unanimous decision was taken that the Usher Hall, scene of the famous concert in 1953 when the Brown band shared the bill with Big Bill Broonzy, was where the plaque should be placed. Dickie Alexander's efforts ensured that this was approved by the town council, who were also prepared to rename one of the bars in the Usher Hall, 'The Sandy Brown Bar'. The design of the plaque was offered for tender and various designs were considered. Under the guidance of David Michie, a design submitted by the Edinburgh College of Art, the work of a talented Greek mature student called Stavroula Fylachtou, was selected.

Funds were raised by a group of jazzers, led by Jack Duff, who collected during the 1997 Edinburgh International Jazz Festival. Several generous individual donations were received, including one from David Binns on behalf of Sandy's former acoustic consultancy practice, Sandy Brown Associates. Stan Greig with Roger Horton, the owner of London's famous jazz venue The 100 Club, organised an evening at the club, when 16 members of Stan's London Jazz Big Band played, without payment, and the entire door takings were given to the fund. The Royal High School Former Pupils Association wished to make a donation but, after discussion, agreed to fund a replica plaque to be placed in the school. A large number of small donations were also received from the general public, demonstrating the wide-spread regard for and pride in, the work of Sandy and Al.

By February 1998, not only was the plaque ready but Paul Adams, of Lake Records in Workington, had issued a CD of the famous Usher Hall concert[199], the first time these recordings had been made available to the public. Furthermore, the fund raising efforts had been so successful that it was possible to have not two but three copies of the plaque made, one for the Usher Hall, one for the Royal High School and one for the '100 Club' in Oxford Street, London.

A problem arose in installing the Usher Hall plaque, as the building was effectively closed for three years for refurbishment, and, with this event delayed, the first plaque actually to be installed was the one at the Royal High School. This took place during the school musical concert in February 1998, when the plaque was unveiled by Flo' Brown. Stan Greig came up from London to attend and a band put together especially for the occasion played a programme that included many numbers associated with Sandy and Al. The band was organised by Ralph Laing, and included Charlie McNair (tpt), Dave Keir (tpt and tbn), Jack

---

[199] See discography Appendix, 'Sandy Brown – The Historic Usher Hall Concert 1952', Lake LACD94

Graham (clt), Jack Duff (rds), Mike Hart (bjo and gtr), Dizzy Jackson (bs) and Bill Strachan (drms). The 100 Club plaque was unveiled at a second session by Stan Grieg's London Jazz Big Band on 5th June of the same year and a large contingent from Scotland made the trip to London for the celebrations. After a lengthy delay, the Usher Hall plaque was finally put in place at a short unveiling ceremony on 1st August 2001. Since then, there has been a further closure of the Usher Hall for major refurbishment and, when I enquired about the plaque in April 2010 with a view to photographing it, it was to discover that this would not be possible as it was not there. However, I was assured that it was safely stored in the meantime at the City Arts Centre and would be re-installed in the Usher Hall in due course.

**Sandy Brown 1929-1975, Al Fairweather 1927-1993
In memory of their contribution to music
(photograph by the author 2011)[200]**

---

[200] This photograph was taken at the City Arts Centre, Edinburgh, in January 2012, by kind permission of David Patterson, Curator of Fine Art. It was expected that the plaque would be returned to the Usher Hall in the near future.

It is extremely satisfying that Sandy's and Al's music was recognised in this way. Satisfying too, that in celebrating their music with a memorial plaque in Scotland's premier concert hall, jazz itself was receiving notable recognition. It is to the great credit of all those who got involved, that the project came to such a successful conclusion. It is particularly to the credit of John Latham, without whose initiative nothing may have happened, and whose personal devotion to the music of Sandy and Al was to find further expression through his production of the Sandy Brown Society newsletters.

The cruise boat, Maid of the Forth, continued to feature jazz in its programme throughout the 1990s and on into the 2000s, the resident band, Maid of the Forth Stompers, playing for the general public rather than dedicated jazz followers. In the early 1990s, banjo player Harald Vox took Bill Salmond's place in the Stompers for a number of years and then he, in turn, gave way to Nigel Porteous. **Nigel Porteous (banjo, guitar, mandolin, bass guitar)** was born in Stirling on 24th July 1942 and, after primary school at Rumbling Bridge, attended Gordonstoun School near Aberdeen. From an early age, he had an ambition to be a jazz guitarist and, in pursuit of this, taught himself to play guitar and also mastered the mandolin. After leaving school, Nigel started work in the family business, a mill in Alva which manufactured Angora fine woollens. This led to him attending a two year full-time course at the Scottish Woollen Technical College in Galashiels, where he completed a City and Guilds certificate, but unfortunately, by the time he had finished his studies, the mill was on the point of closure. However, he was able to make use of his hard won certificate as it helped towards his acceptance into music school in Leeds, where he began a diploma course in jazz and light music.

Nigel had already made a start on playing in public while in the Stirling area, where he had played in local two-piece jazz groups in Bridge of Allan around 1970. While studying in Leeds, he soon found his way around the local music scene and was quickly into action, playing Irish music in the Leeds pubs, where his skills on guitar and mandolin brought him plenty of work. Also in Leeds, he played with a band called the Big Four, which was modelled on the Sydney Bechet and Muggsy Spannier recording group of the same name, and did some broadcasting with this band. He also toured with a sixteen piece band, the Gene Mayo Band, on the Locarno circuit, a gig for which he hastily had to learn to play the bass guitar. Although things were clearly going well in Leeds, an offer in 1973 to play at the Speakeasy Club in Hong Kong, brought his studies to an end and he never completed his music diploma.

Attracted by this chance to play music for a living, he set off for Hong Kong as part of a trio, which included a reeds and piano player called Mike Greensill. His original intention was to stay in Hong Kong for six months but in fact it stretched out to about twelve years, with a break of five years from 1979 to 1985, which he spent in Spain. While in Hong Kong, Nigel was soon recruited by the wonderfully named Kowloon Honkers, a band which, although basically a Dixieland band, also included some show band material in their repertoire. The Honkers was a professional seven-piece band and with them, Nigel was to play at the Sacramento Jazz Jubilee in California, in 1985 and 1988. It was while living in Hong Kong, that Nigel was 'discovered' as a cartoonist, after someone saw him drawing cartoons on beer mats. This led to quite a bit of work as a free lance and eventually to a full time job, working as a creative cartoonist for an advertising company. This was just about the only nine to five job this most laid-back of characters ever had. As a cartoonist, an occupation which he shared with a number of other jazzers including Humphrey Lyttleton , Wally 'Trog' Fawkes, Diz Disley and Monty Sunshine, he adopted the pen name of 'Nurgle'.

Nigel's five year Spanish interlude was spent with a four-piece band, with which he played at many festivals. The band was called Hotstrings and was made up of a jazz violinist, two guitarists and a bass player. Unfortunately, Spain being outwith the European Common market at that time, the band was not allowed to be paid for any of their work and they found themselves playing numerous festival and pub gigs for nothing.

Nigel returned from Hong Kong to Scotland in 1989, settling in Edinburgh, where he soon established himself as a teacher of music, covering the various guitar styles, banjo and mandolin. A player of his calibre was never going to be without gigs for long and he soon picked up work with a band run by the trombonist Paul Munro. This band, which included Jack Graham on clarinet and Roy Percy on bass, had a residency at the Pilton Inn, out near Bonnyrigg and this was soon followed by work for Nigel with the Esk Valley Swing Band. In addition, Nigel himself formed the Bald Eagle Quartet, a band which had clarinet, guitar, bass and drums and played in the manner of the Benny Goodman small groups of the 1930s. The Bald Eagle band played at the Goblin Ha' Inn in Gifford and in the downstairs bar of the Haymarket Station Bar, where they were soon drawing in a respectable number of punters. The upstairs lounge of the Haymarket Station Bar, of course, had been the location of the renowned Basin Street, one of Edinburgh's best ever jazz venues. A change of ownership had brought the Basin Street jazz activity to an end, a move greatly regretted by many Edinburgh Jazzers. However, the success of the Bald Eagle Quartet in the downstairs bar soon persuaded the owners to think again. It was not long before they decided to re-open the jazz venue and were again in the market for jazz bands. Given that it was the success of the Bald Eagle band that had had sparked the re-birth of Basin Street, it was a shade unfortunate that they found themselves unemployed in the reshuffle, the owners deciding that there services were no longer required!

However, for Nigel at least, help was at hand. A near-by pub, the Haymarket Bar on the corner between West Maitland Street and Morrison Street, also featured jazz and their current attraction was Violet Milne's excellent New Orleans styled Spirits of Rhythm. Nigel went along to listen and was soon invited to sit in with band. This led to him depping when required and then, when Brian Weld dropped out, he became a member of the band. Nigel followed this same pattern with the Maid of the Forth Stompers, firstly depping with them on the cruise boat and then, in about 1996, joining the band on a permanent basis. For a number of years he continued, as had been agreed, to give the Spirits first preference when gigs clashed and this arrangement worked well but, in 2002, he left the Spirits and the Maid of the Forth Stompers became his main band.

Gradually he was persuaded to bring his guitar as well as his banjo to gigs and if at first he was a bit reluctant to do this, it was only because it involved him carrying much more gear around. However, his guitar playing vastly increased the band's scope and it soon became an essential ingredient of the band's style. Not one to push himself forward, he rather diffidently began to bring some of his original tunes along to band practices and these, together with some originals contributed by Andrew Lauder, were soon added to the repertoire, adding greatly to the individuality of the band. Nigel was a fertile source of entertainment for his fellow bandsmen. At one gig, his guitar suddenly ceased to function and, after a bit of investigation, it was discovered that it needed the battery in its pre-amp replaced. He briefly struggled to change the battery but, defeated by the technical intricacies of the task, he gave it up as a bad job, switched to banjo for the rest of the gig and put the new battery in his pocket. When we were clearing up at the end of the gig, there were sudden shrieks, indicative of pain, panic and consternation, from the banjo section. The battery had shorted out on the bunch of keys in his pocket, had become almost red hot and all but set him on fire. The clarinetist Ian Boyter tells the story of returning from a gig in the Sheraton Hotel with Nigel in the car. All the way home, Nigel grumbled that he was uncomfortable, his jacket felt very tight and he thought he must have put on weight. When Ian dropped him off at his house, there was a sudden outbreak of Nigel-type consternation and panic as he realized that the jacket he was wearing was not his. Not only was it not his, it was quite obviously a woman's garment, the sleeves finishing half was down his forearms. Ian had to take him back to the hotel where his furtive method of switching the jackets left him fortunate not to attract the attention of the security staff.

After Jimmy Shortreed stopped playing after the 2001 season, there were three or four years when the clarinet chair in the Maid of the Forth Stompers had no fixed incumbent. Mostly, it was Ian Boyter and George Duncan who played but, good players though they were, the band was unsettled. Used to a regular line-up, the band, after Jimmy Shortreed had retired, was unable to develop a new band sound because of the constant changes. Determined to do something about this, I discussed the situation with Andrew Lauder and came to the sad conclusion that there was no one currently available that we could approach. I then remembered Bill Salmond's ingenious method of recruiting – if there was no one around suitable or available, you had to invent someone! It was then that the name **Gerard Dott** came to mind. Gerard had not played since 1987 or thereabouts and had, in the meantime, moved away from Edinburgh, to Eddleston in the Scottish Borders. This seemed not all that far away and, in a spirit of optimism, I took myself off to Eddleston and broached with him the idea of a long-overdue return to active playing. I told him not to give me an answer right away but to think about it and I would phone him at the end of the week. When I phoned him, not at all sure what his response would be, I asked him if he had thought about my proposal. His response was *'I've been practicing all week!'* This was in March 2006 and, with the Maid of the Forth season getting under-weigh at the end of April and Easter holidays intervening, we had little time to get together in advance. In the end, we only managed a single run through and that was only possible because the first of the season's gigs on the boat was cancelled. This meant that Gerard was pitched into action with little chance to become familiar with our material or build up his playing stamina. However, he managed very well and, by the middle of May was back in full swing, as if he had never been away.

The band soon began to settle into a new sound and, over the next few years, developed a repertoire of less usual material, much of it dressed up a little with simple 'top and tail' arrangements. Gerard was responsible for coming up with some of the ideas for new numbers and arrangements and his arrival stimulated a much needed burst of energy in the rest of us, and not only in expanding the musical side. Previously content to have busy summers on the boat and quiet winters, Gerard's arrival had me scuttling about, busily seeking out winter gigs. The Maid of the Forth

507

Stompers joined the band rota at the Edinburgh Jazz and Jive Club, a new Edinburgh venture of which we will hear shortly, and eventually even found a pub residency, at the Grey Horse Inn in Balerno. This was a tiny place and was packed if we managed to attract more than about a dozen listeners. I reckoned that I had found the secret. Back in the early 1980s with the Scottish Jazz Advocates, on two evenings a week, we had regularly filled to capacity an enormous lounge in the Caledonian Hotel at the West End of Princes Street. Nearly thirty years later, I could still boast that we were playing to packed houses, it was just that the venue was a bit smaller. It was a cozy and enjoyable gig with a great atmosphere but it was perhaps a bit unfortunate that the band appeared on the pub website as the Maids of the Forth! The band was also expanded to a six-piece line-up for some on–shore gigs (there was no room for more than four on the boat), bringing in drums and on trombone, George Howden, a recent returner from the south. Winters, thanks to Gerard, were suddenly a lot less like a period of hibernation for the Maid of the Forth Stompers but it was gratifying to reverse the gradual loss of active jazzers and bring back a creatively original clarinet player who should never have been away.

Dave Keir had spent the years, since his return to Edinburgh in the 1980s, mostly playing the instrument on which he had made his name, the trombone. However, he had always considered himself to be a multi-instrumentalist and, sometime in the mid-1990s, he decided to concentrate on his cornet playing. The switch was highly successful and, in no time at all, he had established himself as a technically accomplished and very hot cornetist, making early appearances on this instrument with the Capital Jazz Band. Dave was of course, an extremely experienced jazz musician, in spite of a twenty year break while pursuing his career in teaching, and it soon became clear that he had definite ideas about the type of jazz he wanted to play. This he describes, in his profile on the Sandy Brown Jazzwebsite[201], as being the classic jazz of the 1895 to 1930 New Orleans period (which more or less accords with the

---

[201] http://sandybrownjazz.co.uk/profiledavekeir.html

definition of classic jazz used in this book) and, in 1998, he put together a band designed to play in that style.

In keeping with his chosen model, Dave called the band the **Dave Keir Hot Four** and its original membership was Dave on cornet, with Bob Busby (rds), Jock Westwater (bjo) and Dave's fellow veteran, Dizzy Jackson (bs). The band was immediately successful and was soon into action with residencies at pubs in Rose Street, one of which was Ma Scott's. They were also soon in recording action and, in the autumn of 1999, produced a CD called 'Stomp Stomp Stomp'. This was followed by a second CD, recorded in late 2000 and early 2001, which appeared as 'Redman Blues'. Both of these recordings[202] featured the original line-up and also a taste of Dave's instrumental versatility, with him playing cornet and trombone on the first and cornet, trombone and alto-sax on the second of the CDs. As an interesting side-line, Dave and Dizzy Jackson also got together with two jazzers who were in town for the EIJF. These were George Washingmachine (real name George Washington) from Sydney, who played violin, and a colleague from Dave's London days, the famous guitarist Diz Disley, and a private recording was made for posterity in Jock Westwater's flat. The recording took place the day after the dedication of the plaque in memory of Sandy Brown and Al Fairweather, which means that it was recorded on 2nd August 2001, and it was issued as 'Old Friends and New'[203].

Bob Busby left the Dave Keir band around 2004, when he was replaced on reeds by Jock Westwater's brother, Mike Westwater. Mike got a call from Jock (at one o'clock in the morning!) offering him the chance to join the band and Mike accepted. The band became the **Dave Keir Hot Five** when, at Mike Westwater's suggestion, the Borders based trombone player Gordon Melrose came in. With this line-up, the band continued well into the 2000s and they made appearances at various jazz festivals, including those at Peebles, Keswick, Hawick, Kirkcudbright and the EIJF. Mike Westwater recalls that when the multi-

---

[202] See discography appendix
[203] See discography appendix

instrumentalist, Keith Nicholls, perhaps best known for leading the Midnight Follies Orchestra, came as a soloist to play in Edinburgh, he specifically asked to be accompanied by the Dave Keir Hot Five. Sadly for the Edinburgh jazz scene, the playing of this hot and popular band was to be curtailed by Dave's decision, in about 2006, to move to the south west of England, to be near his family. Dave made a determined attempt to continue to run the band from the south and, although Mike Westwater dropped out to be replaced by Andy Hampton, for a number of years they continued to get together occasionally to play at the Jazz and Jive Club in Edinburgh.

Mike Westwater (reeds), brother of the banjo and guitar playing Jock, was born in Edinburgh on 16th November 1943, educated at Daniel Stewart's College and was to make his living as a civil and structural engineer. He became interested in skiffle and American folk music in his early teens and, after having made himself a guitar, someone gave him a banjo. His uncle had a vast collection of 78 rpm records and, while baby-sitting for his younger cousins, Mike heard his first jazz recordings. His uncle obviously had good taste in jazz, as some of the recordings Mike heard were by the Louis Armstrong Hot Five and Jelly Roll Morton. He then began listening to Acker Bilk's band, which he preferred to that of Chris Barber. However, he soon returned to earlier jazz, seeking out recordings from King Oliver to early Duke Ellington, quickly realizing that he preferred this type of jazz to that of the New Orleans Revival and the British trad bands. He also developed an interest in the music of the Quintet of the Hot Club of France, the wonderful continental band featuring the violin of Stephane Grapelli and the scintillating guitar of Django Reinhardt. Clearly inspired by the latter, Mike played rhythm guitar in a group that included a school friend, **Kenny Ramage (Guitar)**, whom Mike describes as a brilliant guitarist in the Django style. It should be pointed out that this was not the trombone playing Ken Ramage, whom we have already met earlier in this book. I, too, remember the guitar playing Kenny Ramage and he certainly was a very fine player, although I have no idea what became of him and have heard nothing of him for many years. Apart from his own playing experiences, the first live jazz that Mike remembers hearing locally was that of Old Bailey's Jazz Advocates at the Place in Victoria Street and Charlie McNair's band at the Crown Bar.

Mike asked his father for a clarinet for his sixteenth birthday and, his father duly obliging, he proceeded to teach himself to play by listening to 78 rpm recordings of Benny Goodman. He also developed his knowledge of chords from his earlier guitar playing and, aware of the importance of chord structure, cajoled brother Jock into playing the banjo as an accompaniment to his clarinet playing. Apparently, Jock was very reluctant at first but eventually became keen and, of course, went on to establish himself as a long term fixture on the Edinburgh jazz scene. Mike's father, acting on advice from an Edinburgh dance band trumpeter called Frankie Smith who styled himself 'Scotland's Louis Armstrong', arranged for him to have lessons from Harry Laidig. Laidig apparently at that time ran a local Dixieland/Swing band with his sons, which Mike says had been heard by an impressed Charlie McNair. Although fairly informal, the lessons were clearly effective and Mike became a competent reader of written music. Looking back on this, Mike thinks that it was perhaps a 'bum steer' because it drew him into a habit of transcribing solos played by others, rather than simply trying to play them as part of the learning process.

While still at school, Mike began playing clarinet with others of similar musical persuasion who lived nearby, including brother Jock, reeds man George Duncan and Jimmy Elliot, who would go on to play drums with several Edinburgh jazz bands. At University, Mike became friendly with Gerard Dott, who turned up in one of his classes and who invited him to sit in with the Mound City Jazz Band, by then mostly made up of students from the Royal Dick Veterinary College. Mike joined this band, playing both banjo and soprano sax. This was his first saxophone, which cost him £7 10/- (£7. 50 pence in today's money). After a brief flirtation with the Climax band, in which he replaced Gerard Dott but was himself replaced by George Gilmour, Mike left Edinburgh for Argyll, where he played with a multi-purpose band called the Callum Ross Band.

Later, by now based in the Border country, Mike again got involved in jazz and was a founder member of the Borders Big Band and, in 2011, was one of only four original members, after thirty three years with them. The prime mover in this band was the late Dave Young who many Edinburgh jazzers will remember as an excellent trumpeter with the Hawick based Wooltown Jazz Band. Mike had become interested in transcribing and arranging music for the Big Band but, opportunities to play jazz solos being few, he decided to put together a traditional jazz band, which he called the Tweed Valley Jazz Band. Several jazzers active in Edinburgh played with this band at various times, including Jock Westwater, Bill Brydon, Symon Carlyle, Jim Petrie and Bev Knight and it played at festivals in Peebles, Hawick, Kirkcudbright and Keswick, where they recorded in 1997. At the time of writing in 2011, Mike Westwater continues to play with the Borders Big Band and study jazz theory and arranging.

A sad reflection of the passage of time was the fact that, by the late 1990s, the traditional jazz scene in Edinburgh was no longer in its former healthy state. There were, inevitably, fewer traditional jazz musicians still active, fewer supporters around and a consequent decrease in the numbers of bands and jazz gigs, especially in the pubs. Concerned about the situation, the Spirits of Rhythm band leader Violet Milne and jazz enthusiast and record collector Norrie Thomson came up with the idea of setting up a proper jazz club in Edinburgh. This was an innovative step, as the Edinburgh jazz public had been accustomed to having their jazz provided free in the pubs. No one knew what the reaction would be to a pay-at-the-door venture, which the new club would have to be to raise funds to cover their overheads.

In September 2000, the **Edinburgh Jazz and Jive Club** was launched, with the stated purpose of promoting the enjoyment of live traditional jazz in all its forms, whilst at the same time providing a platform for local bands to play on a regular basis. The club was constituted as a non-profit making body and was to be run by a committee of three office bearers and four club members. It was to meet on a weekly basis on Friday evenings from 8.00 to 11.30pm and would feature two local bands each week with a visiting band, that is a band from elsewhere, about once a month. Non-members would be welcome at a slightly higher door price and the club opened its doors in the function suite of the Fairmile Inn, on the city boundary near Fairmilehead. This venue allowed the club to make an encouraging start although, with its long, narrow shape which tended to make the band feel a little separated from the punters, it was not ideal. However, the club met there very successfully until December 2006 when, suddenly and with no warning, the venue closed down, leaving the club without a home. However, the club committee was swiftly into action and, by late December 2006, Heriots FP Rugby Club had offered the use of their clubhouse facilities at Goldenacre. The loss of the Fairmile Inn venue, at first regarded as something of a catastrophe, soon came to seen as a blessing in disguise. The Goldenacre location offered a modern, well set-up clubhouse, which could seat up to a hundred and forty, with a good sized dance floor and was soon welcomed by the club members as excellent for both listening and dancing.

Bands which played in the local band rota included the Spirits of Rhythm, Bill Salmond's Louisiana Ragtime Band, Jim Petrie's Diplomats of Jazz, Brian Robertson's Forth River Ragtimers, Dave Keir's Hot Five and Roger Hanley's Jazz Hounds. Later, after Roger Hanley retired from playing, the veteran bass player Fred Murray took over the latter band and, after re-naming it Fred's Club House Seven, continued in the rota. Another change came when Dave Keir left Edinburgh and the Maid of the Forth Stompers filled the gap, although only during the winter months, when their seasonal cruise boat commitments were in abeyance. A further addition came when some former members of the Climax Jazz Band got together and joined the rota as the Anti-Climax Jazz Band!

It seems ridiculous to write in this final chapter about a musician who was born in 1931 and had been involved in music in Edinburgh, including jazz, in the 1950s, but in fact, it was in the 2000s that **Fred Murray (bass, bass guitar, vocals)**, was to become more involved in the jazz scene than at any other time in his lengthy career. Fred was born in Southampton on 22nd November 1931 and, with his family, moved to Edinburgh in 1940, after they had left Southampton because of war time bombing. Initially educated at the Dean Park School in Southampton, he attended Tynecastle School in Edinburgh before joining and later running, the family tool shop business. Fred did his National Service around 1950 and it was during this period that his interest in music really began to develop, after listening to Country and Western Music on the American Forces Network (AFN), broadcasting from Germany. When he was about seventeen, he had taken up guitar, having some lessons from Bill Oliver, who taught in Rae MacIntosh's music shop and played in the band at the Cavendish Ballroom. After this, when he was about twenty and after deciding that the *guitar did not make enough noise* (presumably it was unamplified), he bought a double bass from Mev Taylor's shop and again had lessons from Bill Oliver.

Although taking an interest in the 1950s skiffle craze, it was dance band work in which Fred became involved but he also made his first move into the Edinburgh jazz scene in about 1954, playing for a while at the Condon Club in India Buildings. There he played in a band, which he recalls as the Chicagoans, with the drummer George Crockett and, on saxophone at the time, Dougie Campbell. Apparently, Fred played with this band in a jazz band competition in Glasgow, in which they were placed second. It was also around this time that I, then a mid-teens schoolboy, first came into contact with Fred. I was interested in skiffle and, with a group of pals, decided that we wanted to play the music. One of them, Colin Oswald, who was the only one of us who actually owned an instrument, happened to live next door to the Murrays in Balgreen Avenue. Strange groaning noises heard through the wall were eventually identified as Fred practicing his double bass in the bathroom next door, a room to which his practicing had been banished on the grounds that it put him as far away from the rest of his family as possible! Although I never played in a skiffle band with Fred, he was approached for advice about annoying details like tuning, advice which, if my memory serves me right, he very graciously provided.

Later dance work included a four year spell with pianist Bert Valentine's band in the Miltonhouse Hotel, a band in which all the music was played from written scores, followed by about seven years playing in the Golden Circle, in Bathgate. The strength of the dance band scene at that time can be judged by the fact that each of these gigs provided Fred with three evenings playing a week. In the 1960s and '70s, Fred continued to play dance music with musicians such as Bill Sinclair (gtr), Ian Reid (drms) and Freddy Martin but, like all the others, found dance band work drying up as the discos started to dominate. He did, however, play at the last televised local heat of the TV show Come Dancing, which was broadcast from the Palais. The Murray family was permitted to stay up to watch Dad on TV and were rewarded with a brief glimpse of Fred's feet.

Fred also played at the Beach Ballroom in Dunoon with the Bert Valentine Band, where they were on a bill that included Kenneth McKellar and Andy Stewart. Top of the bill was the show trumpeter, Eddie Calvert. It was in Dunoon that Fred found himself recruited to play for a week with the visiting Laurie Gold and his Pieces of Eight, a band which played a sort of orchestrated jazz and did a lot of radio work. Laurie was the brother of the more famous Harry Gold and Fred's opportunity came about through a typical piece of band business, the resident bass player apparently having been fired for having a clandestine affair with the singer, who was supposed to be the band leader's girlfriend.

The years rolled by with a scatter of gigs at some of the big Edinburgh hotels, such as the North British, the Royal British and the George, but in his spare time, Fred began to go along to the Basin Street jazz bar to listen to the Spirits of Rhythm, placing this in about the late 1970s or early '80s. The Spirits' bass player at the time was Robin Galloway and, when he left, Fred took his place. Later, he moved with band to the Haymarket Bar and was to stay with them for four or five years, including a trip to the Ascona Jazz Festival in Switzerland. After this there was a gap in Fred's playing career, when the bass was consigned to the attic, which was to continue until about the year 2000, when he was persuaded out of retirement to play with a band assembled by drummer Roger Hanley, to play at the newly opened Jazz and Jive Club. A few years later, when Roger Hanley packed in, Norrie Thompson of the Jazz and Jive Club, anxious not to lose a band from the rota, asked Fred to take it on and Fred said that he would. When asked by Norrie what the band was to be called, Fred told him he hadn't a clue, with the result that the band was christened by Norrie and appeared on the Club rota as Fred's Clubhouse Seven. There it has remained ever since, with a line-up of Kenny Milne (tpt), Bob Busby (rds), John Arthur (tbn), Kenny Henderson (bjo), Gus Mackay (pno), Helen Mackay (vocs) and Fred himself on bass. The band has issued a CD which may be found in the discography appendix. Fred Murray, veteran bass player and vocalist, remains one of the most generous people I have ever met, instantly offering a drink to everyone he meets, endlessly cheerful and as universally popular as ever, after a career in local music that has already lasted almost sixty years.

The Jazz and Jive Club had turned out well, regularly bringing in a respectable if not enormous crowd, perhaps as much attracted by the chance to dance as by the chance to listen. Over the years, the policy of booking guest bands also worked very well and many distinguished visiting bands were featured, some of them almost on an annual basis. The visiting bands policy was a far-reaching one and the guests included bands from Denmark, Sweden, Norway, Germany, France, the Netherlands, the USA, Australia, England and Ireland, as well as from other parts of Scotland. Some guests came as solo artistes including the singer Lillian Boutte and the fine guitarist Marty Grosz. The club also did its bit in supporting the EIJF by featuring guest bands on the two Fridays of the jazz festival each year. The Jazz and Jive Club deserves great credit for its efforts in bringing quality guest bands and individuals to Edinburgh, and for providing a regular venue for the local bands, as pub jazz slowly melted away.

Violet Milne was elected club president, an office she held until the Autumn of 2010, when she decided it was time to step down. It is greatly to the credit of Violet, Norrie Thomson and those who served on the club committee that the Jazz and Jive Club has been such a success. It was a forward looking plan in the first place, without any certainty of support, but it paid off handsomely. Although another unwelcome sign of the times was the increasing need for bands to share musicians, after ten years the club is still going strong. Lang may its lum reek.

The year 2003 marked the twenty fifth anniversary of the EIJF, that is twenty five counting from the festival of 1979 and not including the 1978 mini-festival, which was really just a sort of trial run. Early in the year, Mike Hart contacted me to ask if I would be willing to get involved in organizing a celebration concert to take place during the EIJF that summer. I gave it some thought, met with Mike and agreed to take it on. The purpose of the event was not only to celebrate twenty five years of the EIJF but also to pay tribute to the important part that the local bands had played in the development and success of the Festival. From the start, it was clear that there were would be a number of difficulties. The diminishing number of active jazz musicians meant that several of the current bands, as mentioned above, were sharing musicians, meaning some inevitable duplication. In spite of this, there were a few individual musicians who should certainly have been included but who were not currently active with Edinburgh bands. In addition, two of the most prominent bands from the early days of the EIJF, the historically conjoined Old Bailey's Jazz Advocates/Scottish Jazz Advocates and the Scottish Society Syncopators, were no longer in existence as extant bands. In the case of the former, apart from a couple of re-unions, the band had not had any corporate existence for almost twenty years. The Syncs likewise were no longer really functioning as a regular unit and when Mike did accept bookings under that name, he would put together a band including as many of the former members as possible. In the end, it was decided that the programme would include five currently active and prominent bands: the Spirits of Rhythm; the Diplomats of Jazz; Swing 2003; Dave Keir's Hot Five and Bill Salmond's Louisiana Ragtime Band, plus 're-constructions' of the Jazz Advocates and the Syncopators. It was also decided, on Mike's strong advice, that the Jazz Advocates should appear under their Old Bailey moniker, as this would be likely to attract followers from away back, even though the band had mostly appeared in the EIJF as the Scottish Jazz Advocates. Sadly, Charlie McNair, whose band had been a constant presence in the EIJF and which should most certainly have been included, was already suffering from the health problems that would finally end his jazz career and it was clearly unthinkable to have his band without Charlie himself.

In spite of the lack of the McNair band, it was beginning to look as though we had the ingredients of a good show. The seven bands between them covered a wide stylistic spectrum within traditional jazz, there was variety in the size and sound of the bands and the inclusion of the Jazz Advocates and the Syncs seemed likely to bring in a host of punters whose jazz loyalties stretched back as far as the 1960s. With hindsight, one mistake that I think we made during the planning, was not to give more thought than we did to a further reconstruction; that of the Climax Jazz Band, pioneers of the purist New Orleans tradition in Edinburgh and a band with a long and proud history. However, the majority of the band's longest serving members would be there in any case, scattered amongst the other bands, and the New Orleans style would be well represented by the Spirits and the LRB, while the Diplomats and Dave Keir's band nicely covered classic jazz. Both the Old Bailey band and the Syncs would represent a more arrangement oriented, populist style, with the Old Bailey band also associated with the Dixieland tradition. Providing a very welcome contrast to all the others would be Swing 2003, with their links to the European tradition, particularly to the Hot Club of France and the music of Django Reinhardt. The seven bands scheduled to play however, did not include two prominent and long-serving Edinburgh trumpeters, Gus Ferguson and Brian Robertson. This was soon resolved with Gus included in the Syncs, who would feature a two trumpet format, and Brian added for the occasion to the Spirits, who were currently without a trumpeter.

The title of the 'Silver Jubilee of Edinburgh Traditional Jazz' was adopted. This, of course, was not strictly accurate, it being the EIJF that was celebrating its silver jubilee rather than Edinburgh traditional jazz itself but, as it seemed to have the right ring about it, we settled for that. The running order was worked out by adopting a simple formula: there would be two halves separated by an interval, each half would start and finish with one of the larger (seven or eight piece) bands, with the smaller, mostly drumless bands occupying the in-between slots. This seemed a well balanced way to arrange things and it was further decided that each half would close with one of the reconstructed bands, simply in recognition of their novelty value, neither being active on the current Edinburgh jazz scene. We asked the band leaders to submit their proposed list of tunes, to try to avoid everybody playing Muskrat Ramble and Tin Roof Blues, and also to let us have a short history of their bands, to help introduce each band. Neither Mike nor I could come up with an obvious personality to present the show and we agreed that, in the event of us failing to find a more resounding name, I would be on standby as compere and, in the end, that is what happened and I was MC for the evening. Bill Marshall, who had undertaken similar duties in the EIJF before, was recruited as stage manager and we would be working with Assembly Direct's Steve Martin, as production manager, with Alan Martin in charge of sound. The date was to be 29th July 2003 and the venue, the prestigious Queen's Hall.

In the end it was a great success, with a full and enthusiastic house and a packed programme. In fact, it was really a bit too packed and overran its intended time by a fair bit, lasting for about three hours and forty minutes! In total, thirty five musicians played, with only seven of them playing in two bands on the night[204]. In my view, all the bands did themselves proud, with a good and varied selection of tunes, each band getting a rousing welcome and, no doubt, a special cheer from their own dedicated followers. The show was reviewed by Pat Napier in a write-up posted on the internet which said *'Should anyone ever have been tempted to relegate the trad jazz scene in Edinburgh to a backwater, the big Silver Jubilee celebration would have smashed that idea to smithereens'.* The review

---

[204] To give an idea of the state of Edinburgh traditional jazz in 2003, the full line-up for the 'Silver Jubilee' concert is given in Appendix I

noted that the second half had started with me reading out a list of the Edinburgh jazz musicians who were no longer around, and a depressingly long list it was. I read them out grouped by instrument and each group got an affectionate and, I am certain, sincere round of applause. I also offered a special welcome to Charlie McNair, no longer able to play but present as a special guest.

At the end, Mike Hart, who had managed to assemble an impressive nine of the Syncs former alumni for the show, spoke of how proud he was of Edinburgh's ability to produce so many talented jazz musicians and invited any of them who would like to, to join his band on stage for a final blast on the inevitable When the Saints go Marching In. A good few accepted and my final memory of the night was of a bemused Tom Finlay playing the piano surrounded by five banjo players, all strumming away merrily. Pat Napier was kind enough to call it '...a glorious trip down memory lane'. If memory serves me right, it was the best selling show of the 2003 EIJF.

By the end of the first decade of the new century, there could be little doubt that Edinburgh traditional jazz had made its mark, not only on the culture of Edinburgh and Scotland but also in the wider context of European and world jazz. The sterling efforts of John Latham, with his initiating role, and the many others who had become involved in 'The Lord Provost's Sandy Brown Memorial Society' in the 1990s had, as we have heard, ensured that the great work of Sandy Brown and Al Fairweather was properly commemorated in their native city and elsewhere. In addition, John had also, not only established the Sandy Brown Society in 1996, but had ensured that it was still continuing to thrive in 2012, issuing an informative Newsletter to a large membership every month.

At the end of 2006, Ian Maund had set up the Sandy Brown Jazz website on the internet[205], to make information widely available through the internet about Sandy, his music and his associates. In the way that Sandy Brown and his band developed a 'mainstream' bridge between 'traditional' and 'modern' jazz music, the website aims to

---

[205] **Sandy Brown website** (http://sandybrownjazz.co.uk

span all aspects of jazz through its free, monthly online magazine, *What's New*. In the magazine can be found news, album reviews, articles about new and established musicians, memories and photographs, quizzes, features and 'tasting' sessions for jazz music that you might not have heard before. Ian reports that the website regularly attracts readers and correspondents from around the world. Sandy Brown Jazz can be found at: http://www.sandybrownjazz.co.uk. The website is a marvellous source of information, not only about Sandy himself but also about many of his associates and related information and has been invaluable throughout the writing of this book.

The EIJBF had celebrated its 30th anniversary in 2008 and, however much it had changed and developed over the years, had become recognised as a major European jazz festival. The local traditional jazz bands and musicians had been celebrated in the 2003 Silver Jubilee Concert which recognised not only their considerable contribution to the EIJBF but also a local jazz scene which had burgeoned in the half century and more that had passed, since the Revival of the 1940s. Young and not-so-young Edinburgh musicians, some of them the sons and daughters of earlier Edinburgh jazzers, were highly active and were establishing names for themselves in the realm of modern and contemporary forms of jazz. Then, in the mid-2000s, came another initiative which would reinforce and put on record the reputation of Edinburgh as a major jazz centre.

We heard in earlier chapters[206] how a small group of veteran jazzers had got together on a regular basis in the mid-2000s to share memories and talk about their experiences of Edinburgh jazz since the 1940s. The group was small, with only four members: Jim Keppie, Bill Strachan, Donald 'Chick' Murray and Drew Landles but, between them, they represented a wide range of experience of local jazz. It was not long before informal chat and reminiscence started to crystalise into something with a definite purpose and, by the later 2000s, the idea of both an Edinburgh jazz archive and an exhibition was firmly in

---

[206] See chapters V and VIII

place and the previously informal group became the Edinburgh Jazz Archive Group (EJAG). Sadly, Drew Landles, who had been able to put on the record his memories of playing with the early Edinburgh jazz bands of the late 1940s and early 1950s, died in September 2010 but he did live long enough to see the first successes of the EJAG earlier that year.

There seems little doubt that Janol Scott, had he lived, would have been as enthusiastic and effective a member of the EJAG as he had been of the Sandy Brown and Al Fairweather memorial group, back in the 1990s. Janol and Jim Keppie had been classmates at the Royal High School back in the 1940s and had started attending weekly sessions of the Edinburgh Rhythm Club. This led to them making a start on collecting 78 rpm recordings which were not in great supply in these wartime years. Jim recalls that most were on the HMV label (including some by Jelly Roll Morton) or the Parlophone Rhythm series which included Bix Beiderbecke and, as British post-war jazz began to establish itself, Humphrey Lyttelton's band. These were purchased in Methven Simpson's shop, where they were served by a Miss Wood, or at Clifton's, in which case Betty saw to the transaction. The records apparently cost about 5/4d each and Jim and Janol <u>always</u> insisted on acceptable performances on <u>both</u> sides of the record and quite right too!

Janol Scott died on 2nd November 2007, too early to play a part in the EJAG, but his widow Winnie, later donated to the Archive many items from his sizeable collection, including LPs, CDs and books, and this constituted the Archive's first really significant contribution. In fact, it seems that this kindly donation was a major encouragement to the fledgling EJAG and came at just the right time to provide them with some real impetus and inspiration, so much so that the Edinburgh Jazz Archive was dedicated to the memory of Janol Scott, a life-long jazz enthusiast and collector.

The ideas behind the formation and aims of the EJAG are described by Jim Keppie, under the heading 'Edinburgh

Jazz Archive,' in the Sandy Brown Jazz website[207], to which readers may wish to refer. In pursuing the idea of an archive, it seems clear that there was a feeling that tribute should be paid to, not only Sandy Brown and Al Fairweather, who were now commemorated by plaques at three venues, but to the many others whose contributions to jazz were not so far short of theirs. There were certainly other fine players to remember, including such as the Semple brothers, Alex Welsh, Stan Greig and Dave Paxton from the early days and the many others who had followed in their footsteps. The EJAG deserves a great deal of credit for having the initiative and energy to do something which was crucial, if the story of Edinburgh jazz in the twentieth century was to be recorded before a vast amount of material was lost forever, as the ravages of time took their inevitable toll. The group's original ideas, in fact, were still more ambitious, as Jim explained on the Sandy Brown Jazz website in 2009, where he says:

'The possibility of a Scottish Jazz Archive, which would involve research facilities provision and the collation of material covering at least the major centres in Scotland, was originally mooted in my letter to the Sandy Brown Jazz website in April 2008. While this concept has (for practical reasons) had to be shelved, it is hoped that the arrival of one for Edinburgh alone (sizeable enough on its own) may spur jazz enthusiasts in Glasgow, Aberdeen, Dundee, Inverness and elsewhere to collect and record the evidence of jazz activities in their cities and towns'.

Amen to that, say I. In addition to setting out the idea of an Edinburgh jazz archive, it was through their hard work that agreement was reached with the Edinburgh Central Library to provide the necessary facilities for conserving and cataloguing collected material. The group also set out to gather this material and to encourage others to contribute. This was also explained on the Sandy Brown Jazz website where Jim set out what they were looking for, listing *'...recordings (78's, LP's, CD's), books, journals, photographs*

---

[207] Keppie J, http//www.sandybrownjazz.co.uk/forumarchive.html

523

and other ephemera relating to what was a particularly unique cultural development in the city, mainly from the 1940's onwards'. Significantly, because it was such a determined statement of purpose, he also added *'That said, it is important that we ensure and record the obvious evidence of local jazz provision through to the end of the 20th century and on to the present day and this we would endeavour to do'.*

The EJAG also decided to launch the Archive by putting on the planned exhibition about Edinburgh jazz under the title 'Capital Jazz' and this took place in the Edinburgh Central Library on 31st July 2010, the opening day of the 2010 Edinburgh International Jazz and Blues Festival. It was a resounding success, hailed by a deservedly pleased Jim Keppie, who reported the event on the Sandy Brown Jazz website, saying:

'There was a goodly attendance of jazz enthusiasts and performers from yesteryear and today to view the assembled material on display covering the approximate period 1945-80. This consisted of explanatory texts, photographs, books, instruments and memorabilia as well as books containing memoirs and profile listings of local performers.

Musical support was provided by Ron Carruthers (piano), Tony Howard (guitar), Billy Allison (drums) and John Burgess (reeds) with speeches by Councillor Cairns (Edinburgh City Council), Jim Keppie (EJAG), and Hil Williamson (Edinburgh City Library).

Among those present were Ralph Laing, Mike Hart, Bill Strachan, Drew Landles, Andrew Gilmour, Jim Young, Mike Pollett, Graham Blamire, Jean Mundell, Roger Craik, Winnie Scott (widow of Janol Scott) and Ishbel Semple (widow of John Semple)'.

In his opening speech, Jim had recorded the sincere thanks of the EJAG to Liz McGettigan (Head of Libraries and Information Service) and also the Library officials, Hil Williamson and Garry Gale, for their enthusiasm towards the concept and their willingness to work with the EJAG in developing the whole Archive and exhibition project. The exhibition had launched the Archive very successfully and the hope and intention was that it would continue to grow and develop over the years, becoming a repository for written accounts, photos, posters, recordings and other memorabilia, a treasure house reflecting the quality and history of one the most significant of the UK's jazz centres. This certainly prompted me and probably many others, to encourage other jazz people to consider placing their jazz memorabilia in the Archive when the time comes, just as I intend to myself.

Back in 2009, Chick Murray had suggested that I might be interested in joining the EJAG, with a view to involving me in the writing part, and I went along to a couple of meetings. However, I was not at all sure that I could manage to write in partnership with a retired professional journalist, brought in from outside the group, which was what Chick proposed. In the end, I decided not to commit myself to becoming part of the group, aware that I usually worked better on my own. I was, nonetheless, fully in support of their plans and undertook to give them what help I could in putting together materials for both exhibition and archive. The work of the EJAG has been invaluable. Jim, Chick (in spite of serious health issues at the time), and Bill Strachan put an enormous amount of time and effort into the EJAG projects and, as an additional bonus for me (and, I hope, others!), it was to a large extent their initiative that spurred me into doing what I had always intended doing and getting on with writing this book.

And that is just about that. Deciding when and how to draw this account to a close has been something of a problem but a closing chapter describing the Sandy and Al memorial project, the triumphant Silver Jubilee concert and the advent of the Edinburgh Jazz Archive seems as good a way as any, even if the emphasis was now on the past. Edinburgh traditional jazz was to continue of course but the great years were over. In the hectic 1980s, there had been up to and beyond fifty traditional jazz gigs a week on offer in Edinburgh; at the end of the first decade of the new century, I was aware of only two or three regular spots (and they are fortnightly or monthly) plus the weekly programme laid on by the Jazz and Jive Club. Over the years, I built up a data base tabulating all the Edinburgh traditional jazz musicians and bands, in the period 1945 onwards, that I had been able to identify. The totals, which should be regarded only as minimum figures as there is no guarantee that they are complete, came to almost three hundred and fifty musicians and around a hundred bands. These are impressive figures, although it has to be remembered that they include a number of people and bands whose appearance was brief and transitory.

At the end of the first decade of the new century, the number of active Edinburgh traditional jazz musicians had declined to the point where most bands were sharing at least one and sometimes several musicians with other bands. The Edinburgh traditional jazz bands still in regular action were Bill Salmond's Louisiana Ragtime Band, the Spirits of Rhythm, Jim Petrie's Diplomats of Jazz, Brian Robertson's Forth Valley Ragtimers, Fred Murray's Club House Seven, the Maid of the Forth Stompers, Swing 2011 and, out in Linlithgow, the West End Jazz Band. In addition, there were still occasional appearances at the Jazz and Jive Club of a band under Mike Hart's leadership and a contemporary version of the old Climax Jazz band. Fat Sam's Band remained as professional and international in its appeal as ever. Many of us were crossing the country to fill out jazz bands through in the west, where the decline in numbers was just as pronounced. The diminishing numbers of followers was just as apparent everywhere, although Glasgow seemed to have managed to maintain its free pub gigs rather better than we had in Edinburgh.

What had happened to produce such a marked decline in such a relatively short space of time? The answer is simple. Three upsurges in interest had manned the Edinburgh traditional jazz bands since WWII – the original Revival in the forties and fifties, the trad boom in the late 1950s and early 1960s and, finally and less significantly, the recruitment that stemmed from the virtual demise of the dance bands in the late 1960s and 70s. At the beginning of the new century, the surviving Revivalists were in their seventies or even eighties, many trad boomers in their sixties or seventies and the dance band recruits had not, in the main, been young when they came over to jazz in the first place. The stark truth was that the generations that had driven traditional jazz for six decades were either retiring from active playing or shuffling off this mortal coil and there were next to no younger replacements coming into the music. When I started around 1960, the average age of a jazz band was probably around thirty, in 2000 it was around seventy. In 1964, at age twenty one, I was the youngest in the Old Bailey band, in 2011 I was the youngest in the Maid of the Forth Stompers at sixty eight! So the generations were moving on but the real problem was that there were virtually no youngsters taking their place. This, of course, raises the interesting question, can traditional jazz survive much longer?

It does not seem to me either logical or realistic to expect traditional jazz to ever again feature in the pop charts, that is, amongst the best selling records. With the possible exception of the trad boom years, traditional jazz in the second half of the twentieth century could never be defined as a part of pop culture proper. As George Melly said in his book 'Revolt into Style – the pop arts in Britain', Revivalist jazz differed from genuine Pop culture because it '...*looked back towards an earlier culture for its inspiration, thus admitting that it believed in a 'then' which was superior to 'now' – a very anti-pop concept'*[208]. Revivalist jazz and its various developments between the 1940s and the turn of the century existed alongside, first of all popular music (mostly 'crooners' such as Frank Sinatra, Guy Mitchell and Dickie Valentine) and then, after the mid-1950s, pop music (mostly beat music, Rock 'n' Roll and kiddie-pops). Even in the trad boom era, I do not think that the Acker Bilk, Chris Barber and Kenny Ball records that got into the charts could really be classed as genuine pop music. It seems to me that there were two factors that enabled records of this type to make it into the charts. First of all, the effects of the Revival were still in full swing and the large number of jazzers who were involved would have added up to quite a significant record buying group in their own right, particularly considering that the total record buying public then would have been much smaller then than it is now.

---

[208] 'Revolt into Style - the Pop Arts in Britain' by George Melly, (Copyright George © Melly 1970) Reprinted by permission of A. M. Heath & Co Ltd.

The bands of Bilk, Barber and Ball, and other British traditional jazz bands, had enormous followings at that time and there is no doubt that their records sold like hot cakes among their followers. However, these were basically jazz followers who would have been fairly unlikely to buy many of the other types of records that got into the charts.

The second factor, and this is a bit more like a genuine pop reason for buying records, was the influence of skiffle. Skiffle, and Lonnie Donegan in particular, was extremely popular in the later 1950s. Donegan's records were an almost constant feature of the pop charts at that time and they would certainly have to be considered a bona fide part of the pop culture of the time. However, the close relationship of skiffle with the British traditional jazz bands, remembering that Lonnie Donegan's first hit recording, Rock Island Line, was actually initially released as a track on a Chris Barber LP, brought many skiffle fans into contact with the music of the jazz bands. This was exactly the route by which I and many others first became aware of British traditional jazz and many of us were soon buying British jazz recordings for their own sake. What I am saying is that the appearance of traditional jazz recordings in the charts was simply a function of the sheer size of the jazz public at that time and they were not, nor should they be considered to be, a part of the genuine pop record buying public. It would need another Revival to fuel a similar upsurge in popularity, a highly unlikely scenario in respect of traditional jazz, the originals of which are now so far in the past. We may, in any case, have already witnessed a kind of second jazz revival, with a return to earlier forms of modern jazz like bebop, now that the excesses of free form have melted away and the angry sounds of civil rights jazz seem to have had their day.

A factor that may be missing today from the sort of sociological mix that sparked off the Revival, was the very nature of the troubled 1940s. It would take a sociologist rather than me to explore the part that WWII may have played in fostering the Revival but I have sometimes wondered if there was an element, at least in Europe, of harking back to the music of an earlier, safer and more stable time. I do not think that the trauma and upset of the war itself was a factor in initiating the Revival, as it seems to have been under way by the late 1930s before WWII had begun, but it may be that the unrest and uncertainty of the years leading up to the war played their part. It also seems unlikely to me that young musicians will be attracted to traditional jazz in any significant numbers. Why should they be? For a start, they hear very little of it in the broadcasting media. The few televised jazz programmes are usually scheduled for the middle of the night and the exiguous jazz ration on radio is broadcast mostly on stations that are unlikely to be routine listening for young people. If they are attracted to jazz at all, it would seem much more likely to be towards more modern and contemporary forms of the music, the music of jazz musicians closer to their own age.

It may seem contradictory but another factor that seems to me to militate against youngsters of today coming into traditional jazz is the fact that they have a vastly better chance of formal tuition in playing musical instruments than earlier generations. Today's youngsters, coming through the schools music departments, seem to me to be in a system that is designed to prepare musicians for orchestral music, for which it is no doubt important to produce virtually interchangeable technical experts. What training in jazz playing they receive, if any, will naturally be linked to the sort of jazz that most closely resembles the orchestral model, that is to the formal, music reading, big bands. Those among the young, aspiring jazz musicians with the talent and ambition to be jazz soloists are likewise much more likely to be attracted to the same context, the formally arranged, reading bands which also offer soloing opportunities. It would be asking an awful lot to expect many to break away from the very basis of their training into the informal, relatively unorganised, musical environment of a traditional jazz band. It is not that I have anything against formal training and I certainly would not go as far as to call it a 'clone factory', as did one Edinburgh jazzer with whom I was speaking recently. It is just that I think that formal training does not lead naturally to less formal music of an improvising nature and it is unlikely ever to be a ready source of aspiring traditional jazz musicians.

In fact, I am not at all sure that lack of formal training is such a bad thing in respect of playing jazz. I have already quoted Dave Strutt as emphasising the importance of sound in jazz. While there is no doubting the value of technical expertise, providing it is not used simply to show off technique, I wonder just how much of the individuality of jazz musicians is traceable to their being, at least to an extent, self-taught? Certainly, many great jazz musicians are readily identifiable by their individual, sometimes idiosyncratic, sound and this always seemed to me to be an essential component of their expressiveness, something that gives so much character to their playing. In contrast, well-trained, young musicians of today are a product of a system, the aim of which is, at least to an extent, to produce musicians who all sound the same. This seems to me to the antithesis of playing jazz, where individuality is paramount. There have been many technically more accomplished clarinet players than Johnny Dodds, George Lewis and Pee Wee Russell, many more technically brilliant trumpeters than Bubber Miley, Wild Bill Davison, and Muggsy Spannier, but not many who were more individualisitic. Even technical wizards, like the clarinettists Barney Bigard and Benny Goodman and the trumpeter Clark Terry, however much formal training they received, seem to have used their technical excellence as a basis from which to develop an individual jazz sound. I believe this was because they saw their formal training as preparatory to playing jazz, where they needed to establish themselves as individuals, as would be the norm in those days. It seems to me that these great players overcame the sameness that technical excellence could impose and became great individual jazz musicians almost in spite of it.

The above is, of course, far from being an original point of view. The French writer Jean Pierre Lion, when considering the 1920s career of Bix Biederbecke, made the same point in his extremely detailed book 'Bix – The

Definitive Biography of a Jazz Legend'[209]. Describing what happened when Bix sought formal trumpet tuition from Joseph Gustat, Lion wrote *'After listening to Bix's playing for a few minutes and observing his peculiar fingering technique, the professor advised him to give up any ideas of formal studies of the horn. He comforted Bix in his "faulty" playing – "erroneous" in regard to the playing taught in music schools – realising it permitted the young man to express himself in a unique and surprising manner'*. Lion went on to emphasise the point, writing that Gustat had the sense and finesse to avoid *'putting a wild animal in a cage'*.

So I cannot, in all honesty, pretend that I think traditional jazz has a great future. Although the regular UK publication 'Jazz Guide' still manages to pack up to sixty pages with news of traditional jazz bands playing all over the UK, I fear that the vast majority of them will be of a fairly advanced average age and I suspect the same holds true on the continent. Perhaps the type of traditional jazz that has the best chance of surviving the gradual disappearance of the current crop of active players is the purist or New Orleans style. This form of the music still has the underlying energy that comes from a 'cause', a sort of crusading spirit, and this might, just might, appeal to a future generation of stroppy teenagers. We, or rather our successors, will just have to wait and see.

This book has explored the course of Edinburgh traditional jazz and the people who played it, beginning away back in the 1920s, on through the pioneering years of the Revival, the excesses of the trad boom, the excitements of the Edinburgh International Jazz Festival and finally, up to and beyond the end of the twentieth century. We have met and got to know many of the principle personalities whose efforts and abilities were the building blocks of decades of marvelous music, most of it readily available at little cost. We may have to accept that traditional jazz has almost run its course and that the jazz flame will be carried

---

[209] Lion J P, 'Bix – The Definitive Biography of a Jazz Legend', Revised paperback edition 2007, reproduced by permission of the Continuum International Publishing Group,

on by musicians whose music may not sound much like the jazz we knew. But what a time it has been!

Looking back now, several things stand out. Through the decades there have been endless examples of Edinburgh jazz musicians whose careers were founded on their own, self-taught skills and their intrinsic ability to express themselves at their own level, great or humble as it may have been. Sandy Brown, Stan Greig, Alex Welsh and Archie Semple, who were to play at the top of the tree. Al Fairweather, whose talent and imagination produced, not only his own marvelous playing but some of the most original writing that ever lit up the British jazz scene and yet who said that it had all been a so hard, because of what he saw as his lack of technical skills. Tello who played the hottest jazz you could ever wish to hear and yet who told me that it was a constant battle against the limitations of his self-taught technique. Jazzers like Charlie McNair and Archie Sinclair, whose playing unlocked their talents as communicators and entertainers; great players like Johnny McGuff, Dave Paxton, Ronnie Rae, Kenny Milne and Alex Shaw, deserving of international reputations and yet content to play a great deal of their music on their home patch; and the legions of the rest of us whose DIY, rough-hewn techniques were all our own and yet were sufficient to release whatever creativity we possessed.

A local jazz scene so rich in talent and character that you would have had to go a long way to find the equal of the individuals listed above, when in their prime. The host of bands over the years - the early Sandy Brown and Archie Semple bands, the Climax Jazz Band, Charlie McNair's Jazz Band, the Nova Scotians, Old Bailey and his Jazz Advocates, the Society Syncopators, the Louisiana Ragtime Band, the Spirits of Rhythm, Swing 1980/2001, Fat Sam's Band, the Diplomats of Jazz and the Dave Keir Hot Five and so many more - many of which could hold their own against any local jazz bands, in their styles, in the UK. And the punters, as I have called them throughout this book and to whom it is dedicated, without whose enthusiasm and support there would have been next to nothing to write about. We have witnessed too, the sheer inspirational quality of jazz, the chance hearings that so often switched on individuals to a music that remained with them for the rest of their lives. The magic of a creative art form that could grip someone in an instant - regardless of obstacles of time, education, geography, race, colour or creed - leaving them with a life-long interest and the memory of their own, special, eureka moment.

In the end, what did Edinburgh traditional jazz add up to? George Melly wrote in 'Revolt into Style': *It was inevitable that the spontaneous if mysterious enthusiasm which sprang up all over wartime Britain for an almost forgotten music, Negro jazz of the 20s, should lead eventually to an attempt to reconstruct the music and, by the end of the war, there was already one established band, the George Webb Dixielanders. Within a year or two the revivalist movement had spread to every major city in the British Isles....*[210]. This seems to me to be rather a tunnel-visioned, simplistic view and more than a little London-centric. We have already heard from Jim Walker about what was going on in Edinburgh by that time and about the *'...group of rather older musicians who, around 1945, played at the Edinburgh Rhythm Club, located in the rehearsal room above Methven Simpson's music shop in Princes Street'*[211], the band that included Bob Fairley, Drew and Ma Bruce and Bill McGregor. In addition and perhaps even more significant, is the fact that Sandy Brown had formed his first band in about 1943, when he was still at school and Dave Paxton and George Crockett were certainly both already in action by that time.

Without wishing any disrespect to George Webb and the other early London pioneers, it seems perfectly clear that the Revival was spontaneously springing into life all over the place, and was most certainly not all triggered by what was going on in London. Nor can there be any doubt of the quality of what took place in Edinburgh in the 1940s. Sandy would be around the top of most people's list of the greatest British traditional jazz musicians and Al Fairweather, Alex Welsh, Archie Semple and Stan Greig

---

[210]'Revolt into Style - the Pop Arts in Britain' by George Melly, (Copyright George © Melly 1970) Reprinted by permission of A. M. Heath & Co Ltd.

[211] See Chapter III

533

would not be far away either, right up there with great contemporary jazzers from the south, like Humphrey Lyttleton, Wally Fawkes, Bruce Turner and Ken Colyer.

The succeeding generations too, proved a production line of many more wonderful players, some of whom played professionally, at least for parts of their careers in jazz. But it was not just the great players, although perhaps it was from them that the main strength came. The whole Edinburgh jazz scene was strong in so many ways: so many musicians, so many bands, so many venues, so many punters and over such a long time. We even have the biggest jazz event in Europe in the Edinburgh International Jazz and Blues Festival, thanks to the drive, enthusiasm and relentless hard work of Mike Hart and all the others who made it possible. Only in sheer numbers would London be ahead, because of the enormous scale of the place. However, it has to be remembered that a very significant number of jazz musicians associated with London were in fact not themselves Londoners but were attracted there by the opportunities offered. Putting sheer scale aside, by all other measures, in traditional jazz, Edinburgh has to be rated as one of the great jazz cities of the UK

It has been a pleasure and a privilege to be part of it and to write about it. For me at least, Edinburgh traditional jazz has been a constant factor that lit up my life and brought me many friends and great experiences. I just wish it was possible to go back to the beginning and start all over again.

Appendix I

'Silver Jubilee of Edinburgh Traditional Jazz'

This event was a concert in the Queen's Hall, Edinburgh, on 29th July 2003, celebrating both the 25th anniversary of the Edinburgh International Jazz Festival and the important part played in the success of the Festival by the local bands. The bands, in the running order in which they appeared, were:

1. 'The Spirits of Rhythm'

Brian Robertson (tpt), Ian Boyter (rds), Alan Quinn (tbn, voc), Violet Milne (pno, ldr), Nigel Porteous (bjo), Dizzy Jackson (bs), Kenny Milne (drms)

2. 'The Diplomats of Jazz'

Jim Petrie (tpt, voc, ldr), Bob Busby (rds), Beverley Knight (bjo), Bill Brydon (sousa)

3. 'Swing 2003'

Dick Lee (rds), Stephen Coutts (solo gtr, viol), John Russell (gtr), Roy Percy (bs)

4.   'Old Bailey's Jazz Advocates'

Andrew Lauder (tpt), Hamish McGregor (rds, voc, co-ldr), John McGuff (tbn), Tom Finlay (pno), Mike Hart (bjo, co-ldr), Graham Blamire (bs), Donald 'Chick' Murray (drms)

Interval

5.   'Dave Keir's Hot Five'

Dave Keir (tpt, ldr), Mike Westwater (rds), Gordon Melrose (tbn), Jock Westwater (bjo, voc), Dizzy Jackson (bs)

6.   Bill Salmond's Louisiana Ragtime Band'

George Gilmour (clt), Alan Quinn (tbn, voc), Graham Scott (pno), Bill Salmond (bjo, ldr), Bill Brydon (bs), Kenny Milne (drms)

7.   Mike Hart's Society Syncopators'

Dave Strutt (tpt, voc), Gus Ferguson (tpt), Jake McMahon (clt), Martin Foster (b-sax), John McGuff (tbn), Tom Finlay (pno), Mike Hart (bjo, ldr), Ricky Steele (bs), Bobby Stewart (drms)

Compere - Graham Blamire, **Stage Manager** - Bill Marshall, **Production Manager** - Steve Wilson (Assembly Direct), **Sound engineer** - Alan Martin.

Edinburgh Jazz Discography

This discography covers recordings made, issued and made available to supporters, by jazz musicians and bands associated with the Edinburgh jazz scene. Only recordings made whilst these musicians and bands were mainly domiciled in the Edinburgh area are included. Many of the musicians, bands and recordings are referred to in the preceding chapters.

A great many of the recordings included were funded by the bands or bandleaders and were only available at concerts and other gigs. Few were available through normal retail outlets. Some of the bands gave names to the labels under which recordings were made. Others did not bother and these are shown as 'band issue'. Where the recordings were titled this has been included.

Many of the well known Edinburgh jazz musicians travelled to London and turned professional. These included Sandy Brown Al Fairweather, Alex Welsh, Archie Semple, Stan Greig, Jim Douglas, Dave Keir and Ralph Laing. Recordings made by these musicians, whilst working in London, are well documented in discographies compiled and issued by the Dutch discographer, Gerard Bielderman and his associates.

With very few exceptions, the earlier recordings included have not been re-issued and are no longer available other than, from time to time, through specialised auctions or record sales. However, Paul Adams of Lake Records has undertaken some sterling work in re-issuing some of the early recordings by Sandy Brown, Archie Semple and Alex Welsh.

The entries relating to recordings made in the mid-1940s through to the early 1950s are, in many cases, tentative. As far as possible, the data shown have been confirmed against published discographies, including those published by Gerard Bielderman, John Latham and Norman Simpson. Other reliable authorities have also been consulted.

In recent years, the advances in recording technology have allowed bands and collectors to record both live and 'studio' sessions on portable recording equipment, without the need to hire professional recording companies. This has allowed bands to issue recordings without having to commit to specific numbers of discs. As a consequence of this, musicians and private collectors have recorded many sessions that have never been issued and remain in private collections. None of these have been included in this discography.

The discography does not pretend to be exhaustive. Very few discographies ever are. Should anyone reading this discography know of any recording(s) that should be included but are not, please contact the author (0131 312 8243). Similarly, please advise any errors of omission or commission.

I would like to acknowledge and thank the following people for the help they gave me in compiling this discography – Graham Blamire, Bob Busby, Peter Davenport, Pete Kerr, Kenny Milne, John Russell, Bill Salmond.

Abbreviations Used

alto	alto saxophone
audio-cas	audio cassette
bar	baritone saxophone
b-bs	brass bass (tuba or sousaphone)
b-gtr	bass guitar
bs	string bs
b-clt	bass clarinet
b-drm	bass drum
bjo	banjo
b-sax	bass saxophone
clt	clarinet
c-mel	c melody saxophone
cnt	cornet
cym	cymbal
drms	drums (full drum kit)
e-gtr	electric guitar
flt	flute
flug	flugelhorn
gtr	rhythm guitar
hca	harmonica
ldr	leader
melo	melophonium
org	organ
pno	piano
rec	recorder
s-drum	side or snare drum

solo-gtr	solo guitar
sop	soprano saxophone
sousa	sousaphone
tamb	tambourine
tbn	trombone
ten	tenor saxophone
tpt	trumpet
tba	tuba
voc	vocal
v-tbn	valve trombone
wsb	washboard

Anti-Climax Jazz Band
Jim Petrie (cnt), Alan Quinn (tbn), George Gilmour (clt), Brian Weld (bjo), Kenny McDonald (bs), Kenny Milne (drms)
Recorded: Edinburgh Jazz 'n' Jive Club, October 10, 2009

1. At a Georgia camp meeting	J'n'J CD002
2. Tishomingo blues	J'n'J CD002

Auld Reekie Parade Band
Colin Dawson, Kenny Milne (tpt), Bob Craig, Jack Weddell (tbn), George Duncan (?)(clt) or Dick Lee (?)(clt), Teddy Johnson (ten), Jim Young (sousa), Andrew Hall (s-drm)
Recorded: Edinburgh, 1980

1. St Louis blues	CPLP038

Boab And The Busbymen
Part 1

John Arthur on the 'Fawkirk' Piano and Left Foot; Bob Busby: (1st clt, voc): Track 14: 2nd clt, alto, ten over-dubbed,
Recorded:

1. Shake that jelly roll	private issue CD
2. Wolverine blues	private issue CD
3. In the gloaming	private issue CD
4. Eccentric rag	private issue CD
5. Out of the galleon	private issue CD
6. Chicago buzz	private issue CD
7. Shreveport stomp	private issue CD
8. Funny feather man	private issue CD
9. Every evening	private issue CD
10. Perdido Street blues	private issue CD
11. Love nest	private issue CD
12. A miner's dream of home	private issue CD
13. Gravier Street blues	private issue CD
14. Nothing blues	private issue CD

Sandy Brown's Jazz Band

Archie Semple (cnt), Stu Eaton (v-tbn), Sandy Brown (clt), John Semple (pno), George Crockett (drms)

Yellow Dog blues	private acetate
Stomp, stomp, stomp	private acetate
Shoe shiner's drag	private acetate

Recorded: Edinburgh, 1946

Stu Eaton (tpt), Al Fairweather (tbn), Sandy Brown (clt), 'Ma' Bruce (pno), George Crockett (drms), Dru Bruce (voc - 1)
Recorded: Edinburgh, October? 1946

1. Fidgety feet	private acetate
2. Careless love (1)	private acetate

Stu Eaton (tpt), Sandy Brown (clt), 'Ma' Bruce (pno), Billy Neill (gtr), Bill McGregor (bjo), George Crockett (drms)
Recorded: Edinburgh 1946

1. Yellow Dog blues	private acetate
2. Untitled number	private acetate
3. Doctor Jazz	private acetate
4. Shoe shiner's drag	private acetate

Stu Eaton (tpt), Sandy Brown (clt), 'Ma' Bruce (pno), Billy Neill (gtr), Bill McGregor (bjo), George Crockett (drms), Dru Bruce (voc)
Recorded: Edinburgh, January 3, 1947

1. Careless love (DB-voc)	private acetate
2. Won't you come home, Bill Bailey?	private acetate

Stu Eaton (tpt), Bob Fairley (tpt-1), Sandy Brown (clt), 'Ma' Bruce (pno), Billy Neill (gtr), Bill McGregor (bjo), George Crockett (drms), Dru Bruce (voc)
Recorded: Edinburgh, 25 January, 1947

1. Buddy Bolden blues	private acetate
2. Jazz me blues	private acetate
3. Sad ole blues	private acetate
4. Royal Garden blues (1)	private acetate

5. Joe Turner blues (voc-DB)   private acetate

*Stu Eaton (tpt), Sandy Brown (clt), 'Ma' Bruce (pno), Billy Neill
(gtr), Bill McGregor (bjo), George Crockett (drms)*
Recorded: Edinburgh, July 4, 1947

1. I ain't gonna give nobody none of my jelly roll
                                      private acetate
2. Careless love   private acetate

Sandy Brown's Smoky City Six
*Stu Eaton, Bob Fairley (tpts), Sandy Brown (clt), 'Ma' Bruce
(pno), Dave Mylne (drms), Dru Bruce (voc)*
Recorded: February 20, 1947

1. Atlanta blues (Make me a pallet on the floor)
                                      private acetate
2. Baby, won't you please come home
                                      private acetate

*Stu Eaton (tpt), Bob R Fairley (tpt), Sandy Brown (clt), 'Ma'
Bruce (pno), Bill McGrgeor (bjo), Dru Bruce (voc)*
Recorded: Edinburgh, 1948

1. Buddy Bolden blues   private LP
Further unknown titles   private LP

Sandy Brown's Jazz Band
*Al Fairweather (tpt), Sandy Brown (clt), Stan Greig (pno),
John Twiss (bjo), Will Redpath (bs), Willie Burns (drms)*
Recorded: Edinburgh, October 29, 1949

1. Heebie jeebies   S&M unissued
2. Of all the wrongs you've done to me   S&M unissued
3. Of all the wrongs you've done to me   S&M unissued
4. Of all the wrongs you've done to me   S&M 1001
5. Melancholy blues   S&M unissued
6. Melancholy blues   S&M1001
7. Irish black bottom   S&M Unissued
8. Irish black bottom   S&M1002
9. Alexander   S&M unissued

10. Alexander   S&M 1002

Al Fairweather (tpt), Bob Craig (tbn), Sandy Brown (clt), Stan Greig (pno, voc), Norrie Anderson (bjo), Bill Strachan (drms)
Recorded: Edinburgh, October 27, 1950

1. Chattanooga stomp	S&M LP-5
2. Georgia bo bo (voc-SG)	S&M LP-5
3. Snake rag	S&M LP-5

Al Fairweather (tpt), Bob Craig (tbn), Sandy Brown (clt), Stan Greig (pno), Norrie Anderson (bjo), Bill Strachan (drms)
Recorded: Edinburgh, November 11, 1950

1. Mandy Lee blues	S&M LP-1
2. Georgia grind	S&M LP-1
3. Willie the Weeper	S&M 1003
4. I'm going away to wear you off my mind	S&M 1003
5. Sobbin' blues	S&M LP-1
6. Buddy's habit	S&M unissued
7. Buddy's habit	S&M LP-1
8. Aunt Hagar's blues	S&M LP-1
9. Keyhole blues	S&M unissued
10. Canal Street blues	S&M Unissued
11. Wild man blues	S&M Unissued
12. Heebie jeebies	S&M LP-1

The Historic Usher Hall Concert, 1952

Al Fairweather (tpt), Bob Craig (tbn), Sandy Brown (clt), Stan Greig (pno, drms), Norrie Anderson (bjo), Dizzy Jackson or John Rae (bs), Jim 'Farrie' Forsyth or Bill Strachan (drms), Sandy Currie (announcer)
Recorded: Usher Hall, Edinburgh, February 23, 1952

1. I ain't gonna tell nobody	Lake LACD94
2. Room rent blues	Lake LACD94
3. Keyhole blues	Lake LACD94
4. If I had a talking picture of you	Lake LACD94
5. Squeeze me	Lake LACD94
6. High society	Lake LACD94

7. Buddy's habit	Lake LACD94
8. Gatemouth	Lake LACD94
9. The Entertainer	Lake LACD94
10. Ory's Creole trombone	Lake LACD94
11. Everybody loves my baby	Lake LACD94
12. Savoy blues	Lake LACD94
13. Just a closer walk with Thee	Lake LACD94

Note: the CD information regarding the identity of the bass player and drummer has been questioned

A Sandy Session

Al Fairweather (tpt), Bob Craig (tbn), Sandy Brown (clt), Stan Greig (pno-1, drms -2), Norrie Anderson (bjo), Jim 'Farrie' Forsyth (drms, wbd)
Recorded: Edinburgh, May 3, 1952

1. Lady love (1)	S&M unissued
2. Lady love (1)	S&M LP-3
3. Of all the wrongs you've done to me	S&M LP-3
4. Jazz lips (1)	S&M LP-3
5. Jazz lips	S&M unissued
6. Krooked blues	S&M LP-3
7. King of the Zulus	S&M LP-3
8. Margie	S&M LP-3
9. When you're smiling (1)	S&M unissued
10. When you're smiling (2)	S&M unissued
11. Jazzin' babies blues	S&M unissued

Sandy Brown (pno)
Recorded: Edinburgh, May 4, 1952

1. Maple leaf rag (take 1)	S&M unissued
2. Maple leaf rag (take 2)	S&M unissued
3. Weary Brown	S&M 1004
4. Untitled	S&M unissued
5. Little Rock getaway	S&M unissued
6. King Porter stomp	S&M unissued

Al Fairweather (tpt), Sandy Brown (clt), Norrie Anderson (bjo), Jim 'Farrie' Forsyth (wbd)
Recorded: Late May, 1952

The Lord will make a way somehow   S&M 1004

*Al Fairweather (tpt), Bob Craig (tbn), Sandy Brown (clt, voc),
Stan Greig (pno), Norrie Anderson (bjo), Johnnie Rae (bs), Jim
'Farrie' Forsyth (drms), Mike Hart (drms), David Mylne
(narrator)*
Recorded: BBC Scottish Home Service, Queen Street
Studios, Edinburgh, July 4, 1952

1. Dilly mama yeh (Everybody loves Saturday night)
                                                    Acetate
2. Gettysburg march   Acetate
3. Countin' the blues (Jelly Bean blues)   Acetate
4. Ory's Creole trombone   Acetate
5. Oh! didn't he ramble   Acetate
6. Tears   Acetate
7. Sandy's blues   Acctate
8. I'll see you in my dreams   Acetate

This recording has never been issued commercially
although it has had wide distribution on both acetate and
cassette among collectors.
*The dates shown here are the correct broadcast dates and
have been verified by Tom Lowrie who has the original ticket
stubs from the concert, which show dates and times.*

*Al Fairweather (tpt), Bob Craig (tbn), Sandy Brown (clt), Drew
Paterson (pno), Norrie Anderson (bjo), Dizzy Jackson (bs), Jim
'Farrie' Forsyth (drms), Stan Greig (drms-1)*
Recorded: London, July 11, 1953

1. Dr Jazz   Esquire 333, LakeLACD136
2. Dr Jazz   Esquire 10-310, 333, LakeLACD136
3. Four or five times   Esquire 20-022, 333, LakeLACD136
4. Four or five times   Esquire 10-310, 333, LakeLACD136
5. Wild man blues   Esquire 20-022, 333,LakeLACD136
6. King Porter stomp (take1) Esquire 20-022, 333, LakeLACD136
7. King Porter stomp (take 2) Esquire 333, Lake LACD136

Sandy Brown Blue Five

Alex Welsh (cnt) Sandy Brown (cl, voc - 1), Dizzy Jackson (bs), Alex Imrie (bjo), Stan Greig (drms)
Recorded: Glasgow Rhythm Club, West Nile St, December 11, 1953

1. Trouble in mind	S&M LP-2
2. Johnny is the boy for me	S&M LP-4
3. My man	S&M LP-4
4. Sweet Georgia Brown	S&M LP-4
5. Jenny's ball	S&M LP-4
6. Wolverine blues	S&M LP-4
7. Texas moaner	S&M LP-4
8. Careless love	S&M 10" LP unnumbered
9. Sweet Georgia Brown	S&M 10" LP unnumbered
10. Ole Miss'	S&M 10" LP unnumbered
11. Nobody's sweetheart	S&M issue details unknown
12. Ole Miss	S&M issue details unknown
13. My Monday date	S&M issue details unknown
14. Up above my head (1)	S&M issue details unknown
15. Limehouse blues	S&M issue details unknown
16. Heebie jeebies	S&M issue details unknown
17. Running Wild	S&M issue details unknown
18. High Society	S&M issue details unknown
19. My man	S&M issue details unknown

As far as is known, only one copy of each of LP-4 and LP-5 exist. Unfortunately, all attempts to get access to this recording and for information about it have been unsuccessful. Listening to what is available on taped copies of a few of these tracks, there are at least two sessions involved. One is 'live' and would be the Glasgow Rhythm Club recordings, the other tracks are studio recordings.

Capital Jazz Band

Charlie Malley (tpt), Graeme Robertson (tbn, voc - 1), Jackie Graham (clt, alto), George Cavaye (pno, voc-2), Colin Warwick (bjo), Ken Burns (bs, tba, voc - 3, ldr), Jimmy Henderson (drms)
Recorded: Edinburgh, March 3, 1990

1. Bugle boy march	band issue MC
2. Coney Island washboard (2)	band issue MC
3. Black and blue	band issue MC
4. Blaze away	band issue MC
5. I found a new baby	band issue MC
6. My gal Sal (1)	band issue MC
7. I'm crazy 'bout my baby (3)	band issue MC
8. Hiawatha rag	band issue MC
9. High society	band issue MC
10. Buddy Bolden blues (1)	band issue MC
11. Avalon	band issue MC
12. Yearning	band issue MC

Climax Jazz Band
Jim Petrie (cnt, voc), Jack Weddell (tbn), George Gilmour (clt), Mike Lunn (pno), Jock Westwater (bjo), Roy Percy (bs), Rinus Van De Peppel (drms)
Recorded: De Haagse Jazzclub, The Hague, November 25, 1990

1. Don't give up the ship	Jox 010
2. Tishimingo blues	Jox 010
3. Just a little while to stay here	Jox 010
4. Burgundy Street blues	Jox 010
5. My little girl	Jox 010
6. Old spinning wheel in the parlour	Jox 010
7. South	Jox 010
8. The curse of an aching heart	Jox 010
9. Climax rag	Jox 010
10. Till we meet again	Jox 010

Climax Re-Union Band
Jim Petrie (cnt, voc), Jack Weddell (tbn, voc), Jake McMahon (clt), Tom Finlay (pno), Mike Hart (bjo), Jim Young (bs), Kenny Milne (drms)
Recorded: Fingers Piano Bar, Edinburgh, June 13, 1992

1. Climax rag	band issue MC
2. Red man blues	band issue MC
3. Out in the cold again	band issue MC
4. East Coast trot	band issue MC

5. I'm forever blowing bubbles	band issue MC
6. Down in honky tonk town	band issue MC
7. Bright star blues	band issue MC
8. Girl of my dreams	band issue MC
9. Tea for two	band issue MC
10. Mama's gone goodbye	band issue MC
11. My blue heaven	band issue MC
12. There, I've said it again	band issue MC
13. Sweetie dear	band issue MC

Jim Petrie (cnt, voc), Jack Weddell (tbn, voc), Jake McMahon (clt), Tom Wood (pno), Mike Hart (bjo), Jim Young (bs), Kenny Milne (drms)
Recorded: Sydney, Australia, 1992

1. Somebody stole my gal	CRJB95
2. My little girl	CRJB95
3. All alone by the telephone	CRJB95
4. Baby, I want you tonight	CRJB95
5. Sensation rag	CRJB95
6. Big chief battle axe	CRJB95
7. At a Georgia camp meeting	CRJB95
8. Arkansas blues	CRJB95
9. That's a plenty	CRJB95

Criterion Brass Band
Everybody Loves Saturday Night

Kenny Milne (tpt, ldr), Dave Strut (tpt), Jack Weddell (tbn), George Gilmour (clt), Ian Boyter (ten), Simon Carlyle (sousa), Roy Dunnett (s-drm), Graham Scott (b-drm and cym)
Recorded: Edinburgh, 2001

1. Tell me your dreams	Hot Jazz
2. Everybody loves Saturday night	Hot Jazz
3. Just a little while to stay here	Hot Jazz
4. Ting-a-ling	Hot Jazz
5. Blue Monk	Hot Jazz
6. Down by the riverside	Hot Jazz
7. Mama Inez	Hot Jazz

8. Eh la bas	Hot Jazz
9. The laughing samba	Hot Jazz, J'nJ CD001
10. Ma, he's making eyes at me	Hot Jazz

Bourbon Street Parade

Finlay Milne, Jan Wouters (tpts), Alan Quinn (tbn), George Gilmour (clt), Ian Boyter (ten), Bill Bryden (sousa), Kenny Milne (s-drm), Graham Scott (b-drm), Jennifer Milne (tamb)
Recorded: Fairmile Inn, Edinburgh, 2004

1. Bourbon Street parade	Hot Jazz
2. St Louis blues	Hot Jazz
3. Precious Lord, take my hand	Hot Jazz
4. Jambalaya	Hot Jazz
5. High society	Hot Jazz
6. Beer barrel polka	Hot Jazz
7. St Thomas	Hot Jazz, J'n'J CD001
8. What a friend we have in Jesus	Hot Jazz
9. Over in the gloryland	Hot Jazz, J'n'J CD001
10. Li'l Liza Jane	Hot Jazz
11. Maryland, my Maryland	Hot Jazz
12. Bogalousa strut	Hot Jazz
13. Weary blues	Hot Jazz

Mardi Gras In New Orleans

Kenny Milne, Graham McArthur (tpts), Alan Quinn (tbn), George Gilmour (clt), Ian Boyter (ten), Simon Carlyle (sousa), Mac Rae (s-drm), Graham Scott (b-drm), Jennifer Milne (whistle, tamb)
Recorded: Fireman's Club, Edinburgh, 2006

1. Sing on	Hot Jazz
2. Just a closer walk with Thee	Hot Jazz
3. Does Jesus care?	Hot Jazz
4. Don't give up the ship	Hot Jazz
5. 'Tain't what you do	Hot Jazz
6. Sheik of Araby	Hot Jazz
7. Mardi Gras in New Orleans	Hot Jazz
8. Climax rag	Hot Jazz
9. Tuxedo Junction	Hot Jazz

10. Don't go 'way nobody	Hot Jazz
11. Down in honky tonk town	Hot Jazz
12. Scotland the brave	Hot Jazz
13. The Preacher	Hot Jazz
14. Red rides again	Hot Jazz
15. Four leaf clover	Hot Jazz
16. Chinatown, my Chinatown	Hot Jazz

Diplomats Of Jazz
Dreaming the Hours Away

Jim Petrie (cnt, voc)), Jack Graham (clt, alto), Jock Westwater (bjo), Bill Brydon (sousa)
Recorded: Bute Jazz Festival, date unknown

1. Oriental man	band issue MC
2. Trav'lin all alone	band issue MC
3. Shake it and break it	band issue MC
4. You'll long for me	band issue MC
5. Struttin' with some barbecue	band issue MC
6. Beaucoup de jazz	band issue MC
7. You made me love you	band issue MC
8. Melancholy blues	band issue MC
9. Anytime	band issue MC
10. Gravier Street blues	band issue MC
11. Blame it on the blues	band issue MC
12. Dreaming the hours away	band issue MC

Body And Soul
Jim Petrie (cnt, voc)), Jack Graham (clt, alto), Jock Westwater (bjo), Bill Brydon (sousa)
Recorded: Royal Ettrick Hotel, Edinburgh, February 20, 1995

1. Hey, hey baby	band issue MC
2. Sweet like this	band issue MC
3. I want a little girl	band issue MC
4. Shake it and break it	band issue MC
5. Supposin'	band issue MC
6. I'm not worrying	band issue MC
7. Marguerite	band issue MC

8. Body and soul	band issue MC
9. Snookum	band issue MC
10. What is this thing called love	band issue MC

Jim Petrie (cnt), Bob Busby (clt, alto), Beverley Knight (bjo), Bill Brydon (sousa)
Recorded: Edinburgh Jazz 'n' Jive Club, November 21, 2003

1. Wa wa wa	J'n'J CD001
2. Snag it	J'n'J CD001
3. I can't give you anything but love	J'n'J CD001

The Hut

Jim Petrie (cnt), Bob Busby (clt, alto), Norman Field (clt, c-mel-1), Beverley Knight (bjo), Bill Brydon (sousa)
Recorded: Fairmile Inn
(a) November 21, 2003
(b) April 26, 2004
(c) October 8, 2004
(d) December 12, 2004
(e) March 4, 2005
(f) June 10, 2005

1. Snag it (a)	band issue MC
2. Forty and tight (b)	band issue MC
3. Froggie Moore rag (b)	band issue MC
4. Mandy Lee blues (b)	band issue MC
5. Buddy Bolden blues (c)	band issue MC
6. Love nest (c)	band issue MC
7. Lost (c)	band issue MC
8. Bye and bye (d)	band issue MC
9. Marguerite (4)	band issue MC
10. You're a real sweetheart (1) (d)	band issue MC
11. I'm lonesome sweetheart (1) (e)	band issue MC
12. You're the one I care for (f)	band issue MC
13. Dreaming the hours away (f)	band issue MC
14. Irish black bottom (f)	band issue MC

Jim Petrie (cnt), Bob Busby (clt, alto), Beverley Knight (bjo), Bill Brydon (sousa) - with guest Norman Field (clt, alto, c-mel sax),
Recorded: Fairmile Inn, Edinburgh, March 4, 2005

My Monday Date

1. Martha	band issue CD
2. Keyhole blues	*unissued*
3. Lady love	band issue CD
4. Crying for the Carolines	band issue CD
5. Loveable	band issue CD
6. I can't give you anything but love, baby	band issue CD
7. East Coast trot	band issue CD
8. Blue and broken hearted	*unissued*
9. No moon at all	*unissued*
10. Until today	*unissued*
11. June night	*unissued*
12. What good am I without you	*unissued*
13. You're a real sweetheart	*unissued*
14. San	band issue CD
15. Sweet Ella May	band issue CD
16. Oriental strut	*unissued*
17. Try a little tenderness	*unissued*
18. My Monday date	band issue cd
19. I'm lonesome, Sweetheart	*unissued*
20. Once in a while	band issue CD
21. Sorry	band issue CD
22. Poor man blues	band issue CD
23. Swing that music	band issue CD

Jim Petrie (cnt), Bob Busby (clt, alto), Beverley Knight (bjo), Bill Brydon (sousa)
Recorded: Edinburgh Jazz 'n' Jive Club, June 25, 2010

1. New wang wang blues	J'n'J CD002
2. Cabin in the pines	J'n'J CD002
3. China boy	J'n'J CD002

Fiona Duncan And Her Jazz Friends
Fiona's Fellas

Fiona Duncan (voc), Gordon Dillon (tpt), George Kidd (tbn), Sam Smith (tbn-1), Dick Stroak (clt, saxes), Jack Finlay (pno), Johnny Harper (gtr), Johnny Phillips (gtr-2), Kenny McDonald (bs), Murray Smith (drms) Dave Swanson (drms-3)
Recorded: Craighall Studios, Edinburgh, March 1982

1. I ain't gonna play no second fiddle	FATT FH1000
2. You've changed	FATT FH1000
3. The eagle and me	FATT FH1000
4. Gimme a pigfoot and a bottle of beer (1)	FATT FH1000
5. I can't give you anything but love	FATT FH1000
6. Is you is, or is you ain't my baby?	FATT FH1000
7. Please don't talk about me when I'm gone	FATT FH1000
8. You've been a good old wagon	FATT FH1000
9. Gee baby, ain't I good to you?	FATT FH1000
10. Fine brown frame	FATT FH1000
11. I used to love you (2, 3)	FATT FH1000
12. If I could be with you	FATT FH1000
13. Someday sweetheart (3)	FATT FH1000
14. Dinah (3)	FATT FH1000

Al Fairweather Jazz Band

Al Fairweather (tpt), Bob Craig (tbn), Dave Paxton (clt), Christian Rosendal (clt-1 added), Jock Westwater (bjo), Jim Young (bs), Kenny Milne (drms)
Recorded: Glenelg Hotel, Edinburgh, January 31, 1990

1. Sunset Café stomp	limited issue CD
2. Black and blue	limited issue CD
3. I can't give you anything but love	limited issue CD
4. Rosetta (1)	limited issue CD
5. Canal Street blues	limited issue CD
6. Muskrat ramble	limited issue CD
7. Tin Roof blues	limited issue CD
8. Cakewalking babies	limited issue CD
9. Heebie jeebies	limited issue CD
10. Ole Miss rag	limited issue CD
11. Baby, won't you please come home	limited issue CD
12. An apple for the teacher	limited issue CD

This was a privately recorded session and was made available on a limited basis to members of the Sandy Brown Society only.

Fat Sam's Band
Jive On Down
Gus Ferguson (tpt), Graeme Robertson (tbn), Hamish McGregor (clt, alto, bar, ldr), Nick Robertson (alto, voc), Bill Simpson (sop, ten), Donald Corbett (pno), Tony Howard (gtr), Bobby Millar (bs), Ken Mathieson (drms)
Recorded: Craighall Studios, Edinburgh, January 1986

1. Jumpin' jive *	Salmet 501
2. Jack you're dead	Salmet 501
3. Reet Petite and Gone	Salmet 501
4. Chartreuse *	Salmet 501
5. What's the use of getting sober	Salmet 501
6. That chick's too young to fry	Salmet 501
7. Choo-choo-ch-boogie	Salmet 501
8. Nobody here but us chickens	Salmet 501
9. You run your mouth	Salmet 501
10. Is you is or is you ain't my baby?	Salmet 501
11. Saturday night fish fry *	Salmet 501
12. San Francisco Fran	Salmet 501
13. Five guys named Mo	Salmet 501

Boogie On Down
Gus Ferguson (tpt), Graeme Robertson (tbn), Hamish McGregor (clt, alto, bar, ldr), Nick Robertson (alto, voc), Tom Chalmers (clt, ten, fl), Campbell Normand (pno), Tony Howard (gtr), Donald McDonald (bs), Ken Mathieson (drms)
Recorded: REL Studios, Edinburgh, March 15, 1988

1. Fat Sam boogie	FSC502
2. Flat foot floogie	FSC502
3. You're my meat	FSC502
4. Roll 'em *	FSC502
5. That cat is high	FSC502
6. Minnie the moocher	FSC502
7. Jumpin' with Symphony Sid *	FSC502
8. Caldonia *	FSC502
9. Echoes of Harlem	FSC502
10. Fat Sam from Birmingham	FSC502
11. Moten swing *	FSC502
12. Messy Bessy	FSC502

13. Alright   FSC502

Note: the above two recordings were issued as 'Fat Sam's Band, Volume 1, 1986 -88' on a double cassette and entitled as shown

Swing On Down

Gus Ferguson (tpt), Jimmy Mann (tbn), Hamish McGregor (clt, sop, alto, voc, ldr), Martin Foster (clt, sop, alto, bar), Tom Chalmers (clt, ten, flt), Campbell Normand (pno), Tony Howard (gtr), Donald McDonald (bs), Ken Mathieson (drms)
Recorded: Sonic Studios, Edinburgh, June 11, 1989

1. Miller Madness: Little brown Jug; Pennsylvania 6500; American patrol; String of pearls, Chattanooga choo-choo; In the mood *   FSB502
2. You know it too   FSB502
3. Basically blues   FSB502
4. Shape in a drape   FSB502
5. The Mooche *   FSB502
6. Meet me with your black drawers on *   FSB502
7. All of me   FSB502
8. Spain   FSB502
9. Tougher than tough   FSB502
10. Drop me off in Harlem *   FSB502
11. Night train   FSB502
12. That old devil called love *   FSB502
13. Sure had a wonderful time *   FSB502
14. Bugle call rag   FSB502

Ring Dem Bells
Gus Ferguson (tpt), Jimmy Mann (tb), Hamish McGregor (clt, sop, alto, voc, ldr), Martin Foster (clt, sop, alto, bar), Tom Chalmers (clt, ten, flt), Campbell Normand (pno), Tony Howard (gtr), Donald McDonald (bs), Ken Mathieson (drms)
Recorded: Sonic Studios, Edinburgh, 13 & 14 April 1991

1. Ring dem bells *   FSB503
2. All for the love of Lil   FSB503
3. Sweet Like This   FSB503

4. Stealin' apples	FSB503
5. Black butterfly	FSB503
6. Suey	FSB503
7. I want a roof over my head *	FSB503
8. Oui, c'est samba *	FSB503
9. I found a new baby *	FSB503
10. Lover man	FSB503
11. Everybody eats	FSB503
12. Mood indigo *	FSB503
13. Big 10 inch *	FSB503
14. On the sunny side of the street	FSB503
15. Let the good times roll	FSB503

*Note: * these recordings were issued as 'Fat Sam's Band, Volume 2, 1989 - 91' on a double cassette and entitled as shown*

Live at the Paisley Arts Centre
Gus Ferguson (tpt), Jimmy Mann (tbn), Hamish McGregor (clt, sop, alto, voc, ldr), Jack Duff (clt, sop, alto, ten, bar), Tom Chalmers (clt, ten), Tom Finlay (pno), Tony Howard (gtr), Donald McDonald (bs), Ken Mathieson (drms)
Recorded: The Arts Centre, Paisley, February 1994

1. Sweet Georgia Brown	FSB504
2. T'ain't what you do +	FSB504
3. Hay bab a rebop +	FSB504
4. In my solitude +	FSB504
5. Buddy Bolden's blues	FSB504
6. April in Paris +	FSB504
7. Down by the riverside +	FSB504
8. Davenport blues	FSB504
9. The drippy dripper +	FSB504
10. Mack the Knife +	FSB504
11. Rose of the Rio Grande	FSB504
12. Buona sera	FSB504
13. Embraceable you +	FSB504
14. Just a gigolo / I ain't got nobody +	FSB504
15. Fats Domino Medley: Be My Guest; Ain't That A Shame; I Want To Walk You Home; My Blue Heaven; Blueberry Hill +	FSB504

Live At Fat Sam's Diner
Gus Ferguson (tpt),Eddie Severn (ten-1,), Jimmy Mann (tbn), Hamish McGregor (clt, sop, alto, voc, ldr), Jack Duff (clt, sop, alto, ten, bar), Tom Chalmers (clt, ten), Tom Finlay (pno), Tony Howard (gtr), Donald McDonald (bs), Ken Mathieson (drms)
Recorded: Fat Sam's Diner, Edinburgh, March 1994

1. Cotton Club stomp	FSB505
2. Meet Mr Rabbit	FSB505
3. Stranger on the shore +	FSB505
4. Jumpin' at the Woodside +	FSB505
5. Ain't got nothin' but the blues +	FSB505
6. China boy (1)	FSB505
7. Satin doll (1) +	FSB505
8. The kid from Redbank (1) +	FSB505
9. Shreveport stomp (1)	FSB505
10. Moulin a café (1) +	FSB505
11. Shiny stockings (1) +	FSB505

Note: these two recordings were issued as 'The Best of Fat Sam's Band, Volume 2' on a double cassette and entitled as shown

The Best Of Fat Sam's Band, Volume 1
This is the first CD issued by the band and is a 22 track compilation of SAL501, FSC502, FSB502 & FSB503, marked with an '*', with the following exceptions

20. Shape in a drape (recorded BBC London 'Opportunity Knocks' 1991
21. Ain't nobody here but us chickens (recorded BBC Scotland 1991)
22. Choo-choo-ch-boogie (recorded BBC Scotland 1991)

The Best Of Fat Sam's Band, Volume 2
This is the second CD issued by the band and is a 17 track compilation of, FSB 504 & 505, marked with '+'

Fat Sam's Band, Volume 3 – Live At Fat Sam's Downtown Diner

Tom McNiven (tpt), Dave Batchelor (tbn), Hamish McGregor (clt, sop, alto, ldr), John Burgess (ten, flt), Martin Foster (clt, alto, ten, bar), Andrew Barber (alto, bar – 1), Steve Meeker (ten – 1), Tom Finlay (pno, org), Tony Howard (gtr, voc), Roy Percy (bs, elb), Alistair Morrow (drms)
Recorded: April 15 & 22, 1998

1. Night train	band issue CD
2. It should have been me	band issue CD
3. Change my plan	band issue CD
4. Safronia (1)	band issue CD
5. Flight of the foo birds	band issue CD
6. Alright, OK, you win	band issue CD
7. I love the life I live	band issue CD
8. What's new?	band issue CD
9. Mr Blues is comin' to town	band issue CD
10. Splanky	band issue CD
11. You go to my head	band issue CD
12. Reet petite	band issue CD
13. Sweet home Chicago	band issue CD
14. Theme from Peter Gunn	band issue CD
15. Pink champagne	band issue CD
16. Sittin' on it all the time	band issue CD
17. 'Gators drag	band issue CD

Fat Sam's Band, Volume 4 – Live at Fat Sam's

Bill Hunter (tpt), Dave Batchelor (tbn), Hamish McGregor (clt, alto, voc, ldr), Martin Foster (alto, bar), Iestyn Evans (ten), Tom Finlay (pno), Eric Wales (gtr, voc), Roy Percy (bs), Alistair Morrow (drms)
Recorded: November 17 & 24, 1999

1. Up a lazy river	band issue CD
2. 9.20 Special	band issue CD
3. Big fat mammas	band issue CD
4. Jeeps blues	band issue CD
5. Minnie the Moocher	band issue CD
6. Skin deep	band issue CD
7. Is you is or is you ain't my baby?	band issue CD
8. Honeysuckle rose	band issue CD
9. Bad, bad Leroy Brown	band issue CD
10. Stardust	band issue CD

11. One sweet letter from you	band issue CD
12. Blue Lou	band issue CD
13. Jungle king	band issue CD
14. Fantail	band issue CD
15. Fat Sam from Birmingham	band issue CD
16. Basically blues	band issue CD
17. Buona sera	band issue CD
18. One O'clock jump	band issue CD
19. Flying home	band issue CD

Fat Sam's Band, Volume 5

Bill Hunter (tpt), Dave Batchelor (tbn), Hamish McGregor (clt, alto, voc, ldr), Allon Beauvoisin (alto, bar), Gordon McNeil (ten), Tom Finlay (pno), Eric Wales (gtr), Phil Adams (gtr-1) Mark Austin (bs) ,Roy Percy (bs-1) Alistair Morrow (drms)
Recorded: February 1, 2003

1. The Fat Sam boogie (1)	band issue CD
2. All of me (1)	band issue CD
3. Clementine (1)	band issue CD
4. Lester leaps in	band issue CD
5. Lover man	band issue CD
6. Let the good times roll (1)	band issue CD
7. Stompin' at The Savoy (1)	band issue CD
8. Swingin' the blues (1)	band issue CD
9. Hey now, hey now (1)	band issue CD
10. The angels sing	band issue CD
11. Mama do (1)	band issue CD
12. Opus 1	band issue CD
13. Guitar boogie	band issue CD
14. Have you met Miss Jones? (1)	band issue CD
15. Loch Lomond	band issue CD
16. On the sunny side of the street (1)	band issue CD

Fat Sam's Band, Volume 6 – Airmail Special

Bill Hunter (tpt), Dave Batchelor (tbn), Hamish McGregor (reeds, voc, ldr), Keith Edwards (reeds), Konrad Wiszniewski (reeds), Tom Finlay (pno), Campbell Normand (pno-2)Eric Wales (gtr), Ed Kelly (bs), Alistair Morrow (drms), Tom Gordon (drms-1)

Recorded:
(a) The Spiegeltent, Edinburgh, August 3, 2007
(b) The Jamhouse, Edinburgh, July 31, 2009
(c) The Jamhouse, Edinburgh, August 7, 2009

1. Airmail special (2) (c)	band issue CD
2. Old cow hand (1) (b)	band issue CD
3. Mercy, mercy, mercy (2) (c)	band issue CD
4. The summer wind (2) (c)	band issue CD
5. Salt peanuts (2) (c)	band issue CD
6. Benny's from heaven (2) (c)	band issue CD
7. Isfhan (1) (b)	band issue CD
8. East of the sun (a)	band issue CD
9. Keeping out of mischief now (b)	band issue CD
10. For once in my life (2) (c)	band issue CD
11. Old Fat Sam (a)	band issue CD
12. I'm getting sentimental over you (1) (b)	band issue CD
13. Old man river (a)	band issue CD
14. Harry James Medley: My silent love, You made me love you, I had the craziest dream (1) (b)	band issue CD
15. Cherokee (2) (c)	band issue CD
16. Jump (2) (c)	band issue CD
17. Satin doll (2) (c)	band issue CD
18. Walk between the raindrops (1) (b)	band issue CD

Jack Finlay Trio With Benny Waters
Edinburgh International Jazz Festival, 1986
Benny Waters (alto), Jack Finlay (pno), Kenny Ellis (bs), Bobby Stewart (drms)
Recorded: 1986?

1. Some of these days   1986 Edinburgh Jazz Festival LP

Fred's Clubhouse Seven
Kenny Milne (tpt), John Arthur (tbn), George Duncan (clt), Gus McKay (pno), Kenny Henderson (bjo), Fred Murray (bs, voc, ldr), Roy Dunnett (drms)
Recorded: Edinburgh Jazz 'n' Jive Club, October 10, 2007

1. Buddy's habit	J'n'J CD001
2. You are my sunshine	J'n'J CD001

3. You always hurt the one you love   J'n'J CD001
4. Savoy blues   J'n'J CD002
5. Goin' home   J'n'J CD002

Mike Hart With The Hot Antic Jazz Band
Concert du 10eme Anniversaire du Hot Antic Jazz Band
Michel Bastide (cnt, v-tbn, voc), Benny Waters (alto-1), Jean-Francois Bonnel (clt, alto, ten, cnt, voc), Stephane Matthey (pno), Jean-Pierre Dubois (bjo, gtr, clt), Mike Hart (bjo, voc-2), Bernard Antherieu (bjo-3), Christian Lefevre (bb, tbn), Stephen Joseph (drms, wbd), Jean- Francois Guyot (wbd-4), Dave Bennett (voc-5)
Recorded: Opera de Nimes, France, Friday, March 17, 1989

1. Shine (1,2)   HP-1
2. Nagasaki (1,5)   HP-1
3. I lost my gal from Memphis (1,4)   HP-1
4. Dans les rues D'Antibes (3)   HP-1
5. Petite fleur (3)   HP-1
6. Les oignons 3)   HP-1
7. China boy (1,3)   HP-1

Mike Hart is not featured on any other tracks
This recording was also released in DVD format

Mike Hart's International All Stars
Full House
Mike Daly (tpt), Bob Barnard (cnt-1), John Service (tbn), Hamish McGregor (clt, voc), Jonny Boston (ten, voc-2), Tom Finlay (pno), Mike Hart (bjo, gtr), Roy Percy (bs), Adam Sorenson (drms)
Recorded: The Famous Spiegeltent, Edinburgh International Jazz & Blues Festival, August 4, 2005

1. That's a plenty   Parsnip CD006
2. If you were the only girl in the world   Parsnip CD006
3. Savoy blues   Parsnip CD006
4. Cheek to cheek (2)   Parsnip CD006
5. Wild man blues (1)   Parsnip CD006
6. Keeping out of mischief (1,2)   Parsnip CD006
7. Way down yonder in New Orleans (1,2)   Parsnip CD006

8. I never knew (1,2)	Parsnip CD006
9. Avalon	Parsnip CD006
10. Shine	Parsnip CD006
11. If I had you	Parsnip CD006
12. Topsy	Parsnip CD006
13. After you've gone	Parsnip CD006
14. Sweet Lorraine	*unissued*
15. Strutting with some barbecue	*unissued*
16. Wild man blues	*unissued*
17. Nagasaki	*unissued*
18. Bourbon Street parade	*unissued*
19. My blue heaven	*unissued*
20. High society	*unissued*
21. Royal Garden blues	*unissued*
22. Everybody loves Saturday night	*unissued*

Mike Hart's (Scottish) Society Syncopators
Jazz Tattoo
Gus Ferguson (tpt, voc-1), Johnny McGuff (tbn), Jackie Graham (clt, alto, voc-2), Tom Finlay (pno), Mike Hart (bjo, gtr), Kenny McDonald (bs), Bobby Stewart (drms)
Recorded: REL Studios, Edinburgh, March 9, 1980

1. Go Ghana	Parsnip PR1001
2. My ain folk (2)	Parsnip PR1001
3. Willie The Weeper	Parsnip PR1001
4. New Orleans	Parsnip PR1001
5. Loch Lomond (2)	Parsnip PR1001
6. Rosetta (1)	Parsnip PR1001
7. Doin' the crazy walk	Parsnip PR1001
8. Buddy Bolden's blues	Parsnip PR1001
9. Muskrat ramble	Parsnip PR1001
10. Wolverine blues	Parsnip PR1001
11. T'ain't what you do (2)	Parsnip PR1001
12. Panama rag	Parsnip PR1001

Huntin' Shootin' And Jazzin'
Andrew Lauder (tpt),Dave Strutt (cnt ,tpt, mel) Johnny McGuff (tbn, v-tbn), Jackie Graham (clt, alto), Tom Finlay (pno), Mike Hart (bjo, gtr), Francis Cowan (bs), Frank Birnie (drms), Kenny Henderson (bagpipes-1)
Recorded: Craighall Studios, Edinburgh, March 3, 1984

1. Jubilee	Parsnip PR1002
2. New Orleans stomp	Parsnip PR1002
3. Aunt Hagar's blues	Parsnip PR1002
4. Goin' out the back way	Parsnip PR1002
5. Maple leaf rag	Parsnip PR1002
6. Sing, sing, sing	Parsnip PR1002
7. Trombone rag	Parsnip PR1002
8. Squeeze me	Parsnip PR1002
9. Maryland, my Maryland	Parsnip PR1002
10. Ostrich walk	Parsnip PR1002
11. Apple honey	Parsnip PR1002
12. Bagpipe haggis march (1)	Parsnip PR1002

With Wild Bill Davison and Jim Galloway

Wild Bill Davison (cnt-1), Jim Galloway (sop-2), Dave Strutt (cnt), Johnny McGuff (tbn), Hamish McGregor (clt, sop, alto, bar), Jackie Graham (clt, alto), Tom Finlay (pno), Mike Hart (bjo, gtr), Jerry Forde (bs-3), Francis Cowan (bs), Frank Birnie (drms), Wendy Weatherby (voc-4)
Recorded: Craighall Studios, Edinburgh, March 8, 1986

1. I never knew (1,2)	Parsnip 1003
2. Keeping out of mischief (1,2)	Parsnip 1003
3. Flying home (2)	Parsnip 1003
4. Hard hearted Hannah (4)	Parsnip 1003
5. B.M. rag (3)	Parsnip 1003
6. Save it pretty mama (1,2)	Parsnip 1003
7. Dans les rues D'Antibes (2,3)	Parsnip 1003
8. Big Bill (2,3)	Parsnip 1003
9. Our monday date (1,2)	Parsnip 1003
10. Creole belles (3)	Parsnip 1003
11. A kiss to build a dream on (2)	Parsnip 1003
12. Rockin' in rhythm (2)	Parsnip 1003

Happy Feet

Bruce Adams (tpt),Dave Strutt (cnt, voc), Johnny McGuff (tbn), Jackie Graham (clt, alto, voc), Tom Finlay (pno), Mike Hart (bjo, gtr), Ricky Steele (bs, bb), Frank Birnie (drms), Wendy Weatherby (voc)
Recorded: Fingers Bar, Edinburgh, March 6 & 7, 1987

1. Cakewalking babies	band issue MC
2. Ludo	band issue MC
3. Strutting with some barbecue	band issue MC
4. The right key but the wrong keyhole	band issue MC
5. Cheek to Cheek	band issue MC
6. Willie the Weeper	band issue MC
7. T'ain't what you do	band issue MC
8. Potato head blues	band issue MC
9. Mop mop	band issue MC
10. Sugar blues	band issue MC
11. Happy feet	band issue MC
12. Blues in the closet	band issue MC
13. Dippermouth blues	band issue MC

Rehearsing For A Nervous Breakdown

Bruce Adams (tpt), Johnny McGuff (tbn), Jake McMahon (clt, ten), Tom Finlay (pno), Mike Hart (bjo, gtr), Ricky Steele (bs) Murray Smith (drms), Wendy Weatherby (voc)
Recorded: Fingers Bar, Edinburgh, December 11, 1988

1. Black bottom stomp	band issue MC
2. Second hand Rose	band issue MC
3. I'm sorry I made you cry	band issue MC
4. Poor Butterfly	band issue MC
5. Liza	band issue MC
6. Strike up the band	band issue MC
7. Wild women don't have the blues	band issue MC
8. I found a new baby	band issue MC
9. Tin Roof blues	band issue MC
10. Rehearsing for a nervous breakdown	band issue MC

Rothesay 1993

Dave Strutt (tpt, voc), Dave Fimister (tpt), Johnny McGuff (tbn), Jack Duff (clt, alto, ten), Tom Finlay (pno), Mike Hart (bjo, gtr), Ricky Steele (bs), Murray Smith (drms), Wendy Weatherby (voc)
Recorded: Rothesay Jazz Festival, May 1. 1993

1. I never knew	*Raymer Sound unissued*
2. Maple leaf rag	*Raymer Sound unissued*
3. It ain't no sin	*Raymer Sound unissued*

4. I got what it takes	*Raymer Sound unissued*
5. Cakewalking babies	*Raymer Sound unissued*
6. Squeeze me	*Raymer Sound unissued*
7. Goin' out the back way	*Raymer Sound unissued*
8. Sister Kate	*Raymer Sound unissued*
9. Dinah	*Raymer Sound unissued*
10. Rehearsing for a nervous breakdown	
	Raymer Sound unissued
11. Putting on the Ritz	*Raymer Sound unissued*
12. Potato head blues	*Raymer Sound unissued*
13. Happy feet	*Raymer Sound unissued*
14. Baby, won't you please come home	
	Raymer Sound unissued
15. Just a gigolo	*Raymer Sound unissued*
16. Tea for two	*Raymer Sound unissued*
17. Rose of Washington Square	*Raymer Sound unissued*
18. Sing, sing, sing	*Raymer Sound unissued*

Rothesay 1994

Dave Strutt (tpt, voc), Dave Keir (tbn), Jake McMahon (clt, ten), Brian Kellock (pno), Mike Hart (bjo, gtr), Ricky Steele (bs), Murray Smith (drms), Wendy Weatherby (voc)
Recorded: Rothesay Jazz Festival, April 28, 1994

1. Empty bed blues	*Raymer Sound unissued*
2. Them there eyes	*Raymer Sound unissued*
3. Maple leaf rag	*Raymer Sound unissued*
4. Lazy bones	*Raymer Sound unissued*
5. Too busy	*Raymer Sound unissued*
6. I've got what it takes	*Raymer Sound unissued*
7. Sister Kate	*Raymer Sound unissued*
8. Ory's Creole trombone	*Raymer Sound unissued*
9. Evil hearted blues	*Raymer Sound unissued*
10. 'Tain't no sin	*Raymer Sound unissued*
11. Cal'donia	*Raymer Sound unissued*
12. Keeping out of mischief	*Raymer Sound unissued*
13. Goody, goody	*Raymer Sound unissued*
14. Rehearsing for a nervous breakdown	
	Raymer Sound unissued

Jake's Melody Boys
Traditional Jazz Around The World
Jake McMahon (clt, ldr), Jack Weddell (tbn), Violet Milne (pno), Robin Galloway (bs), Kenny Milne (drms)
Recorded: 1996

1. All I do is dream of you	Jazz Crusade JCCD 3023
2. See See rider	Jazz Crusade JCCD 3023
3. Babyface	Jazz Crusade JCCD 3023
4. True	Jazz Crusade JCCD 3023
5. Underneath Hawaiian skies	Jazz Crusade JCCD 3023

Other tracks on this CD are by the Louisiana Shakers and Jesse's New Orleans Jazz Band

The Jazz Masters
Andrew Lauder (tpt), Jimmy Shortreed (clt, alto), Gordon Cruickshank (ten - 1), Jack Finlay (pno), Graham Blamire (bs, ldr), Donald 'Chick' Murray (drms)
Recorded: Fingers Piano Bar, Edinburgh, March, 1988

1. Chix at six	band issue MC
2. I'ts wonderful	band issue MC
3. How am I to know?	band issue MC
4. Nights at the turntable	band issue MC
5. Good Queen Bess	band issue MC
6. In the wee small hours	band issue MC
7. Shine	band issue MC
8. Black butterfly	band issue MC
9. Liza	band issue MC
10. Coquette	band issue MC
11. Pee Wee's blues	band issue MC
12. Perdido (1)	band issue MC
13. Blues march (1)	band issue MC
14. The Jeep is jumping (1)	band issue MC

Dave Keir's Hot Four
Stomp, Stomp, Stomp
Dave Keir (tpt, tbn), Bob Busby (clt, alto), Jock Westwater (bjo, voc - 1), Dizzy Jackson (bs)
Recorded: Edinburgh, Autumn, 1999

1. Come on and stomp, stomp, stomp	Jox unnumbered CD
2. Dallas blues	Jox unnumbered CD
3. Rhythm king	Jox unnumbered CD
4. Kansas City stomps	Jox unnumbered CD
5. Sobbin' blues	Jox unnumbered CD
6. Piggly Wiggly	Jox unnumbered CD
7. Sunset Café stomp	Jox unnumbered CD
8. Mandy Lee blues	Jox unnumbered CD
9. You're next	Jox unnumbered CD
10. Shake it and break it	Jox unnumbered CD
11. Lina blues (1)	Jox unnumbered CD
12 Ory's Creole trombone	Jox unnumbered CD
13. Angeline	Jox unnumbered CD
14. Weatherbird rag	Jox unnumbered CD
15. Riverside blues	Jox unnumbered CD
16. I'm goin' away to wear you off my mind	
	Jox unnumbered CD

Redman Blues

Dave Keir (tpt, tbn, alto), Bob Busby (clt, alto), Jock Westwater (bjo, voc-1), Dizzy Jackson (bs)
Recorded: Autumn 2000 / Spring 2001

1. Red man blues	Jox unnumbered CD
2. Tears	Jox unnumbered CD
3. Black and tan fantasy	Jox unnumbered CD
4. Love me or leave me (1)	Jox unnumbered CD
5. Chattanooga stomp	Jox unnumbered CD
6. Apex blues	Jox unnumbered CD
7. Walk that broad	Jox unnumbered CD
8. East St Louis toodle-oo	Jox unnumbered CD
9. Mandy make up your mind	Jox unnumbered CD
10. There ain't no sweet man worth the salt of my tears (1)	
	Jox unnumbered CD
11. East Coast trot	Jox unnumbered CD

12. Ole Miss rag	Jox unnumbered CD
13. Alligator blues	Jox unnumbered CD
14. Candy lips (1)	Jox unnumbered CD
15. Bouncing around	Jox unnumbered CD

Pete Kerr's Dixielanders
Al Clarke (tpt), Ken Ramage (tbn), Pete Kerr (clt), Bob McDonald (pno), Jim Douglas (bjo), Johnny Logan (bs), George Crockett (drms)
Recorded: Edinburgh, 1960

1. Stars and stripes forever	Waverley SLP505
2. Ice cream	Waverley SLP505

Al Clarke (tpt), Ken Ramage (tbn), Pete Kerr (clt), Bob McDonald (pno), Jim Douglas (bjo), Johnny Logan (bs), George Crockett (drms)
Recorded: Edinburgh, 1960

1. Coney Island washboard	Waverley SLP506
2. Waltzing Matilda	Waverley SLP506

Pete Kerr's Scottish All Stars
Jazz At The Capital
Mike Scott (tpt), Eddie Lorkin (tbn), Pete Kerr (clt), Mike Oliver (pno), Jim Douglas (bjo, gtr), Ron Mathewson (bs), Billy Law (drms)
Recorded: Craighall Studios, Edinburgh, 1963

1. Peter and the Wolf	Waverley ELP128
2. Night train	Waverley ELP128
3. The old spinning wheel	Waverley ELP128
4. Who's afraid of the big bad wolf	Waverley ELP128

More Jazz At The Capital
Pete Kerr (clt), Mike Scott (tpt), Eddie Lorkin (tbn), Mike Oliver, (pno), Jim Douglas (gtr/bjo), Ron Mathewson (bs), Billy Law (drms).
Recorded: Craighall Studios, Edinburgh, 1964

1. The ugly duckling	Waverley ELP135

2. Sonny Boy	Waverley ELP135
3. Davenport blues	Waverley ELP135
4. Drum break for Billy	Waverley ELP135

Maid Of The Forth Stompers

Andrew Lauder (cnt), Jimmy Shortreed (cl, alto), Harald Vox (bjo,gtr), Graham Blamire (b, ldr).
Recorded: Leapfrog, Edinburgh, March 21, 1995

1. Shine	band issue MC
2. Tishomingo blues	band issue MC
3. Mama's gone, goodbye	band issue MC
4. When somebody thinks you're wonderful	band issue MC
5. Summer set	band issue MC
6. Muskrat ramble	band issue MC
7. I found a new baby	band issue MC
8. Up a lazy river	band issue MC
9. Blues my naughtie sweetie gives to me	band issue MC
10. Wabash blues	band issue MC
11. 12th Street rag	band issue MC
12. Weary blues	band issue MC
13. Chinatown, my Chinatown	band issue MC

Andrew Lauder (cnt), Gerard Dott (clt), Nigel Porteous (bjo, gtr), Graham Blamire (bs, ldr)
Recorded: Edinburgh Jazz 'n' Jive Club, February 2, 2010

1. Always	J'n'J CD 002
2. Stevedore stomp	J'n'J CD 002

Ken Mathieson's Classic Jazz Band

Billy Hunter (tpt), Johnny McGuff (tbn), Dick Lee (clt, alto), Keith Edwards (ten), Martin Foster (clt, bar), Tom Finlay (pno), Ricky Steele (bs), Ken Mathieson (drms ,ldr)
Recorded: The Sound Café, Penicuik, September 19, 2004

1. Chicago breakdown	Demo
2. Shreveport stomp	Demo
3. The pearls	Demo
4. Sweet substitute	Demo
5. Buckini	Demo

Jelly's New Clothes

Billy Hunter (tpt), Ewan McAllan (tbn)), Dick Lee (clt, sop, alto), Keith Edwards (ten), Martin Foster (clt, alto, bar, bar), Tom Finlay (pno), Roy Percy (bs), Ken Mathieson (drms ,ldr)
Recorded: Castlesound Studios, Pentcaitland, 2006

1. Grandpa's spells	CJO-001
2. The pearls	CJO-001
3. Boogaboo	CJO-001
4. Froggie Moore	CJO-001
5. King Porter stomp	CJO-001
6. Jungle blues	CJO-001
7. Mamanita	CJO-001
8. Chicago breakdown	CJO-001
9. Dead man blues	CJO-001
10. Mister Joe	CJO-001
11. Shreveport stomp	CJO-001
12. Sweet substitute	CJO-001
13. Kansas City stomps	CJO-001

Salutes The Kings Of Jazz

Billy Hunter (tpt),Phil O'Malley (tbn), Dick Lee (clt, b-clt, sop, alto), Konrad Wiszniewski (ten), Martin Foster (clt,b-clt, alto, bar, b-sax), Tom Finlay (pno), Roy Percy (bs), Ken Mathieson (drms, ldr)
Recorded: Sound Café, Penicuik, 2007

1. Mahogany Hall stomp	Lake LACD 281
2. Mandy, make up your mind	Lake LACD 281
3. Blues for Kenny Davern	Lake LACD 281
4. Stompy Jones	Lake LACD 281
5. In a mist	Lake LACD 281
6. West End blues	Lake LACD 281
7. Sorry	Lake LACD 281
8. Morning glory	Lake LACD 281
9. Sweet like This	Lake LACD 281
10. Jitterbug waltz	Lake LACD 281
11. Buddy Bolden's blues	Lake LACD 281
12. Bojangles	Lake LACD 281
13. Georgia swing	Lake LACD 281
14. Singin' the blues	Lake LACD 281
15. Down South camp meeting	Lake LACD 281

Ken Mathieson's Classic Jazz Band With Duke Heitger
Celebrating Satchmo

Duke Heitger (tpt ,voc) with Billy Hunter(tpt), Phil O'Malley (tbn), Dick Lee (clt, sop, alto), Konrad Wiszniewski (ten), Martin Foster (clt, alto, bar), Paul Kirby (pno), Roy Percy (bs), Ken Mathieson (drms ,ldr)
Recorded: May 2008

1. Blues my naughtie sweetie gives to me		Lake LACD 286
2. Cornet chop suey		Lake LACD 286
3. When it's sleepy time down South		Lake LACD 286
4. Atlanta blues		Lake LACD 286
5. Song of the islands		Lake LACD 286
6. Wild man blues		Lake LACD 286
7. Down in honky tonk town		Lake LACD 286
8. Eventide		Lake LACD 286
9. Sweethearts on parade		Lake LACD 286
10. I got the right to sing the blues		Lake LACD 286
11. Among my souvenirs		Lake LACD 286
12. Coal cart blues		Lake LACD 286
13. Mahogany Hall stomp		Lake LACD 286
14. What a wonderful world		Lake LACD 286

Ken Mathieson's Classic Jazz Band With Alan Barnes

Alan Barnes (alto) with Billy Hunter (tpt), Phil O'Malley (tbn), Dick Lee (clt, sop, alto), Konrad Wiszniewski (ten), Martin Foster (clt, b-clt, bar), Paul Harrison (pno), Roy Percy (bs), Ken Mathieson (drms ,ldr)
Recorded: Sound Café, Penicuik, Midlothain, 2011

1. I can't believe that you're in love with me
                                                                 Woodville WVCD133
2. Easy Money   Woodville WVCD133
3. A walkin' thing   Woodville WVCD133
4. The Glasgow Suite   Woodville WVCD133
    A little at a time
    DN
    Waltz
    The Clyde
8. Bright future   Woodville WVCD133

9. Stompin' at the Savoy	Woodville WVCD133
10. Honeysuckle rose	Woodville WVCD133
11. Malibu	Woodville WVCD133
12. Symphony in riffs	Woodville WVCD133
13. Doozy	Woodville WVCD133

Hamish Mcgregor's All Stars

Tommy Lister (tpt), Hamish McGregor (tbn, voc), Jackie Graham (clt), Johnny Harper (bjo), Graham Blamire (bs), Charlie Welsh (drms)
Recorded: Craighall Studios, Edinburgh, July 10, 1965

1. Molly Malone	private band recording
2. The Sheik of Araby	private band recording
3. Coney Island washboard	private band recording
4. Sit down you're rocking the boat	
	private band recording
5. I love my mother-in-law	
	private band recording

This recording was made for band members only

Charlie Mcnair's Jazz Band

Charlie McNair (tpt), Bob Craig (tbn), Jackie Graham (clt), Mike Hart (bjo), Dizzy Jackson (bs), Bobby Stewart (drms)
Recorded: Edinburgh, early 1960s

1. The fish man	Waverley Records SLP502
2. Big House blues	Waverley Records SLP502
3. Colonel Bogey march	Waverley Records SLP 504
4. My journey to the sky	Waverley Records SLP504

The Charlie Mcnair New Orleans Jazz Group

Charlie McNair (tpt), Jimmy Hilson (tbn), Joe Smith (clt), Dave Smith & Mike Hart (bjos), Sandy Malcolm (drms)
Recorded: St Andrew's Hall, Glasgow, June 30, 1956

1. Oh, didn't he ramble	Beltona ABL519 *

ABL519 other titles on this 10" LP are by the Clyde Valley Stompers and Alan Mason's Jazzmen

Charlie Mcnair's Jazz Band

Charlie McNair (tpt) Bill Munro (tbn), George Duncan(?) (clt ,alto), Harald Vox (bjo), Colin Archbold (bs), Toto McNaughton (drms)
Recorded: REL Studios, Edinburgh, 1980

Chimes blues   CPLP 038

Charlie Mcnair's Skiffle Group

Charlie McNair (tpt), Mike Pollett (tbn), Joe Smith (clt), Mike Hart (bjo), Sandy Malcolm (drms)

2. Hiawatha   Beltona BL2670
3. Meadow Lane Stomp   Beltona BL2670
Recorded: St Andrew's Hall, Glasgow, September,1955

Nova Scotia Jazz Band
Echoes Of The Mauve Decade

Mike Daly (cnt), John Burgess (clt, ten, ldr), Duncan Finlay (bjo, gtr), Roy Percy (bs)
Recorded: The Music Box, Edinburgh, September 14, 2009

1. At sundown   C-Side 007
2. Up a lazy river   C-Side 007
3. Chinatown, my Chinatown   C-Side 007
4. I want a little girl   C-Side 007
5. China boy   C-Side 007
6. 'Deed I do   C-Side 007
7. Please don't talk about me when i'm gone
                                         C-Side 007
8. Exactly like you   C-Side 007
9. Shine   C-Side 007
10. Do you know what it means to miss New Orleans
                                         C-Side 007
11. Dinah   C-Side 007

Chinatown My Chinatown

Mike Daly (cnt), John Burgess (clt, ten, ldr), Duncan Finlay (bjo, gtr). Kenny Mcdonald (bs)
Recorded: Carlisle, Gateshead & Reeth, June 2011

1. Chinatown, my Chinatown	C-side 029
2. I can't give you anything but love	C-side 029
3. At the jazz band ball	C-side 029
4. I want a little girl	C-side 029
5. Please don't talk about me	C-side 029
6. Way down yonder in New Orleans	C-side 029
7. Royal Garden blues	C-side 029
8. Wrap your troubles in dreams	C-side 029
9. All of me	C-side 029
10. Doctor Jazz	C-side 029
11. Up a lazy river	C-side 029
12. China boy	C-side 029
13. Do You Know what it means to miss New Orleans?	
	C-side 029
14. My blue heaven	C-side 029

Nova Scotia Jazz Band With Forrie Cairns

Mike Daly (cnt), John Burgess (clt, alto, ten, ldr), Duncan Finlay (bjo, gtr), Roy Percy (bs)
John Service (tbn 1, v -2), Forrie Cairns (clt - 3)
Recorded: Music Box, Edinburgh, September 6, 2010

1. Wabash blues (3)	C-Side 008
2. At the jazz band ball (1, 3)	C-Side 008
3. Sweet Lorraine (1)	C-Side 008
4. Five foot two, eyes of blue (1)	C-Side 008
5. Bye bye blackbird (3)	C-Side 008
6. Sweet Sue (3)	C-Side 008
7. When you're smiling (1,2)	C-Side 008
8. Wrap your troubles in dreams	C-Side 008
9. Chinatown, my Chinatown (1,3)	C-Side 008

Old Bailey And His Jazz Advocates

1. *Andrew Lauder (tpt), Archie Sinclair (tbn, voc, ldr), Jackie Graham (clt), Mike Hart (bjo), Forbes Laing (bs), Charlie Welsh (drms)*
Recorded: The Place Jazz Club, Edinburgh

Teddy bears picnic	not known
Beale Street blues	not known

2. *Andrew Lauder (tpt), Archie Sinclair (tbn, voc, ldr), Hamish McGregor (clt), Alex Shaw (pno), Mike Hart (bjo), Ronnie Rae (bs), Donald 'Chick' Murray (drms)*
Recorded: probably1966 as a track for the Edinburgh Students Charity Appeal

Hey, Look Me Over	not known

Old Bailey's Jazz Advocates
Complete With Bum Notes

Andrew Lauder (cnt, tpt), Sam Smith (tbn, voc-1), Hamish McGregor (clt, alto, bar, voc-2, ldr), Tom Finlay (pno), Mike Hart (bjo, gtr), Graham Blamire (bs), Donald 'Chick' Murray (drms)
Recorded: Craighall Studios, Edinburgh, February 10, 1980

1. When the midnight choo choo leaves for Alabam (2)	
	Salmet CS1094
2. Froggie Moore rag	Salmet CS1094
3. Carry me back to Old Virginia (1)	Salmet CS1094
4. Old man river	Salmet CS1094
5. Dapper Dan (2)	Salmet CS1094
6. Rent party blues	Salmet CS1094
7. Honeysuckle rose	Salmet CS1094
8. Teddy bears' picnic	Salmet CS1094
9. Yama Yama Man	Salmet CS1094
10. Sweet Georgia Brown	Salmet CS1094
11. Do you know what it means to miss New Orleans (1)	
	Salmet CS1094
12. Nobody's sweetheart (2)	Salmet CS1094

Dave Paxton

Dave Paxton (clt), others involved and recording date not known

1. Once in a while (?)	S&M?
2. Ole Miss (?)	S&M?

Whether or not this recording ever existed is open to debate. However, a reliable source has vouched for its existence. It is believed to be a 10" disc playing at either 45rpm or 33 1/3rpm.

Brian Robertson's Ellwyn Stompers
Almost Live at the Ellwyn

1. *Brian Robertson (cnt, voc), Eddie Hamilton (clt, voc-1), Graham Scott (pno), Andrew Mulhearn (bjo, tbn), Owen McDonald (bs) guests: Bob Busby (clt, alto), Brian Weld (bjo), Fred Murray (bs) Kenny McDonald (bs)*
Recorded: Ellwyn Hotel, Edinburgh, May 2002

1. Just a little while to stay here	band issue CD
2. A porter's love song to a chamber maid (1)	band issue CD
3. Love letters in the sand	band issue CD
4. Ole Miss rag	band issue CD
5. What a friend we have in Jesus	band issue CD
6. What the Lord has done for me	band issue CD
7. One sweet letter from you	band issue CD
8. Swannee River	band issue CD
9. Smiles	band issue CD
10. St Philips Street breakdown	band issue CD
11. Let me call you sweetheart	band issue CD
12. Frankie and Johnnie	band issue CD
13. Now is the hour	band issue CD

Brian Robertson's Forth River Ragtimers
Down In Honky Tonk Town

Brian Robertson (cnt) Alan Quinn (tbn), George Gilmour (clt), Graham Scott (pno), Brian Weld (bjo), Bill Brydon (bs), Kenny Milne (drms)
Recorded: Edinburgh, April 2000

1. Down in honky tonk town	band issue CD
2. South	band issue CD
3. Bye and bye	band issue CD
4. Exactly like you	band issue CD
5. Panama	band issue CD
6. Precious Lord, lead me on	band issue CD
7. Barefoot boy	band issue CD
8. Lord, Lord, Lord	band issue CD
9. Smiles	band issue CD
10. The old rugged cross	band issue CD
11. Dinah	band issue CD
12. Ballin' the jack	band issue CD
13. Play the blues for me	band issue CD
14. The curse of an aching heart	band issue CD
15. Now is the hour	band issue CD

Climax Rag

Brian Robertson (cnt) Alan Quinn (tbn), George Gilmour (clt), Graham Scott (pno), Brian Weld (bjo), Bill Brydon (bs), Kenny Milne (drms)
Recorded: Edinburgh, March 2002

1. Bourbon Street parade	band issue CD
2. Climax rag	band issue CD
3. Up a lazy river	band issue CD
4. When you wore a tulip	band issue CD
5. In the sweet bye and bye	band issue CD
6. You do something to me	band issue CD
7. June night	band issue CD
8. Only a look	band issue CD
9. Yes, yes in your eyes	band issue CD
10. Out of nowhere	band issue CD
11. Beale Street blues	band issue CD
12. Papa Dip	band issue CD
13. Put on your old grey bonnet	band issue CD

Thriller Rag

Brian Robertson (cnt) Alan Quinn (tbn), George Gilmour (clt), Graham Scott (pno), Brain Weld (bjo), Bill Brydon (bs), Kenny Milne (drms)
Recorded: Edinburgh, March 2003

1. Thriller rag	band issue CD
2. Ole Miss rag	band issue CD
3. When somebody thinks you're wonderful	band issue CD
4. Jealous	band issue CD
5. Dallas blues	band issue CD
6. Lead me Saviour	band issue CD
7. Moose march	band issue CD
8. Melancholy blues	band issue CD
9. In the upper garden	band issue CD
10. Gatemouth	band issue CD
11. Lonesome road	band issue CD
12. Underneath the sheltering palms	band issue CD
13. Oh! you beautiful doll	band issue CD

One Sweet Letter From You
4. Brian Robertson (cnt), John Arthur (tbn), Eddie Hamilton (clt), Graham Scott (pno), Brian Weld (bjo), Kenny McDonald (bs), Roy Dunnett (drms)
Recorded: Edinburgh, January 2009

1. Cakewalking babies	band issue CD
2. Buddy's habit	band issue CD
3. Samantha	band issue CD
4. Weary blues	band issue CD
5. Goin' home	band issue CD
6. One sweet letter from you	band issue CD
7. The postman's lament	band issue CD
8. Yaaka hula hickey dula	band issue CD
9. Somebody stole my gal	band issue CD
10. He touched me	band issue CD
11. At a Georgia camp meting	band issue CD
12. Sister Kate	band issue CD
13. It's nobody's fault but mine	band issue CD

Bill Salmond's Louisiana Ragtime Band
1976
Simon Carlyle (tbn), Dave Paxton (clt), Graham Scott (pno), Bill Salmond (bjo, ldr), Willie Mack (bs), Richard Lord (drms)
Recorded: Edinburgh, c1976

1. In the shade of the old apple tree	band issue MC

2. I'm putting all my eggs in one basket   band issue MC
3. Please don't talk about me when I'm gone

band issue MC
4. Alexander's Ragtime Band   band issue MC
5. Marie   band issue MC
6. Tin Roof blues   band issue MC
7. Milneburg joys   band issue MC
8. At a Georgia camp meeting   band issue MC
9. Lady be good   band issue MC
10. Margie (faded out)   band issue MC

In The Shade Of The Old Apple Tree

Simon Carlyle (tbn), Dave Paxton (clt), Graham Scott (pno), Bill Salmond (bjo, ldr), Willie Mack (bs), Ian Forde (drms)
Recorded: Edinburgh, September 23, 1976
1. In the shade of the old apple tree   Dunedin DLP761
2. Sobbin' blues   Dunedin DLP761
3. Ciribiribin   Dunedin DLP761
4. See See rider blues   Dunedin DLP761
5. Ting a ling   Dunedin DLP761
6. Lucky me   Dunedin DLP761
7. Solitude   Dunedin DLP761
8. Buddy's habit   Dunedin DLP761
9. I double dare you   Dunedin DLP761

Way Down Yonder In New Orleans

Brian Robertson (cnt), Bob Craig (tbn), Dave Paxton (clt), Graham Scott (pno), Bill Salmond (bjo, ldr), Graham Blamire (bs), Mac Rae (drms)
Recorded: St James' Church, Portobello, date not known

1. Panama   band issue MC
2. Oh! You beautiful doll   band issue MC
3. Working man blues   band issue MC
4. Give me your telephone number   band issue MC
5. Big lip blues   band issue MC
6. Way down yonder in New Orleans   band issue MC
7. Together   band issue MC
8. Mabel's dream   band issue MC
9. Sweet Georgia Brown   band issue MC
10. Old fashioned love   band issue MC
11. C jam blues   band issue MC

Linger Awhile
Kenny Milne (tpt), Dave Paxton (clt), Graham Scott (pno), Bill Salmond (bjo, ldr), Tony Sargent (bs), Eric Jamieson (drms)
Recorded: Palladium Recording Studios, Edinburgh, 1980

1. Four leaf clover	Dunedin DLP801
2. Buddy's habit	Dunedin DLP801
3. St. James Infirmary	Dunedin DLP801
4. Lily of the valley	Dunedin DLP801
5. China boy	Dunedin DLP801
6. Untitled blues	Dunedin DLP801
7. Rebecca	Dunedin DLP801
8. Up jumped the devil	Dunedin DLP801
9. Linger awhile	Dunedin DLP801

Edinburgh International Jazz Festival, 1980
Kenny Milne (tpt), Dave Paxton (clt), Graham Scott (pno), Bill Salmond (bjo, ldr), Tony Sargent (bs), Eric Jamieson (drms)
Recorded: Edinburgh, 1980

1. Anytime	CPLP038

Other recordings on this LP by other bands

Live
Alan Quinn (tbn, voc), George Gilmour (clt), Graham Scott (pno), Bill Salmond (bjo, ldr), Graham Blamire (bs), Eric Jamieson (drms)
Recorded: New Orleans Express, Haymarket Bar, Edinburgh, December 18, 1993

1. On the road to home sweet home	band issue MC
2. Red Wing	band issue MC
3. Burgundy Street blues	band issue MC
4. Beautiful dreamer	band issue MC
5. Climax rag	band issue MC
6. Original Dixieland one-step	band issue MC
7. Big Chief Battle Axe	band issue MC
8. Mazie	band issue MC
9. St Philips Street breakdown	band issue MC
10. Wait 'till the sun shines Nellie	band issue MC
11. Ice cream	band issue MC

1995

Alan Quinn (tbn ,voc), George Gilmour (clt), Graham Scott (pno), Bill Salmond (bjo, ldr), Bill Brydon (bs), Eric Jamieson (drms)
Recorded: Craigmillar Arts Centre, Edinburgh, March 25, 1995

1. Ting-a-ling	band issue MC
2. Down by the old mill stream	band issue MC
3. South	band issue MC
4. When you and I were young Maggie	band issue MC
5. Muskrat ramble	band issue MC
6. High society	band issue MC
7. In the sweet bye and bye	band issue MC
8. I'll always be in love with you	band issue MC
9. Savoy blues	band issue MC
10. Clarinet marmalade	band issue MC
11. Rambling Rose	band issue MC
12. Willie the Weeper	band issue MC
13. He touched me	*unissued*
14. Exactly like you (take 1)	*unissued*
15. Exactly like you (take 2)	*unissued*

All I Do Is Dream Of You

Alan Quinn (tbn, voc), George Gilmour (clt), Graham Scott (pno), Bill Salmond (bjo, ldr), Bill Brydon (bs), Eric Jamieson (drms)
Recorded: Queen's Hotel, Keswick, May 15, 1997

1. Original Dixieland one-step	PEK Sound PKC-078
2. Only a look	PEK Sound PKC-078
3. High society	PEK Sound PKC-078
4. I can't escape from you	PEK Sound PKC-078
5. I'm alone because I love you	PEK Sound PKC-078
6. When I leave this world behind	PEK Sound PKC-078
7. All I do is dream of you	PEK Sound PKC-078
8. Let me call you sweetheart	PEK Sound PKC-078
9. Hold me	PEK Sound PKC-078
10. Fidgety feet	PEK Sound PKC-078
11. The first choice	PEK Sound PKC-078

Listen to the Mocking Bird

Alan Quinn (tbn, voc), George Gilmour (clt), Graham Scott (pno), Bill Salmond (bjo, ldr), Bill Brydon (bs), Taff Lloyd (drms)
Recorded: Labour Club, Keswick, May 17, 1998

1. Over the waves	PEK Sound PKCD-109
2. Clarinet marmalade	PEK Sound PKCD-109
3. He touched me	PEK Sound PKCD-109
4. What the Lord has done for me	PEK Sound PKCD-109
5. Franklin Street blues	PEK Sound PKCD-109
6. Don't go 'way nobody	PEK Sound PKCD-109
7. Listen to the mocking bird	PEK Sound PKCD-109
8. Cherry Blossom Lane	PEK Sound PKCD-109
9. Algiers strut	PEK Sound PKCD-109
10. June night	PEK Sound PKCD-109
11. Love	PEK Sound PKCD-109
12. Willie the Weeper	PEK Sound PKCD-109

Memories of George Lewis

Alan Quinn (tbn, voc), George Gilmour (clt), Graham Scott (pno), Bill Salmond (bjo, ldr), Bill Brydon (bs), Kenny Milne (drms)
Recorded: Keswick Jazz Festival, May 21, 2000

1. Collegiate	PEK Sound PKCD-153
2. My life will be sweeter some day	PEK Sound PKCD-153
3. 'Neath Hawaiian skies	PEK Sound PKCD-153
4. Burgundy Street blues	PEK Sound PKCD-153
5. The streets of the city	PEK Sound PKCD-153
6. Panama	PEK Sound PKCD-153
7. Mazie	PEK Sound PKCD-153
8. Rambling Rose	PEK Sound PKCD-153
9. There's yes, yes in your eyes	PEK Sound PKCD-153
10. Climax rag	PEK Sound PKCD-153
11. Ol' Miss rag	PEK Sound PKCD-153
12. Abide with me	PEK Sound PKCD-153
13. Ice cream	PEK Sound PKCD-153

Plays Hymns And Spirituals
Alan Quinn (tbn, voc), George Gilmour (clt), Graham Scott (pno), Bill Salmond (bjo, ldr), Bill Brydon (bs), Kenny Milne (drms)
Recorded: The Fairmile Inn, Edinburgh, March 22, 2002

1. Just a little while to stay here	Dunedin CD002
2. The old rugged cross	Dunedin CD002
3. Lord, Lord, Lord	Dunedin CD002
4. Lead me Saviour	Dunedin CD002
5. His eye is on the sparrow	Dunedin CD002
6. The streets of the city	Dunedin CD002
7. My life will be sweeter some day	Dunedin CD002
8. Nobody's fault but mine	Dunedin CD002
9. Only a Look	Dunedin CD002
10. Lily of the valley	Dunedin CD002
11. Abide with me	Dunedin CD002

Ballin' The Jack
Alan Quinn (tbn, voc), George Gilmour (clt), Graham Scott (pno), Bill Salmond (bjo, ldr), Bill Brydon (bs), Kenny Milne (drms)
Recorded: The Fairmile Inn, Edinburgh, April 8, 2003

1. Someday (you'll want me to want you)	
	Dunedin CD0403
2. The waltz you saved for me / Mobile stomp	
	Dunedin CD0403
3. You brought a new kind of love to me	
	Dunedin CD0403
4. When the swallows come back to Capistrano	
	Dunedin CD0403
5. A shanty in old shanty town	Dunedin CD0403
6. Moonglow	Dunedin CD0403
7. Roll along, prairie moon	Dunedin CD0403
8. Blue again	Dunedin CD0403
9. I can't believe that you're in love with me	
	Dunedin CD0403
10. Save your sorrow for tomorrow	Dunedin CD0403
11. I surrender dear	Dunedin CD0403
12. Ballin' the jack	Dunedin CD0403
13. Rose Room	Dunedin CD0403
14. Beautiful Ohio	Dunedin CD0403

Amazing Grace

Alan Quinn (tbn, voc), George Gilmour (clt), Graham Scott (pno), Bill Salmond (bjo, ldr), Bill Brydon (bs), Kenny Milne (drms)
Recorded: Edinburgh, March 31, 2004

1. Down by the riverside	Dunedin CD0304
2. This little light of mine	Dunedin CD0304
3. What a friend we have in Jesus	Dunedin CD0304
4. Lord, Lord, Lord	Dunedin CD0304
5. Silver Bells	Dunedin CD0304
6. Amazing Grace	Dunedin CD0304
7. Walking with the King	Dunedin CD0304
8. Precious Lord, lead me on	Dunedin CD0304
9. He touched me	Dunedin CD0304
10. In the sweet bye and bye	Dunedin CD0304
11. Do Lord	Dunedin CD0304

Let the Rest of the World Go By

Alan Quinn (tbn, voc), George Gilmour (clt), Graham Scott (pno), Bill Salmond (bjo, ldr), Bill Brydon (bs), Kenny Milne (drms)
Recorded: no details

1. Running wild	Dunedin CD0605
2. This love of mine	Dunedin CD0605
3. Let the rest of the world go by	Dunedin CD0605
4. When we danced at the Mardi Gras	Dunedin CD0605
5. Aura Lee	Dunedin CD0605
6. The very thought of you	Dunedin CD0605
7. Move the body over	Dunedin CD0605
8. When the blue of the night	Dunedin CD0605
9. Washington and Lee swing	Dunedin CD0605
10. Everybody loves somebody sometime	Dunedin CD0605
11. Sensation	Dunedin CD0605

Scottish Jazz Advocates
Live At The Caley

Andrew Lauder (cnt), Sam Smith (tbn, voc-2), Jack Graham (clt, alto), Hamish McGregor (clt, alto, bar, voc-3, co-ldr), Tom Finlay (pno), Mike Hart (bjo, gtr, co-ldr), Graham Blamire (bs), Donald 'Chick' Murray (drms), Fiona Duncan (voc –1)
Recorded: Caledonian Hotel, Edinburgh, c1980

1. Harlem bound	Sacramento Jazz SJS-17
2. Savoy blues	Sacramento Jazz SJS-17
3. Blues my naughtie sweetie gives to me (1)	
	Sacramento Jazz SJS-17
4. Big Bill	Sacramento Jazz SJS-17
5. Louisian-I-Ay (2)	Sacramento Jazz SJS-17
6. Cakewalking babies (1)	Sacramento Jazz SJS-17
7. Chimes blues	Sacramento Jazz SJS-17
8. Keeping out of mischief	Sacramento Jazz SJS-17
9. Cornet chop suey	Sacramento Jazz SJS-17
10. Hard Hearted Hannah (1)	Sacramento Jazz SJS-17
11. Basin Street blues (3)	Sacramento Jazz SJS-17

Transatlantic Stomp

Andrew Lauder (tpt, cnt), Sam Smith (tbn), Jackie Graham (clt, alto), Hamish McGregor (clt, alto, bar, co-ldr), Tom Finlay (pno), Mike Hart (bjo, gtr, co-ldr), Graham Blamire (bs), Ronnie Rae (bs-1), Donald 'Chick' Murray (drms), Dave Swanson (drms-2), Fiona Duncan (voc –3)
Recorded: Craighall Studios, Edinburgh, February 14, 1980

1. African Queen	Sacramento Jazz SJS-22
2. Sidewalk blues	Sacramento Jazz SJS-22
3. Fine brown frame (2,3)	Sacramento Jazz SJS-22
4. Memphis blues	Sacramento Jazz SJS-22
5. Russian rag (2)	Sacramento Jazz SJS-22
6. Mention my name in Sheboygen (3)	
	Sacramento Jazz SJS-22
7. Drop Me Off in Harlem	Sacramento Jazz SJS-22
8. Black bottom stomp	Sacramento Jazz SJS-22
9. I'm coming Virginia	Sacramento Jazz SJS-22
10. Some of these days (3)	Sacramento Jazz SJS-22
11. Snag it	Sacramento Jazz SJS-22
12. Papa Dip	Sacramento Jazz SJS-22

Andrew Lauder (tpt), Johnny McGuff (tbn), Hamish McGregor (clt, alto, bagpipes), Tom Finlay (pno), Mike Hart (bjo, gtr), Graham Blamire(bs), Donald Murray (drms), John McGlynn (drms -1), Ronnie Rae (bs -1)
Recorded: Craighall Studios, Edinburgh, March 3, 1984

All in Perfect Working Order

1. Georgia swing	Teuchter Records
2. Between the devil and the deep blues sea (1)	
	Teuchter Records
3. Kansas City Man blues	Teuchter Records
4. If you were the only girl in the world	
	Teuchter Records
5. Get out of here	Teuchter Records
6. The Chant	Teuchter Records
7. I'm slappin' 7th avenue with the sole of my shoe	
	Teuchter Records
8. Yellow Dog blues	Teuchter Records
9. Moten swing	Teuchter Records
10. Ain't misbehavin'	Teuchter Records
11. Black Bear stomp (1)	Teuchter Records

Jazz at the Connecticut Traditional Jazz Club
Andrew Lauder (cnt), Johnny McGuff (tbn), Hamish McGregor (clt, alto, bar, co-ldr), Tom Finlay (pno), Mike Hart (bjo, co-ldr), Ronnie Rae (bs), John McGlynn (drms)
Recorded: Stamford, Connecticut, June 2, 1984

1. Ostrich walk	SLP20
2. Drop me off in Harlem	SLP20

Other material on this LP by other bands

Archie Semple And His Capitol Jazzmen
Alex Welsh (cnt), Dave Keir (tbn), Archie Semple (clt, ldr), Drew Landells (pno), Jimmy Mooney (gtr), Pat Malloy(?) (bs), George Crockett (drms)
Recorded: Edinburgh, May 4, 1952

1. New Orleans masquerade (take 1)	S&M LP unnumbered
2. New Orleans masquerade (take 2)	S&M unissued

3. Farewell blues	S&M LP unnumbered
4. South	S&M LP unnumbered
5. At a Georgia camp meeting	S&M LP unnumbered
6. Clark and Randolph blues	S&M LP unnumbered
7. Who's sorry now	S&M LP unnumbered
8. Jenny's Ball	S&M LP unnumbered
9. Singing the blues	S & M 1005
10. Who's sorry now	S & M 1005

Alex Welsh (cnt), Dave Keir (tbn), Archie Semple (clt, ldr), Drew Landells (pno), Jimmy Mooney (gtr), Pat Malloy(?) (bs), George Crockett (drms), David Mylne (narrator)
Broadcast: BBC Scottish Home Service, Queen Street Studios, Edinburgh, May 9, 1952

1. Chicago	acetate
2. Royal Garden blues	acetate
3. Mississippi mud	acetate
4. Farewell blues	acetate
5. Singing the blues	acetate
6. There'll be some changes made	acetate
7. Clarke and Randolph blues	acetate
8. After you've gone	acetate

This recording has never been issued commercially although it has had wide distribution on both acetate and cassette among collectors.
The dates shown here are the correct broadcast dates and have been verified by Tom Lowrie who has the original ticket stubs from the concert, which show dates and times

Spirits Of Rhythm
1. *Fraser Gauld (tpt), Jack Weddell (tbn, voc), Ian Boyter (clt, ten), Violet Milne (p, ldr), Brian Weld (bjo),), Willie Mack (bs), Kenny Milne (drms,)*
Recorded: Edinburgh, April 1,1984

3. Big Chief Battle Axe	Spirit LP
4. Let's get drunk and truck	Spirit LP
5. Darkness on the Delta	Spirit LP
6. Sweetheart of Sigma Chi	Spirit LP
7. Red Wing	Spirit LP

Sam Lee (ten, voc-1), Fraser Gauld (tpt), Jack Weddell (tbn, voc-2), Ian Boyter (clt, alto), Violet Milne (pno, ldr), Brian Weld (bjo), Robin Galloway (bs), Willie Mack (bs-3), Kenny Milne (drms, voc-4)
Recorded: Hart Street Studios, Edinburgh, April 7,1984

Everybody Happy?

1. St Louis blues (1)	Spirit LP/CD
2. Dinah (3)	Spirit LP/CD
3. Panama rag (take 1)	Spirit LP/CD
4. Rent party blues	Spirit LP/CD
5. Mr Sandman (2)	Spirit CD
6. Top hat (3)	Spirit CD
7. I love you so much it hurts (1)	Spirit LP/CD
8. My blue heaven (1)	Spirit LP/CD
9. The world is waiting for the sunrise	Spirit CD
10. Caledonia (1)	Spirit LP/CD, J'n'J CD001
11. Exactly like you (3)	Spirit LP/CD
12. Louisian-I-Ay (4)	Spirit CD
13. I can't give you anything but love baby (1)	Spirit LP/CD
14. Panama rag (take 2)	Spirit CD
15. Chinatown, my Chinatown	Spirit LP/CD

This recording was originally issued in LP format but was subsequently reissued as a CD with previously unreleased material included (Spirit CD)

Edinburgh Jazz Festival 1986
Fraser Gauld (tpt), Ian Boyter (ten), Violet Milne (pno, ldr), Brian Weld (bjo), Robin Galloway (bs), Kenny Milne (drms)
Recorded: Edinburgh 1986

1. If I had my life to live over   1986   Edinburgh   Jazz Festival tape

Other material on this tape features different bands

Ascona Jazz Festival
Fraser Gauld (tpt), Ian Boyter (ten), Violet Milne (pno, ldr), Brian Weld (bjo), Robin Galloway (bs), Kenny Milne (drms)
Recorded: Ascona, July 1986

1. Red Wing   FNOM (It) 936

Other material on this LP features different bands

Jazz Hot and Groovy
Dave Strutt (tpt, voc-1), Jack Weddell (tbn, voc-2), Ian Boyter (clt, alto, ten), Violet Milne (pno, ldr), Brian Weld (bjo), Roy Percy (bs), Kenny Milne (drms)
Recorded: Southside Snooker hall, May 6, 1992

1. Dream man (1)	Spirit MC
2. Moose march	Spirit MC
3. West End blues	Spirit MC
4. When we danced at the Mardi Gras	Spirit MC
5. Lover (2)	Spirit MC
6. Bogalousa strut	Spirit MC
7. Just a little while to stay here	Spirit MC
8. Moppin' and boppin'	Spirit MC
9. When your hair has turned to silver (1)	Spirit MC
10. Whenever you're lonesome	Spirit MC
11. Bugle call rag	Spirit MC
12. Magic is the moonlight (2)	Spirit MC
13. June night (1)	Spirit MC
14. Mama's gone, goodbye	Spirit MC
15. Love nest (1)	Spirit MC
16. Boogie in C	Spirit MC
17. Rockin' (1)	Spirit MC

At Nobles Bar
Jack Weddell (tbn, voc-1), Ian Boyter (clt, alto), Violet Milne (pno, ldr), Beverley Knight (bjo), Roy Percy (bs), Kenny Milne (drms, voc-2)
Recorded: Nobles Bar, Leith during 1995

1. Oh, how I miss you tonight (2)	Spirit MC
2. Shine (1)	Spirit MC

3. Trust in me (1)	Spirit MC
4. If I had my life to live over (1)	Spirit MC
5. South of the Border (1)	Spirit MC
6. Chinatown, my Chinatown	Spirit MC
7. Once in a while	Spirit MC
8. Walking with the King (1)	Spirit MC
9. Georgia (1)	Spirit MC
10. Weary blues	Spirit MC
11. On the road to home sweet home	Spirit MC
12. Original Dixieland one-step	Spirit MC

Caledonia
Finlay Milne (tpt, voc-1), Ian Boyter (clt, alto, ten), Violet Milne (pno, ldr), Nigel Porteous (bjo), Roy Percy (bs), Kenny Milne (drms, voc-2)
Recorded: Borrowdale Inn, Keswick, May 19, 1996

1. I can't escape from you	PEK Sound PKC-056
2. Bogalousa strut	PEK Sound PKC-056
3. Darkness on the Delta	PEK Sound PKC-056
4. Panama	PEK Sound PKC-056
5. Blues for Borrowdale	PEK Sound PKC-056
6. Clarinet marmalade	PEK Sound PKC-056
7. Muskrat Ramble (1)	PEK Sound PKC-056
8. Cal'donia (1)	PEK Sound PKC-056
9. Crying my heart out for you	PEK Sound PKC-056
10. Dinah (2)	PEK Sound PKC-056
11. Tin Roof blues	PEK Sound PKC-056
12. The same old love	PEK Sound PKC-056
13. Moppin' And boppin'	PEK Sound PKC-056
14. Bugle boy march	PEK Sound PKC-056

Moppin' And Boppin'
Dave Strutt (tpt, voc-1), Ian Boyter (clt, alto, ten, hca), Violet Milne (pno, ldr), Nigel Porteous (bjo), Dizzy Jackson (bs), Kenny Milne (drms, voc-2)
Recorded: Edinburgh, May 1998 & January 1999

1. Mardi Gras in New Orleans (1)
                        Spirit CD005, J'nJ CD001
2. Absolutely, positively (1)   Spirit CD005

3. Cryin' my heart out for you   Spirit CD005
4. Just a little while to stay here (2)   Spirit CD005
5. My fate is in your hands (1)   Spirit CD005
6. The world is waiting for the sunrise   Spirit CD005
7. I owe it all to you (1)   Spirit CD005
8. Moppin' and boppin'   Spirit CD005, J'n'J CD 001
9. Someday you'll be sorry (1)   Spirit CD005
10. Travelling blues   Spirit CD005
11. See See rider (1)   Spirit CD005
12. I love you (1)   Spirit CD005
13. Indian Summer   Spirit CD005
14. Lonesome and sorry   Spirit CD005

Keswick Jazz Festival 2000

Clem Avery (tpt), Llew Hird (tbn, voc-1), Karl Hird (clt, ten), Ian Boyter (clt, ten), Violet Milne (pno, ldr), Dave Rae (bjo, voc-3), Dizzy Jackson (bs), Kenny Milne (drms)
Recorded: Calvert Trust, Keswick, May 19, 2000

1. Bugle boy march   *PEK Sound unissued*
2. Ole Miss rag   *PEK Sound unissued*
3. Old fashioned love   *PEK Sound unissued*
4. One sweet letter from you (2)   *PEK Sound unissued*
5. Big Chief Battle Axe   *PEK Sound unissued*
6. I want a little girl (1)   *PEK Sound unissued*
7. 2.19 blues (1)   *PEK Sound unissued*
8. Louisian-I-Ay   *PEK Sound unissued*
9. Moose march   *PEK Sound unissued*
10. South   *PEK Sound unissued*
11. Savoy blues   *PEK Sound unissued*
12. All the girls go crazy 'bout the way I walk (2)
                              PEK Sound unissued
13. Corrine, Corrina (1)   *PEK Sound unissued*
14. Swannee River   *PEK Sound unissued*
15. Canal Street blues   *PEK Sound unissued*
16. Bogalousa strut   *PEK Sound unissued*
17. Marie   *PEK Sound unissued*
18. Love songs of the Nile (1)   *PEK Sound unissued*
19. Running Wild   *PEK Sound unissued*
20. On the road to home sweet home *PEK Sound unissued*
21. Royal Garden blues   *PEK Sound unissued*
22. Ice cream   *PEK Sound unissued*

Alan Quinn (tbn), George Gilmour (clt), Violet Milne (pno, ldr),
Brian Weld (bjo), Fred Murray (bs), Kenny Milne (drms)
Recorded: Edinburgh Jazz 'n' Jive Club, Edinburgh, August
14, 2009

1. Rose Room	J'n'J CD002
2. Hindustan	J'n'J CD002

Storyville Five
Edinburgh International Jazz Festival 1980
Donald McDonald (ten), Angus McDonald (tbn), Harald Vox
(bjo), Kenny McDonald (bs), Dennis Morton (drms)
Recorded: REL Studios, West Maitland Street, Edinburgh,
1980

1. Ice cream	CPLP 038

Other material on this recording by different bands

Swing 84
Live at the Cygnet
Dave Strutt (cnt, mel), Dick Lee (clt, saxes, rec), Martin Leys
(gtr, e-gtr), Johan Hoven (gtr), Jerry Forde (bs)
Recorded: Cygnet Jazz Cellar and Restaurant, Edinburgh,
July 31, 1984

1. Nuits de St. Germain des Pres	band issue MC
2. What is this thing called love?	band issue MC
3. Dream of you	band issue MC
4. Frans and Saskia	band issue MC
5. Nuages	band issue MC
6. Dinette	band issue MC
7. Rifftide	band issue MC
8. Crazy rhythm	band issue MC
9. Someday soon	band issue MC
10. Micro	band issue MC
11. Artillerie Lourde	band issue MC
12. Fleche d'or	band issue MC

Swing 86
Live at St John's
Dick Lee (rds), Martin Leys (gtr), John Russell (gtr), Jerry
Forde (bs)
Recorded: 1986

1. Place de Bruckere	*band issue MC*
2. Jersey bounce	*band issue MC*
3. Port Carelle	*band issue MC*
4. September song	*band issue MC*
5. Brazil	*band issue MC*
6. Songe d'automne	*band issue MC*
7. I'll never smile again	*band issue MC*
8. I saw stars	*band issue MC*
9. Lentement Mademoiselle	*band issue MC*
10. Fleche d'or	*band issue MC*

Swing 98
Dick Lee (clt, saxes, rec), Phil Adams (e-gtr), John Russell
(gtr, voc), Roy Percy (bs)
Recorded: 1998

1. Si tu me dis oui	Octavo Oct078
2. Jersey bounce	Octavo Oct078
3. Belleville	Octavo Oct078
4. Songe d'automne	Octavo Oct078
5. Caravan	Octavo Oct078
6. Minor swing	Octavo Oct078
7. Stompin' at Decca	Octavo Oct078
8. Fairweather	Octavo Oct078
9. Anniemation	Octavo Oct078
10. Mood indigo	Octavo Oct078

Swing 99
Get Happy
Dick Lee (clt, saxes, rec), Phil Adams (e-gtr), John Russell
(gtr), Roy Percy (bs)
Recorded: 1999

1. Get happy	Octavo Oct CD009
2. Viper's dream	Octavo Oct CD009

3. Gee baby	Octavo Oct CD009
4. Meditation	Octavo Oct CD009
5. Troublant bolero	Octavo Oct CD009
6. Undecided	Octavo Oct CD009
7. Dream of you	Octavo Oct CD009
8. Linlithgow Suite	Octavo Oct CD009

     (a) Shank's pony
     (b) Bell I: Alma Maria
     (c) Equipoise
     (d) Bell II: Meg Duncan
     (e) Canal dream
     (f) Bell III: Saint Michael
     (g) The Loch
     (h) Train time

Swing 2002

Dick Lee (clt, b-clt, sop, rec), Brian Kellock (pno-1), Phil Adams (e-gtr), John Russell (gtr), Roy Percy (bs)
Recorded: 2002

1. Crazy rhythm	Octavo Oct CD2002
2. Cavalerie	Octavo Oct CD2002
3. Manor de mes reves	Octavo Oct CD2002
4. Del salle	Octavo Oct CD2002
5. China boy	Octavo Oct CD2002
6. Brazil	Octavo Oct CD2002
7. Nuages	Octavo Oct CD2002
8. Duke And Dukie	Octavo Oct CD2002
9. I'll see you in my dreams	Octavo Oct CD2002
10. Fleche d'or	Octavo Oct CD2002
11. West End blues (1)	Octavo Oct CD2002
12. Helensburgh Suite (1)	Octavo Oct CD2002

     Promenade
     Heavier than air
     Hill House
     Comet
     Hurricane

Swing 2005.

Dick Lee (clt, b-clt), Stephen Coutts (gtr), John Russell (gtr), Roy Percy (bs)
Recorded: Linlithgow Jazz Club, Burgh Halls, 2005

1. Limehouse blues	*band issue MC*
2. Moten swing	*band issue MC*
3. Minor swing	*band issue MC*
4. Nuages	*band issue MC*
5. One note samba	*band issue MC*
6. Jersey bounce	*band issue MC*
7. Honeysuckle rose	*band issue MC*
8. Melodie au crepuscule	*band issue MC*
9. Try a little tenderness	*band issue MC*
10. Moonglow	*band issue MC*
11. Troublant bolero	*band issue MC*
12. Stompin' At Decca	*band issue MC*
13. Paper moon	*band issue MC*
14. Caravan	*band issue MC*
15. Sweet Georgia Brown	*band issue MC*
16. Babik	*band issue MC*

Swing 2009

Dick Lee (clt, b-clt, sop, rec), Brian Kellock (pno), Stephen Coutts (gtr, e-gtr), John Russell (gtr), Roy Percy (bs)
Recorded: Dollar Academy Concert Hall, 2009

1. Crazy rhythm	Birnam LCR009
2. Moten swing	Birnam LCR009
3. Limehouse blues	Birnam LCR009
4. Body and soul	Birnam LCR009
5. Brazil	Birnam LCR009
6. Honeysuckle rose	Birnam LCR009
7. Seven come eleven	Birnam LCR009
8. Solitude	Birnam LCR009
9. Liza	Birnam LCR009
10. Caravan	Birnam LCR009
11. Try a little tenderness	Birnam LCR009
12. How high the moon	Birnam LCR009
13. Babik	Birnam LCR009

To: Rebe

Welcor

Elemental Fae

Academy...

#whychoose

"I THINK YOU RENDERED HER SPEECHLESS, Your Highness," Titus murmured, his lips against my hair. "Perhaps you need to help her find her voice."

"Hmm, yes, I think she's feeling quite shy at my finding her naked in bed with you. Again." His gaze lowered to my chest, causing my nipples to harden in response, my body alight with wonder and sensation and confusion. "Any suggestions?"

"Several." Titus's palm slid across my lower belly, the touch a brand against my skin as he pulled me backward. "I introduced Claire to fire play."

"Did you?" Exos stood, his fingers playing over his dress shirt, popping open the buttons with nimble fingers.

This can't be happening.

It has to be a dream.

"You two don't even like each other," I blurted out, then winced at allowing my thoughts to grace my lips. *Are you trying to ruin this?*

Exos grinned. "Maybe not, but we both like you, Claire." The fabric parted around his torso, revealing the toned physique beneath. He was leaner than Titus, but just as muscularly defined, almost in a regal sort of way. Fitting, considering his title. "It's not common for a Spirit Fae to take two mates, but it's not unheard of. Sometimes our affinity for a secondary element is strong, requiring an outlet. Clearly, you have a lot of fire in you." He finished removing his shirt, folding it and setting it on the nightstand beside the bed.

"I'm willing to work with it if you both are," Titus added, his thumb drawing a hypnotic circle around my belly button.

I resisted the urge to pinch myself, certain this had to be my unconscious mind indulging in this inappropriate scenario. But as the mattress dipped beneath Exos's weight, his eyes darkened with desire on my breasts, I realized I'd never felt more alive.

Elemental Fae Academy

Book One

Book Two

Book Three

ᴱLEMENTAL
ꬵAE ᴬCADEMY

THE COMPLETE
TRILOGY

USA TODAY BESTSELLING AUTHORS
LEXI C. FOSS & J.R. THORN

Elemental Fae Academy: The Complete Trilogy

Editing by: Outthink Editing, LLC

Cover Design: Moonchild Ljilja of Fantasy Book Design

Published by: Ninja Newt Publishing, LLC

Print Edition

ISBN: 978-1-950694-69-3

Elemental Fae Academy

Book One

PROLOGUE
EXOS

"HER BIRTHDAY IS NEXT WEEK." Elana sat back in her chair at the head of the council table, her silver-gray eyes brimming with expectation. "Allowing her to stay in the mortal realm is a risk we cannot allow."

"Then kill her," Mortus suggested, his tone flat. "She's an abomination."

"Hear, hear," Zephys agreed. "It'd solve several of our issues."

"But what if she's the one?" Vape was always the voice of reason in these meetings. He sat opposite Elana, his white hair pulled back in a bun, the lines adorning his face showing his near millennia of life.

"Oh, this again." Mortus shook his head. "The curse is a myth."

"Say that to the nearly extinct Spirit Fae," my brother said from his seat at the table. I stood behind him, leaving my seat at his side vacant. There were many who wanted me to join the Royal Council, to take my place in the Fae Court, but I never desired that life. I was a warrior by nature. Not a king, even though my blood indicated otherwise.

"Her mother caused that." A flame played over Blaize's fingers while he spoke. "Just thought I'd point that out. Again."

"We don't know that for a fact," Vape reminded, his tone stern yet gentle. Because this was a delicate topic, one several at the table felt strongly about. Especially Mortus—the fae who fought Ophelia Snow to the death. Ninety

1

percent of the Spirit Fae perished on the same day. Some argued it was a coincidence. Others accused Ophelia of being the destructive force, her betrayal shaking the entire Fae Kingdom.

My instincts told me there was more to the story than met the eye, but I didn't know what.

"Oh, come on. We all know Ophelia was the cause, and this little terror is going to be just as much trouble." Zephys stood. "I don't even know why we're having this conversation. It's a waste of bloody time."

"Sit. Down," Elana commanded, her place at the head of the table affording her the authority of the room. As the eldest, and arguably the most powerful of the fae, she carried significant weight in this discussion. Despite the fact that she used to mentor Ophelia personally, providing her with a somewhat biased opinion.

Still, I believed everyone deserved a chance. Even Claire. "She should not have to pay for her mother's sins," I murmured, knowing my brother would agree. "I vote we give her a chance."

"Good thing your vote doesn't count, then," Mortus sneered.

"But mine does," my brother replied. "And I stand by my brother's words. Claire should not be punished for something she had no control over. We should bring her into the Fae Realm."

"And do what with her?" Blaize demanded. "Keep her in a cage? She's a Halfling. We don't even know what elemental skill she'll possess."

"Clearly spirit," my brother replied, his voice calm. "And likely one other." That was what set our kind—the Spirit Fae—apart from the others. While spirit was our primary element, the majority of us maintained a secondary affinity. For me, that was fire. For my brother, water. Our kind used to hold the most power in the Fae Realm as a result, and still would if the majority of our species hadn't mysteriously collapsed and died in a single day.

Mortus snorted. "Right. She'll be weak with that mortal blood pumping through her veins."

"Or incredibly strong," Vape said in his raspy, old voice. "There's a prophecy depicting a Halfling of five elements. It could be her."

"You and your curses and prophecies," Mortus grumbled, shaking his head. "Show me the proof, old man."

"It's written in the stars" was his cryptic reply. Despite being a water elemental, he seemed to have a foresight ability, something no one else possessed. But for someone of his age, and with his experience, it almost made sense that he would be able to depict patterns in time, to predict an event before it happened.

"We should vote," Elana said, eyeing the parties at the table. Each element had three representatives, which mainly consisted of the royal bloodlines and a few high-ranking fae with stronger affinities to others.

Placards appeared, courtesy of an air elemental carrying them in off a subtle wind and scattering them around the long, oval surface.

"Should we bring her to the Fae Realm?" Elana asked.

Purple meant affirmative. Gold for negative.

My brother tilted his to the violet side, Mortus and Zephys immediately flipping to gold. Blaize surprisingly chose purple. "Call me curious" was his explanation. Several others followed suit, all maintaining a similar opinion, bringing the room to a unexpected agreement on allowing her into the Fae Realm.

"All right, then." Elana clasped her hands over the hard surface. "What will you do with her when she arrives?"

"Send her to the Academy." My brother's suggestion seemed to shock the room.

Mortus's cheeks actually tinged red. "To corrupt our youth? No."

Youth? I thought, nearly laughing.

The fae grew up faster than humans and didn't start attending the Academy until age nineteen. She'd fit right in with the crowd, apart from having grown up without access to her gifts for the last two decades.

Most fae began using their gifts earlier in life, but Ophelia had cast a charm over Claire to stall her elemental progression. It'd been one of the many atrocities the female fae had inflicted on others before her death. And had also been the reason the Council chose to let Claire remain in the mortal realm. She couldn't defend herself here, and there were many who wanted her dead.

Case in point, the furious Spirit Fae to my left—Mortus. I could feel the malevolent intents pouring off his aura. If allowed, he'd kill the Halfling himself.

Claire would need a protector, or several, to survive here. And unfortunately, if her powers manifested as they should, she'd be too dangerous for the mortal world as well. Leaving her rather... stuck.

"The Academy." Vape scratched his jaw, considering. "That would provide her with the ability to learn more about her gifts. She's enrolled in human university now, yes?"

"Yes," Elana confirmed. "But what sector would she attend? Spirit was disbanded after..."

"Her mother destroyed everyone?" Mortus offered. "You can't admit it out loud, but you'll allow her abomination to attend the Academy? To play with the impressionable minds of our realm?" He stood. "This is ridiculous and you know it. I can't be a part of this conversation."

"Then leave," my brother said, his voice hard. Despite Mortus being the elder of our kind, my brother's royal blood superseded the elder male's authority. "My brother and I will represent our kind in your stead."

"You'd like that," Mortus said, his beady black eyes landing on me. "*Your Highness.*" He bowed mockingly. "Enjoy playing with fate. Don't be surprised

3

when she bites back." He stalked out of the room, leaving me sighing in his wake.

That bastard saw me as a constant threat to his position. As he probably should since he clearly couldn't behave as an adult of three hundred years. I wasn't even a tenth of his age, and I behaved more appropriately.

"What do you think, Exos?" Elana asked. "Should she attend the Academy?"

"It would provide her with the tools she needs to hone her elemental gifts," I said slowly. "But Mortus brought up a reasonable point. Who will help her learn about the most important ability of all—Spirit?"

She nodded. "I have an idea for that." A mischievous twinkle entered the elder fae's gaze, one that warned me I was not going to enjoy her suggestion in the slightest. "I'd like you to train her. In fact, I also think you should be the one to retrieve her."

"Why?" I blurted out, unable to hold the word back.

Elana's lips curled. "Because you're the most powerful Spirit Fae I've ever met. And if anyone can protect her, it's you."

"She's right," my brother agreed, glancing up at me with his piercing blue eyes—the same shade as my own. "You're the strongest amongst us. If anyone can control her, and train her, it's you." He lifted his hand to rest over mine on the back of his chair. "She needs you, Exos."

"It's a good pairing," Vape added. "Protection coupled with teaching. Assuming you're up for the challenge?" He raised a white eyebrow, his bottomless gaze boring into mine. The old elemental knew I couldn't turn down a summons, especially when he endorsed it.

I sighed. "Fine. I'll fetch her from the Human Realm. We'll discuss the mentorship when I return."

"Excellent." Elana held out her hands. "Then I believe we're adjourned for now?"

"When this all goes to hell, remember that I voted against everything," Zephys said, walking away from the table. "And if she dies, I didn't do it."

My brother squeezed my hand before releasing it. "You're going to need all the luck you can get, Exos. Try not to die on me."

I smirked. "Anyone who tries deserves their fate. Right, Cyrus?"

He returned my grin. "Right." We bumped fists as he stood. "Happy vibes."

"Happy vibes," I returned.

I'd need them, especially for the road ahead. Because there were very few places worse than hell, and the Human Realm was one of them.

Yeah, lucky me.

CHAPTER ONE
CLAIRE

"TRUTH OR DARE?"

I nearly spit out my drink—some sort of fruity concoction my bestie had given me. Like strawberries or something. Really sweet. Totally not the point. "We're not playing this game, Rick."

"Oh, Claire Bear, we are *so* playing this game." Amie's lips pulled into a wide grin. "And the birthday girl goes first."

I tried to roll my eyes, but the room was already spinning. I wasn't drunk exactly. Just very tipsy. Or I thought that might be my current state. Honestly, I just felt really, really good. Like untouchable. Powerful. *Happy*. But this fruity drink in my hand was so blah. I needed something with more punch, like a shot or something. Maybe—

"Truth or dare, birthday baby?" Rick asked, flashing me one of his sexy-as-sin grins. Alas, he and I shared a preference for men. Not each other.

"Nope," I said. "Not playing."

"But I have the best dare for you," Rick said, a wicked glint in his dark eyes. I'd been on the receiving end of his dares several times over and knew better than to accept.

"Nope," I repeated. "My birthday, my rules." That was a thing, right? Yeah, it should be. "I'm making it a thing."

5

"What thing?" Amie asked, then shook her head, waving me off. "Ignore her, Ricky. She'll play. You know she will. Our Claire Bear can't deny a dare."

"Oh my God." I couldn't believe we were even talking about this. "We're twenty-one, guys, not sixteen."

"Are you saying we're too old for truth or dare?" Brittany sounded aghast. "I'm *not* too old for anything."

"Oh, we know, B," Rick said, patting her hand. "We know."

"And what's *that* supposed to mean?" she demanded, giving me a headache.

"You know what it means, baby girl." He pretended to toss his nonexistent hair, the gelled spikes on his head not moving an inch.

"No, I don't kn—"

"All right," I cut in, not wanting to be in the middle of a banter-fest on my birthday night. "I choose dare." Because it was the only way these two would shut the hell up. "What do you want me to do, Rick?"

"Him." He pointed to a boy—no, a *man*—in a leather jacket at the bar.

My jaw actually dropped. "*What?*" He was so out of my league that we weren't even playing in the same field. And I didn't feel that way due to a lack of confidence. No, I considered myself pretty enough, a solid B on the charts. But that man was drop-dead gorgeous in a bad-boy-rocker kind of way. Strong shoulders, lean waist, gorgeous white-blond hair.

I drew my thumb against my lower lip. Yeah, he was the kind of male women dreamed about, the type who could wreck some lady parts in the bedroom. Or, at least, that was what his confident exterior exuded.

As if he sensed my perusal, he glanced my way, causing me to duck my head.

"Yeah, him," Rick said, a grin in his voice. "He's been checking you out all night, Claire baby. You need to go lay one on him. That's my dare."

"You want me to kiss him?" I couldn't help the squeak in my voice. "At the bar?"

"Wouldn't be your first time," he pointed out. "What was the guy's name? Justin? Jack?"

"Jeremy," Amie supplied.

Rick snapped his fingers. "Jeremy. That's it. You had no problem sucking his tongue right out of his mouth. I want to see you do that to our gorgeous dude over there. Mainly because I want deets. I'm betting he's the dominant type, the kind who takes charge of the kiss and teaches your mouth a good lesson or two."

"Oh God." My face was on fire, my head already shaking back and forth. "Give me a truth instead."

"Nah, this is a good dare." He took a swig of his beer and relaxed into the booth, his free arm going across the back over Brittany's slender shoulders. "I dare you to kiss the blond bad boy. And then report back."

"If you don't do it, I will," Amie cut in, my bestie's eyes taking on an adoring gleam as she studied the bar. "He's *hot*."

Rick snorted. "I love you, A, I do, but the only one at this table with a shot is our Claire Bear. He's had a hard-on for her all night. Trust me. I've been watching."

"Really?" I asked, suddenly feeling far too sober. "He's noticed me?"

"Oh, yeah, constantly." Another sip. "Seriously, go over there and say *hi*. See what happens. It's not like you're dating anyone, C."

I pressed my clammy palms to my exposed thighs, my skirt feeling a bit too short for comfort. The man had returned to his drink, his broad back to me again. Even from behind, the guy oozed sex appeal. Amie was right. He was definitely hot with a capital *H*. "I don't know," I said. "I need another drink or five for that."

The hoop through Rick's brown brow glistened as he arched it. "Since when is this sort of dare an issue for you?"

Since you asked me to kiss what appears to be a god in a leather coat. "I got this," I replied instead. "I just need some more liquid courage. And it's my birthday. I shouldn't even have to ask, right?"

His gaze was knowing. "Yeah, yeah." He lifted his hand for the waiter—a male who'd been eyeing Rick with interest all night. They were totally going to fuck later. "My too-sober friend here needs a round of shots."

"Tequila?" the cute waiter—Drew—suggested.

"Perfect," Rick replied, looking him over. "Definitely perfect."

Drew smiled, his hazel eyes gleaming with interest. "Be back in a moment."

"I hope so."

Brittany scowled as Drew disappeared. "How do you always do that?" she demanded, sounding disgruntled. "Like, he's totally going home with you tonight, and you've barely said anything to each other outside of ordering drinks."

Rick shrugged. "The power of a glance, sweetheart." He winked at her. "Learn how to use your best assets, and maybe you'll perform better."

She grabbed her breasts. "Trust me, I'm using them. This top couldn't be any lower cut."

He eyed her substantial cleavage. "Sometimes revealing less is more. Take Claire Bear. That graphic T-shirt is clingy, showing off the curves without displaying them for the world. And she's grabbed the attention of several men tonight."

"Because she's blonde," Brittany said, gesturing to my long hair as if it were my only asset.

"She's also gorgeous," Amie added. "And tall, with those killer legs."

"That she's exposed beautifully in that skirt," Rick agreed.

My cheeks warmed. "Guys, I understand it's my birthday, but this is starting to get weird. Are you all hitting on me right now? Because I gotta say, none of you are my type."

"I'm totally your type," Rick argued. "You just can't handle my D."

I scoffed at that. "Yeah, that's the reason."

Another wink, this one for me just as our drinks arrived. "Another round, if you don't mind," Rick said before Drew had finished distributing the glasses. "Actually, two."

"On it." Drew was apparently more than happy to continue serving our table—exclusively.

Amie was right.

Rick had a magic touch, or look, or *something*, because this always seemed to happen when we went out.

He clinked his glass against mine, a devious smile flirting with his lips, and I shot the liquid into the back of my throat. It burned so good. I may have just turned the legal age to drink, but this was not my first time in a bar. Most of the clubs near Ohio State University's campus were eighteen plus, and several of them didn't card.

Two more rounds later, a warm, fuzzy feeling settled over me again, easing me back into a comfortable state, one where my reservations dwindled. Mr. Hottie still sat at the bar, not talking to anyone.

Hmm.

Okay. I could do this.

Just walk up to him, flirt a little. How hard could it be?

"Just a kiss, right?" I asked, taking a sip of the water Drew had brought for me.

"Preferably with tongue," Rick replied. "But you do you, boo."

I nodded. "I got this."

"Damn right you do." He grinned. "Go get him, Claire Bear."

I swallowed some more water and stood, testing my heels.

The world spun just a little, but otherwise good. Adding three inches to my five-foot-eight height gave my legs a sexy appeal, lengthening my overall appearance. It also had the skirt at my hips looking indecently short, but it covered the right amount.

Unless I bent over.

Well, that would be one way to draw Mr. Hottie's attention.

I giggled to myself as I approached him. The stool beside him sat empty, giving me the opening I needed. I squeezed in beside him and the vacant seat, resting my elbows on the counter as if I wanted to flag down the bartender. My arm purposefully brushed his in my ploy, sending a zing of electricity across my skin.

Frowning, I glanced at him and met a pair of gorgeous sapphire eyes dusted in golden lashes. Wow, his face up close was a sight to behold. Chiseled perfection. His mouth seemed to beg me to taste him, drawing me in, consuming my vision.

Rick's dare appealed far more than it should.

What would this stranger do if I just laid one on him? Would he kiss me back? Push me away? Gasp?

I leaned closer, enthralled by the mystery of his reaction, addicted to the allure of his lips. He hadn't even said a word, barely even met my gaze, and already I would beg him for a night in bed.

"Who are you?" I marveled, completely in awe of his existence. I trailed my fingers up his jacket-clad arm, needing to touch him, to be near his energy, his pure presence.

He appeared equally as captivated, his throat working as he swallowed. His ocean-blue gaze ran over my features, his tongue sliding out to slick the seam of his mouth. I eyed the movement like a woman starved, desiring him more than I desired to breathe.

What is happening to me?

This instant draw, this attraction, floored me, forcing me to lean in, needing him, *craving* him. I brushed my lips against his, enthused by the feel of him at first touch.

Oh God...

He grabbed my elbow, his grip tight, pulling me closer. Energy hummed between us as my side aligned with his, his warmth a blanket I didn't know I needed.

"Do you often kiss men you hardly know?" he asked against my mouth, his voice deep, seductive. *Sexy as fuck.*

I shook my head. "No."

"Well, that's something, at least," he whispered darkly, his peppermint breath hot against my tongue. I leaned in for another taste, but his grip on my elbow held me in place beside him. "You want to take a walk?"

The words came off as a demand despite the intended question behind them. "Where to?" I asked, completely under his thrall regardless of the warning bells sounding my head.

He's a stranger. Don't leave with him!

But he feels so familiar, so right...

That's the alcohol talking, sweetheart.

Or something else entirely.

Because I didn't feel drunk at all. The daze and confusion of the shots had already worn off, leaving me hot and needy against this too-strong male. His intoxicating scent was like a drug, infusing me with these urges I didn't understand.

"Outside," he suggested, his bottom lip teasing my mouth by remaining just a hairsbreadth away. I clenched my thighs, his deep tenor sending me into a pit of arousal only he could save me from.

"Who are you?" I asked again, completely lost to him. My gaze held his, my breathing erratic. "What are you doing to me?"

"I could ask you the same, princess," he replied, his hand a brand against my elbow. "Let's go for a walk."

Definitely not a question now.

Yet I found myself nodding, accepting this bizarre proposal despite every logical instinct inside me rioting and demanding I say no.

It's just a walk.

You've lost your mind.

It's the right thing to do…

There was just something about him, something I couldn't quite identify. And my friends wouldn't let me go too far, right?

"Just a walk," I whispered.

"Yes." The word was a promise against my mouth, followed by the briefest of touches that left me *needing* more.

"For a kiss," I all but begged.

He arched a perfectly sculpted brow. "Another one?"

"The other didn't count." We'd barely brushed our mouths, let alone *kissed*.

His hand slid up my arm, leaving a trail of goose bumps in its wake. My chest burned with expectation, my legs shaking in anticipation. He wrapped his palm around the back of my neck, holding me tightly as if he owned me, and firmly pressed his lips to mine.

Fire licked through my veins, heating my body in a way I'd never experienced, the energy inside me roaring to the surface to meet his in a foreign mating I couldn't describe, only *feel*. His touch inflamed my very being, his hand anchoring me to him in the most delicious manner.

And then he cursed.

Loudly.

People around us were screaming.

I blinked, confused. Startled by the chaos erupting throughout the bar.

Then I noticed the scorched walls.

Smelled the scent of burning wood.

Felt the hot wave traveling over the crowd as an inferno surged across the room.

My lips parted on a scream, the stranger wrapping his arms around me, sheltering me from the tornado of sensation beating down upon us just as the world went black.

CHAPTER TWO
EXOS

"SHE BURNED DOWN THE BAR?" Elana's question felt weighted, accusatory. "What did you do to her?"

Oh, it wasn't what I did to her but what *she* did to *me*. "Nothing." I couldn't bring myself to tell the truth, to admit that I'd let her kiss me.

What the hell had she been thinking, anyway? Kissing a complete stranger? For fuck's sake.

Right, more importantly, why had I allowed it?

Because she was gorgeous.

Because she seduced me with her elemental gift for spirit.

Because I'd wanted to taste her plump lips all night despite knowing it was wrong.

I shook my head. "I managed to help most of the mortals survive, but there were a few casualties." Including one of her friends, which I imagined would not go over well when Claire awoke.

Shit. I scrubbed my hand over my face, exhausted. It'd taken every ounce of my strength to mitigate the damage. My affinity for fire was negligible at best. And Claire had done a number on that bar, her power exploding out of her and diminishing the establishment to ash.

"Well, on a positive note, we have an adequate cover story for her disappearance." Vape lounged in a chair near the floor-to-ceiling windows of Elana's living area, his casual slacks and button-down shirt suggesting he'd been about to retire for the evening when I'd called.

I hadn't known where else to take Claire, Elana being the only Council member I truly trusted with her safety and the story of the bar. She'd brought in Vape, but no one else, and allowed me to lay Claire upstairs in one of the myriad of guest rooms.

Being one of the oldest fae, Elana owned an exquisite piece of land, her manor adorned in flowers and greenery, all animated by her inner Spirit. Our kind controlled life and death of all beings, including the fae. Unlike the others, like Vape, who mastered a specific element, such as water.

"Yes, we'll spin the bar story to claim her as one of the victims of the tragedy. That'll ensure no one searches for her." Elana stood near a master piano, her hip resting against the hard surface. Her youthful appearance belied her ancient aura. A human would think her maybe thirty, but I knew her to be closer to a thousand years old. It was her ties to Spirit that kept her looking younger, unlike Vape, who showed his age in the creases of his pale skin and the white coloring of his long hair.

"Can you train her?" he asked, his midnight gaze resembling a black pit of wisdom. "Or is she too dangerous for the Academy?"

Goose bumps threatened to pebble over my skin at the memory of Claire's energy. I'd never felt anything like it. "She's powerful," I admitted, palming the back of my neck to diffuse the chill rising at the top of my spine. "But my Spirit can tame hers." It'd taken a great deal of strength—more than I'd ever used before—to temper her gift, but I'd managed it. "I can train her."

What I really meant to say was, *I'm the only one who can train her.*

Elana might be my elder, but my pure royal blood elevated my status, making me far stronger than she could ever be.

Unfair, yes.

But such was life.

Not even my brother could stand up to my affinity for Spirit, which was why the Royal Crown technically belonged to me. However, I'd chosen to abdicate my throne in favor of a warrior life, providing Cyrus with the opportunity to lead.

The arrangement suited us both.

"Then it's settled," Elana murmured, her silver-gray eyes glittering as she smiled. "I recommend the Fire Quad since that's her secondary strength, as well as your own."

"You wish for me to reside with Claire?" I asked, uneasy.

"She needs a protector. I think you're the only one suitable for the job."

I sighed, my hands in my pockets as I leaned against the tree in the middle of her living room. "I'll make the arrangements." Because she was right. Not only was I the only one who could keep Claire's abilities in check, but I also happened to be one of the few who preferred her alive. Most others would use the opportunity to kill her for the sins of her mother.

"She needs more than a single protector," Vape said as if reading my mind. "The girl requires an army of bodyguards."

"Which we don't have." Elana sounded frustrated, likely because our fae brethren were refusing to acknowledge and accept one of our own. She advocated for peace and harmony among the Fae Kingdoms, which was why she'd created the Academy—a place where all the Elemental Fae were forced to bond. Yes, they had separate quads and specific core classes, but there were numerous activities that brought the fae together, such as sporting events where gifts were not allowed and general education courses covering human studies and other useful, employable skills.

"That's a lot to put on one fae." Vape's tone suggested how he felt about that—unconfident. "An important fae at that."

"I volunteered for the job." Not exactly true—more that I was the only one capable of handling this task and wouldn't wish it on another. "I'll keep her safe."

"And what about you?" Vape countered. "Who will keep you safe as one of the two remaining royals of the Spirit lines?"

My lips curled. "I keep myself safe." And I dared anyone who thought otherwise to try to fuck with me. "I'm not concerned."

Elana smiled. "You're so much like your father, Exos. He'd be proud to—"

A shriek upstairs had all three of us straightening.

"Seems Sleeping Beauty is awake," Vape drawled, amusement in his expression.

Crash.

I darted to the windows, peering out into the early morning surroundings, the sun a distant pink on the horizon.

"She knocked down a tree," I said, my brow furrowing. "How the hell did she knock down a tree?" I would have felt her use of Spirit, my own energy having tied itself to hers days ago when I started tracking her. A whirlwind of water and air formed outside, uprooting several trees in its wake and heading toward the house. "Oh, *fuck.*"

I ran up the stairs without a backward glance, vaguely aware of Vape and Elana on my heels, and shoved open the door to the guest room.

Claire stood in the center of a room of roses and vines, her blonde hair tangled, her blue eyes wild as they darted around what she likely perceived as a garden of sorts. She stilled when she caught me standing in the doorway, her hands curled at her sides, her full lips falling open.

My Spirit reached for hers, stroking her with soothing vibrations meant to calm her inner turmoil. This was one of my personal skills—my ability to manipulate and persuade others, to lull them into a state of my choosing.

13

Calm down, I urged, eyeing the dissolving tornado outside.

Thank. Fuck.

It was working.

Her essence was, slowly but surely, responding to mine.

"Is this a dream?" she asked, her soft voice filled with wonder as her shoulders relaxed. She took in the life of the room again, the blooming flowers and the vines slithering up the walls and covering the ceiling in an earthy glow.

I glanced over my shoulder at Elana and Vape. "I'll talk to her."

Elana nodded, understanding that this required delicacy, or we risked overwhelming Claire. Again. "We'll be downstairs, should you need us," the elder murmured.

Vape tilted his head to the side. "One thing first. I sense water. And air."

Yes, I did, too.

And it seemed to be coming from Claire.

She blinked those big blue eyes at me, her brow furrowing. "Who are you?" she asked, her tone holding a hint of marvel. "Why am I dreaming this?"

Yeah, time to have a chat. "We'll be down in a bit." I didn't wait for Vape or Elana to reply before softly closing the door and locking myself in the guest room with Claire. We needed privacy for this discussion.

Claire twirled, her skirt riding high on her long, sexy legs, her arms loose at her sides. She tilted her head back on a smile filled with wonder and excitement. "Oh, it's beautiful here. I feel so alive. So… happy." More dancing, her Spirit clearly drunk on mine. Apparently, I'd soothed her a little too much.

Right. Time to ground her.

"Claire," I murmured, sitting on the bed of flowers she'd awoken upon. The mattress beneath was made of earth, the bed frame crafted from the trees outside. I preferred more modern accommodations, but every fae embraced the elements differently. It seemed Claire liked this style of décor. She bent to touch the roots decorating the floor, her skirt lifting to reveal the curves of her ass.

"Claire." Her name came out a bit strangled this time, my need for her to, well, *stop*, taking over. "Can you look at me, please?"

"Oh, yes." She turned, her gaze traveling over me with unveiled interest. "I will happily look at you. But as it's my dream, I'd really prefer you without clothes so I know what I'm working with here."

I coughed as a jolt of heat seared my insides. "Okay, well, first things first. You're not dreaming."

"Riiiighhhhtt," she drawled. "We're playing hard to get. Is that it?"

"No, we're not playing anything. You're not dreaming. This is the Fae Realm, where I brought you after the fire."

Her brow furrowed. Then she burst out laughing and folded over from the force of it.

14

I supposed, in her shoes, I'd react similarly. The world around her was nothing like the one she'd grown up in, her version of a forest a destructed beast due to humanity's lack of understanding. Fae, however, embraced the wilderness, allowing it into our homes and living peacefully with nature rather than against it.

"Claire, I'm telling you the truth," I tried again, my voice soft. "I meant to ease you into this, to bring you here of your own free will, but burning down the bar forced my hand. Your powers are awakening now that the charm has finally worn off, and you need to be among your kind."

She laughed harder, sitting on one of the roots on the floor, her arms wrapped around her middle. "Oh God, seriously. This is the most fucked-up dream I've ever had."

"Because it's not a dream," I replied through my teeth. "You're in the Fae Realm."

"Uh-huh." She wiped at the tears beside her eyes. "Because fairies are real."

"Not fairies. Fae."

"There's a difference?"

"Yes. Fairies are a myth. Fae are real."

"Oh. Okay. That clears it up." She fought a smile and lost, her lips curling again as another laugh fell from her mouth.

Gods, give me strength and patience; I'm going to need it. "Let's try a new path," I suggested, thinking out loud. "Tell me about your parents, Claire."

All signs of mirth disappeared, her brow furrowing. "What? No. I don't want to talk about that at all."

"Too bad. I want you to tell me about them."

"And I don't want to," she countered. "Fuck off."

"Not a dream, Claire," I told her, yet again. "Can't just make me disappear. Tell me about your parents."

"No."

"Why not?"

"Because I don't want to," she repeated.

"That's a shitty reason. There are a lot of things in this life I don't want to do, such as be here with you now, but we all have a sense of duty, a purpose we can't ignore. And I want to talk about your parents. Specifically, your mother, Ophelia." A cruel tactic, yes, but it seemed to be breaking through some of the fog in her mind, because her pupils contracted, her focus astute.

"I don't want to talk about this," she whispered.

"What do you know about your mother?" I wondered, ignoring the petulant turn of her mouth. "I'm guessing not much since you grew up in the Human Realm." And her father died shortly after Ophelia's demise. "What did your grandparents say about her?" That was who had raised her in Ohio, the mortals seemingly oblivious to Claire's natural birthright. "Because you look just like her, Claire. Did they tell you that?"

"Stop."

I didn't. She clearly needed a push to realize this wasn't a dream, to truly grasp her surroundings and purpose. *To grow the fuck up.* "She placed a charm on you, a hex of sorts, that dismantled your true nature. It finally unraveled yesterday, on your twenty-first birthday. Do you feel it? The gift of energy flooding your veins? Your affinity for the elements? You asked me at the bar who I am, remember? You *recognized* my essence. Because you're one of us. You're a fae. Your mother—"

"*Stop.*" She balled her hands into fists, her gaze narrowed. "Just. Stop."

"I can't." And I wouldn't even if I could. "You need to hear this, Claire. You need to understand *who* and *what* you are. And unfortunately, I don't have a lot of time to ease you into this since you're already in the Fae Realm. Your mother—"

A blast of wind blew me backward into the wall, my head knocking against the vines with a snap that I felt all the way down my spine.

Claire gasped, her hand flexing before her. "Oh God, oh God, oh God." She jumped to her feet, tripping over the root behind her and landing on her ass. "Oh God!"

I wheezed, pushing away from the wall. *Definitely has an affinity for air, too.*

"This… this…" she stammered, her hands feeling around on the floor, her eyes taking on a wild gleam. "This can't be happening. This isn't real. I need to wake up." She pinched her side, causing me to frown.

"Does that ever actually work?"

"Stop talking to me," she demanded, hurling another blast of wind at me with her fingertips.

My jaw snapped to the left from the localized blast, reminding me of a punch to the fucking face. "*Ow.*"

"Oh, fuck! I'm… Shit!" She scrambled toward me, then backward, then froze with her hands beneath her. As if that would stop her.

A knock on the door had her petrified gaze flying sideways as Vape's deep tenor floated through the wood. "Everyone all right in there?"

"Just getting acquainted," I replied through my teeth.

"Sounds like she's kicking your ass, son" was his reply.

I snorted. "Because I'm fighting with both hands tied behind my back."

Claire's eyebrows shot up. "Where am I?"

I couldn't help my resulting sigh. It wasn't like I hadn't said this about a hundred times already. "The Fae Realm."

"The *what?*" she squeaked, shaking her head. "That's not a thing. That's not real."

"It's very real and you're currently inside it." I massaged my jaw, stretching my neck to loosen it. She lifted her hand again, forcing me to add, "Hit me with another blast of air, princess, and I'll retaliate." I wouldn't hurt her, but

I would pin her. Our first lesson? Control.

Her lower lip trembled, but her teeth audibly clenched. "What the fuck is going on?"

Did this woman have a hearing problem? Because I swore we just went through this. "It all relates back to your mother, Cl—"

Energy quaked around me, causing the bed to collapse to the floor, the headboard disappearing into a pile of ashes as flames erupted around us.

Claire screamed.

I cursed.

And tackled her to the ground.

CHAPTER THREE
CLAIRE

THIS ISN'T REAL.
   This isn't happening.
   Everything will be fine when I wake up.
   I just need to—
   "Claire!" The furious growl came from the man on top of me, his striking blue eyes glowing with fury. "Focus on me, on my voice."
   I'd really rather not.
   I just wanted to go home.
   To wake up.
   To escape.
   To be anywhere other than here, with this man who kept talking about my mother, the woman who abandoned me as a child, who shattered my father's spirit. Grandma always said she killed my dad when she broke his heart. He never recovered.
   I hated my mother, couldn't stand to hear anything about her. Childish, yes, but it was how I survived, how I escaped my reality.
   My memories of my parents were nonexistent, having been too young when she left us, too young when my father *died*.
   I shook, tears of the past clouding my eyes. Remembering hurt. Thinking

about them *hurt*. I didn't want to be here. I didn't want to hear about *her*. I just wanted to wake up, to be done with this horrible nightmare.

"Breathe," the man on top of me demanded. "Come on, princess. Listen to me. I need you to calm down, to breathe, to *focus*. Search for the tranquility inside you, call on it, pull it into you and use it."

What the fuck is he even talking about? It could be a different language, for all I knew or cared.

"Claire," he whispered, his lips dangerously close to mine. "Please, sweetheart, I need your focus, or you're going to burn the house down. I'm still exhausted from earlier. Just close your eyes and think of a peaceful place. Describe it for me."

A peaceful place? I thought hysterically, nearly laughing. "Not fucking here!" I shouted, warmth flooding my insides, spilling through my fingertips and raging around me. "Let me go!"

"I can't do that," he said, his palms on my face, forcing me to look at him, to *see* him.

My eyes widened. "You're on fire!"

"I'm aware," he gritted out, wincing. "Just... breathe, Claire. Breathe for me. Slowly."

"You're on fire," I repeated, my heart galloping in my chest. How was breathing going to help? If anything, it'd make this worse, right? Smoke inhalation?

Except, nothing but clean air met my nostrils and mouth.

My brow furrowed.

How is that possible?

And why am I not burning?

I actually felt quite cold, not hot. Because the flames were so intense I was freezing? No, that couldn't be it.

"That's it," he whispered, his forehead falling to mine. "Relax."

"Relax?" Some strangled combination of a laugh and a cry escaped my mouth. "This is... *insane*."

"You're an Elemental Fae coming into her abilities for the first time." The words were low, his voice utterly calm despite the inferno soaring around us. "It's not normal for someone this age to access her elemental gifts. Most fae are taught as children. But I can help you, Claire."

I shivered beneath him, my skin slick, my throat dry. "Help me?" I whispered, my gaze flickering to the wildfire behind him and back to his face. "This is a nightmare. It has to be."

"It's not." The words were a breath against my lips, his body hard and heavy on top of mine. "Please, Claire. Let me help you."

"How?" I asked, unsure of all of this. Of him. Of this place. Of the erratic energy threatening to burst out of my chest. "*How?*"

His nose brushed mine, his fingers sliding into my hair, his mouth trailing over my cheek. His gentle caress set off a flurry of butterflies in my abdomen, a direct conflict from the warning rioting in my mind. The man was *on fire*. Yet he seemed perfectly at ease, his strong form a comforting blanket over mine.

What is happening to me?

My eyelids drooped, exhaustion taunting the edges of my thoughts.

I don't want to sleep.

"Picture your happy place," a deep voice whispered against my ear. "Somewhere that makes you feel calm, at peace. For me, it's the lake behind my old home. So warm and tranquil, and I swear the water tasted of the finest spring you could ever imagine. Swimming is my serenity, where I go when I need to think. What about you, Claire? Where do you go?"

"I…" I swallowed, hesitant. "Camping. Beneath the stars. I love the night sky." *Why am I telling him this?*

"The stars here are beautiful, too. You'll see them tonight." His lips touched my throat, my pulse soaring in response. "Where did you go camping, Claire?"

"In Ohio," I whispered, frowning. My grandparents used to take me to the woods, saying I needed to be closer to nature, to enjoy the fresh air and clear my head. I always loved it, feeling almost at home surrounded by the elements.

Wasn't that what this man had called me? *An Elemental Fae?*

"What's an Elemental Fae?" I asked out loud, my limbs tensing.

"It's what we are." He went to his elbows on either side of my head, causing my eyes to flutter open. He was no longer on fire, the room around us just as green as before.

What the hell is going on?

"Shh, stay in that calm place," he said, his thumb drawing a line across my cheekbone and down to the column of my neck. "I'm strong, but you… You're exhausting me, Claire."

My brow furrowed. "*I'm* exhausting *you*?"

"Yes." He cocked his head, his blue irises taking on a heady glow that stole my breath. "Your… *Ophelia*… was a fae. A pureblood of Spirit. That makes you a Halfling. A very, very strong Halfling."

"Ophelia?" I repeated, frowning.

"The given name of your…" He trailed off, raising a brow.

My mother, I realized. "My mother was a fairy?"

"A fae," he corrected, his lips curling down. "Fairies are tiny little figments with wings, and they don't exist. You're a *fae*. As am I."

"And fae are…?"

"Supernatural beings with affinities for the elements." He sounded so nonchalant, as if this type of topic were discussed every day. "Ophelia was a Spirit Fae, like me. And—"

"Spirit Fae?" I repeated. "What the hell does that mean?"

"A fae who connects with life and death." He balanced on one arm, lifting his palm. "Try not to freak out."

"Okay…"

He eyed me for a long moment, then refocused on his hand. It glowed, energy shivering over my skin, as a gorgeous lily appeared, blossoming into the size of my head, with big white petals.

"How did you do that?" I marveled, awed.

"Life," he said, tucking the flower stem behind my ear. "You, too, have access to the same gift. And with time, I'll teach you how to use it."

Uh, right. He'd lost me again.

"You're saying I can do that?"

"Yes," he confirmed. "In addition, it seems, to several other things." He stared down at me for a long moment, his gaze dropping to my mouth before flicking back up to my eyes. "I'm going to roll off of you now. Can you try to stay calm?"

He really enjoyed that word. *Calm. Relax. Breathe.* "Sure." I could feign calm if it kept the crazy man content.

A flower just blossomed in his fucking hand.

And I'm in a room shrouded in… forest.

I pinched my side again.

Nothing.

This can't be real.

But it certainly *felt* real.

"You're not dreaming," he said softly, clearly catching my not-so-subtle pinch.

I slid away from him, bracing my back against the tree—*yes, a fucking tree*—in the center of the room. "Fae Realm."

"Yes." He drew his knees upward, wrapping his forearms around them. "I know it's a lot to take in, and you still don't believe me, but you'll see."

"And if I want to go home?"

He shook his head. "You can't, Claire. Your powers are too much for the mortal realm. You destroyed that bar."

My brow furrowed. "What bar? When? I don't…" A vision tickled my thoughts. One of him in his leather jacket, sitting on a stool, his lips a hairsbreadth from mine. And then flames, like the ones that had adorned his back only moments ago, encircling us and expanding. "No… That… *No.*" That couldn't have happened. It couldn't be real. "Tell me…" I paused, swallowing. "Tell me that's not… Tell me it didn't…" But I felt the truth of it somewhere deep inside, heard the reminiscent screams as everyone bolted into the night.

Oh God…

"Tell me I didn't…" I couldn't finish, my hand covering my mouth. *Rick, Brittany, Amie…*

21

"I'm sorry," the stranger whispered, his expression one of sorrow. "Your power burst out of you too suddenly for me to anticipate. I tried to save as many of them as I could, but the destruction was too much."

"I destroyed the bar?" I whispered.

He hung his head, as if he blamed himself. "Yes."

"And my friends?"

His eyes lifted to mine, the answer lurking in his gaze.

"Who?" I demanded. "*Who?*"

"The boy," he said.

"*Rick?*" *Oh God…* I pinched my side again, but it was futile. I would *never* dream this. Not even in a nightmare. "I killed Rick?"

"It's not your fault, Claire. You didn't—"

"*Not my fault?*" I shrieked. "You said I burned down the damn bar!" I jumped to my feet, mindful of the roots in this stupid, tiny, forest-laden room. Such a lie. It felt like I was outside, but I wasn't. And the air closing in around me proved it.

I needed to be free.

To run.

To be in the clean air.

Not locked in this little greenhouse with…

Fuck, I don't even know his name!

Fae Realm.

Powers.

Fire.

Burned-down bar.

I spun, not hearing whatever he was trying to say beside me. Not caring to hear another word. This was too much.

I killed Rick.

Did I? What if he's lying?

Why would he lie?

I don't know. I don't fucking know!

His palm was too hot against my forearm. I twisted out of his grasp, needing space, needing *air*. And as if hearing my call, it whirled around me, blowing him into the wall again with a grunt. His pained expression struck me in the heart, causing me to falter.

I don't know him.

I don't belong here.

"I can't," I breathed, staring at the window, watching as the glass blew out with a breath from my lips. "I'm sorry." I followed the breeze on instinct, letting it carry me down to the grass below, not pausing to think about the how or the why, just needing to *run*.

There had to be a way home. A way back to the bar. A way back to Rick. To my friends. My family.

I couldn't stay here. This wasn't my place. This foreign land of endless trees and flowers and vines. *Oh God, where am I even going? It doesn't matter. Just run.* And I did, sprinting through the fields and beneath the canopy of leaves, then across and more fields, past lakes, and continuing into unending nature.

The sun moved overhead, illuminating my journey, aiding my attempt to escape.

But nothing new crossed my path. Only more and more trees, denser with every step.

I whirled around, mystified, tears rolling down my cheeks.

"Where am I?" I breathed, falling to my knees in the thick underbrush. "*Where the fuck am I?*"

I collapsed to my side, my exhaustion finally overcoming me. My legs were bleeding, my feet aching, my heart... *broken.*

"I don't belong here," I whimpered, curling into a ball of despair. Leaves seemed to fold around me, cocooning me from the elements, soothing my spirit in a way I could hardly comprehend. But I allowed it. Because what else was I supposed to do?

"Who am I?" I asked, a sob ripping from my chest.

Claire... My name whispered on the wind, my vision blurred by the flutter of butterflies overhead. *Claire...*

I closed my eyes, not wanting to hear another word, refusing to acknowledge this insanity any longer.

This is not my home.

CHAPTER FOUR
TITUS

WHAT A FUCKING MORNING. My head spun from the aftermath of what felt like a dream that had me in a fog for hours.

Something strange was happening, causing the campus to come alive in excitement. And I wasn't in the mood for excitement, something most would say was out of character for me.

However, after my fuckup with Ignis last night, I had good reason. Sleeping with her had been a huge fucking mistake—not that I'd had much choice in the matter—and now she refused to understand the words *never happening again.* I didn't do relationships, especially not with the likes of her. I just wanted to be alone. Heading to the gym and isolating myself in the guys' locker room seemed to be the only place of solace I could find in this damned school.

Normally, I enjoyed the challenge a Fire Fae like Ignis would bring, maybe even indulge her with a round or two before I moved on, but I'd fallen into a temporary funk that I couldn't explain.

I leaned back against the lockers and let my head *thump* against the unforgiving steel. It was the only place on the premises that wasn't covered in nature and shit. I needed metal and grounding. I needed to focus. Closing my eyes, I focused on the flames licking at my insides and threatening to burst out of me. The air around me wavered, and I knew I risked melting school property if I didn't get my shit under control.

"You okay, man?" River asked, wiping both the sweat and conjured water from his face with a towel.

As a Water Fae, he was the only guy who'd dare approach me in an enclosed locker room. That was predominantly why the shy fae and I had become friends over the past year. In some ways, I seemed to be even more isolated than him. A side effect of being the Powerless Champion—winner of the ring where fighting to the death was common and the use of powers meant execution in the most fantastical manner.

One rule: no powers—hence the title the "Powerless Champion."

It took a certain kind of mental state for me to win in that kind of fighting ring, but that had been me for quite a few years. That was before the accident. Before the Academy. Before a friend like River.

Another spasm rushed through my body that left me feeling nauseous. I felt as if I were being pulled somewhere off campus, like my whole body wanted to run. I never ran from my problems, no matter how big or irritating they were.

Rubbing the back of my neck, I suppressed a groan. Everything hurt as if I'd been back in the fighting ring for weeks, but the days of bashing skulls were behind me. I was trying to turn over a new leaf and control my powers instead of pretending they didn't exist—which had gotten half of my family killed when they finally demanded acknowledgment.

Fuck if that was going as planned.

"I must be sick," I replied to River. I showed him my palm. Instead of veins, embers writhed under my skin like possessed snakes. After so many years of denying myself my powers, they were coming through with merciless greed—or something was calling them to the surface.

Instead of fear, River looked amused. "Must be the curse," he said as he flicked his wrist and sent water splashing onto my skin. Steam hissed immediately and fogged the air, but it felt good.

Waving away the mist, I glowered at him. "Don't tell me you believe in that bullshit, too."

He cocked his brow and strapped the towel around the back of his neck. "So you heard about her?"

Of course I'd heard about her. News of the Halfling was spreading faster than any wildfire I could create. Maybe it was the anxiety surrounding her arrival that set me on edge.

"I have no interest in humans," I said flatly, although the surge of heat in my core suggested otherwise, as if she were somehow the source of all my power trying to burst out of me. Ignoring it, I popped open the locker and snatched my fireproof shirt, stretching the fibers before pulling it over my head. "Why don't you go take a shower?"

It was a poor attempt at tricking River into leaving me alone. The Water Fae didn't need a proper shower, not with his powers fully under control.

Showing off, River spritzed himself with a splash of water and stepped closer to me to evaporate the excess. He grinned before pulling his shirt over his head.

"You know the Halfling is a female... right?" River waggled his brows, no doubt hoping to entice me to go check her out for ourselves. He would be far too shy to approach her, but he was always fascinated by humans. He took every elective and training session he could get his hands on to study the short-lived race.

I rolled my eyes. "I don't care what she is. I don't want to see another girl right now."

Just when I was about to lean back onto the lockers again, River took me by the wrist and yanked hard. He flushed his grip with water that sent fresh steam into the air and protected him against my burning skin. "Stop pouting," he said. "We both know Ignis is waiting right outside, and you've been avoiding her. It's time to confront her and get the bullshit out of the way. Then we can go sniff out the Halfling and see if she's put a curse on you," he added with a smirk.

I narrowed my eyes but allowed River to drag me out of the locker room. He was right. The sooner I faced Ignis and told her to fuck off, the sooner I'd feel better. Something was wrong with me, and I didn't need to be stressing about her right now.

Sunlight made me wince when we stepped out into the cool exterior of the gym. It wasn't like my pad back in the Fire Kingdom, with iron and walls that blocked out the elements. The Academy encouraged all elements to play freely, meaning an exercise and training building would be open for all. Enormous windows spanned the ceiling, allowing wind and light to slip through to caress the great oaks and vines that acted as climbing walls with shifting footholds. I let my eyesight adjust, and three female fae came into focus.

Ignis glowered at me, tall and furious. Her red hair curled around her cheeks in a way that could have made her look innocent if it hadn't been for the tiny flames that licked across her fingertips.

I groaned when I saw that she'd brought reinforcements. The Water Fae, Sickle, and the Air Fae, Aerie, stood on either side of her with hatred blazing in their eyes.

"Thank you, River," Ignis said curtly and waved him away as if she'd ordered him to retrieve me, which she likely had.

River ducked his head and let go of my wrist, but I spotted the mischievous glint in his eyes as he glanced up at me through the shaggy hair covering his face. The bastard thought this was immensely entertaining. "I'll catch up with you at the entrance," he muttered, stuffing his hands into his pockets and shuffling out of sight.

I sighed. "Look, Ignis—"

She stormed up to me and slammed a crooked finger into my chest. Any other fae would have gotten burned by an act like that, but her fire seemed to have grown overnight—after she'd tricked me into sleeping with her.

Damn it.

I was a moron.

"Why have you been avoiding me?" she snapped. "You're mine now, Titus. You and I fucked, which is a binding contract between Fire Fae for at least a month's time."

Well, she wasn't going to beat around the bush about it, was she?

She grinned, no doubt thinking she had me right where she wanted me. I was going to be her trophy for a month? No fucking way was that going to happen.

I matched the fire in her eyes with my own. Maybe if we'd been back in the Fire Kingdom, I'd have to indulge her—no matter if she'd poisoned me with seduction magic or not—but not here, not in the Academy, where freedom was encouraged and elemental customs wavered.

That didn't make my predicament much better. She would fight for this particular custom to be enforced if only to imprison me to her side and add to the growing reputation as a Fire Fae not to be messed with. Taming the Powerless Champion no doubt was on the top of her list of recent achievements and would reduce my pride to the most withering of embers when she was done with me.

The most logical prevention would have been to not sleep with her, and of course I knew better than to stick my dick in this crazy bitch. Just because I had a playboy reputation didn't mean I always acted on it. No one would believe me if I told them that she'd tricked me into sleeping with her.

Seduction magic was a black-market commodity and not permitted on Academy premises, but I still had the sour aftertaste of its recognizable compulsion in my mouth. The bitch had stoked flames that weren't intended for her, which was likely what had left me feeling so off right now. She might have gotten a taste, but never again.

Growling, I gripped her fingers and forced her arm to bend backward. Like most fae, she was graceful and lean, but she was still of the fire element. With the amount of power coursing through her right now, I suspected she might even be a suitable match if we really went head-to-head. I'd already gotten dinged for fighting this year and couldn't afford another mark.

"I'm not interested in entertaining your fantasies, Ignis. You might have tricked me into your bed, but in the light of day, I see you for what you really are." I leaned in, enunciating my words carefully. "Not. My. Type." I let go of her arm. "I'll watch my drinks with a closer eye from now on. Don't think you can trick me again."

Ignis stumbled, overacting the motion as if I'd hurt her. Her eyes brimmed with crocodile tears, and her friends rushed to her side. "You would accuse me of spiking your drink?" she shrieked.

"You brute!" Sickle snapped at me, her voice grating against my ears with the icy edge of her power, making me wince. "How could you treat a kindred fae like Ignis so poorly? What a horrid accusation!"

I narrowed my eyes and crossed my arms over my chest, which was more of a motion to try to keep the growing inferno contained than anything else. "When she acts like a kindred fae, perhaps I'll treat her in the manner worthy of her station."

Ignoring them, I flared my heat, allowing enough of it to singe the air until the fae instinctually backed off, allowing me through.

Normally, I would have been flattered that a powerful Fire Fae would have thought me untouchable enough to have to spike my drink to procure a night with me, but now I just felt angry, manipulated, my pride bruised. Seduction magic might not be permitted on campus, but it wasn't entirely illegal generally because it couldn't force someone into bed unless an ember of desire existed in the first place. It grew passions; it didn't create them.

But I didn't even *like* Ignis, let alone find the devilish female attractive.

No, something felt wrong. My powers were stirring restlessly inside of me, as if on the brink of chaos. And it had started late last night.

Which, from what I had heard, was when the Halfling had arrived in our realm.

Whispers reached my ears, all of the other fae talking about her.

"I heard she's killed already. Should she really be here?"

"Is she bound?"

"Who is her mentor?"

"I heard she's hot!"

Growling, I found River leaning against the entrance and brushed past him. "Since when do you play lapdog to Ignis?"

He shrugged, a little sheepish. "She's a little scary, if you haven't noticed."

"Oh, I've noticed." Damn female had bitten me last night, too. Leaving her claim proudly on my neck. "She's—"

"You," Exos interrupted, his sapphire eyes trained on me. From the state of his shredded clothes, he'd been in a battle or two—on the losing end, for sure.

My eyes widened. The Royal Prince of Spirit Fae was a legend, his connection to Spirit magic the strongest anyone had ever seen, his affinity for fire besting several of my brethren. "Yes?" I asked him, unsure if I should bow or refer to him formally. "Uh, Your Highness?" *What are you doing here?* I wanted to ask.

Then it struck me.

He's here because of the Halfling.

Exos leveled me with a powerful gaze. "I need you to come with me."

I didn't ask questions. When a Royal Fae issued a demand, everyone adhered to it. Especially when that Royal Fae was a legendary Fae Warrior. Like Exos.

He led us—me and River, who had insisted on tagging along—deep into the forest surrounding the Academy, having already shown us the destruction at Chancellor Elana's home just off campus. In a quick debrief, Exos had informed us that he'd been put in charge of the Halfling's protection, and lost her.

Which was why he needed me.

The girl's affinity for fire had left a string of smoky notes in the air, too faint for him to catch. And I was the strongest Fire Fae within immediate reach.

"Keep up. I need your proximity to sense her," Exos said, his feet moving quickly over the exposed roots and fallen leaves.

Great, giant boughs seemed to sway away from Exos as we followed the faint scent of the most powerful fire magic I'd ever felt—and that was saying something. "You're sure she only just came into her powers?" I ventured, struggling to keep myself from sprinting past the fae. Not only was I strong, but I was fast, too, and now that I had her trail, I wanted to follow it.

"Yes, and so far, I sense multiple elements from her. Spirit and Fire, of course, but also Air and Water." He glanced back at River, who trailed behind us. "Is he going to be up to the task? The Halfling is powerful."

I nodded, confident in River's ability. When his head was on straight, he was strong—stronger than even he realized. "He'll be able to help."

Exos gave a curt nod before reaching out a hand to stop us. "Good, because she seems to enjoy playing with fire." He sounded disgruntled over that, which explained some of his singed attire.

"Hold on," I said, my nostrils flaring as I picked up the tendrils of her smoky power. "She's near."

"Lead us" was Exos's reply, his vigilant gaze sweeping the grounds.

My eyes darted across the clearing we'd stepped into. It presented a calm facade, an oasis that now descended into dusk with the softness of purple butterflies lazily lingering over the sleepy meadow. But I sensed the Halfling, her exquisite aura of molten iron mixed with a tornado of power that dared me to take a single step closer.

Exos eyed me warily as I followed the tug that seemed to grow straight from my chest toward a heap of flowers with the shadow of a curled form hidden beneath the colorful earth. Was that her?

I inched closer, studying the sleeping Halfling lying on a makeshift bed of roses. Her skin glowed with inner embers that seemed to react to my presence, making me suck in a breath at her beauty.

Fuck.

29

I'd never seen a creature quite like this. Soft blonde strands draped over a delicate face marred by little brown spots that gave me the peculiar urge to stoop down for a closer look. Fae didn't have flaws, but humans did. It made her endearing, gorgeous, and exotic.

Without thinking, I crouched beside her and trailed my fingers up her arm, smoothing over the volcanic heat that called to me. She shifted in her sleep, her eyebrows knitting with a surge of discomfort before she quieted again, seeming to accept me. My touch went up to her rounded ears, so different from my own.

Then her eyes opened and the most alluring blue irises trapped me in a piece of heaven.

"Hi there, beautiful," I whispered, smiling.

Her pupils shrank like I'd given her a shot of adrenaline, and the ground rumbled.

She screamed in utter terror and surprised me with a gust of wind, sending me flat on my ass. Exos and River shouted something, but I lifted a hand to stop them.

Just in time, too.

A ring of fire erupted around us as the Halfling shot to her feet. Her chest heaved like a bird trapped in a cage, and she flung her face left and right, trying to gather her bearings. "Fuck, I just woke up, so either this is one of those trick dreams or..."

"Not a dream!" Exos shouted unhelpfully from the other side of the flames.

Sighing, I examined the flames the Halfling had sprung into existence. Powerful, yes, but manageable. Sensing the ignition she'd established, I snapped my fingers and sent the fires fizzling into ash.

She startled, blinked at me, then took a step back. "Did you just...?"

"Exterminate your little fire frenzy? Yeah, sweetheart." I grinned. "You're not the only one who likes to play with fire."

"We need to get her back to the estate," Exos growled.

Again, not helpful.

The Halfling seemed stressed by his voice, and energies hummed around her, threatening to explode again. If she called on one of her other elements, I'd be useless.

"Hey," I said softly, lowering myself to one knee. I knew I could be intimidating at my full height, but I wouldn't wish any harm to come to this creature. "We're not here to hurt you, sweetheart."

"Yeah? Tell that to *him*." She pointed at Exos, causing me to fight back a smile.

"I'm not him," I told her, offering her a conspiratorial glance. "I barely know him, actually. But I can see the lack of appeal." Dangerous words to say about a Royal Fae, but I'd deal with the consequences later.

She blinked, startled. "What?"

I cocked my head to the side, allowing my lips to tilt in a way I knew charmed most of the female fae at the Academy. "He demanded I help find you. I'm Titus."

Another blink, this one slower. "Titus?"

"That's me."

She swallowed, looking at Exos and River, then took in her surroundings again. "Where the hell am I?"

"The enchanted boundaries," I informed her, still on my knee, staring up at her. It left me in a far more vulnerable position that seemed to be easing her nerves at least a little.

"I don't know what that means." She shook her head. "I don't know what any of this means."

Exos hadn't given me a lot of insight into what she knew, just that she was a powerful Halfling and her name was Claire, but her knowledge of our world seemed to be very little. "They're the protective borders around the Academy. It's the only area in the Fae Realm where all the elements are allowed to play together, and we learn how to coexist." A load of shit, really. It was all a political game to force the different elements to get along, to live in harmony.

"Fae Realm," she repeated on a breath, her shoulders beginning to shake. "It's all real."

"For fuck's sake," Exos said, his fingers combing through his ash-blond hair.

The pixie of a woman took a step backward, her gaze snapping to his, then to mine, then to his again. "I-I didn't mean to... to..."

"Blow me into a wall? *Again?*" he asked.

Tears gathered in her eyes, her lower lip trembling. "This can't... I don't..."

"How did you blow him into a wall?" I asked, genuinely curious. "Can you do it again? Maybe into a tree?"

"Wh-what?" she asked, her big blue eyes refocusing on me.

"Sorry, it just sounds amusing as hell. Can you do it again?" I didn't really want her to, but I did want to distract her. "Not many fae can take on someone as famous as Exos, so you've intrigued me."

"Exos?" she repeated, her brow furrowing.

"Dude, you didn't even tell her your name?" I asked, shocked and dismayed. "No wonder she kicked your ass."

"I brought you here to help, kid. Not to be a pain in my ass."

"Kid?" I repeated, raising my brows. "I'm twenty-two, *Your Highness.*"

He gave me a look that said he couldn't care less. "Fine. *Man.*"

"Better," I agreed, shifting my attention back to the girl who was observing us with a furrowed brow. Much better than the terrified-little-mouse expression. "Seriously, can you blow him into a tree for me? All I can do is light him on fire, and he'll just extinguish the flames." Not exactly true. I could burn him if I tried hard enough.

"Fire," she whispered, her expression pained.

"Yes," I said slowly, confused. "I'm a Fire Fae."

"She's thinking about the bar." Exos folded his arms. "Which I already told her wasn't her fault."

She crumpled to the ground, her knees giving out beneath her, tears tracking down her face. "A bar?" I asked, inching toward her. "What about it?"

"R-rick," she breathed, her palm covering her heart.

"Her friend," Exos translated. "He... He didn't make it."

The woman let loose an agonized scream, flames singeing the air and igniting my soul. I caught the embers before they could cause any damage, blanketing her in my essence and forcing her fiery abilities to behave as she broke down before my eyes.

"What the hell?" River asked, taking the words right out of my mouth. "What friend? What bar?"

Exos blew out a breath. "Short version: Her powers exploded in the Human Realm. She burned down a building—with her friend inside."

And he couldn't have told us that *before* we found her?

"Fuck," I breathed, rubbing my hand down my face. "*Fuck.*"

CHAPTER FIVE
CLAIRE

I COULDN'T SEE.

Couldn't breathe.

Couldn't think.

Rick's dark eyes flashed before me, his sexy-as-sin grin, his ridiculously spiky hair. I cradled my chest, the burn radiating throughout my body intense. I wanted to scream. To cry. To run. But my limbs refused to move, some invisible weight holding me captive in my cocoon of flowers.

Oh God, I'm covered in... in pollen!

None of this made any sense. The surroundings. The colors. The endless forest. The too-orange sun illuminating the field. The male crouching a few feet away...

His dark green eyes reminded me of the trees framing his muscular form.

I shuddered, curling in on myself, wishing that this would all just go away. That my world would return to normal. That this was all just a drunken nightmare.

Maybe I died in the fire?

I startled at the thought. Was this heaven? That would explain the magic, the odd scents, my bizarre connection to the elements.

"Claire," the one closest to me murmured, his voice deep and soothing and sending a shiver down my spine.

Titus, he'd called himself.

What kind of name is Titus?

"Everyone will tell you it wasn't your fault," he murmured, lying down on his side and bringing our heads to the same level, about five feet of flowers separating us. "But I know those words don't help. I used to hear them all the time. It made me so angry because no one understood. The guilt is suffocating. The agony of loss soul-destroying. And you feel so lonely, so incredibly alone."

Sadness tinged his handsome features, pulling down his brow and his full lips. Dark memories tainted his green gaze, his history etched into the rigid lines of his long, lean body. His elbow drew up to pillow his head of thick, auburn locks, his presence somehow soothing rather than terrifying.

I didn't know him at all.

Yet I felt that strange draw to him, just like I had with the other one. An inkling to trust, to fold myself against him, to escape in the heat of his skin.

"I'm losing my mind," I whispered. "Completely losing my fucking mind."

Titus chuckled. "Yeah? Me, too, sweetheart. Me, too."

I couldn't help the laugh that escaped me. Here this man was, an utter stranger, lying on the ground with me, commiserating over our fall into the land of insanity.

"That's a lovely sound," he murmured. "If a little broken."

"This is crazy." I shook my head, rolling to my back to stare blankly up at the cloudless sky. "I... I don't..." No other words came to me, my mind completely shutting down. I had nothing. No comeback. No comment. Probably about a million questions I had no energy to voice. Just... *nothing*.

"I can't even begin to imagine how alarming this must be for you, to have no idea you're part fae while growing up in the Human Realm. Honestly, I don't know much about it, having spent my whole life ingrained in fae society. I mean, I didn't even want to attend the Academy. The Council forced me, which, it seems, they're going to do to you, too. So, I guess I understand a little bit, but to be raised as a human and stolen to this land, I don't blame you at all for thinking it's crazy."

His tenor, soft and calming, lulled me into a strange sense of comfort. I looked at him again. *Really* looked at him.

He resembled a model sprawled out for a photo shoot, apart from the slight downward curve of his mouth. But he truly resembled perfection in an almost inhuman way. There was a powerful air around him, a humming energy that seemed to sizzle between us as I held his darkening gaze.

Then I noticed his ears.

Not round like mine, but slightly pointed.

My brow furrowed. "Why do you look like an elf?"

His eyes widened. "An elf?" A laugh bubbled out of him, deep and humorous and beautiful. Hmm, yes, I did like the way he sounded, both his voice and his chuckles. "I'm a fae, sweetheart. Not an elf."

"Do you all have pointy ears?"

"We do."

"I don't."

"Because you're a Halfling," he said, smiling. "Your mum was a fae. Your da a human."

The way he said *mum* and *da* had my lips twitching again. *Now he sort of sounds like a leprechaun.* But he was missing the trademark red beard.

"What's funny?" he asked, a smile in his voice.

I shook my head. "Nothing." I couldn't call him a leprechaun. He'd just find me even more nuts. Which, of course, I was, considering my surroundings and the fact that I was starting to believe all this nonsense.

Ugh. What choice did I have? Clearly, I wasn't going to wake up. And I couldn't deny the strange sensations coursing through my veins or the slight memory of the bar flickering in my thoughts.

I burned it down.

I killed Rick.

My gaze fell, my shoulders rounding as another spike of pain splintered my chest.

"Hey," Titus said softly. "Stay with me, sweetheart. We'll get through this."

That sensation to laugh again hit me in the gut, my eyes filling with tears. "I don't even know you. You don't know me. I don't know anything or anyone or what the hell is…" I trailed off, tired of repeating the same words over and over. They did nothing to improve my situation, just leaving me to wallow in the same endless cycle of pity and despair.

"I think you'll find you know me quite well," Titus murmured. "Perhaps not about me, or who I am, but your Fire recognizes mine."

"What?" That didn't make any sense. "What Fire?"

"Your inner flame, Claire." He held out his hand, a flicker of light dancing over the tips. "You're strong. Much stronger than you should be."

"I don't understand."

His smile was sad. "I know, sweetheart. But you will." The flames flickered out, his hand falling to the ground. "We want to help you. To teach you."

"Why?"

"Because you're fae. We take care of our own."

"But I burned down the bar…"

"Which wouldn't have happened if you'd been properly trained," he whispered. "I know what it's like to come into your power too early, to not be prepared. It's terrifying. It's consuming. It kills."

"Yes," I agreed, my voice equally quiet.

"I can help you." He reached for me again, his hand so close but not near enough to touch. "Let me show you."

"How?"

"Lift your hand toward mine," he encouraged me. "You'll see."

Somehow I doubted that but found my arm lifting of its own accord, my sense of curiosity piqued. What did he intend to do? Grab me? He could have done that already. It was three against one. I stood no chance here, even with my bizarre... *gifts*.

"Here." He wiggled his fingers, the tips brushing mine as I rolled closer to him. They were warm. Welcoming. Oddly familiar.

Electricity sizzled between us, sending a zap up my arm that had me pulling back.

"Come on, Claire," he urged, amusement flirting with his mouth. "Let me show you."

"That wasn't it?"

He chuckled. "No. That was mutual attraction, not fire."

My eyebrows shot up. "What?" He couldn't mean that we found each other attractive, right? We didn't *know* each other. I mean, sure, he was good-looking. Actually, no, he was *hot*. But... No. I was not attracted to anything or anyone right now, least of all a pointy-eared man with a too-sexy grin.

"It's a fae thing," he said, a pair of adorable dimples flashing. "Our elements sing to each other when we find a potential mate. That's what you felt. Now come on, don't hide." He held out his hand again, but I was too busy gaping at him to move.

Potential mate? What in the fuck? No. Hell no. "Mate?"

"Elements bond for power," he explained. "No more stalling, sweetheart. Let me show you what I really mean."

"You want to be my... *mate*?"

He sighed. "No. I don't want to be anyone's mate. It's just a part of society. You'll feel it with others, especially since you're multi-elemental. It's about matching power to power. And right now, all I want to do is show you how our essences are linked to one another. Please?"

The way he said that final word, the slight dip in his tone, had me feeling warm all over. None of this made any sense, but somehow, for some peculiar reason, I wanted to trust him. To let him show me whatever it was he desired to show me.

Because I found him likable.

Not in a *mate* kind of way—that sounded too permanent and weird and not at all appropriate for a girl my age.

But in a potential date kind of way. Well, apart from the whole Fae Realm, stolen from my home and life, nonsense.

Okay, so maybe not a *date*.

Just stop thinking, I told myself, exhausted. *See what he wants to do.*

What could it hurt?

Nibbling my lip, I extended my arm, laying my hand palm up in the flower bed. His smile reached his gorgeous eyes as he shifted a little closer to link his fingers over mine. More of that electric energy sizzled up my arm, shocking my system and sending a bolt of heat directly to my lower abdomen.

Okay, he's not kidding about the mutual attraction thing. Because wow.

A totally inappropriate and inexplicable reaction.

Just like I had to that guy at the bar.

My gaze darted across the clearing to the leather-clad bad boy, the one Titus had called Exos. He observed us with no expression, his arms crossed as he leaned against a tree along the edge of the field. Another boy stood beside him, his gaze wide with curiosity.

"Why are they watching us?" I asked, my insides tingling with nerves.

"They're watching *you*," Titus whispered, his fingers lightly tracing mine. "Your power is a marvel, Claire. It's considered a miracle that Spirit Fae—like Exos—can access two elements."

"Okay." I swallowed, refocusing on his alluring features. "I have fire and air?" A guess because I couldn't remember everything Exos had told me, our time together an emotionally laden blur of moments.

"No." Titus drew a line of fire across my skin, the heat causing me to flinch and gape at the same time.

"That... It doesn't hurt."

He chuckled. "Because your fire responds to mine."

"But you just said I don't have Fire."

"Oh, you have Fire." His irises lifted to mine. "An incredible amount of it, too." He shifted even closer, leaving maybe a foot between our prone forms. He continued his path up my arm, the flame dancing upward, heating me in the most amazing way.

"I like that," I admitted.

"I know." He smiled, continuing his touch over my clothed shoulder to my neck, branding my pulse. "Do you feel the connection between us, Claire? The way my fire flirts with yours? Taunting it to the surface? Warming the air around us?"

I swallowed, my lungs feeling a bit tight. "Y-yes."

"That's your power." His voice dropped to a husky tone that caused my heart to skip a beat.

"What about Air?" I asked.

"Hmm, I'm not an Air Fae." He slid an ember across my jaw and upward into my hairline where he pulled the flower from behind my ear—the flower Exos had put there. "I'm not a Spirit Fae, either." He brought the petals to his nose and inhaled. "But you're both."

"That's three elements."

"Yes," he agreed. "You asked why they're staring at you?"

I nodded, my heart thudding roughly in my chest.

"It's because you don't have access to just two elements, Claire." He palmed my cheek, his gaze kind. "You have access to all five."

My eyebrows shot upward. "All five?"

His lips twitched. "Trust me, I'm just as shocked as you are, but I can feel it in your essence. You manipulated this field, bringing all these flowers to life to provide you with a bed to rest upon. The air sings your name. My fire is drawn to your fire, just as Exos's spirit is drawn to your spirit, and I can feel the layer of humidity—water—softening your skin. You're very special, indeed."

"But why?"

"I don't know." He drew his thumb across my cheekbone, his caress warm and far too welcome. "But I can help you. That's all we want to do."

"Help me how?"

"By teaching you." His fingers slid into my hair, threading through my tangling blonde strands and drawing them down to my shoulder. "Control is the only way to live with all that power inside of you. I realize you have no reason to trust me, or any of us, but I'm speaking from experience. If you don't allow anyone to train you, those gifts will consume you beyond reason."

I'd always been one to listen to my instincts, and they told me now that he was speaking the truth. Still, something nagged at me. Not about him, or Exos, or even the other boy, but about this place. This *realm*.

It felt as if I didn't belong. Which was likely related to having been brought here without my permission.

But it went beyond that.

Something about this place seemed *dangerous*.

"What are you thinking?" he asked, his tone genuine and curious. "What caused this frown to form?" He pressed his thumb to the edge of my mouth, his comfort with touching me a little unsettling even while feeling right.

We don't know each other.

But I sort of want to know him.

I shook the thoughts from my head, confused by all the sensations and sounds and *sparks*. "This is all, uh, overwhelming." Not a lie. I just left out the sense-of-danger part. How could I confide that in an essential stranger? In this strange land?

"How about dinner," he suggested.

"Dinner?" I repeated, dubious.

"When's the last time you ate?"

"Uh…" I blinked several times. "I… I don't know."

"Then I'd say dinner is a must." His dimples appeared again, but rather than turn his features boyish, they only seemed to solidify his incredible beauty. "Then maybe we can tour campus together. It'll be quiet, most of the students in their dorms. Maybe you'll see that it isn't too bad here and decide to stay."

Campus? Dorms? Where am I? "Do I even have a choice?" I wondered out loud, referring to dinner and the aforementioned *tour*.

He chuckled. "Depends on your definition of the word. How about we reach that bridge when we're ready to cross it and just take this one step at a time? Dinner first. And I'll answer any and every question you throw at me."

I nibbled my lower lip, considering his proposal. He was right about the *choice*. Did I truly have one when there were no other options?

"Can I, uh, change first?" I asked, noting my soiled state. A long shower sounded appealing. And then maybe some coffee followed by a decent meal.

"Exos can help us arrange that," he said, smiling.

"Exos," I repeated, glancing at the still-emotionless male across the clearing. "Uh, will he be going to dinner, too?"

The man cocked a brow at that, clearly having heard me even from a distance. Which meant he'd heard everything. "Would you prefer I not join you?" he asked, sounding slightly offended.

"Depends on whether or not you're going to be an ass," I said, feeling oddly defensive. He hadn't exactly broken all these details to me in the politest manner, and it was *his* fault I ended up here. And while I was on that path, I could also lay some of the blame for the bar at his feet because he'd been the one to entice me into that kiss.

No, that wasn't fair.

I couldn't blame him for everything. Only a coward would deny all culpability.

But that didn't mean I had to like him.

He snorted as if hearing my thoughts, or perhaps reading them on my face. "Whatever you want, princess," he said. "Just don't fucking blow me into a wall again."

I winced a little at that, feeling bad again. It wasn't like I meant to shove him with my power; it just sort of happened.

"Can we go now?" he asked, his gaze going to Titus. "Because I've had the day from hell and would love a shower."

And I didn't feel bad anymore. "Ass," I muttered.

Titus chuckled beside me. "You know, Exos, I'm starting to see why all this happened. Your bedside manner sucks."

"Do you speak to all Royal Fae in this manner, or am I a special case?"

Titus paled a little. "I... I'm..."

"Yeah, that's what I thought," Exos said, turning away from the field. "Let's go."

Titus cursed softly, his hand falling from my skin and leaving me cold without him. "We, uh, need to follow him."

"Why?" I asked, not understanding the power play here.

"Because Exos says it's time to go." He stood and held out a hand for me.

"And we have to do what he says?" I asked as I accepted his help up from the ground—mostly because I wanted to touch him again.

"Yes." He linked his fingers through mine, something that seemed a little unconscious on his part. His focus was on the third male, with the floppy hair, waiting for us near the tree line.

"Why?" I pressed as we started forward. "Why do we have to do what he says?" Because a part of me *really* wanted to disobey him.

"He's a Royal Fae," Titus replied.

"Okay?" That meant little to me.

He glanced at me. "He's the Royal Prince of the Spirit Fae, Claire."

I nearly tripped over the flowers beneath my feet. "Wh-what?" Was that like... like a European prince or something?

"Technically, he's King of the Spirit Fae," the other man mumbled, his cheeks flushing pink. "He, uh, renounced his throne to his brother, preferring the warrior life. But, well, Exos and Cyrus are the last of the royal line. At least until Cyrus finds a mate, which isn't likely since, uh, yeah, you know, most of the Spirit Fae are dead." He didn't look at me the entire time he spoke, his gaze on my bare feet.

"This is River," Titus said, grinning. "He's a Water Fae."

"Hi." He waved, his focus still on the ground.

"Hi," I replied, concerned that I'd offended him somehow. Or maybe he was just shy? "I'm Claire," I hedged, trying to see him through his mop of dark curls.

"I know." He peeked up at me, his eyes widening when he realized I was staring directly at him. He stumbled backward, almost falling, except Titus caught his wrist and yanked him upright.

"She's not going to bite you, dude."

"I-I know," he repeated. "It's j-just that, well, she's... she's *human*."

Titus sighed. "River has an obsession," he told me, glancing sideways.

"And I need a fucking shower," Exos snapped, appearing again on the path. "Can we please go back to Elana's now?"

Titus straightened, his gaze narrowing. "This woman has been through hell, Exos. Cut her some slack."

"Yeah? She's also put me through hell. What a coincidence." He didn't pay me a glance as he turned to lead the way—again.

"I don't want him to go to dinner," I decided.

"Something tells me he won't be giving us much choice," Titus muttered. "He's been assigned as your protector."

"My protector?" I frowned. "Why?"

Titus just shook his head. "Let's just follow him. We can talk about more over dinner, okay? I promise." His words sent a tingle down my spine as if his vow held power and purpose. Maybe it did.

"Dinner," I repeated. A meal. Followed by a tour. And more information. "Okay. Yeah, I can do that."

Because, again, what other option did I have? Hide here in the meadow forever? Hope for some miracle to take me back to Earth?

An idea nagged at me.

Actually… Maybe I could use this all to my advantage to find a way back home. Play along for a while, learn more about these so-called fae, this realm, my supposed gifts, and perhaps escape.

Assuming that was what I wanted.

I frowned. Oh, hell, I had no idea *what* I wanted anymore.

But I did like the sound of a shower and food.

So, yeah. Going with Titus made sense. At least for now.

"I can sense your indecision," he whispered, his lips against my ear. "Just give me the evening, sweetheart. You'll see." A soft flame warmed our clasped hands. "And if you want, I'll show you how to create fireballs. Maybe you can accidentally throw one at Exos."

A snort from the forest ahead said he'd heard that. He must have just disappeared from view but was clearly still waiting on us to follow.

"A fireball," I mused, pondering the possibilities. "Yeah, I think I like that idea."

"Just try not to burn down any more buildings" was his dark reply.

My amusement died.

Yeah.

Okay.

Maybe no fireballs.

Titus sighed beside me. "Spoilsport," he muttered. "I'll show you how to control it, Claire. You have my word."

I nodded mutely, unable to say anything else.

A shower.

Some clothes.

Food.

Hopefully, one of those things would help me feel human again.

Except I wasn't human, not according to these men.

I'm part fae.

Whatever the hell that really means.

I was too exhausted to dwell on it, my limbs aching, my heart shattered. Titus squeezed my hand again, a jolt of heat sliding up my arm to dispel the ice coating my veins. No words, just a touch, one that seemed to thaw some of the pain. He pulled me close, the warmth from his body a comforting blanket over my skin. I leaned into him, absorbing his essence, his kindness, his strength, and allowing it to fuel my steps.

Maybe I really had lost my mind.

Because some foreign part of me trusted him despite our brief acquaintance. Possibly because he felt like the only friend I might have in this strange land.

Or perhaps something more powerful was at play…

CHAPTER SIX
TITUS

CLAIRE CLUTCHED MY HAND TIGHTLY, her body rigid beside mine. Exos had led us back to Elana's estate and disappeared after showing us to one of the guest suites.

"I... I d-don't understand," Claire stammered. "I blew out that wall."

Ah, that explained the elemental essences lurking in this room. I'd felt it all over the property when we arrived, but it grew stronger as we moved upstairs. "Chancellor Elana must have repaired it."

"Chancellor Elana?" Claire repeated, glancing up at me. "How?"

"She's a very powerful fae and the leader of the Academy." I gave her a small smile. "This is her home." And actually quite rare for a student to visit. In fact, this was my first time entering these famous walls.

Claire frowned. "But I destroyed that wall."

"And I fixed it," a voice murmured from down the hallway. Elana appeared with her light hair wrapped up in a bun atop her head and threaded with flowers. She was a gorgeous woman, the awe of many men, and completely unattainable due to her high status. Rumors said she never mated because she didn't want to share her powers. But it was not for a lack of trying by the male fae.

I bowed my head in reverence. "Chancellor Elana."

"Titus," she returned. "Thank you for helping Exos today."

"It was my pleasure." Not a lie. I rather enjoyed lying in that field with Claire. Wrong, yes, but being near her intrigued me. The power brewing under her skin called to my own, marking her as a potential mate. She wasn't the first to call to my inner gifts, but she was the first to excite me by the prospect. "I was just helping Claire change for dinner."

"Ah yes, it is that time, isn't it?" She stopped in front of us, her slender hands clasped before her. "Why don't you and River stay for dinner? I think it may help Claire feel more comfortable."

Oh. I'd meant to take Claire somewhere on the fire campus and give her a tour as well, but if the Chancellor wanted us to join her here, then we didn't have much choice.

The death grip on my hand suggested Elana's words regarding comfort were true. It seemed I'd become Claire's anchor. "We'll stay," I said, the words meant for both of them.

"Excellent." Elana's smile crinkled the edges of her silver-flecked eyes. "I look forward to getting to know you better, Claire. Once upon a time, your mother was one of my favorite students." Sadness filtered through her softening expression. "Well, we'll catch up over dinner. Oh, and I left you something suitable to wear." She tilted her lips again before floating down the hallway in her long, elegant gown.

"Who is that?" Claire whispered, her eyes rounded.

"Chancellor Elana."

"No, I got that part." She shook my head. "I meant... I... I don't know what I meant. She's beautiful."

"Yes. And very powerful." I'd already said that, but it was worth repeating. "She's a Spirit Fae, like you."

"And she knew my mother?"

"Yes. She was your mother's mentor." A very famous history, considering everything that had transpired after the Academy. But now wasn't the time to discuss all that. "Do you need any help? Or do you want to meet me downstairs?"

"I..." She nibbled her lip and glanced at the dress lying on the bed and then at the doorway beyond that led to the en-suite bathroom. "I, uh, should be all right. But you promise to stay?"

Warmth touched my chest at her show of trust. We hardly knew each other, but her inner flame recognized mine already whether she realized it or not. I drew a line of fire across her cheek with my index finger and smiled. "Yes. I'll be here."

Her shoulders seemed to fall on a sigh, her relief palpable. "Okay," she whispered. "I'll meet you downstairs."

I lifted her hand to my lips and kissed her wrist. "See you then, Claire."

Her lips parted in wonder as I released her. I took a few steps backward, wanting to give her space before I did something stupid like follow her into that bedroom. Her essence was so strong, almost intoxicatingly so. It fucked with my head.

"Titus?" she called after me, concern in her voice.

I faced her at the top of the stairs. "Yes, Claire?"

"Uh, how will I find the dining room?"

I almost told her I'd wait at the bottom for her, but a better idea came to me. A way to test if she felt this connection the way I did. "Follow the heat."

"The heat?" she asked, her brow puckering.

Embers danced over my fingertips as I lifted my hand. "Yes. I'll leave you some hints in the air, and you'll find me." I was sure of it, even if she looked completely baffled by the idea. "You'll see, sweetheart."

I left her gaping after me in the hallway, a smile on my face the whole way down the stairs.

River waited for me at the bottom, his eyebrow raised knowingly.

"Just the lingering effects from Ignis," I said, blaming my peculiar behavior on the seduction magic even if it had worn off long ago. Maybe I was more susceptible to it, or Ignis had given me a double dose. Wouldn't have put it past the bitch. "Where's Exos?" I had a few things I wanted to say to him about his treatment of Claire.

"Changing," River replied. "We're supposed to meet him in the dining room."

"So you know about our dinner plans?"

"You mean the dining edict? Yes." River's voice was soft so as to not be overheard. "I'm not dressed for this." He gestured to his casual attire. "Not for dining with the Chancellor."

"I think her focus is more on Claire more than our jeans," I said, following the aroma of food while leaving a subtle trail of my essence behind for Claire to follow. Sensing that, coupled with the finer scents in the air, she should find us without any problem.

"Um, aren't you worried the human might run again?" River whispered.

"No." I didn't even need to consider it. My instincts seemed to be tied to hers after that little flirtation in the field. I'd sense it if she wanted to run, and that wasn't the vibe I received from her at all. "She's too intrigued to—"

I froze on the threshold of the dining area.

The room was buzzing with *pixies*.

Even though pixies and fairies were myths, elder Spirit Fae like Elana had enough magic to conjure their very own army of servants in whatever form they chose. But to choose a swarm of mythical creatures as house servants sent a message, one I was keen to listen to. Elana was powerful, and she wanted everyone to know it.

A pixie hurried past me, its tiny wings brushing my cheek and leaving behind a kiss of humidity, betraying a hint of water magic mingling with

Elana's powers.

Odd.

Everyone knew Elana only had access to spirit. It was her notorious weakness, being the only Spirit Fae without a secondary element. I must have imagined the intrusion.

The tiny creatures chittered at each other like squirrels while they set the table with gleaming silverware, and several of them teamed up to supply bowls of soup, trays of delicacies, and finely cut slabs of meat that made my mouth water.

"Uh…" A horde of pixies tugged on one of the massive chairs until it was far enough away from the table for me. "Thank you." I glanced back at River as I took my seat, all the while hoping I didn't squash any of the poor things.

River sat beside me, his mystified gaze likely rivaling my own. "I've, erm, never eaten with an elder before," he mumbled, anxiety creeping into his voice. Being in Elana's esteemed presence had me on edge as well, so I could only imagine what River was feeling right now.

I cleared my throat and accepted a glass of golden, sparkling liquid from a trio of pixies. "You're the one who insisted on tagging along," I reminded him. I took a long sip, my eyelids fluttering as sweetness and heat slipped down my throat. Fire water—literally liquid infused with the elements of air and fire—made me feel at home.

Until I remembered my surroundings.

We were about to dine with an elder and a royal. Who knew what sort of edicts would follow? Not to mention this strange connection I felt to Claire. I shivered, the memory of her touch embedded in my skin. It had felt right— *too* right.

A shift in the air had me glancing at the doorway just as Exos made his entrance, his white-blond hair draped across his forehead in an absurdly regal manner. The pompous style matched his all-black suit.

Definitely a prince.

"Glad you're comfortable," Exos said smoothly as he sat directly across from me. He didn't seem the type to often smile, but the way he looked at me now said he was about to drop some serious bullshit in my lap. "I have some things to discuss with you before Claire joins us."

Great.

"Of course," I replied, keeping my voice controlled and respectful. Part of me still wanted to shake some sense into him for his behavior back in the field with Claire, but I knew better. He didn't seem to understand that she needed a tender hand, not a harsh one.

Exos eyed the delicacies as a pixie settled a glass of fire water in front of him, but he only stared at it. "The Halfling needs more boundaries than I'm able to impose," he said, folding his hands and getting straight to the point. "She's stronger than any of us realized."

45

He held my gaze, his ocean-blue eyes so deep that I could almost sense the power that rested underneath the surface. If the Halfling bested this guy, then I knew I didn't stand a chance if I ever lost her trust.

I rested my elbows on the table, leaning forward, and opted for a different approach. "If you don't mind me saying, Your Highness, I think you're treating her too harshly. She's not one of your warriors that you can just bark orders and expect to be obeyed. She grew up in the Human Realm without knowledge of our practices and policies. Obedience won't come as naturally to her as it would to others." There. That was politically correct enough, right?

River nodded beside me in agreement, seeming to find his confidence. "Humans are notorious when it comes to equality and free will, especially in certain regions."

Exos sighed, relaxing in his chair. "Yes, she adopts not only the strong personality of a Spirit Fae but human traits as well. However, she is still *fae*. She will learn to obey her betters."

I agreed with him until that final sentence.

Betters.

All my life I'd been told that had I been born with royal blood, I might have possessed the strength to control my unruly fire. But I wasn't royal-born. I wasn't even high-born. My lineage came from a long line of fae who fought for sport and worked in the hot mines of the Fire Kingdom.

Embers crawled through my veins and singed the tablecloth, demonstrating my frustration. Exos raised a brow in response, noticing my inability to hide the annoyance bubbling within me.

I drew in a deep breath before speaking. "She holds elements you can't control," I reminded him. "Forcing her into obedience won't end well."

He nodded. "That's why I can't train her alone. I need help." He paused, his lips twitching. "Starting with you."

I raised a brow at him. "I've already agreed to help her with dinner. I'm here, right?"

"You are," Exos agreed, finally taking the fine flute of his glass and swirling it, activating the embers lingering in the liquid. "But that's not what I meant. I already spoke with Elana, and she agrees. You're being assigned as one of Claire's bodyguards, and you will mentor her on fire."

Not a request.

An order.

No subtlety to see if I would be up for the task or if I had other plans for my time at the Academy. Just a straight edict that Exos expected me to follow. And apparently, Elana did as well.

My blood boiled with the arrogance of his *demand*, and more so, the power behind his blood that allowed him to lord over me.

"It makes sense with you being the most powerful Fire Fae at the Academy, not to mention your uncanny ability to encourage her cooperation."

He glanced at me over his glass. "It's also a unique opportunity to appease the Council. You could consider it an internship of sorts."

"And if I don't want an internship?" I couldn't help the growl in my voice. This prick thought to own me, to force me into a position of his own choosing without any regard for what *I* wanted.

"We both know what you want," Exos replied, his gaze knowing. "You won't say no, Titus."

To putting my reputation on the line for a Halfling? To having to protect her from what had to be an army of fae who wanted to kill her? To training her how to use her fire?

Well, that last bit appealed to me. But the other parts? I started to shake my head, but a buzzing of excitement caused all of us to glance at the doorway.

"Ah, here we are." Elana clapped as she entered the room, drawing the pixies to her in a flourish of a grand greeting. "The dining area is lovely, thank you." The pixies chirped in happiness, leading her to the head of the table beside Exos's seat.

"Have you discussed our plans?" she asked, her focus on Exos.

"Yes." He set his flute down. "Titus was just accepting."

Accepting, my ass.

"Excellent," Elana replied, her kind eyes lifting my way. "After observing your interaction upstairs, I do think this is best. Claire clearly likes you, and she needs someone she can trust and rely on at her side. You're a good match for her fire as well." The knowing way she said that last bit had a chill running up my spine.

Spirit Fae were powerful beings. They could sense and control all aspects of the life cycle. And she'd clearly noticed the mating potential between me and Claire. Which meant Exos had as well.

I cleared my throat. "If that's—"

A shriek from the other room had me on my feet in a second, the explosion of fire a seduction to my inner flame.

Claire.

I ran into the foyer to find her curled in a ball, the walls around her ablaze with light. River extinguished the inferno with a mist of power while I clamped down on her gifts with my own, calming them on instinct.

She trembled, a cry escaping her throat as a pixie squeezed out of her grasp with an angry chirp. Another wave of fiery power spiked across the room in response, Claire quivering violently on the ground. "This isn't real," she whispered on repeat. "This isn't real. Fairies don't exist."

Exos snorted. "Oh, for fuck's sake." He gestured to her as if to say, *This. I can't deal with this.* And returned to the dining room.

I sighed. His lack of patience made him a shitty mentor. No wonder he needed me.

Crouching beside her, I murmured, "They're not real, Claire. Elana conjured them to help with dinner."

47

"Wh-what?" Glassy blue eyes met mine. "C-conjured?"

I smiled. "Yes, fae magic." I held out my hand for her. "Come on, I'll show you."

She swallowed. "I... I don't..."

"They're harmless," I promised. "Just little pixies. You'll see."

"Sh-she tried t-to pull my dress, and I... I..."

"You reacted," I finished for her. "But everything's fine." I gestured around the foyer. "Not even a charred mark." Thanks to River's hasty reaction. And likely Elana's, too. "Come on, sweetheart. I think you'll like the little fairies once you see them in action."

"Exos s-said f-fairies weren't real."

"Because they're not," he called from the other room.

Her eyes widened. "But it *touched* me."

"Yes, I told you. Elana's powerful." I waggled my fingers. "Will you come to the dining area with me?"

She slowly lifted her palm to mine, allowing me to help her up from the floor. The pretty purple dress she wore fluttered around her knees, her hair damp and combed over one shoulder. I tucked a stray strand behind her ear and caught the fiery ember drifting up her neck in response.

The power inside her seemed ready to explode.

"Hey, do me a favor," I whispered.

Her beautiful blue eyes held mine, her lashes thick as she blinked. "Wh-what?"

"Put your hands up like this." I held mine in front of me, palms outward to face her.

She copied the motion with a frown. "Okay."

"Now I want you to think about everything that's bothering you, all the pain, the anger, the frustration and confusion. And I want you to channel it into your hands like you want to hit someone." At her incredulous look, I smiled. "Trust me. Just pull all that energy into your arms and let it fly through your palms. Like you're gearing up to punch someone in a fight."

"I don't fight," she mumbled.

"But you're angry, right?" I pressed. "Upset? Confused?"

"Of course I am."

"And wouldn't it feel really good to just hit someone?"

"Yes." No hesitation. "But not you. I'd rather hit Exos."

I couldn't help my chuckle. "Well, we'd all enjoy that. But I want you to try to hit me. Pretend I'm him."

She shook her head. "You're not. You're actually nice to me."

Exos entered the foyer, his hands in his pockets. "Then hit me," he said, coming to stand beside me. He must have figured out what I wanted to do, or perhaps realized he deserved her annoyance. "Come on, princess. Let me have it."

Her gaze narrowed. "*You.*" Energy hummed inside her. "You made me destroy the bar."

"You're the one who approached me," he reminded her, an edge to his voice. "*You* destroyed the bar. I *saved* people."

Her hands balled into fists, her gaze narrowing to slits. "You could have stopped me!"

Exos shrugged. "I had no idea you were going to light the damn place on fire, Claire."

"Rick's dead," she continued, not hearing him. "He's *dead!*"

"Yes." Exos didn't flinch, just continued to stare her down. "Come on, princess. Hit me."

"I *hate* you," she said, tears glistening in her eyes. She opened her palms, unleashing an impressive stream of fire that I caught and absorbed before it could hit Exos. Another blast left her hands, weaker than the first one, followed by a third and a fourth until her knees gave out beneath her on a cry. I grabbed her before she could fall, catching her against my torso and holding her tight.

Exos met my gaze, his expression unreadable. "Welcome to the team, Titus."

CHAPTER SEVEN
TITUS

"YOU'LL FIT RIGHT IN AT THE ACADEMY," Elana said, smiling from the entryway. "Shall we eat? The food is getting cold." She gestured for us to follow her, but Claire seemed unable to move.

"In a minute," I replied, running my fingers through her hair.

Elana's eyes grinned as she nodded and disappeared.

"What just happened?" Claire whispered, shaking against me.

"You expunged some built-up power." My lips brushed her forehead, something that seemed to happen without my permission but felt right. "And I absorbed it."

She gasped, pulling back to look me over, her gaze wild. "D-did I hurt you? Exos?"

"We're fine." I cupped her cheek. "I just wanted to show you how to channel your emotions into your gifts, to control it better."

She shook, more tears glistening in her eyes. "I don't understand what's happening to me." She swallowed, clearing her throat and letting out a sad little laugh. "God, I've never felt so emotional in my life. You must think I'm a wreck."

"No, I think you were stolen from your world and placed in a land you never knew existed. Pretty sure I'd feel the same if someone put me in the

Human Realm." I chuckled at the thought and shook my head. "I'd destroy, like, everything."

She blinked. "You would?"

"Oh yeah. My power is barely contained here. Around mortals? I'd be like a firestorm."

Her lips twitched, a funny look gleaming in her eyes.

"What?" I asked.

"Nothing." But that look didn't go away. If anything, it intensified.

"Tell me," I encouraged her, curious as hell.

"You... You sound like a superhero from one of those movies." She giggled, her palm lifting to cover her lips, but a laugh escaped between her fingers. "*Firestorm.*" Her eyes crinkled, her shoulders shaking. "Oh God." A burst of sound came from her, something I enjoyed much more than her shrieking and crying. And I couldn't help joining her even though I didn't quite grasp the joke. I just really, really liked that sound.

"Sorry," she said, wiping the tears from her eyes. "God, I feel insane. All of this. I just don't even know what to do, how to react... anything."

"Well, I vote we start by trying to eat dinner," I suggested, gesturing to the dining area. "Unless you'd prefer fighting more pixies?"

"Pixies?" she repeated.

"The fairies that tried to guide you to the dining room."

"Oh." She scrunched her forehead. "Is that what you meant about a path to follow?"

I shook my head. "No, I meant for you to trace my essence of fire." I trailed a line of fire along her forearm to her hand, causing her lips to part on a big O. "But it seems the pixies were eager for you to join us. They don't want the food to get cold."

"Right," she whispered. "Okay."

"Okay, you want to eat? Or okay, you understand?"

"B-both," she stammered. "I'm... hungry."

I looked her over with a smile. "Yeah, me, too." I held up my palm one more time. "Shall we, Claire?"

She pressed her palm to mine, nodding. "A room of fairies and food. Sure."

I chuckled. "You'll get used to it."

"Yeah. That's what I'm afraid of," she said so softly that I barely heard her. The poor girl clearly thought she was going mad, but after a few days in this realm, she'd realize the reality of her situation. Hopefully.

The seating arrangements in the room had changed with River joining Exos on the opposite side of the table, Elana still at the head, leaving two open seats for me and Claire—beside each other. I pulled out her chair, causing her to smile shyly as she sat, and joined her quickly, my hand finding hers beneath the table to give it a squeeze.

She tightened her hold as the pixies fluttered in to begin delivering food. It seemed they'd replaced the soup with fresh bowls, likely because the old had grown cold. They continued swapping out the dishes until a blend of fresh aromas wafted off the table, the array of foods causing my stomach to grumble in want and my heart to beat in admiration.

Elana was controlling all of this, her power an almost magnetic energy that called to my inner fae and required submission. Because not many could boast such a feast in their homes, especially after repairing the walls.

Claire didn't appear nearly as enthused.

"It's a bit much, huh?" I teased, eyeing the magic sprinkling across the room.

She relaxed, then gave me a small smile of her own. Fuck, she was beautiful. I wanted to make her smile every moment of every day.

Exos remained stoic, his focus shifting to Elana as he asked her something about Claire's schedule. This caused the woman at my side to glance between them, her brow furrowing as they discussed her life without her input.

"Eat, dear," Elana said when she noticed Claire staring at her.

My companion didn't reach out for the food but eyed it hungrily. When she refused to pick her own course, I released her hand to pick up her dish and then plucked a little bit of everything for her to try before setting it in front of her.

"I recommend that one first," I told her, gesturing to the dried pieces of meat. "I love those." I punctuated the statement by heaping several spoonfuls onto my own plate, as well as a few nibbles from other dishes.

When Claire still didn't touch her food, I took a bite of mine to demonstrate that it wasn't poisonous. And then I made an exaggerated moan of approval that caused her lips to twitch.

"Try it," I encouraged her. "It's really, really good."

She shifted in her seat, her mouth pinching to the side. Then she took one of the dried pieces of meat I suggested and nibbled on it, her eyes going wide. She took a larger bite.

I chuckled. "Told you."

She didn't reply, too lost in the flavors of the foods.

"Yes," Elana said quietly. "I think that's best. One day at each campus, and I'll work with the professors tomorrow on her schedule. We should start her in the Fire Quad."

Exos nodded. "I agree. Are her quarters ready?"

"No, you'll stay here tonight. I didn't have enough energy to finish rebuilding the Spirit Dorm."

"You're putting her on the Spirit Quad?" I asked, setting my fork down. River cleared his throat, but I ignored him. He must not have liked my tone, but this was a horrible idea and I wanted them to know it. "It's empty and void of life."

"And therefore safe," Exos added.

"For who? Her or the others?" I shook my head. "If you want her to attend the Academy, you need to have her around other fae. That's how you introduce her to our world. By showing her what the Fae Realm is like and introducing her to fae her own age."

Claire had stopped eating, her eyes dancing between us. "You keep mentioning the Academy and a campus, but what is it? Like a college?" she whispered.

"The Elemental Fae Academy, dear," Elana said, her voice warm. "And yes, it's similar to your university life, but for fae. Everyone in this realm attends from age nineteen to twenty-three, unless there are extenuating circumstances. Like Titus, for example."

"Titus?" Claire glanced at me, frowning. "I don't understand."

"She means I started the Academy late. I'm twenty-two but didn't begin until this year."

"Why?" she asked.

"Because I was born and raised to fight in the Powerless Champion circuit." I shrugged. "I retired and now I'm here."

"After winning," River put in, pride in his voice. "He's the Powerless Champion."

"Like... boxing?" she guessed.

"Nah, that's a boring human sport. Fae fight to the death. And Titus has killed, like, well, everyone who challenged him. His numbers are—"

Exos cleared his throat, cutting off the Water Fae. "What River is trying to say is that Titus started the Academy a little later because of an extenuating circumstance. Just as you will start a little later because of your, well, circumstances."

"You mean my kidnapping?" Claire asked. "Because that's what this is, right? I mean, you *kidnapped* me from my home."

"This is your home," Exos replied. "Your true home. And the Academy is your future."

"And I have no say in this?" Claire pressed. "Because where I come from, that's kidnapping and forcing someone to do something against her will."

"And where I come from, it's rude to argue with your betters."

Her eyebrows lifted. "Betters? Like what? My parents? Because you're not even ten years older than me. And neither is she." She gestured to Elana. "Which is totally irrelevant, by the way, because I will argue with whoever I damn well please." The fire in her had my lips twitching. I much preferred this to the weeping girl I found in the field earlier.

"Exos is royalty," Elana explained softly. "And I'm Chancellor of the Academy. Therefore, in our society, we are considered your betters."

"Because you were promoted at the ripe young age of, what, thirty? That makes you better than me?" Claire snorted. "Yeah, no. That's not happening.

Not least of all because you kidnapped me. And now you want me to attend an academy against my will? Yeah, hard pass."

River choked on his food while I held back a grin.

"You seem to think there's a choice here." The calmness in Exos's voice sent a chill of foreboding down my spine. "Of which, I suppose, there is. Would you like me to explain it to you, Claire?"

"Exos," Elana warned.

"No, no." Exos waved her off, his status coming out in that small gesture. Elana might be the Chancellor, but he was heir to the Spirit Kingdom, making him *her* better in our fucked-up political system. "She wants to hear her choices. Don't you, Claire?"

"I do," she agreed. "Since it's my life, it's my decision. Not that you've given me much of one by forcing me to come here."

He smiled, but it lacked humor. "Yes, well, that's because you can no longer live in the Human Realm without being a threat to everyone around you. The bar proves that."

Her face paled, causing me to curse internally. He had to go there, didn't he? This was clearly a tense subject for her, not that the Spirit Prince seemed to give a fuck.

"I-I didn't mean to do that," she whispered. "I don't even know if it's true."

"If you care for proof, I'll provide it," Exos replied, his voice flat. "But the fact remains that you cannot reside in the Human Realm. You're too powerful, so much so that we can hardly contain you here. Which brings me to your choices, Claire. Are you listening?"

She nodded, her lip between her teeth, her shoulders hunched. "Yes."

"You can attend the Academy and learn how to control your abilities, at which point you may be permitted visitor rights back to the Human Realm. Or, you will be banished to the Spirit Kingdom—the same kingdom your mother single-handedly destroyed in her battle with Mortus. It's void of life and essence, leaving it impossible for you to hurt anyone with your lack of control." He dabbed his mouth with his napkin in a casual gesture as he shrugged. "The third option, of course, is death. Because we can't have a powerful rogue fae wandering the realm. Especially one who lacks training and understanding of our ways."

Claire's mouth opened and closed, her eyes wide, no words coming from her lips.

But of course, what the hell could she say after that calmly delivered edict?

Fucking royal blood, not thinking at all about the consequences of his words. Just uttering them as if he were speaking to a fellow warrior, not a female who had clearly been through hell over the last day or two.

"So what would you choose, Claire? Because I thought the Academy route to be the most humane and practical of options, but if you prefer I drop you in the Spirit Kingdom, we can leave tonight."

"How about we provide Claire with a tour tomorrow of the Academy and let her see what life here would be like before you force her to choose," I suggested, my teeth grating over every word. "And maybe give her a chance to understand the Fae Realm as well while you're at it."

Exos met my gaze, his blue eyes simmering. "Just because I've tagged you for her team does not mean you may speak out of line."

"My job is to protect her. Consider that my current goal." I narrowed my eyes. "Unless you think threatening her life is something I should be overlooking?"

His lips actually twitched. "You are to protect her from others, not from me."

"Maybe she needs protection from you the most," I countered, flames inching beneath my skin.

Elana coughed, dispelling the mood with a wave of her hand. "I think a tour is a great idea. Claire can remain here tonight, then Titus can provide a tour in the morning of Fire Quad. And we'll work out dorm arrangements afterward."

Meaning she wanted to see Claire's reaction to the world before she assigned her sleeping quarters.

"Assuming that is okay with you, dear?" Elana asked, her benevolent gaze finding Claire. The woman was the peacekeeper of our race for a reason, and it showed as she smiled. "Would you like to see the Academy? I think you might find it enlightening. And Titus could take you to the game this weekend, to see the competition of elements. Assuming he's up for it."

I hadn't planned to go, but if it was something Claire wanted to see, I'd take her. "Sure."

Claire glanced sideways at me, her hands clasped tightly in her lap. "Y-you're a student." Not a question, but a statement.

Still, I nodded. "First year, yep."

"A-and I would be near you on the tour?" she asked, her throat working over each word. I rather enjoyed the hopeful glint in her eyes.

"I'll happily show you around campus." I reached over for her hand. "It's really beautiful. You'll love it. Lots of trees and flowers and nature."

She nibbled her lip. "Fairies?"

I chuckled. "No. Those are just here."

"Anything else magical?"

"All sorts of elemental magic, sweetheart." I squeezed her hand. "We're fae. We live and breathe our powers. But the purpose of the Academy is control, so you won't have to fear anyone or anything. Everyone is learning."

"Like a university," she said, repeating Elana's sentiments.

"Yeah, except we learn how to hone our gifts for the betterment of society, while you attended college for, like, a job. And half of the crap you all study is worthless." River's cheeks pinkened as Claire met his gaze. "Sorry, I've studied some of the Human Realm. It's, uh, fun to me."

"What kind of fae are you?" she asked, eyeing him with curiosity. "I can't sense your energy like I do Exos's and Titus's."

Her words had my gaze snapping up to Exos, who merely smirked. Those words, so innocent on her lips, meant far more than she realized. If she sensed Exos the way she did me, it meant he was a potential mate for her as well.

And the slight curve of Elana's lips confirmed she knew it all along.

As did the startled expression River wore.

Fae mated once, for life. But only with one person and always of their element.

That Claire had found a potential connection with two fae, of different elements, was unique. No, it was unheard of.

Maybe she meant she felt Exos's aura the way I felt other Fire Fae who were a potential match to my own magic?

"I, uh, control water," River said, swallowing. "I'm a Water Fae."

"Oh," Claire murmured. "So would you be on the tour?"

He snorted. "Not of the Fire Fae Quad, no. We keep our own quadrants. Too many complications when you mingle the elements."

Her brow furrowed. "But... but I have some?" She looked to Exos. "R-right?"

"You have all five," he confirmed, not meeting her gaze yet somehow knowing she'd leaned on him for the detail. "Which is why I suggested the Spirit Quad." Now he raised his gaze to mine. "Because it would be too dangerous to assign her another place to stay."

"Let's see how the tour goes," Elana interjected, playing peacekeeper yet again. "Then we can decide where she might want to reside. And for tonight, Claire will remain here. Is that all right, dear?"

Claire blinked. "I, uh, okay." She glanced at me. "Are you staying, too?"

"Uh." I glanced at Exos, who nodded. "Yes. I can stay."

"The two of you can work on control," he added. "Might as well start now. I would hate for Claire to blow up a building on campus the way she did earlier." He pushed away from the table. "I need to phone an update to my brother, so if you all will excuse me."

"Is he always this abrupt?" Claire asked as the Spirit Fae left the room.

"I don't know. I hardly know him," I admitted.

"You're not friends?"

I snorted. "He's a royal. He doesn't *befriend* fae like me."

She frowned. "What do you mean?"

"It'd be like the Queen of England befriending a peasant," River interjected helpfully. "That'd be rare, right?"

"I, well, yes." She frowned. "So he's, like, important?"

"He's the most powerful Spirit Fae in existence," I confirmed. "And heir to the Spirit Kingdom."

"He's, like, thirty," she replied.

"Appearances can be deceiving," Elana chimed in, reminding me that she still sat with us. "Well, I'll leave you to your sleeping arrangements. River, you're welcome to stay as well, if your curiosity continues to get the best of you." She winked as she stood. "I require a bit of sleep after all the festivities of today." She paused on the threshold, her eyes going to Claire. "It is lovely to have you with us, dear. I hope you enjoy your tour tomorrow."

Chapter Eight
Claire

RIVER STOOD, shuffling from foot to foot while nibbling his lip. "I, uh…"

"You don't have to stay," Titus told him, a smile in his voice. "You can go back to your dorm."

Relief flooded the Water Fae's gaze. "Are you sure?"

"Yeah, man. I'll catch up with you tomorrow."

"Thank you." He started away from the table, then paused to glance back at me. "It, uh, was good to meet you, Claire." He immediately dropped his focus to the ground and shuffled some more.

"You, too," I replied, confused by his bashfulness.

He gave a little wave and practically ran out of the room.

"Is he afraid of me?" I asked, a little hurt. It wasn't like I meant to keep setting shit on fire.

Titus chuckled. "No. It's being in the Chancellor's place. It's, uh, sort of a big deal. She might not be royalty like Exos, but she's very important in our society. Her home is thriving with elements as well, likely a result of her being a Spirit Fae. He probably senses water somewhere."

"Wait, so she has two elements?" Didn't they just say it wasn't normal to mingle elements? Or did I misunderstand what that meant?

"Uh, no. Well, all Spirit Fae do." He palmed the back of his neck, looking uncomfortable. "Elana actually doesn't, which is considered very rare. But, like, Exos has spirit and fire. And his brother, Cyrus, is a notorious water elemental with a strong affinity for spirit. And you, it seems, have access to all the elements."

"And that's not normal." It was a guess—an educated one based on the last twenty-four hours or however long I'd been here.

"No. It's, uh, unique."

"Sort of like Elana only having one element as a Spirit Fae?"

"Sort of. There's probably been other Spirit Fae in history with access to only spirit; I just don't know of any." His lips twisted to the side. "But you, uh, you are the first and only fae to control more than two elements."

"More than two?" I squeaked, repeating his words.

"Yeah, as I said, Spirit Fae have two. That's the most there's ever been."

And I had five. I blinked. *Five*. "I… What does that mean?"

He shook his head. "I don't actually know," he admitted softly. "But what I can tell you is that the Academy is your best course. They'll teach you how to control the gifts, Claire. And it sounds like you'll be rotating between campuses throughout the week."

I sat back in my chair, flinching as a horde of those colorful insects fluttered into the room. My instinct to kill one earlier, like one would a fly, had overwhelmed me in the lobby. And then I'd screamed when the thing started *yelling* at me.

That kind of shit did not happen in, well, reality.

Except I'd given up considering any of this to be a dream. It was far too fucked up for even me to fathom.

Especially the bits about my mom.

"What, uh, did Exos mean when he said my mother destroyed the Spirit Kingdom?" I asked. He'd mentioned her a few times today, but I hadn't been in the right frame of mind to hear him, let alone understand him.

"You don't know?" Titus asked, sounding surprised.

I gave him a look. "In case it's not clear, I was celebrating my twenty-first birthday at a college bar just… whenever ago. And I knew nothing about fae or fairies or pixies or elemental magic. Until, like, whenever I fell here." My English professor would be appalled by the way I just explained all that, but who could expect any sort of clarity after throwing me into this insanity?

Titus nodded. "Right, yeah. Okay. Are you done eating?"

I eyed my partially finished plate. "Uh, yeah." I couldn't eat any more even if I tried. Not with the gymnastics going on inside my belly. "But that doesn't answer my question."

"I know," he said. "I was just trying to figure out if we should have that conversation here or, uh, elsewhere."

"Like upstairs?" I suggested, liking the idea of being somewhere less out in the open and away from those sparkly, chattering bugs.

"If that's where you want to go." He rubbed the back of his neck. "I don't know where else to go, actually."

"You mean you don't know where else I'm allowed to go," I translated. "I'm not going to run again." At least not yet. Not until I knew more about this place. Otherwise, it was a waste of effort, and Exos's ultimatum about my *options* didn't leave me all that enthusiastic to act out again. Because I didn't doubt for a second that he meant his threat. He very clearly did not like me, and the feeling was mutual.

Well, mostly mutual.

Aside from the fact that I still sometimes wanted to kiss him.

I shook my head. "Let's go upstairs," I said, standing. Because, unlike Exos, I actually *liked* Titus. And also found him hot as hell.

A Titus and Exos sandwich would be, well, amazing. Two powerful bodies thrusting, tongues dancing, hands roaming...

And, oh my God, I needed to stop that line of thought.

Wow.

No.

Not happening.

Ever.

And, Jesus Christ, what was wrong with me to even begin to imagine that? Very clearly losing—

"Claire?" Titus asked, his brow furrowed. He'd stood with me and seemed to be waiting for me to lead.

"Right." I turned and started toward the stairs. To lead him to my room. Which, after that last thought, probably wasn't the brightest of ideas, but it wasn't like Exos would be joining us. Although, I wouldn't exactly complain if he did.

No, wait, yes, I would.

I didn't like Exos.

He was a dick. A dick who just happened to be one of the sexiest men I'd ever seen. As well as Titus, but in entirely different ways.

I groaned, frustrated by the onslaught of images abrading my mind, each of them more graphic than the next.

"Are you okay, Claire?" Titus asked, sounding concerned.

No. "Yes. Just, uh, confused." Not exactly a lie.

His hand caught mine at the top of the stairs, pulling me back to him as his other palm went to cup my face. Eyes the color of an evergreen gazed down at me.

"It's going to be all right," he whispered, his thumb tracing my cheekbone. "I know it's all overwhelming right now, that you feel completely off-kilter in this realm, but I think you'll like it here. Minus maybe the pixies." He tried for a smile that I felt resonate inside of me.

Titus had completely misunderstood my awkwardness, yet his words were exactly what I needed to hear. "Thank you," I said, pressing my hand over his.

"You're welcome." His gaze dropped to my lips, heat flaring between us. It felt different from earlier, his comfort evolving into something more intense. Energy purred beneath his skin, lifting to stroke my own, inflaming a need inside me I didn't understand. It pulled me toward him, hypnotized me, excited me, made me fly. "Fuck, you're beautiful," he whispered, his awe rivaling my own.

I swallowed, tilting my head back—

The clearing of a throat had us jumping apart, my feet causing me to trip right into Exos's hard chest. He caught me with a hand on my hip, steadying me between them.

And what do you know—I'd suddenly become the center of an Exos and Titus sandwich.

My cheeks warmed at the thought, my throat going dry.

"I, uh, I mean, *we* were just going to my room, to, well…" Realizing how bad that all sounded, I stopped talking and gulped at Exos's arched brow.

"Talk," Titus said. "She wants to know about her mother, something apparently you haven't told her yet."

"When I tried, she blew me into a wall." Exos tilted his head at me. "Twice."

Flames seemed to lick across my skin. Perhaps literally. I couldn't tell because I couldn't seem to stop staring into Exos's ocean-blue eyes. That magnetic pull held me in place, paralyzing me before him. Then Titus grabbed my other hip, his chest hot against my back.

Oh, fuck…

I leaned against him, then swayed forward, and back again, unable to decide whom I wanted to touch more.

What is happening to me?

"Are you finally up for listening, princess?" Exos murmured. "Or will you use that impressive wind power of yours on me again?"

"Impressive?" I repeated.

"Very," he admitted, his gaze softening the slightest bit. His thumb swept over my lower lip, his opposite hand tightening on my hip. "So much power." He released me from his gaze as he lifted his eyes to Titus. "Where do you want to sleep?"

"I have no idea," he said, his warm voice tickling my hair. "We were only heading up here to talk about her mother."

"Yes, I heard that the first time." His thumb continued to caress my lip, as if memorizing the feel. "I was asking if you plan to sleep in her room."

"We hadn't gotten that far in terms of arrangements," Titus replied.

"Hmm. Well, I'll be down the hall. If you need a room, the one beside my guest suite is open." His gaze dropped to mine, his mouth curling into a beautiful grin. "And, Titus?"

"Yes?"

"Be careful with this one." His thumb pressed between my lips, lightly catching my tongue before withdrawing and letting his hand fall to his side. "Claire has a penchant for kissing strangers. Don't you, sweetheart?"

My face went up in flames, or at least it felt that way. A vivid memory of the bar pierced my thoughts, taking me back to his first words. *Do you often kiss men you hardly know?*

Exos smiled. "Night, princess."

"N-night," I stammered, my hip tingling as he released me. He didn't turn around as he sauntered down the hallway, his suit clinging to his muscular form and leaving me salivating for the body beneath.

This is seriously fucked up.

I shouldn't be lusting after him. I shouldn't be lusting after anyone. I should be focused on finding a way home.

"You, uh, kissed Exos?" Titus asked, his palm sliding away from me as he moved around to face me, his expression unreadable.

"Um." I cleared my throat. "Sort of. It was a dare."

"A dare?" he asked, raising a brow.

"Like in truth or dare."

He frowned. "I don't understand."

"It's a game. You've never played?"

He slowly shook his head, causing me to smile.

"It's dumb. You're not missing much. But essentially, it's played with a group of friends, and you pick a truth or a dare. A truth might be, like, what's the craziest place you've had sex? And you have to answer honestly. A dare could be something like, go kiss that guy at the bar. That was my dare—to kiss Exos. Rick can be…" I trailed off, the thought of my friend sending a jolt through my heart.

I didn't even get to say goodbye.

Just whisked away to this other realm, without a thought of my past.

Would my friends miss me? Would they come looking for me? My grandparents died last year, leaving me enough money to make it through school. But I had no other family.

Titus cupped my cheek, his forest-green eyes full of emotion. "I'm sorry about your friend."

"Me, too," I whispered, clearing my throat again. "C-can you tell me about my mom?" I asked, needing the distraction. "Tell me why I'm here? *How* I'm here?"

His throat bobbed as he nodded. "Yeah. Of course." He glanced at the corridor of doors before us. "Uh, in your room?"

"Yes, please." I didn't want to be out in the open any longer. I led the way with him trailing behind me, his hands tucked into his jeans as if he were trying not to touch me again. Probably because of Exos's little reveal. The kiss hardly counted, but yeah, I'd been pretty inappropriate that night. Then again, so had he, since he let me kiss him.

I pushed the memory from my head, focusing on the present.

Titus followed me into the room, his demeanor reserved as I closed the door.

He glanced around the flowery space, eyeing the tree in the center of the room and the vines climbing over the walls. "It's definitely Spirity in here."

"What's your place like?" I wondered.

"Black." He smirked. "I like to burn things."

"Apparently, so do I," I grumbled, lowering my gaze. How much damage had I caused without meaning to? Not that I could entirely blame myself. It wasn't like someone had trained me on how to be a... a... *fae*.

Fuck, I really do believe this, don't I?

I shivered, not wanting to admit to the logic flowing through my mind. This sort of shit was impossible. Or it should be. Yet, I couldn't deny all the magic flowing around me, the fact that flames literally shot out of my hands, that I'd destroyed a wall of, uh, vines? I shook my head, trying to clear it.

Titus caught my chin, tilting my head back to stare warmly down at me. "You'll learn to control it, Claire."

"Will I?" I countered. "I didn't even know any of this was real until today, or yesterday, or whenever it was that Exos kidnapped me." It felt like a lifetime ago, my existence forever changed by this new world. "I don't even understand why these powers, or whatever they are, didn't manifest until recently. Or how to begin controlling them."

"It's rumored your mother hexed you," he replied, his fingers gliding along my jaw and down my neck before dropping down to his side. "Exos would be much better at dictating the history, as he sits on the Council of Fae, but I can tell you what I know." There was an edge to his voice when he spoke of Exos, but it didn't reflect in the kindness of his features.

"I'd rather you tell me," I admitted. Something told me Exos would be blunt, and perhaps purposely harsh. And I couldn't handle that right now. I needed someone who would break me into this gently. Someone like Titus.

He palmed the back of his neck and let out a breath. "What all do you know?"

I sat on the bed, which was admirably soft considering the base was made of a tree trunk. "Uh, well..."

I considered the minimal information my grandmother gave me, while toying with the charm dangling from the chain around my neck. An old habit whenever I thought of her, as it'd been one of the last gifts she'd given me before she died.

Pinching my lips to the side, I shrugged. "Honestly, not much. I don't remember her at all. My grandmother said she left when I was a baby and never came home. Then claimed my father died of a broken heart."

He grimaced and leaned against the tree trunk across from me. "Right, we'll need to go back to the beginning, then." He crossed one ankle over the other, his hands tucking into his jean pockets. "So your mother—Ophelia Snow—was a Spirit Fae. Very powerful, as is the case with most female Spirit Fae of a certain birthright. Mortus, another Spirit Fae, was her chosen mate. They never completed the vows because she met your father soon after and created you."

He looked extremely uncomfortable when he finished, but I had to ask: "Chosen mate? Like my mother cheated on this Morty guy?" That didn't sound good.

"Mortus," he corrected. "And basically, yes. When fae mate, we mate for life. There's a power exchange that essentially binds the essences together, and she'd begun that process with Mortus before she met your, uh, father. The rumors say she ventured into the Human Realm on some sort of assignment, then refused to come home after meeting your father. Mortus, being her intended mate, issued an edict that she return and atone for her crimes. So she did, and then she fought him."

A chill shivered down my spine. "And…?" I prompted, my voice barely a whisper.

Titus ran his fingers through his auburn strands and sighed. "When fae agree to a power binding, it's irreversible. To do so causes a disruption in the balance. That's why he called her home, to finish the bond because the elements were already fracturing due to their unresolved vows. Of course, this is all hearsay. I wasn't there when it all happened. But my familiarity with the rituals suggests the truth behind this."

"Rituals?" I repeated. "I don't understand the *bond* part."

He seemed thoughtful, as if searching for the words. Then he pushed off the tree to stand before me, holding out his hand. "Touch me."

I wasn't sure what this had to do with anything, but I pressed my palm to his, curious. "O-okay."

Titus slid to his knees, his gaze kind as he stared up at me. "Close your eyes and just describe the sensations rolling over your skin."

Swallowing, I allowed my lids to fall, confused as to why he'd derailed our conversation. But he clearly had a point to make about something.

"What do you feel, Claire?" he asked, his voice soft. "Tell me what you sense."

"I…" I licked my lips, focusing on the heat spiraling up my arm, the caress oddly familiar after only a few hours of knowing him. "Hot," I whispered. "And…" I bit my cheek, fighting the urge to lean into him, to seek comfort from his known intimacy. Some foreign part of me trusted him despite my mind rebelling against the notion.

I don't really know him.

But I want to.

I like him.

"It feels... natural... to touch you." My cheeks warmed from the admission. It also felt natural to touch Exos.

"Because you feel the connection blossoming between your essence and mine," he whispered, his opposite hand cupping my cheek. "Fae are essence-based. We rely on our links to the elements to guide us, and when we find someone we are compatible with, we gravitate toward that person. My Fire calls to yours, and vice versa. Just as it seems your Spirit is intrigued by Exos. Definitely not common, but nothing about you is ordinary."

"O-oh," I breathed, unable to say more. While his words made sense, they also didn't. He'd essentially just implied that I was attracted to two men.

Two men I hardly knew.

Two men who couldn't be any more different.

Two men who turned me on like no other.

This realm is fucking with my mind, and apparently my libido.

Titus tilted his head to the side, his hands still on me. "Ophelia, your mother, had allowed her affinity to bind itself to Mortus through a series of rituals that the fae undergo when solidifying a mating. But she didn't finish it. Instead, she went to Earth, created you, and only returned when Mortus threatened to go after her. And then she fought him. I don't know the specifics, but I know the outcome."

I gazed into his eyes, waiting for him to continue. When he didn't, I said, "Tell me."

His expression fell, his touch turning cool against my skin. "Ninety percent of the Spirit Fae died of unknown causes that day, destroying the kingdom. Your mother died with them. Mortus lived. And it seems to have awoken a curse, or that's the myth, anyway."

"A curse?" I repeated, my gaze darting back and forth across his face. "What curse?"

"No Spirit Fae has been able to procreate since that day. It's said your mother's betrayal cursed the Spirit Fae, sentencing their species to death."

I gasped. "What?"

"There's more." He looked away, staring at the vines on the wall beside us. "Spirit Fae are life and death, the balance between all the elements. Without them..." He paused, clearing his throat and finally glancing back at me. "Without them, we're expected to die."

Chapter Nine
Claire

I STARED AT THE VINES ABOVE ME, Titus's words repeating over and over in my mind.

My mother cheated on her betrothed with my dad and created me.

Then fought her betrothed to the death.

And created a curse that would apparently kill fae kind.

I blinked. Numb. Cold. Alone. How did one just accept all that information? It wasn't as if I cared much for my mother, having been abandoned by her at birth. But holy shit, what kind of person did this to other people? Er, fae, or whatever. It didn't matter.

My mother had caused a pandemic. On purpose? By accident? I didn't know. But that sort of legacy painted my mom in a horrid light.

It made her sound evil.

"Claire?" Titus murmured, having moved to sit beside me on the bed.

"Still processing," I replied.

"Maybe we should talk about it more tomorrow?" he suggested.

I nodded mutely, not sure I could handle any more tonight. Hell, I couldn't handle any more, period. "You must hate my mother," I realized. "Oh God, everyone will hate me, too." My chest ached at the sudden understanding. I would be condemned with her as the result of her infidelity, not just to

Mortus, but to fae kind.

"Depends on their opinion of the prophecy," Titus muttered, blowing out a breath. "But yeah, I think sleep is probably a good idea."

"What prophecy?" I asked, ignoring his idea despite knowing I was at my limit for information.

"It's a tale, Claire. A myth. It's not true. Honestly, I think the whole curse thing is bullshit, too."

"Then what is it?" I pushed. "Why would it impact someone's opinion of me?"

"Because the prophecy says a fae with access to all the elements will break the curse," he replied flatly. "Or doom us all."

"Oh." I started nodding. "Yeah, that's brilliant. So I'm the daughter of a woman who destroyed the Spirit Fae, and possibly all fae. And I have access to all the elements, which could either rectify the situation or kill you all." I gave a hysterical laugh that bubbled into a sob as I curled into myself. "This is just too much."

I'd never experienced an easy life, having lost my parents before I could walk and being raised by two aloof grandparents who saw me as more of a burden than a gift. But this definitely took the cake.

"And you all want me to go to an Academy tomorrow? With a bunch of people who will clearly hate or fear me?" Another chuckle burst out of me. "Yeah, that's going to go well." Fuck. "*Fuck.*" I wanted to scream. To rant. To run. To fly. To *something*.

"Claire," Titus murmured, his hand on my shoulder.

I brushed him off, but he gripped me harder, tugging me to him.

"*Claire.*"

I ignored him, too busy shaking my head back and forth as I laugh-cried at the insanity of this entire situation. It was as if I'd fallen into a wonderland of crazy people with stories and expectations that made no sense. And this bizarre *energy* that I couldn't control. It swam around me, urging me to use it, to destroy, to create, to *burn*.

"Claire!" Titus yelled, his arms wrapping around me. "*Stop.*"

"Stop what?" I asked on a giggle that sounded maniacal to my ears. The entire world was crashing around me, and he wanted me to, what, relax? Breathe? Focus? Were those the words he was saying? No. It sounded like Exos. In my head. No, my ear. Whatever. I just wanted to hide, to never come out, and ignore everything around me. To disappear.

To leave.

A punch to my gut had me cringing, the power strong and encompassing, yanking me out of my state and back into the present to stare into two glowering blue eyes. Bright with power. Consuming me. Forcing me to yield. To submit. I didn't understand it, tried to fight it, but the magnetic pull was too great, overwhelming every part of my mind and grounding me in the present. His hands were on my cheeks, bands of muscular steel were around my waist, a hot body pressed to my back.

I blinked several times, confused. When did Exos get here? And why was Titus holding me so tightly?

"That's it," Exos breathed, his mouth dangerously close to mine. "Most fae come into their power slowly, but the hex your mo—" He cleared his throat. "You have twenty-one years of pent-up elements slamming into you at once. That you're even conscious is a miracle. It shows a strength very few possess, a strength I admire. But I need you to use that strength to control yourself, Claire. This volatile behavior is what the Council is afraid of, why they don't want you to attend the Academy. But I pushed for you to be allowed, have volunteered to train and guard you myself. And I will not fail. Do you understand me?"

Glittering waves. That was what his gaze reminded me of, so intense, so powerful, so alluring. I fell into him as one would an ocean, allowing the tide to pull me under with a force that stole my breath, and found peace beneath the roaring wake. Blissful and dark and mine.

Another strength came from behind in the form of an inferno, jerking me backward as my soul seemed to fight for control over them both.

Exos had asked if I understood.

But I didn't.

None of this made sense, my mind and body overwhelmed by the dueling sensations and my heart ripping in two. How could I desire two men? Now? Here? In this foreign place?

"She needs sleep," the fiery one said.

"I know," Spirit replied. "Guard her?"

"With my life." A hot vow spoken into my hair.

"I'll be nearby," Spirit whispered, warm lips brushing my forehead. "Try to rest, Claire. We have a lot to discuss tomorrow."

Someone mumbled. Maybe me. I didn't know, couldn't grasp the silky strands of reality floating around me. But oh, my ocean was leaving. That peace. I reached for him, hitting air instead, but a breath into my mind put me at ease.

Still there.

Still with me.

Still easing my pain.

My Spirit.

My other half.

The flames dancing inside me cooled, soothed by the presence of yet another, the one who called to the embers of my soul. I stopped trying to decipher the meaning and gave in to the sensation, trusting those around me to keep me afloat, to never let me drown.

"Good night, Claire," the voice behind me whispered, arms holding me tight. Somewhere in my mind, I noted the lack of clothing, my dress singed into ash around me. But I was too exhausted to verify, too consumed with the need to rest to validate my modesty.

Sleep sounded nice.

Maybe when I awoke, it would be to reality.

Yet somehow I knew this was my life now. My present and future. A fae teetering on the brink of disaster while trying to master elements I couldn't possibly understand.

I might die here.

But I also might live.

* * *

Ugh. Someone had left the heat on too high again. It felt as if I were wrapped up in a scorching blanket, singeing my hairs and leaving a trail of sweat in its wake. This was why I preferred a fan at night, a subtle breeze to help shift the hot air.

Ah, there it was, subtly brushing over my sweltering skin. *More,* I urged, craving the icy chill to cool the flames inching around me, consuming the room.

Wait... I flew upward, my mouth gaping wide at the swirl of power overwhelming the suite.

In the fae world.

Where I now resided.

Surrounded by chaos.

"Titus!" I shrieked, slamming my palm into his bare chest. His eyes flew open, his body going on alert as fast as mine.

He frowned at the maelstrom of elements. "Well, that's, um, different."

"Different?" I repeated on a squeak.

"Yeah, I've never seen anything like that." He shook his head, then grabbed my hand. "Okay, crash course. I need you to concentrate on pulling the elements to you. Think of it like the hop game where you catch the flurries."

I gaped at him. "What?" *Flurries? Hop game?*

"Er, right." He winced. "Uh, do you have an activity where you try to grab things with your mind?" At my blank stare, he sighed. "Okay, focus on the core of the fire, that blue flicker in the middle, and call it to you."

"Call it to me," I repeated. "Right."

"Come on, sweetheart. Trust me and try." His dimples flickered. "Please?"

I must still be dreaming, I decided, giving in to the lunacy of the moment. "All right." I focused on the bright blue of the flame, as he suggested, and bit my lip. *Now what?* Titus had said to call the fire. Okay. But how? Like, was I supposed to talk to it?

Pinching my mouth to the side, I shrugged. *Come here.*

Nothing.

Well, of course nothing. Why would it listen to me?

Except I felt a flicker of something in response. An odd sort of heated string, invisible to my eye but tangible against my finger.

Weird.

I tugged on it, my eyebrows lifting as the flame danced a little in response.

No way…

I tried again, my jaw dropping as the inferno definitely responded. With a twirl of my finger, the blazing colors rotated into a sphere, shrinking as I willed it to resemble the size of a baseball, and landed in the palm of my hand.

"Excellent," Titus praised. "Now use that mist over there to put it out."

Mist?

Oh.

There was a shower happening in the corner of the room, watering what appeared to be a bed of flowers that reminded me of the ones I'd lain on in the field. Coincidence? Maybe.

Another strand tugged at my being as I willed the water to condense and blow toward my hand. My palm sizzled as the elements met, a deep-seated peace overwhelming my senses as all three elements—air, water, and fire—mingled together over my skin.

"Beautiful," Titus breathed, running a finger through the aftermath of my miracle. "I think the flowers can stay."

I gazed at the patch in question, frowning. "Are you saying I did that?"

"You did," he replied, grinning. "Earth and spirit, mingled as one. Not only did you create them, but you also used the soil to help the flowers grow and water to make them bloom."

"And the fire?" I prompted.

"A natural defense. You protected us in your sleep, the air keeping it from burning us or the walls. I'm actually really impressed." He tucked a strand of unruly hair behind my ear. "Exos was right. You're very powerful." He studied my face, as if memorizing my features, his awe a palpable emotion floating between us. "So gorgeous."

"Me or the flowers?" It came out huskier than I intended, my body alight with a different awareness now that the panic had subsided. The intimacy of what I'd just done, with his coaching, stirred something inside me. A dark yearning, utterly inappropriate and yet satisfyingly right.

"You," he whispered, his green irises lowering to my mouth. "You're gorgeous." His gaze continued downward, his pupils enlarging, his lips parting in awe.

It took me a moment to realize why.

My dress had definitely disappeared last night, leaving me naked beside him. And while that should have alarmed me, it didn't. Somehow I trusted him not to act on it, perhaps because he'd held me for the last however many hours without harm. Or maybe because I *wanted* him to see me.

"Titus," I breathed, my fingers running up his bare, muscular arms to his shoulders.

"Claire," he replied, my name a husky melody that seemed to center between my thighs.

"Is this pull normal?" I asked, threading my fingers through his auburn strands. "This instant connection that makes me want to kiss you?"

"It's the fire," he explained, his emerald gaze smoldering as it lifted to mine. "Your element is calling to mine."

"To mate?"

"To test the potential for mating." His palm slid to the back of my neck, branding my skin and causing me to lean closer to him. "It's a call to play, to explore the boundaries and the potential between us."

"What happens if we give in?" I whispered, my lips angling toward his.

"We're bound for a month, where your power tastes mine and vice versa." The words were warm against my mouth, a flicker of fire dancing between us and kissing the air with unspoken promise.

"A month?" I repeated, deciding I liked the sound of that.

"A trial period, yes."

"Like dating?" I surmised.

"Yes, I believe that's what you call it in the Human Realm. A courtship period where we're exclusive to one another."

I frowned. "Just from a kiss?"

He nodded, his free hand going to my exposed hip, holding me. "You would not be able to touch another Fire Fae until our courtship wore off."

"That sounds…"

"Binding," he murmured. "Yes. That's what you've done to Exos."

His words startled me from the stupor overwhelming my mind. "What?"

"You kissed him, thereby initiating the trial." He swallowed, his grip tightening. "And because you are made of various elements, you can entertain more than one courtship at a time."

"Oh," I whispered, my eyes widening. "Is that normal?"

"No." He pressed his forehead to mine. "Not at all."

"Oh," I repeated, my voice hoarse. "Is that why I want you both?"

His deep chuckle vibrated the sensual atmosphere around us, scattering goose bumps along my limbs. "Your elemental gifts crave us both, yes."

"And a kiss binds us?"

"Temporarily, yes. If it's desired and agreed upon by both parties."

Meaning Exos wanted the bond, too. Or had he only yearned to kiss me? I pushed away the thought, preferring to focus on the now, on the way Titus's hands felt against my skin. His breath, a fiery intoxication warming my lips, urging me to close the gap between us, to take what I desired and more. To

71

bind us. To explore him. To taste him. To *feel* him.

I slid onto his lap, my legs straddling his own, my arms wrapping around his neck. "Kiss me, Titus," I whispered, my mouth brushing the words against his. "Please kiss me."

He smiled, his fingers threading through my hair, taking control by angling my head to his liking. "Try not to light the room on fire, sweetheart."

"No promises," I mouthed, the embers already coiling in my stomach. The erection seated firmly between my thighs didn't help, nor did the way his chest burned mine as he tugged me closer, his arm a brand around my lower back.

He led with his tongue, not bothering to ease me into our embrace. It wasn't needed. One touch unleashed the passion between us in an explosion of sensation and lust. My nails dug into his shoulders, anchoring me to him as he dominated my mouth in a way no other man had. It left me breathless, needy, and moaning for more, his experience in this arena detonating all my expectations and laying a new foundation in his path.

Hungers only he could satiate.

A passion only he could cool.

Such fire.

A blaze that trembled over my skin, lighting up every fiber of my being.

"Titus," I moaned, his body owning mine in that moment. He could do whatever he wanted, however he desired, and I would let him. I'd never felt more alive, more energized in my entire life. It was as if he'd introduced me to a new level of existence, one aflame with endless heat and fiery sensations.

And all he'd done was kiss me.

Deeply.

Devouring me to my very soul.

"More," I urged. "Please."

He groaned, the arm around my lower back pulling me closer. "You're killing me, Claire." He tugged my lower lip into his mouth, sucking hard, the hand in my hair tightening. "We need to take this slow."

"Why?" I shifted to press my heated center to his cock, loving the way he felt between my legs. So right. So perfect. So *mine*.

The possessive urge to claim him swept over me, sending a jolt to my system and causing my eyes to widen. I never did this with men I wasn't dating steadily, let alone one I just met. A kiss, yes.

But I required monogamy before sex.

I needed to know the man.

Which was why I'd only been with two—my high school boyfriend and Tucker from last year. And I'd made both of them wait almost six months.

Not six hours, or however long it'd been.

Titus pressed his mouth to mine, slower, less demanding than before. "It's overwhelming," he whispered, his lips touching mine with each word. "You have to ease into it, or the elements will take over. They're very much a part of us, of who we are, of the decisions we make. And nature doesn't always listen to reason. We rely on our minds for that."

Another kiss, softer, coaxing, his tongue gently tracing mine.

I fell into the sensation, my body igniting from within and sending another wave of warmth through my belly.

Fuck, I wanted him.

But I didn't know him.

It was all so confusing, so consuming, so empowering. I shook beneath the onslaught of emotions, my grip on him tightening, my breathing quickening in my chest.

"Titus..."

"It's okay, Claire," he whispered, shifting us so I lay on my back, his lower body settling between my thighs.

His lips remained firm, his tongue a dominant presence in my mouth. Embers seemed to dance over our skin, his palm trailing a fiery path down my side before grabbing my hip to still my movements. I hadn't even realized I was lifting myself against him until he stopped me, his touch a welcome claim.

"You feel like heaven beneath me," he murmured, his lips tasting my cheek before moving to my neck. "Fuck, Claire." He nibbled my racing pulse, sliding down to my collarbone and then back up to my mouth. "We need to sleep, sweetheart."

"I'm not tired," I replied, arching into him on a luscious sigh.

He chuckled, his lips brushing mine. "Trust me, I wish that were true. But we both know you're exhausted, and pushing this any further wouldn't be right."

"It feels right." The words were a soft exhale, my body melting beneath his. "It feels amazing."

"It does," he agreed, his voice husky and hot. "Too damn right." His tongue slid into my mouth again, the taste of him searing me from the inside out.

I couldn't think beneath his onslaught, the sensations too great, the fire brewing inside us a combustible element awaiting our permission to erupt.

I whimpered and writhed beneath him, a wanton woman unleashed beneath a passion I didn't fully understand. His name fell from my lips, a chant and a plea, my nipples chafing against his hot, hard chest. I needed more. I needed him. I needed *this*.

"Enough," a deep voice said, reverberating the walls around us, yanking me from the chains of desire. Dark blue pools met mine as I glanced upward into a face so beautiful my heart threatened to combust.

Exos.

"I told you to train her, not fuck her," he growled, his words dousing me in a wave of cold water. "She doesn't understand our rules, our world, or the bonds that bind. Think with your head, Titus, not your dick."

Titus cursed, his face falling to my neck as Exos stormed out of the room, slamming the door behind him. "*Fuck.*"

I suddenly felt cold despite the blanket of heat on top of me and shivered as he rolled away, his palms digging into his eyes.

"I'm sorry, Claire," he whispered. "I... I... I wasn't thinking."

Neither was I, I wanted to say back to him, but couldn't, too flabbergasted by what just happened.

I'd almost begged him to take me.

Had wanted him to more than anything in the world.

It'd been a temporary escape from the craziness of this realm, of this new life, and he'd almost given it to me.

Except Exos had interrupted.

I didn't know if I wanted to thank him or punch him.

Confused and overwhelmed, and slightly embarrassed, I curled into a ball, tucking my knees to my chest and fighting for the heat of seconds ago to flicker through my veins.

Titus responded by pulling the blankets up around me, his silence a burden at my back.

I didn't know what to say to him. Did he want an apology as well? A compliment? A request for that to happen again?

I had no idea because I didn't *know* him.

Yet I'd been about to let him inside me in the most intimate way.

All to escape a reality I wasn't ready to face.

And because it had felt all too right.

He pressed a kiss to my spine, right between my shoulder blades, then higher against the back of my neck, and slowly slid his arm around my waist.

"Is this okay?" he asked softly, a hint of wariness in his tone. "Or do you prefer not to be touched?"

I swallowed, considering his words, another shudder rattling my limbs. How had I gone from feeling so hot to so cold?

Because he took away his heat, I realized.

He began to remove his arm again, taking with him the last vestiges of warmth around me, and I dug my fingernails into his forearm, desperate to keep him close. Needy, yes. But I couldn't stand the thought of being frozen and alone.

Titus provided a comfort that felt familiar while also serving as a new experience. And I craved both.

"Stay," I whispered. "Please."

He guided me into his body, his arm folding around me in a protective manner as his heated chest enveloped my bare back.

A temporary heaven.

Or maybe it qualified as hell.

I neither knew nor cared, too comforted by his touch to debate any further.

"Sweet dreams, Claire," he whispered.

Dreams, I thought. *Do those even exist anymore?*

My eyes fell closed, the nightmares of my existence sprouting to life behind my eyes in the vision of my mother. A cruel woman destined to destroy the fae.

Except, when I looked her in the eyes, all I saw was a vision of myself.

No, there were no dreams here.

Not for me.

Only delusions of fate.

My fate.

Chapter Ten
Titus

I'M AN ASSHOLE.

Tightening my grip on Claire's hip while she slept, I tried to think of any angle in this situation where I wasn't a bastard, but came up with ashes. Exos had done the right thing by stopping me before I went too far. Claire didn't know me—didn't know this world. I didn't mean to take advantage of her, but damn, the pull between us was so strong.

She destroyed our clothes. That shouldn't have been possible. My wardrobe was customized for Fire Fae. Yet she'd demolished the fibers with the ease of a millennia-old fae. And fuck if that hadn't turned me on even more.

Her power was an aphrodisiac, seducing my fire and exciting a need I could hardly control. Not an excuse or even an explanation, just a fact. But I needed to do better.

She deserved better.

Embers flickered where my skin touched Claire's, reacting to our newly established bond—a bond that would awaken the deepest fiery passions innate to the carnal Fire Fae. Claire wasn't my first courting, but it felt different with her. Almost like I couldn't keep my thoughts straight and our dancing elements went straight to my dick.

Fuck it. Exos was right. I couldn't trust myself to be this close to her. We needed to get up, anyway.

I eased away from Claire and grimaced when she curled into herself and whimpered in her sleep.

"So cold," she mumbled.

"Shh," I whispered, drawing a finger down her cheek and sending more of my fire into her. "Today's a big day. We can't cocoon in our element all morning."

She groaned but didn't open her eyes, as if fighting the urge to wake up. She clutched the charred blanket closer to her chin and turned her face into the pillow.

Holding her through the night had been a selfish pleasure for me. I'd tried to be strong and give her the space she needed, but she'd demanded my touch. Perhaps I'd been weak to oblige her, or maybe I needed her, too.

I wasn't going to fool myself into thinking I meant more to her than what I was: an ally in a world of strangers. Maybe our connection would only make things more difficult for her, or maybe it was the anchor she needed right now.

Or a distraction.

I shoved that thought aside and forced myself out of bed. Elana's guest room of vines and mist and foreign elements seeped into me. I shivered, missing the warm embrace of the Fire Dorms.

Looking down, I smirked as ash fell from my naked body. So much power in the fireball that was Claire. *How did you do it?* I wondered again.

A soft touch across my shoulder blade made me stiffen.

Damn, I hadn't even heard her move.

"Where, uh, are your clothes?" she asked softly, as if reading my mind.

Her fingers continued to explore my back, running over the long scars I'd earned during my time in the ring. Fighting without powers didn't protect me from the harsh edge of a blade.

"You burned them off, sweetheart," I said with a grin, making sure not to turn around. She didn't need to see all of me. Yet. "I don't suppose Elana keeps extra pairs of pants around here?" It was more of a rhetorical question since I doubted Claire knew.

She drew in a soft gasp, and then I realized she was laughing. "Are you going to have to walk out of here naked?"

I finally turned enough to peer over my shoulder and raised a brow. "You sound far too pleased by that idea."

Her gaze dipped, and I knew she wanted to see what I'd been keeping from her last night, but that was our intimate link pushing her—or her grief. I wouldn't take advantage of her again, even if I thought for just a moment that I could help her forget everything.

That maybe she could help *me* forget everything.

Clearing my throat, I forced myself to bring up the one topic that would dispel the moment, to remind her of our predicament.

"Exos might have some clothes I can borrow." The words hurt, but they had to be said. This was the connection between us driving her emotions and reactions. She was too inexperienced as a fae to understand that. Taking advantage of that would be wrong.

She hesitated before her touch retreated, leaving me cold. The impulse to lean back into her overwhelmed me for just a moment before I doused the growing flames in my chest.

"Exos." She repeated the name as if she'd just remembered last night. "I... I'm connected to him, too."

The raw emotion in her voice had me glancing back to find her cheeks flushing pink. Her blue eyes snapped up to find mine, reminding me that she was a Spirit Fae, better suited to one of her own kind.

No.

The very thought of leaving her to fend for herself against Exos—one of the only potential mates left among the Spirit Fae—made me cringe. She may have linked with him, but she needed me to keep him in line.

Gods, I didn't care if she bonded with a fae of every element, as long as I could stand by her side. We shared fire. That was the hottest of all the matings, one no fae could share with her, apart from me.

Taking her hand in mine, tiny flames sparked between us, causing her eyes to widen. "Yes, you've created a connection with him. But *our* bond is strong, even for a courtship," I admitted.

She smiled, making something inside me flip a switch. "Stronger than my bond with Exos?"

She meant it as a tease, but I sensed the tension beneath her words. Even though she couldn't possibly know what it really meant, she clearly felt some guilt at having bound both of us at the same time. Her eyes searched mine, pleading for my approval and assurance.

"Not stronger," I said, drawing the words out slowly as I ran my fingers up the soft curve of her elbow. "Just different."

Her gaze dropped. Not the answer she wanted to hear. "He barged in last night. How did he...?"

I lightly traced her shoulder before cupping her cheek. Her eyelids fluttered closed as she leaned into my touch. She wasn't going to like my response, but Claire deserved the truth. She needed to know what it meant to be bonded.

"He sensed your desire," I said softly. "Whenever you are, well, *aroused*, he'll know. As will I."

She flinched away. "Well, that's embarrassing."

Chuckling, I wrapped a blanket around my waist. I was so busy trying to cover myself to prevent tempting her that I forgot she was completely naked as well. She allowed the charred fabric to pull away from her, revealing lush, sensual skin that glowed with the heat of our connection. She watched me, waiting to see what I would do.

It took every ember of willpower to look away from her. If I indulged myself even for a moment, I'd toss away all my reservations and take her right now.

She's grieving.

She's scared.

She needs you to be strong.

She doesn't understand the bond.

I reminded myself of all the things the Halfling was likely going through right now. Today was going to be rough for her. She needed to see the Academy, and more so, she needed to understand how important it was for her to be here. The alternatives weren't choices at all.

Isolation…

Death…

The sooner she faced the Academy and fae society, the sooner she would be equipped to deal with her new life. My needs were nothing compared to hers.

Before I could look at Claire again and spiral into the depths of our newfound bond, Exos blundered into the bedroom.

Claire snatched her knees to her chest and cried out. "Exos!"

I would have offered her the blanket to cover herself, but there was something in Exos's eyes that said our nakedness was the least of his problems right now. "You two. Get dressed." His gaze flickered to the doorway, and I sensed the low boom of the ground I'd missed a moment before. "Now."

* * *

"News has spread that the Halfling is here." Elana folded her hands in front of her dress and let out a long sigh. Vines budding with blue flowers wound through her hair, a living ornament that made her look ethereal and regal.

I frowned and bit my tongue—hard. The rumor was already on campus. River had been the one to tell me about the Halfling, but the fact that a bunch of unruly students were causing a scene right outside Elana's estate? That didn't just happen. Someone had told them Claire was here.

Not River, because I knew him and he would never do that, but *someone* had.

"What do they want?" Claire asked, her voice taut as her fingers clenched around mine. I shouldn't be indulging her need to touch me, or my need to touch her, but somehow our hands kept finding one another without my permission.

Elana stared at Claire, her expression soft and wise. "Forgive my bluntness, but they're protesting."

79

"Protesting?" she squeaked and dug her fingernails into my skin.

I tugged at my borrowed clothes with my free hand. They were far too tight around my biceps and chest, and the agonizing frills ruffling around my elbows made me feel like a complete moron. Which, I supposed, was Exos's goal when he gave me this pompous outfit.

His wry smile confirmed it. "Don't worry, Claire. Everyone will be so taken aback by Titus in royal garb that you'll be yesterday's news."

I suppressed a retort for the jackass, but Exos was right. This would help take some of the attention off of Claire, which was the least I could do considering her situation.

However, even my comical attire couldn't win Claire's attention. Her gaze was locked on the hall that glittered with motes that had drifted in with the morning sunlight. Low chanting sounded outside the door in our old language, which Claire wouldn't understand, the words making my teeth clench.

Dooms-bringer.

Finish what your mother started.

Fae killer.

"What are they saying?" Claire asked as she tilted her head to the side.

Exos plucked Claire's hand from mine and gave her knuckles a kiss, startling all of us out of our unease. "Nothing of importance, princess." His eyes held hers for a beat before he bowed, releasing her as quickly as he'd grabbed her. "I, uh, need to ready our future accommodations." He refocused on me. "I trust you'll be able to give Claire a proper tour and bring her to the Fire Quad?"

"No one will touch her," I vowed, not because Exos had ordered me to play guardian, but because my blood boiled knowing how many fae wanted Claire dead. Maybe it was just the courtship bond, but instinct told me to shred apart anyone who dared to whisper a threat within her vicinity.

Which was apparently half the entire fucking Academy, if the chants outside were anything to go by.

Exos leaned in, dropping his voice to a whisper. "Don't kill anyone. Just show her around campus. Keep your head on your shoulders." He gave me a once-over. "And your dick in your pants."

That last part was totally unnecessary.

Okay, maybe a little bit necessary after last night.

But for fuck's sake, the jackass really needed to cool it with all the damn orders.

"Come on, Claire," I said, unable to muster anything more respectable than a slight bowing of my head to Exos. "We've been given our *instructions* for the day."

She swallowed hard, but I felt the heat of her trust where her skin touched mine, our hands instinctively finding each other again. It told me that as long as I was with her, perhaps she could face anything, even a protesting crowd of fae.

Elana waved her hand, causing the bangles on her wrist to jingle. The wide doors of her estate opened with low groans, reminding me of ancient trees bowing in the wind.

Sunlight poured into the foyer and illuminated the golden spirals around Claire's face. I wanted to reach out and run my fingers through her silky strands, gather her hair in my fist, and kiss her.

Again.

Fuck. This uncontrollable need to take her was going to be the death of me if I didn't learn how to tamper it. A tour would help. Assuming we could make it through the masses.

"Now or never," I said, more to myself than to Claire.

"I'd rather get the shit show over with now," Claire replied, surprising me with the vigor of her words. She shrugged. "Beats staying in this, uh, forest of a house. Show me your fae world, Titus." She squeezed my hand, her gaze warm and trusting.

A smile twitched at my lips as we stepped out onto the dried leaves in front of the estate. The chanting near the front gates ceased, students' eyes going wide. "Here we go," I said, pulling Claire along at my side.

"There's a lot of them," she whispered.

I snorted. "Yeah. I'm not concerned." I created a fireball in my hand and threw it up in the air, before catching it. Many of the fae at the gates took several steps back, some even going as far as to leave. They all knew me, understood my gifts and how powerful I could be in a full rage.

Begrudgingly, I also had to admit that borrowing Exos's royal attire helped matters. Because they would see *his* symbol on my clothing, which boldly announced my actions to be official orders. And fucking with those orders was a good way to end up in the fire pits.

I tossed a ball at the gates for fun, smirking as several more fae dispersed.

Another flame appeared along the periphery, the signature belonging to Exos, who stood behind us in the doorway wearing a stoic mask.

That caused almost the entire crowd to die, the students not wanting to mess with me or the notorious Spirit Royal.

"Yeah, you'll be fine," I told Claire, winking.

She gaped back and forth between me and Exos. "Did he just...?"

"Yep." I glanced back at him with a nod that he returned before disappearing into the house. "He's just throwing his weight behind mine, not that it's needed with this ridiculous outfit."

Claire giggled, her cheeks pinkening. "You look..."

"Handsome?" I prompted, waggling my brows. "Hot? Sexy as fuck?"

Her laugh was music to my ears, even as she shook her head. "You look hideous."

I covered my heart, feigning a wounded expression. "Claire... How could you? You know my ego is fragile."

She snorted. "Somehow I doubt that."

I slung my arm around her shoulders, tugging her into my side. "You're right. I'm pretty sure even I make this outfit look good."

She patted my abdomen. "Pretty sure you don't."

"Yeah, yeah. You want this tour or not?" I teased. The majority of the onlookers were gone, leaving Claire much more at ease beside me.

"Yeah, I do." She gave me a small smile. "I'm actually a little curious."

"Just a little?"

She ducked her head shyly, her blue eyes sparkling with power. "Scared, too. But mostly curious."

"You have nothing to fear, sweetheart. I've got you." I kissed her forehead, the action so natural, as if we'd been doing this for years, not hours. Not wanting to dig too deeply into that realization, I released her shoulders and held out my hand. "Let's go."

"Okay," she whispered, placing her palm in mine.

The beautiful day unfolded around us as we moved, trees seeming to bow to Claire in her wake. She had no idea what kind of power she exuded in this world, how palpable her essence was to the kingdom surrounding us. Yet, she seemed quite taken with the atmosphere, her free hand curling into the air with each step, her eyes dancing with wonder.

"It's so enchanting," she breathed.

"And you've not even seen the Academy yet," I replied, smiling.

"How far is—" Her mouth fell open as the famous iron gates came into view down the flower-laden hill. "Holy shit, we are not in Kansas anymore."

I blinked. "What?"

"You know, the..." She trailed off and shook her head. "Never mind. It's a line from a well-known movie."

"Oh, human cinema." I smiled. "We don't really have that here, preferring to spend our time outdoors and whatnot." Or at the gym. Or in a fighting ring. "Although, I guess they kind of televise some of our sporting events, but it's not the same. It's all carried by elemental magic, sort of unfolding in replays. And yeah, I'm boring you. Let's head that way."

I pointed to the main entrance, charmed by four of the elements dancing around it. Beyond it were the renowned stone structures of the school, all laced with greenery and adorned in flowers. At least, the main buildings were. Each quad catered to the various elementals. I'd show her the charred towers of the Fire Quad first. It wouldn't be as lively as the Chancellor's home, but just as captivating.

"Are you, like, supposed to be in class right now?" she asked as we walked.

"Nah, you arrived at a good time. It's our downtime right now between courses. Everything starts back up tomorrow."

"Like a weekend," she surmised.

"Similar, yeah. But we do six days on, six days off. Helps keep up the creative flow and allows us to participate in the mandatory intramurals."

"Intramurals?" she repeated, her gaze on the water dancing with fire along the gate as we passed beneath it.

"Fae mingling." I smirked. "It's Elana's way of trying to make all the fae get along, by forcing us to engage in physical activities and other general education courses together. Like Human Studies. We also have a morning or afternoon of obligatory gymnasium activities during our six days on—which, again, includes all the fae."

Her brow puckered. "You don't get along otherwise?"

I shrugged. "Some of us do. Some of us don't. There's a council that guides us, but each kingdom has its own governing structure."

"So… you're like different countries?"

"From what I understand of your world, it'd be more similar to continents." I took a right through a long woodsy corridor between two of the stone buildings. "This is the main campus, by the way. Where the intramural courses are that I mentioned. Then each quad caters to the specific fae, so I'll show you Fire Quad first since I'm most familiar with it."

We stepped into a courtyard where several fae were mingling, all of whom went silent upon spotting us.

Claire gave a little wave that had them all taking several steps backward, their eyes going wide and whispers in the ancient language taking over.

It's her.

I heard she caused the quake last night.

Evil.

Why would they allow her here?

She's going to kill us all.

Claire's cheeks pinkened, her inability to understand their words not mattering. Their tones said it all.

"Enough," I said, irritated.

"It's fine," Claire whispered. "I get it."

"It's not fine." I pulled her across the courtyard, only to find a row of fae waiting along the pathway that led to the Fire Quad.

Fuck.

A trio of fae approached us, their hips swaying and merciless eyes gleaming with mischief.

Ignis and her bratty friends.

"Well, I must say, the Halfling is not what I expected," Ignis said as she curled writhing fire around her fingertips in a blatant display of aggression. "She's so… *blonde.*"

Claire narrowed her eyes, but she didn't seem intimidated. Her gaze dipped slightly to the flames, betraying her moment's hesitation that she'd noticed anything amiss.

"Ah, yeah. I know girls like you," she said, her voice low and full of foreboding. She raised her chin and peered down her nose at Ignis. "You think you have everyone wrapped around your little finger. Well, luckily, there are bitches in the Human Realm, too, and I don't have time for them." She tugged at my hand. "Come on, Titus. I'd much rather watch you play with fire."

Sickle sent a stream flooding in front of Claire, and I jerked her back before she could step into it and get caught in the trap. Aerie laughed, sending a breeze to splash the water onto Claire.

It sizzled on contact.

Good, Claire was pissed.

That meant she would focus on her fire abilities—abilities I could help her with.

Ignis chuckled and stepped close enough to reach me. "Oh, Titus, are you going to let her boss you around like that?" She moved to wrap her fingers around my bicep but hissed when the contact burned her. "Fuck, Titus!" Her eyes went wide, and she bounced her gaze between us, her wild auburn curls fanning out as heat spread across her face. She let out a rude laugh and covered her mouth. "Oh, seriously? You and I fuck, and then the next day, you initiate a courtship bond with a Halfling? Oh, this is too good."

Gods. I'd almost forgotten about the other night, with Claire being so close. Ignis had tried to force the bond, which, by fae custom, meant I owed it to her to try to reciprocate. But clearly, I broke that rule.

"*What?*" Sickle screeched, her voice like nails on a chalkboard. "That's a violation!"

I sighed. *Here we go.*

"Can't expect much from him," Aerie put in. "I mean, you knew he was a player before you let him lure you into bed, Ig."

"He said he loved me."

"Oh, for the love of the gods, cut that shit out," I demanded. "You know I didn't."

Her lower lip wobbled. "And now you deny it?" She shook her head, real live tears popping into her eyes. "Three times, Titus. We made love three times."

"I thought we fucked," I countered, livid. "Which is it, Ignis?"

"How can you be so cold?" She perfected the art of woman hurt. "Oh, because you went and tricked the Halfling into bonding with you. Is it some sort of bet?" Her eyes narrowed. "That's it, isn't it? You're in on the bet on who can fuck her first?"

"Oh, you know he is," Sickle said, confusing the hell out of me. "I heard the stakes are high, too. But initiating an elemental link is a bit of a cheat, if you ask me. The others will disqualify you for it."

"Bet?" Claire repeated, her voice far softer than it was a few minutes ago. Her hand felt like ice in my hand, her arm brittle.

"They're lying," I promised. "I don't even know what they're talking about."

Ignis snorted. "I bet you'll say the same about how you fucked me two days ago, but I have elemental proof." She lifted her shirt to reveal a red handprint on her abdomen. "What can I say? Things heated up."

Claire pulled away from me, her arms folding around herself.

"Aww, not so tough now?" Ignis continued, her tone frigid. "And here I thought you'd be as ballsy as your mum."

"That's enough, Ignis," I growled.

She shrugged. "I don't think she cares. Elements knows her mother didn't when she destroyed the fae race."

"Ignis!"

"What? She's a whore just like her mother, and you're going to stand there and defend her?" She scoffed, tossing her long red hair over one shoulder. "You deserve better, baby. You know you do." She tried to stroke my arm again, but flames erupted around us.

Not from me.

Not from Ignis.

But from Claire.

Tears shone bright in her eyes as flames poured from her hands, sending fae scattering down the pathway to avoid being caught in her emotional outburst.

"Claire," I murmured, reaching for her.

"*No,*" she snapped. "Do not touch me."

I sighed. "Come on, sweetheart. Ignis is just being a bitch."

"Just being a bitch? One you slept with right before...?" She shook her head, unable to finish.

"It didn't mean anything," I vowed. "Not like with you."

Ignis laughed, the sound mean and cold. "Pretty sure you said the same thing to me about, who was it?" She snapped her fingers. "Mae?"

Fucking flames! "Would you just shut the fuck up?"

"What? Worried she might learn about your reputation, lover? A little late for that." She sounded so pleased with herself. If Claire hadn't looked ready to lose her shit, I might have considered teaching Ignis a lesson with my fire.

"Claire." I kept my voice soft. "Can—"

The entire wall went up in flames.

As did the path.

And the courtyard.

Fuck.

CHAPTER ELEVEN
CLAIRE

I HAD LET MY GUARD DOWN. Stupid. So fucking stupid. I knew better.

Titus tried to bond with me over a bet?

He fucked that bitch? Before me?

Everyone hates me.

What am I even doing here?

The fire raged around me, scalding my skin, so foreign and unfamiliar compared to the other flames I'd cast over the last few days. It actually burned me in places, singeing the dress Elana had given me to wear and searing my side.

I jumped away from it, confused.

Why is it hurting me?

Titus roared on the periphery, his body hidden behind the orange-and-yellow wall dancing before me. He seemed to be yelling at me to stop, but I couldn't. I didn't know how. The fire didn't feel right. I tried to call it to me the way he instructed, but all that did was cause it to flare upward toward the building.

Oh no…

People started screaming, the flames climbing and shifting, destroying the vines along the stone walls and creeping into open windows. It reminded me of a snake—lethal and fast.

And I had no control over it.

A hand on my shoulder yanked me backward. I screamed, only to realize I recognized the arm encircling my waist. "Focus for me, princess," Exos whispered, his lips against my ear. "Breathe."

"I-I'm trying."

"I know, and you're doing so good, Claire. I just need you to try a little more, okay?" The words were warm and soothing, causing my shoulders to relax back against him. He kept one arm around me while he used his opposite hand to grab my wrist and pull my hand upward. Then he yanked it back when the fire burned us both.

"It doesn't feel right," I said, shaking my head. "I don't even know what I'm saying." Or what any of it meant. It was pure instinct driving my senses and telling me that I didn't recognize the energy before us.

"Let's try to push against it." He cradled my hand in his, guiding it at an angle. "Right there, baby. I want you to call water and wind, and blast the focal point."

"How?" I asked, exasperated.

He shifted his grip around my waist to tap my heart. "It's right here, Claire. Inside you. Look for it, like you do your fire, and call it to you."

Tears pooled in my eyes, frustration taking over me. He made it sound so simple, but he wanted me to unlock a door I didn't possess the key to. "Exos, I can't."

"You can," he promised, his tone coaxing. Then he yanked my hand back as the flame reached out at us, the heat scorching our skin. Exos's grip tightened, his back hitting the wall behind us as the flames turned our way in a threatening sweep. He started muttering, his own flame glowing in his hand as he threw it at the approaching inferno.

But all that seemed to do was exasperate it.

The blaze yawned, blowing hot air toward us that slick sweat across my skin and caused Exos to shiver behind me.

"We need to find a way out," he said, his voice holding a sense of urgency. "Or that thing is going to destroy us."

I honestly couldn't believe we were even still standing. The fifty-foot tower of fire should have killed us just for being this close.

But something kept it at bay.

Something *protected* us.

I frowned, identifying the thin barrier with my mind while Exos spoke behind me. His statement went over my head, my attention on the odd film of mist that seemed to be pushing against the flames.

When I called to it, the essence responded.

That's mine, I realized, my lips parting. *What can I do with it?*

Exos said I needed air and water. To focus on that cavernous hole above, the source of the flames. I could see it now, the way it swirled dangerously like a whirlpool of lava.

There, I urged, shooting the water upward with a gust of wind, the power roaring out of me from someplace deep within my soul.

Exhilarating.

Powerful.

Lively.

I stole a deep breath, my lungs filling with fresh air, and blew the contents upward with the water, creating a twirl of my own—A breeze infused with cool springs that doused the flames—causing them to sizzle. I repeated the action, a sense of peace falling over me with each exhale, until the inferno fizzled into ash.

Ignis stood across from me, her eyes glowing red, her expression one of abject horror. "That bitch tried to kill me!" she accused while trying to grab Titus's arm. It must have shocked her again, because she flinched away from him, but it was Titus's expression that I couldn't stop staring at. He appeared just as horrified as Ignis.

Her friend with the bluish-blonde hair heaved a huge sigh, a sheet of ice melting beneath my water. "I thought we were gonna die. Not even playin'. Like, I'm fucking exhausted."

"You saved our lives, Sickle," the other girl said, her skirt indecently high as she collapsed against the wall. "Dear Elements…" She shuddered as she put her head on her knees.

"What are you all just standing here for? That bitch needs to be banished!" Ignis went on. "Or did you all just miss that fire tornado that tried to *kill me*! This is mutual ground, Your Highness. You know the rules."

"You provoked her, Ignis," Titus growled.

"I did not!"

"Yes, you did!" He threw up his hands. "You know she's volatile and you pushed all her buttons!"

I winced at his description. *Volatile.*

"She shouldn't even be here anyway! Or have you forgotten what her whore of a mother did? You wait until my daddy hears about this. He will not be happy." She folded her arms, her expression haughty as she stared down her nose at me. "Your days here are numbered, *Halfling*. Mark my words."

Exos's arm tightened around me. "Is that a threat, Fire Fae? Because as you already pointed out, violence on the Academy premises is frowned upon. I would hate to have to report your behavior to *your father*, who happens to sit on the Council. With me."

Her face paled. "He'll never believe you."

"I think you'll find that I am quite convincing," Exos replied, all arrogance. His hold loosened, his hand falling to my hip. "Now, if you'll excuse us, I need to escort Claire to her sleeping quarters."

"Exos—"

"I think you've done enough for the day, Titus," he said, cutting him off. "I'll follow up with you later." His dismissive tone pissed me off before, but right now, it was what I needed. I wasn't ready to talk to Titus, not after everything Ignis had said.

He was with her right before he met me.

It wasn't fair to hold that against him, but I couldn't help it. The woman was an utter bitch, and he'd slept with her.

Right after someone named Mae.

Did he just sleep with all the females on campus?

Was I just a conquest to him? Something new?

No, a part of me whispered.

But what did I really even know about him? He'd almost fucked me last night. Exos was the one who stopped him. Clearly, Titus had a control problem when it came to sex.

Part of me knew the assessment was unfair.

The other part was too exhausted to care.

"Take me to the dorm," I said, voice low, my gaze falling to the ground. I didn't want to see Titus's expression, didn't want to know what he thought. I just wanted to lie down. Fighting those flames had taken a lot out of me. So had this entire morning, or day, or however long it'd been. Actually, no, this whole fucking week had exhausted me.

Exos pulled me with him, away from a sputtering Ignis and her two insipid friends.

Away from the warmth of Titus.

"I don't know what happened," I mumbled, Exos's palm a brand against my hip as he led me through yet another courtyard. *The fae really like being outside.* Except this one was vacant save for a few heads poking out of windows, all eyes on me. When I glanced at a few, they ducked. Afraid.

They all hate me.

"Your emotions created an inferno," Exos murmured. "But you were able to contain it."

"Why did it burn me? It's never done that before." Sure, it singed my clothes to ash, but it didn't *hurt.*

"I don't know," he replied, taking me through a set of black gates lined in fire. The buildings took a drastic architectural turn, the landscape black and charred, all signs of flowers and trees gone. But it wasn't so much barren as it was intriguing, the fountains in the yard flowing fire instead of water. And little flickers that reminded me of lightning bugs buzzed about.

"Wow," I whispered, awed by the sight. "This is..." I had no words.

"Fire," he supplied. "I'm heeding Titus's point that you need to be near the students, and have procured you a dorm here. I'll be staying with you." I missed a step at his proclamation, but he caught me with ease, his lips curling.

"Surprised, princess?"

"Y-you're staying with me?" I stuttered.

"Yes." He gave me a wry glance. "You need supervision. No more burned-down buildings. But hey, the Fire Quad is actually fire-retardant, so that's a plus." While he spoke the words in a teasing manner, they didn't lighten my feelings in the slightest.

Because he was right.

I kept hurting people and destroying everything around me.

Rick.

The bar.

Elana's house.

The path.

I really am volatile, just as Titus said.

"Hey," Exos murmured, gripping my chin and drawing us to a halt outside one of the buildings doors. "I wasn't trying to make you feel bad, Claire. I actually meant it as a positive thing—that we'll be safe here."

I swallowed, trying to look away from his too-blue eyes, but he held me in place, his pupils flaring. "I… I know you didn't. But you're right." The last part was said on a whisper, my throat suddenly tight. "I don't mean to keep hurting people, Exos."

"Oh, darling, I know." He cupped my cheek, pulling me to him. "I can't begin to understand, Claire. Our upbringings are so different. But I can tell you one thing."

I clung to his suit jacket, allowing his comfort, seeking something, *anything*, to make the pain go away. "What?" I whispered.

"Watching you handle that fire was one of the most beautiful sights I've ever seen." The words were against my ear. "Whether you caused it or not remains to be seen. That you were able to dispel it, that's what counts, Claire. It means you're learning control, and far faster than anyone I've ever known." He shifted back to stare down at me. "You're going to be okay. I promise."

"I don't feel okay," I admitted.

"I know." He pressed his lips to my forehead. "But you will. Let's go up to the room. I'll make us something to eat, and maybe you can show me how you created that mist tunnel." He didn't wait for the answer but instead linked our fingers together and slowly led me inside.

Several students with pointy ears poked their heads into the hallway, their mouths gaping wide at seeing Exos. Then freezing as they spotted me behind him.

I didn't try to smile or wave this time. I learned my lesson in the quad.

No one wanted me here. That much was clear.

Well, I don't want to be here, either, I thought at them, my heart skipping a beat in my chest. *None of this was my choice.*

Not Exos.

Not Titus.

Not this entire damn world.

My mother did this to me. A warning would have been appreciated. Some sort of note that said, *Oh, by the way, you're part fae,* would have been great.

But I received nothing. Not even a warning call from the Fae Realm. Just Exos showing up at the bar, kissing me, and stealing me into this world.

Now they wanted me to attend an academy where everyone hated me. Fan-fucking-tastic. Oh, and I had bound myself to two men. One of which was apparently a man-whore, and the other, a dick.

Well, he wasn't acting mean right now.

And Titus, I really didn't know. Maybe he had an excuse? He didn't know me when he slept with her.

Oh God. Of all the fae to sleep with, he chose *her?* What did that say about me? I was nothing like Ignis. Was that his usual type?

Why am I beating myself up over this? I hardly know him.

Yet, I almost slept with him.

"Here we are," Exos said, pushing through a door into a modern living area with all-black walls and furniture. Even the kitchen was painted in ebony shades. However, it maintained a clean feel, the marble beneath my feet reminding me of granite.

Exos closed the door behind me, pressing his thumb to some sort of high-tech lock that shifted beneath his touch. The shades in the room lifted to reveal a view of the forest lining the property, the leaves almost beckoning me out to play.

"Your bedroom is through there." He pointed to an open threshold that revealed a decent-sized bed and dresser. "I'll be in the one here." He gestured to the room across the hall. "I, uh, didn't know what clothes you wanted, so I ordered a selection. And of course your uniforms."

"Uniforms?" I repeated, frowning.

"Yeah, you know, traditional plaid skirt, sweater thing." He shrugged. "Guys wear slacks and button-downs. Pretty standard."

"For a private high school, maybe. But this is supposed to be like a university, right?"

He palmed the back of his neck, looking uncomfortable. "Elana thinks the uniforms help give the fae a united feel. The less competition the better."

"Why?" I wondered.

"Because our elements can either exist peacefully or negatively." He dropped his hand and cocked his head toward the kitchen. "I'm going to fix us some sandwiches. Why don't you go check out your room?"

"Uh, sure," I said, staring at his back as he walked away, dismissing me.

Because he's Exos. A Royal Fae Prince.

And I'm just Claire, a volatile firecracker.

My lips curled down at the side. This whole pity thing wasn't me. I always fought through my hardships. My grandmother used to say I had a spine of steel.

But I didn't feel like that right now.

I felt more fluid. Bendy. Breakable.

And I hated it.

I wanted to fight yet didn't know what to fight against. Or how. Or even who.

Well, I knew one thing. Moping around in this state of hopelessness wasn't going to fix a damn thing. It wasn't me. I didn't just give up. I struggled until I won.

Stubborn to your very core, my grandmother used to say.

I am, I agreed, walking into the room Exos stated was mine. *I just need to accept what is and move forward.*

In this very strange bedroom...

My brow furrowed as I eyed the charcoaled furniture and black sheets. Not my usual style, but being immune to fire was certainly a plus. I brushed my fingertips across the quilt, finding it surprisingly soft. *What is this made of?* I marveled. It reminded me of silk.

I went through the drawers and then the closet. The uniform consisted of a plaid skirt and a sweater, just as Exos had described. But the pinks and purples were beautiful and unlike anything I'd ever seen. I plucked it off the hanger to hold it up to myself in the mirror, enjoying the way it popped against my skin and hair.

"The Fire Fae have special outfits that are flame-retardant for, well, obvious reasons." Exos stood just inside the walk-in closet, a mug in his hand, his shoulder braced against the door frame.

I'd not heard him approach, too lost in the mirror against the wall. "I, uh, okay." My cheeks pinkened to match the fabric in my reflection. "I was just seeing if it would fit."

He grinned. "It'll fit." He held out the mug. "I made you some hot chocolate, if you want it. The sandwiches are baking."

Baking? I pushed that thought away in favor of the item in his hand. "Hot chocolate?" My heart skipped a beat. "I... I would love some hot chocolate." I couldn't remember the last time I'd indulged in a hot chocolate. My grandmother used to make it for me as a child.

After hanging up the uniform, I accepted the warm gift and let the heat seep into my cool fingertips. "Thank you."

"You're welcome." He tucked a piece of my hair behind my ear and took a step backward into the bedroom. "Is this okay? The accommodations, I mean."

"Yeah, it's, well, different. But it's fine."

"Okay, good."

I followed him and sat on the bed with my back braced against the headboard, my dress flaring over my legs. My shoes were in the closet already, leaving my feet bare. I blew across the mug before allowing myself a sip and groaned at the flavors bursting on my tongue. This wasn't like any hot chocolate I'd ever tasted, the whipped goodness decadent and empowering.

He smirked and sat beside me on the bed, crossing his feet at the ankles to reveal a pair of dress socks that matched his elegant attire.

"Do you always wear suits?" I asked, trying for simple conversation.

He shrugged. "Depends on the situation."

"Yeah?" I eyed him sideways. "And when does the situation require you to wear that hideous royal garb you forced on Titus?"

Exos chuckled, shaking his head. "I can't believe he actually put that shit on. I had a pair of jeans and a shirt waiting for him in the other room."

"He was in a hurry after you told us to head downstairs."

"Not *that* much of a hurry," he said, laughing again. "It's a formal outfit that hasn't been worn in probably two or three hundred years. He's probably going to destroy it, which might disappoint Cyrus." He shrugged. "Was totally worth seeing Titus in it, though."

"You're mean," I accused, smiling. Who knew this man had a sense of humor?

He gave me a look. "You can't tell me you didn't enjoy seeing him in that atrocious outfit?"

I hid my amusement behind my mug. "Maybe a little."

"Uh-huh." He nudged me with his shoulder and reached over to press his palm against my mug. Heat flared against my fingertips as he used fire to keep the contents warm.

My lips parted in awe, my own fire igniting to do the same and bringing the liquid to a boil. "Wow," I whispered, staring down at the bubbling chocolate.

"Try stirring it," he murmured, releasing the mug.

"With what?" There was no spoon.

"Air." He studied the drink, his head tilting. "Perhaps water, too, as I added some to the mixture."

I considered his suggestion and exhaled over the top of the rim. It created a tiny ripple that I tugged on and swirled with my mind, the contents shifting with my mental command. "Oh…" It was working. The bubbles smoothed as I whirled the chocolate with another breath, the sweet aroma tickling my nose.

"It's all about control," Exos said softly, his blue eyes simmering as he observed.

"Why is fire so much easier?" I asked, calling for it again to heat my cup and infusing more air to twirl it through my drink.

"It seems to be tied to your emotions. Calling the flames is a natural defense. It's also the most passionate of the elements." Embers danced along his fingertips, jumping into my hot chocolate and joining my atmospheric storm.

I smiled as I absorbed his energy with mine, the feeling so incredibly natural. "Maybe I'm more Fire Fae?"

He shook his head. "No, you're very much a Spirit Fae."

"But I don't seem to be doing much with spirit."

"Because you don't know how to use it yet." His expression darkened a bit. "It's the most powerful element in existence and therefore the most important to understand before you access it. You literally hold the lives of those around you in your hands when you play with spirit."

I stopped playing with the hot chocolate, his words chilling me. "What do you mean?"

"When you have the power to create life, you can also take it. Or…" He met my gaze. "Or you can manipulate it."

"Like telling people what to do?"

He nodded. "But it's more than that. Spirit gives us access to the souls of every living, breathing thing, from the trees outside to the fae in this dorm. And the more powerful the Spirit Fae, the stronger the ability to take control. It's considered a very dark gift, Claire. Most of my kind only use it on a superficial level as a result."

"And you?" I asked.

His expression hardened. "I use it as required as the strongest Spirit Fae in the realm."

"By taking lives," I translated. "Or repurposing them."

"Only in very dire situations. But yes."

I swallowed, finally understanding his purpose here. "That's why you've been assigned to me. To rein me in, or kill me, as required."

"Yes." No hesitation or guilt or apology. "However, my goal is to help you thrive, Claire." He drew his finger across my cheek and down my neck as an alarm sounded in the other room. "Sandwiches." He gave me a small smile before sliding off the bed to leave me with the hot chocolate. It'd gone cold in my hands, my fingers turning it to ice at his words.

If Exos couldn't help me find control over these wayward powers, he would be forced to hurt me.

No, to kill me.

Or worse—possess me.

I shivered. *What if I can't master these abilities?*

Focusing again on my cup, I brought the drink to a boil and tried to access the water inside to stir the contents. When nothing happened, I blew again, re-creating the action from earlier. Then I tried something different by pulling the liquid up with my mind to create a funnel over the rim.

It resembled a tornado of molten chocolate.

I tried tasting it and found the flavor to be the same as it was before, but even more potent. *Magical.* And so, so delicious.

After a few more sips, I coaxed the liquid back into my cup and noticed Exos watching from the doorway with two plates, one in each hand. "I didn't want to interrupt you," he said, his voice huskier than before.

My cheeks heated as I set the mug aside. "I was playing."

"I know." He settled beside me again, handing me one of the dishes. "Your knack for air is growing. I don't have an advisor for you in that element yet, but I'll work on one. Elana mentioned a Vox; apparently, he's tutoring an Earth Fae already and doing a good job with him." He took a bite of the strange green thing in his hand and shrugged. "A task for tomorrow."

I was too busy staring at his food to really hear and comprehend his words. "What is that?" I had one on my plate as well. It reminded me of a lettuce wrap, except cooked. And the stuff inside was definitely not anything I'd seen before.

"Take a bite and find out," he taunted. "You'll see."

I poked the foresty globe on my plate. "Eh…"

"Live a little, princess." He winked and took another bite, then reached around me to grab my hot chocolate and took a swallow before returning it.

The act felt intimate somehow, as if we did this every day.

Yet this was the first time he'd ever been normal with me. Well, as normal as a fae could be, anyway. This sandwich didn't qualify. Neither did the elemental magic tricks.

He arched an eyebrow at me. "If you don't at least try it, I'm going to be offended, Claire. It's not as if I go about cooking for just anyone, you know."

Because he was a Prince. He probably had manservants. Or maybe more of those pixie things that Elana had used.

"Fine." I could at least taste it. The hot chocolate was one of the best I'd ever tasted. Maybe this *sandwich* would join the list? I eyed the globe and picked it up with my hands—like Exos had. The texture reminded me of a moist tortilla, only it was leafy like lettuce.

And so, so *green.*

I took a small bite, expecting the worst, and raised my eyebrows when the taste exploded in my mouth. Spicy but sweet, and delicious.

Yet, mushy.

And not at all what I would call a *sandwich.*

It was more like hummus mixed with crunchy vegetables and beans, heated into a spinach casing with a gooey texture.

Exos waited until I swallowed to ask, "Like it?"

"It's… different."

"It's a sandwich," he replied, acting as if I'd lost my marbles.

"This is not a sandwich," I assured him. "It's like a, uh, melted salad in brick form. There's not even meat on it. Or cheese."

He gave me the most offended look imaginable. "Why the hell would you put meat and cheese in a sandwich?"

I gaped at him.

And giggled.

"Meat and cheese in a sandwich." He shuddered. "Gross."

My giggle blossomed into a laugh that shook my shoulders, the goop on my plate forgotten as I keeled over in a humorous fit. He sounded so displeased by my comment, as if I'd made the most ridiculous suggestion. And hey, maybe to him, I had. Because he wasn't human.

He was a fae.

A fae meant to be my protector and executioner.

I couldn't stop laughing, the hilarity of the moment and situation unraveling inside me. I burned down a bar. *Me. Claire.* What were the chances? Oh, apparently good because I was a fae, too. I battled an inferno today—one I seemingly created. And I fought it with my *breath*.

My body vibrated with uncontrollable mirth. I couldn't stop, the burst of emotion requiring an escape. An outlet. *Something.*

Exos said something, but I couldn't hear him over the thoughts pelting my brain.

I'm a fae.

I control fire.

Wind. Er, air. Whatever.

Water.

Hot chocolate.

And I'm eating goo for lunch. Is it even lunch? Oh, who the hell knows?!

I lost it. Completely lost it. Tears sprouted in my eyes from laughing so hard, tears that turned to sobs. Sobs that *hurt*.

But I deserved it. Because I hurt people.

Rick.

Those girls outside. They may have provoked me, but that didn't warrant me burning them alive over some petty jealousy. Jealousy over a man I hardly knew, yet almost fucked last night.

Oh God… I couldn't stop crying. Couldn't stop laughing. Couldn't stop *being*.

So much for being strong and fighting through my shit, because all I wanted to do right now was curl into a ball and hide.

And I did just that, tucking my knees into my chest while burying my face against my forearms, and let it all out. Every ounce of fear, agony, and sadness, that I'd harbored for days, flew from me in a cacophony of sobs mingled with strangled laughs.

The plate clattered to the floor.

I didn't care.

Exos wrapped his arms around me, his chest to my back, his face in my hair.

I didn't care.

He whispered words of encouragement, his comfort an undeniable force behind me.

I didn't care.

The sun fell outside my window, the tears still flowing.

I didn't care.

I was broken.

Shattered.

Irreparably lost.

And...

I didn't care.

Except that was all a lie. I cared about every minute detail. Which was precisely the problem. I cared entirely too much.

That was what destroyed me.

My actual inability to let it all go, to just accept my fate. And maybe I would eventually. But not tonight.

Tonight, I mourned.

For Rick. For the bar and anyone else I hurt. For my friends that I would never see again. For Elana's house. For the girls I almost hurt outside hours ago.

And most importantly—I mourned for myself.

For Claire. For the woman I used to be. Because she didn't exist here.

It's only me.

CHAPTER TWELVE
EXOS

WATER.

Why am I in water?

I tried to shake off the strange dream, my nose catching in Claire's lavender-scented hair. My arms tightened around her reflexively, some ancient part of me pleased by her nearness—the part that called for our bond.

Falling asleep with her body pressed up against mine had felt natural. Almost *too* natural. But she needed comfort, and I wasn't strong enough to reject her. The spirit essence inside me recognized his mate, whether I liked it or not.

No other Spirit Fae had connected to me the way Claire had, and all through a meager kiss. She'd floored me, knocked me off-kilter, and ruined me for anyone else.

What made it worse was it seemed she required a mate for each element. It wasn't necessarily unheard of for Spirit Fae to have two mates because of our ties to two elements, but most only bonded with one fae. However, on the occasion when a Spirit Fae took two mates, it was one for each element.

And Claire had access to five.

Fuck.

I never saw myself falling into the mating rites, having opted for a life of guardianship. My brother was the one meant to settle down with another and try to create more Spirit Fae.

If he saw me now, he'd laugh. *Cuddling.* An activity I never engaged in, even post-sex.

I almost laughed, then remembered how Claire had giggled over the sandwich and broke down in sobs. Her emotions were all over the map, making it very difficult to predict her reactions. Holding her as she slept was the only comfort I could offer her, and I worried it wasn't enough.

Nuzzling her hair, I sighed. She felt so incredibly right in my arms. I never wanted to let her go, or wake from this strange, warm cocoon. But something nagged at me. The reason I woke up.

I squinted into the darkness, her shutters closed for the night.

Everything seemed all right. So what caused me to stir? Had she moved? Was it a strange dream? I glanced around, searching for the culprit of our disturbance.

Then I *heard* it.

Water.

Had I left the faucet running in the kitchen? Damn. That was exactly what it sounded like.

Easing away from Claire, I made my way into the living room and frowned at the quiet sink. *Where is that noise com—*

The front door began to bow, trickles of water flowing in through the cracks.

"What the fuck?" I breathed, inching closer. Then my eyes widened at the crashing sound just outside. "Oh, shit!" I ran back toward the bedroom, only to have the door slam into my back as a tidal wave swept into the room, throwing me to the ground and then up into a tornado of water.

Claire!

The room filled quickly, my access to air gone before I could utter a word or a warning. I swam toward her, my dress pants and shirt weighing me down. Kicking off my socks as I moved, I managed to meet her halfway, her eyes wild beneath the water.

I gestured at the window and blew a bubble.

She frowned.

Air, I mouthed. *Use your air!*

Because if she didn't burst the glass, we were both going to drown.

Unless I forced her... My spirit drove to the surface, my fight-or-flight responses kicking in, ready to dive into her and take hold of her powers. I hated doing this, the darkness of manipulating others not something that appealed to me, but this was life or—

Claire grabbed my hand and sent an explosion of air at the glass, shattering it. The water pushed us through the opening, sending us sprawling out across the charred ground outside with her on my chest, sputtering.

Several other students were already outside, soaking wet, most in little to no clothing due to the midnight hour. Many were crying. Others gulping in air, terror rendering them speechless.

Fire and water did not mingle well together given their opposite properties.

"Wh-what happened?" Claire asked, her soaked dress clinging to her curves.

"I don't know." I pushed her damp hair away from her face and pressed my lips to her forehead before guiding us both upright. The water seemed to have evaporated, several of the Fire Fae using their gifts against the tidal waves. But the damage was already done.

And from what I could sense, we'd lost at least one life inside. Perhaps two.

"You!" A shriek came from across the yard, the bitchy female from earlier pointing her manicured nail at Claire. "You did this!"

Everyone turned to stare at us, several jaws dropping at the realization of just who had appeared outside.

"I... I didn't," Claire said, her voice soft, barely audible.

"First you try to fry me with my own essence, and now drown me?" the bitch continued, stalking toward us in a tiny pair of shorts and a completely translucent tank top, her fiery hair a mess over her shoulders. "If you want to duel, bitch, let's do it. Right now. Right here."

Gasps fluttered through the air, the challenge a lethal one.

"Sit down and shut the fuck up," I said, pushing to my feet to stand between her and Claire.

"No!" This girl—*Ignis*—clearly had an issue with authority, because she popped her hands on her hips and stared me down. "I'm not standing for this bullshit. That bitch tried to kill me today. *Twice.*"

"It's true," her blue-haired friend said, coming to stand at her side. "I recognize water when I feel it, and that essence came from her." She pointed a finger at a now-standing Claire, her gaze oozing malevolence.

"But I didn't," Claire whispered, her face falling. "I-I don't think I did, did I?"

Ignis snorted. "Oh, brilliant. She doesn't even know if she did it or not? Yeah, like I'm buying that shit."

The blue-haired Water Fae folded her arms and tapped her bare foot on the ground, her gaze narrowed. "You totally did. I can still feel the power rolling off you. So don't bother denying it."

I frowned. While I felt the power still swirling in the air, it didn't remind me of Claire. Just like with the fire earlier. Neither reminded me of her inner spirit, confusing my instincts.

Was she accessing power from a place I couldn't sense?

Was our bond not as deep as I thought?

"What the elements is going on out here?" a deep voice demanded.

Ah, fuck...

The crowd parted to allow Mortus entry, his silk robe cinched around his slender waist. A flicker of surprise entered his elegant features at spying Claire, then his gaze narrowed into tiny black slits. "What the fuck is she doing here?"

"Elana made arrangements for her to stay in the Fire Quad," I explained, my tone flat. I moved subtly in front of Claire, hiding her from Mortus's view. "I'll handle it."

"You'll handle it?" he repeated mockingly, glancing around the water-laden courtyard, the shattered glass windows, and the disheveled state of all the Fire Fae around us. "You're doing a great job of that, *Your Highness.*"

Ignis and her friend smirked, causing my eyes to narrow at them. "What are you even doing in the Fire Quad?" My query was meant for the Water Fae. I didn't know her name. She reminded me of a troll with her made-up eyes and wild blue hair.

"I don't think that's any of your business," she snipped. "But I was staying with Ignis after her traumatic experience earlier."

"Traumatic experience?" Mortus echoed.

"Yes. The Halfling tried to kill me," Ignis said, her tone breaking at the end and causing me to roll my eyes.

"Oh, cut the crap," someone snapped before I had a chance to speak. Titus appeared in a pair of pajama pants and slippers. He resided in one of the other dorms. Either the commotion awoke him, or Claire's distress. Likely the latter, as I felt it trickling through our bond like an alarming beacon. "You provoked her and she defended herself. And how do we know Sickle didn't cause the dorm flood?"

Sickle. That must be the Water Fae's name.

She looked positively affronted by the accusation. "Are you frigid kidding me? I was asleep, you jackass."

"So was Claire," I pointed out.

Sickle carried on with another ear-piercing squeal of an excuse while Ignis fed into the bullshit, and several others started speaking up on their behalves, siding with the mean-girl brigade. Mortus gave me a smug look as the tongue-lashing continued and calls for justice wrung out.

Claire's spirit diminished before me, her emotions turning dark, her shoulders hunched.

I ran my fingers through my hair, irritated as fuck. This had all gotten out of hand far too quickly. It would be a miracle to keep Claire at the Academy now after the two incidents today.

The fae were out for blood—*her* blood. Her innocence would matter little to them all.

"Enough!" Titus shouted, punctuating the command with a roar of fire that hummed over our heads and disappeared into smoke. "Go back to your fucking rooms, dry your shit, and go to bed."

Ignis smirked. "As if I will ever obey your command to go to bed. Again."

He took a step toward her, but I caught him by the arm and pulled him back. "You will do what he says. Now." I allowed her to see the power lurking in my gaze, the ability to force her to do just that, and smiled inside as the color drained from her perky little face. "I won't be repeating myself."

She took a step backward, tears gathering in her eyes.

"Don't even start," I snapped, tired of women crying today. "*Go.*" The word echoed across the quad, sending several fae running toward their dorms, including Ignis and her frigid bitch of a friend.

But Mortus stayed, his beady black eyes blazing with fury. "I told you this would happen. She shouldn't be here, Exos. This little experiment of yours is doomed to fail."

"Thank you for the input." I infused a hint of dismissal in my words, which, of course, infuriated him more.

"You're a pompous little prick, just like your father."

I raised my eyebrows. "You may be my senior in age, but make no mistake." I took a step toward him. "I am your superior in all ways. Now, fuck off before I make you fuck off." While I gave Ignis a glimpse of my power, I allowed this asshole to see it all. My gaze swirled with it, the aura of energy swimming between us and belittling his to ash.

He didn't bow, as one should, but instead stalked off, his shoulders stiff, in the direction of Elana's home rather than in the direction of the Fire Quad faculty quarters.

I sighed, glancing at a still-fuming Titus, who stood beside a shaking Claire. She wasn't crying—thank the gods—but her pale expression and curved shoulders indicated her to be on the verge of it. Or maybe shock.

"I-I didn't..." Her blue eyes flickered to mine, feeling my gaze upon her. "Exos, I-I'm sorry. I..."

I gathered her in my arms before she could finish, my lips in her hair and then pressing to her ear. "It's going to be okay, Claire."

She trembled against me, her head swaying back and forth. "B-but I almost killed you," she mumbled. "A-and I don't even r-remember doing it. Then the fire earlier, it was out of my control, and now this. And I can't do this, Exos. I'm so sorry. I'm making this all worse. Even when I try, I just hurt people. I hurt you." The last three words were a whisper, her broken voice fracturing my heart.

Something was happening here, something nefarious, because I would swear on my life that the flood had nothing to do with Claire. The signatures didn't match. Just like the flames. I *felt* her power in that bar. It didn't match what I sensed today.

Shaking my head, I cupped her cheeks, forcing her to meet my gaze. "We're going to figure this out, baby. I promise."

Her face crumpled. "I heard what they were saying, Exos. They hate me.

Because of what my mother did, what I keep doing." She inhaled slowly, as if striving for control not to cry. "You shouldn't have to do any of this for me, not after, well, everything."

"Oh, Claire. I *want* to do this for you." I brushed my lips against hers, knowing like hell that I would regret this later and not giving a damn right now. "You're mine to protect, sweetheart."

"You barely know me," she replied so softly I almost missed the statement.

"You're thinking like a human, not a fae." I nuzzled her nose, smiling at our ridiculous situation. She had no idea what it meant to initiate the bonds, yet she'd fallen headfirst into our connection. While she might not think she knew me, her spirit did. And that was what I called to me now—her inner strength—the need to embolden her taking hold of my instincts. She needed to know I had her back, that I believed in her, that I knew she could do this.

Stop fighting it, I told myself. *Let her see.*

My mouth sealed over hers, my fingers sliding into her hair to tilt her head to the angle I desired. She grabbed my shirt, her surprise evident in the way she parted her lips. I slid my tongue inside, my grip tightening as I took control and truly kissed her. None of that truth-or-dare shit from the bar. This was a real embrace, the kind of lovers, not acquaintances.

I wanted her to know me, to have my taste in her mouth for the rest of the week, to truly experience our connection and yearn for more.

And most importantly, I wanted her to believe in herself the way I believed in her.

My comments about dropping her in the Spirit Realm were all empty threats, words meant to piss her off and embolden her. But that tactic had not worked as I wanted it to. So this was my new path, my way of showing my support and allowing her to know a piece of me I never revealed to anyone else.

Her spirit brushed mine, the energy warming between us and flourishing into the night. *Yes,* I urged. *Dance with me.*

Power erupted around us, our souls mingling on a wave of existence only Spirit Fae could access. Wonder traveled through the bond, her surprise palpable and sweet and causing me to smile against her mouth.

"There's your spirit, baby," I whispered. Then I deepened our kiss before she could reply and showered her in adoration and encouragement in the only way I knew how—by allowing her access into my heart. It was where our bond originated and anchored, where the elements lived inside a fae. A private resource only mates could access and I granted her entrance into mine, providing her with the most intimate experience known to our kind.

But she needed this to ground her. She needed to *feel* my courage to bolster her own, to borrow some of my faith in her, to see how deep this connection could go if we allowed it.

You're going to be all right.

You can do this.
I'm here to help you.
Trust me.
Let me cherish you.

She couldn't hear my thoughts so much as sense them, the emotion behind them causing her to relax in my arms and return my embrace. So sweet and tentative, but addictive. If we weren't standing outside, drenched from head to toe, I'd take this a step further. But I could already feel the tug from Elana requesting my presence. Just a subtle nudge, one she could do as a Spirit Fae.

There would be another meeting.

And I needed to be there to protect Claire.

I pressed my forehead to hers, breathing deeply, my tongue already missing hers. We would pick this up later, after I assured her safety. "You're going to be all right," I vowed. "But I need to go handle Mortus."

"Why do I know that name?" she asked, her brow crumpling.

I cleared my throat. Titus must have provided her with the history. "Mortus is the fae your mother fought."

Her blue eyes flashed, her body going rigid all over again. "That's who…?" Her mouth dropped. "Oh God…"

I cupped her cheek again, pressing my lips to hers and then to her forehead. "Don't worry, sweetheart. I'll handle him."

"But he must hate me." Her gaze snagged mine. "I'm the product of her infidelity."

"Which isn't *your* fault," I said, wrapping my palm around the back of her neck. "You will not feel bad about actions and decisions that were out of your control. Do you understand?"

She swallowed, but nodded, her pupils dilating.

"Good." I kissed her temple before glancing at Titus. Fire blazed in his eyes, having witnessed the entire exchange between us.

Now you know how it feels, I told him with a look, understanding exactly how this appeared to him. Because I'd experienced the same pang of jealousy and annoyance when I found them naked in bed together. But unlike him, I already understood that Claire may need more than one mate to balance her power. That had happened to my mother, after all—hence Cyrus and I having different fathers.

Of course, that didn't mean I had to accept the same fate for myself.

Regardless, we didn't have time to waste on fighting over her. She needed our protection first and foremost, and right now, he was the only one I trusted who could help keep her safe.

"Can she stay with you for the rest of the night?" I asked.

He didn't hesitate, his response immediate. "Yes."

"This may take a while, which means you'll likely miss your classes today. Claire isn't ready to attend until we lay some ground rules for student interaction." Not to protect her classmates, but to protect *her*. The vicious things that were said to her over the last twenty-four hours were unacceptable and needed to be addressed.

Gods, I did not miss my time here. At all.

"Okay," Titus replied, his gaze falling to a frozen Claire. "I won't let anything happen to her."

"I know." And I did. Otherwise, I wouldn't be handing her over to him. But Claire seemed to need more convincing.

Oh, how the tides had turned.

I shook my head, amused.

And decided to throw Titus a bone.

"Ignis is a bitch, Claire." I tilted her chin upward, forcing her to focus on me. "She used an illegal potion to seduce him. I could smell it the second I found him yesterday. So try to take it easy on him. He's not a complete jackass." I winked to soften the insult.

She blinked. "A potion?"

"I'll let him explain." I pressed my mouth to hers once more—because I could, and wanted to—then finally released her. "Stay with Titus until I return, okay?"

She licked her lips, her gaze bright. "Uh, yeah. Okay."

I smirked, enjoying that dazed look on her face far more than I should. "Try to behave, princess. I'll be back soon."

Hopefully.

It all depended on the Council and how much begging I had to do. No one would believe me if I said it didn't feel like Claire. Which meant I needed a different approach.

Fortunately, I had one.

I just needed them all to accept it.

CHAPTER THIRTEEN
CLAIRE

MY LIPS TINGLED as I followed a silent Titus to his dorm.

Exos kissed me.

Like, well and truly kissed me.

And holy wow, was it good.

He'd awoken something inside me, something lively and buoyant—my spirit. I could feel it thriving through every step, the energy warm and familiar and strengthening my every breath. So much power. So much *life*.

It had shocked me at first, then floored me. He'd allowed me inside him in a way I didn't really comprehend, but I *saw* him. It felt as if I'd known him my entire life, my heart automatically trusting his to guide me.

For once in my life, I didn't overanalyze *why*. I just allowed it. Embraced it. *Enjoyed* it. Perhaps not the right place or time, but what did it matter? It'd happened. It was done. And I didn't regret a second of it.

Except for a little bit now as I stared at Titus's broad back. Mostly because just seeing all that expanse of tanned skin reminded me that I'd spent the previous night in bed with him. Then kissed Exos tonight as if he were my only lover.

Yet, I'd been upset over Titus having fucked Ignis the night before we met?

106

Yeah, that makes me a hypocrite.

Shit. I needed to say that I was sorry. However, I couldn't find the words. Because I didn't feel bad about kissing Exos. It felt too right for me to belittle it with an apology.

This was all so damn confusing. Especially considering my still-brewing attraction to Titus, something that remained evident as I moved past him in the entryway while he held open the door. The bare skin of his abdomen practically burned my arm, the intense heat causing me to trip over my own feet.

He caught my elbow, steadying me, his touch a brand against my arm.

I just kissed Exos. Passionately. I should not want to lean back into Titus now.

Swallowing, I pulled away and waited for him to lead, unable to meet his gaze. Not because I was upset with him, but because I couldn't trust myself not to react.

He made an irritated noise and pushed past me. My elbow felt cold without him, yet my mouth continued to hum with electricity.

I can't have them both.

But I sort of want to have them both.

This is so damn confusing.

Just follow Titus!

I shook off the war waging in my head and trailed after him, my hands clasped tightly before me. We walked up two flights of stairs to the top floor and stopped at the second door.

He didn't say anything as he waved me inside.

Then I couldn't utter a word, too captivated by the view.

His room boasted floor-to-ceiling windows that overlooked a new part of campus, one I hadn't seen yet, all lit up by the moon and stars above. A majestic garden of sorts filled with glowing plants and flowers.

I padded over to the glass, staring down at the enchanted vines curling and growing at impossible speeds and then trimming to allow more flowers to bloom. Every second was a new evolution, the garden shifting and changing at impossible swiftness.

"This building backs up to the Earth Quad," he said, moving to my side. "The vast garden separates us, but there are pathways between. Of course, they're constantly moving to adapt to the greenery, so it's easy to get lost."

"Wow." I stroked the glass as if to touch one of the glowing flowers, entranced by the magic sprinkled throughout the immense field. I couldn't even see the dorms beyond. "This is…" *Amazing? Nothing like home?* I had no adequate words.

"Yeah, it's something," he replied, running his fingers through his hair and taking a step back. "Do you, uh, need something to wear?"

I glanced down at my soaked clothing, my cheeks pinkening at the realization of how revealing this dress had become. "Er, yes. Please."

He nodded and disappeared into a bedroom off the living area. The rest of his space reminded me of the dorm room Exos had taken me to—all modern appliances done in black, stone floors, charred walls, and fireproof furniture.

Titus returned carrying a pair of shorts and a T-shirt. "Here. Bathroom is through there." He pointed to his bedroom.

"No roommate?" I asked, noticing it was the only door.

"No. I don't play well with others." His flat tone had me biting my lip and nodding.

"Right. I'll just go change." I walked quickly through his room, not wanting to invade his private space any more than I already had.

And found him waiting for me on his bed when I exited. His gaze ran over my shirt and shorts, his lips curling at the edges. "You look good in my clothes, Claire."

Oh. My face heated from the dark gleam in his green eyes. "I, uh, thank you?" The last word came out as a squeak, sending another wave of warmth over my skin.

I'm in so much trouble, I realized, my breath catching in my throat. *I really do want them both.* It was so wrong. I couldn't do this, couldn't be torn between them. But they each called to a different part of me. Parts I didn't understand. *My elements.*

Titus exhaled slowly, running his fingers through his thick, auburn hair. "Look, I know I fucked up. Well, sort of." He shook his head. "Look, Ignis is a bitch. She tried to force a bond on me with this seduction potion. And because her power is a reasonable match for mine, she managed to get me into bed. But I can't stand her. I'd never want to be with her, Claire."

I clasped my hands before me, unsure of what to say. It wouldn't be fair of me to judge him, not after my own behavior. Yet hearing his explanation put me slightly at ease. Until I remembered the rest of it. "What about the bet?"

His gaze narrowed. "You honestly think I'd be doing all this just to win some fucking bet?"

Did I? My lips twisted to the side as I considered, which had his face reddening.

"I realize you don't know me very well, but you should at least be able to discern my intentions. I mean, for fuck's sake, Claire. I willingly bonded with you. I'm a competitive man, but not *that* competitive." He pushed away from the bed to walk over to the windows, his shoulders tense as he shook his head. "I might kill Ignis."

For some reason, that last sentence made me smile. I rather liked the idea of throttling her myself. "She's a bitch," I agreed, joining him by the glass.

A horde of violet flowers had formed, each of them releasing crystals into the air that danced around the ever-evolving vines.

We stood in silence for a while, something I hadn't realized I needed until right then. But it gave me a moment to ponder everything and sort through my thoughts. About Exos. About Titus. About this place. About *me*.

I called a flicker of fire to play over my fingertips, smiling at how different I felt—powerful and real.

Ever since I'd arrived, I'd been battling this new reality, fighting Exos, and wanting nothing more than to hide. I lost myself last night to misery. And woke to even more pain. But Exos had done something to me, had awoken some aspect of my being that I hadn't known.

And now everything felt right.

I watched the flame dance across my skin. This truly was a beautiful, unique world. I could be someone brand new here. Someone important. I had the opportunity to prove everyone wrong. The ultimate challenge. I just had to be strong enough to accept it. Fierce enough to master these elements. Wise enough to trust the right mentors.

Such as the male beside me. "I don't believe there even is a bet," I told him, speaking my thoughts out loud. "I think Ignis made it up."

He snorted. "I know she did. I tracked down over a dozen fae who are idiotic enough to consider such a ploy, and none of them had heard a word about it. She's full of shit."

"I'm not sure whether I should be offended by her tactics or flattered. She seems to be going out of her way to ruin me without knowing me."

"She's had it in her head for months that we're going to be a thing. Me and her, I mean. And it's never going to happen." He shivered, clearly repulsed by the idea. "I'm not a saint, Claire. I've dated a lot. But I'm not a cheater." He met my gaze. "I'm devoted to our courtship. Until you tell me otherwise, I mean."

My heart skipped a beat. *Oh God.* "But I kissed Exos." I winced, not meaning to just sputter the words out like that. "I mean, it's… Well, I…" I shook my head, irritated with my inability to form a sentence.

Titus chuckled. "He kissed you, sweetheart." He took a step closer, the heat from his body warming mine as he crowded me against the window. "I accepted that he initiated a connection with you already, Claire." His palm went to the glass beside my head, his opposite hand grabbing my hip. "Just as he's accepted my courtship."

I swallowed. "Oh." It was all I could say, the only word I seemed to know. First, Exos. Now, Titus. These men were going to send me into cardiac arrest if they kept up these seductive antics.

He grinned and leaned into my personal space, his irises capturing mine. "Did you think his kissing you thwarted my claim, Claire? Because I'll take you right now and prove how wrong you are. Your fire is all mine, sweetheart, and that's a part of you that I'm not sharing."

Goose bumps trailed down my arms, my mouth suddenly dry. "So, uh, you don't care that I kissed Exos?"

"Oh, I care." He inched closer. "What I'm saying is I understand and respect your need to date us both. Because what we have isn't comparable. We're fire, sweetheart. And fire is all passion." He licked my lower lip, a trail of flames following in his wake. "Do you forgive me, sweetheart? Or do you need me to grovel?"

Shouldn't I be the one begging for forgiveness here? For almost burning him and Ignis alive? For kissing Exos in front of him after our intimate night together?

"I'm so confused," I admitted.

"May I make a suggestion?" he countered, his hips leaning into mine.

"Y-yes." I swallowed. "Please." I'd do anything to solve the puzzle in my thoughts.

"Stop thinking," he whispered, embers flickering between our mouths. "Just feel." He pressed his lips to mine. So different from Exos's. Not that I should be comparing them, but it was hard considering the short time span that had passed from earlier to now.

Yet, as Titus slid his tongue inside, all my worries vanished. His skilled strokes consumed me, his heat absorbing mine and causing me to arch into him for more. He groaned, his grip on my hip tightening.

"Titus," I breathed, flames erupting over my skin.

He lifted me into the air, bracing my back against the glass as he wrapped my legs around his waist. Then his fist was in my hair, holding me to him as he devoured my mouth, stealing all the air from my lungs.

So hot.

But even as my fire brewed out of control, his tempered the inferno, creating an erotic dance of elements around us. He was right. No one could touch this part of us, not even Exos.

My fire belonged to Titus.

Just as my spirit belonged to Exos.

Acceptance washed over me, my mind too exhausted to fight the truth any longer. I wanted them both, and I would have them both, so long as they would have me. Titus was right. I needed to stop thinking and just live in the moment.

I wound my arms around his neck, my fingers threading through his auburn strands and giving them a tug. He growled against my mouth, deepening the kiss and stirring an inferno in my lower belly.

Exos had ignited a need in me.

Titus was stoking that need to a whole new level.

It left me feeling dizzy and so incredibly aroused. Both of these men touched me in entirely different ways, yet it was all so interconnected inside me in a complex web of elements. It left me craving an outlet, a way to expel some of my pent-up power in a safe environment. And Titus provided me with that, by calling out my fire and wrapping it up in his own. The entire room was alive with light—*our* light.

I felt safe here.

Protected.

Alive.

"More," I whispered, sliding my palms over the bare skin of his back. "I need more, Titus."

He smiled against my mouth. "You want to play with fire, sweetheart?"

I nodded. "Yes." He was my outlet and I needed him. "Please."

"Mmm." His hands fell to the hem of my shirt and pulled it over my head, causing my nipples to stiffen despite the warm air. He kissed me as he lowered my feet to the ground, his grip falling to the shorts at my waist. "Are you sure?"

I didn't know if we were still talking about playing with fire or if he wanted to know if stripping me was okay. Either way, my answer was "Yes."

Warmth caressed my legs as he tugged the fabric down, causing it to pool on the ground at my feet and leaving me naked before him. His gaze ran over me, his pupils dilating. "Oh, I'm going to enjoy this." He lifted me again before I could reply and laid me out over the bed.

My pulse thundered in my ears, my nipples tightening to painful points of anticipation. *What is he going to do now? What do I want him to do?*

I licked my lips, arching as need coursed through me, only to have him walk to the end of the bed to rest his palms on the quilt beside my ankles.

Not what I expected at all. "Titus?"

"Shh," he murmured, trailing his finger over the arch of my foot. "Just feel." A line of fire sizzled along my ankles, sending warmth into my veins and calling my own element out to play. "It's all about the dance." Molten sensation swirled over me, climbing up my legs, each kiss a sizzle against my skin.

"Oh…" I squirmed, my thighs clenching as the flames crept higher. "This is…"

"Fun?" he suggested, leaning over to lick the side of my knee. "Hot?" He knelt on the bed, his mouth trailing the embers up my thigh. "Arousing?" The warmth reached my center, sliding over my slick heat and cascading a series of tremors through my limbs.

This was so *new*. Most boys just fumbled around, touching me as they saw fit, but Titus's movements were deliberate. Skilled. Erotic as fuck.

And the use of our shared element only heightened the moment, eliciting a passion inside me that required release. His name left my mouth on a plea, a worship, a prayer for more. He intensified the pressure of his gift, creating an inferno that encased my body, inflaming the room and igniting my very soul.

"You look gorgeous like this, drenched in my power," he whispered, his lips against my hip and sliding across my lower belly. "I want to taste you, Claire. Can I taste you?"

I swallowed, my heart in my throat, my entire form literally alive with fire and energy. "Yes," I hissed. "Yes." The need to unravel tightened within me, my stomach a bundle of nerves with no outlet, and oh, fuck, was it hot. I could hardly breathe, could barely think.

Just Titus.

Just the feel of his heat caressing my skin, and his lips touching me *there*.

I bowed off the bed, his palm landing on my belly to hold me down with a growl. And all hell broke loose around us. So much fire. So much heat. So much *Titus*.

His tongue slid up and down my slick flesh, his mouth a miracle between my thighs. I wove my fingers into his hair, holding him there as embers drifted up my abdomen to my breasts. Some part of me registered how much this should hurt, but my elements pushed back, creating a sensation unlike anything I'd ever experienced.

Hot and cold.

Lava and ice.

Euphoria mingled with excitement, stirring a catastrophic force inside me that begged to be released. He caught my clit between his teeth, nibbling just hard enough to send a jolt through my limbs and force my gaze to his. The hunger reflected in his forest-green irises sent me flying, my orgasm ripping out of me on an animalistic scream that could likely be heard across the Fae Realm.

And I didn't care, too consumed by the rapture flooding my veins to focus on anything other than trying to remember how to breathe. Ashes seemed to coat my tongue, fire crawling down my throat, and then Titus's mouth was there, possessing me, teaching me how to exist beyond the elements. Helping me to overpower the inferno, to control it, to pull it all back inside and soothe it with a few calming strokes.

Out of this world did not begin to cover what just happened.

I blinked into the dark room, shocked. It felt as if a bomb had gone off inside me, rattling the foundations of the world. Yet, his room remained undisturbed, the garden still glowing outside the windows. "That was…" I cleared my throat, my voice hoarse from screaming. "That was…" Nope. Still didn't have the right word. "*Amazing* seems too dull a description."

He chuckled. "I'm taking that as a compliment." He gathered me into his arms and pressed a kiss to my forehead. "Let me know when you're ready to play again."

"Again?" I could barely feel my arms and legs. Oh, but I hadn't repaid the favor yet. That was what he meant. Rolling to my side, I pressed my palm to his hard abdomen, exploring the muscular dips down to the top of his pants. He caught my wrist in his hand and brought it up to his lips, giving me a kiss.

"When I mentioned playing again, I meant with you, sweetheart. And after you've gotten some sleep." He placed my hand on his chest, over his heart. "It's only three in the morning. I could use a little rest." He brushed his lips against my hair, easing me into contentment.

"Are you sure?" I asked, yawning.

He chuckled. "Yeah, sweetheart. I'm sure." He pulled the blankets up over us, his shoulder acting as my pillow as I snuggled into his side.

"'Kay. 'Cause sleep sounds good," I admitted.

"I know." Another kiss, his arm tightening around my upper back. "Good night, Claire."

"Good night, Titus," I whispered, my eyes drifting closed in a blissful state. I'd wake him later by repaying the favor. But for now, I'd take the reprieve and just... rest.

Chapter Fourteen
Claire

Something soft drifted over my lips, causing me to stir from my cocoon of heat. Piercing blue eyes smiled down at me, causing me to grin in response. *Exos.*

He tilted his head, the motion endearing. "Morning," he whispered.

"Morning," I replied, stretching my legs.

Legs that were intertwined with Titus.

Who was asleep behind me with his chest pressed up against my naked back.

Oh, shit.

Exos knelt beside the bed, placing us at eye level. He brushed a curl away from my face before palming my cheek. "It's okay, Claire." His low murmur scattered a flurry of goose bumps down my arm. "But I am a little jealous that you sleep naked with him and fully clothed with me." His gaze dipped down to where Titus's arm was wrapped around my upper abdomen, my breasts completely revealed thanks to the fallen sheet.

I bit my lip, wincing. "I…" I wanted to apologize but didn't know how. Because I didn't feel remorse for spending the night with Titus, but I did feel bad about doing it so soon after kissing Exos. "I…" I cleared my throat, uncertain of how to proceed. "Sorry."

He leaned closer, his blue eyes smoldering as he refocused on my face. "There's nothing to forgive," he murmured, his mouth brushing mine. "You have five elements, Claire. Powerful elements. You need a balance."

I frowned. He couldn't possibly be implying that I needed five fae to help balance my elements. Right? Because that'd be insane. I could hardly handle the two of these men, let alone *five*.

He pressed his lips to mine once more, his kiss soft and coaxing, while Titus stirred behind me.

Uh-oh...

"How'd it go?" he asked, his voice deep with sleep and sounding sexy as sin against my ear.

"We've reached an agreement," Exos replied, the words fluttering over my lips. "The Council has granted my request to train Claire on Spirit Quad and prepare her powers for the Academy. If we can prove to them that she's stable, they'll allow her to attend classes." He kissed me softly before shifting to glance over my shoulder. "You've been excused from classes due to temporary reassignment."

"Good." Titus's arm lifted from my stomach, his hand shifting to my hip beneath the blankets. "I assume the three of us are relocating today?"

"Yes. The new quarters are being assembled right now." Exos cocked his head, his nose brushing mine as he gave me his undivided attention. "Spirit Quad is abandoned, but that gives us plenty of room to practice. Okay?"

I swallowed, a little hot and bothered by being sandwiched between two incredibly good-looking men. And now they wanted me to live with both of them?

"I think you rendered her speechless, Your Highness," Titus murmured, his lips against my hair. "Perhaps you need to help her find her voice."

"Hmm, yes, I think she's feeling quite shy at my finding her naked in bed with you. Again." His gaze lowered to my chest, causing my nipples to harden in response, my body alight with wonder and sensation and confusion. "Any suggestions?"

"Several." Titus's palm slid across my lower belly, the touch a brand against my skin as he pulled me backward. "I introduced Claire to fire play."

"Did you?" Exos stood, his fingers playing over his dress shirt, popping open the buttons with nimble fingers.

This can't be happening.

It has to be a dream.

"You two don't even like each other," I blurted out, then winced at allowing my thoughts to grace my lips. *Are you trying to ruin this?*

Exos grinned. "Maybe not, but we both like you, Claire." The fabric parted around his torso, revealing the toned physique beneath. He was leaner than Titus, but just as muscularly defined, almost in a regal sort of way. Fitting, considering his title. "It's not common for a Spirit Fae to take two mates, but it's not unheard of. Sometimes our affinity for a secondary element is strong, requiring an outlet. Clearly, you have a lot of fire in you." He finished removing his shirt, folding it and setting it on the nightstand beside the bed.

"I'm willing to work with it if you both are," Titus added, his thumb drawing a hypnotic circle around my belly button.

I resisted the urge to pinch myself, certain this had to be my unconscious mind indulging in this inappropriate scenario. But as the mattress dipped beneath Exos's weight, his eyes darkened with desire on my breasts, I realized I'd never felt more alive.

"You have a lot of power in you, princess. This is one way to help expel some of your energy. We'll absorb it for you. If it's what you want." He lay down beside me and fondled a strand of my hair that had fallen across my cheek. "I felt you come undone through our bond, Claire. Now I want to see it with my own eyes."

My lips parted, my blood heating. "I'm really starting to think this is real," I whispered.

Titus and Exos chuckled, their collective warmth searing me from both sides. Titus's hand slid lower, exploring the apex between my thighs. "Definitely real, sweetheart," he said against my ear.

I shivered, licking my lips. Exos tracked the movement with his gaze before leaning in to trace the same path with his own tongue. *Oh, fuck...* It served as an invitation, one I was hopeless to turn down.

Tilting my head, I accepted his offer and moaned as Titus dipped his finger into my weeping sex. Exos took advantage of my groan, his tongue sneaking inside to begin a dance that set my body on fire. Not in the way Titus had last night, but in an entirely new way. This touch was underlined with spirit, energizing me in a way no one else could.

The combination of elements left me wired and hot and rejuvenated. I felt unstoppable, protected, adored.

How is this my life?

Oh, who the hell cares? Stop thinking!

I had no idea where that last voice came from, but I listened to it and indulged in the sensation flourishing between the three of us. I thread my fingers through Exos's thick, ash-blond hair, holding him to me as he devoured my mouth. My other hand went to lie over Titus's as he explored me intimately, his fingers knowing and sizzling against my flesh.

Fire and spirit dueled inside me, both tugging on different nerves and exciting a maelstrom of activity throughout my body. I shook beneath the onslaught, overwhelmed and consumed by both men and the gift of their touch.

Exos cupped my breast, his thumb brushing my nipple and sending a jolt of electricity through my bloodstream. Then he nipped my lower lip, his eyelids lifting to reveal a pair of glowing irises. "Your arousal is invigorating," he whispered. "I've never felt anything like it."

He kissed me again before I could reply, his fingers pinching my nipple. I arched back into Titus, gasping at the fierce contact. His lips went to my neck, kissing and nibbling, while his hand continued to work beneath mine, his fingers stroking a desperate need between my legs. "Are you going to show Exos how beautiful you are when you come, sweetheart?" he asked against my skin, his voice husky and dark. "I think he's jealous that I saw it first."

I shuddered, the flames inside dying to be released.

Then Exos shifted, his mouth leaving mine to kiss my jaw and then lower to my breast. His hand went to my thigh, lifting it to rest against his hip.

I gasped as his lips closed around my nipple, the heat of his tongue a brand against my skin.

Fuck.

I squirmed between them, the dual sensations sparking a volcano inside my core that throbbed for release. "Exos," I breathed, my grip tightening in his hair.

Titus nipped my neck, his finger driving deep and eliciting a scream from me that resembled his name. I panted both of their names in succession, confused and aroused and needy as hell. I didn't know whom to focus on— Exos at my breast or Titus's hand between my thighs. Both were so, so good. So perfect. So *mine.*

I gave in to that little voice that told me not to think, not to consider the complications of the moment. And I let go completely, enjoying the way they handled me, the way they encouraged my power to flourish between us.

Exos skimmed his teeth across my stiff peak, forcing my gaze to his. A knowing gleam blazed in his irises, his soul seducing mine into an intimate dance that forced me out of this plane of existence.

The tension building inside me unraveled, sending me spiraling into an oblivion of elements that thundered through the room. Incomprehensible words left my mouth, my limbs locking in pleasure, stars bursting before my eyes.

Intense.

Perfection.

Addictive.

I wanted more. I craved a deeper outlet, a more passionate understanding, a *mating.* The realization caused me to tremble, my heart skipping a beat. *What are they doing to me?*

"Balancing you," Exos whispered, licking a path back up to my lips. I must have spoken the words out loud. Or maybe he read them from my eyes. "We'll help you learn how to fly with steady wings, beautiful, when you're ready. But for now, we'll keep you grounded in the only ways we know how."

"I can feel the bond," I marveled, finally sensing it for the first time. "It makes me want more."

"I know." He kissed me softly while Titus slowly drew his hand from between my legs, the dampness of my arousal creating a wet path across my skin. It left me quivering, stirring a desire for another round. I felt insatiable, needy, and undeniably smitten.

"We'll take it slow," Titus spoke against my ear. "Teach you about our world, our customs, our powers. To make sure it's what you really want, Claire."

"Handling both of us won't be easy," Exos agreed, his lips moving against mine. "That's what the courtship is about—learning about the other and deciding if it's what both parties want. For that, you need a stronger comprehension of your abilities and this world. But we have time. And we'll start training immediately."

Titus kissed my shoulder. "He means after a shower."

Exos's lips twitched. "No, I meant now." He kissed me again, his aura calling to mine on an intimate level that left me shaking against him. "Create something with me, princess."

"Like what?" I breathed, captivated by the swirling blue of his irises.

"Anything." He lifted his hand from my leg, holding it between us.

I pressed my palm to his and marveled at the stimulating connection. "More flowers?"

"If you want." An electrical charge caressed the air, causing Titus to shift at my back. He didn't leave but gave me space, allowing me to focus on the energy breathing life into my being.

The energy of Exos.

His spirit enticing mine.

"Think about something you want," he encouraged. "And show me with your hand."

"Anything?"

He grinned. "Within reason."

"Okay." I fell into the ocean of his gaze, drowning in all things Exos. Every inhale belonged to him. Every heartbeat. Every thought. He wanted me to create life. What would he enjoy? A pixie like Elana's?

Or maybe something from my home.

Like a butterfly.

I pictured a winged creature, giving it pink wings with my mind, and felt my heart warm at the idea as my fingertips tingled.

Exos smiled in approval as a butterfly fluttered above our joined hands.

"What is that?" he asked softly. "Your version of a fairy?"

"It's a butterfly." I urged it to fly around the room, its wings glistening with life. "It likes flowers."

"It's beautiful." He released me to tuck my hair behind my ears. "Just like you." He pressed his lips to mine once more, the kiss a possession and a promise wrapped up in one. "See how long you can keep it flying around. My record for a conjured spirit is three months, if you want a goal."

My lips parted. "Three months?"

He waggled his brows. "Consider it your first assignment, princess." He nuzzled my nose and glanced over my shoulder at Titus. "I think I might enjoy playing professor for a few weeks."

"We can teach her all sorts of things," Titus agreed, drawing a finger down my spine. "But I do want a shower first."

"You and me both," Exos said, some sort of understanding passing between them.

I gasped, understanding dawning. *They're still turned on.* "Wait, are you—"

Exos silenced me with his mouth, his tongue a familiar presence that scattered my thoughts. "Pleasuring you in the presence of another, I can handle. Watching you return that pleasure to a man who isn't me? Absolutely not."

"I agree," Titus said. "And I can't just leave the room, either."

Exos nodded. "We'll come up with a way to handle this. For now, I'll settle on a shower."

"There's only one here," I pointed out.

"Titus will go first while you show me what your butterfly can do. Then I'll shower."

"And me?" I asked, raising a brow. "When do I shower?"

Exos nodded. "You're right. You should shower first while we watch, then Titus can go after you, and I'll go last."

I slapped his shoulder. "That's not funny."

"I didn't say I was joking."

"For once, I actually like your demand," Titus added. "Up you go, Claire."

I scowled over my shoulder. "No."

"You can't turn down a royal," he said, smiling. "And he wants you to shower first."

"I thought you wanted a shower?" Exos gripped my chin to pull me back to him, a smile in his eyes. "Or was that you being difficult?" He kissed me before I could retort, causing Titus to chuckle as he rolled out of the bed.

"I'll let you know when I'm done," he said on his way out of the room.

Exos ignored him and continued kissing me, the moment intensifying now that we were alone. He pushed me to my back, his hips settling between mine. "I'm going to kiss you until he returns, Claire."

"Okay," I whispered.

"And I'm going to make you come again." The dark promise sent my heart into overdrive. "With my tongue." He nipped my jaw on his way down, his gaze oozing sin as he looked up at me. "Consider it an introduction to the courtship bond, princess. And you have two of us vying for your attention."

Oh God...

I might not survive this.

Yet, I couldn't bring myself to worry, not with Exos drawing a hot path with his tongue through my slick folds.

This is my new life.

Best to just embrace it.

And I did.

Twice.

Chapter Fifteen
Titus

Two weeks.

Two... fucking... weeks... well, *not fucking*.

I was about to lose my damn mind.

Claire moved beyond the thin veil of the opaque windows as she dressed for our training session. I coveted our lessons together because it provided us with alone time—just us and our fire.

Watching her as she slipped the tight-fitting fireproof garments over her head made the embers in me burn hotter. A feat, considering they were constantly smoldering in her presence.

She glanced in my direction, likely feeling my eyes on her, memorizing every inch of her body. Then she disappeared from view, leaving my fingers curling into fists as the raw need in me demanded an outlet.

As if on cue, Exos appeared at the other window that overlooked the training courtyard just outside the Spirit Quad. He arched a brow as if to remind me that I wasn't the only one with a claim on Claire's body.

Yeah, yeah.

Neither of us could stand the idea of Claire fucking the other, so we'd come to a painful truce. Giving her pleasure took the bite out of our need, but it wasn't enough anymore. And I knew he felt it, too.

Exos's eyes narrowed as though he suspected I might take Claire right here in the courtyard—while he watched.

Not a bad idea, I thought darkly.

A part of me didn't care anymore, but I also knew it would cause a divide that would echo throughout all the kingdoms. I couldn't have Claire—not yet—not until we'd established an understanding of how to make this work.

Sex wasn't necessarily a trigger to deepening a bond, but something told me if either of us fucked Claire, it would deepen our connection to something far more permanent.

Which meant I couldn't touch her. Not like that. Not yet. Not until we all came to a mutual agreement, because it was very clear that Claire would require more than one mate. Perhaps up to five.

She entered the courtyard twirling a baton I'd given her last week. The way she handled it now showed her improvement. The tips bled with tiny flames as she gave me a seductive, mischievous grin.

"If you keep glaring up at Exos like that, he's going to jump down here and join our sparring session. And something tells me it'll be your face he uses for a physical demonstration." Her words were a bit too matter-of-fact for my liking.

I rolled my shoulders back and cracked my neck, making a show of it. "I'm not afraid of the scrawny royal."

I slipped my arm around her waist as she stepped within my reach, and brought her hips against mine so she could feel how hard she'd made me just by standing there showing off the fire that connected us.

Her eyes widened. "I thought you, uh, just took a shower."

As if a hand job could possibly reduce the excruciating need that screamed in me. I let my voice drop, and I didn't care if the demanding huskiness of my tone came off too rough. "I'm tired of showers. Of this place. Of Exos spying on our training." I shot him a look while I said it, which earned me a smirk in response. This was supposed to be my time with Claire, and the bastard knew it.

But he clearly didn't trust me not to take this to the next level. Which I couldn't truly blame him for, as I felt the same way about him.

Claire pouted, her adorable bottom lip plumping out. She thumped her baton against my leg, causing the flames to lick up my sides. "You don't really mean that, right?"

Ah, she didn't understand.

"I would never leave you, Claire. It's just... *hard.*" I nuzzled into the groove of her neck.

"Oh," she said, breathless. She arched against me, pressing her breasts into my chest as my teeth grazed her pulse. Her resulting groan caused my cock to throb between us.

"Fuck, Claire," I whispered, my body on fire—literally.

She twisted in my grip to glance to where Exos tracked our every movement. "Exos is watching."

I know. I can feel his presence.

"You didn't seem to have a problem with that last night," I said instead, grinning when flames erupted around us. She sucked in a breath, the memory of her naked and crying out for more, painting her cheeks a delicious pink. That'd become our nightly routine. And sometimes a morning activity as well.

Claire dropped the baton and gripped my shoulders, her strength surprising me as she pushed me away. The echo of flames burned in her eyes, slowly overtaking the blue that marked her as a Spirit Fae.

Yes, give me your fire, sweetheart.

"I know what you're doing," she said as she narrowed her eyes. "You're trying to distract me, but I'm ready." She retrieved her baton and twirled it before crouching into the battle stance I'd taught her. "I'm going to prove to all the fae that I am not my mother."

A grin stretched across my face as I took a defensive position. Pride swelled in my chest. Yes, Claire was definitely ready to face the Academy.

But was I ready to let her face them without me by her side? Her first class would be on Air Quad—with Exos.

A fireball caught me on the chin, causing me to grunt before stumbling to my knee. I snapped my head back just in time to see Claire's baton coming straight for my face. She'd caught me off guard, but that was because I wasn't accustomed to elements being used against me in a fight. The one handicap of being a Powerless Champion was, well, real fae fought with their powers.

I caught the baton in my grip with ease and smiled at Claire's surprised expression. "Well done, sweetheart, but you'll have to do better than that to beat me."

I intended to yank Claire closer and seduce her some more, when she twisted from my grip in a maneuver I hadn't taught her. One glance up at a smug Exos told me I wasn't the only one who'd helped Claire grow.

My gaze dropped down to Claire, who held her palms together, her brows knitted with concentration as she summoned a new fireball—but it wasn't quite a fireball.

"Claire," I cautioned, hoping she wasn't attempting to combine her elements. She wasn't ready, even if Exos encouraged her. He didn't understand how raw and explosive her emotions were or how they impacted her powers.

Her jaw flexed as she worked on the ball of power. Its gleaming red flames licked around the edges of her fingertips before the other elements came into play in tufts of living color. A magical breeze kicked up and sent her hair flinging over her face, but she didn't move to push the strands away.

A sizzle of water fought against the flames, winning and morphing into something dangerous as an external, circular vortex crashed at her feet and wound circles up her body. It seemed to be climbing an invisible wall, threatening to cut her off from me. Permanently.

"Claire," I tried again, readying myself to intervene.

Except tight roots had bound my ankles to the spot.

Claire had used her spirit to create life, causing the ground to shift beneath us to secure her new creations.

"I'm okay," she said through gritted teeth, her voice distorted by the heavy magic weaving its way up her arms. "I can control it."

No. You can't.

I glowered up at Exos, who merely shrugged, clearly at ease with this display.

Jackass, I growled in my mind. Not that he could hear me. Not that he even mattered.

I refocused on Claire. I wanted to yell at her, strangle her, crash my mouth against hers and distract her from this nonsense, but I knew better. She possessed a fire that rivaled my own, and a passionate ambition that no one could take away from her. I would be a hypocrite to try.

My fingers curled into fists as she worked the fireball and tried to rein in the elements. A small smile played on her plump lips. "I think I'm doing it."

Exos joined us, his blue eyes glimmering in triumph. "That's beautiful, Claire."

Of course he approved.

"Yes, let's encourage her to work with elements we have no power over." Claire's fire might be mine, but the rest of her did not belong to me. If she lost control now, I would be useless to help her.

I did not like to feel useless.

"What's going on?" an approaching voice asked from the edge of the courtyard.

Exos frowned, eyeing the monstrosity growing around Claire. "Prepare yourself, River. We may require your affinity for water in just a moment."

I glanced over my shoulder at a gaping River, having forgotten about Exos inviting him over today. Claire was steadily gaining control over her powers, and while River couldn't reach her elements the same way Exos and I could—thanks to our bonds—he could still help guide her when it came to water.

Good thing, too, because that was the first element to rip free from Claire's careful grasp.

Her smile faded as the churning water around her intensified, spiraling up into the sky like the ground had erupted in a geyser.

"Claire!" I shouted, straining against the vines, which only dug deeper into my skin in response. I winced as the prick of thorns threatened to make my imprisonment even worse.

Of course, I was a stubborn son of a bitch, so instead of obeying Claire's magic, I sent my fire writhing over the vines.

"Don't," Exos bit off.

A single word—a command, one that needed to be obeyed.

My teeth grated together in defiance, but I dispelled the flames only because Exos had an edge to his voice. One I wasn't used to hearing—panic.

Claire had stumbled backward, her body blurring behind a waterspout mingling with violent gusts of air that would soon turn into a full-fledged tornado if not brought under control.

"Now, River," Exos said.

River grunted as he thrust his arms out. An invisible force shifted, twisting the geyser the wrong way to make it lose momentum. A sound of pain came from inside the vortex, making me jerk against my restraints.

"Claire!"

The vortex thinned enough for us to finally see her, causing the blood to drain from my face. Her skin glowed with a silver hue while white flowers came to life and died over and over again at her feet in a panicked cycle of renewal.

Exos stepped inside, braving the whirlwind of power, and gently took hold of Claire's arms. I couldn't hear what he said to her, but her eyes flashed up to him, full of silver and blue power that swirled with distress. He calmed her, then she looked at me and the fireball still in her hand grew.

She let out a long breath before she set the vortex on fire. It was a terrifying sight as the very air around her burst into a swirling inferno, but I immediately understood what Exos had told her to do. By allowing fire—the power she maintained the most control over—to engulf the other elements, she could mingle everything together and draw the energy back into herself.

Clever.

I watched, both with pride and unease at her raw, barely trained strength as she closed her eyes and calmed the storm. The elements slowly drained away and drifted like ash to the ground, sprouting up more white flowers in their wake.

By the time she finished, the entire courtyard was covered in the beautiful blooms.

River let out a long breath. "By the Elements, I almost wasn't able to break through her vortex." He glanced at me, a shaky smile mixed with worry on his face. "I don't know if I'm cut out to be her water mentor, Titus. I'm not able to help her, not like you." His gaze returned to Claire, mesmerized with her just as all the fae should be. "Your bonds are strengthening her far more than I ever could."

Hmm, no, River was definitely not suited to mentor Claire. Nor did they possess a bond-mate compatibility like Claire had with me and Exos. Which, unfortunately, implied she would eventually need a water mate.

Exos already speculated she'd need one for each element.

I sort of hated that he was right.

Claire sank to her knees, her smile indicating it to be from exhaustion, not emotions. Her gaze danced with delight. "I did it. I brought it under control with minimal help."

Just barely. But yes, she did. "Please don't attempt that again, Claire. Not until we've found more mentors to help sharpen your elements."

"Hmm, yes, on this I agree with Titus. We need to find you an air mentor. Fortunately, I have someone in mind." Exos flicked a wrist at me, sending the vines binding my legs unwinding.

My eyes went wide. "Don't tell me you could have done that this whole time."

His resulting smirk said it all.

Royal bastard.

"River," Claire said, ignoring my banter with Exos. "I'm so sorry for losing control like that. Thank you for helping me."

He ducked his head as his face turned pink. "It was nothing, Claire. I'm sorry I wasn't able to do more." He glanced at me. "I'm not like your other mentors."

Her grin widened. "No, I suppose not."

"Yes, as I said, we need to find a suitable mentor for air." Exos glanced up at the sky that had been green and angry just moments ago. "We'll be meeting the candidate I have in mind tomorrow when we visit Air Quad. He's in your first class."

Claire blushed. "Just a mentor, right?"

Exos grinned and brushed his lips against her temple. "That's not up to me, princess."

She leaned into him, her comfort with his presence evident in their interaction. I waited for the spike of jealousy to come, but it didn't, surprising me. Over the last two weeks, I'd sort of learned to accept her bond with Exos. Maybe because it was different, more subtle and mischievous. While with me, she burned with passion and need.

Intriguing.

Exos folded his hands behind his back and straightened, the Royal Fae returning for duty. "The candidate will be tested, of course." His gaze locked on Claire. "As will you. Do you feel truly prepared to face the fae and the Academy tomorrow?"

She smiled and slipped her arm through his, forcing him to buckle against her. "You'll be with me." Her gaze fluttered my way. "I just wish Titus could come, too."

"He has classes," Exos reminded her. "Don't you, Titus?"

I sighed. "I do."

As much as I wanted to be by Claire's side night and day, Exos was right. I had my own classes to attend now that I had permission to resume my academic schedule. So I buried my feelings and the need to protect her, finding the strength in myself to give my trust over to Exos to do that for me.

No matter what conflicts there were between Exos and me, he wouldn't let anything happen to her. Because his feelings for Claire rivaled my own.

He'd give his life to protect her.

Same as I would.

So, this new Air Fae had a lot to live up to. And, as Exos planned on testing him, all I could think was, *Good fucking luck, buddy.*

Chapter Sixteen
Vox

"YOU'RE THE ONE IN CHARGE HERE," I reminded myself, not caring if anyone heard me. Sometimes I needed a little pep talk before approaching Sol in the morning. The damn Earth Fae liked to forget that I was his mentor and he was only permitted in the guest room as a boon. He didn't get along with the Earth Fae—or any fae—but that was why I was his mentor. He needed me.

Right now, he was pissing me off.

Rolling my shoulders back, I inhaled a long, deep breath, held it, and then released it in a drawn-out gust that rattled his door.

Or, should have rattled it.

The damn Earth Fae had made a wall of stone around himself. I could feel it. A weight in the air made me want to sneeze, and my nostrils flared.

"Sol!" I shouted, then reduced myself to beating against the door with my fists. "You're going to make me late for class!" I couldn't just leave him in the Air Dorms unattended. He had to leave.

"Not going!" came the muffled reply of my earthy subordinate. "There's a wild Halfling on campus today!"

As if I didn't fucking know that. That was *precisely* why I needed to be bright and early for class.

I'd heard a rumor that she would be starting on Air Quad today, which meant I didn't have time for Sol's shit. No way was I going to miss this.

I stroked my short beard while I contemplated the best way to beat Sol at this idiotic game. He rarely walled me out like this, but when he did, it really drained my air magic to force him out. My powers needed to be at their height today.

Running my fingers to the back of my neck and securing the loop at my warrior's ponytail, I decided on a new tactic. "Are you telling me you're afraid of a girl?" I leaned in closer, knowing that Sol was right on the other side hanging on every word. "Or are you afraid of the royal?"

A hiss of sound, then a grating of stones as the wall shifted. I grinned.

"Not fucking afraid of that dirtbag!" was the reply.

I let out a low whistle, my powers over air sending the shrill notes vibrating through stone. "Oh really? Because it looks like you've spent the majority of your power making yourself a bunker in order to stay away from the royal. That's not the Sol I know."

I waited, then grinned when the stones shifted again and the slightest sliver of light came through the door. "Nice try, windbag. Not coming out."

I rolled my eyes. "Don't you have any more intelligent insults? Come on, Sol. The Air Quad is the last place you want to be today. They're saying the Halfling will be starting classes here, and if you want to be out of sight, then going back to the Earth Quad is your best bet to stay out of their path."

The wall crumbled, leaving the door to break off its hinges. I jumped back just in time for it to slam down on the place I'd been standing, leaving a very large and pissed-off Earth Fae on the other side. He wore his standard Earth Fae trousers that had gotten wrinkled from him sleeping in them, along with the loose tank around his broad shoulders. He intimidated most fae, but I knew Sol. He was all bark and no bite.

"You know why I can't go back there," he said, his words grating against the marble floors.

Not this again.

I threw my hands up and let them fall, releasing a gust of wind that blew away the dust from Sol's tantrum. Every time I indulged him and let him stay in the Air Quad, he thought he could just wall himself up here and not face the world.

Most fae would have kept their distance from Sol, but my powers made me fast and lithe, enough that I could move out of the way of his brutish strength as needed. Fighting an Earth Fae head-on was the mistake of many. I knew how to dodge, escape, and survive. It was what made me stronger than Sol in any match.

Moving to him, I rested a hand on his shoulder, only to brush aside the loose pebbles that had gathered in the crook of his collarbone. "Listen, Sol. Let's make a deal. I'll find out the Halfling's schedule and make sure you won't be anywhere near her or the royal guarding her, all right?" I gripped him and gave him a light shake. "Oh, also? Use what I have taught you. Don't wall yourself up when they come at you. Evade their attempts to rile you up. You can do it."

Sol set his jaw and looked like he was going to punch me. I angled my feet just in case he did, but then his face erupted in a wide grin and he crushed me to his chest in a hug. "You're right, Vox. You're right."

"Too... tight. Can't... breathe," I managed to squeak out of my crushed windpipe.

Sol laughed and released me, setting me back down. I was a tall fae, but Sol was a titan.

Coughing, I patted him on the arm again. "Okay, so, off with you."

I knew the Earth Fae didn't want to leave. The Chancellor had forced us into this collaboration, avid about multi-element partnerships, and Sol and I certainly had our ups and downs. I might be good for him, a little bit of air in his stubborn sails, but I was also a member of this Academy and needed some time on my own.

"Fine, Vox," Sol said reluctantly and marched past me, sending the walls shaking. He had so much trouble reining in his gifts. It was what made other Earth Fae afraid enough of him to bully him.

I could relate.

I had a history of my own, but I did better than most keeping that under tight wraps. It would take a tornado to reveal what had driven me to the Academy in the first place.

When blessed silence engulfed me after Sol's departure, I let out another long breath, wishing I could spend some time in meditation before starting the day. Today, however, there was no time for contemplation or reflection.

Excitement drifted through the air, palpable and enticing. Whatever energies this Halfling brought with her, it was realm-changing, and I wanted a front-row seat.

* * *

In spite of Sol's delay to my morning, I still arrived early to my conjuring class. This being a more advanced class, I didn't expect to see the Halfling. It made me want to wander outside and see if I could spot her.

"Did you hear we have a new student?" Aerie asked me, one of the Air Fae who often indulged in the latest gossip.

"Quit stirring up motes," I replied. Everyone on campus had heard about the new student. I didn't live under a rock.

"She's tried to kill Ignis twice now. First with her little show of fire power. *Then* by trying to drown her and Sickle and several others in the Fire Dorms. If Sickle hadn't been there, she would have killed Ignis. I saw it all. Well, the first incident, anyway. The second one, I was in the Air Quad."

I resisted the urge to roll my eyes. "Sounds terrifying," I said, placating her. Last thing I wanted to do was goad a fae known to stir up trouble.

"It was!" She kept jabbering, but other students thankfully indulged her bullshit, giving me a chance to meander away.

Pretending to be engrossed in a piece of lint on my suit, I brushed it off before I took my seat, a floating pedestal three desks down that gave me a perfect view of the door. I liked to see who came in and out. Conjuring took place in an enclosed orb where anything summoned—intentionally or accidentally—couldn't escape. It left the doorway as the sole entrance and exit.

With the clock nearly at the late-morning dial, the students started to stream in. Dark hair and uniforms made all the Air Fae look almost the same, but I could spot the small traits that set them apart. They liked to keep their hair short, which was why I'd let mine grow out. The last thing I wanted to be was just another Air Fae.

Then, there she was. I'd been talking myself out of the possibility of seeing the Halfling up close, but she was actually here. A bright glimpse of sunlight and golden hair as she eased into the room with her hands clasped in front of her thighs. The standard Academy uniform clung to her curves, which were far more sensual than an Air Fae's and immediately made my eyes wander from her head to her toes. I could write a song about her grace, undoubtedly innate in the lithe movements of one who wielded the element of air, but there was so much more to her that had me mesmerized.

A flash of dangerous dark-blue eyes broke me from the spell. Exos, the notorious Royal Spirit Fae, instantly took note of me and glowered. "Eyes to yourself."

An order.

I wasn't used to those, but I knew better than to challenge the royal, especially after what he'd done to Sol. The Spirit Fae could manipulate one's very will, and I had no interest in testing the strength of this particular royal's ethical qualms about doing that inside the classroom.

The Halfling fidgeted while the Air Fae took their seats. I tried not to watch her, but it was damn near impossible. She was so utterly fascinating with her round ears and beautiful blonde hair.

Everyone took their assigned seats, leaving the usual circle of empty pedestals around me open. The Halfling took one of the chairs closest to me before glancing between Exos and me, murmuring something I couldn't hear—which was impressive, given that air currents normally obeyed me and I could hear any whispered secret within my vicinity.

"Yes. That's him." The royal nodded, his words soft as he sat behind her, providing him with a clear view of her back and the entryway.

"Hi," the Halfling said, startling me when I realized she was actually talking to me.

"Oh, uh, hi," I said, resisting the urge to glance at the powerful Spirit Fae that was just at the edge of my sight. I didn't care for his proximity, but based on the light tremors of power in the air, that was exactly what he wanted—for everyone to feel uneasy.

Definitely a warrior.

The Halfling smiled shyly, and it felt like sunlight was exploding all around me again. A warm breeze swirled around her that immediately called to my innate element, coaxing me to lean closer, so I did.

The royal cleared his throat. "Distance, Air Fae."

Before I could reply—and with what, I had no idea—the professor entered and tapped a staff against the ground, sending light bursts of air fluttering through the enclosed room.

Professor Helios, one of the more ancient Air Fae, was considered a master of conjuring. He wore his dark hair long, a customary style for one of his age. The thick strands swept around him on an invisible breeze, giving him the illusion of floating. Lengthy robes added to the effect, and he surveyed the class with his inky eyes. Most Air Fae had darker-hued eyes, but not dark enough to overtake the pupil. Professor Helios, however, was powerful—and *old*—so he had an eerie kind of gaze that made it difficult to look directly at him.

He wasted no time and conjured an air sprite to his side. The Halfling let out a soft gasp that made something in me unhinge, but I managed to keep myself in one piece.

The small creature immediately began chittering and buzzed around the Air Fae's head.

"Class, as you can see, we have a new student," Professor Helios said with a sweeping motion. Wind was normally invisible, but when scented with power, it could send color through a controlled breeze. Helios's power was dark, and a shadow swept over the Halfling, making her stiffen. The royal subtly reached out to stroke his fingers through her hair, whispering secret words that I couldn't hear.

Strange. Exos was a Spirit Fae with an affinity for fire, not air. I should be able to hear them.

Unless...

Oh.

Now I saw it. He and the Halfling had initiated a courtship bond. That was what allowed them to speak to one another beyond my intrusion. Fascinating.

An odd surge of jealousy burst through me, causing me to frown. I had no interest in starting a courtship bond with any fae, much less the fabled Halfling. But there was something about her air that called to me.

"Vox," Professor Helios barked, the slice to his words cutting across my ears and making me wince. "You will partner with the Halfling for today's exercise."

A collective gasp, both of shock and relief, swept through the rest of the class.

I hadn't realized I was staring, but the Halfling caught my gaze and offered me a slight smile. *Wait, does she know who I am already? That the professor had just assigned me to her?*

"Vox?" Professor Helios repeated, impatience coloring his tone. "Do you think you can bring our new student up to speed?"

"Yes," I said, clearing my throat as I undid the top button to my suit jacket, hoping I'd feel less suffocated. "Of course."

Professor Helios stabbed his staff into the ground twice, signaling that today's exercises were to begin. "We will pick up where we left off last time. Conjuring figments of our imaginations are great displays of power, and useful, but it all starts with a flicker of our element. Today you will conjure controlled spirals of air at your desk." The creature complained as it flitted around his staff. The professor ignored it. "Keep them controlled, or else this little figment of my imagination will punish you." The air sprite cheered its approval at being involved.

The Halfling's eyes went wide. "Punish?"

I smirked. "Don't mind him," I said, turning to face her as I tried my best to ignore the narrow-eyed royal behind her. "Professor Helios just likes to rule by fear. Thinks that's what'll motivate the students. If you mess up, the worst the air sprite can do is bite you."

She let out a soft gasp. "Bite? Like a mosquito?"

I raised a brow. "Not sure what that is, but yeah, let's go with that."

"Vox," the royal said, startling me. I shifted on my floating pedestal to give him more of my attention. Sunlight struggled to shine in through the translucent barrier to the classroom, but it seemed to bow and waver uncertainly around him, his power a little too *wrong* for this place. He shivered as if sensing how much he didn't fit in here.

"I asked the professor to pair you with Claire. Consider this an audition."

Claire. I'd only heard her referred to as "Halfling" on campus, but I rather liked her unique name.

However, what I didn't care for were Exos's words.

"An audition?" I frowned. "For what?"

He didn't elaborate, instead reaching out to the Halfling to stroke her wrist. "Air was one of the first elements she manifested. After fire, of course. We've been working on controlling her elements, but with her access to all five…" He shrugged, leaving the rest unsaid.

Gods. All five elements in one beautiful, fragile package? I couldn't even begin to imagine how this Halfling had managed to stay in one piece this long.

He couldn't possibly mean for me to be her mentor during her classes on the Air Quad. I must have inferred that wrong. After mentoring Sol for so long, I should have felt like I was capable of anything, but this? Surely not.

My hesitation didn't go unnoticed. Claire moved away from me, just the slightest fraction that most wouldn't have caught, but I did.

"Exos, if he's not comfortable partnering with me, we can find another," Claire mumbled. "Or I can work alone."

Her uncertainty and distrust gave me pause. I didn't know what she'd been through, but I'd never seen such torment in someone's eyes.

Okay. I could handle one class. Maybe not an audition for the future, but today was fine. We'd discuss the rest afterward.

"Claire, is it?" I asked, closing the gap she'd created and rolling my hands on my knees so that they were palm up. A nonthreatening posture to help her feel at ease. "I've heard a lot about you."

Apparently, that was the wrong thing to say.

Heat flared on an invisible breeze that made her golden hair fly back over her shoulders, and her vibrant blue eyes danced with the dangerous spirit powers that sang with the royal's. I sensed that she couldn't manipulate will—or perhaps the royal kept that part of her powers dampened—but a wave of nausea swept over me as she shared a taste of her emotions through the fragile look she gave me.

Pain.

Guilt.

So much *guilt*.

Gods, how was she not splitting at the seams?

"I meant to say, I've been looking forward to meeting you," I amended, realizing the poor girl had likely been swamped with threats and cruelty. While I didn't believe a daughter should be held accountable for her mother's actions, I knew it was a popular opinion.

She narrowed her gaze at me, distrust in every line of her beautiful face. "Why is that?"

I didn't have a good answer for her. For over two weeks, something had put me on edge, so much so that I'd sought out the latest Academy rumors, only to find that there was a Halfling on campus. Ever since I'd known about her, I'd wanted to find her. For what purpose, I couldn't say; I just knew that I had to learn more about her.

That sounded so pathetic. I couldn't tell her the truth, so I opted for what I was best at in these situations.

Divert.

Evade.

Escape.

The class assignment was to conjure air spirals, so that was what I did. The task was easy enough for a fae with my power and control. I let out a soft whistle, and a spiral of air scented with my innate gift colored the element blue. Each Air Fae favored different hues when they worked their powers, but mine seemed to fluctuate with my mood.

This shade of blue meant I was intrigued. And not in a platonic sort of way.

My power is attracted to Claire.

Fuck.

I glanced at the royal to see if he somehow knew. Maybe he could read my mind. I mean, who knew what kind of powers a Spirit Fae like him truly possessed.

However, he didn't react other than to glance at the air spiral flitting around my hand before looking back to Claire.

Her wide gaze was locked on the spiral. I expected her to be afraid, but she seemed fascinated.

An unwanted heat crept over the back of my neck, making me grateful for my warrior's tail and beard. Displaying her effect on me, even if she didn't understand it, was far too intimate for two strangers such as us.

"Go on, you make one," I offered, taking the opportunity to disperse the air spiral.

Her eyes snapped up to mine, making me suck in a breath. Her powers rested just underneath the surface as if they could burst out of her at any moment. So many elements tangled with the beautiful swirling power that was kindred to my own. I sensed her wavering control over her air element and tugged at the wild, snapping strands before I could stop myself.

Her chest leaned forward at the motion as if I'd pulled on her heart. "Oh," she said, the sound more of surprised pleasure than pain. "That's, uh, pleasant."

"What are you doing?" the royal demanded.

Now that I had ahold of her wild power, I didn't dare let go. Each strand was so frayed on the end that I wondered how she wasn't in acute pain.

"Why didn't you come to Air Quad sooner?" I asked before I realized that I was chastising an all-powerful Spirit Fae who could make me squawk like a chicken if he wanted to. "She needs guidance," I clarified.

The royal straightened his spine and narrowed his eyes, then surprised me by uttering a single word. "Continue."

* * *

"Does that feel better?" I asked, hoping Claire could sense what I was doing.

She shifted closer to me until our knees touched. Her skirt ran up her thighs from the motion, giving me a better view of her skin that glowed with power.

Not just power, but also the sweeping blue electricity that was scented with my magic.

Imagining her skirt inching up just a little more had the aura turning a deeper shade of blue that matched her eyes. She sighed, making me slightly dizzy. "Yeah. Actually, it does."

I cleared my throat, my hold on her power tightening. If I let go now, her control would snap, hurting us both. However, the only way to truly strengthen her grasp on air was to provide her with an anchor. She needed an Air Fae in her circle, likely as a mate, to truly master her powers.

Someone strong enough to balance her.

Someone like me.

And, uh, yeah, that was not going to happen. I'd never been interested in courtship, and I barely knew this girl. Attraction was one thing. A mating, entirely another.

She needed another fae. Someone who wanted that kind of connection. I'd mention it to Exos after class.

"Try to conjure an air spiral like I showed you," I said, hoping my tone sounded encouraging. We'd been trying this for several minutes, but she'd yet to create one.

Claire hummed as her eyes fluttered closed.

My power coiled around hers on instinct, the contact intense.

She leaned forward, her shirt dipping with her and providing me with an agonizing view of her graceful neck and cleavage. A better fae would have averted his gaze, but I was weak when it came to a fae who tugged at my strings like this one did. She demanded my full attention.

Then I noticed it—a fire brand.

Fuck, I knew I'd sensed something else off about her. Her fire was too passionate, too practiced and perfected for a Halfling who'd been rumored to kill and injure multiple fae.

She'd bonded with a Fire Fae as well.

Two courtship bonds, one for each element.

That wasn't unheard of for a Spirit Fae, but it was definitely rare. Given what I'd seen of her powers, it seemed necessary to maintain her balance and control. However, I didn't know of a single Air Fae who would be willing to go up against such competition.

Yet, I also knew she required one. Exos had one hell of a challenge set out before him.

"Just focus on that place inside," she said to herself. "I'm a fae," she continued, half chuckling. "I have magical powers. I can summon little air spirals."

"Like the hot chocolate," the royal offered. He kept his touch light and coaxing across her arm. "You're doing great, Claire."

Her brow wrinkled as she focused, and her powers fluctuated beneath my senses. Something new blossomed, a strange, dark force that felt wrong, corrupted.

What is that? Or better yet, who *is that?* It wasn't a power I recognized, the taste of it bitter on my tongue.

Wait, no, I do know that power. It's familiar.

I frowned, trying to identify the owner because it wasn't Claire. "Hold—"

She summoned the air spiral before I had a chance to stop her. I immediately latched on, trying to quell the conjuring, but the angry power reared at the scent of my magic. It was as if the power multiplied by a thousand, hell-bent on wreaking death and destruction to any who dared to get too close to the Halfling.

This wasn't right. I'd mentored other fae before, and I was good at it because I could visualize their inner strength, contain it, and hold on to it until they could contain themselves. Yet when I reached out to grasp the strand of power that burned hot and angry, it wouldn't listen to me.

This magic doesn't belong to Claire.

The air spiral danced over her hand, causing her to smile at the perceived achievement. An innocent expression that morphed into horror as the energy sprung from her grasp.

"Dispel it," I commanded. "Dispel it now!"

Claire's eyes widened and snapped up to mine in confused terror, but it was too late.

The spiral exploded.

Shrieks sounded, and the pathetic air pixie was the first to be sucked in by the wild vortex that crashed through the classroom, sending delicate pedestals catapulting through the thick glass meant to contain even the worst projectiles.

Professor Helios cast a wave of power to try to contain the vortex, but even the ancient fae was no match for whatever the horror had unleashed.

"*You!*" the Professor shouted as his black eyes trained on Claire. "I will not tolerate violent elements in my classroom!"

As if Claire had a choice in the matter. This wasn't her. I was certain of it.

Despite her lack of involvement, I'd seen the kind of power she possessed. She could dispel this, if only I could guide her on how to use it.

The royal braced himself against the winds, and power shimmered around him as he anchored himself to the ground with invisible threads of life. My lips parted at the display of power. I'd known he was strong, but not that he was creative.

"Claire!" he shouted over the roar of the whirlwind that rained down chaos on the classroom. Determination was etched into every line of his face as the cyclone spiraled out of control.

Professor Helios grunted, trying to shove the winds back as a projectile flung dangerously close to his head.

"Claire!" Exos tried again, this time winning her wide-eyed stare. He braced a hand on her shoulder. "Remember what we taught you."

A desk soared through the air and caught him against the shoulder, throwing him to the ground, silencing him.

Ah, shit...

CHAPTER SEVENTEEN
CLAIRE

EXOS!

I'd been so careful, so determined to master my fae elements. But of course, I fucked up again.

And now I'd injured Exos.

I started to kneel, to check on him, when the Air Fae—Vox—grabbed my shoulder. "We can dispel it. But I need you to focus."

Exos had told me this Air Fae might be a good mentor, his ability to control elements and help others noted in his academic records.

The wind whirled around us, catching Exos in its tunnel and dragging him across the floor. *No!* I latched onto him and yanked him back with a strand of fire that had Vox jumping away from me.

The professor screamed words I couldn't hear, causing the tornado to whirl toward him, plunging straight ahead, as though vexed by the command.

What the hell am I going to do?

"Exos!" I shouted, shaking him.

Vox was suddenly there, kneeling beside me. *When had I fallen to the ground?* I'd somehow landed beside Exos, my arms tight around his neck to keep him away from the destructive windstorm roaring through the room.

Oh God...

We're going to die here.

Air was the one element I couldn't seem to master. It always threw me off, always—

"Take my hand," Vox demanded, holding out his palm. "We need to stop it before it destroys the building."

"How?" I asked, raising my voice above the bellowing vortex. The professor seemed to have it contained to an extent, but it was throwing projectiles left and right.

And if one hit the professor...

"Claire!" Vox shouted. "I need you to trust me. You have the power to kill that thing, and I can help you harness it."

Of course I did. Because I fucking created it.

Damn it!

I'd been doing so well with Titus and Exos, and now—

Vox grabbed my wrist. *"Claire."*

I blinked at him, startled. "What...?" I swallowed, my throat tight. "What can I do?"

"Can you feel the darkness?" he asked, his voice too calm for the chaos flourishing around us. "The power? Can you locate and isolate it?"

More shouts came, then screams followed by a crash, and I winced.

"Claire," Vox insisted, demanding me to focus on his voice. "Try to latch onto it. Together, we can destroy it, but I'm not strong enough to do it alone. I need you to try to lasso it with me."

Lasso a tornado.

Right.

Yeah, a walk in the park.

"It's picking up speed!" someone screamed.

"Shit!"

"Run!"

"It's going to take the building down!"

My blood ran cold, the insanity spiraling out of control and trying to tug Exos from my grasp. "No!" I shouted, but the word was lost to the howling winds. My hair tangled before my eyes, the lethal tunnel sucking everything into its inky abyss.

Like a black hole, I realized. *Oh God...*

Vox screamed something over the roar of sound, but I couldn't hear him.

I need to focus.

I need to stop this.

By calling the elements to me.

Just like Exos and Titus always say.

I can do this.

I have to.

Or I'll lose my Spirit, my Exos...

Closing my eyes, I searched within myself—the way Titus and Exos had shown me—and called forth my connection to air. Only, I didn't recognize the whirl of power dancing before me. It felt foreign, tasted wrong, as if it hadn't come from me at all. Not like in the courtyard yesterday when Exos helped me calm my out-of-control elements.

This didn't feel like *me*.

But my power located it, caressed it, explored it, searching for a way inside, trying to find a weakness to exploit.

There, my instincts whispered. *Punch a hole there.*

Using a gust of wind shaped like an arrow, I sent the sharp end into the core, locking onto the heart of the darkness, and gave it a tug.

Sweat dampened my brow from the effort, my breathing escalating, but my gifts took over, leading my every move. I punched another hole with a second arrow, then a third, all while keeping a mental rope tied to each.

Then I yanked them simultaneously with the force of all my power, shredding the vortex from the inside out.

I collapsed from the intensity of it, the back of my head somehow landing on Exos's chest. We'd whirled around from the force of the tornado, landing on the opposite side of the room.

Only, it wasn't my arms around him but his arms around me.

His breath rattled out of him on a sigh that sounded like my name, but the voice was wrong.

I glanced backward to find a handsome face with ebony eyes and a head of long, dark hair. The silver edging his irises was distinctly different. *Definitely not Exos*. The arms around me were leaner, too, but still strong.

What in the world?

I tried to move, to shift away from Vox and find Exos, except something heavy held me down. My hands fluttered over the solid muscle, relieved to find my Royal Fae. He didn't move, still unconscious, but breathing.

I sighed, relaxing my head, causing Vox to inhale sharply.

Shit.

How did I keep finding myself in this position? Sandwiched between hot men?

"Exos," I muttered, giving him a shake.

He didn't move.

Vox's arms loosened beneath my breasts, sending a wave of heat through my body. "Are you okay, Claire?" he asked, his deep voice a rumble beneath me.

"I, uh, yeah. But Exos is—"

"Suffering from a splitting headache," Exos finished for me, his voice low. "While also rather enjoying lounging between your legs, princess. I think I'll stay."

Vox chuckled beneath me. "I think he's fine."

"More than fine," Exos murmured, slowly sitting up and cracking his neck.

It granted enough room for me to squirm out from between the two men, not that either of them seemed too keen on moving, if their matching smiles were anything to go by.

Smiles that quickly shifted to frowns as shrieks sounded from across the room.

Vox was on his feet in a second, his long hair loose around his shoulders. Whatever tie he'd used to secure that thick mass of beautiful brown strands was long gone, thanks to the tornado. Now it billowed in the breeze being cast from Professor Helios—a breeze aimed at me and carrying words of accusation.

"Your Highness," he said slowly. "I suggest you get Claire out of here."

Exos joined him, surveying the mess of the room before holding a hand out to help me up off the floor. My limbs shook with the effort, causing me to frown. Taking down that vortex had exhausted me more than I realized. I actually felt a bit woozy now that the adrenaline of the moment had subsided.

The nausea only worsened as I took in the massacre of the room.

"Oh God…," I whispered, finally *seeing* the destruction. Bodies littered the floor. Some of them were moving. Most were not.

And the one screaming was Ignis's friend. The one with wiry blonde hair who'd joined Ignis in the courtyard where I caused the fire.

Her violet eyes found mine and widened in horror. "*You!*"

Great…

"She didn't do it, Aerie," Vox said, startling me. "It wasn't her magic."

Exos glanced at him in question while my eyebrows rose. *Vox felt that, too?*

The Air Fae—Aerie—screamed, the sound causing me to flinch and my knees to buckle beneath me. Exos caught me by the waist as I pressed my palms to my bleeding ears.

What is that? The shriek had knocked me off-kilter, splitting my head in two, and worsened the ache in my gut. It left me dizzy and unstable, Exos's arm around me the only thing keeping me upright. And even then, the room seemed to be spinning.

I winced as the shriek deepened, worming into my mind. It knocked the air from my lungs, leaving me floating in a cloud of confusion and deafness.

My hands fell as I tried to find them with my eyes.

Why is everything so fuzzy?

I blinked, trying to focus.

"Enough!" Vox roared, a whoosh of wind following the command and sending Aerie into the wall. Or, at least, that was what appeared to have happened. I couldn't really tell. It was as if my vision had shrunk into a teeny, tiny point.

"I'll talk to Professor Helios, but you need to get Claire out of here." Vox's voice registered, but it rang with an authority that surprised me. He seemed like such a nice fae. Not a bossy one. Not like my Exos.

"You and I need to have a conversation," Exos replied, causing my lips to curl. That was my bossy fae. And why did I find that so amusing?

Vox sighed. "Oh, we'll be talking all right. But for now, focus on Claire. She's about to collapse."

I am?

Oh.

Exos hadn't just put his arm around me but had also lifted me into the air. No wonder it felt like I was floating.

Dude, I'm drunk, I realized. Like the entire world was spinning in a mist of intoxication. When did that happen and how?

"Relax, Claire. I have you," Exos vowed.

"Oh, I know," I replied, smiling. "You definitely have me."

"It's the wind tunnel," Vox said, his voice warm and far away. No, close. Wait, where was he standing, again? "Fucks with the sense of balance and thought. She'll be fine in an hour. Just get her some water." Another whoosh followed his words. "Do not move, Aerie."

I swore she growled in reply. Or someone did. And then more yelling ensued, but I couldn't see any of them or anything. The carnage of the windstorm lay dormant beyond my vision. Or perhaps not so quiet. Panic filtered through the air, words I couldn't understand, and chants.

I curled into Exos, craving his familiarity, his security. I didn't want to be drunk anymore, but I couldn't see beyond the fog of my mind. Everything mingled in shades of blacks that were riddled with sounds.

I whimpered.

Lips pressed against my temple. "You'll be okay."

Exos?

Yes. I snuggled into his heat, his scent, his strength.

"What happened?" a new voice demanded, one I recognized immediately as my Titus. I couldn't say when I started thinking of these two men as mine, but I did. They were mine, and I intended to keep them if they let me.

Their tongues and hands, mmm...

"Is she drunk?" Titus demanded.

"Yes, I took her to the bar to celebrate her destruction on Air Quad today. Sorry for not inviting you." Exos set me on a cloud of amazingness. So, so soft. But not warm enough. I reached for his hand, longing for his heat, and found Titus's instead. My lips curled, my fire instantly engaged, and I tugged him toward me.

"Fuck, Claire," he muttered, collapsing on top of me. Or maybe beside me. I really couldn't tell, this wave of confusion shadowing my judgment.

"Yeah, you entertain her there while I go find some water. According to Vox, that'll help cure this wind tunnel messing with her mind." Exos sounded amused, which made me giggle. I liked him amused. He had the best smile.

Like the sun. Except he rarely showed it. Maybe he lived in a cloud, too. Like me. Because I couldn't see a damn thing. But I could definitely *feel*, and I really liked the heat coming from Titus. So muscular. Hard. *Hot.*

"You and I are going to have a long talk about your conversational skills, Royal," Titus growled. "Claire, sweetheart, can you stop—No. Stop that." He grabbed my wrists, causing me to pout. I wanted to pet him. To revel in his *fire.*

No more of this kissing and orgasm crap. I wanted more. To really, truly *feel* him.

To fuck.... yes!

"Claire," he warned. His voice turned to a hiss as I arched into him, signaling with my body what I craved since apparently my mouth no longer worked. Or my eyes.

What is wrong with my head?

So fuzzy.

Oh, but the heat...

"*Claire.*" The pain in Titus's voice had me stilling against him. Had I hurt him in some way? All I wanted was to roll in his flames, to let them bathe over my skin and light my way out of this insane darkness.

"Here." Exos was back. My Royal Fae. My spirit half.

These men were my fae. My Titus and my Exos. Forever mates. Lovers. Oh, but without the fucking. I scowled at that; they really needed to sort this out—

Oh.

Cool liquid slipped over my tongue, exciting my nerves and calming me at the same time. I sighed, my head pillowed against Titus, my hands now being held by Exos.

Sandwiched yet again between two men.

How had this become my life?

"Maybe we should invite Vox," I mused. *Wait, had I said that out loud?*

"He'll be by later," Exos said softly.

Yeah, said that out loud.

Oh, but hey! I had a voice again.

Still can't see, though.

"What the hell is this?" Titus asked as more water slid over my tongue. "Start talking, Exos."

"In case it's not clear, I've had a very rough afternoon and I'm not in the mood for your petulant demands."

"Oh? I'm sorry. You bring home a very drunk Claire, who seems hell-bent on fucking me, and you'd like me to just accept that. All right. Care to leave while I indulge her?"

"Fuck you."

"No, *fuck you.* Now tell me what the hell happened."

I giggled, their banter amusing the hell out of me. And they kept saying *fuck*, which was exactly what I wanted to do. But they had some sort of no-fucking rule going on between them that was driving me *crazy*. Like, how many nights could a girl go to bed naked between two hot men and *not* get fucked?

"Try being one of those males and having to rely on your hand for weeks," Titus growled.

Oh, I said that out loud... My brow crinkled. No. I didn't feel bad about it. "I want sex."

"Dear Elements, we are not having this conversation in your current state," Exos snapped.

"Then busy us both by telling me what the hell happened," Titus suggested, his tone doing this sexy, deep, demanding thing that made my lady parts tingle. "Claire, stop doing that."

Exos sighed. "Here." He gently began massaging my temples, which sparked glimpses of light in the darkness but didn't relieve the ache building between my thighs. I'd much rather have his attentions focused elsewhere. I opened my mouth to say just that, when a tongue slid between my lips, eliciting a groan from deep within.

Which one of them was kissing me?

Exos, my spirit whispered.

Yes... I recognized his dominance, his minty taste, his command.

But rather than excite my nerves and caress the heat building inside, it made me sleepy. Oh, how he drained me. Such a virile, powerful man. I pressed into him, accepting his gift, his presence, his being, and felt my limbs relax.

Such a soft, fluffy world.

Warm.

Safe.

Mmm.

Yes, I would sleep. Just for a little bit. And when I woke, hopefully I'd be able to see again.

CHAPTER EIGHTEEN
VOX

EXHAUSTION WEIGHED HEAVILY ON ME. Dealing with Aerie had been child's play.

Professor Helios, however, had been another matter. Once he'd regained consciousness, he'd been hell-bent on seeking justice for his classroom. And Claire had been the focus of his wrath. Thankfully, Exos had whisked her off to the safety of the Spirit Quad before that could happen.

Of course, now the Royal Fae would have to deal with the repercussions and face the Council. Which meant I'd need to intervene.

That tornado did not belong to Claire. I felt it in every fiber of my being, and not just because my inner air considered her to be a potential mate.

Not happening, I told myself for the thousandth time. Helping her I could do. Falling for a woman with two other mates already? No.

Except all I could think about was how her essence had called to me.

Fuck.

Fuck.

Fuck.

I was mad to even be thinking of her right now. The entire Academy was in an uproar after yet another series of deaths surrounding the Halfling.

Except this wasn't her fault.

"By the Elements," Sol huffed as he stormed into the Earth Dorms carrying a bag. "Vox, what are you doing here?"

Yeah, about that...

I squirmed on Sol's unforgiving excuse for a couch and glowered at the dusty layers of glass that needed a cleaning. There should have been a beautiful view of the shifting gardens, but Sol sucked at housekeeping.

"You really need to get a more comfortable couch," I complained, ignoring his question. "It's not inviting at all."

Sol rolled his eyes and plopped the cloth bag onto the table and began to unfurl it. Steaming, leafy edges of meat pie made my mouth water. Sol tore one of the leaves and broke me off a chunk, handing it to me with a knowing look. "You don't often mope, Vox. Didn't see the Halfling today like you'd hoped?"

I glared at the offering and took a small nibble, not having much of an appetite even though my stomach was roaring for sustenance after the power I'd expensed kicking Aerie's ass. "Quite the opposite," I admitted around the small mouthful.

Sol's brown eyes raked over me as if noticing for the first time that my usually kempt suit was tattered and torn. "Don't tell me you were there for the maelstrom?" His eyes widened when I didn't respond. "Elements, Vox, you could have been killed!" He leaned in and lowered his voice, glancing around as though someone might somehow hear us in the room of solid rock. "Was the royal there, too?" He waggled his fingers at me. "Did he mind-control her to do it?"

I nearly choked on the morsel. "Fuck, Sol. No."

Sol distrusted all Spirit Fae, but Exos more than most. I still didn't know why, but tonight wasn't the night to ask. Nor did I have the energy to prove his thoughts wrong. It would require talking about what happened with Claire, and I wasn't ready to face that yet.

My best friend scoffed at me and wrapped a leaf around a larger chunk of meat, then tore it off with his teeth. He gazed out through the dirtied window, not seeming to care that he couldn't really see through it. "Well, it won't matter much either way," Sol said.

"Why's that?"

He chewed thoughtfully before answering me. "I heard that if there was one more fae death at the Academy, then the Halfling would be expelled and banished to the Spirit Kingdom." He shrugged. "Not a bad thing, because that bastard royal will go with her and I won't have to keep tiptoeing around my own damn campus. She has power over all five elements, you know so she would eventually have earth classes." He shuddered as if horrified by the idea.

My heart skipped a beat. *Banished? Spirit Kingdom?*

No fucking way.

She's innocent.

And fuck if I was going to let anyone send an innocent girl to a damn wasteland.

I slammed my fist on the table, sending dust flying. "For one, *Sol*, you don't fucking tiptoe anywhere. You shake the ground like a beast that can't be contained." I held up two fingers. "And secondly, don't judge someone you've never even met. The Halfling is innocent."

I didn't give Sol a chance to digest my outrage. Instead I caught a glimpse of his wide eyes—and perhaps a little hurt in his gaze—before I tore open the front door with a gust of wind and marched out of the Earth Dorms.

I should have returned to my own quarters, but I found the breeze taking me straight to the Halfling, who I knew would never harm another living soul and didn't deserve the fae's wrath.

Everyone on campus knew she was living in—or rather, *banished to*—the Spirit Dorms. Now I just had to figure out which room she'd chosen in a wasteland of nothing.

* * *

No one ever encroached on the Spirit Quad, and for good reason. The wasteland looked like a scar across the otherwise beautiful grounds. A stark line grooved out in the dirt where the barriers between majestic energies bordered each other. The lively, shifting rock of the Earth Quad kept its distance from the cold, gray, and lifeless dirt that made up the majority of the Spirit grounds. I drew in a deep breath, as if I could gather my air element inside of me in a protective bubble, before braving a step forward.

There.

Ouch.

Okay, yeah, it hurt. It felt like crossing over from life to death because I wasn't meant to be on the Spirit Quad. I hadn't received an invitation, and there wasn't even the slightest breeze here to make me feel at home.

Lifeless, colorless buildings wrapped in dead vines boasted what had once been classrooms teeming with bright-minded students. There was, however, one pop of color that stood out against the corpse-like dirt.

A white flower.

I leaned down to inspect it and grazed it with my fingertips.

Claire.

Another flower marked the path just a few paces down, so I went to it and squinted until I spotted another. Then another still, until I was so deep into the Spirit Quad that I swore I was starting to hear the voices of the dead that had once roamed these grounds.

Oh, not the dead—that's a fae.

I tilted my head to the side and allowed a sliver of my power to carry a breeze to catch the sounds.

There, the dorms.

I ventured in without knocking, not because I meant to intrude, but because I was so intent on discovering what kind of fae might be here other than Exos and Claire.

"You have to fucking do *something*," a muscular fae demanded. Auburn locks licked with tiny flames, and embers burned in the fae's eyes as he challenged the royal that leaned heavily against the wall. He was shirtless, his hair damp, maybe from a recent shower.

"And *you* need to calm down," Exos ordered. He pushed off from the wall and startled me by pinning me with his gaze. "Ah, Vox. Finally, you're here." He waved me over as if he'd summoned me here. "Come in and make yourself at home."

My eyes widened. I was an Air Fae adept in the skills of stealth. I'd passed every shadowstep and secrecy class with outstanding marks, to the point that I was well on my way as a spy for Air Kingdom if I so wanted, yet the royal had noticed me without any effort at all.

The Fire Fae glared at me, causing me to reconsider coming here. I recognized him. Everyone on campus would. He was a renowned fighter. A champion. And lethal as fuck. "Well, you heard Exos," Titus said. "Don't just stand there, Vox. Join us."

Swallowing hard, I entered and awkwardly adjusted my ruined suit. I probably should have changed into something more presentable before venturing over here. "Ah, so, is Claire okay?" I asked.

Smooth, Vox.

"Yes, she's having a nap," Exos said, then gave Titus a raised brow. "And shouldn't be left alone, Titus."

"Should I expect her to wake up intoxicated? Or did your little mindfuck fix that?"

Exos narrowed his gaze. "Did you prefer the alternative?"

Titus growled. "This isn't working."

"I know."

"Then fucking do something about it, *Your Highness.*"

Exos sighed and ran his fingers through his light hair. "Sorry, Vox. You've caught us in a rather *heated* moment, one Titus can't seem to let go." Those last two words were directed at the Fire Fae.

Titus flipped him off in response.

Okay, then. I'd clearly interrupted something. "I can come back..."

"No," they both said at once.

"We have to talk about what happened," Exos added. "About what went wrong."

"She didn't kill anyone," I blurted out, feeling the weight of their stares. "I mean, I felt it. I'm a mentor, and I can sense energies. The energy that created that maelstrom wasn't Claire's."

Exos smiled. "I know. But thank you for confirming my suspicions."

"Again, that whole communicating thing?" Titus waved between himself and Exos. "Still sucking. Now tell me about these *suspicions*."

"Had you given me a moment earlier instead of throwing a fit, I would have."

"Well, fucking tell me now."

"Who is the royal here, Titus?" Exos asked, cocking his head to the side. "Me or you?"

"Oh, this again." Titus threw his hands up in the air. "Claire is passed-out drunk—from something you've still not explained, by the way—and you want to play the superiority game instead of telling me what the hell is going on. Typical."

"What's typical is you losing your temper over nothing."

"*Nothing?*" he repeated, pointing to a door at the end of the room. "*That* is not nothing."

"Aerie sent a target shriek of air into Claire's mind. Specifically, the frontal lobe, causing temporary, well, incapacitation," I explained, hoping to dispel some of the tension. "It's a classic Air Fae attack mechanism. Renders your opponent incomprehensible for an hour or two. Essentially, it makes the victim feel very, very intoxicated."

Titus gaped at me while Exos scratched his chin.

"She'll be fine," I added. "Sleeping it off is the best for her."

"Who do you think manipulated her spiral?" Exos asked, changing the subject.

"I don't know. But I can help you find out."

He arched a brow. "How?"

"By tracking the energy source." It wouldn't be hard. After trying to dismantle the maelstrom myself, I had a pretty good understanding of what it felt like. "As I said, I have a knack for sensing energy." It was what allowed me to help Sol with his affinity for earth.

"You're saying you want to help," Exos translated.

"I'm saying I can, if you need it." I wasn't about to assume a powerful Spirit Fae required my assistance. As he already pointed out, he suspected Claire wasn't the source of power.

He nodded, then glanced at Titus. "I think we found our Air Fae."

"You're assuming he can keep up." Titus folded his arms and looked me over. "You up for the task?"

"Of tracking the energy source? Yeah."

"No." Titus smirked. "I meant, are you up for the task of managing Claire?"

"Oh, uh…" I swallowed. "To help manage her air?"

Titus nodded.

Exos said nothing, his gaze assessing me.

"I just came by to tell you it wasn't her and to offer assistance in tracking down the culprit." No, that wasn't entirely true. A part of me had longed to check up on her. But that was just my mentor side requiring me to make sure the student I'd failed earlier today was all right. "However, yes, she needs a mentor." I'd meant to say that to Exos as well, but the banishing comments from Sol had derailed my focus. All I'd cared about was expressing her innocence so they didn't send her away.

Why do I care so much?

Because she's innocent.

Right.

"She needs *you* as a mentor," Exos replied. "You're a good match for her. I felt it during class. And so you'll mentor her."

He uttered the words as if they were a done deal. "I'll help you find one," I offered. "A mentor, I mean."

"No need." Exos turned, walking down the hall. "She already has one, Vox. You." He paused on the threshold, his blue eyes meeting mine. "Don't leave. I'm just going to grab some proper clothes for us to hunt in."

"But—"

"And I need to wake up Claire. Give me twenty minutes, Vox."

I gaped after the Royal Fae as he disappeared through a door, leaving me unable to argue.

Titus chuckled. "Yeah, he does that. But you'll get used to him."

"I can't mentor her," I blurted out.

"And why's that?" Titus asked, cocking his head to the side.

"I... It's just... I have Sol and classes and..."

He arched an auburn-tinged brow. "I don't know what a Sol is, but so far, all I'm hearing are weak excuses. Sort of disappointing, if you ask me. Exos is clearly wrong. Claire requires someone stronger. Don't worry; I'll talk to him. I mean, he won't fucking listen, but if you're not up for the task, then he'll have no choice. Right?"

"No, that's not what I mean." *Fuck. He's right. They're all just idiotic excuses.* I shook my head and pinched the bridge of my nose. "Her power calls to mine." The truth sort of fell out of my mouth on a breeze of words I couldn't catch. But what else could I say? Another bullshit excuse? No. She deserved better than that. And so did I.

Titus smiled. "Well then, welcome to the team, Vox. I hope you enjoy cold showers."

CHAPTER NINETEEN
EXOS

I RAN MY FINGERS through Claire's thick hair, reveling in the silky texture while I slowly removed my hold over her elements. Manipulating others was the darker side of my ability, and that included being able to put someone to sleep at will.

For Claire, it'd been necessary. Her eyes had been unseeing—*wild*—and her powers had taken on a will of their own. She probably didn't even realize the sheer force with which she'd pulled Titus down onto the bed or the way her fire engulfed him in a sea of hot desire.

Clearly, all of us had some pent-up passion issues at the forefront of our minds.

I sighed and joined Claire on the bed, wrapping my arms around her as she began to stir beside me. Hopefully, her nap had cured the drunken spell Aerie had woven through Claire's mind.

I could kill that Air Fae, I thought, furious. She'd attacked Claire in a moment of weakness, after she'd taken down that maelstrom.

A maelstrom Claire absolutely did not create.

I'd felt the presence of another just before it erupted, stirring chaos throughout the room. There'd been a dark note to it, a sense of spirit that I didn't recognize.

But I knew with certainty that it didn't belong to Claire. My power had tuned into hers over the last few weeks, braiding our essences together and merging our spirits. I *knew* her now. And that destructive energy dancing through the room had possessed an entirely different elemental pattern.

"Exos?" she murmured, her eyes still closed.

"I'm here, princess." I pressed my lips to her forehead and held her tighter. "How do you feel?"

She seemed to consider for a moment before saying, "Hungover. Like, really, really hungover."

I chuckled and reached for the water I'd left on the nightstand for her. "Here." I pressed the rim to her lips and helped her take a few sips while brushing my spirit over hers in a way that had become second nature these last few weeks.

She stretched beside me, a low moan of approval emanating from her throat. "Thank you," she whispered, snuggling into me more.

I returned the glass to the table and folded my arms around her again. "You did well today, Claire." Unfortunately, while I believed that, the Council would disagree. The incident on Air Quad had Claire's fingerprints all over it, which they would most likely use to banish her from the Academy.

"Today?" she asked, her voice sleepy. Then she went stiff. "Oh no…"

"Shh," I soothed. "It's going to be okay." *Because I'm going to figure out who actually created that spiral and break the culprit's neck.*

It occurred to me as well that the other incidents may not have been Claire at all, but the person who had interfered today. The fire and water episodes happened before I fully understood the extent of her powers, so it was hard to say for certain. But given the events on Air Quad, it seemed likely.

"I didn't do it," she blurted out, squirming backward to stare at me. "I mean, I thought I did. I created the spiral, but I don't know how it blew out of control. And when I tried to stop it, I couldn't find my essence inside of it. Like… like… you know, yesterday? With that energy ball in the courtyard? You told me to wrap my fire around it, remember? And I could because I recognized my own powers. But this time…" She trailed off, her expression falling. "I sound crazy, I know, but I swear it wasn't me, Exos."

I touched her chin, gently nudging it upward to capture her gaze. "I know, baby. I felt it, too."

She must not have remembered the part where Vox also claimed it wasn't her. How fascinating that he could sense it without a bond. Either it proved him to be a potential mate for Claire or it was related to his own incredible gifts.

Regardless, it made him perfect for her team.

Which was why he would be joining—with or without his approval.

"You did?" she whispered.

I kissed her softly before pressing my forehead to hers. "My spirit knows

153

yours, Claire."

"Because of the bond," she translated.

"And the last few weeks of training. But, yes, mostly as a result of our connection." I licked her bottom lip and continued to stroke her spirit with mine, eliciting a contented sigh from her. "It's deepening," I told her on a hush of sound. "Can you feel it?" There were different levels to the mating bond, and ours was teetering on the edge of something more permanent.

"I don't really understand it," she admitted softly. "But yes, I can feel it. Is sex what pushes it over the edge?" Her cheeks flushed beautifully with the query, her blue eyes sparkling with life. "That came out wrong. I just... I've wondered if that's why you and Titus are holding back—so we don't accidentally intensify the link."

Her confession surprised me. "You think we don't want to take this to the next level?" It applied to both sex and the mating.

"I, uh, well, yeah." She swallowed. "I mean, I get it. There are two of you, and that just makes this even more confusing, right? And you never really had a choice in our bond, since I kissed you without permission. Not that I knew this would happen. Oh, wait, that came out wrong, too. I don't regret it. What I mean is—"

I captured her mouth with my own, silencing her little rant. While it was adorable, I didn't want to hear her second-guessing the nature of our connection.

Was it my choice? No.

Did it bother me? At first, yes. But now? No.

No, now I wouldn't have this any other way. Her gift for spirit rivaled mine, making her an ideal princess in my court. Apart from the other competing elements, what we had was so unique, so different, so much more powerful than anyone would ever understand.

And it was with that knowledge in mind that I rolled her to her back and worshiped her with my mouth. I unleashed all the emotions I hid from the world, including how I felt about her. Oh, Titus had an idea of how badly I ached for her. But his knowledge only skimmed the surface to the depths of what I kept locked away inside.

A warrior couldn't afford a weakness.

Yet, at some point, Claire had become mine.

She gave new meaning to my heart.

My hips settled between hers, my cock throbbing against her hot center. "Sex is a merging of the bodies," I murmured, my lips moving across her cheek. "The connection is between the elements, and ours is a dance between our souls." I pressed my arousal into the sanctuary between her thighs, providing an introduction to my lustful cravings, and smiled at her resulting moan. If only we were naked, then I could truly demonstrate my yearnings.

Alas, I had a task to complete. One that would hopefully secure her place here and pacify the Council.

To find the one framing my Claire.

My teeth grazed her pulse on my way up to her ear. "You can deepen a bond without sex, Claire. It just has to be a mutual agreement between the fae to continue exploring opportunities. I think, in your terms, it would be the equivalent of going from a few casual dates to dating seriously, or maybe even an engagement. Because once our elements move on to the next phase, it's showing a promise for the future and speaks of a serious intent to mate for eternity."

"How many levels are there?" she asked, her nails scratching down my back as she arched up into me.

I smiled against her neck. "Four."

"And we're on the first?"

"Yes."

"But close to the second?"

"Yes." I took her mouth again—because I could—and slid my tongue deep inside, possessing every inch of her. She groaned, her body vibrating with need beneath mine. I longed to give in, just for one more moment, and so I did.

I gave her everything.

My frustration.

My yearning.

My adoration.

My worries.

The Council would be meeting later tonight, and if I didn't give them a sound argument against expulsion...

No.

I refused.

That was not going to happen on my watch.

Claire's arms wound around my neck, holding me tightly as she reciprocated in kind, her feelings exploding across her tongue. I felt her confusion, her strength, and, most importantly, her craving not just for a physical connection but also for an emotional one.

With me.

A sign of her mutual affection.

She couldn't know that was what it meant, but my power reacted in kind, dancing with hers on a plane only spirit had access to. "That's it, isn't it?" she whispered, awe in her voice.

"Yes." Apparently, that was my word of the night because not only did I keep saying it out loud but my soul repeated it as well.

Claire's energy swirled around mine, causing the hairs along the nape of my neck to stand on end. This was why we didn't need sex to graduate to phase two. The bond required elemental compatibility, coupled with the passion for more.

And there'd never been another fae more for me than Claire. "You're sure?" I asked her softly, nuzzling my nose against hers. "Because if we push this one inch forward, we'll be in the next level, Claire."

"Dating exclusively, right?" she asked, sounding dreamy. Then the words seemed to register, because she froze. "Meaning I can't see Titus…"

"No." I cupped her cheek, pulling her back to me before panic could truly set in. "It would mean you can't see another Spirit Fae. This is about elemental bonding, Claire. You would essentially be declaring your spirit as betrothed to mine."

"Like marriage."

"It's similar, but different. Consider it more of a long-term commitment to ensure that our pairing is what we truly desire. By escalating to the next phase of the bond, you'll have more access to *me*. To my mind. It requires trust, Claire. And then from there, you move into the third stage, in which our elements mingle and flourish off one another—where you could borrow energy from me as I could from you. And the final level is eternity."

She swallowed, some of the alarm melting into curiosity. "Were my mother and Mortus a three or a four?"

"A three," I murmured. "When you reach that phase, there's no going back. The elements are locked into one another—indefinitely."

"Then why the fourth stage?" she asked.

"It's more of a formality, a pledge of fealty that binds the souls. To join your elements, but not the souls, can be quite painful." Which explained Mortus's rage. But I didn't add that part. I could see from the flare of her pupils that she inferred it anyway.

"The third step is binding, similar to an engagement without an escape route if you get cold feet," she surmised. "And the second is a more serious level of seeing someone, like moving in with them. While the first is temporary—like dating—to see if the person your power is attracted to is someone you might like as well."

I kissed her gently, loving the way she'd gone pliant and soft again beneath me. "Very accurate summarization, princess."

"And we're already living together," she continued, her mouth moving against mine. "So, we should move up a level." Her tongue licked across my lower lip. "Right?"

"If that's your desire."

"Is it yours?"

I pulled back to meet her eyes, my palm still resting against her cheek. "Yes." *There's that word again.*

Her blue eyes brightened. "Really?"

I pressed my arousal into her hot center and cocked my head to the side. "You can feel how much I want you, right?"

She slapped my shoulder. "You said this is about emotions."

"It's about everything, Claire," I replied with a laugh. "Do I want to deepen our bond? Yes. Absolutely. But I also very much want to fuck you. The two are not mutually exclusive, but again, the connection isn't about sex. It's about power. And it also happens to heighten the sensations, or so I've heard."

"You've never connected with anyone?"

"Only you, Claire. On any level." I went to my elbows on either side of her head, wanting her to see the sincerity in my expression as I gave her the ultimate truth. "I never wanted to bond with anyone. Nor did I think I would actually find someone who suited my power. I'm one of the strongest fae in the world, and that's not me boasting; it's a fact. Finding a partner who can handle my gift, one my spirit is actually attracted to, was a very impossible notion. Until you."

Tears pricked her eyes, causing me to frown.

That was *not* the response I wanted. At all.

But she pulled me down to kiss her, and the sensation she poured from her mouth to mine floored me.

She didn't just accept the bond; she kicked the fucking door down and yanked me into the next level with her. I felt it in the way our powers snapped together, as if a lock had tied her spirit to mine, securing her place in my heart and mine in hers.

"Claire," I whispered, returning the embrace and worshiping her with my tongue. She clung to me as if she needed me to breathe, her legs winding around my hips, her fingers in my hair.

This kiss sparked a new beginning.

It carved her name into my very being, marking my element as hers and hers as mine. Flowers blossomed around us, the creation of life filling the room with the fragrance of our heightened connection and shaking the very foundations of the building.

That it occurred on Spirit Quad only intensified the moment, bringing all ounces of life back to the formerly dead campus.

The trees rejoiced.

The grounds cried out in pleasure.

And the meadows bloomed.

That was the power we possessed together—a life energy no one could ever touch. *Ours.*

Claire shuddered beneath me, her blue eyes luminescent with vitality. "That's…"

"Amazing," I finished for her softly. "And something we will definitely be exploring more." I laved her plump lip before pressing a kiss to her cheek. Now more than ever I felt a duty to protect her, and that required me to leave her, to find the one trying to cause her harm. "Vox is here," I whispered.

"Why?" she asked, her voice breathy, her expression soft.

"He knows you didn't create that windstorm today, and he thinks he can track the energy signature back to its owner." I drew my thumb beneath her eye, catching the tear she'd shed only moments ago.

Tears of joy, I realized. I sort of liked that. I licked the drop, deciding to taste her emotional gift—*mine. Just like Claire.*

Her gaze widened. "He thinks someone created that thing on purpose?"

"Yes, to frame you. And I suspect the first incident in the courtyard, as well as the water in the dorms, may not have been you, either. So I'm going to go with him to see if we can find the person who created the tornado."

"Me, too," she said, her hands on my shoulders as if to push me away.

I refused to move. "No. You need to stay here with Titus." I pressed a finger to her lips before she could protest. "Claire. He needs you."

This wasn't about my trying to shelter her. If anything, it would be a good lesson for her to learn how to identify the essence of others—especially as Spirit Fae could control them.

No.

This was about Titus.

"He's on edge," I continued. "And to properly protect you, I need him focused. There's only one way to fix it." I'd realized it this afternoon after witnessing the true pain in his features, the barely concealed fire.

While I, too, felt the aching need inside me to claim Claire, my elemental control far outweighed his, and I didn't have a tendency to burn shit down when in a rage.

If we were going to go up against someone powerful enough to manifest powers on Claire's behalf, then I needed everyone focused. Not to mention the general security required to keep our little fae princess alive. Too many people wanted her dead.

I almost liked that she needed more than one mate. *Almost* being the key word. But I couldn't deny that it helped from a bodyguard standpoint.

"Are you telling me to...?" She trailed off, her brow pinched.

I bent to kiss the pucker between her eyebrows before dragging my lips lower to her mouth and whispering, "Yes, Claire. I'm telling you to indulge him while I'm gone. I don't want the details. Although, I'll likely feel it through the bond." I flinched at the thought but quickly swallowed my instinctual reaction.

No one could touch our spirit bond.

Not even Titus.

"It feels... wrong... after we just..."

I silenced her with another kiss, this one coaxing and holding a promise. "You're still mine, Claire. But you're also his. And I respect that, just as I know he'll respect our bond. It's the way of life." I tilted my head to the side, amusement touching my chest. "You're not in the human world anymore, darling princess. We're fae. Our rules are different."

She stared at me for a long moment before yanking me to her once more and rewarding me with her mouth. "Don't do anything without me," she said softly. "If you find the person doing this, I want to know. I want to be there."

"Of course." I brushed my nose against hers. "Reconnaissance only."

"Promise?"

"I vow it." I pecked her lips once more and shifted back to my knees as I sensed a new presence enter the room. I ignored him and decided to have a little fun instead. "Now that I've let Titus and Vox get to know each other, I think it's time we join them to make sure they're both still alive."

Her eyebrows rose, the innocence in her features telling me she'd not sensed Titus's entrance yet. Likely because I'd distracted her with our bonding and other more arousing activities.

"They don't like each other?" she asked.

I lifted a shoulder. "As I said, Titus has some pent-up anger issues. But Vox strikes me as the calm, collected type. Maybe they can be friends."

"As he doesn't harbor a penchant for bossing me around, I think we'll get along just fine," Titus deadpanned.

Claire froze while I chuckled. "Our Claire is awake, by the way."

"I can see that," he replied, the possessive growl in his voice no better than before. The Fire Fae seemed ready to combust, and while I trusted him not to harm Claire, I didn't necessarily trust him not to hurt me.

Leaning down to kiss her one last time, I rolled off the bed and grabbed a shirt from the closet. She hadn't moved, her wide gaze on a glowering Titus. He clearly sensed the heightened bond within her, and his clenched hands said how he felt about it.

I pressed my palm to his chest to back him up a few paces into the wall and caught his fist before it could meet my face. "Vox and I are leaving to track the energy signature. Claire wanted to join us, but I suggested she spend some time here with you. *Alone.*" I lifted an eyebrow with the final word, ensuring he followed my insinuation. "Does that work for you?"

Flames danced in his gaze as he studied my features. Then his shoulders seemed to relax as he gave me a stiff nod.

"I promised Claire we won't act on any information without her. And I imagine we'll be back in a few hours."

Another nod. "Okay."

"Okay." I released him and went to retrieve my shoes. Claire had sat up on the bed during our discussion, her lower lip snagged between her teeth. I bent to tug it between my own, giving her a little nibble. "Try not to burn the dorm down, baby."

Her cheeks flushed an adorable shade of red, causing me to chuckle. It physically pained me to leave her in the hands of another man, but while Titus might not be my favorite fae, I couldn't deny his compatibility with Claire.

And as such, I trusted him implicitly with her life.

He stopped me with a hand on my forearm, his green eyes holding a touch of gratitude in them as they captured mine.

No words were spoken.

Not even another nod.

Just a brief look of understanding before he released me.

"Be careful," Claire called after me, causing me to pause on the threshold.

I glanced back at her, amused. "I'm a Royal Fae, baby. There's no one on this campus who can touch me. Except you." And with that, I met Vox in the hallway. "Let's go, Air Fae. I want to see what you can do."

CHAPTER TWENTY
CLAIRE

TWO MEN.

Fae.

Both mates.

Watching them interact was… *hot.*

Mainly because Titus had this sexy glower thing going on while Exos still managed to alpha him with that shove against the wall. It provoked all manner of inappropriate thoughts, ones that only seemed to intensify as Titus gazed at me from across the room.

"Are you hungry, Claire?" he asked, his voice low.

I couldn't tell if he meant for food or for him. But the answer was a resounding "Yes" either way. Mostly for something of the sexual variety, considering Exos had spent the last however many minutes heating me up, just to leave.

His essence seemed to swim through my veins, his scent forever clinging to me. Because of the bond. He'd been right about it deepening our connection. I could almost sense him in my mind, his resounding amusement at leaving me hot and bothered in his wake.

Or maybe that was my imagination. But it didn't seem too far-fetched a notion.

Titus leaned against the wall. "Are you going to assault me again if I come over there?"

"Again?" I asked, confused.

"You don't remember pulling me onto the bed and rubbing that delicious body all over me while mewling?"

My jaw dropped. "*What?*"

He snorted. "I see Exos failed to mention that part of your drunk little episode." He straightened. "You should eat something."

I frowned as he left. "Okay..."

Is he mad at me? Because of the bond with Exos?

Shit.

I slid off the bed and trailed after him toward the apartment kitchen. Titus stood by the refrigerator, his ass looking mighty fine in a pair of snug jeans. He'd changed out of uniform attire and into casual garb, while I still wore my skirt and sweater—two things that were slightly worn and torn from the Air Quad incident earlier.

My mouth twisted to the side. I remembered taking down the monstrosity and that it wasn't something I created, but I couldn't recall anything after that. *How did I end up passed out in bed? And what did Titus mean about assaulting him?*

"Have I done something to anger you?" I blurted out when he didn't acknowledge my presence.

He glanced over his shoulder with his eyebrows raised. "Do I feel angry to you?" he asked, the question holding a hint of genuine curiosity.

"Uh, well, no, but you're being all... *stiff*." I couldn't come up with a better term.

His lips curled. "That, yes, I definitely am." He returned to his task of placing odd items on the counter. The food in this world was foreign and leafy, and while none of it appeared appetizing, it was mysteriously delicious.

I hopped up onto the counter beside his preparations, wanting to see his expression while we spoke. "What did I do? I don't remember anything after the, uh, tornado."

His emerald eyes flickered up to mine briefly before he pulled a knife from the block behind my back. "Aerie sent a targeted blast of wind into your head. It's meant to incapacitate an attacker."

"Oh." I noticed her in the class earlier, just hadn't realized what she'd done. I almost asked him why she targeted me, but I already knew. "She thought I created the tornado."

"That, and she's just a bitch. She's lucky Exos was there and not me. I'd have lit her ass on fire." The conviction in his tone had me grinning. "Vox said she targeted your mind, something about the frontal lobe. It essentially made you very drunk."

"And I assaulted you?" I pressed, wondering what the hell he meant by that.

His dimples flashed as he finished slicing up the items on his board. "You practically forced me to join you in bed." He tapped me lightly on the nose with the edge of his blade before turning to deposit it in the sink. "Which is why, Claire"—he rotated once more and grabbed my hips—"I'm *stiff*." He tugged me to the edge of the counter, forcing me to wrap my legs around his waist for balance.

I moaned at the feel of his hot arousal aligning with my center and clung to his shoulders as he rocked against me.

"I thought you were mad at me," I admitted, arching into him.

"Oh, I am," he said, his mouth brushing mine with the words. "You drive me crazy, sweetheart. Grinding all over me, telling me to fuck you when you know I can't. It makes me very, very mad. For you."

"I… I told you to fuck me?" It came out on a squeak.

"More like demanded." He nipped my lower lip, then dipped his tongue inside to seduce mine in a dance that left me writhing against him. "Mmm, I'm going to drive you wild, Claire. Taunt you until you beg me to slide inside your slick heat and claim you in a way no other fae has."

Fire licked up and down my arms, eating through my Academy sweater and wasting the fabric away to ash. I gasped as the flames reached my breasts, destroying the fibers along the way until I sat topless on the counter before a smirking Titus. Even my bra was gone.

"Shall we begin, sweetheart?" he asked softly.

"That wasn't the beginning?"

"Not even close," he murmured.

Embers swirled around my nipples, causing them to stiffen beneath the heat. Part of me recognized that it should hurt, but my inner fire caressed the one Titus created, and welcomed the resulting singe.

Just like with Exos, I felt our connection teetering dangerously on the edge of something more. I couldn't explain it, not outwardly. It simply existed. A tangible presence between us, an unspoken contract of fate, just waiting for my mental stamp of acceptance.

"Titus…" I grasped his shoulders, my skin prickling with energy from the wisps of smoke smoldering against my skin. His hands remained on my hips, holding me tightly against his groin.

He smiled. "More?"

I didn't get a chance to reply.

My skirt and panties went up in a whirling blaze of heat—gone in a flash.

I gasped. He'd undressed me before, but never like this. Never with his power roaming over my body, prickling at my nerves, caressing me in sensuality, and destroying all the fabric on me. Even my socks were gone.

"Mmm, that's better." He slid me backward on the counter. "Don't move."

His index finger brushed my knee as he stepped out from between my

163

legs. I shivered at the sensation of electricity humming over my thighs from that little touch, then noticed the flickering energy slowly crawling up my skin.

It held me captive, my eyes refusing to lose focus.

What is he doing?

He's not…

No.

He can't be…

Oh God…

The heat slithered along my inner thigh, the intent clear. And then it caressed my sensitive, damp flesh, inflaming my insides. "Titus…"

"No moving," he repeated, having returned to his food preparations.

"But—" *Fuck, that's intense.* I grabbed the counter to keep from falling over, or running, or jumping, I didn't know. But that little flame circled my clit in the most dangerous kiss, calling my own fire out to play and creating an inferno in the last place I ever thought I'd desire it.

"Beautiful," Titus praised, his green eyes burning with unrestrained desire. "But you need more, sweetheart. I want you so hot that you can't see straight."

I opened my mouth to protest, when the embers grazing my breasts whirled into fiery clamps that pinched my nipples. A scream left my throat, one born of fierce pleasure. Titus's hand against my lower belly was all that kept me upright, my eyes glazing from the rapture his fire had unleashed on me.

"Don't combust on me yet, Claire. I have plans for you." He pushed me backward to prop me against the wall, then returned to his preparations while flames hummed over my skin, skirting over all the places I desired it most without providing any sort of relief.

"You're killing me, Titus."

"Good." He threw everything into a bowl, then drizzled some kind of dressing over it. "You need to eat first."

"Fuck food."

He smirked. "I'll fuck you after food, sweetheart. Trust me." Heat sizzled between my legs, stroking me in a way that reminded me of his tongue and stirring stars behind my eyes.

This was nothing like the other fire play I'd experienced. This was *hot* and full of promise. One that equaled the very heavy erection barely concealed by the zipper of his pants.

Which gave me an idea.

Two could play this game.

I locked onto my elements—an action that was beginning to feel like second nature to me—and pulled my inclination for flames to the forefront.

Subtle, I whispered to the energy swirling inside. *Let's sweep over the jeans and incinerate in one warm wave.*

Titus froze as my power rolled over him, eating through his pants in a thorough sweep and incinerating the fabric to ash. His boxers disintegrated with it, revealing his gorgeous cock.

His eyes narrowed. "Claire..."

"What?" I asked innocently, my flames dancing across his silky skin to form a grip around the base. He nearly dropped the bowl as I stroked upward with my mind.

"*Fuck.*"

Heat spiked in my center as he returned the sensual assault against my sex. I gripped the counter for balance, my vision blacking out for a moment, and then his lips were on mine.

Hungry.

Punishing.

Devouring.

I returned the ferocity in kind, nipping and sucking and moaning. My arms looped around his neck, my legs closing around his waist. He lifted me against him, then slammed my back into the wall beside the fridge, placing his erection right where I wanted it.

"Naughty little fae vixen," he accused, his voice harsh. "You're going to regret not letting me feed you first."

I slid my center against his hardness and sighed, "I doubt it." The last few weeks felt like unending foreplay. Yes, Exos and Titus had gotten me off—*a lot*—but not being able to return the favor had been the ultimate tease.

This was my first time seeing or feeling Titus bare down there.

And oh, how he didn't disappoint.

I clawed at his shirt, needing him to be completely nude, and dropped it on the floor.

Solid muscle pressed against my curves. So hot. So strong. So *mine*.

The connection between us snapped into place without thought, a feeling of finality settling over me as Titus's fire welcomed mine with open arms.

It sent a shudder through him.

Through me.

Through our bodies where they almost joined.

And then he was there, sliding home without warning and completing us on a level of existence foreign to us both.

His name left my tongue to travel over his, and he returned the favor, whispering words of worship out loud and directly into my mind.

What I felt with Exos was incredibly different from this. Still amazing. Still absolutely perfect.

Yet, Titus carried a note of finality, of unbridled promise for always, and I accepted him with a flourish. It felt right. Perfect. Absolute.

Oh, and the manner in which he moved within me... *Mmm.* My head fell back on a groan, the sensation of utter fulfillment thriving through my veins.

Titus's lips fell to my neck, his hands roaming my sides, tweaking my breasts, memorizing every inch of my skin. My nails raked down his back, slipping back up to touch the tendrils of his thick auburn hair.

This was so much more than sex.

Passion fueled the air, our breaths mingling in hot pants, an inferno engulfing us both. But fuck if I could stop it. I let it overwhelm me, shoot me over the edge into a field of stars and light and *bliss*. A place where only Titus and I existed. An embrace overflowing with our kindled energy.

"Claire..." His mouth found mine again, his tongue a benediction against mine, his touch the life connection I craved.

The eruption building inside me seemed tied to him in an impossible way, as if I couldn't explode without him. But his continued thrusts, his strokes, his ministrations, built a maelstrom of sultry power that vibrated through my limbs.

"Please," I whispered, needing a release. He'd created this insanity, this blaze of ecstasy that lurked on the precipice of *more*.

His teeth sank into my lower lip, his hips driving harshly into mine.

Oh, there would be bruises.

My back bore the brunt of his force.

But my legs clamped even harder around him, begging him to increase his speed and drive even deeper.

And he did.

Oh, how he did.

I clutched his shoulders, my body screaming with the need to ignite.

One. Two. Three more...

"Titus," I breathed, detonating from within into the hottest orgasm of my life.

Fire. Everywhere.

A sea of red and orange and some blue.

Amazing.

Overwhelming.

Consuming.

Titus joined me, the force of his eruption sending me into another state of being. Rapture unlike anything I'd ever felt poured over me, spiking my heart rate, cascading my vision into darkness, and sending me down a black hole of oblivion.

Something soft touched my back several seconds, minutes—hours?—later.

A warm voice cooed in my ear.

My heart thumped in time with another.

Complete. Mine. Fire mate.

Cool air flooded my lungs. Warm lips brushed my cheek. And a tear slid from my eyes. *Home*, I realized. *I'm finally home.*

But not in the home I thought I desired.

166

Not Ohio.

Not with humans.

But with my fire. With my Titus.

"I love you, too, Claire," he whispered, his lips against my ear. I didn't know if I claimed to love him out loud or if he gathered it from my mind. Either way, his resulting endearment made me smile. "Rest, sweetheart. I'll bring you something to eat, and we'll do that again."

Yes, I thought back at him. *Yes, please.*

CHAPTER TWENTY-ONE
EXOS

MY LIPS CURLED. "Mmm, Claire's happy." I could almost taste her joy on my tongue, something that warmed me from the inside out.

Vox glanced at me, his hands loose at his sides as we walked. A natural warrior. He arched a brow. "She's happy?"

"Yes."

"You can feel her? Even from here?"

We were wandering the Air Quad, searching for the familiar energy signature. "I can always feel her," I confessed. "Our spirits are intertwined."

"And you're not bothered by another male, uh, you know... making her *happy*?"

"Maybe at first," I admitted. "But she has five elements. I can't satisfy them all, and her fire calls to Titus." As was evidenced by the fact that I'd just felt their very permanent bond snap into place. They'd skipped the second level entirely, landing squarely on the third.

"I guess it's not unheard of for a Spirit Fae to take more than one mate," Vox said. "It's just never something I've considered, and you're a Royal Fae, too. Like, you're expected to, well, you know."

"Procreate?" I offered, smirking. "Claire can still have children, Vox." Although, he did bring up a good point. It was one I intended to discuss with

168

her at length, including all the other complexities that accompanied a Royal mating. Fortunately, I had my mother's experience to lean on when it came to managing multiple mates in a Royal setting. She may have passed years ago, but I remembered the toll it took on her, especially after Cyrus was born.

"Right. Of course. I know. It's just—"

"Becoming my betrothed impacts more than just her," I finished for him. "Yes, I know. That's precisely why she and I won't be moving into the betrothed state anytime soon." I envied Titus for being so much easier on her senses. She would have nothing to consider where he was concerned, and everything to worry about with me.

"And Titus?" Vox pressed.

"Is officially engaged to her fire," I said, smiling. Around anyone else, I would have kept that detail to myself. But as I suspected Vox to be one of Claire's future mates, I divulged the detail.

"Like, as in, right now?"

I turned the corner of the Air Quad and nodded. "Yes."

"You can sense that?"

"Yes. Her spirit is linked to mine, which means I can see her potential bonds to all fae." I narrowed my gaze at him. "Such as you, Vox."

His light eyes widened. "Oh, no. I'm not. I mean, yeah, her air is similar, but I'm not getting involved in that mess. I've never... It's just not... Look—"

"What's more, I feel a duty to vet any potential mates for her other elements. Because only those who are strong enough to protect her should be allowed into the inner circle. I'm sure you understand, right?" I didn't give him a chance to reply, my mind already made up where Vox was concerned. He could try to fight it all he wanted, but we both knew his power had flirted with hers earlier today. And the Air Fae had liked what he felt. "Now, tell me about this energy signature."

We'd been tracking it for almost an hour, but it kept coming and going. Vox had commented on how it didn't feel right.

Based on what I sensed earlier, I agreed. Something about the essence seemed manipulated or forged, yet familiar. I just couldn't put my finger on it.

He cleared his throat and pointed at a nearby dorm. "It honestly reminds me of Aerie's affinity for air. But not quite. As I said—"

"It's been manipulated somehow," I interjected. "I know."

"But that's not possible, right? Like, I should be able to follow it back to the source."

"Could you identify it earlier?"

He shook his head, his long hair escaping the clasp at the back of his neck. "It was dark and ominous."

"And not at all like Claire."

"Exactly."

"But you couldn't determine the source?" I pressed.

"No. Not exactly. But I memorized it."

"Because you intended to hunt it later?" I would admire him greatly if that was his plan. It would show promise in his intentions for Claire.

He pinched his lips to the side. "No, more because I am constantly mapping out signatures."

Ah. Well. Still a useful trait. "Which is why it reminds you of Aerie."

"Right. She has this spirally air wave around her that I sensed in the vortex, but she's not strong enough to have created it. Her aura is also not that *black*."

I leaned against the wall of the dorm he'd pointed at moments ago, scratching my jaw. "Maybe she's working with someone?"

"It's possible, but she seemed just as alarmed by that tornado as everyone else."

"Could be an act," I pointed out. "Gave her cause to attack Claire."

"True. But…" He shook his head again. "It's not completely right."

I understood what he meant. My instincts said we were missing something important, some key component to the explanation. "We need a trap," I decided, thinking out loud. "Now that we know we're dealing with someone manipulating the elements to frame Claire, we need some sort of event to prompt them to act while we observe."

"You want to use her as bait."

"She'll have guards." I looked pointedly at him. "Right?"

"You're really not going to take no for an answer, are you?"

"I only accept viable responses," I told him. "*No* is not reasonable."

He pulled out his hair tie and shook out his long mane of dark strands. Then fixed it up again. A nervous tell, one he seemed to be using to buy time while he puzzled over a response. We both knew he'd already made up his mind. Why else would he be curious about the dynamic between me, Claire, and Titus?

Oh, they might not have an initial bond yet, but their powers had already begun dancing around each other. "You're interested," I said, amused. "You just have to embrace it."

"It's complicated."

"Yes. And fun." I pushed off the wall and glanced up at the star-dotted sky. "Our elements drive us, Vox. Listen to your air, see how it feels, go from there. But in the interim, I need your help in setting up a trap."

"What kind of trap?" he asked warily.

"One where we entice the guilty party to come out to play, then nail his or her ass to the ground. You game?"

His pupils dilated. "You're giving me a choice?"

"No, I just want to know if I need to make this a command or not." Because he would help either way. But I'd prefer him willing. If he had a stake in this game, he'd care more, and I needed to surround Claire with those who *wanted* to protect her.

Vox considered me for a long moment, his expression radiating a mixture of uncertainty and concern. Then he sighed and resolve settled over his features. "All right, Royal Fae. What do you need me to do?"

"So you're in?"

He gave me a look. "I think it's pretty obvious I joined whatever the hell this is when I showed up at the Spirit Quad tonight."

I smiled. "I knew I liked you."

"Yeah, yeah. Tell me what you need."

"For you to whistle around a rumor," I replied simply. Then gave him the words I wanted him to repeat. "Tell everyone. Or better yet, say it in front of Aerie and let her weave the web for you."

"That's one hell of a tale to be telling."

"It's what convinced you to venture over to the Spirit Quad, right? A rumor about Claire's upcoming expulsion?" I hadn't actually spread that one, the students doing it for me. But when I heard the rumor flying about, I wondered how Vox would react. And he had sought me out, as I'd hoped he would, proving he cared and wanted to protect Claire.

"You did that?"

"No, I was too busy caring for Claire. But I was aware of the comments flying around, and I saw the panic in your expression when you arrived. You thought the Council voted to expel her." Which wasn't the case at all. We hadn't even convened yet. Although, a few of them were definitely sending notes of wrath and consequence through the air.

"That's what I heard, yes."

"And you rushed over to proclaim her innocence." Not a question, but a statement. Because that was exactly what he'd done.

He stared at me for a long moment, then laughed without humor. "You're good, Exos. I'm not sure if I like that skill or fear it."

"Stay on my good side and you'll have no reason to fear it." End up on my bad side, well… that'd be another conversation entirely. "So you'll spread the gossip?"

His lips twitched. "Yeah, I'll get it to the right ears and meet you at the gym tomorrow."

"Excellent." I clapped him on the shoulder. "Good to have you along for the ride, Vox. I think you'll make a fine air mate for Claire."

"That's not—"

"Spread the rumors elsewhere, Vox. We both know the future here, and there's no sense in denying it. But good luck with your inner fight. I give you a week, tops, because you will cave."

His spine straightened. "You know nothing about me or my resolve or my desires in life."

"I don't need to, Air Fae." I leaned in, lowering my voice. "All I need is to know Claire, and trust me, you don't stand a chance. None of us do."

* * *

Claire's bare breasts peeked up at me from the sheets as I entered the room, her eyes closed in blissful unawareness. Titus lay behind her, lazily alert and observing my entry.

"Find anything?" he asked softly.

I shrugged out of my shirt and tossed it onto a chair in the corner. "Not really, no. We'll discuss it more in the morning. Did she eat?"

He pressed his lips to her neck and nodded. "Yes."

"Good." I unbuttoned my slacks and kicked off my shoes. "Congratulations, by the way."

His green eyes met mine. "You feel it?"

"Yes."

No hint of guilt or regret entered his features, only pure male pride. "She's amazing, Exos."

"I know." I pulled off my socks and finished removing my pants just as her eyes opened. "Hello, princess."

Her nostrils flared as she took in my black boxer briefs, her lips parting in appreciation. "Exos."

I smiled as I slid into the bed beside her, cupping her cheek. "There are burn marks in the kitchen." I'd noticed them immediately. "But well done on not destroying the dorm."

Claire's skin darkened to a delectable shade of pink. "Thanks, I, uh, think."

Pressing my mouth to hers, I indulged her in a deep kiss meant to arouse. She responded with her tongue and wrapped her palm around the back of my neck to hold me to her.

Titus chuckled, his palm sweeping up her side and back down. "I told you—amazing."

"Mmm," I agreed against her lips. And kissed her again, this time with more fervor than before, allowing her to feel my approval at bonding with Titus and also to provide her with a glimpse into how much I craved her. She needed to know that this arrangement worked for me, that I accepted her as my Claire regardless of the others.

Her spirit was mine.

And only mine.

Just as my spirit was hers.

"How did it go?" The words were a breath into my mouth.

I slid my fingers into her hair, holding her to me. "Vox will make a fine mate when you're ready for him," I admitted. "But I didn't come to bed to talk. We'll do that in the morning." I met Titus's gaze over her shoulder.

"You're welcome to stay, but I'm going to kiss her until she falls asleep."

He drew a line of fire down her bare arm, sending a flicker across her skin. "That's fine. I don't mind finding other ways to relax her while you do that."

"Careful, Titus, or I'll start to think we make a good team."

He chuckled and pressed another kiss to her neck. "Where Claire is concerned, I believe we do."

I smiled, pleased by his reply. It proved my suspicions from earlier accurate. All he needed was a little alone time with our Claire to work himself out. Now that he'd regained his focus and staked his true claim, he would be a formidable ally in protecting our heart. I approved.

"I like it when you two get along," Claire said, a grin in her voice.

"Yeah?" I kissed her again—long and deep. "Shall we show you just how well we can get along where you're concerned?"

She shivered, her blue irises glazed with lust and adoration. "Only if you let me play in return."

"Maybe," I whispered, knowing full well it wasn't our time yet. Not until she fully understood what it meant to mate with a royal. "But I should warn you, Claire. My goal is to make you come so hard you can't do anything other than sleep afterward. As Titus has you all warmed up, it shouldn't be too difficult."

His flames intensified, sliding downward to the apex between her thighs. "I approve, Your Highness."

I nibbled her lip, then started licking a path downward toward her breasts. "Teamwork, Titus. Now let's make our princess scream."

CHAPTER TWENTY-TWO
CLAIRE

"YOU WANT ME TO GO TO GYM CLASS?" I asked, incredulous.

Titus and Exos were sitting at the breakfast table wearing severe expressions. So very different from the ways they looked at me in the bedroom.

My seducers were gone, and in their place were two sexy-as-fuck warrior fae males.

Both taunted my hormones, driving me wild beyond my craziest desires. Just thinking of all the orgasms these two had given me had my face going up in literal flames.

Titus arched a brow. "Does the idea of finding your captor turn you on? Or is it thoughts of last night?"

"Could be this morning," Exos pointed out.

And now my entire body was on fire. "Stop."

"But we like you wet, Claire," Titus replied.

"It's true. We also enjoy your screams."

I gripped the counter and glowered at them. "You were talking about gym class," I reminded them through gritted teeth.

"Your mind went to the bedroom," Titus replied, smirking. "Can't fault us for following."

"Oh my God, you two are impossible." I pinched the bridge of my nose while they both chuckled. Only seconds ago I'd been thinking about how stern they appeared and almost longing for my playful fae mates. Now I wanted to go back to the serious topic. "Tell me again why this is a good idea."

"Fucking you? Or the trap?" Titus teased.

Exos took pity on me and replied, "Because now we know what we're looking for. By luring the culprit into an arena where you can be framed, we can in turn catch the guilty party in the act."

"What if all hell breaks loose and it comes back on me again?" I pressed.

"That's where this comes in." Titus lifted a bracelet. "You'll wear this the entire time. No one will be able to accuse you as a result."

"And what is that?" I asked, eyeing the silvery metal.

"It's what all Powerless Champion fighters wear in the ring." He slid it across the breakfast bar. "The metal works similarly to cuffs in fae prisons—it dilutes your power."

"Meaning you can't create a tornado or firestorm," Exos translated. "So if one occurs at the gym, which I highly anticipate will happen, no one can blame you."

"Okay, but doesn't that also mean I can't stop it," I pointed out.

"Yes. That's why you'll have a team of fae with you during class. Some will be more obvious than others." He smiled. "River and Vox will be incognito but helping."

"And if we have to, we can remove the bracelet," Titus added. "Trust us, nothing is going to happen to you."

Exos folded his arms, eyes narrowed. "However, the same cannot be said about the person framing you."

Titus snorted. "No shit."

"So you want me to attend a gym class and—"

"It's technically an intramural sports activity," Titus corrected. "It's one of the few classes where all fae mingle."

"Right. So gym class," I said again. "And I'm just supposed to roll with it? Go along with whatever we're doing?"

"Yes, but I also want you aware of your surroundings. It'll be a good lesson in defensive magic." Exos pushed away from the breakfast bar and rolled his shoulders. "Ready?"

My eyebrows flew upward. "We're going now?" We'd just finished eating some sort of fried pancake thing. I thought we had at least a few hours to work out the full plan, not minutes.

"We overslept," Titus murmured.

"Is that still the right term when we weren't sleeping?" Exos asked.

"Fair. We overfucked?" he offered.

"Oh my God..." My face was on fire again. "Can we stop?"

"Is that what you want? To sleep alone tonight?" Exos asked, sounding far too serious.

"Ugh!" I threw my hands up in the air. "You know what? You're right. Let's go to gym class."

"See, now I knew she'd be eager for this," Exos said conversationally.

Titus started nodding enthusiastically. "You did. You really did."

"She'll be great."

"Because she's amazing," Titus added.

"Very, yes."

"Are you two done acting like I'm not standing in the same room with you?" I demanded, hands on my hips. "Or are you trying to give me a reason to sleep alone tonight?"

Exos gave me an indulgent look that made me want to punch him. "Oh, baby, you know that'll never happen. If this morning's performance is anything to go by, you'll be begging us to come by midnight."

"I'm leaving now." I started marching toward the front door of the building, their laughter trailing along behind me in a taunting wave of heat and sound.

These men—*fae*.

My mates.

Why had I agreed to this madness, again?

Oh, right. The pleasure. Their sexy energy. The way they knew how to touch me perfectly. Their hypnotic eyes. Gorgeous smiles. Teaching skills. Irresistible bodies. And well-endowed—

I shook my head, needing to clear it before I marched back into the Spirit Dorm and guided them both to our bedroom.

Finding the asshole trying to get me expelled was far more important.

Right. Yes. Focus.

Time to make a fae pay.

* * *

Fae kickball, I thought with a snort. That was essentially what they wanted us to play in gym class today. Except no one wanted me on their team.

It reminded me of a first-grade popularity contest.

With a glare at Exos and Titus—who stood off to the side, watching with those damn serious expressions again—I joined the blue team with Vox and River. Neither of them acknowledged me, which, I suspected, was all part of the plan.

Or, at least, I hoped it was.

It took considerable effort not to pull Vox aside and apologize to him for yesterday. Though it wasn't my fault, but I felt obligated to say something. Maybe even to thank him for believing in me enough to visit last night and going out to search with Exos.

Yeah, that would be good.

I could express my gratitude for what he'd done, for helping again today, and for supposedly joining my mentor team.

All normal-ish things to say. Nothing too emotional or strange, just typical conversation.

Why am I nervous about talking to Vox?

I glanced at his profile. His crisp features definitely drew the female eye, and while I didn't usually like long hair on a man, he definitely wore it well. Lean, athletic lines. Handsome. Okay, so maybe I found him a little attractive, but that shouldn't deter me. I had two equally good-looking men watching from the sidelines. Clearly, my docket was a little full.

But something about Vox's energy called to mine. Like he soothed me in a way the others didn't. Because he understood my chaotic affinity for air? That seemed to be the one element I couldn't master. It ebbed and flowed and fought me at every turn.

Yet, I'd managed to hone the energy under his guidance just yesterday.

That had to be it. I felt a strange connection to him as a result, sort of like he resembled an antidote to the insanity building—

A ball slammed into the side of my head, sending me sideways a step.

"Ow!" I shouted, glowering at the approaching blue-haired bitch to my left. Sickle, if I remembered her name right. "What the fuck?"

"Earth. To. The. Halfling."

Seriously? "What?" I demanded, half tempted to pick up the ball and throw it at her bitchy little face.

Her resulting smile was all teeth. "I asked if you're ready to go to the Spirit Kingdom, where you belong."

I blinked at her. "Wow. That's your taunt?" I glanced around, meeting the gaze of several of my *teammates*. They all appeared as welcoming as she did. Great. I shook my head on a laugh, deciding to play this one low-key and not let her get to me. "Sorry, I just expected more originality in the Fae World. But that wasn't much better than my high school bully."

"You'll wither and die there," she continued.

I rolled my eyes. "Okay."

"And disappear for good."

"Uh-huh." I refused to let this bitch bother me. "Still not impressed. But please, continue. I could use some entertainment."

Ice clouded her blue eyes. "You tried to kill my friends, and you think this is funny?"

"I haven't tried to kill anyone." I folded my arms, bored. "I'm just trying to learn about my fae heritage. That's it."

She snorted. "Your mother was a whore who fucked a human and caused a plague that killed off most of the Spirit Fae. An abomination. And you're the product of it all, a walking reminder of Ophelia's atrocities."

Okay, those words stung a bit. Mostly because they were right. But… "I'm not my mother."

She spit at my feet. "You're right. You're worse. Taking a Spirit Royal for yourself to, what, destroy him, too? And Titus? And how many others? You're an even bigger slut than your mother!"

My palm itched to meet her face, but I swallowed the urge and forced a smile. "Anything else?" I learned a long time ago that the best way to deal with a bully was to not react.

"Yes. I hope they banish you," she seethed, ice forming around us. It prickled against my skin, raising goose bumps along the way. A few of the students stepped back, eyes widening. River, however, stood firm, gaze narrowed.

It couldn't be Sickle.

That would be too obvious.

And she couldn't control air or fire.

Although, the two girls glaring daggers at me from across the gym were capable of controlling those elements.

No.

That couldn't be it.

I'd literally done nothing to them, apart from apparently stealing Titus from Ignis. But he claimed they were never in a relationship.

Hmm, though, she did try to drug him into one. So she clearly has a thing for my mate.

The whistle blew loudly, calling all the players to their respective locations. Our team was in the field first. And that, apparently, was a literal location because grass grew across the floor with each step, bathing the gym in an exterior appearance.

Lily-pad-shaped bases formed a diamond configuration, denoting our field positions, and another whistle sounded.

Sickle maintained a distance—thankfully—leaving me to guard third base. My competitive drive was piqued as a ball shot over my head. I jumped to catch it, then threw it to the first baseman.

He caught it with a surprised look, then grinned at the growling fae who halted mid-run.

"Nice," Vox praised, having skipped over to my side in anticipation of the kick.

"Thanks." Maybe this would actually be fun.

We went a few rounds with me catching more balls, completing several throws, and generally pissing off the other team while enthralling my own.

Several fae even smiled in my direction.

Considering how this started out, I took that as a reasonable sign that at least a couple of fae might actually begin to like me.

At least, until Ignis nearly slammed into me during a field-to-base transition. She tossed her long red hair over her shoulder and sniffed. "You reek of Titus."

"Thank you," I replied, smiling. He winked at me from across the room. "As I'm very familiar with his scent, I'm taking that as a compliment. Now, if you'll excuse—"

She shoved me back with her hand on my shoulder, causing me to stumble. "You might have him fooled, but I see right through your little innocent act. Your mother's blood runs thick through your veins. And soon, you'll end up just like her. *Dead* in the Spirit Kingdom."

My lips parted on a reply as ice drizzled across my skin, forming a ball in my palm.

I gaped down at it, confused.

This isn't mine.

I glanced around, searching for the culprit, and found several people backing away. Including Ignis.

"What are you doing?" she demanded, her eyebrows rising. "Stop that."

"I'm not—"

"You're insane!" she jumped backward, her hands up. "Everyone sees this, right? She's an abomination that needs to be banished!"

"What are you doing, Claire?" some random chick in a skirt demanded.

"Noth—"

"This is how it started yesterday!"

"In the courtyard, too."

"She's unstable."

"A monster."

Energy crawled over my skin, foreign and cold, and began to spiral into a voracious ball of energy.

"River…" I searched for him, finding him too far for comfort.

The mean girl brigade began to approach their team captain, their expressions alarmed, but a sheet of ice blocked their path. Ignis leapt sideways on a yelp, her terrified gaze flickering over her shoulder at me. I did nothing but watch as frozen blades appeared around the room, spiking up from the floor.

Fae screamed.

The instructor—whose name I didn't even remember—shouted.

My name rent the air.

Accusations flew with a fervor.

Stay calm, I told myself. *Exos and Titus are here. It's fine.* I stole a deep breath from within and willed my body to remain warm despite the arctic drop in temperature flooding the room.

Vox was suddenly at my side, his palm on my shoulder. "Do you feel it?" he asked softly. "The negative presence?"

I swallowed, trying to search for whatever he meant and shook my head. "I can't feel anything."

He glanced down at the metal bracelet clamped around my wrist and nodded. "Then the cuff is working."

"Is that a good thing?" I asked, shivering as a frozen sheet blanketed the ceiling of the gym.

"Yes." He nodded toward Elana standing just inside the door beside a man with shockingly white hair. "Looks like Exos invited some of the Council members to the show—Elana and Vape."

Vape. That must be the lanky male with the long, stark strands. Power seemed to emanate from the male's gaze as he studied the room with a serene expression. He said something to Elana before glancing at Exos and giving him a nod.

Something seemed to pass between them. An understanding. Unspoken words. I opened my mouth, ready to ask Vox if he knew what was happening, when an ominous crack sounded through the air.

Golf ball–sized hail fell from the ceiling, crashing into the ground around me. I screamed, falling to my knees, and covered my head just as a lethal ice pick sliced through the air toward Exos's head.

"No!" I made to move, but a wave of fire went up in a flash, incinerating the approaching weapon and leaving a very livid Royal Fae in its wake. He sent waves of power through the gym in a show of dominance unlike any I'd ever seen or felt.

Fire mingling with spirit—the royal declaring his right to the throne.

Everyone froze.

Then several fae fell to their knees on a whisper of sound, his name a chant on the wind.

Chapter Twenty-Three
Claire

I STOOD GAPING AT EXOS, unable to speak, unsure of what to do.

"Who dares to threaten me?" he demanded, his blue eyes scanning the gym. "The last of the Spirit Fae line. A royal."

Several heads turned in my direction, causing him to scoff.

"You all discredit my ability to sense my own mate's power? You think I wouldn't be able to feel any malevolence coming from the future Princess of the Spirit Kingdom?" He tsked. "Such an insult requires punishment, perhaps in the form of a reminder of what a Spirit Fae can truly do."

Shudders rolled through the room, palpable and fear-driven.

"She did it!" someone shouted.

"Who?" Exos demanded.

A petite male with curly dark hair stood slowly and pointed at Sickle. "I felt her water energy roll over me just before it surrounded the Halfling."

"He's right," Vox added, still standing at my side. "I felt it, too."

"Same." The high-pitched voice came from the fae I'd first thrown the ball to at the beginning of the game.

Sickle was frozen on her knees, her expression one of shock. "I... I..."

"I recognized the signature as well," the white-haired male said from the doorway, his voice carrying over the crowd. "It flooded the room. And as you've put the distinctive Powerless Champion cuff on your mate, Titus, it most certainly did not come from Claire."

Several gasps filled the air as Vox lifted my arm. He tugged up the sleeve to reveal the bracelet underneath while I stood stock-still beside him, unable to properly breathe.

Sickle did this?

That just seemed too obvious somehow.

"I didn't do this," Sickle said, her head rotating back and forth. "I would never… I mean… I'm not… This can't…"

"What about the vortex?" Aerie asked, her wiry form shaking beside Sickle. "And the fire? Sickle didn't do those."

"Yet they targeted both me and Exos," Titus broke in. "Odd, considering we're the only two fae helping Claire. Why would she try to harm us?"

"Because she's insane," Ignis muttered from across the room.

"No, I suspect something else is at play." Elana stepped forward in a pristine white outfit, her hands clasped before her. Energy seemed to ripple around her as she moved, the air shifting beneath her, the grassy floor rekindling with life beneath her feet.

Several in the room gave her a wide berth, their reverence palpable as they kept their heads bowed for both Elana and Exos. Even Titus and Vox appeared to defer to them, making me wonder if I was supposed to be kneeling or bowing instead of gaping.

But I couldn't stop.

I couldn't look away.

I needed to see what the hell was about to happen, hear whatever she intended to say. This woman—the Chancellor of the Academy—held my future in her hands. Exos never said that; it was just something I *knew*. And now she seemed to be considering her options, weighing the events of the room in her mind, and stroking the guilty parties with her spirit.

It slithered over me, a darkness that surprised my senses—there and gone in a flash. But it left an inky texture in her wake, confusing my ties to my inner elements.

Wrong.

Intrusive.

Reject.

Exos moved to stand beside her, his hands tucked behind his back, his spine erect in a distinctly regal manner. Titus remained at his station near the side of the room, unmoving, gaze downcast.

But the white-haired one strode forward with purpose, his eerily light gaze sweeping over everyone he passed.

"Stand." Elana's command sent a shiver through the air, but only three obeyed.

Ignis.

Aerie.

Sickle.

"Chancellor El—"

Elana silenced Ignis with a wave of her hand. "No speaking unless I ask you to." She strode around the trio, the atmosphere moving with her as a twirl of pixies appeared on her shoulder. "Mmm, yes, do."

They took off in a swarm, dancing over the three girls who appeared frozen in time, unblinking. I gaped at the display, concerned and confused, while everyone else in the room appeared to be incapable of observing.

What is happening? I wondered.

She's searching their minds for memories, Titus whispered back, causing my head to whip toward him.

What?! She can do that?

As a Spirit Fae, you possess the same ability.

I gaped at his prone form. He'd remained tucked into a revered pose, his eyes hidden from my own. I learned last night that we could somehow communicate in our minds now that we'd mated, but I didn't realize how clear our conversations could be.

Am I supposed to be bowing? I asked, wiping my palms against my skirt.

If you were, you would be. She's controlling the entire room right now, apart from you and Exos.

Why? I wondered. And how did he know she wasn't controlling me? I'd felt her energy slither over my skin. Just thinking about it made me tremble in foreboding. I *never* wanted to feel that again.

Because she can and she's pissed, Titus replied. *But most importantly, because it's a way of exerting power.*

Oh. And you're telling me she's able to search everyone's memories? Why didn't she— or Exos, for that matter—do that before? It would have saved us a lot of trouble, and me a lot of grief.

Who's to say they haven't? he countered. *But from what I understand, it takes a lot of energy. And to dive into someone's mind requires a conflict worthy of the intrusion—such as witnessing a fae using elements inappropriately.*

Hence, today's trap, I realized.

Exactly.

"Interesting," Elana said as her pixies began to chatter. "Very interesting." She clapped and the creatures disappeared. "It would appear none of the incidents were Claire at all, but the three of you trying to sabotage the new student out of petty jealousy."

"That's not—"

"Silence!" Power thundered through that softly spoken word, making even me want to think twice about ever speaking again. Ignis visibly shuddered, her fiery hair falling in a wave over her shoulders as she bent even lower. "What was it you three desired? Oh, yes. For the Halfling to be banished to the Spirit

Kingdom. Well, I do find that to be a suitable punishment for knowingly trying to destroy the reputation of an innocent student. Thoughts, Exos?"

"Perhaps a temporary visit," he suggested flatly. "They are students, after all. And the Spirit Kingdom is not kind to outsiders."

"Temporary," she mused, tapping her lip. "Vape?"

The white-haired male lifted a shoulder in a slight shrug. "As it is an affront on the Royal Fae and his intended, I would defer to his choice on the matter."

"And you, Mortus? I sense you lurking in the corridor. What say you?" she called.

My heart skipped a beat as the tall male with familiar dark features entered the room, his hands tucked behind his back in a similar fashion to Exos. "Does my opinion even matter?" he asked, his tone emotionless.

"As I request it, yes." She gave him her full attention. "Ignis is one of your students, after all."

He glanced at the redhead. "One of many."

"Then you should care what happens to her."

"As I said, one of many." He considered Ignis as one would an inconvenient mosquito. "Well, I suppose a temporary punishment would be adequate. Though, I'll also note that I surmised something like this would happen. The Halfling is not necessarily well liked, and if she is to survive in this world, then she should get used to being attacked."

Ice slithered through my veins at his callous words. Even Vox flinched beside me. But Exos merely chuckled. "I wish anyone luck who attempts to touch my intended betrothed. Not only will they have me to contend with, but also Titus. In fact"—he paused to address the room—"allow this to be a warning to you all. For while I may suggest a temporary sentence to be served in the Spirit Kingdom, I'm also requesting they be stripped of their elements during their stay. As they've proven to use them wrongly, it only seems fitting. Wouldn't you agree, Elana?"

The girls began to cry—silently—while the elders observed, and I wondered what all that would entail. Cuffs like my own? Or something more dire?

"Yes, that suits the crime, indeed," she agreed, a note of admiration in her voice. "Care to do the honors?"

"I do." He shifted forward, hands still behind him but gaze focused on the three bowing females. "As I said, consider this an introduction, for I will not be so lenient on a second offense."

Swirls of energy laced through his words, stringing through the air and wrapping around the women in wispy vines of magic. Their mouths opened on soundless shrieks at the contact, tears streaming from their eyes as Exos weaved the power through them and over them and around them.

Can you see that? I asked Titus, then remembered he couldn't look up.

No, but I feel it.

What is he doing?

Binding their elements, he whispered back to me. *He's essentially making them human.*

I flinched. *Fae can do that?*

Spirit Fae, yes.

Which meant *I* could do that to someone. Take away their will. Control them. Which, of course, made sense. Spirit represented life and death, and apparently, that included a fae's essence as well.

The girls collapsed as he finished, their tear-streaked faces leaving me slightly unsettled. Not that they didn't deserve it. With their little tricks, they'd almost sentenced me to an entire existence alone. And they'd tried to hurt Exos and Titus.

Yes, they more than earned this fate.

"Mmm, I believe justice is to be served, then," Elana murmured, calling on her pixies again. "Take them to the house. I'll escort them personally to the Spirit Kingdom later." She flicked her fingers with the words, and the horde of little fairy things took hold of the trio. They practically dragged the three fae from the room by their hair and clothes while Ignis pleaded after them with her eyes. When she met mine, there was a note of urgency in them that I didn't understand.

Panic that she'd been caught?

Frustration?

A hint of revenge?

But it was too quick for me to study, the girls yanked from the gym with a vengeance.

Elana sighed dramatically. "Well, now that we've settled that, I believe apologies are in order. Claire has been wrongly accused and should actually be commended for her efforts in *stopping* the dangerous elements. I witnessed each account with my mind now, through the eyes of the guilty, and I must say, I'm impressed with your control." She smiled at me. "You've come a very long way in such a short time. I suspect there will be great things in your future, young one." She cocked her head to the side, then peered at Exos. "I have an idea."

"Yes?" he prompted, his expression one of deep admiration. This woman was clearly well loved by the fae. It seemed appropriate. From what little I'd observed of her, she'd earned her status.

"How would you feel about me helping with some of her instruction? Given your recent bond and her attraction to all five elements, she has the potential to help—if not *lead*—our elemental peace initiatives. Thoughts?"

Gasps filled the room, including one from Vox.

But I was too busy trying to figure out what she meant by *peace initiatives* to comprehend the entirety of that statement.

"I think it's up to Claire," Exos replied. "But I agree that it would be an excellent—and very generous—opportunity."

"Might help make up for her rocky start as well," she mused before grinning at me again. "I'll touch base with you next week on what a tutelage beneath me would require, then you can decide for yourself if you're interested. Yes?"

I swallowed. "Um, thank you. Yes, I would be interested." *I think...?* This was not at all how I expected the day to go. But I couldn't necessarily complain about the turn of events, and from the awed noises in the room, she'd just offered me a status of some kind. I only wished I understood what.

"Excellent." Elana clapped her hands once more, eliciting several sighs of relief throughout the gymnasium. "Well, it's been lovely, my beautiful children. I hope we all learned great things today. Should anyone require an audience with me to discuss today's events, you know where to find me."

She left with a flourish of vitality, the ground sprouting wildfires in her trail and a clutter of those pixies forming around her like a guard.

Vape smiled and followed, but not before nodding once at Exos.

And Mortus merely slinked back into the shadows, his presence an ominous shade in the back of the room as everyone seemed to bounce back to life.

I met his dark gaze, felt a chill of ill intention traverse my spine, and suddenly found myself wrapped up in Titus's arms. "You did it," he whispered, his lips at my ear.

"I didn't do anything."

"You remained calm, sweetheart. You didn't let them goad you. And you're one hell of a Faeball player." He cupped my cheeks in his hands and kissed me lightly. "Why didn't you tell us you knew how to play?"

"You mean kickball?" I asked. "Humans play that in, like, elementary school."

His eyebrows shot up. "Really?"

"I told you that," River put in, joining us. "I've said that, like, ten times."

"You did?" He gave him a look. "When?"

"One of the many times you were apparently ignoring my comments about the human world," River grumbled.

"Hmm. Fair." Titus draped his arm across my shoulders, pulling me to his side. "Well, Claire's a natural at it."

I snorted. "It's not a hard game."

"She's really good," someone agreed from the side.

"Yeah, she is," another said.

I frowned after them. "I don't know them."

"Ah, but they know you." Titus pressed his lips to my temple. "Actually, I think your position around here is about to change."

Exos joined our circle, his gaze brimming with pride. "Mortus just gave us permission to move back to the Fire Quad, if you want."

"He did?" I glanced around, trying to find that ominous energy, but he'd disappeared.

"He did," Exos confirmed. "But I told him we're having too much fun on Spirit Quad to move." He lifted a brow. "Unless you disagree?"

I considered it and smiled. "I think the Spirit Quad could use a little life."

His lips curled. "My thoughts exactly." He stepped in to brush his lips over mine while Titus's arm remained solid across my shoulders.

My two fae.

It felt good here.

Felt even better that Vox remained on my other side. I didn't know what that meant, but I would investigate later. For now, I was just glad to have my name cleared of wrongdoing. I still had a lot of work to do to get my elements under control, but at least I could do so without worrying about hurting others.

As Elana said, I'd helped.

No, I'd more than helped. I'd dismantled the bad energy with my own gifts.

"I want to know more about the internship," I whispered to Exos. "What does it mean?"

"It means Elana wants to tutor you personally. Like she did with your mother." He tucked a strand of my hair behind my ear and pressed his forehead to mine. "It would be good for you to have a second spirit instructor, and she's extremely powerful. She could also tell you more about Ophelia."

My heart slid into my throat. "Because she mentored my mom." The gravity of that realization floored me, making me uncertain of how to proceed.

Part of me didn't want to know my mother at all, especially after everything I'd learned. The other part desired more information on what happened, who she was before her relationship with Mortus took a turn, and what similarities I had to her that I should avoid.

"Yes." Exos pressed his palm to my neck, angling my head back to meet his kiss. "Think about it, princess. You don't have to decide now."

"Okay," I whispered. Although, in my heart, I already knew my decision. *Yes.* Because I had to know what she was like, to avoid ever becoming her.

I refused to ever hurt Titus in that way. Exos, too.

"Mmm, we'll discuss it more tonight," he murmured. "I need to go call my brother to update him on our situation, but I'll be quick."

"Promise?" I asked, gazing up at him. "Because I was hoping to get a few sparring lessons in this afternoon."

"Sparring, hmm?" He glanced at Titus. "Seems she wants an upgrade."

Titus snorted. "She just wants to play with spirit because I gave her too much fire last night."

My eyes rolled upward. "Please don't."

"That sounds like a challenge, Fire Fae," Exos replied, looking over him.

"Let's see how exhausted my spirit makes her tonight."

"Ugh, seriously—"

"You're on, Royal." Titus smiled. "We can make a game of it—who can exhaust Claire more."

My cheeks were officially inflamed. "Guys…"

"Sounds like a fun way to spend the rest of the week," Exos agreed, his grin positively wicked. "You ready to join yet, Vox?"

Oh God…

The Air Fae merely shook his head. "I'm just here to teach."

"Teach," Titus repeated. "Right."

"I am."

"Uh-huh. Exos is just here to lay out commands. I'm here to light Claire on fire. And you're going for professorship." Titus shrugged. "Works for me."

"You're incorrigible," I growled, shrugging out from under his arm. "And if you keep it up, I'll be sleeping alone later."

"Sure, sweetheart," he said, snagging my waist and pulling me back to him. "Then you'll just dream about us, but I assure you reality is better."

Reality, I thought with a laugh. What a strange word. Because my reality? Yeah, it was nothing like my dreams, or even my fantasies.

No, this was better.

Even with the teasing, the sharing, the constant confusion, I wouldn't trade my current existence for anything in the world.

Exos winked at me, either hearing my thoughts or seeing them in my expression. "See you in a bit, princess."

It was as he disappeared from view that I pondered over his words. *Call my brother…*

Using what? I wondered. I hadn't seen any phones in the Fae Kingdom. Probably some sort of tree or a bird.

"You ready to go home, sweetheart?" Titus asked, his arms tightening around me.

Home. I smiled. "Yeah." I liked the sound of that. "With you." *And Exos.*

My new world filled with odd mating rules, elements, and, most importantly, love.

A girl could get used to this life.

A girl like me.

EPILOGUE
EXOS

I DIDN'T WANT TO LEAVE CLAIRE, but I needed to talk to my brother. Something about the setup felt off. Too easy. Too obvious. And the energy signatures felt tampered with and wrong somehow.

With quick steps, I ventured across campus toward the nearest communication tower. Fae didn't have technology the way humans did. We used something simpler—our minds. But it required the right condition, hence the tower.

I took the stairs two at a time, the air calming with each step upward. So much energy on campus, all spiked by the mingling of elements. Moments like this, I missed the simplicity of the Spirit Kingdom.

The thought had my instincts itching again.

Did those girls deserve their fates?

Yes, I'd made an example out of them, wanting everyone to know what fate lurks for them should they decide to fuck with my mate. But my spirit had sensed something foul inside them as I wove my energy through their skin—a presence that didn't belong.

One that reminded me of someone.

But who?

I glanced around, the hair rising on the back of my neck.

An essence had just joined mine. Subtle. Dark. Familiar again.

189

No one stood on the stairs. So where was it coming from?

I turned in a circle.

Nothing.

What is that? I crept upward, already reaching out to Cyrus with my mind. He wouldn't answer me right away, would require time to find an appropriate location, but the subtle shimmer of his mind told me he'd received my message.

While I waited, I took in my surroundings once more.

That nagging energy of wrongness thickened. Was it all in my mind? A consequence of that gymnasium? Had I banished those girls wrongly?

No, they were awful beings. I knew that, had sensed it in their auras as I disintegrated their bonds to the elements—one of the worst punishments known to fae kind.

That had to be it. I just felt bad about hurting another, even though those women deserved it. The Spirit Kingdom would not be kind to them—a fate they more than warranted.

Exos? Cyrus whispered through my mind. *Is everything all right?*

I'm not sure, I answered him honestly. *We discovered who was targeting Claire, but I have this odd feeling we accused the wrong fae.*

How so?

I told him about the setup, how Elana used her magic to extract the truth—an exhausting form of spirit magic—and how I sensed a falsehood. *Something isn't right, Cyrus.*

Do you need me?

I think… I trailed off as the dark essence grew around me. No one stood nearby. The sky remained clear. But I *felt* the menacing presence like a scar against my back. *Someone's here.*

Listening?

No. My mental walls were impossible to breach. *But here with—*

A flash in my vision sent me stumbling backward. Harsh. Strong. Quick.

The culprit moved too fast, too unexpectedly. My energy was exhausted after the gymnasium, not yet replete enough for defense. I threw up a wall, but he ghosted through it, startling me. Then struck me upside the head so hard my vision clouded behind a sea of black dots. A second strike forced me to my knees. And a third sent me face-first to the ground.

Exos! someone screamed. Maybe Cyrus. But it sounded mysteriously like my Claire…

Only then I did I realize *who* had joined me up here, the smoky figure taking corporeal form.

But it was too late.

The assailant's name was but a mere whisper in my mind just as everything went dark.

Run, my Claire… Run.

ELEMENTAL FAE ACADEMY

BOOK TWO

CHAPTER ONE
CLAIRE

TITUS'S MOUTH CAPTIVATED ME. So smooth, perfect, and delicious. My tongue craved to meet his, to engage in a sensual dance that would lead to more. But he kept the kiss slow and teasing, his lips tantalizingly tender.

He smiled, the motion knowing. "You said you wanted to wait for Exos to begin our celebrations."

"I did," I admitted, my thighs clenching around his. Climbing onto his lap and straddling his thighs hadn't been part of the plan, but his smoldering green eyes had become a beacon I couldn't ignore. "He's taking too long."

After the episode in the gym—where we finally discovered who was framing me for all the incidents at the Academy—Exos went off to call his brother. Whatever that meant. I had yet to see a phone in this realm. Maybe I'd ask him when he returned.

Titus chuckled and tapped my nose. "So eager."

"I feel liberated. Free. Like I could fly." I threaded my fingers through his thick auburn hair. "And I'm tired of waiting." At this point, Exos could just join us whenever he arrived. It wouldn't be the first time he walked in on me naked with Titus. "Kiss me."

"Mmm, I was," he murmured.

"*Really* kiss me."

He didn't. "When did you become the demanding one?"

"When I acquired two fae mates." One for spirit, one for fire. Apparently, it wasn't unheard of for a Spirit Fae to require multiple connections, as all Spirit Fae bonded to two elements—spirit and another.

Except I wasn't normal.

Somehow, some way, I had access to all five elements.

And I wasn't even a full-blooded fae but a Halfling with a fae mother and a human father.

I still hadn't wrapped my mind around all of it, but I was learning to take it one day at a time and to focus on controlling all my abilities. Something a horde of mean girls had tried to ruin by making me appear unstable to the other fae.

Fortunately, we'd stopped them.

Hence the reason I wanted to celebrate.

I kissed Titus again before he could reply, this time with tongue, and he responded with a growl. His grip on my hips tightened, his leisurely movements disappearing as he took control of the embrace and reminded me of his inner strength.

Fire.

I reveled in it, bathed in the glory of his heat. It soothed mine in a way no one else could because he was my chosen mate. For eternity. My flames called to his, engaging him in a passionate gyration of power that warmed the room. Embers floated around us, kindled by our coupling, and stirred a smoky flavor in the air around us.

"Fuck, Claire," he whispered.

"That's the idea." I tugged his lower lip between my teeth, sucking hard. "Take me to bed, Titus."

I didn't want to do this in the living area, not when others could interrupt us. Not that many would. The Spirit Quad was a wasteland—a consequence of ninety percent of the Spirit Fae dying after my mother— *No.* I refused to think about it. Not now. Not while Titus was doing *that* with his hands.

Traveling up my sides.

An inferno trailing in their wake.

Oh, for the love of the fae... I loved when he did this, displaying complete control over his power and incinerating my clothes along the way. It showed restraint. It seduced and taunted my fire to come out to play. And it heightened the moment.

Titus's palms went to my ass as he stood. My legs tightened around his waist, my lips never leaving his. He kissed me back with a fervor, his excitement hot and evident between my thighs.

We'd only just moved to the next level of our relationship, a place where our fiery souls promised each other eternity. There was still a step beyond this one, something about a ritual with words similar to wedding vows. I didn't know, would reach that stage when we were both ready. But for now, I would delight in the present and learn everything I could about my intended fire mate.

Such a stark contrast to Exos.

And yet, I adored them equally. For entirely different reasons.

By the time my back hit the mattress, my clothes were already gone, thanks to Titus's precise use of energy. He'd burned away every inch of the fabric from my body. I began to return the favor, when power sliced through my heart, eliciting a sharp cry from my mouth.

Titus pulled back, his gaze full of alarm. "Claire?"

The pain struck again, this time to my mind, cascading my vision in shades of white and black as if someone had slammed a fist into my head.

I pressed my palms to my temples, fighting to understand, but the ache only grew. An emptiness formed a cavern deep inside, creating a black void of nothing.

"Claire!" Titus shouted, his hands on my shoulders. But I couldn't see him. Could hardly feel him. All I sensed was this immense torment of loss. As if something had been ripped from my very spirit.

Oh God... "Exos!" I sat up abruptly, my head connecting with Titus's hard chest. I still couldn't see, the fog behind my eyes a mist my senses refused to navigate. "He's... *Oh*... Something's wrong. Something's wrong with Exos, Titus. Something's... I don't... It hurts!" I clutched my head again, whimpering as fractures of light pierced my pupils. "He's *hurt*."

"Claire..." Titus cradled my face, his familiar presence cascading heat over my quivering form. Exactly what I needed, a call to return to the present, to the bed, to his mostly naked body.

I blinked at him, my cheeks damp from tears I hadn't realized I'd shed. Somehow I *knew* time had passed without my knowledge, as if I'd lost consciousness when something hit me—no, *Exos*—upside the head. I tried to reach out to him, to sense his presence, our link, but I felt empty and alone. My heart raced. "He's... he's *gone*."

What does that mean?

Did he sever our bond?

No. He wouldn't do that. I had felt his emotions, strong and vibrant and true.

So what happened?

"Where is he? Where did he go?" Frantic sparks clawed over my skin, scattering goose bumps up and down my body. Coldness unlike any I'd ever experienced solidified in my veins. "He's... Titus... *Where is he?* Why can't I feel him?"

A sob caught in my throat, worry and panic overwhelming whatever he said in reply. Pounding flourished in my ears, and the room began to spin again, my entire existence being swallowed up into a void of confusion and despair.

"*Where's Exos?*" I repeated again and again and again. He wouldn't leave me. Not after everything. Right? Our spirits were bonded, not quite as deep as the one I had with Titus, but still just as powerful.

"*Claire.*" Titus's voice finally penetrated the rhythmic beating clogging my ears. "Breathe."

I inhaled sharply, my lungs weeping with joy from the much-needed air. I swallowed, exhaled, and repeated. It overwhelmed me, sending shudders through my limbs, eased the dark edges of my vision, and grounded me once more in the present.

The torment inside lessened to a dull ache, my connection to Exos wounded and almost completely dissolved. More tears came, the pain of loss destroying my heart.

I couldn't control it, couldn't stop it. Like a dam had opened and refused to be sealed off. My limbs were stiff, and my body strained in an anguish my mind hardly comprehended.

Part of me wanted to fight. To go find Exos. To figure out what the hell had happened.

But the other part of me—the one that drove my motivations—just felt broken.

Because my spirit is gone.

My soul.

My other half.

Flames roamed over me, Titus reminding me of his presence, his adoration, his *love*. I collapsed into him, and his lips went to my hair, his arms a cage of comfort around me.

Seconds, minutes, hours, later, I finally remembered how to think, how to *exist* again, and I looked at him once more. Concern radiated from his handsome face, his gorgeous eyes flooded with protective energy I longed to bathe in.

"Can you feel him at all?" Titus asked, his deep voice soothing and soft.

I shook my head. "I… I don't think so."

He massaged my wrists, considering. "Sometimes those Powerless Champion cuffs can leave a residual essence behind that hinders your ability to connect properly to your elements. It's one of the downsides. Maybe that has something to do with it?"

"But I took them off right after we left the gym." I'd only worn them to gym class because we had suspected someone might try to frame me again. And they had. However, this time I'd worn physical proof of my innocence—the cuffs that blocked me from my powers. "They didn't make me feel weird at all, just human again." Something I admittedly indulged in, at least temporarily. The elemental fae world was overwhelming, strange, and not at all like the reality I grew up experiencing.

I shook my head, clearing it and focusing. "It's not the cuffs," I said, certain. "Something... something has happened."

Titus considered for a long moment, then nodded. "All right. You said he was going to call his brother, right?"

"Yes."

"Then let's go to the tower. I doubt he's still there since it was hours ago, but we can see if you can pick up on his essence. Okay?"

"Hours ago?" I repeated, my eyebrows lifting.

"Yeah... It's almost midnight, Claire. You lost consciousness for a while, then woke up screaming before passing out again. It's been, well, an eventful afternoon and evening."

So I'd been right about time escaping me. I swallowed. "What do you think happened?"

"I'm not speculating. Not until we go to the tower." He slid off the bed, fully clothed and more than proving that we'd lost several hours. "Vox is here, so he can probably help. He brought an Earth Fae with him—Sol. River is here, too."

Oh, good. An audience for my breakdown.

I groaned, feeling like hell turned over. Titus must have been worried if he called everyone here. Not that I blamed him. A part of me felt, well, *dead*. I shivered at the realization, refusing to accept that fate for Exos.

He can't be... He was too strong. Too otherworldly. No, there had to be another explanation. I just didn't know *what*.

"Uh, Titus?" Vox's familiar tone came through the door. "You need to—"

"Move." The deep tenor sent a chill down my spine. It reminded me of Exos, but not quite. And the face that appeared in the doorway a second later was a near spitting image of my Spirit Fae, only with lighter blue eyes that glistened with a silvery hue in the light.

Titus immediately fell to his knee, his head bowed. "Your Highness."

The fae didn't even look at him, his enigmatic focus entirely on me. "Hello, Claire."

I pulled the sheets up to cover my bare breasts, my throat working as I attempted to formulate a response. His athletic build, light hair, and aristocratic jaw told me exactly *who* this was even before Titus knelt.

Cyrus.

King of the Spirit Fae.

Exos's younger brother.

There was only one reason he could be here, and it wasn't to deliver good news.

CHAPTER TWO
CYRUS

"WHERE IS HE?" the Halfling demanded. "Where's Exos?"

"Claire," the Fire Fae beside her whispered urgently. "*Bow.*"

Titus. Powerless Champion.

The famous fae appeared less menacing than I anticipated, perhaps due to his position on the ground. Still, I knew of his speed and strength. He was certainly not one to be underappreciated.

"Where's Exos?" Claire repeated, her vivid blue eyes boldly holding mine.

"Forgive her, my liege. She's unaccustomed to our ways and hasn't been fully trained on formalities." Titus maintained his formal position, as I assumed those in the other room did as well. But Claire remained unmoving, her gaze imploring mine for an answer.

I could see why Exos fancied her—golden locks, a gorgeous face, and curvy assets designed for a male's hands to pet and squeeze. Yet it wasn't like my brother to be so careless. Rather than telegraph his coordinates through our familial bond, he'd sent me here. To *her.*

Which suggested he put her above his birthright.

Fascinating.

And equally disturbing.

"Can you locate him through the bond?" I asked, ignoring her question and Titus's apology. In this situation, we could ignore the formalities.

"The connection broke," Titus replied.

Claire's lower lip wobbled, her dismay over the abrupt loss evident. I folded my arms, unimpressed by the useless emotion. "So reestablish it." My brother wasn't dead, just unconscious. I could feel his spirit thriving through the links, and as they were clearly beyond the first level of courtship, she should sense him, too. "Get over the shock, pull yourself together, and find him. Now."

She gaped at me. "But he's gone."

"No, he's not. He's taking a fucking nap." Not by choice, it seemed, but that didn't matter. "But I'll be sure to let him know how little faith you had in him to survive after we find him."

Her full lips parted on a gasp, her eyebrows lifting. "You know nothing about me or what I just felt. He's not *napping*; he's gone."

I rolled my eyes. "You're not worthy of him at all, are you?" I finally looked at the Fire Fae, whose hands were fisted at his sides, his annoyance evident in the tension lining his muscular form. "Why do you allow her to act this way? She's an emotional mess and useless." Better yet, why the hell had my brother fostered such behavior? "You're unfit to be his mate."

Her palm cracked across my cheek so fast I was almost impressed. "Fuck you!"

"Claire!" Titus was on his feet, his hand wrapped around her wrist, pulling her back.

I massaged my jaw, intrigued by both her reaction and the lack of a sheet covering her breasts. All right, so I could definitely see why Exos had chosen her. At least physically. Because she was perfectly proportioned in every way, and well groomed, too.

"Let me go!" she shouted, squirming in the Fire Fae's grip. "I'll show him unfit. And how dare you judge what you don't know, asshole. You don't know anything about me or Exos or what we had. You—"

"*Have*," I corrected her, bored again. "Past tense implies something is irrevocably broken. Your bond is very much present." I could feel it in the air swirling around her in a protective pattern.

Which was precisely why my brother had sent me here.

Ah, Exos, I thought, understanding dawning. My brother could have given me his last location but instead sent me to guard his mate. Fuck. She must be in danger if he used the final reserves of his energy to point to her.

"He's alive?" Some of the fight had left her posture and tone.

"Clearly, you're useless to me," I surmised, irritated.

"She's new to all of this," Titus replied, his jaw clenched so tightly the words came out stilted. "Have some compassion."

I laughed. "Is that what this coddling behavior is called? How quaint."

Claire growled, the sound adorably erotic coming from her mouth.

"You're an asshole."

"Fuck," Titus breathed, looking heavenward. "Please, she doesn't understand our—"

"Is she incapable of owning her own actions?" I wondered out loud. "Is that why you continue to speak and apologize on her behalf?"

Emerald fire glowed in the depths of Titus's gaze. "She's my mate."

"That's clear," I replied flatly, the depth of their connection heavy in the air. "I asked why you continue to treat her as an insignificant fae who can't speak for herself."

"If Exos is alive, then where is he?" Claire cut in, her eyebrows arched in challenge. "I can't feel him, even though you say I should be able to, so where is he?"

"That's precisely why I'm here, little queen." I cocked my head to the side. "And you're the only one who can answer that question."

"How?"

"By finding your spirit." What the hell had my brother been teaching her all these weeks? How to fucking cry?

She held my gaze, the action unprecedented. "You can feel him."

This was growing tiresome. "Have you not been listening to a word I've said?"

"I've heard every damn one," she snapped, the tone one I wasn't accustomed to hearing from a female. "I want you to tell me that you can feel him."

"Of course I can. He's my damn brother." I took a step forward, ignoring the tensing Fire Fae at her side, and grabbed her chin. "And he's your fucking mate. So honor him well, little queen, and *find him*."

She shook off my hold with a glower. "You're nothing like him."

I snorted. "Three weeks ago, I would have disagreed wholeheartedly. But seeing how weak he's allowed you to be has me wondering otherwise."

"Get out of my room." She pointed to the door. "Now."

Titus appeared to be readying himself for a fight. It would be one he'd lose, but male fae were protective of their mates. Hence, my current location. *Fucking Exos.*

"Get dressed and meet me in the living room. You have five minutes before I come back in here and carry you out—naked or not." I allowed my eyes to roam over her once more, this time in a slow perusal that caused her skin to flush in the wake of my gaze. "Well, at least you offer my brother something for his trouble."

"Out!" she shouted, scrambling for the sheets.

I chuckled and left her growling obscenities behind me. Exos would be furious when he found out, but I didn't care. All I wanted was his safe return, and someone needed to rouse the spoiled princess from her worthless emotions.

The three fae I'd stormed past in the living area all leapt up and knelt again, causing me to shake my head. "You're supposed to be her guardians?" *Pathetic.*

"No, Sire," the Air Fae replied, his lean, athletic form rising from the ground first. "Prince Exos requested I mentor her air abilities, but I haven't agreed yet. Sol is one of my other mentees, and River is a friend of Titus's."

"And your name?" As he appeared to be the most important of the fae in this room, I wanted to know his identity. It would help me discern why Exos had entrusted him with Claire's safety.

"Vox," he replied.

Ah, yes. "You're a royal descendant." And one of the top students in his class. Exos had mentioned him briefly.

He grimaced. "I am, but I'll never vie for the throne."

"No, you won't," I agreed, sensing his power level. It was impressive, yes, but nowhere near that of the ruling king. "And you?" I glanced at the Earth Fae, whose presence rumbled the earth with slight vibrations. "You've not been assigned to Claire?"

"No," he gritted out, not looking at me.

I nodded. "Well. It seems my brother was more concerned with bonding than establishing appropriate guardians." My gaze fell to the Water Fae. "Your power is no match for Claire's."

He shook his floppy hair, his demeanor underlined in fear and frailty. "I've only helped temporarily; Exos has not assigned a water mentor to her yet."

Because he was too busy getting his dick wet.

When I found my brother, I'd throttle him. This behavior wasn't like him at all. Sure, he'd entertained females before—several, in fact. But not like this.

And to bond to one?

I sighed, irritated beyond measure. Perhaps fate had worked in our favor, because the Halfling's life obviously required order.

As if hearing my thoughts, she appeared in the living area in a pair of jeans and a tank top, her close proximity to Titus telling. She trusted the Fire Fae more than anyone else in the room, which I expected considering their bond.

"All right, let's get a few things straight," I said, needing to seize control of this tenuous situation. "Vox? Your consideration is over. You're officially one of Claire's guardians and her air mentor."

The Air Fae bristled, clearly not used to taking orders, which confirmed my suspicions. "Surely there's another who could—"

"I sense your power, Vox," I said, cutting him off. "You're a suitable match and you will begin immediately. Starting by relocating to the Spirit Quad. Tonight."

"You can't just decide that for him," came a rumbling voice.

I turned all of my attention to the source of rebellion, finding an insolent Earth Fae staring me down. I hadn't received this much resistance since, well, since Exos turned down the crown. I'd slipped into my royal role after a volatile calamity hit our people and they needed a leader. I wasn't questioned—ever.

"And who are you to question my authority?" I snapped, storming up to him and letting my spirit energy roll over my skin. Thanks to my secondary affinity for water, a wave was exactly what it looked like, and I didn't pull back the cascade of power that washed over me. I didn't get angry often, but my brother was missing, unconscious, and our only hope of finding him before something worse happened rested in the incapable, beautiful hands of a Halfling who didn't have proper guidance. Or a suitable guard.

Brown eyes that swirled with the copper of the earth narrowed up at me, followed by a rumble of power that soothed my inner ire.

Well, hello there, traces of a third royal line.

Maybe my brother wasn't such a moron after all.

"Sol, *Your Highness*," he grated in reply.

My spirit energy probed him, causing him to flinch.

I immediately withdrew, sensing the damage in his spirit.

By the Elements...

This Earth Fae had been hurt by my kind, and badly, too. Raised scars tore across his core, a place only a fae of my skill could sense without being bonded.

How are you alive? I wondered, awed. These wounds came from the womb, meaning Sol had lived with this pain his entire life. Most fae would go mad from such an assault, yet he remained intact. Strong, even.

Yes, you'll do just fine.

But I couldn't establish my authority over him in the same manner as I had with Titus and Vox. No, commanding a fae like Sol would backfire in an instant.

I took a step back, giving him room and noting the cracks along the ground that had formed beneath our feet. Yes, this one was strong, and the way he'd stood up for Vox was a testimony to the fae's character.

"Sol," I repeated his name, making sure to slightly bow my head. Earth Fae reacted to subtle body language. I wasn't going to try to control him. Only a moron would try to squeeze blood from a stone. No, I had to nudge this fae in the direction I wanted him to go and allow his own momentum to do the rest. "Why are you being mentored by an Air Fae?"

"Because my control is absolute," Vox replied. His tone and posture indicated a hint of insolence, one I only allowed because I could. "If I'm going to be living here, then I still need to be able to maintain my duties to Sol."

I didn't have to ask what he meant by that. Clearly, the two fae had worked together for quite some time, and if Vox was the reason Sol had healed so spectacularly, then I would be a fool to separate them.

Turning to the Air Fae, I crossed my arms and arched a brow. "Does that mean you agree to become Claire's mentor and guardian?" I asked. He didn't have a choice, but I'd pretend for Sol's sake.

Vox stared at me for a long time before he answered. "If you agree to let Sol stay with me, then yes."

I almost smiled. *Excellent.*

"Very well," I said instead, acting as though it were a concession on my part. I wouldn't have to give the Earth Fae orders at all. He had enough power to keep Claire in check if her earth element got out of control. "Do you agree to help protect the Halfling?" I asked Sol, inserting a hint of boredom into my tone.

Sol mimicked my pose, his thick arms crossing over a broad chest. "I agree to protect Vox, who will be helping Claire."

"And protecting her," I added, glancing at the long-haired Air Fae. "She needs guardians."

Vox sighed. "She's safe on campus."

"Is she?" I countered. "Because Exos would probably state otherwise."

"Ignis and her friends tried to kill her," the Water Fae added quietly.

"They've been detained," Vox pointed out.

"Yet my brother has gone missing. How?" I gave the Air Fae my most condescending stare. "You and I both know the Academy isn't safe at all; it's just a guise of friendship crafted by Elana on her holy quest for peace." I looked at the Earth Fae. "Do you feel we're at peace, Sol?"

He scoffed at that. "Fuck no."

"I stand validated," I murmured, shifting my focus to the Water Fae. "You're dismissed. I'll handle her water training from here on out."

My secondary affinity for water wasn't unknown. My Spirit Fae mother had notoriously mated with a Spirit Royal and a Water Royal. I was the product of her mating with the latter, which gave me a uniquely powerful ability to manage two elements. If anyone could help train the little Halfling, it was me. And as I required her cooperation to find my brother, it seemed I had no choice.

Which left me with one final task for the evening. "While the rest of you prepare your new quarters, I will work with Claire. It seems she requires a lesson in the bonds and how to appropriately use them."

Cerulean fire licked through her irises. "I'll work with Titus, thanks."

I smiled. "Oh, no, little queen. You'll be working with me. Because unlike Titus, I won't go easy on you. Now follow me." I wrapped a rope of water around her waist and gave her a firm tug that elicited a squeal from her lips.

Titus took a step forward as if to catch her, but I cut him off with a glance. "You've done enough. It's my turn now, Powerless Champion. Be useful and help Sol and Vox find a room." The auburn-haired male knew better than to question my authority, even if the fiery energy rolling over his skin said he felt otherwise.

"It's fine," Claire said, her palm on his chest. "I've got this."

The queen coming to the aid of her knight.

Hmm.

Perhaps there's hope for you yet, little Claire, I thought, pleased. "Now." I gave her another tug for emphasis and grinned at her resulting growl. *Oh, yes, I'll make a worthy queen out of you if it's the last thing I do.*

CHAPTER THREE
CLAIRE

EXOS, IF YOU CAN HEAR ME, I hope you'll forgive me because I'm about to murder your brother.

He didn't reply.

Because I couldn't feel him.

But this jackass in front of me seemed to think I could, so I stomped after him into the late-night hours outside while using a flame to incinerate his water into steam.

Cyrus eyed the power exchange with interest, his lips quirking at the side. "Impressive, little queen."

"My name is Claire," I told him flatly, hands on my hips.

"I'm aware," he replied, glancing up at the stars littering the sky. "I need you to close your eyes and focus on your bond with Titus. Tell me what he's doing."

"He's helping Vox and Sol find their room, as you commanded, *Your Highness*."

His mouth flattened into lines of disapproval. "I'm trying to help you, *Claire*. Shut your fucking eyes, search for Titus, and tell me exactly what he's doing."

Gah, I wanted to smack him again. Kick him. *Hurt* him. "You're such an asshole."

"And you're a weakling, but here we are. I need you to find my brother, and the sooner you do that, the sooner I'm gone. So shut your damn eyes and focus on Titus."

A scream built in my throat, one underlined in profanities and insults all designed for this *Royal Fae* jackass. I was *not* weak. *Fucking prick.* I slammed my eyes closed and found Titus, his emotions a tangle of concern and annoyance. He wanted to peek out the windows to check on me but was instead helping Vox and Sol find a room near mine. A part of him was thankful that Exos had sent a cleaning crew through the dorm, readying several beds in preparation for others to move in.

He'd wanted to grow my mentorship team and find guards, something I knew, and Titus seemed to respect the decision.

"He's two doors away from my room, showing Vox the bathroom that connects to another room, which he's recommending for Sol." I opened my eyes. "And he's considering whether or not he needs to come out here and flame your ass."

Cyrus chuckled. "I wish he would. It's been a while since a worthy fae challenged me. I'm honestly bored."

Flames flickered over my fingers, the urge to send a fireball into his chest consuming. But a wave of his hand cooled my fiery energy, water perspiring over my skin in the shadow of his power. "Save your rebellion for someone in your league, little queen," he said, his gaze holding a touch of ice that sent a shiver down my spine.

While Exos's gaze resembled the darkest depths of the ocean, Cyrus's irises were coated in a glimmering silver blue that painted him in an almost otherworldly glow.

Gorgeous, my brain supplied. *But only on the outside.*

"I want you to repeat what you just did, but locate Exos," he said, tucking his hands into the pockets of his suit pants. "Tell me where he is."

"Did you mishear the part where I told you the connection is broken?" I asked, irritated beyond belief by this male's arrogance and lack of regard. Okay, yes, crying all evening had been a poor use of time, but I *felt* Exos's spirit disappear. It had destroyed me. What the fuck did he expect me to do? Run around looking for an enigma?

God, I hate this, I thought, suddenly exhausted. *Where are you, Exos?*

"Try" was all Cyrus said.

Try, I repeated sarcastically. *Yeah, fine. I'll try.*

I shut my eyes for show, then focused on the part of me tied to Titus. His warmth flowed back, caressing me with his energy and love and basking me in the familiarity of his fire. My lips almost curled, the relief he provided palpable.

But I needed to prod a little deeper, search for the distorted link that left an anchor of pain in my heart.

Exos, I whispered, my relief dissipating into agony. The jagged edges of our connection cut deep, the pain spiking inside me and shredding my spirit into two halves.

Tears gathered in my eyes, threatening to fall as I tugged on the snapped tether binding our spirits. Only, the rope didn't slacken the way I expected it to, didn't reveal the frayed end I'd anticipated.

No, it held.

My lips curled down, confused.

What was it holding on to?

I followed the thin line with my mind, creeping across the dark chasm of my soul, to the obsidian that lay beyond, unmoving.

Unconscious, my mind supplied. *Exos is unconscious.*

What was it Cyrus had said? His brother was taking a nap?

Well, not exactly.

"It's like he's locked in a coma," I whispered. "Unmoving. Unthinking. Asleep, but not by choice." I poked a little harder, trying to nudge him to alertness, but his spirit remained curled into a ball, soundless and alone.

"Can you see anything around him?" Cyrus's deep voice penetrated my thoughts, an unwelcome twinge that caused me to grimace.

I really dislike your brother, I told Exos.

No reply.

Sighing, I glanced around the depths of our connection, searching for any kind of clue as to where he was resting. "It's too dark," I said, shaking my head. "Like he's underground."

"Good. Can you smell anything? Hear anything?" Cyrus had lowered his voice into a soothing tone, one he probably thought helped, but only served to irritate me more. Introducing my fist to his face would be a remarkable experience and far more fulfilling than the slap against his cheek.

Regardless, he was right.

Exos is alive.

And knowing that settled my soul.

I sighed, content with his known existence while also worried about where he might be.

Damp.

Dark.

Dungeon.

I shook my head, not recognizing anything from the sights to the smells to the sounds. "He's definitely underground." My nose twitched, the scent of moss and rust apparent. The murmur of machinery followed, some sort of constant crank, and the cackle of a male voice. I pressed deeper, trying to hear more, only to be shoved out by an unseen force so heavy it sent me to the ground in a whoosh.

Cyrus grabbed me, his hands foreign on my exposed shoulders, his words gibberish over the rising volcano inside me. *So hot. Too hot.* I gasped, energy swimming over my skin and clawing at my being. I couldn't discern what was happening, the inferno overtaking me until a sudden wave took me deep under water.

Choking, I sputtered, coughing up a mouthful of the sea, Cyrus's palm a steady beat against my back.

"*What the fuck?*" Titus demanded.

I couldn't stop gagging, ice suffocating me from the inside out. If Cyrus answered, I couldn't hear him, the sounds of the ocean thick in my ears. Everything swam before me—the moon, the stars, the buildings.

Exos's spirit brushed mine, a brief hint of concern in that soft touch, only to disappear behind a wall of ivy I couldn't penetrate.

Someone is trying to break our link, I realized, my eyes flying open. My mouth tried for words, but all that came out was more water.

Titus was shouting.

Cyrus was hitting my back.

Chaos, I thought deliriously, trying to regain control of myself and my surroundings.

Deep breath, someone said.

I listened.

Now exhale.

I did.

Cyrus appeared above me again, his irises glowing with power and determination. His spirit felt foreign, unwelcome, his charming face one I never wanted to see again.

He smiled as if hearing my thoughts, his thumb brushing over my cheek. Only then did I realize I was in his lap, cradled against him like a baby.

Ugh. Not where I wanted to be. At all. I tried to squirm, but his arms were too strong, his grasp harsh.

"You tried to burn me alive, little queen," he murmured, amused.

What? I did no such thing.

"So you tried to drown her in response?" Titus demanded, sounding furious. "You almost killed her!"

"I merely reminded her of her place," Cyrus replied, his eyes still on mine. "Or rather, I informed whoever attempted to control her that I won't be going down so easily." He searched my face, spirit swirling in the depths of his gaze. "Whoever has my brother is tied to spirit and is very powerful indeed."

I blinked. Was that what I felt force me out of Exos's mind? The person trying to distort our link?

Cyrus nodded. "Yes, someone tried to use your bond to get to me." Had I spoken out loud? Or were the comments in my eyes? "Which explains why my brother tried to cut you off," he continued. "That's the pain you felt hours ago—Exos trying to close the link, to keep you safe." He ran his fingers through my hair and sighed. "That's going to make it more difficult to find him, but I understand his choice."

"So a Spirit Fae has him," Titus translated.

"It would appear so, yes. A powerful one." Cyrus continued to pet me, confusing me greatly. Mostly because I *liked* it.

No. No way. I would *not* be attracted to this jackass.

First, he was Exos's brother.

Second, he was a dick.

Third, I really needed him to stop looking at me as if he cared. As if I amused him in some way.

He chuckled. "I'm starting to see the appeal," he murmured, that head of his tilting. "She's much more pleasant when silent."

Yeah, I hate him. I started to squirm again, but those arms of steel held me in place. "Let me go," I managed, my voice a rasp I hardly recognized.

"No." He glanced up at Titus. "There are very few Spirit Fae in existence who could subdue my brother and reach me through her bond."

"Mortus," Titus replied.

Cyrus nodded. "He is a potential candidate, yes, but he's not strong enough on his own. Regardless, I suggest we keep an eye on him."

"Or corner him and demand he tell us what he knows."

"That would be the rookie approach, of course. But I play in the land of fae politics, Fire Fae. We need to go about our business as if everything is normal, continue training Claire, and prepare her for the battle to come. If we accuse anyone too early, we risk Exos's life, and that's not a mistake I'm willing to make."

"How is tracking down Mortus and demanding Exos's location going to risk your brother's life?" Titus demanded, taking the words right out of my head. Well, sort of. I had a few additional curses and commands woven between my thoughts. Like, *Let me go, you asshole. I'll talk to Mortus myself and get Exos back.*

"Mortus is old and wise and won't break easily. By the time we learned anything from him, Exos could be dead. There's also the possibility he's innocent and knows nothing at all."

"Can't you just mind-fuck him like Elana did to the mean girls?" I asked, my voice slowly recovering from whatever the hell had happened.

"Mortus is too powerful. While I could break him eventually, it would take weeks, if not months, and a lot of energy." Cyrus shook his head. "Going about our business and putting him at ease is the smarter play, because ultimately, he'll lead us to Exos. Assuming he's the culprit, of course."

"I heard a man laughing," I whispered, recalling the cackle of sound.

"Another clue, but not enough for us to be certain. And as I said, he won't break. So even if I charge him with kidnapping my brother, we still risk not finding Exos in time."

Which meant fae could die. I'd never actually asked how that happened, too busy trying to learn all about this new world. "Is that why I could smell rust?" I wondered aloud, more to myself than to Titus and Cyrus. "Fae don't like iron, right?"

Silence met my query, followed by a soft voice saying, "It's a common myth on Earth."

River. He must have felt the use of water outside.

I finally looked around, noting the destruction Cyrus and I had caused. Singed ground, a new pond in a formerly dried-up crater, all the flowers destroyed, and the buildings charred.

Well, shit.

"Iron does not kill fae, little queen," Cyrus said, his voice oddly gentle. "A fae dies when the spirit dies, which will happen to Exos if he's left underground too long without a lifeline."

"How long?"

"A few months. For a fae as strong as Exos, maybe a year," he admitted as he finally shifted me off his lap.

I scrambled backward to get away from him as fast as I could and didn't stop until my back met Titus's legs. Instant satisfaction rolled over me, the rightness of his touch causing my shoulders to slump.

"Well, I think that was enough for one night," Cyrus said, not looking at me. "You'll take her to classes tomorrow. Resume her schedule. In the meantime, I'll keep an eye on Mortus." His demeanor seemed to shift, as if I'd hurt his feelings with my stark rejection.

Impossible, obviously. Because the fae was a colossal jerk.

Titus bent down to help me stand, his arms circling my waist. "Are you okay?" he whispered, his lips at my ear.

"She's fine," Cyrus replied, some of his earlier distaste returning. "Stop coddling her, Fire Fae. She needs to learn how to fight, not cower." His cold gaze met mine. "You're powerful, Claire. Hiding from it only makes you weak, and weakness will get you killed. It's time to grow up and assert your place in our world. Otherwise, you'll die."

With that beautiful proclamation, he stalked off toward the Spirit Dorm.

"I really don't like him," I muttered when he was out of hearing range.

"Yeah, I take back every negative thing I ever said about Exos. He's definitely the more likable of the two." Titus brushed his lips against my temple. "Come on. Let's get you dried off."

The Earth Fae and Vox stood just inside the entrance, their expressions grim.

"Why don't you go grab some of your things," Titus suggested softly. "We can regroup after class tomorrow."

Vox nodded. "Is she going to Fire Quad?"

"Yes." Titus ran his fingers down my spine, causing me to shiver. "I'll be with her all day."

The Earth Fae snorted. "Good. That means we don't have to worry about her."

I frowned, unsure of how to take that. We hadn't even met yet. Not formally, anyway. "Sol, right?"

His brown eyes met mine, a hint of hesitation in his gaze. "Yes." No elaboration. No welcoming comment. Nothing to go on. Just a flat response accompanied by a grimace.

Great.

"I'm sorry to meet you under these circumstances," I told him softly. "Hopefully, I can improve your opinion of me later. You know, when I don't resemble a drowned rat." I pointed at my head for emphasis.

Vox's lips twitched. "It's not your best look."

"Thanks," I replied, returning his grin. "But I like leaving lasting impressions. Obviously. I mean, I created that disaster of a vortex when we met the other day. Tonight, I met Sol after surviving what felt like a tidal wave. So tomorrow, maybe I'll just go up in flames during class and burn off all my clothes. Should be fun, right?"

"Your uniform for Fire Quad is fireproof," Titus reminded me, smiling. "But I would enjoy that show."

Sol didn't seem nearly as amused.

But at least Vox chuckled. "Never a dull moment with you, Claire," he said softly.

I nodded. "Well, thank you both for, I guess, moving in."

"Not by choice," Sol pointed out, his arms folding across his thick chest. The fae was built like a linebacker, his well-over-six-foot height dwarfing mine.

I swallowed thickly, glancing up to meet his gaze again. "I... I can talk to Cyrus and excuse you from the guard, if tha—"

"That's not going to happen," Cyrus said, walking in with just a towel wrapped around his hips.

Yeah, he and Exos were definitely brothers.

Chiseled.

Perfection.

With a dusting of hair that led—

"My brother may have allowed you to make the rules before, but I can assure you, I am not Exos." His icy gaze captured and held mine, a warning radiating from his pupils. Leaving me speechless, he shifted his focus to the others. "Sol and Vox, go grab your shit. I expect you back in an hour. We'll go over some things for tomorrow. Titus, give Claire a bath, fuck her, do whatever it is you need to do to feel content with your mate. I don't want to

211

see her again until after her classes." He gave a wave as if he expected us all to follow his orders.

And shockingly, the fae did.

Sol muttered under his breath, yanking Vox out the door without saying goodbye, and River trailed along with them.

Titus gave me a calculated look, his vexation stirring embers between us. "The sooner we find Exos, the sooner that jackass leaves."

"It's like you read my mind," I replied.

"I did," he admitted. "Now, how do you feel about starting a fire in the bedroom? One that might spread a few doors down?"

My lips curled. "Seriously, it's like you're in my head, Titus." Because that sounded like a fantastic idea.

"Glad we're on the same page, sweetheart." He wrapped his arm around my shoulders. "Let's give him a shower. One littered in ash."

"I love you, Titus."

"I love you, too, Claire."

CHAPTER FOUR
SOL

"I TOLD YOU THAT YOU SHOULD HAVE stayed away from the Halfling," I muttered as I ripped clothes out of his dresser and tossed them onto the bed. "Now we're stuck in the thick of it. She's a loose cannon, and the Spirit Fae she attracts are no better."

Vox sighed and cast a breeze over his tousled things, brushing away loose stones I'd managed to conjure. I tried not to irritate him with debris everywhere, but my power and I never got along very well. It was part of an illness I'd been born with.

An illness caused by the Spirit Fae.

And by the Halfling's mother.

Vox's black eyes glimmered with a ring of silver that made him stand out from other Air Fae. "You're just being possessive. Now I have another student, but you want me all to yourself."

I frowned because that was partially true. I didn't like the idea of sharing Vox. He'd helped me come so far, and more than that, I was on a mission to help him as well. "If you graduate with honors, you'll be able to clear your family name."

Vox flinched. He did not like to talk about his royal ties—much less how an entire side of his family had been shunned and denied their heritage. He

213

insisted that he wanted nothing to do with the royals, didn't care about his heritage or fortune. All he wanted was to prove his place in society and become a professor at the Academy someday. It was a lofty goal, but it would take more than graduating with honors for that to happen. It was a miracle he'd been accepted into the Academy at all.

It was why he'd been stuck with me in the first place. What better way to sabotage a disgraced fae from graduating with honors and making his dreams come true than by pairing him up with an impossible case?

Except, Vox actually helped me and we made a good team.

Vox ignored me while he carefully folded each shirt before placing them into a neat suitcase. It drove me mad how meticulous he was with everything. We shouldn't even be packing. We should be telling the king to go shove his orders up his ass.

But he hadn't ordered me.

No, he'd ordered Vox, making this the Air Fae's decision.

Of course, that didn't mean I had to be quiet about my disapproval. "You know that no good can come of this."

Vox shrugged. "Maybe you're wrong. Claire isn't so bad."

I rolled my eyes. "You're attracted to her. I get it, but I'm not talking about Claire. I'm talking about the king."

"I'm not attracted to her, even if my magic thinks I am," Vox mumbled, plucking another stone that had somehow made its way into the suitcase. Perfection ruined, he took out one of the shirts he'd already folded and started over, making a low scream build in the back of my throat. "She's just vulnerable, Sol. If she uses earth power around you and you're forced to step in, then you'll see what I'm talking about." A wry grin took over his face. "I'll bet you an entire month of credits that when that happens, you'll fall for her—hard. You know what they say." He winked. "The bigger the Earth Fae, the harder they fall."

I snorted. "That's an easy bet. My magic isn't a wimp for a pretty face like yours is. You're on." I thrust out my hand.

Vox took it and we shook on it, my crushing grip encasing his lithe fingers. The Academy gave out credits once a day for standard purchases—namely, meals, amenities, and frivolous purchases I never bothered to save up for. I preferred to spend my credits on food and more food. Credits could also be earned through high scores in classes and winning intramural games between fae, although I never wasted my time on either of those. I had plenty of food to keep me happy.

Speaking of, I was starving. "Are you done packing yet? We can hit the cafeteria for a snack on our way back." It was open twenty-four hours a day and would be pretty much vacant right now. Especially on a school night.

Vox groaned. "Really, man, the cafeteria is for those who can't afford their own ingredients or kitchen supplies. I have more than enough credits to feed both of us."

I eyed the damage I was already causing to the bedroom floor. "Maybe we should eat at the cafeteria today, since I owe you for property damage again."

Vox glowered at me. "What's the point of making a bet with you if I have to spend all of my credits on you anyway? Let's get out of here so that the tab is on the Spirit King's bill and not mine."

Finally, he was talking sense.

My earth magic was raging inside of me, dying to get out. Doing some damage that the king would have to pay for sounded like fun to me.

After a snack, of course.

Chapter Five
Exos

FUCK. MY HEAD ACHED, the world spinning behind my closed eyes.

I sensed *him* lurking in the darkness, waiting for me to wake.

No, that wasn't right.

Not *him.* Except, yes, it was a male, but something wasn't—

"He's stirring," a voice said.

I know that voice.

Why do I know that voice?

Fuck, I was dizzy. *What have they done to me?*

They, yes. Focus on the they.

Where's Claire?

I tried to reach her and frowned. She was far away, her soul cut off from mine. *Why? Oh, because I built a wall. Why did I do that?*

My mind spun, searching for a reason, the voices growing outside my cell.

Dungeon.

I'm underground.

Why?

Because someone had knocked me out.

My eyes fluttered, my brain working, memories surfacing.

Oh, fuck...

I shot upright, needing to warn her, to tell her what I'd learned. "Claire!"

A blast of spirit energy hit me square in the chest, knocking me backward into the stone, my head landing harshly against the rock.

Claire, it's not who we thought. It's—

CHAPTER SIX
CLAIRE

EXOS!

I flew upward, hand to my racing heart.

Titus stirred beside me, his abdomen rippling as he stretched in his sleep. He murmured my name and sighed, his lips curling.

God, he was beautiful.

For a few blissful hours, he'd helped me forget, provided me with a pleasure that still hummed through my being.

Until Exos called to me.

I rubbed my chest, tentatively plucking at the wounded bond and wondering what he'd been trying to tell me. It sounded like a warning, a sharp plea for me to listen, only to be silenced by something harsh.

The connection between us thrived, more alive than before but still tainted by a dark, disturbing presence. *Who are you?* I wondered, careful not to provoke the essence. It weighed over our bond like a thick cloud, menacing and cruel and filled with malicious intent.

Something about it seemed familiar, reminding me of the out-of-control vortex from Air Quad earlier this week. But that was impossible. Aerie had cast that havoc, laying the blame falsely at my feet.

So how do I know you? I slid from the covers, my skin tender from Titus's affection. A glance at the clock had me swallowing a groan. I'd slept for maybe two hours. It would have to be good enough because I was wide awake now.

But Titus could sleep another ninety minutes or so before he had to wake for class.

Maybe I'd have breakfast ready for him.

I smiled at the thought of something *normal* to do. Then remembered there was nothing *normal* about fae food. Frowning, I put on a pair of silky shorts and a camisole top, then wandered into the shared kitchen of the dorm to see what I could find.

No eggs.

No bacon.

Not even potatoes.

"What the fuck am I going to make without the staples?" I grumbled, unfamiliar with pretty much every item in the fridge. *What I wouldn't give for some cheese and peppers to put in an omelet.* Ugh, my stomach rumbled in agreement at the thought.

"Uh, want some help?" a soft voice asked from behind me.

I whirled around to see Vox standing in the doorway in a pair of pajama pants, his long hair mussed and hanging around his bare shoulders. I blinked twice, stunned by the sight of his surprisingly ripped torso. His slender appearance had placed my expectations on the scrawny side, but Vox possessed the body of a runner—lean and athletic, without an ounce of fat on him.

He raised a dark brow. "Claire?"

I shook my head, clearing it. "Sorry, you startled me." *Understatement. More like he shocked the hell out of me.* I coughed to unblock my suddenly thickened throat. "I, uh, wanted to make an omelet. But there aren't any eggs."

"Eggs?" he repeated, his brow furrowing. "In the morning?"

"When else would you eat them?" I wondered aloud.

He stared at me for a long moment and shrugged. "Not in the morning, but all right." He started shuffling through cabinets until he found two cartons and set them on the counter. He inspected the inside and smiled. "These'll do. They're fresh, too."

"Why aren't they in the fridge?"

"Why would you put eggs in a fridge?" he countered.

I considered and finally sighed. "I've heard it's not common in Europe. I guess it's like that." Whatever. I wanted eggs and he provided them. "What about cheese?"

"Why would you pair eggs and cheese?"

"Because it's delicious?" I suggested.

With a dubious expression on his face, he opened the freezer and found a bright orange brick. "Here."

Gross. "That's not cheese."

He glanced at it. "Uh, yeah, it is." He set it on the counter. "Anything else?"

"Mushrooms, onion, and bacon."

"That's disgusting," he accused, looking appalled. "Not that I know what bacon is, but why the hell would you defile a mushroom with cheese and eggs?"

"Have you tried it?" I asked.

"Of course not. It sounds awful."

A laugh bubbled past my lips, causing my shoulders to shake. And then I erupted in a fit of giggles I couldn't seem to stop.

He thought an omelet sounded awful. This fae. One who probably ate that hideous-looking green mush that Exos favored. I couldn't stop laughing, the humor of it all bursting inside me in a wave of much-needed release.

This entire world, all these men, were completely unfathomable, yet real. And they didn't want to eat an omelet.

"What the hell did you do to her?" a gruff voice demanded, causing the cabinets to shake around us. "Did you break her?"

"She wants to make some sort of atrocity with eggs and cheese," Vox explained, shuddering.

I laughed harder in response.

"Why the fuck would you put eggs and cheese together?" Sol demanded, sounding affronted by the very idea.

"Oh, and she wants to add mushrooms and onion, and something called bacon." Vox gagged at the notion and Sol joined him.

I swiped the tears away from my eyes, thoroughly amused. "Get me some mushrooms and onions, then park your asses there." I pointed to the stools by the bar. "I'm going to blow your mind."

"Park my ass?" Sol repeated, glancing at Vox. "Can you believe this chick?"

The Air Fae's lips twitched. "I gotta admit, I'm officially curious." He started rooting through the kitchen and handed me a single mushroom that was the size of a head of lettuce. "Onion, onion, onion," he repeated, searching the freezer. "Nope. No onion. But I can add it to my grocery list for later today."

"Maybe check the pantry?" Wasn't that where onions went?

Both men looked at each other, then at me. "What?" they said in unison.

"Never mind," I sighed. "What about pepper? Like, the vegetable, not the spice."

"Why would pepper be a spice?" Vox asked, already looking.

He handed me two orange bell peppers a moment later, causing me to smile. "Finally, something normal." It wasn't cold, but it smelled right. "And pepper can be a spice on Earth."

"Humans are weird," Sol muttered, taking his seat at the counter. "Pretty, but weird."

My lips quirked. "You think humans are pretty?" I found a knife and started chopping the pepper, much to the horror of Vox observing.

"Well, you're the only one I know," Sol said, lifting one broad shoulder in a shrug. Unlike his counterpart, he wore a shirt, but something told me he'd be a solid brick of muscle under those clothes.

Not that I wanted to think about it.

Or about Vox.

I had a beautifully sculpted Titus waiting for me in the other room. Hopefully, he didn't mind my making breakfast for them all.

"How do I melt this cheese?" I asked, looking at Vox.

He visibly gagged again. "In a pan?" He grabbed a skillet from under the stove. The presence of familiar items lightened something inside of me, as did the familiarity of being in a kitchen surrounded by foods I mostly recognized.

Well, except the eggs had a strange purple consistency to them as I cracked them open.

And the cheese was very much not cheddar.

Sol and Vox both watched in obvious disgust as I mixed all the items together in the skillet, neither of them saying a word.

Right, so it didn't look like an omelet at all when I finished. More of a purple hash with the strong aroma of vegetables. But the gooey cheese made me smile.

"Do you have any tomatoes?" I asked.

Both men looked ready to vomit.

"Never mind," I said slowly, twisting my lips to the side. "Humans would call this—"

"What the hell is that smell?" an aristocratic voice demanded as Cyrus came into view wearing a suit from Exos's wardrobe. Of course they wore the same size.

"Claire made breakfast," Vox whispered, his nose scrunched up in clear disgust.

Cyrus came around the counter to study the pan. "That's repulsive, Claire."

"Then it's a good thing I didn't make it for you," I snapped, my amusement melting into immediate annoyance. "Actually, if none—"

Sol tapped the bar, cracking the solid granite. "I want to try it."

Vox swung around on his stool and gaped at his best friend.

"What?" the Earth Fae said, looking a smidge chagrined. "It's food. I like food."

Cyrus snorted. "Such a simple-minded creature. I'll pass."

"Considering I didn't make you any, that's perfectly fine." I grabbed a plate and cut a piece of the omelet off for Sol, then slid it across the counter to where he waited with a napkin.

He stared at it and shrugged. "Cool." Then picked it up with his hands to take a bite.

"Uh, you're supposed to use a fork..." I pinched my lips to the side, unsure of where they were located, but Sol seemed to be doing fine without a utensil.

In a blink, half the portion was gone. "It's fucked up, but oddly good." He held it out for Vox to take a bite.

And much to my surprise, he did, his wariness disappearing into one of wonder. "Huh. I never would have put those ingredients together." He glanced at me. "Okay, Claire. I'll have a plate."

Pride prickled my chest as I cut him a slice and handed it to him—with a fork.

Except, like Sol, he ignored it.

The last two pieces were for me and Titus, leaving Cyrus alone. Where the jackass belonged. Not that he seemed to care as he prepared himself some sort of green, leafy shake. "Now that is *repulsive*," I muttered, watching him feed a variety of plants into the blender.

"Then it's a good thing I didn't make it for you," he parroted, narrowing his eyes.

I snorted, picking up the two plates I'd just prepared for myself and Titus. "Charming, as always."

"Oh, you've hardly gotten to know my charm yet, little queen." His gaze dipped to my cleavage and lower. "I suggest you wear something more appropriate for class."

"Thanks, Dad," I replied in a sugary tone.

Vox and Sol observed the exchange, their expressions ones of dread and shock. I smiled at them, noting their clean plates. "See? Eggs and cheese can be good, right?"

"Not my first choice," Vox admitted softly. "But not nearly as horrible as I anticipated."

Sol lifted one of those big shoulders. "I don't know. I liked it. Better than cafeteria food."

Cyrus snorted. "Not a resounding compliment, in my opinion." He backed me into the counter behind me, then reached around for a straw, his gaze holding mine the entire time. "If domestication is your preference, I'll have some of my mother's recipes sent over so you can do your job properly."

If my hands weren't full of food, I might have slapped him again. "Move," I demanded.

He cocked his head to the side. "Say 'please,' little queen."

I smiled, another idea coming to mind as I sent a blast of energy into his chest, knocking him into the counter where Vox and Sol sat with open mouths. "*Please*," I said, my voice sickly sweet.

Cyrus didn't appear annoyed or angry, just amused. "Careful, Claire, or I'll have to tell Exos you were flirting with me."

I scoffed at that. "Assuming you're alive when we find him."

Vox gasped, while Sol chuckled.

"Yeah, okay. I like her," the big guy murmured. "This'll do." He pushed away from the counter. "Don't forget onions for tomorrow, Vox. I want to try the human's version of an egg pie again, but to her requirements. So find that con stuff, or whatever you called it."

"Bacon," I supplied.

He snapped his fingers, causing the entire building to shake around us. "That, yes. Whatever bacon is." He clapped Vox on the back. "I'm going to get ready for class." He disappeared down the hall, whistling as he walked.

His size had intimidated me at first, but now I kind of liked the giant. I stared after him fondly until Cyrus stepped into my view. "Go feed your mate, little queen."

"Claire," I corrected him, angry all over again. *I'm not fucking little.*

"Sure," he replied, sipping his green slush. "Have a good day, *Claire.*"

"Eat shit, Cyrus," I returned with a smile and rotated on my heel.

Rather than rise to the bait, he chuckled, the sound following me all the way to my room. I hated how it warmed my skin and caused my belly to tighten. The asshole could at least have the common decency to be ugly. But no, he had to go around looking like Exos in his three-piece suit and ooze sex appeal.

Bastard.

"Enjoy class," Vox murmured as he passed me, his control of air seeming to send the words to my ears alone. "And nice gust in the kitchen back there," he added, his dimples flashing. "I couldn't have done it any better myself."

My cheeks heated at the compliment. I'd sent that wave of energy out of me without thinking, wanting the jackass royal to move. But it was nice to know I'd done it correctly. "Thanks," I said softly.

He reached around me to open the door, something I hadn't tried to do yet, thanks to the plates in my hands. "Don't tell Titus what's in that if you want him to eat it," Vox advised. "Tell him afterward."

"Will do," I replied. "See you later today."

"Yep." He gave me a nod and a wink, leaving me to my plans for breakfast in bed.

Titus sat waiting for me, his back against the headboard, his auburn hair mussed with sleep. I'd wanted to give him more time to rest, but in reality, cooking had gone by faster than I realized. Still, he didn't appear all that fazed, his green gaze tracking me across the room as I approached. "I don't like waking without you in my arms," he said, his voice deep and sexy.

I set the plates on the nightstand and crawled into the bed, straddling his strong hips. "I wanted to cook for you."

"Why?" he asked.

"Because it's an activity I used to enjoy doing and I needed a distraction."
Some of his seductive energy slithered away. "Exos?"

I nodded. "He reached out to me, but before I could reply, he was gone."

Titus reached up to cup my cheek, his thumb tracing the hollows beneath
my eyes. "We'll find him," he vowed. "But Cyrus is right about keeping up
appearances. We need to go about our business as usual and lull Mortus, or
whoever has done this, into a false state of comfort."

"And if that doesn't work?" I asked, biting my lip.

"You'll continue to search for him through the bond, but more carefully
than last night." He pulled me closer, his lips brushing mine. "Next time, I'll
help instead of that royal prick."

I smiled. "I would like that much more, yes." I kissed him again. "Mmm,
there are a great many things I would like, actually."

"Yeah?" he asked, his tongue sliding into my mouth for a taste. "Like
what, Claire? What would you enjoy right now?"

"Mmm." I sucked his bottom lip between my teeth and released it with a
pop. "I made you breakfast."

His brow furrowed. "I know."

"I want you to eat it," I whispered, kissing along his jaw to his neck.
"Please." I licked the column of his throat, creating a wet path that led to the
strong planes of his chest. "You eat while I indulge myself in an appetizer." I
gazed up at him as I continued my trail, kissing and nipping and memorizing
the ripples of his abdomen on my way down to the prize below.

"Claire," he whispered, embers flickering in his pupils. His thick arousal
sat heavy between his legs, the crown beading with liquid welcome.

"Eat your breakfast, Titus," I said, my lips hovering above his cock. "And
I'll enjoy mine."

I sampled his excitement, moaning at the salty taste of him, and took him
deep into my mouth. He cursed, his fingers threading through my hair as he
encouraged me to continue. Titus and Exos had tasted me so many times, but
I'd never returned the favor. And this morning seemed like a perfect
opportunity to do so.

"*Fuck*," he breathed, his grip tightening as I swallowed more of him. He
was too big for me to take completely, so I wrapped my hand around the base
and squeezed. Rather than eat his breakfast, he stared at me with admiration
and desire, his stark need soaking me between my thighs.

This was supposed to be about him, but my body reacted accordingly,
stirring a moan deep in my throat that vibrated his shaft.

Titus growled, thrusting upward and forcing me to take more of him. He
cursed, his lack of control evident in the way he tried to pull away, but I
refused to allow it, needing to feel the empowering motions of his hips. I
raked my nails across his thigh, my opposite hand still wrapped around the
base, and groaned as he shot upward again.

"Your mouth is fucking divine, Claire." The harsh texture of his voice stirred a sensation in my lower stomach that only he could satisfy, but I ignored it in favor of providing him pleasure, my thighs squeezing together to keep my own needs in check.

Fire slowly trickled from his being to mine, the flames heating my skin and taunting my own to come out and play.

Passion smoldered between us, an inferno rising as it always did when Titus touched me. My pajamas disintegrated while the sheets remained, a show of fiery control from my mate, one that turned me on even more.

He tugged on my hair, pulling his hardness away from my mouth and yanking me upward to meet his kiss. My back met the mattress, Titus's hips settling between my thighs, and in one thrust, he filled me to completion. I groaned, my nails digging into his shoulders to hold him to me as more flames painted the air.

He set the pace—a bruising, hard, punishing one that had my back bowing upward to meet him in our frenzy to fuck.

Blissful escape.

Ecstasy.

Hot.

Fuck, he mastered me as easily as his flames, his body knowing mine in a way no one else could. He used our shared element to intensify the sensations, covering my skin in a blanket of heat that left me screaming beneath him in the best way.

Harder.

Faster.

More.

My chants were a litany he returned in kind, giving me what I wanted until an explosion erupted between us and caused white lights to dance behind my eyes. His name was a curse and a blessing, his presence mine to adore, and our mating bond rejoiced between us.

"My Claire," he whispered, his lips soft against mine, his tongue an addiction inside my mouth that I would never get enough of. He kissed me tenderly, adoringly, lovingly. His palms stroked up and down my sides, his cock an inferno inside me, and so damn hard despite our shared orgasm.

"I'll never get enough of this," I said, drawing my nails down his back and scoring his skin with fire, claiming him as mine.

He chuckled, his mouth falling to my ear. "Claiming me, Claire?"

"Yes," I hissed, arching into him once more. "You're mine."

"And you're mine," he murmured, nibbling my pulse. "We have time for another round before class. Unless you still want me to eat?"

"You can eat on the way to class," I decided, no longer caring about my omelet. I'd make him another tomorrow. "Fuck me again, Titus."

"As you wish, my Claire."

CHAPTER SEVEN
TITUS

I RAN MY FINGERS THROUGH MY HAIR, a strange sensation churning my gut. If I didn't know better, I'd call myself nervous. But I was never nervous. Not even for my Powerless Champion matches.

Yet sitting here, beside Claire, and knowing I was the only guardian in her presence for class, did something to me. It put me on high alert, inspecting everyone in the room with a regard I never considered before.

I almost missed Exos and his constant vigilance.

Not that I would ever admit it.

I needed a distraction, and the lecture at the front of the room was not cutting it. Although, Claire seemed to be enjoying it. She sat on her little stone pedestal in the middle of the cement yard, her fingers clasped over the desk before us.

An angel dressed in a sinfully perfect uniform. I'd never noticed it before, having not cared that everyone wore the same outfit. But Claire, mmm, her legs looked amazing in that skirt.

Providing me with the perfect idea for a distraction.

I sent a heat wave to the beautiful apex between her thighs—a part of her I was never going to grow tired of, even if I did fuck her twice this morning.

Her eyes widened, as she clenched her legs together and shot me a glare.

I grinned and pointed at Professor Vulcan, who was droning on about how to use fire in controlled bursts.

Pay attention, I mouthed.

She thrust her middle finger up at me in response. I frowned, unsure of what that meant. I would have to ask River about human gestures.

The class itself was mind-numbingly boring, at least to me. Neat piles of straw dotted the outdoor arena with a marker for difficulty. I could set them all ablaze in two seconds flat, but the goal of the exercise was to burn a particular target without igniting the surrounding ones.

Control Concentration was my least favorite course.

Hmm, but how would Claire perform with the task? Would she be able to do it while distracted?

I smiled, intrigued by my own wickedness.

Normally, this would be a good exercise for her—without the distraction. But if she really needed to conjure a controlled flame, it wouldn't be in an environment of complete silence where she could focus. Someone had taken Exos and was powerful enough to keep him sedated, and if they came after her, she would need to be ready for them.

I'd been training with Claire for weeks. Power came easily to her, but control? Not so much. And while I loved to make her lose control, it was time she learned how to master her powers.

"Claire," Professor Vulcan said, making her flinch. "Why don't you and your guardian take point and make the first attempt."

Claire's face paled as she glanced at me. I knew that look. She definitely didn't want to be in the spotlight, much less go first in an exercise she'd never done before.

The rest of the class had been curiously watching us the entire time, a sea of Fire Fae who were edges and hardness against Claire's delicate form. She surveyed the group, most of them with tattoos or spiked hair that might come off as intimidating to a human. I liked my people; they were blunt, real, and passionate. Claire would learn more about them, and they'd get to know her and love her like I did. All she needed to do was be her beautiful self.

I took her hand and gave her a reassuring smile. "I'll show you the exercise. It'll be fun."

Professor Vulcan glowered at us. He resembled a flame himself, his hair standing straight up with a red streak down the middle. He stepped aside and crossed his muscular arms. "Only one demonstration, Titus. I need to assess the Halfling's control before I place her in more classes."

Claire swallowed hard. "So, this is a test?"

I sent a trickle of flame behind her ear, and she swatted at it.

"Don't worry, sweetheart. You can't fail a test here. This is about embracing your fire." I kissed her on the cheek and she stiffened, her eyes darting to our audience.

Everyone was staring.

Most of the students had done this exercise before, but they wanted to see what Claire could do. She suffered from a bad reputation born of her mother's doing and was then framed for stirring elemental chaos on campus. But she was innocent, proved to be a victim herself, and she'd survived. What she didn't realize was the respect that came with her survival. I saw it in the eyes of our fellow fae. They wanted to admire her for coming through the firestorm alive.

I needed to give Claire all the courage to feel accepted here. All she had to do was believe in herself.

I pointed at a distant patch of straw with a red flag poking out the center of it. "See that middle marker? I'm going to ignite it without touching any of the other piles nearby. The goal here is control, Claire." I teased her skin with a caress of heat, causing her to arch an eyebrow at me.

"You? Control?" She glanced pointedly at the goose bumps creeping across her arm. "Uh-huh."

I responded with another brush of warmth, stirring a shiver from her. "Doubting my ability already, sweetheart?"

Her eyes narrowed, her focus falling to me instead of our audience. "Show me what you can do."

"We both know what I can do," I said, flexing my mental muscles and locating the marked pile. "Ready?"

"Stop teasing and do it," she said, her feistiness coming through.

I waggled my brows and ignited the straw with barely a thought.

She eyed the field and nodded. "Not bad. So I'm supposed to light another on fire?"

"Yep," I said, withdrawing my flames. "Any pile you want, just make sure it's one of the marked ones and nothing else."

She sucked her lip between her teeth, her gaze wandering the field and the various targets.

I wondered which one she would pick. She should be conservative and choose the closest marker for her first try, but of course, that wasn't my Claire.

She extended her hands, and flames licked at her fingertips. Stripes of blue wound through her fire like an elemental rope, sizzling with barely contained power.

That's new, I thought.

The other fae murmured in reaction to the display. I leaned in closer to Claire and pressed my lips to her ear. "Is that water?"

She glanced at the flicker and frowned. "Yeah."

"Can you rein it in and use just your fire?"

Her lips twisted to the side. "I don't know."

That was the problem—Claire's powers controlled her, not the other way around. Which created an issue when she engaged non-fiery elements while surrounded by Fire Fae. If her water magic grew out of hand, I couldn't help. And it would likely take the entire class to restrain her if she unleashed whatever was dwelling inside.

Which meant I'd have to speak to Cyrus about it since the element taking control of her now appeared to be water.

Great.

If only he hadn't dismissed River...

Except we all knew that was the right move. Cyrus's renowned familial ties to the Water Fae King made him exceptionally powerful and proficient in the element. Even if it wasn't the side of his nature he chose to acknowledge most. He was too busy serving as the Spirit King.

Alas, he'd volunteered to take on her water mentorship, and given the strengthening blue swirl around her fire, he'd better get started sooner rather than later.

"It's all right," Claire murmured, her voice low and taut with renewed concentration. The winding strands of water extended over her flame, making a sort of tunnel for her to aim with.

Is that supposed to be an elemental gun?

Well, shit.

She pointed to the final marker in the distance, one even I would have had trouble hitting, much less without burning anything around it.

"That one," she said, marking her target, and then heat emanated from her in a building storm that made my eyes widen and very inappropriate sensations run straight down to my groin. Damn, she was hot. *Literally.*

The inferno built until she was satisfied with her aim, and an explosion rocked the ground, sending a ball of fire directly at her target. It streaked across the arena, bypassing all of the other piles of straw without harming them. The tight collection of flames hit the final target, making the straws explode in a vertical strike that lit up the sky.

A hush fell over the Fire Fae students.

Then they roared their approval, making my chest swell with pride.

"Holy shit!"

"Did you see that?"

"She's fucking amazing!"

Claire beamed and lowered her hands, her powers retreating inside of her with a measure of control I hadn't expected. "I did it," she breathed with relief as if she hadn't anticipated a positive outcome. She shook her head as a low chuckle escaped her. "Every time I used my powers in public before, it felt like they always swept out of my control, but that wasn't really my fault, was it? It was Ignis and the other girls messing with me." Her blue eyes glimmered with a hope I hadn't seen in her before. "Maybe I *can* do this."

I gripped both sides of her face and pulled her in for a kiss. Hovering my mouth over hers, I tasted her embers and licked my lips in anticipation. "You can do anything, Claire. Anything you want, and I'll be right by your side admiring every inch of you."

I no longer cared who was watching. I crushed my mouth to hers, and she parted for me, allowing my tongue to slide inside and taste the lingering effects of her power and her elation.

When I released her, the Fire Fae had gotten even more out of control. They loved passion and clapped their hands, cheering us on for more.

"All right, that's enough," Professor Vulcan griped, even though I could see a gleam of approval in his eyes. "Claire, I'll discuss a schedule with Elana in the morning. You need advanced training, not intermediate. Well done."

CHAPTER EIGHT
VOX

BACON CAME FROM PIGS.

Pigs.

Fuck. That.

Why would anyone want to eat a pig?

River had assured me it was a delicacy in the Human Realm after I asked him about it, but I would not be entertaining that in our shared kitchen, no matter how adorable Claire may have looked earlier in those little shorts and tiny tank top.

Or the way I'd felt after she used magic on Cyrus.

The feeling of her element brushing against mine had stuck with me all day. Not only did we share magic, but she seemed to like cooking, too. I had to admit sharing a joy of cooking—even if her tastes were questionable—made me want to like her.

But yeah, nope, not going there.

I only went to River to ask about bacon because Sol wanted to try a proper egg pie in the morning. Not because I wanted to please Claire. And fortunately, we didn't have *pigs*. But we did have fatty meat from the hide of a troll, something River assured me would be similar. Although, he also suggested I not tell Claire what it was and just call it bacon.

231

It's an innocent lie, he'd promised.

Well, we'd see tomorrow morning when she cooked another monstrosity for breakfast.

Sol's eyes lit up when I stumbled into the Spirit Dorm. "You brought food!" he cheered, sending the floor cracking as he stormed over to me and snatched up the weight as effortlessly as if I'd been carrying feathers.

"Careful with that," I grumbled as he threatened to rip the bags and send the ingredients scattering.

Sol whistled as I sent a wave of magic to brush the pebbles of the broken floor he'd left behind over the threshold. I was used to cleaning up after the Earth Fae, and I knew how to keep him happy.

There were five mouths to feed now, and no one else seemed to know how to cook. Except maybe Claire. But all I'd seen in the kitchen were ingredients for quick meals like shakes and finger patties. Sol would become intolerable without a real meal, and I needed him to cooperate when it was time to teach Claire some earth magic.

Proving my decision to buy some real food a good one, Sol began plucking out the ingredients, stopping when he saw the troll fat. He gave me a raised brow.

I put it in the icebox. "It's for the Halfling's experiment tomorrow," I offered with a shrug. "River said it was like bacon." I pointed at him. "But don't tell her what it is."

Sol hummed and went back to rummaging through the groceries. "More egg pie sounds good to me." He held up a salted red weed most fae hated. "Oh, good, you bought some scurbuttle snacks!"

"Do I want to know what that is?" Claire asked, sweeping into the kitchen with a smile on her face. Titus trailed in after her, both of them looking pleased.

Seeing their shared glance of satisfaction reminded me of my interaction with Claire this morning, how we'd shared a moment of air magic, whispers, and then...

Then I'd heard the way Titus had made her scream.

"You definitely don't want to know what that is," Titus informed her, slipping his arm around her waist.

She leaned into him just enough that her body formed to his. I wondered if she was aware of how sensual she was in the subtle movement.

Claire's bright gaze found mine, and then her smile dimmed. "Everything okay, Vox?"

Shit, I sucked at hiding my emotions. I cast my gaze down and continued to unpack the groceries as I tried to think of a response. Every time she opened her mouth, all I could hear were those delicious sounds she'd sent filtering through the air currents just for me. I knew she hadn't done it on purpose; it was her air magic reacting to mine. It was natural. We were compatible, at least in our elements, but that didn't mean I had to give in to my primal instincts like some kind of animal.

"I think he heard us this morning," Titus supplied, his smug grin saying he was damn proud of that. "You weren't exactly quiet."

Claire turned as red as the scurbuttle weed. "Oh God," she said, covering her full lips with her hand. "I'm so sorry, Vox. I didn't even think—"

Titus cut her off with a kiss and sent a lingering flame running down her shirt, making Claire squeak with surprise. "You're cute when you're flustered."

"You're not helping," she whispered loudly.

"I'm not ashamed, sweetheart," Titus replied. "And neither are they."

"Oh God…"

"Hey, why don't you help me cook dinner," I offered, trying to put her at ease and to prove I was fine. That everything was fine. That this whole fucked-up situation was, well, *fine*.

Besides, Claire and I were going to be spending a lot of time together— Titus included. I knew better than to try to dampen a Fire Fae's passion, and by the look on Claire's face when she'd walked in those doors, he was what she needed right now with Exos missing and his asshat of a brother coming in and ruining all of our lives.

Oh, fuck, I hope he doesn't join us for dinner.

Claire brightened, the light in her eyes returning. "Okay, that sounds fun." She looked to Titus and he laughed.

"Don't need my permission, sweetheart." He stretched, making a show of putting his arm around her shoulder. "I'll go shower before dinner and leave you all to it." He grinned at me with a knowing glance. "Didn't get a chance to this morning."

Right, because Sol had been in our shared bathroom, so in a moment of desperation, I'd stolen Titus's shower in order to take off the edge Claire's screams had given me. The Fire Fae had warned me there would be a lot of cold showers included with this job…

Fuck.

If Claire had put two and two together, she didn't comment.

"So, what's for dinner?" she asked.

I was grateful for change the subject. I pulled out the largest item from the sacks and used my air magic to lift it up.

"Dragon steak," I announced with a grin. River had said this would impress Claire, and after the way Cyrus had treated her, I wanted to do something to take her mind off things.

Her eyes went wide. "Dragon?"

I nodded. "It's supposed to taste like something you call beef," I said, sending a wave of air to settle the slab onto the cutting board on the counter.

"Are you going to add eggs and cheese to it?" Sol asked around a mouthful of his snack.

Claire smiled. "I think we can save that for breakfast."

I gave her simple tasks of cutting vegetables and grinding fresh spices. She seemed to enjoy the job, and I felt a pang of regret for her. All of this was so new and different for the Halfling, but I was able to give her something that maybe made her feel like she was back home, doing monotonous things she used to do as a human, such as chopping up ingredients in a kitchen. I supposed it didn't matter what world or race one was a part of—food still needed preparing.

It wasn't until I had closed the oven door on a decorated pan of dragon steak and gotten to work on a patty salad that I felt Claire's magic testing mine. I stopped folding the leaves over strips of filling to glance at her.

"I understand if you don't want to be here," she said, her words soft and for my ears alone. Her bright eyes fixated on me, rooting me to the spot. "I didn't mean to uproot you and Sol, and I'm sure when Exos comes back, I can explain that Cyrus made a mistake." Something in her gaze said she hoped I would disagree with her, and I wasn't sure if I wanted to.

I glanced at Sol, but she'd done the trick skillfully enough that he hadn't heard her. He chomped down on the last of his snack and fluttered his eyes closed, blissfully enjoying the simplicity of a tasty treat.

Yes, I knew what Sol needed. He needed to be around fae strong enough to help him. Fae like me…

Fae like Cyrus and Exos with royal lines stronger than mine.

Perhaps even a fae like Claire.

She edged closer to me, her fingers grazing my arm in a way that made my magic snap taut against hers. She sucked in a breath but didn't back away.

"The king's orders are never disobeyed," I said, trying to put ice and steel into my tone like Cyrus was so good at doing. He seemed to have a knack for pushing the Halfling away, and that was one skill I needed to work on. If I was going to be her guardian, I didn't want to end up mating with her. Not because I disliked her, but because it was just too complicated.

She flinched at my tone, and even though she backed away and left me feeling guilty, I knew it was the right thing to do.

"Right," she said, her teeth grating at the mention of Cyrus. "Well, at least he won't be getting any dragon steak. Right?"

I nodded. "I didn't get enough for him." A lie, but Sol would help cover that up with his mighty appetite.

She crossed her arms and seemed pleased by that. "Honestly, I vote we never let him have any of the meals we cook together."

Together.

Why do I like that?

I cleared my throat and continued folding the salad patties. "Agreed."

We worked on the last of the meal in amiable silence, Sol displaying one of his rare bouts of patience until the dragon steak and patties were done.

We all sat around the table, and Titus joined us, his skin steaming as he used his magic to dry himself. He grinned as he settled next to Claire and gave her a kiss. "It smells delicious."

Claire laughed and leaned into him, but her eyes were on me. "It was all Vox, really."

Sol grabbed his steak with both hands and ripped into it. He chewed and swallowed the enormous bite, then smacked his lips. "Delicious," he agreed.

I took one of the leaves from my salad patty and used it to pick up my portion of steak. "Bon appétit," I said with a grin.

We dug into our food, and for the first time in a long while, I didn't feel uncomfortable around other fae. Food always had a way of bringing everyone together, which, I guessed, was why I'd learned to cook in the first place. I didn't exactly have the most stellar social skills, so I let a good meal do the work for me.

By the way Claire looked at me—like I'd just given her a piece of her life back—maybe it worked a little too well.

"So, tomorrow," Titus said, putting down the last of his leaves with a satisfied sigh. "I'm off to Fire Quad without you, sweetheart."

She appeared slightly uneasy at the notion. "And where am I going?"

He lifted his glass and gave Sol a salute. "Earth Quad."

Sol's eyes went wide. He was well into his second slab of dragon steak, and he paused midbite. "What?" he said, his mouth still full.

I chuckled and began clearing the table. "Titus is right. Claire hasn't had any earth training, and you're the only one who can show her around the Earth Quad." I grinned at Sol's open horror. "Welcome to escort duty, big guy."

"Well, fae on a spit," he cursed, dropping the tainted piece of meat. "That's why you brought home dragon steak."

"No." Because I didn't know her schedule. "But I assumed you'd need something positive in order to remain here."

"Damn it. I knew a great meal was too good of a thing coming from you, Vox." He crossed his arms and glowered at me.

I sent him a whisper of wind so my words only made it to his ears. "Remember, a month of credits!"

Excitement lit his eyes. Even if it was a silly bet that Claire would make him admit he'd met his match, it was one way to get him to agree to take the Halfling to class.

He nodded.

Challenge accepted.

CHAPTER NINE
CLAIRE

EARTH CLASS WAS NOT WHAT I EXPECTED.

Sol had painted a picture with his size, giving me the impression that all Earth Fae were, well, ground shattering. I mean, the man's fist could crack stone.

So when we entered the outdoor arena surrounded by trees and buzzing life, I blinked. And as the students who were half of Sol's size began to stroll inside, I blinked again.

Several of the girls glanced at him and blushed while saying hello. He engaged in pleasantries, but I sensed his unease and wondered why he kept himself apart from the group who clearly wanted to engage with him.

However, I followed him as he meandered along the outskirts, each step shaking the ground beneath him. No one else seemed to carry such weight or energy, some of the other males appearing downright petite compared to Sol. Almost sickly.

How strange.

"Hi, Sol," another female fae said, her dark hair the color of midnight stones and her eyes a gleaming azure shade.

"Aflora," he returned, his lips curling fondly.

"Have you decided about the Solstice Ball yet?" she asked, her hands tucked behind her as she swiveled on her feet.

"You know I hate those events." He said the words with a smile, his affection more brotherly than flirtatious. "But I've heard Glacier wants to take you. Say yes to him."

"I'll wait for you," she said instead and gave him a little giggle before flouncing off through the flowers with a jump in her step.

Sol sighed, shaking his head. "Damn Solstice Ball."

"What's a Solstice Ball?" I asked.

"This big holiday dance where everyone gets dressed up. Happens around the Festivus season, seven weeks from now." He sounded completely disgusted by the idea. "It's like couple purgatory."

"Why?"

He cut me a sideways glance. "Did you miss the part about dressing up?"

"That sounds fun to me."

He looked me over and snorted. "Yeah, I suppose you'd enjoy wearing a ball gown and slippers. But me in a tux? No, thanks."

"Then wear normal clothes," I suggested.

He chuckled. "That would certainly shock the masses."

"Then do it," I encouraged him, smiling. "I'll go with you. And I'll wear jeans."

His amusement melted into shock. "You want to go to the ball with me?"

"Sure." It seemed like the least I could do after all this forced guardian crap. And it hadn't taken a genius last night to determine how much he didn't want to take me to class today. Maybe something like the ball would show him I wasn't so bad. And besides... "It sounds fun."

"Fun," he repeated, sounding dubious. "You really want to go?"

"Yeah, why not?" I smiled. "I mean, only if you want to."

"What about Titus?" he asked. "Wouldn't you prefer to go with him?"

"He's not mentioned it." But perhaps that wasn't what Sol meant. Was he trying to come up with an excuse for us not to go? I glanced at the girl with dark curls, watched as she laughed with a beauty most men would adore. "Do you want to go with Aflora?" I wondered out loud. Because if he did, I'd understand. I mean, we weren't dating. We were hardly even friends. But I sort of wanted to be friends. Maybe.

Sol followed my gaze, his expression turning into one of adoration as he slowly shook his head. Not necessarily the kind of look a man gave a woman he wanted to fuck, but perhaps Sol was different?

"Nah. Aflora has a childhood crush on me, but I'm not right for her. It's because she was one of my sister's best friends," he explained, running his fingers through his copper-colored strands. His earthy brown eyes flitted shyly to mine, then dropped to the ground. "I, uh, lost my sister a few years ago."

"Oh, Sol, I'm sorry." That wasn't at all what I expected him to say.

He lifted a shoulder. "It's the plague, you know. Spirit Kingdom is next to Earth Kingdom, so, uh, it spread." His mouth twisted. "That's why everyone looks, uh, small."

"You mean this isn't normal?"

"It didn't use to be." He grimaced, palming the back of his neck. "Sorry. I didn't mean to talk about this, just thought you might want to understand why I'm so much larger."

"I was wondering," I admitted. "I… I don't know much about the plague. But I know my, uh, mother somehow caused it."

He nodded. "That's the story, but I think it was general corruption amongst the Spirit Fae."

"What do you mean?"

Sol shoved his hands into the pockets of his navy slacks, his shoulders hunching. "I shouldn't talk about it."

"Why?" I wondered. "Because it's me? Or in general?"

His mouth twisted. "It's, well, both." His earthy gaze met mine, the light green flecks hidden in his brown irises coming to life beneath the sun above. "We're not supposed to talk about it." That last part was a whisper, his expression contrite. "I shouldn't have said anything."

"I'm glad you did," I admitted. "No one will talk to me about my… what happened. I mean, Exos gave me the basics, told me how my mother left Mortus during the third stage of the bond and then refused him after returning to the fae world all those years later. And somehow that started a plague. But that's all I know."

Sol lifted his face to the sky, the glow tanning his features and lending him a handsome appearance. I could see why many of the Earth Fae females wanted his attention. He seemed completely oblivious to his charming looks, which made him all the more attractive.

"That's the story they want us to believe," he said quietly. "But my mother told a very different tale." He glanced at me, then at the students assembling on a variety of tree trunks throughout the courtyard—tree trunks that weren't there seconds ago. "Class is starting."

Meaning he didn't want to talk about this anymore. I understood. We hardly knew each other, and he didn't trust me. Given my introduction to this world and the events of the last few weeks, I couldn't fault him for disliking me. Maybe I'd read his responses to the ball completely wrong. It wasn't so much shock at going as it was shock at me asking him to go.

Note to self: don't bring it up again.

"Okay," I said, recognizing that he needed space. "I'll go find a, uh, seat." I took a step and tripped over a piece of earth that wasn't there a second ago.

Sol caught me by the arm before I could hit the ground and yanked me upright. "Shit, my bad. I thought you sensed that."

I frowned, looking down at the two tree stumps that had magically appeared without my knowledge. "How…?"

"This is where I usually sit. I made you one, too, thinking you wanted to, well, you know, but you can join the others. That's cool. I mean, you can do whatever you want. I'm not, this isn't, well…" He palmed the back of his neck again and shook his head. "Yep."

My lips threatened to curl at his stammering, my heart warming in his presence.

He's nervous, I realized.

That made two of us.

"I'd like to sit with you, if you don't mind." I gave him a small smile. "You're the only one I know, and I'm not very familiar with earth magic yet."

He nodded and considered me for a long moment. "This class is all about creating life from the soil. It's a self-educated course, which is why everyone is spread out. Most work in pairs or quads, learning the feel of the earth and producing art."

"There's no professor?" All the courses I'd attended so far had someone in charge, but looking around, I saw none.

He shook his head slowly. "Most of our elders are, well, sick. There are a handful on campus who lead the more advanced courses, but you have to pass the intermediate levels—like this class—before you can join. And most don't make it that far. But I'm close." His brow furrowed. "I just need better control."

I glanced at the pair of tree stumps and chose the one closest to me. "Well, you seem to be doing okay."

"That?" He snorted. "That's simple." He pulled a paper from his bag and handed it to me. "That's what you have to create to pass."

I stared at a sketch of an intricate tree with fruit hanging from the limbs and vines wrapping around the base. Then I glanced around to see other students had already started growing their trunks while sitting on top of them. "Is this the first day?"

He chuckled. "No, we're halfway through the semester."

What? "Then where are all the trees?"

"Oh, we move them after class to the nearby acres." He gestured to the forest around us. "They're all thriving in their own way."

"But why?" I asked, baffled. "I thought the purpose was to create the drawing."

"You have to make it within the course hour," he clarified, smirking. "Anyone can make that with enough time. It's the speed that matters, and the tree in that drawing has close to a hundred or so years of existence on it. Not an easy task, especially when you lack control." He sat across from me and pointed at the ground. "Let's start with the basics. Press your palm to the earth and tell me what you feel."

I immediately felt guilty. I'd expected a professor or someone to teach me, not Sol. He had his own work to do. "You don't have to waste time on me. If you just point me to where the textbook is, I can start reading. I clearly have a lot of catching up to do."

He narrowed his gaze. "Put your palm on the ground, Claire."

I swallowed and did what he said, mostly because he was a muscular giant and that look on his face brooked no argument. And his tone, well, it sort of reminded me of Exos's tone.

My heart gave a pang at the thought, my connection to him humming in response.

Still alive.

I closed my eyes, wishing I could follow the path to him, to find—

"What do you feel?" Sol asked, his deep voice drawing me back to him and the task I'd been assigned.

Heartbroken, I wanted to tell him. But I knew that wasn't what he desired to know.

So I pushed my reservations aside and allowed him to help me. It was the least I could do since he'd chosen to take the time to help me when he didn't have to.

Life fluttered beneath my hand, the tickle of grass against my skin a tease to my senses. I tilted my head, following the thread of the element into the soil beneath and luxuriated in the earthy notes filling my nostrils.

It felt almost refreshing. Cool. Hypnotic.

I sighed in contentment.

Fire breathed passion. Air stirred sensation. Water encouraged tranquility. Spirit warmed my heart.

"Earth is invigorating," I breathed, swimming in the undercurrents of power.

"Yes," Sol agreed, his voice thick with an emotion I couldn't see because my eyes were still closed. I had the picture of a tree in my head, the one with fruit dangling from the limbs. Mmm, what I wouldn't give for a peach. That wasn't what I'd seen in the photo, but I craved the sweetness of summers past. My grandmother used to bake the most delectable pie. I could almost remember the smell if I concentrated enough.

My lips curled as I found the ingredients in the earth, not for the dessert, but the core ingredient—a peach pit.

It seeded beneath my palm, growing roots to secure itself to the soil, and pushed through the grass. "I miss peaches," I whispered, my brow furrowing. "I miss home."

"Me, too," Sol agreed, his words a breath on the wind. "But I can never go back."

"Why?" I asked, my creation growing in my mind, boasting vitality and scenting the air around us. "Why can't you go home, Sol?"

"Because there's nothing left," he grumbled. "The plague has taken everyone I love. There's no one for me to go back to."

"Why is it spreading?" I asked, not understanding. "If Ophelia is dead, how are more fae falling ill?"

"Because it's not her." Sol's tone sounded pained, causing my eyes to flutter open in concern. His eyes were on the tree I'd unknowingly blossomed, the leaves budding as if in the heat of spring. Several other students were gaping at my creation, most of them staring in awe. "That's very impressive, Claire. But it's not the assignment."

My branches sprouted with life, my desire to taste a peach taunting my tongue. It all came so naturally, so unexpectedly, that I giggled when the first hint of little green pits developed on the tree.

"What is it?" a soft voice asked.

Aflora.

Her wide blue eyes gazed lovingly at my creation, her lips parting as a peach fully developed before her.

"A fruit tree from my childhood," I said.

"It's beautiful," she praised. "May I touch it?"

I nodded, biting my lip, uncertain of what else to say. But the petite fae seemed too lost in the masterpiece hanging over my head to care for words. She stroked the tree with adoration, several others wandering over to join her.

Sol watched without a word, a strange spark of energy in his earthy gaze.

Had I messed this up? I wasn't trying to garner attention, or to even create a tree; it just sort of happened. "My control needs work, too," I mumbled, wringing my hands in my lap.

He didn't reply but stood to reach the highest branch and plucked a fresh peach. Several fae watched as he sampled the fruit of my labor, their expressions anticipatory. He took another bite, chewing, his brow furrowed. "It's sweet."

"It's a peach," I replied, confused.

"I like it." He shrugged and grabbed another to toss to Aflora. She caught it with a furious blush and skipped away, her long black hair waving in the wind. A few others held out a hand, and he tossed each of them a peach from the branches above, then dropped one into my lap before taking a second for himself. "The fruit in the assignment is supposed to be dry and bland, not sweet. I prefer your creation."

"Why would anyone want to eat a bland fruit?" I wondered aloud, taking a small bite of my peach.

So, so good.

I sent up a request for more, and the tree responded immediately.

This is so much better than a vortex, I thought.

"Apparently, it's good for cooking," Sol said, grimacing. "Not my favorite. This is much better."

His magic brushed mine as he took control of one of my branches and forced it to lower to him so he could pluck several more peaches. The tree groaned as he released his mental hold, the leaves and sticks flying upward with a snap that shook the earth.

He cringed. "Sorry."

I soothed the earth, healing the fractures he'd caused within my creation, and smiled. "You're powerful."

"Yeah." He waved his hand, causing a new stump to form and grow. "Vox is helping me learn how to foster and maintain it, but I grow stronger every day. It's like I'm constantly absorbing energy, but I'm only one fae and I don't have anywhere to release it all."

My element reached out to his without thinking, blending into his life force as if searching for a way to ease him like I did the tree.

He flinched, his gaze widening. "What are you doing?"

"I-I don't know," I admitted. "It's just sort of... I fixed the tree and now..."

"You can't fix me, Claire," he snapped. "Stop." The ground quaked as he shoved my element away from his, the power of his strike sending me backward off my stump. He cursed. "Shit. I'm sorry. I shouldn't—"

"Well, that's one way to train the little queen," a haughty voice interrupted. "Intruding on one's elements without permission is a punishable offense. I'd have knocked her out for it."

Gasps littered the air in his wake, the Spirit Fae having just appeared out of nowhere.

How did he do that?

Sol stood, his arms folding across his chest. "What the hell do you want, Royal?"

Tremors traversed the earth, the other fae backing away with fear in their eyes. *Fear for Sol,* I realized. Because he'd just squared off with the King of Spirit Fae.

Damn it.

I jumped up and brushed the grass from my hair and uniform. "Why are you here, Cyrus?" I demanded, wanting the focus on me, not on Sol.

"I need you to sign some documents," he said, not taking his gaze away from Sol. "Your challenge is noted and not accepted, Earth Fae. When you have better control, we'll talk."

What? How had Cyrus interpreted a challenge from Sol's question? I'd essentially demanded the same thing, albeit with a tad more respect, but still. "What challenge?"

Cyrus finally glanced at me. "He's proving I chose the right Earth Fae guardian for you, is all." He glanced back at Sol. "Isn't that right?"

The giant of a man merely glowered at him. "I make my own choices, Spirit King."

"Good. I wouldn't have it any other way." Cyrus reached into his suit jacket and pulled out a few pieces of paper. "I need you to sign these, Claire."

"What are they?"

"Documents for your internship with Elana."

I frowned. "But I haven't decided to do that yet. I was supposed to talk to Exos before he, uh, left." The last word was a whisper. I couldn't say *disappeared*. We'd agreed to not tell anyone what really happened, although I still didn't agree with why.

"There's no decision to make. You're going to work with Elana." Cyrus held out the papers. "Sign."

I mimicked Sol's stance and folded my arms. "No."

He cocked a brow. "So you don't want an opportunity to learn more about your mother? To discern truth from fiction?" His gaze flickered to Sol. "To find out why the Earth Fae believes it's a corruption of my people that created the plague, and not Ophelia?"

Sol blanched, his demeanor shifting from shock to fury in a blink. "Get the fuck out of my head!"

He took a menacing step forward, only for Cyrus to send up a waterspout between them. "I'm not in your head. I just happened to be observing Claire's course today and heard every word you said."

Sol raged behind the water, his words cut off by the increasing flow that kept Cyrus safe from the wrath the Earth Fae unleashed. Except then the ground began to shake in earnest, a sinkhole pulling the geyser underground and spreading to the tips of my shoes.

"You'll hurt Claire," Cyrus warned, his words underlined in power. "I don't wish to fight you, Earth Fae, but I will if you continue to endanger the future queen. *Control it.*"

I grabbed my tree, terrified of the show of power and the violent energy swimming between Cyrus and Sol. Then I met the big guy's sorrowful gaze over the water and saw his shoulders collapse. The ground calmed, his expression falling as he turned.

"Sol...," I started but didn't know how to finish. Not that he was intent on listening to me anyway. He disappeared into the trees lining the courtyard where several others waited for him. Aflora wrapped an arm around him, guiding him away without a backward glance.

"He has a lot of potential," Cyrus mused, staring after him. "He's one of the strongest of his kind left. He just requires control."

"Why does he think Spirit Fae are corrupt?" I asked. It wasn't like I could break Sol's confidence since Cyrus had eavesdropped the entire fucking time.

"Everyone believes your mother incited the plague by breaking one of the most sacred vows between mates, but there are several—myself included— who think it was a cover for something far more sinister. And it seems Sol is one of the enlightened few who suspect similar foul play. His kind are dying, and your mother is the source of blame. But she's dead. So how can that be?"

He raised a brow at me as if I might hold all the answers.

I swallowed, uneasy. "Are you saying I might be the cause?"

He stared at me for a long moment, all traces of arrogance fleeing his expression. "I'm saying it's an unsolved mystery that holds a variety of possibilities, including ones involving you." He held out the papers and shrouded us in a wall of mist. I opened my mouth, ready to ask him what he was doing, when he softly said, "I need you to accept this internship, Claire. Not just because of what Elana can teach you, but because of what you might observe under her tutelage."

My eyebrows lifted. "You want me to spy on Elana?"

"And anyone who crosses her path, yes." A blunt reply, one I could appreciate. His gaze drifted to my tree and then back to me. "She mentored your mother. Now she wants to mentor you. I find the correlation between the two to be suspect, don't you?"

I hadn't until now. "I thought it was my access to all the elements that intrigued her."

"Oh, most definitely that. But the question we need to ask, little queen, is *why*? Wouldn't you like to discover the answer? Because I know I would." He leaned closer. "Someone powerful enough to subdue my brother is holding him hostage, and as powerful as Mortus is, he's no match for Exos."

"But Elana has the ability to overpower him," I translated in a whisper.

"Indeed," he replied, studying me intently. "Did you sense her in his spirit?"

I shook my head. I hadn't, but I wouldn't know what I was looking for even if I tried. "She exonerated me," I said instead, confused. "Why would she do that if she wanted to hurt Exos?"

"A better question would be, why didn't she use her gifts to exonerate you before?" he countered, arching a brow. "Something isn't adding up, Claire. And this internship provides you with an opportunity to learn more. If you're up for it."

"If she's the culprit, isn't giving her access to me dangerous?"

"Yes." No hesitation. "Which is why a guard will escort you to every session."

"Yeah, but if she could subdue Exos…"

"They don't stand a chance against her," he finished. "But it might give you just enough time to escape should you require it." He sighed then, leaning back against my tree and gazing upward at the branches. "It's all conjecture on my part, Claire, but I have to consider everyone as a suspect. And you're the only one being provided direct access to Elana. She's very likely innocent. However, I learned a long time ago not to trust anyone except family."

Which meant he didn't trust me, either. Hence his comment earlier about all the possibilities of the plague.

I'm a suspect in his eyes. How many others felt the same?

The icy gaze that fell upon me said he knew what I was thinking and refused to put my thoughts at ease in any way. "What'll it be, Claire? I'm late for a meeting."

Did I really have a choice? If Elana had Exos—which I strongly doubted—then I had to at least try, right? If anything, I'd learn more about myself and my mother and the history of this world. And maybe I'd garner stronger control.

Nothing to lose, really.

I cleared my throat and nodded, taking the documents and his pen. "All right."

"Good girl." He eyed my tree again and snagged a peach from a lower branch. "Thanks for lunch, little queen. I'll see you after the Council meeting."

I signed where indicated and handed the papers back to him. "Council meeting? Like the ones Exos attends?"

"Mm-hmm." He smirked. "I'll take you one day. You'll hate it."

"Are you going to tell them about Exos?" I asked, hopeful that maybe they could help us.

His gaze shuttered, darkness shadowing his light eyes as the watery wall collapsed around us. "Absolutely not."

With that, he disappeared as quickly as he'd appeared, leaving a trace of mist in his wake.

How did he do that?

CHAPTER TEN
CYRUS

"WHAT NEWS DO YOU BRING US?" Elana asked, her place at the head of the council table brimming with power.

I'd debated all day if I wanted to announce Exos's disappearance and ultimately decided against it. With Mortus sitting across from me, it seemed even more prudent I say nothing at all and play along. They all believed I'd tasked my brother with something spirit related, temporarily taking his place by the Halfling's side.

Showing weakness to these fae would be detrimental indeed.

So I relaxed into my chair and shrugged, feigning boredom. "Claire is progressing in her classes as expected. She's proven quite capable with fire, her spirit is growing, and the other three elements are not far behind." I didn't bother mentioning she was one of the most powerful water elementals I'd ever felt or that she'd managed to shove me across the room with a single gust of wind.

This Council was out for blood.

I would not be offering up Claire's for sport.

"All five elements," Vape marveled, his shock of white hair cascading around his shoulders like a waterfall. "The prophecy—"

Zephys slammed his hands on the table. "Don't bloody start about the prophecy again." He glared at Vape, then turned his attention to me. "And your brother? Why did he choose now to leave her? Haven't they bonded?"

I tilted my head, keeping Mortus in my line of sight. "I'm not my brother's keeper," I replied flatly. It was the truth, after all.

Blaize watched me expectantly as he played with a flame over his fingertips, rolling the element with a gentle control that took a Fire Fae years to master. "Yet, you sent him on an errand of some kind. Yes?"

"A family matter required his attention. In return, I offered to help Claire improve her affinity for water." I lifted a shoulder, my gaze sliding to Mortus. "I'm sure he'll return soon."

"Excellent," Elana said with approval, ignoring the brewing tension between the Council members. "I've had the pleasure of witnessing her powers firsthand, and I'm thrilled at her development." She grinned and splayed open her hands expectantly. "And the tutorship I offered?"

I slid the signed document across the table. "Claire will be meeting you once a week. Thank you for offering her your mentorship. She's thrilled." Or she would be when I informed her that I'd finalized the opportunity.

Mortus scoffed. "No good is going to come of this. If she's anything like her mother—"

"You'll kill her, too?" I asked, arching a brow.

The Spirit Elder wasn't used to me talking back to him so directly, but I wanted to surprise him. I needed him to drop his guard just for a second.

"If she poses a threat, yes, I will do what I must for fae kind."

"And I'll be right there beside him," Zephys agreed. "I voted against this. You have nothing to lose, Cyrus. Your people have already been obliterated by the curse Ophelia unleashed upon us, but what about Obsidian's people?"

The Earth Fae Elder rolled relaxation stones across her palm. "We have managed to stifle the illness expanded from the Spirit Kingdom. It will breed out in a generation or two."

Obsidian didn't like to take sides or vote and often opted out of decisions for things she felt were out of her control. She dealt with problems as they came to her.

"You should be more concerned," Zephys growled. "This Halfling will bring about the curse again, and it could be your people who suffer." She shrugged, which only enraged the Air Elder. "Come on, Obsidian. Get your head out of your arse."

She narrowed ebony eyes at him. "Trying to predict the way the earth moves will not help us prepare for tomorrow. If the curse hits us, we will respond to it."

Mortus snorted. "She's right about one thing. We are ready for whatever comes." His black eyes flashed with challenge. "I hope you're keeping an eye on the Halfling when you return to the Academy, because there are others who know what trouble she'll bring."

There you are, I mused.

I tilted my head in mock innocence. "Is that a threat, Mortus?"

He launched to his feet. "If I was threatening you, then you would know it, you insolent—"

I slammed my hands on the table, standing and leaning toward him. "You'd what?" I demanded, wanting him to snap, to provide me with the opportunity to shred apart his soul and find my brother. "Come on, Mortus, what would you do?" I pressed on him with my spirit, allowing him to *feel* my challenge deep inside. "*I am your king,*" I reminded him, my words underlined with enough power to make the entire room cringe.

My spirit wove around his, prodding, sensing for a weakness, anything that could tell me what he'd been up to. His enlarging irises told me he felt it, knew what I was doing, and the shiver that rolled across his skin said it scared him.

Good.

Unfortunately, Elana ruined the moment by sending a fine mist of water over the table as if she were spraying a herd of cats for misbehaving. Interesting timing for her to intervene, as if she sensed I was closing in on something important.

And since when could she create water? Elana was notoriously powerful in spirit, but she had no other elements under her control. A very rare state for a Spirit Fae, but a well-known fact where Elana was concerned.

Did I imagine it? Because it was already gone. *Maybe it was pixie dust, not water?*

"This meeting is meant to be informative," she stated flatly. "I will not have bickering."

"Then what purpose does this meeting truly serve, Elana?" I inquired, over the charade of this bullshit. "None of us like each other. It's all a power play, and as I sit at the top, I'm a constant opponent." I moved away, pushing my chair in. "If there's nothing else of import, I'll get back to my temporary assignment."

She sighed. "Cyrus…"

"I understand what you're trying to accomplish here, Elana, and I admire you deeply for it. But not everyone on this council feels the same." I glanced pointedly at Mortus and Zephys and finally at Blaize. "You all want to condemn an innocent woman for the atrocities of her mother. Perhaps you should consider investigating the sins of your own parents to determine your ability to lead."

My name trailed behind me as several argued my words, but I didn't listen.

I'd attended the council as a formality and to remind Mortus of my place.

Task accomplished, I had a new item on my list. *Protect Claire.*

Because I'd seen the indignation in the Councils' eyes. One slip and she'd pay the price with her life. I refused to allow that to happen on my watch.

Where are you, Exos? This power game grows tiresome without you. And your little queen is quite the handful.

Just thinking of Claire had my lips curling. Oh, she loathed me, and I, of course, encouraged it. But she needed the tough love to grow.

All this coddling bullshit would destroy the woman. She needed to realize her potential, and the only way to do that was by pushing her to achieve greatness. As no one else seemed keen to do it, I'd taken on the task.

And when we found my brother, he'd take over what I'd started.

Easy. Hopefully. Maybe...

I shook my head. There was no alternative. I needed her to be strong so I could use her to find Exos. Whatever she did with that strength was her choice and didn't impact me in the slightest. Not even a little bit.

If I told myself that enough, I'd grow to believe it. Because she wasn't mine, and she never would be. Exos owned her spirit, and I refused to interfere with that. But even I could grudgingly admit as I tilted my head up to observe the stars above that my brother had chosen well. I didn't get it at first, but two days with her showed me why.

She's a good mate for you, Exos, I thought to him. *I vow to keep her safe. Always. For you.*

And maybe a little bit for me.

But Exos didn't need to know that part.

No one did.

CHAPTER ELEVEN
EXOS

CLAIRE... I could feel her trying to find me, her essence an intoxicating presence in my soul that I longed to stroke. But I had to push her away. It was the only way to fight the shadow holding me hostage.

A shadow whose thirst for Claire crawled inside me, sinking its inky claws into our bond and inching ever closer to my mate.

No! I shoved it back, but it grew more powerful—*hungrier*—with every second. It reminded me of a black hole, spinning and sucking, *needing* to feed off the spirit energy thriving around us.

If that thing hurt Claire, I'd never forgive myself.

And I needed all my strength to battle the presence overtaking my being.

I will not become your puppet, I growled, determined.

We'll see, the foreign presence taunted, pressing deeper.

Fuck you, I seethed.

Laughter filtered through my conscious, the perpetrator amused.

Are there two? I wondered, dazed. *It* felt too energized to be a lone entity. Too consuming. Too... *familiar.*

The identity kept swirling in and out of my thoughts, too powerful for me to hold on to for long. Which was precisely why I had to close myself off from both Claire and the evil being threatening to take control of my spirit.

I slid into the recesses of my mind, preparing my blockade, hell-bent on strengthening my reserves before I came out swinging.

But it would take time.

Days.

Weeks, maybe.

A month.

And I had to say goodbye to my Claire. At least for a little while.

I sighed as the last ledge of the barrier began to form, my heart aching for the bond I had to lock away. Not broken, just closed. For now. Until I was strong enough to protect us both.

Don't give up on me, Claire, I whispered to her. *I'll reach out again soon. I promise.*

Darkness descended on the message, following the chain to the woman I'd allowed into my heart. I screamed in rebellion, using the last vestiges of my power to cut the fae off and blast the asshole backward.

An "Oomph" followed, telling me I'd won.

For now.

A temporary victory, one that would only enrage the being more.

Who are you? I wondered, infuriated that I couldn't identify the familiar brush of power.

Ah, it didn't matter.

As soon as I recharged, I'd destroy whoever tried to subdue me. I was the rightful heir to the Spirit Kingdom. I'd denied it all my life, but now it was time to embrace it. All I needed was to harness that strength and use it.

Soon, I swore. *Soon.*

The last vestiges of my cage assembled, I shut my eyes and closed myself off from everything and everyone.

The battle had not yet begun.

But when it did, I'd land on top.

I always did.

CHAPTER TWELVE
CLAIRE

A Little Over a Month Later...

THE PIXIE CHIRPED AT ME IN DELIGHT, causing my lips to curl. "I have no idea what you're saying," I told it. That only seemed to make the little fairy more excited. She began to dance, her dust flying around her and causing me to laugh.

A second appeared beside me, this one conjured by Elana, and the two began chattering in their little language while flying in hypnotic circles across the dining area.

This had become my favorite part of our sessions—the creation of life through magical means.

Elana's energy warmed mine, her smile one of approval as I called another pixie into formation with my mind, this one a male. The two females immediately drew near, their intrigue evident.

"That's new," Elana murmured.

I lifted a shoulder. "I have a few males to draw on for inspiration." Five, to be exact. Six if I included River. Sol, Vox, Titus, and Cyrus had become permanent fixtures in my life, with Exos a nightly feature in my dreams. The only female I'd grown close to over the last month was Elana, but I couldn't exactly call us friends. She was more like the fairy godmother I never knew I needed.

She laughed as the females began to chase the male around the room. He squeaked out some kind of command they didn't appear interested in following, and beat his wings harder to get away.

"Is that how you feel daily?" Elana mused. "With all those male fae circling your powers?"

My cheeks reddened. "They don't chase me around." They just, sort of, followed me everywhere. Titus waited downstairs for our session to end, and we'd likely be intercepted by Vox or Sol on the way back to Spirit Quad. "They're a little protective."

Not in an overbearing kind of way, but in a responsible manner.

Their defensive energy had heightened over the last month while I continued to master my elements. It was as if they didn't like the attention I brought upon myself, but I couldn't help it. The whole point of the Academy was to learn.

"You have five elements," Elana murmured. "It's not surprising you're attracting mates from different sides."

"Oh, it's not like that." At least, I was trying very hard for it not to be like that. Titus kept me well satisfied, and my spirit still very much belonged to Exos. "We're all just friends."

The words came out stilted, but I had to believe them.

While Exos once said I'd likely need a mate for each element, I was determined to prove him wrong. Five men? I almost laughed.

Or maybe I wanted to cry.

Shaking my head, I focused on the pixies and created another male to join the foray, which caused all three to halt their dance about the room.

Louder chirping sounded as the original male squared off with the newcomer.

Hmm, seemed the little guy didn't like competition.

It made me frown. Titus never acted like that. Actually, none of the guys did.

So yeah, just friends. That was why Sol never brought up the Solstice Ball again and why Vox seemed to only open up to me while in the kitchen. And Cyrus, well, he was just an ass. Nothing new there.

The pixies continued yipping while I yawned.

"Tired?" Elana asked, her gray eyes holding a touch of motherly concern.

I nodded. "I didn't sleep well last night." *Or the night before. Or the night before that. And, well, for the last four or five weeks.*

Exos came to me every night, causing me to awaken with a broken heart every morning. I could feel our connection wilting with each passing day, the bond corroding over time. Cyrus said it was a result of Exos closing me off, that if we didn't rekindle the relationship soon, it would wither and die and we would never be linked again.

My chest ached at the thought.

But I had no idea how to find him. He'd shut me out with a few whispered words about not giving up on him. Well, that would never happen. However, it would have been nice to be given a clue about his situation.

"Are you all right, Claire?" Elana studied me in that uncanny way of hers. "You're making great strides in your control. I mean, that evidence is dancing on the table."

I forced a smile at the show and shook my head. "Yeah, I'm fine. It's just been a long month."

"Exos," she said, giving a knowing nod as my gaze flew upward to hers. "I had wondered why he would leave in such a crucial time of your relationship. Perhaps you should call him home?"

Such an innocent question underlined in genuine concern.

Cyrus thought she might be behind Exos's kidnapping, but after five sessions with her, I knew he was wrong. This woman cared too much about peace and finding harmony among the fae to harm another. She often cried when we had to dismiss the pixies, and they weren't even real.

I sighed. "I miss him." *But I can't tell you why or where he is.* Because even if I knew her to be innocent, I couldn't bring myself to betray Cyrus's trust. He was busy working this case from other angles, not that he seemed to be getting anywhere.

But if anyone cared for Exos as much as I did, it was Cyrus.

So I would trust him until he gave me a reason not to.

"Call him home," she said again. "Or tell Cyrus to." A knowing glimmer creased her eyes into a smile. "Or I can tell him to, if you prefer. I know how intimidating Cyrus can be."

"Oh? I think he's positively charming," I deadpanned.

She laughed outright. "Isn't he just?" She swiped a tear from the edge of her gaze and shook her head. "He's a stubborn one; that's for sure."

"Understatement," I muttered. "I'm sure he means well, but yeah, he's a force of nature."

Elana nodded. "Yes. He's definitely his father's son. Strong-willed and dominant and unfailingly loyal." She finished her tea and set it off to the side with an indulgent smile. "You may not want to hear it, but you're very much like your mother, Claire. The history everyone speaks about her is tainted in so many ways." She lost some of her sparkle, her features falling. "The Ophelia I knew was determined, smart, and so very talented."

I leaned forward, intrigued to hear more about the mother I didn't know. Elana had mentioned her in passing a few times but never provided much context. This was the first time she'd indicated any doubts about my mother's legacy. "What do you mean by 'tainted'?" I asked.

She sighed, waving her hand and dissolving the pixies to dust on the table.

Normally, this was when she shed a tear, but she seemed too distracted by the past to see the present.

"There's so much about those days that remains unclear. I mean, for one, they never found your mother's body. And Mortus sometimes swears he can sense her."

"Wait… I thought he killed her?" Why would he talk about sensing her if he knew she was dead? Did he believe in ghosts or something?

"Oh, he claims to have killed her, yes. But no one actually found her remains." She pinched her lips to the side, and then sighed. "Honestly, I don't know why I even bother speculating. It was an impossible fight for her to survive, and her body likely dissolved beneath the energy backlash of a failed bond. But the plague that followed doesn't really make any sense. Fae dropped to the earth in waves, their souls snatched from their bodies as if sucked up into the clouds. It was all very *suspicious*, for lack of a better term."

Elana swallowed, her hands clasping tightly over the ornate table of her dining room. Ghosts danced in her gaze, painting a haunting history one had to live through to understand, and it scattered goose bumps down my arms.

"Chaos rained down upon us, Claire. For weeks. It's truly hard to say what did and did not occur." Her silver eyes met mine, her expression grim. "Your mother's infidelity is absolute and you're living proof, but circumstances of that decision seem, well, harsh."

"The plague is spreading to the Earth Fae." I'd witnessed it with my own eyes. Two Earth Fae students had gone home ill in the last month, leaving Sol even more aloof each time. He seemed to blame himself for surviving, and I saw the worry in his gaze for each of his classmates. I wished there was something I could do, even if it was just to talk to him, but whenever I brought it up, he changed the topic to training or some sort of instruction. Then he'd find a way to excuse himself.

"It is spreading, yes," Elana confirmed quietly. "They blame the Spirit Fae, but there's not many of us left to take credit. Which is why I'm so focused on harmony—because I believe the cause isn't a shattered bond at all, but distrust amongst fae kind. Rather than work together to survive, we've divided our elements into kingdoms and fight for power amongst ourselves. It's why you're so important, Claire. You hold the key to bring us all together."

"Because I have all five elements," I whispered.

"Exactly." Her shoulders relaxed, her lips curling. "It's not a discussion for today, dear Claire, but you must see your potential. There are those who wish to destroy it. I would prefer we cultivate it. It could be the key to saving us all."

I wasn't sure how I felt about either alternative. One clearly equated to death, while the other hinted at the possibility of being used.

"Chancellor." Titus's voice came from the doorway, his tone modest, while his fire warmed my skin.

"Yes, yes, it's time." Elana waved her hand, standing.

"I didn't mean to rush you," he said, sounding contrite.

"Oh, no, we've already gone over. It seems to be a continuous habit." She winked at me. "Same time next week?"

I nodded. "Yes, please."

"Excellent." She beamed at Titus. "You can have your mate back now, Fire Fae. Be good to her."

"I will, ma'am," he promised, his arm settling around my lower back as I stood.

Elana gave a wave, showering the room in dust that grew into an army of new pixies. "We have a dinner to prepare, little ones," she announced, her focus having already shifted to the next task at hand.

Titus and I left in the middle of her instructions, his lips curled in amusement. "You should do that in the Spirit Quad. They could cook all our meals."

"I think Vox enjoys the kitchen too much to allow that to happen," I teased. "But maybe they could help us clean?" The boys were messy. Especially Sol, who seemed to track loose stones everywhere he went.

"True." He brushed his lips against my temple, guiding me out of the house and down to the trail that led us back to campus. "How was your lesson?"

"Good." I frowned, thinking about what Elana had revealed. "Actually, it was enlightening."

"How so?"

"I don't think she has Exos." I'd told Titus about Cyrus's suspicions last month, not wanting to keep anything from him. He'd agreed with the logic, saying that, while dangerous, it made sense to get closer to her to see what I could learn. And today seemed to have taught me more than the last several weeks combined. "Did you know my mother's body was never found?"

He considered for a long moment and slowly shook his head. "I've never heard that."

"Elana said Ophelia's body was never found and that Mortus claims to sense her sometimes," I said, thinking out loud as I played the scenario through my thoughts. "What if Ophelia is still alive?"

Cyrus chose that moment to materialize, his water element heavy in the air. "Well, that's an interesting theory," he replied, causing Titus to scowl.

"I fucking hate when you do that," he muttered.

"Ditto," I agreed.

Both men cocked their brows.

"It means I agree with Titus," I clarified.

"Of course you do," Cyrus said, smirking. "Regardless, I need you to come with me, and we can continue discussing your little theory along the way."

Little theory. What an ass. "Titus and I have plans." We didn't, but it was the principle of the matter. "So go mist off somewhere else." I started walking again, but Cyrus's response froze me midstep.

"I have a lead on Exos, Claire."

CHAPTER TWELVE
EXOS

CLAIRE ROTATED SO QUICKLY THAT TITUS had to grab her hip to keep her from falling over. "*What?*"

"I don't like repeating myself." She'd heard me just fine. "Will you come with me or not?"

"*We* will come with you," Titus said while Claire's mouth moved silently over words I couldn't hear.

"No." I met the Fire Fae's gaze. "Only Claire."

"Why?" he demanded.

"Because we need to go to Spirit Kingdom." And only a Spirit Fae could survive there without lasting consequences.

Titus's answering expression said he knew it, too, his face going white at the prospect. "You can't be serious," he breathed.

"It's a solid lead." Mainly because I'd followed Mortus there the other night and there could only be one reason he'd chosen to venture into the dead kingdom—Exos. "We've searched the Academy grounds, and we've even combed through the enchanted forest. Where we haven't been is the Spirit Kingdom. And it would explain how my brother was able to cut himself off from everyone." There were elements in the dead realm that could facilitate such a trick. It would also mean he might be harvesting leftover energy to put up a fight.

"You need her to help you sense his presence." Titus sounded horrified.

"I do," I admitted. "I tried myself last night and came up empty-handed. Maybe Claire will find something different."

"At the risk of her own life," Titus managed to say, his teeth clenching. "The Spirit Kingdom is a wasteland."

"True." *On both accounts.* "So I guess the question is, how much is the little queen willing to risk for her spirit mate?" I arched a challenging brow at her. "Are you strong enough, Claire? Or would you rather leave him to suffer until it's too late?"

"That's not fair," she whispered.

"What's not fair is my brother lying in the ground somewhere," I argued. "He's dying, Claire. And every day we pretend he's fine is another day closer to his demise. So either—"

"You're the one who said we should go on like nothing happened," she snapped, squaring off with me. "*You* won't go to the Council. *You* won't corner Mortus. *You* are the one killing him, Cyrus. Not me." She sent a blast of air straight into my chest, sending me a step backward. "Don't you *dare* talk to me about his death as if I'm the one causing it. You're not the one going to bed every night and dreaming of him and waking every morning trying to find him in the connection he turned off."

I rubbed the spot where she'd assaulted me and grimaced. "You might not agree with my methods, but I—"

"I don't agree with you popping up and acting like I won't do everything I can to save him. You want me to go to the Spirit Kingdom? Fine. I'll go. But I don't need you to provoke me into it. I want to save him just as badly as you do, if not more. So fuck you and your mind games, Cyrus. Either take me or mist off."

Titus gaped at her, shocked by her outburst.

But all I could do was smile.

That was the fighter I required. The woman beneath the elements who would do what was needed to save those under her care. No tears. No excuses. Just a warrior ready for battle.

And maybe my methods made me an asshole, but they'd worked.

"All right," I said, holding out my hand. "We need to go now."

"Fine." She glanced at Titus and sighed at his expression. "I'll be fine."

"You have no idea what you're walking into, Claire," he said, his anger creating a line of invisible fire across his aura. "And you just allowed Cyrus to bait you into going."

"He had me at 'Exos,'" she replied, her smile sad. "If he has a lead, I have to follow it. And I would do the same for you."

"I'd never ask you to."

"And neither would Exos." She cupped his cheek and went to her toes to

259

kiss him deeply, the moment one meant for two lovers. I found it oddly satisfying. A strange sensation, since she wasn't mine to care for, but I rather liked seeing her content. Something told me Exos would approve, too. "I'll be okay."

"It's a death trap," Titus whispered. "The Spirit Kingdom is where they send fae to die."

"Then it's a good thing I'm brimming with life." She kissed him again, then stepped back. "And I have the Spirit King as my guide."

A smart-ass remark about her trusting me graced my tongue, but I didn't allow it to escape. I really did need her cooperation if this was going to work, and as I had it, I wasn't about to lose it.

"If anything happens to her—"

"You won't have to worry about killing me, Titus," I interjected. "My brother will do that for you should harm befall her."

He stared me down for a long moment before nodding. "Bring her back, Spirit King."

I held out my hand for hers and smiled. "If I have it my way, it'll be Exos who brings her back."

CHAPTER FOURTEEN
SOL

"SHE'S SO SMALL," I muttered. Not necessarily as small as Aflora or my little sister had been, but definitely smaller than me.

"Who?" Vox asked as he worked on fixing my latest damage to the Spirit Quad.

What had once been a dining table was now a pile of splinters that Vox meticulously worked to reassemble. It took incredible power and concentration for the Air Fae to align each broken shard back together.

I hadn't meant to break it. Frustration had gotten the better of me, and, well, yeah.

"Who?" Vox repeated, a hint of impatience in his tone.

"Oh. Claire." Who else could I be talking about? "She's just so much smaller than me."

"And?" he prompted, finally looking at me.

"I just…" I palmed the back of my neck, uncertain of how to word it. Maybe it was easier if I just said nothing at all. I mean, Vox didn't need to know. He probably had his own issues to deal with where Claire was concerned. "Never mind."

"Oh, no. I want to know why you said that. Why are you thinking about her height?"

"It's not so much her height as it is her overall size," I huffed. "She's so small."

"Yeah, you said that." He folded his arms. "Why do you care?"

"Don't you?" I demanded. "I mean, you hear her at night just like I do. You have to think about it." And there were the words I didn't mean to say. By the shock on Vox's face, they also weren't the ones he expected.

"You're talking about... like..." He made a gesture that left me frowning. "What the fuck is that supposed to be?"

"You know."

"No, I really don't." It had looked like... well, I didn't know. He'd scissored his fingers like he wanted to give her a haircut. "You've had sex before, right?"

He blanched. "Sol!"

"What?" I demanded. "Come on, with that little gesture, it's a valid question."

"We're not having this conversation."

"You're the one who asked me what I was thinking about. Now you have an answer." One he appeared to be judging me for, which was completely unfair. "You can't tell me you've not thought about it, because I've noticed the abundance of showers lately."

"Oh, Elements," Vox said, looking up at the ceiling.

"All I said is she's small, okay?" I grumbled. "I realize you don't have to worry about that, but I do."

"What happened to not wanting to mate with her?" Vox prompted.

"I... I don't want that." *I think. Maybe. Fuck. I don't know.* I shook my head. "It was just a thought, okay?"

"About her size in bed."

"And how I could break her," I growled. "Never mind. Just keep doing whatever you're doing."

"Whatever I'm doing is cleaning up the damn mess in the kitchen," he snapped. "Because *you* broke the table. I suppose that's fitting, considering your concerns."

"Hey, that's not fair."

"Isn't it?" Vox demanded. "You know what? You should fix it."

"Why are you being such a dick?" This wasn't like my best friend. Sure, he had bouts of temper in the past, but this seemed deep-rooted, as if there was something else going on. "What's wrong?"

"I can't fix dinner, Sol. Because we have nowhere to eat it. *That* is what's wrong." He waved at the mess, creating an air vortex that swept it all away and out the open door. "And why in the fae are you thinking about fucking Claire?"

My eyebrows shot upward. "Are you telling me the thought hasn't ever crossed your mind?"

"Of course it has," he replied, his cheeks darkening. "I mean, I hear the same things you do."

"So why are you giving me a hard time about it?"

"Because neither of us wants to mate with her!" Vox exclaimed, a gust of wind amplifying the lie he was trying to tell himself. I hadn't been exaggerating about the showers, and he knew it.

"We don't?" I asked, testing the thought aloud. "Because if you wanted to, and I wanted to, then maybe it could work."

And maybe Vox would stop being such an uptight dirtwad and I could get my head on straight again. The Spirit Quad would be grateful; I'd certainly done enough damage to it over the last month.

Vox balked at me, making me frown. "Why are you looking at me like that?"

He threw his hands up. "It's weird, okay?"

"Weird," I repeated. "Mating with a gorgeous woman is weird. Okay," I grumbled and turned to face the swirl of air that was keeping the table somewhat assembled in the shape it should have been. Fine cracks lined its broken seams, and I forced my earth magic to reach out and command it to remember its form. It was once wood, born of the earth, and had known life and seasons long before it'd been smashed by my careless whims of power.

"We'd be sharing her," Vox said after a long bout of silence, his voice softer than before. "Don't you think that's weird?"

I shrugged. "Honestly, no." Did I want to be intimate with other men? Not really. But if I trusted anyone to share a woman with, it was Vox. "If anything, you'd help me with my control so I wouldn't hurt her." The words came out on a mumble meant mostly for me, but Vox's affinity for air would have made them loud in comparison.

My best friend froze. "What?"

I sighed. "You heard me just fine."

"You've thought about... the three of us?" He sounded so alarmed I had to laugh.

"Dude, it's not like I fantasize about you. Just, you know, how it would all—" I shook my head. "You know what? Forget I ever brought it up."

"Forget that you want to have a threesome with Claire?" Vox asked, the wheeze in his tone irritating me.

You know what? Fuck this table. I smashed it into little bits, much to Vox's horror, and created something from the ground instead.

Something I knew Claire would love.

Recalling her magic from class, a tree not of this world rooted into the floor, its earthly spirit thriving as I searched the fine grains. It grew, reaching out fresh limbs and blooming with some of Claire's impossibly fuzzy, sweet fruit. What had she called them?

Peaches.

I re-created their essence in my palm and sent several seeds scattering, telling them to remember Claire's element.

"*Sol!*"

Vox had been yelling at me for quite some time, but it was only when he slammed a wall of air into my chest that my eyes flung open, my energy ripped free from the magic and peaceful thoughts that had taken me under.

I stared at the result of my creation. What was supposed to be a dining table was now a long slab of wood with branches sticking out of the ends. Long roots burrowed into the broken tiles of the floor, and an engraving of Claire's peach tree decorated the polished surface. Sister trees sprouted out of the sides and leaned against the ceiling, heavy with fruit.

I smiled.

Vox balked at me. "What in the five elements has gotten into you, Sol? Now the entire floor is ruined and we have trees in our kitchen."

Titus chose that moment to walk in, sparking embers across his fingertips that looked like tiny explosions. He'd already been wearing a scowl when he'd entered, but when he saw my handiwork, he stopped midstride. "Well, somebody's redecorated."

Heat scalding my skin from embarrassment, I took a seat at one of the overgrown stumps at the table and plucked a peach from a lower branch. "You were making dinner, weren't you, Vox?" I reminded him. "You wanted me to fix the dining room, and, well, I did." Simple as that. I sank my teeth into the delicate fruit, relaxing instantly.

Vox glowered, then deflated—literally. A puff of air sent his loose hair floating around his head, the band having broken free in his attempts to reassemble the table. "Fine. I'll cook. Maybe some food will calm down whatever's gotten into you." He glanced at Titus, who had steam wafting off of his skin. "And you, too, apparently."

Titus took a nearby stump and glowered. "I don't want to talk about it." Flames slithered over his skin like snakes, making me flinch.

"Don't burn down the trees," I chided. "I made it for Claire because she likes peaches. And I do, too."

Titus hummed in approval, some of his fire dying. "Assuming she makes it back, I'm sure she'll love them."

There was so much resentment in his voice that I stopped eating. Juices from the peach ran down my wrist, and I wiped it on my pants. "Assuming she makes it back from where?" It struck me then that if she wasn't with Titus, she had to be with Cyrus. Or maybe Elana.

Titus growled and clasped his fist in his hand. "Cyrus took her to the fucking Spirit Kingdom." His eyes flashed with rage. "He claims to have a lead on Exos, but I call pixie shit on that."

"But classes start up again in a few days," I said, confused. "Why would he take her there? She could be gone for weeks. And then she'll miss the ball."

That last part wasn't meant to escape, but I hadn't been able to stop thinking about it for over a month. I never actually said *yes*, and she'd not brought it up again, so I didn't know if we were going or not. But I sort of wanted to take her.

No, I *really* wanted to.

Which was definitely a problem because we were supposed to be just friends.

Except my fantasies were decidedly *not* friend-based.

The silence overwhelming the kitchen had me looking to Vox and Titus. They were both gaping at me.

"Claire's been dragged off to the undead wasteland of a realm, and you're worried about the ball?" Vox asked, sounding incredulous. "Since when do you care about those things?"

I creased my lips together and frowned. I'd already said too much, and Vox was right. Claire was in danger, although I highly doubted even the Spirit Kingdom could dampen her life. Still, this was no time to worry about stupid Academy social events.

Even if I was starting to look forward to it.

"Yeah, Sol," Titus said, his flames receding as a spark of amusement flashed across his face. "Why do you care about the ball?"

"Did she ask you?" Vox interrupted, an odd note in his voice.

"So what if she did?" I demanded, taking another bite of the peach. "Titus didn't ask her to go, and she said she'd go with me and we'd wear jeans." We just never finalized our plans, but she still planned to go with me. *I think.*

"Formal attire is required," Vox reminded me. "You can't wear jeans."

"Well, she said we're wearing jeans, and I'm good with that." And there wasn't shit he could do about it.

Vox's brow furrowed. "I'm going to win our bet. You're falling for her."

I snorted. "Dude, I haven't lost yet. We're not mated, just friends. Besides, what was I supposed to do? Tell her she can't go to the ball?" Even I could hear the defensive quality of my tone, but fuck if I would admit it out loud. It was a ball. Who cared if I wanted to take her?

"If you don't want to adhere to the social customs, you should let someone take her who actually wants to dress up," Vox grumbled, slamming his knife down into the slab of meat with a gust of wind. He cursed when he couldn't get the blade free from the cutting board.

Titus leaned back against one of the peach trees and smirked. "Are you two seriously bickering over who gets to go to the ball with Claire? Why don't you just both take her?"

Vox stopped trying to yank his knife free, and I stared at the Fire Fae. "You're not upset?" It was his mate, after all.

Titus shrugged. "Look, when she gets back from whatever nightmare Cyrus puts her through, she'll need a distraction. I think the Solstice Ball is a great idea, but I can't go. Banned, remember?"

"Oh yeah." Vox chuckled. "You burned down the pixie orchestra at the last ball. That was hilarious."

Titus frowned. "Only because some Water Fae were being dicks. I wasn't in the mood for their shit." He shuddered as if the idea of any Water Fae revolted him. I wanted to remind him that Claire had control over water as well, but I didn't want to be the next thing he burned. "Anyway, you both should take her. It'll help get her mind off things after Cyrus inevitably comes back empty-handed." His jaw flexed. "If I didn't know better, I'd say this is all a ruse on his part to make her stronger. He's been a complete ass since day one."

None of us were about to disagree with him, but the idea of both Vox and me taking her to the ball had me distracted. I couldn't dance—not without destroying half the ballroom—and Vox could pull off a ballroom suit a lot better than I could. He could show her the good time she deserved without me trying to turn her down and probably hurt her feelings in the process.

"So, what are we supposed to do while they're gone?" I asked, having grown accustomed to teaching Claire at earth class. The other students looked forward to watching her magic. It had been so long since we'd had an Earth Fae with her kind of power and control—she didn't realize it, but we were learning from her.

Titus glanced up at the peach tree. "I think I have an idea."

CHAPTER FIFTEEN
CLAIRE

"THIS IS YOUR CHILDHOOD HOME?" I asked, marveling at the white marble walls and obsidian floors. It was so clean. So stark. So *bare*.

Cyrus leaned against one of the pristine pillars, his icy gaze holding me captive. "This isn't just our childhood home; it's our current one, too. It's the Royal Palace of the Spirit Kingdom, Claire."

I'd gathered the royal part by the grandiose appearance outside, but it seemed so unlively. Even the moats along the stone walls seemed still. "There's no one here." I grimaced as soon as the words left my mouth. "I mean, it's—"

"Death," he finished for me. "Yes." He pushed away from the stone column and walked toward a balcony overlooking the grounds, his hands tucked behind his back.

I glanced at the old paintings hanging from the walls as I followed him, noting the portraits of all the stoic fae. That seemed to be where Exos and Cyrus obtained their hardness from, or maybe it was a result of growing up in this massive home alone.

Wisps of dead trees, still waters, and vapid land met my perusal outside. Even the setting sun seemed dim, the world around us awash in blacks and whites and little splashes of color. Except for what appeared to be a city in the distance, the glowing embers of a fire catching my gaze.

"Springfall," Cyrus murmured, following my gaze. "It's the only Spirit Fae community left in existence." His hands had slid into his pockets, his expression closed off. "We have a residence there, one in the heart of the court, but Exos and I prefer staying here. It keeps us focused, reminds us of our failures and the journeys that rest ahead."

"Sounds lonely," I admitted.

He nodded. "It is, but it's also necessary."

"How do you help your people by living in isolation?" I wondered out loud, not following the logic. "Surely they would prefer to see you. And why are there no Spirit Fae at the Academy?" I'd started to assume there were no Spirit Fae left, but the colony of light appeared sizable, even at a distance.

"There are no fae of age to attend the Academy, Claire."

I frowned. "Are they too young?"

"Claire," he said, forcing my attention back to him. "You're the youngest Spirit Fae in existence. No others were born after you."

My lips parted. "Because of the plague."

He nodded. "Yes." He tilted his head. "Has my brother not spoken of this? Of the importance of your mating and what it means for our people?"

I swallowed and slowly shook my head. "We've… It's been… Well, I mean—"

"A simple *no* would suffice," he interjected, his tone suggesting his displeasure at my rambling.

But it wasn't like there'd been an abundance of time for Exos and me to discuss all of this. Between my recruitment—if I could even call it that—into the Academy, and all the insanity that followed, plus his disappearance, we hadn't gotten around to what it meant for him to be a royal. Or, really, anything about Spirit Fae history other than my mother's impact.

"My people will pray for your fertility, Claire," he said, his gaze returning to the glow of Springfall. "You'll be our only hope at creating an heir to the Spirit Kingdom."

My mouth worked without sound, his words not at all ones I expected to hear.

Fertility?

Heir?

"*What?*"

He glanced at me, his lips curling down. "Why else would you mate with my brother if not to perform royal duties?"

My eyes widened, my head moving back and forth. "You can't be serious. I just met your brother."

"And yet, you're in the second stage of mating with him." He faced me fully, his annoyance evident in the lines of his handsome face. "Are you truly so selfish that you would only engage in the bond for your own self-fulfillment?" His blue eyes raked over me in disgust. "Never mind. Of course you are."

He turned again, as if to walk away, but I grabbed his arm and yanked him back to me. "At least give me a second to process your accusations before giving up on my reply," I snapped. God, this fae was such a fucking prick! "What is your problem with me?"

His perfect eyebrow arched. "Would you care for a list?" He didn't give me a chance to reply before he started in on me. "You're weak. You're a Halfling, not a full-blooded fae. You're not of the royal line. You're unfaithful and parading around like a regular whore. You're—"

My palm cracked across his face, my anger erupting into a fire along my skin and threatening to singe him to ash.

"You know nothing about me!" I shouted, done with all of this. "You asked me here to find Exos. So why the fuck are we here? What lesson are you trying to instill in me before we search for your brother? Because I'm done with your very wrong analysis of my character. Yes, I'm a Halfling— one with access to *five* elements. Fuck your bloodlines and imperious notions on what is best for your brother. Because he chose me, too, or did you forget that little detail of our bond?"

Fuck, I was furious.

I wanted to smack him again.

Kill him.

Something.

It took serious effort to take a step back from him. For I didn't trust myself not to burn him alive for his crude evaluation.

"I am not a whore," I whispered, the words costing me severely in emotion. Never had I felt so belittled in my life, and after everything I'd been through in the last few months, that was saying a lot. "You don't know me at all, *Your Highness.*" I mock-bowed and left him on the balcony.

Only, he caught me after a few feet, his arm wrapping around my lower abdomen to yank me backward into his chest. "You're wrong." His lips were at my ear. "I've done nothing but study you for the last month, Claire. I *know* you."

I slammed my foot back into his shin and tried to sweep his legs out from beneath him in the way Titus had taught me. Cyrus released me, but just long enough to whirl me in his arms and capture me again.

My fiery handprint on his cheek pleased me greatly, and I wanted to add another.

So I fought him with all I was worth to hit him again. But he blocked each punch, his skill admirable and infuriatingly good.

"Why are you doing this?" I demanded, enraged and exhausted and confused as hell. "Where's the lead on Exos?"

"I'm preparing you for it," he said, catching my fist again with ease and

269

shoving me backward.

I charged him with a growl and almost clocked his face, only to find myself pinned yet again by his arms. Dropping low, I went for his knees and grunted as my back hit the ground. Cyrus landed on top of me with ease, his hands catching my wrists above my head.

My chest heaved beneath him, exerted from the impromptu battle. Yet he wasn't even sweating. The damn fae barely seemed fazed at all!

"I fucking hate you," I told him, squirming in earnest and not moving his body a fucking inch. *Gah!* "I wish they'd taken you instead of Exos!"

"Me, too," he admitted softly. "I wish it every day, but it's a waste of time and energy. What we need to do is find him."

"Then find him," I snapped. "Stop wasting *my* time with all this bullshit and look for him."

"I'm not wasting your time, Claire."

"Like hell you're not," I seethed, writhing beneath him to drive the point home. "Calling me a whore, telling me I'm not worthy, and criticizing—"

His mouth sealed over mine, silencing me.

I was so shocked at first that I didn't react, my brain frying beneath the onslaught of power in that single brush of his lips.

What...?

No.

I bit him. *Hard.* Irate that he thought to take such a liberty with me.

He hissed, his grip tightening on my wrists.

"Fuck you," I snarled. "If this is your way of proving I'm a whore, then seriously, *fuck you.*"

He had the good grace to look chagrined, but only for a second. And the asshole still didn't move. "I followed Mortus last night into the death fields. I think that's where he's keeping my brother. But what you need to understand is those grounds harbor tortured souls who play on fears and are notoriously degrading. They thrive on making a fae feel so small that he wishes for death. All the tormenting thoughts you've had about yourself will come to life out there. Consider my words an introduction to the experience."

He finally released me, popping to his feet before I could try to hit him again.

"I don't think you're a whore, little queen. But I know all about the social standards on Earth and how they've programmed your mind. Don't let the death fields use those thoughts against you, or you may never recover." He straightened his jacket, his stance stiff. "We leave in an hour."

I gaped after him, deflated.

That had all been a test? No, a preparation of sorts. Including the kiss? *What the hell?*

I shook my head, dazed.

Why does your brother have to be such a fucking dick? I asked Exos. *I mean, for fuck's sake!*

Of course, he didn't reply.

I ran my hand over my face. Only then did I feel it—the stirring of another bond. A seduction of sorts, my element reacting to a potential match. The liquid sensation settled over me, followed by a bolt of horror as I realized what had just occurred.

That hadn't been any ordinary kiss.

No.

Cyrus had just tied me to him under stage one of the courtship.

Fuck!

Chapter Sixteen
Cyrus

WHY THE FUCK DID I JUST KISS HER?

To shut her up.

No.

Damn it.

I blew out a breath and glowered at my reflection in the mirror. I kissed her because I hated the agony in her expression that my words had caused. But it wasn't like I *meant* them. I just wanted to prepare her for the task ahead. Warning her would have defeated the purpose. She needed to feel those comments like a punch to her gut to understand the weight of the death fields. Otherwise, they'd destroy her.

But kissing her had not been part of my plan.

And now, my water element was rejoicing.

Not spirit, because my brother owned that part of her. So I'd taken the one that called to me most, the hot liquid boiling throughout her gorgeous form.

I gripped the counter, livid with my lack of restraint. I knew better than to indulge a female of equal power. Yet, I'd given in to the urge and taken what wasn't mine to take.

"I'm an ass," I said, shaking my head. Especially because I rather liked the way it felt to be connected to her.

I frowned at the foreign bond, evaluating it. Being a descendant of two royal bloodlines, I possessed equal power in both spirit and water. So establishing a bond with my water element didn't shock me, but it was far more fluid than I anticipated. I could *feel* her links to the others, the way her fire burned for Titus, how her spirit mourned for Exos, the intrigue her earth had in Sol, and the admiration her air felt for Vox.

Am I supposed to be able to sense all of that? I wondered. *More importantly, can I use it to access Exos?*

The thought had me freezing in place.

A practical course, yes.

But how would that impact Claire? She already loathed me. I could sense that much in our initial bond. Oh, her water element was very attracted to mine. But the woman, well, I'd done myself no favors by kissing her.

"Fuck," I muttered, my shoulders hunching again.

Pragmatism nagged at me, whispering the rightness of the situation, how I could use it to my advantage in locating my brother. It was only an initial bond. Temporary, at best. Once I completed the task and saved him, I would release her of our obligations to one another, and she'd be free to mate with another Water Fae.

That sounded easy enough. And she'd be so thrilled with having Exos back that she wouldn't care. In fact, she'd be relieved to see me gone.

So how do I use this link? I wondered, exploring it further. If she felt me prodding around, she didn't react, but I certainly felt her fury at what I'd done.

I sighed.

This was going to be painful.

The things I did for my brother.

CHAPTER SEVENTEEN
TITUS

I DROPPED THE PEACH TO THE GROUND, stunned.

What.

The.

Fuck.

Was.

That?

"Titus?" Vox asked, hovering over another tree that Sol was struggling to get to twist just right into formation. We'd been at it for hours. When Claire came back home, she'd have a peach orchard of a paradise in the back of the Spirit Quad.

If Cyrus would give her death, then we would give her life.

"Did you guys feel that?" I asked, stumbling back into one of the finished trees. A few peaches thumped to the ground and burst a sweet scent into the air. My flames had a mind of their own and threatened to burn the precious life pressing against my spine.

Sol grabbed me by the arm, abandoning his project and making Vox curse as the boughs slapped him in the face. "Something's wrong with you," the giant observed.

No shit.

"It's like... she's *drenched*." Claire was always my burning flame, but now something had doused her with an unexpected tidal wave that had hit me just as hard.

And she was pissed off about it, fighting it as hard as she could as her flames called for me, seeking for anything to evaporate the hopeless ocean that threatened to consume her.

But there was something even I could feel that made her hate herself. She had allowed it, even if it was brief. It'd been enough.

Sol frowned, dropping me to a sandy spot of the courtyard where I'd been working to make the soil fertile with touches of fire. My flames immediately spiraled out and sank into the ground, crystalizing the fine grains. It was as if my element was trying to reach out to her, to protect her from...

Him.

"Is Claire okay?" Vox asked, sweeping his hair back into a warrior's tail and securing the strands. "Do we need to go after her?"

It warmed my fiery heart that the Air Fae wouldn't think twice about marching into the Spirit Kingdom. I shook my head. "Even if we could survive in that shithole, it wouldn't be for long. And..." My eyes narrowed as my fingers curled into fists. "As pissed off as Claire is, she won't need our help."

"Why's she pissed off?" Sol asked, crouching to look me in the eye.

Just saying the words aloud made me want to set the world on fire.

"Cyrus pushed the first stage of a mating bond on her. And I'm going to fucking kill him."

Sol's eyes went wide.

Vox looked stunned, then a slightly hysterical laugh escaped him. "Even the Spirit King can't resist her," he mused, shaking his head. "I feel for Claire. She has her work cut out for her if she really is going to put up with a mate like Cyrus."

"What if he's not just trying to mate with her?" I snapped, embers sparking from my fingertips and threatening to catch the nearby brush on fire. "That asshole is up to something, and if he uses her, or hurts her in any way..."

Sol slammed a fist into the ground, sending a quake thundering through the entire quad. "I'll help you smash him," he said, a wide grin spreading across his face. The Earth Fae looked overjoyed by the idea of finally getting to challenge the prick. "Together, we'd be a match for him."

I'd been tolerating the ass until now, but if the Spirit King thought he could use Claire and throw her away, I would take Sol up on his offer.

Assuming Claire didn't murder him first.

Chapter Eighteen
Claire

Fire licked across my knuckles, my ire at Cyrus growing with every step. He had barely said a word since we left the palace, only telling me to keep my head high.

Prick.

He bonded with me without permission.

And now he wanted to act like it hadn't happened?

Well, fuck him.

Titus once told me this stage lasted a month. I'd have to ask him if there was a way to reject the link sooner. Maybe it would hurt. Oh, I hoped it would. Cyrus, specifically. Because the bastard—

"You can only sever a connection early when both parties are willing," Cyrus murmured. "Just as, coincidentally, you can only create one between willing partners." He glanced over his shoulder at me as he led me down a gravel path toward the darkness beyond. "So what angers you more, little queen? That I bonded with you without asking? Or that you accepted the bond?"

I glared at him. "Don't read my mind."

"Then stop telegraphing so loudly," he returned.

If I had a gun, I'd shoot him in that perfect ass of his. Maybe I could set fire to his pants instead. After we found Exos.

Which reminded me… "How do you think your brother is going to feel about this?"

He shrugged. "I assume he'll be too relieved at being freed to care. Besides, you wouldn't be the first fae we've shared."

I stumbled over the flat ground, causing him to whirl around and catch me by the waist before I fell on my face. We stayed like that for a long moment, him holding me precariously in the air while I remembered how to breathe.

You wouldn't be the first fae we've shared.

Oh God.

Fuck.

I didn't like the picture that came into my thoughts with that comment. Mainly because it was one of me sandwiched between them. And no.

No. No. No. No.

My head was shaking with the thought, eliciting a deep chuckle from Cyrus. "You humans and your sensibilities. I've always found it amusing. Fae are far more passionate creatures, little queen. Why else do you think Exos approves of your mating with other males?" His lips feathered over my temple as he righted me beside him. "We'll talk more about that later. I need you focused."

Focused.

Yeah.

Like that was going to happen.

He'd just admitted to *sharing* women with Exos. Which… was fucking hot. And so, so, so wrong.

"Stop fretting," he whispered, his palm sliding to my lower back. "Do you see the dark patch up there?" He pointed with his opposite hand, highlighting a particularly ominous-looking hole in the landscape ahead. "That's the entrance to the death fields."

I swallowed. "Okay. What exactly is a death field?" He'd mentioned the taunts, but that really didn't tell me anything. I mean, how did a field *talk*?

"I believe you would call them cemeteries," he murmured, his touch a brand against my spine. "But these are Spirit Fae tombs. Tormented Spirit Fae."

"The plague," I whispered.

"Yes. It's where we buried the dead."

Hence, death fields, I translated. *Right.* "But their souls still live?"

"To an extent." He started walking again, the pressure along my lower back forcing me to move alongside him. "Most fae live several hundred years, but Spirit Fae are known to live longer. We embody life and death, after all. But most of the victims lying in that field died far too young, long before their spirits were ready to leave."

He continued in silence, his heartache a palpable presence in the link we'd forged. Deep inside, he felt responsible, like he'd let his people down. The guilt of it washed over me, the hardship of having to lead a dying breed and the helplessness that accompanied it. He and Exos were the last of their kind, the last Royal Fae, and if they didn't continue their legacy, his entire kingdom would die.

"It does something to a fae to have their bodies die before their souls are ready to move on," he added, his voice gruff. "And that's what the death fields have become. That's what Titus feared, what everyone fears. The words I said to you are just a taste of what you'll hear here, Claire. These spirits are desperate and deteriorated, and all they do is writhe in a sea of despair."

"Can nothing be done for them?" I asked, feeling the desolation creeping over me with every step closer to the vapid hole before us. Maybe it was all in my mind, maybe it was from the link with Cyrus, but I suspected it was more. I could almost hear their screams.

"We've tried." His palm flexed against my back, his demeanor shifting. "They were originally buried in family plots, but the darkness spread, infecting those nearby and driving what few remained insane. It's why we created this place, why we reburied them all here, as far away from Springfall as possible. But they've only grown harsher, more restless, and there are those who believe the sickness will spread once more."

I stopped midstep, glancing up at him. "Am I putting myself in danger by crossing that threshold? Can I become sick?"

"Yes." He didn't hesitate, the answer certain. "As can I. But if you ignore the taunts, realize they're just words and not reality, you'll be okay."

"I don't understand."

He fully faced me. "The sickness they carry is a darkness of spirit, one that corrupts and controls, but if you ignore them and the cruelty they spread, you won't fall victim to their plight."

"So it's not like a contagious disease," I clarified.

"Not like your human world, no. It's a corrosion of life." He glanced at the paling sky, his expression thoughtful. "Think of it like being told you're worthless your entire life and finally believing it. What happens?"

"You become depressed."

"Well, yes, but I mean beyond that. Surely you've heard of a self-fulfilling prophecy. Where if you believe something enough, you'll make it happen."

I nodded. "Yes."

"That's what these tormented essences do. They warp you into believing you're evil, despicable, a failure, until all you want to do is die. And then maybe you forget to eat. You forget how to *live*, thereby killing your body while your spirit remains."

"That's a horrible way to go," I whispered.

"It's a horrible thing to observe," he countered.

"But I thought the Spirit Fae all died in one day," I said, recalling the story Exos once told me. "That my mother and Mortus fought, and nearly ninety percent of the Spirit Fae died as a result?"

He tilted his chin once. "Yes. But it was as if they all lost the will to live at once, and just stopped. Their spirits rose, leaving their bodies to rot, and that's what we buried. Only, the souls eventually came back, but their hosts were no longer viable, leaving them in this constant state of turmoil."

"So could they ever be rejoined?" I asked, picturing hundreds of zombie bodies being repossessed by dead spirits. That sounded... bad.

Fortunately, Cyrus negated the idea with a swift shake. "No. There's nothing that can be done for them now. We just have to wait for their spirits to move on, except they seem unable to, as the circle of life has been so vastly disrupted. As I said, you're the youngest of our kind. No other females have been able to conceive since that day, and what's worse, it's spreading."

"To the Earth Fae."

"Indeed," he agreed, giving me a nudge to move forward again. "One trip to the death fields won't hurt you, Claire. You just have to remember to tune them all out, and don't believe anything you hear."

I took several steps before a thought struck me so hard in the chest I stumbled again. "You think Mortus has been keeping Exos here?" The words came out on a gasp, Cyrus's grip on my hip the only thing keeping me upright.

He gazed down at me with a tired expression, one that bespoke of his own fears—ones he'd clearly been hiding even from himself.

"You tried to find him last night," I realized out loud, reading the true exhaustion and knowledge in his gaze, felt it creeping along our bond as he fought futilely to hold it back. "You couldn't sense him above the chaos of the voices."

He didn't reply because he didn't have to. I sensed everything I needed to through our fresh link—the guilt, the exasperation, the utter notion of failure, and the most important one of all, regret.

"You don't want me to have to do this." It was right there at the forefront of his thoughts, the hatred at what he needed to do, but his loyalty to Exos outweighed his regard for me. And it was something I had to respect, to understand, and I did. "You're doing the right thing, Cyrus."

"Am I?" he asked, cupping my cheek. "Was binding us the right thing?"

It provided me with fresh insight into his decisions, helped me respect some of his choices even if I didn't agree with them. "I guess we'll find out," I said, placing my hand over his. "Take me into the death fields, Cyrus. I'll let you know what I sense."

He dipped his head to whisper his lips over mine. "Thank you, Claire."

A tenuous agreement formed between us, one founded in a like-minded goal—to find Exos.

As we walked, I wondered if this openness between our minds was normal, because I hadn't felt that way with Titus during our first stage. Same with Exos. But I could read Cyrus clear as day, and he'd made it obvious he could access me just as easily.

"It's not," he admitted, again hearing my thoughts, or perhaps openly assessing them. "But water is a fluid element; it's clear and concise and always consistent. It makes sense that our bond would resemble those qualities."

I could understand that—the purity and clarity of water thriving between us.

It was the complete opposite of the opaqueness at the end of this path, standing maybe ten feet away. I gulped at the sight of it, my heart hammering against my ribs.

Power lurked beyond that threshold.

Not the good kind, but the bad. I could feel the inky quality rubbing along my skin, giving me the sensation of wrongness and urging me to turn around.

Something isn't right here, I thought to myself. But still I kept moving, my need to see if I could even pick up a trace of Exos forcing me onward. Because if he resided in this field, it was a wonder he still breathed.

"He's strong," Cyrus whispered. "He always has been. But if he pushed you out, it was for a reason."

"And you suspect this is why."

"Yes."

"Where did you follow Mortus to?" I asked, needing to focus, to ground myself. Because already I could feel my soul being twisted as if invisible hands had entered my being to stroke me from within.

And we weren't even inside yet.

"I'll show you," Cyrus said, his touch falling away from my back, to my arm, and down to my palm, where he linked our fingers. "Don't let go of me, Claire."

"I won't." I squeezed his hand for emphasis and allowed him to lead me over the threshold. Moss instantly encased my feet, sliding over my shoes and up my socks. Yet when I looked down, I saw nothing but gravel.

Strange.

Cyrus continued moving, and I struggled alongside him, my ears clouding with a buzzing energy that hummed inside my mind.

Not words, no.

Just a constant sizzling that left me squinting into the foggy chasm. I blinked to clear it, but that didn't help. All I saw were writhing creatures, smoke and brimstone, and a darkness that threatened to swallow me whole.

I tried to ask Cyrus to explain but found myself alone, his hand no longer in mine.

Whirling around, I sought his presence, only to see miles and miles of clouds in all directions. The ground began to shake, my name a chant on the wind.

Cyrus...

I couldn't sense him.

Couldn't breathe.

What's happening?

The moss was climbing again, still invisible, but there. It drove through the fibers of my clothes, seeping into my veins and painting my blood in shades of black.

I shook in time with the ground, my soul screaming at me to run. But I didn't know where to go. I couldn't remember where I'd entered, couldn't focus on anything other than the impending doom surrounding me.

Tears streaked down my face.

My heart raced.

The world blinked in and out.

And all I could do was fall, fall, fall... into nothingness. And everything. And bittersweet darkness.

My home.

CHAPTER NINETEEN
CYRUS

FUCK!

Now I knew what Mortus had been up to last night. He'd set a fucking trap. And not for me, but for Claire.

I wrapped my arms around her, tugging harshly against some unknown force. It seemed to be sucking the elements right out of her, as if starving for her life. And it was fucking killing her.

Her skin turned ashen, her breath stuttering between blue lips. It'd all happened so quickly, her body whirling around in a violent circle as her life drained before my eyes.

"Claire!" I shouted.

Nothing.

Not even an acknowledgment.

Just a limp, boneless body collapsing into mine.

I had to get her out of here. But that force had its claws so deep into her, preventing me from moving. So I did the only thing I could think to do. I misted.

Water overwhelmed my senses, transforming me into a breeze that allowed me to traverse kingdoms via magical means. Only, I'd never taken another being with me before.

Come on, I urged, thickening my energy and forcing it to overwhelm Claire. A hint of her water responded, as if a hand was forming from within her and reaching for me. I grasped it with my mind, locking our element together in a whirlpool of power.

My chest ached beneath the force of it, a connection forming that surpassed time and space, but it was the only way to free her from that violent hold.

I felt it now. The inky abyss sucking her into a black hole of malevolence, stripping her of her gifts, and cascading her to the darkest depths of the ocean floor.

Not on my watch, asshole! I shoved the shadow back with a tidal wave so strong that the being—trap—*thing*—unlatched, releasing Claire to my superior strength, causing me to stumble backward in mist form.

I didn't think; I acted.

My power wrapped around her in earnest, forcing her to disintegrate into water molecules that I could manipulate, and I took her with me to the only place I knew would help.

We collapsed in a bedchamber I never used.

In a kingdom I rarely visited.

The cascade of falls graced my vision, a fountain running in the corner with renewed vigor at my presence, as an unconscious Claire lay in my arms.

Crashing booms echoed outside the chambers, the guards sensing the presence of a powerful fae and rushing to defend their territory. The doors flew open, a Water Fae with broad shoulders and thick thighs plowed inside.

"Who are—" His mouth actually fell open at the sight of me on the floor with a nearly dead female clasped tightly to my chest. "My Prince." He dropped to his knee, head bowed. Most referred to me as their *king*. Here they called me *Prince* for my water birthright, one I'd rejected. But today I needed *his* help.

Everyone followed suit, their dismay clear.

But none of them possessed the presence or power I needed.

"My father," I rasped. "I need my father."

Chaos erupted around us. Shouts ensued. But all of my focus was on the too-cold woman in my arms.

Guilt pounded through my thoughts. I should have known Mortus wouldn't lead me to Exos so easily, that he knew I was following him last night.

Damn it to the Elements!

"Claire," I whispered, rocking her helplessly and feeling her life escape between my fingers. This wasn't supposed to happen. Exos trusted me to guard her, to *protect* her, and I'd led her to her own fucking slaughter.

And I still didn't know what caused it or how that shadowy thing had sucked the life from her. The death fields embodied so many nightmares, but nothing like that. It had reminded me of a vampire, something so starved for the elements that it'd hooked itself into Claire and drank freely of her power.

How?

What monstrosity had Mortus created? And why had it only attacked Claire?

"Son?" My father's voice held a note of concern, his confusion written into the lines of his face. His formal attire suggested I'd interrupted something important, but the way he came to his knees before me said he didn't care. "Is this…?"

"Claire," I breathed. "I took her to the death fields, looking for Exos, and something attacked her. It sucked the elements right out of her. I don't… I don't know what to do."

He placed his palm on her forehead and closed his eyes. "She's weak," he agreed.

An understatement. I could see the tendrils of her soul threatening to leave her body, the fear etched into her essence palpable. *Hang on, little queen,* I whispered. *I'm going to fix this.*

Somehow, some way, I would uphold that promise to her. I had to. Exos was counting on me. Claire, too.

"Your bond is strong," he marveled, tilting his head to the side. "Very strong for being so fresh."

"It was an accident," I admitted, ashamed now more than ever. She deserved so much better. "We briefly kissed and it formed."

His blue eyes—the same color as my own—focused on me, his brow crinkling. "You're in the third stage, son."

I blinked. *"What?* No. We just… It's new… I mean…" *What?* I checked the connection, mortification and horror swimming through my veins. "Oh, Elements…" He was right. When I grasped for her element to mist her here, we'd *bonded.* Irrevocably binding our souls, proclaiming unspoken vows of eternity.

It was deeper than her link to Exos.

He's going to kill me.

Fuck, Claire *is going to kill me.*

"You must finish it," my father urged. "It's the only way. I can feel the others she's reached out to, but there's no time to bring them here. She'll die."

"Finish it?" I repeated, my heart skipping a beat. "Finish the bond?" *Without her permission?*

"She needs your strength, Cyrus. Without the lifeline, she'll never recover. It might already be too late."

Sprites, this is bad. Very, very bad.

"You don't have time. Either you save her or you don't. But wallowing in your fate will cost the girl her life." There was the father I knew—direct and to the point without a hint of remorse. He might as well have said I dug my own grave by initiating this link to begin with.

Which, yeah, he'd be right.

"What if she rejects it?" I asked, noting the very real chance of that happening.

"Her elements rule her now, and there's no better water match in this world than the rightful Water King," he replied, a challenge in his tone, daring me to contradict him. For once, I didn't take the bait. This wasn't about my conflicting destiny or the fact that my power outweighed his and all other Water Fae. This was about saving Claire.

"Tell me what I need to do," I said, my choice already made.

I couldn't leave her to suffer, couldn't allow her to die because of my mistake.

Maybe I deserved a future of unrequited love.

At least Exos would be happy.

And Claire.

This was not the right recourse—bonding an unconscious female was the epitome of taboo—but what choice did I have? She needed a lifeline, and I was the only one available.

"Prepare the ceremonial chambers," my father demanded, causing fae to scatter. "This has to be done right and quickly."

I nodded, knowing what he meant. The best way to guarantee that Claire's element accepted mine was to make her feel at peace.

She was so cold and small in my arms, her skin a now bluish tint.

I hated seeing her this way, hated more that I'd caused this through my own urgency to finish this task. Mortus may have set the trap, but I knew better than to step into it.

I'm sorry, Exos, I thought, knowing full well he couldn't hear me.

He wasn't anywhere near those death fields. I felt it now through the bond with Claire that Exos remained somewhere safe and untainted. Had I taken two minutes to prod her a little deeper earlier, after our initial connection, I would have sensed that.

But instead I'd led her astray.

"Come," my father said, his palm a brand against my shoulder.

I cradled Claire against my chest and stood, following him without a word, knowing what this meant.

Not only would I be taking on an unwilling queen, but we were mating under the element of water. Which stirred an entirely different problem, one I would acknowledge later. Because if I thought about the ramifications now, I'd run. And Claire didn't deserve that.

Fuck, she didn't deserve any of this.

She was not the son of two powerful bloodlines. My future was never hers to bear.

Although, now she would have no choice.

And I hated myself all the more.

I'd wanted to push her to greatness, but not like this, not by forcing her to become the Water Fae Queen.

My father's mate—Coral—met us in the hallway, her black hair spun high on her head and clipped with pink shells. A beautiful woman, one admired by many. But the way she looked at me bespoke of our history, her trepidation of getting too close to the true heir of the Water Kingdom throne.

She was my mother's replacement after the plague took her life.

And I'd never given her a chance to be anyone else.

"Cyrus," she said, bowing her head in a manner of respect she bestowed on few others.

"Coral," I returned, the usual acid in my tone gone in favor of the female curled into my core.

She eyed Claire with interest, her lack of questions suggesting she'd already been informed of what was happening.

Time seemed to be escaping me by the minute, Claire's life hanging on by a thread I desperately held on to. I could feel the presence of the others, all lending their elements to her in a vain attempt to bolster her reserves. With every passing moment, I sensed the veracity of my father's claim.

Claire needed a fully bonded mate to provide her with the strength she required to survive.

And while she'd probably prefer it to be Titus, not even he could bring her back now.

She needed royal blood.

My blood.

A room adorned in plants and life opened before us, the altar situated at the foot of a giant waterfall. I'd only been here once—the day my father took his new bride in the mating-bond ceremony.

It was one of the worst days of my life, rivaling the funeral of my mother.

And I'd not set foot in these palace walls since.

That would change today, my obligation to the Water Kingdom bearing down on me with the weight of a thousand waves.

I laid Claire on the podium, brushed the blonde hair from her face, and bent to press my forehead to her icy one.

"Hang on, little queen." There were preparations required, the need for a fae priestess to initiate the ceremony. All I could do now was pray we weren't too late.

Because my father was right. I could feel it now, the need to finish this, to give her what she required. But it was on Claire to accept it. To accept *me*.

And after our tenuous relationship, I wouldn't be surprised if she told me to mist off.

In which case, Elements help us all…

CHAPTER TWENTY
SOL

WHAT THE HELL WAS THAT? I thought, bleary-eyed and dazed.

I slept like a rock—literally—but the explosion that flashed behind my eyelids had me shooting straight up in a cold sweat.

Heat raked across my skin, making my element react and crust over a protective layer of earth.

Where is it coming from?

I rushed to the source, my entire room bathed in a glow of red, and found an inferno shooting into the sky in front of the Spirit Quad.

Titus.

I knew the Fire Fae was powerful, but he roared with terrifying fury with arms outstretched and muscles taut as his element left him all at once, seeking and devouring everything in its wake.

Something pinched inside my chest, and I grabbed at it as if a needle had just pricked me. Then it struck again, this time harder, and cracks spread out at my feet in protest.

"Sol!" Vox came billowing from the house in a rush of wind that caught the inferno and sent tiny tornados swirling across the destroyed landscape. "What's happening?" His wild black eyes with that distinct ring of silver grew wide as he took in the scene. "Sol, you have to stop Titus from whatever he's doing. He's going to die if he keeps that up!"

This had to be the same force that took Exos, that wanted Claire dead, and now it was after us.

"I'll get to him," I promised and set my feet apart. I'd never done this before, but now was not the time to fear what I was capable of. I opened the gate that I kept tightly locked on my talent. No hesitation. No fear at what I might destroy. If I didn't stop Titus, his flames would consume him and then melt us all.

My power rushed out of me and made the world tremble, but Titus wouldn't be deterred. His inferno lifted him up and made him throw his head back, and he pushed even harder on a scream, his skin turning white-hot and his eyes ablaze when they flung open to take note of me.

"Claire!" he roared, the name a plea.

My gut twisted that something might have happened to her, but I couldn't help Claire right now. Titus was the one about to rip himself in half, and I had to get him under control.

Control, the one thing I feared losing, slipped over me like a breeze, and I glanced back to see Vox with his arms spread and his hair flung out around him like an ancient god of the fae. Few knew his true power, but I did. It was why he'd been assigned to me and also why I trusted him.

He wasn't afraid to contain the earth.

The wind listened to him, swirling the fires aside and giving me the energy I needed to keep my own unruly power in check.

Bless you, Vox.

My skin took on an impenetrable armor, and the heat lessened to a manageable level. I stormed up to Titus and grabbed him by the neck. "You need to stop!"

"Claire!" Titus repeated, the name a vow.

Then I felt it.

I felt *her*.

That ache inside my chest grew and became a clawing need. It was coming from Claire.

My eyes went wide. *She's dying.*

"Impossible," I breathed. Claire and I hadn't made a connection, hadn't bonded even on the lowest level, but she was inside my soul, reaching out to me, begging me for my element.

No wonder Titus was losing his shit.

I turned to see Vox concentrating on keeping the inferno in check, as well as stabilizing my energy, but Claire could do that for me.

If I just gave in, we could help each other.

The fires loomed, building walls that crept closer to the edges of the quad and threatened to reach the trees bordering Earth Quad. These weren't normal flames. They would consume everything in their path, and nothing would stop them. Titus had lost control, being the only bonded mate that Claire could reach out to, and she'd taken too much.

It was as if something had sucked the very life out of her, forcing her to latch onto those closest to her, to help her reinforce her elements.

Without the added strength, she'd die. I could feel it in my very soul. There was no choice here. Either I let her in or I allowed her to perish.

And damn it, I couldn't let that happen.

"Vox!" I yelled, sending my voice booming across the distance between us. "It's Claire! Let her in!"

He flinched and his winds twisted. "Are you insane? I can't let you go; you'll be even worse off than Titus!"

I knew Vox's fears. If my control slipped, even for a second, I could split the world in two.

Titus grabbed my shoulder and squeezed, his hot fingers a brand even against my armor. His eyes glowed with rage and fury and desperation. "Give her what she needs," he begged. "She's dying. I can't give her enough." He sounded so broken. So alone. So anguished.

And it was all the encouragement I needed. I closed my eyes and felt her spirit slip inside as if it had always meant to be there. The sweet flush of peaches filled my senses, and her earth warmed over me like an embrace. I fell to my knees, relieved when Vox's steadfast control retreated as he followed suit.

The world trembled, burned, and my ears suffered the howl of a thousand hurricanes.

But Claire would live, if only for just a few moments longer.

It would have to be long enough.

Because I felt it now, the water energy joining the others.

You better save her, Cyrus, I thought. *Or there will be hell to pay when you return.*

CHAPTER TWENTY-ONE
CYRUS

CLAIRE WAS NO LONGER BREATHING, her body limp on the altar. Warm water flowed around her, most of it controlled by my magic, as I fought to keep her alive long enough to complete the ceremony.

It wasn't supposed to be like this.

She should be awake and willing, not knocking at death's door. Fuck, my betrothed should at the very least *like* me, but we were nowhere near that level of comfort. I was just a means to an end for her. A nuisance she wanted to get rid of at her earliest opportunity.

And I couldn't blame her for that.

Yet I wouldn't change a thing.

Other than not taking her into the death fields.

But her training? The way she'd strengthened under my harsh treatment? That was my doing by being the enforcer she needed. The others were too soft on her, drowning the fighter inside. I provoked her to the forefront, and I hoped like hell that little warrior met me now.

"We must begin," my father said as the priestess arrived.

"This is unprecedented," the petite fae replied, taking in the scene before her. "We value consent as one of the highest principles."

"With life right above it," I told the tiny, white-haired woman. "If it's not meant to be, her element will reject mine. Now stop delaying."

I stroked my thumb across Claire's frozen cheek, willing the hot springs around her to heat her blue skin. It didn't work. Because that wasn't what she needed.

Her elements were drowning, seeping from her body to the netherworld. She needed an anchor.

I would be that anchor if she accepted the bond.

The priestess took her position before us, her frail hand lifting to hover over Claire's heart. A chant began, one hummed in the old language. I closed my eyes, allowing the whispers to infiltrate my being, taking me to a place in the fae heavens where energy pulsed bright and consuming.

Claire, I breathed, searching for her spirit, willing her to come forth, to join me in the plane and allow me to give her what she required to survive. *Come to me, little queen.*

I clasped her hand in the ceremonial room, squeezing tight, while my soul roamed the fields in pursuit of her. She wasn't gone yet. I could feel her life hanging in limbo, her fae half striving to hold on just a little longer as if it knew what I would offer.

And there.

Sitting by the spring, her eyes a gorgeous blue, I found her.

She played her fingers across the water, watching it form on her fingertips before floating up to the beaming sun. *It's beautiful,* she marveled, oblivious to the chaos looming over her prone form.

You're beautiful, I admitted, swallowing. *Do you know why you're here?*

She shook her head, sending those alluring golden curls in waves down her exposed back. This flowy dress she wore was unlike any I'd seen her in, but I wanted to buy her hundreds just to see it again. Because she was stunning. Strong. Luminescent.

I like it here, she whispered as if the words were a secret only for me. And maybe they were.

It's one of our most sacred places, Claire. Not even I have ever set foot here.

Why now? she wondered, her voice holding a musical quality I longed to hear from her icy lips.

The priestess guided us here for our vows.

Mmm. She looked around, her expression one of awe and expectation. The water element in her was taking over and driving her instincts, knowing the reason for all of this even while the human inside had no idea.

I need you to repeat the vows, I told her, hearing them from the priestess now. *Can you do that for me?*

She murmured her approval, her bright blue eyes smiling up at me. The utter devotion in that gaze nearly undid me. I had to remember it was her element staring at me like that, not Claire. Because she never gazed at me in that manner. And likely never would.

291

"I, Claire…," the priestess started.

And I began translating each word for my betrothed, needing her to hear them from my lips, not from those of a stranger.

I, Claire, accept the power that binds me to Cyrus, born of Spirit and Water. To cherish and respect, through all of the eras and time that may fall before us, until our souls do us part. I give unto him my fluidity, my grace, my tranquility, and accept his in return. My element is now his just as his is now mine, to the fae heavens may we never part. And I shall never forsake him for another, my water forever belonging to him and to him alone.

She repeated each word, the pledge engraving her name into a piece of my heart that I would never get back. Tears filled my eyes by the end, the very real ramifications finally settling over me as my own oath began.

I, Cyrus, former King of Spirit and heir to the Water Kingdom, accept the power that binds me to Claire, future Queen of the Water Kingdom. To cherish and respect, through all of the eras and time that may fall before us, until our souls do us part. I give unto her my favor, my serenity, my purity, and accept hers in return. My element is now hers just as hers is now mine, to the fae heavens may we never part. And I shall never forsake her for another, my water forever belonging to her and to her alone.

A binding energy flourished around us, swimming through our veins, flooding my thoughts and my heart, and forever tying me to a woman who never wanted me. And to a kingdom I never desired.

But I wasn't given time to consider the future, the spring around Claire bubbling over into a wave of molten lava that threatened us both. I grabbed her and misted back to my quarters, the ceremony complete, and held her against me as her energy consumed mine.

Take what you need, I encouraged her, feeling her lethal yearning.

My heart raced as our elements locked, her water greedily absorbing mine as I cocooned us in a sea of warmth and allowed the waterfall in my chambers to soothe her ears and lull us both into a comatose state.

I'd done my part.

Now it was on Claire to survive.

But a warrior lurked within her, one my presence seemed to provoke best. And that warrior was now raging in my head, seeking out every reserve and drinking me dry.

I succumbed to the darkness, my last thoughts for Claire. *You'll have to do better than that, little queen. Take everything. Take more. And don't stop until you can breathe.*

CHAPTER TWENTY-TWO
EXOS

MAGIC STIRRED AROUND ME, a desperate pull at my senses, and yanked me from my hole with a fierceness few others could possess.

Claire.

She was all around me, her spirit weeping with words I couldn't understand. I flew upright, the barren cell around me unfamiliar and cold. *Where am I?*

Another wave of need hit me hard in the chest, sending me to the floor on a groan. It felt as if my heart were splitting in two.

No. My spirit.

My eyes flew open. Something had happened to Claire. Her death slithered around me, her need for my energy clawing at my insides and begging me to save her.

Only, another was there instead of me.

Water.

The hot spring scented the air, a new bond falling into place.

Cyrus.

I would recognize that power anywhere. He'd taken his rightful place in the Water Kingdom. And it seemed Claire was his chosen queen.

Fuck.

My throat refused to work. My body stiff from disuse.

What's happening?

I felt it then, the fraying link to Claire, unraveling from being without one another too long. A tear fell from my eye, a foreign concept, one I'd never experienced, not even at my parents' funeral.

But for Claire...

I collapsed in anguish, my spirit withering at the erosion between us. *Claire*... I needed to find her, to rekindle our bond.

I'd waited too long to escape. Hid from that dark essence for far more time than I'd anticipated.

Where is it? I wondered, searching the shadowy recesses of my cell, noting the low lighting in the dingy corridor. No one spoke. Nothing moved. *I'm alone down here.*

I stood, my legs protesting beneath me, and shook the iron bars. They didn't move. *But I'm awake*, I realized. *That gives me an advantage.*

All I had to do was wait. Someone would come by soon, and I'd manipulate that person into releasing me.

Don't forget me, Claire, I whispered. *I'm coming for you.* Because I had to warn her. I just couldn't remember about who or what. But someone, *something*, was down here with me. *Who?*

I shook my head, dazed from several weeks—over a month—of shutting everything down.

Why had I done that? Better yet, why can't I remember anything of import?

I swallowed, my throat parched from disuse. I just had to escape, then everything would be fine. It had to be.

Another ache settled over me, Claire's essence drawing on mine, and I allowed it. Whatever had happened, she needed it more, and I had enough left to fight.

Whoever put me down here was going to die. Horribly.

And I couldn't fucking wait.

CHAPTER TWENTY-THREE
CLAIRE

Several Days Later…

EXOS STROKED MY CHEEK, his breath warm against my neck. I snuggled closer, adoring his strength and the crisp scent of water clinging to his skin. *Mmm, that's new.* He usually smelled of sunshine and man, but today he held a cleaner scent, reminding me of the rain forest.

"How are you feeling?" he asked, his voice huskier than usual.

I smiled. "Refreshed." Oh, how my throat burned.

A straw slid between my lips as if he knew. "Drink, little queen."

My brow furrowed even as I complied. *That's a new nickname.* Exos usually called me *princess*, sometimes *baby* when he was turned on. My thighs clenched at the prospect, missing his touch and the way our element danced when together.

I drew my finger down his bare abdomen, creating a stream of water along his skin. I'd meant to use fire, but this worked, too.

Exos groaned as I pushed him back, my tongue already traveling downward to lick up the mess I'd made.

"Claire…," he cautioned.

"Shh." I needed this. Needed *him.* My body ached with weakness, my heart not fully whole.

I don't want to think, I decided, indulging in the motions instead of my thoughts. I could analyze my body later. For now, I wanted to mate. To complete the bond we'd started. To consummate our link.

Some part of me questioned that logic.

A hint of the Claire of old.

But the Claire of new pushed worry and concern out the window, the fae inside me flourishing to the forefront.

"*I need,*" I said, not necessarily understanding what I required, just that I did.

"Open your eyes," he demanded, that voice harsher than Exos's usual tone. He pushed me to my back, his lower body settling between mine and causing me to arch up into him.

Something was different.

A fluidity in our movements I'd never felt before.

Oh, I *liked* it.

"More," I begged.

"Look at me first." He trapped my hips as I tried to move upward, his hands on my face, a trace of cool water sliding across my lips that I licked off on a moan.

My eyelids fluttered, a dull light illuminating the male above me. So cruelly handsome with aristocratic lines etched into his stern jaw and perfect nose.

But the eyes were all wrong.

Not Exos.

"Cyrus," I breathed, confused, but not alarmed. A sense of safety fell over me, his essence so well known and welcomed that I could never push him away. I cupped his cheek and tilted my chin enough to brush my mouth against his. "Kiss me." Two words I never thought I'd say in his company, but they fell from my lips like a prayer.

It wasn't Exos I needed, but Cyrus. I felt incomplete without him, a puzzle piece missing from where we were joined.

"Oh, Claire," he whispered, his forehead falling to mine. "You don't understand yet."

"Make me understand. Show me." I drew my nails down his bare back, adoring the way his muscles flexed beneath my touch. "Please, Cyrus."

"You're killing me." He swallowed, his arousal thickening between my thighs. "The urge to… It's wrong, little queen. So fucking wrong."

"Then make it right." I kissed him again, this time with more force, and licked his bottom lip. "I need you."

I couldn't explain why.

Didn't understand how I'd ended up in bed beneath him.

But fuck my mind. My body ruled me now. And water.

I wrapped him in a sheet of my power and smiled as he caressed me in kind. So much peace in that seductive touch. It elicited a sigh so deep that I swore I left the world for a moment before I returned.

"Cyrus," I breathed, arching into him once more. "*Please.*"

His growl vibrated my chest, causing my nipples to bead against him beneath the shift I wore. I wiggled, wanting it off, yearning to *feel.*

And then his mouth took mine in a kiss unlike any other. It subdued me in a way that left me whirling beneath him. His tongue became my new addiction, my only way to breathe, as he took me underwater and caressed me with his very soul.

"I'm going to hell," he whispered.

"Only if I can go with you," I replied, wrapping my arms around his neck as he ripped the gown from my body. His clothes soon joined the torn garments on the floor, allowing me my first glimpse at the beauty that was Cyrus.

All seamless lines of perfection, a swimmer's body encased in a power I longed to stroke.

I went to my knees with him, both of us naked and admiring and petting and memorizing. His fingers wove into my hair, his lips capturing mine once more, as his opposite hand dipped between my legs. "So fucking wet," he praised.

I gripped his shaft, marveling at the size and girth, and smiled. "So damn hard."

He chuckled, his teeth running over my bottom lip before he sucked it deep into his mouth. "I'm sorry, Claire."

"Why?" I asked.

"I just am," he murmured, his mouth taking mine again and silencing my reply.

He released my hair to grasp my hips, yanking me forward and returning me to my back. His tongue slid across my cheek, to my ear, and down my neck to my breasts. I wove my fingers through his hair, reveling in the sensations his mouth unleashed on my stiff peaks. He used his teeth, causing me to writhe, while his hand disappeared between my legs again.

Gentle wasn't in Cyrus's nature.

And yet, every touch was smooth and thorough, reminding me of waves caressing my skin.

A sense of rightness overwhelmed me, causing my water element to dance to the surface and play with his. Raindrops prickled our skin, vacillating between hot and cold, each one eliciting a new sensation between my legs.

"Cyrus…" Each pelt against my being churned the ache inside me, creating a whirlpool I couldn't control. It kept building and building, overtaking me and consuming my every breath. "*More.*"

He kissed his way up my body, each brush of his mouth stirring a moan from my throat, until I swore I would scream.

"I can't say no to you," he said against my ear, his arousal aligning with mine. "I'll give you what you need, Claire."

"Yes," I hissed, bowing off the bed as he slid inside me.

So slick.

So wet.

So perfectly *us*.

I wrapped my arms around him, holding him possessively and swearing to never let him go. His head fell to my neck, his harsh curse fueling my desire. My legs wound around his waist, my body pumping in time with his, as he edged us closer to the waterfall of oblivion.

Threading my fingers in his hair, I forced his mouth back to mine, kissing him as if I required him more than oxygen. And maybe I did. Because I swore we were swimming underwater.

All I could hear were our hearts beating in tandem with one another.

The slide of his body over mine.

And the consuming warmth building between my thighs.

His name fell from my lips, only to be caught by his. One of his hands fell to my hips, urging me to keep up with his quickening pace, while the other cupped my cheek.

Icy blue eyes met mine.

Pain blending with pleasure.

And that look alone sent me cascading over the falls into the blissful waters below. He followed on a bellow, my name a hum within his mind, as something powerful snapped into place.

Contentment settled over me.

Complete, my heart whispered. *We're now complete.*

You own me, Claire, I heard him say in my mind. *Until the end of time.*

I yawned, too exhausted to reply, and kissed him softly instead. His tongue played over mine in lazy strokes, our bodies still joined below. The rightness of it all lulled me into a slumber, a smile permanently etched into my lips.

Peace.

I finally knew peace.

* * *

I woke two more times to the same treatment. Cyrus's body a healing solvent I didn't know I needed. Each session I felt stronger, invigorated, and pleased.

But I sensed unrest deep within. My other elements dissatisfied by my prolonged slumber.

Soon I would emerge from this watery cocoon.

Someone needed me.

I only wished I knew who.

Rest, I heard someone say. *You'll find me when you're ready.*

Mmm, I loved that voice. *Okay.*

I'll be waiting...

Okay, I repeated, snuggling into the hot male at my side. *I miss you.*

I miss you, too, princess.

"We'll go back to them soon," a deep voice murmured, lips close to my ear. "Maybe even tomorrow. Sleep and we'll evaluate your strength then."

"Mmm, 'kay." I nuzzled his skin, adoring the fresh scent and allowing it to overwhelm my senses. "I trust you."

And I did.

Because he was mine.

And I trusted what was mine.

"We'll see" was his reply. "Sleep, little queen."

I yawned, nodding. Who was I to argue with a king?

Chapter Twenty-Four
Cyrus

MY FATHER JOINED ME ON THE BALCONY of my rooms, his light hair tied back at the nape. Most Water Fae preferred to wear their hair long, enjoying the way it flowed like water over their shoulders. I preferred to keep mine shorter, as was customary of my spirit side. That might have to change in the years to come.

Another concession, I thought. *All for a female I never desired to love.*

Yet glancing over my shoulder now to see her blonde curls against my navy pillows had me thinking otherwise. Claire was special. Very, very special.

"How is she?" my father asked, following my gaze.

Well fucked, I mused, eyeing her swollen lips and resting form. The silky sheets hid her body from view, but I knew the rest of her was just as well sated as her mouth. "She's recovering," I said out loud instead. "Slowly, but steadily."

He nodded. "Her healing will improve and strengthen even more once she's near her other elements."

I agreed. "Yes. I'm thinking of moving her tomorrow." While she still slept most of the day, her moments of lucidity were powerful. And, well, demanding. Every time she opened her eyes, she reached for me and wouldn't focus on anything else—like eating—until I fucked her senseless. "I had no idea the mating bond could be so… stimulating." Not that I was complaining. I rather benefited from Claire's neediness.

"Your bond is making up for what should have been months of courtship," he murmured. "I'm not surprised it's asserting certain requirements on you both." His expression lacked the amusement in his tone, his gaze taking on a faraway gleam as he rested his elbows on the balcony railing. "I'll save you the lecture, son. We both know what this means."

I appreciated him not wasting my time with words. My mind was littered with enough of them already. "I can't ascend until I've found Exos." Because I couldn't rule two kingdoms.

He remained quiet for a long moment, the breeze from the seas below ruffling the collar of his suit and blowing the fabric of my loose pants. It felt nice being surrounded by life and energy. Yet my duty to the Spirit Kingdom hung over my head, weighing me down. I couldn't just turn my back on them. Even after I accepted my rightful place here, I'd advocate for the kingdom I considered my true home.

"I wish you would have come to me," he finally said. "About Exos, I mean."

"You know why I didn't."

"Yes. But you know I can keep a secret from the Council, Cyrus." He glanced sideways at me. "I think this week proves it, don't you?"

I swallowed, bowing my head in agreement. "Yes." While the news of my mating with Claire had spread on a tidal wave throughout the kingdom, the circumstances that required it were never mentioned. And my father had even gone as far as to tell Elana that we were on a honeymoon of sorts, which was why Claire needed to miss her internship and some school.

I supposed it wasn't entirely a lie. We'd spent all week in bed together, after all.

But my father had done what he could to protect us both, and I appreciated his loyalty. Even more so because he didn't tell anyone about Exos's disappearance.

"Do you still believe him to be in the death fields?" he inquired.

I shook my head. "No. He's awake now." I'd felt him through Claire, a thriving presence pacing in a cage, waiting. It took serious effort not to request she communicate with him, or allow me to penetrate her spirit to find him, but her rest came first. Both to me and to Exos.

And my brother would kill me if I broke that unspoken pact.

Never in my life could I have imagined putting another before my kin, but Claire changed everything.

She's my mate.

I vowed to protect her, to cherish her, to comfort her in times of sickness, and most importantly, I promised to put her needs above my own.

"When she's in a better mental state, I'll ask her to reach out to my brother," I said, having decided this days ago. "What's important is that he's alive. He'll be able to assume his duties as the Spirit King once we've found him, and then I'll face the consequences of my mating."

"Consequences," my father repeated, snorting. "Still so reluctant to accept your true place."

"The Spirit Fae need me more than the Water Fae." It was an old argument, but still relevant. "You're not even two hundred years old. They're fine beneath your rule."

"But there will always be contention until the most powerful rises to the top, son. That's what you fail to understand. You worry about your spirit half while neglecting your fae here, and while many may understand the choice, fae will always respond to power. And you possess the strongest water element of any in the history of our kind." He glanced again at the beauty in my bed. "With Claire being a close second."

Those were the right words to say. I liked that he acknowledged her gift. Even ungroomed she surpassed the royals in this palace. "She's amazing, isn't she?"

"I had my doubts," he admitted. "But I can feel her potential now. If you're not careful, she'll surpass even you."

"And wouldn't that be a wonder for the Fae World to see?" I mused, intrigued by the prospect while also knowing it to be impossible. Oh, Claire possessed superior abilities to most. However, her connection to water didn't quite rival mine. Even with training, I'd still remain the king of this kingdom.

Oh, but Claire would become queen to several kingdoms. And *that* was what made her more powerful than even I was.

"When do you leave?" he asked, again staring at the incoming waves crashing into the black sand beach below.

"Tomorrow," I decided out loud. "Being around Sol, Vox, and Titus should improve her health enough for her to hear Exos clearly." It would also lessen some of the tension I felt building in the bonds, her other mates longing for their Claire. She still didn't yet understand that she'd bonded with Sol and Vox in her desperation for survival, her elements reaching out to those she trusted most and latching onto their reserves to bolster her own.

When she awoke, she'd be controlled by her fae half.

I truly hoped the human beneath could accept it.

I knew enough about her former land to understand how hard it would be for her to embrace. But her elements would give her no choice. She needed a mate for each element, and she officially had them.

A circle of nature.

One I never thought to be a part of, but I had no choice now. As a fully bonded partner, I would remain no matter what the recourse.

And my heart would always be faithful to her, even if we'd never exchanged the emotional platitude of words. This was how our kind functioned. And as long as she welcomed it with an open mind, our unit would function seamlessly.

"We'll talk after you find your brother," my father said, clapping me on the shoulder. "I'll handle the politics here in the interim."

"Thank you." I looked at him then, needing him to see the full extent of my gratitude. "I mean that. Thank you for everything."

"You're my son," he replied, his lips curling faintly at the edges. "Thank you for trusting me with this."

I tilted my chin, acknowledging his concession.

Our relationship was tenuous at best. But we were about to get a whole lot closer.

Oh, Claire, I thought, turning back to the bedroom and her stirring form. *You have no idea how complicated this is about to become.*

Her beautiful blue eyes blinked open, the sleepy quality inside stealing my breath for just a moment.

And then she reached for me, that sultry purr in her throat telling me exactly what she desired.

My father excused himself silently as I lowered myself over my bride and captured her mouth in the kiss I knew she craved.

One more night alone.

Then I'd share her once more.

But for tonight, she was mine.

My Claire.

CHAPTER TWENTY-FIVE
VOX

A WEEK.

A *fucking* week and we still hadn't heard anything.

My fingers went to my chest, the ache still there, reminding me that I hadn't imagined the horrible night where Titus had gone supernova in front of the Spirit Quad and Sol had very nearly lost control of his power.

The night Claire had taken over.

Her presence a breath inside me, begging me to help her, to let her in. And I—

"Vox!" Professor Helios snapped, making me flinch. His bushy brows furrowed with impatience. My reputation as his best student had taken a hit over the last month. I'd been too damn distracted.

She's ruining me. In the best way. And the worst.

My half-hearted attempt at today's exercise resembled exactly how I felt. A weakened air pixie floundered on my desk, sending dust motes drifting around her head as she feebly squeaked up at me in protest. She shuddered, wilted, and then disintegrated into ash.

"I didn't say you could dismiss your project," the professor deadpanned, but I recognized the note of concern in the way the air flitted around him.

The other students whispered, their magic sending words flying all over the classroom in wisps I shouldn't have been able to hear, but everything had changed since that night with Claire. Aside from the obvious—our forced bond. But in addition to that, my powers seemed to be going haywire. Claire had weakened me by absorbing so much of my element, and it left my magic clawing at me with a lack of control I wasn't used to experiencing.

Is this how Sol feels all the time?

"*Vox.* What in the motes has gotten—"

A knock at the door interrupted the professor's reprimand, and I was relieved until I spotted Elana's bright eyes and friendly smile.

Shit.

"May I speak to Vox for a moment?" she asked.

The stunned professor bowed. "Of course, Chancellor."

The whispers started up again, and I tried to ignore them, but my magic wouldn't allow me a moment's peace. It was as if the elements wanted me to be on full alert until Claire returned and finished what she'd done to me.

"Do you think it's about the Halfling?"

"Didn't you hear? She's the Water Queen."

"Oh, I know. It's insane. Cyrus and Exos?"

"Well, Vox mentors her, too. And I swear I sense her on him."

"Does anyone know what that explosion last week was about?"

"I heard…"

I rolled my shoulders, shrugging off the murmured rumors, and met Elana outside.

She shut the door with a soft *click* before turning to me and giving me that too-friendly smile again.

"Vox," she greeted, her gaze sweeping over me and no doubt taking note of the dark circles under my eyes, my loose hair, and the way air seemed to distort around me with my uncustomary lack of control. She took a step closer, invading my air currents in a way that made me stiffen. "I've mitigated most of the rumors about last week's incident, but you're going to have to tell me what's going on. It's getting worse and, forgive me, but you all look like rocks uprooted after a storm."

Everyone had seen Titus shooting fire into the sky, the tornados I'd conjured to contain him, and Sol's quakes that had shaken the entire Academy. There was no way we could hide what had happened—but we couldn't explain it. Not without consulting Cyrus and Claire first.

"When the Spirit King returns, we'll give you an update," I assured her for the millionth time.

Her head tilted. "You're tired, Vox. Is Claire all right? Is there anything I can do?"

Elana's eyes were kind, but I sensed her frustration. It rivaled my own. Claire wasn't here at the Academy, where we could keep her safe. And the only news we'd received were rumors on the whispering winds that she'd…

I couldn't even repeat the offense in my mind.

Water Queen, my conscious said anyway.

A sharp pain jolted through my skull, and I pressed my thumb to my temple.

Elana moved closer, motioning to rest a hand on my arm, but my air shoved her away. She flinched, a hurt expression crossing over her eyes.

"Sorry," I breathed and let out a long breath. "I think I should just go back to the Spirit Quad and rest."

She considered me for a moment as she absently tested my air currents with her own magic, tiny dew droplets riding the breeze and glimmering around us like crystals. The effect seemed unconscious on her part, just an extension of her ever-growing power. Which perplexed me because I didn't know she had an affinity for water. It was well known that Elana only had access to spirit, unlike the other of her kind, who all maintained two elements.

"If I don't see improvement in the next few days, I will need to intervene," she warned. "Whatever it is you all are going through, you do not have to do it alone."

Wrong. This had nothing to do with her. This was between Claire and her guardians.

However, I nodded to appease her. "We'll get it under control," I promised, uncertain of how we would accomplish it, but knowing we needed to.

The tension in my chest stung again and I rubbed at it. Whatever Cyrus was doing to Claire was strengthening her, and I hoped that meant she'd return soon.

Because when she did, she had some damn explaining to do.

* * *

If I'd hoped to get some reprieve by returning to the Spirit Quad, I was in for a disappointment.

Without Claire, the place seemed to fit its reputation. The Spirit Quad had lost what little bit of life she'd sprung back into it, the ground outside a desolate wasteland of cracked, burnt soil and overturned stones.

My affinity for air cleared my path, flinging away debris as I approached the front door and made my way inside. I found Titus brooding over a cooling plate of leftovers.

I winced. Admittedly, my cooking had taken a hit ever since that night. I just didn't have it in me. "Not hungry?" I asked him, leaning against a darkened stump that had once been a dining table.

Titus didn't look up. Instead, he glowered at the tepid soup. "It's too cold." Meaning he couldn't heat it up.

I sighed and rubbed at my chest again. "My powers are on the fritz, too.

Whatever Claire did to us—"

Titus was in my face, eyes wild with awakened embers, before I had a chance to even think about finishing that sentence. "This isn't Claire's fault," he snapped.

Normally, I'd find the Fire Fae intimidating, but I didn't have the patience for his short temper today. I sent a gust of wind reeling and aimed at his chest.

He grunted as the force knocked him back. My powers didn't seem to work unless I was emotionally invested, like right now with Titus in my face, which wasn't like me at all. I wouldn't admit how much that lack of control unsettled me.

"Where's Sol?" I asked. "Perhaps he's better company right now."

Titus ground his teeth before replying. "Out back. But if you think he's better company than me, good fucking luck." Titus shoved past me, his embers burning my Academy robes as he went.

I doused the tiny flames with a snap of wind and thought about going after the Fire Fae, but a fight was what he wanted.

Actually, you know what? Fuck it. I want a fight, too.

My vision went white, and with it, a tornado burst into existence. Every display of weakness I'd had over the past few days transformed into what was really hiding under the surface. My royal lineage had been dormant, suppressed under years of careful control, but something had cracked, allowing it to escape.

Titus bellowed and didn't have time to stop the force from launching him into the air. He hit the wall—*hard*—and landed with a thud. He popped back onto his feet and grinned.

"A challenge? Who knew you had it in you?" His smile was feral. "Let's take it outside and burn off some steam. Or better yet, let's go *find* her."

The fae wasn't even fazed by my attack.

He just wanted a sparring partner. A way to let loose.

I dismissed the tornado with a flick of my wrist, sending siding and damaged wood crashing to the ground. Our kitchen was even more hopelessly ruined. Not that I cared.

Okay, maybe I did a little.

Damn it!

"We can't just go barreling into the Water Kingdom without permission. We are Academy students," I reminded him. "We don't have the clearance or the right to trespass." It was Elana's dream to unite the fae, the Academy being a grand gesture in that regard, but borders were tighter than ever since the plague hit.

Titus growled. "I'm so fucking tired of these excuses." Fire burst up his arms, then quelled, and then flamed again. "Claire is stuck there, and if Cyrus isn't going to tell us what the fuck is going on, he can't blame us for going after her. Can't you feel that she needs us?"

Yes, of course I could feel her.

That was the problem.

"I'm not going anywhere without Sol," I said, my air rumbling over the ground in tiny somersaults.

"I think you'll find him far more willing than you realize. Ask him." Red veins spidered down Titus's arms as if a volcano built inside of him and was just itching to get out. "Actually, you know what? Fuck that. If you and Sol aren't at the front door in five minutes, I'm leaving without you assholes."

Cursing under my breath, I snatched up the tepid soup—which had remained miraculously untouched—and marched toward the back of the quad. Even if it was pathetic food, it was still food. And I needed something to bargain with.

"Sol!" I bellowed.

I hadn't checked on the peach orchard since that night, but stopped, alarmed, when I saw the unexpected decay. What Sol had spent days putting his energy into, a thriving forest of life and sweet fruit, was now a graveyard. Wilted trees hung with rotten fruit, and a sour scent spiked the air.

I found Sol slumped against one of the larger trees that had a scar down its center and leaned precariously to the side with half of its roots upended. Sol didn't seem to notice and tossed pebbles across the dirt.

"Sol," I tried again, my voice softer as I approached him. "You all right, buddy?"

He glanced up at me, and he looked just as tired as I felt. "It's all ruined," he lamented. "When Claire gets back, she's going to be so disappointed. She didn't get to see what it looked like... before." He turned his attention back to the ground, and his shoulders sagged.

I set the bowl of soup next to him. "You sure you don't want to eat something?"

He wrinkled his nose at the bowl. "I'm good, thanks."

Sitting down, I sighed. "Well, we're a sorry pair, aren't we?"

Sol scoffed. "That's what happens when we find a beautiful mate and Cyrus keeps her all to himself."

My fist curled at the thought. I forced myself to loosen my fingers. "We didn't find a mate." I palmed the back of my neck, noting the knots there and wincing. "She didn't give us much of a choice."

Sol's eyes, the color of the earth with flecks of green, glanced at me, full of disdain. "Is that what you really think? She chose us, Vox."

"Actually, she didn't." The memories of the last few weeks had me jumping to my feet. I started pacing, my air working overtime to brush aside the countless stones Sol had scattered across the courtyard. The pungent smell of rotting fruit wasn't helping my mood, either. "Maybe she chose you, but she didn't choose me," I continued, needing him to understand. "Think about it, Sol. She asked you to the ball. I'm just a convenient Air Fae for her to suck dry. I'm a fucking mentor with benefits."

And I was not pleased about it.

"Don't talk about her like that," Sol warned as the ground trembled. "She was dying, Vox. And she would never force a mating bond. Claire isn't like that. She needs us just as much as we need her, and I know you can feel her inside of you." He rubbed a fist over his heart, in the same spot where my own chest ached with a need I couldn't understand. "Trust your soul for once, not your head."

I scoffed and opened my arms at the expanse of destruction around us. "You mean you're taking it so well?" I marched over to him and bent to stab a finger into his chest, which hurt when my knuckle popped, but I didn't care. "Look at this place, Sol. You're falling apart without her because *she* bonded to *you,* and she's not even fucking here!"

"Enough!" came a voice with enough power to make both Sol and me flinch.

Authority.

Demand.

I turned, only to have every air molecule inside of me wilt with both relief and fury.

Cyrus stood with an unconscious Claire in his arms, and all I wanted to do was punch him in the face.

CHAPTER TWENTY-SIX
CYRUS

WHAT A FUCKING MESS, I thought while laying Claire down in her bed. The silky blue robe she wore contrasted with the cotton surrounding her. I slid it from her shoulders, removing it entirely, and allowed her to nest into the familiarity of her own sheets.

She murmured something unintelligible, lost to her dreams, but I immediately felt her content at the energy strengthening around her. Returning her to the Academy had been the right call.

Even if I had three very angry fae at my back. They were oblivious to Claire's nakedness, mostly because I blocked their view of it.

Once the blankets covered her completely, I turned to face the fuming mob.

Titus seemed ready to push forward, to take over, but I shoved him back with a water punch to the chest. "Outside," I demanded, not wanting to disturb Claire. She needed more rest.

All three of the men appeared ready to argue, but one pointed glance over my shoulder at the sleeping beauty had the trio marching toward the exit.

"You have a lot of explaining to do," Titus snapped as soon as we exited the building.

"What the hell did you do to the kitchen?" I asked instead, having noted all the destruction along the way. At least Claire's bedroom appeared safe and clean.

"Are you fucking kidding me?" Titus was apparently ready to kill me. I couldn't blame him. It wasn't like I'd explained much yet. "What the hell happened to Claire?"

"That's an excellent question," I replied, folding my arms. "One I'm still trying to figure out myself. Some sort of entity latched onto her in the death fields and drained her elements." What perplexed me most was that it hadn't touched me at all, only Claire. "It nearly killed her."

"Clearly." Vox rubbed his chest, his brow furrowing. "She mated with all three of us."

"I know." I'd felt it. "She required the strength. Without it, she would have died."

"Which is why you mated with her as well?" Titus pressed, clearly sensing our intense connection.

I nodded. "You were too far away to help, and Exos, well, he's still missing. So I completed the ceremony and lent her my elements." It had left me drained, but functioning. Unlike these three. They all appeared to be swept away with the waves, their exhaustion palpable. "What the hell have you been doing all week?"

A laugh burst from Titus, one born not of amusement but of disbelief.

And Sol followed suit.

Same with Vox.

"Have you all lost your minds?" I demanded, alarmed.

"You're joking right?" Titus chuckled again, the sound broken and oddly maniacal.

"What the hell is wrong with you?" I demanded.

"Oh, fuck you," Vox said, uncharacteristically confrontational. I saw it then, the anger lingering in his gaze. Sol's eyes held a glimmer of it, too.

They all appeared desperate.

No... they were furious.

Titus lost his cool first, the fire bursting out of him and nearly hitting me square in my chest.

"Seriously?" I shouted, infuriated by the ridiculous attack. Even though I was weakened by Claire, he was no match for me. Except Vox joined him next with a howl of wind that swept my hair back and pushed me several feet into the dead courtyard.

A courtyard that was sinking quickly into a hole created by the Earth Fae.

"Okay," I said, calm despite the three-way attack. "I can see we have some aggression issues to work through." I shoved them all back with a wave that swept the three of them off their feet. "You want to play with me? Let's do this. But I expect your best, not this cockamamie bullshit attempt." I lifted my hand in a *come get me* gesture. "And when I win—which I will—I expect a little more respect while we discuss next steps."

None of them acknowledged me.

They just attacked.

Idiots.

But I supposed I deserved it. I hadn't exactly been forthcoming over the last week, what with being too busy saving Claire. And fucking her senseless.

Yeah, all right, I'd be mad, too.

So I allowed Titus to get one good fire punch in, the stroke of it singeing my cheek. I gave Vox his chance to slap me with a clap of wind. And I granted Sol one powerful shake beneath my feet.

Then I went to work, schooling the three of them simultaneously with a shock of water that temporarily doused their fight. It wasn't good enough to knock some sense into them, though, because they came at me with a renewed vigor, determined to drown me in their anguish and frustration.

And while I may have deserved some of it, I wasn't about to accept all of the blame.

"I saved Claire," I reminded them all. "Without me, she would have died."

"Without you, she wouldn't have been in danger to begin with," Titus tossed back over the roaring winds. "*You* are the reason she almost died!"

"And you left us here with no word," Vox added. "No idea of how she was doing, while expecting us to give her everything."

"What they said," Sol agreed.

Well, at least they were all working as a unit.

"*I* didn't almost kill her. Whatever trap Mortus left for us was the culprit." That was the argument I'd given myself for the last week. It almost satisfied me. Almost. "How is our fighting benefiting Claire?"

"I don't know, but I feel a hell of a lot better right now." Sol's words vibrated the earth, the giant finally allowing his powers out to play.

While I appreciated the show of force, I would have preferred it to not be directed at me.

"You feel better because Claire is back," I informed them, my words carried over the wake of another wave that sent them all to the ground. *Again.* "Now stop wasting my time and let's talk about this like—"

A blast of fire knocked me backward a few feet, the flames burning a hole in my suit.

"Okay." I brushed off the embers. "Right. We'll work this out the unintelligent way, then." I showered them all with hail, which earned me a whip of sound to my ear—Vox attacking strategically. "Remember, I tried to warn you," I said, infusing a hint of disappointment into my tone.

And then I let them truly feel the brunt of my power.

They would all bow by the time I finished.

I was, after all, a Royal King, and they were about to find out what that meant.

CHAPTER TWENTY-SEVEN
EXOS

CLAIRE, I whispered, sensing her stronger state. *Baby, I need you to hear me now. I can't wait any longer. You feel it, don't you? Our connection fraying? Another day or two and it'll be too late. I need you to find me now.*

Silence.

I paced in my dark cell, frustrated. I'd hoped by now that someone would check up on me down here. Alas, no. I was just as alone as the first day I awoke—whenever that was.

At least the inky presence had disappeared. Well, mostly. The culprit had left some residue in my mind, blocking the memories I desired most. While I recognized the energy signature, I couldn't recall the owner, and it was pissing me the fuck off.

I couldn't even recall who knocked me out to begin with, yet I firmly remembered the sensation of being blasted from behind.

Claire, I tried again. *Baby, please.*

Still nothing.

I growled and kept moving, doing everything I could to keep my body in prime condition. A month of lounging had resulted in slight deterioration, but not much. Fae could withstand far worse treatment, including an extended time period without food.

313

Of course, that didn't make me any less hungry or thirsty.

Fuck, what I wouldn't give for a crackle pie right now. Juicy, thick, and oh-so decadent. I sent images of it to Claire for fun, wondering if I could wake her with thoughts of food.

Or even better…

I thought about running my hands over her body, our spirits dancing on a plane only we could reach, and drew kisses down her sternum to the sweet place between her thighs. *I love the way you taste,* I whispered. *Mmm, I miss it, Claire. When I see you again, I'm going to devour every inch of you and kill anyone who gets in my way.*

A flicker of something came back to me.

Intrigue.

I smiled. *So sex is how I get you to talk to me, is it?*

A sleepy unintelligible murmur traveled through our link, amusing me despite my surroundings.

You want me to continue? I taunted. *Talk to you about how I plan to fuck you for the first time? How I intend to make you scream for hours upon hours?*

Exos… She sounded so tired.

Yes, baby, I'm here, I whispered to her. *I'm sorry for waking you, but I need you to find me. Can you do that for me, Claire? Can you track me by using our link?*

No reply.

"Fuck," I groaned, slamming my fist into the wall. If I didn't get her up soon, our link would die. Permanently.

So I tried again.

And again.

Her name blossoming into a prayer inside my mind, my heart begging her to hear me, to focus, to come for me.

I'm not giving up, I told her. *You will hear me. Now wake up, Claire. Wake. Up. Right. Now.*

CHAPTER TWENTY-EIGHT
CLAIRE

MMM, I LOVED THIS DREAM.

Exos's hands swam over my skin, heating my sides, my breasts, my throat. And Cyrus remained a cool presence at my back, his fingers trailing along the warmth to leave ice in their wake.

Hot and cold.

A torture underlined in delicious energy and followed by lips tracing every inch of my form. Both men were powerful, their elements playing with mine and building an inferno between my thighs.

They wanted to enter me at the same time.

Oh, it was wicked.

Could I let them?

Would I enjoy it?

Yes, they whispered in unison.

Oh God... I shuddered, the sensations overwhelming my mind and forcing me into awareness as I exploded in the silence of the night.

Alone.

With my hand between my legs.

"Shit," I breathed, convulsing wildly from the orgasm I hadn't expected to be real. "That's new..." I collapsed onto the bed, the black sheets familiar and scented of Titus, not Cyrus or Exos.

I frowned. Why did that feel wrong? I'd dreamt of silky blue sheets, a stream running near the foot of the bed, and a handsome Water Fae with a talented tongue.

And Exos.

My heart panged at the thought, our connection hanging on by a bare thread. What happened when it severed?

Once broken, it cannot be reengaged, Exos's voice was fluid in my mind and underlined in sadness. *You have to find me, Claire. Before it's too late.*

But where are you? I wondered, terrified at the thought of losing him. *You cut me off. I can't feel you anymore.* It hurt so much to say, to know that this was just another dream. *I hate this.*

I'm here, baby. I've been here all week.

I frowned. *What? All week? When? How? Where?*

And why did I smell like Cyrus?

I looked around the familiar room, searching for something, a hint, anything to explain the last few days and why I felt so weak.

Use our connection, Claire, Exos demanded, his royal tones causing my lips to twitch with the familiarity. *I'm not far. I feel you. Which means you can feel me. Follow the link. Find me.*

I pinched my side, needing to ensure that I was actually awake. Because everything seemed foggy, as if I'd been living underwater for days or weeks.

So strange.

Claire. Exos's voice sounded strained. *Please. I need you to find me.*

I will, I vowed, sliding from the bed. *I just need to tell the others that I can hear you again.* And to confirm that this was real, not a dream.

Cyrus can help, he replied. *I can sense his bond, which means he can sense mine.*

Bond? I froze with my hand on the doorknob, the memories crashing over me in a wave that left me shaking. *Oh, fuck...*

I hadn't just bonded to Cyrus, we'd *mated.*

And then we fu—

I shook my head, clearing it.

Except that didn't help at all. Vivid images of how he took my body assaulted my conscious all at once and had my thighs clenching with need despite the orgasm that had awoken me.

I have a serious problem, I decided. *I'm addicted to sex.*

I'm very much okay with this problem, Exos returned, sounding amused.

That wasn't meant for you, I said, my cheeks flushing red.

But I heard it anyway. And he didn't sound at all apologetic about it.

Who else had heard it? Cyrus? Titus? And what else was happening? *Is that Sol and Vox?* I asked, a tiny shriek in my head. *Don't answer that.*

Because I didn't need him to.

I felt all five of them inside me, their elements soothing mine and replenishing my energy reserves. Something had happened that caused me to establish connections to all of them. I just couldn't remember *what* brought me to that point.

I definitely recalled the outcome, though. All the nights and mornings and days in bed with Cyrus. The petting. The kissing. The pleasure.

It made no sense. I hated him.

And yet, deep down, I cared for him.

Talk about a conundrum. My emotions were all over the place, yet my elements had never felt more stable. For once, I actually felt a semblance of control. Like my powers were finally grounded and just awaiting my command.

Claire, baby, I love that you're finally embracing your fae half, but I need you to find me, Exos urged. *Please.*

Right. I could play with these sensations later.

For now, I needed to focus on Exos and how to locate him. Which required a better understanding of how to track the link.

I closed my eyes to envision my connections—all five of them.

Insanity, I marveled while prodding each one tentatively. Four were in a cluster, suggesting them to be nearby. The fifth was close, but not with the others.

You're not far, I whispered to him. *But I don't recognize the land you're in.*

Show Cyrus. He'll help.

Okay. I never thought I'd want Cyrus's help with anything, considering our tumultuous relationship, but I sensed his adoration now through the bond.

Totally unreal.

Never in my wildest dreams could I have imagined this.

And yet, here I was, bonded to *five* men.

I had no choice but to embrace it. Primarily because it gave me a sense of completion I hadn't realized was missing before. Now I didn't want to go back. I *liked* this semblance of control, this power, this flourishing energy surrounding my soul.

You were destined to be a queen, Exos agreed, his voice soft. *Now go find Cyrus.*

I twisted the handle on the door and went into the living area, searching for the four elements I felt nearby. *Outside,* my mind prompted. A strange place for them all to be while I rested inside, but maybe they were having a meeting of sorts.

Or maybe they were trying to kill each other.

I gaped at the scene before me—Cyrus with a wall of water protecting him from the fire and air Titus and Vox were throwing at him, and a stream beneath his feet to keep him elevated above the hole in the ground.

"What in the world are you all doing?" I asked, my voice far raspier than I intended. I cleared my throat and tried again, but my words were mere whispers despite my alarm.

I sent a note of panic through the links—an instinctual response that had four pairs of eyes swinging my way, all of them rounding at the sight of me standing outside.

And the elemental battle ceased.

"What the hell was that?" I demanded on a hoarse whisper of sound.

A fountain of water appeared before my lips, Cyrus offering me the drink I hadn't realized I needed. I sipped from the cool spring and sighed, content, and tried again. "What's gotten into you guys?"

"Uh, Claire…" Chagrin painted Titus's features, his voice trailing off.

Vox and Sol appeared too speechless to explain.

And Cyrus just seemed to be amused.

Whatever these fae had been up to, no one wanted to speak. Okay, fine. I'd focus on the more important task at hand, then. "Exos is awake and talking to me, and I have a hint of his location. He's close, but not on Academy grounds."

All traces of enjoyment left Cyrus's features. "What did he say?"

"That if I don't find him soon, the link will be broken." I cringed with the words. "We need to find him today." And given the location of the moon overhead, I estimated we had about twelve hours. How I created that timetable, I didn't know. I just knew it was right.

"Has he mentioned Mortus?" Cyrus asked, seeming to be the only one capable of speaking.

"No." I thought the question at Exos and heard a snort travel through the line.

Yeah, I sense his presence down here, but something's not right. Tell Cyrus I think Mortus is being influenced.

I conveyed the message.

Cyrus scratched his jaw. "Interesting. I imagine Exos doesn't know by who, or he would have said." He glanced at the trio of gaping fae. "Seriously. It's like the three of you have never seen a naked woman before. Pull yourselves together. We have work to do."

I frowned at his statement. It seemed to come out of—

Wait…

I glanced down, a gasp leaving my throat. "Oh, shit." I'd wandered out here without clothes on. Heat climbed up my neck, a squeak leaving my lips. "*Oops.*"

"Not complaining," Cyrus said, lifting a shoulder. "And these guys aren't, either. Or they wouldn't be if they had enough brains to fucking talk."

Vox and Sol spluttered.

Titus merely smirked. "You look healthy, Claire."

"Doesn't she?" Cyrus mused, his icy gaze roaming over me knowingly and stirring a warmth deep inside.

Oh God. I'd practically mauled him this week in my *need.* Who knew sex could be so healing? Even now, I craved more.

With all of them.

This is bad.

"I'm going to, uh, yeah." I ran back inside, the desire to roll myself up in a sleeping bag and never come out overwhelming my thoughts.

Five traces of arousal mingled with enjoyment inside of me.

Even Exos knew.

You men are going to be trouble, I growled.

And you'll love every minute of it, Exos returned.

We'll see, I grumbled, finding one of Titus's robes that hit me well below my knees.

Can you be naked when you find me? Exos wondered, a teasing note in his voice. *Because I could use a little relief, Claire.*

My face went up in flames. *Exos.*

Claire.

I puffed out a breath. *You're incorrigible.*

No, princess. I'm bored and I miss you.

I miss you, too, I said, my shoulders falling. *I'm coming for you, Exos. I promise.*

Oh, I know, baby. And soon you'll use those words beneath me in bed.

One-track mind, I accused.

Says the woman who ran naked into an elemental battle between four males. But hey, at least you captured their attention.

I'm going to start ignoring you now, I lied, my lips twitching despite my mortification.

Then I'll just speak louder, he vowed. *I'm not going to stop until this link dies or you find me.*

I flinched. *It won't die. It can't.*

Then start searching. Because we're running out of time.

I nodded, hand on the doorknob yet again, this time with my body properly clothed. *Don't give up on me, Exos.* I spoke the words with purpose, recalling the night he said the same thing to me. Now it was his turn to trust me, to have faith in me to locate him before it was too late.

Never, he whispered. *I'll never give up on you, Claire.*

CHAPTER TWENTY-NINE
TITUS

SEEING CLAIRE AGAIN HAD TAKEN AN ENTIRE week's worth of frustration and rage right out of me, but seeing her like *that*…

Fucking fires.

Resisting the urge to burn down the door, I waited for Claire. In spite of what Cyrus believed, I wasn't an idiot. I sensed the change in her—a big one—perhaps a change I would enjoy exploring, but she wasn't just mine anymore.

She belonged to all of us.

Claire appeared and paused, taking me in with those bright blue eyes that now glittered with an overflow of Cyrus's power.

I wanted to fall to my knees and worship her.

"You're so beautiful," I whispered, awed.

She slipped into my arms, and every muscle in my body relaxed, knowing her as my mate. She tilted her head back and smiled.

"Titus," she said, my name having a new flow on her lips that made my core tighten.

I wanted to give her space to adjust to the fae inside her overriding her human half, but I couldn't resist as she tugged against my flame from somewhere deep in my soul.

My lips found hers on instinct, the taste of her grounding me as her mouth parted for mine.

Safe.

Home.

Mine.

A wave of heat slammed into me, showering me in a deep-seated craving we shared—our fire yearning to complete what we'd begun.

Soon, I vowed. *Soon.*

Her teeth sank into my lip, and her nails ran down my back, leaving a trail of embers that deliciously burned and danced with my own magic.

"While I appreciate that you've stopped throwing fireballs at my head, can we focus?" Cyrus rudely interrupted. "Claire's vitality is what needs to be rejuvenated, not your own."

He was right. Claire's hand already dipped to my pants, sensing the need in me for her touch. I grabbed her wrist before she could slip her fingers past the waistband.

She pouted and narrowed her eyes at Cyrus. "It's not all about me."

The amused smirk on Cyrus's face said otherwise, not that I doubted he hadn't enjoyed their past week together. The residual impact from full mating rituals was well known, and while I was envious, I also knew Claire would have been ravenous in her near-death condition. It was a tall order for any man to take on.

Cyrus responded with his element instead of his typical smart-ass retorts. A glimmer of liquid swept across Claire's lips like a kiss, a show of power that surprised me in both its precision and gentleness. Her tongue slipped out to taste it, and she fluttered her eyes closed with delight.

Not to be outdone, I followed the trail of magic with my own, concentrating to sweep blue heat across her delicate skin. She gasped, her lashes lifting as the steam mixed with our breaths, her blue irises flashing with a knowing flame that absorbed my energy. My hand fisted in her hair, angling her to my desire to give her everything she wanted—everything she needed.

"Yes," Cyrus said, his tone approving as Claire stopped trying to give me what I yearned for and greedily drank in the elements swirling around her. "Just like that."

A blush crested Claire's cheeks and she smiled.

Energy danced in her gaze, and I realized I'd never seen her like this—balanced, like a new fae born into the world who understood her powers and how to control them.

No hesitation.

No emotions running her into the ground.

Just knowledge and acceptance.

Cyrus had done what none of us had yet to accomplish—he'd given her what her elements craved. And while she was sated with regard to water, she needed *more.*

Challenge accepted.

I poured my flames through the bond, adoring the way it lit up her features and the sigh that feathered from her beautiful mouth. But I wasn't enough, and the flicker of her gaze to the hall told me as much.

Claire craved her circle and the balance it provided.

"Sol and Vox are in the kitchen," I murmured, guiding her away from the bedroom before I yanked her inside and burned her clothes off.

If we—her mates—did this right, it would prove far more satisfying in the long run.

Claire glided beside me, her movements graceful as water mixed with fire along her footsteps.

Elements, she has no idea how powerful she is. She's intoxicating.

Sol's arms were crossed, his large form leaning against a broken peach tree that had grown from what was left of the dining table, while Vox stood with both fists knuckled down onto the cracked wood.

They both stopped midsentence and locked gazes on Claire the moment I brought her into the room. If it hurt me in my soul not to be fully mated with her, I couldn't imagine what her call was doing to them.

By the look of utter conflict on Vox's face, he was fighting it hard. Sol, on the other hand, loosened his stance and gave Claire a warm smile.

With a small nudge to her back, I sent her toward the Earth Fae. "Go on, sweetheart. Don't be afraid."

She gave me a playful nip of fire that ran over my lips. Her fae side was powerful, dominating her in the best of ways, and she was rolling with it.

Fucking finally.

"Sol," she said, marveling at the peach tree. "Did you do this?" If she felt embarrassed by her earlier display of nudity, she didn't show it. Had perhaps forgotten it beneath the onslaught of elements cascading over her skin. Or maybe she was just embracing it, like everything else.

"Uh." He cleared his throat, then shuffled his feet. "Yeah. Actually, I made some more outside, but they kind of, well, didn't do well this week." He grimaced, causing Claire to frown.

"Because of me?" she asked, so quiet, her steps retreating backward toward mine. "Did I hurt you all?" She glanced at me, then at Vox and Sol, and finally at Cyrus.

"You required a lot of energy to heal, little queen," Cyrus replied. "But we're all fine and ready to give you more of what you need now." He ran a rope of water over her neck for emphasis, one I trailed with fire.

Sol glanced at Cyrus as if seeking permission to participate. The royal nodded, and the scent of peaches filled the air as earth energy rolled over her skin.

Claire sighed, her eyes falling closed beneath the abundance of power. I wrapped my arms around her, holding her to me while pouring more fire through our bond. She absorbed it with ease, thriving on the balance we represented.

Vox watched the exchange with guarded interest. His magic hummed at the ready, waiting to reel Sol in at the slightest hint of danger. No matter his reservations, he wouldn't allow Claire to be hurt.

Hmm, perhaps we would convince the Air Fae to come around after all.

The kitchen and dining area shifted around us, repairing itself as Sol drenched Claire in more power. He shuddered, whispering, "Claire, I feel you."

"Me, too," she hummed, the element intensifying until she focused on Vox. He was the only one not adding his elements to the melody. It felt like an incomplete song without him and Exos to add the final notes to the balance.

"Vox," I said, irritated. "Stop being stubborn."

Claire shook her head. "No. Don't force him, Titus." Even though her words said that she permitted his insolence, I felt her tugging on his elements, making his mouth part ever so slightly. I would have missed it had I not sensed his desire twist in response through the bond that linked all of us.

I grinned. That was my Claire. She wouldn't be denied over a little bit of stubbornness, especially when she could feel that Vox wanted her.

Cyrus added another flurry of water to the air, easing some of the tension. "This is exactly why we returned," he said, regarding all of us with an air of authority.

The royal seemed... different. Still pompous enough that I swore a stick was permanently lodged up his ass, but there was a softness to him that hadn't been there before. Or perhaps it had been, and he'd just buried it so far that even he hadn't known it existed.

He shifted his focus to me, all of the authority of a king in his eyes, but which king? He didn't seem to fit the cold hardness of the Spirit Kingdom anymore. "How do you feel, Claire?" he asked softly, still holding my gaze.

She ignored him, her attention on Vox. Whatever she was doing seemed to have the Air Fae entranced. He took a step forward to graze his fingers across her cheek. She didn't move a muscle, as if she would scare him off if she so much as breathed.

The moment his magic brushed her skin, her eyes fluttered closed and she shivered. "More," she whispered.

He complied, stroking a breeze through her hair and then down along my robe.

Silence fell.

The four of us exchanged elements, with Claire at the center. She took it all, energy vibrating around her in a powerful wave that reminded me of an impending inferno.

And then her eyes flashed open. "Exos." She whirled in my arms, the look of victory on her face making me want to kiss her. "I feel him, Titus. I *really* feel him."

Cyrus nodded as if he wasn't surprised. "The elements are grounding you and building up the circle that binds all of us to you, including Exos. Your fae side craves the elements, craves completing what's begun. Now where is he?"

Her gaze became distant, and a flutter swept through our connection. She turned to Cyrus, my arms still wrapped around her. "He's safe. And close."

Cyrus's eyebrows lifted. "At the Academy?"

"No. But nearby." Her nose scrunched. "Beyond the enchanted trees, I think. If I follow the link, I can find him. He's calling to me. Strongly."

None of us could disagree with that. Her need for all of us to be with her burned, and her connection to Exos was so precious, yet it had become so fragile. Even I could hardly feel the faint strand that should have been strong, a united front with Claire as our common anchor.

"Then let's go," I said, indulging in the deluge of magical energy that tingled against my skin. Every part of me thrived, flexed, and purred, ready to fuck or to fight. Perhaps both. And if I felt like this just being near Claire and four of her elemental mates, I couldn't imagine how glorious she'd be when Exos completed the circle.

"No." Claire's blue gaze blazed with an authority I hadn't seen in her before. Droplets teased along her hairline as she shifted her attention to Cyrus. "Exos says you need to distract Mortus. While he doesn't think Mortus is the actual culprit, his essence is all over the cell. So he's suggesting you distract him so I can reach Exos without interference."

Cyrus hummed in thought. "Could be fun." The bastard clapped me on the back, his water magic sizzling against my heat and sending a plume of steam into the air. He grinned. "Titus?"

Irritation prickled along my spine. Cyrus had far too much confidence in Claire. Yes, she was powerful. Yes, she was amazing, but if that bastard of a fae thought I'd let her leave my sight again, he was a moron.

"Fuck off," I snapped, shoving him away and wrapping myself around Claire once more. I ran my fingers up her jawline and cupped her face. "I'm going with Claire."

"Because that won't draw attention at all," Cyrus drawled, sounding unamused and somehow saying I was an idiot without even trying. "Everyone knows you're one of her mates. Mortus will be watching you just as much as me. No, we're going to have to stick together." A gush of water pushed me away from Claire and doused me with cold reality, making me growl.

Ignoring me when I sent flames scalding over my body, he narrowed his gaze on the remaining two fae. "Vox. Sol. You're our secret weapons. Mortus doesn't know Claire has bonded to you, so he won't be tracking you yet. Not like he'll be doing with Titus and me, anyway. And besides…" He met my gaze once more. "We'll keep him distracted, right?"

Vox stiffened. "Weapons?" he repeated, apparently focused on that part of the equation, not the ridiculous plan Cyrus had just crafted.

"Yes," Claire agreed, a smile in her voice as she slid out of my arms to stand in the center of the ring, her back to me as she faced Vox and Sol. "My guardian weapons, right?"

The Air Fae's obsidian gaze swirled with that ring of silver, a light breeze rushing from him to Claire as if she'd called for his magic touch. If he noticed it, he didn't react. Instead, he nodded.

Finally. She's tamed the Air Fae.

Except I still felt his resistance. Which meant Claire did, too.

"You're really going to let her go off with two barely bonded fae?" I challenged Cyrus, not liking this idea one bit. Sol could handle it. Vox? I had my doubts. "This is reckless."

Claire spun around, her eyebrow arching. "*Let* me?"

Growling, I couldn't contain my flames anymore. A line shot across the floor, aimed at the source of my problems. *Cyrus.* If he wanted to force Claire to stay here, with us, where it was safe, I had no doubt he could. Letting her go off with Vox and Sol was a bad decision.

He swept his hand through the air, dousing my flames. "Stop. Coddling. Her." His magic shoved me, sending me skidding back a few steps. "But I appreciate the challenge, Fire Fae. It gives me an idea as to how we'll distract the masses. Let's see what the Powerless Champion is capable of against a Royal Fae." His blond brow arched high. "Unless you're afraid?"

Sol's entire countenance brightened. "Did you just challenge Titus to an elemental duel?" Then his brow furrowed. "Wait... We'll miss it." The big guy shrugged. "Ah, well, I must like you, Claire, because that's a sight I'd love to see."

Claire seemed conflicted, but a whisper through the connection from Exos put her at ease, and she shook her head. "You two behave," she said, looking at me and Cyrus. Then she smiled at Sol. "And I like you, too, Sol."

The Earth Fae seemed quite pleased by that pronouncement. "Yeah, totally worth missing the fight. We all know Cyrus will win anyway."

"Hey." A fireball formed over my palm. "I can take him."

"Prove it," Cyrus replied, sounding bored.

He was goading me and I knew it. But I couldn't resist an opportunity to put the bastard in his place. "All right. You're on, jackass. But don't get too cocky. I've never lost in the arena."

The only place in all the realms that I felt at home, other than in Claire's arms, was in those bloody, dusty pits where the crowds chanted my name.

Cyrus wouldn't know what fucking hit him.

Chapter Thirty
Claire

THEY'LL BE FINE, I told myself for the hundredth time. Exos had promised as much when he suggested I let them burn off some steam and have some fun.

Hopefully, he was right.

I am, he murmured now, his voice a caress against my spirit.

Energy hummed over my skin, causing my lips to curl as I walked with Sol and Vox through the outskirts of the forest that lined the Academy. I felt invigorated, full of life, *happy.* All strange sensations for someone who had almost died, but for the first time in my existence, I was at ease.

Balanced, Exos whispered. *You're balanced, Claire.*

Yes, I agreed, feeling the veracity of his proclamation in my blood. My links to all the elements had grounded me, providing me with a newfound existence.

Except for that sense of unease coming from air.

No, from Vox.

I glanced at him as we walked, noting his stiff posture. There weren't any threats nearby. Titus and Cyrus were making sure of that by causing diversions on campus. I just hoped they were getting along.

Well, while the Air Fae didn't seem thrilled by our new connection, Sol appeared to be content enough. The ground wasn't even shaking beneath his steps. If anything, he appeared lighter, too.

His lips curled as he caught me looking at him. My cheeks pinkened a little, embarrassed to be caught staring, but it really was a wonder to see him moving so fluidly over the grass.

"You haven't broken anything," I murmured.

He chuckled. "No, and it feels damn good." He rolled his shoulders and glanced up at the sun overhead. "Actually, I feel incredible."

"Me, too," I admitted, smiling in earnest now. "Like I could fly." I skipped into the field on a whirl, the elements dancing to my steps and stirring a mixture of power into the atmosphere around me. It left me sighing in fulfillment.

Apart from my link to Vox. That felt brittle, as if a slight miscalculation in movements would shatter the tentative link.

I frowned. "What's wrong?" I asked, suddenly feeling very conscious of his discomfort. "Have I hurt you?" Because I knew I'd drained the others while trying to climb back into existence. Poor Cyrus had taken the worst of it, then nursed us both back to health in the waves of passion.

Did I just pity the man for having to fuck me all week? I thought, snorting to myself. *Yeah, that's a hardship.*

Although, I'd been pretty demanding.

But none of that was the point right now.

What I wanted to know was why Vox hadn't looked at me once since we started this walk. Why his shoulders remained tense. Why his mouth was compressed into that hard line. Why he still hadn't answered me despite my asking him a direct question.

"Vox," I tried again. "What's wrong?"

"Nothing." He kept moving, ignoring me completely.

Our link determined that single-worded reply to be a lie.

I blinked at Sol, arching a brow. "You're okay, right?"

"Never been better, little flower," he replied, his brown-green eyes gleaming with adoration. "I mean, the last week wasn't easy, but having you back, it's like..." His lips slid to the side and he shrugged. "It's like you returning has completed a part of me I didn't know was broken."

"That's exactly how I feel," I marveled, relieved he sensed it, too. "Exos says it's because I'm balanced. Like all my powers are finally aligned, allowing me to see them all clearly." I created a butterfly in my palm to demonstrate and encouraged it to flutter away with a slight breeze. Only, it turned into a gust that caused me to grimace. "Okay, so not perfect, but you get the idea."

Sol held out his hand and created a pile of dirt, then threw it at Vox, who was walking several steps ahead of us.

"What the fuck?" Vox snapped, turning around to glare at the giant.

"Oh, I'm sorry. Did that hit you?" Sol asked with false innocence.

Vox narrowed his silver-rimmed gaze and sent a gust of wind over Sol's shoulder, which only seemed to enrage him more.

"You missed," Sol said, a study in nonchalance.

"Uh, guys…," I interjected, wanting to steer us back onto the path of finding Exos. With every step, his essence grew closer. This was definitely the right way, even though I had no idea where we were in this field. It was somewhere beyond the enchanted forest, in what Cyrus had called "neutral territory." Apparently, these lands separated the Academy from all the kingdoms, which left them often vacant and not commonly traversed. Hence the overgrown grass, which really resembled out-of-control weeds.

Another whirl of wind went sailing through the air, knocking me on the shoulder and causing Sol to growl. The earth shook beneath us as he retaliated in kind and sent the Air Fae to his ass.

My eyes widened.

I was used to Vox schooling Sol in powers. Not the other way around.

"I see," Vox said, jumping up to his feet in a lithe motion and wiping the dust from his pants. "So you get a little control and turn your back on the one who's been helping you for the last two years. Fine. Maybe I should just go and let you two chatter on about your newfound *balance*."

Wow, I'd never heard Vox like this. He sounded so bitter and almost cruel. "Seriously, what is your problem?" I demanded. "Is it because I forced the connection on you?"

I didn't remember doing it, had no say in my elements trying to save my life, but I could understand that upsetting him. I just hadn't realized how much it would bother him.

"I mean, I'm sorry. To you both, I mean. I… If I'd known what was going to happen…" Would I change it? I bit my lip. *No*, my elements all said in unison. No, I wouldn't change it at all. Which meant my apology really meant nothing because it lacked truth.

Well, this is fun. I wiped my palms against my jeans and stared off into the distance while the two males observed me in silence. *Really helpful, guys.* Although, yeah, they deserved an explanation. Not that I really had one, but I could at least try.

I cleared my throat, opening my mouth but then closing it, and considered how I wanted to say this.

Then I caught sight of Vox's irritated expression.

And Sol's hurt one.

Right.

No more thinking.

"I-I don't remember what happened," I started and immediately regretted the words as their faces fell. "But I understand *why* it happened," I quickly assured them. That seemed to intrigue them both. "When Exos first brought me down here, I was a mess. He told me fae existed, that I had access to all these elements, things kept happening around me that I didn't understand, and I kept feeling these inappropriate feelings for multiple men."

I shivered as I recalled those early days between Titus and Exos, and felt their responding warmth through the bonds.

"It had terrified me," I admitted. "Where I come from, you don't date more than one guy. There are actually some pretty horrible names associated with human women who date around. And that's the world I grew up in." This was something Cyrus seemed to understand more than the others. He'd made a comment about it before the death fields, one that resonated with me.

"I don't think you're a whore, little queen. But I know all about the social standards on Earth and how they've programmed your mind."

He was right.

My upbringing dictated my outlook.

But now that I felt the connections, allowed my fae half to reign while healing my body, I understood.

"Things are different here," I continued, swallowing thickly. "My feelings for you all are more accepted. And so, it makes sense to me why my elements reached out to you both. My energy recognizes both of you as potential mates, and moreover, I've developed a trust with each of you. So in my time of dire need, my elements called to yours." The connection couldn't be entirely one-sided—something Cyrus's bond had taught me. So if Vox and Sol hadn't craved the link on some level, they wouldn't have been open to it, and they certainly wouldn't have reciprocated.

I met Vox's gaze, noted the closed-off nature of his expression, and sighed. "If you don't want this, I'll understand, and we can end our bond after the preliminary time requirement." Which, I knew, was around a month. "I won't push you into something you don't want." I glanced at Sol. "Either of you." I pinched my mouth to the side, debating what else to say. "I can't really apologize because I acted on instincts alone, and, well, I don't regret it, even if I probably should."

"You better not," Sol said, folding strong arms over his muscular chest. "Because I don't."

"Don't what?" I asked, confused.

"Regret it," he clarified. "Once I realized what was happening, I let you in. It felt right." He lifted a shoulder. "And it still feels right. I don't need to know more than that."

So accepting and honest. Sol might be a giant of a man, but inside existed the biggest of hearts, and I felt it now, beating in time with my own.

None of this was what I expected for myself.

But something happened to me this week. I just woke up ready to embrace it all. No more chaos. No more fighting. Just feeling and reality and an unequivocal need to accept it.

That's your inner fae, Claire, Exos murmured, his presence thriving around me. *You're finally allowing her to breathe.*

And it feels amazing, I admitted, smiling. But Vox didn't seem to agree.

"Tell me what you need," I said to him. "An apology? A better explanation? I can't promise either, but I can try."

"Is this still about the ball?" Sol demanded, his dark eyebrow arching. "The fact that she asked me and not you?"

Irritation tainted the air surrounding Vox. "It's not the ball. It's everything. She mated with Exos and Titus because she wanted to. Even with Cyrus, it seems. And she at least asked you to the ball. I'm just a mentor, the one she latched onto in a time of need. Which I get, and it's fine, and it's my own damn fault for not embracing the connection sooner. But it is what it is. Can we find Exos now?"

His assessment left me reeling.

Because, for one, I didn't mate with Exos because I wanted to. It'd been on accident. Same with Cyrus. And I hadn't chosen Vox only out of *need.* Although, I could see why he felt that way.

Who knew the Air Fae was so emotional? Exos drawled. *Kiss him, Claire. That'll solve it.*

I nearly fell over. *What?*

You heard me, princess. Kiss the man. Exos spoke the words as a demand, but a hint of amusement underlined them.

I don't—

Claire, male fae thrive on action. And all of yours thus far have Vox feeling left out. Just kiss him. Trust me.

Had my behavior made him think I wasn't interested? Maybe. I had been quite reluctant. A brat, really, considering how patient all these men were with me.

All right. Time to fix that. To put all the confusion to rest and move forward.

I stepped closer to Vox, caught the wild frays of his energy, the uncertainty swirling around him, and the general hurt beneath the surface. My element reached out to soothe his, to brush the harsher strands and mingle our elements in an intimate manner. "Vox," I murmured, moving into his personal space. "I initiated the bond with you because our powers are a match. And"—I took a final step—"I like you." Perhaps we weren't at the same level as I was with Exos or Titus, but I sensed the potential. If he'd let me in and gave me a chance.

Which meant I needed to show him my interest, to ground him the way he'd grounded me last week. I went to my toes and brushed my lips over his. Just a tender stroke, one meant to entice and invite, and wrapped my arms around his neck. The second kiss was a little more forceful on my part, begging him to react. And by the third, his lips finally reciprocated, the shock of my touching him receding into a passionate flurry of wind.

"Claire?" he questioned, his mouth against mine.

"Vox." I smiled. "Please kiss me." I could feel his desire to thrumming through my veins; otherwise, I would have backed off by now. But it was a tangible presence, tangling with my aura in the most alluring of ways.

Vox and I were more alike than he likely wanted to admit. He seemed to fear his magic overruling him, just as I had feared my fae half.

"Give in to your instincts," I whispered. "I did." Sometime over the last week, with Cyrus's help, I'd accepted my magic and my nature, my most inner desires, and my passion. And it'd only made me stronger.

One of his hands hand fell to my hip, gripping tightly. The other thread through my hair, tugging my strands into his fist as he positioned me where he wanted.

And then he took me.

Not hard. Not rushed. Not fast. Just thoroughly. Expertly. As if his mouth was designed just for mine, his tongue knowing and skilled, and stole my breath away. It was the perfect kind of embrace, one where the wind lightly brushed us both, whirling us into a cloud of perfection and yearning. Only, a hungry presence at my back confused my senses, earthy tones mingling with mine and heightening the moment to one of irresistible lust.

Vox turned me in his arms, right into Sol, who was waiting to catch me— with his mouth.

My heart skipped a beat at the synchronization, at the feel of having two strong and capable men holding me as if I were their reason for being, and at sensing their undeniable longing for more.

I shuddered, my elements flourishing to life.

This was what I needed. How I wanted to exist. What I required for breath.

My mates.

All five.

Creating a harmony of energy inside me, begging to be stroked and tempered, and my fae reacted in kind, each of them sending me what I needed to harness my control and allow me to just be.

I lost track of time between Sol and Vox, their rotating mouths and hands leaving me hot and bothered in the middle of nowhere. But my missing link pulled me from the haze, my elements even more honed and alive and ready.

"He's near," I whispered, opening my eyes to find Vox's striking eyes glazed with passion. With his willingness traveling through the bond, I felt even more empowered, everything around me falling into sharper focus.

"Where?" Vox asked, his palm running up and down my arm, as if addicted to my energy.

And maybe he was. I felt the same about him, my fingers still woven through his thick, long hair. My other palm had reached up behind me, clasping Sol's neck, his palm around my throat, not in a threatening manner

331

but in a protective one. I relaxed back into him, absorbing his strength, and closed my eyes to *feel* the earth and search for the presence beneath the ground that should not be there.

The elements responded, bowing to my growing power, their worship intensifying with every breath.

This world is mine now, I thought, authority thickening my veins and rooting me in my power. It surpassed everything around me. Everyone. "I can feel so much," I whispered, sensing the expanse of land beneath my feet, stretching all the way to the Academy grounds and beyond, to where Cyrus and Titus were creating havoc of their own.

I smiled.

Cyrus was certainly enjoying himself.

And Titus, well, he was done playing nice.

Exos, my soul breathed, venturing in the other direction, to the ancient crypts few knew existed. When I spoke the words out loud, Sol and Vox looked at each other in confusion, but I didn't doubt my instincts. "This way," I said, allowing the energy to guide me.

See you soon, Exos murmured, pride sliding through our bond.

Yes, I replied. *Very soon.*

Chapter Thirty-One
Cyrus

I WANTED A CHALLENGE.

And the best way to earn a Fire Fae's respect was through violence.

So I'd give him what he desired—an ass beating.

Crystalline lights sprung to life, Earth Fae working with Water Fae to conjure what would normally be underwater plants that glowed bright enough to light up the entire arena. Despite classes being in session, it hadn't taken long to gather a crowd. Word of the challenge had spread quickly.

Elana was going to be furious.

A double bonus in my mind.

That old fae was hiding something, as she always seemed to be doing, but one of these days, I'd get to the bottom of it.

Chatter and anticipation swam around us, creating tidal waves of excitement throughout the Academy's small stadium. It was large enough to house the current active students but paled in comparison to a proper arena—something Titus had already commented on.

Bets were being made throughout, the fae engrossed in the battle before them.

And wouldn't you know? Mortus stood among them with several Academy teachers at his side. They'd no doubt recruited their fellow professor to join in on the fun. It wasn't every day a royal fought a Powerless Champion.

His snarl told me how much he disapproved.

I winked at him in response.

"As far as a diversion goes, this isn't half bad," Titus conceded under his breath.

"Was that a compliment, Fire Fae?" I asked, arching a brow at him.

He snorted. "Just a concession before I hand you your ass."

"We'll see," I replied, amused. "Ready?"

"I've wanted a reason to destroy you since you set foot on Spirit Quad." He grinned at me, a blaze already burning in his eyes. "Trust me when I say, I'll enjoy this."

"Too bad those magical barriers above have to remain." They were what kept fae from killing each other. This wasn't a true Powerless Champion ring, and Elana valued the lives of her students.

Except she still hadn't arrived.

Interesting.

"Consider them your only protection," Titus replied, smirking. "Let's do this, Royal Ass."

I smiled. "Aww, you've given me a nickname. How adorable."

He made a rude gesture that had several fae gasping and left me chuckling.

Oh, this was going to be fun.

A hush fell over the crowd as a petite Water Fae hurried over to hand me a selection of bracelets. She bowed formally, causing the tiny shells dangling from her pointed ears to bounce.

"It's the rules," she whispered apologetically, her words barely audible. This was a true element-on-element duel, which meant I couldn't use my spirit energy against Titus. One element in direct opposition with the other was required—a true test of magical power.

Water against fire.

Perusing the selection, I chose the strongest bracelet that would seal my spirit energy with its merciless diamond cores. Even that would only dull my ability, and I suspected it would do absolutely nothing to Exos.

Still, it resembled a cuff of sorts that diluted my strength and brought my affinity for water to the forefront. Which had admittedly already been there, waiting for me to take my rightful place as king.

And maybe I could be ready—soon—with Claire at my side.

Snapping the bracelet onto my wrist, my vision jolted with a flash of red, then waves crashed in on my senses as my spirit energy retreated, leaving me dazed. The crowd cheered, sensing the shift of energy and signaling that the show was about to begin.

A single moderator hovered at the edge of the arena, raising his voice for the crowd to hear with a gust of air elemental power. "We have an unprecedented duel today! I present Cyrus, King of the Spirit Fae, Prince of

Water, pitted against Titus, our very own Powerless Champion in his first Elemental Duel!"

The crowd cheered, making my ears throb as I fought to adjust to the utter lack of spirit in my chest. It felt wrong, and yet, oddly right. Especially as oceans of warmth rushed in, reminding me of how Claire had drowned me in the most delicious of ways.

"May the victor earn this quarter's title of Academy Elemental Champion! Begin!"

Really? I don't even qualify, I thought with a snort. *Not a student, remember?*

But then a horn sounded, forcing me to focus on the task at hand while my senses struggled to adjust to my lack of spirit. This was my first time shutting out the element, and I hadn't expected it to be so... overwhelming.

Titus took advantage of my disorientation and sent an inferno barreling toward me at full speed.

My magic reacted before I did, rushing out of me all at once and meeting Titus's flame with a raw power of my own.

The arena's magic hummed to life, monitoring our life signs and extent of power. Elana and I, and the other Council members and Academy professors, had erected this barrier, so I knew it could contain even my magic at full force.

An ocean with rising elemental seahorses that rode the waves erupted from my fingertips, spilling out to fill the stadium in seconds and dousing Titus's flames in a single sweeping motion.

The Fire Fae gaped at me but only allowed his shock to settle for a moment before he crouched and drew his magic into himself, building a blazing tornado that sizzled against the mass of water and burned his pants—pants that should have been fire resistant. Yet it left his bare torso alone, suggesting his ultimate control of the raging energy.

Titus wasn't a royal, but his magic had Claire's passion infused into him, making him far more powerful than I would have given him credit for. He looked like the ancient god Vulcan, erupting molten lava that billowed from his feet in a wave of its own that rivaled my oceans, making my seahorses neigh in dismay before steaming into nothingness.

"That all you got, little king?" Titus taunted, twisting my nickname for Claire against me. I wasn't the Water King yet, and if I was defeated in the arena by a Fire Fae, I'd never hear the end of it from my father.

But it would make for a better show.

And it just might give Mortus, and anyone else watching, the false opinion that my link to Claire had somehow weakened me.

Hmm.

Perhaps we needed to use this duel to our advantage and paint some false perceptions.

I grinned as his lava crept toward me. The soft red glow made the air turn bloody and gave Titus a terrifying appearance. By the gleam in his emerald eyes, he blamed me for putting Claire in danger.

Maybe I blamed myself.

Still, I had to make this look good. To ensure that everyone believed Titus had earned this win.

I changed up my attack, twisting my body to create a current that swept against Titus's lava and forced it to harden. He grunted from the blow as fine whips of water lashed against his bare chest, leaving trails of bright blood in their wake. He took the punishment, growling as flames erupted and threatened to consume him in his rage.

That's it. Lose control. See how that works out for you.

Titus should have sidestepped my onslaught and let me wear myself out. The strain was already pounding in my skull, my reserves threatening to admit they were empty, but that wasn't Titus's style. He rushed at me head-on and barreled through the thickest part of my waves, expending his energy as he billowed fire to evaporate a path directly at me.

His fist, a ball of flames, aimed straight at my face.

I dodged his punch and allowed his momentum to slam him into the wall of water at my back, making him buckle and lose his balance.

I pinned Titus to the soaked, sandy pit. His heat glazed the surface with raw energy until it melted smooth, and he clawed against it, my waters rushing in, targeting his flames and making his fingers slip against the fresh glass. "You better make this look good, Titus."

"What?"

"You heard me." I released him, only to be surprised as he shut off his flames completely. Without heat for my waters to target, the resulting wave crashed over both of us, causing me to lose my balance.

Titus moved fast—too fast—and swept my legs out from under me, sending me to the ground.

I raised a hand to send my waters crashing into him, but did so half-heartedly. Oh, to the audience, it would look like I tried, his armor of fire sizzling against my element. And that was all that mattered.

He rushed in, hard and fast, and his fist connected with my jaw, leaving a sharp crack to ring through the arena.

A hush settled over the crowd, stunned.

The king had been struck.

The unfamiliar pain that jolted through my body made me feel alive. No one ever got close enough to strike me, much less do any real damage—no one except my brother.

I twisted and sent one last rope of water at Titus, flinging him away from me, but it was more for show than anything else.

Mortus's obsidian eyes gleamed from the audience, exactly as I desired. If the pompous prick thought he could find my weakness by watching me fight Titus, then he was in for a disappointment.

My only weakness was my greatest strength, and she was far away, saving my brother from darkness.

Exos, I hope Claire is in your arms now and you're safely on your way back to us.

Without my spirit, I couldn't sense him, but I sensed Claire. Her healthy glow caused me to smile, which probably resembled a grimace to the crowd.

I wiped the back of my hand over my mouth, and it came back bloody.

Staggering to my feet, I crouched into a warrior's stance and grinned. "Powerless duel?" I taunted him.

Titus rolled his fingers into fists and readied himself, all signs of his embers dying in the wind along with my water. "You want a beating?" He shrugged his shoulders. "All right."

He came at me, fast and without mercy, blow after blow landing, but I got in a few of my own.

"That all you got?" he taunted.

"I could do this all night," I replied, meaning it.

I dodged and then blocked, taking the hit hard on my forearm before connecting my elbow with his jaw. Titus's entire body jerked up against the blow. It would have left any other fae reeling, but he recovered with impressive speed. My admiration for him grew by the second.

His eyes glowed with embers, but he didn't use his fire on me. Instead, he took the next hit in the gut, his core clenching hard to absorb the blow, and used the opening to wrap his fingers around my throat, twisting me so that my back arched and put me off balance.

"Having fun yet?" he growled, his rage palpable.

Whether it was from the fight, or at me, I didn't know. Likely both.

It didn't take a genius to understand his fury. I'd mated with Claire, and in his mind, I didn't deserve her.

And maybe he was right.

But I couldn't change what happened, nor would I want to.

I clawed at his fingers and spat, then crashed my arm down hard against his wrist and broke his hold. He cursed when I retaliated and swept behind him, wrapping an arm around his neck and putting him in a chokehold of my own. It would be so easy to call for his defeat as I weakened his airway.

Alas, I needed him to win.

So I said something I knew would set him off.

"You realize I only mated with Claire to save Exos, right?" I spoke the words without any emotion, needing him to believe them. And I infused the knowledge that I had considered that tactic several times into my expression. "Seems I've won."

Titus roared, his fury snapping at the reins as his fire ignited, forcing me to release him. His elbow connected with my rib cage and sent all my air rushing out of me. I stumbled back and fell right along with Titus as he launched over me, knee on my chest and hand on my throat again. "Submit," he demanded. "Or I'll *end* you."

Not bad, I thought. And as his fist nailed my jaw, igniting a series of lights behind my eyes, I decided this was good enough.

Conceding to him served so many benefits.

Including enhancing our elemental circle, something Claire badly needed.

And so, for her, I smiled. "I submit." The words triggered the arena's magic and froze us both in place, signaling the end of the battle.

Titus's gaze narrowed, his palm releasing my throat. "You goaded me. Again."

"Did I?" I asked, my voice hoarse.

"Bastard."

I lifted a shoulder. Or tried to, anyway. The Fire Fae was big and on top of me.

"You let me win," he added, a hint of respect coloring his features.

"Why would I do that?" I infused a bit of innocence into my tone, but it really came out as more of a rasp.

He shook his head, amused. "Next time, don't hold back."

"Next time?" I wasn't sure I wanted another public duel. But sparring, I could do.

"Oh yeah. Next time I'm beating you in earnest, Royal Fae."

"Wait, I thought I was your little king?" I managed to sound hurt. "I mean, here you are, straddling me and all…"

He punched me again for good measure, causing me to laugh as he practically leapt off me. "If I wasn't exhausted, I'd challenge you again."

I bounced up to my feet, grinning. "It's like you're flirting with me, Titus."

"For fuck's sake, man." Vehemence colored his tone, but he was grinning, too. "Seriously, we're doing that again."

"Sure." I gave him the requisite bow to acknowledge my defeat. "I look forward to it."

Movement in my peripheral vision showed Mortus backing away as if he'd seen enough—or perhaps he finally sensed what we'd been trying to distract him from.

Claire had found Exos, his location just beneath her feet. And Mortus was already too late. He couldn't mist, the power purely my own.

But what bothered me more was Elana's absence.

This seemed like the kind of event she'd try to stop.

Alas, she was nowhere in sight.

Where are you, Chancellor? I wondered. *And what have you been up to?*

Titus clapped me on the back. "If you ever claim to have mated with Claire to save your brother again, I really will fry you."

I met his burning gaze with a grin. "Don't worry, Powerless Champion. Exos would kill me first."

CHAPTER THIRTY-TWO
EXOS

CLAIRE'S VITALITY GREW WITH EVERY STEP, my spirit soaking her in and allowing it to fuel my being. That was the sustenance I needed. Not food. Not water. Just *her*. It brought my spirit to the forefront, dousing me in an energy that thrived through my veins.

I'd channeled so much into our bond these last few days, locking onto the frays of our connection and holding desperately to the ends. Now that she was nearing my position, I felt the link strengthening again, remembering the beauty of her presence.

It made me come alive in a way I hadn't felt in a long time.

As soon as she was close enough to touch, I would deepen my hold on her and encourage us to the third level so nothing like this could happen again. Oh, it could still shatter—Ophelia and Mortus had proven that in the harshest ways—but I wouldn't have to fear time or space deteriorating our connection.

I agree, Claire whispered through my mind, her spirit so attuned to mine that it was as if we were one being now. Part of it stemmed from the energy I'd forced into our bond while begging my mate to find me, but a larger reason for our enhanced connection was Claire acceptance of her fae half.

She felt complete. I could sense it in her spirit, her contentment with grounding all her elements. She may not have meant to bond to the Earth Fae

339

or Vox or Cyrus, but there wasn't an ounce of regret within her. Not even her human half—the one gaping in horror at the idea of *five* mates—could overcome her fae mind now.

And I fucking loved it.

You're close, I murmured, sensing her above me.

Yes. She went silent for a moment, her other elements taking over as she focused. My lips curled as the walls shook around me, Claire using her affinity for earth to manipulate the ancient tombs. A blast of energy—air—shook the foundation above.

Found the door, she said, a hint of pride in her tone.

I felt that. I smiled. *Try not to collapse the roof over my head, princess.*

Her amusement trickled through her spirit, as did Vox's astonishment at her display in power. Having such a close connection to the Air Fae was a bit strange, but as a Spirit Fae, I often connected to the auras of others.

But the Earth Fae was very new to me.

Sol.

I only knew his name because of Claire. The power beneath his tough exterior rivaled some of the strongest fae in existence. This must be the fae Elana mentioned that Vox was tutoring in control. Interesting.

From a guardian standpoint, I approved. And I imagined Cyrus did as well, hence his presence in Claire's life.

I ran a palm over my face, thinking of all the things I needed to discuss with my brother. He would want to know who knocked me out and put me down here, but I couldn't remember. My memories were hidden beneath a thick wall of ink, one I hoped Cyrus could help me demolish. Because the answers were right there, at the back of my mind, hidden behind that mossy black substance. I'd prodded at it all week, trying futilely to demolish the block. Whoever had put it there was powerful in the darkest way.

Mortus seemed too likely a suspect, even though I sensed his presence all around this place.

No, I suspected something more sinister.

Someone had been using him as a puppet.

But the question remained: *Who?*

A gust of wind sailed through the room, blowing out the torches on the walls. I relit them with a wave of my fingers, the fire second nature. Claire's presence hummed on the breeze, her eagerness thickening my blood.

"Exos?" she called, her voice the most beautiful sound in my existence.

"Over here, baby." I clasped the iron bars, hoping she could at least see my hands from where she stood.

Her energy warmed my being as she approached.

So close.

Almost there.

My Claire.

My breath stuttered out of me at the sight of her, all those golden locks illuminated by the flame in her palm. Her blue eyes seemed lit from within, her smile rivaling mine. "There you are," she breathed, studying my prison cell. "Back up."

Vox and Sol came to stand behind her, their postures protective. Especially the Earth Fae's. And the look he directed at me said I was the threat in his mind.

I tilted my head as I stepped away from the bars—per Claire's request—and met the male's gaze. "You've been hurt by one of my kind." I could see it in the scars lurking in his spirit.

"Understatement," he grunted.

My lips curled. "I bet you and Cyrus get along famously."

Both Sol and Vox snorted at the mention of my brother, which only amused me more. Cyrus only knew how to rule, his royal blood providing him with the authority and power to do so. And he excelled at it by not putting up with petty bullshit.

Like past grievances that didn't apply to either of us.

Hmm, but with Sol, I bet he took a measured approach, not demanding he do anything at all while allowing him the false perception of making his own choices.

I shook my head. Cyrus was good. Very, very good.

Claire's elements whirled around her, a mixture of water and air building in her palm. "I'm going to blast the hinges," she said, focusing.

"Damn," Sol replied, arms folded. "I'd sort of like to see you burst through this door like you did upstairs."

"And hit the Spirit Royal in the face?" Vox asked, arching a brow. "Would definitely leave a mark."

Sol smiled. "Exactly."

"We've only just met and already you're making threats." I tsked. "And here I hoped we could function as a happy unit."

"Yeah? Talk to your ass of a brother about that." Sol's animosity clouded the air, suggesting I'd missed some sort of altercation.

"Shh," Claire murmured, her eyes closing. "I need to *hear*."

Energy singed the air, blowing her hair away from her face and painting her spirit in a warm glow that rivaled my own. I braced myself against the wall, sensing the building power, and grinned as she expertly honed in on the hinges of the door with a shock of ice. They froze instantly, then rattled beneath her onslaught of wind, cracking and inevitably shattering to the floor.

Sol reached over her with an open palm and sent the door crashing to the ground with a harsh shove.

Claire jumped over the iron and ran right for me. Her lips were on mine before I could speak, her arms winding around my neck and yanking me down to her for a hungry kiss. Our bond sparked to life, humming in approval at our shared touch and solidifying once more. We both knew how close we'd been to losing one another, how our connection nearly faded away into nothing. But neither of us had dwelled on it, too determined to fix the problem.

And that was the way it should be.

The way I always wanted it to be.

Claire responded in kind, accepting the third stage of our link with a bold thrust of her tongue into my waiting mouth. We had so much to go over, so many items to discuss, but it all paled in comparison to the near sense of loss.

Never again, she whispered. *I'm never losing you again.*

Took the words right out of my mind, baby. I deepened our kiss and grasped her hips to lift her into the air. Her legs wrapped around my hips as I braced her back against the wall and well and truly devoured her.

I missed you. The words were spoken by us both, simultaneously, over and over and over. Her body sung to mine, her mouth openly receiving my worship. Each swipe of her tongue invigorated my soul, giving me the strength I hadn't realized I needed and bringing me back to full health in an instant.

"Claire," I whispered, reverent. I wanted to do so much more than kiss her, but this wasn't the place. And we had an audience.

A *hungry* audience.

I could feel their desire for her through the bond. They were only in the initial stage, their courtship fragile, while her other three mates were already promised for eternity. That had the potential to create another imbalance, one Claire had only just fixed. But it was too soon for her to promise herself to them as well. I could sense it in her mind that she wanted more time to get to know them, to make sure it was what *they* wanted.

And with Sol, I could feel his absolute craving, his unwavering loyalty crafted over the last month of knowing who he considered to be his *little flower.* I rather liked that nickname and wondered if he'd spoken it out loud to her yet or not, because it seemed to be a recent blossom in his mind.

Hmm, but Vox, he remained uneasy. While he liked Claire, he wasn't yet satisfied with her motives. Primarily because he'd spent their entire relationship pushing her away, and he seemed to think he'd done too good a job.

I almost laughed.

It definitely showed he needed more time to get to know Claire, because once he did, he would see the stubborn female that lurked beneath.

She sighed against me, her sense of rightness palpable. "Take me back to our bed, Exos," she whispered. "Please."

My lips curled against hers. "Not even going to let me eat first?"

She froze, her eyes flashing wide, her nails an anchor against my shoulder. "Oh… Oh *God,* you're right! I'm mauling you when you probably—"

I silenced her with my mouth, pressing her harder against the wall and aligning my thickening arousal with the sweet spot between her legs. "Baby, I'm fine and only teasing."

A whine left her as I kissed her again, this time with all the fervor built up from the months of knowing her and *not* consummating our relationship. Oh, I'd tasted her—several times—but I'd yet to experience the sweet bliss of my cock sliding into her waiting heat.

And unfortunately, I had to wait even longer before I could fuck her.

Because I needed to work with Cyrus to determine the real threat.

It wasn't the mean girls who set up our Claire and made her appear too unstable to exist, but someone else. And the presence was at the tip of my thoughts, still hiding behind that sticky wall that didn't belong there.

Claire palmed the side of my head, her lips leaving mine, her gaze narrowing. "I feel it," she said, clearly having followed my thoughts. "It's..." She prodded it with her spirit, her brow furrowing. "I think—"

A piercing shriek had me flinching and almost dropping her.

Sol was suddenly there, his hands on Claire, trying to rip her from my arms.

I shook my head to clear it, holding on to her tightly, as the sound continued.

And then I realized it was coming from her.

"Let go!" Sol shouted.

I did immediately, my palms going to my aching skull as I doubled over from the negative energy scalding our connection.

Claire wept against Sol, Vox's hands roaming over her form for signs of injury.

"What did you do?" Sol demanded.

Even if I could have managed to speak, I'd have had no response to that. Because I didn't know. She was fine, and then she wasn't.

And *fuck* my head hurt.

I gripped my hair and fell to my knees, trying to solve the chaos going on in my mind. It felt as if I'd been splintered, the dark mass thriving inside and hissing in fury.

No. Not fury.

Hunger.

What. The. Fuck.

A hand on my shoulder had me flinching, but Vox held on tighter, his mouth moving with soundless words. All I could hear were Claire's screams.

Was that an apology on his lips?

I didn't—

His fist connected with my skull, sending me into a pit of darkness that was all too familiar.

Claire...

No response.
She'd cut me off.
And I had no idea why.

CHAPTER THIRTY-THREE
SOL

"WHY DID WE COME ALL THIS WAY to save this Spirit Fae bastard again?" I asked on a growl.

Vox rubbed his knuckles where he'd punched the royal in the face, knocking him out cold. The force needed to knock Exos out had required the use of Vox's wind.

Too bad I hadn't been able to get in my own hit.

The Spirit Fae would look awesome with an earth-infused blemish.

Yet one glance at Claire's pained expression as she rested against my chest, unconscious, stilled my violent desire. Whether I liked it or not, this was one of her mates.

Which meant I could never kill him.

"Because you believe in this mate circle-of-elements thing, right?" Vox muttered flatly, replying to my comment about retrieving Exos. "I doubt he did that on purpose. Whatever that was, it felt... wrong."

I nodded, having sensed it, too. An inky, dark void that had reached out just for Claire, clawing over my connection to her to embolden its strides. I hadn't liked how it felt at all, especially with my complete inability to stop it.

"We need to get them both back to the Spirit Quad," Vox surmised, glancing at me with that silver-rimmed gaze that burned with determination.

He'd finally opened up to Claire, even if just enough to feel what he could be for her, what she was to all of us. True mates compatible on the most intimate of levels.

He glanced down again at Claire in my arms. My grip on her instinctually tightened, wanting to protect her by using my own body as a shield against anything that would try to come at her again. "You're going to have to let her go," Vox murmured, giving me a sidelong smirk. "Before you crush her, that is."

I loosened my grip. "I can carry her. She hardly weighs anything."

Vox chuckled and pointed at the lopsided royal on the ground. "Well, he doesn't, and I'm not carrying him all the way back to the Spirit Quad." He glowered at me until I cursed.

"Then drag him," I suggested through my teeth.

Vox narrowed his eyes. "When Claire wakes up, she's going to expect Exos in one piece, and if I drag him through a day's worth of forest, she's not going to be very happy with us. Especially if she knows you refused to carry him."

Shit. He had a point.

"Fine," I grumbled and shifted Claire into his arms.

Vox used his air currents to settle her weight against him, making me envious of how, even in sleep, she wrapped her arms around his neck and nestled under his chin. Vox's breath caught at the movement.

"Don't get too comfortable," I warned him. "Whatever that thing was, it was waiting here for us. And whoever put it in Exos's head might be back to finish the job."

Vox glanced into the darkness around us and shivered. "Right. Let's go."

I stormed on ahead with Exos slung over my shoulder, making no attempt to still my power or make the royal comfortable.

He would already have a headache when he woke up. No one would question a few bruises.

CHAPTER THIRTY-FOUR
CYRUS

A TRAP.

The scent of it soiled the air as the Earth Fae dumped my brother's body at my feet. I cocked a brow at the giant. "You know, at some point, we're going to need to work through your Spirit Fae issue."

He snorted, but it lacked heat as his eyes were on Claire in Vox's arms. Her head rested against the Air Fae's chest, her eyes closed in a fitful sleep.

I'd felt her panic as if it were my own, the terror an ice cube down my spine. It had sent me misting back to Spirit Quad with Titus hot on my heels, only to find the dorm empty.

Once I'd pinpointed her location, I sensed Vox and Sol already on their way back and advised the fiery redhead to calm down and wait.

He'd responded with a fireball to my head.

One that I'd doused in a tidal wave that had left him sputtering.

If I'd learned anything from today's experience, it was that Titus served as an excellent sparring partner. Once Exos woke up, I would share the news.

Hmm, but this trap...

I crouched before his prone form and palmed the side of his head.

"I wouldn't do that," Vox warned. "That's exactly how Claire ended up unconscious."

347

Well, I'm not Claire, I thought, ignoring his caution and driving my spirit essence into my brother's psyche to have a look around. Something in his essence stirred a foul note in the air, adding a hint of pollution in his aura that shouldn't be there. Claire must have gone searching as well, her instincts driving her to heal her mate. But unlike my little queen, I knew not to touch things that didn't belong.

Like that inky abyss crawling about in my brother's mind.

"Hmm," I murmured, assessing the scathing energy hissing about at my presence. It almost appeared to have scales, the dark magic reaching out with claws, searching for the spirit it truly craved.

Claire.

"Exos was left alone on purpose," I said, my eyes closed as I continued to dance with the foreign presence inside my brother's mind. "The culprit wanted Claire to find him."

Which explained why she'd been able to suddenly pick up his location when she couldn't only a month ago. I'd wrongly assumed it was the enhancement of her elements. But no. It was all part of this wicked being's plan.

That was two traps I'd fallen for.

There would not be a third.

"My brother's mind has been infected with the same essence that attempted to overcome Claire in the death fields. That's why she reacted. And from what I can see, she fought back when it tried to grab on to her again." The evidence lurked in the bubbling texture—they appeared to be wounds of a sort, similar to the ones marking Sol's aura. Only, unlike Sol's, these weren't scarring. "I think she damaged it permanently"—which impressed me a great deal—"but she also hurt Exos."

"Can you blame her?" Vox demanded, sounding defensive.

"Not at all." I unwove myself from Exos's essence and opened my eyes. "And he won't, either." The harm to the foreign presence might be irreparable, but Exos would be fine. Once I helped him remove that entity, anyway. I ran my fingers through my hair and sighed. "I need to take Exos home to deal with this. We can't risk that infection spreading to Claire."

"Infection?" Sol repeated, his skin losing color. "Like the plague?"

I'd not really considered the similarities, but I supposed they were there.

Unknown essence.

Element devouring energy, rendering the body useless.

But it worked slower, didn't deteriorate the shell so much as the soul within.

"Not quite," I said slowly, still considering. "But I see what you're saying." I really needed Exos back up and running to bounce some ideas off of. He was the one who tended to see through puzzles; I merely dictated how to unravel them. "It's not the same, because I can remove it," I added. "But I need to do that away from Claire."

Because I didn't want to risk it seeking her out again.

Wait...

"It's attracted to Claire," I continued, rubbing the back of my neck. "That thing in the death fields only attacked her, not me. And it just did it again through Exos's mind. So no, it's not the plague but seems to be something designed just to hurt her." Which sounded insane, but the facts were right there before us. "It's not even hurting Exos, just appears to be muddling his memories."

"So get it out of his head and report back with whoever did this to him." Titus—the man of profound reason—repeating what I essentially already stated.

"That's the idea," I replied. "But I can't guarantee it won't seek Claire out again as soon as Exos wakes up. I mean, it didn't before, but now that they've enhanced their connection, it's possible it will go straight for her." Which—of course—was why Exos had closed himself off for so long. To protect Claire from that foreign essence. He must have thought it was gone, thereby reaching out to her.

"Do you need him awake to remove it?" Vox wondered, still holding Claire tightly to his chest.

"Yes." Whatever black magic put that thing in my brother's mind was going to take a lot of elemental fae power to remove. "But if you keep Claire occupied with her other elements, then it won't be able to access her as easily."

Titus folded his arms. "Occupied?"

"Distracted," I tried again. When all three males stared at me for more, I muttered a curse under my breath and tried for the third time. "Ground her in air, earth, and fire, guys. Fuck her. Spar with her. Make her use magic. I don't care how you do it, just consume her in her non-spirit elements so she's too busy to reach out to Exos. Got it?"

Sol's jaw was on the ground.

Vox appeared as brittle as a glass vase.

And Titus merely smirked. "Yeah, that I can do."

Well, at least one of them had the confidence to satisfy her appetite for the elements. "When she wakes, comfort her and tell her Exos is fine. Explain what we're doing. Then initiate whatever *distraction* you want, but make it good." I met Titus's gaze on that one. "I'm going to need time. You feel me?"

"We can exhaust her," Titus promised, a wicked gleam in his emerald gaze. "You weren't the first to taste her, Fae King. I'm very familiar with her appetites."

If he meant to bother me, he didn't. My mother had two mates. My father had re-mated after my mother died, but not after several potential bonds crossed his path first. I was not shy when it came to sex or sharing a woman.

And I went into this fully aware that Claire needed five mates.

So all I could do was smile. "Good. See that it's done. And help these guys, would you? They're still gaping at me like fish out of water."

Sol growled. "I know how to handle a female."

"Excellent," I replied, bending to pick up Exos and tossing him over my shoulder before meeting the big guy's gaze. "Then handle Claire. She's quite fond of oral sex. Start there."

Of course those were the words she chose to stir on.

I shook my head with a laugh. "See? Even the comment causes her to wake." I started walking, needing to get my brother away from her before she reached full consciousness. "Have fun, boys."

CHAPTER THIRTY-FIVE
CLAIRE

THE FRESH SCENT OF THE OCEAN tickled my senses. *Cyrus,* I sighed.

Yes, little queen, he murmured, his amusement a seductive stroke against my inner thighs.

I never thought we'd be in this situation, where I desired him, but I didn't see the point in fighting it. Did he piss me off? Yes. But he also made me scream for hours on end in the best way. And I craved so much more.

Ah, alas, you'll need to rely on your other mates tonight, he whispered. *I need to tend to Exos.*

My eyes flew open. *Exos?*

He's okay, Cyrus promised. *Whoever captured him planted a trap in his mind, similar to the one in the death fields.*

Yes. I blinked up at Vox, who was gazing down at me in bemusement. "Hi," I squeaked, confused. Titus stood at his side, with Sol behind me, but it was Vox's arms holding me in the air.

Let them take care of you, Cyrus urged. *I'll look after Exos.*

How? I wondered.

"Are you all right, sweetheart?" Titus stroked a flame across my cheek, heating my cool skin.

By destroying the foreign entity in his mind, Cyrus replied. *Go be with your mates,*

351

little queen. We'll return to you soon.

"Claire?" Titus sounded concerned.

I cleared my throat. "I... hold on." *Don't let that thing attack you, Cyrus. It's strong.* The second I'd felt it trying to tug me under, I'd lashed out at it with everything I could. That it'd left me unconscious afterward had me a bit concerned. *I need more training on defensive elements.*

Hmm, yes, you do. But in this case, the essence appears to be designed for you, Claire. It merely hissed at my presence in his mind.

Designed for me? I repeated, my skin heating from where Titus caressed my face and down to my neck, his gaze holding mine. *This is confusing.* Because I felt Cyrus in my head, but Titus, Sol, and Vox were very much here, their hands all on me now.

Go engage your other elements, Cyrus said, his tone holding a demand. *We'll update you when we know more, but for now, I need you to focus on the others while I help my brother. Trust me, little queen. Trust me to fix this.*

I do. I meant it. If I trusted Exos's fate to anyone, it was Cyrus. *I just...*

Don't think, just do, he encouraged. *Embrace your fae, Claire. You'll enjoy it more.*

"Is she talking to Cyrus?" Sol's rumble vibrated my back, his palm clasping the side of my neck. That was the second time he'd caught me in a protective stance. I rather liked it.

"Yes," Titus replied. "I can't hear them, but I feel his water bond heavy in her mind."

"He's telling me about Exos," I explained, swallowing. "Whatever that thing is, it tried to suck me back into a black hole again, but I fought it."

And you did so well, Cyrus whispered, pride evident in his tone. *I'm going to leave you now and tend to Exos. I'll be thinking of you, my little queen, and how you sound when you come.*

Heat suffused my skin. *Cyrus.*

His chuckle slid up and down my spine, sending splashes of yearning to every nerve receptor before he pulled away from my thoughts.

My thighs clenched as a surge of warmth ruined my panties.

Damn Water Fae.

Whoever claimed hate and lust were related emotions deserved an award because, boy, were they right. I didn't want to be attracted to Cyrus, and I sensed he felt the same way, but here we were, mated for life.

You adore me, he teased.

I thought you were leaving, I grumbled.

I am, but I had to make sure you were in the right frame of mind to indulge your other elements. And now that you are... enjoy.

Another hot flash graced my skin, setting me on fire—literally. Vox dropped me into Titus's waiting arms, where he soothed the flames with a few of his own. I doused myself in water in an attempt to cool myself off, but it didn't help. If anything, it made me burn hotter.

I groaned into Titus's chest.

"Claire?" Sol's grip on my nape tightened, his earth essence somehow blocking the inferno cascading along my spine.

"I just need a moment," I managed, my throat dry.

"I think you need longer than a minute," Titus whispered, his lips at my ear. "Let us take care of you, sweetheart."

Ugh, it would be so easy to give in to him. But what about Exos? It seemed wrong to, well, *play*, while he suffered from whatever had corrupted his mind.

I'll be fine, he whispered, his conscious barely brushing mine. *Let them distract you, princess. Only Cyrus can help me now, and we will destroy this thing. See you soon.*

He left before I could reply, his essence stroking my heart along the way.

A distraction, I realized. That was what they were trying to do, to keep me occupied while Cyrus and Exos worked through his mind. Because whatever had consumed him was a threat to me.

I understood now.

They needed me otherwise engaged, to prevent my links to them both from interfering.

"Maybe you should take her back to your room?" Vox suggested, his lips twisting, his uncertainty written in the lines of his shoulders.

Sol grunted. "Not a chance. We're in this together and I need you. Remember?"

Vox met the eyes of the Earth Fae, who seemed to be forever at my back—a protective rock who wouldn't budge.

How times have changed, I thought, a little delirious but also extremely intrigued. *What would the three of them do to me in bed?*

My thighs squeezed together again, tighter, and Titus's knowing gaze twinkled with interest.

"She's not ready," Vox replied. "I mean, this is all so new. And three of us? Let's just let her do what she's used to and play this slow."

I frowned. *Why is he rejecting me?* "Who are you to tell me I'm not ready?" I poked him in the chest.

"I think he's still sour over the ball," Sol said, a teasing note in his voice.

Vox narrowed his gaze. "Could you not bring that up right now?"

"What's the big deal about this ball?" I asked, flabbergasted. "I mean, I'll take you both. Heck, I'll take all three of you."

"Not me," Titus replied, his tone amused. "I'm banned, but you should absolutely take Vox and Sol."

"Banned?" I repeated. Then shook my head. That wasn't the point. Vox kept rejecting me, and I didn't understand it. "We'll all go."

"Oh, don't change your plans on my account," Vox drawled, clearly unimpressed with my offer.

Seriously? What more does this guy want?

I kissed him earlier. Wasn't that enough to prove I liked him? Or did I need to do more to convince him this wasn't just a temporary thing for me?

The realization of this being *it*, our circle finally being complete, sent my heart racing.

I don't want anyone else. These are my fae. And damn it, I'm keeping them.

My fire died, replaced by wind. Vox's nostrils flared as my power wrapped around him, forcing him to acknowledge me. I reached for him, my fingers sliding into the loose strands of his thick hair as I yanked him down for a kiss.

Mine, I thought at him. *You're mine.*

CHAPTER THIRTY-SIX
VOX

CLAIRE HAD KISSED ME BEFORE, but not like this, not with complete abandonment of her other elements. She might as well have dropped all her clothes for the impact it had on me, leaving me stunned.

Titus and Sol both stiffened at the sudden change, but they didn't interfere. Instead, they encouraged her, their touches soft against her back as she embraced magic that sang only for me.

Her melody whispered through my senses, singing a song of the ancients that called to my element and made me ache for her.

Her magic knocked at my soul, and this time, I let her in as I gave in to the need to taste her. I would have been a fool not to graze my tongue across hers and indulge in the song she played so sweetly just for me.

"You're mine, Vox," she whispered, tangling her fingers into my hair as she pulled me down to her again. "*You.* No other Air Fae, Vox. You are who I trust and who I want. I choose *you.*"

My lips hovered over hers as her breath mingled with mine, but she didn't close the gap. Instead, she waited for my move.

I chose to explore what she offered. This was a true mate bond, one unlike anything I'd felt in all my years. I'd come across a handful of fae who'd tried to tempt me, who might have guessed at the raw power I hid from the world, but the truth was that I didn't trust anyone enough to set it free. I had royal blood in my veins, and that made me dangerous. I stayed in control because I kept that power in check, but what Claire offered me was a life without restraint.

Freedom.

Her air flirted with mine as her fingers went to my school robes, coaxing them past my shoulders with a breeze that had my skin pebbling.

"You're not the only one who's afraid," she murmured, the blues of her irises darkening. She was allowing her affinity for air to come out and dominate her, pushing her fae half to the surface. The element felt hungry, starved even, and was entirely focused on me.

A gust of wind lifted her golden hair, sending the curls sweeping away to reveal her nape before lashing out to rattle the walls with warning. Titus glanced at me, but the power wasn't mine, and I was afraid to add more of my element to her reserves. While she craved it, I recognized the same lack of control I'd seen in Sol. I'd always treated that as a weakness, something to be contained and monitored.

Reaching around her, I gripped Titus by the wrist and brought him closer, placing his hand on her hip. I did the same with Sol and watched her visibly relax as their touch worked magic into her, grounding her with balance.

This was how ultimate power was meant to be controlled—not contained, but sated.

"I've been wrong all this time," I marveled, reevaluating all my previous notions. "Power isn't meant to be suppressed."

"It's meant to be set free," Claire finished for me, smiling as her fingers swept loving touches over my face.

"What do you want to do, sweetheart?" Titus whispered, his fire roaming over the thin fabric of her tank top.

"I…" She swallowed, her gaze holding mine. "This is new for me."

"Us, too," Sol replied, a chuckle in his voice. "I mean, not the female part. The, uh, group part."

His slight hesitation seemed to put her at ease, because her eyes twinkled. "I like the way you all make me feel," she admitted, glancing around before refocusing on me. "I want to explore more." Her fingers returned to my face as she kissed me again, her nails sliding to the back of my neck to hold me as if she thought I might let her go.

Not that I ever could.

Not with her tongue stroking mine like *that*.

But she was right.

I wanted more, too.

I deepened our embrace, allowing her to feel my yearning, and smiled as Titus's fire slowly tracked down her spine—singeing the fabric in his wake.

Claire didn't shy away from it, or perhaps didn't notice it. And when Sol gripped the loose strap on one shoulder, she didn't stop him. Titus took the other, and together they unveiled her perfect breasts to my view.

I exhaled slowly, feathering my breath across her skin to swirl around her dusky nipples.

"Vox," she whispered, the word a plea.

This time, I obeyed.

My lips followed the traces of my exhale, running a wet line down her nape and over the crest of one breast. She arched into me, and I sucked her taut peak into my mouth, eliciting a cry from deep within her throat.

An explosion of air followed, whirling around us.

She needed more. So. Much. More.

My hands fell to her hips, pushing her back into Sol's solid form. He immediately grasped her shoulders, causing her lids to flutter closed.

Power.

The best kind of distraction.

"Titus," I said, running my fingers along the top of her jeans.

He smiled, sending a flicker of flame down the seams on either side of her legs. She sighed beneath the energy, completely unfazed by him undressing her. She'd tilted her head back to receive Sol's kiss, her mouth parting for him. One of his palms slid to grasp her throat, holding her to him as he indulged her thoroughly.

I concentrated on her exposed curves, swirling energy around her stiff peaks and teasing her pale skin. Then I sent the breeze lower to peel away her now loose pants.

"Claire," I breathed, shocked to find her bare beneath.

Beautiful.

Smooth.

Perfection.

She shivered, only to sigh as Titus ran a wave of heat over her skin. His power mingled with mine over her breasts, an indication for me to move lower—and I did.

I went to my knees, kissing her along the way.

Her fingers wove into my hair again, her opposite hand seeming to reach for Titus.

A cohesive unit, coming together, in one elemental tornado.

I never would have expected this. Never thought to desire it. But now I knew that I'd never dream of anything but this.

"Taste her," Titus urged me, then took her away from Sol for a kiss of his own.

I met the Earth Fae's burning gaze over her shoulder, saw the raw need flourishing inside him, the desire for him to watch me indulge Claire.

And I couldn't resist.

Both for him and for me, and even for her.

Fuck. She tasted like those fruit trees he kept planting. *Peaches.* And, oh God, I needed more. I slid my tongue through her folds, drinking my fill of her sweetness and reveling in the tremors my strokes elicited from her core.

Her moan thickened my cock.

Her throaty purr excited my heart.

And the way she gave herself over to the three of us had my soul soaring.

For the first time in my life, I felt free.

Complete.

Where I needed to be.

And it was on my knees, worshiping this goddess of a fae with my tongue.

Chapter Thirty-Seven
Claire

I'D NEVER FELT ANYTHING LIKE THIS BEFORE. So many elements tugged at me, begging me to devour and to be devoured.

Titus caressed me with licks of tantalizing flames across my bare chest.

Sol kissed me again, this time harder, his palm locked around my neck.

And Vox.

Oh, *fuck*, Vox.

His tongue unraveled me below, causing my hips to undulate in the most wanton of ways. And while part of me couldn't believe I'd just indulged myself in a foursome, my fae side overruled.

This was my life now. Where I should be. With these males. And I wouldn't have it any other way.

The world around me began to crumble, pleasure overcoming right and wrong, as Vox's mouth sent me soaring into the clouds of ecstasy. So different from the others, and yet just as consuming in an entirely unique way. His air magic caressed mine, intensifying our connection and amplifying the moment, and when I finally opened my eyes, it was to find him grinning up at me. The silver band around his irises practically glowed, so full of power—power I felt bolstering my own.

And then I was kissing Sol again. His grip felt possessive and right around my throat, but I craved more. His opposite palm finally went to my breast, his hips pressing into my backside. The impressive length of his erection sent a thrill down my spine, spiking my curiosity. He was a big man. Rock hard, too. And I wondered how far that trait stretched...

My palm slid backward, exploring his muscled thigh, making me wish the men were as naked as me.

Titus seemed to sense my unspoken desire, because I *felt* him remove his shirt, the heat of his skin basking against mine. Then he took one of my nipples into his mouth while Vox continued to play between my legs, and the room spun once more.

So much pleasure.

So much sensation.

So much *power.*

I felt it swirling around me, the energy invigorating my soul. *I no longer feel human,* I realized. I felt... *fae.*

And I... I loved it.

Sol released me to Titus, his tongue sliding inside as his hand replaced the one previously grasping my throat, and Vox's mouth left my warmth below.

They didn't give me a moment to question it, all three of them guiding me toward the bedroom. Clothes seemed to be disappearing as we moved. And it should have terrified me, but I didn't feel an ounce of fear. Only acceptance.

My mates.

It had to be fae magic overruling reason. But Cyrus was right. In this world, I could indulge without judgment.

Yes.

The soft mattress of my bed met my back, Titus stepping away to unfasten his jeans without removing them.

Sol had lost his shirt.

Vox, too.

But all of them still had on their pants, their hungry gazes roaming over my body.

"This feels unfair," I said, narrowing my gaze.

Sol's lips quirked upward. "Not from where I'm standing, little flower." He pressed his palms to my knees, spreading them wide. "It seems more than fair to me."

"Yeah?" Titus tried to play a similar game with me in the kitchen once. He'd lost. And Sol would, too.

He jumped as I sent a shower of fire over his pants, destroying the fabric while leaving his skin unscathed.

I started to smile until I realized I'd removed *all* of his clothes.

Oh. My. God.

I had expected him to be large, but... *damn.*

Sol made no move to cover himself. Nor did he seem put off by my expression. If anything, it only deepened his smirk as he crawled onto the bed—directly over me.

"Rushing things?" he asked, his lips brushing mine.

"She does that," Titus said, kneeling on the bed beside us while Vox circled to the other side.

Vox ran a finger across my cheek, his gaze kind. "Don't be afraid."

Oh, I wasn't afraid.

I was in awe.

My hand slid between me and Sol, unerringly finding his shaft and giving it a sturdy stroke. His smirk fell on a hiss, his forehead dropping to my neck. *"Claire."*

"As I said, she's good at rushing," Titus murmured, his flame dancing along my lips. "And here I thought the three of us could indulge you for hours."

Oh, yes, please. "Who says you can't?" I asked, batting my eyes at him.

His lips curled. "So needy, my Claire."

"*Our* Claire," Vox corrected, a stroke of cool wind meeting my wet flesh below.

I arched in response, my grip on Sol tightening and eliciting a growl from deep within his throat. *"Fuck."*

Vox's energy slithered through the bonds, his protective instincts warming the connection between me and Sol. *Testing his control,* I realized, marveling at how attuned the two of them were to one another. I explored the link, curious, and paused as Sol's intense need consumed my senses.

Oh, wow...

He needed a lot more than my stroke.

Which gave me a wicked idea.

Because that cock... *mmm.*

I nudged him to his back, which took some effort considering his size, and kissed a path down the muscular planes of his chest and abdomen. His copper eyes watched my progression, his irises inflaming into dark pools of need as he realized my intent. Even Vox watched, transfixed by my motions, his own desire palpable.

And Titus.

My beautiful Titus.

He stood naked now by the bed, his palm lazily stroking his erection as he observed my descent.

I held his gaze for a long moment, recalling a conversation between him and Exos about them being okay with sharing me so long as they didn't have to watch me provide pleasure to the other.

But he seemed fine now. Aroused, even. More so than I'd ever seen him.

And his smile gave me the courage I needed to continue.

This is... amazing.

I had no other word for it.

Maybe *dream* would do. Because for a moment, I struggled to believe any of this was real, until my mouth closed around the bulbous head of Sol's cock. Because that had to be real. It was too big, too thick, to be fake.

And, oh my, this would be fun inside me later. Maybe not tonight, but at some point. Hopefully.

For now, I indulged in tasting him.

Stroking my tongue up and down his massive length and trying to take as much of him as I could into my mouth.

He groaned, my name a warning on the air as energy sizzled around us. Vox was already there, stroking the power, issuing his brand of control, but it wasn't what Sol needed.

I met his gaze—a gaze that had turned a metallic copper as his element seeped from him in broken, golden tendrils. I'd opened some sort of deeper connection, one tied directly to our consummating of the first level of our bond, and he seemed to be struggling to maintain it. The ground trembled, warning that if Sol didn't find an outlet soon, he would release the magic into the world.

Magic meant for me.

With a firm grip on his shaft, I ran my tongue up the length of him, eliciting a deep noise that made my insides curl with pleasure. His hands fisted at his sides as he struggled to keep control, tugging hard on Vox's energy that kept that door latched closed and not blown wide open.

Hmm, that won't do.

I sensed what he needed, understood it on a supernatural level after bonding with water, spirit, and fire.

Sol needed to unravel.

To push his element into mine and receive some of my earth magic in return.

And the only way to do that was to make him feel comfortable. To ease him into the earthquake waiting to erupt.

I took as much of him in my mouth as I could fit, running the length of him into my throat and then licking my way up and over the head, lapping at the salty droplet that formed.

"Claire," he warned, his control slipping as the ground shook again.

Not enough, some part of me whispered. *More.*

And not just from Sol.

No.

I needed Vox.

His wild eyes met mine, his thirst palpable. He *liked* what I was doing to Sol, and given the way he stroked himself through his pants, he was imagining me doing the same to him.

Only, that was not where I wanted him.

Fuck, this is wanton, I thought. But I pushed the human voice down, chasing my elements through the fae realm instead.

And said what I needed to say.

"I need you inside me, Vox."

His eyes flashed with hesitation, but Titus sent a gust of heat to slap some sense into him. "Trust her," he said, no doubt in his voice. He knew what I wanted to do. He sensed how my elements were screaming at a fever pitch, and I could leash all of my mates to my desires if they just gave in to me. It didn't matter how powerful they all were.

I could show them freedom like they'd never known.

How, I couldn't say.

I just knew I could.

Vox swallowed but slipped out of the remainder of his clothes, revealing a lithe, muscular body that made my mouth water. Dark hair unfurled over his shoulders, and dark eyes watched me with unmatched attention. Even his cock was graceful, arching just slightly at an angle that I knew would feel heavenly inside of me.

He joined us on the bed, his hands clasping my hips. "You're sure?" he asked, his eyes alight with a fresh need that rivaled Sol's.

Sol, who was looking down at me in awe as he balanced himself on his elbows.

Oh...

Could I contain them all?

"Yes," I breathed, pressing my backside into Vox as I took Sol deep into my mouth.

"For the love of the fae," Vox whispered, his arousal meeting mine.

And then he was there.

Entering me.

Filling me to completion.

And unleashing a pleasurable storm inside of me, reminiscent of a hurricane. His knowing fingers found my clit as he set a rhythm, one that rivaled my mouth. He breathed out a gust of rapture, his magic sweeping over me and sending my hair flying.

I captured that power and pushed it into Sol.

The giant of a man groaned when I stroked down hard, following my fingers with my mouth. I reached for Titus as my tongue tasted the earth, copper and peach mixing with the blissful motes of air that fueled my body as Vox increased his thrusts, sliding in and out of me, his control losing its distinct edge as he panted, his pleasure slipping through our bond as he let go and trusted me to hold on to the three strands of elemental power that sank their teeth into me.

Yes.

I found Titus's cock ready for me, hot against my fingers that had been cooled with Vox's power. I pumped him hard, twisting to follow my movements with my mouth. Titus groaned and his fire burst into the air, engulfing all three of us in a cocoon of warmth and making my skin glow red.

Vox reached around my middle and hauled me against his chest, his lips going to my neck as he continued to thrust into me, his pants hot against my ear as his air took on Titus's element.

With me as the conduit, they could share their power and gain the balance that settled into my very being.

Sol sensed what I was doing and loosened his control another fraction, stirring a quake in the most intimate of places between my legs and forcing me closer to the edge of oblivion. His fingers wove through my hair as he joined me on that ledge, his yearning taking over, and danced with me on the precipice.

So close.

My body screamed with the need, my elements roaring through my system.

But it was Titus grabbing my breast that sent us all crashing over into a maelstrom of euphoria. Male groans rent the air, the ground literally shifting around us as fire consumed the room, only to be wrapped up in Vox's tornado of an element, and grounding us in a heaping pile on the bed.

I shook, my limbs practically numb from the intensity. My lips swollen. My body well used.

"Claire," Titus breathed reverently, pulling me toward his sweaty chest. "You're…"

My skin glimmered with a contortion of elements. Fire, wind, and earth sent a rainbow of color cascading through the room, and my breath misted the air with sparkling power. My ears itched at the tips, and I palmed at one absently, finding it pointed.

My inner fae had finally taken over.

I'm no longer Claire.

I was passion, wild, taming the three elements that threatened to explode. And I craved more.

I wanted Sol inside me next. Titus in my mouth. And Vox in my hands.

I said as much out loud, eliciting masculine chuckles through the bedroom, which gave way to heated gazes and warm touches. Because they wanted it, too.

Mine.

You are all mine.

Chapter Thirty-Eight
Exos

I'M REALLY FUCKING TIRED of being knocked out and manipulated by other entities in my head. I glowered at my reflection, talking to the foreign essence maintaining residence in my skull.

"Yes, that helps," Cyrus drawled, sounding bored.

"You're not the one with black magic in your damn mind," I reminded him, my voice a low growl of annoyance.

We'd tried several old spirit methods, most of which involved Cyrus sending blasts of elemental energy into my brain. By the time we finished that, my neural cavities resembled the aftermath of tunneling pixies in the Earth Fae mines.

I swallowed another gulp of my spritemead and slammed the mug down on the counter. "Again."

"Are you saying that because you're drunk off the mead, or are you a closet masochist?" Cyrus's icy gaze sparkled with challenge, his goading meant to distract me from the pain he was about to unleash on my spirit.

"Don't flirt with me. Just do—*fuck*!" Lights flashed behind my eyes, sending me to my knees. Oh, if I ever found out who put this nasty piece of darkness in my head, I would enjoy killing them. Over and over and over again.

I massaged my temples and tried futilely to help Cyrus. He used my power to bolster his own, causing me to cringe as he detonated a particularly harsh attack inside my being.

The inky thing roared back at him, clinging to me with sludgy claws that made me gag.

"Almost there," Cyrus said, totally full of shit. I could feel how thick the thing in my skull was, and he hadn't even sawed through half of it.

Cyrus yanked out so sharply that I gasped.

"I have it," he said.

"No, you fucking don't," I rasped, hating him almost as much as that muck in my head. "It's still there, id—"

A spiritual punch to the black wall left me winded, and a second had me curling into the fetal position. I wanted to demand him to stop, but he seemed hell-bent on whatever method he'd enlisted and he was drawing on so much of my energy that I couldn't block him even if I wanted to.

My vision swam, the walls of our home blurring.

But I felt the crack splintering through my mind.

A whine came from inside, escaping through my throat, as Cyrus mentally beat the darkness to a pulp. Until it sputtered and sizzled and died in a pool of inky fluid that he sucked out of my spirit and sent to the floor beside me.

"Dark Fae magic," he growled, spitting on the dying substance. "Whoever did this is playing with forbidden arts."

Of a land none of our kind ever ventured into, I thought, unable to speak above my panting breaths.

"No wonder it felt like a fucking vampire," Cyrus continued, his disgust evident. "Because that thing was created by one. And I think that thing in the death fields may have been a Dark Fae, or the spirit of one."

What he said made sense.

Except I didn't understand why.

Until suddenly I did.

Because my memories were finally free.

I sat up despite the ache in my skull and forced my mouth to function. "Mortus." It came out croaky.

"He took you?"

I nodded, then shook my head, and then nodded again, trying to clear my throat.

"Yes, that clears everything up, brother. Thank you." Cyrus, the perpetual smart-ass, handed me my spritemead. "Drink that. You make more sense while drunk."

Jackass. I snatched the mug from his hand and gulped several swallows while he watched with a touch of impatience.

Right. Because one could just recover immediately after hours of mental torment and allowing another to use his energy.

I took another sip just to piss him off and smiled when he rolled his eyes.

"It was Mortus," I clarified, wiping my mouth with the back of my hand. "But he's being controlled."

"By...?" Cyrus prompted, waving a hand.

"Ophelia." I met his widening eyes. "Claire's mother has turned Dark Fae, and it would appear that she's very much alive."

"You're sure?" he asked, his voice holding a hint of disbelief.

I dipped my chin in the affirmative. "Now that I can properly think again, I recognize the essence. It feels so much like Claire, but darker."

"And she's fixated on our little queen as well," Cyrus added, his eyebrows lifting. "That's why it holds similar properties to the plague, but different."

"It would seem it's all connected, yes."

"And that Ophelia somehow survived, and by bringing Claire to the Academy..."

"We awoke a dormant beast," I finished for him. "Yes."

"Fuck," he breathed, glancing at the acid-like substance eating through our stone floor. I flicked a flame over it, needing the shit to burn and disappear. "This is bad."

I snorted. "Understatement of the century, brother."

"Has she been controlling Mortus all this time?"

"It's possible." The fae never had seemed right, but I'd chalked it up to his dark history. "But I'm more interested in figuring out how an Elemental Fae turned Dark Fae." They were usually born, their world far different from ours. They required blood to survive—hence, vampires. And they lived without sunlight, something our kind thrived on, which was why trapping an Elemental Fae underground for too long could kill one.

"That is an odd development," Cyrus agreed, scratching his jaw. "But who knows what happened while she was up in the Human Realm?"

"True," I agreed. The Dark Fae liked playing with humans; the whole blood and drinking thing really got them off. I blew out a breath, rubbing my face. "Dude, I need a shower."

"No shit?" Cyrus feigned shock. "It's only been a few weeks."

"When I'm done, I want to see Claire." I could feel her happiness through the bond, her lazy energy telling me exactly how her other mates had distracted her. My heart warmed, my spirit rolling in her bliss. "Do you regret it?" I wondered out loud, pausing at the exit of the living area.

Cyrus glanced up at me, his own spritemead a breath away from his lips. He didn't need me to clarify, his thoughts almost always in tune with mine. "I expected to," he admitted. "But no. No, I don't."

"Would you change the way it happened?"

He chuckled. "I'm pretty sure it was the only way it could have happened."

I nodded, understanding immediately. "She didn't like you."

"Not one bit."

"Good," I replied. "She needed someone to break through the human shell and unleash the fae beneath."

His lips curled. "You're welcome."

So arrogant, my brother. But I couldn't help my resulting laugh.

Because yeah. We all had him to thank. Seeing that Claire had finally embraced her inner fae.

I sighed, both overjoyed and distraught.

Because I wasn't sure which news I wanted to break to her less—that her mother was alive and causing chaos or that Claire had awoken a fae circle so powerful that it proved all the prophecies about her correct.

My precious Halfling was no longer a princess.

No.

Soon, she would be crowned Elemental Fae Queen.

She just didn't know it yet.

EPILOGUE
CLAIRE

A WARMTH CARESSED MY HEART, causing me to stir among the heavy limbs in my bed. Or was it our bed? I really didn't know anymore. We all had our own rooms, including Titus, but he never slept in his quarters, only mine. So it felt like a shared space. And now it was littered with male limbs.

Vox in front of me, Sol yet again at my back, and Titus between my legs using my thigh as a pillow.

I can't move, I thought.

A chuckle ran through my mind, the sound adoring and so very missed. *Exos.*

I'm here.

I sighed, my lips curling. *I miss you.*

Then come get me, he murmured. *I'm in the hallway.*

I shot upright, causing Sol to grumble and Vox's eyes to fly open. "What is it?"

Titus nuzzled into my leg, then shifted a little to release me. "Exos is back," he said, his voice deep with sleep. "Go ahead, Claire. We'll be here."

Sol's hand moved from my upper thigh to his own leg, his nonverbal way of granting approval to move. And Vox rolled to his back. I tried to slide over him to get out of the bed, but he caught me by the hip. His fingers threaded through my hair as his mouth captured mine in a mind-bending kiss

369

reminiscent of the hours we spent in bed.

How is this my life? I wondered, awed.

When he finally released me, I almost forgot what I wanted to do. Then I felt Exos's tug again, a patient presence underlined in authority.

"I'll be back," I whispered.

"I know," Vox replied, nipping my bottom lip. "I'll be here."

He kissed me again, gentler this time, his tongue lazily stroking mine, before helping me to stand. Titus and Sol had already passed out again, completely at ease. Vox shifted to his side, tucking his arm under his head, as he watched me pad to the door.

I slipped into Titus's robe—an item I really needed to procure for myself—and met Exos in the hallway. He wore one of his elegant suits, his blond hair stylishly gelled, as if he were about to attend a meeting of some kind.

Yet the clock on the wall said it was just after four in the morning.

"There are some formal ceremonies I need to attend," he explained, sensing my confusion. He cupped my cheek and brushed his thumb over my bottom lip. "Will you come with me?"

"Are you… Is everything okay?" I asked, leaning into his touch.

He nodded. "Cyrus destroyed the essence in my mind."

Yes. I'd felt as much when he reached out to me. He felt clean. Like my Exos. And now that I saw him, I could see he was completely back to normal. Fae certainly healed quickly. "What was it?" I wondered out loud.

"Something I want to talk to you about," he admitted. "Which is why I want you to come with me today."

"Where?"

"To the Spirit Kingdom."

I shuddered, not ready to experience that again. But I had to ask: "Why?"

"It's time to take my rightful place as the Spirit King. And I'd like you by my side when I do it."

I blinked. "What? What about Cyrus?"

"He'll be there, too." Exos leaned down to replace his thumb with his lips and kissed me softly. "There's so much we need to explain, Claire. And I would prefer to do it in the Spirit Kingdom. Please."

"What about the others? And the Solstice Ball?" That had to be coming up soon. And why was I fixated on that above everything else? "I promised to go with Sol and Vox," I clarified, deciding that was a good reason. Well, we hadn't really finalized it. But it was definitely happening.

Exos's lips curled. "I'll have you back in time for the ball, Claire. In addition to your classes, as I understand you've missed a few."

"Been a little busy trying not to die," I pointed out.

"Yes, I understand the feeling." His palm slid to the back of my neck. "Please come with me, Claire. I need you to understand what it means to be a Royal Fae." *Because you're becoming one,* I heard him whisper, the words a haunting statement in my mind.

"I…" I glanced at his suit and frowned. "Do you want me to wear my Academy clothes?"

He chuckled. "No. I have a gown for you, princess. One that will make you look like a queen."

I swallowed. "You'll tell me what to do?"

"When have I not?" he teased, nipping my lower lip.

"True," I agreed, amused. "Okay. But I need to tell the others."

"Of course. Just one thing first."

I stared into his ocean-blue eyes. "Anything."

"Mmm, I was hoping you'd say that." He pulled me even closer, one hand tightly holding my neck while his other pressed into my lower back. And then his mouth took mine in a kiss underlined in power.

My soul rejoiced, my heart beating in time with his, as he lifted me into the air to press me into the hallway wall. I wrapped my legs around him for support, not caring at all how it split my robe open to reveal my intimate flesh.

Exos rocked his hips into mine, his hardening cock hitting me right where I desired him most.

I missed this.

Missed *him.*

And I told him that out loud, his name a conviction I'd whisper for eternity.

His palm slid from my back to my breast, squeezing and kneading and eliciting sounds from my throat that I was sure would wake the others.

But no one disturbed us.

This was just me and Exos, his hard body against mine, his mouth tasting and licking and memorizing. And oh, how I wanted to remove the suit.

Yet it seemed sexier to have him clothed, especially as the robe hit the floor and left me naked and wanting against him.

"If we had more time, I'd take you completely," he whispered, his voice harsh and sexy at my ear. "But for now, I'll be satisfied with hearing you scream my name."

I panted, shocked that my body could respond this way after so many hours of pleasure. However, Exos always knew what I needed, his touch a hypnotic caress that left me shivering and quaking for more.

And now was no different.

He pressed into me, the head of his hard cock engaging my clit through the fabric of his pants and sending me shattering on a wave of ecstasy that took me to another plane of existence.

Our plane.

The one only our souls knew how to access.

371

I stayed there for several minutes, reveling in the feel of *us*. He kissed me softly, knowingly, our bond singing in approval as our link strengthened all the more.

"My Claire," he breathed.

"My Exos," I agreed, smiling against him. "You can take me anywhere you want. You know that."

"I do, but it's nice to have your cooperation for once."

I smiled. "A lot changed while you were gone."

"I can see that," he mused as he tucked a strand of my hair behind my ear, his finger running up the pointed tip that still felt so foreign to me. "I approve."

"Good." I tugged his lower lip into my mouth. "Because I like the new me. I feel stronger. More in control."

"And that will only continue to grow, Claire." He pressed his forehead to mine. "You have no idea what destiny is laid out before you, but I'll help you in every way I can. We all will."

"That sounds ominous."

"It is," he whispered. "More than you know."

"So tell me."

He sighed, one palm cupping my cheek while the other clasped my hip to keep me balanced between him and the wall. "It's your mother, Claire."

"I know what she's done, but I won't make the same mistakes." I felt it deep in my core that I could never betray my mates the way my mother had done with her own.

"No. Not that." His blue eyes took on a serious quality, his grip tightening. "Your mother…" He paused, sighing. "Your mother is the one who tried to kill you with dark magic. She's also the one who used Mortus as a puppet to capture me."

My lips parted. "But she's dead." Which sounded like a ridiculous statement considering what he just said. Except, everyone told me… My eyes widened. "Elana said a body was never found."

He nodded. "Because there wasn't one to find."

Holy fae… "My mother's alive."

ELEMENTAL
FAE ACADEMY
BOOK THREE

PROLOGUE
CLAIRE

MY MOTHER'S ALIVE.

I repeated that phrase over and over again in my mind and out loud until someone shook me out of my stupor. No, not someone. The ground. *Sol.*

I blinked and met the concerned gaze of the Earth Fae. He stood stark naked before me, his muscular form momentarily grabbing my attention before I frowned at the males standing around me.

All of them were naked except Exos.

And no one seemed to be noticing this apart from me.

I cleared my throat. "Uh, guys..."

"What do you mean, Ophelia is the one who orchestrated your kidnapping?" Vox demanded, his arms folded over his lean torso. While Sol was built like a solid linebacker, Vox had a runner's build. And Titus, well, he reminded me of a wrestler. No, a boxer.

Why were they all naked, again?

Right. We'd been in bed.

And then Exos came and revealed—

"My mother is alive," I whispered. "And you're all very naked."

Titus smirked. "You didn't mind that a few hours ago."

Honestly, I still didn't. But it was damn distracting.

"From what Cyrus and I have discerned, Ophelia is very much alive and using Mortus as a puppet. It's the only explanation for what has happened." Exos glanced up at Sol. "It also explains why the Earth Fae are slowly dying."

"Because she's the cause of the plague," my earth mate replied softly.

"We think she's using Dark Fae magic," Exos added. "And Claire coming to the Academy is what has led Ophelia to come out of hiding."

"Dark Fae magic?" I repeated.

"Vampires," Titus muttered, shuddering. "Vile fae. They live on human blood and play with the dark arts."

"Vampires are real?" I squeaked. "Like Dracula?"

Exos sighed. "They're not vampires the way you've been taught. But yes, other types of fae exist."

"What other types?" I demanded. "Werewolves? Skinwalkers? Demons?"

"Don't be ridiculous, Claire," Exos replied, shaking his head. "What matters is Ophelia is using dark magic to weaken the Elemental Fae."

"Seriously, are werewolves real?"

He just gave me a look. "No."

"Demons?"

"Also, no." He shook his head, his expression softening. "We can talk more about the types later. I promise it's nothing alarming."

"Says the fae who just revealed vampires exist," I muttered.

He tucked a strand of hair behind my ear. "Before we get to all that, I need to ascend, and I want you with me, Claire. As my mate."

Wait... "Like... fully mated?" I asked, my heart skipping a beat.

He nodded. "Yes."

"Yes," I parroted back at him, not even needing to think about it. "Yes." Because I refused to lose him again. Ever. And this would make our bond permanent. Unbreakable. Impenetrable. "Yes," I said again.

His lips twitched, his blue eyes glittering with amusement. "Well, at least I know how to make you agreeable. Just put you in a hallway of naked men."

I narrowed my gaze. "Don't ruin the moment, Exos."

"I wouldn't dream of it, princess." He pulled me into a hug while the others murmured around us about my mother and what that all meant.

"Do you think taking her to the Spirit Kingdom is a wise move?" Vox asked, his tone holding a hint of something I couldn't quite define. Not jealousy, exactly, but a touch of longing underlined in concern.

"She'll be there with me and Cyrus. We won't take her anywhere near the death fields." Exos pulled me to his side, his arm securing my shoulders. "But it's her decision if she wants to go back there."

I swallowed, recalling what happened the last time I visited the Spirit Kingdom. The stark desolation of the lands, the way the death fields had nearly claimed my soul, and that little flicker of light in the distant village housing the only remaining Spirit Fae.

Ninety percent of them had perished because of my mother, leaving them with only two royals left—Cyrus and Exos. My mates. My loves. My fae.

Allowing Exos to ascend on his own wasn't really an option.

It would also mark me as a coward.

No. My mother had taken enough from me, from *them*. She wouldn't take this, too.

"I'm going," I said, feeling the confidence of those two words all the way to my bones. "It's where I'm meant to be. Where I'm needed." I had to show the fae world that I wasn't afraid. I might be Ophelia's daughter, but I wasn't *her*.

Vox, Titus, and Sol all studied me with resignation in their gazes. They could feel my decision through the bonds, my spirit's need to finalize my connection to Exos palpable to everyone in the hall.

"Hurry back to us, little flower," Sol murmured, giving me a small grin. "I'll make sure your peach trees are ready."

"And I'll see what I can do about cleaning up around here," Vox added.

Titus winked. "Meanwhile, I'll supervise and keep them out of trouble."

Sol snorted and Vox shook his head. "If anyone will be supervising anyone, it'll be me," Vox declared.

I think they'll be just fine for a few days, princess, Exos whispered into my mind.

My lips curled in amusement as all three of them began bickering in a playful manner. *Yeah,* I agreed. *I know.* I hated to leave them behind, but they couldn't enter the Spirit Kingdom.

We won't be gone long, Exos promised softly. *A week at most.*

And when we returned, I would have two full mates. Water and Spirit. With three more to go.

I kissed them all goodbye before taking Exos's hand.

It was time to face my future. My mother. And all fae kind.

My name is Claire Summers and I accept my fate.

Whatever that may be.

Chapter One
Claire

"HANDS ABOVE YOUR HEAD, PRINCESS." Exos loomed over me in an all-black suit that clung to his form in unfair ways—ways that forced me to obey him.

I stretched my hands above my head and gripped the bars of his headboard. "Happy?"

His ocean-blue eyes ran over my naked body and smiled. "Yes. Very." He slowly unraveled his tie while keeping one knee beside me on the mattress, his opposite foot on the ground.

We were supposed to be going to our mating ceremony, but Exos had pulled me in here instead. Not that I was complaining. However, I did want to move to the final level with him. I almost lost him once. That would not be happening again.

"Mmm, the beauty of spirit is how solitary it is," Exos murmured as he drew his silky tie along the center of my torso up to my collarbone. "We don't require an audience, Claire."

I frowned up at him. "What do you mean?"

He slid the silk around my wrists, tying the fabric into a sturdy knot. "This is our ceremony, Claire." He leaned down to kiss me, silencing whatever comment I could have uttered back to him. But he had to *hear* my shock, just as he'd clearly overheard my pondering about him taking me here rather than to the ceremonial room.

"Every element is different. Some require the formality, and while Spirit used to indulge in a similar tradition to the others, we gave up on it years ago. Not enough of us left to fill a room." He righted himself, slid the jacket from his shoulders, and walked over to a corner desk to drape the wool fabric over the chair.

"We'll be celebrated tonight after the coronation," he continued, returning to the bed to smile down at me. "But this morning and this afternoon are for us and us alone." He punctuated the words with a tug against the silk binding my wrists.

I glanced up to see them secured to the headboard—something he must have done while we kissed. Clever fae. It left me naked and bound before him.

His grin told me he more than approved.

"We're going to bond, Claire," he said, his tone holding a delicious depth to it that scattered goose bumps across my flesh. "We're going to bond all day."

My lips formed an O, but no sound escaped me.

Because he had started unbuttoning his shirt and I only had so many functioning brain cells around a disrobing Exos.

For months, he'd explored my body without allowing me to return the favor. Well, this last month hadn't been his fault. My mother had held him captive underground.

Because she was apparently alive.

A train of thought I was so not going to consider right now.

No, I much preferred the sight of male sin before me.

I nearly swallowed my tongue, Exos's body an art crafted by the Fae gods. His shirt fell to the floor, his muscles rippling along the way, and his hand landed on his belt. "Are you ready to recite your vows, Claire?"

Uh... I licked my lips. "Does it involve saying them around your cock?" Because I could totally get behind that. While I'd seen Exos naked before, I'd never been gifted the opportunity to memorize him with my tongue. And I would very much enjoy doing that right now.

His lips curled. "The ceremony only works if your words are intelligible, baby."

"Then you probably should have left our clothes on."

"What would be the fun in that?" he countered, the leather sliding from the loops of his pants. "I thought you enjoyed a good challenge. Isn't that how we met? You were dared to kiss the man at the bar?"

"The very handsome man," I clarified, recalling the night we met. It seemed like a lifetime ago.

"Do you regret it?" he asked softly, kneeling once more on the bed, his

379

pants unbuttoned but still zipped. He cupped my face, his eyes holding mine. "Do you regret kissing me?"

I swallowed and shook my head. "No." I still mourned Rick, my friend who had died in the resulting fire, but I no longer held myself responsible for the massacre.

Mastering my powers had provided me with a new view of the world, a deeper understanding of my control. There was nothing I could have done differently that night, apart from not kissing Exos. But even then, I'd been a ticking time bomb.

"You're mine," I said, wishing my hands were free to grab him. "I'll never regret claiming you."

His lips curled. "That's good, Claire. Because I'm about to make you mine. Forever." He glanced over his shoulder. "Cyrus? Can you help us with the vows?"

My eyes widened as Exos's brother entered the bedroom in a suit, his light hair mussed in that way I adored. He smirked, his hands tucked into his pockets. "You just had to one-up the mating ceremony, didn't you?"

Exos gripped my thighs while casually replying, "You chose your platform; I picked mine. And in my opinion, a bed is far more appropriate than a ceremonial altar." His sapphire gaze slid to mine as he gently spread my legs to expose my intimate flesh. "I prefer my method of worship."

Cyrus snorted and stopped beside the bed, his icy blue irises grinning down at me. "I think I prefer your method, too." He tilted his head. "You ready to say your vows, little queen?"

My mouth went dry as Exos positioned himself between my splayed thighs. He couldn't mean to—

I arched off the bed as his lips closed around my clit without warning.

"*Fuck*," I breathed.

Cyrus tsked. "That's not how the vows go. It starts with, 'I, Claire, accept the power that binds me to Exos, born of Spirit.'" He arched a blond brow. "Now try again."

Exos slid his tongue through my folds, his gaze holding a wicked glint as he watched me.

"I... I..." *Oh God.* I writhed, unable to focus, my veins flooding with liquid fire. This wasn't fair. How either of them expected me to focus—

Cyrus palmed my breast, his touch eliciting a long, needy moan from my throat.

It was official.

These two were going to kill me.

"Focus, little queen," Cyrus whispered, his lips brushing over mine. I hadn't even felt him lean over the bed. My senses were all focused between my legs and on my breasts. "You don't want to lose Exos again, right?"

I shuddered, shaking my head. Those words registered in my thoughts, the notion of severing my connection to Exos a very real threat. Because it had almost happened.

"Then repeat after me." He lifted just enough to capture my gaze and hold it. And he repeated the first sentence of the vows.

"I, Claire," I began, my fingers clenching as Exos did something sensuous with his tongue. "Accept the power that binds me to Exos, born of Spirit."

Cyrus smiled and uttered the next part.

"To cherish and respect, through all the eras and time that may fall before us, until our souls do us part." This was the same as my mating to Cyrus. However, the circumstances were very different. I'd spoken the vows in a dreamlike state within the Water Kingdom. Now, oh, Exos was making this extremely difficult.

Keep going, he encouraged through our bond. *I'm just warming us up.*

Some warm-up, I thought back at him while Cyrus spoke the next part.

"I give unto him the center of my essence, the heart of my being, my very spirit, and accept his in return," I recited, my voice far breathier now than it was when we began. Because Exos's warm-up? Yeah, it was turning into something far bigger.

Cyrus kissed me again before delivering the final words.

Which I parroted in a sultry voice I barely recognized.

"My element is now his just as his is now mine, to the fae heavens may we never part. And I shall never forsake him for another, my spirit forever belonging to him and to him alone."

"Mmm," Exos murmured, the vibration pushing me near the edge of oblivion.

And he sat up.

I half growled, my thighs quivering from the pending climax he'd denied me. But then he started speaking, the vows ones he clearly knew by heart. A warm aura settled over us, our spirits mingling intimately on a plane only we could access together. It was the place where our elements bonded, where promises were made and feelings were realized.

With each word he uttered, I felt the finality of our joining clicking into place, tying me to him indefinitely.

I sighed, the burning in my veins subsiding beneath a euphoric wave of rightness.

Mine.

Mine, he agreed in my mind, his palm settling over my heart.

Cyrus placed his hand over Exos's, creating a powerful burst of energy that swirled around the three of us.

Two finalized bonds.

Water and Spirit.

Royal ties on both ends.

Titus, Vox, and Sol came to life in my mind, their elements aware of my

381

deepened ties to spirit. But I didn't feel any animosity or jealousy, just a sense of understanding and acceptance.

I was a Halfling with access to all five elements. I needed my fae mates to ground me, to complete the elemental circle we'd all started.

And two of those threads were now absolute.

Nothing could come between us.

Not even my evil-as-fuck mother.

Exos stretched out on top of me, his mouth sealing over mine. A kiss to bind us together forever. I felt it all the way to my toes, the finality of our embrace. And the welcome of a new future.

My tongue met his in a dance filled with promise and intent. All the heat he'd awoken between my legs roared back to life with a vengeance, my need for him consuming my every thought.

Please, I whispered to him. *Please, Exos.*

After months of him exploring me sexually, I needed him to let me return the favor. I craved his intensity, his touch, his intimacy.

He cupped my breast, his touch similar to Cyrus's and yet so entirely his own.

Cyrus, I thought, remembering his presence.

Only, he was no longer standing beside the bed.

Try not to kill my brother, little queen. He's still recovering. His words caressed my mind, his touch fluid and strong and commanding.

Pretty sure he can handle himself. As Exos was proving with his mouth.

Cyrus mentally slid away with a chuckle that warmed me all over. A warmth Exos seemed to follow with his hands as he traced my curves. "My brother had you for a week, Claire," he said softly, nipping at my lower lip. "Today you're mine. And only mine."

I had no reply for that.

Which was good because he didn't give me a chance to even try before taking over my mouth again.

His hips settled between mine, his pants an unwelcome barrier. But my wrists were still bound, holding me hostage as he took his sweet time kissing me. I could taste myself on his tongue, a flavor that only heightened my arousal and need for him.

All these months of foreplay.

Culminating in a fiery moment of passion.

One he seemed hell-bent on prolonging.

"Exos," I moaned. "You're killing me."

"Seems only fair to give you a dose of how I've felt these last few months." He pressed a kiss to my throat before dipping down to tease my breasts. "I've burned for you, Claire. So fucking hot. And now you're mine." Those dark blue eyes glimmered up at me. "*Mine*, princess."

"Yours," I agreed, my hips arching in a desperate plea for friction.

He sucked my nipple deep into his mouth, the act almost punishing but also deliciously appeasing. Such a twisted and convoluted sensation.

Exos repeated the action with my other peak before drawing back onto his knees to admire my bound form. "You're turning a beautiful shade of pink, Claire."

"Because I'm on fire," I admitted, squirming. Fuck, if my hands were free, I'd pleasure myself at this rate.

Which was probably why he tied my wrists above my head.

Evil mate.

"Fuck me," I demanded.

His full lips quirked up. "Oh, I'm going to do more than fuck you, baby." He slowly slid down his zipper. "I'm going to devour you—mind, body, and spirit."

I had no idea what he meant by that, but I welcomed all of the above.

My acquiescence with his plans only deepened as he revealed his perfect cock. Long, lean, and strong, just like him. He swept his thumb over the head and brought the essence to my lips.

He didn't even need to issue a demand.

I sucked the pad into my mouth without a word and moaned as his masculine flavor touched my tongue. *Yes…* I've been craving him for so long. Too long.

And finally he was naked.

Hard.

Ready.

But not moving, his gaze riveted on my weeping center.

"Exos," I hissed, my body strung so tight it felt ready to shatter.

He stroked his shaft, his expression thoughtful. "You look beautiful like this. Hot. Needy. So fucking wet."

Oh God, if he kept talking to me like that, I'd burst. And wouldn't that be a feat?

His smile told me he knew, too.

"I missed you, Claire," he whispered, crawling over me. "Do you want to feel how much?"

"Yes." I swallowed and repeated, "Yes."

His lips ghosted over mine as he positioned his hips right where I wanted him. "I've wanted this from the moment I first saw you," he admitted softly. "I fought it at first only because you needed time to acclimate, but there wasn't a second between us that I didn't think about this. About having you."

He pressed against my entrance, his body shuddering over mine and revealing the truth of his words.

"I've never wanted someone so much in my life." He spoke the words against my mouth, his heart beating hard in his chest against mine. "And now you're truly mine."

Exos slid all the way inside, sheathing himself to the hilt with a thrust so powerful I gasped.

A sense of completion washed over me, sprouting goose bumps up and down my limbs. *That* was the finality of our vows, marrying our spirits in eternity. I thought I'd felt it earlier, but this was the consummation.

And as he began to move, I felt our souls stitching together in an unbreakable knot, sealing our fates for eternity.

I groaned, the wholesome feeling consuming me, leaving me light and buoyant and full. My hands ached with the need to touch him, something he must have sensed because he released the binds while capturing my mouth beneath his own.

My nails scored his back, drawing my name into his very flesh as he claimed my body below. He wasn't soft or tender. No. Exos was all strength, his movements done with purpose and fulfillment. Every upward stroke hit me deep, and every flex of his hips grazed my clit.

He was skill personified.

Experienced in the best way.

Flawless and thorough and *amazing.*

My spirit seemed to detach from my body, sprinting toward our plane to find his element, to join in a gyration of heat and intensity.

With each shift and touch, I flew closer to the edge, my limbs tense and shaking.

And then I was falling on a scream I swore reached the stars.

Exos caught the sound with his tongue, feeding off my pleasure while giving me more, his pace increasing as he chased me into oblivion.

Where we met and moaned and reveled in a rapture I felt with every fiber of my being.

Joined. That was how I felt. This had gone beyond fucking and directly into the art of making love. Exos had redefined it, adding his own flavor to the twist, his own technique to the act of bonding.

I shuddered beneath him, nowhere near done.

And from his continued movements, I knew he wasn't either.

"Take me to the stars, Exos," I whispered.

He smiled. "Oh, Claire, I'm going to take you to a whole new galaxy."

And he did.

With each thrust, kiss, lick, and caress, he introduced me to the novel world of spirit. Our own personal paradise where only we belonged.

For eternity.

CHAPTER TWO
CLAIRE

THE GOWN EXOS SLID OVER MY HEAD felt too heavy, too suffocating. I didn't want to wear anything, every part of me too alive from Exos's touch. But attending his coronation naked would raise a few questions.

Unlike our mating ceremony, there would be more than just Cyrus at the ascension.

Exos's lips ghosted across my bare shoulder. "You look beautiful, Claire." The silky material hugged my curves, the color the same shade as his dark blue eyes.

I met his gaze in the mirror and smiled. "You look pretty handsome yourself."

He chuckled and fixed his tie. Considering how we'd spent the afternoon, we both cleaned up pretty well. The shower had helped. But seeing Exos dressed in an all-black suit just had me wanting to return to the bed again.

He grabbed my hips and pulled me back into him. "After the formalities are finished, I'll take you up on that thought." His lips brushed my racing pulse. "Maybe Cyrus will join us."

My lips parted. "Cyrus?"

Exos nipped my earlobe and released me with a vague hum. I tried to grab his hand, but he was already on his way to the door. He opened it to reveal his brother waiting in the hallway in an identical suit.

Despite spending my afternoon with Exos, my hormones did a little dance. Because, holy Fae, the two males were sin personified.

And their matching grins said they knew it, too.

Cocky males.

I heard that, Cyrus replied, holding out his arm. *Come here, little queen.*

I smirked and shook my head. *You're incorrigible.* But of course I went to him anyway. Because he was Cyrus. In a suit. And he smelled like the mist from a fresh waterfall.

He hugged me close, his lips pressing into my temple. "Mmm, I see my brother took good care of you today."

Exos closed the door to his room with a snort. "I took more than *good care* of her."

Cyrus laughed. "Yes, I felt that through the bond." He kissed me again before sliding his arm to my lower back. "Shall we? The crowd has already started to gather in the town square. Feather is managing the roast, while several others have created an assortment of side dishes. Gale handled the spritemead, which I'm sure shocks you."

"Gale? Spritemead?" Exos feigned surprise. "And here I thought he hated alcohol of all kinds."

Neither name meant anything to me, but the fondness in Exos's and Cyrus's auras told me they meant something to them.

"Are they Spirit Fae?" I wondered out loud. It seemed an appropriate deduction since we were in the Spirit Kingdom, but I also knew over ninety percent of the Spirit Fae had perished after my mother unleashed a plague a little over two decades ago.

"Yes. Gale helped raise us after our mother died." Exos threaded his fingers with mine, walking to my left, while Cyrus's arm remained snug around my waist, his heat a blanket against my right side. "Feather is the oldest matron of the Spirit Fae, but only about fifty human years old. She looks closer to twenty-five, like the rest of us."

"The plague took out all the eldest fae among us," Cyrus clarified.

"And it's happening again with the Earth Fae," I added, swallowing. "At least, that's how Sol described it."

Exos nodded. "Something similar is happening to his kind, yes. But rather than wipe them out in a single day, it's taking years."

"Almost like something—or someone—is feeding off their energy," Cyrus murmured, his expression falling into serious lines.

"Someone like my mother," I translated.

"Maybe." He cleared his throat, his arm tightening around my waist. "But that's a discussion for tomorrow. Tonight is a joyous occasion. My brother has finally decided to grow the fuck up."

Exos snorted. "Okay, Prince of Water. If that's how you want to play this."

"Who served as Spirit King for the last decade because his brother preferred playing warrior?" Cyrus pretended to think about it. "Oh, right, me."

"Playing warrior." Exos shook his head, but his grin said he didn't mind the jibe. "I'll play warrior with you later and see how you fare."

My eyebrows rose. "That sounds like an innuendo." One I would really enjoy watching unfold.

"Because you have fae cock on the brain." Cyrus glanced over my shoulder as we descended one of the palace's many stone staircases. "I'm starting to think you left our little queen unsatisfied, brother."

"She's insatiable," he drawled.

Cyrus grinned. "Tell me about it."

"If you both keep talking about me like I'm not walking between you, I'll make sure you're both very *unsatisfied.*"

They laughed, their confidence a palpable cloud around us. "We'll see," Cyrus mused. Yeah, he sounded pretty sure of himself. And, well, I couldn't blame him. Not with them both resembling gods in their matching suits. They would have me naked and panting in seconds if they put their minds to it. Especially if they worked together.

Just thinking about it had me clenching my thighs.

An Exos and Cyrus sandwich? Uh, yes, please.

I'll keep that in mind, Cyrus replied.

Stop playing in my head, I muttered, my cheeks heating from how easily he read my thoughts.

Stop telegraphing so loudly, he returned.

"I rather like how open she is to sharing," Exos said out loud. "Something to consider later."

"Can we not do this right now?" Because if they kept it up, I wouldn't be able to keep a straight face in front of the other Spirit Fae. Hell, I wasn't even sure I could stand before them at all without melting into a puddle of need. Mating Exos had left my body primed and ready and *needy.*

It'd taken almost a week in bed with Cyrus to work it out.

I'd only indulged in an afternoon with Exos.

To say I wanted more would be an understatement.

Don't worry, princess. I'll take care of us both, Exos whispered, squeezing my hand. *But I need to ascend first, to stabilize the Spirit Kingdom.*

Right. Because Cyrus had essentially renounced his throne when he mated me in the Water Kingdom. He was the king's only heir, leaving him with no choice but to ascend now that he'd chosen a mate for his water element.

And Exos had to become the Spirit King.

Making me the mate to not one but *two* Royal Fae.

Just another day in the life of Claire Summers, I thought with a snort.

My heels clacked against the marble ground as we reached the first floor

LEXI C. FOSS & J.R. THORN

and started toward the main hall.

This place was a vacant maze where sound echoed due to the lack of people. Stepping outside almost relieved me, until I felt the cruel pull toward the death fields.

Fortunately, we were headed in the opposite direction, toward the town in the distance.

Cyrus stopped beside a vehicle—or I assumed that was the purpose of the strange three-wheeled contraption. It looked like the kind of thing I saw back in the Human Realm, with a few distinct modifications.

Like the open-air seating.

And the lack of a steering wheel.

It looked like what would happen if a car mated with a motorcycle.

"Hop in, princess," Exos said.

"Hop in," I repeated. "Right." A magical fae car wasn't the most exciting thing I'd been introduced to over the last few months, so why not? I allowed him to help me onto the soft, leather-like seat while Cyrus climbed in behind me. "I didn't realize fae had cars."

"Not really a car," Exos replied as he slid over to sit beside me. "More like a teleporter."

"A wh—"

The wind whooshed from my lungs as the contraption began to spin. I grappled for something to hold on to, which turned out to be Exos's arm, and held on for dear life as the scenery morphed into a cloud of dust.

Within seconds, we were surrounded by tiny cottages and cobblestone streets. I blinked. *We're in Bavaria*, I thought, bewildered. Thoughts of my high school geography class populated my mind, flashing images of Southern Germany left and right.

No, little queen. We're still in Spirit Kingdom.

Looks like Germany to me.

Well, sometimes fae travel to the Human Realm and create inspirations. Where do you think supernatural tales came from? Cyrus nibbled the back of my neck before jumping out of the teleportation transporter thing. He held out a hand. "Claire."

"Cyrus," I replied, allowing him to help me find my footing. "What do you call that thing?"

"A convenience." He smiled. "Much faster than walking."

"But that's not how we got here from the Academy."

"No, we used another method of transportation," Exos said as he came around the front of the teleporter thing. "Portals take us between the kingdoms, and the realms, too. Same idea in terms of technology and power, but different execution."

There was still so much about this fae world that I didn't know or understand. So I just nodded as if it all made sense, when it very much did not.

Exos cupped my cheek and pressed a brief, sweet kiss to my lips. "We have all the time in the world to teach you, Claire." He brushed his nose against mine before pulling away. "So let us introduce you to another aspect of our world—the coronation."

Chapter Three
Vox

SAYING GOODBYE TO CLAIRE after she'd turned my world upside down hadn't been easy, but I'd done it for her. I'd put on a smile and given her a tender kiss and sent her off to the Spirit Kingdom, a place that I couldn't go, but I would have tried in a heartbeat if she'd asked.

I might have looked calm on the outside, but Claire had awakened a tempest in my soul. It slipped out more often now, especially when I was thinking about her... which was all the time.

The dishes I'd just cleaned went flying off the counter and shattered onto the ground in a dramatic cascade of broken porcelain as my air magic slipped from my grasp. An invisible gust spun around the kitchen, rattling the light fixtures, before I squeezed my eyes shut and suppressed the outburst.

When I reopened my eyes, Sol and Titus were both staring at me.

Sol straightened and set down the sandwich he'd been working on. "Doing okay, Vox?"

I shrugged, trying to play it off as a fluke—something I'd done a little too much these last few days. "Too much soap," I offered as an excuse. "It's slippery."

Titus chuckled. "Soap doesn't send three pounds of rice flinging across the entire dorm."

Oh, oops.

I turned enough to see that my slip had not only sent the dishes flying but had also uprooted the pantry box with ingredients meant to last us a week—ingredients that were now scattered all the way down the hall.

I sighed and shuffled to the closet for a broom.

"Why don't you just use your element to push it out the door?" Sol asked with an edge to his question.

It was what I normally would have done, but my powers were out of control and he clearly knew it.

I shrugged again. "Just craving some exercise."

The ground trembled, signaling Sol's irritation with me. "I hate it when you close yourself off, Vox. Just admit that you're frustrated Claire's gone. Then we can talk about it."

Titus chuckled and snapped his fingers, lighting a perfectly blue flame on his fingertips as he heated up a cup of tea that had gone cold. "That's all we've been doing for days, Sol. Claire's gone to shack up with Exos and we're not invited. What else is new?" He waggled his eyebrows. "It's not like she could forget the night we gave her. She's going to be thinking of us the entire time."

I wished I possessed an ounce of Titus's confidence, but opening myself up to Claire had done something to me that I feared couldn't be undone. Did Claire really know the impact she had on me? Was I honestly ready to embrace it?

The memory of her naked before me made my core tighten, and for a moment all I could think of was how she'd tasted—and how all I wanted was more of her. How she made me feel *free*.

No, I could never go back to *before* that night.

Which meant I had to face the consequences of opening myself up to the bond with Claire.

Her mating to Exos and his coronation would only make her pull on me stronger. She was already something unprecedented—a Halfling with access to all five elements. She was able to tug at every secret I thought I'd buried out of reach, and as her mate-bonds grew, so would she, and that would only force me out of my shell further.

Not something I was ready to embrace.

Titus surprised me by snatching the broom from my grasp. He glowered and then pointed at the table where a pile of remaining sandwiches waited. "Sol has a point, Vox. I'm tired of your moping. Sit and eat something before you get skinny." He appraised my lean body. "Well, maybe too late for that."

My eyes narrowed. *Skinny? Yeah, I'll show him skinny.*

I peeled off my shirt and arched a brow. "Claire seemed to like this just fine the other night."

Titus smirked, his green eyes running over me. "Yeah, I guess you're not bad. No need to get your ponytail all in a twist."

I snorted. "Whatever." I marched over and sat across from Sol, who was grinning at our exchange and my lack of a shirt.

Okay, so maybe that'd been a bit of a brash reaction. But Titus had turned up the temperature in here anyway, bringing the Spirit Dorm to a boiling point. So it felt good to remove some clothes. And yeah, maybe I also missed Claire.

Bantering with the mate-circle always seemed to help a little. These guys understood how I felt about Claire being gone. But they didn't know what was really going on with me. I could tell them, but there was nothing they could actually do. The control was on me. Besides, Sol barely understood his royal ties and Titus wasn't a royal at all. Even if Cyrus and Exos were here, I'd rather swallow a spiked fruit than ask for their help.

So I'd figure it out on my own.

Or maybe with Claire, when she returned.

"The Solstice Ball is coming up soon," Sol said as I picked up one of the sandwiches.

I rolled my eyes, tired of this topic. He'd brought it up several times over the last few days. "Will you relax already? Exos said he'd have Claire back in time for the stupid ball."

"He's excited about it, okay? Don't undermine the one good thing our titan has in his life," Titus said, sending a flame down the hall to burn the spoiled food rather than sweep it up. I wrinkled my nose at the sour scent it created and moved my hand to send a gust out the door, then thought better of it and hunched my shoulders as I endured the stench.

"I don't understand why he had to take her so quickly," Sol complained, his shoulders drooping as he stared at the half-eaten sandwich on his plate. "Or why this coronation had to be in the Spirit Kingdom." He curled his fingers into massive fists, and his stony gaze challenged me. "Is he really trustworthy? You had to knock him out because that *thing* was inside of him. What if it's still there?"

That *thing* was Claire's mother. I shuddered with the memory of the dark essence that had almost taken Claire's life, the shadow energy that had possessed Exos.

Did I trust Exos? Yes.

Did I trust him to protect Claire against Ophelia? Also yes.

But something told me Ophelia had tricks up her sleeves that none of us were prepared to face yet. So I understood Sol's concern, and shared it myself.

Titus sent another controlled wave of flame that manipulated the air, pushing the burnt remains down the hall with a heat-infused gust. "Cyrus wouldn't have let Exos anywhere near her if that darkness was still inside of him. I don't trust the asshole Water Royal farther than I can throw him, but I know he wouldn't make the mistake of putting Claire in danger again."

That was big talk coming from Titus. I raised a brow, wondering what kind of bond the two fae had formed after their bout in the Academy's arena. I supposed Cyrus had earned our trust after all that went down, at least as far as Claire was concerned.

I nodded my agreement. "Claire should be there for the coronation and be a part of such an important day in her mate's life. It'll just make their mate-bond stronger and also strengthen her control over her spirit element." As much as I disliked being apart from her, this was exactly what Claire required—and what the mate-circle needed to protect her.

Sol's jaw clenched. "Do you know something we don't know? How is dragging Claire back to a dying land where she almost died herself a *wise* move?"

I cocked my brow at the disgruntled Earth Fae. "You know what the coronation does, right?" Sol wasn't familiar with his royal line, but I figured even he would know what a coronation really meant. Maybe I was wrong.

Titus finished up his "cleaning" and joined us at the table, looking intrigued. He brushed his hands together and left a flutter of soot over the table that I'd just wiped down before our meal. "I remember she was much stronger after mating with Cyrus, who is as royal as one can get. Is that what you mean?"

I shook my head. "Cyrus is only king because Exos originally turned down the crown. Don't get me wrong, he's still strong—almost impressively so—but Exos will be even more powerful as king."

"So what's going to happen?" Sol asked, concern etching a pattern into his forehead.

My lips twitched. "Nothing bad. Bonding with Exos will ensure she never loses him again. And, by participating in his coronation, she's embracing a royal line of power. She'll no longer have to draw from the outskirts of the element like most fae do because she'll have access to the source directly through Exos."

That kind of power was what made royals so respected and feared. Accessing the raw core of an element was something only true elemental kings could do. As Exos's mate, Claire would be able to piggyback on that ability. Most considered it a dangerous connection—hence the reason only the strongest of fae could ascend.

I'd been in contention for that power once.

I'd immediately denied it.

Air was the most volatile of all the elements and could cause destruction that would decimate the fae in unskilled hands. I would never want to rule such an energy source. Ever.

"How do you know so much about this?" Titus asked, leaning on the table. "I know you have some royal blood in you, but you don't talk about it much."

"For good reason," I muttered, but these were Claire's bond-mates. Both Sol and Titus watched me expectantly, their concern palpable. They were beginning to feel like family. Like they were mine just as much as Claire was mine.

Keeping them in the dark seemed wrong.

And so I did something I'd never done before.

I opened up about my history. Just a little bit.

"My grandfather was given access to the royal source of the air element," I admitted. The source wasn't necessarily a secret; it just wasn't common knowledge as to *how* the royal lines were so powerful. "It's a boon that can be granted by the king. My grandfather, well, he thought he could control it. Until he couldn't."

I shuddered at the memory of tornados exploding across the main city just a day after he'd bragged to everyone about his new powers. Several fae lost their lives that day, casting dishonor over my family line as a result.

"Long story short, he abused his access to the source, which labeled my family as weak and lacking in control. So you can imagine why I'd want to prove them all wrong." Consequently, I refused to allow myself to go anywhere near my royal ties to the source of my elemental power. To do so would be to repeat my grandfather's mistakes.

"What happens when Claire is exposed to the source of spirit magic through Exos?" Sol asked, his eyes growing wide.

Claire wasn't like me. I'd seen how she embraced her elements with a natural grace that put my abilities to shame. She'd grown fearless these last few months and would only thrive with the power that came from the source. "She'll be fine," I assured him. "I have no doubt about that."

Another short burst of air escaped my grip and sent my hair unfurling from its loose warrior's tail and put out the small flame dancing across Titus's knuckles.

Yeah, Claire would be fine.

But me? That I wasn't so sure about.

Chapter Four
Claire

I STOOD BETWEEN CYRUS AND EXOS as we faced a crowd of a hundred or so young-looking fae in the center square. The setting sun left everyone dressed in warmer clothes as cool wisps of air seemed to descend upon the small town from the outskirts. It left a chill along my skin, reminding me of the nearby death fields.

Yet everyone around me was smiling.

Not at Exos or Cyrus. But at me.

Apparently, I was the one they all credited for Exos's decision to ascend. He squeezed my hand as Cyrus recited something in the old language, the words weaving a magical web in the air that I could almost taste.

Power. A lot of power.

It hummed through the air, weaving into our essences and stringing us even closer together. Exos's grip tightened, his body tensing beneath the cascade of energy. It vibrated through his spirit, intensifying his aura.

My lips parted. *Exos...*

It's okay, baby, he whispered. *I'm ready for it.*

Ready for what? It felt like a tornado spinning around and around, sucking us into a dark vortex of vitality.

The source.

The source of what? I demanded, my hair whipping around my face.

Spirit. He sounded pained. *Cyrus is relinquishing his hold over it. We've shared it for...* He trailed off, his features pulling tight.

I cupped his face, everyone else forgotten. *Talk to me. Tell me how to help you.*

You already are, he breathed into my mind. His arms wrapped around me as he pressed his forehead to mine.

I closed my eyes and embraced his spirit with my own. Wind swirled and roared through my ears, the universe seeming to fall apart piece by piece. But I had my Exos, my mate, my Spirit King. He kissed me tenderly, the magic warming our blood and souls.

Royal Fae manage the access to the core of our element, he explained softly. *I've always shared the ownership with Cyrus, but he's giving me everything. He can't maintain a hold over spirit and water. It would be too much for anyone to bear, even one as powerful as him.*

Does it hurt? I asked, my tongue sliding along his lower lip. *Is that why you didn't want to ascend?*

No. I'm the rightful heir, so it all feels natural to me. I only denied my position to help Cyrus. He refused to embrace his water element. Because of you, Claire, he's finally ready. Exos smiled against my mouth, his pride and gratitude caressing my heart. *You've changed us both for the better.*

Now you're just sweet-talking me, I replied, my fingers slipping into his thick hair. *You realize I've already committed for life, right?*

I do, he murmured, his eyelashes fluttering as he opened his eyes. "Mine forever."

"Ours forever," Cyrus corrected from beside us, his tone amused. "Not to intrude on the moment, but Gale wants to know when we can start drinking."

I frowned. "We're done? Already?"

Exos chuckled. "Yeah, it's not a difficult transfer when a royal already has access to the elemental source. It has to be done on the grounds of the element—which is why we're in Spirit Kingdom. But as I was already the rightful heir with direct ties to the source, it didn't take long. Cyrus's ceremony will be a bit grander since he's refused his water ability most of his life."

My Water Fae mate grimaced. "I prefer not to think about that right now." He clapped his brother on the back. "Tonight's about you, Exos. We all know how much you adore being the center of attention, so shall we get started?"

A few of the nearby Spirit Fae laughed, clearly hearing the sarcasm in Cyrus's commentary. Exos just shook his head. "You're incorrigible, brother."

"So you and my little queen keep saying," Cyrus drawled, winking at me. "Want something to drink, Claire? Maybe a glass of mead?"

Exos's mouth preoccupied mine before I could reply, his tongue parting my lips and capturing my undivided attention. Oh, his kisses literally removed me from this plane. I wound my arms around his neck, holding him close, and gave him everything. All my adoration. My trust. My heart. My soul.

His element stroked mine, eliciting a flurry of butterflies across my skin. I giggled as they appeared in corporeal form, their pink wings fluttering in excitement.

Several fae gasped around us, awed by the display of power.

But Exos merely smiled. "Always creating life, my Claire." He pressed another kiss to my lips before releasing me. "Let's have some mead before Gale drinks it all."

Someone snorted loudly. "It's ye brother who'll drink it all, lad."

Cyrus pressed his palm to his heart. "Me? Never."

A few laughs echoed through the main square, causing Exos's mouth to tilt upward even more. "It's a joyous occasion," he announced, lifting his eyes to the crowd. "Let us celebrate new life and a renewed destiny, and drink to a prosperous future for the Spirit Fae."

"Hear, hear!" everyone cheered, the sounds of excited chatter breaking out amongst the town. It wasn't long until the spritemead made its rounds, all the fae indulging in mugs of the potent liquid. And a fire blazed to life— courtesy of Exos's secondary ability—in the cobblestone center.

Pixies and other fairylike creatures buzzed about, delivering plates of snacks, while a female with long blonde hair tended to what appeared to be a roasting boar above the fire.

It all unfolded so naturally, so beautifully, that I wondered how often the town's people indulged in such festivities.

"Not regularly," Exos whispered. "Not anymore, anyway."

"Morale is down," Cyrus added. "Way down."

We sat on a wool blanket a few yards away from the flames. Other couples had joined us nearby but kept to themselves while they enjoyed the appetizers brought to them by the flickering "staff."

"Maybe you need to do this more often," I suggested, glancing around. "They seem to be enjoying themselves."

It was laid-back, but the vibe felt happy, almost relieved to have a reason to socialize. I couldn't imagine how lonely these fae were with how much loss they'd suffered over the years. And that none of them could have children, well, I assumed that only worsened the mood.

Most areas of the Spirit Kingdom were like Spirit Quad at the Academy— desolate and dead. This was honestly the most life I'd seen since visiting these lands. I wanted to see more of it, to learn more about all the fae who survived, to find a way to help them grow.

There had to be a reason the fae couldn't procreate, some sort of lasting impact on the spirit element. My mother would know. Maybe it was good she hadn't really died. When we found her, we could demand answers.

"A hunt?" Cyrus asked, eavesdropping on my thoughts as he was wont to do. "I'm down for that." He bumped my shoulder. "But you still have classes, little queen."

"I think locating my mass-murdering bitch of a mother is a little more important than school," I muttered, staring at the flames. "She tried to kill me. Hurt Exos. Killed thousands of fae." Each statement made me angrier and angrier. "And she's still alive somewhere, probably plotting her next move."

Something dastardly and evil.

I could feel the knowledge of it in my blood, the very real burn of an impending doom.

Cyrus wrapped his arm around my shoulders and yanked me into his side. "Nothing is going to happen to you, Claire. Not on my watch."

"Or mine," Exos added, his hand grabbing mine.

I shook my head. "It's not me I'm worried about." *But everyone else.* "She almost killed you, Exos."

He canted his head, his lips curling. "No, baby. She didn't come close to killing me. I'm a lot tougher than that." He released my hand to cup my cheek and leaned in to kiss me. "And we're mated now, princess. So you'll never have to worry about losing me again."

Cyrus's lips met my neck, his kiss working its way up to my ear. "You're stuck with me, too, little queen."

Fire licked a path down my spine, my stomach tightening in anticipation.

Only to have a female clear her throat. "Your Highnesses," she greeted as both men looked up at her.

"Feather," Cyrus replied, grinning. "Thank you for organizing the roast. Orc is Exos's favorite."

My eyes widened. "*Orc?*" Like the giant horned-goblin things? "Orcs are real?" I demanded, looking at Exos.

He kissed my temple. "Not the way you think. But Cyrus is right. I love a meaty orc. When do we eat?"

I suddenly wasn't very hungry. All I could envision were those gross-looking things from that famous movie about the ring. Weren't they, like, dead elves or something? "Where does spritemead come from?" I asked, cutting off whatever Feather had just said. "Sorry," I added, my cheeks heating.

Cyrus squeezed my shoulders a little. *Honey and grains, little queen. Made by the fae with all-natural elements.*

Well, that's okay, then. But orc? Yeah, I'll pass on that.

Feather asked Exos if he wanted to do the honors of slicing off the first piece. He heartily agreed, leaving me beside Cyrus to watch. I cringed, shaking my head back and forth the entire time.

Nope.

Not happening.

Don't care at all how hot Exos looks in that suit. A girl has to have limits, and I am not eating that.

When he returned with three plates and a dimple on his cheek, I sort of felt obligated to at least try the odd meat. No, I felt coerced. Seduced. Compelled. Whatever the word. And I had to admit, it didn't smell all that bad. It reminded me a bit of roast beef, at least in terms of scent.

"You use the algae wrap to eat it," Cyrus explained, picking up the leafy green on his plate. He used it to break off a hunk of the orc and put it in his mouth, then waggled his eyebrows as he chewed.

Anyone else, and I would have gagged.

But it was Cyrus.

And somehow, he made the entire damn thing look elegant and far too sexy.

Exos did the same, minus the eyebrow move. He just smiled afterward and promised to find me something else if I didn't want to try the meat. Which was apparently a delicacy, according to Cyrus.

Because yeah, why wouldn't orc be a delicacy?

When in the fae world, I thought to myself as I broke off a piece of the leafy green wrap. *How the times have changed.*

One of these days, I was going to force the guys to find me a pizza. No, a hamburger. Maybe both. And ice cream. Oh, that sounded decadent. But instead, I had a weird piece of roast beef–looking meat wedged between two grassy leaves.

I closed my eyes and forced myself to take a bite.

Warm and smoky. Not chewy. Hmm.

I wrapped up another piece and tossed it into my mouth.

Okay. This isn't bad. Actually, it's pretty good.

After a few more bites, I found Exos and Cyrus both watching me with hungry expressions. "What?" I asked, wiping my lips.

"You keep moaning," Exos replied.

"Loudly," Cyrus added, his gaze falling to my mouth.

"Oh." I swallowed. "Uh, the orc is, uh, good." I picked up my spritemead and downed the rest of my mug, needing a distraction.

Exos took it from my hand as soon as I finished.

And Cyrus wrapped his palm around the back of my neck and pulled me in for a kiss, his tongue wasting no time in exploring my mouth. *More than good,* he corrected, referring to my comment about the orc. *You taste amazing, Claire.*

He released me on a pant, my chest rising and falling from the much-needed oxygen that disappeared as Exos took hold and sealed his mouth over mine.

Right. Okay. I can get used to this.

Cyrus chuckled and Exos growled, the combining sounds making my heart skip a beat. These two males were going to be the death of me one of these days.

And what a beautiful death it would be...

But as soon as the kissing began, it slowed to a stop as Cyrus and Exos tucked me between them. My body protested while my chest expanded on a sigh of contentment. One of them picked at the remainder on my plate, bringing bites to my mouth and to their own, as we sat in silence to observe the still-roaring fire.

Peace settled over me.

Satisfaction.

Rightness.

This was the life I was always meant to lead. I just hadn't known it existed until very recently. But now that I'd embraced it, I didn't know any other way of being. This was just me. My world. My fae. And I would do anything and everything to protect it.

Even from my own flesh and blood.

My eyes began to drift closed, the hour darkening the sky as all the fae continued to mingle in soft waves of conversation. Exos and Cyrus murmured around me, conversing together and with others, while I rested tranquilly between them.

I felt protected in their arms. Happy. Thankful.

But something nagged at the back of my mind. An uncertainty I couldn't quite identify. The sensation of being watched. Which, yeah, everyone at the bonfire had their eyes on me. However, this was different. An almost surreal sensation, one I shouldn't be able to sense yet did.

And I swore for half a second that it was my mother's presence I felt. Except it lacked the darkness I expected. Worry and urgency floated in its place. A message I couldn't hear. Lost to a connection we never—

"Claire," Cyrus whispered, his mouth hovering over mine. "Wake up, little queen."

Light pierced my gaze, startling me to my new surroundings. We were back at the palace in Exos's room.

"How did we...?" I swallowed, my throat dry from what felt like hours of sleep.

"A little too much mead, it seems," he teased, kissing me softly as he slid into the bed beside me.

Warmth caressed my back as Exos wrapped his arm around my waist.

Only then did I realize the three of us were naked.

Very, very naked.

Cyrus pressed a kiss to the corner of my mouth. "Mmm, we'll let you sleep." He nuzzled my nose. "You need it."

Exos sighed against the back of my neck. "Something to look forward to another night."

"Indeed," Cyrus agreed, his icy blue eyes glittering with promise. "Sweet dreams, little queen."

"Yes, sweet dreams, darling Claire," Exos breathed against my ear. "We'll return to the Academy tomorrow."

Snuggled between them, I had a hard time denying the pull of their words. While my body desired something different, my mind felt exhausted from something I couldn't identify.

That message, I thought, yawning. Seeking it out had left me tired. But I couldn't for the life of me remember why or whom I'd been trying to connect to.

A query to solve tomorrow.

For tonight, I allowed myself to fall into the safe haven of my two royal mates. And dreamt of what it would be like to experience them both… at the same time.

CHAPTER FIVE
TITUS

LIFE WITHOUT CLAIRE SUCKED.

I should have been in class, but there was no way I could focus right now. Instead of causing trouble and picking a fight with my fellow Fire Fae, I decided it was safer for the Academy if I just stayed here and took my frustration out on the dusty practice arena in front of the Spirit Dorm.

I'd only just gotten her back.

Now she was gone. *Again.*

It didn't matter that there was a good reason for her absence. A hole existed in my heart where her essence should have been, and demanded that I do something about it.

I spun a magicked bo staff and sent a blaze of fire running a jagged line through the sand, leaving behind a streak of melted glass. The staff itself threatened to buckle under the heat, but it would hold up for a few hours more. It was the third one I'd gone through this week. I really needed to get some better weapons.

My growing power should have frightened me. Claire was changing me—changing all of us. Her lingering power surrounded me on our familiar training grounds and gave me a small sense of comfort.

Gods. I just wanted to see her again.

I put on a good show for Sol and Vox, but I missed her more than anything. Every kiss and touch had strengthened our bond. But that connection strained when I was apart from her for too long.

My eyes flashed open, my instincts flaring.

Someone's coming.

I didn't know how I knew, but I sensed the approaching presence. A subtle shift of heat and magic, disturbing unseen elemental currents that ran through the Fae Realm. Maybe it was Mortus trying to recruit me for the more advanced classes again, or Professor Vulcan come to chide me for yet another absence.

"Whoever it is, now's not a good time," I growled to the shimmering air roiling with heat. "I'm in no mood." I twirled the training staff and let the flames etching across the magicked wood grow hotter. Nothing too fancy or exciting or all that intimidating.

I really need more practice with elemental weapons to help protect Claire. The real world used fire and other magical essences, unlike the Powerless Arena.

A teasing hint of water misted over my bare chest, causing steam to fog the air, and I raised a brow.

Cyrus misted in front of me with a grinning Claire in his arms. She launched from him with a laugh and jumped into my aura of flames, causing my weapon to fall with a clatter against the ground. She merged with my element, seamlessly transitioning from water to fire as the living magic enveloped her as its own.

"Hey, you," she said, her voice husky as if she was high on elements and sex.

Which, given the way Cyrus smirked at me, was probably accurate.

"Hey," I replied, unable to stop the pleased grin that spread across my face as I tucked my hands under her perfectly rounded ass and held her against me.

Cyrus invaded the flames, sending the heat sprawling away from him with an effortless wave of water that wrinkled my nose. His lips went to her neck as if he couldn't stop touching her.

I understood that feeling.

"I have business to attend to, little queen," he whispered in her ear, then gave her a nip. His silver-blue eyes locked onto mine. "I trust Titus can handle your needs while I'm gone."

My pleased grin turned sinister. Maybe it was insulting that Cyrus was literally using my dick as a way to keep Claire occupied, but I didn't care.

Not when she wiggled in my arms like that.

"What kind of business?" Claire asked, her lids heavy as she stroked a line of fire up my neck. "Hmm, because I wonder what it would feel like to mix water and fire," she added, glancing at me with a mischievous glint as a cool mist of her magic ran down my abs, sending steam between us. Her fingers followed the cool touch, playfully bringing warmth back to my protesting skin.

The effect was fucking amazing.

Cyrus chuckled, and I realized that I'd groaned—loudly.

"Why don't you practice for me? Seems like Titus may enjoy it." Without answering her question, he misted away, leaving me and Claire alone in the training yard.

I didn't give her an opportunity to go after him. I didn't know if she could mist now, but I wasn't going to risk losing her attention again. I claimed her mouth with mine and scooped her up against me.

"I missed you," I told her between breaths.

"I missed—" She tried to reply, but my tongue was busy exploring hers as I all but sprinted us to the Spirit Dorm.

She laughed when I tossed her onto my mattress with a bounce. "I think that was a new record of getting me into bed," she said, fisting the sheets and bringing them to her nose. She inhaled and her eyelids fluttered closed. "Mmm…"

Seeing her take in my scent made my already rigid cock stand to attention. The inferno in me was primal, and it wanted to *claim*.

I was already shirtless, but my pants were a sudden restriction that needed to be removed. Instead of slipping them off, my flames ignited and seared over my skin, burning what was supposed to be a fireproof garment.

Claire's eyes flickered with blue fire as her element responded to mine, and her gaze dropped in appreciation. "We really need to invest in some better fireproof wear for you," she said as she tilted her head and licked her lips.

Sensing what she wanted, I stepped to the edge of the bed and groaned as she wrapped her plump lips around the head. I fisted my fingers through her gorgeous hair, urging her to take me deeper while cautioning her at the same time.

"Careful, Claire. I won't be able to last long if you keep doing that," I warned, flames licking down her shirt and leaving a trail of ash as my element played with her nipples.

She gasped, then ran her tongue defiantly up my shaft, making my legs go weak. Her gaze snapped up to mine, full of fight and challenge. The embers in her eyes glazed over with a sparkle of ice, and she let out a long breath directly against my cock, one of cool mist that mixed a foreign element into our play. She skimmed her tongue over the delicate skin, sending a new blast of heat that had my cock throbbing as startled nerves ignited back to life.

"Fuck, Claire," I growled, then grabbed her by her hips and unleashed a wave of fire over her, burning all remnants of her clothes. I spun her so that her back was to me, then I wrapped one arm around her chest and cupped the space between her legs with my opposite hand. She tossed her head back onto my shoulder and grappled at my arms as I pinched her clit. "I'll punish you for that little ice trick," I vowed, my tone playful.

She writhed against me, her need palpable. "You'd better punish me harder," she said as her ass rubbed up against my throbbing shaft in clear provocation.

I shouldn't have obliged her, not yet, but my hips adjusted to match her entrance and then I was inside her, thrusting hard—just as she'd requested.

"Titus," she cried as her body clenched around mine.

She was different now that Exos had ascended to the spirit throne. I could sense the shift in her, the aching need that demanded she connect with all her mates. Perhaps part of her desire for me was because Exos's second element was fire and it would be a natural progression for her to seal the bond with me next.

In time, I would claim her completely, but the fires that threatened to consume us frightened even me.

So I enjoyed the burn and lost myself as I tipped over the edge with her into blissful oblivion.

* * *

Well, the room was destroyed, but I didn't care. In fact, I admired the licks of fire scars across the walls followed by permanent streaks of ice that refused to melt.

Claire lazily rested against my chest as her fingers explored mine. "I think we need to have sex in a metal stronghold," she mused on a chuckle. "This is getting ridiculous."

"I kind of like the look," I said, grinning at the pattern of destruction that was uniquely beautiful in the way ash and ice spiraled over one another across the damaged room.

When she sighed, not out of satisfaction but a subconscious sound of discontent, I shifted to look into her eyes. "What's wrong?"

She blinked up at me. "What? Oh, nothing." She grinned, that discontent disappearing behind her love for me. She ran her fingers over the short stubble of my chin and pressed a kiss to my lips. "You gave me exactly what I needed, Titus."

I stroked her hair from her face. "And what's bothering you that you needed a fire-fuck to get your mind off of it?" I pressed a kiss to her forehead. "Don't hide your problems from me, Claire. I'm more to you than that, aren't I?"

Her eyes widened. "Of course. You mean more to me than anything. I didn't mean it that way; I just—"

I chuckled and sealed her mouth with a kiss. "I'm just teasing, sweetheart. What's on your mind?"

She trailed her tongue across my lower lip, trying to distract me.

I tsked, running my thumb across her cheek, and gazed into her eyes. "None of that, Claire. Talk to me."

A small smile quirked at the side of her mouth. "Stubborn," she grumbled, then rested her head against my chest once more. "It was just a lot to take in, you know? The whole Spirit Kingdom and meeting all of the Spirit Fae." Her eyes fluttered closed as if she were reliving the past few days. "I glimpsed what they should have been like, but I know that Exos's coronation was a rare cause of happiness among them." Her fingers clenched into a fist. "My mother took so much from them, Titus. And I don't feel like she's done."

I wrapped my arms around her and held her tight. I would protect her from whatever would come, give my life for her if that would take away even a fraction of her pain. "You don't need to be afraid, Claire. I'll make sure nothing happens to you."

She hesitated, then burrowed into my neck.

She didn't say anything, but I knew her true fear.

It wasn't her own life she was worried about. My Claire wanted to save the world.

And I loved her for it.

Chapter Six
Claire

Just days ago, I stood in the middle of Spirit Kingdom while Exos ascended to his throne. And now I was back at the Academy meeting Elana for our biweekly training.

Somehow, it felt wrong. Like I should be doing more than just attending classes as usual and acting as though I didn't know my mother had tried to kill me. But every time I tried to say something to Elana about it, my lips seemed to seal shut.

Which only made this session all the more uncomfortable.

My saving grace was knowing Sol stood just outside waiting for me to finish. At least returning here meant I had all my mates in one place again. Although, Cyrus kept leaving for his mysterious meetings in the Water Kingdom. And Exos had returned to his Spirit Fae twice in the last few days on business.

It made me wonder what life would be like when all my mates graduated.

Would I have to travel between the kingdoms to see them all?

I frowned. *Cyrus really needs to teach me how to mist.*

"Everything all right, dear?" Elana asked, her silver eyes kind in her assessment.

"Just thinking about the coronation," I replied. Not necessarily a lie. It was related to my future, right?

But Elana didn't look all that convinced, her brow pinched in a way I didn't care to see.

So I said the first thing I could to deflect the subject back on her.

"You weren't there. I assume because it's not mandatory to attend that sort of event?" I phrased it as a question, which was totally lame. However, the way her face clouded over suggested I'd touched on an interesting topic. "Mortus wasn't there either."

She nodded slowly, the pixie she'd conjured disappearing into mist. *Water,* I realized, fighting another frown. *She just used water.*

Something I wouldn't have questioned except that Elana supposedly only had access to spirit. So how was she using water now? Had she somehow manifested the element and not told anyone? Maybe it was a fledgling power. Or—

"I hated missing the coronation," Elana said, interrupting my thoughts. "But the Academy required me to stay here. Mortus, too. All the young lives at this school are my responsibility, and I take that responsibility seriously."

My brow furrowed. The way she said that made it sound like the Academy could be in danger.

Because of my mother? I wondered. *Does she know that Ophelia is still alive?*

It was on the tip of my tongue to ask, but my voice refused me. Literally. Like, I couldn't part my lips. It felt as though someone had clamped an invisible hand over my mouth. Urgent whispers flooded my thoughts, all of them unintelligible.

I'm losing my damn mind.

That was it.

I clearly needed more sleep. Less sex. Something. Because apparently, I no longer had control over my brain or my body.

Elana had said something while I was lost to the invisible force controlling my body. She stared at me expectantly. "Sorry, I missed that," I admitted, my mouth working just fine over those words.

My mentor gave me another one of those concerned looks. "Are you sure you're all right, Claire?"

"Mm-hmm." I cleared my throat. "I'm just a little tired. It's been an exciting week." Understatement of the fucking century.

Her silver eyes told me she didn't believe me, but she allowed the topic to drop. "Well, how about we focus on something new today? Instead of pixies, I mean."

"Sure. What did you have in mind?"

She swept her hand in a wide circle and conjured an ethereal bowl of water. *No. Correction. That is definitely not water.*

"You've established a firm hold over life, the side of spirit that comes naturally. However, there is another side to your power you've yet to explore, and I think it's time to teach you what it really means to be a Spirit Fae." Elana locked a cold grip on my wrist, making me suck in a breath.

There was only one other side of life that I could think of.

Death.

Power flooded into me, fluxing back and forth as my mentor tugged at my spirit essence that wasn't ready for this invasion. "What are you doing?" I asked, my voice going up a pitch.

Elana gave me one of her kind smiles in an effort to soothe me, but every hair stood on end as the temperature in the room plummeted. "Relax, Claire. This is a normal progression to your training that I promise you are ready for."

I didn't feel ready.

And this certainly didn't seem all that *normal.*

The bowl of misty liquid rippled as Elana concentrated. "Think of your power and what it is capable of. Spirit transcends this world, and that is a beautiful thing." Her element tugged at mine again, just enough to extract a sliver of my connection to Exos—to the source.

A translucent face formed, one with dead, silver eyes that looked right through me.

Elana smiled. "My, this is one of the older Spirit Fae I haven't had the pleasure of talking with yet. Well done, Claire."

I didn't feel like I'd done anything at all.

Trying to extract my grip from Elana's, I found myself bound to her and an icy power linking us as the spirit finally focused his gaze on me. It tried to smile, but the motion seemed forced.

"Why don't you try speaking to him?" Elana asked. "Introduce yourself."

The last thing I wanted to do was talk to the spirit of a dead fae. It seemed inappropriate. Intrusive. *Wrong.*

"Um," I managed to say around my tongue, which had gone dry. "Hi. I'm, uh, Claire. Who are you?"

The spirit tilted its head, the motion slightly unnatural with his unblinking stare. "You?" he asked, not seeming to be able to comprehend my question.

"Use your power," Elana encouraged. "Ancient spirits are accustomed to rest, not conversation. He'll need some help."

Help. Right.

My lips twisted to the side. I didn't see the point in disturbing an ancient fae's rest like this, but clearly, Elana wanted me to learn something.

Use your power, she'd suggested.

Okay.

I concentrated on the writhing form, on the agony teasing the edges of his lopsided mouth. My brow furrowed. *What happened to you?* I wondered, noting the way he flinched every few seconds as if reliving his death over and over again.

Was that why this felt so wrong to disturb him? Because it tortured him to call upon his spirit?

"Pain?" I asked, using a single word with a coaxing strand of my power underlining the question. This all felt so strange and foreign. I needed to know if the spirit was suffering as a result of our intrusion.

Elana frowned. But I ignored her and focused on the visage before us.

His eyebrows—what was left of them—pulled down. He opened his mouth to say something, but then Elana ripped her hand from mine, dissolving the spell instantly and sending out a shock wave of mist and energy.

"Spirits need to be comforted and coaxed," Elana chided, clearly irritated with me. She brushed her hands together and sighed, transforming back into the patient and kind mentor in a second, the change a startling one. "You're a sweet creature, Claire. But your human side has too much empathy. Spirits can't feel pain, I assure you. It may seem like they can, but that's just because they mimic the life that came before. When conjured, they are tools just like any other power offered by the elements."

My spine went rigid. *Tools?* Elements weren't tools. At least not to me, or to my mates. Our gifts were to be respected and embraced—not used as mindless *tools*.

"I see," I murmured, not sure what else to say.

Elana seemed to sense my discomfort, and she summoned a few familiar pixies to clean the table of the sparkling spirit dust. Warmth and life seeped back into the air, bringing with it a sense of rightness. I almost sighed in my relief, except the cool claws of reality seemed to be clinging to my heart.

That soul… he felt pain. I was certain of it.

"I don't mean to frighten you, sweet child. You have to understand that I'm a thousand years old. I've seen life and death run its course hundreds of times, and I have grown to accept its finality." Elana twisted a ring around her finger. "It's easier that way."

Guilt spiked a hole through my chest.

Of course Elana must have lost so many friends and family members over the years. I was being too hard on her to expect her to have the same level of empathy that I did. What did I really know of loss or spirits? Rick's death still held its bitter weight in my soul, but that was one death, whereas Elana must have experienced many. "I'm sorry," I said. "You're right." I gave her a weak smile. "It was just… unexpected. That's all."

She nodded. "Sometimes lessons are best learned without warning." She rose to her feet and brushed spirit dust from her dress. "I've traumatized you enough for today. Return to your mates, Claire, and think about what I've said. You have a great gift, and if you choose to embrace it, you can help the Spirit Fae and the rest of the realm in ways no one else can. I would love to explore your spirit magic further on our next visit. We don't have to continue to explore this side of your power if you are averse to it. However, if you are willing, there is much I can teach you."

The hope in her gaze said she truly believed me to be capable of great things. Although, I wasn't sure I could ever get behind summoning spirits as part of my training. "I'll think on it," I promised. "Thank you, Chancellor."

Elana beamed and guided me to the front hall, indulging me in meaningless chitchat that I tuned out, too consumed with the day and everything that had happened.

All I wanted to do was return to my mates. To Sol, who waited just outside and promised me life—not death.

I smiled to myself. *Yes. My Earth Fae is exactly what I need right now.*

CHAPTER SEVEN
SOL

FINALLY, IT WAS MY TURN WITH CLAIRE. I knew having four other mates kept Claire busy, but I hadn't gotten to spend time with her like this since before she left for the Spirit Kingdom.

I paced back and forth in front of Elana's mansion, not realizing that I was grinding a crack in the stone until I tripped over a jagged edge. How long was Elana going to keep Claire in there? Was everything all right? Should I go in?

Before I made a fool of myself and barged into the Chancellor's home, Claire appeared with a knot to her brow and her gaze distant. I waved a hand in front of her face.

"That bad?" I asked.

She blinked up at me as if she'd almost forgotten I was there. I'll admit, that stung a little, but then she smiled and slipped her fingers around my neck to pull me down for a kiss. Her lips brushed mine, and I tossed out any notion that Claire could ever forget about me.

"Better now," she promised, then curled into my chest. "I just don't think Elana was good for me today. I need to relax."

I grinned and wrapped an arm around her tiny waist, careful not to put too much weight on her. It made me nervous to be this close to Claire without

Vox as my backup to make sure I didn't break her, but I couldn't use him as a crutch forever.

Baby steps.

"I know the perfect place to relax," I told her, grinning.

She glanced up at me, curiosity bright in her blue eyes. Her irises had an occasional rainbow sparkle to them now that she had embraced her fae half, and I adored the small curve of her newly pointed ears. "Consider me intrigued," she said.

I led the way toward a field between the Spirit Quad and the Earth Quad. I'd tried—and failed—to grow Claire an oasis of peach trees on more than one occasion. I finally figured out that it was all about placement. Too much shit went down on a constant basis to have such delicate things out in the open in the Spirit Quad. Not with Vox sending tornados out the window when he sneezed and Titus setting things aflame because, well, that was just what Titus did.

No, Claire and I needed a place only for us.

Just for earth and sky and sweetness.

The punch of flowering peach trees hit us before we crested the hill to the small grove hidden in the forest.

Claire's eyes lit up and she sucked in a breath. "Sol, did you make this? It's gorgeous!"

My heart grew three times its normal size. I'd created and lost so many groves in an attempt to impress Claire. They never seemed good enough or were destroyed before she'd gotten a chance to see them. Then I had worried she would think it was stupid or a waste of energy.

But seeing her expression now? Yeah, it was worth all the effort.

She grabbed my hand and dragged me into the oasis, the crunch of forest under her shoes morphing into the soft patter of her footsteps over the smooth stones I'd placed for a path. My own thunderous footfalls drowned out her excitement, but she didn't seem to mind.

Claire let go of me toward the middle and skipped to one of the trees, running her fingers up through the leaves and wrapping her delicate fingers around a peach. She snapped it free and brought it to her nose. She closed her eyes and drew in a long, deep inhale. When she let out the breath, her eyes fluttered open and she smiled at me. "Sol, really, this is lovely."

Encouraged, I waved a hand and sent a wall of forest trees aside to show the rest of the grove that I was still working on. "It's not done yet, but I was hoping you could help me. I mean, I was hoping we could work on it together."

She approached the clearing where small mounds of dirt waited for life. I craved more of her magic, of the sweet fruit and mystery that only Claire could provide.

So the place didn't look too bare, I had sent pink and purple fae flowers around the perimeter. It gave the place a pop of color, and Claire grinned as she stepped over the boundary. "It's like a fairy circle," she mused.

We'd told her a hundred times that fairies weren't a thing, but I shrugged and agreed. She could call this place whatever she wanted. "Sure."

She chuckled and handed me the peach. "In the human world, we have these stories in which there are fairy circles. If you get trapped inside, then the fairies will take you to their world and never let you leave."

I bit into the sweet flesh of the peach and chewed as I considered the idea of a fairy circle. I swallowed and nodded. "You've got me. I'm not letting you leave." I offered her the remaining half of the peach. "But at least you won't starve."

She took it, then ran a finger over my mouth where a hint of peach lingered. Her features softened, and I leaned down to her unspoken command to adore her. She met me with a tender kiss, her tongue running over my lips, and then she parted for me when I couldn't resist a taste for myself.

She was so much fucking better than a peach.

My hand went to her collarbone in a possessive grip, but I forced myself to pull away. That tension was still in her body, and I wasn't going to ignore the signs that my mate had something on her mind.

"What's wrong?" I pressed.

She licked her lips, her gaze lowering to take in the bulge forming at my crotch.

Well, I couldn't help that.

She was my mate and we were alone, and all I wanted to do was show her how much she meant to me, but I would always put her needs before my own.

"I should be asking you the same question," she teased, but a darkness in her eyes said that she was weary and troubled.

Without giving her a chance to stop me, I scooped her up, running my arm across the back of her legs, and slipped her against my chest. She squealed as she went airborne, and the peach in her hand went flying as she clung to my neck. "Sol!"

I marched her to the biggest tree in the oasis. Peach trees dotted the long path I'd made, but there was one surprise at the end.

The fae called it a World Tree, and it would be where Claire and I would one day consummate our vows. Assuming, of course, that she intended to someday have me as her true mate.

For now, it would be where I would share secrets with her, where she would be free to open up to me, and where we'd both feel safe from anything that chased her.

This was our place.

Her eyes went wide when she took in the long silver branches that made the tree appear otherworldly. "What is that?" she asked against my cheek.

"A World Tree," I said, proud of the creation. I'd come a long way in my studies and my powers since Claire had taught me not to be afraid of what I was capable of. "It's just one branch of many that come from my magic's source."

Vox hadn't been pleased when I showed him this the other day, saying it was dangerous to tap into my royal blood.

The look on Claire's face now, however, told me he was wrong.

Large roots sprawled out from the base, making a perfect bed with soft moss, and I laid Claire down onto it before joining her. She nestled up against me and slipped her fingers under my shirt, exploring the muscles across my chest.

"You're full of surprises, Sol."

I gave her a kiss on the crown of her head. "And you're full of worry. Spill it, or I'll tell Cyrus that you're holding back."

She laughed. "No, you won't."

She was right. Talking to Cyrus didn't fall on my favored list of activities, and everyone knew it. Not my fault the Royal Fae was a pompous ass. Oh, he gave me space. But I saw through his antics.

Fucking waterfall.

I brushed the hair from Claire's face and pressed my forehead to hers. "I'm here for you, little flower." That was what she felt like—a delicate bloom that could fly away on the wind if I breathed too hard. "Talk to me. Did something happen?"

Her fingers continued to explore my skin, making the earth tremble as my need for her grew. "It's Elana, I guess. She introduced me to the other half of my element today, and it sort of didn't go as planned," she admitted, then sighed. "Actually, no. Honestly, I think it's my mother that's bothering me more."

"Oh?"

She bit her lip, the motion distracting me before she continued. "Everything just feels off. I can't really explain it, just a sense of wrongness. But I know it's her."

"Off how?"

She sighed and draped her leg over mine. I couldn't help but notice that it put her hips dangerously close to my reach. If she kept that up, I was going to be useless in this conversation.

Her glittering blue eyes met mine, holding me captive. "It's just, I think I keep hearing her. In my head. But unclearly." Her gaze darted around our oasis. "She feels very *here*."

I stiffened and immediately unlatched the door I kept over my roaring power, sending the ground around us rumbling. But I only found Claire and her bond-mates in blissful harmony, nothing dark. "I don't feel anything."

"I didn't mean *here*," she murmured, smiling. "But with me somehow."

She shook her head. "Honestly, I think I'm just exhausted from everything. It's probably all the sex." Her eyes glittered with intent as she slid her hand across my shirt, parting the buttons to expose my abs along the way. She let out a long breath of appreciation. "Sometimes I can't believe all of this is real."

I couldn't take it anymore and ran my hand over her hip and down her thigh, squeezing while putting my thumb just close enough between her legs to give her a hint of anticipation. Her breath hitched as I massaged her knotted muscles. "It's very real, little flower. We'd do anything for you."

Her expression sparkled with delight, then turned mischievous. "Even dress up in a real suit for the Solstice Ball?"

I grimaced, but my heart leapt that she'd brought it up. "I thought we'd agreed on jeans."

Her fingers ran lower across my abdomen, causing my muscles to clench. "You'd look good in silk, I think." She licked her lips and then leaned in, replacing her touch with her tongue.

I rumbled my agreement. If she wanted silk, I'd wear the damn silk. Fuck, I'd go naked. I didn't care, not when she was doing...

That.

I groaned when her mouth came dangerously close to my beltline, and the ground trembled as my powers threatened to lose control.

"I can't, little flower," I said through gritted teeth.

Gods, I wanted to, but I felt my control slipping. Either we needed a full mate-bond to keep me grounded or I needed Vox here with us. Regardless, I would never do anything that put Claire in danger.

She didn't argue, her understanding written into her features. "You shouldn't be afraid of your gifts," she whispered, nestling back up into my neck as she wrapped her leg around my hip again and pressed her entire body into mine.

My aching cock underneath the thin layer of my clothes protested when her thigh pressed into my shaft, but she stilled when I gripped her hip to keep her from moving.

"I'm not," I promised her. "I'm just careful with you."

She chuckled and lazily swept her fingers over my chest. I indulged her mouth with a tender kiss. "Perhaps later, then," she suggested, delight in her voice. "If you need the others with us to feel safe with me, then they'll be happy to oblige, I'm sure." She gave me another kiss, this one more forceful. "But promise me that one day it can be just us. Maybe your World Tree with our earth and our love." She adored all her bond-mates, but it made me feel like an entirely new fae that Claire wanted me all to herself.

My hand went to its possessive hold on her neck again as I tasted her. "That's a promise I can keep, when we're ready." When the bond between us was so strong that even the earth would move on command.

She poked me on my nose. "And you're taking me to the ball."

I nodded, nipping her lower lip. "You have a deal, little flower."

CHAPTER EIGHT
CLAIRE

I PINCHED MY LIPS TO THE SIDE. *Something's missing.* I just couldn't put my finger on it.

My makeup was subtle, my hair was tousled in long blonde waves down my back, and my blue dress had the most amazing sweetheart neckline. It accented my curves in all the right places without being too clingy. The fabric also matched my eyes, which was a plus.

But something wasn't right.

I tapped my chin, my gaze on my reflection in the mirror. This sense of uncertainty weighed upon my shoulders, holding me captive in my three-inch silver heels.

What is it? I wondered. *What am I not seeing?*

The edges of the glass dimmed a fraction, flickering beneath the fluorescent lighting. I just couldn't stop staring at myself and wondering what—

"You look gorgeous," a warm voice murmured from behind me. A pink butterfly kissed my cheek following the words before settling on my pointed ear like an ornament.

I blinked at my reflection, everything suddenly right. "How strange, yet oddly beautiful."

"You or the butterfly?" Exos mused, coming up to stand at my back. He wore one of his trademark suits, making our attire match for once. Except somehow he still wore the formal outfit better than I did. Benefits of being the king, I supposed.

"Everything," I replied, shaking my head and shifting to face him. "Ignore me. I've felt a little off all day."

He cupped my cheek and drew his thumb across my lip, his gaze thoughtful. "Off how?"

I knew that look. If I didn't give him an answer, he'd press me for one. And we didn't have time to play that game right now. Besides, Exos was my mate. He'd understand, or maybe even be able to put me at ease.

"I just feel like I'm missing something," I admitted. "That's weird, right? I can't think of anything I might need tonight other than what I'm wearing."

Exos's sapphire irises smoldered as he reviewed my appearance, his full lips quirking at the corner. "Oh, I don't know. Are you wearing panties?"

My cheeks heated. "Exos."

"Are they blue like this dress?" he pressed, his hands finding my hips. "Shall I lift your skirt to see?"

I laughed and shook my head. "One-track mind."

"Can you blame me, Claire?" He eyed my neckline. "You look amazing in this dress. It makes me want to attend the ball with you and the others, just to have a reason to stare at you all night."

My heart skipped a beat, my tongue sneaking out to dampen my lips. "So I look okay?"

"More than okay, princess. You're stunning." He bent to brush his mouth over mine. "Vox and Sol are going to have a hard time not bringing you home early. I give them two hours max before they can't take it anymore and need you naked between them."

I shivered at the heat of his words and the picture they painted. "Would you join us?"

"If you wanted me there, yes." Another kiss, this one longer, more sensual. "I would do anything for you, Claire."

My blood warmed, lighting a flame deep within my soul that burned for Exos alone. My spirit mate. My king. My love. I wrapped my arms around his neck and held him close, not caring at all about my makeup. All that mattered was his tongue and the way it embraced my own.

I would do anything for you, too, I whispered to him.

I knew how he felt about sharing me. He'd commented once to Titus that he didn't mind sharing in my pleasure, but watching me with another wasn't an activity he particularly wanted to experience.

And yet, with Cyrus, he seemed rather open to it.

Maybe our bond had changed his view.

You changed my view, he corrected, his palm flattening against my lower back.

Seeing you happy makes me happy. When you smile, I smile. He pulled back just enough to nuzzle his nose against mine. "I love you, Claire."

"I love you, too," I whispered, closing my eyes. Everything about the moment felt right again. This was what I was missing—my mates. Being apart from them left me feeling empty and alone. They were my life now, my circle, my completion. I sighed against Exos, resting my cheek on his chest as I hugged him hard. "Thank you."

"For what?"

"For helping me feel better."

"Anytime." He kissed the top of my head. "It's been a whirlwind these last few months. Try to have some fun tonight. You've earned it."

"I can't believe I'm going to a ball," I marveled, amused. "Of all the things to do. I seriously thought dances were over after high school."

"Welcome to the fae world." He squeezed me once more before loosening his hold. "I'll take you dancing sometime, just the two of us."

I cocked a brow at him. "You dance?"

His lips curled. "Oh, Claire. You have no idea." With that, he released me and led me to the door. "Vox and Sol are waiting and I can feel their impatience."

Yeah, I could feel their nerves as well through the bond. I couldn't talk to them the way I did Titus, Exos, and Cyrus, but emotions traveled easily between all of us. Such as Sol and Vox's annoyance at Titus's amusement. My fire mate found their formal attire comical, something he'd clearly remarked on a few times in their presence.

I turned toward my makeup to touch up my face, only to find myself being led toward the door with Exos's palm against my lower back.

"No sense in reapplying lipstick, Claire. The guys will just destroy it." He pressed his lips to mine for emphasis and opened the door before I could protest.

Sol and Vox stood in the hallway, their expressions morphing from nervous to clear appreciation as they caught sight of my gown.

"Oh, wow," Sol said, awed. "You remind me of the azure meadows in the heart of Earth Kingdom, only even more alluring." He stepped forward and captured my hand, bringing it to his lips. "Hi."

Butterflies took flight in my stomach at that little word, the way his deep brown gaze twinkled with it almost shyly. I went to my toes to kiss him properly on the mouth. "Hi." I took in his crisp black-and-white tux. "While I love you in jeans, you do wear this rather nicely."

His lips twitched. "Yeah?"

"Yeah." I kissed him again before turning to a mute Vox. The silver around his black irises seemed to thicken as he gazed at me, giving him an unearthly regal glow.

He swallowed.

Twice.

And cleared his throat.

"Try using your air," Titus called from a few steps away. "I hear that helps with speaking."

Exos chuckled at my back. "Can you blame him for being a bit speechless?"

"I certainly don't," Cyrus mused, joining us. He looped his arm around my waist, tugging me to him without acknowledging the others, and captured my mouth in a hungry kiss that left me shaking with need against him. "Now you're properly warmed up." He winked and nipped at my bottom lip. "Your natural blush is so enticing, Claire."

"It is," Vox agreed, his voice sounding a bit hoarse. "She's magnificent. *You're* magnificent."

Now it was my turn to be speechless.

Between Cyrus's embrace, the heat radiating from Exos, Sol's compliments, and Vox's nerves, I felt a bit overwhelmed.

The only one who didn't seem to be flustering me was Titus, but catching his gaze from the other room, I understood why. He served as my rock, the one grounding me to the moment and lending me strength where he knew I would need it.

He blew me a kiss and winked.

All of these males played a different role in my sanity, bolstering my courage, taking care of me, and respecting me in ways I never could have anticipated.

I was seriously the luckiest woman in the world. No, in all the worlds. However many there might be.

I shook my head on a laugh. That was a topic for another day.

Tonight I wanted to have fun, just as Exos suggested.

I would spend the evening with two of my intended mates, forget about everything else, and just enjoy myself. Because my life? Yeah, my life was pretty fucking amazing.

And I had all my mates to thank for everything.

"Let's go to the ball," I said, eyeing Sol and Vox. "I can't wait to dance with you both."

CHAPTER NINE
EXOS

"WHAT'S WRONG?" Cyrus asked as soon as the door closed behind Claire.

I twisted my lips to the side. "Something's coming." I felt it rising all day, this sense of wrongness settling over my shoulders and knocking my world off-kilter. "She sensed it, too."

"Hence your distraction," Cyrus murmured.

I nodded. It hadn't been part of the arrangement for me to go to her in the room, but I'd sensed her need for emotional relief. "She deserves a night of fun without her mother hanging over her head." Or whatever this dark, doomful energy meant.

"I don't feel anything," Titus said, joining us in the hallway. He'd overheard our conversation, not that I'd tried to hide it from him. As Claire's mate and one of the strongest fighters I'd ever met, he needed to be involved in the discussion.

"It's a disturbance in the spirit." I folded my arms and leaned against the wall. "It feels like a gray cloud lingering on the horizon that refuses to leave. Claire mistook it for something she was forgetting. But I recognize it for what it is—a bad omen."

"Someone is playing with magic that doesn't belong here," Cyrus translated. "Dark Fae magic."

Yes, that was exactly what I felt. "Do you sense it, too?"

"Only through Claire," he admitted. "But it reminds me of Kols."

I snorted. "Feels harsher to me."

"But you know what I mean."

"I do." The energy signature was similar in origin, marking it as belonging to the infamous Midnight Fae, which we commonly called Dark Fae.

"Who or what is a Kols?" Titus interjected.

"A Midnight Fae Royal," Cyrus replied. "Cocky bastard, but a hell of a lot of fun at parties. You'd love him."

Titus's auburn brows rose to meet his hairline. "You're friends with a Midnight Fae?"

"'Friends' might be a bit of a stretch." It wasn't like I called upon Kols regularly. We just saw each other at the occasional political function.

"For you," Cyrus clarified. "I adore the bastard."

I shook my head. "Of course you do." They had similar personalities, despite their clear fae differences. "You should reach out to him, see how things are going over there." Last I heard, there was some sort of war breaking out between the two classes of Midnight Fae.

"Yeah, once we solve our problems with Claire's mom, I'll follow up." Cyrus slid his hands into his pockets. "Unless you think this is all somehow related."

"Nah, Elemental Fae can't use dark magic." Only the Midnight Fae had access to darker energy. Some believed it was their affinity for human blood that enabled them to reach the harshest recesses of the fae power. More likely, it was tied to their overall nature more than anything else.

I shook my head. "It might feel like Midnight Fae energy, but I don't see how that could be possible. Regardless, we need to look out for Claire. I want her to have an enjoyable evening."

"Which is why you didn't tell Vox or Sol," Titus added. "You want them all to have a good time."

"Yes." I knew Vox wouldn't be able to enjoy himself if he was too busy watching out for Claire. Same with Sol. "It's better if we just watch from afar. I don't think anything will happen, but I want to be there just in case."

Titus rolled his neck, his excitement palpable. "Works for me." The Fire Fae was clearly born for this kind of job. "Let's do this."

"So eager and ready to fight," Cyrus murmured. "Some might say you're burning a bit hot for it, really."

"What can I say?" Titus drawled. "My last opponent didn't give me much of a challenge, so I'm looking to up my game."

"Hmm. Maybe next time your opponent won't go so easy on you."

Titus snorted. "Are you saying you lost on purpose?"

"You know I did."

"You two fought?" I asked, interrupting their bickering. "And Titus won?"

"I let him win," my brother admitted. "Claire wouldn't have been all that happy with me for killing her fire mate."

Well, that was true. Still… "I can't believe you let him win." I glanced between them. "I want to see a rematch."

Titus grinned. "Happily."

Cyrus sighed dramatically. "So eager for another beating." He peered at the Fire Fae. "Were you dropped on your head often as a child? Or were you always this dumb?"

Titus narrowed his gaze. "Were you born an ass? Or did all that power just go to your head and turn you into a colossal prick?"

My brother laughed outright. "I was definitely born this way."

"That's what I thought." Titus pushed away from the wall. "Are we going to continue standing around here flirting or go protect our woman?"

I smiled. "I knew I liked you, Titus."

"I'd say the same, but I'd be lying," he replied, leading the way to the door.

"I'm telling you, he's not the brightest mate of the bunch," Cyrus mock-whispered. "Unless he's on fire, in which case, he burns rather bright." A flame broke out across my brother's hand with the words—a flame that sizzled and died beneath a light spray of water.

Smoke billowed around Titus not a second later as he defended himself from Cyrus's retaliation.

And an elemental blend of fire and water broke out around us.

I sighed. "Yeah, this is how we inconspicuously attend a ball to guard Claire."

The two males chuckled. "I promise we'll behave," Cyrus said. "Mostly."

"Mostly," Titus agreed, smirking.

Oh, Claire.

The things I do for you...

Chapter Ten
Sol

"WHAT IS *THAT*?" Claire asked, her focus on the Earth Fae's carriage waiting for us in the Spirit Quad.

"It's tradition," I said, rubbing the back of my neck. I mean, Claire deserved the full Solstice experience, and I damn well planned to give it to her. And that included providing the transportation most fae were accustomed to receiving for the ball.

Her mouth quirked up on the side, her amusement palpable. "It's a pumpkin carriage."

I reviewed my work, trying to grasp her meaning. The rounded orange undercarriage was left open at the top with fine vine framework to keep its shape. I supposed it sort of resembled a pumpkin, but I wasn't quite sure why she jumped to that conclusion.

"Sure. I guess it resembles half of one." I had taken pride in doing this for her, despite the work required to create such a delicate design. *Oh well.* "If that's what you want to call it, then that's what it is." I held out my hand to help her onto the first step.

She giggled and placed her palm against mine. "All I need now are some glass slippers and talking mice."

Vox paused at Claire's side and gave me a worried look over her head.

"Glass would be quite dangerous to walk on, and mice don't speak here." His eyes seemed to ask me if the mice in the Human Realm spoke, something I didn't know. We'd have to ask River later. Titus's Water Fae buddy seemed to know everything about mortals.

"Guys, I'm joking." Claire settled onto the bench and tucked her dress under her thighs, leaving little to the imagination as the fabric hugged her curves. "It's from an old fairy tale." At our blank stares, she sighed. "Just get in here."

She didn't need to tell me twice. I bounced into the opposite seat, needing more space in the small vehicle and to balance the weight. Vox cleared his throat as a small breeze swept between us. He seemed nervous and unsure of himself, which was decidedly unlike him.

I arched a brow. His power seemed to be unraveling as a result of the mating, something he hadn't exactly admitted out loud. But I could see it in the way he handled himself, especially now. Yet he said nothing. Part of me wanted to call him out on it. Claire was our mate, and if his powers were on the fritz, she needed to be aware of it.

However, as someone who had spent an entire life in his shoes, I understood his hesitancy. He would tell us when he was ready. As long as it didn't wind out of control, I would allow it. But the second I even suspected he might put Claire in danger, I'd call him on it.

Vox wiped his hands on his pants before slipping into the carriage and next to Claire. His gaze went down her delicious curves, and another stronger breeze swept her hair away from her shoulders, revealing cleavage that I wanted to bite into like one of her ripe peaches.

Claire chuckled. "If the two of you keep looking at me like that, we're not going to make it to the ball with our clothes on."

Vox's gaze snapped up to her face, and he offered her a smile. "You're gorgeous, Claire. You're going to be the envy of everyone at the ball."

Her natural blush deepened. "And you both look quite dashing in your suits. I'm glad we decided on formal wear." She glanced at us, and this time I took note of how *we* were affecting *her*. We'd all been intimate together before, but tonight felt like it was supposed to be special, that it needed to be perfect.

I cleared my throat and leaned onto my knees, taking one of Claire's hands and pressing a kiss to her knuckles. "I agree with Vox. All the fae are going to drop at your feet."

With the tense moment broken, Claire smiled, her magic conjuring tiny pink butterflies. It was a new trait, one that I liked and made her seem all the more ethereal. Her free hand strayed to Vox so that we were all connected, then she glanced around the carriage. "So, uh, how do we get to the ball? I don't see any horses or anything."

That was Vox's cue. Usually, an Earth Fae would hire a troll, or some other creature of burden, to take us to the ball. But we didn't need one with an Air Fae present.

Vox grinned, and this time he appeared more confident now that he was touching Claire. She seemed to ground him and embolden his courage.

A strong gust of wind caught at the carriage, sending it rolling along the path to the ball.

Claire jolted as the wheels moved, and amusement warmed her features. "Oh, I see."

Vox normally would have had to concentrate for the amount of elemental power it took us to ride all the way to the ball, but he was strengthened by his connection to his mate.

I felt the same with her.

My unruly energy found its roots in her soul, something that only intensified as she closed her eyes and allowed the three of our elements to blend into an intoxicating web of rightness.

I almost didn't want to leave when the carriage came to a halt outside the bustle of the castle used for the Academy's entertainment events. However, when Claire gaped up at it, I knew she was going to love every minute of this.

I exited the carriage first, followed by Vox, and we both held out our hands for our mate.

Several fae paused on the stairs to watch, causing Claire to freeze. Air magic swept up her golden locks, sending them tumbling over her shoulders in an alluring wave. My earth gave her skin a bronze glow, and then there was still the immense buildup of her time with the others. Her eyes glowed blue with Cyrus's water, her tongue flicked out with a touch of Titus's fire, and a fresh sprinkle of pink butterflies tangled up in her hair like a crown, reflecting Exos's coronation and her eternal connection with the source of spirit.

Her impact stole my breath away, as it did for any fae who'd stopped to observe the new arrival.

Aflora was the first to break the frozen moment. "Sol!" she exclaimed, skipping up to us and flashing Claire an adoring smile. "I see that you've brought the Halfling."

Claire chuckled. "I do have a name, you know."

Aflora's eyes widened. "Oh, I didn't mean to offend. I just, uh..." She bit her lip. "I'm terrible at this."

Claire grinned. "I'll let you in on a secret," she whispered as she descended the carriage. "I'm terrible at this, too."

My lips curved, pleased by their interaction. "She prefers 'Claire,'" I said softly.

"I do," my mate agreed.

"Claire," Aflora repeated, her pale cheeks pinkening as she studied the makeshift crown in Claire's hair. "I love your ornaments." She reached up to touch one and jumped back when it moved.

"Butterflies," Claire explained. "They're my favorite."

427

"They're beautiful," Aflora replied, awed.

"Thank you." She licked her lips and glanced at Vox, who squeezed her hand in encouragement.

This was probably the longest conversation Claire had ever experienced with another fae on campus, aside from her mates. I couldn't have picked a better representative. Not only was Aflora kind, but she was well liked by our people. They would see her interaction with Claire as a vote of confidence.

"I, uh, love your dress," Claire attempted.

Aflora giggled and smoothed out the soft petal frills. "Really? I made it myself."

"Wait…" Claire eyed the fabric closely. "Is that… It's alive?"

Aflora's icy blue eyes lit up. "Yes!" She shifted in a circle, pointing out all the nuances of her vibrant red gown while Claire studied it in awe.

Vox and I subtly led them toward the ballroom, the two girls lost in a discussion about other clothes Aflora had made for herself using the roots of her earth. She was a powerful fae, which was to be expected with her royal bloodline. Her father had been king, once upon a time. Leaving her as the only heir to the throne. But as a female, she couldn't accept it. Only male fae could access the source directly.

Claire sucked in a breath as we pushed open the oversized ballroom doors. "Oh…"

Delicate melodies filtered throughout the huge chamber, filling every corner with the best music magic had to offer. Elana had gone all out this time, as had the other professors and student committee who'd put together this year's Festivus celebration.

Aflora stepped back into the balcony shadows with a wink, fully aware of what was about to happen. And I gave the male at the top of the ballroom stairs a card to announce us.

He cleared his throat, adjusting the rune on his necklace that amplified his voice. "Solstice Celebration, I announce Sol of the Earth Fae, Vox of the Air Fae, and their consort, Claire, Halfling of the Five Elements."

A hush fell over the crowd as Claire went rigid under the scrutiny.

"You didn't say they'd announce us!" she hissed under her breath.

I chuckled and tucked my arm around her tiny waist. "Would you have come if I had?"

She glared at me, but I took a step forward, my weight forcing her to follow me down the stairs and into the crowd. The other fae didn't shy away from her, but rather eased closer to welcome us all.

Some of the Earth Fae swept in to touch the butterflies in Claire's hair, all of them naturally drawn to signs of life. The Fire Fae nodded in admiration. The Air Fae bowed when Vox passed, giving Claire respect out of association. Even the Water Fae took turns joining us for idle chatter, curious about their new princess.

Aflora leaned closer to Claire and lowered her voice. "Do you like the plants?" she asked, pointing up at the delicate vines and blooms that lined the ancient walls and spiraled up columns that speared to the top of the high ceiling. "I added some of those peach trees you taught us."

Claire smiled, taking note of the fuzzy fruit being enjoyed by some of the fae. Glacier, who I assumed was Aflora's date, approached us with a half-eaten treat in his grip. "I presume I have you to thank for this delicacy? Do tell, is there more like this where you come from?"

Aflora beamed and nodded emphatically. "Yes, I'd love to hear all about the many human trees you could teach us!"

"Have you tried them?" Glacier asked Aflora, offering his piece. "They're quite delicious."

Aflora blushed. "Yes, of course. She grew some during Earth Class." She glanced at Glacier's companion, who joined us with a handful of the fuzzy fruits in tow. "I see that River is new to them."

The Water Fae, who I remembered was Titus's friend, joined us with a beaming smile on his face. "This is incredible!" He tucked his chin when he noticed Claire giving him a raised brow. "Oh, hi." He glanced at Aflora. "Did I hear someone say Claire was going to teach us more about human trees?" The Water Fae had a vast knowledge of human facts, but he seemed as enthralled as Aflora to hear it from the source.

Claire giggled and started talking about apple trees, which bled into a discussion on other fruits and how they were grown. River seemed most fascinated by the fact that humans took years to grow their trees, with no magic at all. A crowd formed, everyone hanging on her every word. Even the Fire Fae seemed enraptured.

I met Vox's amused gaze and shook my head.

So much for this being a special night for the three of us. It seemed the school had finally embraced Claire as their own, and now they wanted to know every detail about her.

Aflora stood at her side the entire time, offering a friendship I would have to thank her for later. I knew she did this out of loyalty to my sister, whom we both lost in recent years. Kamsa would have appreciated this a great deal. She always thought I would end up with Aflora, but while the younger female fancied me, I'd only ever been able to see her as a sister. And it seemed she was starting to realize that her crush had been unfounded as well.

The music changed, causing several of the fae to grab their partner and head for the dance floor. I took that as a cue to truly begin the evening with my date.

I glanced at Vox and corrected myself. *Our date.*

Glacier bowed and offered his arm to Aflora. "Shall we dance?"

Aflora shrugged. "If you can stop stuffing your face with peaches, perhaps."

"For you? Anything." He kissed her cheek, to which Aflora fluttered a shy gaze at me, then looked away.

An Earth Fae and a Water Fae. Not a typical pairing, but there weren't many Earth Fae left for our kind to date.

Claire smiled as they walked away. "They seem nice." She glanced around the ballroom. "Everyone seems to be nice, actually."

Vox bent his elbow the same way Glacier had. "You belong here, Claire. They all know that, even if they were reluctant to admit it at the beginning."

Claire relaxed and took Vox's arm, then glanced at me to see how to manage. She finally decided on resting her palm on my wrist. My bicep was far too massive for her to loop her arm around.

"So, who gets the first dance?" Claire asked, seeming to enjoy the dilemma. "You can't possibly ask me to choose."

Vox loosened his collar, then snagged a fluted glass from one of the passing server's trays. "Perhaps a drink first." He handed her the bubbly drink, then grabbed one for me and himself.

I raised my glass. "A toast to the best Solstice Ball ever."

Claire grinned. "Agreed."

Vox saluted with his drink, then tipped it back, downing the whole thing. I had hoped the Air Fae would have calmed his nerves, but now that we were here, it seemed he was getting all worked up again.

Claire sipped from the rim, and the butterflies in her hair fluttered. "Mmm. That's delicious."

"Careful," I warned. "Solstice brew is strong."

She gave me a sly smile. "I doubt it can hold a candle to spritemead. If I can handle that stuff, then I can handle some Academy booze."

I chuckled. "Very well. Don't say I didn't warn you." I clinked my glass against hers. "Maybe it'll help you pick who to dance with first."

Claire relaxed, her expression one of joy and happiness, a sight that warmed my heart. The other fae were accepting her, the ballroom was breathtakingly beautiful, and her contentment brightened the air.

A perfect evening.

Eventually, she nodded. "Very well. I've made up my mind. I'll dance with Sol first." She placed her empty glass on a passing tray. "I mean, the whole ball was your idea to begin with. It only seems fair."

If Vox was dejected, he didn't show it. In fact, he looked relieved as he handed her over to me. "I'll be waiting for my turn," he promised, giving her a brief kiss before backing away.

I frowned at him, but Claire tugged me toward the dance floor before I could protest. Something was definitely up with Vox. He seemed trapped in an eternal struggle between his clear intoxication with Claire and his reservations of how she made him feel.

Claire stood on her tiptoes to reach me as she wrapped her arms around my neck. She seemed to sway a bit, the drink having loosened her muscles and leaving her in a pliable state.

I chuckled. "I warned you that it was strong. Are you going to dance or just let me carry you around on the dance floor?"

She tilted her head back and grinned at me. "Where I come from, that qualifies as dancing." She moved with me, humming to the music. "Oh, Sol, this is just perfect. I feel like I'm in a dream." She glanced over her shoulder, noting Vox, who watched us with that soft ring of silver to his eyes. He smiled and waved. "Vox isn't mad at me, though, right?"

I smoothed her hair from her face. "No, of course not. He's just nervous." At least, I hoped that was the cause of his odd behavior. Maybe his control over his power had slipped more than I realized.

Claire murmured something, her eyes glazed with pleasure, and giggled when the song transformed into a more rambunctious beat. It didn't fit the mood, and Vox looked like he dreaded having his turn. Considering the new pace, I couldn't blame him.

"I think I'll go to the bathroom. Give Vox some time to prepare." She hiccupped and covered her mouth, smothering a giggle. "Okay. Perhaps that Solstice brew was a bit much."

I pointed to the end corridor. "The facilities are that way. Do you want me to take you?"

She waved me away. "I'm fine. I'll be right back."

I waited until she had disappeared from sight before approaching Vox. "The fuck is wrong with you?"

The Air Fae frowned. Although, he didn't seem surprised at my anger. "You don't understand what it's like, Sol." He glanced up at the trees and vines lining the walls. A cool breeze had kicked up during the last song, and even I had noticed how leaves floated through the air, the decorations slowly deteriorating under the damaging winds. "I can't even control myself here, during what is supposed to be a joyous occasion." He scoffed and ripped the band from his warrior's tail, sending his hair flying around his face. "I'm losing control, Sol. I'm not used to this."

Well, at least he admitted it out loud.

Still, I couldn't help feeling a bit irritated by his statement. "Really? I wouldn't know anything about losing control?" I narrowed my gaze. "How about you try that again?"

He rolled his eyes. "You know what I mean. You've had all your life to learn how to deal with it, but it's new for me, and it shouldn't exist at all. I should be in control."

"Claire is what you need," I reminded him. "And damn your control. Your ass is tighter than an orc's. You really need to get over yourself."

The Air Fae smirked. "That's a lovely picture."

I retrieved another Solstice brew and made him drink it. When he was done, I shook him by the shoulders. "Now, are you going to pull yourself together and show Claire a good time? She's counting on us. It's important that she feels welcome here. I don't want anything to make her feel like she doesn't belong, especially not your broody-ass self."

Vox chuckled and pushed my hands off him. "Yeah, all right. Stop hounding me already."

We both nursed a fresh drink while we waited for Claire, but when the next song started and she still hadn't returned, an unsettling feeling grumbled in the pit of my stomach. It wasn't until an unfamiliar surge of fear swept through the mate-bond that I realized Claire might be in trouble.

"Did you feel that?" I asked, shoving my drink to a fae next to us.

Vox's eyes locked on the corridor. "She's in trouble."

We hurried through the gathering of female fae, ignoring their shrieks when I ripped the door open. "Claire?" I called, my rumbling voice rising in panic.

The room was empty.

Claire was gone.

CHAPTER ELEVEN
CLAIRE

Five Minutes Earlier

PERFECT.

Everything was perfect.

And yet, I still had that strange nagging suspicion that I was missing something. It'd crept back up my spine on the way to the bathroom, and as I stared at my reflection in the mirror once again, I felt it hitting me square in the chest.

What is it? I demanded.

No one stood nearby, the restroom empty.

I hiccupped again from the bubbly brew Vox had given me. The pear-like taste still lingered in my mouth. *So good.* I wanted more. Just as soon as I figured out this sensation of loss.

Gripping the counter, I studied myself. "You're losing your mind," I muttered. "Here you are at a beautiful ball with two gorgeous men, and you're talking to your reflection." Good thing no one else was in this bathroom to hear me, or they would have agreed.

"Claire..."

I jumped at the sound of my name, spinning around and searching for the source.

No one.

Nothing.

Not even the beat of the music from the ballroom reached me here.

What the hell?

Had I imagined it?

I crouched down to look beneath all the doors, wondering if I somehow missed a person, when I heard my name again. It came on a whisper against the back of my neck that sent me rotating upward onto my feet.

Vacant space.

"What the fuck?" I demanded, the hairs along my limbs standing on end.

It had to be an Air Fae of some kind playing a trick. But why?

I narrowed my gaze on the exit and marched toward the door, fully expecting to find some asshole in the hallway. But it was as empty as the bathroom.

"Claire..."

I blinked to my left, toward the source of the murmur. "Where are you?"

No answer.

Fine. Someone wanted to play with me? They'd deal with the full weight of my elements.

The door closed behind me as I wandered down the stone-walled corridor toward what appeared to be an open terrace. Earth and fire swirled around me, ready to engage my command on a second's notice.

But as I stepped out onto the cobblestone patio, I found a myriad of unoccupied benches and a garden beyond them. The floral scents called to me, hypnotizing my senses and shrouding me in the comfort of home.

I remember this, I thought, delirious and lost in a memory of my grandmother's garden. She loved Oriental lilies, would tend to them every summer and fill the house with the ones she pruned.

Who knew the same flowers grew here? I meandered toward them, curious. Because I hadn't seen these anywhere on campus.

"Claire," a feminine voice said, clear now.

A chill skated down my spine. I knew that voice. Had heard it in my dreams.

I spun around, a scream lodged in my throat as a ghostly image of my mother appeared with her hands raised in the air. "I don't want to hurt you," she said urgently. "Please, just hear me out."

"Hear you out?" I repeated, my voice squeaking at the end.

I needed to run.

To fight.

To do something other than stand here and gape at her.

Yet my feet refused to move because, holy shit, my mother had appeared in spirit form. I tried to engage my own element, to battle her in whatever way a Spirit Fae fought, but my heart refused me.

Exos!

"Please, Claire," my mother whispered. "Everything you know is a lie. You can't trust Elana. She's the one who—" Her essence flickered, disappearing into the night, and with her the scent of my grandmother's favorite flowers.

I spun around, searching for whatever trick she'd set up for me, only to find myself alone beneath the moon.

"Claire!" Exos's voice thundered through the night as he pushed through the doors I'd touched only moments ago. I collapsed at the sight of him, my knees hitting the ground as if whatever spell I'd fallen under had been lifted.

And cried out in surprise.

Not because of the impact of my legs against the cobblestone, but because of the very real memories assaulting me. My grandmother. Her flowers. And the sense of dread and loss piercing my heart.

My mother was alive. And she appeared to be trying to communicate with me in spirit form. Her words reverberated in my head as all my mates were suddenly there, surrounding me with questions, but their voices were lost to the wind of my thoughts.

You can't trust Elana.

That statement resonated the loudest. Because I felt the truth of that claim all the way to my very soul. Something wasn't right with that woman. I sensed it when she called upon the dead. An eerie, violent energy that no one should possess or use.

I didn't sense that from my mother. Her features and tone and words resembled concern and fear, not anger and harshness.

Everything you know is a lie.

Not everything, I thought back at her, taking in the horrified expressions of my mates. *I know them. I know their love.*

But something told me that wasn't what my mother meant.

Strong hands on my shoulders shook me. *Cyrus*. I met his cool blue eyes, noted the irritation in his gaze, and narrowed my eyes. "Why are you looking at me like that?"

He snorted and released me. "She's fine."

I shook myself, taking in all five males yet again. Sol and Vox look horrified. Cyrus appeared pissed off—no shock there. Although, Titus seemed just as angry. And Exos, well, his expression radiated tired patience. "What happened, Claire? What would possess you to walk out here alone and unescorted?"

My eyebrows rose. "Are you implying that I can't wander around by myself?" Totally not the point, but a worthwhile question.

Cyrus gestured to my body on the ground as if to say, *Do I even need to answer that?*

Right. One moment of weakness and the men all turned me back into a damsel in distress. I supposed I did look rather ridiculous on the patio ground in this gown. But I'd just seen an apparition of my mother. I was due a bit of a freak-out.

Everything you know is a lie.

With those words ricocheting through my mind again, I shoved myself upward—without the assistance of my mates—and brushed my palms against my gown. "We need to talk," I told them all.

"Really?" Cyrus deadpanned. "I had no idea."

"Stop being an ass," I said, not in the mood for his brand of tough love.

"Stop being a brat," he countered.

My eyebrows rose. "Are you serious right now?"

"Deadly," he snapped. "You can't just go wandering around on a whim, Claire. Unless you've forgotten the threat of your mother's existence? That she nearly killed you and Exos?"

"I've forgotten nothing."

"Could have fooled me." He folded his arms. "What the fuck were you thinking wandering out here alone?"

There it was again, the subtle hint that I couldn't protect myself and needed their help to stay alive. "Following a voice," I replied. "Which happened to belong to my mother. Except she appeared as some sort of ghostly spirit thing. And I'm fine, by the way, thanks for asking."

"I can see you're fine, Claire. Your mental state, however, remains to be seen."

My lips actually parted, his insult a slap against my face.

"Cyrus," Exos muttered.

"What? You all agree with me. What she did was careless and stupid. Acting in this manner puts not only herself in jeopardy but also the rest of us. What would happen to the Spirit Kingdom if she died, Exos?" he demanded.

"Not the time, brother."

"Not the time," he scoffed. "Well, we had better pick a damn time because our little queen is just wandering around without a care as to herself or the impact her demise would have on the rest of us."

"What the hell are you talking about?" Because he clearly meant something beyond the typical grief that accompanied death. "Also, I'm fine. I can protect myself. Thank you."

"Can you?" he countered, stepping into my personal space, his icy eyes glistening with power. "Can you really?"

"Cyrus," Exos hissed.

But his brother ignored him, as did I. Instead, I sent a wave of power into Cyrus, forcing him back several paces.

He wrapped a cord of liquid rope around my waist to yank me along with him. I stumbled, found my footing, and severed the thick substance with a sweep of air mingled with fire. Then called upon the earth to break through the stone and wrap around his ankles.

Cyrus countered by creating a geyser that held him a foot off the ground, the hot spring too powerful for my tree roots to break through.

So I smiled, whirled my finger, and called on my water and air. Together they formed a tornado that nearly took Cyrus down. But he leapt forward, wrapped his arms around my waist, and misted me back to Spirit Quad, where I found my back pressed up against a wall.

I growled as his lips claimed mine. If I couldn't feel the very real worry traversing our bond, I might have bitten him. But sensing the weight of his fear had me melting into him on instinct, my need to convince him that I was fine outweighing all the words he'd said.

Because he was right.

Going out there alone had been a really stupid thing to do.

I knew that, especially after everything that had happened.

My arms wove around his neck, holding him to me as he devoured my mouth with his own. Cyrus's kisses were all-consuming heat and adoration, and I returned every ounce of that emotion with my tongue.

It wasn't until I felt the others approaching that we finally broke apart, Titus's fire a burning flame against my soul as he glowered at my water mate. "I hate when you do that."

Cyrus wrapped his arm around my shoulders, holding me at his side. "I would apologize, but I wouldn't mean it."

"So much for a fun night at the ball," Sol muttered.

My heart sank. "Oh, Sol…" I walked across the courtyard into his open arms and hugged him tight. "I'm sorry. I didn't mean to ruin our evening. I just…" I glanced backward at Cyrus. "I wasn't thinking. I heard my name and followed it." Which could partly be blamed on the alcohol, but also on my curiosity. "It didn't sound like her until I was outside and surrounded by the lilies."

"What did she say?" Exos asked, his voice holding an edge to it.

I sighed. I'd let them all down, something I secretly vowed not to do again. Not when it resulted in all these disappointed expressions. "I'm sorry," I said again, this time to all my mates. "It was a stupid thing to do."

"Yes," Exos agreed. "Now I want to know what she said."

I swallowed, glancing around, and dropped my voice to a whisper meant for their ears alone. "She told me that everything I know is a lie and not to trust Elana. Then she disappeared before she could elaborate."

Cyrus snorted. "Well, that's informative. I haven't trusted Elana in nearly twenty years."

My brows rose. "What?"

"Instincts," he replied. "I've never bought into her holistic-fae approach. It's always felt too contrived, and I swear she's hiding something."

"Yet you told me to accept her mentorship." I frowned. "Why?"

"Keep your friends close and your enemies closer, little queen." He winked at me. "Remember that."

"She's definitely hiding something," Exos added. "But I don't think she's evil."

"What did she have you do the other day that made you so uncomfortable?" Sol cut in. "The day I picked you up from her house?"

"Can we do this inside?" Vox interjected, sounding tired. "Sound carries out here, and I don't want to waste energy on covering a conversation that could happen in the dorm."

I nodded and followed them all into the common area inside the dorm. Cyrus took the chair, Titus across from him in the opposite recliner, while Vox and Sol took over the couch with me between them.

Exos was the only one who remained standing. "What did Elana teach you?"

I cleared my throat and glanced at Sol, who gave me a reassuring nod. "Tell him."

"She, uh, conjured a spirit. A dead fae." I twisted my hands in my lap, wincing. "I didn't…" I swallowed and tried again. "It didn't feel right, but I thought it was just my mood. You know, with my mom and all that."

Cyrus's face told me my reaction had nothing to do with my mother and everything to do with Elana. "She raised the dead?" His icy gaze narrowed at Sol. "And you knew about this?"

Sol appeared just as uncomfortable as everyone else in the room. "I only knew Elana introduced her to the other half of her ability. I didn't realize that meant raising spirits from the ground."

"You should have told me." Exos sounded frustrated. "That's not how spirit magic works."

"How would I know that?" I countered, my shoulders falling. "She's my mentor and the damn Chancellor. She's supposed to be good. Right?"

Cyrus and Exos shared a look, both of them shaking their heads. "Yeah, she should be good, but lately, there have been signs of her hiding something." The statement came from Cyrus, his gaze still on his brother. "She manipulated water at the last Council meeting."

Exos's brows rose. "And you're telling me this now?"

"Been a little busy, brother."

"Clearly." He ran his fingers through his blond hair, cringing. "Disturbing the rest of a spirit… What was she thinking? Did it say anything to you?"

My mouth went dry with the memory of the male's head appearing, his stark sense of pain. "Not really. He seemed, well, preoccupied. Like he couldn't focus. And I think he was in agony."

"Sounds about right," Exos muttered. "Why would she teach you something like that?"

If I had the answer, I would have given it, but his guess was as good as mine at this point.

"Has she done anything else? Made you uncomfortable in any way?" That came from Titus, who had been quiet and observing from his chair.

I shook my head. "Nothing I can think of off the top of my head, but I've never been very comfortable around her. I always assumed it was her position of power and the fact that she could banish me to the Spirit Kingdom with a flick of her wrist." Which reminded me… "What happened to Ignis and her friends?" They were the mean girls who tried to make it appear as though I had no control over my elements. "If Elana isn't who we think she is…"

"Then she may have manipulated them into their dirty work," Exos translated. "Yes. I thought it might be the work of your mother after we realized she's still alive, but Elana would be more than capable of that."

"So what happened to them?" I pressed, frowning.

"I don't know. Elana was the last to be seen with them." He frowned. "And I didn't sense their presence in the Spirit Kingdom, which is strange since I bound their power. I should have a link to them, but I don't."

He shared another of his cryptic glances with Cyrus. "It's a good thing school is out of session for a few weeks," Cyrus mused at him. "Gives us time to sort this out."

"Yes," Exos agreed. "But where? We can't afford to separate. Not now."

Cyrus nodded. "Agreed. The Water Kingdom will be too chaotic with my father breathing down my neck."

"And they can't go to the Spirit Kingdom," Exos added.

Both of them looked at Titus. His auburn brows rose. "I don't have a palace, if that's what you're asking me."

"What are you asking?" I interjected, trying to follow their cryptic conversation. We went from Elana to, well, I wasn't quite sure.

"For a place to spend the holidays," Vox explained. "I'm the best candidate."

Everyone looked at him, but it was Cyrus who grinned. "Indeed you are, Vox. Thanks for volunteering."

A hint of frustration and fear blossomed in my bond with Vox, but he didn't let it show as he nodded. "I'll make the arrangements."

"What about Elana?" I demanded. "And my mother?"

"We'll figure it out," Sol said, lacing his fingers with mine and giving me a gentle squeeze. "Together."

The others nodded their agreements. "And we'll make it a little easier for Ophelia to reach out again," Exos added.

Cyrus seemed to tense but didn't argue or comment.

"Do you think that's a wise idea?" Titus asked, sounding wary.

"Only one way to find out," Exos replied. "But my instincts tell me it's the only way. We need answers, and it seems Claire's mother is the guardian of those answers."

My heart skipped a beat, the idea of seeing her ghostly form again didn't appeal to me in the slightest. But Exos was right. She might be able to tell us more.

Like where the hell she'd been these last twenty years.

Or why she'd tried to kill me.

I shivered, the memory of my near death too fresh to ignore.

Sol kissed my shoulder, his touch surprisingly soft with his big form. "It's going to be okay, little flower. I promise."

My throat constricted, his words exactly what I needed but also reminding me how horribly wrong our evening had gone. "I'm sorry about the ball."

His lips quirked up. "I'm not. We danced, you were beautiful, and now we're home. The perfect experience, if you ask me. Minus one minor detail."

"Yeah? What's that?" I wondered, feeling his amusement warming our connection.

"You're still clothed."

Those three words captured the attention of the entire room.

And lit my body on fire, diminishing all the sense of dread clouding my spirit. "What are we going to do about that?" I asked, my voice dropping to a whisper.

"We're going to remove your dress," he said, his palm circling the back of my neck. "And then we're going to devour you, Claire."

CHAPTER TWELVE
CLAIRE

"ARE WE AT THE TWO-HOUR MARK ALREADY?" Exos mused, glancing at his wrist. "Fascinating." A devilish glint entered his gaze as he looked at me. "Strip, beautiful."

I gaped at him. "*What?*"

"You heard him." Cyrus pushed off the chair, his icy blue irises trailing over me in a seductive wave of energy. "Strip."

"My mother just appeared in an apparition, and you all want sex?" This was the clear downside to having five male mates.

"We can still discuss that while you're naked," Titus casually pointed out. "In fact, I feel it would drastically improve the conversation."

Exos nodded. "My thoughts exactly."

"You're all incorrigible," I said, standing.

Only, Sol tugged me back down, his palm going to my thigh and trapping me on the couch. "This isn't about us, little flower," he murmured. "This is for you."

"Being naked is for my own benefit?" I nearly laughed. "Right."

He tilted his head. "I think we need to demonstrate, Vox."

The Air Fae beside me grasped my opposite thigh, his lips brushing my neck. "You really do look amazing in this dress, Claire," he whispered against my escalating pulse. "If you want to keep it on, I can work with that."

"What about—"

"There's nothing we can do about Ophelia at the moment," Cyrus said, cutting me off. "What we can do is continue enjoying the evening we intended to indulge in prior to her making an appearance."

"And what evening did you intend us to have?" I asked, my throat going dry.

Sol's mouth trailed across my jaw until he hovered right over my lips. "Well, I had intended to remove your dress." His hand slid down to my knee, where he bunched the fabric upward in knowing, measured movements. "Slowly," he added, punctuating his point by the tedious rise of my gown up my legs.

"While we planned to watch," Cyrus murmured. "It's Sol and Vox's night, but the three of us couldn't deny your beauty in that dress."

"Which is why we all agreed on observing," Titus added, a flicker of heat in his words. "And maybe more."

"Depending on your mood," Exos said, his strength and courage brushing my spirit in a tender stroke. *Vox and Sol went all out for tonight, their desire to spoil you superseding reason. It would be a shame not to celebrate their hard work, princess. Don't you agree?*

You're talking about the carriage, I whispered, whimpering out loud as the fabric of my dress inched up my thigh.

Among other things. Finding a suit to fit Sol wasn't easy.

But he looks so good in it, I replied, trailing my palm up his thick thigh.

Sol's lips captured mine, his tongue a welcome presence in my mouth as he continued to lift my dress higher and higher. Vox's palm moved to my bare limb, slipping between my thighs and upward to my heated center.

I moaned as he cupped me through the lace, my body responding to them all in different ways.

Fire in my veins for Titus.

Liquid warmth for Cyrus.

A writhing spirit for Exos.

Aroused scents permeating the air for Vox.

And an earthly quiver jolting my body for Sol.

Oh Fae...

They were right yet again. I needed this, a moment to forget, to just be me, to ground us all with the elements and experience the bonds Mother Nature intended me to have.

My fingers wove into Sol's thick russet hair, holding him to me as I devoured him in kind. My opposite hand went to rest over Vox's between my thighs, urging him to do more than just cup me.

Fabric rustled.

My dress flying over my head.

Lace ripping.

A cool breeze teasing my exposed skin.

They had me naked so quickly that I could scarcely breathe, but I trusted them implicitly. These were my mates. My fae. My men. They would never hurt me.

No, they wanted to take care of me.

I released Sol's nape and lowered my grasp to his groin. They were all wearing too many clothes, a complaint I voiced out loud, which earned me a few warm, masculine chuckles in response.

But I heard them complying.

Their zippers music to my ears.

This was what I needed, a chance to play with my elements, to weave our souls even closer in the mating circle, to take us that much closer to completion.

With all five.

Oh, this had never happened before. Only three. And they'd nearly killed me with pleasure. But I would handle this, for them, because I wanted it. Wanted *them*.

Sol shifted, his suit disappearing beneath his hands and leaving him primed, naked, and ready. I didn't wait. Didn't ask. I just straddled him, taking him inside me on a rumble of vicious need.

The entire room vibrated, his control hanging on by a thread. However, that was exactly what he needed to break. I could feel it in the way our bodies came together, the underlying desire to bestow his trust in me, to allow our connection to deepen, and for my power to literally ground his.

"Use me," I whispered. "I can take it."

His palm splayed across the base of my spine, his mouth brushing mine. "Claire…"

"I'm here," Vox said, his chest pressing to my back and shooting a current through us that stole my ability to think and breathe. I tossed my head back against his shoulder, my breasts heaving. He wrapped an arm around my center, stabilizing me between them.

Energy hummed between the three of us, Vox and Sol holding each other's gazes and communicating some unspoken words.

Cyrus stepped up to the couch wearing nothing but a pair of dress pants, his rippled abdomen on display and begging my fingers to explore. He caught my hand and brought it to his lips, then guided it backward to Vox's groin.

"Touch him," Cyrus encouraged. *Show him how you feel.*

I squeezed Vox's shaft with my palm while my thighs clenched around Sol, causing both males to groan in satisfaction.

But it was the approval in Cyrus's gaze that nearly undid me.

He was such an enigma in my life, constantly mentoring me in his own way. To the point where I wanted to kill him at times, but in moments like this, I loved him more than I could even articulate. And his smile said he knew it.

His fingers circled my hips before moving backward to my ass. "She's not ready for this yet," he murmured. "But someday soon."

I shivered, the implication of his words making me want *someday* to be *today*.

Vox went to his knees on the couch beside us, providing me easier access to stroke him.

And Sol thrust upward.

I curled over into his broad chest, the pleasure of that single move sending me closer to the edge of oblivion.

Then Titus trailed a kiss of fire down my back that had me vibrating with pleasure.

All of them were teasing me in their own way. Even Exos, who seemed to be using his spirit to touch mine intimately, caressing me from the inside out.

I lost myself to the rapture, indulging in all the elements, reveling in Sol's big body trembling beneath mine, and feeling Vox's response beneath my hand.

More... I bent to take Vox's cock into my mouth, needing to taste him.

"Fuck," he breathed, his fingers weaving through my hair.

Sol repositioned us all on the couch. He entered me from behind with a thrust that had me seeing stars, my ass up in the air as I bent over Vox's pelvis with my fingers digging into his thighs.

Power rippled around us.

Energy thriving and urging me to deepen our bonds to the next level.

Until it all snapped into place, zipping through my bloodstream and soul.

Vox and Sol were mine.

Third-level bonding.

Intended for forever.

And it felt amazing. Perfect. *Right.*

Vox's grip tightened, his beautiful, athletic form tensing as he pistoned into my mouth. Sol's palm stroked up and down my back, his pace brutal and sensual at the same time.

Fire licked up my limbs, Titus adding his own element to the mix, and glided to my core to flick my clit.

I groaned, his hot touch shooting me into the stars on one of the most intense orgasms of my life. Exos joined me there, his spirit catching mine and cradling me in our special way.

While Cyrus's water blanketed my skin, cooling my body from the outburst of my pleasure.

All of it culminated in Sol and Vox erupting inside me, their essences an addiction I would never get enough of. I swallowed all of Vox, sucking him for more long after he was done, while my core continued to squeeze Sol, refusing to let him go.

But my mates weren't done. Nowhere near it.

Titus soon took Vox's place, his long, perfect member protruding proudly near my lips as Cyrus slid into me from behind. Only Exos remained off to the side, his pants securely fastened while he observed with hungry eyes.

I fell into the hypnotic pull of his irises as Titus and Cyrus set a pace.

You look beautiful, Exos murmured. *And very well fucked.*

My throat worked, my mouth tightening around Titus as another orgasm mounted swiftly between my legs.

What about you? I asked, my mind delirious with the impending ecstasy.

Oh, I'm quite content to watch, princess. I never thought I would be excited by this, but it's hot as hell.

I moaned, Cyrus's fingers doing something to my breasts that captured my undivided attention. Titus's grasp on my hair tightened, his muscles tensing in the way I loved. He wouldn't last long like this, something his expression told me as I sought out his gaze.

I ran a flame up his neck and along his jaw to his lips, giving him a fiery kiss. He returned it by sending another cinder of heat between my legs to stroke my clit, making me think of his tongue.

Fuck... I wasn't going to last either if he kept that up, especially with Cyrus adding water to the mix. The two of their elements combined against my most sensitive place drove me hard over the cliff and sent me soaring into the clouds.

Their pace increased as they chased after me, their groans music to my ears.

I all but collapsed between them, my body weak from being so thoroughly taken by the four of them, leaving only Exos leaning against the wall, his arms crossed over his bare chest, those maddening pants still buttoned.

His control floored me.

I beckoned him with my eyes, my body too exhausted to move. He merely smiled. *We'll play later, baby,* he promised. *When you're ready for another round.*

My heart skipped several beats, my breathing labored as I whispered, *I love you.*

I love you, too, he replied, pushing off the wall. He approached and bent to brush a kiss over my swollen lips. "You never took off your shoes."

I blinked at him. "What?"

He gestured with his chin to my heels, and sure enough, they were still strapped to my feet. "Hottest thing I've ever seen."

The other males grunted in agreement, causing me to laugh.

All I could do was shake my head. "You all are going to kill me with sex."

"But what a way to go," Titus mused, his thigh flexing beneath my head. Somehow I'd ended up using his lap as a pillow.

Cyrus drew his palm down my backside, which was draped over his legs.

445

Sol and Vox were on the floor, their heads leaning back against the cushions of the couch near my midsection.

What a picture we all made.

A proper… six-some.

I laughed, the sound bursting from my lips on an unexpected wave of happiness.

Titus gazed down at me, arching an auburn brow. "Did we fuck you too hard, sweetheart?"

"Nope. I'm fine." *I just had a six-some. No big deal.*

Technically a five-some, Exos corrected, grinning. *I just watched.*

You did more than that, I told him. *I felt your spirit.*

Because it's yours, he replied. *As are all the other men in this room, Claire. We're all yours.*

"We can't do this in Air Kingdom," Vox suddenly said, causing several of the males to laugh. "No, I'm serious. My parents are already going to have issues. If we do *this*…" He flinched. "It won't go well."

"Oh, I don't know," Cyrus drawled. "I think that went extremely well."

"Something we actually agree on," Titus replied.

"Seriously, we cannot do this in Air Kingdom," Vox tried again.

"Sure," Cyrus murmured. "We'll keep it in mind."

Vox sighed, shaking his head. "I'm so fucked."

"No, that would be Claire," Exos corrected, winking at me. "And we'll figure it out, Vox. It's just a week of holiday celebrations. How difficult can it be?"

"You've clearly not met my parents," the Air Fae grumbled.

My heart warmed at the idea of meeting his parents and learning more about my air mate. It sounded like a great way to spend the holidays. Whatever holidays they were.

I frowned. "What are we celebrating, exactly?"

"Fae Festivus," Titus said.

"And what's that?" I asked, curious.

"Oh, Claire," Exos murmured. "You're in for quite a treat."

Part II

"The Fae Festivus is a time for bonding among the elements. Raise a toast to the gods above, thank them for our beautiful gifts, and be merry. Cheers."

—Exos

Chapter Thirteen
Vox

NOTHING ABOUT HOME HAD CHANGED. Not the way the wind plucked at my hair, or how dizzy I became when I looked over our spire's balcony, and certainly not my family.

"Tempest, quit your fussing!" my father roared at my mother, his temper already out of control.

He didn't like it when I visited, but rather than own up to it, he took it out on everyone else. Especially my delicate mother, who would never face his rage head-on. Instead, she bent to his wrath like a willow leans with a strong breeze, somehow never breaking under the strain.

Ignoring my father, my mother cupped my cheeks and gave me a kiss just above the line of my trimmed beard. "Vox, darling. Am I fussing?"

She always liked to put me in the middle. A blockade against my father's winds.

Shifting my gaze to the angry Air Fae, I took in my father's scowl as he stood in the foyer surrounded by baggage for two—Claire and me. Sol, Titus, Cyrus, and Exos would be coming in a few days. That had been my only condition that Cyrus would agree to.

By the look on my father's face, it wasn't going to be enough.

"No, Mother, you're not fussing. And even if you were, I haven't been

449

home in quite some time," I reminded my father, not that he seemed to care.

"You could have given us more warning," he growled, crossing his arms over a perfectly pleated white suit. "Or better yet, you could have just done what you do every year and not come home." He narrowed his gaze. "You've made it clear that your family disappoints you."

I didn't let his challenging stare deter me. Yes, my family disappointed me. And if there was somewhere else we could have gone for the holidays, I would have suggested it in a heartbeat. But Claire needed all her mates right now, and Air Kingdom made the most sense. The grounds were protected and well populated, and being here offered us the space and opportunity to spend the Festivus together as a unit.

Our only other options had been the Academy or Cyrus's home. The former posed a problem because of Elana, and the latter would have likely forced Cyrus and Claire to focus solely on coronation planning.

No, we needed a place to lie low, enjoy ourselves, and allocate adequate time to analyzing Elana's and Ophelia's motives without any potential interference. This place provided us all with an opportunity to determine our next steps beneath the sanctuary of my home. Because Elana couldn't visit Air Kingdom without an invitation, and Ophelia, well, she wasn't welcome anywhere.

Yes, this was where we were meant to be.

My father would just have to deal with it.

"It would be improper for me to spend yet another Festivus season on campus or in another realm," I said to him now. The sooner he accepted I was here to stay for a few days, the better.

My mother nodded with eager agreement, her white curls flowing over her shoulders as an effortless wave of her power swept around her gentle form. "I agree, Notus. It will do our standing well to have Vox home."

"And your intended mate? A *Halfling?* What in the Four Winds were you thinking?" My father—Notus—snapped, his black eyes going wide. He cared so much about what the other royal Air Fae lines might think.

Elements forbid I hadn't brought home a privileged Air Fae brat. *Because that's who I've always dreamed of mating. Not.*

My father scoffed, adding, "No. It's worse than just the Halfling. We now have to deal with multiple bond-mates like some kind of barbaric Spirit Kingdom family. How many did you say there were?"

"Give the boy a break," came a scratchy voice from the hall. My grandfather, the one who had brought shame to our family, entered with a smile. His notorious jagged scar tugged across his left eye, running through a milky white iris that served as a reminder of his sin. "I've settled the Halfling with the best view of the spire."

He had secured this particular spire in his youth in one of the more desirable crags that overlooked the clouds and distant cliffs below. It contained strong winds meant to power a family's elemental well—or push unwary guests off the edge to an early death.

I swiped my face with my hand. "You can't leave her out there by herself," I said, worry creeping into my voice. "She's not from here." And my mate had a tendency to wander off alone.

"Of course she's not from here!" my father bellowed, his temper spiking again. "She's not fae!"

"Half-fae," I corrected.

He scoffed. "It's more shame that you bring on this family, Vox. I won't tolerate it."

As much blustering as my father wanted to do, this was my grandfather's house. When he passed, then my father could have a say in such matters, but until then, I never paid him much heed.

"Sounds like you need to go burst some wind," Malichi grumbled, waving away my father's rage. He swept a frail arm around me and tugged me along with him. "Come, boy. Your grandfather has missed you."

We left my parents behind bickering over the baggage. Father threatened to toss it all over the edge of our property, and Mother began the tedious work of soothing him with promises that Cyrus and Exos were powerful royals that could offer a boost to our reputation. He'd come around, but this was precisely why I hadn't brought all my other bond-mates right away. My family needed time to adjust to the idea.

"What's it like?" my grandfather asked, his good eye sparkling with delight. "Being mated to a Halfling?"

Shrugging his arm from my shoulders, I wrinkled my nose at the cool, nostalgic breeze that swept scents of clouds and mist through the wide halls. Sunlight streamed in from skylights that lined every corridor, making the spire feel like there was no place to hide from watchful eyes.

I hated being home.

"You've been mated before, Grandfather," I said, not wishing to discuss Claire with the Air Fae. "You don't need me to tell you what it's like."

He chuckled. "That's not what I meant, my boy." He swirled an invisible breeze around his finger. A subtle practice act of what was left of his power that he insisted on keeping up, even though the Air King had taken away his access to the source of our element. "She has access to all five elements, so I hear. Do you feel them, too?"

I tilted my head in thought. Yes, I was connected to the other elements because of Claire and my bond-mates, but it didn't give me power over them in the way my grandfather likely hoped. "Only Claire has that power," I assured him. "Don't get any funny ideas."

He dismissed the breeze, sending his beard puffing from the tiny shock wave. "Can't blame an old fae for trying to think of ways to redeem the family line. If our own royals won't speak to us, then maybe your bond-mates have some connections."

I wanted to tell him that was impossible. Exos and Cyrus had their own problems, and Sol definitely had other, more important things to worry about than my "family honor." Our royal line would never be anything but a shameful reminder of what happened when powerful Air Fae lost control. It was what we deserved until we could prove otherwise.

The extravagant display of wealth when we reached the viewing platform reminded me that my family was hopelessly vapid and could never meet my expectations.

Claire, however, stood on the very edge with her arms spread and her hair flinging in the violent wind.

My heart leapt in my throat and my tongue went dry. "Claire?" I said, hoping we wouldn't startle her over the spire's cliff. "Don't you think you're a little close to the edge?"

She spun on her tiptoes, teetering in a way that made me dizzy. Wind swirled around her, and I realized that she leaned back, staying aloft by invisible threads of power that kept her from falling. "Vox! This is amazing!"

While she did indeed look amazing, my hands clenched with the need to grab her and tug her away from the cliff. "Claire…"

My grandfather chuckled. "Fine mate you've got yourself there, my boy." He gave me a lewd wink. "I'll leave you two to enjoy the view." He waved a hand as he turned. "And don't worry about your parents. I'll talk to them. This is still my home, and we are more than equipped to handle a few guests for the festivities. You just enjoy yourself this evening."

My grandfather shuffled away while my gaze remained locked on Claire. I extended a hand. "Claire, I know you're powerful, but you can't fly. Come here before you fall."

"Oh, Vox," she said with a soft pout, allowing me to take a breath when she stepped away from the edge and walked into my waiting arms. She wrapped herself around me and gave me a tender kiss. "You never told me how much magic there was here. I can feel it everywhere. It's incredible."

I held her tight, my heart thundering from the very real fear of losing her. She was a true fae sometimes—wild and free. And she had no idea how easy it would be to fall from the windows of this spire.

"The Air Kingdom is located in the highest lands available in the Fae Realm," I said and led her to a bench on the translucent floor. The picturesque view below depicted low-lying clouds intertwining with rocks and trees. "It's also the closest we can be to the source of our element. That's what you sense, Claire. And through our bond, you'll be able to access that source while you're here."

I palmed the back of my neck. It hadn't occurred to me that by mating with Claire, she would gain access to my power and bloodline. All my walls wouldn't protect her. She'd have to build her own.

Claire rested her head on my shoulder and squeezed my hand. "Tell me what it was like to grow up here," she mused, her gaze locked on the expanse beneath us. "Your mother seems nice."

I snorted. "She just knows you're mated to two kings and wants your approval."

My mate shrugged. "Or maybe she cares about you and wants to make me feel welcome."

I highly doubted that, but I didn't debate it. "I apologize for my father, and my grandfather. They can both be a bit, uh, much."

Claire chuckled and burrowed her nose against my neck, leaving tender kisses that forced the knots to unwind from my shoulders. "No family is perfect."

I winced. No one knew that better than Claire. "I'm sorry," I admitted. "I shouldn't complain."

She nipped my ear as her hand drifted over my thigh, making me forget why I'd been so upset to begin with. "Nonsense. Complain away. I want to hear why you hate it here so much, because then maybe I can do something about it."

"I never said I hated it here."

"You didn't have to," she replied, eyeing me knowingly. "I can sense it."

Of course she could.

I sighed. Titus and Sol already knew about my history. But I hadn't yet told Claire. I supposed now was as good a time as ever.

So I told her the story about my grandfather and how he obtained his scar. How the Air King gave him access to the source, only for my grandfather to take advantage of it. "He killed people," I told her. "And not because he's vile or malicious, but because he was arrogant and lacked control."

I continued by telling her how it brought shame to our family, how despite being of the royal bloodline, we were no longer permitted to touch the core of our power.

"My connection with the source is stronger than anyone else's in our bloodline. As such, my father seems to think I can restore our family's good name," I concluded. "But I know my limits, and I have no desire to follow in my grandfather's footsteps. Hence my need for control."

Claire studied me for a long moment, and I half expected her to express disappointment in my history. Instead, she murmured, "Hmm, but denying your gift isn't how you stay in control."

"I'm not denying it."

She gave me a look. "I can feel you fighting it, Vox. And if you continue to deny your abilities, it'll eventually explode out of you. That's how people get hurt."

The shadow of memory in her gaze told me she was thinking about the night she burned down the human bar. It was a bit different since she didn't know about her gifts then, but I understood her implication.

"I'm not fighting it," I clarified slowly, "so much as trying to find new ways to tame it."

"Seems similar to me." She studied me. "You've felt… stressed."

I huffed a laugh. "Yeah, that's one way to describe it."

"And coming here didn't help," she added.

"No, maybe not. But I'm determined to enjoy our Festivus regardless. I even ordered food for us to cook together."

Her blue eyes twinkled. "Bacon and eggs?"

Not exactly bacon… "Yes," I said instead, still not having the heart to tell her the truth about the origin of her precious pig meat.

"So this is like Christmas," she mused. "Right?"

"Uh, sort of?" I knew the humans celebrated a holiday around a giant fat man with cookies, but I didn't really understand the point of it. "It's the same time of year."

"Excellent." She seemed quite pleased by the similarity, so I didn't add any corrections. "I have an idea."

"Oh?"

She nodded. "But first, we need a tree." She jumped up, clapping her hands in excitement. "And ornaments." Claire spun around, her joy palpable. "Oh, Vox, this will be so fun." Another clap. "This is going to be the best fae holiday ever; you'll see."

"Sure," I agreed. *But why the hell do you need a tree?*

CHAPTER FOURTEEN
CLAIRE

BEAUTIFUL, I thought, evaluating my work.

All my mates were in the other room with instructions not to enter until I was ready for them. I could hear Titus chuckling at something Cyrus had said, their banter becoming friendlier every day. Which was perfect because I needed them in a good mood for this to work.

I tugged on the writhing garland—a vibrant green strand I'd created using my earth element. My gift came in handy for the flowerlike ornaments as well, while my spirit controlled the red butterflies fluttering around the branches. A different shade from my usual pink, but I wanted proper Christmas colors.

"Okay," I breathed. "I think that's about it."

Wiping my clammy palms against my blue dress—an early present from Exos—I made my way toward the guest area where all my mates had taken up residence. Everyone had arrived last night and had given me all day today to work on this surprise.

The open windows lining the hall gave me a glimpse of the cheerful activities below as the entire city celebrated the Solstice holiday with lights and beautiful melodies. The scents and sounds weren't exactly the same as Christmas, but close enough.

My tree and holiday brunch would do the trick of melding it all together.

Titus met me by the door with a suspicious twinkle in his forest-green eyes. "Why are you grinning like that, sweetheart?"

I blew a kiss at him in response, not ready to reveal my surprise yet. I needed Vox to confirm something first. "Your parents are gone, right?"

He raised a dark brow from his seat upon the couch. "Yeah, they're out for dinner with one of the commissioners." His lips twitched to the side, his expression contrite. "Sorry they didn't invite you, but they insisted you would have found it boring."

I laughed. "I'm sure that was their reason." We both knew the truth. Some of the Air Fae found me to be an enigma and someone they wanted to know. Others, however, were horrified by the idea of a Halfling wandering among them. That I had five mates only made it worse.

Fine by me. Besides, Vox's parents were right. I would have found dinner with some snobby commissioner terribly boring, and I really wanted to spend some quality time with my men.

Titus looked me up and down. "Are you bored, sweetheart? I can think of a few things that might entertain you." He accentuated his proposal with a waggle of his eyebrows.

"Hold that thought. I have a surprise first," I said, about to burst out of my skin. I'd been planning this for what felt like days.

"I like surprises," Sol offered, always the first of my mates to jump on board when I had a crazy idea. He wrapped a massive arm around my shoulder and kissed the crown of my head. "Does it involve eggs and cheese?"

I chuckled. "It's not food, well, not just food." I tugged him by the arm, leading him toward the hall. "Come on. I'll show you."

Cyrus and Exos shared a quizzical look before shrugging and following along. Titus looked hopeful that my "surprise" would involve being naked, and Sol's stomach growled. Vox poked him in the abs. "I just fed you an hour ago. How are you still hungry?"

My mates bantered and tried to guess what I'd been doing in the sitting room all day. The only one with any idea of my intentions was Vox since I'd needed his help in gathering supplies. But he didn't know how I used everything. Nor did he know about the presents I slid under the tree this afternoon.

"I just want to know what you did with that poor tree," Vox murmured.

Sol pegged him in the shoulder, making the Air Fae wince as pebbles clattered to the floor. "Don't be rude. Claire's excited, so I'm excited. Plus, she said there's food."

Vox gave me a playful smirk. "Well, you heard the ogre; show us your surprise."

Sol *hmphed* but seemed satisfied and crossed his arms.

I grinned at them all and paused just outside the door. "Ready?"

They all gave me expectant looks.

"Merry Christmas!" I exclaimed, pushing through the threshold and admiring my twelve-foot-tall evergreen tree.

Berries and pinecones added pops of color with a shimmering string of fae-glamour as my blinking lights. Fae didn't exactly have ornaments, but I found items around the house that worked in addition to my floral adornments.

I winced as the big light at the top flickered and died.

Ugh, I'd fixed that three times today, and of course it chose now to burn out again.

With a shake of my head, I snapped my fingers and set the blue flame alight again just an inch above the tree. My water element flowed just beneath it, helping to protect the branches from burning. *A star*, I mused. *Perfect.*

I turned with a smile, excited to see their reactions, and froze.

Abject horror radiated from Sol's expression.

"Why did you kill a perfectly good tree and decorate its corpse?" he demanded, taking in the strings of fae-lights and the ominous fire burning at the top. "It's a bit morbid, Claire."

"I, uh, it's—"

"Why are there prayer orbs hanging from the branches?" Vox asked, his voice hitching at the end.

"Prayer orbs?" I repeated. "What—"

"And are those my mother's fertility leaves?" Vox gaped at the middle where I'd set a pair of beautiful red palms I'd found downstairs. "That's… that's just wrong."

"I don't know," Titus said, his brow furrowed. "It's kind of cute. She's using the dead tree to protect her bags." He gestured at the gifts beneath the tree. "They're a bit shiny, though."

"That's certainly an interesting use for water," Cyrus put in, eyeing the top of the tree.

"Is it supposed to be an elemental project?" Sol asked, his palm on the branch as he outwardly mourned the life of the evergreen. "Can we replant it outside? Restructure its roots?"

"Um… I guess, but—"

"It's a Christmas tree," Exos cut in, shaking his head. "Come on, it's a popular holiday treat for humans."

My shoulders sagged. "Yes."

"It's beautiful," Exos praised, wrapping me up in his arms and kissing the top of my head. I sensed him admonishing the others in the room with his eyes, his annoyance stark in our bond. "Thank you, Claire," he added.

"Yes, thank you," Cyrus murmured. "It's… unique."

"But we can plant it again later, right?" Sol pressed.

"Yes," I said, giving up. "We can plant it after brunch." Because, clearly, they were not going to enjoy the tree in the same way I had.

"Brunch?" he repeated.

"Food," Vox clarified. "I'm just going to go return my mother's fertility leaves to her room. I'll be right back."

I banged my head against Exos's chest while he chuckled. "That was a strange adornment, Claire," he murmured against my ear.

"Vox's grandfather said I could use them." The elder male had been positively jovial when I asked to borrow it. "Now I understand why."

Cyrus laughed outright. "Oh, I bet he was all for it."

I allowed the fire to die above the tree, no longer caring about the stupid star. At least the food would be appreciated. Because yeah, I could see why the Christmas tree tradition might be a bit weird. Especially to an Earth Fae like Sol.

Probably should have thought about that before creating the evergreen and decorating its dead branches.

With a grumble, I righted myself, determined to still enjoy our brunch.

Which Sol had already found in the dining side of the sitting area.

He was eyeing the holiday delicacies with a hungry gleam. The embers I'd set alight kept the food warm while I finished decorating the tree.

"Humans usually feast for Christmas, so I tried to organize something for us to enjoy that sort of spans both holidays," I explained.

"It all smells amazing," Sol said, giving me a small smile.

Well, at least I'd done something right.

The others joined Sol in admiring the dishes. And Vox returned with a relieved expression, then eyed all the platters of food. "Wow, now I see why you wanted all those ingredients."

I smiled. "Thank you for finding me what I needed. Your grandfather helped, too."

He stared at me. "He did?"

"Yep. He helped me with the cookies and sandwiches. But the dragonsteak was my idea." I pointed to the stick of meat wrapped in bacon. "I also made eggs and an orc roast." But I had no clue how that turned out. I just kept cooking it and hoping for the best.

All the males nodded and began filling up their plates.

Except for Cyrus and Exos, who appeared to be eyeing the dragonsteak skeptically.

I frowned at them. "What's wrong?"

"Nothing," Exos said slowly. "It's just, uh, not something we've seen before."

"It's bacon swirled around a dragonsteak stick," Vox supplied helpfully, his eyes latching onto Exos as he gave him a tight smile. "Eat it. It's good."

Exos blinked at him. "It's a what?"

"A bacon-wrapped dragonsteak," I clarified. "Trust me, you'll love it." I'd already snacked on a piece earlier today.

"Bacon," he repeated as if tasting the word.

"It's from a pig," Sol said helpfully, already halfway done with his first plate. "Human thing."

"Claire calls it bacon," Vox added.

Exos just stared at him. "You told her this was bacon?"

"Because it is bacon," Vox replied through his teeth. "Eat it, Spirit King. Claire made it."

Cyrus burst out laughing, his amusement a heavy wave of entertainment. "I'm not touching that," he said between chuckles. "I love you, little queen, I do, but it's not happening."

"Then I'll eat it," Sol replied, taking all of the dragonsteak for himself.

"You would." Cyrus wiped tears from his eyes.

"I don't understand why this is so funny," I said, glancing between them all. Even Titus seemed amused. "What aren't you telling me?"

Exos appeared to be the only sober one in the room, his gaze kind as he said, "That's not bacon, princess. It's troll fat."

Another round of laughter ripped from Cyrus's mouth. Titus joined him.

Vox just looked defeated. "You're both assholes," he hissed, the words directed at Exos and Cyrus.

"I'm not the one who told her troll fat was bacon," Exos drawled. "That's on you."

"River promised me it was the same thing. And it's not even that bad, as long as you don't think about it."

"Troll fat?" I repeated, still catching up with Exos's statement. "I've been cooking *troll fat*?" No, not just cooking it. Eating it. "Oh God..." I was going to be sick.

Titus caught me around the middle before I could run from the room, his lips against my neck. "Trolls look like pigs, sweetheart. They're gross little things that roll around in mud. Same kind of meat, just a different species."

"Gross," I muttered, cringing.

"Now you see why we won't be touching that," Cyrus mused, taking one of the sandwiches instead.

"I like it," Sol said, on his second helping of food. "You all are seriously missing out."

"I'm sorry, Claire." Vox hung his head. "I couldn't get you bacon, so I improvised."

"And gave me troll fat," I translated. "Which I wrapped around dragonsteak. For Christmas dinner." I blinked a few times and then burst out laughing at the absurdity of it all. Welcome to the fae world, where nothing matched human reality. Like my sad Christmas tree.

I giggled and shook my head, wiping tears from my eyes.

"Now I can't wait for you all to open your presents. It'll be one joke after another." Especially since Vox's grandfather helped me. For all I knew, I'd actually be giving them fertility gifts.

I laughed again, my stomach hurting from the effort.

But the men had sobered, their attention falling to the boxes beneath the tree.

I waved them on, too humored to help at this point.

Vox did the honors of distributing the boxes. Which they all praised for being beautiful. When I told them they actually had to unwrap them, they all started laughing right along with me.

Wow, we came from different lands.

Yet somehow that made this Festivus all the more unique and special, because they were teaching me about their traditions while I showed them my own. It didn't escape my notice that had my mother actually been around while I was a child, my experience would have been completely different today.

For one, I wouldn't have put fertility leaves on a tree.

I also would have known it was troll fat, not bacon.

Still, I wouldn't have changed any of my mates' reactions for the world. Vox's excitement at unwrapping his new fae flute—an item his grandfather had recommended—would stay with me forever. Same with Sol's genuine pleasure over the seeds I'd created of all the fruit trees from back home.

Titus loved the bo staff I'd created for him using my earth skills. I'd melded it with fire and water, ensuring it would last more than a few practice sessions beneath the weight of his hot power.

"Can I slap Cyrus with it?" he asked. "Give it a good test run?"

"No," my Water Fae said with finality. He palmed his own gift—a ring forged from my elements. I'd created an identical one for Exos as well, which he had already slipped onto his finger.

Eventually, I would make ones for Sol, Titus, and Vox. When our matings were complete.

"Humans wear symbolic bands to indicate their relationship status." My cheeks heated, uncertainty swirling in my thoughts. "I mean, I don't know if it's really like marriage here, but I'm mate-bonded to the two of you on the deepest level and, soon, hopefully, to all of you. I just... I want to show that to the world, somehow." I shrugged. "Maybe it's silly."

Cyrus wrapped me in his arms and kissed me. "It's not silly, little queen. It's heartfelt and true."

Exos agreed with a smile, then glanced at the others. "We should make a gift, too."

"What did you have in mind?" Titus asked, arching an auburn brow.

"She says a ring symbolizes love," Exos murmured. "How is metal made?"

"By joining the elements," I said, my head against Cyrus's chest. "Or that's how I did it, anyway." It took some serious effort and a lot of trial and error, but I finally figured it out.

"On it," Titus said, his hand glowing as he held out his palm.

"Here," Cyrus murmured, triggering a mist that joined Titus's element.

Vox's hair began to blow as he focused on the whirl of magic, and the foundation of the room rumbled as Sol engaged his own element.

Exos grinned and held his palm over Titus's, then slowly closed the gap between them.

If it hurt, they didn't show it. Instead, they all seemed to be enjoying themselves, their magic mixing and blending until they released it all at once, leaving me winded in their wake.

And then Titus revealed what they'd created—a tiny ring glimmering with all the colors of the elements.

Much fancier than the ones I'd crafted.

"I need to up my game," I marveled as Exos plucked the item from Titus's palm.

My Spirit Fae grinned, holding the item out for my review. "Here's a piece of all of us, Claire. Just for you."

"Always for you," Cyrus whispered, his lips against my ear.

With tears in my eyes, I slipped it over my finger and smiled. "It's perfect."

"Merry Christmas," Exos mused.

"Merry Christmas," the others echoed.

Peace slid over me, making me feel at home and alive all at once. "Happy Festivus," I replied.

This was the way life should be.

Happy, loving, filled with joyful moments.

But deep down I knew this would be short-lived, could feel a darkness calling for my attention. Yet I shoved it away, promising to acknowledge it another day.

Because something was coming.

I could feel it in every fiber of my being, and the look Exos gave me over the cheerfulness in the room told me he felt it, too.

CHAPTER FIFTEEN
EXOS

A SOFT CRY STIRRED ME FROM MY REST.

Claire.

I sat up, searching for her in our makeshift sleeping quarters. She lay absolutely still between Vox and Sol, her eyes closed and her little hands curled into her chest.

Then she whimpered again, not out loud, but into my mind.

A bad dream, I realized, creeping over to her.

Cyrus stepped into the room with an arched brow, my brother having chosen to stand guard for the night while everyone else rested. We agreed to alternate evenings. The Air Kingdom might be safe, but something lurked on the horizon. Claire's other mates couldn't feel it, their lack of a connection to spirit impeding their ability to sense the darkness looming over all of us.

A tear leaked from the corner of Claire's eye, her expression otherwise soft.

I gently clasped her ankle, searching for a connection to her mind and found the source of her pain.

Ophelia.

She stood alone in a cold cell, shivering and mouthing unintelligible words to Claire.

I frowned at the apparition, trying to discern dream from reality when those cruel eyes locked on me and narrowed.

Reality, I decided, closing my eyes to focus on falling into Claire's mind...

"You don't belong here," Ophelia said, her voice sharp and cold and reminding me of our stark surroundings. Wherever she'd taken Claire, it was icy and unwelcoming.

"I could say the same to you," I replied, cocking my head. *"What are doing to my mate, Ophelia?"*

Her eyebrows lifted. *"Mate?"*

"Don't play coy. You know what Claire means to me and can sense our bond. What is it you want, Ophelia?" I demanded.

She blinked at me, the action slow and deliberate. I glanced around the cell, noting the rotting bars and moldy stones. Somewhere with water, which made sense. Ophelia was a Spirit Fae with access to the water element.

But why would she choose this as her desired meeting location?

"Where's Claire?" I asked, searching for the source of whimpering I still sensed in my mind.

"She's fine," Ophelia said. *"It was you I wanted to talk to."*

I arched a brow. *"Interesting. I thought I didn't belong here."*

"You don't. Or I thought you didn't." She shook her head, a hint of madness lurking in her expression.

She resembled a much older, far more tired Claire. Something that shouldn't be possible on a fae so young. It appeared as if someone had siphoned all her beauty and youth from her, leaving her frail and gaunt.

"Why am I here, Ophelia?" I prompted, drawing her focus back to me and away from whatever thought had captured her mind.

"You care... about my Claire?" she asked, sounding uncertain.

"She's my mate."

"Not just a ruse?" Her head tilted in an eerie way. *"She says you're using Claire for power. But I don't sense deceit."*

"She who?" I wondered.

"You know who," Ophelia replied cryptically. *"She's orchestrated all of this, you know. I never should have listened to her. I thought... I thought she would leave me be. Freedom is a dream, young king. She lied."*

"Who lied?" What started as a coherent conversation had melted into confusion.

"She did," Ophelia murmured, her voice taking on a dreamy quality. *"Part Dark Fae. Part Spirit. She's using my Claire. You'll see. You'll all see soon."* She began to hum a broken song, the sound hauntingly beautiful. *"She's coming. I need more—"*

A harsh zap had me grabbing my head and stumbling backward, the dark cloud in my mind sucking energy from me on a gush of sound that brought me to my knees.

Cyrus's voice rose above the chaos, his hands on my shoulders as he blasted me with his water element and knocked the leech loose from my spirit.

"Fuck!" someone shouted.

But I was too busy reeling beneath the unexpected attack.

The bitch had tried to siphon spirit off me, using me to connect to the source.

I gripped my hair, ready to pull it from my head when I heard Claire screaming from the bed. It snapped me out of the last vestiges of my dream state and sent me flying toward her, only to see her gazing upward with tear-ridden eyes. She grabbed me by the shoulders and yanked me onto the mattress, her arms weaving around my neck. "I thought... I thought..." She hiccupped, her voice in hysterics, her body trembling beneath mine. "I thought she took you from me..."

"I'm right here, princess," I whispered, meeting Cyrus's furious stare. "I'm fine."

"You're a fucking idiot is what you are," my brother seethed. "You let that thing in your head again!"

"She was in Claire first," I argued. "Better she latch onto me than her."

Claire shook her head. "No. No. No. She wasn't hurting me. She was trying to tell me something... something about Elana. But she had to go, and borrowed energy so she can come back."

Vox and Sol gaped at Claire. Titus, too. In fact, we were all gaping at her.

"How do you know that?" I asked, my voice a rasp of sound.

"She told me," Claire said. "She whispered an apology right before she latched on, saying she needed the strength to make a future connection."

I just stared at her.

"Does she often visit your dreams?" Cyrus asked, his voice a lethal calm that I recognized.

Claire shook her head. "This is the first time."

The tension radiating from my brother seemed to dissipate a fraction. "If she's reaching out on the spirit planes, then she's growing in strength," he muttered.

"She was in a cell," I said, frowning. "Not the spirit planes."

"What's the difference?" Vox asked, his fingers running through Claire's hair.

She hadn't yet released my neck, so I shifted with her in my arms, sitting up and cradling her in my lap. Claire buried her face against my throat, her face wet with tears. "Spirit Fae can access the spirit planes. It's where we pull life and death. But Ophelia created an entire background for her visit, suggesting she might have taken us to a real place."

"A cell," Claire whispered. "She's being held there."

"How do you know?" I wondered out loud.

"I just do," she replied, shivering. "It was so cold there, Exos. So... dead."

I met Cyrus's gaze again. "It reminded me of the death fields, only slightly more lively."

He shook his head. "This is insane. You're saying Ophelia dream-walked and took you to a cell, to what? Share stories? Warn you?"

"She wanted to test Exos," Claire breathed. "She doesn't trust him."

"Yeah, well, the feeling is quite mutual," Cyrus assured.

He wasn't wrong, so I didn't comment. Instead, I palmed Claire's cheek and pressed my lips to hers. "Are you okay?"

She nodded. "She didn't touch me, but I felt her siphoning energy from you. I... It scared me."

I nodded, understanding, and pulled her against me once more. "I'm all right, baby."

"What does she want?" Sol asked. He'd moved up to lean against the headboard, his bare chest on display for the room. "What's her goal? Why does she need to trust Exos?"

"She seemed to be worried about my intentions with Claire," I replied, my brow furrowing. "Honestly, it didn't make a lot of sense. She kept talking about a Dark Fae, or someone who was part Dark Fae."

"Part Dark Fae?" Cyrus repeated. "That's... not a thing."

No, it most definitely wasn't. Elemental Fae did not mate with Dark Fae, or any other kind of fae for that matter. We stuck to our own kind for a reason. To do otherwise would tip the balance of power. "We need to talk to her again."

Cyrus's expression conveyed his response before it left his mouth. "Absolutely fucking not."

"I wasn't asking permission, Your Highness," I replied. "Oh, wait... I'm king now."

His ice-blue eyes narrowed. "Don't be a conceited dick."

"Pot, meet kettle," I tossed back at him. Similar to *spirit, meet element*, but I preferred the human phrase because it sounded ridiculous. It also irritated Cyrus. Win-win.

"You two are like twins," Titus marveled, pulling on a pair of sweatpants. "Claire, sweetheart, what do you want to do?"

"I want to talk to her again," she said without hesitation.

"Then there we go," Titus said, waving at her. "You two might be kings, or whatever the hell you are right now, but she's our queen."

"I agree," Sol put in.

"Me, too," Vox murmured.

Cyrus shook his head. "You're all playing with fire."

Titus's palm blazed to life as he grinned. "And what fun it is, Water Prince."

My brother snorted and doused the flame with a spray of mist. "Fine, I can see my intelligence is outnumbered here. So how do we go about talking to her again?"

"I have an idea," I admitted. "But it'll take me a few days to get it worked out. In the interim, bolster Claire's elements. She's going to need them."

* * *

It took effort to convince Claire to fall back asleep, but it was the middle of the night and she needed rest. Especially for the festivities to come. The fae did not play around during the Festivus season. There would be a bonfire, dancing, and endless nights of drinking ahead. Which would hopefully help her relax, at least a little.

Although, she seemed rather content in the bed with Sol, Vox, and Titus.

Those three certainly knew how to wear out our mate.

With a small grin, I stepped into the hallway where Cyrus stood waiting.

"Have you lost your fucking mind?" he demanded, his irritation coming through just fine despite his low whisper.

"I don't think Ophelia is a threat," I admitted. "She seemed a bit insane, but not in a cruel way. There was no darkness in her aura, just a hint of desperation that escalated when she latched onto my power. Like she's been starved and needed my energy to survive."

Cyrus narrowed his gaze. "Go on."

Those two words showed how well he knew me. I never stopped analyzing and theorizing, something he was guilty of as well.

I palmed the back of my neck, blowing out a breath. "If someone's kept her locked up all these years, then that could explain why she latched onto Claire in the death fields. She would have been so hungry for spirit that she'd have done anything to absorb it. Including attack her own daughter. Which explains the energy depletion on Claire's part."

My brother considered my words and stroked the stubble dotting his chin. "That would also explain why she tried to go through your bond to get to her."

"They're related by blood. That links their spirits."

He nodded, then frowned. "But why starve Ophelia?"

"To feed off her own power?" I suggested. "She looked ill, Cyrus. Like a thousand-year-old fae, if not older. When she's, what, maybe fifty years in total? Not even?" I shook my head. "Something isn't adding up here."

"That something seems to point to Elana," he added.

"Half Dark Fae, half Spirit. That's what Ophelia said." Of course, she was probably stark raving mad, but it was worth bringing up again. "What if she's talking about Elana?"

"She's a Spirit Fae."

"With access to only spirit." A trait that was exceedingly rare for our kind. Although, lately, I'd begun to question whether or not it was true, because I'd sensed her water element rise on more than one occasion. As had Cyrus. "Who were her parents?" It wasn't something I'd ever thought to investigate or to know, but now it seemed imperative that we found out.

466

"I can ask my father," Cyrus murmured. "He wants to talk to me about coronation stuff anyway." He grimaced over the words.

"At some point we need to tell Claire what it means to be queen," I pointed out. She sort of understood, but not really.

His lips curled down. "Yeah, that's a conversation I'm not looking forward to."

"She's strong," I said softly. "Intelligent, too. She'll understand."

"Oh, I know. It's just not something I want to talk to her about." He ran his fingers through his hair. "One problem at a time. We'll focus on Elana, see what we can find out about her history, while you work on your idea to contact Ophelia again. But I want defense mechanisms in place. And this time, I come with you. Because I don't trust that woman near you or Claire."

I grinned. "Spoken like a protective little brother."

"By, like, eighteen months," he retorted. "And someone has to keep your wits about you. Going into her mind like that without even asking for backup." He shook his head. "If I hadn't been so busy kicking that fae out of your head, I'd have kicked your ass for being so stupid."

"Aww, I love you, too," I drawled, tugging him into a hug.

He returned the embrace, squeezing once before letting me go. "Don't do that again."

I smirked. "We both know I can't agree to that."

"Stubborn prick," Cyrus grumbled, then held up his hand. "Yeah, yeah— pot, meet kettle. Picking up human terms." He shook his head. "Tell Claire I'll be back soon."

He misted without another word, leaving me chuckling in the hallway. Half brothers, we might be, but he was also my best friend. And I meant what I said. I loved him. Just as I knew he loved me.

I couldn't think of anyone better to have my back.

Stay safe, I thought at him. Not that he needed it. Cyrus was probably the strongest of all of us, something he already knew. Although, I bet Claire would one day give him a decent challenge. And wouldn't that be a sight to behold?

With that fantasy in mind, I returned to her and sat in the chair near the foot of the bed to guard her dreams.

CHAPTER SIXTEEN
VOX

THIS WAS BULLSHIT.

Claire and everyone else had wandered off to one of the bonfires to ring in the solstice with spritemead and sparkling pixielings, while I was stuck here being grilled by my parents. Again.

"You've had your fun," my mother was saying with a tempered kindness as if I were a faeling all over again. She handed me a prayer orb, reminding me how Claire had "desecrated" the sacred objects without even realizing it. "It's time to come back to reality, Vox. Pray to the elements for forgiveness and move on from the Halfling. She has no place in our family."

Apparently, she'd given up on the idea that Claire might help restore our family name.

Shocking.

"I'm *bonded* with her, Mother," I reminded her for the thousandth time. "We're already committed on the third level. We won't be breaking it. Can I go now?"

"By the Four Winds," my father barked, sending a violent breeze through the sitting room. "I don't care what level of bond you have with the girl; it's foolish and she needs to be removed." He took a blue gem from his pocket and showed it to me. "This will call the guard, and they will escort Claire from the kingdom. All I have to do is break it. Do you really want to force my hand?"

The hairs on the back of my neck stood on end. "You really want to test the wrath of the Spirit King and the Water Prince?" Cyrus had returned this morning after spending three days in Water Kingdom. The wariness in his expression told me he'd endured similar dealings with his parents. Well, maybe not too similar. His father at least liked Claire, from what I understood.

My father gave me a grim stare. "We only recently had some of our political privileges reinstated, and your bond with the Halfling is threatening those arrangements."

"What privileges?" I asked, his claims being news to me.

"If the Halfling has befuddled your loyalties, then she needs to be dealt with," he added, ignoring me as he always did.

"She's *befuddled* nothing," I snapped, my words stirring a breeze that caused the items hanging from the Christmas tree in the corner to jingle. "I love her, Father. I realize that's an odd concept for you, but that's how I feel. We will move to the fourth level, with or without your approval."

Distant thunder sounded as my father's black eyes glimmered. "After tonight, I forbid you to see her again."

"And here we go," I drawled, irritated beyond measure. "Do my words not even reach your ears?"

"She's half-human, right?" he interjected, again acting as though I didn't have a voice. Which maybe I didn't. "That means you'll only have to wait a short time before she succumbs to her mortal weakness and you can take a new mate."

"Never happening," I countered.

But he once more continued as if I hadn't spoken. "You will stop your folly at the Academy and focus on your studies. And if you don't listen to me, then you'll force me to do what needs to be done."

Excommunication.

The irony.

"I'm not ending my relationship with Claire," I replied, keeping my voice calm even while my heart raced. "So do what you need to do, *Father.*"

"Don't be a fool!" he roared.

"Oh, so you heard that," I said, mostly talking to myself. "Good."

"You don't understand, Vox," my mother cooed. "We've been given responsibilities again in the kingdom, and that includes watching for threats— threats like the Halfling. It's a preliminary step, but if we prove our loyalty, we will continue to climb and maybe reinstate our family name."

Which was all they ever cared about.

I fought not to roll my eyes. "Claire isn't a threat—"

"I'll not have you ruining everything with this ridiculous fancy of yours!" My father clenched his fist around the jagged jewel in his palm. "Your mother is right about one thing. The Halfling has no place in our family."

"Maybe she's not the only one who doesn't belong in this family," I returned, my own element swelling in my chest with an uncharacteristic rage that only my "well-meaning" parents could incite.

A pained look crossed my mother's expression. "Vox, sweetheart. You don't mean that."

"Oh, no, actually, I do." I swept my hand, releasing a sliver of my power that sent the Christmas tree bowing and prayer orbs flinging to the ground. "I've tolerated the two of you and your ridiculous ambitions all my life. I've kept my head down and done my best to redeem the family by subduing my own power, but now I realize how fucked up that is."

"Vox!" my mother cried, covering her mouth.

"You will not speak to your mother that way!" My father flung his free arm wide, sending a gust meant to slap me and sting my flesh like he'd done so many times before.

I'd always endured his punishment.

But not today.

I retaliated and opened the gates to my element—gates I'd kept locked for far too long. The force was strong enough to send the gem hurling from my father's grip until it jammed into the ceiling.

Fear should have trampled down my spine, but all I felt was invigorated. Finally, I was embracing my true path.

No more webs meant to lock down my ability.

No more internal chastisement for unleashing too much energy.

No more *bowing* to those who pretended to be my betters.

My father wanted to own my every action. Well, no longer would I allow it.

My mother screamed when my control slipped and twin tornados released into the room, sending furniture and drapes catapulting into the air.

My father blocked the worst of the debris with the last of his power, enduring the onslaught and keeping him and my mother safe. My parents stared, dumbfounded, until the winds dissolved, sending the wayward items clattering to the floor.

The mixture of hope and horror on my mother's face said it all.

I possessed more power than they realized because I'd hidden it, kept it bottled up inside and refused to allow it out to play.

Until Claire.

She'd unraveled my power, our mating bond emboldening my royal ties to the source—royal ties I'd spent two decades blocking.

And I'd spent the last few weeks terrified of it.

Now I embraced it.

My parents gaped at me until a light knock sounded at the door. My grandfather poked his head into the room, and his dark eyes went wide at the destruction. "I thought I heard a crash..."

"This is your fault!" my father yelled, finding a new, suitable target for his rage. He pointed a finger in accusation. "You shamed our family, and now your only grandson chooses to follow in your footsteps!"

Unaffected by my father's outrage, the old fae stepped over broken prayer orbs and smashed plates to give me a pat on the back. "Your beautiful mate came by to check on you, saying she felt a disturbance. I promised her I would investigate." He took another long look at the room, then locked his gaze onto my father's. "You should be ashamed, son. Have you learned nothing from our excommunication? You've tried so hard to win a place back into society that you've forgotten what it means to be an Air Fae, to be family."

"Don't lecture me, old man," my father said.

"Enough." I was done. I didn't want to have this conversation anymore. There was nothing they could say or do to change my mind. "Claire is looking for me, and her concern means more to me than yours. So if you wish to ever speak to me again, you'll consider your next actions wisely. I leave for the Academy tomorrow—with my mate and my bond-circle."

I expected my father to fling another weak attempt at punishment at my face, or go for the gem lodged in the ceiling, but for the first time in my life, his dark eyes shifted down. "If you leave us now, you will not be welcome back," he warned.

Fucking fine with me.

I turned on my heel and left my parents with their prayer orbs and judgment. It tore me up on some deep level to make this choice, and I hated them even more for it. But if I'd learned anything, it was that "family" did not mean pursuing blind ambition at the cost of my soul.

True family was where I could be free.

* * *

My grandfather followed me as I stormed out of the spire to where Claire stood waiting on the doorstep. Her blue eyes sparkled with concern. "Vox, is everything all right?"

I ignored the question, needing more than words right now.

Threading my fingers through her tousled hair, I pulled her into a kiss. It was hard. Fast. Filled with emotions I couldn't hide. And powerful.

She melted into my embrace, her slender arms sliding around my neck as I parted her lips with my tongue.

Heat blossomed between us, carried on a robust wind stirred by the mixing of our shared element. A roar of sound tunneled through my ears, the whipping sensation one I reveled in and adored.

This.

This is what I needed.

471

What I craved.

What I desired.

My Claire.

My mate.

"I want you to be mine," I whispered. "To keep me for always. To ground me. To soar with me. To love me as I love you."

Her reply was lost to my mouth, my need to devour her overriding everything else. She clung to me with the same intensity as I did with her, our lips engaged in a dance no one could interrupt. Not even my grandfather, who stood behind us clearing his throat.

I no longer cared about propriety.

No longer worried what my family might think.

Fuck any and all reputation tied to my parents. I was my own person, destined to create my own future.

And I chose Claire.

Her legs wound around my waist as I lifted her and pressed her back into the wall of my parents' home. "Vox," she breathed.

"Claire," I returned, nibbling a path down her neck.

She ran her fingers through my tousled hair, which had come undone during the explosion of wind. "What happened?"

"I'm following my destiny," I told her. "I've chosen you." My raging element instantly quieted with her presence to stabilize my power, but it was time to stop denying what my heart needed.

What she needed from me.

Titus leaned on a nearby pillar and watched the exchange. I gave him a nod. "Titus, can you tell the others that I'll be stealing Claire away for the remainder of the night?"

He gave me a knowing grin. "Only if she agrees."

"What am I agreeing to?" Claire asked softly, her lips swollen from my attention.

I palmed her cheek and captured her aroused gaze. "I want to complete our mating. If you'll have me."

"Tonight?"

"Tonight," I agreed. "Here. In my kingdom. With my grandfather as my witness." It was why I didn't mind him following me. I needed a royal to help with the vows, and while he might be an outcast, he still maintained his bloodline.

The look he gave me now said he understood. And his smile told me he approved.

Old, he might be. Dense, he was not.

"Really?" Claire beamed at me. "You want to finalize our mating?"

"I do," I told her, brushing my lips against hers once more. "I've never wanted anything more in my life."

It wasn't because of my parents or their harsh words. Although, their callousness did prove my choice to be the correct one. Without their push tonight, I might have waited a little longer.

But now I saw no choice in putting off the inevitable. I wanted Claire. I'd always wanted her. And I didn't want to spend another moment without her as my true mate.

"Yes," she said, smiling. "Yes."

Our lips met again, this time in a slower embrace filled with every emotion we shared between us. My frustration at my parents. Her fear of the future. My utmost respect and adoration. Her devotion and love. Our affinity for air. Our intertwined future with all the other elements. Our promise to always remain faithful to each other in our own special way.

Mine, I thought. *My Claire.*

I just needed the world to know it. To bind us in the most traditional of ways. To cherish her for eternity.

"I'll let the others know," Titus said, sounding amused. "Besides, I hear Sol is going to try some of your city's famed blast mead." He chuckled. "It's too bad you both will miss it."

Claire grinned against my mouth. "I want to hear stories later."

"Anything for you, sweetheart," Titus promised, blowing her a kiss.

She blew him one back, her arms never leaving my neck and her legs still wound tight around my waist.

Titus shoved off of the pillar, staggering once. Perhaps the Fire Fae had enjoyed some of the powerful mead himself. "If I sense anything strange, I'm coming to find you." He gave Claire a semi-stern look, then he sauntered away.

"What did he mean by 'strange'?" I asked.

Claire shook her head. "I'll tell you later. I promise."

I stared her down, but Claire merely smiled.

Reluctantly, I let it go.

I didn't want to live another moment without Claire as my mate. And there was only one way to secure our future together for good.

"Grandfather," I said, never once looking away from Claire as I grazed my thumb over her lower lip. "You still have priest status, yes?"

The old fae chuckled. "I do. The king can't take that away."

I nodded. "Good. Claire and I wish to wed. Isn't that the human term?"

She laughed. "It is, but I want to know what happened up there first. I've never felt emotions like that from you. You were... angry. Like someone had betrayed you."

"I was," I admitted, allowing my element to unravel and sweep around us. The distant melody of the Festivus celebration was a pleasant contrast to my father's thunder.

I took Claire's hand and wrapped it around the ring that hung about my neck. She'd created it after our Christmas celebration, stating she wanted me, Titus, and Sol to have one as a symbol of her commitment to us all. It served as her promise to mate each of us.

"My father threatened to take you away from me. To say he disapproves would be an understatement, but the thing is, I don't approve of him. I don't approve of anything he or my mother have done to try to regain power. They're exactly what's wrong with our family name." I glanced at my grandfather. "No offense."

"None taken," he replied. "You're right. They've not learned a damn thing from my mistakes, but I can see that you have."

"Power is not something you acquire; it's something you cherish, regardless of how much or how little you possess," I said softly, thinking of Claire and her abundance of elements. "But this isn't about status or ascending. This is about love. This is about devoting my future to my mate, no matter the consequences." I palmed her cheek. "This is about me binding myself to you in an impenetrable connection."

Because I had no doubt that if I returned to the Academy and resumed my life with my bond-circle without having stronger ties in place, my father would find a way to tear Claire and me apart, third-level bond or not.

Claire blinked up at me with both concern and wonder in her gaze. "I don't want to force you into anything. If your family is pressuring you, perhaps I could go talk to them and—"

"No, Claire." I fisted her hair, forcing her to hold my gaze. "You are my family; do you understand? I won't deny what you mean to me any longer. Nor will I deny the power thriving inside me."

Her eyes went wide, and then a smile broke out on her face. "Are you serious?"

I captured her mouth with mine, and she bent to me, opening for me and intertwining her elemental gifts with my own until my skin tingled with her never-ending power.

My grandfather cleared his throat. "Now, now. Can't have you two mate-bonding right here on the spire's doorstep."

"Where, then?" Claire asked, breathless from my kiss.

I grinned. "I know just the place."

CHAPTER SEVENTEEN
CYRUS

"SHE'S HAPPY," I murmured, tapping my spritemead against Exos's mug.

"You mean distracted," my brother clarified.

"Mmm," I agreed, sipping the seductive liquid and sighing. "Mating Vox is a good play. It'll only strengthen her to have more of that royal blood in her."

Exos nodded. "Sol should be next."

I eyed the drunk Earth Fae, who sat several yards away with a laughing Titus at his side. "Either will do," I said, considering their elemental affinities. "But yes, having a stronger tie to Sol's bloodline would benefit her."

And given what we both felt was coming, enhancing Claire's abilities was more than needed.

"What did your dad say about Elana?" my brother asked softly, keeping his voice low and pitched for my ears alone.

We hadn't been able to chat much today with all the festivities, and it'd been our top priority to keep Claire happy. She hadn't slept well in my absence. Yet Ophelia never appeared. It was almost as if she kept trying to manifest but couldn't.

"My father did not have kind things to say about Elana." Which was an understatement. He pretty much cringed the second I brought up her name and didn't stop huffing until we were done talking about her. "I guess it's rumored that her mother had an affair, but no one knows with whom. But she didn't look anything like her father. Some claimed Elana's single spirit ability was a consequence of her mother's infidelity. From what I gathered, our brethren were not kind to Elana."

"Which could explain why she chose the path she did. She wants unity among the fae to bring us together and remove negativity and competition from our world."

"Or, she's full of shit and up to something," I countered. "Which is what my father claims. He says he's never trusted her, that he's sensed her growing affinity for water for over a decade, and he feels strongly that she's hiding something."

"Sounds like you," Exos drawled.

"He is my father, after all." Something I'd denied most of my life, choosing to ally myself with the Spirit Kingdom first and foremost. I half expected my father to hold that against me, but he said he respected the loyalty because he knew the Spirit Fae needed my guidance more.

The old man wasn't half bad.

I might even eventually like him if he kept this up.

Shaking my head, I returned to our conversation at hand. "Regardless, I'm inclined to agree that Elana is hiding something. I just can't figure out why she'd go through all this trouble, or for what."

"So you think she might be keeping Ophelia captive?"

"It's possible." I rubbed my jaw, considering. "I just don't know why." I glanced at him. "How close are you to summoning her again?"

"Close. I'm planning to work with Claire on it tomorrow."

I nodded. "Good. I want to be there."

"Serves as a good lesson," Exos added, shrugging. "As Spirit Queen, she should know how to call upon the fae spirit."

"It's not exactly a beginner course," I replied, cringing. "I'd not even call it advanced." It was more like a superior skill that very few Spirit Fae had mastered. It required a great deal of elemental power, typically drawing from the source. "Still, I agree. It'll be a good training exercise." Because it was the same method we drew upon to control another fae, which may come in handy one day and save her life.

"Elana knows how to do it," Exos pointed out.

"I know." I'd observed her manipulate others countless times. "She always does it in a way that paints her in a positive light."

"Like when she forced the truth out of those girls at the Academy and supposedly sent them to the Spirit Kingdom?" Exos suggested.

"Yeah, exactly like that. Comes in, plays the role of savior, and rids the world of evildoers."

"Only, I'd bet you a bucket of spritemead those girls were actually innocent." He lifted his glass, knocked back the drink, and relaxed on our bench against the rocky cliff behind us. "Not that I picked up on it at the time."

"No, from what the others implied, they looked pretty guilty."

"Almost as if someone set them up," Exos murmured.

"Indeed," I agreed, leaning back on my elbows, my mug nearly empty. "I think we have a lot of detective work to do, brother."

"My favorite kind," he mused.

My lips curled. "Mine, too."

CHAPTER EIGHTEEN
VOX

FESTIVITIES ECHOED AGAINST THE CRAGS, and the air grew thin as we climbed the seemingly endless stairs to the top. But the exhaustion was worth it because I knew we wouldn't be disturbed here.

"How far is this place?" Claire huffed, her breath coming in short gasps.

I chuckled and took her hand. "Do I need to fuss at Titus for not keeping you in shape? He's far too easy on you if a couple of stairs are your match."

She glared at me. "Easy for you to say. You have the body of an athlete and grew up in this thin air. I don't think you ever run out of stamina."

I grinned. "Quite right, Claire. I can go all night."

Her eyes widened. "Did you just make a joke?"

"Here we are!" my grandfather announced, ignoring our banter. He waved his hand and undid the magical binds that kept the sacred ceremonial chamber locked. The doors popped open and revealed a platform that overlooked the city and the cliffs below. It provided an even more breathtaking view than that at my grandfather's home.

He let out a long, appreciative sigh. "I haven't been to this place in centuries. Perhaps the last time was when I mate-bonded to your grandmother." His smile turned somber, and a reminiscent breeze swept over the sacred space.

"I miss her, too," I admitted and took Claire's hand as I guided her onto the platform. This one had safety rails, something I appreciated as it alleviated my concerns about losing control of my power during the ceremony. I wasn't sure what to expect, but I knew this would be the moment where I had to embrace my true nature and acknowledge myself as a Royal Air Fae.

Claire clung to my robes as she took in the vast scenery.

The kingdom glimmered with lights, alive with celebration and joy. The music could barely reach us at this height, but another melody caught my ears. One of wind and nature's harmony as the element twirled and played at the top of the ceremonial spire.

Claire focused on the starless sky above, its tapestry blocked out by a long sea of rolling aura lights. "It's beautiful," she breathed, lifting her fingers as if to touch the masterpiece. "What is it?"

"Wind's source," my grandfather said with pride. He moved to a single pedestal that housed sacred texts, even though he didn't need it. We all had the vows memorized by heart. To mate-bond was the most important day of our lives as a fae, and I didn't take this lightly.

"Nothing is more beautiful than seeing you here with me," I said, brushing away Claire's hair from her face. My fingers didn't touch her skin but hovered just out of reach as my element kissed her cheek.

She smiled. "What made you change your mind?" she asked, seemingly bewildered by my readiness to mate-bond with her. "I'm not blind, Vox. I've sensed your hesitation from the very beginning. I thought you would never go beyond the second stage of mate-bonding, but then the other night, I thought maybe I pushed you into the third bond..." Her gaze drifted to the aura again. "Are you really ready for this?"

I didn't tease this time. I wrapped my hands around her waist and pulled her close to me so that I could feel her breath on my face.

"I've been a fool." My admission echoed out across the great expanse even though I'd barely uttered the words. The energy in my chest stirred, and anticipation made every inch of me feel electrified.

"Yes, I've fought the bond," I continued. "But not because of you. I fought because deep down I knew what it meant for my power. All my life, I've prided myself on my control, and you, my darling Claire, unwind all my practiced restraint. It terrified me at first, made me feel like I'd lost a key part of myself. However, I realize now that you were teaching me how to live. How to breathe for the first time. How to truly *feel*."

I cupped her cheek and brushed my lips across hers, loving the taste of her, the sensation of her in my arms, the irrefutable reality of her finally being mine.

"I love you, Claire," I told her. "So yes, I'm ready. I've never been more ready for anything in my life." And I meant every single word.

Claire answered me with a kiss of her own that ignited a storm inside of me. A storm that confirmed this was where I belonged.

My grandfather creaked the old book open. "Repeat after me…"

Claire spoke the words first, her lips hovering just over mine.

I, Claire, accept the power that binds me to Vox, born of the Four Winds. To cherish and respect, through all of the eras and time that may fall before us, until our souls do us part. I give unto him my promise of freedom, my warm breeze, my calm before every storm, and accept his in return. My element is now his just as his is now mine, to the fae heavens may we never part. And I shall never forsake him for another, my wind forever belonging to him and to him alone.

The elements roared to life when she completed the last phrase, and she gasped, her finger running over my cheekbone. "Vox, your eyes."

I didn't have to ask her what she meant, because her eyes had transformed as well. For just this moment in time, she was an Air Fae, embracing all that it meant to become one with me and to approach the source of my power. Her irises glistened with a wild silver band that grew as the winds surrounding us picked up.

I felt that power in my chest, and I did what I never could have done without Claire.

I embraced it.

I, Vox, accept the power that binds me to Claire, a Halfling who completes me like no Air Fae could. To cherish and respect, through all of the eras and time that may fall before us, until our souls do us part. I give unto her my promise of freedom, my warm breeze, my calm before every storm, and accept hers in return. My element is now hers just as hers is now mine, to the fae heavens may we never part. And I shall never forsake her for another, my wind forever belonging to her and to her alone.

The blast that hit us swept us off the platform. It didn't matter that there was a rail; we went flinging over it and into the skies. Claire gasped and clung to my neck.

"I thought you said we couldn't fly!"

We couldn't, but we weren't flying.

We were being accepted by the source of the Four Winds into a sacred realm only royals could go.

"Don't be afraid," I assured her and turned her so that her back was to my chest. Our feet dangled, but an invisible force took us up into the thin air where the surging aura lights waited. Jewel tones filled the horizon, and a bed of clouds formed under us.

I lowered Claire onto the soft element, finding it tangible and real. She marveled as she swept her hand through the cottony substance. "I've never seen anything like this."

Her eyes had gone completely silver now, and my element called to hers. My yearning for her to complete what we'd started overwhelmed me. We had to appease the energy swirling around us, to become one in the most sacred of realms.

"Claire," I breathed, her name a desperate plea as if I were in pain even from this small separation. We needed to complete the bond.

Her silver eyes gleamed knowingly, her fingers sweeping in an arc that sent wind tangling her power through my hair, undoing my warrior's tail, and lifting the dark strands over my shoulders. She tugged at my clothes as I did the same to hers, sending my desire to shift her sleeves off her shoulders. My lips went to her delicate skin, then I tasted her neck with my tongue.

"Vox," she said, fluttering her eyelids closed as my hand went underneath the thin veil of her dress to pull away the fabric that separated us. I wanted us to be skin to skin, to feel every inch of hers with my own.

Her hair waved around me when my touch found the delicate folds between her thighs, slipping my fingers into her wetness and rolling my thumb over the soft nub that waited for me. I claimed her mouth as I drank in her moans.

"Vox," she attempted again, arching her back against the bed of wind and mist. "We're on a cloud. Floating. This… I should be terrified. But…" She trailed off on a moan.

We dangled above the kingdom where the air grew thinner and only magic kept us aloft, but I trusted the source more than I ever had in all my life. It wished us to become one, to bless our union. I had only heard about such pairings in Air Fae myth, but it assured me that I had made the right choice beyond a shadow of any doubt.

Claire was mine.

"Do you trust me?" I asked, pressing my cock to her waiting heat.

"Yes," she whispered. "Always."

She sighed as I slid inside her, my hips setting a rhythm meant to please and enhance our joining. I clamped my teeth over her taut nipple, eliciting a shocked groan from her throat, one I reveled in and adored.

"More," she urged. "Take me, Vox."

I did, picking up the pace and driving into her with a craving only she could satisfy. My power circled us, the wind kissing every inch of her skin as I worshiped her breasts and thrust deeper into her with each intake of her gasping breath. I ground my hips in a way that brushed her clit, making her silver eyes roll into the back of her head as she approached pure bliss.

Her body tightened around me, just needing one more push to be sent over the edge.

I gave it to her, caressing her with a gentle breeze and driving myself to the hilt. She cried out, my name a chant on the winds and forcing me to tumble over the cliff into my own release.

We are one, I thought, moaning her name out loud.

But the source wasn't done with us yet.

It wanted more.

I wanted more.

And so did Claire.

She writhed underneath me, her hands going to my hair as she pulled me down for a kiss. "Whatever you just did to me, promise me you'll do it again." Her silver eyes flashed with renewed desire.

And so I did, my powers whispering back to life, commanded by my mate to worship every inch of her until there was nothing left but sky, wind, and her sweet cries drifting on the breeze.

Chapter Nineteen
Claire

MY HEART FLUTTERED AT THE SIGHT of Cyrus and Exos waiting for me in the hallway, their stances relaxed despite the task ahead. They'd dressed slightly more casually today in button-down shirts and slacks. Apparently, this was their idea of being comfortable.

I couldn't say I minded. They resembled walking models, especially with the sleeves of their dress shirts rolled up to the elbows like that. If their aim was to distract me from our goal, they were off to a fabulous start.

Exos's lips pulled up into a grin as he wrapped his palm around the back of my neck, pulling me in for a long, sensuous kiss. I barely had a second to breathe before Cyrus grabbed me and repeated the greeting, his mouth a warm welcome I adored.

"Well, if that's how this activity is going to go, then I'll happily play along," Titus drawled from the doorway behind me.

He stood in nothing but a pair of flannel pants, his upper body flushed from sleep.

"I wish it were that enjoyable," Exos said, taking my hand and tugging me into the space between him and Cyrus. "Alas, it's going to be a long day."

"You say that like you don't enjoy fucking with the spirits of others." Sol appeared beside Titus, his expression matching his harsh tone. "Oh, but wait, that's what your kind does best."

Ouch. I frowned at him. "What are you implying? That I want to play in the spirit realm and hurt people?" Because that was far from the truth. We were only doing this today to obtain answers from my mother. "Don't you think I'd choose another route if I had a choice?" My mother hadn't reached out again since that fretful night. And frankly, I wanted our next contact to be on my terms, not hers. This was the best way to accomplish that.

"Not all of us enjoy inflicting torture on others," Cyrus added quietly. "I can see the scars on your spirit. What we are doing today won't touch another in that manner. I swear it."

Sol narrowed his gaze at my water mate. "It'd better not." And with that, he stomped off, his agitation clear in the way the stone reverberated beneath his steps.

I flinched, my chest aching as if he'd shot an arrow through it. "He thinks I would do that?"

"No, he thinks we would." Exos kissed my temple. "Trust me, his anger isn't directed at you."

"Could have fooled me." He hadn't even looked at me, much less replied to my commentary.

"I'll talk to him," Titus promised, pushing away from the door. "He's probably just hungover from all that blast mead last night." He waggled his brows. "Vox and I will fix him right up with some breakfast. He'll be as good as new when you get back."

"Pretty sure it's more than a hangover," I grumbled. Sol had always appeared to be on edge around Exos and Cyrus, but I never knew why. And Cyrus's comment regarding Sol's scars was news to me. I didn't even know what he meant.

How does one scar a spirit? I wondered.

We'll explain it today, Exos replied with another kiss against my head. *It's one of the darker parts of our power.*

Like raising the dead? I asked.

I sensed his scowl more than saw it. *No. That would be dark magic.*

"Come on," Cyrus encouraged, wrapping his arm around my shoulders. "We have a long day ahead."

I blew my fire mate a kiss that he caught and brought to his heart before sending me one in return. With a smile, I allowed Cyrus and Exos to lead me down the hall. "Where are we going?"

Exos threaded his fingers through mine while saying, "Vox suggested a place where we won't be disturbed."

My lips curled at the thought of my air mate. It'd been hard to leave him in bed this morning, but he looked so at peace between the—

"You're still here?" a deep voice demanded as we entered the foyer.

Exos turned toward the source with an arched eyebrow. "Indeed we are.

Is there a problem, Notus?"

Vox's father narrowed his ebony eyes at me, ignoring Exos entirely. "Haven't you done enough to disgrace my family, Halfling?" He practically spit the name at me as if it were a curse. "You've already ruined our name and stolen my son. I think it's high time you left."

My eyebrows met my hairline. "Wow, you're charming in the morning." And a complete dick as well. "Vox told me about your reservations regarding our relationship, and I'm truly sorry you feel that way. But I've done nothing to ruin your family name. As for taking your son, I believe he made that choice all on his own."

"I did," Vox agreed, seeming to appear behind us with the wind whipping around him as he called upon his gift to empower his stance.

Notus's lips parted at the demonstration of air energy. "You're accessing the source."

"Because of Claire," he replied flatly. "My *Halfling* mate. The one you've chosen to belittle and disregard because she's not the royalty you've always craved. How interesting that the elements seem to favor her."

My cheeks heated as he awarded me with an indulgent smile.

"Yes, it does seem to me that Claire could have only helped with the family name," Exos said, his tone regal and filled with authority. "But after the hospitality we've received here, I can assure you that will never happen." He glanced at Cyrus. "I suggest we move our lesson to another kingdom, as we're clearly no longer welcome here."

"I'm sure my father would accommodate us," he drawled, not missing a beat. "He'll also be incredibly intrigued by this turn of events."

Exos nodded as Notus sputtered out nonsense. I almost wanted to hear what he had to say. But then again, he wasn't worth our time. He'd made his opinion clear, and there wasn't a damn thing we could do to change it.

"I'll inform the others of our change in plans, and we'll meet you back at the Academy tonight," Vox said, ignoring his father's rambling apology—or I assumed that was what he was trying to say. Maybe it was just another insult. At this point, I no longer cared to listen. Vox was happy, and that was all that mattered to me.

"It will likely be tomorrow," Cyrus said. "We'll need time to recover before we travel again. Fortunately, my father is a hospitable host." That last comment was tossed in Notus's direction. "We'll meet you there, Exos."

The world dissolved around us as Cyrus engaged his misting ability and teleported us with the ease of a practiced fae. I hadn't learned how to do this yet but loved the way it felt—like effortlessly swimming through a refreshing stream. Except we always arrived dry.

We materialized in the center of Cyrus's bedroom to the welcoming sound of the waterfall in the corner. I vaguely remembered it from my time here, that tranquil song of moving water while we made love over and over in his silky sheets.

He stole my mouth in a kiss, confirming his mind had ventured to the same memory, as he replayed those heated nights with his tongue against mine. I arched into him, adoring the sensations he stirred inside me and longing to indulge in so much more.

But a stern knock on the door shattered the moment.

Cyrus sighed, his fingers running through my hair. "Exos won't be here for another hour, pending fae transport."

"Because you can't mist him, right?" It wasn't something he ever actually clarified for me.

"Only Water Fae can mist, little queen." He tapped me on the nose and pressed a final kiss to my lips. Then went to tug open the large wooden door, revealing his father on the other side.

"Back so soon?" the king drawled.

"What can I say? I love this place," Cyrus deadpanned. Then he informed his father of Notus's poor accommodations and continued into what we had planned for today. His father didn't appear alarmed, telling me Cyrus had disclosed his suspicions about Elana already.

Instead, all the king did was nod. "Let me know if I can be of any help." His blue eyes—the same shade as Cyrus's—focused on me. "It's good to see you healthy, Claire."

We hadn't properly met the first time, a result of my near-death state. However this man had not only helped save my life, but had also encouraged Cyrus to mate-bond with me. "Thank you, sir," I said, my throat going dry. "For the, uh, compliment, and everything else."

Smooth, Claire, I chastised myself. *Really smooth.*

The Water King grinned, his amusement palpable. "Trust me, it's you I should be thanking." He glanced at my mate. "You finally made my son grow up."

Cyrus scoffed. "I grew up a long time ago."

His father sobered a fraction, nodding. "Well, that's true. But I have her to thank for you accepting your rightful place." There was an edge to those words—an edge that had Cyrus standing up a little straighter.

"I'm not here for that right now," he replied through his teeth.

"I know. But we'll need to set a date soon, Cyrus. The imbalance of power must be rectified." The look he gave his son wasn't nearly as friendly as it was moments ago, but was instead a stern, fatherly admonishment. "Soon," he repeated. He then took his leave with a casual, "I'll ask Coral to make dinner arrangements."

"What does he mean by 'the imbalance of power'?" I wondered out loud after the door closed.

Cyrus ran his fingers through his hair, blowing out a long breath. "Our mating has tipped the scales." He stepped forward, wrapping his arms around my waist and gazing down at me with a smile in his eyes. "We're strong together, Claire. Stronger than everyone else in this kingdom, including my father. But with that strength comes a price."

"Your coronation," I translated.

He nodded. "Yes, however, it can wait." He pressed his forehead to mine. "We have more important things to worry about first."

Like my mother, I thought. *And Elana.* "Your coronation is important, too," I pointed out. "And Exos's ascension hasn't changed much, right? Will yours be much different?"

He gave a little laugh and shook his head. "Oh, little queen, you have no idea." He slid his palm down my arm to my hand and tugged me along beside him out onto the balcony rimming his suite. Waves crashed against the shores below, bleeding into streams that roped through the city surrounding us.

A giant city.

Bigger than the Spirit Kingdom and Air Kingdom combined.

My lips actually parted at the sight, having not seen any of this during my last visit. Or, at least, I didn't remember it. "Wow, Cyrus, it's beautiful."

"It's the biggest kingdom of all the fae," he added, grabbing my hips to guide me backward into his body, where he pressed his chest to my shoulder blades. "This will all one day be ours, Claire. But with great power comes great responsibility."

"And you never wanted the position," I realized out loud. "That's why you chose the Spirit Kingdom."

"Not entirely. The Spirit Fae needed me more than the Water Fae did, but they have Exos now. Leaving me to take over my responsibilities here, with you." His lips brushed my cheek before he settled his chin on the top of my head, his substantial height dwarfing mine when he held me like this. "Being queen of this world will require sacrifices, Claire."

I stiffened, not liking that term—*sacrifice*. "What kind of sacrifices, Cyrus?"

He sighed, his refreshing scent teasing my nostrils as he held me close. "For one, we'll be required to produce an heir. And, as you have several mates, dividing time between kingdoms will prove difficult. There might be instances where I have to remain here while you venture to Spirit Kingdom with Exos. Both of our lives will require certain formal functions, ones meant to unite our fae kind. I won't lie to you, Claire. It's going to be difficult."

I turned in his arms, lifting my gaze to his. "But we'll make it work."

"That was never a question," he replied, a small smile curving his beautiful lips. "How do you feel about the heir part of the conversation?"

The idea of giving Cyrus children made me feel all warm inside, but it did raise a pertinent question. "How will we know it's yours?"

"We'll know," he murmured.

"How?" I pressed, actually curious now. And then a horrifying thought hit me. "Wait, should I be using protection?"

He chuckled. "No, little queen. We have it well handled on our side."

"What does that even mean?"

Another chuckle as he shook his head. "Fae males control reproduction, at least for Elemental Fae. You won't become pregnant until one of us decides it's time, which, trust me, will be a group conversation."

I blinked at him. "Male fae…" Yeah, I couldn't finish that.

"We're not human," he added, drawing his finger over my pointy ear. "And neither, my darling, are you."

Right. That part I accepted. "But you can control it?"

His lips curled again. "Yes, little queen. I can control quite a few things. Would you care for a demonstration?"

My eyes widened. "Now?"

He laughed outright. "I'm not going to impregnate you, but it's good to know where you stand on the pregnancy discussion."

"I mean, I'm not against it. But, uh, I don't… I mean, it's not time yet. Right? I'm only—"

His mouth silenced mine, his kiss a seductive caress that had me melting into him on instinct. Minutes passed. Maybe hours. I always lost time when Cyrus touched me, but somehow we remained clothed, our tongues doing all the talking while the soothing sound of waves rolled in the distance.

My Cyrus, I thought, adoring his touch.

My Claire, he returned, his palm flattening against my lower back. *I love you.*

I love you, too, I whispered, my arms winding around his neck. *Whatever you need, I'm yours.* And I meant it. If it was an heir he desired, I'd give it to him in time. If we needed to mist around the kingdoms to keep everyone happy, I'd do that as well. Whatever he required, I'd give him. Just as I knew he would do the same for me and the others.

My mate-circle.

My life.

My loves.

CHAPTER TWENTY
TITUS

THE ACADEMY FELT EMPTY WITHOUT CLAIRE.

No, it felt wrong.

Mostly because she was about to undergo a dangerous journey without me. I trusted Exos and Cyrus to watch over her, but I hated that I couldn't even help.

And worse, they'd left me to play babysitter to a cocky-ass Vox and a sulking Sol. The former was acting like a faeling who had just discovered his powers for the first time, while the latter wouldn't stop muttering about "damn Spirit Fae."

Why had it become my responsibility to keep this mate-circle together and happy?

Rubbing my temples, I grumbled, "Isn't that Exos's job?"

Vox paused his chopping of the ingredients in the kitchen—from his position on the couch—and sent a controlled gust to slice into the vegetables on the counter. He grinned, proud of his new trick, and focused on me while his meal essentially prepared itself through the use of air alone.

Hence, cocky-ass Air Fae.

"What's Exos's job?" Vox asked. "Making dinner? Why would that be his job?"

"Exos," Sol repeated, his lip curling in annoyance. The ground rumbled, sending a fresh crack up the Spirit Dorm's columns. He clenched and unclenched his fists as his eyes flashed with building rage.

"What the hell is your problem?" I demanded, already exhausted and we'd barely spent an hour back at the Academy. "It's like you're about to implode, and you"—I pointed at Vox—"keep throwing invisible knives around. If one of those nicks me—"

A gust spirited between my legs, causing me to jolt in surprise. *Fucking Air Fae.*

Vox grinned. "No idea what you're talking about."

I gathered a fireball and aimed it at Vox's carefully prepared meal. "Don't make me burn it to teach you a lesson."

Vox readied a stance, seemingly intrigued by the challenge. His eyes took on a flash of silver when I released the attack, yet the fire fizzled out in midair before it had a chance to hit. Only a gentle brush of wind betrayed that Vox had done anything at all.

I sighed. "I liked you better when you were broody." The bump to his power—and his confidence—that Claire's influence gave him was getting on my nerves.

Sol slammed his fist against the table, sending it breaking down the middle, as he shot to his feet. "I can't think straight with the two of you idiots around," he growled and then shoved past me, sending a painful jolt through my shoulder.

I gave Vox an arched brow.

"Don't look at me." He raised his hands in surrender. "Sol's been in a sour mood all day. He's probably just hungover."

"It's more than that," I said, turning and following the Earth Fae outside.

Sol stormed to the practice arena as jagged spires of rock shot into the air all around him. The shiver of power that permeated the soil made my hair stand on the back of my neck, but I trailed after him anyway.

Just an angry Earth Fae... I can handle this.

"Sol," I snapped, hoping to jolt the fae out of whatever funk he was in. "What's got you so worked up?"

He ground his teeth together and his jaw flexed. Vox took position at the edge of the yard to watch us, his eyes bright with a strong band of silver that said he'd intervene if I needed it.

By the way the ground shook, it was likely.

Sol slammed his foot, and another column of earth shot up, spraying dust and pebbles everywhere. I lifted my hand to shield my face with a column of fire.

"Spirit is dangerous!" Sol roared. "You don't know. You don't understand. You weren't fucking there!" He let loose a guttural scream as he sprinted for me with a balled fist.

I dodged the impact—barely. And I noted the light gust of air that had helped me move out of the way in time. Without it, I might have lost my head.

"Fuck, Sol!" That was way too close. "Did you just try to punch me?" I demanded.

The Earth Fae's chest heaved with so much pent-up rage that I was surprised he could stand. I'd seen that look before, the one that bespoke of years of repressed anger and grief. It was the kind of expression that often came out in the Powerless Arena.

"Sol," I tried again as I retrieved the bo staff Claire had given me from our weapons stash. I'd just put the gift here when we arrived this afternoon, hoping I'd get a chance to play with it later. Might as well give it a whirl now. It lit up with an aggressive wave of blue heat as I twirled it in my palm. "Why don't you tell me what's going on?"

Sol looked between Vox and me as if there were answers just out of reach. "I…" He grabbed his head and groaned. "Claire can't go there. She can't experience what I did. She won't… She *can't* survive."

"She's a Spirit Fae," I reminded him. "She'll be fine."

"No, no. You don't get it. Neither one of you does. You didn't… They all died. Every single one of them *died*." Sol fell to his knees, denting the earth on his way down. "And it hurt."

I eyed Vox to see if he could tell me what the hell Sol was talking about.

The expression of horror on the Air Fae's face told me he did. "Your family," he breathed.

"All of them," Sol whispered, the sound broken. "You don't know what it's like to have them in your head, in your *soul*, and not know what they did. All you feel is immense *pain*. And I don't even know who did it. Who touched me. Who left me with all these scars."

Oh, shit. I mean, I knew the Earth Fae had some issues with control, and yeah, he was a bit of a grump at times, but I just thought that was part of his misguided charm. But this? Yeah, this wasn't something I would have guessed.

Sol groaned as if in pain, and the ground shook again, this time forming spiky craters that spiraled down into the earth. "A Spirit Fae ripped us apart from the inside. And the plague, it killed them, but somehow, I survived. And I don't even know why."

The plague. He's talking about the plague. The Earth Fae had experienced the worst of it—second to the Spirit Fae. Yet Sol seemed to be untouched by it. Hence his size, strength, and ability.

But what he described made it sound like he'd been a victim, too. Just of a different variety of torture.

He blew out a breath, his shoulders hunching as a cascade of cracks ran through the training yard that threatened to reach the dorm.

If the giant kept this up, he was going to demolish the entire quad.

491

"Okay, Sol, you need to take a deep breath, man. Claire is with Cyrus and Exos. I know they're assholes, but they've proven themselves. She's in good hands, buddy. Or I'd be just as pissed as you. Got it?"

Sol narrowed his gaze at me and ground his teeth again, sending a rumble to unseat my balance.

Right, so that approach didn't work well.

I stabbed my staff into the soil and poured my fire into it, melting rock back into place.

"Look, if you love Claire, you have to stop this. She's a Spirit Fae. You can't just rip—"

When the heat of my fire reached Sol, he launched to his feet with an explosion of earth and power.

Okay, maybe fire was a bad idea.

The Earth Fae roared as he stormed toward me, his massive legs building momentum in a terrifying blur of speed I wouldn't have credited to the titan.

I dodged him—this time without Vox's help—and twirled my bo staff, creating a fire shield to separate us. Sol twisted as he tried to reach for me, but the position put him off-balance.

Hmm, the bigger they are, the harder they fall. And Sol clearly needed some sense knocked into him. I swiped my bo staff at his ankles in an attempt to topple him over.

The staff met rock-hard calves, and the crack reverberated up my arm, making my teeth chatter.

Sol grabbed the weapon, ignoring the flames that engulfed him as he pulled me closer.

Not good.

I ducked when another punch went flying past my head, and I slammed a palm to the ground, pouring my fire into it. Sol staggered as rock melted and resolidified around his ankles, trapping him.

He swung wildly, this time catching me once in the ribs. It would have broken something had Vox's air not softened the blow, something I'd have to thank him for later.

Another fist, then another, and all I knew was fury and pain as Sol unleashed his rage. The winds couldn't stop him forever, and Vox's shouts echoed through the training yard, but the Earth Fae wasn't listening.

I raised the bo staff and poured all of my heat into it, thinking of Claire and the passion our fires burned together. The flash blinded me and Sol, causing the giant to roar with outrage as he snatched up the instrument and snapped it in half.

The impact stole my breath.

That had been a gift from Claire, and he'd just... *snapped it.*

Sol seemed to freeze, stunned as the halves of my weapon clattered to the glassy ground.

"You broke it," I whispered, unable to mask the hurt in my tone. Claire had given me that staff as a present, and now…

I blinked.

"How could you do that?" I demanded. "How could you do that to Claire? To me? What the hell is your problem?" I shoved him back, the rock giving way to his feet as he stumbled.

Sol seemed as broken as my staff, his earthy gaze falling to the ground. "Fuck." He fisted his hair and blew out a long, harsh breath. "*Fuck.*"

Yeah, understatement of the afternoon. "Seriously, what the hell is wrong with you?"

The giant shook his head. "Everything and nothing." He gripped the back of his neck and finally met my gaze. "You don't understand what it's like to watch everyone around you die and have no idea why you survived. But I feel the marks of it every day—whatever that Spirit Fae did to my soul that damaged me so much that not even the plague wanted to touch me."

"But Claire isn't like that," Vox whispered. "You know she's not. And neither is Exos or Cyrus."

Sol visibly shivered, his shame painting his cheeks a dark red. "I know. I… I just don't know who did it. Or why. And now they're teaching Claire how to do the very thing that nearly destroyed me. The thing that I'm convinced created the plague among my kind, not that I have any fucking proof."

He kicked a glassy stone with his shoe, his tension mounting again. But rather than unleash it on me, he just puffed out his chest again with another of those violent sighs.

"You know the worst part?" he mused, more to himself than to me. "I don't even remember most of it. Just what I see in my nightmares. I couldn't even tell you who did this to me. That person could still exist, could be stalking our Claire, and I'd have no idea."

He bent to pick up the pieces of my staff, his shoulders falling again.

"It's not her fault. I know that. It's not anyone's but the asshole who did this to me. It's just… It's hard." He pressed the two halves together, his earth magic flaring to life. "Give me some fire and wind," he said, focusing on the splintered frays. "Help me meld this back together."

My eyebrows lifted as he smoothed over the wood, gluing it together with a flicker of power that lifted the hairs on my neck. I added my flames to the seam, helping to melt the embers as Vox guided them with his wind.

And in seconds, the staff was as good as new. Just with a few added flavors to the mix, making it not only a gift from Claire, but a product of the three of us as well.

Sol tossed it to me. "You might need Cyrus to add some water to the weak spot to ensure your inferno doesn't rip it apart again. Otherwise, it's solid."

"Thanks," I said, somewhat pleased to have my weapon back. I twirled it once to test the balance and infused it with my heat, watching as it effortlessly flashed a blue shade. "It'll do."

He gave a nod. "Good." He glanced up at the sky and then back at us. "Just so we're clear, if anything happens to Claire during this spirit lesson, there'll be hell to pay."

I grinned. "On that, we agree."

"Good," he repeated, brushing some rubble from his shoulder and rolling his neck. "Then how about we try all that again, Fire Fae? I have a lot of anger to burn off, and you seem somewhat capable of holding your own."

"Somewhat capable?" My brows inched upward. "You really want to use those words?"

"Prove me wrong and I'll change the phrase," he taunted.

I grinned and tossed my staff to the side. Weapons weren't required for friendly sparring. And, well, I didn't exactly trust him not to snap it again. Especially as it hadn't worked all that well on him the first time. "Bring it on, Earth Fae."

Sol grinned, and for the first time today, it reached his eyes. "Your funeral, Fire Fae."

Vox sat on the sidelines, a giant smile on his face. "Let me know when it's my turn. I think I'll enjoy this game."

Of course he would.

Cocky-ass Air Fae.

CHAPTER TWENTY-ONE
CLAIRE

"ALL RIGHT, CLAIRE. I need you to close your eyes." Exos's warm tones echoed through Cyrus's bedchamber, his voice sounding much farther away due to the chaotic beat drumming in my ears. "And breathe for me," he added softly, his palm sliding up and down my bare arm.

Cyrus sat to my other side, his hand bracing my lower back while Exos led the exercise.

I swallowed and focused on the comfort of their presence. It was so peaceful here with the soft flow of the waterfall trickling into the makeshift fountain in the corner. Magic existed all around us, kissing the air with a blissful mist that soothed my soul.

Slowly, my heart rate returned to normal.

Inhale.

Exhale.

Repeat.

I couldn't tell where the words originated from, but whether from me, Exos, or Cyrus, it didn't matter. I followed the advice, easing my spirit and relaxing between my two mates.

One of them brushed my hair with his fingers.

The other placed a kiss against my shoulder.

And I felt the cushions press into my spine as they eased me backward into the bed of pillows on the ground.

"Look inside yourself, Claire. Search for the tendril of spirit that mates us as one," Exos instructed softly. The proximity of his voice told me he'd lain down as well. His palm went to my stomach, the heat of his skin branding me through my thin strapless dress.

Cyrus rested on my other side without touching me, giving me the space I needed to connect to his brother.

With a deep breath, I tugged on my elemental strand that bonded me to Exos. I felt his grin more than saw it and sighed as he brushed his lips against mine. "Follow the link, baby. Come play with me."

He made it sound so simple.

Truly, it was.

I trailed the cord to our special place, the one where only our souls could dance.

Only, Cyrus's presence lingered there, too.

A dark blue wave on the horizon, rippling powerfully and quietly.

Exos found me first, his spirit familiar with mine and reaching for my hand as if we stood beside one another. And maybe we did. Just as apparitions of ourselves.

This is the spirit plane, he explained softly. *But it's our safe place, Claire. One that our souls constructed just for us. Out there, where Cyrus waits, is the spirit realm that houses the source of power.*

I saw it then, the blinding light in the distance that flickered with intensity, beckoning us to come closer. Like an addictive ray of sunshine that taunted our aura, begging for a chance to bathe our skin in hypnotic energy.

It's dangerous, Exos continued. *The allure can overwhelm an untrained fae. Particularly one not accustomed to standing so close.*

Yet Cyrus appeared unfazed.

As did Exos.

But I felt the draw, the thirst to explore and indulge in a forbidden essence. To consume myself in the core and never let go.

It was intoxicating.

With each step, my desire grew. My heart began to thump almost painfully in my chest, the yearning to lose myself in the vitality of this plane almost overwhelming my ability to think.

Until Exos stepped into my path, blocking my view. *Focus on me, Claire.*

I blinked up at him as if awoken from a dream. The craving still persisted, a lethal draw to move around him and run toward the vibrant rays. He cupped my face, his touch grounding my instincts. I leaned into him, absorbing his strength and knowledge, trusting him to lead me through the perimeter toward Cyrus and away from the magnetic ball representing life.

This is a plane only Spirit Fae can access, and most can only move so close to the center before being drawn back to their corporeal form, Exos murmured. *However, my birthright places us almost directly on the source whenever we venture into this realm of being. It's why you must be careful never to do this alone, not until you're better trained on how to handle the pull.*

I understand, I replied. And I did. This was not a place I wanted to visit without Exos by my side. I could feel him anchoring me in both mind and spirit, his touch a final weight to keep me locked at his side.

From here, you have access to all life, Claire. Do you remember our conversation about the Dark Fae?

Not just Elemental Fae, but all types of fae. It's why our kind is often revered and feared by other supernatural beings. Because at the end of it all, we control the vitality of fae kind.

I stumbled at his words, my lips parting. *All of them?*

He nodded. *But most have employed protective runes to prevent Spirit Fae from interfering in their lives. Not that it's really needed. Only the strongest bloodlines can reach across barriers to the other species of fae.*

Exos paused on the path, his arm stretching toward a translucent tendril of smoke. He gave it a tug, pulling a darker aura toward us.

This leads to the Midnight Fae, the ones you call vampires. They have wards in place to identify a breach from our lands, which I could circumvent with a lot of concentration. But there's no point in altering their lives, as they are so different from our own.

He released the dark string and reached for another, lighter one, the color a pristine white.

Fortune Fae, he mused. *They foresee the future and don't require any runes at all. Because they would see me coming before I even tried.*

Exos selected a handful of others, naming the different types and associating them with their colors before releasing their strands. They all seemed to wave around us, humming near the vibrant core, waiting to be manipulated.

But it was the elemental ones that seemed to writhe around him as he stroked his fingers through the air.

Their souls recognize our power, he mused. *Unlike the others, there's nothing foreign about our touch and they almost welcome our interference, our source of vitality.* He caught one that hummed close to my side, the yarn appearing almost frayed at the edges. His brow furrowed as he studied the patterns, his gaze flickering to Cyrus. *A powerful Spirit Fae did this.*

Yes, Cyrus agreed.

Did what? I asked, gently stroking the cord and recognizing the earth energy vibrating protectively within the threads.

Do you recognize it? Exos countered, releasing the soul to my hands and smiling as the essence twined around my arm like a loving vine, sliding upward to rest near my heart.

A tear caught in my eye as the name breathed into my spirit. *Sol.*

Mmm, Exos hummed in confirmation as he captured a flash of light in his palm. The ball unwound into the flicker of a flame that he released onto my shoulder.

Titus, I recognized immediately. *And the one hovering by your head is Vox.*

Yes, it's like he's supervising me even from afar, Exos mused, teasing the spirit with a puff of air.

Can they feel us?

He shook his head. *They might sense we're near, but they can't access this plane.*

Their spirits are entirely vulnerable to our influence, Cyrus added, his palm cradling a liquid strand of powerful waves.

Your father, I realized.

Yes. He settled the essence on his shoulder, his gaze watching as Vox floated closer to me. *Those of our bloodline gravitate to our presence automatically. And it seems your mates have found you as well.*

But they can't feel us, I said, disturbed. *That's a terrifying concept.*

It is, Exos agreed. *Which is why entering this plane should only be done with a purpose.*

To do otherwise would be an abuse of power, Cyrus added. *But this is where one would go to manipulate another being, because access to the soul allows you to control the mind.*

This is how Elana questioned Ignis and her friends, Exos added. *She went into this plane to access their souls and force the truth to the front.*

And also how she made everyone freeze in the gym. I shivered, recalling how everyone bowed and remained that way until she released them. *She commanded so many souls.*

A show of power. Exos raised his arm, and a swarm of energy latched onto him in an instant, including the souls that had been clinging to me. *It takes practice, but calling upon the spirit of others isn't a difficult task.* He released them as quickly as he'd summoned them, his expression radiating a regal brightness that took my breath away.

Perhaps now you understand why so many fear us, Cyrus whispered.

I swallowed, nodding. *Yeah.* Because that was terrifying. Exos hadn't even needed to think to call all those lives to him. It struck me then how easily he could command the fae, manipulate their minds to his will, and take over the entire elemental world. Maybe even more.

Yet he remained poised and in control.

Always.

No wonder you're so stubborn, I marveled. *Both of you.*

Exos chuckled. *Ah, Claire, we could say the same about you.*

He pulled me to him, his fingers running through my hair, or what felt like my hair, anyway. We were really just apparitions of ourselves, but I sensed him touching me back in Cyrus's room, his body a blanket of protective heat beside my own.

Let's try calling your mom, he suggested softly. *As Cyrus said, our bloodline reaches out to us automatically, as do any of our mates. So she should be hovering nearby.*

Somehow I doubted it would be that easy. *How do I find her?*

Think about her, Exos replied. *Picture her in your mind. Call her to you.*

Okay. I considered the ball, the way she'd appeared to me in that wispy form, and wondered if that resembled her current state. So elderly and frail and not at all like the photo I saw of her as a child. But nothing happened, the only souls swimming around me belonging to those of my mates. I smiled as Titus brushed my cheek, his fire leaving an ember behind like a kiss.

Sol continued to weave around me as if trying to root himself in my soul. Maybe he was, too. We weren't yet fully bonded. *Soon,* I promised him. *My Sol.*

And then there was Vox, who continued to hover near Exos, ever vigilant.

My lips curled at how perfect they all were, my circle of fae mates. Even here they acted as I expected.

Until a disturbance rumbled between us, causing them all to flicker around me in a shield of protective warmth.

Cyrus moved to my side, Exos on the other, their expressions hard.

Tell me this is normal, I said, grabbing their hands as another tremble threatened my footing.

I'm not in the habit of lying, Claire, Cyrus replied, his fingers tightening against mine. *Your mother is trying to answer your call, but something is stopping her.*

Something powerful, Exos added, his arm lifting as he commanded the spirit to appear. I felt it rather than heard him, the power erupting from him harsh and all-consuming. It threatened to steal my breath away, causing my heart to jump wildly in my chest.

Exos...

Let him concentrate, Cyrus murmured, his grip resembling concrete as wind whipped around us in a violent maelstrom of energy.

I sensed the fight in Exos, his dominance taking over as he broke through the binds that held my mother's soul captive. Each mental snap made me cringe, the visual in my head one of agony and despair.

You're hurting her, I breathed, shaking from the onslaught of her pain. *Exos, you're hurting her!*

I know, he gritted back. *But I have no other choice.*

Cyrus wrapped his arms around me before I could retaliate, his embrace a waterfall of sincerity and love that ejected me from the spiral of anguish and into one of peace and tranquility. I blinked in confusion, his mist a cloud I didn't expect to see or feel. But oh, how I adored him. How I needed that brush with reality, the reminder of our bond.

Ready? he asked.

For?

His mouth captured mine for a split second before everything evaporated to reveal a vapid space of white and nothing else.

I blinked. *Cyrus?*

Nothing.

Exos?

No reply.

I twirled in a circle, finding myself alone in a world of endless *white.*

Oh no. This can't be good.

I spun again, my eyes opening and closing wildly, my heart practically bursting in my chest. *Exos! Cyrus!*

Why had they left me?

Where was I?

How was I supposed to get out of here?

This was still the spirit plane. I felt it in every fiber of my being.

But I was standing in the middle… of the source? Maybe?

My feet sprinted on my behalf, taking me this way and that as I fought to find a way out, any path I recognized. Yet everything looked the same. Just white. No souls. No mates. No life.

I opened my mouth to scream, but no sound escaped me.

Just soundless inexistence.

Think, Claire, I demanded. *There has to be a way out of this. A way home.*

To my mates.

Yes.

I just needed to think about them. They would come. My loves. My life. My circle.

My breath evened as I envisioned them, demanding they respond, that they find me and free me from this pristine cavern.

"Claire?"

Not the voice I expected to hear.

I turned toward my mother. She stood in a translucent state several feet away, her blue eyes wide with surprise.

"How did you bring me here?" she asked, glancing around as if in a hypnotic state. "How did you break her spell?" And then her expression morphed into one of horror, her eyebrows lifting in astute alarm. "You didn't. Oh, darling, no. Dark magic is not for our kind. Promise me you'll stop. Promise me you won't do it again!"

"I didn't," I replied, my voice strained. "I haven't touched dark magic."

"Then how did you break the binds?"

"I didn't," I repeated. "Exos… He called you to the spirit plane."

"Oh no," she whispered, shaking her head. "Oh, no, no, no. She'll know, Claire. She'll have felt the interference! You must run before she finds you. Run, Claire! Run now!"

"Who will find me?" I demanded. "You're not making any sense."

But my mother seemed to be fading, her expression one of absolute terror.

"She's coming. Oh, she's coming. Run, darling. Don't let her find you. Ru—"

The ground roared to life, swallowing me into a hole of sound and sensation and eliciting a scream from deep within as I was forcefully sucked into a vortex of swirling color. Life. Death. Water. Pink. Fluttering wings. It all wavered around me in a blanket of confusion, swathing me in the sea of reality and spitting me back out onto Cyrus's bedroom floor.

I came alive with a gasp, my lungs on fire, my heart racing against my ribs.

Cyrus and Exos let out a cry of relief, their hands running over me in protective strokes.

"Holy fuck," I breathed, my voice raspy and harsh. "What a trip." Because wow, that was intense. It was as if I'd seen a millennium of life in that tunnel, all whipping around me in a whirlwind of activity too fast for my brain to comprehend.

"What the hell were you thinking?" Exos demanded.

"What?" I gaped at him. "What do you mean?"

"You stopped breathing, Claire," Cyrus snapped. "For ten fucking minutes."

My eyes widened even further. "*What?*"

Exos sat back on his heels, shaking his head.

Cyrus rubbed his face with his hand.

Pissed-off energy mingled with relief between them, their grips on my arms almost bruising.

"It was all white," I whispered, trying to recall what happened. "And then my mother appeared." I told them what she said, how she made no sense at all, and they just stared at me in obvious alarm. "Say something."

They both shared a long look.

But it was Exos who finally broke the tense silence. "You went into the elemental core, Claire."

"Right into the damn center of it," Cyrus added, his tone somehow furious and surprised at the same time.

"And somehow survived." Exos grabbed my shoulders and yanked me into him. "Don't ever do that to me again, Claire." His mouth captured mine before I could reply.

So I whispered, *I don't even know how I did it.*

Never again, he repeated.

Which I would promise if I knew how it happened in the first place.

But he wasn't hearing any of it, his lips too busy memorizing mine as if he thought he'd never kiss me again.

Cyrus clasped the back of my neck, tugging me away from Exos and kissing me with the same vigor, his emotions a tidal wave of need against my senses.

Each lick engraved his name upon my soul.

Each nip a reminder of our bonds.

Each caress a promise for a long future ahead.

By the time he released me, I couldn't form a coherent sentence, let alone think.

Which seemed fine by them.

Because Exos was already tasting me again, his tongue mating violently with mine as Cyrus ripped off my dress.

What is happening? I wondered, my mind spinning beneath the onslaught of their seductive energy.

We almost lost you. Exos sounded frantic. *We thought we lost you, Claire.*

I'm right here, I promised.

Prove it, little queen. Cyrus bit my shoulder, causing me to groan and arch back into him. *We need you to prove it.*

CHAPTER TWENTY-TWO
CYRUS

SHE DIED.

Claire. Fucking. Died.

Her heart stopped.

Her lungs ceased to breathe.

Her svelte form refused to move.

And her soul…

I shuddered and buried my nose in her hair, her neck, needing to *feel* her, to believe she was actually still here. "I've never been so terrified in my life," I admitted, my mouth trailing along her neck. "Fuck, Claire. Don't ever do that to me again."

"I didn't—"

Exos's mouth captured hers, silencing her response.

Not that it mattered.

Nothing she could say would alleviate the pain of our momentary loss, the agony of having her ripped from my arms for what resembled eternity.

Exos and I had awoken frantic, unable to sense her at all. She'd just disappeared. Her spirit gone.

Never had I felt so lost and weak all at once. Neither of us had known what to do, where to go, how to find her and bring her back.

My sweet Claire.

My little queen.

My heart.

I breathed her in once more, tasting every inch of her skin with my tongue. Her breasts. Her flat stomach. The apex between her thighs.

Fuck, I loved her scent. Floral and sweet and, oh, that delicate place that wept for attention. I licked her deep, adoring the way she cried out into Exos's mouth.

Alive.

She's alive.

I repeated the words over and over again, reveling in her strength, her spirit, the soft beat of her heart.

"Make her come," Exos urged. "I need to hear her scream."

"Mmm, happily," I agreed, circling her clit before sucking the bud between my teeth.

Her back bowed off the floor, her limbs shaking from the onslaught of sensation writhing through her veins. Confusion warred with yearning in her features, her body bending to our will on pure instinct and need.

More.

We all needed so much more.

However, she required gratification first.

A small hint of the evening to come.

Because after almost losing her, we had no choice but to celebrate her life. To lavish her with our love, to rejoin all our souls and reignite the bonds between us. Oh, they still existed. Still flourished after her first returning breath. But it wasn't good enough.

As Exos demanded, we needed to hear her scream.

And scream she did, her orgasm slamming into her body on an excruciating wave of power that I felt through our connection.

The others would, too.

Which, I knew, they needed just as much as we did, because they had to have sensed her detach from this plane. Just as they would have experienced her return.

"More, Claire," Exos breathed. "Give us more."

She moaned, her breasts flushing from her residual pleasure and calling to Exos's mouth. He laved her nipple, eliciting another delicious sound from her throat as I drew her arousal downward with my tongue.

Our sweet Claire was too lost to the assault of our lips to understand my goal, too wet from her climax to realize where my mouth was headed even as Exos rolled her to her side to grant me better access.

It wasn't until my touch reached the heart of her backside that she jolted. First with my tongue and then my fingers, preparing her for what we all needed.

504

My name fell from her lips, whether in warning or question, I couldn't tell. But she soon succumbed to the moment, her beautiful form writhing beneath Exos's mouth as he worshiped her sweet pussy with every ounce of skill he possessed.

Life breathed into the air between the three of us.

Claire's life.

Her spirit rejuvenated. Joyful. Alive. *Here.*

But still, I needed more.

She'd *left.*

Stopped breathing.

Her energy *gone.*

Never again. I wouldn't allow it, would thread my soul with hers if I had to, just to keep her with us forever. And I knew Exos felt the same, could sense it in the way he caressed her now. So frantic, alarmed, and uncontrolled. All heat and emotion. Arousal. Yearning.

A craving she nearly left us with for eternity.

A deep sadness.

A perpetual loneliness.

No. I refused to accept such a fate.

Mine, I thought, biting her rump and smiling at the imprint left there.

"Cyrus," she groaned, searching for me over her shoulder. With one hand in Exos's hair, she tried to grab me with her other, but the angle was all wrong. I nipped her backside once more before pressing kisses up her spine to the back of her neck, my fingers still lodged deep within her. Scissoring. Expanding. Preparing her for something I doubted she'd ever experienced.

But our Claire wasn't shy. No. As soon as I was close enough, she grabbed the back of my neck and forced me to kiss her.

Exos chuckled against her damp heat, high from the taste of her ecstasy— a sign of *life.*

We were drunk on it.

Fueled to take her to additional heights.

To fuck her into an oblivion of mutual satisfaction.

Sharing women wasn't unusual for us. It also wasn't typical. We'd been known to experiment and play. But to have Claire between us now put all that previous experience to shame.

Because she was our heart.

Our mate.

The one we adored more than existence itself.

"We're going to take you, Claire," I whispered against her mouth. "Together."

"Mmm, and you're going to love every second of it," Exos agreed, licking a path up her stomach to her breasts. "I can't wait to hear you come with both of us lodged deep inside you, baby. It'll be the most amazing sound."

"Yes," I agreed. Her screams resembled vitality, assured us both she still breathed. And her pleasure was still ours to give.

I withdrew my fingers, certain of her readiness, and nudged her backside with my cock.

"Do you understand, Claire?" I murmured, my lips at her ear now as she arched back into me. "Do you understand what we're about to do to you?"

"Oh God…" She shuddered, her eyes falling closed as she pressed into my groin once more. "Yes…"

I smiled against her neck, tonguing her racing pulse. "Good." I positioned myself at her entrance—the one no one had dared enter before—and pushed just enough to test her acceptance.

She shivered, her body flushing all over.

And Exos distracted her by sucking her nipple deep into his mouth while his fingers grazed her damp folds.

I slid in a little more, my balls tightening as she squeezed my shaft in response. "Easy, Claire," I murmured, gently kissing her throat. "It's better if you relax."

"Mmm," Exos agreed, switching breasts and biting down on her stiff peak.

She cried out, her focus temporarily shifted, and I used the distraction to thrust deeper inside her. "Oh!" She jerked against me, causing me to glide home, where I stayed and allowed her to acclimate. "*Fuck…*"

"We've not even started yet," Exos mused, causing me to chuckle against her nape.

Because yeah, we really hadn't.

And when we did? Oh, sweet Claire would be in for the ride of her life.

Exos licked a path up her throat to her chin and hovered over her mouth. "There's only one mate I'll likely ever be able to truly share you with like this, Claire." He kissed her softly while I buried my nose in her hair, inhaling deep. "But we can do this whenever you want."

Which we both knew would be often.

But I'd let her admit that when we were done.

I nibbled her ear, exhaling slowly as Exos pressed his arousal to hers. "Ready, little queen?" I asked, meeting Exos's gaze.

He wouldn't hurt her.

But he wouldn't be gentle either.

I caught her hip just as he thrust into her waiting heat, her cry one of surprise mixed with ecstasy and maybe a hint of pain. We weren't lacking in size, and having us both inside would be a bit overwhelming the first time.

An expletive fell from her lips, followed by a mewl of pleasure as we began to move—slowly at first, introducing her to the experience.

Then Exos set a pace, one I met with ease, my mouth falling to her neck as my breathing turned harsh. Because fuck, that felt good. To be inside her. To feel her quivers. To scent her arousal. To embrace her soul with my own.

With each thrust, I embraced her vitality. Heard her moans. Experienced her gratification. She squeezed my cock, groaned our names, whispered commands, and engaged us both in a hedonistic display that would grace my dreams for decades to come.

She was perfect.

Gorgeous.

Mine.

I couldn't imagine a more exquisite feeling than having her writhe between us with abandon. Words left her mouth that were so fucking dirty and beautiful that I could hardly believe my ears. She demanded more. Harder. Faster. Again. And we gave it to her and more.

She came on the hottest surge of power, our names an engraving into the stars above.

But we weren't done.

It wasn't until she released again that I allowed myself to follow, with Exos quickly on our trail, the three of us lost in a euphoric cloud of wantonness.

A cloud that continued.

On and on.

Our need to worship Claire, to celebrate her existence, too strong for just one climax.

No, we fucked until we couldn't move, our hearts hammering in our chests, our bodies depleted and shaking from the exertion.

A wildness had taken over, driving our movements, forcing us to the point of no return.

We collapsed together in a pile of limbs with Claire giggling between us.

I glanced sideways at her, noted her gorgeous pink complexion, and smiled.

She looked so animated and joyous that it almost hurt my heart. But I used the last vestiges of my strength to tug her to me for another kiss and sighed as she relaxed against my chest.

Exos wrapped his arm around her waist, nuzzling her back, our positions having switched at some point during the fuck fest. I couldn't be the only one to experience that sweet ass of hers, after all.

Now it all resembled a blur of sensation and sex and absolute bliss.

One I would happily experience again, once my dick awoke from a long nap.

Claire nuzzled into my pec, her cheeks still pink. I drew my fingers through her hair, unknotting the strands. "Don't ever leave us again, little queen. Please."

"I didn't mean to," she whispered, her eyes drooping. "I don't even know how I did."

Which was even more concerning than her actual disappearance.

Exos's eyes said the same as he met my gaze. "We need to talk to Kols.

Find out what the hell is going on."

"He might not know," I pointed out. "But I agree. If anyone can shed some light on this darkness, it's him." Because that was what I felt when Exos had unraveled the binds holding Ophelia's soul hostage.

Dark Fae magic.

Evil shit.

And somehow his slicing through the ropes had sent Claire directly into the source, a consequence we absolutely needed to avoid in the future. Assuming they were related. Which, I was willing to bet, they were.

"I'll arrange it," I said, referring to Kols. "In the morning." When I could properly move again.

Claire wasn't even listening, her eyes having fallen closed after uttering her last word.

But Exos was alert. He nodded, then kissed her nape. "Good night, princess."

She didn't even stir.

I smiled. "Yes. Sweet dreams, little queen."

Part III

"When one becomes half
And five become one,
A plague will descend upon
the fae.
Only death is the cure."

–Gina

CHAPTER TWENTY-THREE
CLAIRE

OF ALL THE PLACES TO MEET A MIDNIGHT FAE, Cyrus chose a Manhattan nightclub. Like, in New York City. With humans. Alcohol. And obnoxious music that grated on my nerves.

I winced as a particularly harsh bass kicked up to the roar of the crowd, everyone gyrating to the hypnotic tune. At least it wasn't as loud at the bar, which allowed for conversation.

Not for the first time, I glanced at my entourage and demanded, "When is this guy going to show?" Because I was more than ready to head back to the peace and quiet of the Elemental Realm.

Cyrus sipped his bourbon and grinned. "And here I thought this place would make you nostalgic."

I snorted. "This is not what I miss about my world." Pizza? Absolutely. Loud parties? No.

Exos wrapped his arm around me, pulling me closer to him and kissing my temple. "It won't be much longer."

"He's right," a feminine voice chimed from behind the bar. "He should arrive in the next few minutes."

My brow furrowed as Cyrus and Exos broke out in matching grins. "Well, would you look at that?" Cyrus mused, reaching for the woman's hand. "A

511

Fortune Fae playing bartender in the city. I never would have prophesied such a thing."

Cyrus paused just before touching her, and the woman gave him a knowing smile. She extracted a strange playing card from her pocket that gleamed. "Hmm."

Her dark eyebrows danced, and he caught her hand in response.

She laughed as he pressed a kiss to her wrist. "You always were a charmer, Cyrus," she said, her tone sultry and immediately getting under my skin.

No. It wasn't the tone. It was her whole package. She had curves in all the right places. A tight top that emphasized said curves. Perfectly straight near-black hair. Soft blue eyes. And a smile that captured the attention of half the bar.

Including that of my mates.

I hated her on sight alone.

Hated her even more as Exos took her hand and kissed her in the same place Cyrus had. "What brings you to the Human Realm, darling?" he asked, gaze flickering with curiosity.

She sighed and shook her head. "Bureaucratic bullshit." She waved her freshly manicured fingers around and focused on me. "You must be Claire." The woman even had dimples when she smiled. Too fucking perfect.

"I am," I replied. "And you are…?"

"Not your competition," she mused, her gaze twinkling. "But I am glad you finally tamed these two. They caused quite the stir in the Fortune Kingdom a few years back. Who was it? Aurora and Cassandra, right?" She giggled. "You two are bad, bad boys."

"Now, now, Gina." Cyrus flashed her an indulgent look. "Don't go putting thoughts in my mate's head."

"Oh, she doesn't need my help with that," the female—Gina?—replied, winking at me. "I can see she's well acquainted with your antics already."

"Who are you?" I asked again, this time with a little more force.

"Gina." She positively beamed at me. "I'm so glad you're finally here. The plague is spreading, you know. But you'll fix it all up in no time. Just have to rid yourselves of that dark piece that doesn't fit."

Cyrus folded his arms on the bar, his amusement dying behind an intense mask. "Elaborate."

"Oh, I would, future Water King, but I've already revealed too much. And with my luck—which does appear to be running out—I'll be discovered sooner rather than later." She sighed dramatically. "The future refuses to bend."

"Who is the dark piece?" Exos tried again.

But Gina merely smiled. "You already know, Spirit King. As does your beautiful mate. And if I may…" She made a show of leaving the playing card on the table before capturing my hand without warning. Her blue eyes flickered into a creepy clear shade. She blinked, the color returning to normal as she gave me a squeeze. "So much pain, Claire. Two decades of it. But you have the power to heal them all, to restore the balance. I'm rooting for you." She leaned in and lowered her voice. "Just remember who you are, Claire. Your mates aren't the only ones counting on you." Her attention drifted over my shoulder, her expression lighting up. "Ah, he's here. You all behave now. Can't have you drawing more attention to me."

She whirled around, frolicking—and that wasn't an exaggeration—to the other side of the bar with a flourish of her very short skirt.

Like she really needed any help drawing attention.

Fortunately, Cyrus and Exos didn't seem to notice the length or her magnificent legs. They were too busy standing to greet the newcomer who I assumed was Kols.

And wow, was he gorgeous.

Tall. Athletic. Brown hair tinted with a hint of red that glimmered beneath the low lighting of the club. And eerily beautiful golden irises that flickered with power as he met my gaze.

Fuck, this guy is potent. I could see it in the grin that graced his full lips.

"Charm her, and I'll kill you," Cyrus said flatly as I pushed off the stool.

Kols chuckled, the sound warm and masculine. "Too late, Water Prince." He held out a hand. "I'm Kols."

"Claire," I replied, pressing my palm to his.

"I know," he murmured, kissing my wrist the same way Exos and Cyrus had done to Gina. This time it was their turn to scowl.

Exos wrapped a possessive arm around my back, tugging me into his side. "Good to see you, Kols."

"Is it?" the Midnight Fae asked, releasing my hand. He glanced around the room, the slight arch of his neck showcasing a line of inky black tendrils moving just beneath the collar of his dress shirt. Like Exos and Cyrus, he wore a suit, sans tie. However, he'd chosen all black, while my mates were in crisp white shirts and ebony jackets.

When he finished his perusal, I noted the hungry gleam in his eyes.

Vampire, I remembered, shivering.

His lips quirked as if hearing my internal thought. And maybe he could. Wasn't that a supposed trait—their ability to read minds? Or was it mind control? I'd have to ask Exos and Cyrus more about it later.

"Let's grab a corner booth," he suggested, nodding toward the darkest side of the club where a group of people had just stood to vacate.

Did he do that? I asked, my heart fluttering in my chest.

Yes, Cyrus said. *Kols isn't just a Midnight Fae; he's also a prince. Like me.*

Meaning he's powerful, I translated.

Incredibly gifted, yes. Cyrus took my hand and led me forward, while Exos remained on my opposite side with his arm draped around my waist. If any of the humans noticed our little triad, they didn't react to it. But Kols certainly eyed our touch with amusement. He slid into the booth first, followed by Cyrus, while Exos and I took the opposite side.

"Was that Gina I saw up at the bar?" Kols asked, curiosity deepening his voice.

"Yeah." Cyrus glanced at the stools we just vacated. "She's hiding from something."

"Isn't she always?" Kols mused.

Cyrus lifted a shoulder. "Seemed a bit more serious this time, but I'm sure she has it handled. Besides, she seemed more interested in leaving us with cryptic words."

"Typical Fortune Fae." Kols's eyes glimmered as he steepled his fingers on the table. "So how can I be of service? As I assume this isn't just a meeting for fun."

"Not this time, no," Cyrus agreed, indicating they'd met for fun in the past. Given his easy candor with Gina, I could only imagine what that meant.

I mean, my mates were all experienced. And I knew I wasn't their first lover. While I could accept that, I didn't want to think about their pasts. Especially not with a beautiful fae like Gina.

"We suspect one of our elders is using dark magic," Exos said, jumping right to the point. "And we're hoping you can help us confirm that."

Kols grinned, a flicker of flame circling his pupils and dying beneath a blink of his long, elegant lashes. "Sure. Can you replicate it? Or detail what you felt?"

Cyrus looked at me. "Can you describe what happened when Elana summoned the dead?"

Kols eyebrows lifted. "A death spell?"

Cyrus and Exos nodded.

"Do tell," Kols murmured, leaning forward, his intrigue palpable.

I cleared my throat, unsure of where to start. So I went with the beginning, about how Elana had taught me about spirit magic, creating pixies and things of that nature. Then I told him about our last session, about the spirit writhing in the strange liquid and the pain I felt from his spirit. Just the memory of it made me shiver with wrongness. "It was like he couldn't speak," I added. "But I sensed he wanted to say something."

Kols nodded. "My guess is she threaded a mutation into the magic, one that disabled his ability to form sentences. Because a proper summoning allows the soul to speak. It's also possible she infused some of her spirit element into the act, thereby compelling his silence."

"So you agree it's dark magic?" Cyrus pressed.

"Oh, absolutely. I didn't need all the gory details to tell you that. Necromancy is popular among a certain sect of my kind, while frowned upon by the rest of us. Aswad is a particular advocate for raising the dead." He grimaced. "But yes, it's absolutely dark magic. Which means your Elana must have some Midnight Fae heritage because one does not just become a necromancer. One must have an affinity for the death call first."

Cyrus and Exos shared a look.

I knew what they were thinking because I thought the same. "Part Dark Fae, part Spirit. Isn't that what my mom told you?"

Exos nodded. "Yes."

"That's impossible," Kols cut in. "Mating between the species is prohibited. It tips the scales of power."

"Such as being able to raise the dead and control it, too," Cyrus suggested, arching a brow.

"Wait, what do you mean by 'prohibited'? Why?" I asked, frowning. "We're all fae, right?"

"Yes, but with unique bloodlines. Tampering with those bloodlines creates... abominations." Kols cringed, his gaze darkening to a black cloud that sent a shiver down my spine. "The Dark Wars are not a time I ever wish to live through."

"Dark Wars?" I repeated, even more confused.

"A black point in Midnight Fae history," Exos explained softly. "Commingling between the fae altered the balance that we all pull from to survive. Imagine vampires with the ability to control water or fire."

"Well, that's not a difficult trick," Kols murmured, a light flame erupting over his fingertips. There and gone in a second. "But it was worse than that. Magic requires an equilibrium between light and dark. If it's disturbed, mutations occur, and power is distributed rather unevenly."

"Which creates chaos and allows dictators to rule," Exos added.

"That explains her obsession with the Council," Cyrus mused, causing Exos to arch a brow at him.

"Meaning?" my spirit mate pressed.

"If her origins were revealed, she'd be executed without ceremony. However, if she convinces us all to work together and asserts herself as the leader of the Council—which she has—that puts her on a pedestal as the fae who created it all. If you ask me, it's only a matter of time before her true intentions rise."

I pinched my lips to the side. "So you think it's all a ruse and she's using her connections to all the fae for her own benefit somehow."

"By siphoning energy from them," Kols said, leaning back in the booth. "I mean, if she's already playing with the dead, why not manipulate the life source of others while she's at it?"

My eyebrows shot upward. "She can do that?"

He flickered another of those flames across his knuckles and winked. "Child's play, sweetheart. Especially if she's of the necromancy line."

"Water." Cyrus laughed, the sound lacking in true humor. "I've sensed her use water more than once, but she's notoriously a single-gifted Spirit Fae."

Kols spread his hands as if to say, *Case in point*. "She's siphoning it off another."

"But why?" Exos demanded. "Why would she do this?"

Cyrus scratched his chin. "Only one way to find out."

"If she's practicing dark arts, I doubt it will be as easy as having a conversation. But I might have something that could help you," Kols said, grinning. "Your elders won't like it, though."

"What is it?" Cyrus asked, arching a skeptical brow.

"A book." His lips quirked up even more. "Sort of like a beginner's guide to necromancy. I'd be breaking a dozen Midnight Fae laws by giving it to you, but I suspect it'll assist you in more ways than one." Power radiated from him as he spoke, reminding me of how the elements seemed to swim around Cyrus and Exos.

"A Midnight Fae text," Exos mused. "Exactly how many rules are you breaking by handing that over to us?"

Kols chuckled. "How many are you breaking by accepting it?"

Cyrus and Exos just smiled.

"Why would there be rules about a textbook?" I wondered out loud.

The three of them laughed, Exos's arm wrapping around my shoulders to pull me in for a hug. "Fae politics, princess," he murmured. "Dark magic is purely Midnight Fae. Just as we own the elements."

"But sometimes you have to break the rules," Cyrus drawled.

"And I'd say now is one of those times," Exos agreed. "When can we get the book?"

"Tomorrow," Kols replied, his gaze drifting out to the club. "I'll be busy tonight."

Right. Vampire. Nightclub. Sort of cliché, but also appropriate. "So are we done?" I asked. Because as hot as he was, I really didn't want to see him snacking on humans.

"So eager to get us home," Exos teased, his lips trailing up my neck. "Do you want us to share you again, princess?" The words were spoken against my ear, causing my stomach to twist in anticipation and my cheeks to heat.

Cyrus smiled from across the table, clearly aware of what his brother had just said.

Fortunately, Kols appeared too busy scoping out his next meal to pay attention to us. "Right, well, I'll be in touch," he said, pushing away from the table. His gold eyes met mine, twinkling with mischief. "I would tell you to have a nice evening, Claire, but I can already see Exos and Cyrus have it covered. So I'll just say, lovely to meet you, gorgeous. Enjoy."

CHAPTER TWENTY-FOUR
EXOS

"SO DO YOU TWO OFTEN VENTURE to the Human Realm to meet up with other fae?" Claire asked as we escorted her to a well-known New York City portal.

She'd been rather disappointed by the uneventful transport, stating she thought it would be magical with fairy dust or pixies or some crazy flying horse. Instead, it was an elevator in an older building with a special keypad that teleported us between the realms at will.

"Not often," Cyrus replied, his arm draped across her shoulders. I'd given her my jacket, wanting to cover her shoulders and protect her from the cool New York air. It was winter, after all. And she'd worn one of her usual dresses with knee-high boots instead of a sweater and a coat. Fortunately, she had her fire to keep her warm, but she seemed to appreciate the chivalrous act as she hugged my jacket around her.

"But you seem to know the other fae well," she said slowly. "Like Gina."

My lips quirked up. "Jealous, Claire?" I teased, kissing her on the neck before opening the door to the building we needed.

"No." Her answer was quick. Too quick.

I shared an amused glance with Cyrus and gave him a look that said, *You tell her.*

LEXI C. FOSS & J.R. THORN

"She's an old friend," he explained. "And not that kind of friend, Claire. Fucking a Fortune Fae would not be enjoyable. She'd know all my moves before I made them."

A laugh leapt from my throat as I nodded in agreement. "He's right. Takes all the surprise out of it." I nipped at my mate's neck again, pressing my chest to her back and wrapping my arm around her waist. "Just think how boring last night would have been had you already known what was going to happen, Claire."

She shuddered, her body melting into mine. "I... That wouldn't be..." She swallowed, her weight collapsing into me even more. "Yes."

I chuckled against her throat as Cyrus mused, "That wasn't a complete sentence, little queen." He pressed the button for the elevator in the lobby. "But I'll allow it."

"As for us visiting the human world, it's infrequent. But as Royal Fae, we are well acquainted with the others. It's how we know Kols and Gina. Their families hold status in their respective fae kingdoms, and occasionally, we are required to meet for social functions."

"To maintain the balance," Cyrus added.

"Exactly," I agreed. There was still so much Claire didn't understand about the supernatural world, the laws that governed us all, how we cohabited in peace, and our long histories of times where we didn't maintain that perpetual peace. We were just so wrapped up in the current problems within the Elemental Realm that we hadn't had a moment to talk about the others. But Kols and Gina, they both had their troubles within their own ranks. Just as the numerous other types of fae did.

We all just chose to mostly focus on ourselves, only coming together when needed.

The elevator chimed, and Cyrus entered the sequence of numbers required to return us to the Academy as I ushered Claire into the waiting car.

"Can you mist from here?" she asked.

Cyrus considered it as he joined us, just as the doors closed. "I can mist anywhere, but between realms is harder. Within our elemental home, I'm closest to our source. It's easier. Here, it would require a lot of effort that I'd prefer not to expend because who knows when I might need my magic."

It wouldn't necessarily deplete, but I understood what he meant. Accessing the core of our gifts from this far away took strength and energy, weakening our ability to fight like we could on our own ground. Best to retain as much of our element as possible in case of the need.

Light flickered around us as we began our journey, the sound a quiet *whoosh* softened by the metal car transporting us to the Academy. Kols would use this contraption as well, but it would take him to the Midnight Fae Academy. "Is Kols in his final year?" I asked, thinking out loud.

Cyrus shrugged. "No idea. That fae doesn't talk about himself a lot."

I snorted. "True." For as many times as I'd met him, I barely knew him. He seemed to hide behind a mask of nonchalance and elegance. A typical royal, really.

We came to a stop, the metal clinking and beeping and dissolving before our eyes to reveal the heart of the Academy. My muscles loosened on instinct, the familiar elements bathing us in warm welcome.

Claire spun in a circle, her smile one of the most beautiful sights I'd ever seen.

Until a familiar presence spoiled our fun.

I turned toward it, eyebrow already arched. "Mortus," I said, his name resembling more of a curse than a greeting. I hadn't seen him since he knocked me out and threw me in a cage. I knew now that it wasn't actually him, that someone had been controlling him, but that didn't make me any more relieved to see the bastard.

"Where have the three of you been?" he demanded, eyeing Claire.

"I don't believe we have to report our whereabouts," Cyrus said coolly, wrapping his arm around our mate. "Unless you're questioning the intentions of your Spirit King?" He nodded at me.

"He's right," I agreed. "We don't owe you an explanation at all."

"The two of you maybe, but Claire is a student. And all students were due to report back this morning." Mortus straightened his spine. "Unless you believe she's above the rules?"

I smiled. "We both know she is, Mortus. But if you must know, we were on official Spirit business. Nothing to concern yourself with, old man. We're fine."

His black eyes narrowed into slits, flames practically shooting from his ears. He turned with a dramatic flare of his long black coat and stomped off in the direction of Elana's home.

"Fucking prick," Cyrus muttered. "He'll tell her where we've been."

"And all she'll find is evidence of a nightclub visit," I replied. "I'm not worried. Claire's part human. She can't fault us for wanting to reacquaint our mate with her home world."

"Yes, because going to clubs is how I spent my time," she deadpanned.

"I met you in a bar," I reminded her, snagging her waist with my arm and guiding us toward the Spirit Quad. "It's a logical assumption."

She snorted. "Uh-huh." Her elbow dug playfully into my side. "I did more than drink and party."

I kissed the top of her head as we walked, chuckling. "I know, princess. If that was all you did, you wouldn't be quite so stubborn."

"Ha ha." She attempted to elbow me again, but I caught her and pulled her up into my arms, carrying her across the quad.

"Our poor drunk Claire keeps running into me," I said conversationally to Cyrus.

"Shouldn't have given her that cherry cocktail, E." He reached over to tickle her side, causing her to squirm in my arms on a laugh that warmed my heart. "What will we do with her?"

"Oh, I have some ideas," I drawled. "But I think the others might want to join in."

"Mmm, a welcome-home party," Cyrus mused. "Yes, that sounds entertaining indeed."

"Ugh, I swear you all are going to break me," Claire muttered, then laughed as Cyrus tickled her again.

"You love it," he murmured, eliciting more giggles from her and making it rather hard to continue walking while carrying her. But hearing those sounds from her lips made it worth the effort it took to stay upright and moving.

"Okay! Okay! I give!" She practically chortled with the words, and Cyrus took her from my arms to hug her close.

"I love you, little queen," he said, brushing his lips against her forehead as he allowed her to stand once more, this time with his arm around her. "Now let's hurry back. I can practically feel Titus's irritation at our late arrival, and I can't wait to goad him a little."

Claire rolled her eyes. "The two of you are going to end up killing each other one of these days."

"Or fucking," I put in, smirking at my brother. While he typically bedded women, I knew of a few males he'd entertained in previous years. Cyrus always was one to experiment and play.

He merely shrugged, neither confirming nor denying it. "One or the other."

"Wait…" Claire turned to walk backward, her gaze on Cyrus. "Did you just admit you'd fuck Titus?"

Another shrug. "He could use a dominant hand." His expression darkened a fraction, his icy gaze twinkling with deviousness. "Why? Is that something you'd enjoy?"

Her stumble answered the question without words. As did the beautiful blush painting her cheeks.

Oh, Claire.

Our innocent little princess.

The things we would teach her in the years to come.

Maybe we'd even teach her a few things tonight...

CHAPTER TWENTY-FIVE
CLAIRE

MY ENTIRE BODY TINGLED, courtesy of Cyrus and Titus. Oh, they didn't fuck each other last night, but they definitely had fun putting me between them.

Of course, I spent half of it imagining what they would do to each other.

Vox and Sol, too, for reasons I couldn't explain.

But not Exos. No, I suspected Exos would never touch any of them. A point he drove home by merely watching last night rather than joining in. I could sense his arousal the entire time, yet he never once approached, preferring to almost supervise like the last time all of us engaged in an orgy in the living room.

God, who was I becoming?

A sex fiend, obviously.

"What are you thinking about over there, little queen?" Cyrus mused, his blue eyes knowing. "You're looking awfully flushed."

"Nothing," I lied. I squirmed in my seat and tried to focus on the papers in my lap.

Kols had delivered the dark-magic texts to Exos this morning—as promised. Only, he'd provided us with more than the one book we discussed, saying we might be interested in defensive magic as well. So Cyrus had that text while I perused the dark arts for something resembling what Elana had done. Exos sat beside me on the couch, one arm stretched out across the back over my shoulders and his other palm on my thigh as he read with me.

"There," he murmured, fortunately concentrating better than me. "It mentions liquid summoning."

I skimmed the passage he pointed at and nodded. "It's similar to what she did, yeah. But she seemed to have more control somehow."

"Perhaps she altered it with spirit," he replied.

"Sounds ominous," Titus said as he approached with a tray of mugs. "I'm not Vox, but I tried my best." He set the drinks on the table and picked one up to hand to me. "I may have added something special to this."

I peered inside to see embers rotating on the top.

No, not embers.

Burnt marshmallows.

My lips curled. "You made hot chocolate."

"Or a version of it, anyway," he replied, sending a flame dancing over my cheek in a kiss. "I had to improvise a little from the recipe Vox left out because we're low on ingredients. Used some sort of fruit milk instead of the creamy stuff you like."

I sipped it, noting the spicy undertone, and sighed. "It's perfect." It tasted nothing like the hot chocolate I grew up with, but I didn't mind. This was better. Sweeter, stronger, and it warmed my insides. Mmm. Yes. "Perfect," I repeated, taking another sip.

"I'm glad you—"

A sharp pain to my abdomen had me dropping the mug, which tumbled to the floor after splashing hot liquid all over me and the couch. But I felt none of it, the pang inside me too great to feel or hear anything else.

Sol! I cried out, our link quaking uncontrollably as his agony flooded my soul.

I leapt up, threw the blanket and book—which, thankfully, caught the majority of the spill—and took off for the Earth Quad with Cyrus, Titus, and Exos sprinting along behind me.

They were saying things.

Telling me to slow down.

But I couldn't stop even if I wanted to.

My mate was in trouble and needed my help, his anguish unlike anything I'd ever experienced.

Classes had restarted today, and I'd spent my time in fire class with Titus. Sol had gone to his usual courses, but the Earth Quad was huge. He could be anywhere, except for maybe the dorms.

Where? I demanded, calling upon my spirit to follow the thread to his soul. *There.*

He knelt in the middle of an orchard with an unconscious woman in his arms, his tears streaking down his face.

Aflora, I realized as I took in the dark hair and petite form. "What's wrong? What happened?" I landed on my knees beside him, my hands running over his bulging biceps. "Talk to me."

"She's…" He broke off on a growl laced with such agony that my heart fractured in two.

I saw it then, the blue lines traversing her skin, flooding her veins with a plague her small body couldn't fight. It blanketed her skin in a sheet of white laced with sweat.

"Claire," Titus whispered, the strain in his voice drawing my attention to him and then to the field around us.

"Oh God…" Aflora wasn't the only one.

There were at least twenty, all lying in the grass as if on their deathbeds.

And the trees moaned with their loss, the branches drooping in sorrow before my eyes.

My hands ran over Sol, searching him for signs of the infection, but he remained as sturdy as ever, his soul flourishing beneath my touch. "How?" I demanded. "How are you unaffected?"

But he didn't answer, his heart breaking before my eyes. "Don't do this to me, Aflora. Don't you dare die on me." He sounded so anguished, so terrified. And I understood then that she was the only family he had left—his final root to the Earth Fae. It wasn't a romantic connection but a familial one that mattered more to him than I realized before.

His mother had raised her as her own, a detail I picked up from our bond, something he'd never before mentioned. No wonder they had such a close relationship. She wasn't just his sister's best friend, but his sister as well.

Sol had already lost his parents and the sister Aflora once called her best friend.

"Don't do this to me," he repeated softly. "Please don't do this to me."

Tears pricked my eyes, the once beautiful female wilting in his arms like a dried-up leaf.

This can't happen.

I glanced around the field, noting all the others in similar positions.

Exos and Cyrus were with a few of them, offering words of encouragement that did nothing to stir life into them.

This plague—or whatever the cause—had reached the Academy, and it was taking them all.

"No," I breathed. "No." I wouldn't accept this.

My mother was involved with this once, or so the rumors said. And I had a way to contact her. She would give me answers.

She *had* to give me answers.

To stop this.

To fix this!

Sol had already lost too much. He would not lose Aflora. Not today.

Where are you? I demanded, standing, searching, peering into the spirit network for my mother's soul. *I know you're here. I want answers. You* will *answer me.*

The Academy fell away as I floated to the place Exos had taken me, near the electric source. But I didn't care about the core this time. No, I wanted my mother.

Come to me. Now. I threaded the words with power, urging her to comply. *Now!* I shouted.

There would be none of this hiding bullshit.

She had information I needed, and we didn't have time to spare.

Claire? My name was a whisper on the wind, one I followed with my air element, searching for the owner of that voice.

Too far away.

Too cloudy.

Come here now! I screamed, tired of this game, these tricks, the damn hide-and-seek. This ended today.

Energy swirled around me, the elements answering my call and thrusting me into the heavens on a surge of power so great it knocked the breath from my lungs and blinded me with its light. I shielded my eyes, pushing through the thick ropes of spirit threatening to drown me, and shoved to the other side.

To darkness.

I coughed, sputtering from the acrid stench littering the air, and blinked a dozen times to clear the flash from my retinas.

Only to find myself in a cell lined with iron bars that burned.

Literally.

With fire.

What the fuck? I spun around, my feet splashing in unspeakable fluid. I gagged, the air reeking of foulness and death. *Where—*

I jumped as a hand landed on my arm, the touch as cold as ice. "Claire?"

My mother's voice.

I whipped my attention to her, startled.

And gaped at the terrifying sight before me.

She resembled a walking corpse, her bones protruding from all angles, her hair a ghastly white, and her eyes... They were as colorless as the night. "M-Mom?"

"Well, isn't that sweet," a third voice said, sounding decidedly cruel and all too familiar. "A family reunion at last."

I slowly looked to my right, through the fiery bars, and met the eyes of my mentor. "Hello, Elana."

CHAPTER TWENTY-SIX
SOL

"CLAIRE!" Exos's shout pierced my ears, drawing me from my sorrows and introducing me to a new horror.

An unconscious Claire.

A shock wave of spirit magic spilled from Exos and Cyrus, slamming into my chest and sending a vibration down my spine.

They were kneeling beside us in an instant, Exos cradling Claire's head while Cyrus leaned to listen for breath. Titus paced, flames burning along every inch of his skin as he cursed.

The ground began to quake around me, my ire mounting by the minute.

Aflora still lay in my arms, her earth magic swarmed by a sea of darkness as she absorbed the brunt of the plague-like energy swirling in the air. Her royal line provided her with the direct source to our element, denoting her as the perpetual gatekeeper of our magic. And she was playing her part, acting as a shield to the rest of our kind.

A shield I couldn't help her reinforce because the plague refused to touch me.

And my bloodline wouldn't allow me to step into her shoes, not without claiming her as my mate.

Which I couldn't do.

But Claire…

"It's hurting her, too," I realized out loud. The darkness swathed her essence, a spiritual element I shouldn't be able to see. However, through my bond with Claire, it was right there. Tangible. Stealing the life from my mate right before my eyes.

I stirred a bed of grass with my element and placed Aflora in it, wrapping her in my power before turning to help Cyrus and Exos.

Except, I didn't know what to do.

"She's not breathing again," Cyrus said, his tone underlined with fury. "It's the fucking spirit source!"

"Then fucking fix it," Titus ordered, his flames inching higher.

"No, it's different this time." Exos placed his forehead against hers, closing his eyes and focusing. "Her spirit is here, at the Academy, just not inhabiting her body."

I snapped my gaze up to him. "What the fuck does that even mean?" I demanded, finally finding my voice.

Because this was ridiculous.

All of it.

Why is this happening?

"I don't know what it means. It's never happened before," Exos said slowly, lifting his head. "But she's alive. I'm certain of it."

"Claire!" Vox shouted, his voice carrying a desperate plea on the wind as he ran to us. His element swirled around him, lifting him off the ground so that his feet barely touched it as he sprinted. His wild eyes burned with a silver ring as he fell to his knees beside Cyrus. "Bring her back," he said urgently. "Bring her the fuck back!"

Exos grasped Vox's shoulder. "She's not dead," he promised him.

"She's just not breathing," Cyrus said through clenched teeth. "But Exos can feel her spirit."

"Where?" I demanded. We were running out of time. I could feel the earth magic seeping away from the realm, threatening to take the last of my family line with it.

Aflora might not be my blood sister, but she was every bit my sibling. We grew up together. Learned earth together. Grieved the loss of my mother and sister together.

And now something was trying to take her and Claire from me.

It was unacceptable.

Wrong.

Cruel.

This is not happening on my watch.

Exos frowned, his gaze flicking from our Claire to some invisible point in the distance. "She's not far. But I think she's underground."

Which meant she would be weak.

Elemental Fae couldn't access the source from beneath the earth. If left there for too long, fae died.

"We need to split up," Exos continued, standing and taking charge like the king he was. Normally, I'd tell him to fuck off. Today? Yeah, today I craved his leadership. Because my head was not in a good place. It was clouded with memories of death.

"Sol and Vox, you two come with me," Exos said.

"What about the Earth Fae?" I asked, glancing at Aflora and then the others. "I can't just leave them." I was the only one still awake. What if one of them needed my strength?

Not that I knew how to lend it.

But I'd damn well figure it out.

Like I was trying to do when Claire arrived.

"Claire's underground, Sol. You might be the only one who can find her when we get close enough." Exos glanced at Vox, squeezing his shoulder again. "And you're fully bonded with our mate. You can help me pinpoint her location."

My shoulders fell.

Because he was right.

Titus finally stopped pacing, his gaze finding mine. "I'll help with the Earth Fae," he promised. "And Cyrus will look after Claire."

For once, the two of them didn't bicker.

Cyrus merely nodded, his fingers running through Claire's hair. "I'll keep searching on the spirit plane," he said softly. "She'll find us. She has to."

Titus knelt beside Aflora, eyeing the nest I'd created. "I won't let anything happen to her, Sol."

I nodded, my throat clogging with emotion.

Never in my wildest dreams would I have predicted such a decision—my mate or my family.

But my mate was my family, too.

An impossible choice. One someone would pay for, for making me endure it. I shoved to my feet, the soil shuddering beneath the weight of my frustration.

"Is that soot?" Titus asked, gesturing to the tendril creeping up Aflora's arm.

I eyed it with a grimace. Because yeah, it certainly looked like the remnants of a fire.

"We don't have time," Exos pressed, dragging my focus to him. "We have to find Claire. I can sense her agitation, the wrongness embracing her spirit. She needs us. Now."

"I'll look after Claire and the Earth Fae," Cyrus vowed. His blue eyes swirled with his element, giving them a striking azure glow. He reached out and sent gentle streams of water to feed the weeping trees and give them the nourishment my people needed to fight off this illness. He glanced at me, his expression determined. "I won't let you down, Sol. You're not going to lose them. Not today."

For once, I allowed myself to have faith in a royal.

Titus gave me a reassuring nod. "We've got this."

I believed him.

Not because of the severity of his expression or the way he said it, but because I *knew* him. Claire's chosen mate. Member of our circle.

As a unit, the six of us were powerful.

And we would prove that today, a certainty I felt all the way to my soul. *We're coming for you, Claire.*

I followed Exos and Vox through the Earth Quad, rage burning in my chest with each step because we couldn't walk in a straight line, forced to avoid the writhing Earth Fae that were dying all around us. My instincts begged me to stop and help them, but my soul's priority belonged to Claire.

My mind reeled from having to face this darkness again, from watching others suffer while I survived. It wasn't right. None of this was right.

The ground trembled as I stormed along behind Vox and Exos.

Vox glanced back at me with concern knitting his brow. "Save your power for whoever is behind this."

He wasn't telling me to contain my gifts, not anymore. Vox had changed and so had I.

But he was telling me to be smart about it.

Cracks radiated out from each heavy footfall as I embraced my element. "Don't worry," I said through gritted teeth. "There's plenty where this came from." When I finally had a target for my fist, I'd revel in breaking every bone in the culprit's body.

Because someone had to be behind all of this. Plagues didn't just happen. No, there was someone pulling the strings, and my instincts told me that puppet master was after my Claire.

Exos paused when we reached Elana's mansion. It didn't surprise me that this was where he sensed Claire's spirit, but it did confirm what we were all already thinking.

Dark vines guarded the entrance, a maze of twisted earth magic that stood in our way.

"Well, that's new," Exos mused.

I didn't share his amusement.

"Get out of our way," I commanded, storming through the earthy blockade. Vines snapped beneath my command, the earth rumbling in favor of its approaching master—*me*. Some of the plants retaliated, pinching me with familiar energy as if all my people were here, protecting Elana as their queen.

Why?

The magic and energy were wrong here. I sensed a well of power beneath the ground—a lot of it.

Vox and Exos followed on my heels.

"She's here," Exos said, certainty underlining his tone.

But I didn't need him to tell me that.

Because I felt her, too. Imprisoned underground. Scared, but not alone. *There.*

I knelt, intending to rip out the ground with my power, when pain spiked up and down my spine. Claire's ethereal screams echoed up through the layers of earth and hit me straight in the chest. The ground began to quiver and quake, forming jagged cracks and spikes of harsh rock.

"Get back!" I roared just as the columns of Elana's manor splintered and the floor gave way. Vox swept us all out into the safety of the forest with a blast of wind just as the walls of her home came down.

"Claire!" we shouted as one.

But none of us could be heard over the roar of energy and power swirling up into the clouds.

The manor... was gone.

CHAPTER TWENTY-SEVEN
CLAIRE

Several Minutes Earlier

"WELL, THIS PRESENTS A SLIGHT PROBLEM," Elana mused, glancing at my corpse of a mother. "You just had to reach out, didn't you?"

"What is this place?" I demanded, whirling around and flinching as more of that slime on the floor touched my shoe. Well, sort of, anyway. I wasn't exactly corporeal, but even in spirit form, I definitely *felt* my surroundings.

Like my mother's icy fingers grasping my arm. "Go, Claire," she urged. "Go!"

But I couldn't.

I didn't even know how I got here, let alone how to leave. So I focused on Elana instead and repeated my question with a haughty arch of my eyebrow.

It earned me a chuckle from the bitch on the other side of the bars. "You think to command me, child? That's adorable. You couldn't even summon a spirit properly." She tsked. "Oh, Claire. I had such high hopes for you. What will I do now?"

Eat shit and die? I thought. But yeah, that wasn't the best reply to this situation. So instead I folded my arms and assumed a casual position, similar

530

to how I imagined Cyrus or Exos would do if they were in my shoes.

"You could start by explaining yourself," I suggested. "I mean, we both know my mother's evil. But you told me she was dead." A thought occurred to me then, one I ran with without looking back. "Actually, you told me her body was never found and suggested she might be alive. Why? Because you had her in custody?" I tilted my head, feigning confusion. "Why hide her? Why not tell everyone you have the source of the plague?"

Assuming my mother even caused it, I added mentally. *Which I'm seriously starting to doubt.*

The way my mother's expression fell with my comments confirmed my instincts, but I still wanted an explanation for all of this.

Answers regarding the plague. A way to help the Earth Fae. Why it's happening all over again now. My lips flattened. *Wait a minute...*

Why it's happening again now, I repeated to myself, my senses picking up on something I'd missed before.

Elana.

She was surrounded by spirits, their smoky tendrils chaotic and terrified as they tried futilely to swim away. As if she was sucking them all into her with a summoning spell...

"How did you get here?" Elana demanded, ignoring my questions.

Does she know I can see all those souls slithering around her? I wondered. She had to at least expect it since I was in my spirit state. Hmm, but it would be best not to confirm it.

So I sighed, acting agitated. "Exos keeps trying to teach me how to navigate the spirit planes." Not necessarily a lie. "He told me to seek out a soul I knew, and I thought I was going to Sol, yet somehow ended up here." Well, that wasn't exactly true, but it carried hints of the truth.

Enough to lend confidence to my tone, anyway.

"I have absolutely no idea how to get back to my body," I added truthfully. "But since I'm here, I'd love to know what's going on." I arched a brow, glancing at my cowering mother and then back at Elana. "Did you find her lurking around campus? Because we've suspected she had something to do with Exos's disappearance last month."

Elana's eyebrow rose in a perfect example of surprise. "What disappearance?"

I fought the urge to scoff, *As if you don't know.*

Instead, I said, "Someone took him and siphoned off his energy. He said it felt a lot like Ophelia." I glanced at my shivering mother, her hand no longer on my arm. "You tried to kill my mate. You're going to pay for that." An empty threat, but I imagined myself saying the words to Elana, so they came out just as lethal as I desired.

My mother opened her mouth as if to reply, only to wince as her jaw snapped closed.

A strand of energy trailed from her lips to Elana as if she wore a muzzle tied to a leash. Could I see that because of my current state? Or had my powers grown?

Elana smiled one of her trademark indulgent smiles. "Actually, I did find her recently. I just haven't decided what to do with her yet."

I bet, I thought. "What was she doing?" I asked, wanting to see how far this lie would go.

Elana waved a hand as if brushing the question aside. "What matters is that I've caught her and we can seek justice. I was just in the process of trying to find out what she's done to the Earth Fae, in fact. This would serve as a suitable lesson for you, if you'd like to join our interrogation."

Man, she's good.

Still playing the part of perfect mentor despite the obvious red flags.

But hey, why not play along? It wasn't like I knew how to leave, and maybe I'd glean some important details along the way.

"I'd love that," I said, not lying. "As I clearly have no idea what I'm doing."

"I don't know, Claire. You seem to be doing very well to me. Appearing in this form outside of the spirit planes, as you are now, requires a great deal of power. It's something not even I can do." A hint of envy flashed through her gaze, but she blinked it away behind her caring mask. "I have great hopes for you."

Uh-huh. To do what? I wondered.

"Well, where were we, Ophelia?" Elana continued, her mask slipping just a hair as she focused on my mother.

Fear radiated from my mother, her fingers clenching into fists as she fought the tendril of spirit hovering against her mouth.

What do you really want to say? I thought at her, tempted to brush that strand away, to reveal her true words.

It looked easy.

Just flick it with a talon of my own.

"She's lying!" my mother screeched as the rope disappeared, my heart skipping a beat in the process.

Shit. Did I do that?

But I didn't have time to worry because my mother took center stage, words spewing from her on a wave of truth that unsettled my very soul.

"It's not a plague. It's Elana. She's feeding off the Earth Fae like she did the Spirit Fae. It's dark magic, Claire. She siphons the elements, borrows them, kills them. It's not me. But I figured out what she was doing when she forced me to bond to Mortus, using spirit compulsion. I broke free by going to the Human Realm, but I met your father, and then she came for me. I had to leave you, Claire. I had to leave both of you behind. But she's framed me for all of this."

It all came out so quickly, so harshly, that Elana didn't have time to stop her.

Mostly because I seemed to have her strand caught in my mental fist.

Something her thunderous expression told me she'd noticed.

Oops.

Sorry, not sorry?

I swallowed as the calm-mentor veneer disappeared, revealing a darker expression, one that caused the hairs along my arms to dance in warning. Her lips peeled apart into a sneer that had me instinctively reaching out to Exos. Only, I couldn't find him. Or Cyrus. Or Vox. Or any of my mates.

Oh, they were there. But not. Like I'd somehow left them in my current state, similar to when I'd ventured into the blinding white light.

Shit.

I should have evaluated that earlier, but I'd been distracted by my mother and Elana.

Now, however, it became far too clear that I was on my own to find a way out of this.

"I could try to deny it, but what would be the point?" Elana took a step toward the bars, her eyes on my mother. "You've been such a disappointment to me, Ophelia. Over and over and over again." She tsked, the sound reminding me of nails on a chalkboard.

An ice dagger shot from her hand toward my mother's chest, one I instinctively manipulated with my fire to melt before impact.

Elana snarled, sending another that I quickly deflected before creating a sheet of flames meant to protect my mother from further assault.

"You've been holding out on me," my former mentor accused, changing tactics and focusing on me. "If the fae knew how powerful you've grown…" She trailed off, tapping her jaw. "Well, I imagine we'd share an execution chamber. It's what the fae do to those they consider different. It's all about the balance, trying to avoid wars between the supernaturals, because they all fear true power. Which you and I both possess, Claire. In abundance."

She took a menacing step forward to wrap her fingers around the bars, completely unfazed by the heat flaring from the fire shield I'd created.

"I know what it's like," she murmured. "Not being accepted by your own kind, being called derogatory names like Halfling or Weakling. Being a Spirit Fae with access to only one element painted me as insignificant to most. They either teased me or pitied me." Her lips flattened. "It wasn't an easy existence, knowing I couldn't tell anyone my true nature. Knowing if anyone found out my father was a Midnight Fae that I'd be burned alive. It's not like I chose my parents, but the fae don't care, Claire. They discriminate against anyone they fear."

I swallowed. Because what she described matched what Exos, Cyrus, and Kols had told me. *Abominations*, they'd said. And I was fully aware of how the others had treated me as a Halfling, like an unwanted roach among a sea of butterflies.

But they're different now, I told myself, recalling the ball. *They were... nice.*

Because they liked me?

Or because of my ties to my mates?

"You know it's true," Elana said, astutely reading my thoughts. "They wanted to banish you to the death fields just for existing, Claire. But I'm the one who made sure that didn't happen. I'm the one who protected you, offered to mentor you, *vouched* for you. Because I don't believe in prosecuting someone just because of her birth. I *value* your power, Claire. I want to see how high you can climb."

"Don't listen to her," my mother interjected. "She just wants to use you, Claire. Like she—" She cut off on a gurgle, water spilling from her mouth.

Fuck! Her lungs were overflowing with liquid. I focused on the element, calling it to me and begging it to bend to my control. But Elana had a firmer grasp, her age and experience far surpassing my own.

"Ophelia, you've well and truly served your purpose here," Elana said, her tone holding a wicked edge that frosted the air with power. "When I present your remains to the fae, they'll bow at my feet in worship, thanking me for finding the one who *plagued* their kind. Maybe I'll do it just in time to save the Earth Fae from their fate."

My mother's eyes went wide, her expression a plea that slashed my heart.

No!

We weren't finished here yet.

I needed answers.

And it seemed my mother possessed them all.

She began to convulse, drowning on the liquid clogging her airways. But the element refused me, Elana's grasp on it decidedly strong.

An element she shouldn't even be able to touch, I thought, frowning. *Unless it's not water at all, but something else entirely. Something like dark magic.*

My gaze widened.

Shit.

I couldn't fight her Midnight Fae side. But I could use my own gifts to fight her.

Like earth.

Roots danced beneath the concrete floor, begging for my attention. I caught two of them and thrust them upward right beneath her feet to dislodge her stance.

She tripped to the side, her concentration momentarily distracted.

I mentally latched onto two more roots, sending them upward to grab her, only she dodged and sent a flicker of smoke to encircle the limb. It immediately snapped, the agony from the ground nearly bringing me to my knees.

But I wasn't done.

Stones and dirt and *earth* responded to my call, dismantling her floors and creating a bumpy terrain that threw her off guard. She fell with an *Oomph*.

And my mother sputtered beside me, finally able to breathe.

I knelt beside her, unsure of how to free her. The bars were iron, thick, encrusted in fiery magic. And not the element I adored, but a harsher essence that seemed to answer to Elana alone.

She leapt up with a roar, a horde of inky strands writhing around her. *Earth Fae.*

They were scrambling, screaming, trying to escape.

But she was sucking on them harshly, absorbing more and more of their power.

Is Sol among them? I wondered, my heart catching in my throat. *Aflora? How many others?*

I had to do something, *anything*, to stop this madness.

It couldn't continue.

I wouldn't let her take down the Earth Fae as she had the Spirit Fae. Sentencing a faeling to death because of her bloodlines and abilities was wrong, yes. But Elana's response, her torment, her violent reactions, made it all so much worse.

There had to be another way.

I refused to accept her path, to agree with such a fucked-up mentality. *This can't be the solution.*

My arms spread wide, my elements joining and thrashing inside me, urging me to intervene, to *fix* this. To help the Earth Fae trapped around her aura. To free my mother. To find another method of coexistence. To take down the bad influence who threatened the source of elemental good.

Heat engulfed my being, my fire stirring passionate and hot.

Ice cascaded down the walls and along the iron, penetrating the brutal energy and winding around it in wintry ringlets.

Rocks rumbled beneath my feet, answering to my call and vibrating with vengeful need.

A breeze kissed my cheeks, whirling in rapid circles up and down the corridor, searching for a way to break me free.

And my spirit thrived, my essence reaching out to all the dying souls floating in this dungeon, to lend strength for survival and *life*.

Vitality, I realized, calling upon the source as I closed my eyes. *They need vitality.*

Chaos erupted as Elana chanted foreign words, her own magic battling mine and springing deathly hollows all around us.

Visages of ghosts, howling in pain, painted the ghastly dungeon. Their mouths gaping in hunger as they slowly began to crawl into our reality, their presence disturbing the balance between life and death.

Everything began to shake.

The foundations of the building around us unable to hold because of such power and *wrongness*.

I grabbed my mother, calling the roots to fold around us, to craft an impenetrable hold, and demanded the souls beneath the earth to latch onto my essence.

They swam in waves, eagerly leaving Elana for the safe haven I created, my water flowing in a spring above my roots to hold the falling debris off of us.

But there was too much.

The power too great.

Energy hummed around me, my mother cringing beneath the violent onslaught. I couldn't hold us much longer, had to do something, to save us all.

Darkness cascaded over my vision, leaving me to swim in a sea of black.

I screamed, my throat clogged with soil. Roots. Trees. Flowers. Plants. Life exploding around me, through me, consuming every inch of my being.

"Claire!"

My mates were calling for me.

My mother, too.

I thrashed violently, fighting off the vines holding me down and the smoky cloud drowning my spirit. Warm hands grasped my bare shoulders, shaking me.

Lips met my cheeks, my hair, my neck.

My name rent the air.

Words followed.

It was all a jumble, my body tangled in a frenzy of limbs and heat and elements.

Water.

Fire.

I basked in the familiarity, lost to the soothing sensations.

Until my eyes flashed open to find the sky looming above my head.

And two very pissed-off male mates.

Chapter Twenty-Eight
Titus

ENERGY HUMMED THROUGH THE AIR, seeming to zap Claire's body back to life.

And her eyelids flew open.

I gaped at her, shocked by the sudden change.

Cyrus, however, growled low in his throat before saying, "I need you to stop fucking doing that, Claire."

"I second that statement," I said without missing a beat. Her lack of breath had scared the shit out of me. If Exos hadn't been absolutely certain her spirit still thrived...

No, I couldn't think about that right now. We had more important things to worry about, like the Earth Fae stirring around us. An earthly essence filled the air, reinvigorating them and causing several of them to moan.

Although, Claire didn't make a sound. Her brow furrowed as if confused. Then she bolted upright. "I have to stop Elana!" She tried to launch to her feet, only to be wrapped up in Cyrus's arms.

"You need to tell us what the hell is going on," he corrected, his bedside manner as on point as always.

She shook her head, shoving him away, only to collapse back into him. Her chest heaved as she sucked in fresh breaths, her pallor a bit too pale for my liking. "Easy, Claire," I murmured.

Cyrus steadied her, his expression smoothing into lines of concern. "Your body needs a moment to adjust. You know, because your spirit somehow *detached*. Again." He brushed a kiss over her cheek, the spot glowing blue with his element as he gave her the power she needed.

I knelt beside them and grasped her hip to lend her some of my fire. It slowly breathed color back into her features, heating her otherwise cool skin.

"Elana," she managed to say, her voice hoarse. She cleared her throat to try again. "She has Ophelia. She's draining her. Draining them all." She swallowed and tried to stand again. "Need to go. Now."

"You need to absorb more energy," Cyrus said, wrapping his arms more firmly around her.

Earth Fae began to whimper all around us, their heads shifting as questions spilled from their lips. None of them were coherent, all lost to the plague that'd taken them down.

"They're recovering," Cyrus said, eyeing the Earth Quad with interest. "What did you do, Claire? What did you find?"

"*Elana*." Claire shoved away from us with far more force than Cyrus or I anticipated, allowing her to leap to her feet. She bolted before either of us had a chance to grab her.

"Claire!" Cyrus shouted, his voice catching on the wind as I took off after her in a dead sprint. I sensed him following on my heels. I had no doubt he was as frustrated as me. Our mate had a tendency to run toward danger without thinking. I wasn't going to let her leave my sight.

We worked our way through the recovering Earth Fae. Roots and vines wound over their limbs and lifted them up, the males seeming to grow larger and the females sprouting blossoms in their hair.

"Is this your doing?" I asked Cyrus. He'd been trying to infuse life back into them while we guarded Claire, but without much luck.

He shook his head as he kept pace at my side. "No. Whatever was infecting them disappeared." He paused to head right, following Claire. "I felt the dark presence lift right before Claire woke up."

Sprouts formed in our mate's footsteps as she sprinted, suggesting that she might be the one healing the Earth Fae.

I frowned, unsure of sure how I felt about that. She couldn't save everyone. If she expended all her energy, she'd have none left for herself.

We reached Elana's mansion—or what was left of it—and found Sol ripping chunks of rock from the earth. A boulder bigger than my head flung past, and I ducked. "Hey!" I shouted. "We have Claire. You can stop digging."

"There's something down there," Sol grunted, tossing another boulder over his shoulder.

Focused on his task, Vox helped Sol, sweeping away debris with controlled gusts as Exos pointed toward a single spot. "There!" he shouted.

We stopped just in time to find Sol unearthing a wad of vines and roots. Goose bumps spread over my flesh when I faintly sensed Claire's magic inside the ball of elemental power.

Claire dove into the pit and gripped on to Sol as tears streamed down her face. "Is she alive?" Claire glanced back at me and bit her lip. "Titus, can you burn away just the top layer? Please be careful. We have to get her out of there."

Her who? I wondered.

Claire clung to what was left of Sol's shirt as her eyes pleaded with me. *"Titus. Please."*

Right. I didn't know what she wanted out of that heap, but it clearly meant something to her. And if she didn't want to dismantle the ball herself, it was because she didn't trust her own control.

Cracking my knuckles, I prepared myself for the task ahead. In my current state, I was going to have trouble doing this without making something explode. But I'd do it for Claire and for whomever she protected inside the bundle of earth.

Deep breaths.

Sweat broke out over my forehead as I concentrated.

Slowly now...

I crafted my flame into a thin rope that I sent through the air with as much precision as I could manage. It landed on top of the nest like a saw, which I used to cut through the top layer.

Then the second.

As well as the third.

Until finally a ghostly hand fell free of the opening. Working around that, I slid the fire wide, carefully lancing the side.

And a corpse-like body fell out.

Claire caught the woman whose bones protruded from every angle and hugged her to her chest. "Help me," she said, looking at Exos. "Help *her.*"

He jumped into the crater Sol had created and scooped her into his arms, his eyes running over the ghastly remains. "She's energy-starved. Weak. It's going to take a lot of work, but we're not too late."

Cyrus knelt beside the hole to take Ophelia—or who I assumed was Ophelia, as it was hard to tell with her decrepit form—into his arms.

Sol lifted Claire out of the cavern while Exos climbed out himself.

And the Earth Fae hoisted himself onto land. "How are my people?" he demanded, looking at me.

"Recovering," I said. "Cyrus said the plague is gone."

"Not a plague," Claire cut in. "*Elana.* She was using dark magic to siphon their energy."

"Why?" Exos demanded, his focus on Ophelia and not Claire. But his question was on point, as always.

"She went on about being an abomination, said the Council would kill her if they knew about her birthright. She said they'll kill me, too, when they realize how powerful I am." She swallowed on that last bit, then shook her head. "I think she was trying to recruit me."

Cyrus and Exos shared a long look.

Then the Spirit King glanced at me, Vox, and Sol. "Cyrus, Claire, and I have a lot of work to do. Ophelia is hanging on by a thread after whatever Elana did to her. I need you to check on the other fae throughout the Academy, make sure they are all okay. Because that power surge I just felt? It was fueled by the fae on these grounds."

I nodded. "Whatever you need. We're on it."

"Good." He glanced at Claire. "Let's go back to the Spirit Quad. It'll be a quiet, safe place for us to begin the energy transfusion. But I need you to be very careful, Claire. No more source visits without me."

"She shouldn't even be able to do that," Cyrus muttered at his side.

"A conversation for another day, brother," Exos returned, already walking. "Let's go."

Sol seemed to think twice, his desire to snatch Claire written all over his face, but he drew a deep breath and squared his shoulders. "I'll be on Earth Quad."

"And I'll check Water and Air Quad," Vox said.

"That leaves me with Fire Quad." I took off at a run toward the chaos, unsure of how to truly help but determined to find a way.

Tufts of earth had overturned every which way, leaving scars across the ground on my jog to Fire Quad. Weakened fae staggered and held their heads as if dazed, while others screamed for answers.

Utter insanity.

But one fae caught my attention above all the others.

Mortus.

The old fae staggered back a step, his expression one of bewilderment and confusion.

I reached out to steady the professor and noted his lack of fire. "Mortus," I said slowly. "What's wrong?"

He blinked, his dark eyes focusing and unfocusing all at once. "I... I don't know." He leaned in and lowered his voice. "C-could you tell me...? What year is this?"

CHAPTER TWENTY-NINE
SOL

WHEN I CAME UPON THE EARTH QUAD, I paused to assess the damage.

Not as bad as I'd feared. Likely due to Cyrus's glittering blue streams he'd woven through the grounds. Previously wilted trees now stood up straight and boasted fresh leaves and fruit, along with solid branches that reached for the sun. And the soil breathed with vitality, happy to have absorbed liquid nutrients from the Water Prince.

I spotted Aflora tending to another Earth Fae in the shade of one of the larger trees. She pressed her palm to the trunk and drew in its copper power, glowing as she fed on the source of our element, and gifted it to the petite female beside her.

Relief lightened my chest.

She's alive.

"Aflora," I said, and she glanced up at me, her blue eyes flashing with specks of emerald magic. I smiled and rested a heavy hand on her tiny shoulder. "You shouldn't be using your magic right now. Just moments ago you were unconscious."

Almost dead.

My gaze ran down her neck, searching for those black streaks. Aside from some lingering soot, I couldn't detect the illness that had taken her so suddenly.

She shrugged me off. "I'm fine, Sol." She flashed me a confident smile. "Can't keep this Earth Fae down."

I frowned, not wishing to downplay how close to death she'd come.

The female fae beside her groaned as black lines retreated under Aflora's magic.

"There," Aflora murmured, seemingly pleased as she rested the Earth Fae against the sturdy trunk. "Draw on its power," she instructed. "You'll feel better in no time."

Even though Cyrus had bolstered the Earth Fae, Aflora's miraculous recovery didn't settle well with me.

I glanced around the quad again, noting how many of the others resembled the female fae Aflora had just treated, all of them leaning on the coppery substance of earth for survival.

But someone had given them a kick start.

Was it something Claire had done, or was Aflora's grasp on the source stronger than I had previously imagined?

Aflora wiped her hands together as she stood and rolled her eyes. "Why are you looking at me like that?"

I pinched some of the soot remaining on her shoulder and rubbed my fingers together. "It doesn't feel right, Aflora. You need to reserve your magic, not spend it."

She chuckled. "Well, aren't you the bossy one? I knew there was a royal in there somewhere."

Now it was my turn to scoff. "You're the princess, Aflora. In time, it'll be you who leads our people back to the fruitful civilization it's meant to be." I knew she had always thought we'd do that together, but I could never mate Aflora. Not just because she was like a sister to me, but also because of the scars on my soul. I didn't know who or what had put them there, but it kept me walled off from the darkness that infected my people.

Not that it mattered. I wasn't a leader. I'd spent my entire life trying to figure out my own shit. However, I was making progress thanks to Vox, Claire, and the rest of my mate-circle. Today confirmed that, as it was the first time I'd been able to trust someone else to carry my burdens with me.

I'm no longer alone.

Aflora and I made our way through the recovering Earth Quad, and I marveled at how the fae seemed to be stronger than before, as if experiencing another bout with darkness had shaken them loose from the long years of suppression and now they could take in a full breath for the first time.

I told Aflora what I knew so far, about Elana and how we suspected her to be a Midnight Fae Halfling. Claire mostly confirmed it with her comment about dark magic, but I didn't know what else was said.

"Death magic?" Aflora squeaked. "Do you think she'll bring the dead here?"

"I don't know," I admitted. "But we need to be ready." I surveyed the stronger Earth Fae, noting their growing vitality, and nodded.

It might be enough.

Enough for an army.

CHAPTER THIRTY
VOX

I'M GOING TO KILL THAT BITCH, I thought, picturing Elana.

She'd absorbed air from several of the fae. Enough to create her giant vortex that had swallowed her entire home.

It left debris and terrified fae all over campus. I'd met with several of the professors, told them what had happened, and warned them that this was only the beginning. Because Elana? Yeah, she was alive. I knew because I'd seen her energy go up into that damn cloud before everything vanished.

A neat trick, sure.

One I'd love to replicate with fire and watch her burn alive.

A task for another day. Because I needed a damn nap first.

No, I needed my Claire.

All the Air Fae and Water Fae were managing themselves beneath the supervision of professors, leaving me without much left to do other than go home.

Using a gust of wind, I propelled myself back to the Spirit Quad and nudged open the doors.

Claire startled against Exos's chest, her gaze flying to mine.

Cyrus merely slammed his palm down on the table to stop the papers from flying, his gaze on an open textbook.

"Necromancy doesn't even begin to describe what Elana did today," Cyrus said. He flipped a page and frowned. "Kols gave us a shitty book. I swear this thing is useless."

Based on Cyrus's sour mood, I decided not to even ask what he meant by that and went to my mate instead.

Claire rubbed her eyes as Exos helped her to her feet. "How'd it go?" she asked groggily as she slipped effortlessly into my arms. "Are the Air Fae all right?"

I nodded as I tucked my chin beneath her ear and indulged in her elements surrounding mine. "Only a few were weakened by the momentary leech of power," I said, reluctantly pulling away. "Elana seemed to focus mostly on the Earth Fae, minus her finale at the end."

"I hope Sol's okay," my mate lamented. Her pain swept through our bond, and I clutched her to my chest.

"He'll be all right," I promised, although I knew the Earth Fae was thoroughly shaken. I cupped Claire's face. "Everyone is okay, Claire. Thanks to you." And whatever the hell she'd done to Elana. I wanted to hear more, but I also didn't want to press her right now. She looked ready to collapse with exhaustion.

Her lips curled into a small smile as she rested her hands over mine. "I hope so."

I brushed my lips over hers. "Trust me."

She began to nod just as Titus and Sol entered the dorm.

"Fucking Mortus," Titus said by way of greeting, rubbing his temple. "I left him in the care of some of the other Fire Fae, but we're going to have to do something about him. The guy has absolutely no recollection of anything after mating with Ophelia."

My eyebrows rose. "What?" That was news to me, but the lack of surprise from the others suggested they already knew.

"Did he say what the last thing he remembered was?" Claire asked.

Titus shook his head. "His last memory is of his time here. As a student."

Exos whistled. "That was over two decades ago."

"So he's been under Elana's control all this time?" Claire looked stricken. "That's horrible."

"It's the power of a Spirit Fae," Sol muttered, collapsing on the sofa. "How's your mom?"

Cyrus finally parted from his texts and rested a fist on the table. "We've stabilized her for now. She'll remain in a coma until she's recovered enough to break free of what Elana did to her." He shrugged. "We can cure her body, but she'll have to be the one to cure her mind."

Claire shivered and leaned into my chest. "How much do you think she can tell us about Elana?" Her fingers slipped under my shirt and ran slow circles around my abdomen as if the contact gave her comfort. I released a sliver of my connection to the source into Claire's touch, attempting to rejuvenate what she'd depleted.

"She'll have many of the answers we seek," Cyrus confirmed. "But it'll take time."

"If that's even possible," Exos added with a frown. "Two decades of torture. Do you really think she can bounce back from that?"

"Only one way to find out," his brother replied.

Which meant we were going to have to wait, and time was the one thing we didn't have on our side. I pressed a light kiss to Claire's hair. She smiled up at me, no words needed to express that she knew we were all here for her, that I loved her.

"Let's hope she wakes up soon," Titus said, joining Cyrus at the table.

Claire frowned. "And what are we planning to do in the interim? Just wait for Elana to attack us again?"

"Yes," Cyrus said, his tone that of a king. Final and with no room for argument. "Except this time, when she returns, we'll be ready for her."

Titus smirked as a flame danced across his fingertips. "Now you're speaking my language."

Cyrus smiled. "I've been speaking it for years, Fire Fae. You just weren't very adept at listening."

"Sounds like you want to start sparring right now, Water Prince," Titus drawled.

"Now you're just trying to seduce me," Cyrus replied, closing his textbook. "But we can dance tomorrow, Powerless Champion. See how you hold up *with* your element." He waggled his brows in challenge. "You'll need it, after all."

"So will all the others," Exos interjected.

"Sounds like we have a new course for the Academy," Titus said, grinning. "One I'll very much enjoy leading."

Cyrus snorted. "More like co-leading."

"Sure." Titus grinned. "We can call it that."

"Regardless." Exos stood, interrupting their little bickering match. "When Elana returns, we're taking her down," he said, his tone brooking no argument. "Together."

"Together," everyone agreed.

Part IV

"At the core of every element is a light so bright it blinds those with unworthy intentions. I can only hope it finds my heart pure and gifts me with the strength to survive. For a war is on the horizon. One we all desperately need to win."

–Claire

CHAPTER THIRTY-ONE
TITUS

One Week Later

"AGAIN," Cyrus demanded, eyeing River's form as he created a water whip and lashed it through the air. When we announced our intentions to train some of the fae in preparation for Elana's return, several students—and professors—had jumped at the opportunity to learn.

Others had fled for their kingdoms, the Academy on a permanent break until the situation here could be sorted.

Apparently, finding out the lead Council member and Chancellor of the Academy was an evil bitch turned everything into a shitshow. Who knew?

But Cyrus and Exos were confident she'd be back. If anything, to retrieve Claire.

I wasn't as certain because I didn't understand Elana's motives. Sure, she was an abomination. She hated the way people treated her and decided to bolster her power to seek revenge. Seemed a bit extreme to me, but then again, I'd never been on the receiving end of such cruelty.

Exos claimed it really messed with her mindset.

Cyrus said it might stem from a lack of Midnight Fae training, which led to her misguided use of her death magic.

My opinion? She was just a power-hungry bitch out to rule the fae.

Claire seemed to agree with me.

I struck my bo staff against hers, countering her attack and smiling as flames danced between us. "Now, now, Claire," I taunted. "Don't let those emotions rule your movements."

"Don't know what you're talking about," she replied, sending a liquid wave over my weapon and cooling my fire. She readied another fighting stance as the flames in her eyes glazed over with the azure glow of her water element. A breeze shifted between us, gathering moisture from the air to form a barrier that slithered across the ground. Her powers had definitely grown, but I noted the lack of control when it came to earth and fire.

That was her primary weakness.

And weaknesses weren't acceptable when it came to a battle with Elana.

Claire's elements naturally strengthened through her bonds with her mates. By engaging the final level with Exos, Cyrus, and Vox, she'd created a shift in her balance of power. It was almost lopsided in favor of her completed links. Meaning she needed more fire and earth to truly feel grounded.

Meanwhile, Elana drew energy from all of those around her, which meant that Claire had to be ready for anything.

And her current state suggested she wasn't.

Which concerned me.

"Focus," I said, vaulting over the floating stream to her side. I faked a blow to her head, forcing her to raise her weapon before I snatched my staff back and caught her in the ribs. She buckled at the impact, even though I'd held back. "You're distracted."

Her jaw ticked as a powerful gust shoved me off-balance. She launched at me, using her staff against my throat to pin me to the ground. "My mother is in a coma. Elana is off doing fuck knows what while we prepare for an attack we don't even know is going to happen. We not actually sure if she really intends to come back or do something worse. Hell, we don't even know what she's truly capable of yet. So yeah, I think I have every right to be a little *distracted.*"

"Titus is right," Cyrus interjected, approaching us and leaving River in charge of Water Fae training.

Claire frowned as she swung her leg over me and allowed me to stand. Cyrus offered an arm and I took it, grateful for the backup. It wasn't often that we found ourselves on the same side.

The Water Prince gave me a knowing grin. I'd pleased him with our sparring session this morning. Whether I wanted to admit it or not, we worked well together and our opposing elements created a spark that I'd never felt with another male.

As much fun as it would be to practice more of my fire on Cyrus, Claire was the one holding back, and all of us knew why.

Cyrus was just the first to say it out loud.

"You need to complete your bonds to the elements, Claire. You're clumsy when it comes to fire and earth. I paired you with Titus as a test, and it's proven my theory correct. You're having to rely on your other elements to fight him because they are easier to access." He brushed a kiss across her cheek, proving his point when droplets swarmed around her in an effortless display of her gifts. "You need to complete your mating bonds, little queen. It'll strengthen you."

Claire's expression showcased a mixture of emotions, her hand clenching around her staff. "It feels wrong to indulge in my bonds when so much is happening."

She glanced at Mortus. He was supposed to be leading the other Fire Fae but instead lingered on the outskirts while the high-level students took turns building fireballs and launching them into the air. He still had that distant look of horror on his face, as if he couldn't quite wrap his mind around the two decades he'd lost.

"How am I supposed to concentrate when so many are suffering?" she added quietly. "It seems selfish."

"No, little queen. It's practical." Cyrus took Claire's hand and placed it in mine. Flames linked our fingers together, our elements ready to take the next step. "Denying the bonds isn't going to solve anything. It'll only make matters worse."

"He's right," I agreed. "You need our elements to bolster your own, and it's not selfish to strengthen yourself, sweetheart. It's a good way to prepare for the inevitable."

"Assuming Elana even comes back here," she muttered.

"If she doesn't, then we'll go after her. When we're ready." Cyrus lifted a brow. "And in your current state, you're not ready."

She blew out a breath, her irritation palpable. Then she glanced at me and her gaze softened. "This isn't at all how I imagined mating you, Titus," she admitted, her words tinged with regret. "You deserve better." The way she said that implied she thought I only meant to do this because I had to, not because I wanted to.

"Claire," I murmured, drawing her into my embrace. "We don't have to be in a fancy room in the Fire Kingdom for me to declare my love for you." I brushed my fingers over her shoulder, and her skin glowed red in response. "My fire has always belonged to you."

To prove my point, I claimed her mouth and ran my tongue across hers, this time not holding back as I poured my element into her. She could handle the raw truth of the passion she brought out in me.

We were both ready for this step and had been ready for a while now. There just hadn't been the right moment. And maybe now still wasn't perfect, but I didn't care. I just wanted her. I always had, from the first time I'd laid eyes on her in that field.

My beautiful Claire.

She melted into my touch and kissed me in return. Flames licked at my hair as she nudged open that well in my soul where my fire burned. Claire stoked those flames unlike anything else I'd ever experienced, and I knew mating with her would decimate my world in all the right ways.

The ground trembled beneath our feet—courtesy of Sol. A subtle reminder that we were still in the training yard and had a very real audience.

Claire giggled as she pulled away and waved at her earth mate. A number of Earth Fae practiced building shields as trunks and branches shot from the ground, although they'd all stopped when Sol had formed a brutish wall of solid rock in demonstration. He grinned at Claire. "Titus isn't the only one who has something to offer."

Maybe, but tonight Claire was mine. I made sure of that as I stabbed my staff into the ground, allowing my fire to inch across the earth to melt Sol's stone block. It'd worked well enough during our last encounter, where I'd temporarily trapped him during his little smash tantrum.

But the Earth Fae was ready for my trick this time.

Powerful roots wove across the ground, making a lattice against my molten attack. He grinned. "Nice try, Fire Fae."

"Nice tactic," I mused.

The surrounding Earth Fae seemed to agree as they mimicked the motion with their own magic, trying to accomplish a similar style of defense.

I grinned. Sol might not see himself as a royal among his people, but he was a leader where it mattered.

Claire smacked me in the ribs with her staff and grinned when I expelled a startled breath. "Now who's distracted?"

I retaliated by sending a tuft of fire underneath her clothes that bit at her nipples. She squeaked and tried to soothe the burn with water, but I wasn't going to allow her to cheat her way out of playing with my flames this time. I nodded to Cyrus and his eyes darkened. He was a source of power for Claire, but he could dampen that connection, even if it took some effort.

Claire's mouth parted as I took advantage of the momentary lapse of her power. Her skin heated, and my inferno wrapped around her, forming an embrace on every sensual curve.

"No fair," she breathed, her tone aroused and willing.

"I think you're ready," Cyrus murmured, approaching us. "As we don't necessarily have a Fire Fae available to complete the vows, I suggest we use Exos as a stand-in. His royal title and affinity for flames should do the trick."

"Wait, you want to do this now?" Her eyebrows rose.

"Why not?" Cyrus countered, already leading the way. "It'll give you two time to celebrate afterward." He flashed me a knowing wink over his shoulder, causing my lips to curl.

"It's like you're trying to get into my good graces, Cyrus," I said, pulling Claire along beside me.

"Maybe I am," he replied, a smile in his voice.

Claire glanced between us, her brow furrowing. "I thought you two hated each other."

"Fine line between love and hate, little queen." Cyrus opened the door to the dorm. "After you."

I met and held his gaze for a long minute before guiding Claire inside. Something was definitely there between us, a weird spark I didn't quite understand. Most days, it resulted in me wanting to kill him. Today, however, it burned a little on the aroused side—a place typically only Claire could touch.

A consideration for later. It was probably just the mating circle fucking with my instincts.

Exos sat inside, his nose in one of those dark-magic textbooks. His Midnight Fae friend had sent a few more, along with a few suggestions.

Hence the training outside.

Kols. who was apparently a Midnight Fae Prince, told us to prepare for anything. Because if Elana was truly messing with death magic, she was capable of a hell of a lot more than burning her own house down. He even mentioned the possibility of spirit minions, whom Claire had immediately called zombies.

Cyrus inched a brow upward when his brother didn't react to our entrance. "Exos."

"Yeah, I know." He shuffled some of the books around and stood. "We don't exactly have a ceremonial space on campus, so how do you feel about your bedroom, Titus? It's already pretty well decorated by you and Claire."

Her cheeks reddened at the cause of those decorations, and I smiled. "Does that mean I can mate her naked?"

"I'd enjoy that," Cyrus mused, glancing at his brother. "Reminds me of her spirit mating."

Exos's lips curled in memory, his gaze flickering with wicked intent as he looked at Claire. "I love this plan."

She sputtered out an unintelligible response that earned several chuckles from the room. I moved behind her while fondling the hem of her shirt. "It'll help keep you focused," I whispered against her ear, inching the fabric up her skin.

"Focused?" she squeaked out. "*How?*"

I kissed her racing pulse, drawing the shirt higher and over her breasts. "Trust me." Because it was already working. She wasn't thinking about Elana at all now. Just the two hungry males watching as I tugged the cloth up and over her head.

Goose bumps trailed across her skin, followed by a swathe of heat as our element danced across the surface.

She barely seemed to notice me removing her shoes, socks, and pants, too lost to the sensation all three of us stirred inside her. Part of me thanked Cyrus and Exos for that, knowing how badly she needed to remain grounded in the moment without concern for what was happening outside or in another realm.

This moment was about our mating.

And I accepted that Cyrus and Exos were very much a part of that.

I unsnapped her bra and slid the straps from her shoulders, revealing her hard nipples to the room. Then sent a strand of fire across the lace of her panties, singeing them at her sides and causing the rest to fall to the floor. "Beautiful," I said against her ear, running my hands up and down her sides. "Ready, sweetheart?"

She swallowed, her back relaxing into my chest as she placed her palms over my grip. "Yes."

I smiled. "Good."

Exos turned away first, heading toward my room.

Cyrus followed, but not before running his gaze over Claire one more time. I couldn't exactly blame him. Our mate without clothes served as the best kind of distraction.

I lifted her into my arms and carried her to the bedroom, not releasing her until we stood beside the bed. She clung to my shirt, then crinkled her brow. "Wait."

Wait? My heart skipped a beat, uncertainty an evil presence in my soul, until I felt the stirring of her power.

A flame erupted down my spine as she effortlessly sawed through my supposedly fireproof shirt. As it disintegrated to the floor, I wondered—not for the first time in her presence—if I needed to invest in a new wardrobe.

My pants were next, her fire coming awfully close to my stiffening dick.

She stroked a flicker of heat across it, reminding me of a kiss, before teasing the head and completing the job.

"If I have to be naked, so do you," she said, her palms resting against my abdomen as she lifted a challenging brow while the rest of my clothes turned to embers at our feet. Even my shoes.

"I'm starting to wonder if she needs the bond to help her focus, or just sex," Cyrus commented conversationally.

"That was impressive," Exos agreed. "Maybe it's both?"

I wrapped my hand around the back of her neck, pulling her to me. "I suggest you start the vows, Exos. Before our mouths become too busy to repeat the words."

The vows came quickly and efficiently, each statement breathed against each other's mouth.

I, Claire, accept the power that binds me to Titus, born of Fire. To cherish and respect, through all the eras and time that may fall before us, until our souls do us part. I give unto him my heat, my passion, and my internal flame, and accept his in return. My element is now his just as his is now mine, to the fae heavens may we never part. And I shall never forsake him for another, my fire forever belonging to him and to him alone.

I promised her the same, my soul igniting as the finality of our bond slipped into place. The room grew hot from the fire flaring between us, causing Exos and Cyrus to excuse themselves before the true inferno began.

An inferno that I assured Claire would blaze all night long.

One she happily accepted.

Over and over again.

CHAPTER THIRTY-TWO
CLAIRE

EVERY PART OF ME ACHED from Titus's attentions. He'd more than lived up to his pledge to fuck me all night. And then some.

A glance at the clock showed it was well past noon, meaning we'd only slept a handful of hours. Not that I minded. Titus had provided me with the escape I needed from the reality looming over our heads.

I turned in his arms, smiling as he trailed a molten rope of fire over my naked thigh, inching up and up.

"Mmm," I moaned. "You're going to make it so I can't even walk later." My eyelids fluttered closed, reliving the all-consuming sex that had left me both sore and empowered. Our vows had come hot and quick, pledging our souls to one another in an endless cascade of fire and bliss.

Titus kissed my cheek, then grinned against my skin. "Did I wear you out, sweetheart? Or can I wake you properly?" He punctuated the request by sliding his fire inside me—*down there.*

"*Fuck,*" I groaned, arching into his touch, my body alighting from the inside in response to his hot intrusion. Rather than burning me, I reveled in the way I absorbed the power as it fueled my spirit. "More."

He inflamed his elemental touch and grabbed my hip to keep me from moving.

Mate-bonding with Titus was everything I had imagined it could be and so much more. His raw need slithered over me, trailing a sea of molten lava in its wake up and down my spine.

An eternal flame.

That was my Titus.

He wasn't royal, but he didn't need to be. His passion more than made up for his lack of a noble bloodline.

"You've really been holding back on me," I accused, sensing his yearning pooling beneath his skin like liquid fire.

"You have no idea, sweetheart." He nuzzled my neck, his lips caressing my pulse. "This is only the beginning."

My mouth parted when his heat licked at my swollen clit. It both hurt and soothed, causing me to crave another stroke. I would always want more from my Fire Fae.

And it seemed he felt the same, if the erection pressing up against my thigh was anything to go by. Titus possessed an impressive stamina, something our mate-bonding had only seemed to strengthen.

"I will fuck you over and over again," he said, confirming my thoughts. His palm slid to my lower back, branding my skin. "I will consume every inch of you until the two of us melt together as one."

Oh, I'd long ago melted. Warmth and liquid heat pooled all around us, adding more scars to the floor and bedroom walls. It was a miracle we hadn't burned the entire building down.

Titus's fingers trailed back to my hip and down to the slickness between my thighs. The world turned red as his flames devoured me from the inside out, his touch a searing stamp of our promises to one another.

"Yes, that's it, Claire," he breathed, his mouth hovering over mine. His kiss belied the intensity brewing below, an intensity he bolstered by pushing me to my back and replacing his fingers with his hard cock.

I gasped as he slid inside me, his claiming pure and passionate and so fucking hot.

"More," I demanded, lifting my hips into his and urging him to take me deeper.

"Always," he returned, nipping my lower lip.

And then he was kissing me.

Hard.

Fast.

Perfection.

He rivaled the rhythm with his lower body, taking me to new heights with every stroke. "I love you," I chanted. "I love you, Titus." Maybe it was in poor form to announce such a thing in the heat of our passion, but that was what defined us—our fire.

"I love you, too, Claire," he whispered, his tongue dancing along my lower lip. "My mate."

"My mate," I repeated, squeezing my thighs around him and sighing as he slowed the pace. What had begun as a rough taking morphed into gentle lovemaking, his body worshiping mine in the best way.

Because he knew.

He always *knew*.

Exactly what I needed and how.

Tender strokes.

Followed by intense, deep thrusts.

Erotic and emotional.

Arousing and heartfelt.

My Titus. My fire mate. My love.

CHAPTER THIRTY-THREE
EXOS

"AT THIS RATE, she won't be physically capable of mating with Sol tonight," Cyrus said, joining me at the table. He scanned the page of the text I had open and whistled low. "Well, would you look at that."

"It's like they wrote this about Elana," I muttered, reviewing all the ways a Midnight Fae could absorb the powers of others. "Kols says it's not practiced often."

"I imagine not. It sounds painful for both parties involved." He was still skimming. "A lot of sacrifice required."

"Which explains the plague that took out our kind." Because all of this magic necessitated death, typically in the form of absorbing a soul and gifting it to the Midnight Fae gods as payment. "She used this spell"—I found a previously opened book, turned it to the right page, and gave it to Cyrus—"and her spirit magic to create a vortex of power. It's how she created the death fields."

"They're all the souls she's refused to release from this plane," my brother finished for me, his eyebrows lifting. "Shit."

"Yeah," I agreed, blowing out a breath. "It proves she's coming back, because those souls still exist."

"And she needs them to practice her fucked-up magic," he surmised,

559

taking the words out of my mouth—again.

I nodded. "Exactly."

He collapsed into his chair, meeting my gaze. "We need to tell Claire."

"We need Claire to finish her mating to Sol first." Because if these texts were right, Elana had amassed more power than any other fae in our realm. And our only hope was that Claire could use the five elements to take her down. "She needs earth to complete the circle."

"Then I should probably tell Titus to stop exhausting her," Cyrus suggested, his lips curling.

I shook my head. "You keep flirting with him and he's going to retaliate."

"Good," Cyrus replied, standing. "I can't wait to see how that works out for him."

"We both know you'll end up on top," I said, returning to my texts.

"But he doesn't know that," my brother mused.

"Who doesn't know what?" Vox asked, entering the dorm's lounge with Sol following close behind.

"Sol doesn't know that he's mating Claire tonight," I announced smoothly before Cyrus could comment on the sensual game he had in store for Titus.

The Earth Fae froze, his eyebrows lifting. "What?"

"She needs to complete the circle," I said, feeling like a broken record. "She needs her earth."

"And she's okay with this plan?" Sol pressed, no doubt fully aware of the fucking going on in the other room.

"Of course," Cyrus replied, his tone one of confident ease. "I was just about to go ask her for a time. But perhaps you can tell me instead and I'll just relay the details?"

Sol's mouth opened and closed several times.

I closed my book and leaned back, folding my arms. "What's wrong, Earth Fae? Afraid of the competition Titus is providing in the other room?"

The giant scowled. "*No.*"

"Then what's the problem?" I demanded, not having time for this. We had a hybrid fae on the loose with an undetermined return date.

And she was definitely going to return.

Those texts proved that not only did she need the death fields but she also needed to remove any and all powers that stood in her way of accessing those fields. And now, I just happened to be that power. The second I'd learned of her energy source, I'd used my spirit to seal it off from all external parties. Only I could enter that field now. Until someone removed me from the equation.

No one knew I'd set myself up as the bait yet. Mostly because I'd just done it this morning. Cyrus would be the first one I told, as soon as we figured out this final mating.

"Nothing's ready," Sol grumbled. "I've not even asked her if that's what she wants."

I frowned. "Why wouldn't she want to mate you, Sol? You're already on the third level. That makes you engaged by her human standards."

His cheeks tinted a red shade. "Yeah, I know, but I wanted to ask her... properly."

Cyrus smiled. "The closet romantic. Let me guess—peaches were going to be involved?"

The ground rumbled beneath us as Sol narrowed his gaze. "Yeah, well, unlike you, I value consent."

And all the amusement in the room died.

"Excuse me?" Cyrus said slowly. "Are you trying to accuse me of something?"

"It's not an accusation. It's the truth. You mated Claire while she was unconscious, without a voice."

"To save her fucking life," Cyrus retorted, taking a step forward. "Or are you saying I should have just let her die? Because if that's the case, then you're not worthy of her at all."

"I'm more worthy of her than you are, *Spirit Fae*." The words tumbled from Sol's mouth, followed by a vibration of the foundation of the building, his power mounting by the second. "At least I'll never manipulate her into anything. Won't threaten to break her fucking soul. But you can't promise that, can you? Water Prince or not, you're still a Spirit Fae at heart. And Spirit Fae *hurt*."

Right. One step forward, twenty steps backward.

I pushed away from the table to stand in front of Cyrus before he could physically react.

It didn't stop the whip of water that lashed out and struck Sol across the cheek. Or the words that seethed from my brother's mouth. "I have been patient with you, Sol. Very fucking patient. But your misconception regarding Spirit Fae? It ends today." He shoved him again with another strand of liquid, then wrapped it around his throat. "Spirit Fae are not the only ones who can inflict pain and harm. Shall I demonstrate?"

I opened my mouth to tell him to stop, when a root burst through the floor and circled Cyrus's waist. Squeezing. Hard.

"Stop!" Vox shouted.

But the two fae were lost to their elements now.

Sol had already conjured another thick branch, this one coming through the window from the outside, and went directly for Cyrus's chest.

While my brother lashed out at it with a tidal wave, snapping it into pieces.

Chaos ensued as Vox tried to blast them apart with air, and I used my fire to incinerate both the water and roots infiltrating the dorm.

They were going to take this fucking place down.

"What are you doing?!" Claire screamed, her body clad in a sheet as she took in the wreckage of the living area. Her power flew out of her, smacking all of us in the chest as she forced us to different sections of the room.

Spirit, I recognized.

Not her other elements.

But her spirit.

She'd used it to force our compliance, and the look on Sol's face bespoke of just how much that hurt him.

Shit.

"What the fuck is wrong with all of you?" Titus demanded, coming up behind Claire in a pair of boxers and nothing else. "We have an unconscious Spirit Fae, who happens to be Claire's mother, resting in the other room, and you all are trying to take down the damn building on our heads!"

Cyrus had the grace to appear contrite.

Vox just looked frustrated.

And Sol, he was utterly broken.

I sighed, rubbing my hand down my face. This was not a team ready for Elana's pending arrival. It was a clusterfuck of emotions and twisted-up pasts. I focused on the core of the pain—Sol.

"I don't know what happened to you or who did it," I told him. "But I can promise it wasn't me, Cyrus, or Claire. And this animosity you carry toward our gifts? It has to end. Now. Either you trust us or you don't. It's as easy as that."

Claire froze, understanding seeming to punch her in the chest. "Wait." She cleared her throat and turned to face Sol. "You think we would, no, that *I* could ever use my power against you? In a negative way?" She released all four of us in an instant, her touch against my spirit gone in a flash. "You think I could hurt you? Intentionally?" She blinked, but not fast enough to hide the tears blossoming in her gaze.

It had me wanting to take a step toward her, to pull her into my arms.

But this wasn't my hurt to fix.

This hurt belonged to Sol.

"Do you not know me at all?" she whispered, her heart breaking before our eyes.

Cyrus gave Sol a thunderous look, as though he wanted to rip him limb from limb.

Vox merely sighed and shook his head.

And Titus appeared ready to join Cyrus in his rampage.

"Claire," Sol started, taking a step forward.

But she took one step back, her head swaying back and forth. "I... I don't know what to do with this. I thought... I thought we..." She trailed off, swallowing. "I need... I need a minute."

Her shoulders hunched as she turned away from everyone and left the room.

Titus took a step to go after her, but I called out, "No. Don't."

He glanced back at me as if I'd lost my mind. "Are you fucking kidding me right now?"

"Sol needs to do it," I said, gritting my teeth at how hard it was not to follow Claire myself. "He needs to fix this." I looked at him. "You're either in our circle or you're out, Sol. No more waffling. No more distrust. You fucking fix what you just did, or you leave. Your choice."

I couldn't stand there to see what he'd do.

Couldn't think beyond the beating of my heart.

Because if he didn't go to Claire and heal the pain I felt radiating from her soul, I'd fucking kill him.

Which meant I needed space, too, before I did something we'd all regret.

I grabbed my brother—who was seething just as much as I was—and forced him to follow me outside. "I need to talk to you."

"Now?" he demanded.

"Now." I had his shirt gripped in my fist as I all but yanked him outside. Sol's bullshit notwithstanding, we had Elana to worry about and a trap to discuss. One I now regretted igniting because it meant she'd be here sooner rather than later.

And after that show in the living area?

Yeah, none of us were ready.

Which meant we needed a plan B.

"I want to talk about contingency plans," I told him.

He snorted. "Why?"

I met his storming gaze. "Because we're going to need them for when Elana realizes I've cut off her access to the death fields."

His eyebrows lifted. Then a curse tumbled from his mouth.

"Yeah. My feelings exactly," I muttered, running my fingers through my hair. "We're going to need backup."

He huffed a laugh. "Brother, at this point, we're going to need a fucking miracle."

For once, I hated that he was right.

CHAPTER THIRTY-FOUR
SOL

WELL, NOW I'D REALLY FUCKED THINGS UP. I'd never seen Claire look at me like that, and I stood like an idiot in the destroyed living room.

Fix it.

Exos's last order to me before he dragged his brother out of the room, although a part of me wanted Cyrus to try and take my head off. Prove me right. Prove what the Spirit Fae were really capable of.

Yet, if all Spirit Fae were evil, then that meant Claire was evil, too.

In my heart, I knew she wasn't evil at all. And neither was Exos or Cyrus.

Which left me with one option—to figure this the fuck out. And, as Exos had said, fix it.

Clenching my fists, I gathered the courage to go after my mate. I'd hurt her deeply, and raw emotions ripped through the bond-mate circle. An apology wouldn't be enough, but I had to start somewhere.

"Are you just going to stand there?" Vox demanded, not hiding his disgust. He was used to my tantrums, but this time I'd gone too far. And even I knew it.

"I don't know what to say to her," I admitted as I stared down the hall. "I love her, but..." *She's part Spirit Fae.*

"But nothing," Vox said with a snap of wind across my face. "If you love her, then that's all you need to know." He pointed down the hall. "Like Exos said, you're going to fix this, or you're going to get the fuck out."

It stung to hear Vox give me an ultimatum like that. We'd always been close, but on this there was no room for negotiation.

Vox was right.

They all were right.

All of her mates were more than capable of calming Claire down. I was the only one not fully mated to her, which made me feel least qualified for the job. Still, I'd created this mess, so I was going to fix it, even if I had to bare my scarred spirit to her.

If I were being honest with myself, I'd admit that was what frightened me most—that she might see how damaged I really was.

But maybe that was exactly what I needed to do.

Show her everything. Trust her with not only my heart, but my very soul.

I found Claire in the next room with her back to me, the white sheet draped precariously low across her waist as she clutched the fabric to her chest. She stared out the window, up into the sky.

"Claire..." I swallowed, mostly because her shoulders stiffened upon hearing my voice. Not the kind of reaction I desired or liked from my intended mate. I moved closer, stopping just within touching distance. "Claire, I'm—"

She spun on me and growled before I had a chance to finish. Her eyes blazed with raw power from her bond with Titus.

"I don't want an apology," she said, stabbing a finger to my chest. The tiny digit held enough earth magic to stagger me back a step. "Actions speak louder than words, Sol. I would expect you to understand that by now, but clearly, you don't. Or you couldn't possibly think I'd ever intentionally hurt you."

"You're right," I whispered, hanging my head low and splaying my palms open in surrender. "You're right," I repeated. "Actions do speak louder than words, Claire. And if I let you understand my history, you'd understand just how true that is."

That seemed to soothe some of her ire, just enough to let a hint of curiosity through. "Then tell me."

"I could," I whispered, realizing in that moment exactly what I needed to do. How I could truly gain her trust and prove myself to her in kind. "But I'd rather show you, Claire." She required more than words. I understood that better than anyone. So I'd give her everything.

My love.

My trust.

My very soul.

"There are two sides to a Spirit Fae," I continued. "I want to show you the darker side. No, I *need* to show you, Claire." I knelt beside the bed, pleading with her. "Help me stop hiding who I am. *See* me, Claire."

She studied me, her expression softening another fraction. "I do see you, Sol. I always have."

"I'm not talking about my exterior." I swallowed. "I'm talking about my soul." I closed my eyes, my forehead meeting the mattress. "I need you to truly look, Claire. Go into my spirit and witness what was done to me. The pain. The torment. The marks I can feel but can't actually see. The torture I can't remember but have spent countless nights reliving in a sea of darkness and screams."

My throat began to burn.

My heart pounding in my chest.

The memory of that night a haunting image just out of my reach.

"Do you know what it's like to know something happened but not be able to detail it?" I wondered out loud, lifting my head to meet her gaze. "I remember the pain, the screams, my mother begging and my sister crying. Yet, I can't tell you how it all unfolded."

I paused, needing a breath.

Then forged ahead.

Because she needed to understand. It was the only way to explain my fear and my inherent reactions to her element.

"All I know is, a Spirit Fae plagued us that night. The fae reached into my soul and shredded it, did the same to my mother and my sister, and I had to watch them gradually die for over a decade as a result. No one believed me. But I saw the signs, Claire. I knew what was happening to them and couldn't do a damn thing to stop it."

I trembled, their pain ingrained into my mind. The visual of them so ghastly and pale on their deathbeds.

"Something happened that night, Claire," I whispered. "Something that haunts me to the very core of my element and has left me without access to the source, even with my supposed royal ties. And you can see the scars of it on my spirit."

I reached for her hand, which, thankfully, she allowed me to take.

"Look at me. Beneath the surface. Find my spirit and tell me what you see. Because it kills a part of me to know those marks are there and to not be able to prove it to my own eyes. Be my eyes, Claire. Please. Tell me what you see." I brought her palm to my chest and closed my eyes, waiting.

"Sol..." My name sounded so broken from her lips, but I refused to back down. I hadn't realized how much I needed this until now.

"Please, Claire," I whispered. "I'm ready. Use your spirit and tell me who I am. Tell me what you see."

She brought her other palm to my face, and I leaned into her touch, craving the truth. I trusted her to do this, to explore me without harm, to learn my spirit and all the broken pieces of me.

Because that was how I felt beneath it all.

Shattered.

Alone.

Lonely.

She had my heart, but what we both needed all this time was for her to access my soul. I'd kept it locked away and out of reach, protecting that final part of me that was so wounded long ago.

It was finally time for me to stop hiding.

For her.

For *us*.

Her breath fanned my lips a second before she kissed me. So soft and tentative as I felt the first stirrings of her power brushing against mine. I didn't retreat. I didn't even flinch. I merely accepted this as our fate. Welcomed her into me. And unleashed everything I owned for her to explore.

Warmth spiraled through my center, blossoming in my chest as I *felt* her spirit brush mine. No icy talons or sharp stabs of pain. Just a pleasant comfort. My Claire, caressing me in a way I never could have anticipated.

It stole the breath from my lungs.

Escalated my pulse and subdued it at the same time.

Left me depleted and exhilarated all in a single second.

Vitality, I realized. *She's gifting me the comfort of her vitality.*

And it brought a tear to my eye, the soothing touch not one I expected. "Claire," I whispered, my throat clogging with emotion.

"Shh," she murmured, her fingertips trailing over my cheek to my neck. "I can't mend your scars, but I can relieve some of the tension in them."

I shivered as her actions followed her words, an invisible weight lifting from my shoulders with each passing moment. The intimacy of the moment alleviated all my worries. Filled me with hope. Replenished my every desire. By the time she pulled away, I felt so full of life I thought I might burst.

Instead, another tear fell from my eye, one she caught with her finger. And she sighed. "Oh, Sol, I can't even imagine the pain you endured to receive such damage."

"That's not even the worst part for me," I admitted. "I can deal with the pain. It's not knowing how it happened that haunts me." My eyelids opened to find her gazing at me with so much love it made my heart hurt. "I survived, Claire. That's the biggest punishment of it all—having to watch the plague take my mother and my sister while leaving me healthy and alive in their place. And never understanding why."

"While only knowing a Spirit Fae caused it all," she added, her voice whisper-soft. "How old were you when it happened?"

"Seven." I swallowed. "My sister was only five. She lived for over a decade with that darkness inside her, stunting her growth and abilities, until finally she died. And you know what she said to me that day?"

It hurt to repeat, to relive the memory, but Claire needed to know. I had to tell her everything I could. To help her understand why her element terrified me.

I cleared my throat, pushing the emotion down into my chest, where it festered and burned. "She... she told me she was thankful," I managed to say, my voice hoarse. "She was thankful it was finally her time to die. Because she knew it wouldn't hurt anymore. And she'd be with my mother again. Her only regret was leaving me."

To live a lonely existence while always wondering why it all happened.

What I did to deserve such a cruel fate.

"Sometimes I think I received the worst punishment of all," I whispered. "Because I survived. Because I had to bury them both in the earth. And live on. Without them." My history was the reason Aflora meant so much to me. She was there through it all, living the agony at my side.

She was possibly the only one who understood.

Until Claire.

"Oh, Sol," my mate said now, her arms encircling my neck and pulling me up onto the bed to join her. She didn't cry or cast pity my way, two things I was grateful for. Instead, she curled into me and gave me her strength, her spirit caressing mine in a kiss of life.

We lay like that for what might have been hours.

Me lost to the memories of my past.

Claire soothing my fractured soul.

I relaxed into our embrace, feeling closer to her than ever before, with my hand drifting up and down her bare side. *Content*, I realized. *I'm truly content.*

Because she was mine.

And I was hers.

Not officially, though. Not quite.

"I know I've not been the best mate," I started, deciding that might be the understatement of the century. "Trusting Exos and Cyrus will never come easily to me. But deep down, I know they're not evil. I know they'd never do this to a person out of spite. It's just the mere idea that they could that unnerves me. And you possess the same ability."

"I do," she murmured, her fingers tracing patterns into my shirt as she rested her head against my shoulder. "But the thought of harming another in that way sickens me, Sol. I would never do it. And certainly not to you."

"I know." I tightened my hold around her, squeezing her. "I know, Claire."

"Cyrus and Exos wouldn't either."

"I know that, too. But whenever I feel spirit energy in use, it... it makes me ill. Because all I remember is how it was used against me in a way I can't recall. All I hear are my sister's dying words. All I see are my mother's gaunt features and her lips trying to form one final smile." I closed my eyes against the pain. "I don't know if it will ever go away."

"How did you feel when my spirit touched yours?" she asked softly, peeking up at me. "Did that hurt you?"

I shook my head. "No. It felt…" I searched my brain for the right words. "Soothing. Good. Natural."

She studied me for a long moment, then propped herself up on my chest. "Then maybe that's what you need to heal. I would never wish to replace your memories, but we could add new ones, positive ones, that you can draw upon whenever you feel spirit in use."

Her soul kissed mine with her statement, whether on purpose or not, I wasn't sure. But I felt her presence there, the warmth of her nearness and acceptance, her calming energy surrounding mine. It elicited a shiver from deep within, the ease with which she accessed my soul both unnerving and sensual. A conflict of interest that would likely take years to fix. However, her idea held merit.

"I would be willing to try," I said, my voice much softer than it'd ever been before. "But only with you." Exos and Cyrus meant well, something I understood on a fundamental level, but the notion of allowing them access to my soul had all my walls flaring.

Still, I could admit that I owed both of them an apology.

Especially Cyrus.

My comments earlier were unfounded and unfair. I knew he had no choice but to mate Claire. Was thankful he'd done it to save her life. And it was very clear to me that she didn't regret it at all. Even if I didn't understand her attraction to the royal prick.

Her lips curled, amusement flashing in her eyes. "I can feel your animosity toward Cyrus. He's not that bad, you know."

"I know." I frowned. "But he's still a dick."

"It's part of his charm," she replied, smiling. "And he respects your boundaries, Sol. I've been with him on the spirit plane, have seen how he avoids touching your spirit. Exos, too."

"You found my soul on the spirit plane?"

She shook her head. "No. You found me. You all did. Like you were protecting me from myself and the source itself." She rested her chin on my sternum. "Exos and Cyrus were very careful not to touch any of you, or any of the other souls drifting around. I don't know who did this to you, but it definitely wasn't them."

"I know," I said. "Logically, I know. But in the moment…"

"It's hard not to fall on old memories," she replied. "Yes, I understand. But it's something we can work through, Sol. Together. If you want."

I didn't hesitate. "I do, Claire. I want forever with you, too. The whole fight started because Exos demanded I mate you, but it felt wrong to do something without talking to you first. I wanted to ask you formally. I had it all planned with peaches, too." It seemed ridiculous now. Childish. But with all the chaos of late, I wanted to give her that moment of peace and sweetness. To escape to our special place and discuss forever together.

"Peaches?" she repeated, her eyes smiling. "I do love peaches." She moved up my body to press her palms into the pillows on either side of my head, her bare breasts hanging over my chest as she angled herself over me. It didn't seem intentional on her part, but I was definitely enjoying the sexual connotation behind her words, coupled with the visual.

Her expression, however, fell serious. Her gaze intent.

"I want forever with you, too, Sol," she said. "But it requires accepting all of me. Including my spirit. And Cyrus. And Exos. I need to know you can do that."

I lifted my palm to cup her cheek while my other arm slid around her back, holding her. "I already do, Claire. My mind may fight my intentions, but my heart has accepted you all for longer than I can admit. My soul will take longer, at least with Cyrus and Exos. However, you're mine, Claire. And I'm yours. If you'll have me, that is."

She canted her head. "Forever?"

"Forever," I repeated. "Everything I have is yours, if you will have me."

Tension eased from her features, her lips curling as she bent to brush her mouth against mine. "Then I will take you, Sol, every single piece, and I'll put you back together again."

She kissed me again, this time with more sensuality and intent.

"Tomorrow?" I asked softly, not wanting to spend another day without finalizing our bond but also knowing I needed time to create the perfect oasis for our ceremony. To show her I truly meant what I said.

"Tomorrow," she agreed, falling into my embrace. "But for tonight, I want you to kiss me, Sol. Show me I'm yours."

I threaded my fingers through her hair, holding her above me. "Only if you return the favor by claiming me in return."

Her spirit settled against mine. "Oh, Sol, you've been mine for a while now."

I smiled against her mouth. "Good. I wouldn't want to be anywhere else."

"Stop flirting and kiss me, Sol."

"I thought you'd never ask."

I took her mouth with my own, unleashing all my emotions into our embrace and allowing her unfettered access to every part of me.

My soul had never felt more alive.

All because of my Claire.

My little flower, the one who'd finally given me the chance to bloom.

Chapter Thirty-Five
Sol

EVERYTHING HAD TO BE PERFECT. Especially after all the shit that went down yesterday.

I needed to reaffirm to Claire that I loved her. To prove that she was my rock. And to make sure she knew I was in this for eternity. Not just with her, but with the entire circle.

Surveying the oasis I'd created brought a grin to my face. I'd spent all day on this project, and it was perfect. All of Claire's favorite plants and trees covered the grounds, stirring notes of sweet fruits throughout the air. Flowers of all shapes, sizes, and colors lined the walkways, and the sprout of the World Tree I'd called into the center now towered high into the sky.

Across from it sat a fountain—one Cyrus had created to commemorate the occasion. He meant it as a peace offering, which I'd accepted and returned by giving him a bucket of peaches. He nibbled on one now from his spot on the path, his icy gaze grinning in approval. "Almost done, Earth Fae?"

"Yeah." I knelt and inspired a few more flowers to bloom, then nodded. "I'm ready."

"You are," he agreed, clapping me on the back. "Or Exos might kill you."

I snorted. "He could try." And probably succeed. But he wouldn't do that to Claire.

"Let's go," Cyrus said, leading the way.

I left the grove behind with a sense that everything was going to go perfectly tonight. Claire loved life and earth and adored the stillness of everlasting promises our element offered, just as much as I did. She'd taught me how to embrace the source of my power, and now I would share my world with her.

I couldn't fucking wait.

Returning to the Spirit Quad, Exos cocked a brow. "Does our giant have a skip in his step?"

Vox grinned as he adjusted his warrior's tail. "I'd say so. Wonder why that could be?"

I opened my mouth to tell them both to fuck off, but the music of Claire's giggles cresting the corner made me pause.

A red glow preceded her as she made her entrance, flames forming a thin dress down her delicious curves as Titus rested a hand on her hip. He never took his eyes from her, glued just as I was to the raw beauty of her power.

"May I present our glowing mate?" Titus pressed a sensual kiss to her neck, then waggled his brows playfully.

Claire brushed him away and smiled shyly at me. "Hey, Sol."

Her nerves were palpable, likely a result of being bathed in Titus's passion, but it didn't bother me at all. She was my mate, my heart, my rock. And she radiated such joy that I couldn't help but be grateful to Titus for making her smile like that.

I offered my hand to her, feeling massive when she slipped her tiny fingers into my waiting palm. "Hello, little flower."

Her cheeks deepened in a ruby blush as she transitioned her power to accommodate mine. Fire made way for bronze, and her dress took on a metallic hue.

Beautiful.

I bent to taste her plump lips and Claire lifted her chin. Just a quick kiss, meant to—

An icy chill swept through the Spirit Quad, causing us to freeze.

Silence.

Followed by an agonized scream that split straight into my skull.

"Mom!" Claire shouted, eyes wide as she spun and tumbled out of my grip. Her dress melted to ash as she ran toward the bedroom where we kept Ophelia isolated. Titus was hot on her heels, his shirt flowing off his body to wrap around hers, as our mate seemed completely oblivious to being stark naked.

All of us stopped in the hallway, and Claire entered first.

Ophelia shrieked, flinging herself into the corner of the room, her eyes wide with raw terror. She still resembled more of a corpse than something alive, her stringy hair a ghastly veil that framed her gaunt face.

"Elana!" she screeched and pressed herself further into the corner, curling her knees up to her chest as she made herself small.

Claire glanced at the five of us. "Don't frighten her. Please."

My jaw flexed. Claire might believe Elana was behind all of this, but until I saw substantial proof of that, Ophelia remained on my guilty list.

The bitch had tried to kill my mate, something Claire seemed to have forgotten. But she insisted on taking the gentle approach.

Fine.

Obeying, I nodded and eased into the shadows where I could keep an eye on her should Ophelia go from cowering corpse to crazed killer.

But Exos took a step forward, unwilling to hide. As Spirit King, I supposed he had the most right to that claim. This was the female who supposedly demolished his kind. I got it.

Titus and Vox lingered in the doorway while Cyrus joined me in the shadows, his spirit humming at the ready. Between him and his brother, Ophelia wouldn't be able to pull any tricks on us.

And if she did, well, I could always smash her face in.

Claire glared at me when the ground rumbled, and I pulled my power back into my body, biting the side of my cheek to keep myself in check.

"Mom, it's me. It's Claire," my mate said, her voice low and sweet as Titus's shirt billowed around her thighs. She seemed to frown at it, momentarily distracted. And my lips parted as she burned away the garment, replacing it with an array of fluttering pink butterflies.

"When did you learn to do that?" I wondered out loud.

Her lips quirked up. "Aflora taught me a few wardrobe tricks." Her amusement was short-lived, her focus quickly returning to her mother. "Mom?"

Ophelia blinked up at Claire, her expression competing between terror and awe. "C-Claire?" My mate reached out to comfort the creature, but the moment of lucidity passed and Ophelia's face twisted with horror. "No! Stop it! I can't take it anymore!"

A shock wave of spirit flashed out and slammed into my chest. Exos and Cyrus were ready and held off the attack. Exos shoved out with raw power, making Ophelia's eyes roll back in her head.

"Sleep," he commanded.

Ophelia collapsed, and Claire caught her just before her head slammed against the wall. She glared back at the Spirit King. "Was that necessary?"

Exos didn't flinch or respond to her censure. "It's as I feared. Her mind can't handle the two decades of torture Elana has put her through. We're going to have to get answers a different way." He shared a look with his brother. "We could go into her mind…"

"No," Claire said with finality. Exos might be a king, but Claire's gaze burned with a regal authority of her own. She held power over the five elements, not to mention our hearts. "We're going to do this my way, Exos. Nobody is touching her mind *ever* again."

When Claire struggled to drag Ophelia's limp body back to the bed, I left the shadows and gently took the woman from my mate's arms, then draped the frail female over the sheets as carefully as I could.

"Thank you," Claire whispered, taking my hand and guiding me out of the room. "Call me if she wakes up," she called over her shoulder, the words a demand, not a request.

I couldn't help the grin that formed at the edge of my mouth. I loved hearing Claire boss around the royal brothers.

And their responding smiles said they felt the same, even if they didn't agree with her.

Vox and Titus followed us into the living area, where Claire began to pace.

"That went well," the Fire Fae said, crossing his arms and settling his gaze on Claire. He looked as if he wanted to go to his mate, to comfort her, but Claire was too shaken for the unbridled raw emotions Titus inspired in her right now.

She needed something solid, a rock she could hold on to.

As if hearing my thoughts, she stopped by my side. I wrapped an arm around her shoulders, hugging her close and kissing the top of her head. "It's going to be okay, little flower."

She nodded, then melted into my embrace. "I know. But I need to be here when she wakes up again. There are things she can tell us, things that can help us, and I don't know if she'll talk to anyone else." She flicked her gaze to Exos and Cyrus as they entered. "And she won't be able to if they just knock her out every time she screams."

"She's suffered intense pain and torment, Claire," Exos replied, unapologetic. "Her mind is unreliable, which means defensive energy is our only approach until we can ease her into her new reality."

"He's right," Cyrus agreed. "I can't even begin to understand what she's endured these last two decades. And I can't decide whose situation is worse—hers or Mortus's."

"They're equally bad," Titus muttered. "Have you seen how lost he is out there?" He gestured to the makeshift sparring grounds outside. They were empty right now due to the evening hour. But his point was made.

"It's bad," Exos agreed. "They're both in rough shape."

"Which leaves us without additional information on Elana," Cyrus added. "Luckily, we've learned a lot from those books. Such as the source of her power."

"Which is?" Claire asked, her brow furrowing.

"The death fields," Exos replied, glancing at his brother. "The spirit energy she's imprisoned there is used for sacrifices to the dark arts, particularly death magic. Fortunately, she can't access it anymore."

"And unfortunately, that means Exos is her new target," Cyrus added, narrowing his gaze at the Spirit King. "I gave you a day, brother."

"And I said we would discuss it after the matings were done," he gritted out through his teeth.

"We're on a time clock here and—"

"Wait," Claire interjected, cutting off Cyrus. "You set yourself up as bait?" Her voice broke on that last word. "And didn't tell us?"

"I needed a way to guarantee she'd come here," he said. "Now she has one."

"Which would be great if we were better prepared to receive her attack," Claire countered.

He didn't appear at all fazed by her combative tone. "My choices were to shut down her access or allow her to continue feeding her dark energy, and the latter didn't feel like a great option. So I did what was best for the Spirit Fae—what was best for all of us."

"What do you mean by 'feeding her dark energy' with the death fields?" Vox asked, his dark brows furrowing.

"The Spirit Fae plague wasn't a plague at all," Exos explained. "It was a way for her to trap the souls of dead fae, to use as fuel—*sacrifices*—for her death magic."

"You're certain?" I asked.

He nodded. "And from what I can tell, it's what she's been doing to the Earth Fae. She's been slowly stealing their lives and putting the remnants of their souls in the fields. Refusing to grant them access to the afterlife."

Vox frowned. "As Spirit King, can't you just release them all?"

Exos shook his head. "No. Not without undoing her magic. The best I could do was block her access to the souls by placing a spirit shield over the entry point."

"Which will make her come after you." Claire dampened her bottom lip, considering. Then sighed. "You still should have told us."

"You've been a little preoccupied with your matings, princess," he replied softly. "Which was more important to all of us."

"But how am I supposed to mate Sol tonight with my mom being in a spirit-induced coma and the very real threat of Elana's impending arrival?" She glanced up at me, her eyes filled with sadness. "It won't be fair to mate you tonight with my mind preoccupied by everything else."

I pressed a kiss to the crown of her head. "I understand, little flower." It broke my heart not to complete the bond with Claire, especially when she needed my earth to fully ground her. But Claire was right; these distractions would damper our joining and ruin what should be a joyous experience. "We'll postpone the mating until after things have cooled down."

"But she needs to complete the circle," Exos interjected. "It'll strengthen her."

She shivered in my grasp like a leaf about to tear itself from its tree, defying his words. "Not in this state," I argued. "Mating tonight while all of this is weighing upon us will taint the bonding."

Exos eyed us both, then blew out a long breath and shook his head. "Damn it." He glanced at Cyrus.

"He's right," his brother said softly.

"I know," Exos agreed, scrubbing a hand over his face. "I know."

"We'll figure this out," Cyrus vowed. "All of us. But first, I suggest Claire spend tonight with Sol to at least absorb what she can through the bond."

I nodded. "I'll give her whatever she needs."

"But you need your element, too." She tugged on my shirt, demanding my attention. "You only give me what you can, Sol."

"Okay." I kissed her forehead. "But I have a lot of power."

Her gaze narrowed. "Sol."

"What? I do." I lifted her up into my arms, loving the way her butterflies seemed to flutter around me in response. "I'll prove it."

"Yeah, go prove it," Titus encouraged. "But try to get some rest with Sol. We'll watch over your mother in case she wakes again."

Vox, Exos, and Cyrus all nodded in agreement.

"No more fainting spells," she said, aiming the words at the two Spirit Fae.

"Yes, ma'am," Exos drawled, winking at her.

I started walking toward my bedroom before she could argue, not wanting to waste another moment of our time together. We might not be mating tonight, but we could bond in other ways.

Claire seemed to agree, because her dress dissolved the moment her body hit my bed, the oversized mattress large enough to accommodate my size. My gaze raked over her.

She curled under the sheets like a seed settling into the earth. Her blue eyes seemed to glow in the dim light awarded by the window. "Sorry," she murmured. "The butterflies were starting to itch."

I smiled, peeling away my clothes and joining her, to add warmth to the cool sheets.

She settled against my chest and draped a leg over my thigh.

"I'm here for anything you need," I said, stroking her bare shoulder.

She tucked her chin against my neck and breathed in, then exhaled, and her breath swept goose bumps across my skin.

"Fuck, Claire, don't do that, or I'll be here for *more* than you need right now," I said as my cock reacted to what she did to me.

She giggled and snuggled closer, wrapping her arms as far as she could around my chest. "Sorry." She didn't sound very apologetic.

I took three long breaths and tried to bring to mind images that would calm the rumble in my chest.

Hmm.

Glacier—hate his face. He's so not good enough for Aflora. But I knew better than to tell her that.

Oh, Titus melting my stone around my ankles. The bastard had made me look like an idiot.

"Do you think Vox will join us?" Claire asked, interrupting my attempt at a mental distraction. Because just the thought of Claire between Vox and me had me rock hard.

I shifted my weight. "Do you want him to?"

She pondered the question, then rested her head on my chest, her hair splaying over me. "I think I just want to rest. For now. It's been a long few days. Weeks. Months." She laughed softly. "You know what I mean."

I did. But I wouldn't change any of it for the world.

"We can rest," I agreed, stroking my fingers through her hair.

She fell quiet for so long that I thought perhaps she slept.

But I felt her eyelashes moving against my skin, her mind clearly racing.

"What are you thinking about, Claire?" I asked, drawing my thumb down her spine and back up again.

Her breath feathered over my skin, reminding me of a warm solstice breeze. "She was so scared, Sol," Claire whispered. "I... I could feel what Elana did to her." She made a fist and shivered, the sensation reverberating against every inch of me. Because I knew what she meant, understood how spirit could scar the soul. "Elana's going to pay, Sol. For this. For what she did to the Earth Fae. For everything."

I tucked her closer into my side, wishing to shield her from the darkness her words evoked.

But Claire was right.

Elana would pay for what she'd done.

And soon.

CHAPTER THIRTY-SIX
CLAIRE

FIRE LICKED ACROSS MY SKIN, burning a path along my soul, branding me in death.

I fought beneath the restraints, my hands bound behind my back.

Elements whirled around me. Chaotic. Frenzied. Unbalanced.

And the winds roared overhead.

"She's coming, our queen," a dark voice whispered, the cackle that followed eliciting a trail of goose bumps down my arms. Only to wither and die beneath the fire.

"She's coming," it repeated, singsonging in my thoughts. Inky wisps of smoke twirled along my nostrils, leaving behind an acrid stench. "She's not alone."

Another tendril wrapped around me, bathing me in the scent of the dead.

"We're coming," an echo taunted. "Run, run, while you can. We're coming for you."

I flew upright on a scream, my body drenched in sweat. "She's coming!" I shouted, sounding like the remnants of my nightmare.

But it wasn't a nightmare.

I knew deep down it was very real.

Those creepy-crawly *things* were on their way here.

A hot arm wrapped around me, eliciting another shout from my lips, my fight instincts roaring to life.

"It's me!" Sol said, jolting away from the flames flashing across my body.

"Shit."

He waved his hand around, the skin burned from my carelessness. I immediately soothed it with water and spirit, mending his wound without even realizing my intention. He gaped at it in shock. "How did—"

Exos threw open the door, Cyrus right beside him. "What the hell is going on?" my spirit mate demanded.

"She's coming," I said urgently, apparently unable to say anything else.

"Elana?" Cyrus asked.

Vox and Titus appeared behind them, looking half-asleep.

Which, yeah, it was the middle of the night. But… "We need to prepare. Right now."

They all shared a glance, and I knew what they were thinking: *How do you know it's not just a dream?* Well, I *knew.* I couldn't say how. I just *knew.*

"Trust me," I urged. "Please. We need to prepare the grounds. She's bringing the dead with her." I couldn't explain how I knew that either. Or what those things would look like. But their stench still lingered in my nostrils.

Real.

Lethal.

Things.

My mates nodded as one, choosing to believe my instincts. "Right," Cyrus said first. "We all know what to do. Let's sound the bells. See you all on the main grounds."

And so it began.

The beginning of the end.

I felt it in every fiber of my being.

Tonight was the night.

I'm ready.

CHAPTER THIRTY-SEVEN
CYRUS

THE MOON BLURRED beneath an uncustomary cloud, confirming Claire's claims. The elements were warning us of the future lurking beyond the horizon. Death drifted in the air, the earth uncharacteristically silent.

"Soon," I whispered to Vox, aware of the currents lingering around my mouth, awaiting my command.

He nodded from the other side of the quad, acknowledging he'd heard my warning, and relayed it to his fellow Air Fae.

A chill swept goose bumps up and down my arms, leaving behind an inky sensation of doom.

Water Fae stood at my back, awaiting my signal.

While Sol and Titus hid with their respective ranks.

We had a good idea of what to expect, thanks to the texts from Kols and to Claire's previous death experiment with Elana. It seemed the old Chancellor was playing with animated corpses. And from what Claire described of her dreams, those were exactly what we could expect to arrive any minute now.

Exos stood at the top of a tower, Claire lingering at his side.

He was the bait and she was his knight.

How the chess pieces had shifted. But our mate had demanded a front-row seat, her powers the strongest among all of us thanks to her access to all the elements. If only we'd been able to complete her mating to Sol.

Alas, there wasn't time.

Not with the approaching army of dead coming for my brother.

Mortus cleared his throat, and I glanced sideways at the shell-shocked professor. "Yes?"

"I can feel her," he said softly, grimacing. "Like a leech searching for the souls it's touched before."

That didn't surprise me. We'd agreed before this began that I'd be knocking him out if I suspected for a second that Elana had ahold of him. Hence his position beside me.

I poked his spirit with my own, found it as shattered as before, and nodded. "She'll either swoop in quickly to take you over or she'll leave you to the wolves." My bet was on the latter. Mortus had served his purpose, his mind and body resembling a broken puppet after Elana's manipulations. There weren't many resources left for him to offer her at this point.

Ophelia was in the same boat.

Which was why we left her unconscious at the Spirit Quad. A handful of Fire Fae had agreed to guard her. Not that we expected it to be needed.

No. Elana wanted Exos.

And my brother was standing at the highest point, essentially offering himself up for her to kill.

Anyone else, and I'd call him an idiot. Fortunately, I knew better than to question Exos's strategy. I trusted him. As did Claire.

"Titus and Sol are ready," River announced, meeting me on the field to take his position.

"Good."

We'd set a little trap for Elana, one Sol and Titus had constructed together. The rest of us were merely the lure, to ensure that her minions came to the right spot.

She's here, Claire said suddenly. *I can't see her, but I feel her darkness everywhere.*

I followed her line of thought to the spirit plane and noted the dimness approaching the source. *Yes*, I agreed, pulling back to focus on our surroundings. "She's here."

"Where?" River asked.

I shook my head. The darkness lent her a supreme advantage, something she played on as more fog and clouds filled the sky, removing the moon from our view.

"It's time," I whispered, nodding at Vox.

He bowed his head in acknowledgment, communicating to his squadron.

The hairs along the back of my neck rose.

A whistle of foreign energy glided through the air.

Followed by the acridness associated with the dead.

There! Claire shouted into my mind. *By the forest line.*

I narrowed my gaze, seeing the shift of smoke. But another glimmer near the opposite edge of campus caught my focus just as Vox said, "Behind us."

She's approaching from all angles, I told Claire, saying the same out loud. *She means to divide our forces.*

A smart tactic. One that would work if we weren't all in communication in some manner. "Luring these monsters isn't going to work. River, tell Sol and Titus to move to their secondary plans. They'll understand what that means. Go. Now."

"On it," River said, taking off for the rock tunnel manufactured by the Earth students. It appeared to lead underground, but didn't. The clever fae had carved it into a hill, one that rested above sea level, thereby allowing the fae inside to maintain their access to the elements while hiding beneath a sturdy shelter.

I rolled my shoulders, preparing for the inevitable. Darkness continued to fall as the smog painted over the light above, shrouding us in a sea of black.

But I had a contingency plan.

One that would light up with my signal.

Closing my eyes, I called upon the source of both my elements, weaving them together in an intricate web of life and ripples of tranquility.

Sprinkle and grow, I whispered to the intoxicating mess of magic. *Breathe new vitality into the sky. And shade our land in hues of blue.*

I released it on a breath, smiling as the sensation grew into a spark of watery light above our heads.

The display of a royal.

The power of a king.

"Vox," I said, opening my eyes and glancing at him. "Wanna dance?"

His lips curled from across the field. "Hell yeah."

Air tangled with my elements, stirring a vortex into the night sky that absorbed the darkness threatening our lands while leaving my energy to shine.

That was the sign.

"Let's begin," I said, raising my hand and showering my fae with gifts from the source itself. "Go!"

CHAPTER THIRTY-EIGHT
CLAIRE

DROPLETS KISSED MY SKIN, Cyrus's power infusing my own and eliciting a smile from me despite the dire circumstances. *I love you,* I whispered to him.

I love you, too, little queen. Now focus on protecting my brother.

My smile grew. *Already am.*

I had my palm pressed to Exos's lower back, our spirit energy growing mutually between us and cascading over the lands in search of the villain we sought. We had one goal: to dismantle her soul.

But she remained elusive, hiding behind her ebony ocean of death. It clouded our affinity for life while seducing our darker side, causing us to fight an upward battle as we strove to hold on to the vitality that grounded us.

Exos had chosen this position for visibility, not just for us but for Elana, too.

"She'll scatter her minions across the grounds and come for us alone," he'd said as we climbed the tower. *"Which is exactly what we want. Kill the source, everything else dies with it."*

His plan hinged on our ability to take out Elana alone.

And if that failed, we would move on to another plan involving all my mates.

I brushed my damp palms against my cotton pants. Titus had given them to me, claiming they were light and fit for a fight, while also fireproof thanks to a magical surface treatment. Same with my long-sleeved shirt. Both were meant to protect me.

As was the staff in my hand and the blades strapped to my hips.

They didn't bring me nearly as much comfort as my elements did. Especially as the first sounds of attack drifted upward into the air.

I swallowed, the acrid air unsettling my insides. My soul instinctively reached out to check on my mates, worried for them as they battled below.

But I found only excitement lacing our bonds.

Pride from Cyrus.

Fierceness from Sol.

Determination from Vox.

And a sense of happy resolve from Titus as he chanted threats in his mind at the deathly creatures crawling overhead. His power ignited, warming my skin, as Sol collapsed the earth on a horde of incoming skeletal beings. Fire poured over them all, melding the land around them to form an ensnaring rock.

"Brilliant," Exos praised, his amusement palpable. "I knew those two would come to terms and work well together. Now let's see about getting them some help, shall we?"

I nodded, refocusing on the task at hand. *Find Elana.*

But her presence was everywhere and nowhere at the same time, her soul withering just out of reach. I frowned at it. "How does she keep doing that?"

"She's old," Exos said, his presence closest to the source. "And she's developed some cunning tricks over the centuries."

I growled, frustrated, and dove back into my spirit.

So much darkness.

Not at all like the last time I ventured into this plane.

Shadows lurked in corners, taunting my presence and providing false leads. *Hmm, but that one in the distance keeps fading and appearing as if striving to hide but failing.* I trailed after it, determined to identify the master of the creation.

Or maybe mistress.

Where are you, Elana? I wondered. *Come out, come out, wherever you are.*

The ground shifted, rocking our tower. I clung to Exos and a nearby pole, my focus still on the spirit realm and that fleeing form. *You can't escape me,* I thought at it, pursuing it faster. *I'm going—*

A piercing scream yanked me back into reality, my eyes flying wide. "Mom!" I shouted, recognizing that yell from the last few days of overhearing her night terrors.

Exos caught me around the waist before I could begin the descent. "It's a trap," he said, his mouth against my ear.

"How do you know?" I demanded, my mother's agonized shouts slicing my heart. "They're hurting her, Exos! We have to do something!"

Exos's arms tightened around me. "Think, Claire! We have a plan. We can't deviate."

"But they're killing her!" I could see it in the way her aura flickered in the spirit realm, a sense of her demise looming over my very soul. I had to go to her, to help her, to *free* her. I'd only just gotten her back, and for her to die now wouldn't be right.

She deserved a second chance.

She needed to clear her name.

Everyone hated her, accused her of a sin that she never committed.

If she died, she'd leave us with the knowledge of her failure.

Another shriek fractured my heart, her light blinking in and out in the soul plane, begging me for help. I couldn't ignore her. I had to go to her, to help her, after all the years of leaving her to suffer. Never again. Not now that I had the power and knowledge to do something.

Exos's words were drowned out by the escalated beating of my heart, the sound whooshing in my ears as if I were underwater. His arms fell away. His touch seeming to go right through me as the world dissolved into a shield of clarity and peace.

Only to be wiped away by the sight appearing before me.

My mother on her knees.

Elana's hand wrapped around her throat.

A yawning vortex of energy swirling around them both as Elana literally absorbed my mother's soul right before my eyes.

"Enough!" I shouted, blasting her with every bit of power I could muster and sending Elana across the Spirit Dorm into a nearby wall.

I misted, part of me realized.

But I had more important problems to worry about.

Slithering skeletal minions turned on me, furious that I'd dared to touch their mistress. With a wave of water, I sent their remains scattering. Then created a fiery shell around my mother, protecting her unconscious form on the floor from future harm. Earth would have been better, but I didn't trust that element yet. Not with my mating bond still outstanding.

Air, water, spirit, and fire would have to do.

I used the first to create a tornado, sucking up all the pieces of Elana's minions and blowing them out into the Spirit Quad. Then I focused on the bitch herself.

Except she was nowhere to be found.

I frowned, whirling around, searching for Elana.

She'd been there just a second ago.

Realization dawned as the scene rippled before my eyes, disclosing the truth for the split second I needed to discover what was happening.

It's all a mirage...

With that thought, the world calmed and revealed the real Spirit Dorm.

585

The flames died around my mother. She still lay unconscious with sleep—a sleep Cyrus and Exos had subjected her to only hours before.

And the only destruction around us was the one I'd caused.

None of it was real.

But where were the Fire Fae set to guard my mother?

With a sickening feeling, I wandered outside, hoping against hope that it hadn't been them I destroyed.

And I found them all lying on the lawn.

"Oh God…" I pressed my hand to my mouth, falling to my knees.

Those skeletal things were fae…

And I killed them.

My heart hammered in my chest.

Fuck. Fuck. Fuck. I punched the earth, furious at myself for allowing my emotions to take me under. The ground rumbled beneath my strike, cracking. *Stand up*, I told myself. *Stand up and find that bitch. Finish it.*

My legs wobbled with the effort.

"I'm sorry," I whispered, a tear tracking down my cheek as I breathed the word to the five fae on the field. "I'm so—"

Claire! Exos's scream ripped through my being, his agony a slap to my senses.

I looked for his tower and found it wavering in the night, electricity flickering all around him.

Exos! I took off at a run, leaving my mother behind. It physically hurt, but my soul drove my actions, forcing me to make the impossible choice. *I'm coming!*

But he didn't respond, his spirit lost in a duel I should have been engaged in with him, at his side.

How could I be so stupid?

Elana played the one card she knew I wouldn't ignore.

Using my mother against me yet again.

Hatred fueled my steps. Vengeance darkened my heart.

A watery haze overcame me once more, power erupting through my veins. And I arrived on an explosion of elements to find Exos unconscious at Elana's feet.

Unconscious but alive.

Because I felt his life thriving around me.

He'd taken Elana to battle in the spirit plane.

Only, she seemed to be in both places at once. Her arms seemed to lower in slow motion, the blade in her hand on a perfect trajectory to hit Exos's chest.

"No!" I sent a fistful of water into her face while grabbing hold of the metal with my fire and melting it right from her hand. A drop of it sizzled against Exos while the rest scattered on a breeze I shot sideways.

Elana roared, coming for me in a split second of speed I hadn't seen coming, sending us both over the side of the tower.

Vox's scream assaulted my ears, his howl seeming to circle around me to soften my descent, just as the earth cushioned my fall.

A fall that should have killed me and Elana both.

Only, she was again nowhere to be seen.

Another mirage!

I rolled to my side and up to my feet, furious, and spun around. "Where are you?" I demanded. "*Where the fuck are you?*"

"Where's Exos?" Cyrus breathed, having misted to my side.

I pointed upward.

And Cyrus disappeared, only to reappear with my unconscious spirit mate in his arms.

"What happened?" he demanded.

I shook my head. "She's creating fucking visions."

Hell, for all I knew, Cyrus could be one. Except I felt in my soul that he wasn't, our bond thriving from our nearness.

Speaking of... I pressed my palm to Exos's chest, focusing on our connection to find him in the spirit realm. *There.*

He stood before the source, encased in power as Elana blasted him with magic that didn't belong here. It shook the core, disturbing the balance and causing Exos to fight for his footing.

I pulled away slowly, considering our options.

"We need to find Elana's body," I told Cyrus. "She's here somewhere. But we need to find her fast." Because from what I could see, Exos didn't have long until one of her foreign balls of energy pierced his armor.

And I didn't want to know what would happen then.

"I might be able to help with that," a soft voice said.

Mortus.

He held up his hands. "I promise she's not in my head. But I have certain memories of the last two decades. Or I think that's what they are. Honestly, they feel like dreams."

"Your point?" Cyrus demanded.

Mortus cleared his throat. "I, uh, I think I know where she is."

CHAPTER THIRTY-NINE
CYRUS

I DON'T TRUST HIM, Claire whispered into my thoughts.

Neither do I, I admitted. *But I don't sense any compulsion of his spirit.*

It could still be a mirage. She folded her arms, her eyes narrowing at Mortus. "Where do you think she is?" The skepticism in her tone wasn't lost on me or Mortus.

He flinched before replying, "There's a place in the forest, just beyond campus, that leads to an array of hidden tunnels."

My brow furrowed. "You want us to go underground? Where our elements don't work?" I snorted. "Yeah, that's going to happen." Plus, I wasn't even sure those tunnels existed. I'd never heard of such a thing, or seen them, and I knew these grounds forward and backward. When I said as much out loud, Mortus shook his head.

"I found them last week," he admitted, his voice low. "I kept dreaming of them and had to see if they were real. And, well, they are."

"And you didn't think to tell us that?" Claire snapped, taking the words out of my mouth.

He lifted his hands as if surrendering. "I... I didn't know they would be important. I... You don't know what it's like to not know what you've done, or who you are, or whom to trust, or to wake up in a world that's aged without you." His eyes met mine. "I remember your mother like it was yesterday, Cyrus. Like we just shared a spirit course together last week. I... I don't..." He shook his head, a deep sadness overrunning his typically stern features.

A twinge of pity radiated from my chest, only to be squashed by the weight in my arms.

My brother grew weaker with every passing second. I felt it as his soul fought with everything he had, against a force that was far more powerful than it should be, especially when faced with the wrath of the Spirit King. "Show us the entrance," I said, not yet seeing an alternative. If Mortus's words proved right, then we'd call upon Sol to unearth the entire maze.

Assuming he could take a break from slaughtering the dead.

Skeletal creeps had overrun the grounds, and they were fast little fuckers, too. Worse, they kept putting themselves back together. It didn't matter how many times Vox's team blew them apart; the damn bones seemed to just morph into new creatures that continued to cause havoc.

Shrugging off a foreboding chill, I gestured for Mortus to get moving. We'd be taking Exos with us because I didn't trust anyone to watch over him apart from me and Claire, and her mates were otherwise engaged. "Tell Vox and Titus where we're going."

"Already done," she replied, following Mortus. *I still think this is a bad idea. Do you have a better one?* I asked her.

No. She cast me a look, then glanced at Exos, her shoulders falling as guilt pierced our connection. *I shouldn't have left him.*

What do you mean? I demanded. *When did you leave?*

She informed me of what happened with her mother while we walked, her mental voice holding a touch of sorrow when she reached the end about the Fire Fae she'd accidentally destroyed.

Casualties are a consequence of war, I whispered, brushing her cheek with a mist-like kiss. *And fae are tougher than one might expect. They may have survived.*

You think?

We'll find out after we deal with Elana, I promised, my arms beginning to shake from the weight of carrying my brother.

At least he'd chosen a tower near the edge of the campus.

It meant we hadn't needed to walk very far until Mortus showed us the entrance—an entrance that was mysteriously void of the death creatures haunting the Academy grounds.

What do you think? Claire asked, eyeing the twisting trees.

An observer would see only that—two giant trunks mating at the earth to form a beautiful V with vines dancing up and around to decorate the limbs.

But Mortus pulled aside the shrub at its base to reveal an entrance only large enough for a person to crawl through.

I think there's no way in hell I'm letting you wander down there alone, I replied, frowning.

Which left me with a significant issue resting in my arms.

You can't carry Exos through that, she replied, noting the problem already spinning through my thoughts.

I know. And there was no way in hell I'd leave Exos under Mortus's care. *Can you reach out to Titus and Vox, ask one of them to bring Sol?*

Claire shook her head. *There isn't time, Cyrus. And I've already taken you away from the fray. The others need them.* She took a step forward to investigate the trees and the cavern they revealed below. *There's only one choice here.*

I disagree.

I know you do, she tossed back. *But you're also wrong.*

"*Claire.*" I laced her name with a warning.

"Take care of Exos," she said, stepping out of my reach. "I'll be back."

"Claire!" I set Exos down, prepared to grab her, but the little minx had already slithered into the damn hole. "*Fuck!*"

I'll be okay.

Not when you get back out here, you won't, I seethed, pacing before the entrance and ignoring Mortus's muttering. He offered to look after Exos, which was not happening. *Fuck, Claire! I'm going to beat your ass raw.*

That sounds arousing, she returned. *You promise?*

This isn't funny. Get back here.

I'm fine, she promised.

I glanced at Exos, then at the ground, and then back at Exos. "Blast the elements!" I hated the choice she'd left me with—leave my brother and help her, or trust her and guard him.

But she was underground.

Where she couldn't seek the elements.

Going fuck knew where.

Claire, I growled.

Stay there, she demanded, infuriating me more. *I might need your element.*

Which I couldn't access if I followed her into the tunnels. *I'm going to throttle you, woman!*

Promises, promises, she singsonged. *Now stop flirting and tell me how to kill Elana when I find her.*

CHAPTER FORTY
CLAIRE

CYRUS'S ROAR OF FRUSTRATION sent a chill down my spine.

Yeah, I'd pissed him off.

But we were out of time. One look at the spirit realm and he'd know that. Exos had put up one hell of a fight, but the darkness swarming around Elana was beginning to overpower him. I suspected it was because of me. Exos couldn't go full Spirit King without jeopardizing my access to the source, thereby weakening me. And the stubborn male would never allow that.

I knew, because I'd do the same.

We all sacrificed sanity for love.

Hence my presence in this ghastly tunnel.

Fortunately, it'd opened up after the entrance, allowing me to walk along the rocks rather than crawl. But I had no idea where this led, and the light down here was nonexistent.

A very small flame flickered over my fingertips, the passage not entirely underground. Or maybe that was wishful thinking, because I felt my elements draining with each step.

I paused, frowning. *Cyrus?* I asked, realizing he hadn't replied to my question about how to kill Elana.

Static flowed back at me.

Not good.

Either I was wrong about the depth of this maze or something had happened.

What if Mortus turned on him? I wondered, glancing backward, my feet caught between moving toward Elana to save Exos and retreating to check on Cyrus. *She's the source,* I thought, taking a breath. *If Mortus is under mind control again, it's because of Elana. The best way to save them both is to proceed.*

Killing her would protect them all.

I just hoped I wasn't too late.

Picking up my pace, I continued onward, searching with the flickers of my spirit energy for Elana's signature.

Nothing.

As if she were dead and buried. Because she couldn't access her elements down here?

My lips curled downward. Hmm, that wasn't right. Otherwise, she wouldn't be engaged in a battle with Exos right now.

Which meant that not only was she using her natural gifts but they were also strong.

I hastened my stride into a jog, determined. This had to lead to somewhere, a meadow or a field. An outside source that granted her access to the elements.

Unless we were completely wrong about this being her hiding place, in which case we were all royally fucked.

No.

I refused to think like that.

My heart warmed as I pushed on, my instincts taking over as I allowed the elements to guide me. A twinge of life here. A taste of earth there. And a fire that burned brighter with each step.

Yes.

This is the right way.

Somehow, I just knew. As if it were my fate leading me to the ultimate duel.

All my mates had gone quiet.

But I wasn't listening for them now.

Elana was who I sought, her black heart twisted with foul energy that didn't belong. Brushing my fingertips against the dirt-laden wall, I sensed it. A wrongness blossoming in the earth. Death lingering in her wake.

Closing my eyes, I began to walk again, tracing the tendrils of magic that soured my elements.

Until I entered an underground clearing filled with plants and flowers and a slotted roof with access to the air above.

I smiled, breathing in the core of my strength, my mates immediately rioting in my mind—their joint concern one I soothed with a thought to each of them. *I'm fine.* And what was more... *I found her.*

Lying on a stone.

Surrounded by snarling minions.

If this is another mirage, I'm going to lose my ever-loving mind, I thought, using my air magic to scatter the minions into pieces. Then engaged my earth to tie them to the ground, forbidding them from piecing themselves back together.

Elana came alive on a gasp, the threat of my presence yanking her out of the spirit plane. Something Exos and Cyrus both confirmed in my head, so I knew this was real.

Third time's the charm, I thought, smiling. "Hello, Elana."

Where are you? Cyrus demanded.

I stirred a geyser above us, shooting it high up into the sky as a signal of my location. *Here. And the demon is awake,* I added as Elana leapt to her feet.

"Mortus," she spat, clearly irritated.

I knew better than to let her talk or to gain the advantage.

So rather than listen to the words spewing from her lips, I created an ice pick and aimed it at her heart.

She diminished it with a wave of her hand, her control of water surprisingly strong. A similar weapon came back at me, one I barely blocked as I called on my fire for a shield.

Liquid rained from above, dousing my flames in an instant, and Elana sighed. "Harming children has never been an enjoyable activity, but it is an easy one."

My chest ached as she hit me with an invisible wave of power, knocking me backward and almost out of the small clearing. I called a gust of air to force me back into the center, requiring my elements, but Elana tripped me with a black tendril of thick smoke.

Shit! My ass hit the rocks, shooting pain up my spine.

"Ah, Claire," Elana murmured. "How young you truly are."

Ice pelted me from all sides, slicing through my clothes without preamble and digging into my skin.

I shrieked, spinning away from the foreign sensation that wasn't water yet resembled it.

But it didn't heed my call.

My fire tried to burn it away, creating an acid-like liquid that scalded my skin and elicited a scream from my throat.

Claire!

I couldn't tell which of my mates was shouting. Cyrus? Vox? Titus? A mixture of them all?

I curled onto my side, fighting the pain and relinquishing my hold on the elements just for a chance to breathe. Somehow Elana was using them against me. Turning my powers into harmful substances that hurt me rather than offering me protection.

"We could have been so good together, you and I," Elana continued, her icy power swathing me in a blanket of foreign energy. "But it's too late for that now. I see that the way to breaking Exos's hold is through your heart. Without you, he'll crumble. And I can take what is mine to take."

Exos, I breathed, sensing his pain through the bond.

Elana had come close to destroying him.

With my demise, she would complete the job. I felt it to the very core of my being. Because breaking our bond would distract him long enough for her to finish the job. And then she'd go after Cyrus. My other mates. The entire Academy. Everyone in the Elemental Fae Realm.

I sensed her plans in the dark power wrapping around me.

Her malevolent intentions to take everyone down who might stand in her way.

She'd gone mad with her vengeance. What had begun as a simple desire to protect herself—to not allow others to find out about her Midnight Fae half—had blossomed into this need for destruction.

With every soul she absorbed, she'd eaten at her own spirit. Diminishing it to dust beneath her craving for more power.

I almost felt bad for her. This couldn't have been her original intention, but now it consumed her.

Hatred.

Violence.

A desire to kill.

It all swam around her in inky waves, her heart no longer that of an Elemental Fae, but of a being overrun by her own dark energy.

Whoever Elana once was, she no longer resembled that woman now. She merely wore the facade on the outside, her mind a constant game of chess as she devised her next play.

Calculated.

Cunning.

Cruel.

Not an ounce of remorse inside her, not even for the lives she would take today. For the very academy she ran for all these years. A means to an end.

How I ever saw sympathy in her eyes was a miracle. A concept her savage spirit had crafted to lend to her plans. Which all led to the ruination of Elemental Fae kind.

I saw it all unfolding in the blink of an eye. Her devastating schemes. The way she used the death fields as a source of unbending power. The way she fed those fields with more souls—souls she'd taken through the use of death magic.

It sent a shiver down my spine.

"How can you even live with yourself?" I wondered out loud, shaking my head. "All those fae… you've taken them all." I saw with clarity what had happened to Ignis and her friends, how Elana had controlled them like she'd done with Mortus, forcing the girls to frame me for elemental crimes against their will. And then their resulting screams as Elana tossed them into the Spirit Kingdom, allowing the fields to swallow them whole. All the while absorbing their magic for herself—a magic Exos had bound, and then released upon being knocked out by Mortus.

Everything played out in full detail.

Unraveling all the moves I hadn't seen her make.

Setting my mother's decrepit soul in the mess of the others, allowing her to lie in wait, knowing full well that Cyrus would take me there. Elana's resulting laughter as Ophelia latched onto me as a source of life, our bloodlines calling to one another by instinct. My former mentor had reveled in that moment, enjoying the way I suffered at the spirit of my own mother, the manner in which I almost died.

However, I survived, a fact that intrigued Elana even more.

Mated Cyrus—a move she hadn't anticipated, but adored.

Meanwhile, Exos provided a challenge, one she tried to break by putting Ophelia in the cell beside his. Allowing her to feed on me through my connection to Exos. Only, the stubborn male cut me off, a fact Elana had respected and hated at the same time.

My head spun with the truth of it all, the explanations none of us had seen.

I blinked up at the devil incarnate in absolute horror, words lining up on my tongue that were meant to scathe. Only, she gazed at me with blank eyes, her entire form frozen, her magic a stagnant energy in the air.

It dissipated in a second, her rage coloring her cheeks in a putrid red shade. *"You dare enter my mind?"* she demanded, lashing out at me with a whip of power that scalded my insides.

I sucked in a breath, the air icy and cold. *What?*

My mouth couldn't form the word.

I'd entered her mind?

Of course, I realized. *That* was how I'd seen all her pieces, the perpetual chessboard calculating her every move.

Including the one I *knew* she'd make next.

I engaged my fire on instinct, flaring it bright in her eyes to catch her off guard while I dove into the spirit realm and directly for the source. It was the only way to overcome her dark hold.

I needed to fight her with *light*.

Exos brushed my spirit as I raced past him and leapt for the white energy I craved. It bathed me in a heat that could melt the sun. But my access to the other elements kept me grounded.

My fire roared to life in a protective wave.

My air whirled me in a motion that kept me moving even while everything else threatened to stop me.

My water soothed my aching bones, filled my soul with peace.

And my earth rooted me to the reality I needed to fight in.

All four combined with the most powerful of them all, bringing me to my feet on a surge of elements that sent Elana back several paces. I cocked my head, curious by her widening eyes.

Fear, a part of me recognized, my mind oddly detached from my emotions so that it seemed like a foreign concept. Yet I knew I liked it. Craved more of it.

I wrapped her in a rope of bronze laced with fire, not pausing even as she screamed.

Evil existed inside her.

Evil that needed to be eradicated.

Spirit Fae adore life and vitality. This one craved death. And it was my duty as Spirit Queen to give her what she desired.

The source of all the elements swarmed me, lifting me from the earth and to the field above. A field I vaguely recognized as the first place I met Titus.

Filled with flowers.

And happiness.

And a blossoming sun on the horizon.

How beautiful and perfect for the burial of this foul being.

"Spirit is both the essence of life and death," I said, not recognizing my voice at all, but hearing the power behind it, realizing that I myself somehow inhabited the core of the spirit.

No, not only spirit.

Air.

Water.

Fire.

Just not earth. Although, I sensed it waiting for me, welcoming me with flowery petals of warmth and sunshine.

How beautiful, I mused. *Hmm, but not yet.*

No, I had other sources to appease first. Specifically, spirit. It raged for the life before me, craving the death of such a vile fae.

"You abused our power," I seethed, again not recognizing my voice. So deep. Still feminine, but echoing as if for miles. Commanding. I liked it. But I did not like the woman cowering before me, tied up by my elemental rope.

"Claire…" The uncertainty in that familiar voice had me glancing sideways to where Cyrus stood. Exos at his side. I couldn't say who had spoken, but thought it might have been the Water Prince.

Mmm, my mates, I sighed, happy to see them both alive. The energy inside me rippled in its pleasure, bowing to the masters of their source, before refocusing on the task at hand.

Because today, I was queen.

And this poor excuse for a fae no longer deserved to live.

"The elements have spoken," I said, tightening the vines around her. "And you, Elana of Spirit Fae, will abuse us no longer."

Vitality rippled out of me, swathing her in a bright, white cloud. It absorbed her soul into its depths, taking her to a place where she would never escape or even be reborn. Her spirit too vile for any reconsideration.

And in its wake, it left the shadow of a Midnight Fae.

One that crumpled to the earth in a pile of black ash.

A breeze teased the remains, whirling them into the air as flames erupted, engulfing every speck and removing the existence of her form in all ways.

The elements taking their due.

Destroying every last bit.

And eliminating the death magic from the lands.

I sensed it in the frosty kiss of the air, the finality of her passing erasing any and all evidence of her previous existence.

Including the death fields.

Exos fell to his knees, the power lancing through his chest, but the source inside assured he would be fine.

Cyrus, too.

They would all survive.

But the spirits needed to ascend, and so I closed my eyes and willed it so. Freeing thousands upon thousands of fae from Elana's cruel captivity.

Fly, I encouraged them. *Fly and be reborn once more.*

For that was the cause of sterility among the Spirit Fae. Not a plague, but a curse maintained by Elana. Every spirit she fed to the darkness couldn't be reborn. And she wouldn't allow any of the others to move on, to complete the circle of life.

A tear slid from my eye at the understanding of it all, the workings of the universe laid out inside me as if it was my destiny all this time to absorb every detail.

Spirit.

Life and death.

The elemental core of our very existence.

I bowed before it, respecting the gifts given to me, thanking it for my creation, and promising never to abuse the energy thriving inside me.

Each element embraced my very soul, accepting the vow and returning me slowly to the new reality I'd created. The world I'd blessed. The kingdom I'd just saved.

To my mates.

My loves.

My fae.

CHAPTER FORTY-ONE
EXOS

CYRUS CAUGHT CLAIRE before she hit the ground, his ability to mist making me envious and grateful at the same time. Because she was out cold, her form a dainty feminine ball of power tucked against my brother's chest.

Icy blue eyes flashed up at me, his expression rivaling my own. "Did that just happen?" he demanded.

I swallowed twice before I could muster up a response. And it had nothing to do with how weak I felt from dueling Elana in the spirit plane. "I, uh, yeah. Yeah, it did."

Our mate had absorbed four elemental sources, her body flaring with a light that would have killed an ordinary fae. Yet she'd worn it like a queen, her hair glittering a white shade of power. I stepped forward to fondle the ash-blonde strands, the only remaining hint that what we'd just witnessed had truly come to pass.

Well, along with the vitality flowing all over the Academy grounds.

"She demolished them all," I marveled, gazing down at her beautiful face. "She did what we couldn't."

Because Elana's powers were far stronger than any of us could have anticipated. The way she used the elements against me—including my own—had weakened me beyond repair until Claire's timely intervention.

"I don't know how she did it," I continued. "But she absorbed all four cores of her bonded elements, even flirted with earth there for a moment. And then they spoke through her."

Cyrus brushed his lips against her forehead, smiling. "Because she's our queen."

"Yes." I combed my fingers through her hair again, preparing to say more as Mortus stumbled into the clearing, his expression one of bewilderment and confusion. It seemed to be his permanent mask these days, the poor bastard.

"Thank you," Cyrus said to him now, nodding his head once. "Your help today has not gone unnoticed."

"She's gone," he whispered, staring at the hole in the earth created by our Claire. "She's truly gone." He didn't sound sad, exactly. More broken. As if he'd hoped that Elana's disappearance would heal him somehow. It would take a lot more than that evil woman's death to mend the wounds she left behind on his soul.

Claire began to stir, her energy humming around us in a calming wave that soothed my heart.

"At least she didn't stop breathing this time," Cyrus mused.

I chuckled. "There is that." I pressed a kiss to her cheek and released her hair. "Mist her back to the quad. The others will need to see that she's all right."

Cyrus nodded his agreement, disappearing and leaving me alone with Mortus. His black gaze lifted to mine, a hint of worry fluttering in the depths as he swallowed.

"I should punish you," I said, walking toward him. "For everything you've done."

"I know." He swallowed again. "I would accept it, too, my king."

Pausing before him, I considered my options for the thousandth time this week. He'd kidnapped me, hurt me, and committed countless sins over the years, all beneath the compulsion of Elana.

Many would call for his castigation, regardless of his control over the acts.

Same with Ophelia—who, as far as I could tell, was completely innocent in her crimes. But two decades of rumors would be hard to assuage.

However, it did give me an idea.

"Walk with me," I said, leading him along the trail back to the Academy grounds. This place brought back memories of my first days with Claire, her emotions running high due to the guilt over killing her friend and the very real impact of being uprooted from her world.

Seeing her performance this morning had proven just how much she'd grown.

How powerful she'd become.

My lips curled, knowing I played a small part in her ascension. Or maybe a large part. Regardless, the majority of it was Claire. Her determination, strength, and stubbornness were what won over the elements. That they chose to favor her with their gifts merely indicated the powerful future ahead of her.

A future I was thankful to be a part of.

My access to the source burned bright inside me, pleased with my acceptance of my mate, while also fortifying my position as king.

But everyone knew a king was nothing without his queen.

Mortus stumbled over a root, the early morning sun not yet brightening our horizon. I teased a flame into the air, highlighting the ground as we moved, my mind spinning over the idea that had come to me moments ago.

"Do you feel any connection to Ophelia?" I wondered out loud.

I felt his wince more than saw it. "Yes," he admitted, his voice gruff.

"What level?" I pushed aside a low branch and watched as he moved through the passageway I'd created.

He paused to allow me to lead once more, a sign of both submission and reverence. Good. It was high time he recognized me as his king.

Of course, all those hostile moments on the Council weren't him at all, but Elana playing him like a puppet.

I nearly sighed, agitated with her once more. The image of Claire shredding her with elements, however, appeased my inner vengeance. Elana had more than deserved the pain of being ripped apart by the spirit source. Had I been able to do such a thing, I would have in an instant. But it was Claire whom our spirit chose as the conduit.

"I... I'm not sure what level we're on," Mortus eventually said, drawing me back to the path we were walking upon. "I can sense our link, but it's frayed to hell."

"Because she broke the vows of a third level," I murmured, nodding.

"No." Mortus cleared his throat. "Because it was compelled, not willingly given. On both sides."

"Interesting." I mused over that in silence for several minutes, pleased to see the grounds appearing through the forest ahead—the dimming moon still shining across the lively grass. "Elana compelling you two to bond defied the elements, which caused the rift of power." I almost admired the clever bitch. Almost. But I despised her a hell of a lot more. "And she used that distraction to her advantage by sucking the souls of all the Spirit Fae in attendance on that fateful day."

"During our ceremony, yes," Mortus said.

"You remember?" I asked, glancing at him.

He shook his head. "Not exactly. But enough people have told me what happened."

We stepped onto the path that led back to the Academy, a warm energy caressing the fields and leaving a hint of Claire's sweet scent behind.

She smiled into my thoughts, our connection thriving stronger than ever.

You're okay, she whispered.

Thanks to you, my queen, I replied softly, my lips curling. I didn't ask if she was awake. I already knew, could feel her vitality sweeping through the air all around us.

What happened to 'princess'? Her amusement touched my chest, causing my heart to beat in time with hers.

My princess became a queen, I told her. *No, a goddess of the elements.*

I don't know how it happened, she admitted. *It just... did.*

You were favored by the source, Claire. Thereby completing the prophecy our Council once feared. *When one becomes half and five become one, a plague will descend upon the fae. Only death is the cure.*

For so long, our kind thought it meant the end to the Elemental Fae race. But that wasn't it at all. Claire was the cure—the one to bring death upon the plague otherwise known as Elana.

No one ever told me the prophecy. I could picture her frown matching her internal voice. *Why did you all keep it from me?*

Because it never mattered, I replied. *You chose your fate, Claire. Not some prophecy proclaimed by the Fortune Fae.*

It might have helped to know I was destined to absorb a bunch of energy and kill Elana, she countered, her sassiness causing me to chuckle.

Would it have made a difference? I wondered back at her. *Truly? Because I think you would have done exactly what you did regardless of some words hanging over your head. Or perhaps you would have acted differently and changed fate.* I shrugged even though she couldn't see it. *Either way, you were exquisite, my queen.*

She seemed to be mulling over my comment, just as Mortus was with my earlier statement about Elana using his compelled bond to create a distraction.

"I want you to help Ophelia," I told him as we walked through the Academy's iron gates. "Help her heal and I'll consider your debt repaid."

He glanced at me, his shock written in the lifting of his eyebrows. "You think I can help her?"

"I think you might be one of the only ones who can, Mortus." I paused on the precipice of the quad, admiring the joyous chaos unfolding among the fae with their savior, Claire, at the center. Cyrus, Sol, Titus, and Vox stood around her like warriors protecting their queen. But Claire wouldn't be deterred, her magic spreading among the masses to offer healing and acceptance to everyone around her.

Just like the queen I knew her to be.

"Why?" Mortus asked, drawing me back to our conversation—one I was ready to end in favor of embracing my mate. "Why do you think I can help her?"

"Because of the bond," I replied. "I can see your spirits, Mortus. They're linked in a fractured way, suggesting that not only can you assist her in healing but she can also return the favor and mend you. If you allow it."

"If *she* allows it," he returned.

I hid my smile. "Yes, I imagine she'll be quite stubborn." Like mother, like daughter. "Hence, it's a fitting punishment, don't you think?" Winking at him, I took my leave with a casual, "I couldn't go too easy on you, old man," tossed over my shoulder. "May the fates be with you." Because he was going to need all the luck he could get.

The circle parted for me as I approached Claire and the pink butterflies swarming around her. One kissed my cheek, earning me a flirty little smirk from the queen in the center.

I hauled her into my arms, reveling in the spirit energy overflowing from her center, and kissed her hard for all to see. She giggled against me, her arms winding around my neck. *Arrogant king,* she accused.

Glorious queen, I whispered back at her, nipping her lower lip. *Have I told you today that I love you?*

Only once.

I smiled against her mouth. *I love you, my Claire.*

I love you, too.

Thank you for being the queen we all need, I added, pressing my forehead to hers. "Goddess Claire."

"Our future Water Queen," Cyrus said, adding his own flavor to the mix.

"With air royalty flowing all around her," Vox mused, his breeze kissing her cheek.

Titus pressed a palm to her lower back. "And a fire that burns brighter than the sun."

"All that's missing now is earth," I said, glancing at the giant beside us.

He wrapped his hand around Claire's neck, his earthy gaze flaring with intent. "Not for much longer."

She smiled up at him, the sun in her blue eyes. "Not for much longer," she repeated, accepting his mouth against hers as a binding promise.

And stirring more of those beautiful butterflies all over the quad.

We won, I thought, taking in the light glistening on the horizon. *And today is a new day to shine.*

Part V

"In the aftermath of destruction, new life breathes restoration and hope into the most compelling of futures. And I couldn't be more proud."

–Ophelia

CHAPTER FORTY-TWO
CLAIRE

"I, CLAIRE, ACCEPT THE POWER that binds me to Sol, born of Earth," I said, holding my intended's gaze. "To cherish and respect, through all the eras and time that may fall before us, until our souls do us part."

His smile grew with each word, the World Tree beside us seeming to hum its approval.

Sol pressed my hand to the base of our tree, the roots thriving with my mate's power. The influx made me suck in a breath as raw life surged through my veins.

The musk of earth enveloped me, exploring and glorifying in our pairing. My missing piece. The one source I couldn't access. My final connection.

We didn't have an Earth Fae priest to guide us through our vows, only the element itself. The earth touched my heart and gave me the words I needed to say. Although, I had most of them memorized by now.

I opened my eyes to find Sol gazing down at me in wonder as vines danced all around us, sprouting flowers from my world as well as from his in a flurry of color. My other mates kept their distance but would witness this bond with us, the final seal on all five elements.

Inside the oasis Sol had crafted.

With the afternoon sun shining overhead.

Healing energy flourished around us, the campus grounds restoring themselves from the hurt inflicted upon them by Elana's dead army. We lost lives today. They would not be forgotten. I felt the breaths of their souls warming the spirit plane, their circle of life flowing the way it should, and blessing the union occurring today.

The one to my earth mate.

Flowers whispered the words on a breeze, encouraging me to continue my vows.

But I already knew what was needed; I'd merely chosen to bask in the beautiful moment, to absorb the elemental bliss dancing around us.

"I give unto him my unyielding promise, my vitality, and the seed of my heart, which, together, we will nurture and grow, and accept his in return. My element is now his just as his is now mine, to the fae heavens may we never part. And I shall never forsake him for another, my earth forever belonging to him and to him alone."

He palmed my cheek, his opposite hand remaining above mine and pressed to the base of our tree as we lounged in the flower bed he'd created for this moment.

Water trickled nearby, courtesy of Cyrus's fountain.

Flames twirled in an arch several feet away, one we'd walked beneath to reach this special place in our oasis.

A light breeze filled with love tousled our hair.

And the Spirit King blessed our union in the plane harboring our souls.

My earth mate grinned, his happiness an aphrodisiac that heightened the moment almost as much as his vows did. Each word was low, purposefully uttered, and rumbled across the ground beneath his intense power.

I shivered.

Smiled.

Leaned into him for more.

And closed my eyes as the sweet embrace of energy from the earth flowed over me, encasing me in the element I so craved.

It was the piece I needed all this time, its healing essence making me one with this world.

Fire.

Water.

Air.

Spirit.

And finally, earth.

Sweet, sweet earth.

I sighed, reveling in the finality of the bonds, my lips seeking Sol's with a hunger only he could sate. My mates would protect us, would give us this moment, would allow us to prosper beneath the bright blue sky.

Our bond slid into place like two pieces of stone carved for one another.

The butterflies clothing my being fled, revealing all of me to Sol's gaze. "Don't make me wait," I whispered, my fingers sliding through his thick hair as I pulled him down on top of me, my head cradled by the flowers decorating the tree roots. "Take me, Sol. Don't hold back."

His mouth responded without words, his tongue parting my lips to devour me.

I love you, he said into my mind, his voice a welcome presence that had me clinging to him more.

I love you, too.

His clothes seemed to disappear beneath my hands. Or perhaps magic. I couldn't tell, too eager to consummate our mating, to slide that final piece into my soul.

It'd been missing today when I danced among the elements.

My earth felt so far away and still did.

Something was holding us back.

A broken quality that required healing.

"Sol," I whispered, my thighs parting to accept him. "Please."

I needed all of him. His heart. His mind. His *soul.*

I opened everything of me to him in return, urging him to let go, to find his peace and accept our mating. But I could feel his struggle, the part of him with errant control that required soothing. Jagged spikes littering his spirit, caused by an unknown fae.

My heart longed to soothe them. To smooth out the rough edges and help him recover.

He pressed his forehead to mine, his breath harsh. "What are you doing to me?"

"Loving you." I laved his bottom lip, my gaze finding his. "You're mine, Sol."

His palm encircled my throat, his erection prodding the entrance of my waiting heat. "And you're mine."

"I am," I agreed, my back bowing off the ground as he slid all the way inside me, his penetration perfect, demanding, and so very powerful. "Take me," I urged again. "Give me everything."

Because I needed to feel him. His strength. His force. His pain. His happiness. His fears. No more hiding. No more fighting for control. We were in this together now, and I showed him that with my element, the ground quaking beneath us in affirmation.

More flowers blossomed.

Life sang all around us.

Peaches ripened.

Trees sprouted fresh leaves.

And not just here, but all over campus, our power lending healing energy where the Academy required it most.

"Mate me, Sol," I told him. Because I felt him holding back. Knew this wasn't the best he could do.

He trembled, his restraint causing the ground to shake beneath me. "I don't want to break you, Claire."

I drew in some of his magic, mixing it between us so that there wasn't just Sol or Claire, but two branches of a single tree that needed nourishment. "You can't," I assured him. "Fuck me, Sol. Show me that you trust me."

His eyes widened, the bronze irises flecking with the emerald magic of his vitality and life. "You really are a goddess," he whispered, his expression one of reverence as our bodies joined below in a matrimony as old as time itself.

I felt like a nymph come to life.

Bedded in flowers and earth, my screams echoing off the branches around us, vines growing and flourishing beneath the power our bodies created as one.

He pulled out, then drove in hard, making the World Tree shake under the impact. My body blossomed with pleasure as I took his brute force. I was just as much an Earth Fae as any other element, and my body attuned itself to his.

"So delicate and strong," he praised as he thrust again, this time with more confidence.

I clawed my nails down his arms, leaving marks that sparkled under the sun. I closed my eyes and threw my head back, enduring the pleasure that filled me up from the inside. "More," I pleaded, and Sol gave it to me, pounding into me until my words turned into screams of ecstasy.

His climax pushed me over, his seed filling me and providing the final claim to my body that sent me over the edge.

Sol, my foundation, my rock.

I love you.

A momentary stillness of peace overcame us as Sol's spirit brushed against mine, linking us together for eternity.

Complete, I thought with a sigh. *Finally.*

Peace settled inside me, only to be disturbed by the fracturing of Sol's essence all around me. A wall tumbling beneath the power of our mating.

Sending us spiraling into the depths of a nightmare.

Of a sequence of events long buried.

By the source itself.

CHAPTER FORTY-THREE
CYRUS

Several Minutes Earlier

"SHE'S HIGH ON HER ELEMENTS," I mused to Exos from our posts outside of Sol's little oasis.

Our little queen had decided to consummate her earth bonds directly following the ceremony, her ethereal energy still high and floating around her in this intoxicating cloud of vitality.

"How long do you think it will last?" I continued, pondering out loud. "Or is this a permanent change?"

He chuckled and shook his head. "I don't know. I imagine it'll become a mixture of both."

I nodded. "Good. I would hate for her to lose that fiery temper of hers."

"No, she'll probably just set you on fire instead," my brother replied conversationally.

"And I hope to be there to watch," Titus added, approaching from the side. He'd run off to check on Claire's mom and the Fire Fae stationed to guard her. From his expression, I could tell we had a problem. "Did you send Mortus to talk to Ophelia?"

"Ah, yeah." Exos palmed the back of his neck. "I'm hoping he can break through to her, you know, using the bond."

"Well, she's screaming," Titus replied. "But not out of fear." His lips curled just a touch. "Seems she's not Mortus's biggest fan."

"No idea why," I drawled.

"Yeah, well, I'm gonna give them some space to work out their differences." A flame flickered across the Fire Fae's fingertips. "I'll only intervene if needed."

I looked him up and down, amused and a little aroused. "You endear yourself to me more every day, Fire Fae."

He snorted. "Not a chance in hell, Water Prince."

Exos just shook his head. "You should know better than to give my brother a challenge. He always wins."

"Yeah? Like that time in the powerless ring?" He feigned a thoughtful expression. "Oh, right, I won that, didn't I?"

"Because I let you win," I reminded him.

"So you say." He arched a brow. "I'm ready for a rematch—a real one— when you are."

"Can we focus on putting the Academy back together first?" Vox interjected, a breeze floating around him as he landed before us. The Air Fae had developed a knack for flying, one that intrigued me. I still preferred my misting, but I'd never seen a fae manipulate air currents the way this one did.

"What's the damage?" Exos asked, his expression turning serious.

"Sixteen known deaths. Several dozen injured and recovering." Vox palmed the back of his neck. "Fighting in the main quad was smart, as it isolated the majority of the damage, but there's quite a bit of it."

Exos frowned. "I thought Claire's date with the source released enough vitality to restore the grounds."

Vox shook his head. "She rid the Academy of those dark remnants, but the buildings themselves are in bad shape." He glanced at the oasis. "And, well, what they're doing right now is revitalizing the agonized earth elements throughout campus. So mating Sol was a good call."

"She made that choice, not us," I said, admittedly amused by our little queen's decision. She truly had blossomed into the epitome of a fae creature, following her elemental heart before her human mind. And I couldn't be more proud.

"Regardless, it's helping. But they're going to need a lot more than earth to restore the Academy." Vox sounded tired. "We need to work together as a unit."

"You say that as if it's a tedious task we can't handle," Exos replied, his lips twitching. "I think we've proven to perform as quite the unit, yeah? So maybe we should put on a little show for the Academy."

"Spoken with the arrogance of a king." I waggled my brows. "When do we start?"

My brother's smile was infectious. "Right now." He met Vox's gaze. "You stand guard for a bit, make sure no one sees our mate in the throes of passion. Titus, Cyrus, and I will go have a play on the Academy grounds."

"There's a squadron of Air Fae awaiting orders." Vox folded his arms. "I'm sure you won't have any trouble taking command."

"I think I can handle them," Exos agreed. "And if not, I'll give them to Cyrus."

My lips curled. "Today just keeps getting better and better."

As if Claire agreed, I felt her ecstasy through the bond, her waves of pleasure stirring goose bumps up and down my arms. *Mmm, my little queen.* How I adored her climaxes, even the ones not gifted by me.

The pause from the others confirmed they'd felt it, too.

All four of us were aroused by what was happening beneath that World Tree.

It would be so easy to join them, to add our own personal touch to the mix, but Sol had earned this. It was his time with Claire, and none of us would interrupt such a beautiful moment.

"Yeah, a distraction sounds great," Titus said, breaking the silence. "Let's, uh, go."

"Feeling a little hot?" I teased. "Allow me to help with that."

Mist pebbled across his skin, sizzling beneath his own power. "Not happening, Water Prince," he gritted out between his teeth.

But I caught the subtle flush to his cheeks.

Oh, this would be fun.

Whether anything would ever come of it remained to be seen. Merely taunting him satisfied me immensely.

But it was Claire whom I adored and loved. If she ever wanted to play, I'd happily indulge her. And despite Titus's opinions to the contrary, I suspected he'd gladly succumb as well.

Fortunately, we had a long and prosperous future ahead to work out the finer details.

Another rumble of the earth sent us all running ahead on a chuckle.

Until the rumble turned into a quake.

And our Claire screamed.

Directly into our minds.

CHAPTER FORTY-FOUR
CLAIRE

FALLING.

Pain.

Suffering.

The World Tree guided me through the chaos of Sol's heart, a place where black, spiked vines wrapped around a pulsing core.

Trapped memories that festered and bled, leaving an acrid stench in my nostrils that reminded me all too much of Elana and her evil.

Even in death, she haunted me.

I reached out and touched the darkness, bleeding my vitality into it and forcing the inky sickness to unravel and release its hold on my mate.

The memories unfurled in a tumult of agony, taking me under in its sea of sorrow that had dwelled in my Earth Fae's heart for far too long.

And when I opened my eyes, I was no longer Claire.

But Sol.

* * *

A Spirit Fae with silver eyes towered over me at the front door, her hair pulled up tight at the top of her head. She kinda looked important. But she wasn't supposed to be here. "You gotta leave," I told her. Mom wasn't home, but she'd be back soon.

The lady didn't smile.

She sort of growled.

Her presence was dark and wicked and not quite right. I didn't like her.

"Get out of my way, child," the woman sneered, lashing at me with magic.

Spirit magic.

Mom once warned me about the Spirit Fae. She said they could control other fae. Fae like me. But most didn't. Most were good. At least according to my mom.

But I could tell this lady was bad. And not just 'cause of the way she looked at me. Her black cloak seemed weird, and she smelled funny.

"Move," she demanded once more.

"No," I said, folding my arms. "I'm not gonna." My mom said not to let any strangers in the house while she was out with my little sister. She called me the man of the house. And this lady wasn't gonna come in no matter what.

She sighed. "Why do children never listen?" Her hand cracked the side of my face, sending me into the nearest wall with a loud thud.

I gasped.

My legs wobbled.

Black spots messed with my eyes.

'Cause that hurt! A lot.

But the scream from Aflora in the living room hurt more.

"No!" I shouted, trying to find her. She was supposed to be hiding. I told her to when I saw the weird lady standing outside. But Aflora was always soooo difficult, refusing to listen. Even to my mom, who was supposed to be her mom now. I didn't really get that. But now wasn't the time.

Mom put me in charge of Aflora.

She was too small to fight on her own.

I ran into the other room, the ground seeming to vibrate beneath me, and found my new sister against the wall with the evil woman's hand locked around her throat. Aflora clawed at the lady's arm like a wild animal, her stark blue eyes flaring with fear and fury.

"Finally," the woman said. Smoke twirled around her finger in a tendril of foreign magic that didn't belong here. "Your parents did a good job of hiding you, little girl, but I have you now. The final Earth Fae Royal. Mine to devour and destroy."

The smoke turned into a thick rope, swirling in the air and unsettling the earth magic in the room.

It was very wrong.

It didn't belong.

I wanted it gone.

With a stomp of my foot, the ground shook beneath the woman, knocking her off-balance. Aflora squirmed at exactly the right moment, jumping away from the crazy lady and sprinting toward me in the doorway.

"You want to touch my sister, you gotta go through me." I called for a root to wrap around my feet, forcing the earth to hold me upright as Aflora hid her little body behind

mine. She grabbed my sides, her fear shaking us both like leaves in a breeze.

The Spirit Fae turned, her gaze narrowed. "You're a brave but foolish little boy. No royal blood. No Academy training. Nothing that's worthy of my time." She flicked her wrist, sending a wave of magic infused with darkness to stab into my chest.

Pain shot through me, causing me to bend forward, but my roots kept me standing. Darkness spread from the black dagger lodged into my chest.

"Sol!" Aflora cried out, her grip on me tightening as her earth essence clung to mine.

It burned.

Fought off something on my behalf.

And grew.

Too much.

Too bright.

The source, I realized. Aflora somehow had access to it, even though she was a girl. They taught us in school that it was a boy's power. Yet somehow she was giving it to me. And I latched on with all my might, needing the energy not to save myself but to save her.

Because deep down I knew this lady was here to destroy my new sister.

And as man of the house, I couldn't let that happen.

The lady roared in disapproval, causing my lips to curl. 'Cause that just meant I'd done something right. Or maybe it was Aflora.

Either way, this lady had chosen the wrong house to barge into.

She scowled as another burst of fresh power rooted itself inside me, protecting me and forming a barrier around the darkness that had iced over my heart. It burned cold and painful, but layers formed over my insides as I straightened once more.

"What is this?" the woman demanded, slashing another wave of magic at me again.

This time it pinged off of the shield the source had built for me—for me and Aflora—a barrier that nothing could penetrate, not even the darkness the Spirit Fae sent my way.

"You can't have my new sister," I said, curling my fingers into fists as the ground around us began to shake. I'd always been strong, but now renewed energy flooded in without any sign of stopping. It frightened me, but I didn't let that show on my face.

The evil lady growled, the darkness swimming around her in that odd black cloak. "If I can't have your new one, I'll take your old one. And your mom, too. Unless the source seeks to protect them, too?"

As if hearing the lady's words, my mom came running into the house with my little sister at her side. Both their eyes wide. "Elana," my mother gasped. "What are you doing here?"

"I was trying to tie up a loose end, but your son has shown exquisite strength." She narrowed her silver eyes at me. "Much to the cost of everyone else around you."

I gulped. That sounded bad. But everything should be okay now, right? Mom was home. She'd make this evil lady leave.

She sighed loudly, her cheeks puffing with the motion. "Well, it seems the Earth Fae's source is still beyond my reach. For now." She stroked her black cloak. "No matter. I'm a patient woman, and I'm happy to do this the hard way." She grinned, the expression making me sick to my stomach. Because it was me she grinned at. Not my mom. Not my *sisters. But me. "Mark my words, boy. Your family. Your friends. Everyone you've ever loved will wither and die before your eyes. You won't even know why, or how. You'll just know that this all started with you."*

She extended a crooked finger, making a shiver go through my bones with the force of her prophecy. She wasn't a Fortune Fae, but I felt the weight of her promise just as much as any dark premonition the ominous fae could supply.

I said something.

Or thought it.

But the words were lost to sudden darkness that overcame the room.

Only to be disturbed by a scream that came from deep inside my house.

My concentration faltered as I turned toward it. Aflora gripped my wrist, trembling, all the fight bleeding out of her as fear filled her eyes. "Sol, what's going on?"

I tried to reply.

But I couldn't.

I... I couldn't remember.

Wasn't there someone here? Someone bad?

I turned again, spinning toward that dark, weighty feeling of spirit magic and wrongness. Nothing.

Dread crept over me in a sickening wave as I took Aflora's hand. "Let's go inside," I told her, the words tasting wrong in my mouth. I thought we were already inside?

My torso burned hot as if I'd been branded with fire, but I straightened as Aflora looked to me for confirmation. She felt it, too. Something terrible had happened, but neither of us knew what or why.

I scratched at my aching chest, which felt like it might split in two, as I went inside and found my mother and sister collapsed on the floor with strange, dark veins writhing under their skin.

And froze as Aflora screamed.

Because somehow, I knew, this had all been my fault.

I just didn't know why.

CHAPTER FORTY-FIVE
SOL

I WOKE WITH A START, feeling lighter than I ever had before despite the dark weight of my memories pressing at my soul.

Because I remembered everything.

Every detail of how it felt.

It was never a Spirit Fae that scarred my soul, but the earth source itself. To protect me against Elana's dark magic. To help me guard Aflora. To strengthen me with direct access to the element, then block me from ever taking on too much.

And then it had blocked my memory of everything that happened to hide the truth from me until I was ready to face it.

With Claire by my side.

She blinked up at me with tears streaming down her cheeks. She'd been there, revisiting my memories with me, the source as our guide. Leaving me with the full access of a royal fae, my element finally feeling balanced inside me for the first time in my life.

All because of Claire.

She was my balance, my mate who could absorb the weight of my past and guide me into the future. To help shoulder my burden, stabilize my growing power, and keep me grounded.

"Do you think Aflora knows?" Claire breathed, her blue eyes still ripe with tears.

I shook my head. "No. She has no recollection of that night." And something told me the core of our element wasn't ready to tell her yet.

Because that night with Elana was only the tip of the iceberg on Aflora's past.

How I knew that, I couldn't say. I just did. Courtesy of the source, most likely. It would tell her in time, perhaps when she found a mate of her own. I would be there for her, as a big brother, but I sensed it wouldn't be me she needed when that time came. Or our element would have given us both the truth long ago.

Sighing, I snuggled my mate to my chest and held her tight.

Vines, blooms, and an array of foliage and soil caked in all around us, having formed a cocoon during the healing. I sensed concern emanating from the mate-circle. It was strange to feel them so clearly now that I'd been fully bonded to Claire. Testing out the connection, I sent out a wave of reassurance that we were okay.

An echo of relief returned, but they were watching over us until we were ready to unearth ourselves from our bonding cocoon.

"That's new," Claire mused, nuzzling my neck.

"What is?"

"The five of you being able to communicate," she replied. "Or whatever that was."

"You couldn't do that before?"

"Oh, I could. I can speak to all of you mentally. But the circle has never been able to communicate collectively, at least not as clearly as that."

"Interesting." I drew in a deep breath, for the first time feeling whole. Not just because of Claire and my element, but because of them all.

How wrong I'd been about Cyrus and Exos. I could sense it now, their powerful energy a hive of strength for our mating circle.

Titus was the fire that inflamed all our passions, heightened our emotions, and resembled the glue between us all. Even though I doubted he'd ever admit it.

And Vox represented the practical branch, his intelligence and cunning providing us all with the voice of reason and control. Our personal Air Fae philosopher. I would enjoy having this close access to his mind.

A fun task for another day.

Because now, I just wanted to be with my Claire. To revel in our pairing and the element surrounding us.

"Part of me wishes Elana wasn't dead," Claire admitted. "Just so that I could kill her all over again."

I chuckled and stroked my mate's hair, untangling the small blooms that had grown within the strands. "She's gone, thanks to you. And now I know what really happened that day." My chest was still heavy with the memory, but it felt good to know, to actually remember.

Claire stroked my cheek as she gazed up at me. "Elana was trying to make her way through the royal lines. What do you think she was aiming to accomplish?" She frowned. "Other than spreading death and disease."

"She wanted the source," I said, caressing my mate's shoulder. It was the only explanation. "And she didn't just want one element; she wanted them all. I suspect she desired ultimate control over our kind, which would require the power of all five elements."

Claire flinched. "I guess that's why I was so attractive to her as a protégé." I nodded. "Indeed."

Claire let out a long sigh as she nuzzled into me and closed her eyes. "Does it still hurt? What the source did to protect you."

I rubbed at my chest. "For the first time since I can remember, the pain is dulled. It's still there." There would always be scars. "But it's not cutting into me anymore. It feels like I can finally heal now." Mostly because I had my access to the source again, the shield it had created no longer a barrier between me and my power.

"What was it like—seeing what happened to me?" I wondered out loud. "I could feel your presence but didn't see you."

"Because I was you," she said quietly. "I lived through the memory as if I were a seven-year-old Sol."

"There's a scary thought," I mused. "Not a good place for you to be, Claire."

She giggled and shook her head. "I doubt it'll be a common occurrence, unless there are more memories locked up in that head of yours?"

"Hopefully not," I replied. Of course, I wouldn't know for sure, but at this point, I doubted any of the others mattered. "But I suspect there are several hidden in Aflora's mind."

Claire glanced up at me. "What do you mean?"

I shook my head. "It's an instinct awoken by my contact with the source. It's done something to her, or perhaps her parents are to blame. But there's a history there."

"Like why she came to live with you?"

"Yes, like that." Because it was never really explained to any of us. "Our mothers were best friends, but I never actually met Aflora's parents. I assumed all this time that they died from the plague, but given Elana's struggle against me and the source—as a seven-year-old—I have to wonder how true that is."

"And if perhaps they hid her for another reason entirely," my mate added.

"Yes." Which meant Aflora's story wasn't finished yet. Not nearly. "We shouldn't try to unlock her memories, though. Or even hint at them." Because she had never displayed any of the signs that I had. Aflora was funny, light-spirited, and a stubborn thorn when she wanted to be. I didn't want to do anything to change that.

Claire squeezed her arms around me as far as she could. "I agree. The elements will tell her when they're ready." She kissed my chin. "Let's sleep, just for a little while longer, before you dig us out." She glanced at our makeshift roof, a smile curving her lips.

I chuckled, looking up through the tangle of vines that blocked the sky. "Or we could just stay here forever."

Claire awarded me with a soft laugh. "My other mates might not appreciate that."

I hummed. "Perhaps not."

We held each other, reveling in our love while I also reveled in the light suffusing my soul.

All thanks to Claire, my mate, my heart, my rock. She'd chased away my darkness. For good.

Chapter Forty-Six
Claire

Two Weeks Later

I STUDIED THE FINAL BUILDING on our tour and nodded. "It's done."

"Yeah," Exos agreed, his palm at the base of my spine. "Good as new."

"Minus the Chancellor's house," I added. We hadn't bothered to reconstruct that monstrosity. "And the Spirit Quad is looking a little less dusty." *And a lot more alive,* I thought as a butterfly fluttered by my nose.

Sol had helped me spread seeds all over the campus, creating new life in every corner to help improve the vitality among campus. He'd also assisted Cyrus in creating a series of fountains—a combination of Sol's rocks as the foundation and Cyrus's water element for the visual art. Vox had managed reconstruction with his squadron, the Air Fae using their wind to lift heavy Earth Fae–crafted boulders for the Fire Fae to weld together.

It took a literal village, but the Academy had never looked so beautiful. "What's the verdict from the new Council?" I asked my spirit mate. There'd been an emergency gathering among all the royals—new and old—this morning to discuss the fate of the school. While I was invited, I'd chosen not to attend in favor of helping Sol, Titus, and Vox around campus. My elements craved a release more than a political meeting.

"We'll reopen in the next term, which would be similar to a human university in the autumn." He brushed a wisp of my hair behind my ear and pressed a kiss to my cheek. "They've agreed to allow the four of you to graduate early, but there are some conditions that come with the allowance."

With the Academy not reinstating itself this year, it left Vox, Titus, Sol, and me in limbo. So Exos and Cyrus had agreed to ask for a waiver that allowed us to call our education complete. It seemed strange since I'd only attended the Academy for a few months, but the whole purpose was to master my elements. And the last few weeks had more than proven that task to be accomplished.

"What are their terms?" I asked.

"Well, first, they've asked me to take over as temporary Chancellor and Head of the Council," he said, his tone suggesting just how he felt about that. "Apparently, I've shown great leadership in my young years."

My lips curled. "They're not wrong, Exos."

"Yes, that remains to be seen." He heaved a breath, his acceptance of the requirement evident in that gesture alone. Exos was a man of duty. If the fae requested his leadership, he would give it, if nothing else but to protect those he loved. Like me and Cyrus and our mate-circle.

I pressed my palm to his chest, allowing him to fold me into his arms. "What else do they want?"

"You," he replied softly, his ocean-blue eyes glittering with challenge. "Specifically, your connection to the elements. They say it makes you a fine Advisor to the Council—a title they made up this morning that essentially means you'll function as a conduit between them and the core of our powers. Any decision they make, they want to run by you for approval."

"Approval from the elements," I translated, frowning. "They make it sound as if I can speak to them."

"Can't you?" Exos countered, palming my cheek and drawing his thumb across my lip. "You have access to all five sources. It's likely that your instincts would tell you if the Council made a decision that went against our elemental cores."

I swallowed, considering.

A shallow dive into my spirit showed a series of bright stars awaiting my command, all flashing their approval, knowing I would never do anything to abuse them.

"My goddess Claire," Exos mused, having followed me along that path, his spirit right beside mine, his mouth at my ear. "As you said, love, they're not wrong." His lips against my temple drew me back to the quad, my gaze capturing and holding his.

"What else do they want?" Because in that brief touch of our spirits, I sensed there was more. These were just the two biggest concessions.

"Vox, Sol, and Titus," he murmured. "The Academy is in need of strong

621

mentorship. Particularly the Earth Fae, which is why they want Sol to take on a teaching role among his kind. As for Vox, Professor Helios is on the verge of retirement. They feel Vox is a suitable replacement but want him to mentor beneath Helios for a few years first. And Titus is the perfect replacement for the intramurals professor who fled before the battle."

"So all three of them have to stay at the Academy." I wasn't sure how I felt about that. "What about me, you, and Cyrus?"

"I plan to reside here as well, having already proven to be able to effectively manage the Spirit Kingdom from afar. Not to mention, I want to be here when the Spirit Quad reopens. There's going to be a lot needed to get it ready again. Fortunately, we have some time before the life cycle kicks in again." His eyes lit up with the words, his relief flooding our bond.

Already, two Spirit Fae had fallen pregnant in the last couple of weeks, proving Elana's hold over the death fields had been the cause of infertility.

"And Cyrus, he can mist between the Academy and his Water Kingdom. As can you," he added, his palm sliding from my cheek to the back of my neck. "You can live here with us and still see Cyrus whenever you want. Which, I assume, will be often because I don't see him going more than a day without your touch."

"Where will we stay?" I wondered out loud. "The Spirit Dorms?"

He chuckled, shaking his head. "No, baby. I was thinking of building a place for us out in the field."

"In the forest?"

He nodded. "Unless you have another idea in mind. But I'd prefer to live off campus grounds." His lips brushed mine before drifting to my ear. "Your rapturous screams are for your mates and no one else, Claire. Therefore, privacy is a must."

Exos nipped my escalating pulse, the heat of his breath raising goose bumps along the back of my neck.

"What do you think, Claire?" he asked, his voice dropping to a whisper. "Would you like to stay at the Academy? Help mentor some students and continue learning about your elements?" He kissed my cheek before pressing his forehead to mine. "If you think about, it's the perfect place for you, surrounded by all the Elemental Fae. You'd thrive here."

I shivered, my arms loosening to allow me to clutch his shoulders. "I want to be where my mates are," I told him, locking my gaze on his. "I want to be where *you* are, Exos. And if that's here, then I'll be here. If that's in Spirit Kingdom, then I'll be there. If we all stay with Cyrus in Water Kingdom, I'm okay with that, too. I just want all of us to be together."

"Spoken like a goddess," he mused, pride beaming from his gaze. "I think they'll all vote to stay where you are, Claire."

"But being here would make them happy," I added.

He nodded. "I think so, yes. Vox has always wanted to be a professor. Sol would thrive on the idea of helping his fellow Earth Fae through mentorship. And I don't see Titus balking at the idea of taking over fae intramural athletic activities."

My lips twitched. "No, I don't see him rejecting that either." In fact, I pictured him loving every minute of it. All of them would enjoy the opportunity. "And what would I be doing all day?"

"What you already do," Exos replied. "Leading us all."

"To where, the bedroom?" I teased.

His amusement tickled our bond. "If that's where you want us to go, we'll happily follow."

"Uh-huh." I smiled up at him. "I want to help you."

"Me?"

I nodded. "With Academy responsibilities. While also being the conduit, or whatever you called me, for the Council."

"Advisor," he corrected, his grip tightening. "And I accept, Claire. You're my queen, baby. We belong beside each other. Always." His lips touched mine for too fleeting a moment, leaving me with a craving deep inside for more. The hardness pressing into my lower abdomen through his suit pants told me it was a yearning he shared. But the seriousness in his gaze warned that we weren't done discussing important matters.

"Your mother," he started, his hand finding my hip while the other remained against my neck. "While the Council is convinced of her innocence, they're concerned about her mental state. Which is the other reason they recommend we remain on campus. Because they want to keep Ophelia here for the time being."

"Why?" I wondered out loud. "She's a Spirit Fae. Can't she live in Spirit Kingdom?"

"She could, but the fear surrounding her is too great. Believing the truth is entirely different from accepting it, and unfortunately, the Spirit Fae have villainized your mother for so long that it will take time for them to see her in a new light." His thumb stroked up the column of my throat. "Her mental state is too fragile to handle them right now."

I sighed. He was right, of course. Most mornings she woke up screaming. Once she remembered her location and everything that had happened, she was usually fine. But some days, she walked around with a distant glow in her eyes, one that reminded me very much of death.

"Mortus has agreed to remain as well, to continue trying to heal her," Exos added.

"Because that's going splendidly," I muttered.

Allegedly, they were archrivals in school, something being forced to bond only made worse. Because the link still remained, awaiting their true consummation. For years it was believed she'd died and Mortus had just chosen not to take another mate. Apparently, it was all a charade, because the

Spirit Fae couldn't bond with anyone else while my mother still lived.

They were forever engaged.

Mortus seemed to be more accepting and apologetic than my mother.

At least at first.

But a few words from her, and his ire spiked, creating this strange energy between them that left me decidedly uncomfortable.

"They'll work it out," Exos mused. "I have faith in that."

"Glad you do, because I think they're going to end up killing each other." When my mate informed me of his decision to pair Mortus with my mother for her recovery, I feared it would do more damage than good. But the only time she really seemed to come alive was when she bickered with him over old wounds from two decades ago. "They fight like teenagers."

Exos chuckled. "Reminds me a bit of Titus and Cyrus. All that tension and animosity. I do wonder what will come of it."

"We both know how I intend to resolve that problem," my water mate informed us from behind me. I hadn't sensed his approach, too wrapped up in Exos's aura. But I sighed as Cyrus pressed his chest to my back, his lips against the top of my head. "Mind if I steal our little queen for a moment? We have state business to discuss."

"Ah, the coronation." Exos waggled his brows. "I did catch on to your father's impatience this morning. Best not to leave the old man waiting much longer, brother."

Cyrus buried his face in my hair while murmuring his agreement, his arm sliding around my middle as Exos took my mouth in a kiss underlined in promise. The heat from them both kick-started my heart, reminding me of the night the three of us shared together what felt like too long ago.

I wanted to experience that again.

To revel in them both.

To lose myself to their touch.

Soon, little queen, Cyrus promised, his warm exhale sliding over the back of my neck and Exos's hand. *Soon.*

Now works for me, I replied, my tongue eagerly engaging in the sensuous battle Exos had just initiated. He meant to tease. Well, I happily returned the favor, arching into his groin and moaning as he deepened our embrace.

He grinned against my mouth. "Playful little minx," he whispered, then spun me into his brother's waiting arms. "Try to keep her warmed up for me, Cyrus. I'd like to continue that when you're done."

My water mate spread a possessive palm against my lower back while his opposite hand gripped the back of my neck, just like his brother's had. "She'll be ready," he promised, his lips gently claiming mine. *Mmm, we need to talk about the coronation. But kissing you is far more enticing.*

His tongue engaged mine in a slow, sensual dance that stirred butterflies in my lower abdomen. When Cyrus kissed me like this, I felt fragile, worshiped, and very much *his*. Mist spun around us, our element playing in time with our mouths. It left me feeling giddy, eliciting a giggle from within that he swallowed with a groan.

How are you so perfect? he marveled, his hands falling to my hips to lift me in the air.

I wove my legs around his waist, my arms encircling his neck. *The elements made me this way*, I teased. *And I remember a time when you didn't think I was all that perfect.*

He nipped my lower lip in reprimand. *Nonsense. I adored you from the beginning.* Uh-huh.

You were my stubborn little queen then, just as you are now. He took a few steps, halting when my back hit the trunk of a tree. It provided him with the leverage he needed to hold me between his body and the earth behind me.

I groaned as he pressed his growing arousal into the pillow between my thighs, making me wish I'd chosen a skirt today instead of pants. Or perhaps it was better this way. Cyrus and I couldn't be trusted in this state, too consumed with devouring each other to care about propriety.

With the Academy no longer in session, my father wants to do the coronation next week, he whispered into my thoughts. *He states that I can no longer use your studies as an excuse to delay.*

Okay, I replied, sucking on his tongue and threading my fingers through his thick hair. *Just tell me what to wear.*

He pulled back, his eyebrows lifting. "This is a big deal, Claire."

"Mm-hmm," I agreed. "So you need to tell me how to dress." I went to try to kiss him again, but he held me at bay with an incredulous look.

"This will make you the Water Queen."

"I know."

"And things will be expected of you."

"I'll need to give you an heir," I translated. "Yes, you told me that."

His eyebrows shot up. "You make it sound so easy, Claire."

"Isn't it?" I countered, arching an eyebrow right back at him. "I'm your mate. You're the future king. That makes me the future queen. We'll need to provide leadership over the Water Fae, and eventually, we'll need to produce a son. How am I doing so far?"

"It's a lot of responsibility, Claire. And easier said than done."

"Aren't all things easier said than done?" I asked him, my lips curling. "But I'm sure you'll enjoy the procreation part. We can practice as many times as you want, my future king. And when we're ready, I'll carry your heir and raise our child with you and the others. You just have to work out with Exos who gets to impregnate me first. Let me know what you decide."

He openly gaped at me. "Who are you and what have you done with my little queen?"

"She turned into an elemental fae goddess," I replied conversationally.

"Now she listens to her elemental instincts." I tightened my hold around him, drawing his mouth closer to mine. "And right now, they're telling her to devour her water mate. Then follow him to his coronation next week and wear a pretty crown at his side."

"Fuck," he breathed, his exhale reminding me of an ocean breeze. I wanted to revel in it, taste him, indulge him forever.

"You're mine," I told him softly. "And I'll be whatever you need in return. It's as simple as that, my Water Prince. Now kiss me. I'm tired of talking about politics and want to fuck instead."

He released a surprised chuckle. "My needy little queen," he mused.

"You promised to satisfy me for eternity, Cyrus."

"Indeed I did," he agreed, his mouth lingering over mine. "I'll ascend next week, then."

I nodded. "Yes. You will."

"Then I'd better get to satisfying my future queen," he said quietly. "She's a stubborn little thing."

"Demanding, too," I added.

He smiled against my lips. "That she is."

"Kiss me, Cyrus."

"Happily, my queen," he whispered, his mouth taking mine.

All talk of the future was swept away beneath a wave of lust and erotic intention. The Water Prince seducing his Water Princess beneath a sea of matrimony and bliss.

Forever and always.

To the moons and back.

Over and over again.

EPILOGUE
CLAIRE

"MAY I PRESENT QUEEN CLAIRE?" Cyrus announced, opening the bedroom to his quarters.

I glanced at him sideways. "You can stop saying that now." He'd been doing it all evening, ever since accepting the Water King crown. "This is supposed to be your night, not mine."

"Oh, but it is my night," he murmured, his palm resting against the small of my back. "And I intend to celebrate accordingly."

"Yeah?" I asked, allowing him to guide me through the threshold and into his bedroom. "What did you have in mind, Your Highness?"

"Mmm, I like those words from your mouth, Claire." He pulled me to him, kissing me long enough to have me consider the need for breathing. "Say it again."

"Your Highness," I repeated, batting my eyes up at him.

He chuckled, closing the door behind him with his foot. "That gives me delicious ideas for later, when I have you on your knees."

"You'll make me kneel?" I feigned shock. "How degrading, King Cyrus."

"You'll enjoy it," he promised, his palm sliding down to smack my ass. Hard. "Besides, we love when you go to your knees, little queen."

"We?"

He smiled. "I told you that I intended to celebrate accordingly. And I would prefer to go down in history as a giving king." His gaze lifted over my head. "What better way to start my reign than to share my coronation night with those I value most."

"I love that dress on you, Claire." Titus's warm voice caressed my exposed spine, his heat radiating from somewhere behind me.

We were all waiting on the balcony, Sol explained into my mind. *Cyrus wanted it to be a surprise.*

I smiled. *Consider me surprised.*

While all my mates had attended the coronation, there'd barely been a moment for me to spend with them. Exos hadn't lied when he warned me Cyrus's ascension would be a grand affair.

Several Elemental Fae were in attendance, including Aflora. She'd worn a flower dress fit for an Earth Fae Queen but didn't seem quite herself. I suspected it had something to do with Glacier. From what I'd gathered, he was supposed to be her date and had chosen to stay with his parents the whole time instead.

Sol was right about him. The jackass didn't deserve Aflora. I'd wanted to talk to her, but Kols had distracted me with a giant hug. I'd known the Midnight Fae Royals would be in attendance. His easy candor still caught me off guard. However, it was a brief encounter because not two minutes after embracing me like we were best friends, he'd left me to pursue Exos and Cyrus's Fortune Fae friend—Gina. I'd only seen her in passing, just long enough to receive a glimpse of a smile and the approval radiating from her expression.

Cyrus said it was typical, that Gina probably stopped by to ensure the future she prophesized had come to fruition. And it must have, because I didn't see her again after that. Mostly a result of me being too wrapped up in meeting fae from all over the world to notice much else.

One thing was for sure: I still had a lot of learning to do about this fae world. Because there were a hell of a lot of kingdoms I'd never heard of.

But now was not the time for such explorations.

Not with the growing warmth at my back as all my mates entered the room from the balcony outside.

Cyrus's palms skimmed up my arms to the dainty blue straps at my shoulders. "Hmm, I don't think Titus wants to destroy your beautiful gown, little queen. Shall I help you remove it for him? Before his passion burns out of control?"

I shivered and pressed a kiss to his jaw. "Whatever you wish, Your Highness."

His lips curled. "Oh, Claire." He hooked his thumbs beneath the sapphire fabric. "If that's how you want to play, then that's how we'll play." He slid the silky strands to my biceps and lower, the Grecian-style dress falling with his movements to pool at my waist. His gaze followed, the icy ring around his pupils thinning as he took in my exposed breasts. "Do you know why I chose this gown, little queen?"

"Because it flows like liquid over my skin," I replied.

His lips curled. "Yes. And because I knew you wouldn't be able to wear anything beneath it." With a slight tug, he caused the garment to fall to the floor, leaving me clad in only a pair of silver heels. "Knowing you were naked beneath that dress was the ultimate tease for all of us." He pressed his lips to mine, then turned me to face my suit-clad mates. "Again," Cyrus murmured softly. "May I present Queen Claire?"

Four pairs of hungry gazes roamed over my body as if seeing it for the first time, their arousals all slamming into me at once.

Standing naked in a room surrounded by five males in formal wear was certainly one way to seduce a woman. Because fuck, I could hardly stand beneath the need assaulting me from all angles.

Cyrus grasped my hip with one palm, his chest a comfort against my back, and dipped his opposite hand into the damp heat between my thighs. "Mmm." He nuzzled my neck. "Our Claire is quite ready, gentlemen. Shall we indulge our little queen?"

Exos leaned against the wall beside the fountain, in his hand a glass of bronze-colored alcohol. "Yes," he agreed, clearly not in line to be the first to touch me.

No.

My spirit mate liked to watch.

He'd be the last one inside me. Make us both wait for the joining of our souls.

Titus would be first.

Vox and Sol sharing second.

Then Cyrus.

And maybe Exos would join then.

A trail of fire caught my focus, the flame inching downward to meet Cyrus's hand. The Water King didn't move, instead adding a kiss of water to the mix that left me quivering in his arms. Titus stepped forward, shrugging out of his jacket as he moved. "You're making me thirsty," he said casually to the male behind me.

"Am I?" Cyrus asked, his finger gliding with ease through my folds as Titus's flame followed.

I trembled between them, my body lost to the sensations below. And we hadn't even started yet.

Holy Fae, these men are going to kill me, I thought, grabbing Cyrus's wrist as he thrust two fingers inside me. I gasped, the penetration harsh and oh-so right.

"Poor Claire," he mused at my back. "How will she survive us all?"

Sol and Vox both removed their jackets.

Titus kicked off his shoes.

And Exos remained calmly composed, sipping his drink and watching me with desire bright in his dark blue eyes.

A cool breeze tweaked my nipples, drawing my gaze to Vox. He smiled and canted his head. "I foresee a lot of screaming in her future."

"Indeed," Cyrus agreed, his fingers leaving me and stirring a whimper from deep within my soul.

Until Titus went to his knees before me.

My knees buckled as his mouth sealed over my clit, but Cyrus caught me with his arm around my middle, his opposite hand lifting to my paint my lips with my arousal. "Don't lick, little queen," he said. "That's for Sol to taste, not you."

Oh, dear mother of the elements...

Sol stepped forward, his palm going to my throat as he angled me to receive his kiss.

And kiss me he did.

The heat of his tongue a brand against my own, mingling with the juices Cyrus had left for my earth mate to enjoy.

Titus grazed me with his teeth, forcing me to divide my focus between them.

One of my hands went to Titus's hair, the other to Sol's cheek, and all the while, Cyrus remained a steadying presence at my back, holding me upright while my other two mates devoured me.

Vox's groan had me opening my eyes to find his lips wrapped around Cyrus's fingers, sucking them clean. And fuck if that wasn't the hottest thing I'd ever seen.

My men playing together?

My thighs clenched around Titus in response.

Yes. More of that, please, I thought, groaning against Sol's mouth.

A consideration for later perhaps, Cyrus replied, his lips brushing my neck and nibbling at my racing pulse. *Tonight is about worshiping you, our queen.*

While you lead them as the king, I whispered back to him.

He smiled against my neck. *Yes, little queen.*

I understood then that he'd worked this all out with my mates, his dominance coming out to play in the way he knew best. While allowing us all to flourish under his command, to indulge and enjoy.

And I wouldn't have it any other way.

Sol pulled away, allowing Vox to take his place.

Titus remained between my thighs, his tongue bringing me ever closer to the edge of oblivion as he teased my wetness with his fingers.

"Do you remember what happened the last time we were in this room?" Cyrus hummed against my ear.

I arched back against him, Titus's mouth doing something that sent a violent tremble up and down my spine. Vox continued to kiss me, making a verbal response impossible, so I answered in my mind with a hissed, *Yes.*

"Do you want to experience it again, little queen?" he asked softly, his arm tightening around me while his other hand drifted from my hip to slide between us, down to my ass. "Do you want all of us to fuck you, Claire? To take you to new heights? Together?"

I swallowed, my lips leaving Vox as I panted at the picture Cyrus created. "That's impossible to do," I breathed, considering how many of them there were. I only had so many, uh, options.

My water mate chuckled, his breath warm against my neck. "We'll have to take turns." He nipped my earlobe. "But only if you want to, Claire."

Titus tilted his head back, his forest-green gaze glazed over with lust, his lips damp from my core. My limbs tightened at the image, my lower belly curling painfully with the need for release.

"I want you all," I said, my voice hoarse with desire. "However you want. Wherever you want. Just, now. Right now."

Cyrus chuckled. "You heard our queen. She wants us all. Let's take her."

Sol and Vox began unbuttoning their shirts.

Titus went the easy route of burning his to ash, his cock bouncing against my lower belly as he stood before me. His mouth found mine, his abs pressing into Cyrus's arm.

"Hold her," my water mate demanded.

Titus wrapped his arm around my lower back as Cyrus disappeared, his opposite hand going to the back of my neck. Mmm, he tasted like me and fire combined, his mouth a heated ember I longed to lose myself in. And so I did, kissing him back with everything I owned, until something cool and damp slid between my ass cheeks.

"Shh." Cyrus pressed a kiss to the top of my spine. "Just helping you prepare for your mates."

I jolted as he slid a finger inside me back there, my body going directly into the wall of muscle that was all Titus.

And I forgot the world again.

My lips finding his in a passionate embrace underlined in an inferno I felt building throughout my entire body.

Hands began to caress me.

Mouths and tongues tasted my skin.

Vox and Sol, my elements recognized.

I moaned, the sound swallowed by Titus as he and the others guided me toward the bed.

Except for Exos. He remained as poised as always, still in his suit, waiting. The heat in his gaze resembled a brand as I crawled onto the mattress, that tumbler grazing his lips while he took yet another sip. Cyrus stepped into my view, his tie unknotted, his jacket gone, but he remained almost as clothed as his brother.

"Titus is going to fuck you, little queen. Sol wants your mouth. And Vox is going to slide behind you. Do you think you can handle that?" His words stirred a maelstrom inside me.

Three men?

At once?

Oh Fae… Why am I nodding? Because I wanted this. Because the wickedness of his words had set me on literal fire. Titus traced the flame along my arm, his lips curling. "That's one way to express your approval, sweetheart."

I swallowed, my gaze finding his. "Why aren't you inside me yet?" I sounded breathless. Needy. Aroused.

"Feisty," he murmured, lying down beside me, his green eyes darkening with yearning. "Take what you want, Claire. Ride me to your heart's content."

"Here, love." Vox held out his hand, pulling me up and helping me to straddle Titus. "Get comfortable." He pressed a kiss to my shoulder, his strong body kneeling behind mine for support while I took Titus inside me.

My fire mate hissed in response, his palms grasping my hips to guide himself deeper and all the way to the hilt. "Fuck, Claire."

"You said to take you," I reminded him, sliding myself up and then down.

He growled my name, causing my lips to curl.

I love that sound, I told him.

And I love when you moan, he returned, his fingers drifting along my lower body to strum my clit. *Yeah, just like that.*

I nearly collapsed onto him, my body strung so tight from all the kisses, nips, and strokes, but Vox caught me around the middle, his arm strong. "Ready for me?" he asked against my ear. He tweaked my nipple with his air element, causing me to arch back against him, presenting myself in the most wanton manner.

The head of his cock nudged my ass. With one arm still wrapped around me, he used his other hand to part my slick cheeks to find my entrance.

Only Exos and Cyrus had fucked me back there.

But Vox, he didn't penetrate fast or hard.

No, he took his time, his shaft easing in and out. In and out. Setting a rhythm that had my breaths coming in matching inhales and exhales. Calming me. Soothing me. Seducing me.

Titus incited heat and passion

Vox bathed me in sensuality.

And Sol grounded me, my rock, my giant with the tender smile. He caressed my cheek, capturing my attention, as he stood beside the bed. "Can you angle this way, little flower?" he asked softly.

The way Vox and Titus had positioned me on the bed put me at the perfect height to take Sol in my mouth. I just had to bend a little. But that bead of moisture on the tip of his arousal had me hungry for a taste.

So I responded by licking him, his fingers sliding into my hair to support my movements, not rush them.

Vox and Titus set a pace, not fast or painful, but smooth and enticing. I felt so full. So owned. Absolutely consumed.

Air caressed my skin.

Fire blossomed in my veins.

And earthy scents filled my senses.

Perfection.

My mates.

My elements.

All bonding as one while my water mate and spirit mate watched, waiting their turn. They were both in my mind. Praising me. Telling me how gorgeous I looked between my mates. Promising me a night of unending pleasure. And as the first orgasm crested through me, I knew they would uphold everything they vowed and more. Their hearts beating in time with mine.

I swallowed Sol's rapture, moaned as Titus's hot essence filled my insides, and sighed as Vox caught his release on a breeze that stirred every hair on my body.

And then Exos and Cyrus were there, taking their positions and driving me into an oblivion lined with the stars.

I lost myself to all of them, their hands, their mouths, their unbridled passion and desire. Over and over again we danced, the night soon blossoming into morning, where we finally fell asleep in a pile of limbs and adoration.

All six of us.

My mates.

Forming a circle of elements bound by love. Respect. Joy. And ecstasy.

Joined in a union no one could ever penetrate.

For eternity and beyond.

In our very own happily ever after.

The End

THANK YOU SO MUCH FOR READING CLAIRE'S STORY!

We had so much fun crafting this world and meeting all the fascinating voices thriving inside of it. As you can imagine, there were scenes in our heads that couldn't fit into the books. One such scene was Titus and Cyrus's Powerless Champion rematch, and the aftermath of their battle. Another involves Sol and Vox, and a lesson in sensual control.

If you're interested in reading more about Titus and Cyrus, and don't mind a little MMF action, visit: https://www.lexicfoss.com/elemental-fae-academy-bonus-scene. The story is free with Lexi's newsletter subscription.

If you're interested in reading more about Sol and Vox's encounter, which also includes Claire, visit https://authorjrthorn.com/elemental-fae-academy-bonus-story. The story is free with J.R. Thorn's newsletter subscription.

But that's not all.

This world grew so large that we have two more academies to play with as a result.

Lexi is following Aflora to Midnight Fae Academy, where she's been enrolled against her will due to an unsanctioned vampire bite. Mixing fae magic is dangerous, and this bite may have just created the most dangerous weapon yet. Because Aflora has secrets. Secrets she doesn't even know about yet...

J.R. Thorn is diving into the world of the Fortune Fae, where tarot cards predict the future, except Gina doesn't want to accept hers. The cards are calling her an Omega, and in a world run by Alphas, that's a dangerous classification. She's on the run for her life, with a hot alpha right on her tail. What happens when she's caught?

You met Aflora in Elemental Fae Academy. Now she's about to meet the Dark Fae of the world, and she's not at all happy about it…

Welcome to Midnight Fae Academy.
Home of the Dark Arts.
Vampires.
And cruelly handsome fae.

A forbidden bite led to my capture and recruitment.
There are no flowers here. No life. Only death.

I'm an Earth Fae who doesn't belong here.
They can play their little mind games all they want, but I'm going to find a way back to my elemental world. Even if it kills me.

Except Headmaster Zephyrus is one step ahead of my every move.
Prince Kolstov won't stop cornering me.
And Shadow—the reason I'm in this damn mess to begin with—haunts my dreams.

My affinity for the earth is dying and being replaced by something more sinister.
Something powerful. Something deadly.

The Midnight Fae believe this is my fate. They claim that I was "recruited" for a purpose. To battle a rising presence. Or to die trying.

I don't owe them a damn thing. But if I have to pass their trials to find my way home, then so be it. I survived a plague and far worse in the Elemental Fae realm. An ominous energy? Please. What a joke.

Give it your best shot. I'm waiting.
And don't you dare bite me. Or I'll make you regret it.

Author Note: This is a dark paranormal reverse harem trilogy with bully romance (enemies-to-lovers) elements. Despite Aflora's opinions on the matter, there will definitely be biting. Shadow, aka Shade, guarantees it. This book ends on a cliffhanger.

You met Gina in Elemental Fae Academy. Find out what she's really up to in Fortune Fae Academy…

I never asked to be an Omega.

I'm a Fortune Fae—I see the future. But I didn't see this coming.

My Alpha will stop at nothing to possess me and has dragged me all the way to Fortune Fae Academy to join the other wide-eyed Omegas-in-training. He believes I'll survive--and I hope he's right.

He also believes I'll kneel at his feet.
He couldn't be more wrong about that.

I don't need three broody Betas and an asshat Alpha telling me what to do. When I graduate the Academy as an ascended Omega, I'm rejecting my mate-circle and getting the hell out of here.

Except there's one slight problem. My Alpha has seen the future too… and he knows something I don't.

Whatever he thinks is going to happen, his cruel smirk says I'm not going anywhere.

Fortune Fae Academy is Book 1 in a Reverse Harem Omegaverse Romance. Be warned there are obsessive males who will stop at nothing to claim their fated mate. As this is a series, book 1 ends on a cliffhanger.

ABOUT LEXI C. FOSS

USA Today Bestselling Author Lexi C. Foss loves to play in dark worlds, especially the ones that bite. She lives in Atlanta, Georgia with her husband and their furry children. When not writing, she's busy crossing items off her travel bucket list, or chasing eclipses around the globe. She's quirky, consumes way too much coffee, and loves to swim.

www.LexiCFoss.com
https://www.facebook.com/LexiCFoss
https://www.twitter.com/LexiCFoss

ABOUT J.R. THORN

J.R. Thorn is a Reverse Harem Paranormal Romance Author.

Learn More at:
www.AuthorJRThorn.com

Addicted to Academy? Read more RH Academy by J.R. Thorn: Fortune
Academy, available on Amazon.com!

**Welcome to Fortune Academy, a school where supernaturals can feel at
home—except, I have no idea what the hell I am.**

Lightning Source UK Ltd.
Milton Keynes UK
UKHW040840140622
404366UK00006B/35/J